S0-CXW-613

Special Edition

Using

StarOffice ®

This convenient tear-out booklet is designed to give you a quick introduction to getting started with the latest version of the StarOffice suite. Look here first if you want to get up and running fast. For more detailed information, please refer to the respective sections in *Special Edition Using StarOffice*.

Launching StarOffice for the First Time

Although the StarOffice installation process is similar across platforms, how you launch StarOffice varies slightly according to platform, operating system, and setup.

Windows Users

Select Start, Programs, StarOffice and choose the StarOffice 5.1 icon. The Help Agent Tips window automatically opens on the first launch, as does the Internet Setup wizard (see Figure 1).

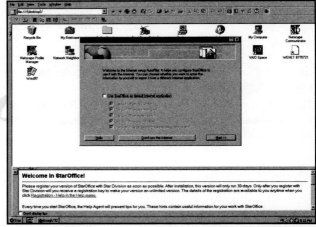

Linux Users

The steps for launching StarOffice vary depending on your system configuration. This book assumes that you are launching StarOffice from within X, with StarOffice located in your usr directory. Note that you must launch X

Figure 1

and the window manager before you can launch StarOffice following these steps:

1. Make sure you are in your `usr/Office51/bin` directory. This is where the script for starting StarOffice is installed in the default installation.
2. Type `./soffice` at the X Window prompt.
   If you want to launch StarOffice as a background application to the xterm window you are launching the program from, add a space and an ampersand (&) afterwards (`./soffice &`).
3. Press Enter.

It takes a minute or longer to launch StarOffice for the first time, as it runs through its initialization protocol.

Your desktop will look similar to the Windows version desktop shown in Figure 1. However, special to the Linux version, a printer setup utility is provided, which can be launched by double-clicking its icon on the desktop. (Note that StarOffice supports only PostScript printers on Linux; if you have a non-PostScript printer, you'll need to use a translation program like Ghostscript.)

Setting Up Your Internet and Email Accounts

After launching StarOffice, you're greeted by an Internet setup wizard (refer to Figure 1) that simplifies your setup process. If you currently use Netscape Communicator and/or MS Internet Explorer and MS Outlook Express for email and browsing, you can choose to import existing inbox and browser settings. You can also choose to set StarOffice to handle any or all of your Internet chores by default (which include Web browsing, email and news accounts, and FTP); or, you can continue to use your existing programs from within StarOffice.

If you have not registered already, you will also be prompted with a dialog that asks if you want to register now. Choose Yes and a wizard steps you through the registration process. You can register online, by fax, or by mail. Your best choice is to register online as your registration is handled by an automated process that typically only takes a few minutes. If you've already completed the Internet wizard, you'll be all set to go.

Note If you want to defer configuring your Internet connection until later, click Don't Use the Internet. You can run the AutoPilot again at any time by choosing File, AutoPilot, Internet Setup. (You can also use this AutoPilot to change your settings.)

If you connect to the Internet through a modem, telephone line, and ISP, you must have a dial-up networking program installed on your system that you've set up to dial your ISP. This section assumes you are either connected to a LAN or have already set up your dial-up networking.

The first step in completing the Internet AutoPilot is to choose if you want StarOffice to be your default program for handling any or all of your Internet needs. If you want StarOffice to handle any of your Internet chores on a regular basis, click the Use StarOffice as Default Internet Application option.

This option sounds more global than it is. Once you select it, the grayed-out list of choices in the lower part of the dialog becomes active, enabling you to select only those chores you want StarOffice to handle.

You can set StarOffice to be your default for any of these five tasks:

- Web browsing
- Email client for POP3, VIM, and IMAP accounts
- News client
- FTP client
- Safe HTTP connections (secure HTTP)

Make your selections by clicking the checkbox(es) next to the option(s). When you're done, or if you don't want StarOffice to handle any of Internet chores at all, click Next to move to the next dialog box.

If you run either Netscape Communicator, or MS Internet Explorer and/or Outlook Express, the Internet AutoPilot automates the process of importing existing email inboxes and outboxes and browser settings from these programs.

Select Apply All Settings Automatically if you want the wizard to import your existing settings, and click Next. StarOffice will automatically import all Internet settings from your selected program, existing mailboxes, and news folders.

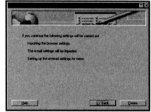

Figure 2

You're almost done! The AutoPilot presents you with a screen that summarizes what actions StarOffice is about to take (see Figure 2). Clicking Create gives it your permission to proceed.

Introducing the StarDesktop

The StarDesktop is the central location where you perform all your tasks and it is a key part of the StarOffice interface. On first launch, the program automatically creates a default StarOffice desktop. Under Windows, this desktop incorporates the same program icons and documents as your Windows desktop. Note also that icons on your Windows Start menu show up in the StarOffice Start menu. Under Linux, if you have a desktop folder, it will incorporate this folder; otherwise, it will use the StarOffice desktop (/usr/Office51/Desktop) as your default desktop. The suite does not replicate your window manager menus within itself.

→ For information on customizing your desktop and creating and working with multiple desktops, **see** "Managing Multiple Desktops," **page 123**.

Notice the two icons, an arrow and a stickpin, on the upper left border of your window and on the upper border of the Help Agent at the bottom of your screen. These icons are controls for floating desktop windows. (Look ahead to Figure 3 to see them identified.) Clicking the arrow hides or reveals the window—so if you want to clear your desktop, click the arrow to hide the Help Agent. Clicking the stickpin "pins" the window to the desktop. Otherwise, it floats on top and therefore may cover some of the desktop contents.

Clicking the arrow on the upper left reveals (or hides) the Explorer, a key component of the StarOffice desktop.

Exploring Some Elements of the StarDesktop

Your desktop is made up of a number of elements, shown in Figure 3. The title bar contains controls for resizing and closing the program window. Click the Maximize/Restore button to reduce the program to a resizable window, and you can drag it anywhere on your system desktop.

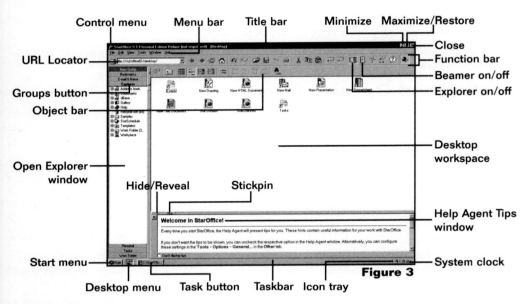

Figure 3

The Task bar displays all active tasks as icons. Click any icon in order to view and edit the active task. On the right in the Task bar you see a task tray which shows, among other things, the e-mail indicator and the time of day.

The area between the Start and Desktop buttons represents the Quickstart bar. It can be used to quickly start an application, open a document or folder, and so on. Just drag the respective object into the area between the buttons to enable this feature.

In the left corner is an icon that represents the StarOffice program. Clicking it opens a menu that offers the same commands as the buttons.

Introducing the Explorer and Beamer

In the Explorer, you can manage and organize all the elements in StarOffice. You can open the Explorer by clicking the Explorer icon on the function bar (sixth icon from the right). If it is open but hidden, click the Show icon (right-pointing triangle) at the left border of your desktop.

You can choose to display objects in the Explorer in one of three views: Hierarchical, Small Symbols, or Large Symbols. To set the Explorer to Hierarchical view, right-click the Explorer group title bar and select Hierarchical from the context menu.

When your group is set to display on Hierarchical view, the Beamer displays the contents of most types of Explorer entries when you select and click or extended-click them. Displaying files in the Beamer gives you access to special drag-and-drop features.

To turn the Beamer on and off, click its icon in the function bar, or choose its name in the View menu. You can also turn the Beamer on (but not off) by pressing Ctrl+Shift+B.

The Explorer is your usual starting point for creating what you might think of as new interface objects—that is, objects that enable you to connect with and perhaps (if you choose) store some outside source of data and information. These include links to other directories, email account Inboxes, your email and news Outbox, StarBase databases (which are most frequently used to import data from external sources), and FTP accounts.

Working Across the StarDesktop

Where StarOffice stands out from the pack of Office suites is in its tight integration of applications and Internet programs into one desktop—a desktop designed to blend into office networks and the Internet as well as work smoothly across platforms.

This integration includes the sharing of commands, tools, and desktop utilities across applications, which makes learning to use StarOffice relatively quick and easy.

Creating and Opening Documents

Because StarOffice is a task-oriented program, you begin work on the desktop by creating and opening files and documents, not opening applications. Simply double-click the desired document in the Beamer or on the desktop and StarOffice will automatically open the required module so you can start to work with the document.

Starting a New Task

To start a task, you can open new documents from a number of locations on your desktop workspace, or you can create documents by using templates and the AutoPilot Wizard.

To start a new task or create a new StarOffice document, you can choose from these options, among others:

- You can open the Start menu from the task bar and click the desired document type icon to start a new document.
- You can choose File, New from the menu bar and then select a document type from the submenu.
- You can open the Tasks group in the extended Explorer by clicking its title bar. Then you can click the desired document type icon to start a new document.
- You can choose File, AutoPilot for help with creating text, presentation, and Web documents and templates.

Flying on AutoPilot

AutoPilot is a document- and template-creation wizard that helps you quickly create polished, formatted versions of the most common document types—Letter, Fax, Agenda, Memo, Presentation, and Web Page—by stepping you through a limited set of formatting and layout options.

If you have templates and documents created in Microsoft Word, Excel, or PowerPoint, you can use the Microsoft Import wizard, a special AutoPilot wizard that imports your Microsoft Office document templates and/or documents into StarOffice formats in a few easy steps. Just select File, AutoPilot, Microsoft Import from the menu bar. (For more details, see the section "Importing Microsoft Office Documents and Templates" in Chapter 4, "Working in StarOffice.")

To create new documents and templates with the AutoPilot, select File, AutoPilot, and then the type of document you want to create. StarOffice walks you step by step through a series of dialogs that assist you in creating a template according to your needs. If you make a mistake or change your mind, retrace your steps with the Back button and make changes. Click Cancel to cancel the entire process and return to the desktop.

After you've entered all the necessary information, choose Create. StarOffice opens a blank document based on the template. With ordinary text documents and presentations, it also automatically creates and saves a custom template in the `Standard` subfolder of the `Templates` directory, using the name you entered during the creation process. It saves this template even if you do not save the document created with the AutoPilot. With Web (HTML) documents, you must click the Save Template option box to save your custom template.

→ For more information on working with the AutoPilot for text documents, **see** "Creating Documents and Templates with the AutoPilot," **page 253**.

→ For more information on creating and working with text templates, **see** "Working with Templates," **page 308**.

→ For more information on working with StarCalc templates, **see** "Creating StarCalc Templates," **page 579**.

→ For more information on working with HTML (Web page) templates, **see** "Creating a New HTML Document," **page 946**.

Opening Existing Documents

StarOffice includes filters for opening documents and file types created in many other programs and on other major platforms, as well as for opening older versions of StarOffice documents.

To open existing StarOffice and non-StarOffice documents, you have these options, among several others:

■ You can click the Open File icon on the function bar or select File, Open from the menu bar or to open the Open dialog, which is similar to the Save As dialog (look ahead to Figure 4). You can navigate anywhere on your system from here. After you've located your file, you can select it and click Open.

■ You can double-click a document or file in the Beamer or on the desktop.

■ You can open the Start menu and move your mouse pointer over the Documents entry. It opens a submenu listing the last 30 documents you have opened—not just in StarOffice but anywhere on your system. Just click a document to open it.

Saving and Closing Documents

StarOffice's Save commands come in the standard flavors:

■ **Save**—Save saves the active task on your desktop. Save is also known as *fast Save* because you can save on-the-fly by using the Ctrl+S key combination or by clicking the Save button on the function bar.

■ **Save As**—Save All saves all open documents.

■ **Save All**—Using Save All and Save automatically overwrites the previous version saved under the same name.

If you choose either Save or Save All and have not yet assigned a filename to the open document(s), StarOffice automatically prompts you with the Save As dialog (see Figure 4). Using this dialog, you can name your current document and select a file type in which you would like to have your work saved, as well as assign a password.

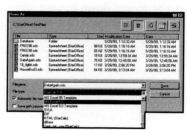

Figure 4

Formatting and Using Styles and Templates

In every application, you create objects that have attributes, discrete aspects of an object's appearance. Formatting is defining the attributes of an object. StarOffice gives you unsurpassed control in formatting your objects.

The most efficient way to apply attributes is to create and apply a style, a saved collection of formatting attributes that you can apply again and again. Because styles are managed centrally from one dialog box, you can change a style's attributes in a few minutes. Changes you make apply globally to all objects of that style in your document, enabling you to reformat in a flash.

Creating templates, collections of styles for all aspects of formatting a document, is the most efficient way of managing documents.

Navigating in StarOffice

Using StarOffice's integrated desktop, you can easily navigate among or within open tasks.

Quick Desktop Navigation with Keys

Although StarOffice makes full use of the mouse, you can often navigate more quickly by using keys; you might need to use keys if you are using command and control programs.

Moving Among Tasks

Each open document on your desktop is represented by a respective button in the task bar. You can switch to any task by clicking its button. When you have multiple task windows open on the desktop, you can also press Ctrl+Tab to cycle through them in a forward direction. Press Ctrl+Shift+Tab to cycle backward.

Using Arrow Keys in the Explorer and Beamer

If you are in Hierarchical view, your up- and down-arrow keys move you up and down entries in the Explorer, as they also do in the Beamer. If your currently selected Explorer entry has a plus sign next to it (which indicates it has subfolders or other contents), press the right-arrow key to open its list of contents and the left-arrow to close the list again. If your currently selected item is already closed or doesn't have any contents, pressing the left-arrow key returns you to the top entry in the Explorer. Because the Beamer displays only individual files, pressing the left-arrow key always returns you to the top of the Beamer list.

If the Beamer (Ctrl+Shift+B) and Explorer (Ctrl+Shift+E) are both open, pressing Tab moves you between the two windows.

Using Arrow Keys on the Desktop

When you have folders open on the desktop in Details view, you can use the up- and down-arrow keys to move up and down the list. When you're in Icon view, you can use the left- and right-arrows to move among the objects.

Steering Through Documents with the Navigator

Whereas the Explorer and Beamer are navigational tools for the desktop and the world outside StarOffice, the Navigator is a tool for quickly moving around inside StarOffice documents and quickly moving data between documents (see Figure 5). It's a dockable window that you can keep open on your desktop as you work. Because the Navigator is a tool unique to StarOffice, you might not find it intuitive to use initially. When you become familiar with its easy drag-and-drop and point-and-click interface though, you'll never want to work without it again.

Turning the Navigator On and Off

The Navigator command is grayed out until you have a navigable document type open on your desktop. When you have a document open, click the Navigator icon on the function bar, press F5, or select Navigator from the Edit menu to open the Navigator. To turn off the Navigator, click its icon on the function bar again, deselect Navigator from the View menu, or click the Close button in its upper-right corner.

Exploring the Navigator

The Navigator keeps track of all special objects (such as tables, graphics, and links) you have insert-

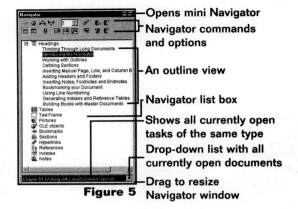

Opens mini Navigator

Navigator commands and options

An outline view

Navigator list box

Shows all currently open tasks of the same type

Drop-down list with all currently open documents

Drag to resize

Figure 5 Navigator window

ed in your documents. In text documents and presentations, you can also view and manage your outlines in the Navigator, including rearranging sections.

The display is similar to that of the Explorer in Hierarchical view. If a category has a plus sign to the left, it means further contents are available. Just click the plus sign to reveal them.

Navigating In and Between Documents

Click the name of any object the Navigator tracks, and you jump to its location in your document. You can also enter a page number, slide number, or column and row reference into the spin box on the Navigator toolbar and press Enter to jump to the specified location. Click the arrow next the drop-down list box at the bottom of the Navigator to see a list of open document of the same type (for example, all open text documents). To see the elements of a given document in the Navigator, just click the desired document in the drop-down list. You can then drag and drop elements from the selected document to the currently open document.

Finding Help in StarOffice

When you're new to StarOffice, it's a good idea to turn on the Extended Tips feature. Using this features enables you to see a short description when you place the mouse pointer over a screen element or command. To activate this feature, select Extended Tips from the Help menu (you'll see a check mark to left of the command, indicating that the item is turned on)

Both beginners and seasoned StarOffice users should leave the Tips option in the Help menu activated. This not only enables you to see the name of an icon when you rest the mouse pointer over it, but also to pick up other context-sensitive information such as line or column numbers in spreadsheets when you're scrolling through a document and other useful information.

Additional Help is available via the Help Agent, which is automatically activated for the more "complex" dialogs. The Help Agent is an extended help feature that enables you to search for terms and even ask questions by using the question mark icon. To turn the Help Agent on or off, select the item from the Help menu or click the Help icon on the function bar (second icon from the right, with the question mark).

Finally, you can activate the General Help either by selecting Contents from the Help menu, or by clicking the right-most icon in the Help Agent.

Special Edition
Using
StarOffice®

Michael Koch

Sarah Murray

with

Werner Roth

que®

A Division of Macmillan USA
201 W. 103rd Street
Indianapolis, Indiana 46290

CONTENTS AT A GLANCE

SPECIAL EDITION USING STAROFFICE®

Copyright © 1999 by Que

International Standard Book Number: 0-7897-1993-2

Library of Congress Catalog Card Number: 98-89542

Printed in the United States of America

First Printing: September 1999

01   00   99   3   2   1

TRADEMARKS

WARNING AND DISCLAIMER

Executive Editor
Dean Miller

Acquisitions Editor
Maureen A. McDaniel

Development Editor
Maureen A. McDaniel

Managing Editor
Brice Gosnell

Project Editor
Gretchen Uphoff

Copy Editors
Chuck Hutchinson
Kitty Jarrett
Pamela Woolf

Indexers
Rebecca Salerno
Bruce Clingaman

Proofreader
Andy Beaster

Team Coordinator
Cindy Teeters

Technical Editors
Frank Becker
Lasse Becker
Michael Herger
Matthew Borowski

Interior Design
Dan Armstrong
Ruth Harvey

Cover Design
Ruth Harvey

Layout Technicians
Brandon Allen
Timothy Osborn
Staci Somers

Contents

IV Getting Graphical—StarDraw and StarImage

V   Presenting Results—StarImpress

ABOUT THE AUTHORS

Michael Koch has eight years of magazine and book publishing experience, and makes his living as a publishing consultant, editor, and technical writer of computer and computer game books. An avid StarOffice user, Michael has held positions with GW Press, IDG Books, and Prima Publishing, and now works out of his home in Oakland, CA, where he enjoys living in the center of the most beautiful place on earth (the Bay Area), only occasionally looking back to his native Germany. *Special Edition Using StarOffice* is his first book with Que Publishing.

Sarah E. Murray has many years of journalistic, academic, and technical writing experience, including a two-year stint at Autodesk and freelance projects for Netscape, Fujitsu Computer Products, and Sun Microsystems. She set aside her anthropology dissertation and new stand-up comedy routine to write this manual instead—well, it seemed a good idea at the time! She normally lives in Berkeley, CA, although for the duration of this project she has mostly lived in Michael's kitchen, along with a slew of computer boxes, computers running StarOffice on Linux and Windows, and an ever-simmering pot of chicken soup.

Werner Roth is a research assistant at the Computer Science department of Universität Paderborn, Germany. He dedicates his time on the job to find new ways of educating Computer Science students and introducing ordinary people to the mysteries and possibilities of computers and computer software. Werner has been a loyal StarOffice supporter ever since the days of StarWriter 2.0. A founding member of TEAM StarOffice, the power user group that evangelizes StarOffice on the Net and in classrooms in Germany, Werner is the co-author (together with other members of TEAM StarOffice) of two StarOffice 5.0 books in Germany. He also maintains a Web site (`http://www.wernerroth.de/staroffice/`) full with tips and hints on how to get the most out of StarOffice.

ACKNOWLEDGMENTS

Books may be written by authors, but they come to life through the collaborative efforts of a slew of dedicated individuals who for some reason or other one morning woke up and decided to join the lucrative world of book publishing. Well, not quite, but the first part of this statement certainly holds true—books are the result of tremendous team efforts from authors to editors to sales. In that spirit, we would like to thank our friends at Macmillan: Grace Buechlein for giving us the opportunity to work on this book; Dean Miller for authorizing our checks and keeping his cool as deadlines rushed by; Maureen McDaniel for her expert guidance and editorial advice; Gretchen Uphoff and Pamela Woolf for being so kind to our prose; and the many unknowns and extras we never met, but know have been part of the creative process in getting this book out on time. We'd also like to thank Steve Schafer at Macmillan Digital for getting us critical research materials.

At StarDivision, we would like to thank Frank Loehmann in Hamburg, Germany, for expediting materials when we needed them, and Oliver Petry and Dirk Meisner in Fremont, California, for their help and advice (and for convincing us that there's nothing you can't do with StarOffice—you just need to know how). Thanks also to Frank and Lasse Becker, certified StarOffice experts (at least in our book) and tech editors extraordinaire (and their compadres at `teamstaroffice.org`). More tech editing kudos go to Rachel van Maanen, a Computer Science student at R.M.I.T University in Melbourne, Australia, who kept a critical eye on the StarBasic chapters while still deciding if she wants to become a systems analyst or a crocodile wrestler. Finally, we'd like to thank the contributors of the various StarOffice newsgroups who inspired us to look at the program in ways we would have never thought of before.

Closer to home, Michael would like to thank Sandra and Dan Gookin for their friendship and for pushing him into the right direction; his friends and family for excusing his absence during a period of grueling writing; his mom for keeping a steady flow of chocolate and truffles coming from Germany; and Deb, without whom he wouldn't be where he is today.

Sarah would like to thank Norm and Janet for both putting her up and putting up with her during the crucial early phases of this project; their next door neighbor, Pete, for serving as irritant and inspiration in continuing to make technical writing better serve people's needs; Welcome, for her nutritional advice and other friendship services extraordinaire; her brothers and father for their warm long-distance support; and Kris, for feeding her, in all senses, when she really needed it.

TELL US WHAT YOU THINK!

As the reader of this book, *you* are our most important critic and commentator. We value your opinion and want to know what we're doing right, what we could do better, what areas you'd like to see us publish in, and any other words of wisdom you're willing to pass our way.

As an assitant publisher for Que, I welcome your comments. You can fax, email, or write me directly to let me know what you did or didn't like about this book[md]as well as what we can do to make our books stronger.

Please note that I cannot help you with technical problems related to the topic of this book, and that due to the high volume of mail I receive, I might not be able to reply to every message.

When you write, please be sure to include this book's title and author as well as your name and phone or fax number. I will carefully review your comments and share them with the authors and editors who worked on the book.

Fax: 317.581.4666

Email: office_que@mcp.com

Mail: Dean Miller
          201 West 103rd Street
          Indianapolis, IN 46290 USA

INTRODUCTION

It's so hot it's cool, it's free, and it's a prime contender for a place of honor in the MicroScare Hall of Fame. Introducing StarOffice 5.0, the award-winning office suite from StarDivision, a German-based software development house that is garnering the attention of many industry insiders.

StarOffice is arguably the most feature-complete office suite available today, and if you're looking for an alternative to you-know-what, you need not look any further.

Visually slick, Web-enabled, and Microsoft Office-compatible, StarOffice can do word processing (StarWriter), spreadsheets (StarCalc), presentations (StarImpress), vector and bitmap graphics (StarDraw and StarImage respectively), formulas (StarMath), email (StarMail) and newsgroups (StarDiscussion), Web browsing and HTML editing, and databases (StarBase) in one fully integrated environment.

And if you familiarize yourself with the application's programming and macro language, StarBasic, you'll discover that there's virtually nothing StarOffice can't do—okay, except, at the moment, handle fully relational databases across all platforms. (Relations are implemented only on the Win32 platform.) This is the weakest link in an otherwise outstanding package whose price-point can't be beat. StarOffice is free for personal use and cost-of-ownership for businesses is comparatively low due to StarDivision's attractive site licensing models and the program's intuitive, context-sensitive tools and menus.

Clearly, StarOffice is a more-than-worthy challenger to the hoary old Office suite. It's not perfect—what software package ever is?—but it has an amazingly rich range of features, including some unique ones like the Navigator and the Stylist, which Microsoft is reportedly busily copying for inclusion in (the optimistically named?) Office 2000 suite.

StarOffice's strength does not just lie in features, however. Built around a task-centered logic, StarOffice puts the focus of an office suite where it should be—on you and what you need to do, not on the applications you use.

In the course of carrying out a common business task—say, creating a spreadsheet for a formal presentation that combines a company logo, a company mission statement, and current financial figures—you may end up needing to create pictures, text, documents, complex charts and numerical calculations, as well as slides and other visual aids.

Conventional office suites would require you to open four or more applications and perhaps master a different interface and set of tools in each one.

StarOffice has none of that.

Guided by the principle of "Make Your Ideas Work," the program's integrated desktop puts all the tools you need to carry out a full range of tasks at your fingertips—but only when and where you need them.

In short, StarOffice works the way you work—and the way other office suites promise, but don't.

WHO SHOULD USE THIS BOOK?

Special Edition Using StarOffice is designed for intermediate to advanced computer users.

It's the right choice for corporate personnel, people running a home business, students, instructors, computer support staff, small businesses, non-profit organizations and anyone else interested in getting up to speed on StarOffice. Since the free version comes with limited documentation, individual users may find this book particularly useful as it offers a more in-depth introduction of the program than is currently available in in English. Corporate IT specialists considering making the switch to Linux but concerned about available end-user applications may also find this book a useful introduction to the power and flexibility of StarOffice across platforms.

HOW TO USE THIS BOOK

Special Edition Using StarOffice consists of eight parts, broken down by application and common features.

PART I: INTRODUCING STAROFFICE

Part I, "Introducing StarOffice," gives you a basic introduction to this office suite as well as an overview of the common tools and features in StarOffice.

Chapter 1, "A Star Is Born," introduces the StarOffice program suite, complete with a feature review of each individual module.

Chapter 2, "Stepping into StarOffice," gives you a tour of the StarOffice desktop, your central command post for all your work in StarOffice, as well as the online Help system.

Chapter 3, "Getting Ready for Work," takes you through the steps of setting up your online accounts and configuring your StarOffice work environment.

Chapter 4, "Working in StarOffice," introduces you to common tools and features that are shared among program modules and explains the basics of opening, saving, and closing files in StarOffice.

Chapter 5, "Managing Folders, Files, and Mail," introduces you to file and desktop management principles that will help you manage your work more efficiently.

PART II: CREATING DOCUMENTS—STARWRITER

Part II, "Creating Documents—StarWriter," takes you into the heart of the StarOffice word processing module that is giving MS Word a run for its money.

Chapter 6, "Creating and Editing Text Documents," introduces you to the StarWriter workspace and toolbars. It takes you through the basics of entering, editing, and selecting text as well as saving, closing, and opening documents.

Chapter 7, "Formatting Text Documents," explains your character, paragraph, and page direct formatting options, including numbered and bulleted lists, as well as the AutoFormat function.

Chapter 8, "Using Styles and Templates," covers the essentials of working with styles and templates and shows you how to be more efficient by using them.

Chapter 9, "Working with Tables, Charts, and Fields," tells you how to create, edit, and format tables in StarWriter and make the most of using fields, including mail merge.

Chapter 10, "Working with Long Documents," details the challenges and tools involved in creating complex and long documents, including using the Navigator, outlines, indexes, and master documents.

Chapter 11, "Desktop Publishing with StarOffice," describes ways you can add a desktop publishing flair to your documents by using multicolumn layouts and inserting graphics and objects into documents.

Chapter 12, "Proofing and Printing Your Documents," discusses StarWriter's proofing and spelling tools, search and replace, previewing, printing, and faxing options.

PART III: WORKING WITH SPREADSHEETS—STARCALC

Part III, "Working with Spreadsheets—StarCalc," introduces StarOffice's workhorse, StarCalc, which offers all the calculating and analysis power you would expect plus a bevy of database management features.

Chapter 13, "Creating Spreadsheets," gives you a tour of StarCalc's tools and workspace. It also gives you thorough grounding in basic data entry, selection, and navigation techniques, and steps you through the basics of opening and saving files.

Chapter 14, "Editing Spreadsheets," explains the hidden mysteries of worksheet cells and introduces basic editing techniques and tools in StarCalc, including its superior drag and drop features and Navigator, StarOffice's roaming office assistant.

Chapter 15, "Formatting Spreadsheets," discusses issues to consider when formatting spreadsheets and explains how to use the many cell, row, and column formatting options you have in StarCalc.

Chapter 16, "Using Formulas and Functions," explains how to create and work with formulas in StarCalc, introduces some of StarCalc's many built in functions, and shows you how to use the Function AutoPilot.

Chapter 17, "Creating Lists and Databases with StarCalc," discusses the benefits of using StarCalc to manage lists and databases and introduces you to the tools you'll need to do so.

Chapter 18, "Analyzing and Charting Data," introduces you to some of StarCalc's more advanced data sorting and analysis features, including pivot tables and the DataPilot, StarCalc's unique data analysis wizard, and takes you through the steps of creating charts with StarChart.

Chapter 19, "Preparing and Printing Reports," explains page formatting and page styles and takes you through the steps of preparing a report for printing, including dressing up your document with graphics, setting your print range, and previewing your page layout.

PART IV: GETTING GRAPHICAL—STARDRAW AND STARIMAGE

Part IV, "Getting Graphical—StarDraw and StarImage," tells you all you need to know about StarOffice's drawing and image manipulation modules.

Chapter 20, "Getting Sketchy with StarDraw," provides a basic introduction to vector versus bitmap graphics, explains their uses, and details your options when working with vector graphics, including using the geometric drawing tools, drawing lines, shapes, and curves, and creating 3D objects.

Chapter 21, "Creating and Modifying Images with StarImage," covers image conversion and manipulation options in StarImpress and shows you how to work directly on the image in numerous image formats.

PART V: PRESENTING RESULTS—STARIMPRESS

Part V, "Presenting Results—StarImpress," tells you how to make the most of presentations with StarImpress.

Chapter 22, "Getting Started with StarImpress," introduces you to the basics of presentations, including planning, creating, saving and opening presentations.

Chapter 23, "Enhancing Your Presentation," explains how to enhance your presentation with 3D, font, transition, and animation effects.

Chapter 24, "Previewing and Presenting Your Presentation," tells you how to preview and print presentations, produce on-screen slide shows, and create speaker notes and audience handouts.

PART VI: SPREADING THE WORD—STAROFFICE ON THE WEB AND AT WORK

Part VI, "Spreading the Word—StarOffice on the Web and at Work," introduces you to StarOffice's Web features and Groupware capabilities.

Chapter 25, "Getting Started with StarWriter/Web," describes how you can use StarWriter as an HTML editor and covers basic HTML editing and formatting techniques, including adding hyperlinks and objects.

Chapter 26, "Enhancing HTML Documents," shows you how to take advantage of StarOffice's integrated desktop to create great-looking Web pages for personal and business use.

Chapter 27, "Publishing Your Work on the Web," goes into details on uploading and downloading files and setting up a StarOffice FTP account.

Chapter 28, "Teaming Up at Work," gives you tips on how to best utilize StarOffice in a workgroup or network environment, including making the most of time and document management features such as StarSchedule and revision marks in documents.

Chapter 29, "Communicating with StarMail and StarDiscussion," tells you all about using StarOffice's email and newsgroup modules, including how to create email mail merges, handle attachments, and manage mail and news effectively.

PART VII: WORKING WITH DATABASES—STARBASE

Part VII, "Working with Databases—StarBase," introduces you to one of StarOffice's newer modules, the StarBase relational database.

Chapter 30, "Working with Databases in StarBase," explains StarBase's central role as integrated data manager in StarOffice and your database import and export options. It also introduces you to the four types of StarBase objects and gives a brief tour of their tools and menus.

Chapter 31, "Creating Stand-Alone Database Tables," takes you through the steps of creating flat list database tables with both the AutoPilot and from scratch, introducing you to some important database design issues along the way.

Chapter 32, ,"Creating Tables with Relations," takes off from Chapter 31 to introduce basic relational database concepts, including primary keys and data normalization, and discuss creating relational tables in the native StarBase format (available only on the Win32 platform).

Chapter 33, "Working with Data in Tables," discusses not only entering and editing data in StarBase tables, but more importantly how to get that data where you want it in your StarOffice text and spreadsheet documents.

Chapter 34, "Creating Forms for Easy Data Entry," shows you how to create queries with the AutoPilot as well as modify them afterwards, and touches upon StarBase's implementation of SQL (Structured Query Language), a computer language used to query external data sources.

Chapter 35, Getting Answers with Queries and Fields," introduces you to StarOffice's form building tools and explains how to create new forms in StarBase.

Chapter 36, "Creating and Printing Reports," demonstrates how to generate database reports in StarBase using the AutoPilot. It also discusses the attractive alternative of creating reports and report templates by importing StarBase data and fields into ordinary StarOffice documents.

PART VIII: AUTOMATING YOUR WORK—STARBASIC

Part VIII, "Automating Your Work—StarBasic," introduces you to StarOffice's macro and programming language, StarBasic, and shows you how you can create your own macros, organize a library of programs, and customize your desktop by using the macros and commands already included with the program.

Chapter 37, "Familiarizing Yourself with StarBasic," introduces you to StarBasic and StarOne, its cousin, and plunges you into creating and editing macros to automate your work. It also explains the StarOffice object hierarchy of macros, modules, and libraries and offers tips for organizing your StarBasic macros and programs.

Chapter 38, "Understanding StarBasic Structures and Statements," takes you more deeply into StarBasic's programming statements and structures. The chapter is packed with detailed examples of code that you can enter for yourself.

Chapter 39, "Programming with StarBasic," discusses programming with StarOffice objects, using StarWriter and StarCalc as examples. It also explains how to assign macros to events and takes you through creating an entire application in StarBasic—creating a custom dialog box as an alternative to StarWriter's AutoComplete feature.

APPENDIXES

The appendixes offer a potpourri of useful information to help you get StarOffice up and running and put it to work for you.

Appendix A, "Installing StarOffice," goes over the basics of installing StarOffice on both single user and network systems, and explains the StarDivision registration process, which must be successfully completed for the program to function past its 30-day trial period.

Appendix B, "File Formats and Extensions," lists all the file types StarOffice imports and exports, as well as all the file extensions of native StarOffice file formats.

Appendix C, "StarOffice Program Directories and Files," gives a selected list of program files, their locations, and tips about which files you might edit to directly manage aspects of your StarOffice environment.

Appendix D, "Default Keyboard Shortcuts," lists the default keyboard shortcut assignments for each program module.

Appendix E, "StarBasic Error Codes," provides a complete list of undocumented error codes in StarBasic.

CONVENTIONS USED IN THIS BOOK

StarOffice enables you to use both the keyboard and the mouse to select menu and dialog items: you can press the Alt key plus letter your keyboard to open menus and menu items, or you can open a menu and select an item by clicking it with the mouse. A typical command sequence may read: Select File, Open, or press Ctrl+O.

This book assumes that your mouse is set for right-handed operation. You use the left mouse button for clicking toolbar buttons, menus, and dialog options. You use the right mouse button for bringing up shortcut menus. Unless otherwise noted, click means clicking the left mouse button, and right-click refers to using the right mouse button.

Note that your screen may appear slightly different from the examples in this book. StarOffice gives you numerous ways of customizing and changing the look of your desktop and interface. Although we've tried to keep StarOffice's default settings as much as possible, there may be discrepancies between what you see on your screen and what you see in the screen shot—nothing to worry about, though.

This book also uses several eye-catching icons that you ought to familiarize yourself with:

Note

This icon highlights a special point of interest about the current topic

Tip #1001 from
Michael & Sarah

This icon helps you work smarter and faster by pointing out killer techniques or shortcuts.

Caution

Sometimes it's best to be careful. This icon alerts you to those instances.

→ This icon sends you to other places in the book for more information on a current term or topic.

Note

These icons highlight platform-specific issues. For the most part, StarOffice works the same across platforms. These icons highlight the few occasions where something on one platform may not work, or may work a bit differently, on another.

 StarOffice comes with numerous toolbars and buttons that you can click to execute a command. This book uses button icons in the margins, indicating which button to click to execute the currently discussed task.

INTRODUCING STAROFFICE

CHAPTER

1

A STAR IS BORN

In this chapter

applications, plus an integrated FTP client. It also manages to unite all functions for working with text, graphics, spreadsheets, or databases into one integrated work environment. With optional add-ons, you can connect a PalmPilot and Dragon NaturallySpeaking software. And when you familiarize yourself with the application's programming and macro language, StarBasic, you'll discover that there's virtually nothing that you can do in other Office suites that StarOffice can't do at least as well if not better—with the exception of handling fully relational databases across all platforms. (Relations are implemented only on the Win32 platform.)

StarOffice has been designed with its own internal implementation of object linking and embedding (OLE), which allows information to be carried seamlessly from one application to another—even to store that information in an area where any StarOffice application can grab it at any time. If necessary, you can have your spreadsheets transparently dump their data into your text documents without having to switch programs, or you can embed a chart into a spreadsheet and have it update its columns whenever you edit the tabular data, to name but a few options.

WHAT'S INCLUDED IN STAROFFICE?

Because appearance matters a great deal, often the first thing people notice about any program is how it looks—the user interface. StarOffice gives you complete control over your user interface. Most of StarOffice's frames and toolbars can be "torn off" and placed or docked anywhere within the master frame. If you like, you can also switch off everything and maximize your workspace to the hilt.

When you start StarOffice, you'll find that working with the interface is not dissimilar to working on a Windows 95 machine. The StarOffice shell is similar in form and function to Windows 95's Explorer. And the integration between the different StarOffice "modules" is very well implemented to say the least.

The *StarDesktop* is a major factor in the design of this Office suite. It has its own icons, folders, and directory tree, and it ensures consistency across platforms. When you open a document in StarOffice, it appears in its own private taskbar, which resembles the Windows taskbar, including a Start button and system tray. Although you cannot detach a document window and have it float outside the StarOffice desktop, you can choose whether you want to run StarOffice as an integrated desktop. If not, StarOffice floats on your desktop like any other Windows application. If you're not used to the Windows paradigm, you might find working in StarOffice a bit confusing at first. However, after you orient yourself in "StarSpace" and learn to navigate the desktop, you will find that your workflow and speed improve tremendously. StarOffice's navigation is simplified through the Beamer and Explorer—frames that you can toggle on and off and which show directory structures and directory contents. These features are useful when you want to drag and drop files or links to files in other places.

The *Explorer*, found on the left-hand side of your application window, enables you to organize your work and your work's peripherals (including clip art, images, sounds, and so on) in such a way that you can easily access them without leaving your document. You can assign it to link to anywhere you like. You can also create folders that link to other areas on your system or network. For example, you could conceivably create a new folder called apps in the Explorer, link it to your application directory on the hard drive, and then use StarOffice like a program-launching shell in conjunction with the Beamer.

The oddly named *Beamer* serves as your center for importing data. You can open tables and queries in the Beamer, and you can drag and drop data, merge fields, and form controls into open documents. No complicated dialog boxes, no searching through menus for the right command! You can also insert data with database fields. You can consolidate and copy tables through drag and drop in the Explorer and on the desktop. The Beamer is located at the top of your application window. If the Explorer is set to Hierarchical view, it can display the contents of whatever Explorer folder you have selected in the open Beamer.

The Explorer and the Beamer, when used together, enable you to quickly assemble and reuse pieces of documents over and over again. Not surprisingly, the Explorer and the Beamer are fairly consistent StarOffice features that you can toggle on or off at your whim, regardless of what kind of document you are working in at the time.

Each StarOffice component has all the features you would expect from a program of its type, plus a lot more:

- **StarDesktop** is the center of your work in StarOffice. Together with the Explorer and the Beamer, it allows access to all available program and system resources. In addition to several features that help with your daily work in StarOffice, StarOffice 5.1 offers you extra highlights for working in utmost comfort. Tapping into various configuration options, users can easily create their own personalized work environment.

- **StarWriter** is a powerful word processor that comes with a host of features, including numerous styles, autoformatting capabilities, a spelling checker with multilingual and custom user dictionaries, and (for an Office suite) a superb capability for handling multiple formats in the same document, complex multichapter documents, and booklet-style layouts. If you acquired the Personal Edition Deluxe, this module can open and save even more files and documents created in Microsoft Office, WordPerfect, Lotus 1-2-3, and AmiPro. The module also doubles as a Web browser, which enables you to edit both Hypertext Markup Language (HTML) source code and Web pages in WYSIWYG (What You See Is What You Get) format with all the advantages of a word processor. As a browser, StarWriter supports Cascading Style Sheets, frames (even when editing), Java, JavaScript, and proprietary Netscape Navigator and Internet Explorer HTML features and plug-ins.

- **StarCalc** looks and works very much like Microsoft Excel. All the features are there, including macros (not Visual Basic for Applications, though), advanced formula construction, Microsoft Excel 5 and 95, Lotus, and dBASE compatibility. StarCalc also enables you to create lists or clearly present your data and create impressive 3D charts, and an easy-to-use scenario manager helps analyze data according to various factors. Plus the module is fit for the new millennium, with four-digit data handling and complete Y2K compliance. It also handles Euro conversions with typical European flair.

- **StarImpress** is Star Division's answer to Microsoft's PowerPoint. It imports PowerPoint files reasonably well and includes vector graphic and special effects tools that enable you to create impressive presentations and object animation, as well as import documents and objects from other StarOffice applications. Graphic tools include flowchart-style shapes, and a wizard walks you through the process of creating a Web-based slide show. You can save your presentation in HTML format, allowing you to easily create a copy for a World Wide Web home page. Each slide of your presentation will be saved as a picture on an HTML page (so any multimedia or animation your presentation may have had will not be kept in the transfer), and an index page will automatically be created, allowing Web users to easily access all of your presentation's slides. Just upload the converted HTML to a Web site, and you're ready to go.

- **StarDraw** has the power of a vector graphics program that enables you to create a wide range of 3D graphics and Bézier curves very quickly (in fact, its functionality might be compared to CorelDRAW). Using StarDraw, you can create drawings of varying degrees of complexity. You can add color, text or textures to your shapes and 3D objects, create buttons and icons for your Web pages, or design a multipage interactive document. You can create organizational charts and technical drawings. In general, every object you create in StarDraw can be inserted into any other StarOffice document as a graphic object. And since StarDraw is an OLE-compliant application, you can use OLE to move images between Draw and other StarOffice modules. In short, StarDraw can enhance your creative freedom. Like the rest of StarOffice, StarDraw is fully integrated into the package as a whole and able to import some legacy graphics formats.

- **StarImage** is a graphics utility similar in scope to Paint Shop Pro with the capability to transform, filter, and otherwise perform basic image editing tasks. It includes many conversion and manipulation functions, including bitmap tools to control brightness, contrast, and other image attributes; it also enables you to work directly on the image in numerous image formats, including BMP, JPEG, GIF, TIF, XBM, EPS, and PNG. As is the case with the other StarOffice modules, StarImage is fully tied into the rest of the suite and can import some legacy image formats. It's also quite fast and has several handy effects and filters.

- **StarChart** is an efficient applet for chart creation. Using StarDraw, you can create and import charts of any size into your text, table, drawing, and presentation documents. StarDraw renders charts in 3D format, and generates simple pie, bar, and line diagrams. If you want to present complex data in even more visually impressive ways, use StarDraw.

- **StarBase** is StarOffice's built-in data manager. It's been considerably improved in version 5.1 with a switch to the new Oterro database engine made by rbase. In addition, many bugs have been fixed, and ODBC and JDBC support have been improved on both Windows and Linux platforms. If you want, you can create relational databases in the native StarBase format on the Win32 platform. However, StarBase is not intended to be a fully robust relational database management system (RDBMS), so you must take off your Microsoft Access glasses when you look at StarBase's features! As a data manager, StarBase enables you to create mail merges and import data into your StarWriter and StarCalc documents in a snap. The built-in Address Book is a StarBase database (in dBASE format), so playing around with the Address Book is a great way to learn StarBase's tricks. You can create and import tables in dBASE format; import data in text format; and connect to ODBC, JDBC, Oracle, and DB2 client/server databases. If you have the Microsoft Jet Engine and DAO installed, you can import Microsoft Access 97 databases as well.

- **StarMail** and **StarDiscussion** are the suites' email and news clients, respectively. Both modules are totally integrated into the StarDesktop. With release 5.1, these email and news functions have been improved and extended, with *security*, *comfort*, and *reliability* being the development watchwords. No other office suite offers you comparable ease of email use or flexibility in addressing, storing, and exporting email and news postings.

- **StarSchedule** is a robust scheduling and task management tool that you can use alone or as part of a workgroup environment. StarSchedule does an excellent job of keeping track of events and to-do lists, enabling you to combine both, together with your database Address Book, into a single screen. With StarSchedule, you can define a one-day or recurring event, check your free time and appointments, or update your to-do lists. In addition, it features a reminder system that not only supports the usual "pop-up" dialog alerts (with or without sound), but also sends email reminders to yourself at a prescribed time (up to two days before an appointment or event)—a welcome feature when you're on the road or dividing your time between two or more computers. Naturally, you can also directly synchronize data with hand-held digital assistants such as the 3Com/U.S. Robotics PalmPilot.

- **StarMath** is a powerful and user-friendly formula editor that enables WYSIWYG editing and comes with numerous symbol sets and operators.

WHAT'S NEW IN STAROFFICE 5.1

Committed StarOffice fans and the ABM (Anyone But Microsoft) crowd will find lots to like in the latest version of the award-winning software, and newcomers to the StarOffice world will find much to like as well. Compatibility and efficiency were Star Division's major goals for this release. In StarOffice 5.1, for example, you can open and save in earlier StarOffice file formats. This version also offers the following new conveniences:

- New and more efficient AutoPilot wizards—including an Internet Setup Wizard (Windows only), a Microsoft Import Wizard for documents and templates, and an HTML Export Wizard for presentations and graphics—make it a breeze to get online quickly and without hazzle or create professional-looking documents.

- Version 5.1 provides (near) seamless collaboration for Microsoft Office users, not only with document import and export, but also with templates.

- The option to integrate external browsers rather than use the built-in StarOffice browser enables you to surf the Internet with the most up-to-date technology. StarOffice 5.1 supports MS Internet Explorer 4.0 and 5.0. Netscape Navigator integration is planned in the near future.

- Perfect interaction with the operating system enables you to import existing bookmarks into your StarOffice work environment, as well as define the program's email client and news reader as default applications for mail and news.

- Version 5.1 comes with completely revamped Open and Save As dialog boxes. The focus has been on optimizing and improving the navigational and file management options. You can now access directories and files more quickly and with greater focus than ever before.

- The new Explorer provides single-click support and more organized, easier, and quicker access to files, functions, and objects.

- The improved uniform approach to working with documents of any kind makes working in StarOffice more intuitive.

- The StarOffice help system, including the Help Agent and Extended Tips feature, guides you step by step through your work process so that you can quickly reach any goal with ease.

- Efficient tools to convert bitmapped images to vector graphics or to 3D objects give you creative freedom and variable design options.

- New effective 3D diagrams and descriptive share charts give you the option to visualize your data even more impressively.

- Version 5.1 provides improved security for your personal mail with standard PGP encryption support (Windows only).

- This version provides for individual configuration in a matter of seconds.

- The advanced groupware functions make it easy to work in a team environment, share documents and data, and coordinate events and tasks among network users.

Other improvements include an enhanced database, the completely revised Formula Editor, and the substantially enhanced performance when printing graphics.

ADVANTAGES OF USING STAROFFICE

StarOffice was designed from scratch to be ported across many platforms and to solve the problem of different user interface "experiences" at the same time. As a result, it feels like a window manager within a window manager. It has its own desktop, scripting language, file management system, and taskbar, and it comes with a slick-looking interface that is more than just skin deep. You'll enjoy many benefits when working with StarOffice.

MICROSOFT OFFICE-COMPATIBLE

You can import existing Microsoft Office documents and templates to create spreadsheets, presentations, and documents in StarOffice; then you can save all your data in Microsoft (as well as other) formats or as HTML files to post on Web servers. Although it is not 100 percent perfect, compatibility between StarOffice and Microsoft Office is often better than compatibility between different versions of Microsoft Office. (In general, it's impossible to create 100 percent working import/export filters since different Office suites are using different approaches. In our humble opinion, however, StarOffice provides the best Microsoft filters available.)

SEAMLESSLY INTEGRATED WORK ENVIRONMENT

StarOffice is the first Office package to unite all functions for working with text, graphics, spreadsheets, slides, mathematical formulas, and databases into one common, visually slick user interface. The modules that make up StarOffice have standardized, context-sensitive toolbars and menus and consistent commands and dialog boxes. After you learn one application, you can easily familiarize yourself with the others. Best of all, with StarOffice you no longer have to start several applications while working on a project. The suite does everything in one place. If you have worked in Office suites like Microsoft Office, for example, you certainly have experienced the frustration of working in one application and then having to find another application, clicking on its icon or menu entry, and waiting for it to start. With StarOffice, you don't need to wait. Everything is in one single application, which represents StarOffice itself. You can simply start with one project (or document) and have StarOffice put the items and commands you need on your desktop automatically when you need them.

WEB AWARE

StarOffice is not only a fully integrated Office suite, but it is also essentially an Internet application. Many aspects of the product make access and communication across the Internet almost invisible. The function bar at the top of the screen features browser controls that enable you to browse both the Web and your desktop and files. In the adjacent URL text box, you can type an Internet address or the location and name of a locally stored file. The path to a file you are working on is accessed as if you were on the Internet. Local files are accessed using the FILE: protocol, whereas documents stored on Internet servers can be accessed with the FTP and HTTP protocols, for example. The history list of recently opened documents mixes both the Web pages you've visited next to your spreadsheets, letters, and memos. From StarOffice's point of view, the difference between a file on your own hard drive and a file on a server somewhere on the Internet is slim.

In addition, you can easily select text and then add a hyperlink to the text by using the hyperlink bar, which also doubles as a gateway to your favorite Web search engines. The product also recognizes references to objects on the Internet, such as URLs or email addresses. When you click on an address, StarMail is launched. Email is fully integrated, so you can create mass emailings with mail merge in a few easy steps.

One of the suite's neatest tricks is its capability to open and publish documents directly to and from Internet FTP and HTTP servers. Star Division supports industry standard technologies such as Internet protocols and services and is open for established industry standards. In general, if HTML is your bag, StarOffice definitely takes the gold. Its HTML integration is unsurpassed, and its image manipulation and creation capabilities will no doubt come in handy when you're doing any serious Web publishing. Last, but not least, the built-in browser is almost on par with Netscape Navigator and Microsoft Internet Explorer 4; it supports Java, JavaScript, plug-ins, frames, and blinking text and is integrated with StarWriter's impressive HTML support.

Note

In its current incarnation, StarOffice's browser is still a little slow compared to other commercial browsers.

RESOURCE EFFICIENT

Aside from the convenience and time you save by working in an integrated environment, you also can save system resources with StarOffice's single-user interface—provided you're not working on an old PC and attempt to start other programs from StarOffice, in which case the integrated desktop is a speed and resource killer.

GROUPWARE ENABLED

All major modules in StarOffice include both email and groupware integration, allowing you to send your presentations easily to any person or workgroup. StarOffice also has excellent multiaccount email features built in and comes with a useful news reader. The program also reveals its European heritage (the parent company is German) with its multilingual spelling checker and strong support for international keyboards and characters. The StarOffice Server extends StarOffice into a full-blown network application. It is perfectly suited for those who want to take full advantage of network possibilities, regardless of whether you work with PCs, NCs, or heterogeneous systems.

COST EFFICIENT AND AFFORDABLE

Migrating to StarOffice involves minimal cost for personal and business users thanks to Star Division's attractive license offers. Because StarOffice can be used on various operating systems, and because it can quickly exchange documents in all important formats, including Microsoft formats, migration to StarOffice reduces cost of ownership, offering enormous advantages for both business and private use.

REDUCED COST OF OWNERSHIP

Perfectly aware that businesses and individuals have made investments in other Office suites, Star Division is working to reduce total cost of ownership of its Office suite through revolutionary licensing models. For example, private users can download a fully functional StarOffice Personal Edition for free from the Star Division Web site at www.stardivision.com. For the educational market, Star Division offers two licenses

(K-12 and Campus) at an affordable price, which also entitles registered users worldwide to free updates and free upgrades for future versions. For businesses and corporations, StarOffice offers a choice of three site licenses (Small Business, Business, and Enterprise). In addition, Star Division is expanding its support and service network to solidify its market position as the leading office solution provider. For the German market, it is already offering consulting services and the new StarOffice Certified User Program (CUP); similar plans are in the works for the international market.

EASY CUSTOMIZATION

StarOffice is easily one of the most customizable programs available. Each application within StarOffice has its own set of tools and customization features, allowing you to create a working environment best suited for your situation. For example, each application comes with its own set of toolbars. These toolbars are tailored to the kind of work you do. StarWriter, for example, loads toolbars focusing on formatting documents if you use a text document template, but it loads toolbars focusing on Web design if you use an HTML template.

In addition, you can easily show or hide the icons associated with a toolbar function (via the toolbar's configuration and context menus), edit the menu items, assign keyboard shortcuts to your favorite commands, and even save entire configuration schemes so that different users can share the same computer without one of them having to compromise his or her preferred working style. (By the way, the toolbar icons are actually 16∞15 bitmaps, stored in the Office51\config\symbol directory, so you can stick your own bitmaps there and use them in your menu bars.) In addition, you can automate your workflow by creating macros with StarBasic.

DISADVANTAGES OF USING STAROFFICE

Now the bad news. Despite all StarOffice's features, some components of the program are not yet as powerful as those of its competitors—first and foremost Microsoft Office and Corel's Office suite—which started out as separately marketed programs long before the idea of an Office suite came along. By the way, this factor may also prevent those established suites from integrating their components together in StarOffice-fashion as easily as StarDivision has. So there is a trade-off. For example, StarWriter comes with a solid spellchecking program but does not include a grammar checker, and its revision marks feature is somewhat temperamental and incompatible with Microsoft's or Corel's. Also, if one application crashes the whole suite is off, and you typically have to reboot to be able start the suite again. In its favor, however, one has to commend the suite's ability to restore documents lost by a crash—it's quite good.

As of this writing, the documentation is still undergoing translation into English, so the online help system is still under construction (to say the least), and what little there is could benefit from a better localization job. However, the Tool Tips and Extended Tips that guide you through the various buttons and their functions don't leave you totally stranded. Besides, you also have this book to nudge you on.

Furthermore, many users are disappointed by the lack of a distinct database. However, as mentioned earlier, StarBase is not intended to be a fully robust relational database management system (RDBMS). Instead, it's meant to be used as a data manager that enables you to create mail merges and import data into your StarWriter and StarCalc documents in a snap, as well as filter and query Oracle, SQL, and other huge databases. And although Linux users are generally delighted to have such a powerful suite, many among them have repeatedly requested a native LaserJet driver instead of StarOffice's default PostScript driver. Under Windows 95/98 or Windows NT, StarOffice uses the standard Windows printer drivers.

Also, although StarOffice does a reasonably good job of importing documents, the Import/Export functions can never be 100 percent perfect for all the more complex and obscure features of Microsoft Office, for example. Microsoft constantly changes them to prevent compatibility and to force upgrades. (From that perspective, StarOffice is often more compatible with Microsoft Office than Microsoft Office is among its different versions.)

Despite these shortcomings, the bottom line is that if you're looking for a single Office suite that will run natively on most major platform and tie the entire company and all its divisions together, this is the one. If you're just looking for a great Office suite and don't want to base your operating system choice on what kind of applications you want to run, this is the one. Also, the suite supports most, if not every, major language straight out of the box, so it's perfect for a company dealing with international offices or for anyone who does business internationally (and StarOffice does run quite nicely on a laptop). And by the end of the day, StarOffice is much more intuitive to use than its competitors, which is mainly due to the fact that the tools you need aren't hidden in out-of-the-way menus that you stumble on by chance or luck.

StarOffice Versus Microsoft Office

StarOffice may emulate the look and feel of Microsoft Office and the Windows operating system; looks, however, can be deceiving. The following is a list of advantages that StarOffice has over the Microsoft Office suite:

- **Low cost**—StarOffice is significantly less expensive than Microsoft Office and provides a meaningful alternative to Microsoft's practice of increasing the cost of Office with every new release while tightening the licensing restrictions every year.

- **Easy migration**—Using the new StarOffice Microsoft Import Wizard, Windows users don't have to be afraid of losing their valuable data and templates. StarOffice can convert Microsoft Word, Excel, and PowerPoint documents and templates on-the-fly.

- **Better stability**—Even the Windows versions of StarOffice crash much less often than Microsoft Office. On other platforms, crashes are extremely rare. Greater stability means higher employee productivity.

- **Better performance**—StarOffice's high performance means you do not have to upgrade your computers to the level required for Microsoft Office 97 or Office 2000. Better performance means higher productivity—for you and your employees.

- **Freedom of choice**—You can use the best environment for your specific jobs yet maintain consistency. Microsoft Office is designed to prevent you from using non-Microsoft products or even older versions of Microsoft products, even when they may better suit your needs. StarOffice, by contrast, is available for Windows 95/98, Windows NT, OS/2, Linux, and a few other UNIX dialects. Thus, no matter which operating system you have, you can take advantage of its features.

- **Java-enabled**—The StarOffice Java client is compatible with the new component architectures and "thin clients," including network computers (NCs). With StarOne (programming API) and StarOffice Beans, you are ready for emerging low Total Cost of Ownership (TCO) environments. Microsoft Office, by contrast, is still mired in the monolithic programming practices of 1984—despite all the recent fanfare of an HTML companion file format and Web collaboration features of Office 2000.

CHAPTER 2

STEPPING INTO STAROFFICE

In this chapter

LAUNCHING STAROFFICE FOR THE FIRST TIME

Although the StarOffice installation process is very similar across platforms, how you launch StarOffice varies slightly according to your platform, operating system, and setup.

Note

Whatever your platform, you are greeted with an opening screen that prompts you to register the program, and to configure StarOffice for use with the Internet. For instructions on registering, see Appendix A, "Installing StarOffice." For instructions on stepping through the Internet setup process, **see** "Getting Online," **p. 85**. You may want to refer to "Getting Online" before you launch the program, as stepping through the Internet wizard requires you to have some information ready as well as make some decisions about how StarOffice will handle your Internet chores.

WINDOWS USERS

Open the Start Menu and click the StarOffice 5.1 icon. Alternatively, open the Office51 or StarOffice 5.1 folder and double-click the StarOffice 5.1 icon.

Your desktop will look similar to Figure 2.1.

Figure 2.1
The StarOffice desktop for Windows, with the integrated desktop turned on. The Help Agent Tips window automatically opens on the first launch, as does the Internet Setup wizard.

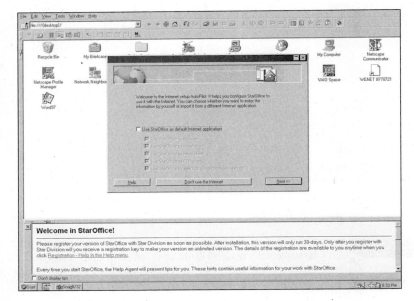

LINUX USERS

The steps for launching StarOffice vary depending on your system configuration. This book assumes that you are launching StarOffice from within the X Window System, with

StarOffice located in your usr directory. Note that you must be running X to launch StarOffice.

There are two common ways to launch StarOffice. Follow these steps to launch StarOffice directly from within the X Window prompt:

1. Make sure you are in your usr/Office51/bin directory. This is where the script for starting StarOffice is installed in the default installation.

2. Type ./soffice at the X Window prompt.

   If you want to launch StarOffice as a background application to the xterm from which you are launching the program, add a space and an ampersand (&) afterwards, like this: ./soffice &.

3. Press Enter.

PART

I

CH

2

Most modern Linux distributions automatically launch your window manager when you launch X. However, if your system is not configured in this way, you will need to launch your window manager from within X before you launch StarOffice. To launch your window manager (in this case, fvwm) first, and then launch StarOffice from the window manager desktop, follow these steps:

1. Type fvwm at the X Window prompt.

2. Press Enter.

3. Double-click the StarOffice icon on your fvwm desktop; or, if you do not see a StarOffice icon, open a new shell, navigate to your /usr/Office51/bin directory, type ./soffice, and press Enter.

Note that it takes a minute or longer to launch StarOffice for the first time, as it runs through its initialization protocol.

Your desktop will look similar to the Windows version desktop shown in Figure 2.1. However, special to the Linux version, a Printer setup wizard is provided, which can be launched by double-clicking its icon on the desktop. (Note that StarOffice supports only PostScript printers on Linux; if you have a non-PostScript printer, you'll need to use a translation program like Ghostscript.)

Note

Throughout this book, all illustrations and examples for Linux are for StarOffice run in X Window, using fvwm as the window manager, under the Red Hat implementation. For more information, see Appendix A.

Don't worry if the opening screen for your operating system doesn't look exactly like the one shown here. The look of your desktop depends on which edition of StarOffice you have and how your system has been configured.

New to version 5.1, you're greeted by an Internet setup wizard that considerably simplifies your setup process. If you currently use Netscape Communicator and/or MS Internet Explorer and MS Outlook Express for email and browsing, you'll have the option of just importing your inbox and browser settings from your program of choice. You can also choose to set StarOffice to handle any or all of your Internet chores by default (which include Web browsing, email and news accounts, and FTP); or, you can continue to your existing programs from within StarOffice. The wizard also prompts you to enter your basic Internet account information.

While the wizard makes the process easy, there are some complex issues involved in choosing one option over another. If you are already familiar with StarOffice and how it handles Web browsing, mail, and news, you're likely familiar with the issues already and can easily follow the wizard. If you're new to StarOffice, we recommend that you refer to "Getting Online" in Chapter 3 before proceeding.

→ Getting online is covered in detail in "Getting Online," **p. 85**. For more information on troubleshooting installation and registration problems, **see** "Appendix A," **p. 1353**.

> **Note**
>
> If you choose to have another browser serve as your default, StarOffice will continue to greet you on startup with a screen that asks if you want to set StarOffice as your default browser. If this screen annoys you, uncheck the option Always Perform This Test at the Start of StarOffice, and it won't display any more.

You will also be prompted with a dialog that reminds you that your program will expire in 30 days and asks if you want to register now. If you choose Yes, a wizard will step you through the registration process. You can register online, by fax, or by mail. Your best choice is to register online, as your registration is then handled by an automated process which typically only takes a few minutes. If you've already completed the Internet wizard, you'll be all set to go. If you were unable to complete your Internet setup, you can defer registering for now. It's recommended that you print or fax your registration only if you will not be connected to the Internet at all.

If you choose No, you will continue to be prompted to register every time you start StarOffice. Note that if you don't successfully register the program within the 30-day period, your installed version of the program will expire and you will need to re-install the program from your CD or file.

> **Note**
>
> If you have problems opening the program and you installed it from an intranet or CD-ROM, run the Setup program from the StarOffice directory on the hard drive. Windows users should select Repair in the opening installation screen. Linux users should launch setup from the usr/bin directory using the -repair option, like this: ./startup -repair. If you downloaded StarOffice from the Internet and continue to have problems, you might need to download another copy.

WHAT HAPPENED TO MY DESKTOP?

For users who are familiar with other office suites, opening StarOffice for the first time can be startling. The program does not open to a blank document, spreadsheet, or drawing board, but to an integrated desktop that offers you a complete set of tools for creating and managing your work.

Under Windows, when the integrated desktop is on (as it is when you initially launch the program), StarOffice incorporates Windows menu items and elements of your Windows system. If you click the Start menu, for example, you'll see your familiar Windows Start menu of program selections.

Under Linux, how StarOffice behaves depends on the window manager you use and selections you made during installation. In the implementation used in this book, the fvwm menus are not incorporated into the StarOffice menus. They are hidden initially, but clicking the taskbar button that says fvwm makes the fvwm taskbar visible. Regardless of your window manager, though, StarOffice behaves strangely for a UNIX/Linux program: It does not allow you to drag windows outside of the StarOffice window. This is not a bug, it's a feature; it's part of Star Division Inc.'s efforts to maintain interface consistency across platforms.

Note

KDE menu integration is installed as an option by default. If KDE is already installed in your system, your KDE menus will be integrated automatically during installation. If you install KDE after installing StarOffice, you'll need to run the KDE setup separately from the `/usr/Office51/bin` directory. CDE menu integration is available as an option with custom installation. For more information, see Appendix A.

Some of the StarOffice tools are standard—such as Cut, Copy, and Paste functions—but others are unique to StarOffice. Understanding the desktop and its tools is the key to using StarOffice effectively.

Not all these tools are visible at one time. What you see on your screen and menus changes as you move between different kinds of tasks or select different kinds of objects on which to work.

Note

In some Linux configurations, the StarOffice screen may be too large to fit on a single desktop. You will need to resize your window to match your screen resolution. This can be done in the StarOffice desktop.

Regardless of your operating system, the StarOffice desktop is the control center of the StarOffice workspace—the equivalent of the bridge on a starship. Everything you need in StarOffice can be launched, opened, or located right here.

Note If you find it disorienting that StarOffice takes over your desktop, you can turn off the Integrated Desktop by clicking the Integrated Desktop command on the View menu (Ctrl+Shift+I). (When you have documents open, this command is also available under a different name, Desktop mode, on the Window menu.) StarOffice becomes a window on your system desktop and can be resized, moved, and reduced to a taskbar button just like any other window.

Note The StarOffice online Help uses Desktop mode and Integrated Desktop interchangeably. These are just different names for the same command (Ctrl+Shift+I).

UNDERSTANDING THE DESKTOP WORKSPACE

On first launch, the program automatically creates a default StarOffice desktop. Under Windows, this desktop incorporates the same program icons and documents as your Windows desktop. Note also that icons on your Windows Start menu show up in the StarOffice Start menu. Under Linux, if you have a desktop folder, it will incorporate this folder; otherwise, it will use the StarOffice desktop (/usr/Office51/Desktop) as your default desktop. It does not replicate your fvwm menus within itself.

Tip #1 from
Michael & Sarah
You can customize the Start menu by creating links to or copying items into the Office51\config\start directory.

The incorporation of your usual desktop icons on your StarOffice desktop makes access to other commonly used programs easy from within StarOffice.

Gaining access to these folders and programs is easy. If you double-click a folder, StarOffice opens a window on the desktop that displays the folder's contents. If you double-click a program icon, it runs as a window on top of the StarOffice desktop. You can change the contents of this desktop workspace and customize it in many ways. You can also select another folder to be the default desktop, or you can have multiple desktops. However, you must always have one designated default desktop. That desktop is always active while the program is running. You can think of this desktop as the root desktop.

→ For information on customizing your desktop and creating and working with multiple desktops, **see** "Managing Multiple Desktops," **p. 123**.

Figure 2.2
The initial StarOffice for Windows workspace, with the Integrated Desktop turned off. The StarOffice desktop is visible, but you might see your system desktop instead.

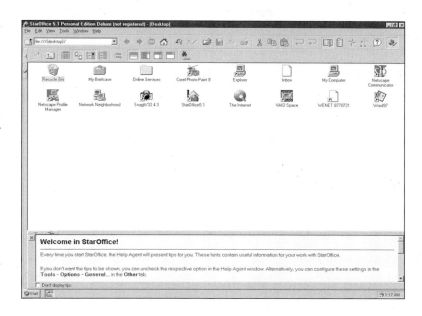

The contents of your desktop workspace change continually as you open and close documents and folders, and as each document or window you open is placed on top of your desktop workspace in succession. You can have as many as 255 documents open at one time; however, it is not recommended that you open this many because it slows your system performance quite a bit—unless you have mega megabytes of RAM!

However, your default desktop is always there.

You'll also notice that there are two icons, an arrow and a stickpin, on the upper left border of your window and on the upper border of the Help Agent at the bottom of your screen. These icons are controls for floating desktop windows. (Look ahead to 2.3 to see them identified.) Clicking the arrow hides or reveals the window—so if you want to clear your desktop, click the arrow to hide the Help Agent. Clicking the stickpin "pins" the window to the desktop. Otherwise, it floats on top and therefore may cover some of the desktop contents.

Clicking the arrow on the upper left reveals (or hides) the Explorer, a key component of the StarOffice desktop which is discussed in detail in "Using the Explorer and Beamer," later in this chapter.

ORIENTING YOURSELF IN STARSPACE

Now that you've stepped into StarOffice, the first step is to look around and familiarize yourself with the layout and basic functions of the desktop tools.

It's a good idea to read this section in front of the open program so that you can explore as you read along.

ELEMENTS OF THE STAROFFICE DESKTOP

Your desktop is made up of a number of elements. Figure 2.3 identifies some of these elements, each of which is discussed in more detail in this section.

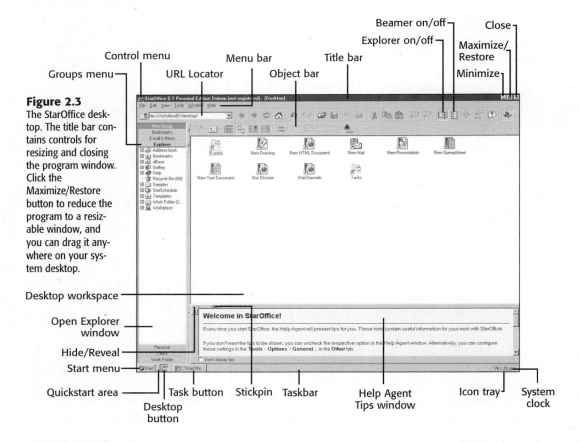

Figure 2.3
The StarOffice desktop. The title bar contains controls for resizing and closing the program window. Click the Maximize/Restore button to reduce the program to a resizable window, and you can drag it anywhere on your system desktop.

Note

The title bar, which is shown in Figure 2.3, is displayed only if the Integrated Desktop feature is turned off.

The title bar lists the version name and number of StarOffice. If you have not yet registered your program, the bar reads [not registered]. The title bar also lists the name of the currently active window on your desktop, as you can see in Figure 2.4. Figure 2.4 shows StarOffice with an open StarWriter document and the Integrated Desktop turned off, which means that the program control buttons (Minimize, Maximize/Restore, and Close) are visible in the upper-right corner. If the Integrated Desktop is turned on, you will not see these buttons for the StarOffice program, only for tasks, and you must use the Control or File menus to exit StarOffice.

Task Minimize,
Maximize/Restore,
and Close buttons

Figure 2.4
New documents or tasks open on your desktop in a task window, which can be resized, moved around within StarOffice, and combined with other tasks into one window. Click the task window Maximize/Restore button to make your task into a resizable floating task window.

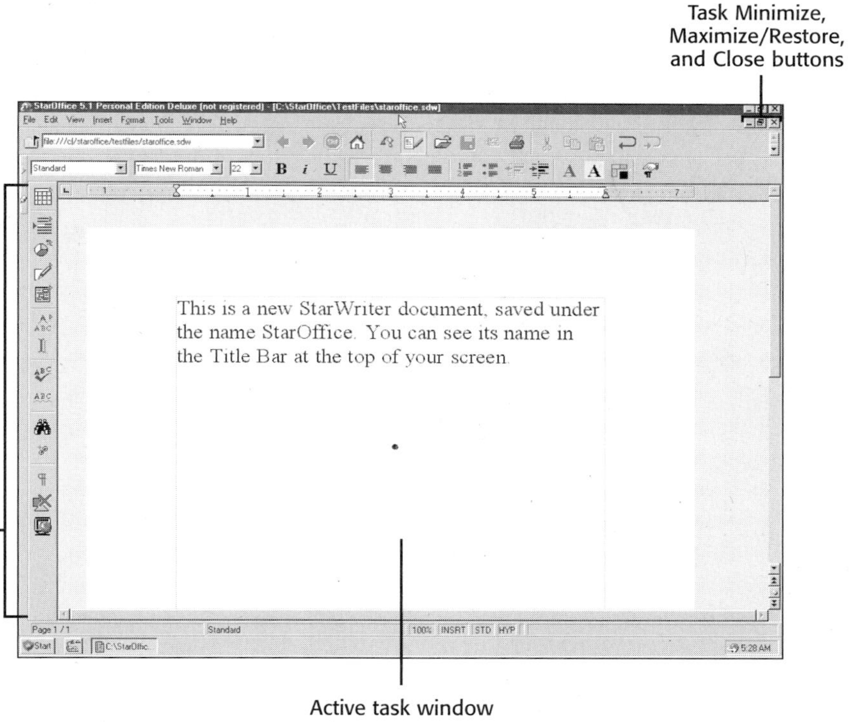

Main toolbar —

Active task window

As you open new documents, they are automatically assigned the default titles of Untitled1, Untitled2, and so on. This appears in the title bar until you first save a document, when your assigned filename appears. If you later assign a title to the document using the File menu Properties command, the title bar shows the assigned title rather than the filename.

You can manipulate your program and tasks windows in a variety of ways:

- In the right corner are buttons that enable you to control the size and location of the StarOffice window, and close the program.

- Clicking the Maximize/Restore button causes your StarOffice window to either fill your entire screen as a docked window (Maximize), or float as a window of the previously set size (Restore). When the program is in Restore mode and floats as a window, you can move and resize the window with your mouse.

■ To move the window, position your cursor on an empty spot anywhere on the desktop and drag the window to the desired location.

■ To resize the window, move your mouse to the borders of the window until your cursor changes appearance to a double-headed black arrow. Then, drag the side or corner to the desired size.

The program remembers only your most recent window size; therefore, as you resize the StarOffice window throughout a work session, the Restore button automatically adjusts to return you to the last window size you created.

■ Clicking the Minimize button reduces StarOffice to a button on your operating system desktop taskbar, and clicking the Close button closes StarOffice and returns you to your operating system.

■ In the left corner is an icon that represents the StarOffice program. Clicking it opens a menu that offers the same commands as the buttons.

THE MENU BAR

Just below the title bar is the main menu bar, which lists the titles of current desktop menus. The commands that are available on these menus vary, depending on the type of document or object you have open on your desktop. Some commands might be listed but grayed out, which indicates that they're not suitable for your task and are therefore temporarily unavailable.

When you have a window or document open on the desktop, the menu bar also displays Maximize/Restore, Minimize, and Close buttons as it does with the title bar. These buttons function in a similar manner, except that they affect open windows and documents rather than the StarOffice program window as a whole.

Tip #2 from
Michael & Sarah

Your default desktop has no Maximize, Minimize, and Close buttons because the desktop is not a task, and can therefore never be closed or resized independently of the program window.

The menus are logically organized to help you find commands quickly without memorizing their locations. Some of the more frequently used menu commands are also assigned to buttons on the function and object bars and to program context menus, which open with a right-click.

Tip #3 from
Michael & Sarah

To speed up your work, you can assign your own frequently used commands or macros to buttons on toolbars. For more information about customizing toolbars, see Chapter 3, "Getting Ready for Work."

To open a menu, click its name or press the Alt key in combination with the underlined letter in the menu name. To select a menu command, click it. Some commands also have keyboard shortcuts. These shortcuts are indicated to the right of the command.

→ For a list of the most commonly used keyboard shortcuts, **see** "Appendix E," **p. 1429**.

THE FILE MENU

The File menu, along with the desktop and Explorer (described later in this chapter), is the launching pad for your most common work tasks.

On the File menu, you can open new documents of all types with the New command, create documents with template wizards using AutoPilot, or open existing documents that are saved to files with the Open command. The File menu also contains all the basic commands for managing documents that you have open on your desktop, including saving, sending as email, and printing.

THE EDIT MENU

The Edit menu contains commands for deleting, changing, and moving data, as well as for inserting objects, images, and links. It also contains the very important Undo command (Ctrl+Z), which undoes your regrets and mistakes up to 20 steps back.

Tip #4 from Michael & Sarah	Change the default number of undo steps in the Tools, Options, General, Save dialog. You can set undo to any number from 0–100.

The Address Book command opens a dialog box that speeds the process of entering and finding contacts in your StarOffice Address Book database. The Address Book is a dBase III database that is fully integrated into the StarDesktop and helps automate common office tasks, such as creating form letters and mass emails.

→ For an introduction to working with the Address Book, including tips on importing an existing Address Book into StarOffice, **see** "Introducing the Address Book," **p. 180**.

Caution	If you alter the structure of the program's Address database, this dialog box no longer works with the address book.

→ For a complete visual presentation of the various StarOffice menus and submenus, **see** "Appendix D," **p. 1413**.

THE VIEW MENU

The View menu enables you to turn on and off the display of the Explorer, Beamer, and toolbars. You can also switch between a full screen view (which gives you an uncluttered desktop with no visible menus or toolbars) and a normal desktop view, and you can turn the Integrated Desktop on and off.

PART
I

CH
2

THE TOOLS MENU

The Tools menu contains commands for customizing the applications and tools on your desktop. The Macro and Configure commands enable you to create and edit macros and to associate macros and StarBasic modules with program elements. The Options command opens a master dialog box. On the left is a list of program functions and modules. Click the + sign to open a list of dialog boxes that enable you to set options related to the function or module. Click on a dialog box name to make the dialog box appear. Some of the options you can modify include your StarOffice Internet and browser settings, your default workspace look and feel, and defaults for your StarOffice module work environments.

→ For in-depth information about configuring your desktop and document defaults, **see** Chapter 3, **p. 75**.

→ For more information about working with macros in StarOffice, **see** Chapter 37, **p. 1239**.

THE WINDOW MENU

The Window menu contains basic commands for managing your desktop windows, as well as a dynamic list of currently open windows. One way to place a currently hidden, open window on top of the desktop is to click its name on this list. The window that is currently on top is identified with a bullet character.

THE HELP MENU

The Help menu contains commands that enable you to turn the Help Agent and help tips on and off, and to open the User's Guide. It also contains three other very important commands:

- **Registration**—Enables you to register your StarOffice program (see Figure 2.5)
- **StarChannels**—Takes you to the area of the StarDivision Web site where you can download program patches and updates
- **About StarOffice**—Contains information about the version of StarOffice you are running

If you change key parts of your user data, you must re-register the program or it will expire. See Appendix A for more information.

EXPLORING DESKTOP TOOLBARS

StarOffice also makes many commands immediately visible as tools on the toolbars that border your desktop. Some of these tools are shortcuts to commands that are found on the menus, but others are only found on the toolbars.

Figure 2.5
Choosing Registration from the Help menu launches a wizard to guide you through the registration process. After you've successfully registered, the Registration command is grayed out.

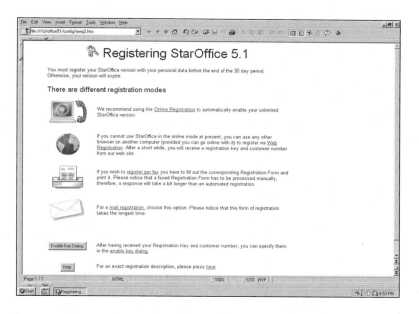

Tools are activated with a single-click. All toolbars can be made into floating toolbars by pressing Ctrl while double-clicking in an empty area of the toolbar. To reattach a toolbar, press Ctrl and double-click again in the same area. You can also press Ctrl and drag the toolbar toward the edge of the desktop at which you want to dock it. As you approach the desktop edge, the toolbar previews its docked size and shape in outline form. When you release the mouse button, it automatically attaches.

If you want to learn the names of tools, turn on Tips in the Help menu. When you move your mouse pointer over a tool, a tip pops up with its name. You can also right-click in any toolbar to open a toobar context menu. In turn, you can open a submenu that matches all the toolbar icons to their names.

THE MAIN TOOLBAR

The Main toolbar appears only when you have an open document on top of your desktop. This toolbar appears by default at the left of the workspace. Its contents change, depending on what you're working on, because each document type has its own tools.

Tip #5 from
Michael & Sarah

An extended-click on main toolbar buttons with a small green arrow on them opens tear-off floating toolbars that you can drag anywhere on your desktop.

There are also three general desktop toolbars that are always available:

- Function bar
- Object bar
- Hyperlink bar

THE FUNCTION BAR

By default, the function bar is always visible on program startup. To turn the function bar off or on, click the View, Toolbars, Function bar command (see Figure 2.6). When the bar is turned on, a check mark appears to the left of its name.

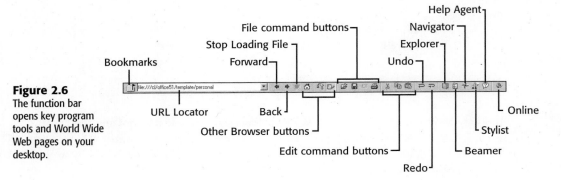

Figure 2.6
The function bar opens key program tools and World Wide Web pages on your desktop.

The function bar is the one toolbar with tools that remain constant across tasks and applications. Generally speaking, the function bar contains three types of commands:

- Commands that turn on and off the display of critical desktop components such as Explorer, Beamer, Help Agent, and Navigator
- Common editing and file commands such as saving, opening, printing, and sending email
- Browser functions that enable you to browse the Web from your desktop, including a URL Locator and Forward and Back buttons that enable you to scroll through recently opened documents, Web pages, and windows

> **Note**
>
> URL stands for *uniform resource locator*, and usually refers to a World Wide Web address. To visit a Web site, you need to know its URL, just as you need to know a store's street address. StarOffice uses *URL* more broadly to refer to any address on a computer, including local path names.

Tip #6 from
Michael & Sarah

For a detailed glossary of Internet terms, search in the Help Agent or the online Contents Index for `Terminology Descriptions: Internet Glossary`.

Tip #7 from
Michael & Sarah

If you've reduced StarOffice to a window, you might not have enough room to display all the function bar tools at one time. If this happens, a double arrow appears on the far right of the function bar (as in Figure 2.7). Click the black arrow head to make the missing part of the bar visible.

PART

1

CH

2

Figure 2.7
Reducing StarOffice to a window on your desktop reduces the visibility of tools, but they're still there. Here, clicking the arrow head on the function bar's double arrow reveals hidden tools, including the Explorer and Beamer.

THE URL LOCATOR, WEB BROWSING, AND LOCAL DRIVES

The URL Locator is the most visible sign of StarOffice's integration, not only with your operating system desktop, but also with the wider world of computers beyond your desktop. After you've configured StarOffice for Internet access, surfing the Web is as simple as typing a Web address in the locator and pressing Enter.

→ For information about setting up your Internet account from within StarOffice, **see** "Getting Online," **p. 85**.

However, the URL Locator is more than a Web browsing tool. StarOffice treats your local drives as part of an Internet or intranet network. It therefore refers to both local pathnames and Internet addresses (including FTP, Web, and email addresses) as URLs, and enables you to search for both using the URL Locator. The syntax for entering a local path is

`file:///c¦/[foldername]/[filename]`

For example, if you want to open a file on your desktop called `fundraising`, which is located on your C: drive in a folder called `volunteer`, you type the following in the URL Locator, and then press Enter:

`file:///c¦/volunteer/fundraising`

Tip #8 from
Michael & Sarah

The symbol that is used to separate the C from volunteer in this example is called a *pipe*, and it looks similar to a colon. Its location on keyboards varies, but it is usually on a key near the edge of the standard keyboard, and often on the same key as the backslash symbol.

THE OBJECT BAR

The object bar is also visible, by default, on startup. To turn it off and on, click the Toolbars, Object bar command on the View menu. When the bar is turned on, a check mark appears to the left of its menu name.

In general, the object bar contains commands that enable you to change and manipulate the object that is currently open on your desktop. The contents of the object bar vary a great deal depending on your current task. Figure 2.8 shows the desktop object bar, which you use to move around in directories, view files, and view and change file and folder properties.

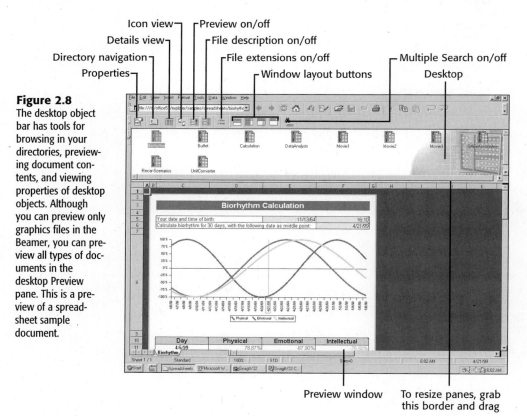

Icon view
Details view
Directory navigation
Properties

Preview on/off
File description on/off
File extensions on/off
Window layout buttons

Multiple Search on/off
Desktop

Figure 2.8
The desktop object bar has tools for browsing in your directories, previewing document contents, and viewing properties of desktop objects. Although you can preview only graphics files in the Beamer, you can preview all types of documents in the desktop Preview pane. This is a preview of a spreadsheet sample document.

Preview window

To resize panes, grab this border and drag

However, when a document is open, the object bar contains formatting tools that can change the look and layout of your text. When a spreadsheet is open, the object bar contains a formula entry box, the AutoSum tool, and the Sheet Navigation box.

This book follows StarOffice's own logic and discusses the object bar for each program module in the context of introducing program modules and explaining how to execute specific tasks. Therefore, this section introduces only the desktop object bar as it appears when you have a folder open on your desktop. The desktop object bar enables you to carry out basic desktop management tasks:

- On the far left (refer to Figure 2.8) is the Properties button, which opens the Properties dialog box for the selected object. Next are the Up One Directory button, for browsing, and the Originals button, which can help you locate the original source file of a link.

- The next buttons, Icon Display and Details Display, change the display of objects on your desktop. Their neighbors to the right turn on or off document previews and display of document properties, respectively. When document previews and document properties are turned on, additional window panes open on your desktop; you can resize these panes by grabbing their borders and dragging.

- To show file extensions when you are displaying objects as icons, click the button with an asterisk. This button is grayed out when list display is turned on because file extensions automatically display in List view.

- The next four buttons change the arrangement of your desktop's frames when you have document preview or document properties turned on.

- The last button on the right turns the Multiple Search feature on and off. Searching in StarOffice is described in detail in Chapter 5, "Managing Folders, Files, and Mail."

THE HYPERLINK BAR

The hyperlink bar is not visible at startup. To turn it on and off, click View, Toolbars, Hyperlink bar (see Figure 2.9).

Figure 2.9
The hyperlink bar can be turned on in any document; it helps create and keep track of hyperlinks, which are used in preparing documents that are to be used as Web pages.

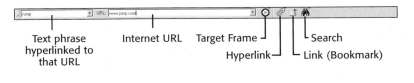

Text phrase hyperlinked to that URL · Internet URL · Target Frame · Hyperlink · Search · Link (Bookmark)

The hyperlink bar contains tools for quickly creating and navigating among hyperlinks in documents. Highlight text in your document, and type a URL in the URL Locator; your text is now hyperlinked to that address. If you press Enter, you instantly see the Web page on your desktop. The drop-down list on the left of the URL Locator lists the phrase that you've highlighted so that you can both keep track of the sites that are associated with your hyperlink words or phrases and jump around your document hyperlinks by clicking them on the list.

You can also drag and drop URLs from the URL Locator into your documents to create hyperlinks. (After dropping, you must press the spacebar or Enter before it will become a hyperlink.) You can also create bookmarks to Web sites or local paths by clicking the Bookmark tool. A bookmark for the URL displayed in the hyperlink bar is automatically created in the Explorer Bookmarks folder.

→ For more information about using the hyperlink bar when you are creating Web documents, **see** Part VI, "Spreading the Word—StarOffice on the Web and at Work," **p. 917**.

Note

Despite sharing its name with the Hyperlink toolbar Bookmark tool, the function bar Bookmark tool does not automatically create a bookmark. Instead, it enables you to drag and drop URLs into the Bookmarks folder or an open document.

Clicking the Binoculars icon on the end opens a list of all the Web search engines that are specified in the Tools, Options, Internet, Search tab; with a quick click, you can be sleuthing on the Web. On the bottom of the menu, click the Address Book or Bookmark name to drop a URL into the Address Book URL field or to create a new bookmark.

→ For information on changing the default menu list of search engines, **see** "Getting Online," **p. 85**.

Note

To get on the Web, you must first be connected to the Internet through a network or a dial-up connection.

USING THE MOUSE ON THE DESKTOP

Although many commands and tools are available through toolbars and the main menus, StarOffice makes maximum use of the mouse to put commands at your fingertips and make working intuitive.

CLICKS, DOUBLE-CLICKS, AND EXTENDED-CLICKS

Highlighting, selecting, dragging, and dropping all use mouse clicks and double-clicks in ways you're surely familiar with from other Windows or X Window programs. However, some functions in StarOffice are activated with the less familiar *extended-click*.

An extended-click is a single, long click with the left mouse button. A tool with extended-click response usually responds to a regular click as well—but it executes a different command.

Tip #9 from
Michael & Sarah
If you have trouble getting extended-clicks to work, try changing your mouse click speed.

For example, a click on the desktop function bar Back button takes you back to the document or Web page you previously opened from the URL Locator. However, an extended-click opens a submenu with a history list of the most recently entered filenames and URLs. Just click a path or URL in this list to return to the selected location.

The simplest way to learn where extended-clicks apply is to explore the desktop when Help, Extended Tips is turned on.

DRAGGING AND DROPPING

Often, the most efficient way to work in StarOffice is to drag and drop with your mouse. Not only can you copy and move data and objects this way, but you can also create links, insert objects, and insert data from databases into documents. Drag and drop works between documents as well as among documents, the Beamer, and the Explorer.

→ For more information on the Beamer and Explorer, **see** "Using the Explorer and Beamer," **p. 43**.

Some of the many ways in which you can use drag and drop are summarized in Table 2.1.

TABLE 2.1   SELECTED DRAG-AND-DROP FUNCTIONS IN STAROFFICE

Do this...	And the result is...
Drag file, folder, link, or email from one Explorer location to another.	Moves the selected object to the new location.
Ctrl+drag file, folder, link, or email from one Explorer location to another.	Copies the selected object to the selected location.
Ctrl+Shift+drag file, folder, link, or email from one Explorer location to another.	Creates a link between the object and the selected location.
Drag file or link from the Explorer into the desktop.	Creates a copy of the file or link into the current desktop directory and opens it on the desktop.
Drag text, spreadsheet, HTML document, or Web page file from the Beamer into an open document.	Creates a link to the file.

continues

TABLE 2.1   CONTINUED

Do this...	And the result is...
Drag a graphic or presentation filename from the Beamer into an open document.	Opens an Insert Slide, Objects dialog box. Objects you select are inserted as copies into the open document.
Drag an image file or formula from the Beamer into an open document or other desktop task window.	Opens the image file in StarImage or formula in StarMath.
Ctrl+Shift+drag an image file, presentation, or formula from the Beamer into an open document.	Creates a hyperlink or link to that object.
Drag a Gallery image, sound, or graphic from the Beamer into an open document.	Inserts a copy of the object into the open document.
Drag a URL address from the URL Locator into an open document.	Creates a hyperlink (an Internet address) or link (a local path) to that address.
Drag and drop an email account from the Explorer or an open task window into the desktop.	Opens your Inbox in a task window.
Drag and drop an entry from the Address Book into an open document.	Copies the data to the new location.
Drag or Ctrl+drag a table from one database to another.	Opens a Copy Table dialog box that enables you to copy the table definition and data or definition only, or to append the table.

The varieties of drag and drop are so great that the best way to learn is to try things and see what happens. If something unexpected happens, immediately invoke the Undo command (Ctrl+Z). The shape of the pointer also often gives it away—when you drag and see only a gray outline, the object is moved; when you see a gray outline with a plus (+) sign, the object is copied; and a gray outline with an arrow shows that a link will be created.

Tip #10 from
Michael & Sarah
Generally, drag-and-drop functions in StarOffice work the same as in the Windows Explorer.

If you want to know exactly what has happened after you've dragged and dropped something, open the Edit menu and look at the Undo command, which specifies the action.

Tip #11 from
Michael & Sarah
Want to see two tasks side by side? Combine them into one task window by dragging and dropping one task button on top of the other. To separate them again, drag the top Task button away.

Note

Although you can drag and drop between StarOffice and other applications, sometimes parts of the data or the object are missing, or system crashes occur. If you have problems, try opening your non-StarOffice files in StarOffice, dragging and dropping within StarOffice, and then reopening them in other applications as necessary.

RIGHT-CLICKS AND CONTEXT MENUS

Context menus contain most of the commands that are essential for managing your desktop. If you can't figure out how to do something in StarOffice, usually the best way to find out is to position your pointer where you want to be or to highlight the object with which you want to work, and then open the context menu by right-clicking.

Context menu commands are discussed throughout the book with the objects and tasks to which they are related. Check the Index to locate the discussion of a specific command. Also see Appendix D, "Default Keyboard Shortcuts," for illustrations of all the program context menus. Explorer context menus, which are crucial for creating and managing desktop objects (including StarBase databases), are discussed in the next section.

PART

I

CH

2

USING THE EXPLORER AND BEAMER

If your desktop is like the bridge of a spaceship, the Explorer is similar to the captain's chair, the seat from which you direct the operations, survey your universe, and begin new projects. The Beamer is your second mate—your assistant in carrying out a variety of important tasks. Although the program does not launch with the Explorer and Beamer visible on your desktop, they are integral parts of working in StarOffice. (The Explorer is open, but hidden on the left side.) You will probably frequently work with one or both of them open all the time.

Table 2.2 shows the various objects that you can find in the Explorer and briefly describes their function. Each is described in more detail later in this chapter.

TABLE 2.2   DEFAULT EXPLORER OBJECTS

Explorer Icon	Object Name and Function
Address book	The Address Book is a StarBase database you use as a contact manager.
Workplace	The Workplace displays your system's drives or volumes and directories. It also appears as a group.
Work Folder	The Workfolder is either a link to your system work folder or the Workfolder in the Office51/Explorer directory. It also appears as a group.

continues

TABLE 2.2 CONTINUED

Explorer Icon	Object Name and Function
Samples	The Samples folder contains subfolders and files with sample databases, drawings, formulas, presentations, spreadsheets, and text documents.
Bookmarks	The Bookmark folder contains hyperlinks to Internet sites. It also appears as a group.
Gallery	The Gallery contains clip art and sounds that you can insert in your documents.
Recycle Bin (15)	The Recycle Bin stores files deleted from within StarOffice until you empty it.
StarSchedule	StarSchedule is your personal appointment planner and calendar within StarOffice.
Help	Help contains links to sections of the online Help system, and a Help bookmarks folder so you can create your own links as you go along.

Table 2.3 shows the various objects you create and store in the Explorer via the Explorer context menu. These objects enable you to connect with external data sources like Internet accounts and databases.

TABLE 2.3 OBJECTS CREATED IN THE EXPLORER

Icon	Name and Function
	A POP3 mail account Inbox downloads email from POP3 servers.
	An IMAP mail account Inbox downloads email from IMAP servers.
	A VIM account downloads email from VIM intranet mail systems.
	Your Outbox stores all sent and unsent emails.
	A news account enables you to subscribe to and read Usenet news groups.
	An FTP account enables file exchange via the Internet.
	A Link enables you to jump to the folder or file you designate as its target from the Explorer.
	A StarBase database enables you to connect to external sources of data or to create your own dBaseIII and StarBase-format databases.

Icon	Name and Function
	A `Search folder` enables you to bring distant files and folders to your StarOffice desktop.
	A `Web subscription` enables you to receive messages when the contents of Web pages you designate change.
	The `Templates folder` contains StarOffice templates and any you create with the AutoPilot

The Explorer has been improved since version 5.0 and has a number of new features, most visibly, the capability to create *groups* that enable you to better organize your desktop. To recognize its new features, it's now called the extended Explorer. You now also can choose to display files in the Explorer (whereas in version 5, files displayed only in the Beamer) by selecting the Display Documents command on the Group context menu.

In addition, you can choose to display objects in the Explorer in one of three views: Hierarchical, Small Symbols, or Large Symbols. Objects in groups respond differently to your mouse actions when a group is set to Hierarchical view versus the two symbols view; some special functions are available only when a group is set to Hierarchical view. This section therefore focuses on discussing using the extended Explorer in Hierarchical view.

→ For more information on the effects of choosing different views of groups, **see** "Working with Groups in the Explorer," **p. 49**.

Note

To set the Explorer to hierarchical view, right-click the Explorer group title button and choose Hierarchical View from the context menu.

In the Hierarchical view, double-clicking an object in the Explorer opens it on your desktop. Clicking the plus sign to the left of an Explorer object shows you the contents of its subdirectories. If you open the Workplace icon at the bottom, you'll see a branching list of all your volumes and drives.

When your group is set to display on Hierarchical view, the Beamer displays the contents of most types of Explorer objects when you select and extended-click them. Displaying files in the Beamer gives you access to special drag-and-drop features. For example, when the Address Book is open in the Beamer, you can drag and drop Address Book entries or merge fields into an open document. Likewise, you can show the contents of any folder in the Explorer in the Beamer, double-click the files in the Beamer to open them, and drag and drop the contents of the Gallery theme into an open document.

Note

For the contents of an object to display, the Beamer must first be open before you extended-click the object in the Explorer.

Tip #12 from
Michael & Sarah

Display one folder's contents on your desktop and another in the Beamer, and you can easily copy files and create links with drag and drop.

The Explorer is your usual starting point for creating what you might think of as new interface objects—that is, objects that enable you to connect with and perhaps (if you choose) store some outside source of data and information. These include links to other directories, email account Inboxes, your email and news Outbox, StarBase databases (which are most frequently used to import data from external sources), and FTP accounts. (The Tasks group, StarOffice desktop, and File, New menu, on the other hand, are where you are more likely to start new tasks and documents.)

MANIPULATING THE EXPLORER AND BEAMER WINDOWS

When you first launch StarOffice 5.1, the Explorer is open but hidden on your desktop. Click the gray arrow on the left edge of your desktop to reveal it.

If the Explorer is off, you can open it by clicking its icon on the function bar, pressing Ctrl+Shift+E, or selecting Explorer from the View menu. Open the Beamer by clicking its icon on the function bar (to the right of the Explorer icon), pressing Ctrl+Shift+B, or selecting Beamer from the View menu. Your desktop will look similar to Figure 2.10.

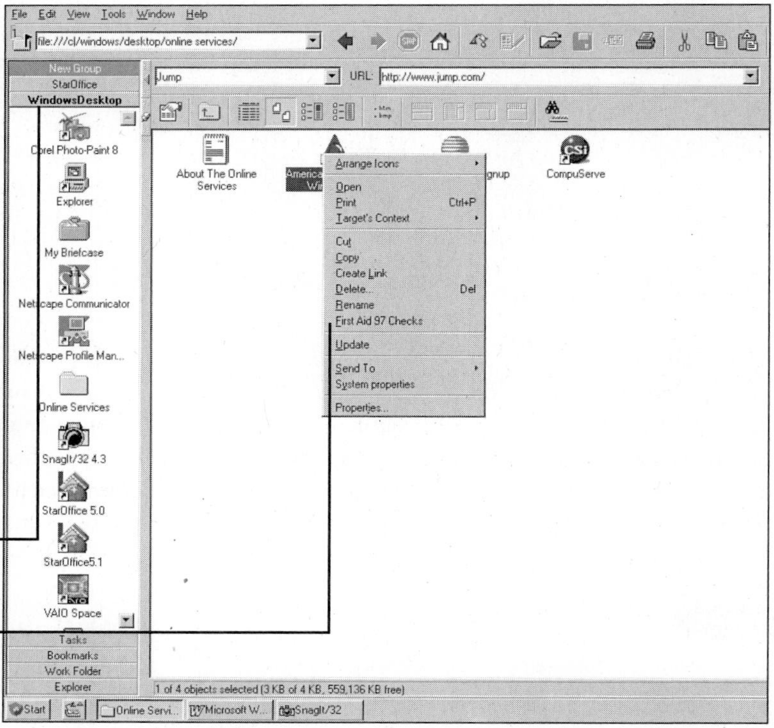

Figure 2.10
Open Explorer groups by clicking the title bar that displays the Group name. In the default Hierarchical layout, open Explorer objects by double-clicking them. You can select and right-click objects to open a context menu for managing them (either unopened in the Explorer, or opened on your desktop, as seen here).

Click here to open group.

Right-click to open context menu.

The Explorer and Beamer are both dockable floating windows. They open initially in a floating, docked state.

To fix them to your desktop, click the Stickpin icon. They will then automatically fit neatly beside your desktop workspace rather than floating over your open tasks.

Just as with the Explorer, you can alternately hide and reveal the Beamer by clicking the small arrow on its border.

To resize the Explorer, drag its right border; to resize the Beamer, drag its bottom border.

To undock a floating window, press Ctrl and double-click a blank area inside the window.

PART
I
CH
2

To dock a window again, press Ctrl while dragging the window by its title bar toward the edge of the desktop where you want to dock it. As you approach the edge, the outline of the window will change to preview its docked shape. When you see the outline, release the mouse button.

More information about working with dockable floating windows is given in the section "Other Floating and Dockable Windows" later in this chapter.

EXPLORER CONTEXT MENUS

From the Explorer, you can search for files and folders, move between StarOffice and your locally available drives, and manage objects with drag-and-drop features. Most importantly, you can create and manage most types of StarOffice objects—including databases, news, FTP and email accounts, folders, and links—using commands on the Explorer context menus. You can open a context menu by either right-clicking in a blank area or selecting an object and right-clicking. The commands that appear depend, to some extent, on the type of object (if any) you've selected, although some commands are common across object types. Figure 2.11 shows the context menu that opens when no objects are selected.

To create a new object, place your cursor in a blank area of the Explorer (or select the folder that you want the object to be placed in), right-click, and choose the New command. You'll see the submenu that appears in Figure 2.11.

To change an existing object's name or set rules on when and how it updates and displays on your desktop, select it and choose the Properties command.

Table 2.4 lists the Context menu commands that are specific to file management and desktop tasks. These commands appear for folders and links and may be found on the menus of other types of objects as well. Note that special StarOffice objects such as the Recycle Bin, Gallery, and Help have a different and limited set of context menu commands that relate to their special functions.

Note

The commands that appear also depend on the plug-ins that you have installed on your system.

Figure 2.11
The Explorer context menu is your starting point for creating email and news accounts, databases, folders, saved searches, and Web subscriptions. Some commands, like the Paint Shop Pro and Corel commands here, are for other programs on your system so what you see will depend on your system configuration.

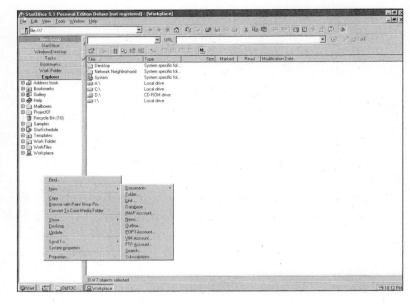

TABLE 2.4 BASIC DESKTOP CONTEXT MENU COMMANDS

Name of Command	Purpose
Open	Opens object's contents on your desktop.
Find	Constructs on-the-fly Boolean searches that can look anywhere on your system or network to retrieve objects to your desktop. (This command was called Search in version 5.0).
New	Creates new objects, including documents of all types (repeating the File, New commands), saved searches, and Internet newsgroup subscriptions.
Cut	Deletes object from Explorer and places it in general-purpose buffer or on the Clipboard.
Copy	Copies object into general-purpose buffer or Clipboard.
Create Link	Creates a link to the selected object (the target). The link can be cut and pasted or dragged and dropped elsewhere, or left in the Explorer.
Show	Sets how objects display in the Explorer.
Desktop	Designates a chosen location or folder as a desktop, or returns the object to ordinary status.
Update	Updates the contents of the selected object (if the Include in Update option of its Properties, Contents tab has been selected).
Synchronize	Synchronizes data in the cache with data on your local server (for use on networks).

Name of Command	Purpose
Send To	Sends active document as email or fax; directs file or folder to disk drive.
System Properties	Displays basic properties of the selected object, including folder name, location on your system, and folder or file attributes.
Properties	Displays and enables you to change a broad range of properties of the selected object (including some that appear in System Properties dialog box).

→ For a thorough discussion of the context menu Search, Show, Update, and Properties commands for folder and file management, **see** Chapter 5, "Managing Files, Folders, and Mail," **p. 191**.

→ For instructions for setting up email accounts in the Explorer, **see** "Creating Mailboxes," **p. 96**.

→ For a discussion of the context menu Desktop command, **see** "Managing Multiple Desktops," **p. 123**.

WORKING WITH GROUPS IN THE EXPLORER

New in 5.1 is the capability to create *groups* in the Explorer. In previous versions, the Explorer could get cluttered very quickly, especially if you clicked the Workplace icon to open your drives and volumes to manage your entire network or drive structure. By designating folders or drives that you frequently access as groups, you can easily open them with the click of a button while bringing into view only those objects you need at the moment.

The following groups are created automatically for you at first program launch:

- Tasks group, which repeats the selections of new tasks you can create with the File, New menu
- Workfolder group, whose contents will depend on your system configuration
- Email and News group that contains either new, empty StarOffice email inbox and news accounts, or your imported inbox and news accounts from another program
- Bookmarks folder, which contains either StarOffice default bookmarks or your bookmarks imported from another program

The best way to manage your work in StarOffice is to create a group in the Explorer for each of your current projects. Then, you can store all the documents and templates you need for a project in one place (whether as originals, copies, or links) and always have instant access.

Tip #13 from
Michael & Sarah

If you need to pull together documents from disparate locations to use in a project, create a saved search in the Explorer. A saved search enables you to create rules that search any volumes, drives, or directories you specify and retrieve items based on criteria you set. For more information on creating saved searches, see "Retrieving Distant Files and Folders," in Chapter 5.

Note that while you can technically create a group with special Explorer objects, such as the Gallery, and the Recycle Bin, they won't display any individual files in their group window. You can display the objects' contents only from the Explorer group.

CREATING AND NAMING NEW GROUPS

To create a new group, right-click the New Group button at the top of the Explorer. You have two choices: to create a new group as a (blank) folder, or to create a new group as a link to an existing folder. You can link to folders anywhere on your system.

If you select Add Group as Folder, a new group immediately appears with the default name of New Group.

If you select Add Group as Link, a two-tabbed dialog box opens. If you already know the exact pathname of the folder for which you want to create a link (which is called the *target folder*), enter it in the text input box on the General tab. If you don't know the exact pathname, skip the General tab and go right to the Bookmark tab. Click Directory, which opens a file browsing dialog box. Navigate to the location of the folder, click it to enter its name in the text input box, and click Select. Next, enter the Group name in the Name text box. That name automatically fills in the General tab name box also. Click OK, and your group, with all its objects, now appears in the Explorer.

Tip #14 from
Michael & Sarah

A shortcut for creating a new group as a link is to drag and drop an existing folder onto the New Group button.

To change a group's name, right-click its title bar and choose the Rename Group command. Its name on the Group button will become highlighted; type in your new name. Renaming a linked folder has no effect on the name of the source folder; it affects only the name you see in your Explorer display. You can also rename a group by choosing Properties from the context menu and entering a new name on the General tab.

Caution

Although your group may be only a link to a folder, the objects inside the target folder are only links if you originally created them as links. If you delete them, you're deleting them from the source, not just from the Explorer display. If you find that you've accidentally deleted something in this way, open the Recycle Bin on your desktop and use the context menu Restore command.

REARRANGING THE ORDER OF GROUPS

To rearrange the order of groups, grab a group's button and drag it to its new location.

REMOVING GROUPS

To remove a group, open the group context menu. Depending on whether your group is an actual folder in the Explorer or only a link to a folder stored elsewhere, you will see either

Remove Group or Remove Link to Group. If your group is a folder in the Explorer and you choose Remove Group, everything in the group will be deleted. If your group is a link only, deleting the group deletes the link only and has no effect on the target folder.

Changing a Group's Source Folder

If you have created a group as a link, you can change the group's target folder by choosing the Properties command from the group context menu, and assigning a new target URL (in other words, pathname).

Changing Your Explorer Layout

New to version 5.1, you can change the layout of objects in the Explorer by right-clicking the group name to open its context menu. You have three choices of how to display objects: Large Symbols, Small Symbols, and Hierarchical. "Symbols" are more typically called icons. The Hierarchical view is the default Explorer view in which folders and drives are displayed in a branching, hierarchical structure.

Your choice affects not only the objects' appearance but also how you launch programs and open objects. In Hierarchical view, a single-click opens the subdirectories on a folder or drive and a double-click opens a folder on your desktop or launches a program. In the Large Symbols and Small Symbols views, a single-click opens an object or launches a program. Also, in Hierarchical view only, you can choose to display the contents of folders in the Explorer by choosing the command Display Contents on the group context menu. You can also only display contents of folders and other objects in the Beamer when your group is set to Hierarchical view. (In fact, so many of StarOffice's special desktop management features are available only in Hierarchical view that it doesn't make much sense to set the Explorer group to anything else.)

Figure 2.12 shows the Group context menu and the open Tasks group in Large Symbols display.

Databases and the Explorer

In version 5.0, databases could only be created from the Explorer context menu Users found that too confusing, so version 5.1 includes the new database command on the File, New menu. However, a database is still fundamentally different kind of object than a document—it's more like a folder, as it is a container for a number of database objects—and you therefore still work with it in the Explorer. After you have created a new database, you can create tables and other database elements using File, AutoPilot; or you can import database objects from external sources. For more information, see Part VII, "Working with Databases—StarBase."

Default Explorer Contents

You should investigate the Explorer because it comes with a number of files, folders, and objects that can make your work easier; furthermore, it reveals some of StarOffice's talents and gives you a head start on creating your own projects.

Figure 2.12
Change the display and response of objects in the Explorer with commands on the Group context menu. In both icon views, programs launch and folders open with but a single-click.

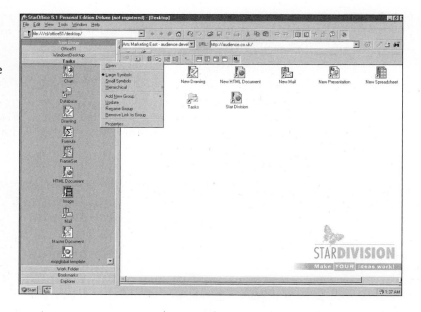

THE ADDRESS BOOK

The Address Book is a searchable dBase III StarBase database for use as a contact manager. It's fully integrated into the desktop, and is available from many text document templates and AutoPilot wizards.

From within text, HTML, and mail document context menus, if you select a person's name and click the Who Is? command, StarOffice immediately pulls up his or her address on your desktop. You can then select the contact information to insert. By selecting a contact's name or other information and choosing AutoBrowse, you can bring up a contact's Web site on your desktop while you're working. You also use the Address Book (or another data table of your choice) to create mail merge form letters and emailings.

→ For information on creating form letters and document mail merges, **see** "Creating Form Letters with Mail Merge," **p. 360**.

→ For more information on creating mass emailings, **see** "Creating Mail Merges with StarMail," **p. 1062**.

The easiest way to add, edit, and locate entries is with the dialog box that is opened with the Address Book command on the Edit menu (shown in Figure 2.13). This dialog box has been considerably improved over version 5.0, and an annoying bug that reversed the country and state fields has been fixed, making the address book fully functional for U.S. users.

→ For general discussion of using the Address Book and information on importing contact databases from other applications, **see** "Introducing the Address Book," **p. 180**.

Note

To ensure that no one accidentally deletes the Address Book, it is protected. If you try to delete it, an error message appears, denying your access to the folder in which it is stored.

If the Beamer is open, pressing F4 opens the Address Book in Table view in the Beamer, where you can also view and edit entries or drag and drop addresses into open documents (see Figure 2.13). Version 5.1 has a new Lookup Record button on the Beamer toolbar that enables you to easily search for records directly from the Beamer table display as well.

Lookup Record button

Figure 2.13
The Address Book database is managed in the Explorer and Beamer as well as from the Edit, Address Book dialog box.

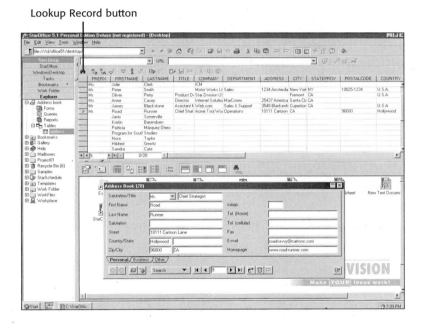

THE BOOKMARKS FOLDER

The Explorer Bookmarks folder is designed to be your site for storing bookmarks in StarOffice. If you're a Windows user who had MS Internet Explorer installed when you installed StarOffice, this folder is a link that was automatically created to your Internet Explorer Bookmarks folder. If you are a Linux user or a Windows user without MS Internet Explorer, your Explorer Bookmarks folder will be the StarOffice Office51\Bookmarks folder. If you're an MS Internet Explorer user, you can create a link to the StarOffice Bookmarks folder in the Explorer, if you'd like access to this collection of preset bookmarks, or you can copy any that interest you to your Bookmarks folder in the Explorer.

Besides appearing in the Explorer, your default bookmarks folder also has its own Bookmarks group.

The StarOffice Bookmarks folder contains shortcuts to useful Web sites and links to locally stored StarOffice documents that contain information about its StarOne programming environment. It also contains shortcuts to the Java RunTime console and monitor, and to Web sites that discuss using the Java programming language

The Bookmark tool on the hyperlink bar automatically drops the currently displayed hyperlink bar URL into this folder, making it the easiest place to create new bookmarks while browsing. However, you don't have to stick with the default assigned Bookmarks folder. It's easy to set another folder as your default through Tools, Options, Path dialog box. The name of the entry is Bookmarks; click Edit to edit the path. The folder that you choose will then appear in the Explorer.

Caution

If you delete or move the Bookmarks folder, the Hyperlink toolbar shortcut tool no longer works.

These shortcuts are just like any other links or bookmarks that are created in the program; they can be moved, copied, and deleted. You can also add your own bookmarks to existing folders or create your own bookmark subfolders.

Note

In version 5.0, there was a bug that prevented you from renaming a bookmark without losing the link. In version 5.1, you can rename bookmarks without problem.

Note

Bookmarks, links, and shortcuts are essentially the same kind of object. Each is a type of reference to a file that enables you to jump to the file's location or open the file when you click the bookmark, link, or shortcut.

THE GALLERY

The Gallery is filled with cool photos, bitmaps, drawings, sounds, animated images, and backgrounds that are ready to be inserted to lend pizzazz to your Web pages, presentations, reports, and anything else you create in StarOffice.

You can preview all the images and sounds in the Beamer, as well as drag and drop them from the Beamer into open documents. For more information, see "Previewing Files, Sounds, and Images in the Beamer" later in this chapter.

To add your own graphics or sound files to the Gallery, select the Gallery folder, open the Gallery context menu, and select the Import command. When you're browsing the Web, there's also a handy context menu command that enables you to easily copy or download any graphic file and add it to the Gallery.

EXPLORER HELP LINKS

Access to help is sprinkled all over the desktop, including here in the Explorer, which provides a different way of accessing the User's Guide. To see the contents of the User's Guide, click the plus (+) sign to the left of the Help icon to open the Help folder. Continue clicking plus signs until you see a chapter title that interests you. Double-click on the title, and its contents appear in a desktop window.

THE RECYCLE BIN

When you delete most objects from StarOffice, they are not immediately discarded from your hard drive: they're stored in the Recycle Bin in case you find that you still have some use for them. They remain in the Recycle Bin until you explicitly delete them with the Delete command.

PART

I

CH

2

> **Caution**
>
> The Recycle Bin is one example of how StarOffice's total integration can affect the amount of disk storage the program requires. Be sure you set aside enough room on your partition or hard drive to accommodate the Recycle Bin. Also be sure to empty it periodically so you don't build up trash on your hard drive. You can also choose a folder located elsewhere to serve as your trash folder via the Tools, Options, General, Paths dialog–but you'll lose the special safety features of the Bin.

The number of objects that are currently stored in the Recycle Bin is always visible in parentheses to the right of its name in the Explorer.

To delete objects from the Recycle Bin, follow these steps:

1. Double-click the Recycle Bin icon in the Explorer, which opens a desktop task window that displays its contents.
2. Select the items that you want to delete.
3. Select Delete from the function bar or Edit menu.
4. StarOffice gives you yet another chance to save the file from total destruction. To confirm that you want to delete the file and complete its disposal, choose Yes or press Enter.

Objects that you have moved to the Recycle Bin cannot be dragged and dropped as can other objects on your desktop. To return objects that are in the Recycle Bin to their original locations, select the object, and then choose the Restore command on its context menu.

To empty the Recycle Bin, choose the command of the same name from its context menu.

SAMPLES

To give you a taste of StarOffice's possibilities, a number of sample documents that were created in the program have been included. Some of the samples (for example, Logo

Workshop in the StarOffice Pro edition), even show you, step by step, how the final product was created.

Note

The samples that you have might vary, depending on which edition of StarOffice you have installed.

You can use these samples as templates for creating your own projects. For example, a sample database to keep track of a video collection is included. You can customize this database to organize your own video collection.

StarSchedule

Manage your schedule, set automatic reminders for upcoming events, and plan projects from your desktop with StarSchedule. Although StarSchedule can be used to keep track of just one person's calendar, its power is revealed when it is used on a network, where you can keep track of project team or department schedules while enabling all team members to access the schedule. The StarSchedule Servers folder enables you to add or delete servers that have access.

You can set automatic reminders to pop up on your desktop, or schedule emails to be sent automatically to all members of a mailing list.

Part of StarSchedule's beauty is its simplicity—no more bloated, cluttered desktop calendars, just a clean, intuitive interface. Open the StarSchedule on your desktop and double-click Tasks; a task list opens. Add your tasks, and they automatically appear when you open the Events calendar (by double-clicking). You can then drag and drop tasks onto the calendar or click in the calendar and type directly. If you click a date on the overview calendars to the right, your Events page automatically changes to match.

→ For details on working with StarSchedule, **see** "Getting Organized with StarSchedule," **p. 1020**.

Workfolder

When you first launch StarOffice, the program automatically creates a folder or link called Workfolder and places it in the Explorer. It also automatically makes Workfolder an Explorer group. Depending on how your system is configured, it may create an empty new folder or create a link to a folder you've already designated in your operating system as your default storage location. This folder is also the default storage location for your documents in StarOffice. It is placed on the desktop for your convenience, to help you get up and running quickly in StarOffice. Some of the desktop navigation buttons have handy shortcuts to the Workfolder, so it's a good idea to reassign the path of the Workfolder rather than delete it altogether. To reassign its path, use the Tools, Options, General, Paths dialog box. Search for the type Work Folder (the last item in the Paths list), and click Edit to change its path.

Workplace

Double-clicking the Workplace icon opens a window that shows all your available local drives, all available network drives and servers (if you are connected to a network), and a complete network map. You can then navigate around your drives, conduct a multiple search, and view and edit the properties for selected objects using the tools on the object bar and
• the Workplace context menus.

Tip #15 from
Michael & Sarah

Workplace in StarOffice is the equivalent of My Computer in Microsoft Windows.

Further Explorations with the Beamer

The Beamer (shown open in Figure 2.14) was introduced briefly at the beginning of this section as the Explorer's assistant, but it's time to take a closer look at just what it can do. The Beamer is like a lantern that shines a bright light on what you find with the Explorer, revealing details of files. You can manage individual files via commands on the main Beamer context menu and the document context menus. As mentioned earlier, it's also where the Address Book table displays if you press F4. With the Address Book open, you can drag and drop names, addresses, and phone numbers from the Address Book into open documents. You can also display any other StarBase table in the Beamer, and drag and drop field names into documents to create merge fields.

To turn the Beamer on and off, click its icon in the function bar, or choose its name in the View menu. You can also turn the Beamer on (but not off) by pressing Ctrl+Shift+B.

If the Beamer is open, an extended-click on a folder or other object in the Explorer window displays a list of that object's contents and its properties—such as last date modified—in the Beamer. Click on a property's title bar to change the sort order; drag its right or left border to shrink or expand its length. Double-clicking some title bars automatically reduces their size. You can also choose the Property display fields that you want to see using commands on the Beamer context menu Insert command.

To select a single file, click its name; to select a list, click the first item in the list, and then press Shift and click the last item. Press Ctrl while clicking to select multiple noncontiguous items.

After you select an item, you can conduct a search based on that item. Note that you can't create saved searches in the Beamer—you can only do that from the desktop or Explorer—nor can you display the contents of saved searches.

Note

The Remove command does not delete files from the Beamer; it only deletes the property title display that you currently have selected in the Beamer.

Figure 2.14

Actions that you can carry out in the Beamer include printing and deleting files, updating a file, and assigning a file's default document template. In this figure, the Beamer context menu, which enables you to manage the file properties' fields that display, is showing. Open this context menu by placing the pointer in a property title bar and right-clicking.

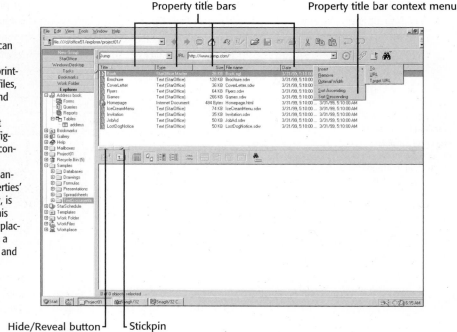

Property title bars

Property title bar context menu

Hide/Reveal button ⌐ Stickpin

PREVIEWING FILES, SOUNDS, AND IMAGES IN THE BEAMER

Besides being a local file manager, the Beamer is also a preview window in which you can view or listen to Gallery clips (see 2.16). What's even nicer is that you can also drag and drop a graphic or sound file from the Beamer into an active document.

To preview the contents of a Gallery folder, extended-click its name in the Explorer when the Explorer is set to Hierarchical view. This opens a strip of previews called *thumbnails* (because of their small size). To see a file in larger view or to hear a sound file, double-click it. Double-click again to return to the Beamer's thumbnail browsing view. To move through the files in the folder, use the Beamer scrollbar.

Other objects can be dragged and dropped from the Beamer as well. For example, you can insert a text file into another document by dragging it from the Beamer onto an open text document page.

OTHER FLOATING AND DOCKABLE WINDOWS

The Explorer and the Beamer are not alone; StarOffice has a number of other special floating, dockable tools windows that you can keep open while you work. These include the Navigator and the Stylist, both of which open from the function bar (but are available only when you have a document open on your desktop). The Help Agent is a dockable window, and if you use it often as you're learning the program, you might find it easier to work with it docked so it doesn't cover your work area. The Tips window that opens at program launching is special part of the Help Agent that only displays tips. It's not useful as you work so you may want to dock the real Help Agent there instead, which gives you a context-sensitive program. Other special tool windows can only be opened from within specific document types and include the Function List in StarCalc and the Form Navigator.

Figure 2.15
The Beamer acts as a thumbnail viewer and player for Gallery multimedia files, which include 3D animations to put your Web pages in motion, sounds, and graphics. When you find a file you want, drag and drop it into your document.

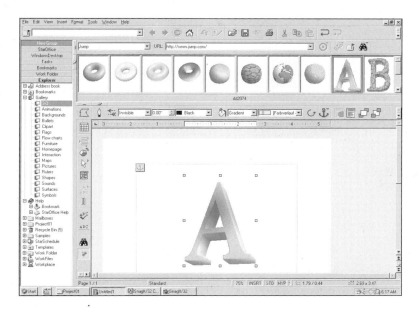

PART

I

CH

2

You can manage these windows on your desktop much like you do the Navigator and Beamer. When a window is floating, as the Navigator is in Figure 2.16, you can grab it by the edges and resize it so it doesn't take up as much screen real estate.

Double-clicking the title bar toggles the window between the title bar and open views. You can drag and place the title bar anywhere on your desktop. (Note, however, that you cannot dock a window when it is in title bar form; the window must be open.) Ctrl+click works to dock and undock windows, and clicking the Close button in the upper-right corner closes them.

FLOATING TOOLBARS AND DIALOG BOXES

There are two other types of floating objects that you'll encounter that are not dockable and have some other important differences from floating dockable windows as well.

The main toolbar has a number of tools that each boast a small green arrow on the right. These are double-function buttons. An extended-click opens a toolbar—a mini-toolbar, really—that can be detached and moved anywhere on your desktop. Some buttons on object bars also open tear-off floating palettes or toolbars—for example, the background color palettes in StarCalc and StarWriter. Another mini-toolbar, the Navigation toolbar (refer to

Figure 2.16), opens from within the Navigator or by clicking the Navigation button in documents. (Look ahead to Figure 2.17 to see the Navigation button identified.) Unlike the main program toolbars, these floating toolbars cannot be resized or docked. Click the Close button (the X) in the corner to close them.

Figure 2.16
The desktop, with the Explorer and Navigator open as floating windows, and the Navigation floating toolbar open.

When you close a mini-toolbar that resides on the main toolbar, the Tool button that displays reflects the last tool you selected. A regular click activates the displayed tool. If you need a different tool, extended-click the button to open the entire toolbar and select the tool you need.

Virtually all dialog boxes also open as floating dialogs that can be reduced to title bars and moved anywhere on your desktop. They cannot be resized. Although you can move a dialog box off your desktop, in many cases you can't do any other work until you've closed the dialog box.

UNDERSTANDING TASKS AND TASK WINDOWS

StarOffice is task-oriented, and most of your work takes place in *task windows*.

You can have up to 255 tasks open on your desktop at once —and many open tools windows—so learning how to manipulate and manage multiple task windows and organize the tools on your desktop are keys to efficient use of the program.

Note

To get the most out of StarOffice's desktop, it's best to have a monitor with at least a 17″ viewable area, set to 1024×768 resolution or higher. If you run at lower resolutions or on a small monitor, you'll find that your desktop gets very cluttered and you cannot see all your tools at once.

Tip #16 from
Michael & Sarah

Keeping many windows open hogs system memory. To avoid system crashes, keep open only as many windows as you really need.

WHAT IS A TASK?

A *task* is anything you open in a task window on the StarOffice desktop.

There are six basic types of tasks in StarOffice:

- Creating and working with documents
- Scheduling and managing tasks and events
- Writing, reading, and sending email and news
- Creating and managing databases
- Managing files, folders, and other objects
- Browsing the Web and viewing HTML documents

In StarOffice, *document* refers not only to text documents, but also to spreadsheets, drawings, images, presentations, Web pages, and other types of files that you create.

When you open a new document, double-click an object in Explorer, or drag a file from the Beamer onto your desktop, and a new task window automatically opens.

Tip #17 from
Michael & Sarah

To open an object in the Explorer in a new task window without closing the active task window, press Ctrl while double-clicking.

WORKING WITH TASK WINDOWS

When you open a new task window on the desktop, it is automatically added to the list of open tasks in the Window menu, made the active window, and placed on top of any other open tasks. However, just as you can slide papers and folders around on a real desktop, you can rearrange the order and appearance of task windows.

Even though when it opens it is docked to your desktop, you can make it into a floating window (as in Figure 2.17) by clicking the Maximize button in the upper-right corner. As a floating window, it can be dragged anywhere, resized, and reduced to a floating title bar, much like the Explorer and Beamer. By clicking the Stickpin, you can also pin your task to the top and ensure that it is always visible.

Figure 2.17 identifies the basic elements of a task window and shows an open Task window context menu.

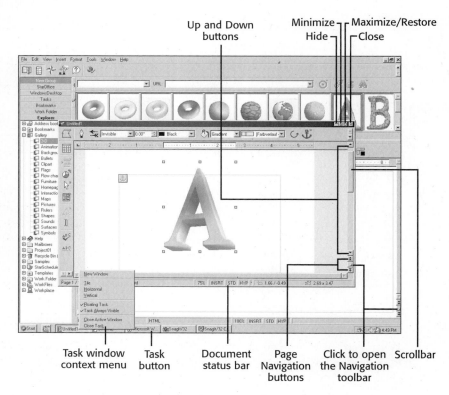

Figure 2.17
Although the specific tools that border task windows differ depending on the task at hand, all task windows can be manipulated in the same ways. The Task window menu you see is opened by right-clicking the Task button. Also try right-clicking document status bar fields; often, useful shortcut menus appear.

Up and Down buttons
Minimize
Hide
Maximize/Restore
Close

Task window context menu
Task button
Document status bar
Page Navigation buttons
Click to open the Navigation toolbar
Scrollbar

Tip #18 from
Michael & Sarah

Ctrl+Tab cycles you through all open task windows.

THE STATUS BAR

Whenever you have a task window open, a status bar (refer to 2.18) appears at the bottom of the window, displaying basic information about the document and its current settings. The specific information you see depends on the type of task.

All status bars are divided into various sections. If your mouse pointer turns into a double-headed arrow when you move it over an area's borders, you can drag and resize that section. In many of these sections, right-clicking opens a fly-away shortcut menu, while double-clicking opens a dialog boxes—just click around and explore!

The status bar displays for specific document types are discussed in the sections on each document type. Check the Index and Table of Contents to find specific page numbers.

MANAGING TASKS WITH THE TASK BAR AND TASK BUTTONS

You can manage task windows using any of the following:

- Commands on the Window menu
- The taskbar
- The Task window context menu
- The Close, Maximize, and Minimize buttons in the upper-right corner of all task windows

PART

I

CH

2

Tip #19 from
Michael & Sarah

The most important commands are located on the taskbar and Task window context menu.

Of these, the taskbar and its associated context menu is the easiest to use and has the widest range of commands. The taskbar also contains other items that assist you in managing your desktop, including the Desktop button (which enables you to switch between different desktops and open the desktop contents menu), the Start button (which opens a menu that enables you to start programs, tasks, and documents from anywhere on your system), a quickstart area, and task tray icons. This section describes these elements in more detail and explains how to use the task buttons to manage open tasks.

When you open a new task, a button for that task is automatically placed on the taskbar at the bottom of your StarOffice desktop (see Figure 2.18). This Task button can be used in many ways to rearrange the order and appearance of tasks on your desktop.

Right-clicking a task button opens the Task window context menu (refer to Figure 2.17), which gives you a range of commands for arranging task windows.

With the New Window command, you can open a copy of your selected task in a second window; this is handy if you're working on a long document or in a spreadsheet where you want to see two different worksheets at once. The Tile, Horizontal, and Vertical commands arrange the open task windows in preset patterns. Floating Task is a toggle that alternately floats and docks a task, whereas Task Always on Top leaves a task on top even when it isn't the active window.

Tip #20 from
Michael & Sarah

If you're dragging and dropping a lot of files or data between two open task windows, make one into a floating task window and set it to Task Always on Top (or click the Stickpin icon). Then both are always visible, and you can use your entire desktop for working—even with the Explorer and Beamer open.

Figure 2.18
You can have tasks layered on top of one another with only the tasks buttons of inactive tasks visible (as shown here), or you can use the Maximize/Restore button to change documents into floating tasks so you can overlap and see multiple tasks at once (refer to Figure 2.17).

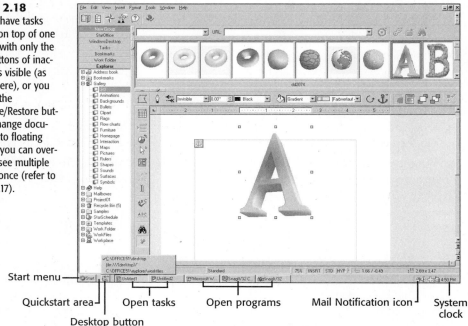

Start menu — Quickstart area — Desktop button — Open tasks — Open programs — Mail Notification icon — System clock

If only one copy of a task is open, Close Active Window (Ctrl+W) and Close Open Task have the same effect—they close the task—but if you have multiple copies open, Close active window closes only the active copy of the task.

Note

If the integrated desktop is on, you see a unified taskbar. If it's turned off, you have separate Windows and StarOffice taskbars. If the Windows taskbar is in the way, click it in an empty area and drag it to the side.

Note

Some users experience problems with StarOffice's taskbar hiding beneath the FVWM2-95 taskbar. If you have this problem, try editing the App-Window line in your `sofficerc` file (in your StarOffice directory) so that it reads as follows:
`App-Window=0,0,16,1024,752;0.` (This assumes you're running at 1024×752 resolution.)

Besides managing task windows individually, you can also combine tasks into one window by dragging and dropping one task button onto another. There are three basic ways you can combine open tasks:

- If you drag and drop one task button onto another, it combines the two tasks into one window (although each remains a separate file).

- If you Ctrl+drag and drop a task button (Task 1) onto another (Task 2), a copy of Task 1 is combined in a single window with Task 2. This copy is separate from Task 1 and is no longer updated.

- If you Shift+Ctrl+drag and drop a task button (Task 1) onto another (Task 2), a linked copy from Task 1 is created and combined in a single window with Task 2.

This feature makes many tasks much easier to accomplish. Here are some possible uses:

- Drag and drop a StarCalc spreadsheet Task button onto a StarWriter Task button. You can then easily drag and drop a table of StarCalc data into a StarWriter document.

- Drag and drop your mail Inbox into an open StarWriter document. You can then easily drag and drop individual mail messages into StarWriter documents, which is much easier than exporting them as ASCII files!

- Drag and drop the Task button of one open copy of a document onto the Task button of a second open copy. You can then easily view two parts of your document at the same time.

- Drag and drop the Task button of an HTML document in Source Code view onto the Task button of the same document in Online view. You can then easily see the effect of changes you make in the source code to the final document as seen onscreen.

- Drag and drop the Task button of a StarBasic session onto the Task button of the document for which you are creating macros or scripts. You can then see the program code in one window and the results for the document in the other.

THE START MENU   From the Start menu (shown in Figure 2.19), you can launch new StarOffice tasks, manage your system, and run system programs.

Figure 2.19
The StarOffice Start menu offers a different entry point into online Help with links to task-oriented headings, and to the new task commands.

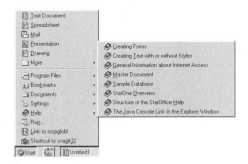

Tip #21 from
Michael & Sarah

You can customize the appearance of the Start menu by adding or deleting entries in the Config\start menu folder in your StarOffice directory.

The Documents folder contains a list of the last nine documents you worked on, enabling to you open recently used documents with a single-click.

Tip #22 from
Michael & Sarah

If you right-click the Start menu, a fly-out menu opens from which you can open your Programs folder (Windows users), or your /bin folder (Linux users) onto your desktop. If you're on a network, you can also open your network systems folders from here.

Tip #23 from
Michael & Sarah

Here is a quick way to customize your desktop: Open your Programs or network folder from the Start Menu, and Ctrl+Shift+drag links onto your StarOffice desktop for any programs or administration tools you want to launch from your desktop.

Tip #24 from
Michael & Sarah

Choose the Show Large Symbols command on the fly-out menu to increase the font size of items on the Start menu.

THE QUICKSTART AREA   You can create your own quickstart buttons for single-click launching of any object by dragging it from your desktop and dropping it onto the quickstart area (the small area between the Start menu and the Desktop menu on the taskbar; refer to Figure 2.18). This is particularly useful for objects that you frequently open, such as your email account inboxes or a project schedule.

To remove an item, right-click it and choose Remove.

THE DESKTOP MENU   Just as you might have one desktop at home and another at work, you can create multiple desktops in StarOffice. By default, the StarOffice Desktop folder and your systems Desktop folder are both designated as desktops. You can also create your own desktops by selecting a folder in the Explorer or in a task window, right-clicking to open the folder's context menu, and then choosing the Desktop command.

These desktops are managed through the Desktop menu, which opens with a right-click (see Figure 2.20). To select a different desktop as your default, click its name in this menu.

While you can have as many folders as you want designated as desktops and waiting in the wings, only one desktop can be *on stage*—that is, selected as your default—at a time.

> **Note**
>
> If you want to designate a linked folder to be a desktop, you won't see the Desktop command on the main context menu; you'll need to open the Target's context submenu.

An extended-click opens the Desktop Contents menu, which shows all the items you have stored in your currently selected desktop.

Figure 2.20
You can change the items that appear on the Desktop menu by choosing a different folder to serve as your desktop. Here, the Workfolder has been chosen as a desktop, making it easy to locate and launch documents while working on other tasks.

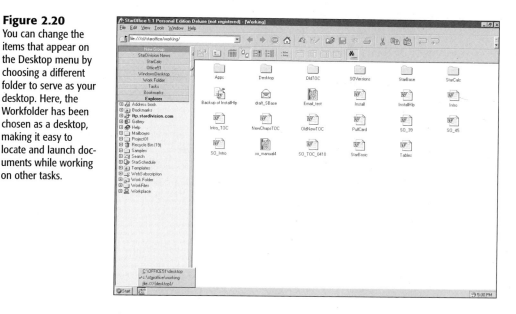

A click on the Desktop icon in the taskbar toggles you between the current default desktop and your most recently opened task.

→ For more information on creating and working with multiple desktops, **see** Chapter 3, "Getting Ready for Work" **p. 75**.

THE ICON TRAY AND CLOCK   The Taskbar icon tray displays two StarOffice-specific icons: the system clock and a Globe icon, which changes appearance when you have new mail. If you double-click the clock, your StarSchedule desktop calendar opens.

Note

The New Mail Notification icon works only when you have set up your StarOffice Internet connection and created an email account Inbox.

The other icons that appear depend on your computer's configuration.

Note

If the Integrated Desktop is turned on, your Windows system icons appear in the StarOffice icon tray. If not, only StarOffice-specific icons appear. You can turn the Integrated Desktop on or off by selecting Integrated Desktop from the View menu.

Tip #25 from
Michael & Sarah

Make the User's Guide Help window a floating task, and then select the Task Always Visible command to keep Help open alongside tasks while you're learning the program.

CLOSING TASK WINDOWS

All open desktop windows close in the same way, whether their contents are a document, Web page, email, or the contents of a folder you have opened. (The one exception to this is the designated desktop, which always remains open as long as the program is open.)

There are three ways to close an open task:

- Click the Close button in the upper-right corner of the desktop window. (If you have integrated desktop turned off, be careful to click the *lower* Close button because the upper Close button exits StarOffice.)
- Select Close from the File menu. Do not select Exit because this exits StarOffice altogether.
- Right-click the Task button in the taskbar, and select Close Task.

ADJUSTING YOUR VIEW

Besides manipulating desktop windows, you can also change your view of the desktop, turn on and off the display of various desktop tools, and zoom in and out of tasks. These actions are carried out with commands on the View menu or with context menus.

MAKING MORE SPACE ON YOUR DESKTOP

One of the disadvantages of having an integrated desktop is that your workspace can get very cluttered. When you need to see more of a task, you can make it fill up your display by selecting Full Screen view from the View menu. Click the Monitor icon that appears to return to the regular Desktop view.

TURNING TOOLBARS ON AND OFF

Another way to make more space on your desktop is to turn off the display of unneeded tools. To turn on and off the status bar, click its name on the View menu. To globally turn on and off the display of program toolbars—including the function and object bars—open the View, Toolbars submenu, and then click the name of the toolbar that you want to hide (or reveal). Note that the Main toolbar may be selected (as indicated by a check mark next to its name) but still not be visible because it displays only when you have an open document on your desktop.

To turn off the display of a toolbar within a particular context, position your mouse in a toolbar and right-click. This opens the toolbar context menu, which lists only those toolbars currently open. Click to deselect or select a toolbar. If you've turned them all off, you'll need to use the View menu commands to turn them back on again.

ZOOMING

The View menu Zoom command becomes active only when you have a document open in a task window. Clicking Zoom opens a dialog box that enables you to either select a preset zoom value or enter your own value. You can select any value between 20–400.

The value that you select is in effect for all documents you open in that application until you change it again.

FINDING HELP IN STARSPACE

StarOffice offers superior functionality and ease of use in most areas; unfortunately, however, the English online Help system is not yet one of them. Because the program documentation is relatively weak (although the version 5.1 Help is more complete than previous versions), you are pointed to some other useful resources.

HELP AGENT, TIPS, AND EXTENDED TIPS

When you launch StarOffice for the first time, the Help Agent tips window automatically opens and Help Tips are turned on. The contents of this tips window are static during a work session, changing only when you exit and then re-open the program. The main Help Agent window opens automatically when you execute certain program commands, but you can also open it yourself at any time by selecting the Help, Help Agent command.

If you find the Help Agent annoying, you can turn it off globally by deselecting the Start Automatically option in the Help Agent portion of the Tools, Option, General, Other dialog.

The Help Agent is a searchable help file that displays context-sensitive help as you click on different commands and tools. It also contains a number of tips that are not found in the User's Guide.

Figure 2.21 shows the Help Agent and identifies its tool buttons and window controls.

You can reduce the Help Agent to a floating title bar by clicking the Minimize button, or you can dock it to your desktop to keep it open but out of the task's way, just as with the Beamer and Explorer.

Help Tips give you the names of StarOffice tools and buttons in dialog boxes. When Help Tips are turned on, move your mouse pointer over the tool button or dialog box command whose name you want to know, and a tip with the name pops up on your screen. After you move the cursor away, the tip disappears. If you turn on Extended Tips, explanations of the tools and how to use them appear. Although Tips and Extended Tips can be simultaneously selected on the Help menu, this is misleading, as only one functions at a time for a given button. If no Extended Tip exists, the tool name appears.

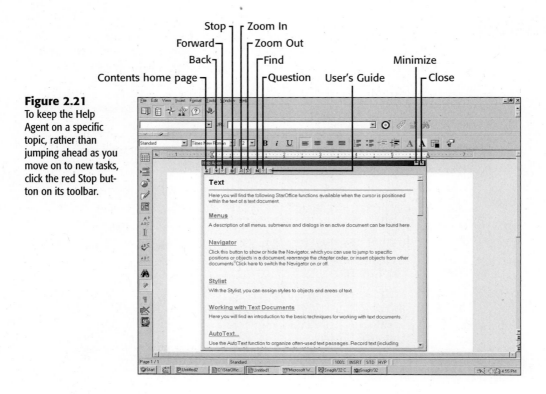

Figure 2.21
To keep the Help Agent on a specific topic, rather than jumping ahead as you move on to new tasks, click the red Stop button on its toolbar.

THE HELP POINTER

The Help pointer gives you immediate, brief, context- sensitive help with StarOffice tools and dialog boxes that is more detailed than Help Tips. To activate the Help pointer, press Shift+F1. Your pointer shape changes and becomes an arrow with a question mark attached. To get help, move your mouse pointer over the tool button or dialog box command about which you want to know more, and help pops up on your screen. It disappears after you move the cursor away. Click anywhere in the desktop to turn the Help pointer off.

USER'S GUIDE (CONTENTS)

The User's Guide is a searchable hypertext manual that provides a basic introduction to the StarOffice desktop and program modules. Open it by selecting the Help menu Contents command, or by selecting Help on the StarOffice Start menu. The User's Guide contains a good reference guide to StarBasic, with alphabetical dictionaries of all the available functions and an overview of StarOffice's API programming structure (called StarOne).

Note

The online Help describes StarOffice's functionality as it exists in the Windows version. Not all these functions are available on Linux. (Most notably, the StarBase format database, the native format that enables users to create relational databases, is available only on the Windows32 platform.) Therefore, if the functions described here or in the StarOffice Help are not available, don't assume it is a program error.

The User's Guide Help system has the same Find, Contents Home Page, and Zoom In and Zoom Out buttons as does the Help agent. To move forward and back in the User's Guide, use the Forward and Back buttons on the desktop function bar.

Tip #26 from
Michael & Sarah

You can print sections from the User's Guide with the File, Print command.

The User's Guide Help window main toolbar has two other buttons: one for bookmarks and one for annotations (see Figure 2.22).

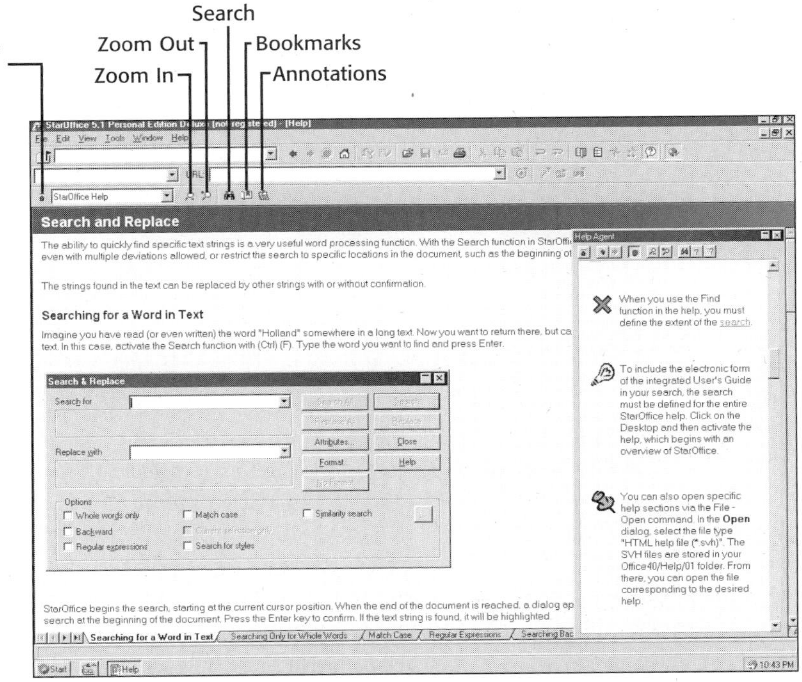

Search

Zoom Out ─┐ ┌─ Bookmarks

Home page of ─── Zoom In ─┐ │ ┌─ Annotations
User's Guide

Figure 2.22
The online User's Guide gives a basic overview of StarOffice. You can have the Help Agent open simultaneously with the User's Guide.

Clicking the Bookmarks button creates a hyperlink to the section that you are currently browsing in a Bookmark folder inside the Explorer Help folder. (Note that this folder is different than the main Bookmarks folder.) Clicking Annotations opens an annotations window into which you can enter notes—for example, your own tips or explanations. After you click OK to confirm the annotation, the Annotation icon appears to the left of the section title. When you're browsing in that section again and click the Annotation icon, your earlier note pops up for review.

Specific sections of the User's Guide also appear as menu items on the program Start menu.

INTERNET RESOURCES

StarDivision, Inc. maintains a Web site that offers some basic support for installing and using StarOffice. Most usefully, it offers information links to StarOffice Internet newsgroups it maintains. These newsgroups address the use of specific applications and troubleshoot general installation and desktop problems. The newsgroups are lively, and both StarOffice personnel and eager power users offer translations from German documentation on many topics that are still undocumented in English. As of the time of this writing, the URL was `http://www.stardivision.com/support/ek_news.html`. Old newsgroup postings can be found on the Deja News Web site at `http://www.dejaneww.com`. The StarOffice desktop and Bookmarks folder contains bookmarks for single-click travel to StarDivision Web sites that can also guide you to the newsgroups and other help resources. The StarDivision and StarOffice overview links jump you to the general home page and an overview of the program, respectively. Click Support at the top of the page, and then follow the links to find a list of StarOffice newsgroups in English.

Note

StarDivision Web Help is only available after you've configured your Internet account in StarOffice. For information on configuring StarOffice for the Internet, see Chapter 3.

For German readers, there's an abundance of StarDivision documentation available online.

Tip #27 from
Michael & Sarah

German readers who are interested in StarBasic might want to download the 1,200-page StarBasic 4.0 manual in `.pdf` format from `ftp.stardivision.de`. (The reference is still useful, although much has changed. There is no more recent detailed reference available, at least not for public distribution. If you have specific questions, post them to the StarBasic newsgroup.) The document is in the basic folder (not pub). Log in as `anonymous`; you'll be requested to enter your email address as a password.

OTHER STARDIVISION PROGRAM SUPPORT

When you've exhausted your program and Internet help resources, StarDivision's U.S. office maintains a telephone support line from Monday through Friday, 8 a.m. to 8 p.m. (PST) at (510) 505-1490. You're entitled to 30 days of free support after registration. The company says that most questions can be answered within six minutes. If a representative cannot help you right away, you will receive a written response from customer support within 48 hours.

StarDivision also offers different types of support contracts to personal, commercial, and institutional customers. If you are considering installing StarOffice on an office or networked system, you should explore these options.

If you have downloaded the program for free, keep in mind that the company cannot afford to devote its resources to giving free support indefinitely to non-paying customers. Make good use of your initial free support, if you need it, but be considerate and be aware that many of the most common questions have answers already on the newsgroups. Alternatively, if you find the program worthwhile, consider paying for a support contract.

TROUBLESHOOTING

Suddenly, I can't find the Explorer and Beamer tools on my function bar. Help! Where did they go?

You probably turned off the StarOffice integrated desktop, reducing the width of your StarOffice display window; and there's no longer enough room to display all your tools at once. A double-headed arrow should have appeared at the right end of your toolbar—click the black arrow, and the rest of your tools should appear.

Every time I try to exit StarOffice, my system crashes!

Some versions of fvml in Red Hat conflict with StarOffice and cause a system lockup, if you exit the program by clicking the Close button on the title bar. Try exiting using the Control menu Close command, or use the File menu Exit command instead.

I keep getting a message on startup that the plug-ins manager couldn't be loaded and I should run Setup with the -repair option. I run setup as instructed, but continue to get the message.

StarOffice is looking for Netscape or Internet Explorer plug-ins already installed on your system to incorporate into its own browser and file management system. If you don't have either of these browsers currently installed, it won't find any plug-ins to manage and will generate the message you see. StarOffice will run fine without the plug-ins for most desktop tasks, but you will be unable to open certain types of email attachments or Internet documents unless you have the proper plug-ins loaded on your system.

I can't see my desktop workspace, the Beamer and Explorer cover things up.

Click the stickpin icons on their borders to pin them to the desktop. When they're not pinned, they float on top of the desktop workspace. Click the arrow button to hide the window entirely.

I can't find my deleted files.

StarOffice maintains its own separate Recycle Bin. Check the StarOffice Recycle Bin, which can be opened by double-clicking its icon in the Explorer.

I can't drag my files out of the Recycle Bin.

As you've discovered, drag and drop doesn't work on objects in the Recycle Bin. To restore an object to its original location, select the object, right-click to open its context menu, and choose Restore.

I can't get folders to display their contents in the Beamer.

If a folder contains only other folders, its contents won't display. Only files display in the Beamer. If a folder does have files, an extended-click does the trick. (A double-click opens the folder on your desktop in Hierarchical layout, a single-click in either of the symbols layouts.)

I can't find the Explorer context menu New command.

You're opening a context menu when you have a non-folder object selected. Select any folder object, or position your cursor in a blank area of the Explorer and right-click.

I can't open more than one task window at a time.

You're probably opening objects from the Explorer or Beamer by double-clicking them. Try pressing Ctrl when you double-click, or selecting an object, right-clicking, and choosing the Open command.

I click on hyperlinks in the Help Agent and Contents and don't get anywhere.

The original program documentation is in German and the English program documentation is not yet fully translated. These hyperlinks indicate sections not translated in time to add to the version you have. While the English version of 5.1 has a few hundred pages of additional English Help files, it still does not offer the full range of help that the German version does.

I want to set a graphic as my desktop background, but I need to see what's in the file to be sure it's the right one. All I see is a big box with an X in it!

You need to select the Preview option in the dialog box, and then you can see thumbnail images of any graphic files you select while browsing around your directories.

Every time I open StarOffice, I see things on my desktop that I don't want. How can I change what appears on my desktop on launching?

Change your default desktop. You can designate any folder you want as a desktop by selecting it, opening its context menu, and clicking Desktop.

CHAPTER 3

GETTING READY FOR WORK

In this chapter

SETTING YOUR GENERAL OPTIONS

After you've installed StarOffice, it's a good idea to customize your workspace. Everyone has certain preferences when it comes to using menu commands, buttons, and directories, and StarOffice enables you to customize your workspace to match your work habits and aesthetic sensibilities. If so inclined, you can change toolbars, buttons, and menus; default directories, paths, and custom commands; as well as the appearance of your desktop.

Most users will want to start out with setting their general options for working in StarOffice. These options enable you to modify your personal data, paths to important files, overall desktop appearance, as well as the default save, print, and color settings. You can set these options in the General Options dialog box (see Figure 3.1). To access the General Options dialog, select Options, General from the Tools menu on the menu bar.

Figure 3.1
The General Options dialog box gives you access to the basic types of customization that users typically want to do (or should do) right after installation.

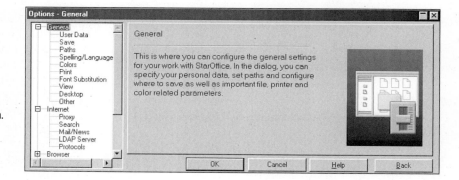

MODIFYING YOUR USER DATA

The User Data dialog boxlists your contact information—including name, company, address, phone, and email—which you were asked to provide during the setup process.

Tip #28 from
Michael & Sarah

> To take full advantage of all that StarOffice has to offer, be sure to keep your contact information up to date. StarOffice includes a series of templates that use fields to plug in all or part of your contact information (depending on the template you use), which it retrieves from this dialog box.

To update your user data, place the cursor in the text box you want to change and start typing. You can move between text boxes by pressing the Tab key and reverse by pressing Shift+Tab.

If you've changed certain key portions of your user data when you choose OK to confirm your new user data, StarOffice warns you that you'll need to re-register the program or it will expire in 30 days. Choose Yes in the warning box to complete entering the new data. Choose No if you've changed your mind, and then choose Cancel in the User Data dialog.

It's best to re-register at the same time you change your user data so you don't have an unhappy surprise when you try to start StarOffice one day. To re-register, choose Help, Registration, and select the Register button. If you're online, it takes just a few seconds. If you don't have an Internet account or online registration fails for some reason, you'll need to mail or fax your registration to StarDivision.

SETTING YOUR SAVE OPTIONS

While computers are great tools, it's frighteningly easy to lose work when you're using them. Power outages, computer crashes, a slip of the fingers on the keys—and there it is, a whole afternoon's work gone. Has this ever happened to you? Then you know you can never save your work too often.

You should regularly save open documents on your desktop by clicking the Save button on the function bar or pressing Ctrl+S. For an added level of security, you should also set the Automatic Save and Backup options in the Options, General, Save dialog box (see Figure 3.2). Taking the time to set these two options in the beginning might end up saving your nerves and neck as well as your work! Just click the Automatic Save Every check box and set a fixed time interval in the Minutes spinner box. You can also choose if you want to be prompted to confirm each save (default) or not. If you prefer not to be interrupted by constant Save dialogs while working, you should deselect the Prompt to Save option. StarOffice will now save your open documents every x minutes (where x is the time interval you specified), replacing each time the previously saved version of your document.

PART

I

CH

3

Figure 3.2
The Save dialog box enables you to set a number of global options related to saving files and undoing mistakes.

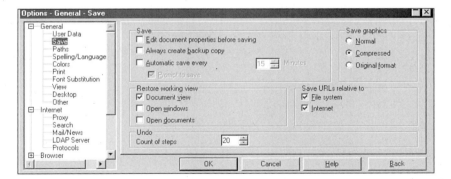

If you prefer to keep a backup copy of your documents and files, you should select the Always Create Backup Copy check box. Every time you save a new version of an open document, StarOffice automatically saves the previous version with a .bak file extension in the backup folder of the StarOffice directory.

Note

You can always change the default path for saving backup files in the Path dialog box in the General Options category. However, be sure the folder you want to designate already exists or you will get an error message. You can create a new folder from inside the Select Path dialog box that opens when you click Edit—the second button from the right creates a new folder (directory). To open a file with a .bak extension, double-click it from inside the Explorer.

In addition to the Automatic Save and Backup options, you can also set the Undo Number of Steps, which determines how many steps you can backtrack (by pressing Ctrl+Z, for example) to undo changes in your document. The default value is 20, but you can set this number anywhere from 0–100.

If you're the worrying kind, you might be tempted to set the number at 100. Keep in mind that these undo steps take up space in RAM and temporary swap files on your hard drive, and might also slow down system performance. If you have less than 64MB of RAM, you should probably set this number at 50 or less.

However, StarOffice handles Undo differently in StarWriter than you might be used to, because it treats individual additions—such as a space—as an action, so 20 backward steps might be smaller steps than you imagine.

If you're particularly uptight about keeping track of different versions and contents of a document, you can also check the Edit Document Properties Before Saving check box. Each time you save a document with the Save As command, the Properties dialog box appears, enabling you to update and save the document information. Information you enter in the Properties dialog box can later be entered as fields in your document. This is a particularly useful tool for working in project teams and managing document storage and retrieval for an office, as you can easily track such things as document authors, keywords, and document titles through fields in headers and footers.

→ For more information on working with fields in text documents, **see** "Working with Fields," **p. 350**.

The Restore Working View options affect what information StarOffice saves about your task window arrangements when you exit the program. If you choose the Open Windows or Open Documents options, it will save and reopen your last desktop windows arrangement and your last open documents or folders, respectively.

CHANGING DEFAULT LOCATIONS FOR IMPORTANT FILES

All program paths for default file searching and storage are set through the Paths dialog box in the Options, General category. StarOffice enables you to create your own directory structure.

Note

The default location for bookmark storage is `\Explorer\Bookmarks`. While you can change this path (to store them in another program's directory), keep in mind that you must store your bookmarks in a folder in the StarOffice Explorer, or create a link to that folder in the Explorer, to have them available on your StarOffice desktop.

Paths you might consider changing include the Recycle Bin (`\Store\Trash`), the Internet and network download path (`\download`), the Mail/News Storage paths (`\Store`), and the Backup copies path (`\Backup`).

To change a path, select the type you want to change, and then click the Edit button in the Paths dialog box (see Figure 3.3). Enter the new pathname in the Path text box on the Select Path dialog, or select a folder from the list box. You can click the Up One Level button to move up to the next level in the folder hierarchy. An extended-click opens a submenu that displays the hierarchy of the next highest directory up to the workplace. You can also click the New Folder button to create and name a new folder within a hierarchy. When you're finished, click Open to assign the new path to the selected type.

PART

I

CH

3

Figure 3.3
Glancing through the list of default program paths in the Paths dialog box can help you understand StarOffice's organization and file handling. You can change any path by selecting it and choosing Edit.

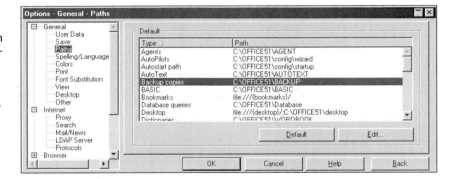

SELECTING SPELLING AND LANGUAGE OPTIONS

The Spelling/Language dialog box in the Options, General category enables you to set global spelling and hyphenation rules that will be used on all your StarOffice documents (see Figure 3.4). In addition, you can set the default language used for spellchecking and manage installed and custom dictionaries.

Check this box to ensure that footnotes, text
boxes, and other non-body text are spellchecked

Figure 3.4
The Spelling/
Language dialog box
is where you create
and manage custom
dictionaries as well
as set global options
related to
hyphenation and
spellchecking.

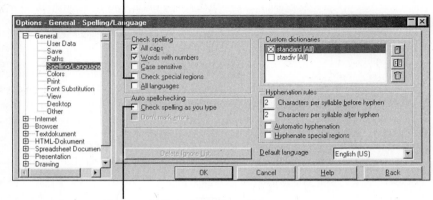

You can also turn this on and off on the main toolbar

Table 3.1 lists the various options you have when spellchecking your documents.

TABLE 3.1   GLOBAL SPELLCHECK OPTIONS

Option	When Selected...
All Caps	Uppercase words are included in spellchecks
Words with numbers	Words that contain numbers are included in spellchecks
Case-sensitive	Capitalization is checked
Check Special Regions	Headers, footers, footnotes, and other areas of text outside the text body are included in spellchecks
All Languages	All installed dictionaries are used to perform spellchecks

Tip #29 from
Michael & Sarah

If you use many foreign words in your documents, or if you frequently write entire sentences or paragraphs in another language, you might want to select the All Languages check box. StarOffice will catch your spelling errors as long as you've installed the dictionaries for the languages in question. You can install up to three language dictionaries in StarOffice. For more details on managing your installed dictionaries see "Understanding Dictionaries in StarOffice," in Chapter 12, "Proofing and Printing Your Documents."

If you want StarOffice to automatically mark your spelling errors with the AutoCorrect feature as you type, select the Check Spelling as You Type check box in the Auto Spellchecking section. When you select this option, the Don't Mark Errors option becomes available, allowing you to turn off the automatic highlighting of your spelling errors.

Note

> While you can turn Auto Spellchecking on and off with a button on the main toolbar, you can only set the Don't Mark Errors option in this dialog.

In the Hyphenation Rules section, you can turn automatic hyphenation on and off. If it is off, StarOffice will hyphenate words based on the hyphenation rules entered here.

When you installed StarOffice, the installer program gave you the option to install up to three language dictionaries and set a default language. You can change the default language at any time if so inclined. As long as the dictionary for the language you choose has been installed, StarOffice will continue to catch your spelling errors.

Note

> The drop-down menu lists a huge number of languages, even though you are only given the option to install three (or less). (Note another minor localization glitch: It also lists some languages available only in the European versions—such as Finnish. Given Linux's current popularity, who knows? Maybe we'll soon all be speaking and spellchecking in Finnish!)

Note

> While the program allows you to set any language you want as your default, be aware that you might not currently have it loaded on your system. You won't know you've made an error until you check your spelling. For more details on switching your installed dictionaries see the section "Installing New Dictionaries," in Chapter 12.

At this time, there is no way to purchase additional dictionaries from StarDivision, although a top product development manager says they are working with their third-party dictionary providers on this.

Tip #30 from
Michael & Sarah

> Be sure to set the language you use most often as the default language.

Besides being able to choose three language dictionaries, you can also create and manage custom dictionaries from this dialog. *Custom dictionaries* are specialized dictionaries that (if turned on) are checked in addition to your currently selected language dictionaries. Since you cannot add to or alter the language dictionaries, custom dictionaries allow you to create your own dictionaries of commonly used words and acronyms, which speeds up spellchecks.

The program comes with two custom dictionaries. The Standard dictionary is the default that StarOffice uses to record words you add when running the Spelling command. The StarDiv custom dictionary contains a number of words and terms specific to computing and the Internet.

> **Caution**
>
> The program depends on the Standard custom dictionary for spellchecking, so don't delete it!

→ For more details on the custom dictionaries, **see** "Installing New Dictionaries," **p. 474**.

CREATING CUSTOM COLORS

Although not in a league with professional publishing and imaging programs such as QuarkXPress, Adobe PageMaker, and Adobe Photoshop, StarOffice 5 comes with some pretty sophisticated graphics and color capabilities, including the capability to mix your own RGB and CYMK custom colors for onscreen and online display or output, respectively. These colors are available to you in all StarOffice modules.

→ For more details on RGB and CYMK colors, **see** "Understanding Color Models and Modes," **p. 796**.

To create custom colors, follow these steps:

1. Select Colors in the Options dialog, General category. A color palette opens, shown in Figure 3.5.

Figure 3.5
The Colors palette, with two custom colors added to the bottom of the palette. On the left, you'll see the palette of standard system colors; on the right you'll find a series of preview and editing tools.

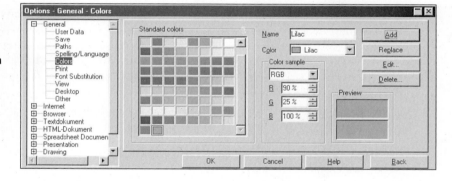

2. Next, click a color on the Standard Colors palette, select RGB or CYMK in the Color sample drop-down list box, and then change the percent value for the individual colors (Red, Green, and Blue or Cyan, Yellow, Magenta, and Black).

3. Click a color on the Standard palette to form the base for your mixing. Your results are shown in the Preview area in the lower window, while the upper window shows the original base color before you applied changes.

4. Once you're satisfied with your choice, label the color by typing a name in the Name text box, and then click the Add button. The color is immediately added to the Color menu, but will not appear on the palette until you click its name in this menu.

You can also choose to replace the Standard palette color with your custom color, or you can edit or replace your standard and custom colors.

The Reset button returns all colors to the values they had before you made any changes in your current session. Cancel cancels all changes and exits the dialog.

SELECTING GLOBAL PRINTER ALERTS

You can set three global printer alerts through the Print dialog box in the Options, General category. These commands are particularly useful for users on a network.

Check the Document Printer Not Found option if you are working with a document on more than one machine or across a network, but need to print it to a specific printer. After you select the printer that the document is associated with, StarOffice sends you an alert if anyone tries to print the document from a machine that is not connected to the specified printer.

If the Paper Size and Orientation options are checked, you will be warned when the size and orientation you have selected for your page(s) do not match the current printer settings for your attached printer. You can then open the Printer Settings dialog box to change your printer's settings, as appropriate, without wasting time or paper.

SELECTING FONT SUBSTITUTIONS

StarOffice has its own font substitution table built in. It automatically applies this table anytime you open a document created in another program that contains fonts you don't have currently loaded, that StarOffice does not handle, or when you export files. However you can also choose to apply your own font substitution table, which makes substitutions within your StarOffice documents and desktop. Certain fonts used on the desktop, in the Explorer, or for the display of data in StarBase tables are determined by system settings that you can't change directly. However, by creating and applying a font substitution table, you can achieve the same effect and see the fonts you want onscreen.

You create a font table through the Substitute Font dialog boxof the Options, General category (see Figure 3.6). To apply your own table, check the Apply Replacement Table check box in the upper left of the dialog. Only when this option is checked can you create your table.

The Font box on the left contains a drop-down menu listing all fonts currently available on your system. Scroll down the list until you find the font you want to replace. Click to select it. Next, select the font you want to replace it with from the Replace With drop-down menu, which also lists all currently available fonts.

Once you have selected both fonts, the two previously grayed out buttons on the right become active—the Add (green check) and Delete (red X) buttons. To add this font pair to your table, click Add.

Figure 3.6
The Font substitution table sets substitutions internal to StarOffice documents. Be sure to choose the green check mark to add your entries to the list.

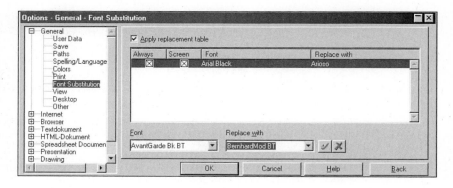

Tip #31 from
Michael & Sarah

The pair appears in the table with two additional check boxes. Click Always to always apply this substitution option. Click Screen to have the substitution affect the screen fonts as well as printer fonts.

DEFINING THE APPEARANCE OF YOUR DESKTOP

The General Options View dialog box enables you to define the general look and feel of your desktop windows, the size of your buttons, the spacing between icons on your desktop, the mouse positioning, and the Beamer controls. For example, you can give your desktop a Macintosh, X Window, OS/2, or StarDivision look and feel, each of which has its own style of title bars and colors for common elements. The Window Drag drop-down list box enables you to choose if task windows appear as full windows or outlines (frames) when you drag them. You can also leave this choice to your operating system (OS).

Tip #32 from
Michael & Sarah

Dragging windows with their complete contents visible requires more memory and processor power. If you have a small amount of RAM or are experiencing frequent memory faults, set Window Drag to Frame Only.

Tip #33 from
Michael & Sarah

If you want StarOffice to start a little bit faster, select Don't Show from the Logo drop-down list in the Display section. This turns off the program splash screen that you normally see during startup.

SETTING MISCELLANEOUS OPTIONS

The Options, General, Other dialog box enables you to set your 3D view and influence the behavior of the Help Agent. For those of you worried about Y2K, it also enables you to determine how two-digit dates are handled by the program.

The 3D View option enables you to decide how StarOffice displays three-dimensional objects created in 3D charts or StarDraw. If you have at least 64MB of RAM and a Pentium-speed processor, select all these options. It will significantly improve onscreen appearance and printing.

By default, the Help Agent is set to start automatically when you invoke many program commands. Some people find that the Help Agent hovers around annoyingly when they are working. If you are one of them, deselect Start Automatically and you will be spared its sudden appearance. The Help Agent tips window displays at the bottom of your window the first time you launch StarOffice. If you're not content with just hiding it on your desktop, you can turn it off globally here, as well as reset the Tip list to the beginning of its cycle.

Note

The tips referred to here are tips given in the Help Agent, not the Tips and Extended Tips you turn on through the Help menu.

Documents created in StarOffice do not face the Y2K problem because StarOffice stores year dates internally as four-digit numbers rather than two. However, many other documents have not been created on systems with four-digit date year handling. Two-digit year date handling, as you're probably aware, can cause problems at the turn of millennium as two-digit dates are no longer sufficient to distinguish between, say, 1905 and 2005. StarOffice's two-digit date handling option enables you to set the start year, which defines how two-digit years are interpreted by StarOffice.

The default setting is to begin at 1930 and end at 2029, which means that StarOffice will interpret the date 01/01/30 as January 1, 1930, but the date 01/01/29 as January 1, 2029. This doesn't entirely solve the Y2K dilemma, but it does loosen the noose a bit. It's recommended that you set the start date as close to the current date as possible—but think carefully about the date you choose, as this will affect all date handling of spreadsheets you import into StarCalc. Let's say, for example, you set the start date as 1960 but you were born in 1955. If you've imported an Excel spreadsheet that automatically calculates how many years until you can collect social security, you'll find that you haven't even been born yet and have to work another 101 years!

Note

The dates you select here also affect how file dates are interpreted; so, consider the age of non-StarOffice computer files that you regularly access.

GETTING ONLINE

To take advantage of all that StarOffice has to offer, you need to connect your desktop to the outside world. While you can choose to run third-party mail, news, FTP, and browser applications, StarOffice has good built-in Internet programs. The advantages of StarOffice's total Internet integration are particularly great when running StarOffice on a network.

If you run StarOffice all the time and remain online, you can do it all right from your desktop—automatically download new email from your server, browse the Web, send a draft document as email to a colleague—not to mention synchronize your schedule with colleagues on a common StarSchedule calendar! There are some technical issues to consider, though, so read on before making any decisions.

If you connect to the Internet through a modem, telephone line, and ISP, you must have a dial-up networking program installed on your system that you've set up to dial your ISP. This section assumes you are either connected to a LAN or have already set up your dial-up networking.

You now have two choices for Internet setup:

- New to 5.1, you can use the Internet AutoPilot, a wizard that guides you through the process. The AutoPilot starts automatically the first time you launch the program and can also be started anytime by choosing the File, AutoPilot, Internet Setup command.

- You can enter settings and create mail and news accounts manually. Internet and browser settings are entered in the Tools, Options, Internet and Tools, Options, Browser dialog boxes (respectively). Mail and news accounts are created via context menu commands in the Explorer.

While the AutoPilot makes getting online easier, it's still a good idea to understand how to create and configure accounts manually as you may want to create additional Inboxes or change settings that you can't access via the AutoPilot. There are also some technical issues to consider in configuring your account and choosing your default Internet programs. It's therefore recommended that you read the entire "Getting Online" section.

> **Note**
>
> If you have multiple mail accounts to manage, setting them up can be confusing in StarOffice because of the way the program uses Inboxes and Outboxes. If you have more than one email account, refer to "Managing Multiple Mail Accounts" in Chapter 29, "Communicating with StarMail and StarDiscussion."

SETTING UP YOUR INTERNET ACCOUNTS WITH THE INTERNET AUTOPILOT

An Internet AutoPilot (shown in Figure 3.7) greets you when you first launch the program to ease you through the intial steps of configuring your Internet accounts in StarOffice.

If you want to defer configuring your Internet connection until later, click Don't Use the Internet. You can run the AutoPilot again at any time by choosing File, AutoPilot, Internet Setup. (You can also use this AutoPilot to change your settings.) Alternatively, you can set up your Internet account and create your own mailboxes and news accounts manually in the Explorer, with methods that are described later in this "Getting Online" section.

Figure 3.7
When you launch StarOffice for the first time, an Internet AutoPilot stands at the ready to guide you through your Interent setup. If you want to use StarOffice as your system-wide default program for some or all of your Internet chores, check Use StarOffice as Default Internet Application.

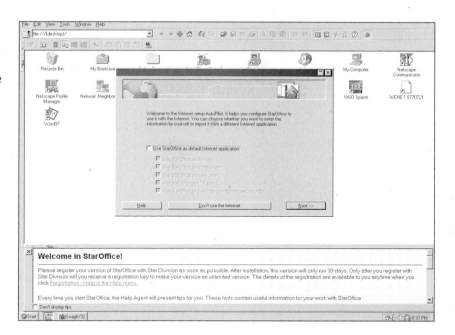

CONSIDERATIONS IN CHOOSING YOUR DEFAULT INTERNET PROGRAMS

The program you choose to serve as your default browser is not that important if you are only online intermittently and open your Internet programs each time you connect. It becomes more important if you are continuously connected, whether through a local area network (LAN) or intranet, or a dedicated connection to an Internet Service Provider (ISP). Your default program will run in the background all the time, managing your Internet and network services.

If you're running StarOffice from your local drive, keep in mind that StarOffice is comparatively memory-hungry, so consider your needs carefully. If you need only to be connected to email and you have less than 64MB of RAM or a less powerful processor, you might be better off running a less demanding program (such as Pine (Linux) or Eudora Lite (Windows)) as your default email client. You then won't need to run StarOffice or have it online all the time. On the other hand, if you're using StarOffice as your regular desktop work environment, you'll save memory and take advantage of its integration if you use it routinely for all your connection needs instead of opening other programs on top of the StarOffice desktop.

If you are running StarOffice off a server on a regular workstation installation, memory demands will not be an issue.

You should also be aware that StarOffice mail and news files can get very large very quickly—larger than you may be used to with other programs. If you choose to use StarOffice for these tasks, make sure you have ample space on the partition or drive where you're storing these files. The default path is Office51\Store; you can change this path in the Tools, Options, General, Paths dialog box.

SELECTING YOUR SYSTEM DEFAULT INTERNET PROGRAMS

The first step in completing the Internet AutoPilot is to choose if you want StarOffice to be your default program for handling any or all of your Internet needs.

If you want StarOffice to handle any of your Internet chores on a regular basis, click the Use StarOffice as Default Internet Application option.

This option sounds more global than it is. Once you select it, the grayed-out list of choices in the lower part of the dialog box becomes active, enabling you to select only those chores you want StarOffice to handle.

You can set StarOffice to be your default for any of five tasks:

- Web browsing
- Email client for POP3, VIM and IMAP accounts
- News client
- FTP client
- Safe HTTP connections (secure HTTP)

Note

Secure HTTP is an extension to HTTP which provides a number of security features, including Client/Server Authentication, Spontaneous Encryption, and Request/Response Nonrepudiation.

This section focuses on using the AutoPilot. Later sections in "Getting Online" offer more detailed technical explanations of Internet accounts.

Once you select StarOffice to be your default Internet application for a specific task or type of file, StarOffice will be your system-wide default. For example, if you select StarOffice to be your default browser, anytime you open an HTTP file on your system or activate a script to access the Web, StarOffice will automatically start (if it isn't already running) and open the selected file or URL.

If you don't choose StarOffice as your default Internet application, you can still use any StarOffice's Internet capabilities from within StarOffice.

Equally, if you do choose StarOffice as your default application, you can still open and use other applications for those tasks. However, be sure StarOffice is offline to avoid conflicts.

Make your selections by clicking the checkbox(es) next to the option(s). When you're done, or if you don't want StarOffice to handle any of Internet chores at all, click Next to move to the next dialog box, shown in Figure 3.8.

IMPORTING SETTINGS AND MAILBOXES FROM OTHER PROGRAMS

If you run either Netscape Communicator, or MS Internet Explorer and/or Outlook Express, the Internet AutoPilot automates the process of importing existing email inboxes and outboxes and browser settings from these programs (see figure 3.8). Importing these settings and files is not the same as integrating these programs into StarOffice and its menus, however. When carrying out tasks with StarOffice menus and commands, you'll still use the StarOffice modules for browsing, email, FTP, and news accounts—unless you open the other program within the StarOffice desktop and run it as you would normally.

Note

New to 5.1, you have the option of integrating the MS Internet Explorer browser into StarOffice's desktop. This option must be selected at the time you install StarOffice, and MS Internet Explorer must be already installed on your system. If you have already installed StarOffice but want to use this feature, you'll need to deinstall StarOffice and reinstall it as a custom installation.

PART

I

CH

3

Regardless of your selection, if you have MS Outlook Express on your system, you can send mail through it directly from the desktop using the Explorer Send command.

Figure 3.8
Any existing installations are listed on the second screen of the Internet Setup AutoPilot. Select the program whose settings you want imported. If you choose to apply all settings automatically, settings for all Internet chores will be imported from that program. Choose Apply Single Settings and you can pick and choose among programs.

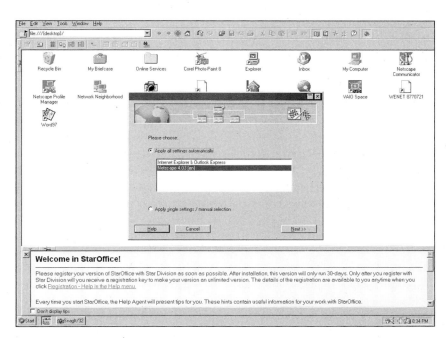

If you choose not to import settings and mailboxes from these other programs, you can set up new, separate accounts and mailboxes within StarOffice.

Tip #34 from
Michael & Sarah

It can be useful to maintain different mail or news accounts in different programs. In case you want to exchange files between them, it's handy to know that StarOffice imports MS Outlook Express and ASCII files directly from the Explorer, and exports only in ASCII format. You can also always import Netscape or MS Outlook Express mailboxes again using the AutoPilot (although the imported mailbox will overwrite the existing one for that account). StarOffice's Address Book is a dBase database file that will import easily into many contact managers and email programs, including MS Outlook Express. Netscape doesn't do as well either importing or exporting address books.

IMPORTING SETTINGS AUTOMATICALLY If you select one of the two programs and the Apply All Settings Automatically, and click Next, StarOffice will automatically import all Internet settings from your selected program as well as any existing mailboxes and news folders.

Note

StarOffice will not import any subfolders you have created in your Outbox(es). StarOffice's Outbox is built differently. You can't create subfolders in its Outbox, only direct your sent mail to regular folders via filters set in the Outbox properties, where each message exists as an individual document file.

If you've taken the automatic route, you're almost done! The AutoPilot presents you with a screen that summarizes what actions StarOffice is about to take, similar to the screen shown in Figure 3.9. Clicking Create gives it your permission to proceed.

Figure 3.9
Whether you take the automatic or manual route, once you've finished making your selections, the AutoPilot greets you with a final dialog box that summarizes your selections and asks for your permission to proceed.

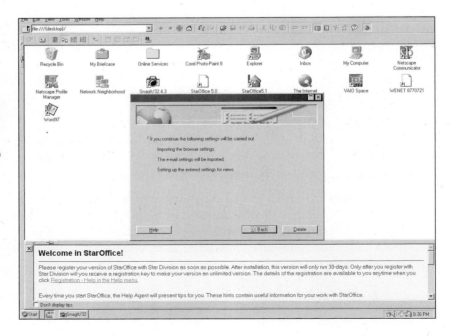

Skip ahead to the section "Creating Your Accounts with AutoPilot" to see what happens next.

→ For information on working with StarMail (email) and StarDiscussion (news groups), you should begin with "Orienting Yourself in StarMail and StarDiscussion," **p. 1046**.

ENTERING SETTINGS MANUALLY   If you're the sort who likes to have more control over your setup, you can choose the Apply Single Settings / Manual Selection option (refer to Figure 3.8). This will step you through three additional dialogs—one for your browser, one for email, and one for news—that enables you to pick and choose how your Internet settings are configured.

Taking the manual route gives you two options:

- Importing all your settings automatically, but mixing and matching between Netscape and MS Explorer or Outlook Express
- Entering some or all of your settings directly

If you choose the latter option, you should be prepared with the following information:

- For manual browser setup (LAN users): proxy settings for your browswer, if any. Ask your system administrator for your network's settings.
- For manual email setup: your incoming (POP3, IMAP, or VIM) and outgoing (SMTP or VIM) mail server names; your user or login name; and (optional) your password.
- For manual news subscription setup: the address of the news server

After you've selected the manual option and clicked Next, you'll see the dialog box shown in Figure 3.10 that prompts you for browser settings.

You can choose to have no browser settings configured at this time, to enter your settings manually, or to import them from Netscape or the Internet Explorer. You need only choose to configure your settings manually if you're on a network and need to enter settings for a proxy server. Otherwise, choose No Browser Settings or import them from an existing program. Regardless of which option you choose, you'll want to check and adjust an extensive set of browser configuration choices later via the Tools, Options, Browser series of dialog boxes.

→ For more information on configuring your browser, **see** "Fine-tuning Your Broswer," **p. 105**.

When you're done establishing your browser settings, click Next to move ahead to the email settings dialog box. You'll have the same set of choices: applying no settings at all, importing from available programs, or entering your email account information manually. If you choose to enter your settings manually and click Next, you see the dialog box shown in Figure 3.11, which prompts you to enter your basic account information.

PART

I

CH

3

Figure 3.10
If you take the manual route, you will first be greeted by a dialog box requesting you to select browser setting options.

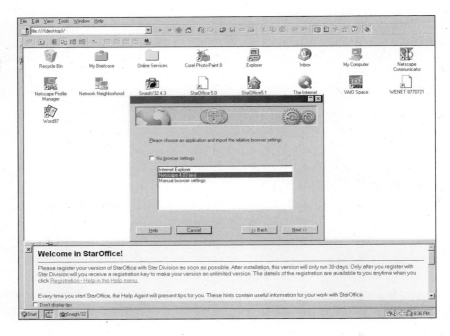

Figure 3.11
If you choose the manual settings option, you enter your email server information and your user name and (if you like) password in this email settings dialog box of the AutoPilot Internet Setup wizard.

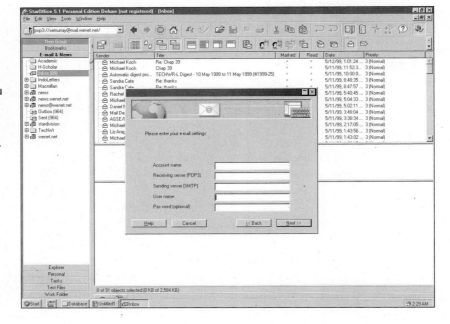

Just click in a text entry box and start typing. You can enter any name you like as your account name, which is simply the name your account will display in the Explorer Email/News group. The remaining information you should have from your ISP. Note that you don't have to enter your password here. If you choose not to, StarOffice prompts you to enter it every time you log on from within the program.

Later, you can create as many additional Inboxes from the Explorer as you like. However, you can create only one Outbox. The reasons for this are explained in "Creating Mailboxes" later in this "Getting Online" section.

Note

If your username requires you to use the @ symbol, be sure you enclose your full name in carets, like this: <roadrunner@acme.com>. Otherwise, StarOffice will choke on the @ symbol.

Click Next when you've finished typing, and you'll be faced with the next-to-last dialog box (shown in Figure 3.12), where you can enter news settings. Here again, you enter an account name and a server name—but this time a news server name. You can enter the name of any publically accessible news server; it doesn't have to be the one run by your ISP or network. For example, in Figure 3.12, the StarDivision server, stardivision.starnews.com, was entered.

Figure 3.12
The next-to-last step of your AutoPilot journey is to enter the name of your news server and assign a name to the account.

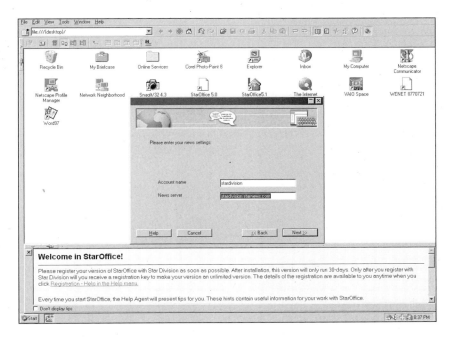

Once you've entered the required information, click next to take you to the final dialog, which looks similar to the one shown earlier in Figure 3.9. Check the summary of your selections, and if you're satisfied, click Create to complete the setup process. If you want to make any changes, just click Back to step back through the process. Click Cancel to abandon all settings and return to the desktop.

CREATING YOUR ACCOUNTS WITH THE AUTOPILOT   After you click Create, depending on how large your mail and news files are, it may take StarOffice a few minutes to complete its work.

It will automatically create a mail Inbox and Outbox for you in the Explorer Email/News group, enter relevant browser settings in the Tools, Options, Browser series of dialog boxes, and enter your basic Internet connection information in the Tools, Options, Internet series of dialog boxes. To open your mail or news account, first open the Email/New group in the extended Explorer by clicking the group title bar. If your group is set to icon view, click the mail or news account you want to open on your desktop (or Ctrl+click if you want to open it on top of other open documents). If it's set to Hierarchical view, double-click (or Ctrl+ double-click) to open it.

Tip #35 from
Michael & Sarah

If you have your mail and news group set to Hiarchical view, you can display a list of individual messages or news items by selecting the Display Contents command on the group's context menu.

MODIFYING AND CUSTOMIZING YOUR INTERNET CONNECTION

While your default and/or imported Internet settings may be just fine for you, there are many settings you can modify and customize to better suit your network needs. In case you experience connection problems, you may also need to make adjustments to these settings.

To enter or change Internet settings, open the Tools, Options master dialog box and click the plus sign next to the word Internet. You'll see a list of five dialog boxes, each of which is discussed briefly below.

MODIFYING AND CUSTOMIZING MAIL AND NEWS SETTINGS

Figure 3.13 shows the Tools, Options, Internet Mail/News dialog box. This dialog box saves your default Internet connection information. These settings are used to determine how all outgoing mail is routed, as well as email sent from the desktop (that is, without opening a specific account Inbox). Changing these settings will not delete or otherwise change any existing Inboxes you have; it will only change the routing of mail.

Figure 3.13
You can set email format defaults and speed news loading by checking the Autoload option on the Mail/News dialog.

You can choose here to set defaults for email file formats. Messages are always sent in ASCII format; you can also choose to send them in any of three additional formats: HTML, RTF, or StarOffice. Creating mail in these formats allows you to format your message in more sophisticated ways, such as applying bold face or italics. If you select one or more of these options, the default will be set to send your message in both ASCII form and the selected format(s). (However, you can change your options for a specific message from within the StarMail composition window.)

Only select an option if you know you need it. Many email accounts and newsgroups accept only standard ASCII text messages, and your HTML, RTF, or StarOffice copy might not be readable by your recipient. Choosing one of these formats also increases the size and transmission time of your message substantially. Besides, it's not polite to clog up someone's mailbox with fancy-formatted mail messages they can't read.

→ For a discussion of these different formats and their uses, **see** the section "Creating and Sending Mail," **p. 1053**.

If you check the Autoload option, the contents of news postings automatically appear in your viewing window when you open your news Inbox and begin to scroll. If you check Automatically Mark Mail as Read, you can set your mail to be marked as Read after a time delay you specify—anywhere from 0–999 seconds.

CHANGING PROXY SETTINGS

You can change proxy settings in the Tools, Options, Internet, Proxy dialog box. Some networks use a proxy server as a kind of cache in order to ensure network security and improve performance.

If you work on a network, ask your MIS computing support guy or gal or your ISP support contact about your proxy configuration. If you are told that you do not have one, select None. Otherwise, enter the settings as instructed.

ADDING WEB SEARCH ENGINES

The Tools, Options, Internet, Search dialog box contains the names and site addresses of Web search engines that you can call up from a handy shortcut menu that you open with the Find button on the Hyperlink toolbar. A number of common search engines are already listed. You can delete these entries and/or add new ones.

ADDING LDAP DIRECTORIES

The Tools, Options, Internet, LDAP Server dialog box contains names of Web directory services (the Web version of phone books) that you can search from the StarOffice Address Book dialog box. The only default entry is the Four11 Directory. Once you locate an address in one of these directories, you can automatically add it to your own Address Book as well.

MODIFYING YOUR INTERNET PROTOCOLS

The Protocol dialog box contains options that define how you connect to servers. The Domain Name Server (DNS) translates a human readable Internet addresses such as (www.stardivision.com) into the real Internet Protocol (IP) address (209.0.29.180). If the option is set to Automatic (the default), StarOffice automatically reads the DNS server's address from your operating system settings. If the option is set to Manual, you can manually enter a DNS IP address as provided by your ISP. Most users will want to leave this option set at Automatic.

Tip #36 from
Michael & Sarah

> Your default Internet settings and ISP information are all saved in the soffice.ini file (Windows) or sofficerc file (Linux) located in your root StarOffice directory (Office51 is the default). They can be checked and edited manually by advanced users.

HTTP and FTP servers are servers you use to connect to the WWW and FTP sites, respectively. You can be connected to more than one HTTP or FTP server at a time; this allows you to download something from one site while you're browsing a Web page from another. The defaults are four HTTP sites and two FTP sites. Don't increase these defaults unless you have a good reason, because the more sites you connect to at once, the more likely your browser or FTP connection is to crash.

Note

> HTTP stands for *Hypertext Transfer Protocol*, and FTP stands for *File Transfer Protocol*. They are two languages (protocols) used for communication between computers on the Internet.

CREATING MAILBOXES

When you send and receive *snail mail* (computer lingo for that quaint artifact, a stamped, paper letter), you can use the same mailbox for incoming and outgoing mail. When you send and receive email in StarOffice, you use separate Inboxes and Outboxes.

Your Inbox receives and (if you download your mail from the server) stores mail people send you. This Inbox also directs your outgoing mail under certain conditions. (See "Setting Up Multiple Accounts" in this chapter for more information).

Your Outbox processes all your outgoing mail. Messages you write and defer sending while offline are stored in the Outbox until you go online again. Copies of every message you successfully send are automatically saved here as well.

Note

All incoming and outgoing mail and news files are saved in the \Office51\Store folder (with the .scs extension). You should frequently browse through your saved mail in the Inboxes and Outbox and delete old mail that you no longer need in order to free up space on your hard drive. If you need to keep a lot of your old mail or news messages, keep an eye on the size of this folder, as it might quickly outgrow the size of your assigned partition for StarOffice. If necessary, assign a different path (on a different partition or hard drive) using the Mail/News Storage category of the Tools, Options dialog.

PART

I

CH

3

You create Inboxes and Outboxes from the Explorer context menu New command (see Figure 3.14).

Figure 3.14
The Explorer context menu contains commands for creating email account Inboxes and Outboxes. You can also create other Internet accounts from here—FTP accounts, news group accounts, and Web subscriptions.

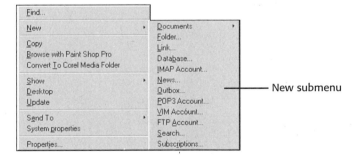

New submenu

If you used the Internet AutoPilot to set up your accounts initially, a Mail/News group was created for you automatically in the Explorer. If you don't have such a group, it's a good idea to create one as it's easier to manage your mail and news if it's in the same place. However, when you create mailboxes manually, you can put them anywhere you like.

Tip #37 from
Michael & Sarah

Storing all your mail in one big Inbox or Outbox gets unwieldy pretty quickly. By setting rules to sort and filter your mail, you can store incoming and outgoing mail messages in different folders anywhere on your network or directory. Create and apply rules through the Inbox and Outbox context menu Properties command (Rules and Views tabs).

→ For more information, **see** the sections "Using Filters to Manage Files," **p. 197** and "Techniques for Managing Mail and News," **p. 1075**.

CREATING AN ACCOUNT INBOX

What StarOffice separates on the Explorer context menu as POP3 Account, IMAP Account, and VIM Account (refer to Figure 3.14) are really just three different routes to the same end: creating an email account Inbox. This Inbox is the mailbox that receives and (if you choose) stores all your incoming mail for a specific account. There are three separate commands because each type of account works with a different mail protocol and can be assigned slightly different properties.

Note

Linux users who were frustrated with the lack of IMAP support in version 5.0 will be glad to know that improved IMAP support for Linux is one of the major features of the 5.1 release. However, if support for a particular IMAP Server is critical for your ability to use StarOffice as an email client, check before you commit to using StarOffice, as it still does not support a full range of IMAP Servers.

Because POP3 accounts are the most common type, we'll use creating a POP3 account Inbox as an example here. The process and principles of creating an account Inbox are pretty much the same, regardless of its type

Before you create your mail account Inbox, you need to know:

- The type of mail protocol your ISP or server uses to manage mail
- The names of your incoming and outgoing mail servers
- Your email and newsgroup password(s) (optional)

Note

POP3, IMAP, and VIM are the three most common protocols for managing incoming mail. POP3 is popular with commercial ISPs oriented toward individual dial-up connection, whereas individual users download mail and store it on their own hard drives. IMAP is used by many UNIX and Linux computing environments, as it assumes mail is being stored and managed on a central server. VIM is the mail protocol used in Lotus Notes and cc:Mail, and is used on many corporate intranets. If you aren't sure or can't guess what protocol you use based on this information, ask your ISP or network administrator.

→ For in-depth discussion of using StarMail to send and receive mail and manage newsgroups, **see** Chapter 29, "Communicating with StarMail and StarDiscussion," **p. 1045.**

After you have all your email account Inbox information at your fingertips, follow these steps:

1. Select the group and/or folder where you plan to store your account.
2. Right-click to open the Explorer context menu.
3. Open the New submenu.
4. Select the name of the mail protocol your server or ISP uses to manage mail (POP3, VIM, or IMAP). This opens a new account Inbox dialog box. Figure 3.15 shows a new POP3 Account Inbox dialog.

Figure 3.15
The General, Send, Receive, Headers, and Contents tabs are common across the VIM, POP3, and IMAP new Inbox commands. Each type of account may also have its own unique tabs.

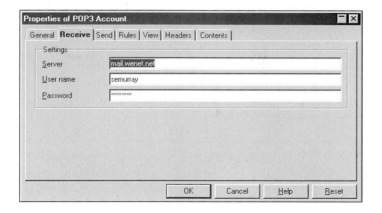

5. Click the Receive tab. Your server name, username, and password information have already been automatically copied and entered from your user data and any existing Internet settings.

   If you want to create an Inbox for a different account, select the current information and type over it. Replacing this information here has no effect on the information you saved in the Tools, Options, Internet, Mail/News dialog box or your user data.

   You can leave the password blank if you're concerned about security. As long as you haven't saved your password in the Internet dialog box or an Outbox, you'll be prompted for your password each time you connect and it won't be saved.

6. The Send tab enables you to determine how outgoing mail is routed. If you only have one email account, your Outbox settings will determine how your outgoing mail is sent (As Outbox Settings option). If you have multiple mail accounts, you will want to select the User-defined Settings option, click the User-defined settings button, and enter the appropriate information for your second account. For more information, see the section "Managing Multiple Mail Accounts" later in this chapter.

7. Click the General tab and enter a name for the account. If you don't assign a name, StarOffice automatically names it after your mail server.

8. The Rules and View tabs enable you to create filters to manage your Inbox messages. (Learn about using these commands in Chapter 5, in the section "Using Filters to Manage Files" and the section "Techniques for Managing Mail and News" in Chapter 29.)

9. The Headers tab enables you to determine what header information displays when you read incoming mail.

10. Click the Contents tab (see Figure 3.16). Here you can set your Inbox to automatically check your mail server and download your mail at an interval you specify, as well as update every time you click the Update command in your Inbox's context menu.

Figure 3.16
If you're online all the time, you can set your email to automatically update by a period of minutes or hours on the Properties, Contents tab.

These options are active only for news accounts.

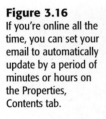

Tip #38 from
Michael & Sarah

If you're not continuously online, you might want to set the update time interval to 0. Otherwise, if you forget go offline from within StarOffice (by clicking the Online button on the function bar so it does not look pressed), StarOffice will keep looking for a connection, taking up system resources, and generating connection error messages.

11. You also set your mail storage options here—a very important setting. To set these options properly, you need to understand what happens when you open your Inbox to read your mail.

    When you open your Inbox, StarOffice copies the headers of your mail messages (the To, From, and Subject lines, along with some technical information) from your mail server into a temporary file called a *cache* and makes these headers visible in your Inbox. When you double-click a header to view the message, StarOffice fetches the message contents from the mail server and allows you to view them. The message contents are not stored on your machine—they're stored on the mail server.

    If you select Remove Messages from Server, every time you connect to your incoming mail server (here, the POP3 Server) and read your mail, all messages will automatically be deleted from your mail server after you've read them. POP3 accounts are designed to be used this way.

    If you select Store Document Contents Locally, complete copies of your incoming mail messages will be downloaded and saved on your hard drive.

Caution

If you select Remove Messages from Server and do not select Store Document Contents Locally, every time you finish reading an incoming mail message, it is automatically sent to the Recycle Bin.

12. Click OK to confirm your entries. Clicking Reset returns the settings as they were on opening the dialog box and leaves the dialog box open. Cancel returns the settings to their original state and closes the dialog.

You are now the proud owner of an (empty) email account Inbox.

To download, read, and reply to mail, double-click your Inbox icon in the Explorer. Your account Inbox opens on your desktop, displaying any messages, and you are in StarMail.

Tip #39 from
Michael & Sarah

If you have the You Have New Mail! icon turned on in the status bar and are online continuously and update automatically, a Globe icon in the icon tray will signal when you have new mail. You can turn this icon on and off in the Tools, Configure, Status Bar dialog.

If you open your Inbox when you're not connected to your ISP or network, you might get a Connection Failure error message, or you may be prompted with your system's dial-up networking dialog—the program seems unpredictable this way. If you are connected but are not in Online mode, the program sends you a message and asks if you want to go online. Once you are connected and online, StarOffice logs in to your server and downloads your mail.

You can also check your server for new messages at any time by clicking Update on the context menu, or clicking the Globe icon in your icon tray and choosing Update from its context menu.

→ For more information on reading and replying to email, **see** "Creating and Sending Mail," **p. 1053**.

CREATING AN OUTBOX FROM SCRATCH

If you used the Internet AutoPilot to set up your Internet accounts, you had an Outbox created for you automatically and you don't need to create another one. If not, you'll need to create one manually from the Explorer. You cannot send mail until you have an Outbox.

You cannot create multiple Outboxes for multiple accounts. While technically you can create additional Outboxes, in reality these only enable you to apply different sets of filters to your one and only Outbox.

→ For the steps required to set up your mail account to route mail through a different account, **see** "Setting Up Multiple Accounts," **p. 103**.

→ For the steps required to send outgoing mail through a different account, **see** "Managing Multiple Mail Accounts," **p. 1067**.

If you create your Inbox manually, StarOffice asks you on completion if you want to create an Outbox. It's a good idea to reply Yes and proceed because you can't send any email until you create an Outbox. To create an Outbox, you need to know the protocol your system uses to send mail and news to your ISP or network server.

SMTP and NNTP are the dominant Internet protocols for sending mail and news, respectively. VIM is the other major protocol, and sends both mail and news. If you don't use Lotus Notes or cc:Mail, you can assume your system communicates with SMTP and NNTP.

PART

I

CH

3

Here are the steps to follow to create an SMTP Outbox from scratch; if you create your Outbox directly after creating your Inbox, you'll begin at step 3.

1. Select the folder where you want to store your Outbox settings.

2. Select Outbox from the Explorer context menu New submenu.

3. Enter a name for your Outbox in the General tab.

4. Click the SMTP tab. Your server, username, and password should have already been copied from your Internet settings. If they have not, enter the name of your outgoing mail server, your email username, and (if you choose) your email password. (Your server name will be something like smtp.wenet.com.) If you don't enter your username and/or password here, you will be prompted with a dialog box to supply them every time you connect. These settings determine the default route for all your outgoing mail.

Caution

If you enter your password, others might be able to access your account without your permission or knowledge.

5. If you entered an email address as part of your registration or Internet setup, that address has automatically been entered into the Sender field of the SMTP tab. This address appears in the Sender field of email messages you write from your default Inbox or from your desktop. (If you have multiple Inboxes, your default Inbox is the Inbox that uses the email address in your Tools, Options, Internet, Mail/News data.) If you want return mail sent somewhere else, enter your return email address in the Reply To box.

Note

Surround your email addresses with caret brackets, for example: <jlopez@wenet.com>. If you don't use these brackets, StarOffice will choke on the @ symbol in your address.

Note

You don't need to worry about any of the other tabs right now. The Rules and View tabs will help you manage your outgoing mail later, and the NNTP tab relates to newsgroup subscriptions. You've entered all the information you need to send outgoing mail.

6. Choose OK to complete the creation of your Outbox. Choosing Cancel cancels the creation of the Outbox and returns you to the desktop; choosing Reset returns the Outbox to its initial settings on opening and leaves the Outbox dialog box open.

If you use the VIM protocol, ignore the SMTP tabs. Enter your information on the VIM tab and click OK. Otherwise, the procedure is the same.

After you choose OK, your Outbox appears in the selected Explorer folder. You're now ready to send mail from your desktop. You can send mail from your Inbox or Outbox by selecting the New, Mail command from the File menu, or by clicking the New Mail icon on the StarOffice desktop.

To read and manage copies of your sent mail and news postings, double-click the Outbox to open it on your desktop.

Tip #40 from
Michael & Sarah

To open your Inbox and Outbox at the same time, double-click to open the Inbox on the desktop, and then press Ctrl while double-clicking the Outbox.

→ For more information on sorting, filtering, and managing your Outbox mail, **see** "Techniques for Managing Mail and News," **p. 1075.**

PART

I

CH

3

SETTING UP MULTIPLE ACCOUNTS

StarOffice manages multiple email accounts through account Inboxes. You can create as many account Inboxes as you want. (The program documentation, by the way, often refers to account Inboxes as *mail servers* because they contain information for receiving mail from a server.)

Why would you want more than one Inbox? Perhaps you have more than one email account. If you work on an intranet, for example, you might have one email account on your company intranet for work mail and another account at a personal dial-up ISP account that you sometimes call from work. Or maybe you maintain separate business and personal accounts.

CREATING MULTIPLE ACCOUNT INBOXES

Setting up multiple accounts is easy. Begin by following the steps in the earlier section "Creating an Account Inbox." Then follow these steps:

1. Assign the Inbox a different name than any existing Inboxes.

2. Input the name of the mail server for this second account in the Receive tab along with the username and (if you choose) password. If there is already a username and password, delete them and enter your new information.

3. On the Contents tab, select the options you want for updating and storing your mail for this account. (Refer to the section "Creating an Account Inbox" earlier in this chapter for more information.)

4. Click the Send tab. Here you'll enter information that directs mail you send from this second account through the correct outgoing mail server.

5. The Send tab by default has the As Outbox Settings option chosen for both the SMTP and NNTP accounts, as. When this option is selected, StarOffice automatically uses the settings in your Outbox to route outgoing mail; you don't want this option. Choose instead the User-Defined Settings option for both (see Figure 3.17).

6. Click the User-Defined Settings button on the lower right. This opens a new dialog, shown in Figure 3.17, called Properties of Send Protocol.

Note

> Selecting the User-Defined Settings options is the key to sending your mail through a second account. When—and only when—this account Inbox is opened on your desktop, this option over-rides the default Outbox settings that normally guide the routing of your outgoing mail and sends them according to the settings in the Properties of Send Protocol dialog box (shown in Figure 3.17).

Figure 3.17

The settings in the Properties of Send Protocol dialog box are used to send mail when: 1) the User-Defined Settings option is selected on the Send tab of the account Inbox Properties; 2) you have the account Inbox open on your desktop; and 3) you create mail using the StarMail New Mail tool button.

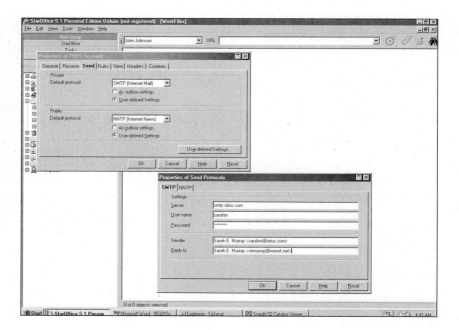

This dialog box has two tabs: one for your SMTP account settings and the other for your NNTP account settings. Delete any existing information that is not relevant, and enter the correct server names, and (if you choose) username and password. Change the sender and return address (Reply) as appropriate.

When you've finished, choose OK to confirm your settings, which returns you to your Inbox dialog. Choose OK in your Inbox dialog box to confirm. You've now successfully set up a second email account!

Note

> Regardless of how your outgoing mail is sent, all copies of your outgoing mail are saved and stored in the same Outbox.

→ For more information **see** "Managing Multiple Mail Accounts," **p. 1067**.

CREATING MULTIPLE OUTBOXES

An Outbox has two different functions:

- It contains the default outgoing mail server address for routing your outgoing mail and news postings, along with your username and password (if you've saved it) for that server.

- It stores unsent mail and news postings and stores and filters all copies of sent mail.

You can create as many Outboxes as you like. However, all the Outboxes you create will have the same settings because you can have only one default outgoing server in StarOffice. If you create a new Outbox and enter new server information, username, and password in the SMTP and NNTP or VIM tabs, this information automatically overwrites the existing information in all your other Outboxes.

To send outgoing mail through a different server, you don't need to create a second Outbox. You manage this by creating a second account Inbox, as described in the section "Creating Multiple Account Inboxes."

However, creating multiple Outboxes can help you deal with the mammoth task of sorting, filtering, and filing all your sent email. By using the Rules and View tab options of your Outbox properties, you can create different views of your sent mail, and create filters that copy or move outgoing mail to different folders and locations.

The steps for creating a second Outbox are simple.

1. Select Outbox from the context menu New submenu.
2. Give your new Outbox a unique name.
3. Ignore the SMTP, NNTP, and VIM settings unless you want to change your default Outbox settings. Settings you enter here will overwrite settings in any other Outboxes.
4. Set any rules or viewing options you want on the Rules and View tabs.
5. Choose OK.

FINE-TUNING YOUR BROWSER

A *browser* is a program that reads documents created in HTML and can communicate via the Internet hypertext text protocol (HTTP, the first part of every WWW address). StarOffice has a built-in browser fully integrated with the program's file searching and file management tools. Just type or paste a WWW address into the URL Locator, press Enter, and voilà! The Web page appears on your desktop, where you can view it or email it like any other StarOffice document. Pretty cool! This browser, together with StarWriter, is also what you use to create, edit, and view HTML documents.

Feature-wise, the StarOffice browser stacks up quite well against Netscape Navigator and Microsoft Internet Explorer. You can define a wide range of browser characteristics, including the size of your caches and how cookies and security are handled. If you installed the Java RunTime environment, it also works with Java applets and JavaScript.

When you start StarOffice for the first time, you have the option of setting StarOffice as your default browser. If you do, StarOffice will be the program that handles all your future Web browsing on your system. Even if you choose not to set it as your default, however, you can still use it to browse from your StarOffice desktop.

Note

New with 5.1, you can integrate MS Internet Explorer 5 into your StarOffice desktop. IE5 must be loaded first, so if you want to integrate it but have already installed StarOffice, you'll need to uninstall it, install IE5, and reinstall StarOffice.

All your browser characteristics are set in dialogs in the Tools, Options, Browser category (look ahead to Figure 3.18). Note that settings in the Browser HTML dialog box also determine the file format of HTML documents you create and export from StarOffice.

The most important dialogs to check during setup are Cache, Scripting, and Other, so you'll look at those first.

SETTING MEMORY AND HARD DRIVE CACHE SIZES

WWW pages are complex documents that can contain graphics, video clips, sound, and text. It takes time for such complex documents to travel across your network connection or phone line. To speed and smooth your viewing, browsers store recently visited Web pages both in system memory (RAM) and on your hard drive in *caches* of documents.

You can set the size of your caches on the Cache tab of the Browser dialog, as well as clear each cache of stored documents and determine how often StarOffice compares a document in the cache with the actual Web site. If you want, you can also do without a cache at all by entering the name of your machine or server(s) in the No Cache For box.

As shown in Figure 3.18, the default cache sizes are 10 documents stored in RAM, with 10240KB (10MB) of space set aside on the hard drive. You can set your RAM cache from 0–999 documents and your hard drive cache from 0–500,000KB (500MB).

The sizes at which your memory and hard drive caches are set affect the speed of your browsing. Another consideration is that if cache sizes are too low or too high, you might experience crashes. You also don't want to set your caches too high because you don't want to take up all your system resources—you need RAM and hard drive space for your other applications as well.

Figure 3.18
The Cache dialog box in the Options, Browser category allows you to control the size of your RAM and hard drive caches for Web documents. The top Clear button clears the RAM cache; the bottom Clear button clears the hard drive cache.

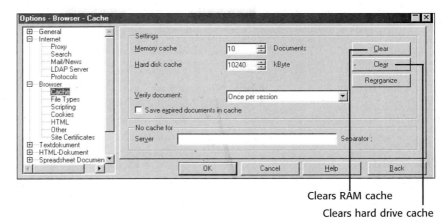

Clears RAM cache

Clears hard drive cache

After you've loaded a Web page into your StarOffice Web browser and it's saved in a cache, StarOffice doesn't necessarily keep going back to the original site to see if anything's changed. If you want StarWeb to always compare a page in the cache against the original on the site, select Always in the Verify Document drop-down menu. If you select Never or Once per Session, you'll need to click the Reload button on the function bar to freshly reload the page from the original site.

CLEARING DOCUMENTS FROM YOUR CACHES

Because StarOffice caches Web documents as you browse, you can build up a lot of clutter that you don't want. Also, if you're having memory management problems or your system has been crashing frequently, you might want to clear your RAM cache at intervals while you're browsing. You can manually clear all files currently stored in your RAM or hard drive caches with the two Clear buttons on the Cache tab. Even though the buttons have the same name, they serve different masters—the top Clear button clears the RAM cache, while the bottom button clears the hard drive cache (refer to figure 3.18).

ENABLING JAVA

Java is a computer programming language that runs on all machines regardless of their operating system. Many Web sites have mini-programs called *Java applets* that run when you visit or carry out specific actions on the site, and will work properly only if your browser can run Java.

StarOffice works with Java if you have installed the Java RunTime environment (an option at initial installation), and if Enable is selected in the Java section of the Other dialog, shown in Figure 3.19.

Figure 3.19
The Other dialog box in the Options, Browser category is where you enable plug-ins and Java, and change your default home page. The Browser Identification box contains information Web sites need to work with your browser.

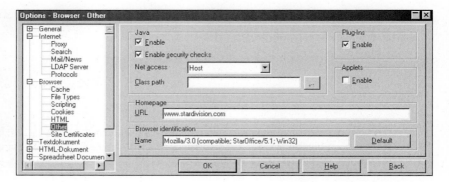

Tip #41 from
Michael & Sarah

Selecting the Enable Security Checks option is a good idea if you're running Java programs because StarOffice then checks the source of the program and alerts you if it seems suspicious.

Because a Java applet is a program from a foreign source entering and running on your computer, it can pose a security risk, especially if you are on a network. As a safety feature, you can determine the type of access applets have to your network—None at All, Host (the same access as your computer), or Unrestricted (total access to the network). Unless you have a specific reason to allow unrestricted access, you're best advised to set this to Host or None.

SETTING YOUR BROWSER HOME PAGE

The function bar has a button called Home that instantly takes you to the page designated as your home page. Your default home page is the main StarDivision page at www.stardivsion.com. In the Other dialog box, you can change your default home page to any page you like—just delete the StarDivision address and enter your new URL into the URL box (refer to Figure 3.19).

SELECTING HOW SCRIPTS ARE HANDLED

Some Web sites have *scripts*, miniature programs, attached to them that are designed to run on your machine when you connect. While most scripts are benign and do things such as help process online orders or register you for a site, some scripts are nasty and carry computer viruses or do things you might not want. With the Scripting dialog box in the Options, Browser category, you can control, to some extent, how scripts are handled by your browser.

StarOffice recognizes two types of scripts: JavaScript, which is the most common Web scripting language, and StarBasic scripts, which are used on StarDivision's sites (as well as other sites created with StarOffice). JavaScripts are in the same family as Java applets (discussed earlier in the section "Enabling Java").

If you select Enable JavaScript, StarOffice will run all JavaScripts it encounters during browsing.

With StarBasic scripts, you have a greater level of control. You can choose to not recognize them at all, to run scripts only from a list of authorized sites that you maintain, or to run all encountered scripts. The default option is to run scripts from authorized sites.

Caution

Because your local drive is treated just like another node on the Internet, you must have either the From List or Always Execute options checked to run StarBasic scripts on your computer. A script on your own computer is listed as `private:nameofscript`.

Note

Some sites will not function properly if you do not execute their scripts.

MANAGING PLUG-INS

A *plug-in* is a program that works together with your browser to extend its capabilities to open different types of files. Common plug-ins include the RealAudio player, which enables you to listen to radio over the Internet or even watch TV, zip programs that automatically unzip downloaded program files, and document-viewing programs that allow you to open email file attachments.

At installation, StarOffice checks your system to see if you have a Netscape or MS Internet Explorer installation. If you do, it automatically uses these plug-ins in StarOffice as well. You can view the list of currently loaded plug-ins and add new ones on the File Types tab.

Note

If you do not currently have a browser installed, you might receive an error message on startup saying that StarOffice could not load its plug-in manager and prompting you to run Setup with the `-repair` option (Linux) or choose the Repair option on the wizard (Windows). Running repair will have no effect because you don't have any plug-ins for StarOffice to find. StarOffice will still run without plug-ins, but some browser functions will be unavailable and you may not be capable of opening some types of email attachments.

A plug-in automatically opens any files with file extensions that have been assigned to the plug-in. The File Types list shows all the file types StarOffice currently handles. You can change the association of a specified file type with a plug-in or add new file types by entering the MIME type and file extension, and then choosing the plug-in and plug-in filter you want to open that type of file. Choose Replace to replace a current file type association, or choose Add to add a new one.

Select Open with Plug-In, and then click the drop-down Filter menu to see the complete list already in your version of StarOffice.

Note

For plug-ins to work, Enable must be checked in the Plug-Ins area of the Other dialog box in the Tools, Options, Browser category.

You can also associate StarBasic macros and StarOffice application modules with specific file types by choosing Other from the Open With drop-down menu, or browse on your local drives and attach executable programs stored outside the StarOffice directory by choosing External from the Open With menu.

CHOOSING COOKIE-EATING OPTIONS

A *cookie* is a piece of data that a Web site sends to your browser. It stores certain information about you that the site wants every time you connect (for example, perhaps your browser type, name, and email address). Cookies speed up connection time. They have roused some controversy about privacy because you don't actually see what's in a cookie. However, cookies can't reveal any information you have not already given to the Web site.

If you select Accept on the Cookies dialog box (Tools, Options, Browser category), StarOffice will always accept cookies. If you select Confirm, you will always be asked if you want to accept a cookie, whereas Ignore ignores all cookies. Also, all cookies currently saved in your cache display in the list. You can select cookies and either delete them with the Delete button or choose to ignore them with Ignore.

Caution

Showing a fierce kind of hospitality, some Web sites don't allow access if your browser doesn't accept cookies.

SELECTING HTML DOCUMENT FORMATTING

In the browser HTML dialog box (Tools, Options, Browser category), you can determine how HTML pages are imported and exported from StarOffice, as well as the displayed font sizes of Web pages. The export settings affect the appearance of HTML documents you create in StarWriter\Web as well as documents you export in HTML format.

Because Web pages have to display on many different kinds of systems, they don't handle fonts in the same way as regular documents. Instead of having specific fonts embedded in them, they refer to font sizes that range from Size 1 (smallest) to Size 7 (largest). You can set the font size StarOffice assigns to each of these sizes and thus determine how large the type of a Web page is onscreen. The maximum font size is 50 points.

HANDLING SECURITY WITH SITE CERTIFICATES

Many people now shop over the Web and send confidential financial information, such as credit card numbers, which need to be kept secure. Remember those secret decoder rings from childhood? Well, one way of securing this information from snoopers is to *encrypt* it—provide your computer with a secret decoder ring through a site certificate system—so you can send valuable information safely. There are a number of third-party companies that manage site certificates for Web sites, each with their own encryption system. You can determine what type of site certificates StarOffice accepts by editing the list of these companies on the Site Certificates tab.

MANAGING AND IMPORTING BOOKMARKS

Browser bookmarks are managed from the Explorer Bookmarks folder.

When you install StarOffice, it tries to locate any existing bookmarks you have and automatically places them in the Bookmarks folder. If you have bookmarks that don't make the cut, you can create a link to them in the Bookmarks folder or somewhere else in the Explorer so you have all you need at your fingertips.

→ For more information on the Explorer Bookmarks folder, **see** "Default Explorer Contents," **p. 51**.

For more information on the Explorer Bookmarks folder, **see** "Default Explorer Contents," **p. 51**.

CONFIGURING YOUR DOCUMENT OPTIONS

You can also find dialog boxes in the Tools, Options dialog box that enable you to set all kinds of options related to how you work with the seven basic StarOffice document types (text, HTML, spreadsheet, presentation, drawing, formula, and image). Setting these options is mentioned where appropriate in the individual chapters or sections that deal with StarWriter, StarCalc, StarImpress, StarDraw, StarMath, and StarImage.

You can also turn on the Help Agent, which guides you through most of these options as you click your way around the dialog box tabs. Be sure to turn on Extended Tips in the Help menu as well; moving your pointer over options will then make visible basic descriptions of tool functions.

SETTING PROGRAM TEMPLATE DEFAULTS

Almost every program module in StarOffice—StarWriter, StarCalc, StarDraw, StarImage, StarImpress, StarMath, StarChart, StarMail, and StarWriter\Web—has a default template, called the Standard template. There are also default templates for a Master document (a special kind of document you can create in StarWriter), and a Frame document (a special kind of Web document). These templates define the basic properties of a new, blank document of that type, including fonts, colors, styles, and document margins. A template also includes the definition of the default desktop work environment for that document type—toolbars, menus, keyboard shortcuts, and so on.

You cannot delete the Standard templates nor can you edit them directly as files (although you can add your own custom styles and customize your workspace from inside a document). However, you can assign a document template of your own to serve as the new Standard template in the stead of any of the program default Standard templates. The template you assign will be the template that opens every time you choose the File, New command or double-click one of the new task icons from the StarOffice desktop.

To make your own template the default, follow these steps:

1. Open the folder that contains the document you want to set as the template, either on the desktop or in the Beamer.
2. Select the file.
3. Right-click and choose Set Default Template. A submenu will open that lists the matching StarOffice template.
4. Select the template icon.

CUSTOMIZING YOUR DESKTOP

Because StarOffice offers so many ways to customize your workspace, sometimes settings commands are spread out across various menus and dialogs, such as those for changing the look of your desktop, which can be found in three places:

- The Desktop context menu
- The Options, General, Desktop dialog
- The Options, General, View dialog

Methods for achieving other kinds of desktop customization, such as adding and deleting items from the Start menu and setting non-StarOffice programs to start when StarOffice is launched, don't involve commands. However, they do involve understanding StarOffice's directory structure and special program directories, things that may not be intuitively obvious to a new user.

This section guides you through desktop customization specific to the general desktop environment. It does not exhaust the customization possibilities, but once you understand the general principles and procedures, you will quickly be able to customize almost anything you encounter in your StarOffice workspace.

SETTING DESKTOP PROPERTIES

Every object on your desktop, including your desktop, has properties that you can see and change through the Properties command on the context menu. (Be sure you've selected the correct object first.) The desktop Properties dialog, like all other StarOffice objects, has Rules, View, and Contents tabs which allow you to create viewing and saving filters, and determine if the object can be updated with the context menu Update command. Using the options on these tabs is discussed in detail in Chapter 5.

CHANGING YOUR BACKGROUND COLOR AND GRAPHIC

Buried deep in the back of the Properties dialog box is also a tab for changing the look of your desktop background, (see Figure 3.20). With the Background tab, you can change the background color of your desktop and assign a graphic to display.

Figure 3.20
The Background tab of the Properties dialog, with the Background set as Graphic.

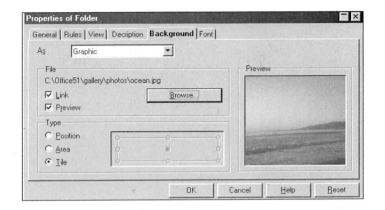

Note

To open the Desktop context menu, make sure the default desktop is visible. Place your cursor in the desktop and right-click it. Then choose the Properties command and click the Background tab.

At the top of the tab, next to the As label, is a drop-down box where can choose to set the color (fill) or background graphic. (You can apply both a color and a graphic if you want, but you choose each in separate dialogs.)

If you select Color, a Color Palette dialog box appears with a Preview window on the right. The default setting is No Fill. To select a color, click it. Choosing OK exits the Properties dialog box and returns you to your freshly colored desktop.

Tip #42 from
Michael & Sarah

You can create your own custom desktop colors by blending colors in the Colors dialog box in the General category of the Tools, Options dialog box.

If you select Graphic, the choices are more complex. Your first decision is whether you insert the graphic as a copy or link the graphics file to your desktop. It's usually best to link it, as this requires less space and ensures your desktop display automatically updates when changes are made to the original graphic.

You also have three choices of how to position the graphic:

- **Position**—Placed in a position you choose
- **Area**—Expanded to cover the entire area of the desktop
- **Tile**—Repeated in tiles to cover the entire desktop

If you select Position, a grid appears with a red dot it the middle and purple dots around the perimeter. Click the purple dot that best represents the area where you want the graphic to be placed. If you leave the red dot in the middle, the graphic will be centered.

By default, the dialog box tab previews graphics in Wireframe mode. Click Preview to see a thumbnail of the graphic. If you don't know the exact pathname of the file, click the Browse button and search your directories for the file you want to use. Be sure to click the Preview button here as well if you want to take a look at the file.

Once you're satisfied with your selection, click OK to accept the graphic and return to the desktop. If you don't want to accept the changes, click Cancel to cancel all changes and close the dialog box, or click Reset to return your original settings and experiment some more.

StarOffice includes a number of sample drawings as well as many graphics in the Gallery that you can use as backgrounds—and of course, you can also create your own background with StarDraw or StarImage.

Besides applying a graphic or background to your desktop, you can do the same to any folder or object that opens on your desktop. This includes your Explorer groups. There is no global way to set the background for desktop objects; you must set the properties individually for each object (unless you're a clever programmer).

SETTING DESKTOP ICON DISPLAY

In the Options, General, Desktop dialog, you can set the appearance and behavior of icons on your desktop. If you select Free, you can freely move the icons around. If you select Snap to Grid, they are arranged in alignment with the invisible grid that StarOffice uses to determine object locations in the program. If you select Auto Arrange, StarOffice automatically arranges icons on the desktop so they are equidistant from one another and line up from left to right, top to bottom. You determine the spacing that is used in the Icon Spacing spin boxes in the next section. Note that the changes you make here affect the display of objects only when you are in Icon view, not List view.

CUSTOMIZING THE START MENU

The Start menu is really just a special folder within the Office51\config directory. Items that you move, copy, or link to the Start folder will appear on your Start menu the next time you launch StarOffice. The More folder in the same directory contains the items that appear when you choose More from the Start menu.

SETTING PROGRAM START-UP OPTIONS

Right below the Office51\config\start folder is a folder named Startup. If there's a particular program you always want to start simultaneously with StarOffice, create a link to the program here. (It's not a good idea to move the actual program file here, as that may interfere with a variety of system and program settings.)

In practice, some programs won't start up properly. It's a good idea to add links one at a time, restarting StarOffice each time, to see if it works. It's also not a good idea to start up too many programs simultaneously.

OTHER CUSTOM FOLDER OPTIONS

Besides the Startup and Start folders, there are some other folders in the Office51\config directory that enable you to place shortcuts, templates, links, files, and folders where you want them on your desktop:

- Tasks
- Helpmenu
- Groups
- New
- Quickstart

The Tasks folder contains items that appear in the Tasks group in the Explorer. The Helpmenu folder contains items that appear on the Help submenu that opens from the Start button. Groups, as you might expect, contains all the group folders you create in the Explorer. You can easily create groups from within the Explorer, but it's also handy to be able to just drag and drop an entire folder (or a link to a folder) here and have it appear. The New folder contains items found on the File, New menu, whereas the Quickstart folder contains items that will appear in the quickstart area of the taskbar. (For more information on the quickstart area, see "Understanding Tasks and Windows" in Chapter 2.)

PART

I

CH

3

CUSTOMIZING DESKTOP TOOLS AND MENUS

In previous generations of software, the goal was to be *user-friendly*. StarOffice goes beyond being friendly; it wants you to be like family, come in, take a look around, and start rearranging the furniture. To that end, it makes customizing all your desktop tools amazingly easy.

You do most of your customizing via the Configure dialog box. You can open the Configure dialog box either from the bottom of the Tools menu or from the toolbar context menu. In the case of toolbars, where you can construct your own from scratch rather than just add and subtract elements, you also use the Customize dialog. Alternatively, you can do on-the-fly toolbar customization using the Visible Buttons fly-out menu (new to 5.1).

Note

In version 5.01 (the filter update), it was a known bug that creating custom menu configurations could cause StarOffice to crash every time you attempted to open a menu—which means you couldn't configure your menus at all. This bug has been fixed in version 5.1, so feel free to experiment. If you encounter problems with any customization such that your program does not run properly, exit StarOffice, delete the soffice.cfg file from the Office51\config directory, and relaunch the program. StarOffice will automatically generate a new, clean soffice.cfg file, and your program should run without problem.

USING THE CONFIGURATION DIALOG

When you choose the Configure command, a multitabbed dialog box appears. (You can look ahead to see an example in Figure 3.21). There are five tabs: Menu, Keyboard, Status Bar, Toolbars, and Events. The basic procedure is similar for all five tabs, although there are slight variations for each tab. For example, the Status Bar and Toolbar tabs don't allow you to assign commands, only turn on or off the display of specific tools. (You assign tool buttons through the Customize dialog.) With events, you cannot save a configuration file, only assign events to the standard StarOffice configuration file.

This section gives a quick overview of the general procedure for configuring your desktop tools and discusses the differences between each tab. The following section takes you through the process of assigning or reassigning keyboard shortcuts step by step. Since the process of assigning menu commands or events is essentially the same, for step-by-step guidance, refer to the section on keyboard shortcuts. The instructions on saving and loading configuration files in the keyboard shortcuts section are also relevant to the Status Bar and Toolbar tabs, which are discussed in sections following the one on keyboard shortcuts.

For those of you already familiar with the concepts of direct and style formatting in documents, those concepts offer a good metaphor for understanding your choices in this dialog. You can make new assignments in the dialog box and choose OK, which changes the settings of the Standard program template (the equivalent of direct formatting). Or, you can make new assignments in the dialog box and choose Save, which saves a new configuration file under a name you choose (the equivalent of creating a new style).

→ For more details on style formatting and templates **see** Chapter 8, "Using Styles and Templates," **p. 291**.

You'll find the same two sets of buttons on the lower portion of all the tabs. Aligned from left to right on the very bottom are OK, Cancel, Help, and Reset. These buttons are common dialog box buttons across the StarDesktop. OK confirms your selections and completes your interaction with the dialog; Cancel cancels the entire operation; Help opens the Help Agent, which gives you (more or less) context-sensitive help tips; and Reset returns the dialog box settings as they were when you opened the dialog box.

Stacked in the lower right of all but the Events tab are the Load, Save, and Reset buttons. These get more to the meat of this dialog's special function:

■ Load opens the \Office51\config directory and enables you to load a configuration file that contains custom menu or keyboard shortcut settings for that program module.

■ Save saves the current menu or keyboard shortcut settings in the dialog box as a configuration file in the \Office51\config directory, under a name of your choosing. Saving a file in this way enables you to load the file at a later date, giving your desktop a custom design.

■ Reset is misnamed here, as it doesn't do what Reset does in most other StarOffice dialogs, or at the bottom of this very same dialog. Rather than resetting the values to those in force when you opened the dialog, it resets them to the StarOffice program defaults. (This button is usually logically called Default elsewhere in the program.)

In the Keyboard, Menu, and Events dialogs, you'll also see a list at the top of keyboard shortcut keys, menu names and items, and events, respectively. Below each list you'll see a list of function categories (or StarBasic modules) on the left, and commands (or StarBasic macros) contained within the category on the right. In the case of keyboard shortcuts, you'll see a third pane to the right, which lists the currently assigned keyboard shortcut, if there is any for a specific command.

Basically, you want to browse the Category list to find a category that seems to describe the command(s) or macros you want to assign. All available program commands are listed in the Keyboard and Menu lists, as are all StarBasic modules and any macros and program modules you might have created yourself. The Events list displays only StarBasic and program modules. Then, browse the Commands list. When you find a command that you want to assign or reassign to a key combination, add to a menu, or assign to a program event, make sure its name is highlighted. Then look to the buttons in the upper-left portion of the dialog box to guide your choices.

In the case of keyboard shortcuts, you'll click the Assign button. Note that if there is already a different command assigned to that key combination, it will be replaced by your chosen command.

In the case of menus, you can choose to add a new entry (New), replace an existing entry (Modify), or create a new menu entirely (New Menu). Choosing Delete deletes the item currently selected in the Menu list without adding anything new from the Command list. The up and down arrow buttons move the currently selected item in the Menu list up or down in the order of the menu. The dotted line symbol is a separator that creates a thin border on your menu to help visually organize your commands.

In the case of events, you first can choose between three types of commands: those in StarBasic, those in StarScript, or those in JavaScript. (The JavaScript category is empty unless you have your own scripts that you've copied into the config directory.) The default is StarBasic; a slew of built-in macros are listed and available here for assignment. When you find a macro you want to assign, click Assign. The Remove button then becomes active and, obviously, you click Remove to cancel the assignment of the macro to the event.

When you finish making your selections, choose the appropriate command at the bottom of the dialog—Save or OK—and your new settings will either be saved to a new configuration file, or applied immediately to your current program module desktop.

> **Note**
>
> Assignments are module-specific not program-wide. Changes you make and save with the OK button are saved to the default template for that module.

CUSTOMIZING YOUR KEYBOARD SHORTCUTS

Assigning a command to shortcut keys or changing the default assignment of a shortcut is extremely easy in StarOffice. You'll be surprised at the large number of program commands available for assignment. You also can assign your own StarBasic macros to a shortcut.

It's helpful to turn on Extended Tips in the Help menu before you start—you'll then get brief descriptions of these program commands as you move your mouse over their names in the command list.

Also, it's important to understand that while some keyboard shortcuts are commonly assigned across StarOffice, assignments are actually application-specific. Therefore, the specific assignments you'll see in the Keyboard list described will vary, depending on what type of document you're in when you open the Configure dialog. This means you can create different custom keyboard assignments for each document type.

→ For a complete listing of default keyboard assignments, **see** Appendix E, "Default Keyboard Shortcuts," **p. 1429**.

Here are the steps to follow:

1. Select the Tools, Configure command. A Configure dialog box opens (see Figure 3.21).

Figure 3.21
The configuration options in StarOffice are so extensive that only some of your configuration options are found in this Configure dialog box. However, this is where you can customize program menus, some aspects of toolbars, status bars, and keyboard shortcuts, as well as assign events to specific actions.

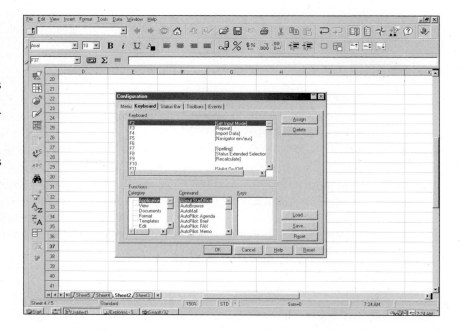

2. Click the Keyboard tab. On the top of this tab is a list in the Keyboard section that displays all the current keyboard assignments. Notice that all the keys and key combinations available for assignment are listed and many of them have nothing written next to them. On the bottom of the tab is the Function section, which has three lists:

   ■ **Category**—A list of categories of commands (many of them are menu names as well, although not all).

   ■ **Commands**—A list of all commands within the currently highlighted category.

   ■ **Keys**—The current key assignment (if any) of that command. There are a huge number of program commands listed that you can assign to keys.

Any StarBasic libraries you've created appear at the bottom of the Categories list, and those commands can be assigned like any other. There are a few StarBasic commands included with the program in this list as well that you might want to browse.

3. Scroll down the Keyboard list to find the key or key combination to which you want to assign a command and highlight it.

4. In the Function section, select a category of commands you want to browse or select from.

5. Scroll down the Commands list until you find the command you want to assign.

6. Click Assign. You'll see the name of the command appear in the Keyboard list and the keyboard shortcut appear in the Keys list in the Function section.

At this point, if you change your mind, you can restore the assignments as they were when you opened the dialog box by either choosing Delete while your new entry is still highlighted in the Keyboard list, or by choosing the Reset button (Esc) at the bottom of the dialog. You can then make another selection following the same steps as earlier.

If you choose Cancel, not only are your changes canceled but the dialog box closes as well.

You can continue assigning keys until you've assigned all you want. Once you're satisfied with all your assignments, you have two choices:

■ **You can choose OK to confirm them and return to the desktop**—Your assignments don't take effect until you choose OK. Choosing this permanently changes the default keyboard assignments by writing them to the `soffice.ini` (Windows) or `sofficerc` (Linux) configuration file.

■ **You can choose to save your keyboard assignments to a file with the Save command**—The Save command prompts you to save in the StarOffice Configuration directory, which is probably the best place for you to do so. Leave the Automatic File Extensions options checked so StarOffice is sure to recognize it as a configuration file when you want to open it. When you save in this way, the original StarOffice defaults are not changed because you have created a new, separate configuration file listing your assignments.

You can then apply your new keyboard configuration with the Load command any time you want. This enables you to create as many custom keyboard configurations as you like, so you can create different configurations for different jobs

If you want to return to the default program keyboard assignments, load the `soffice` file from the `\config` directory.

CONFIGURING THE STATUS BAR

You can also configure the status bar via the Configure dialog box. Open the Configure dialog box via the Tools menu or by right-clicking in a blank area of any toolbar.

The status bar is the bar that appears at the bottom of your task window. Besides informing you of the status of your document or desktop folder in StarOffice, it also contains the hidden treasures of shortcut context menus and shortcuts to dialog boxes. Get to know your status bar, as it will help you work smarter, not harder.

Just as with all other aspects of StarOffice, status bar assignments are specific to each module, so the choices you'll see on the Status Bar tab will vary. Therefore, make sure you have the document type open on your desktop whose status bar you want to configure.

When you open the dialog, you'll see a list of all status bar items available for that program module. All items marked with an X are currently selected and on display. Those items without an X are not selected. If you have turned on Extended Tips, hovering over a name with your mouse will pull up a brief description of that status bar item's function. If you're still unsure what an item really does, you can test it by selecting or deselecting it, clicking OK, returning to your document or desktop, and seeing what appeared or disappeared. (It's easy enough to change the configuration back again.) Be sure you double-click and right-click in a field to test its function. Be aware that some fields may not have any noticeable function until you begin entering data into a document or carrying out specific operations.

CUSTOMIZING TOOLBARS

New to 5.1, you can turn off and on the display of tools on-the-fly using the Visible Buttons fly-out menu. Customizing couldn't get much simpler. This menu is the place you should begin if you're looking for a tool that you just can't find visible on your desktop but you think should be there.

To open the Visible Buttons fly-out menu for a specific toolbar, place your cursor in a blank area of the toolbar and right-click. Move your mouse over the Visible Buttons menu command, and a fly-out menu will open (see Figure 3.22). This menu contains all the currently visible buttons on your selected toolbar and their names, as well as a number of buttons that are not currently turned on but activate commands relevant to that toolbar's function. To turn a button on or off, select its name in the menu.

Note

There is no Visible Buttons menu for the desktop object bar. The buttons you see are the buttons you get.

If you want to customize your toolbars in ways that are permanently saved to either your Standard template or a configuration file, there are two different dialogs you use. The first is in the same Configure dialog box that you open to configure menus, keyboard shortcuts, and the status bar as well as assign events to program actions. The second is a Customize dialog box specific to toolbars.

The Toolbars tab in the Tools, Configure dialog box is where you turn the display of specific toolbars in a program module on and off. By default, all available toolbars for a module are turned on. You can turn off a toolbar display by clicking its check box to deselect it. Bars that are indented in the list represent toolbars that do not display continuously but appear in a specific location when the context is appropriate.

The Customize dialog box is where you get down and dirty and can create your own tool-bars from scratch or reassign the toolbar assignments of existing toolbars.

You can open the toolbar Customize dialog box only from the toolbar context menu. Right-click in an area of any toolbar and a context menu like the one on the left in Figure 3.22 appears. Choose Customize to open the Customize dialog box. It's useful, however, to first select the Visible Buttons command and open the Visible Buttons submenu (like the one on the right in Figure 3.22), where you can see each button currently assigned to the selected toolbar and its name (which is the name of its assigned command).

Figure 3.22
The toolbar context menu opens the tool-bars Customize dialog box (look ahead to Figure 3.23) as well as this handy Visible Buttons fly-out menu, which enables you to customize your tool-bar on-the-fly and see the association between command names and button icons.

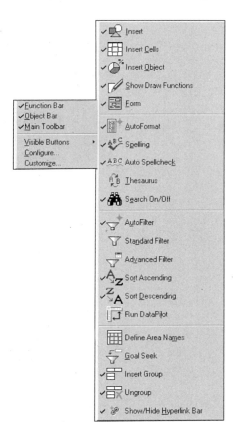

When you choose Customize, a dialog box like the one in Figure 3.23 appears. (The specific dialog box you'll see will likely be different.)

Figure 3.23
In the Customize
Toolbars dialog box,
you can not only add
and delete tool but-
tons from existing
toolbars, but also
assign your own
macros and
programming
modules to buttons.

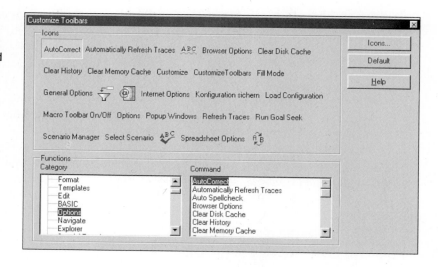

In the bottom are a Functions Category list and a Command list. The Functions Category list organizes available commands into categories. The Functions Command list shows all the available program commands, prebuilt StarBasic macros and scripts, and any macros and program modules you may have created yourself within a given category.

In the top portion is an Icons list, which displays all the toolbar button icons that by default are assigned to the commands in the currently selected category. You'll notice that many buttons (like many of those in Figure 3.20) don't have pretty pictures assigned to them.

Don't despair—you can assign any existing program button bitmaps to a command by click-ing the Icons button and browsing through a thumbnail album.

To add a new tool button to your toolbar, follow these steps:

1. Browse the Functions Category list to locate the category that interests you.

Tip #43 from
Michael & Sarah

Many StarMail commands are in the Explorer category, as they're considered general desktop commands.

---

2. Browse the Command list to find the command you want. Notice that when you select a command in this list, the icon associated with it appears pressed in the Icons list above.

3. If you don't like the default picture assignment, click Icons and browse the available Icons list to find one you like. Click the icon to select it and choose OK to assign it; then return to the Customize dialog. The Default button returns the tool button assignments to the program default settings, so have no fear of messing about with them.

4. Drag the button onto the toolbar where you want it available. Space will be made to accommodate it. If you add a tool button to a toolbar that already fills the entire length or height of your screen, it will be added but hidden, and a double-headed arrow button will appear. Click the dark arrow of the pair to reveal the invisible portion of the toolbar.

5. If you want to remove a button, drag it off the toolbar into any blank space on the desktop, and then release the mouse button. Poof! It disappears. (Just from the toolbar, not from the program.)

You can also save your toolbar configurations to a separate configuration file if you like—although not from the Customize dialog box. You must open the Configure dialog box to do that. Otherwise, changes you make here in the Customize dialog box will be saved to your current Standard template and will appear any time you create a new document of that type or open an existing document that uses the same template.

CREATING AND MANAGING MULTIPLE DESKTOPS

You must always have at least one default desktop while StarOffice is running. However, you can create as many desktops as you like and switch between them during your work session.

CREATING MULTIPLE DESKTOPS

From a user's point of view, a *desktop* is a space on your screen with icons for launching programs and documents. From the program's point of view, a desktop is a folder that either has the name Desktop and is stored in the StarOffice and OS directories; or it is a folder you have made a desktop by selecting it and applying the Desktop command on the Explorer context menu.

In order to make a folder become a desktop, check the Desktop entry of its context menu. You will see a check mark to the left of the command. Its Folder icon in the Explorer is also replaced with the Desktop icon. A right-click on the Desktop icon in the taskbar (shown in the margin) reveals that your newly designated desktop has been added to the menu of available desktops. Also, the items in the Desktop folder have been added to the Desktop menu (which opens with an extended-click). (If the folder is still empty, so too will be your desktop and the Desktop Contents menu.)

WHY USE MULTIPLE DESKTOPS?

Why have multiple desktops? Imagine you're using StarOffice for both personal and business use. You can create one desktop that has templates and programs you regularly use for personal matters, and another with templates and programs you regularly use for work.

Then designate them both as desktops. Both will appear on the Desktop shortcut menu as desktop choices (see Figure 3.24). When you select one as the default (Active) desktop, all the objects it contains also automatically appear on the Desktop menu. This means you can always have the tools and documents you need most readily available, even as you cover your desktop with multiple tasks. And you can easily switch back and forth between the two different desktops without disturbing the arrangement of your open tasks.

Figure 3.24
A right-click on the Desktop icon opens the Desktop menu, from which you can set your default desktop. A regular-click opens the Desktop Contents menu, which displays the contents of the default desktop's folder.

When you exit the program, the default desktop is the desktop that opens on next launch. So, by creating your own desktops, you can also choose the tools that appear when you start your next StarOffice session.

SWITCHING BETWEEN MULTIPLE DESKTOPS

To set a different desktop as the default, open the Desktop menu and click its name. The contents of both your desktop and the Desktop Contents menu instantly change.

You can only have one desktop from this menu selected at a time. However, because a desktop is just a specially designated folder, you can also open the contents of any folder you have designated a desktop in the usual way—by double-clicking it in the Explorer.

When a folder designated as a desktop is opened in this way, it is opened as a regular task window with a Task button on the taskbar. In its incarnation as a task window, it can be manipulated just like any other task window.

To demote a desktop to a folder again, select the folder in the Explorer, right-click to open the context menu, and click the Desktop command again. The check mark disappears, and the magic of being a desktop is over.

You cannot deselect either the StarOffice desktop or your OS desktop as desktops. StarOffice automatically places these folders on the desktop path on first program launch, and then searches for these folders every time you start up. While you can add and delete objects from the StarOffice Desktop folder, it's best not to delete the folder itself. If you do, be sure you also delete its path entry in the Tools\Options\General\Paths tab or StarOffice will be confused the next time you launch the program.

IMPROVING STAROFFICE'S EASE OF USE FOR THE PHYSICALLY CHALLENGED

If you have physical limitations or disabilities that make the conventional StarOffice setup less than ideal, no worries! You can make a host of small changes to improve StarOffice's ease of use. This section offers you some ideas. However, it does not exhaust the customization possibilities so it's recommended that you explore on your own as well.

Table 3.2 points you to options that improve the visibility and usability of desktop tools like toolbar buttons and menus.

TABLE 3.2 OPTIONS TO IMPROVE USABILITY OF DESKTOP TOOLS

Option Name and Action	Location	Result
Increase the value in the Scaling spin box to more than 100%	Tools menu, Options, General category, View dialog box, Display section	You can see menus and dialog boxes more easily as both the size of dialog boxes and the system font size increase.
Select Large Buttons	Tools menu, Options, General category, View dialog box, Buttons section	You can see toolbar buttons more easily.
Deselect Flat Buttons option	Tools menu, Options, General category, View dialog box, Buttons section	You can tell toolbar buttons apart more easily.
Deselect Menu Follows Mouse Pointer option	Tools menu, Options, General category, View dialog box, Tools section	Your menus remain open once you've opened them (rather than following your mouse movement); you can use certain types of command and control software more easily.
Select Dialog Center from the Mouse Positioning drop-down list	Tools menu, Options, General category, View dialog box	You save wrist strain as the mouse pointer automatically positions itself

continues

TABLE 3.2   CONTINUED

Option Name and Action	Location	Result
		over the default command in dialog boxes.
Select Colored Tab Controls option	Tools menu, Options, General category, View dialog box, Tools section	You can see and distinguish the tabs of tabbed dialog boxes more easily as they appear in a multicolored array instead of gray.
Add buttons to your toolbars with the Customize command	Toolbar context menu, Customize command; to access, place your cursor in the toolbar you want to customize, right-click, and choose Customize	You can put all the tools you regularly use on your desktop, reducing the need to use mouse or keyboard.
Select icons and text, or text only, as the displayed contents of your toolbar in the Contents drop-down list	Tools menu, Configure command, Toolbars tab, Contents section	You can see toolbar buttons more easily; also, choosing text display makes it easier for some command and control programs to recognize commands.

➔ For more information on customizing your toolbars, **see** "Customizing Desktop Tools and Menus,"
p. 115 in this chapter.

Caution

Sometimes rescaling your view can cause your system to become unstable, especially if you increase the scale to a large number. If you find you're unable to start StarOffice after rescaling or the program runs but keeps crashing, remove the `soffice.cfg` file from the `Office51\config` directory. (Or, if you have saved the rescaling to a different configuration file, remove that file.) Do this when the program is not running. You can either delete the file or save it to another location. Then, restart the program. StarOffice automatically generates a new default configuration file that enables the program to run. (Or, it takes its settings from the `soffice.cfg` file instead of your custom configuration file.) You lose all your custom configurations, however. If you understand how to edit configuration files and have saved your old broken file, you may be able to simply edit out the scaling configuration and reuse the file. Otherwise, you need to recustomize your desktop.

You should also take full advantage of StarOffice's automated features such as AutoText and AutoFormat to make your work easier.

If you have repetitive stress injuries (RSI) to your hands or arms and cannot type, or have other physical disabilities that require you to speak into your computer, you can install the optional Dragon NaturallySpeaking API that enables you to use Dragon NaturallySpeaking on the Windows platform. If you did not choose a custom installation this during your initial installation of the program, you need to run Setup from the Office51 directory, Choose Modify and follow the installation wizard instructions.

TROUBLESHOOTING

What do I have to do in order to access the Internet?

First of all, you must have a network connection to a LAN or intranet, or an Internet account with an ISP and a dial-up networking connection.

The easiest way to inform StarOffice of your Internet account information is to use the Internet AutoPilot, which helps you get online in a jiffy. It launches automatically the first time you start StarOffice. If you chose not to complete the AutoPilot when you first launched StarOffice, you can start it anytime from the File, AutoPilot menu. Follow the steps in the section "Setting Up Your Internet Accounts with the Internet AutoPilot" in this chapter.

If you want to set up your account yourself, refer to the relevant parts of the "Getting Online" section in this chapter.

Once you've checked these settings, click the Online button on the StarOffice function bar so it looks pressed in. Now, you're ready to browse! Click any Web bookmark in the Explorer and your dial-up networking dialog box will open as StarOffice seeks an Internet connection. Take whatever actions you usually do to connect. After you're connected, you can browse by entering Web addresses (URLs) in the URL Locator field on the function bar and pressing enter.

If you want to download files using FTP, read Usenet newsgroups, or send and receive email, you need to have within StarOffice an FTP account, news account, and email account Inbox and Outbox respectively. If you used the Internet setup AutoPilot on first launching the program, you may already have an email Inbox and Outbox and/or a news account in your Email and News group in the extended Explorer. If you did not, the simplest way of setting up an email account and/or news account is to select File, AutoPilot, Internet, and step through the dialog boxes, selecting only those new options you want to add. Complete details on creating a StarDiscussion news account are given in the section "Beyond Mail: Joining Newsgroups with StarDiscussion," in Chapter 29. Creating an FTP account is discussed in Chapter 27, "Publishing Your Work on the Web."

How does email access work in StarOffice?

To receive email, you must set up an email account Inbox. If you completed the Internet wizard on opening the program for the first time, you should already have an account Inbox in your Email and News group in the extended Explorer. If for some reason you did not, or if you want to set up a second Inbox, you'll need to create it in the Explorer. Right-click the folder in which you want to store your email and choose the New command. From the sub-menu, choose the type of email account you want to create—POP3 (the most common, and the type you surely have if you connect through an ISP), IMAP, or VIM. To send email, you must first create an Outbox via the same context menu New command. If you completed the Internet AutoPilot, you already have an Outbox and don't need to worry about it. For detailed instructions on completing these dialogs, see the section "Getting Online" earlier in this chapter.

I'm a Linux user and I don't like the look of the StarOffice desktop and windows. How can I change it?

Select Tools, Options and click View in the General category. You can change the appearance of dialog boxes and buttons using the Look & Feel drop-down list box in the Display portion of the View dialog. One of the options includes their attempt at an X look-alike—Xwindows.

I've created an IMAP account, but every time I open my mailbox, nothing happens.

While StarOffice 5.1's IMAP support is much improved over that of version 5.0, it still does not support all IMAP servers. If you're unable to use a POP3 connection to access email at all, you're probably out of luck. You should try contacting the company to confirm if they support your particular type of IMAP server. If you don't know the details about your server, ask your network administrator.

I'm a Linux user, and my POP3 connection hangs every time I try to download my mail. I have to kill the process. What can I do to use StarOffice as my email client?

There are a variety of reasons you might be experiencing problems. One common cause is that you have not entered a fully qualified domain name for your server. Try editing your etc/hosts file and entering the fully qualified domain name. Linux connection problems can be complex, however, and it also must be said that StarOffice is not as stable on Linux as on Windows. If this does not solve your problem, check out the StarMail newsgroup, which has lots of good discussion about email connection issues.

How can I integrate PGP with email?

PGP integration is new to 5.1. However, you must have installed the optional PGP integration pack during installation. If you did not, run Setup from the Office51 directory and choose Modify. When you click Next, a dialog box with the title Select StarOffice 5.1 Modules appears. Scroll through the list of Optional Components until you see PGP_Support. Click the Blocks icon to the left so it appears colored in. Click Complete and follow the steps home. Once you install the PGP module, a PGP icon will appear on your StarMail object bar.

How can I import my existing email files into StarOffice?

Using the Internet AutoPilot, you can import entire mailboxes from Netscape Communicator and MS Outlook Express. Importing in this way overwrites any existing messages you have in your default Inbox and Outbox, however, so it may not the best route if you already have some stored messages. (If your messages are stored on a server, however, you can always just synchronize with the server again to download new copies of your messages.)

From the Explorer, you can import ASCII and MS Outlook Express files. So, first be sure your file is in a suitable format, and then select your email account Inbox (the Inbox in which you want the messages to appear) in the Explorer. Right-click and choose File, Import. Navigate to the directory where the file you want to import is located, and the rest should be clear from the dialog box.

I keep getting the error message, "Read Error, could not resolve host name..." when I try to connect to the World Wide Web.

You're trying to get online but do not have Online mode activated and/or are not connected to your Internet server. You must activate your dial-up networking program and connect to the Internet, and also click the Online button at the end of the StarOffice function bar.

I created custom keyboard assignments, but now they don't work!

What application or document type were you in when you created them? Keyboard shortcut assignments are application-specific (although some are attached to the desktop and are common across all applications). You probably created them while in, say, a StarWriter document and are now trying to use them in StarCalc or StarImpress. This capability to attach keyboard assignments to specific applications is part of StarOffice's "the tools you need when you need them" approach to desktop organization.

I don't want my System folder set as my default desktop, but I want to be able to open it on my desktop.

Create a link to the System folder in the Explorer. You can then open it as a task window on the desktop. Keep in mind that in 5.1, you can also create a System group that links to your System folder.

CHAPTER 4

WORKING IN STAROFFICE

In this chapter

DESKTOP INTEGRATION IN STAROFFICE

The basic word processing and spreadsheet applications StarOffice provides are similar to those you find in any major Office suite today. Where StarOffice stands out from the pack is in its tight integration of applications and Internet programs into one desktop—a desktop designed to blend into office networks and the Internet as well as work smoothly across platforms.

This integration includes the sharing of commands, tools, and desktop utilities across applications, which makes learning to use StarOffice relatively quick and easy. For example, if you learn to use the table AutoFormat feature in StarWriter, you already know how to auto-format tables in StarCalc—even if you've never opened a spreadsheet in your life.

This chapter gives you an overview of StarOffice's common dialog boxes, tools, and desktop organization and a glimpse of the integrated desktop at work. It's packed with tips and tricks to maximize results and minimize your work in StarSpace. Later chapters go into detail about how to best accomplish specific tasks when you're using these tools in the individual application modules.

CREATING AND OPENING DOCUMENTS

Because StarOffice is a task-oriented program, you begin work on the desktop by creating and opening files and documents, not opening applications.

CREATING NEW DOCUMENTS

To start a task, you can open new documents from a number of locations on your desktop workspace, or you can create documents by using templates and the AutoPilot Wizard. In StarOffice, *document* refers not just to text documents, but to many other document types as well.

Table 4.1 lists the types of documents you can create in StarOffice.

TABLE 4.1   USING DOCUMENT TYPES IN STAROFFICE

Use This Document Type	To Create
Text	Letters, faxes, reports, and other text documents
Spreadsheet	Financial reports and analyses, lists, and some types of databases
Presentation	Slides, transparencies, handouts, and outlines for oral presentations
Drawing	High-resolution illustrations
HTML	Simple Web pages and other kinds of documents that use hyperlinks
Mail	Email letters
Frameset	Complex Web pages that combine multiple files and documents onto one online page

Use This Document Type	To Create
Master document	Master document for long documents, to simplify tasks such as generating an index and a table of contents
Chart	Graphical representation of numerical data
Image	Simple graphics suitable for publishing on the Web or customized screen elements such as buttons and icons
Mathematical formula	Complex mathematical formulas requiring special fonts and symbols sets

CREATING DOCUMENTS FROM SCRATCH

To create a new StarOffice document, you can choose from these options, among others:

- You can choose File, New from the menu bar and then select a document type from the submenu.

- You can choose File, AutoPilot for help with creating text, presentation, and Web documents and templates.

- You can choose New, Documents from the Explorer context menu and then select a document type from the submenu. The choices are the same as those on the File, New submenu.

- You can open the Tasks group in the extended Explorer by clicking its title bar. Then you can click the desired document type icon to start a new document.

- You can open the Start menu from the task bar and click the desired document type icon to start a new document.

CREATING DOCUMENTS FROM STAROFFICE TEMPLATES

If you create a document by choosing File, New, you open a generic, blank document based on the StarOffice Standard template for that document type. It's the equivalent of a blank piece of paper.

You can also create a new document based on a template. A *template* is a prebuilt form for creating a specific type of document—for example, a memo or a loan calculator. A template can include custom styles, prebuilt tables, background graphics or graphics placeholders, formulas, and fields that draw data from your user data or Address Book database. In StarOffice, it can also contain custom desktop configurations.

Using a template, you can create a professional-looking document more quickly and easily. You're not bound by a template's design; you can change parts of a document created from a template just as you can in any other document.

StarOffice includes templates for a wide range of tasks, ranging from an academic paper to a loan and mortgage calculator to perfectly sized zip disk covers. These templates are

PART

I

CH

4

organized by category and task, not by StarOffice application, and they include templates for tasks carried out with StarWriter, StarWriter/Web, StarCalc, and StarImpress.

Tip #44 from *Michael & Sarah*	Exploring these included templates is a great way to see some of the tasks you can perform in StarOffice. You can also always cut and paste elements you like from a template into your own document or template. Using the Style Organizer, you can drag and drop styles from a template into your current document or template as well, a technique explored later in this chapter in "Managing Styles and Templates."

To create a new document from a template, choose File, New, From Template or press Ctrl+N. Then start browsing for the desired template.

→ For more details on using the New templates dialog, **see** "Working with Templates," **p. 308**.

 PREVIEWING AND OPENING TEMPLATES FROM THE DESKTOP The Templates directory appears in the Explorer, and one way to browse the templates is to open a templates folder on your desktop. If you click the Preview option on the desktop object bar, you can see full-sized previews of the templates.

Note	Even if you have turned on the Display Documents option in the Explorer Group context menu, individual templates are not displayed in the Explorer. You must open a template folder in the Beamer or on the desktop to see its contents.

If you see a template you want to use to create a new document, double-click it. A blank document based on the template opens on the desktop.

Caution	If you want to place a shortcut to start a template from your own custom desktop, make sure that you select the option blank on the Internet tab of the document's Edit menu Properties dialog.

Caution	If you want to edit the template directly rather than create a document based on the template, select the template, right-click to open its context menu, and select Open As Template.

CREATING CUSTOM TEMPLATES A template is a special type of document file and has its own extension, *.vor. If you have created a document that you want to use as a model for other documents of the same type, you should save it as a template.

The simplest way to save an open file as a template is to use the Templates command from the File menu. First, make sure the file is the active document on your desktop (that is, it is the document on top and/or contains the cursor). Then select File, Templates. Next, select the category (folder) where you want to store your template. Finally, type a name for the template in the New Template text box, and click OK. Your active document (complete with text, styles, and everything else) is saved as a template in the Templates directory and will be available to you the next time you open any of the templates dialog boxes.

You can also save a file as a template in the Save As dialog box. To do so, just select the appropriate StarOffice 5.1 Template type from the File Type drop-down list. You can save a template anywhere you like. However, it's a good idea to either save your template in the Templates directory or create a link to your template in the Templates directory. You can then access your template via the File, New, From Template and File, Templates dialog boxes.

→ For more information on working with templates, including manually importing templates and styles created in other programs, **see** "Managing Templates and Styles," **p. 167**, in this chapter.

FLYING ON AUTOPILOT

AutoPilot is a document- and template-creation wizard that helps you quickly create polished, formatted versions of the most common document types—Letter, Fax, Agenda, Memo, Presentation, and Web Page—by stepping you through a limited set of formatting and layout options. It simultaneously creates a custom template for you based on your selections.

New to version 5.1, a special AutoPilot Wizard imports your Microsoft Office document templates and/or documents into StarOffice formats in a few easy steps.

CREATING NEW DOCUMENTS AND TEMPLATES WITH AUTOPILOT   To create new documents and templates with the AutoPilot, select File, AutoPilot, and then the type of document you want to create. StarOffice walks you step by step through a series of dialogs that assist you in creating a template according to your needs. If you make a mistake or change your mind, retrace your steps with the Back button and make changes. Click Cancel to cancel the entire process and return to the desktop.

After you've entered all the necessary information, choose Create. StarOffice opens a blank document based on the template. With ordinary text documents and presentations, it also automatically creates and saves a custom template in the Standard subfolder of the Templates directory, using the name you entered during the creation process. It saves this template even if you do not save the document created with the AutoPilot. With Web (HTML) documents, you must click the Save Template option box to save your custom template.

→ For more information on working with the AutoPilot for text documents, **see** "Creating Documents and Templates with the AutoPilot," **p. 253**.

→ For more information on creating and working with text templates, **see** "Working with Templates," **p. 308**.

→ For more information on working with StarCalc templates, **see** "Creating StarCalc Templates," **p. 579**.

→ For more information on working with HTML (Web page) templates, **see** "Creating Web Pages in StarOffice," **p. 946**.

PART

I

CH

4

Note

You can also create StarBase database elements with the AutoPilot. Working with StarBase elements is different from working with ordinary documents, however, so it is not discussed here. For information, refer to Chapter 30, "Working with Databases in StarBase."

IMPORTING MICROSOFT OFFICE DOCUMENTS AND TEMPLATES If you're making the switch from Microsoft Office, you can get up and running quickly by using the Microsoft Office Template and Document Import Wizard on the AutoPilot menu. You can import and convert Microsoft Word, Excel, and PowerPoint templates into StarOffice templates, as well as import and convert existing Microsoft documents into their corresponding StarOffice document types—all in one fell swoop. (Your original templates and documents remain unchanged.)

Note

StarOffice has a fine set of filters for Microsoft Office documents, so you don't need to import your documents to open them in StarOffice. You can work with them directly in their native formats if you like.

Begin by selecting the Microsoft Import command from the AutoPilot menu on the File menu. You then see a dialog box like the one shown in Figure 4.1.

Figure 4.1
The opening screen of the Microsoft Importautopilot greets you in somewhat broken English, but the import process itself is smooth and trouble-free.

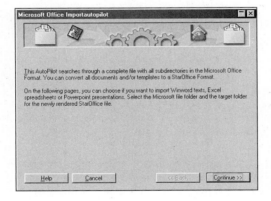

Click Continue to move to the next dialog, which looks like the one shown in Figure 4.2.

This dialog box is the key to your import process. You need to complete three steps for each of the three programs:

1. Determine whether you want to import templates for that program and change the listed template path, if it is not correct. You can also choose to search subdirectories of your selected template import directory.

2. Determine whether you want to import existing documents created with that program and change the listed directory path, if it is not correct. StarOffice will import only documents stored in that directory (and its subdirectories, if you have selected that option).

3. Determine the path for the target directory into which your imported documents will be placed.

Figure 4.2
In the second dialog box of the Importautopilot, you can select the options for importing MS Word, Excel, and PowerPoint templates and documents.

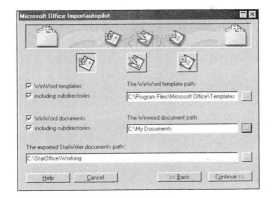

By default, the Importautopilot is set to import all existing Microsoft Office templates and documents in the listed directories and their subdirectories. StarOffice uses the same filters to import documents and templates as you use when you open an individual document via the File menu's Open dialog. You might want to test the filters on selected documents before importing them *en masse* to see whether your documents import acceptably. Of course, your original documents still exist in case the imported version is not usable.

 Caution

Some features, such as revision marks in Word and certain Excel functions, may not translate. If you speak German, you can find a list of the import/export status of every feature at www.stardivision.de, Star Division's German site.

The settings you see initially are only those for Microsoft Word. To confirm or change the settings for MS Excel and MS PowerPoint, you must click their respective buttons in the upper part of the dialog box.

You don't need to list a target path for imported templates because StarOffice automatically creates folders for them in the Templates directory.

After you have confirmed the settings in this dialog box, click Continue. You then see a dialog box like the one in Figure 4.3 that summarizes your selections. You would be wise to scroll through the summary to confirm your selections.

PART

I

CH

4

Figure 4.3
The third dialog box of the Importautopilot summarizes the options you have selected; here, you can change the names of the folders for the imported templates.

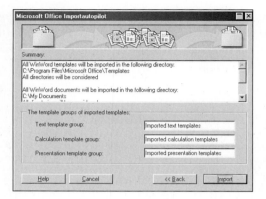

Note

When the summary says `All Directories Will Be Considered`, it means you have selected the Include Subdirectories option for the relevant program, not that the Importautopilot will import templates and/or documents from anywhere on your local drives.

Note

You are essentially making copies of all the selected templates and files. Be sure you have enough room on your hard drive or partition to import all the templates and/or documents you select.

The default template folder names are listed here—Imported Text Templates (for Microsoft Word templates), Imported Calculation Templates (for MS Excel templates), and Imported Presentation Templates (for MS PowerPoint templates). You can change these names, if you like, by selecting the default names and typing over them.

After you have confirmed your settings, click Import to begin the import process. Importing takes a few minutes, so be patient. StarOffice first searches your selected folders and counts the number of templates and/or documents that have the appropriate format; you can see the number on the dialog box. (If you see an alarmingly large number and are worried about your drive space, click Cancel to stop the process.) It then imports them.

Tip #45 from
Michael & Sarah

Want to see just what the import wizard did? Open the URL Locator history list on the function bar right after the AutoPilot completes its work. You'll see a list of the last 100 templates and/or documents that were imported.

OPENING EXISTING DOCUMENTS

StarOffice includes filters for opening documents and file types created in many other programs and on other major platforms, as well as for opening older versions of StarOffice documents.

→ For a complete list of non-native file types handled by StarOffice, **see** Appendix B, "File Formats and Extensions," **p. 1395**.

Note

The free version of StarOffice (Personal Edition) comes with a limited set of import and export filters. To obtain the complete set, you must purchase the Personal Edition Deluxe or the Professional Edition.

Tip #46 from
Michael & Sarah

Normally, when you're opening files using the desktop shortcuts described next, your new task replaces your currently active task (if there is one), which is closed. To place your new task on top of existing ones, press Ctrl while opening the file. This trick works with entering paths into the URL Locator field, as well as clicking and double-clicking files in the Explorer and Beamer.

To open existing StarOffice and non-StarOffice documents, you have a number of options:

- You can select File, Open from the menu bar to open the Open dialog (look ahead to Figure 4.4). You can navigate anywhere on your system from here. After you've located your file, you can select it and click Open.

- You can click the Open File icon on the function bar, which opens the same dialog box as the File, Open command.

- You can double-click a document or file in the Beamer or on the desktop.

- You can type the file's complete path into the URL Locator field and press Enter.

- You can open the URL Locator drop-down history list and click a path listed there. (Your last 100 opened URLs are listed there, which includes locally stored files and Internet addresses such as Web addresses and news servers.)

- You can open the Start menu and move your mouse pointer over the Documents entry. It opens a submenu listing the last 30 documents you have opened—not just in StarOffice but anywhere on your system. Just click a document to open it.

PART
I

CH
4

Tip #47 from
Michael & Sarah

A handy shortcut for opening files is the recently opened files list at the bottom of the File menu. Just click a filename to open it. The default number of files listed is four, but you can change this number by adding a line to your `soffice.ini` (Windows) or `sofficerc` (Linux) file. Open the file in a text editor such as Notepad or VI. Then search for the

continues

continued

heading [soffice-Picklist]. This section records your browsing and file opening history. Next, go to the end of the section, and add the line

Pick=*x*

where *x* is the number of recently opened files you want to appear on the File menu. Finally, save the file and exit. The change goes into effect the next time you start StarOffice.

OPENING DOCUMENTS FROM THE OPEN DIALOG

A common way to open documents is to use the Open dialog (Ctrl+O), which you access from the File menu (see Figure 4.4). This method presents a number of advantages. You can navigate anywhere on your system. You can select the specific filter you want to use in opening your file. You even can choose to open your file in read-only form, in case you want to look but not touch.

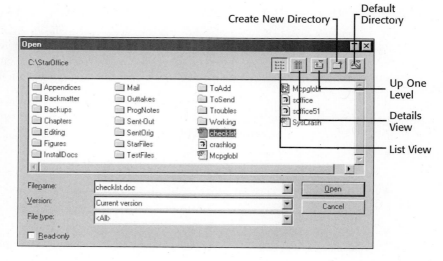

Figure 4.4
The Up One Level and Default Directory buttons at the top of the Open dialog enable you to navigate anywhere on your system. You can extended-click them to open handy shortcut fly-out menus.

FEATURES OF THE OPEN DIALOG You might think you have nothing to learn about an Open dialog, but StarOffice's Open dialog actually has a number of unexpected features. Those that relate to navigating around your system and opening files are explored here, whereas those that ease file management are explored in Chapter 5, "Managing Files, Folders, and Mail."

→ For more information on managing files from the Open dialog, **see** "Managing Files and Folders from the Open and Save As Dialog Boxes," **p. 192**.

The first time you open the Open dialog in your current StarOffice session, it opens to your designated work folder. After that, it opens to the last directory in which you opened a file.

The upper portion of the dialog contains navigational buttons.

The main portion of the dialog is filled with a list of files and their attributes. You can see more details on the files, such as last modification date and file size, if you click the Details View button. (Figure 4.4 shows the dialog in the default Icon view, and Figure 4.5 shows it in Details view.) You can also resize the dialog itself by grabbing a corner and dragging—pretty unusual, but also useful in these days of long filenames. The ability to resize the Open dialog box is also one of the features that enable you to manage files and mail in this dialog box.

The lower portion of the dialog contains text boxes in which you or the program enters information about the files you want to open. The Version text box relates to the StarOffice Versions feature, which enables you to save different versions of the same document in a single file.

→ For more information on working with versions, **see** "Working with Versions," **p. 1007**.

By default, all file types are displayed, but you can target and speed your search by selecting a specific file type from the File Type drop-down list.

USING WILDCARDS TO SEARCH FOR FILES   You can enter a portion of a filename by using a wildcard character (*) or an extension by using a wildcard character (*) and then press Enter to list only those files that match your search criteria. For example, if all files related to a specific project begin with the letters *ARC*, you can enter arc* in the Filename box and press Enter to see only those files listed. If only one file in the folder matches your search criteria, StarOffice opens it on your desktop.

PART

I

CH

4

Caution	
	Don't place an asterisk at the beginning of your search string because it is interpreted to mean "Search for all files."

Use the question mark character (?) to stand in for a single instance of a character. For example, if you're looking for Microsoft Word files that have the number 9 at the beginning and four digits afterward, you would search for 9????.doc.

OPENING FILES   To open a file from the Open dialog, double-click it, or select it and click the Open button. Files are placed on top of any other open tasks.

If you only want to read a document, you can ensure it isn't accidentally changed while open by selecting the Read-only option in the lower left of the Open dialog.

Tip #48 from	
Michael & Sarah	If you're unable to open a document, your template may be corrupted. You can load the document without its template, however. Just press Ctrl+Alt+L, click OK in the resulting dialog box, and choose Open. StarOffice checks the formatting and replaces any corrupt styles on-the-fly with its standard format.

NAVIGATING IN THE OPEN DIALOG The basics of navigating in the Open dialog are likely familiar to you from other programs. However, as usual, StarOffice has a few unlikely tricks up its sleeve.

You can navigate anywhere on your local and network drives by double-clicking folders to see their contents or using the navigation buttons at the top of the dialog to move to higher levels or other areas of your directory structure.

The Up One Level button moves you up your directory structure one folder at a time. If you accidentally go too far, just double-click the folder or icon that you want to open again.

The Create New Directory button creates a new folder in your current location, which means you can easily manage your files at the same time you open and save them.

In Microsoft applications, you can set frequently visited folders as "favorites" and quickly navigate to them. In StarOffice, you can do something similar but better by using the Default Directory button. A click on the Default Directory button takes you to your designated work folder. This button works not just in the Open dialog, but in many other dialog boxes you use, so it's a good idea to set your most commonly used directory as your work folder. Doing so really speeds your navigation.

Tip #49 from *Michael & Sarah*	You can change the directory assigned to the Default Directory button by editing the entry for Work Folder in the General category Paths dialog box, opened from the Tools, Options "master dialog" box.

Some of the Open dialog's unlikely tricks relate to the small green arrows sported by the Up One Level and Default Directory buttons. The arrow is StarOffice's signal that an extended-click on these buttons opens something special—in this case, handy fly-out menus with navigational shortcuts. Both give you access to the Workplace (which lists all your drives and volumes) and a shortcut to the root level of your C: drive. The Default Directory fly-out menu (shown open in Figure 4.5) gives you further choices that include the StarOffice Templates folder, the Explorer, the Explorer Groups folder, and all your designated desktops.

Designating directories you use frequently as desktops is an easy way to ensure speedy navigation. Just select a folder in the Explorer or Beamer, right-click, and choose the Desktop command.

Tip #50 from *Michael & Sarah*	Clicking the Filename drop-down list in the Open dialog opens the same history list of your last 100 accessed documents as opens from the URL Locator field. Just click a document on the list to open it on the desktop.

Figure 4.5
The Default Directory shortcut menu offers a wider range of selections than the Up One Level shortcut menu, and it is more customizable.

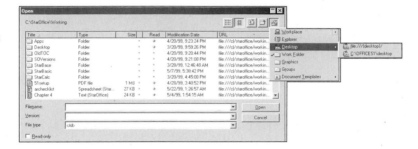

DISPLAYING AND SORTING BY FILE PROPERTIES

When you save a file, a number of properties are saved with it, including its title, path (URL in StarOffice lingo), type, size, and modification date. When you select Details view in the Open dialog, you can display these properties in the Open dialog to help you identify and manage your files (refer to Figure 4.5).

By default, files are sorted alphabetically from A to Z by title, but you can sort on another field by clicking its name on the field title bar. Clicking again on the field title bar reverses the sort order.

PART

I

CH

4

Tip #51 from
Michael & Sarah

You can also drag and drop files within the Open dialog to create a custom list order. This capability can be handy when you're opening multiple files.

Many fields are hidden from view—including Filename and URL. To insert a hidden field, place your cursor on a field name, and right-click to open a context menu. Choose Insert to open a submenu of available fields. You can also remove a visible field by choosing the Remove command. The Optimal Width command, just as it suggests, sizes the field column to fit the widest entry and no more. Don't bother with the two Sort commands; they do the same as clicking the field names, which is much quicker.

Note

By default, the title of your file appears in the Open dialog. The title is a property set in the Document Properties dialog box, which you open from the File menu. If you don't assign a title yourself, usually StarOffice assigns your saved filename as your document's title. Sometimes it uses other names, like the name of its document template.

The Open and Save As dialogs are linked, so any changes you make to one apply also to the other.

You might be surprised to see the long list of properties, many of which are traditionally used only in connection with email and news accounts. This connection reflects two aspects of StarOffice's serious Internet integration: StarOffice applies many techniques for labeling and managing email and news messages to ordinary folders and files, and you can actually manage your StarOffice email and news accounts from this dialog box.

→ For more information on managing email and news from the Open dialog, **see** "Managing Files and Folders from the Open and Save As Dialogs," **p.192**.

USING FIND TO SEARCH FOR FILES   If you're not sure of the location of the file(s) you want to open, click the StarOffice Start menu and choose the Find command. In Windows, choosing this command opens a submenu with three choices: the StarOffice Find command and two Windows system search dialog boxes. In Linux, you should see the StarOffice Find command but some users report that the menu integration of this menu command doesn't work and they see no choices. It doesn't matter, as you can access Find from the Explorer context menu.

You can also open Find by right-clicking in the Open dialog and choosing Find from the context menu.

Find enables you to construct a complex Boolean search on-the-fly for files anywhere on your system.

Tip #52 from
Michael & Sarah

You can also construct and save searches with the context menu's New, Search command, which creates a special search folder on your desktop.

You can construct a search with Find in two basic steps. On the Criteria tab, specify the characteristics of the file(s) you are searching for by selecting conditions from the drop-down list and entering the text string you are searching for—for example, a filename—in the Expression text box. If you click the Regular Expression option, you can use a wide range of wildcard characters that enable you to search for files that share characteristics that are similar but not exactly the same. If you want to search for multiple files, click the Multiple Search tool on the desktop object bar.

Caution

Be sure to click Add when you're crafting new criteria statements. Entering them in the text boxes at the bottom of the dialog box is not enough.

→ For a list of regular expressions and a discussion of their use, **see** "Using Regular Expressions," **p. 153**, in this chapter.

On the Location tab, navigate to the directories, drives, and/or volumes where you want StarOffice to search, and click the Add button to add them to your list of searched sites.

After you have completed these two steps, click Show to begin the search and show the results. A new window opens on your desktop to display the results; if no files or directories are found, the desktop window is empty.

If you want to modify your criteria, select the statement you want to modify. Its statement appears in the text boxes below. Make your changes as desired, and then click the Modify button.

To delete a criterion, select it and click Delete.

After you make changes, you might need to click Update to refresh the display. The Update command searches only for new files and folders that match your criteria; it does not match the contents of your Find folder against those of the target directories and drives you are searching.

Clicking Synchronize, however, does just that. Because it matches the contents of your desktop folder against the target directories based on your criteria, some items may disappear from your folder if you have changed the criteria and those objects no longer match them.

SEARCHING FOR FILES WITH SPECIFIC EXTENSIONS   If you want to search for files with a specific extension, you first need to make sure you have clicked the Show File Extensions button on the desktop object bar. (To reveal this tool, you must have a folder open on your desktop.) Then open a Find dialog box, and enter as your criteria `Title Contains`. (You can use `File Type` in place of `Title` as well.) In the Expression text box, type a period (.) followed by the extension—for example, `.sdw`.

On the Location tab, enter your location. Be sure to select the Search Subfolders option if you want a broad search.

Note that neither `*.sdw` nor `*sdw` will work.

→ For more information on using the Find command and its cousin, Search, **see** "Retrieving Distant Files and Folders," **page 206**.

OPENING MULTIPLE FILES   To open multiple files, you select the files you want to open using either Shift+click (which enables you to select a contiguous list of files) or Ctrl+click (which enables you to make non-contiguous selections). When your selections are complete, click Open or press Enter.

Depending on the number and size of files you have selected, loading all your files might take a few minutes. They are placed one on top of the other on your desktop. You then can use the Window menu or press Ctrl+Tab to move among your documents.

OPENING DOCUMENTS FROM THE DESKTOP

Besides using the File menu's Open dialog, you can also preview and open files directly from your desktop by using the Explorer and Beamer, or by opening a folder on your desktop. The shortcut you use to open the file varies. If you have set the Explorer to one of the symbols views, you open a file by single clicking its icon. Otherwise, you open a file by double-clicking its icon.

It doesn't matter if the file was created in StarOffice. If not, StarOffice opens the file in the correct application based on the file's extension. If the document does not have a file extension that StarOffice recognizes, you need to open it by using the File menu's Open dialog, where you can specify the correct file type manually.

Using drag and drop, you can also insert a file from the Beamer as a section in an open document.

Tip #53 from	In general, you cannot open a file on the desktop by dragging and dropping it from the Beamer. However, you can open a spreadsheet in this way if you drop it on top of an open text document.
Michael & Sarah	

PREVIEWING FILES To preview files, you must first open a folder on the desktop by selecting it in the Explorer and double-clicking, or right-clicking and choosing Open. If you double-click, the currently active task (if there is one) is closed and the folder opened in its place. If you right-click and choose Open, the folder is automatically opened on top of any currently active task.

Next, click the Preview button on the desktop object bar. Then select the file you want to preview. After a moment for loading, it appears in the preview window as a read-only copy.

Note	If you want to preview graphics files, you need to import them into the Gallery. You can then display your folder in the Beamer, which can function as a thumbnail viewer.

OPENING FILES FROM THE EXPLORER Now in version 5.1, you can display and open documents directly from the Explorer in one of three ways:

- If your group is set to either of the Symbols views, you can click a document to open it.
- If your group is set to Hierarchical view, individual documents are listed only if you also select the Display Documents command on the Explorer context menu. (Place your pointer on the group title bar, right-click, and choose Display Documents.) Just double-click a document to open it.
- In all three views, you can also open a document by selecting it, right-clicking, and choosing Open from its context menu.

OPENING FILES FROM THE BEAMER If you open the Beamer and click a folder in the Explorer when it is set to Hierarchical View, the folder's contents are displayed in the Beamer. To open a file, select and right-click it; then choose the Open command.

OPENING MULTIPLE FILES You can open multiple files in an Explorer group set to Hierarchical view or the Beamer. To do so, first select the files you want to open by using Ctrl+click (for noncontiguous files) or Shift+click (for a contiguous list). Then right-click and choose Open from the context menu.

OPENING FILES AS TEMPLATES If you want to open a copy of a document as a template, select it, right-click, and choose Open as Template from its context menu.

OPENING A LINKED FILE'S TARGET Frequently, you do not have original files stored in your Explorer groups, but only links to files saved elsewhere. You can open a link just as you can open a file. However, you cannot open a link as a template. You can easily open the original file as a document or as a template. To do so, select your link, right-click, and choose the Target's Context command. From the submenu that opens, choose either the Open or Open as Template command.

INSERTING FILES AS SECTIONS   StarOffice's drag-and-drop features are extensive and increase your efficiency considerably. A nice shortcut for inserting one text document into another as a section is to drag it from the Beamer and drop it into the other document when the document is open on the desktop. Sections are a complex feature that can involve data links, so you might want to consult Chapter 10, "Working with Long Documents," before using this feature.

→ For more information on sections, **see** "Defining Sections," **p. 378**, and "Hiding and Protecting Text with Sections," **p. 1009**.

Note that you cannot undo a section insert by choosing Edit, Undo (or pressing Ctrl+Z). To delete or otherwise manage sections, you must use the Edit menu's Sections dialog box.

SAVING AND CLOSING DOCUMENTS

StarOffice's Save commands come in the standard flavors: Save, Save As, and Save All.

Save saves the active task on your desktop. Save is also known as *fast Save* because you can save on-the-fly by using the Ctrl+S key combination or by clicking the Save button on the function bar.

Save All saves all open documents.

PART

I

CH

4

Tip #54 from
Michael & Sarah

If your current document has not yet been saved or has been changed since your last save, an asterisk appears in the status bar as a reminder.

Using Save and Save All automatically overwrites the previous version saved under the same name.

If you choose either Save or Save All and have not yet assigned a filename to the open document(s), StarOffice automatically prompts you with the Save As dialog (see Figure 4.6). Using this dialog, you can name your current document and select a file type in which you would like to have your work saved, as well as assign a password.

Note

The Save and Save All commands are grayed out until you assign a name to an open document.

The Save As dialog box offers you a number of important choices for saving your files, as you'll learn in the following sections.

Figure 4.6
You can save in a variety of formats in the Save As dialog. Just select a file type from the File Type drop-down menu.

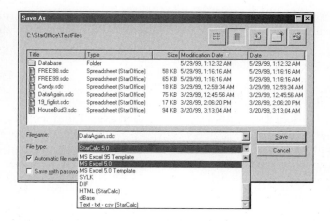

SAVING FILES WITH A PASSWORD

You can select the Save with Password option in the lower left of the Save As dialog box if you want to secure your file with a password. If this option is checked, choosing OK in the Save As dialog box opens an Enter Password dialog that prompts you to enter your password. After you have entered a password and clicked OK, a second dialog prompts you to retype the password and confirm it. When you click OK in the Confirm dialog box, your file is password-protected.

Tip #55 from
Michael & Sarah

Don't forget your file password! You cannot open a file whose password you don't remember or know.

UNDOING PASSWORD PROTECTION

Undoing password protection is simple—if you remember the original password. In this case, you can open the document (which requires the password) and then save with Save As again. This time, save without checking the Save with Password option.

SAVING WITH AUTOMATIC FILE EXTENSIONS

By default, the option Automatic File Name Extension is checked in the Save As dialog box. StarOffice therefore automatically assigns the correct file extensions to all files saved within the program, including those saved in non-StarOffice formats.

Many programs manage and recognize files by using specific file extensions, and StarOffice is no exception. For example, StarWriter documents have an *.sdw extension, whereas StarCalc documents have an *sdc extension. These extensions help programs search for and manage files more effectively, and make opening files easier. (On the Windows platform, the extension also enables you to open a document in its source application by double-clicking a document icon.)

If you want to assign your own file extensions, or if you have no file extensions at all, deselect this option. Deselecting it is recommended for advanced users only.

→ For complete lists of StarOffice file extensions and foreign file formats supported in StarOffice, **see** Appendix B, "File Formats and Extensions," **p. 1395**.

SAVING AND EXPORTING FILES IN DIFFERENT FORMATS

The Save As command enables you to choose the format in which your document will be saved. By default, StarOffice saves in StarOffice document types for new documents. If you open a document that was saved in a different format—say, Microsoft Word—StarOffice automatically selects that file type as the format in which to save. However, if you have made changes to your document that might not survive if you save it in a non-StarOffice format, you are prompted and asked to confirm your Save format.

All the supported file formats for a document type are listed on the drop-down menu in the File Type box in the Save As dialog. To select a file type, click to open the drop-down list, scroll to find your choice, and click to select it.

To save presentation and drawing documents in non-StarOffice formats, you must choose the Export command on the File menu.

→ For information on exporting presentations, **see** "Exporting a Presentation, Slide, or Object," **p. 909**.
→ For details on exporting drawings, **see** "Saving and Closing a Graphic," **p. 775**.
→ For information on saving and closing bitmapped images, **see** "Saving and Closing Images," **p. 806**.

AVAILABLE FILE TYPES

The file types available to you depend on how many filters are available in your edition of StarOffice and how many you chose to install during the initial installation.

→ For a list of available file formats and extensions, **see** Appendix B, "File Formats and Extensions," **p. 1395**.

SAVING AND EXPORTING EMAIL AND NEWS

You can choose to save StarMail messages or StarDiscussion postings as files in the StarMail .sdm format. If you have composed messages using formatting, saving them this way preserves your original formats. If you store mail and news on your local drives, you can also move individual messages and postings to other folders through drag and drop or any other conventional desktop file management techniques (although you lose threading).

To save your Inbox, Outbox, or news account in one large file as a backup, use the Explorer context menu's Export command. To access this command, first select your Inbox, Outbox, or news account. Then right-click, and select File, Export from the context menu. Your mailbox or news folder is exported as an ASCII .mbx text file that can be opened in all word processors.

→ For basic information about managing mail and news, **see** "Using Filters to Manage Files," **p. 197**.

→ For advanced information on managing your StarMail and StarDiscussion accounts, including a more detailed discussion of importing and exporting files, **see** "Techniques for Managing Mail and News," **p. 1075**.

WORKING ACROSS THE DESKTOP

If you understand the logic of StarOffice's common tools and design, you'll be able to work more efficiently and creatively, no matter what your task.

ISSUING COMMANDS

You can issue commands in numerous ways in StarOffice. For example, you can do any of the following:

- Click commands on menus
- Highlight commands on menus and press Enter
- Click toolbar buttons
- Click buttons in dialog boxes
- Press Enter in a dialog box, which activates the button that is the current focus (indicated by a darker, bolded line around the button)
- Enter keyboard shortcut combinations
- Press Alt in combination with a command's underlined letter on its program menu
- Run a macro, StarBasic, or Java script

If you are using speech recognition and/or command and control software with your computer, you can configure StarOffice so that menus remain open and do not follow your mouse pointer; you also can make other adjustments that make using StarOffice easier.

→ For more information on customizing StarOffice if you are physically challenged, **see** "Improving StarOffice's Ease of Use for the Physically Challenged," **p. 125**.

UNDERSTANDING MENUS

Menus are a fundamental part of any program with a graphical user interface (GUI), and StarOffice is no exception. You can, of course, execute commands on menus, which is their main function. Just as important, though, by laying out the program commands for you in an organized, logical, and visual display, menus are great tools for learning the program. Don't be shy about just clicking a command to see what happens (after you've saved your current file, of course). In most cases, you can easily undo any unwanted action by pressing Ctrl+Z.

You can customize your menus by choosing Tools, Configure. You can't change the length of the menus, however; you can only delete or change their listings.

→ For more information on customizing menus, **see** "Customizing Desktop Tools and Menus," **p. 115**.

OPENING MENUS WITH KEYS

You can open menus with your keyboard by pressing Alt in combination with the underlined letters (known as *hotkeys*) in a menu or submenu. This same trick enables you to execute many commands with the keyboard as well.

UNDERSTANDING STAROFFICE CONTEXT MENUS

Context menus are the menus that appear when you right-click in a workspace, or select an object and right-click. In StarOffice, unlike some other programs, these menus do not offer shortcuts only. Many important commands appear *only* on the context menus.

Context menus exist all over the place, but because they become visible only when you act, you might easily forget them or be unaware that one is available. When you're learning a new application module, you might want to open a document and just start right-clicking different areas of your workspace, both when you have objects selected and when you don't.

Because context menus give you only the commands that are appropriate for your particular object or location, the commands you see vary considerably. If you're looking for a specific command that you can't find on a context menu, the fact that you don't see it is probably a sign that you do not have the proper object selected to access that command.

UNDERSTANDING "DISAPPEARING" MENU COMMANDS

The commands offered on the regular StarOffice menus, just like those on the context menus, vary depending on your current task, location, and selected object. Don't be surprised if a command you have seen before on a menu suddenly isn't there any more; it's just a sign that your current task is not relevant to that command.

UNDERSTANDING DIALOG BOXES

StarOffice's dialog boxes share many common buttons and features. For example, most dialog boxes have Close and Minimize buttons in the upper-right corner. Clicking Close closes the dialog box, whereas clicking Minimize reduces it to a floating title bar that you can move anywhere on your desktop.

The Open, Insert, and Save As dialog boxes share a number of unique features that enable you to manage files from them, features that are explored in Chapter 5, "Managing Folders, Files, and Mail."

A number of common buttons found in StarOffice dialog boxes are listed in Table 4.2. Pay special attention to the entries on the Reset, Standard, and Default buttons because they have somewhat idiosyncratic StarOffice meanings that you're not likely to grasp immediately on your own.

PART

I

CH

4

TABLE 4.2 UNDERSTANDING COMMON DIALOG BOX BUTTONS

Click This Button	If You Want To
Cancel	Cancel all settings and selections in the dialog box and return to the desktop.
Help	Open the Help Agent displaying help appropriate to your current dialog box or tab.
Open	Open the item(s) you have selected in the dialog box.
Close	Close the dialog box and register your changes.
OK	Register your changes in the dialog box and return to the desktop.
Add	Add the selected item to a list in the dialog box.
Delete	Delete the selected item from the dialog box.
New	Open a New dialog box so that you can create a new object of the type you have currently selected.
Modify	Modify your current selection in a list based on entries or selections you have already made elsewhere in the dialog box.
More	Enlarge the dialog box to offer additional options.
Update	Update all selected files and folders on your local drives without synchronizing them with the network server.
Synchronize	Synchronize the selected files and/or folders in a search with the network server. If you have files and/or folders stored locally that have since been deleted from the server and you choose Synchronize, your local copies are deleted as well. Conversely, if you have deleted files and/or folders locally that remain on the server, they are copied to or displayed on your local drive(s).
Default	Cancel any changes to an object or text element and revert to the currently defined styles in the default template for that document. Despite its name, this button does not return settings to the program default—only your currently defined default template or style.
Reset	Erase all changes you have made in the dialog box during your current session and reset them to the value they had when you opened the dialog box.
Standard	Return settings relevant to the dialog box to those of the program Standard style or template—what most programs would call returning to the default styles.

Caution

Be careful when you use the Default, Reset, and Standard commands because all your changes are lost in one fell swoop, without any request for confirmation.

You can navigate with your keyboard in dialog boxes as well as with your mouse. Press Tab to cycle forward through the buttons and Shift+Tab to cycle backward. If you are in a row or column of buttons, you can also use your arrow keys to move among them; however, this trick doesn't move you to non-button items in the dialog box. For that, you have to use the Tab key instead. If a drop-down list is selected, use the up- and down-arrows keys to move up and down the choices in the list.

When a button is the focus—that is, the active button—simply press Enter to activate it. The button with focus is always outlined in a darker, bold border with a dotted box around the text of the command.

GENERAL DESKTOP KEYBOARD SHORTCUTS

You can speed your work by learning the StarOffice keyboard shortcuts. Just as with menu commands, the shortcuts available to you depend on your current task.

→ For a complete list of program keyboard shortcuts, **see** Appendix E, "Default Keyboard Shortcuts," **p. 1429**.

→ For instructions on customizing keyboard shortcuts, **see** "Customizing Desktop Tools and Menus," **p. 115**.

USING REGULAR EXPRESSIONS

Many StarOffice dialog boxes give you the option of using regular expressions for searching or filtering. *Regular expressions* are a set of symbols that you can use to construct complex searches or filters based on partial matches or other complex conditions. You might be familiar with using the wildcard character, the asterisk (*), to search for partial matches. Using regular expressions gives you more power and flexibility than using the asterisk. However, using them is not as simple and requires some time and practice. Note also that some of the expressions perform erratically (although implementation of regular expressions has been much improved over earlier versions).

Table 4.3 lists the regular expressions accepted. (This list is also printed on the pullout card that accompanies this manual.)

Note

In Table 4.3, terms in bold represent examples; you should replace them with your own search string. Terms not in brackets indicate exact characters you must use to find the desired object or string.

TABLE 4.3   WORKING WITH REGULAR EXPRESSIONS IN STAROFFICE

Character or String	Use
.	Acts as a wildcard character. The search term `gr.nt` would find both `grant` and `grunt`. You can use more than one period in multiple locations in a search string.
^Begin	Finds the entered word only if it is at the beginning of a paragraph. Special objects or contents (for example, anchored frames or notes) are ignored.

continues

PART

I

CH

4

TABLE 4.3 CONTINUED

Character or String	Use
End$	Finds the entered word only if it is at the end of a paragraph. Special objects or contents (for example, anchored frames or notes) are ignored.
*	Indicates that the character placed before this symbol can appear in unlimited instances or not at all. Used together with the . (period) character, this character enables you to search for variations on a sentence or phrase structure. For example, Sales figures .* have would find Sales figures for the month of May have risen and Sales figures have been promising for the second quarter. The combination .* represents unlimited or no characters.
+	Indicates that the character placed before this symbol must appear at least once but can appear in unlimited instances. Note that spaces are counted as characters, so Ctrl.+drag would find Ctrl + drag but not Ctrl+drag.
\z	Finds all instances of the specific character entered after the slash. This expression is case sensitive only if the Match Case option selected.
\t	Finds tab spaces. This expression can be used in Replace With as well.
\n	Finds a StarOffice newline symbol.
\>start	Finds the search term if it is at the end of a word. The example shown here would find quickstart but not starting again.
\<patch	Finds the search term if it is at the end of a word. The example shown here would find dispatch but not patching.
^$	Searches for blank lines.
$	Searches for the end of a paragraph.
^	Searches for the beginning of a paragraph.
&top	Use in Replace With box only. Appends the word or string to the end of the string entered in the Search For box. If you enter table in the Search For box, the example would replace all instances of table with tabletop.
[xyz]	Finds all instances of each character between the brackets. The example shown here would flag tax, yes, and xylophone.
[1-9]	Finds all instances of each character between the specified numeric or alphabetic range. Note that it recognizes only one-digit numbers. For example, 1-45 would find all individual instances of the numbers 1, 4, and 5 but would not find the number 43.
[a-gw-z]	Finds all characters or numbers between the two specified ranges. The example shown here would find all instances of each character a through g and w through z. With numbers, [1-27-9] would find all individual instances of the numbers 1, 2, 7, 8, and 9.

Character or String	Use
`[^w-z]`	Excludes all instances of the specified range of characters or numbers from the search.
`\xXX`	Finds all characters with the hexadecimal code XX.
`\XXX`	Finds all characters with the Octal code XXX. (This code always consists of three digits.)
`'note'`	Ignores all characters or numbers between the single quotation marks.
`have¦were`	Searches for alternative words in the same position in a longer phrase or sentence. This expression is used to build a complex search string such as `Sales figures .* have¦were`.

→ For information on constructing and using filters, **see** "Using Filters to Manage Files," **p. 197**.

→ For more information on using Find and constructing saved searches with Search, **see** "Retrieving Distant Folders and Files," **p.206**.

NAVIGATING IN STAROFFICE

Using StarOffice's integrated desktop, you can easily navigate among or within open tasks. Despite what you might think, the Navigator is not the primary tool you use to do this; the Navigator is used to navigate within one document, transfer data between different documents of the same type, and navigate between selected objects or sections of documents of the same type. You have more than enough ways to navigate among all your open tasks, however.

QUICK DESKTOP NAVIGATION WITH KEYS

Although StarOffice makes full use of the mouse, you can often navigate more quickly by using keys; you might need to use keys if you are using command and control programs. We discuss navigational keyboard shortcuts within specific document types in other chapters when introducing the basic tools for each application module's workspace. The following sections describe a number of generic shortcuts that work across the desktop.

MOVING AMONG TASKS

When you have multiple task windows open on the desktop, you can press Ctrl+Tab to cycle through them in a forward direction. Press Ctrl+Shift+Tab to cycle backward.

USING ARROW KEYS IN THE EXPLORER AND BEAMER

If you are in Hierarchical view, your up- and down-arrow keys move you up and down entries in the Explorer, as they also do in the Beamer. If your currently selected Explorer object has a plus sign next to it (which indicates it has subfolders or other contents), press the right-arrow key to open its list of contents and the left-arrow to close the list again. If your currently selected item is already closed or doesn't have any contents, pressing the left-arrow key returns you to the top entry in the Explorer. Because the Beamer displays only individual files, pressing the left-arrow key always returns you to the top of the Beamer list.

If the Beamer (Ctrl+Shift+B) and Explorer (Ctrl+Shift+E) are both open, pressing Tab moves you between the two windows.

USING ARROW KEYS ON THE DESKTOP

When you have folders open on the desktop in Details view, you can use the up- and down-arrow keys to move up and down the list. When you're in Icon view, you can use the left- and right-arrows to move among the objects.

NAVIGATING WITH LINKS, BOOKMARKS, AND HYPERLINKS

In the context of the StarDesktop, links, bookmarks, and hyperlinks are essentially the same kind of object: a reference to the location of a specific file or part of a document that, when clicked, opens the file on your desktop or takes you to the location of the text. You can use them as desktop navigational shortcuts.

Note

> StarOffice links are the same as symbolic links in Linux or shortcuts in Windows, Windows 98, and Windows NT. In technical terms, the text block, file, or folder link refers to is called its *target*; you will see this term used on the Explorer context menu of links and in the Help files.

In StarWriter, a *bookmark* is also a special kind of marker that you can insert into your document for quick navigation; it's the local text equivalent of an Internet anchor.

Note

> The term *link* also can refer to a piece of text or data that is a copy of information from an original document embedded in another document as either an OLE object or a DDE object. When a link appears in the form of linked data like this, clicking the data does not jump you to the original. These types of links are discussed in the section "Sharing Data Between Documents" elsewhere in this chapter.

CREATING BOOKMARKS

URL addresses are an eyeful to remember. That's where bookmarks come in. They're handy icons created to store Web page addresses (URLs) with useful names—like StarDivision Web site. You then just click the icon to return to the target Web page.

StarOffice includes bookmarks to a variety of Web sites to get you started cruising. You also can have imported bookmarks from existing Microsoft Internet Explorer or Netscape browsers. One way or the other, you have a Bookmarks group in the Explorer that contains bookmarks.

You can create a bookmark to the current URL in the URL Locator by clicking the Bookmark tool on the function bar. A hand pointer appears, indicating that you can drag the URL and drop it into any folder, group, or open document on the desktop. (If you insert it into a document, it appears as a hyperlink rather than a bookmark.) Because StarOffice names locally stored paths following URL conventions, you can create bookmarks (in other words, links) to any local file or folder by using the same Bookmarks tool. Clicking a bookmark opens the selected URL on your desktop.

You can also create bookmarks by using the Hyperlink toolbar's Bookmark tool (called Link). To do so, turn on the Hyperlink toolbar in the View, Toolbars menu. The Link command is active only when a URL or pathname is entered into the Internet URL text box (the text box to the right). Click it, and a bookmark is created automatically in the Bookmarks group in the Explorer, using the name you enter in the URL Name text box (the text box to the left), if there is one. Otherwise, StarOffice names the bookmark after the Internet URL. You can move the bookmark to another folder via drag and drop.

Tip #56 from
Michael & Sarah

You can change your default Bookmarks folder in the General category Paths dialog box, which you open from the Tools menu's Options "master dialog."

PART

I

CH

4

CREATING LINKS TO FILES AND FOLDERS

You can create links to an individual file or folder on your desktop by selecting the object and Ctrl+Shift+dragging it to the location where you want the link to be stored. You'll notice a curving arrow as part of your pointer; it is the symbol for a link.

To create a link to a distant file or folder, position your cursor on the desktop, right-click to open the Explorer context menu, and select New, Link. A dialog box opens, enabling you to navigate to your file's or folder's location. Click to select the file or folder, and choose OK. A link is then created wherever your cursor was positioned (the desktop, the Beamer, or the Explorer).

Open the link as you would any other file or folder; it automatically seeks and opens the target.

Creating links is usually a better way to bring documents and files stored on a network to your desktop rather than copying them. Because you are always working on the original, you don't need to worry about comparing files or versions. Updating a file or folder is as easy as selecting it, right-clicking, and choosing Update.

If you need to circulate multiple copies of a document, check out the Versions and Changes features of StarWriter and StarCalc that enable you to exchange documents easily among a team.

→ For more information on revising documents in a team environment, **see** "Exchanging and Reviewing Documents," **p. 1002**.

CREATING GROUPS AS LINKS

You can create an Explorer group that is a link to another part of your directory structure. If you're working on a network, creating such a link is often the best way to bring distantly stored files to your desktop. For example, you can create a link to a parent directory that contains subdirectories you use frequently and then easily open those subdirectories in the Explorer.

To create a new group as a link, right-click the New Group button at the top of the Explorer group's structure, and select New Group as Link. Click the Bookmark tab and then the Directory button to navigate to the folder's location. When you've located the folder, select it. Finally, enter a name for the group, and click OK.

STEERING THROUGH DOCUMENTS WITH THE NAVIGATOR

Whereas the Explorer and Beamer are navigational tools for the desktop and the world outside StarOffice, the Navigator is a tool for quickly moving around inside StarOffice documents and quickly moving data between documents (see Figure 4.7). It's a dockable window that you can keep open on your desktop as you work. Because the Navigator is a tool unique to StarOffice, you might not find it intuitive to use initially. When you become familiar with its easy drag-and-drop and point-and-click interface though, you'll never want to work without it again.

Figure 4.7
The Navigator isn't just for navigating; it's also for quickly creating links, copies, and hyperlinks among documents of the same type.

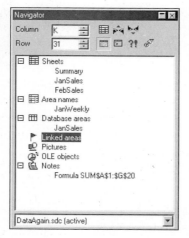

TURNING THE NAVIGATOR ON AND OFF

The Navigator command is grayed out until you have a navigable document type open on your desktop. When you have a document open, click the Navigator icon on the function bar, press F5, or select Navigator from the Edit menu to open the Navigator. To turn off the Navigator, click its icon on the function bar again, deselect Navigator from the View menu, or click the Close button in its upper-right corner.

EXPLORING THE NAVIGATOR

The Navigator keeps track of all special objects (such as tables, graphics, and links) you have inserted in your documents. In text documents and presentations, you can also view and manage your outlines in the Navigator, including rearranging sections.

The display is similar to that of the Explorer in Hierarchical view. If a category has a plus sign to the left, it means further contents are available. Just click the plus sign to reveal them.

The Navigator is available in StarWriter and StarWriter/Web, StarCalc, StarDraw, and StarImpress. A special Form Navigator that keeps track of controls in forms becomes available only when you have a form on the desktop; it is activated by a different icon.

Hold your mouse pointer over an object type in the Navigator for a moment, and you'll notice a box pop up telling you how many of that object type you have in your current document.

NAVIGATING IN AND BETWEEN DOCUMENTS

Click the name of any object the Navigator tracks, and you jump to its location in your document. You can also enter a page number, slide number, or column and row reference into the spinner box on the Navigator toolbar and press Enter to jump to the specified location.

Note

Note that the document title list in the Navigator does not enable you to jump from one open document to another. To switch to another document, click its icon on the taskbar, press Ctrl+Tab, or use the Window menu.

As usual in StarOffice, the contents of the Navigator window change depending on the context, so you see different tool buttons depending on the type of document in which you're working. Table 4.4 lists the common buttons. Tools specific to each document type are discussed in their respective parts.

TABLE 4.4   IMPORTANT NAVIGATOR TOOLBAR BUTTONS

Tool Button	Function
Toggle	Moves you between a full view of all objects tracked and a view of only the selected category of objects.
Mode	Changes your drag-and-drop mode between Link, Hyperlink, and Copy.
Contents/List Box On/Off	Closes or opens the Navigator list of objects. If the list is closed, the Navigator becomes small. This feature is useful in non-StarWriter applications where the mini-Navigator is not available. In StarWriter, it's more useful to open the mini-Navigator.

CREATING LINKS, HYPERLINKS, AND COPIES

The Navigator does more than enable quick navigation. You can easily create links and hyperlinks to other documents of the same type, or copy elements from other documents of the same type, by dragging and dropping from the Navigator—regardless whether that document is open on the desktop.

If you have two documents open on the desktop and want to move data from one into the other, follow these steps:

1. Make the document into which you want to copy or create the link (document 1) your active document.

2. Open the drop-down list of documents in the Navigator, and click the name of the document from which you want to copy (document 2). All its tracked objects appear in the Navigator (but your active document remains the same).

3. Click the plus sign (+) next to the category of objects you want to copy.

4. Select the object you want to copy, drag it from the Navigator into the document, and drop it where you want to insert it.

To insert elements from a document that is not open into an open document, you first need to open the document's folder in the Beamer so that your file is visible. Then you can open the Navigator and drag and drop the file into the Navigator. All its elements appear just as if the document were open. At this point, you can proceed as with the preceding example.

BASIC EDITING AND FORMATTING

Selecting, moving, deleting, and copying text, data, and objects are tasks common to all applications, and StarOffice gives you all the tools you would expect, and then some, to carry them out. As with most other tasks in StarOffice, the desktop cry is "Remember the context menu!"

BASIC SELECTION TOOLS

Selection techniques for objects differ from those for text and numbers. The following sections briefly address selection in StarWriter and StarCalc, and the section "Selecting Objects" elsewhere in the chapter discusses selecting objects.

SELECTION MODES

In both StarWriter and StarCalc, you have three selection modes: Standard, Additive, and Extended. These modes correspond to normal selection with the cursor and mouse, Ctrl+selecting with the mouse, and Shift+selecting with the mouse, respectively.

To change from one mode to another, click the appropriate field in the document status bar; you see STD, ADD, or EXT in that field, depending on your currently selected mode. Standard is the default. When you're in one of these modes, you can use the keyboard, mouse, or any combination to select text and objects in your document.

Caution

You must manually turn off a selection mode. It does not automatically turn off after you've completed a selection.

SELECTING WITH THE KEYBOARD

After you have positioned your cursor where you want your selection to begin, you can select a block of text or cells by pressing Shift and using the four arrow keys.

SELECTING WITH THE MOUSE

Selection with the mouse, for the most part, matches common conventions: You place your cursor where your selection is to begin, hold down your mouse button, and drag until the desired area is highlighted.

The selecting functions with the mouse are slightly different than the Microsoft conventions. Whereas a double-click selects a word or string just as in Microsoft programs, a triple-click selects only the line where the cursor is placed, not the entire paragraph. In the case of a spreadsheet, a triple-click selects all data in the cell.

UNDOING SELECTIONS

You can undo a selection by pressing the Esc key (which also escapes a command sequence you may have started).

You can also click your mouse anywhere outside the selection.

PART

I

CH

4

BASIC EDITING TOOLS

StarOffice's basic editing commands follow Windows conventions, as you'll learn in the following sections. However, some of these commands, like Undo and Repeat, behave in ways you might not expect, so be sure to at least glance over this section.

CUT, COPY, AND PASTE

You have two types of cut, copy, and paste commands: for editing text and objects within documents and for managing files, folders, and other objects on your desktop.

For use within documents only, Cut, Copy, and Paste are available on the Edit menu and the function bar. They follow Windows conventions, including using the familiar keyboard shortcuts of Ctrl+X for Cut, Ctrl+C for Copy, and Ctrl+V for Paste. Cut or copied objects and data are placed on the program Clipboard or in the buffer and held until you either paste the current contents or replace them by cutting or copying something else. Cutting, copying, and pasting from within documents can be undone (and redone and repeated).

To manage folders, files, and other objects within the desktop, Cut, Copy, and Paste commands are available on the desktop context menus. Although these commands have the same names as those on the Edit menu, they are actually different functions within the program, so the keyboard shortcuts do not work. Objects deleted through the context menu's Cut command are placed in the Recycle Bin.

UNDO, REDO, AND REPEAT

Undo, Redo, and Repeat are located at the top of the Edit menu, and you can find shortcuts for Undo and Redo on the function bar.

You can also invoke Undo on-the-fly by pressing Ctrl+Z. The default number of steps you can undo is 20. Note that Undo steps in StarOffice are very short—for example, in StarWriter, Undo undoes only one letter at a time instead of an entire word. You are well advised to change the default when you set up StarOffice for the first time.

| Tip #57 from | You can change the number of Undo steps in the Save dialog box in the General category |
| *Michael & Sarah* | of the Tools, Options "master dialog." The maximum number you can undo is 100. |

Undo, Redo, and Repeat work only within documents, not on actions performed in the Explorer or Beamer, or in task windows that display the contents of folders. Undo also does not undo deletions of mail messages from your Inbox or Outbox. In most cases, deleted objects, including links, are stored in the Recycle Bin until you actively delete them.

SELECT ALL

Select All (Ctrl+A) selects everything in your active document, including special text areas in text documents such as headers and footers. You can then easily cut or copy the entire document.

DELETE

The Delete key is programmed to delete your currently selected object or the item at your current cursor location directly, without placing it on the Clipboard or asking you for confirmation.

If you delete StarOffice objects, they are placed in the Recycle Bin. However, you can carry out many non-StarOffice tasks from the desktop, and some of the non-StarOffice objects you delete might not be placed in the Recycle Bin—for example, files deleted from zip disks.

You can customize the Delete key to perform another action by using the Keyboard tab in the Tools, Configure dialog box.

Note that the Delete command used on the context menu for objects in the Beamer and Explorer does not function in the same way as the Delete key; deleted objects are stored in the Recycle Bin.

OVERWRITE MODE

You can switch to Overwrite mode in StarCalc, StarWriter, and StarWriter/Web. In this mode, the characters you enter from the keyboard "write over" any existing characters in the same location. To change the mode, press the Insert button on your keyboard, or click the field that says INSERT in your document status bar. Clicking this field changes the mode from Insert, the default, to Overwrite, and you should see the abbreviation OVER appear in the field. You can press the Insert button or click the field again to return to Insert mode.

SEARCH AND REPLACE

StarOffice's Search and Replace function (Ctrl+F) is an extremely powerful and flexible feature. The specific Search and Replace options available to you vary depending on the application, but the basic principles are the same.

Tip #58 from *Michael & Sarah*	Even after you have closed the Search and Replace dialog, you can continue your search by pressing the key combination Shift+Ctrl+F.

In StarWriter, you can also control the search direction with the Navigation floating toolbar. You open it from the Navigator or by clicking the round button in the lower right of the document window.

→ For more information on using Search and Replace in StarWriter, **see** "Using Search and Replace," **p. 460**.

→ For more information on using Search and Replace in StarCalc, **see** "Using Search and Replace in StarCalc," **p. 547**.

p. 460

p. 547

SEARCH BASICS

When you're ready to search, type the word or phrase for which you want to search into the Search box of the Search and Replace dialog. If you only want to locate a string, not replace anything, leave the Replace text box empty.

Click Search to begin the search. How the search is conducted depends on the options you select in the lower part of the dialog box. Table 4.5 lists the most basic options that are found across all applications; you might see other options in your specific application.

TABLE 4.5   BASIC SEARCH AND REPLACE OPTIONS

Option	Description
Whole Word	Looks only for whole words. Sale would not return sales.
Match Case	Looks for words with the same pattern of upper- and lowercase letters. Buddy would not return buddy.
Backward	Searches backward in the document.
Current Selection Only	Searches for matches only in the currently selected block of text. This option is grayed out if nothing is selected when you open the Search and Replace dialog.

PART

I

CH

4

SIMILARITY SEARCHING

By checking the Similarity Search box, you can search and replace deviations of words or phrases, based on rules set in the Similarity Search dialog box. You could enter the word practice in the Search For box, for example, and using Similarity Search find practiced, practicing, and practical. You cannot search and replace formatting characteristics with Similarity Search (although Attributes is still available), nor can you use regular expressions.

To use similarity searching (also known as *fuzzy searching*), first select the Similarity Search option. Then open the Similarity Search dialog by clicking the button with ellipses to the right of the option's label. In the dialog that appears, you can set the rules for how the search will be conducted. You can choose from three categories of fuzziness:

- Words that have the same number of characters but have different characters in some locations—for example, *beat* and *bear*
- Words that have the same characters as your entered word but also have additional characters—for example, *bear* and *bearing*
- Words that share characters with your entered word but have fewer total characters—for example, *bread* and *bead*

These three types correspond to the three spinner boxes—Exchange Characters, Add Characters, and Remove Characters.

If Combine is checked, the three rules are treated as a single rule when searching, and items that fulfill any combination of the three conditions are returned. For example, with the default settings of 2 for each category, combining the rules would return creed for breaded. (It has two fewer letters and has two substitutions).

Tip #59 from
Michael & Sarah

Search and Replace keeps history lists of searched and replaced terms in drop-down menus in the Search For and Replace With boxes for single-click re-searching.

SEARCHING WITH REGULAR EXPRESSIONS

If you select the Regular Expressions option on the Search and Replace dialog, you can extend your search capabilities considerably. Be forewarned that this feature is still rather buggy, however, and doesn't always work as advertised.

Searching with regular expressions is particularly useful when you're working in text or HTML documents because you can search for the beginning and end of words, as well as search for alternative phrasings.

Refer to the section "Using Regular Expressions" earlier in this chapter for a complete table of expressions and brief examples of their use.

FORMATTING, STYLES, AND TEMPLATES

In every application, you create objects that have attributes. An *attribute* is any discrete aspect of an object's appearance. For example, a text's font and color are attributes, as is the presence of a border around a text box or an image's size. *Formatting* is defining the attributes of an object. StarOffice gives you unsurpassed control in formatting your objects.

The most efficient way to apply attributes is to create and apply a style. A *style* is a saved collection of formatting attributes that you can apply again and again. Because styles are managed centrally from one dialog box, you can change a style's attributes in a few minutes. Changes you make apply globally to all objects of that style in your document, enabling you to reformat in a flash.

You can control a range of document attributes through styles. For example, in StarWriter documents, you can apply a style to an individual character or word, a paragraph, or a page.

Creating templates is the most efficient way of managing documents. *Templates* are collections of styles for all aspects of formatting a document.

APPLYING FORMATS AND STYLES

Generally speaking, if you want to format a specific object, you can select it and right-click to open a context menu with a range of formatting commands. The application's object bar also offers shortcut tools for formatting. Applying formats in this way is *direct formatting* (called *hard formatting* in the StarOffice Help system), which means applying attributes one at a time, directly to a select object or set of objects.

It's more efficient to apply formatting through styles, however, and to save your styles in templates. StarOffice provides two program-wide tools that help you create and manage styles across applications: The Stylist and the Style Catalog (Ctrl+Y).

INTRODUCING THE STYLIST

The *Stylist* is a dockable window that you can keep open on your desktop while you work. It's context sensitive and automatically displays the set and type of styles appropriate for your current selection and document.

To turn the Stylist on or off, click the Stylist button on the function bar, or press F11.

To apply styles, select the text or object you want to format, and click the style name in the Stylist window.

You can select a style name and right-click to open a context menu with commands for modifying the style.

Figure 4.8 shows the Stylist as it appears in StarCalc and StarDraw and identifies the functions of its toolbar buttons (the numbers correspond to the following numbered list).

PART

I

CH

4

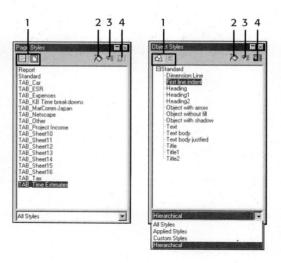

Figure 4.8
The Stylist is a stylish tool that makes creating, applying, and managing styles easy.

1. Click an icon to switch the type of style listed in the Stylist window.
2. Click to update the style applied to the currently selected text or object based on direct formatting you have applied to it.
3. Click to create a new style based on your currently selected text or object.
4. Click to enter Fill mode, which turns your cursor into a style applicator. Wherever you click, the currently selected style is applied.

USING THE STYLE CATALOG

Using the Style Catalog, you can create, modify, and manage styles but not apply them. This feature is somewhat redundant because you can carry out the same tasks by using the Stylist, and you're better off doing so unless you need to use keys rather than the mouse. (You can't navigate the Stylist toolbar using keys.) The one unique feature of the Style Catalog is that you can open the style and template Organizer by clicking the Organizer button.

→ For details on using the Style Catalog in StarWriter, **see** "Managing Styles with the Style Catalog," **p. 306**.

Tip #60 from
Michael & Sarah

Use the Style Catalog instead of the Stylist if you need to navigate with keys, use a command, or control a voice recognition program.

MANAGING STYLES AND TEMPLATES

Every document you open in StarOffice has a template attached to it. A template is a collection of styles that determine the appearance of a document. It's like the document's skeleton; the document can't stand up without it.

SEARCHING FOR ATTACHED TEMPLATES

When you open a document, StarOffice searches for the document's template. If StarOffice can't find the template, it notifies you and asks whether you want the program to continue to search for the template every time you open it. If the template no longer exists, choose No. Otherwise, try to locate the template and place it in its original location. Alternatively, you can force StarOffice to search for templates that may have been moved elsewhere by modifying the soffice.ini or sofficerc file (located in the Office51 directory). Find the [Common] section of the soffice.ini file, and enter SearchTemplate=1 at the end of that section.

MANAGING TEMPLATES

Whereas you open new documents based on templates from the File, New, From Template dialog box, you manage and edit templates themselves in the Document Templates dialog box (see Figure 4.9). You open this dialog by choosing Templates from the File menu.

PART

I

CH

4

Figure 4.9
You can create new templates from open documents instantly, as well as edit existing templates in the Document Templates dialog box.

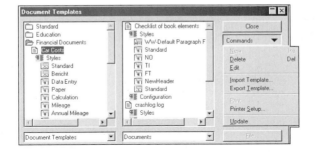

To open a template for editing, select it in the Templates list, and click the Edit button. When it opens on your desktop, you can edit it like any other document. By default, it is set to save as a template file (.vor). Be sure you do not change the file type in the Save As dialog box; otherwise, StarOffice will no longer recognize it as a template.

IMPORTING TEMPLATES AND STYLES MANUALLY

In the Organizer dialog box, you can import templates and styles from documents or templates created in many programs, including Microsoft Word, WordPerfect, and Microsoft Excel. You can import templates in their entirety by using the Import Template command, or you can selectively import styles by dragging a style from one pane of the Organizer into a template in the other pane.

Note

If you are using the downloaded StarOffice Personal Edition, you have only a limited set of filters.

You can open the Organizer from two locations:

- The Style Catalog dialog box, which you open by choosing Format, Styles and Templates.
- The Templates dialog box, which you open by choosing File, Templates.

Just click the button that says Organizer.

→ For information on importing styles using the Organizer, **see** "Modifying Styles," **p. 303**, and "Managing Styles with the Style Catalog, **p. 306**.

Tip #61 from
Michael & Sarah

Ever had to type a style sheet? If so, you know it's not a fun job. With the Organizer, you need never type a style sheet again. Just double-click the template or document whose styles you want to print. Then select the Styles icon, click Commands to open the Commands drop-down menu, and choose Print.

UNDERSTANDING STAROFFICE STANDARD TEMPLATES

The StarOffice Standard templates are not ordinary templates. They are generated by programming scripts from within the StarOffice program. As a result, the Standard templates can perform a lot of useful tricks, such as automatically distinguishing between text and numbers in StarCalc. Special links to call up these scripts and generate a new document are located in a number of subdirectories within the Office51 directory, including the config\new and config\start directories.

Caution

Don't delete links to the Standard templates, or you won't be able to open new blank documents. If you accidentally delete some, see whether you have them in another directory. If so, you can copy them, or you can run the StarOffice setup program and choose the Repair option.

EDITING THE STANDARD TEMPLATES

You can edit three standard templates directly: the templates used to reply to email and news postings using the Reply (Ctrl+R) command, rplytxt and rplymail; and the default StarWriter template, Standard.

The rplytxt template is used when you reply in ASCII-only format, whereas the rplymail template is used when you choose any additional formats (HTML, RTF, or StarOffice). The Standard StarWriter template is used when you create a new text document by choosing the File, New command or any of its companions.

You can find these templates in the Wizards folder of the `Templates` directory. (However, you can't locate them through the Edit menu's Templates dialog box or the Organizer; you must search via the Explorer or the File menu's Open dialog.) The simplest way to edit a template is to display the contents of the `Wizards` folder in the Beamer, select the template you want to edit, right-click, and select Edit as Template from the context menu. Then you can make any changes you want and save it before exiting, as you would with any other template.

Tip #62 from
Michael & Sarah

You can create email signatures with AutoText, but you must insert a signature manually each time you write email. If you're lazy and want to have a signature file permanently appended to your email replies, add your signature to the two reply mail templates. You still need to use AutoText, however, to append a signature to email created by choosing the New, Mail command or the StarMail New Mail button.

CHANGING THE DEFAULT TEMPLATE

Because the Standard templates are not like other StarOffice templates, you cannot edit most of them directly. However, you can set your own template to be the default template used to open new documents by choosing File, New.

To set your template as the default, follow these steps:

1. Navigate in the Explorer to the folder in which your template is stored.
2. Open the Beamer.
3. Extended-click the folder to display its contents in the Beamer.
4. Select the template file, and right-click to open its context menu.
5. Move your mouse pointer over the Set Default Template command to open the submenu, and click the document type that appears.

RESTORING THE STANDARD TEMPLATE AS THE DEFAULT

To restore any of the program Standard templates as the default, follow these steps:

1. Navigate in the Explorer to the `Office51\config\new` folder.
2. Select the document type whose template you want to restore.
3. Right-click to open its context menu.
4. Select Restore as Default.

RESETTING STYLES TO THE STANDARD TEMPLATES

Some dialog boxes have a button called Standard. Clicking this button returns the relevant style settings to those of the Standard template—that is, the program defaults at the time you installed StarOffice.

PART

I

CH

4

USING COMMON PROOFING TOOLS

StarOffice comes with dictionaries in three languages that enable you to check your spelling and language usage in most StarOffice modules where you can insert text.

Tip #63 from
Michael & Sarah

StarBase does not have spellchecking, but you can open many types of databases in StarCalc and use its spelling tools.

By choosing Tools, Thesaurus, you can check the meaning of words as well as find synonyms.

You can check spelling with either the automatic spellchecker, AutoSpellCheck, or the Spelling dialog box opened from the Tools menu. StarWriter also has an AutoCorrect feature that automatically corrects spelling errors and changes formatting according to entries and selected options in the AutoCorrect/AutoFormat dialog box, opened from the Tools menu.

When the spellchecking tools are available in an application, you can turn them on by clicking tools on the main toolbar; AutoSpellCheck is the one with the wavy line underneath the letters. You can also turn them on via the Tools menu.

Although one language is set as the default, you can check your documents in one, two, or three languages. You can also create a style that has a specific language associated with it.

→ For more information about working with the installed dictionaries, **see** "Checking Your Spelling," **p. 464**, and "Understanding Dictionaries in StarOffice," **p. 474**.

The specific proofing options you have may vary depending on your document type.

→ For more information on using proofing tools in StarWriter, **see** "Proofing Your Work," **p. 460**.

→ For more information on using proofing tools in StarCalc, **see** "Proofing Your Work," **p. 702**.

Besides using the installed dictionaries, you can also create any number of your own custom dictionaries. If you have activated any custom dictionaries, they are checked in addition to the installed dictionaries you have selected. Two custom dictionaries are also included in your default installation: stardiv and standard.

If you don't create any custom dictionaries of your own, words you add while spellchecking are appended to the standard dictionary.

You can control the dictionary to which spellcheck words are added by turning custom dictionaries on and off.

You can create and control custom dictionaries via the Tools, Options, General, Linguistic dialog box, and the Spelling dialog (which you open by selecting Tools, Spelling, Check, More, Options).

SHARING DATA BETWEEN DOCUMENTS

One of the benefits of working in an integrated Office suite is the ease with which you can share data between applications. StarOffice again stands out from the pack here, making data exchange a snap with drag-and-drop technology that operates everywhere you go—dialog boxes, the Explorer and Beamer, the Navigator, and the taskbar.

You can also share data in more conventional ways, using the Paste and Paste Special commands to create dynamic data exchange (DDE) and object linking and embedding (OLE) links, as well as pasted copies of data.

You can also insert data from StarBase databases with ease via the Beamer and a variety of specialized commands.

→ For a general introduction to inserting data into documents from StarBase, **see** "Using StarBase as a Data Manager," **p. 1087**.

→ For details on inserting StarBase data into text documents, **see** "Moving Data into Text Documents," **p. 1160**.

→ For details on inserting data into StarCalc from StarBase, **see** "Importing and Exporting Data," **p. 636**.

If you share data through linking, you need to understand the technology behind it so that you can store your files correctly and avoid file corruption.

PART

I

CH

4

UNDERSTANDING LINKED DATA

Although you'll find some of the same vocabulary used, linked data is somewhat different from links, shortcuts, bookmarks, and hyperlinks. The latter objects all jump you to a specific location when you activate the object. Linked data originates from one document (its source or target) but appears also in the second document where the link has been inserted (its destination). Ultimately, though, the link is created in the same way: StarOffice records a pathname (URL) as the target for the link.

Caution

If you link data, you must be sure you do not delete, move, or rename the source file. If StarOffice can no longer find your source files, your destination file might be damaged when you open it.

Two standards are common for linking data between different programs and documents, and StarOffice supports both: dynamic data exchange (DDE) and object linking and embedding (OLE). You can also insert graphics and sections as ordinary links.

You can make changes to the linked data in your destination document, but these changes have no effect on your source document. On the other hand, every time you update a DDE link, your destination document is updated with data that reflects the source. Any changes you have made to the data in the destination document—including formatting—are overwritten.

Tip #64 from *Michael & Sarah*	If you have a table or text that is a DDE link, and you need to format it differently than in the source document, you can create and apply styles. That way, you can quickly reformat after an update.

The techniques you use to share data vary depending on the type of link you want to create and the types of documents you're working with. However, you manage all linked data centrally (whether text or graphics) through the Edit menu's Links dialog box. With DDE links, you cannot delete the linked data directly from your document but only via this Links dialog box.

DYNAMIC DATA EXCHANGE (DDE)

In a dynamic data exchange (DDE) link, the data in the destination document remains dynamically connected to the source data and can be updated at any time.

LIMITATIONS OF DDE You are limited in the ways you can manipulate DDE linked data. For example, if you insert a portion of a StarCalc worksheet into StarWriter, it is inserted as a table. You cannot delete or add rows or columns to this table, although you can edit the table's contents.

METHODS FOR CREATING DDE LINKS You can create DDE links among StarOffice documents by dragging and dropping or using the Navigator. If you want to create DDE links with data in non-StarOffice documents, you can copy the source data, use the Paste Special command on the Edit menu, and select DDE Link.

OBJECT LINKING AND EMBEDDING (OLE)

Object linking and embedding, usually referred to as OLE, was originally developed by Microsoft as a way of sharing data among its Office applications. You might say it was an early (and somewhat clumsy) effort to create an integrated desktop where there was none.

An OLE object retains links to its original application. When you double-click an OLE object, it opens in its original application so that you can edit it using the tools you used to create it in the first place. The original application is said to be *embedded* within your current document.

Unlike a DDE object, an OLE object is not usually linked to its source data; it is just a copy. For example, if you insert a portion of a StarCalc worksheet into a text document as an OLE link, the data is no longer linked to the original StarCalc worksheet.

CREATING OLE LINKS AMONG STAROFFICE DOCUMENTS   In StarOffice, StarChart charts, StarImage image files, and StarDraw drawing files are native OLE objects. That is, they are always inserted into other StarOffice documents as OLE objects.

You can also choose to insert portions of a StarCalc spreadsheet, a StarWriter document, or a StarImpress presentation as an OLE object. To do so, either choose Insert, Object, or copy the selected text or object and use the Paste Special command.

You can easily resize and move OLE objects, unlike DDE objects, by using standard object mouse and drag-and-drop techniques.

→ For an overview of working with objects, **see** "Working with Objects," **p. 176**, in this chapter.

However, you're often better off using DDE links (if you want your data to remain linked to the source so that it can be updated) or using the formatted text option in the Paste Special dialog box (which gives you more flexibility in formatting and handling your object).

Caution

As in many other programs, OLE is still rather unstable. If you create large documents which have many OLE objects, you may encounter problems with your files, such as crashing, corruption, or inablity to open the document file. Be sure to save multiple backups of any such documents.

PART

I

CH

4

To create an OLE link, copy the text or object, and then switch to the destination document. Select Edit, Paste Special. The first choice on the list in the resulting dialog box is to paste your selection as a StarOffice data type; the specific phrase used depends on the type of object you have selected. For example, if you have a StarWriter selection on the Clipboard, it says `Text(StarWriter 5.1)`. Highlight that choice, and click OK.

CREATING OLE LINKS FROM NON-STAROFFICE APPLICATIONS   You can also use OLE to copy data from some non-StarOffice applications into StarOffice. To insert an object as an OLE object, select it, choose Copy from the source application's Edit menu, and switch to the StarOffice document that is the object's destination. Choose Paste Special from the Edit menu, and then choose OLE Object from your list of choices.

In general, though, OLE is relatively inflexible compared to StarOffice's rich palette of data sharing and editing possibilities. You have almost all the tools you might ever need at your fingertips in StarOffice, so it is rare that you need to embed another application into a document.

Note

Microsoft Office does not support copying StarOffice data and pasting it as an OLE link into MS Office documents.

ORDINARY LINKS

When you insert pictures using the Insert, Pictures command, in most cases you see an Insert Pictures dialog box. In this dialog, you have the option of inserting your graphic as a copy of the original file (the default) or as a link. This type of link is most commonly used with graphics files. You can also insert document files as links into a StarWriter document.

INSERTING GRAPHICS AS LINKS   If you are creating a document with many graphics files, inserting your files as links is strongly recommended. The document then doesn't store the picture inside it, only a reference to the picture's location. The reference takes up much less room in your document. It also prevents your document from developing problems that can arise when a document is too large.

Graphics linked in this way are not dynamically connected to the source file. You can change your graphics file in any way you like, and those changes will remain even after you update your document.

WORKING WITH LINKS AND LINKED DATA

You edit and work with linked data using different techniques and commands than you use with data you create from scratch in your document.

> **Note**
>
> You cannot edit or otherwise modify DDE linked data or linked text you insert into a StarWriter document directly unless you break the link. You must edit the source file.

Your link control center is the Edit Links dialog box, shown in Figure 4.10. If you create linked text sections in StarWriter documents, you also use the Edit menu's Sections dialog box.

Figure 4.10
The Edit Links dialog box lists the complete pathname of all links in your document. You can use the Modify command to change a source file's path or substitute a different file.

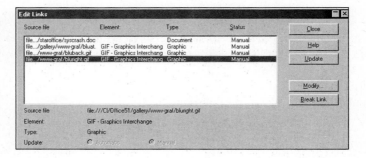

MAINTAINING FILE INTEGRITY WITH LINKED FILES

The pathname that StarOffice records for your link is the address of the source data you want to display in the destination document. If you change the location of the source file—that is, if its address changes—StarOffice can no longer find it, just as if you change your address, the Post Office can no longer deliver your mail. (Although it's more like the Post Office moving and taking all your mail with it.) Avoid changing the location. You can permanently damage files that you open if their links are not available.

To maintain file integrity, you must make sure that any linked files are always available to the receiving document. Ideally, you should place linked files either in the same folder as your document or in a subfolder in the document's directory.

If you need to move and/or rename a source file, you should immediately open the receiving document and select Edit, Links. Then select the (old) pathname of the link, and click Modify to open the Insert dialog box. In the dialog, navigate to the source's new location, select it, and click OK to substitute this new path for the old.

You can also substitute a different file for the original source file by using Modify—but only if both files were created in the same application. Otherwise, you need to insert the new file freshly by using the Insert command.

UPDATING LINKS

When you create links, your source and destination documents are not in constant contact with one another. The data in your receiving document is refreshed only when the file is *updated* against the source file.

By default, StarOffice prompts you to update all links when opening and closing the destination document. However, you might need to update links while you're working to ensure that you have the most current data.

FINDING UPDATE COMMANDS   You can update links from inside an open document by using the Edit menu's Links dialog box or by choosing Tools, Update. You can update a file in the Explorer or Beamer by selecting the file, right-clicking, and choosing Update from the context menu.

EFFECTS OF UPDATING   When DDE links are updated, any changes you have made to your destination DDE data, including formatting, are overwritten by data from the source document. If StarOffice cannot find the source document, it leaves your data as is.

When graphics links are updated, StarOffice just checks and confirms that the file is still where its path promises. When linked text sections in StarWriter are updated, the section is refreshed to reflect any changes you have made to the source document.

When OLE links are updated, StarOffice checks and confirms that the source application is still where its path promises. Updating has no effect on the data in OLE links.

Caution

If you move a source file from its original location, StarOffice does not give you a warning that the file cannot be found when you choose Update. Updating may cause the program to crash.

BREAKING A LINK

If you break a link, the data remains in your destination document but is no longer linked to the source. It becomes a copy of the source data. (In the case of a graphics file, keep in mind that this can increase the size of your document substantially.)

PART

I

CH

4

To break a link, choose Edit, Links. In the Links dialog that opens, select the filename of the link you want to break, and click Break Link.

To reestablish a link, you must reinsert the source file into your destination document.

WORKING WITH SECTIONS

If you insert sections as links in a StarWriter document, you can manage the links with the same Edit menu's Links dialog box. However, you also can manage the individual sections via the Edit menu's Sections dialog box.

→ For more information on working with sections in StarWriter, **see** "Defining Sections," **p. 378**.

WORKING WITH OBJECTS

You'll find two different kinds of objects in StarOffice: draw objects, which are component pieces of vector drawings such as lines, circles, and rectangles; and inserted objects. Inserted objects include a diverse range of things that on the surface don't appear to have much in common, including graphics files, text boxes, form control fields, and charts and other OLE objects. They do have something in common, however: StarOffice bounds all these objects with bounding boxes and enables you to manipulate and format them in essentially the same way. Understanding their similarities will help you quickly become effective working in StarOffice.

→ For more details on working with inserted objects, **see** "Rehearsing Objects," **p. 421**.

→ For detailed information on creating and working with Draw objects, **see** "Working with Graphic Objects," **p. 736**.

→ For an explanation of vector graphics, **see** "Understanding Computer Graphics," **p. 733**.

UNDERSTANDING INSERTED OBJECTS

An inserted object is placed inside a bounding box that structures the object's size. This box is attached to your document with an *anchor*, represented on the screen by a gray square with an anchor symbol. The anchor ensures that your object doesn't get pushed around by the regular data in your document. Your ability to move your object is constrained by the attachment point of your anchor.

You have two different ways of working with your object. You can manipulate and format your object's invisible bounding box, or you can manipulate and format your object's contents. For example, if you insert a text box, you can change the text box's size, move it to another location, and change the color and thickness of the box's border. You can also click in the text box and enter, edit, and delete text.

The way you work with contents of different objects is different, but the way you work with an object's bounding box is the same with all objects across StarOffice application modules.

INSERTING OBJECTS

You can insert an object into a StarOffice document in three basic ways:

- You can copy something from one application and paste it into another as an OLE object.
- You can drag and drop a picture from the Beamer or an object from the Navigator into another document.
- You can use commands on the Insert menu.

→ For a brief overview on inserting pictures from the Beamer, **see** "Previewing Files, Sounds, and Images in the Beamer," **p. 58**.

→ For details on inserting graphic objects, **see** "Working with Graphic Objects," **p. 440**.

Table 4.6 lists and briefly describes the types of objects you can insert from the Insert menu.

TABLE 4.6   INSERTING OBJECTS FROM THE INSERT MENU

Select This Command	To Insert This Type of Object
Text Box	A box into which you can insert text that is separate from the main body of your document.
Table	A table.
Horizontal Line	A horizontal line to act as a divider. Horizontal lines are pictures; this command is just a shortcut to speed creating Web pages, which often use lines to visually organize the page.
Picture	A graphics file from the StarOffice Gallery or saved elsewhere on your system.
Object	An OLE object, Java applet, StarMath formula, or a plug-in program.
Chart	A StarChart chart.
Floating Frame	A frame to use in structuring Web pages that use framesets.

You can insert horizontal lines and pictures as copies or links. Inserting them as links takes much less room in your document but means you must ensure the graphics file is available on any system where the document will be opened.

By choosing Insert, Object, OLE Object, you get the widest selection of options for inserting OLE objects, including inserting them from non-StarOffice applications.

→ For more information on working with charts, **see** "Charting Data," **p. 666**, and "Inserting Charts," **p. 348**.

COMMANDING OBJECTS

To work with an object, you must first select it. When you select it, your object bar automatically adjusts, bringing the correct object manipulation tools to the desktop. The tools vary slightly among object types. Figure 4.11 shows three object bars—for an OLE object (a chart in this case), a text box, and a graphic. The tools that repeat across the bars are identified only once, on the OLE object bar. Note that when you select an object, the object's type is displayed in the Style box on the far left of the object bars.

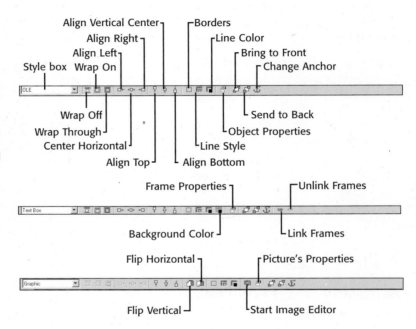

Figure 4.11
The object bar contains tools for aligning and positioning an object, changing its properties, and setting its wrap characteristics. If a tool is grayed out, it may not be available for the type of object you currently have selected.

Objects also have their own context menus and Properties dialog boxes, which, for the most part, provide the same basic options.

As always, to open a context menu, you select the object and right-click. Object context menus offer shortcuts for the alignment and wrap commands on the object bar (Arrange, Alignment, Anchor, and Wrap). Just below those four commands, separated by a thin line, is the command that opens the object's Properties dialog box. The name of this command varies according to the type of object: Object for an OLE object, Picture for a graphic, Text for a text box, and so on.

The object Properties dialog boxes consolidate a comprehensive assemblage of settings with which you can control an object's appearance. Because all objects used in StarOffice are embedded objects, they share, with minor variations, the same basic dialog tabs: Type, Options, Wrap, Hyperlink, Borders, Background, and Macro. Get to know an object's dialog box. Its tabs enable you to control an object's overall appearance and behavior.

SELECTING OBJECTS

Selecting objects is easy if you understand the difference between working with an object as an object and working with its contents.

To select any object as an object, click its border. When the bounding box is selected successfully, green boxes, or *handles*, appear on the corners and midpoints of the object's borders.

The technique for selecting an object's contents varies depending on the type of object with which you are working. In all cases, however, you must not select the object's bounding box. If necessary, you can deselect it first by clicking anywhere outside the object.

To enter text in a text box, you place your mouse pointer over the center of the box and click. The text entry cursor should appear, blinking merrily. You can then type and enter text as usual.

To open an OLE object, such as a chart or formula, you double-click somewhere inside the object's boundaries. The application or dialog boxes from the application open on your desktop, and appropriate tools appear on the toolbars.

To work with a bitmap graphic, you need to open it in StarImage. To do so, click the Start Image Editor button on the toolbar, or select Image Editor from the object's context menu.

Note

If you edit a graphic you inserted as a link, the link is broken, and a copy of the graphic is inserted in your document.

RESIZING, MOVING, AND COPYING OBJECTS

After you have selected an object so that its handles show, you can resize and move it through drag and drop.

To move the object, place your cursor in the center of the object, click, and drag to the new location.

To resize the object, grab one of its handles and drag. When you start dragging, a directional arrow alerts you to the dimension you are able to resize with that particular handle.

Tip #65 from
Michael & Sarah

To maintain an object's proportions when you're resizing, press Shift while dragging.

To copy an object, press Ctrl while dragging it.

MAKING SENSE OF ANCHORS

Anchors "tie" an object to a specific cell, character, or paragraph in your table, spreadsheet, or document. Anchoring your object ensures that as you change your layout and add new data, your object is not moved out of proper relation with its associated text or other data.

By default, StarOffice anchors inserted objects to the paragraph nearest your cursor. You can drag your object around freely within the page margins, and the anchor automatically shifts to the paragraph nearest its new location.

You can change an object's anchor point via the context menu's Anchor command, the object bar Change Anchor tool, or the Type tab in the object's Properties dialog box. The Properties dialog box gives you the most fine-grained control over the anchoring and positioning of your object.

If you want to position an object outside the normal page margins, you must anchor it to the page or a character.

If you anchor an object as a character, it remains in place where you positioned it, just as a letter in a word remains in place even as you add new words and letters around it.

FORMATTING OBJECTS

You format an object as an object in its Properties dialog box. You open this dialog by clicking the Properties button on the object bar, or you can right-click your object and select the name of your object type (Picture, Text Box, Object, and so on) from its context menu.

The following are the basic properties shared across most object types:

- Position, size, and anchor point (Type tab)
- Border (Border tab)
- Wrap (Wrap tab)
- Background (Background tab)

DELETING OBJECTS

To delete an object, select its bounding box so that the green resizing handles are visible. Then press Del or Ctrl+X. Delete clears the object from your document entirely, whereas Ctrl+X stores it on the program Clipboard or buffer for reuse.

INTRODUCING THE ADDRESS BOOK

The Address Book is a built-in contact manager stored in the Explorer. It already includes a table in dBASE format called *address;* it is the default table for storing your contact information. You can create forms, queries, and reports based on this table so that you can manage, filter, and print your contacts in various ways.

→ For a basic introduction to StarBase databases, **see** "Introducing StarBase," **p. 1086**, and "Using StarBase as a Data Manager," **p. 1087**.

→ For details on entering and extracting contacts, **see** "Using the Address Book," **p. 1011**.

→ For details on creating mail merges with the Address Book, **see** "Creating Letters with Mail Merge," **p. 360**.

→ For details on creating email merges, **see** "Creating Mail Merges with StarMail," **p. 1062**.

SETTING A DIFFERENT ADDRESS BOOK AS THE DEFAULT

If you want to set a different database table as your default Address Book, select the desired table in the Explorer, open its context menu, and click the Address Book command. (This process is just like designating a folder to serve as your default desktop.) The next time you activate the Address Book command from an application, this table will be opened in the Beamer. It is also the table called automatically when you choose mail merge commands.

WORKING WITH THE ADDRESS BOOK

You can enter and extract data via the Address Book dialog box, which you open through the Edit menu. It displays one Address Book record at a time. Using this dialog is the easiest way to add, edit, and search for individual entries. A few other tools are at your disposal only from this dialog (see Figure 4.12).

Figure 4.12
Using the Address Book dialog box is the easiest way to retrieve single addresses into your documents and enter new contacts.

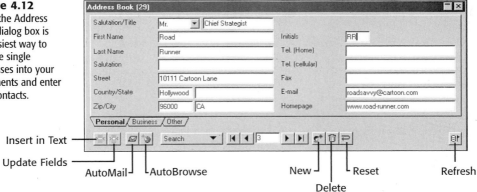

You can also open the address table in the Beamer. In this view, you can easily create form letters by dragging and dropping Address Book fields into an open document. You can also filter and sort your data by using the tools on the Beamer toolbar and easily locate and insert multiple records by using the new Lookup Record tool.

In both views, you can move forward through a record's fields by pressing Tab and backward by pressing Shift+Tab.

You can drag and drop addresses only in Table view; to insert addresses from the dialog box, you need to click the Insert Text button or, if you are in StarMail, click AutoMail.

In StarMail and StarNews, you can select email addresses in the Header pane, right-click to open a context menu, and select Add to Address Book to automatically add email addresses to the Address Book.

MODIFYING THE DEFAULT ADDRESS BOOK DATABASE

Because the default Address Book table exists as a database file (`address.dbf`) in dBASE format, you can modify its structure. However, if you change the structure of the database file or assign a table that has a different structure as the default Address Book, you can no longer use the Edit menu's Address Book dialog box. It's therefore best to create queries that sort, filter, and present the information as you specify rather than edit the default address table's structure.

→ For more information on creating queries, **see** Chapter 35, "Getting Answers with Queries and Fields," **p. 1201**.

WORKING WITH MULTIPLE ADDRESS TABLES

Although you can have only one table set as the default Address Book at a time, you can switch among multiple tables that you use as Address Books. The best way to create additional Address Books is to copy the program *address* table and rename it.

→ For steps on how to copy the address table structure, **see** "Copying the Address Table's Structure," **p. 1013**.

IMPORTING AN EXISTING ADDRESS BOOK

If you have an existing Address Book that you want to use in StarOffice, it must be saved in a database format that StarBase can read and placed in the Address Book database or another StarBase database. (By default, the Address Book database is stored in the Office51\Database folder.)

Your first choice of format should be dBASE. If you cannot save or export your address book in dBASE format, you should export or save it as a delimited text file (.txt or .csv). You then need to open it in StarCalc and save it as a dBASE file.

Note

Text databases are read-only in StarBase. You can edit them only in StarCalc.

After you place your table in your database directory, follow these steps to get access to it:

1. Open the Explorer.
2. Select the database into which you're importing the table.
3. Right-click and choose Properties from the context menu.
4. Click the Tables tab to bring it to the top. You should see a list of all dBASE tables (files with the *.dbf extension) stored in the same directory as that database.
5. Click the check box to the left of the table's name so that an X appears. Clicking this box selects the table to appear in the database in the Explorer.
6. Click OK.
7. Back in the Explorer, click the plus sign (+) next to the Tables folder in your database. A list of available tables appears; your imported table should appear in this list. To open it on your desktop, double-click its name.

The quickest way to import your data is to append your existing table to the default address table. First, you must create a new database in the Explorer. Then you must export or save your existing Address Book from the application in which you created it in dBASE or delimited text file format. Next, assign the name address to this exported copy of your existing Address Book; giving it this name is the key to the process because you can only combine two tables that share the same name.

→ For details on creating a new database in the Explorer, **see** "Creating a New Database in the Explorer," **p. 1092**.

Finally, copy the Address Book table you are importing to the directory in which you created your new database, and follow the same steps given earlier in this section for revealing the table in the Explorer. Completing these steps imports your table into StarOffice; you then need to append this imported table onto the existing address table.

When you append data to a table, only data in fields that match the field names of the receiving table are imported. You therefore might need to edit the field names of your existing Address Book so that they match those of the Address Book address table. You don't need to delete extra fields.

To edit your existing Address Book, select its name in the Tables folder of your database, right-click, and choose Table Design. Your Address Book opens on your desktop in Edit mode.

→ For details on modifying your table structure, **see** "Creating and Modifying Tables in Design View," **p. 1122**.

When your existing Address Book table is ready, open both your new database and the Address Book database in the Explorer. Select your imported table, and drag and drop it onto the Tables icon in the Address Book database.

A Copy Table dialog box appears, offering you three choices:

- Definition and Data
- Definition
- Append Data

Choose Append Data, and your data is automatically added to the end of the existing address table. If your existing Address Book has fields that the StarOffice address table does not, you see a dialog box informing you that data from these fields will not be imported.

Choosing Definition and Data would make a copy of your entire table, whereas choosing Definition would create a blank copy of your table.

WEB AND FILE SURFING WITH AUTOBROWSE

AutoBrowse is a feature that automatically opens the URL entered in that address record onto your desktop. It is also available from the File menu, where it can be used to automatically open a URL you have selected in a document. This URL can be an Internet address (if you are online), but because StarOffice equates pathnames with URLs, it can also be a locally stored file. For example, if you enter into the URL field the pathname of a price quote letter you sent to a contact, clicking AutoBrowse automatically opens that file on your desktop.

SENDING AND PRINTING DOCUMENTS

You find the same flexibility in handling printing across StarOffice. You can print open documents on your desktop, or you can print files directly from the Explorer, Beamer, or desktop by selecting the Print command (Ctrl+P) from the context menu. However, sending documents to a conventional printer is only one of many ways that you might output your StarOffice document in a final product. With the File, Send commands and the Explorer context menu's Send commands, you can also output your document as email, a fax, or a file copied to portable disk media.

Note

The File menu's Print and Print Setup commands are grayed out unless you have an open document on the desktop.

SETTING UP YOUR WINDOWS PRINTER

StarOffice automatically reads any existing printer settings in your Windows Printers folder in the Control Panel when you install the program and enters the settings for your default printer into the Print dialog box. You should still check the settings in the Print Setup dialog box the first time you start StarOffice to be sure they are correct.

Note

If your Print Setup dialog box settings are different than those of your current default printer in Windows, you might experience printing errors or incorrect printing output.

SETTING UP YOUR LINUX PRINTER

If you have a PostScript printer, you're in luck because StarOffice includes a printer setup utility that has a large number of PostScript print drivers that will help you get up and printing in no time. All you need to do is double-click the Printer Setup icon on your StarOffice desktop and choose your printer from the list in the dialog box that opens.

If you have a non-PostScript printer, you must use a translation program such as GhostScript to filter your PostScript output from StarOffice into a language your printer can understand. Most distributions of Linux include GhostScript or a comparable program. Taking you through the process of configuring GhostScript is beyond the scope of this book; however, you can consult your distribution's manual, your man pages, or any other documentation you may have. Typically, you'll want to choose the generic PostScript print driver as your printer choice from within StarOffice to direct the output to GhostScript.

→ For more details on installing your Linux printer, **see** "Installing Your Printer: Linux," **p. 1382**.

PREVIEWING YOUR PRINT JOB

In StarWriter, you have a Page View/Print Preview command available on the File menu that enables you to see what your output will look like, as well as to print thumbnails of your documents via the Options dialog box. In StarCalc, you have a less flexible Page View command that enables you to see what your selected print area(s) will look like when they print.

Tip #66 from	Want to tweak your document in Normal view and see what it will look like in Print Preview? To do so, open your document, and then select Print Preview to open a second instance of the document in Preview mode with its own task button on the taskbar. Then drag the Preview mode task button on top of the Document view task button, and drop it. You can see the two views side by side. To separate the views again, just click and drag from the task button—the preview task button reappears—and drop it on a blank spot in the taskbar.
Michael & Sarah	

You have only a limited set of commands available in Preview mode, and they all relate to setting your print options or manipulating your view. Don't forget to right-click to access the context menu.

→ For details on previewing documents in StarWriter, **see** "Previewing Documents," **p. 475**.

→ For details on previewing spreadsheets in StarCalc, **see** "Previewing Your Worksheets with Page View," **p. 709**.

→ For details on previewing presentations in StarImpress, **see** "Previewing A Presentation," **p. 892**.

To close out of Preview mode, click the Close Window button on the toolbar, or select Close Window (Ctrl+W) from the task button's context menu.

PART

I

CH

4

PRINT BASICS

The most difficult aspects of printing are usually configuring your printer to print correctly. After you've crossed that hurdle, the rest is easy.

To print a file or a portion of a file that is open on your desktop, select the area you want to print (or select nothing if you want to print the entire document). Then choose File, Print. A Print dialog box appears, similar to the one in Figure 4.13. Your default printer is visible in the Printer Name drop-down list. To use another installed printer or print driver, you can select its name from the list.

Select your print range in the Print Range section. The default is to print all pages.

Your current page location appears automatically in the Pages options box, but when you select the option, you can enter other page numbers and ranges. Note that the punctuation you use to separate page numbers differs from Microsoft Office conventions. To print single, noncontinuous pages, you must separate page numbers with a semicolon (;). To print a range of pages, you must enter the first page number followed by a hyphen (-) and the last page number. For example, 3;7;10-15;23 will cause pages 3, 7, 10 through 15, and 23 to print. If you enter 4-, StarWriter will print the document starting at page 4.

Figure 4.13
You can set print options for all document types except spreadsheets from the Print dialog box. You also can select a printer and adjust your printer's properties.

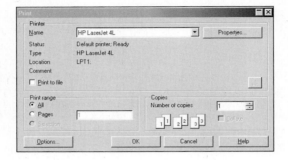

The Selection option is available only if you have already made a selection in your document.

Next, select the number of copies you want to print in the lower right of the Print dialog box.

If you need to adjust your printer's properties, click the Properties button in the upper right. The properties you have available vary depending on your printer.

With all programs except StarCalc, you can also click the Options button to set a variety of print options. In StarCalc, you set printing options on the Sheet tab of the Format menu's Page dialog box. Figure 4.14 shows the Printer Options dialog boxes for StarWriter and StarImpress.

Figure 4.14
The options available to you change according to your document type, but basic layout of the Printer Options dialog box is the same.

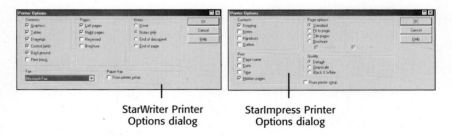

StarWriter Printer
Options dialog

StarImpress Printer
Options dialog

After you've set your properties and options, choose OK in the main Print dialog box, and let the printing begin.

→ For more information on printing in StarCalc, **see** "Selecting What to Print," **p. 704**, and "Printing Your Results," **p. 710**.

→ For more information on printing in StarImpress, **see** "Printing Your Presentation," **p. 906**.

→ For more information on printing in StarImage, **see** "Printing Images," **p. 810**.

→ For more information on printing in StarDraw, **see** "Printing Graphics," **p. 776**.

SENDING DOCUMENTS AND MAIL FROM THE DESKTOP

Today we seem to be receding ever further from the ideal of the paperless office, but at least electronic communication and document exchange is easier than ever before. If you want to do your part to lessen the paper load, you can send your document directly to your audience via email or fax. To send your document as email, choose File, Send, Document as Email. You can choose to send it as email text or an attachment.

→ For more information on sending mail from the desktop, **see** "Mailing Documents and Web Pages from the Desktop," **p. 1059**.

Tip #67 from *Michael &* *Sarah* 	If you have Microsoft Outlook or Microsoft Outlook Express on your system, you can also send mail through that account by using the context menu's Send To command.

To send your document as a fax, choose Print, and then select your fax driver as the printer in the Print dialog box. Alternatively, you can select the file, right-click, and choose Send To, Fax Recipient from the context menu.

Tip #68 from *Michael & Sarah*	Another option for in-house document exchange is saving documents in HTML format and posting them to the company intranet or emailing them as HTML files (because many email programs have browsing capabilities as well, as does the StarDesktop).

PRINTING FROM THE DESKTOP

You can print text documents, StarMath formulas, presentations, spreadsheets, and Web pages directly from the Explorer or desktop without opening them. However, you cannot print individual graphics or image files unless they are open within an application.

To print from a file, select its filename in the Explorer or task window, and then select Print (Ctrl+P) from the context menu or File menu. (Right-click the selected file to open the context menu.) You can select multiple files to print by using the usual Ctrl+click and Ctrl+Shift selection shortcuts.

Note	If you print spreadsheets or presentations from a file, the entire file prints; you do not have the opportunity to select specific portions.

If you choose Print from the context menu or press Ctrl+P, your file prints directly to the printer, just as if you had clicked the Print button on the function bar.

If you choose File, Print, the Print dialog box opens, enabling you to change the current print settings.

PRINTING TO FILE

You can print a document to a file, which creates a file in the printer language of your selected printer. You then can take this file to a typesetting shop, or you can put it on another computer with the same printer and the correct print manager program and print it directly.

You usually choose this option if you are creating an output file to take to a professional print shop or service bureau. However, it can be useful if you need to print a document on another computer that doesn't have StarOffice.

To print to a file, choose File, Print as usual. Then select your target printer from your printer list. (You might need to install a new print driver.) Click the Properties button to adjust any properties as necessary; ask your print shop or service bureau for guidance. Setting your page size and other document properties correctly is important because you can't change anything in a print file.

Then select the Print to File option. Next, click the button with ellipses (…) to the far right of the option box. Clicking this button opens a browsing dialog box that enables you to navigate to the directory where you want to save your file. When you are in the right directory, enter a filename for the print file. Leave the automatic file extension option turned on. Finally, choose Save. The process of saving the file make take a few minutes, depending on the speed of your system, the target printer, and the size of the file.

TROUBLESHOOTING

My cursor is acting strangely, and I can't select things the way I want.

If you use your status bar shortcut menus a lot, you can easily turn on Additive or Extended selection modes accidentally. When one of these modes is on, you can't use your cursor and mouse as you normally do; your click is interpreted as indicating a selection. Just click the selection mode field in the status bar (look at the bottom of your document window) until you see the abbreviation STD, not ADD or EXT.

Your mouse could be behaving strangely for non-StarOffice-related reasons as well. If the problem continues, or you are already in Standard selection mode, check to ensure your mouse is snugly plugged into your computer. If you installed a new mouse driver, that driver and StarOffice or your system might be incompatible; conversely, if you have an old driver, it may not work properly either.

On the Windows side, the generic Windows mouse driver usually works, although you might lose the ability to program your mouse buttons. On the Linux side, drivers are a more complicated issue because many mouse devices and other peripherals aren't officially supported on Linux by their manufacturers. Check with your mouse manufacturer for more assistance, or (Linux users especially) cruise the newsgroups for information.

I have links in my document, but the Edit menu's Links command is grayed out.

Try placing your cursor in one of the linked areas or selecting one of the linked areas. With documents inserted as sections in StarWriter, sometimes Links doesn't appear if no other linked files are included in the document. You can manage your sections via the Edit menu's Sections dialog box and update them by choosing Tools, Update. Or, if you really want to use the Links dialog, you can insert a dummy linked graphic temporarily, select the graphic, and open Links.

I've made changes to my graphic that I don't like, and I want to return to the original appearance. However, when I click Update, nothing happens.

Graphics files work differently as links than does alphanumeric data. When you update, your linked copy is matched against the target original for certain key information, but changes you make to the size, colors, and certain other attributes are not undone. If you want to return to the original, and you are too late to use the Undo command, you need to reinsert the original graphics file.

I can't enter text in my text box.

If your text box is selected as an object (with the green resizing handles visible), you can't enter text. Click outside the object somewhere on the desktop. Then position your cursor over the center of the text box, and click. Your text insertion cursor should appear, and you can enter text as usual.

I press F4, but a different table opens in the Beamer, not my Address Book.

By default, the table that opens in the Beamer when you press F4 is whatever table has been defined as your current Address Book or, if you have an active document with merge fields, whatever table is the source of those fields. To define a different table as your Address Book, select the table you want in the Explorer, right-click, and choose Address Book. A check mark appears next to the command. To change your current database, choose Edit, Exchange Database. Then scroll through your list of available tables and queries, and select the one you want. From this point forward, this table will open in the Beamer when you press F4 until you select another table as your default database.

I need to save my file as a WordPerfect file, but I can't find WordPerfect in the File Type list.

If you are using the free Personal Edition downloaded from the Internet, you don't have access to WordPerfect filters. If you are using another edition, you just need to run the Setup program from the Office51 directory and choose Modify. In the window where you can choose application modules and elements, select and open the Text Filters list. There, you'll see a wide range of WordPerfect filters.

CHAPTER 5

Managing Folders, Files, and Mail

In this chapter

DESKTOP MANAGEMENT WITH STAROFFICE

The advent of computers occasioned a lot of marketing talk about the paperless office of the future. Well, not only are we still really drowning in paper, but we're also virtually drowning in electronic files.

How to manage the deluge? When you understand StarOffice's underlying logic, you'll find it's easier than you thought.

StarOffice's motto of "do everything in one place" is expressed in something as mundane as the Open and Save As dialog boxes, from which you can not only navigate to find distant files, but also create links, copy and delete files, and create new folders. Try that with MS Office!

On a deeper level, StarOffice once again shows its origins in the Internet age by extending email concepts to files and folders. You can use commands likeMark, Subscribe, and Read to almost any object you store on your computer and then create powerful Boolean filters that sort and handle not just your email and news, but also your files and folders.

This chapter gives you a quick overview of the program's underlying logic for storing and managing objects and shows you how to use the most important tools for organizing your desktop.

MANAGING FILES AND FOLDERS FROM THE OPEN AND SAVE AS DIALOGS

The basics of opening and saving files are discussed in Chapter 4, "Working in StarOffice," in the sections " Opening Existing Documents" and "Saving and Closing Documents." In this section, the focus is on using tools and drag and drop in the Save As and Open dialog boxes to manage your files.

NAVIGATING IN THE SAVE AS AND OPEN DIALOGS

The Edit, Open and Edit, Save As dialog boxes (shown in Figures 5.1 and 5.2) have some small differences but share the same basic tools and organization.

The main portion of both dialogs is filled with a list of files and their attributes. By default, the dialog is set to List view; clicking Details view changes to a Beamer-like display that reveals details like file type, size, and modification date.

By default, both these dialogs open to the folder called Work Folder in the Explorer. You can then navigate anywhere on your system by using navigational buttons on their tool-bars—the Up Directory button on the left and the Default Directory on the right.

The Up One Level button moves you up your directory structure, one folder at a time. If you accidentally go too far, just double-click the folder or icon that you want to open again to move down a level. Extended-clicking this button opens a fly-out menu that displays all your current drives and/or volumes and your most recently visited directories.

Figure 5.1
The Open dialog box, by default, searches for and displays all file types, but you can target and speed your search by selecting a specific file type from the drop-down menu.

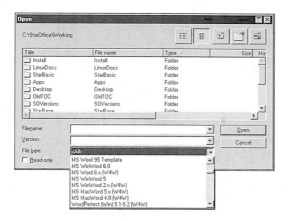

Figure 5.2
The Save As dialog box automatically displays the current name of the file you're saving and, unlike the Open dialog, shows only files of the same type as your active document. Extend-click the Up Directory button, and up pops another shortcut menu.

List　　　Details　　　Up One Level

Create New Directory

Default Directory

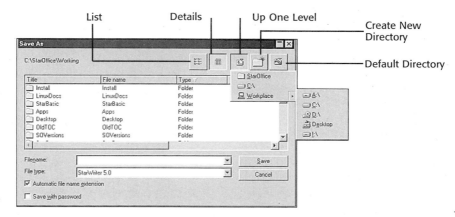

The New Directory button creates a new folder in your current location, which means you can easily manage your files at the same time you open and save them.

Clicking the Default Directory button takes you to your designated Work Folder (set in the Tools, Options, General, Paths dialog box). If you extended-click this button, a fly-out menu with other directory options opens.

PART

I

CH

5

Tip #69 from
Michael & Sarah

You can navigate entirely with keys in the Open and Save As dialogs. Press Tab and Shift+Tab to cycle forward and backward, respectively, through the dialog box buttons and lists. Press Alt+ Down Arrow to open the directory icon pop-up menus and the file lists in the Filename, Version, and File Type text boxes. Press Esc to exit the pop-up menus and lists.

Because the Open and Save As dialogs are like mini-Beamers, you can actually manage files from them in a number of ways. Doing so might seem a bit strange at first because in most programs you must exit the application to manage files, but it's a much more intuitive way of working—after you get over the old, bad habits instilled in you by less-thoughtful program design.

Tip #70 from
Michael & Sarah

> StarOffice gives you a choice for mail handling   you can save all your messages in one large inbox or outbox (which, if exported, is an ASCII format .mbx file); or you can save or export individual messages as .sdm (StarMail format) files. (Or, you can do both.) Once you save mail messages individually, you can't use the great tools on the inbox and outbox toolbars and context menus   but with the new Details view, you have access to most of the same tools in the Open and Save As dialog boxes. These dialogs become your de facto inbox and outbox for saved mail.

CREATING NEW FOLDERS

You can create a new folder by using the New Directory button in both the Open and Save As dialogs. If you're wondering, "Why would I want to?" the answer is StarOffice's drag and drop, combined with the power of the document context menu, which you can access from these dialogs as well as the Beamer.

MOVING, COPYING, AND DELETING FILES

From within the Open and Save As dialogs, you can use the usual drag, Ctrl+drag, and Shift+Ctrl+drag combinations to move, copy, and make links, respectively. You therefore can save a copy of your new proposal and place a link to it on your boss's desktop at the same time, with no need to exit your task and return to the desktop. To create a new folder, just click the New Directory button, and a dialog appears prompting you for a name. Enter the name, or click Cancel to exit without creating the folder.

CHOOSING WHERE TO SAVE YOUR FILES

Obviously, you can choose where to save your file in the Save As dialog by navigating through your directory structure. The larger question, however, is where is it best to save your file? Although that's a question only you can answer, keep in mind that with StarOffice's links, you can save a file anywhere and create multiple links to it, rather than save multiple copies on multiple desktops or even save copies in multiple folders on your own local drives.

Tip #71 from
Michael & Sarah

> If you work on a network, take advantage of the server backups your company or business surely creates. Save all critical documents on the server, not your local drive, and just create links. You can create links directly from the Open and Save As dialogs   just select the file, right-click, and choose Create Link.

Caution

If you're working with links to files located on a server, be sure you're in Online mode. Otherwise, you see and work in a file stored in your computer's cache, not the most current copy on the server.

Note

Although you can open files from linked folders in the Open dialog, you cannot save files to linked folders in the Save As dialog. You must navigate to the original folder location.

Tip #72 from
Michael & Sarah

You can also link one locally stored document to another from within a document by inserting a hyperlink using the Hyperlinks toolbar. It looks just like any other hyperlink. Clicking it automatically closes the first file (with appropriate prompts) and opens the hyperlinked file on the desktop.

Caution

Be careful not to create links either to or from removable media such as floppy or zip disks. If the media isn't in your system when you click a link, you may experience system instability.

SAVING FILES ON A NETWORK

 If you're on a network, be careful that you're always working in Online mode. (If you're online, the Online button in the Function bar appears pressed.)

If you're not online when you try to save a file to a network drive, what you see will not be what you get. StarOffice displays only the directory map stored in your cache, not the current real map, because it isn't able to update.

SAVING FILES FOR USE ON A WEB SITE

If you're saving HTML files to be posted on a Web site, you might want to save your files with *relative* rather than *absolute* pathnames.

An *absolute* pathname is a file's or link's complete address that uniquely and precisely specifies its location—just like your street, city, and country address absolutely and uniquely identifies your house. An absolute address for a file might look something like

`file:///h¦reports/june/sales1`

where `file` indicates that the object is a file on a local drive (rather than a Web page, for example, identified with the HTTP prefix), `h` is the local drive, `reports` and `june` are folder (directory) names, and `sales1` is the name of the report.

A *relative* path specifies only the correct directory relations for a file rather than indicates the specific drive on which it is stored. For example, a relative path for the same report would be the following:

`reports/june/sales1`

PART

I

CH

5

Why save a file with a relative pathname? Saving it this way is useful if you're creating documents to be used as Web pages, as long as you create a directory structure on your Web server that exactly matches the directory structure on the drive where you're creating the content. The relative path tells the system where the file for the Web page is located in relation to the home page or another page on the system, without specifying any particular hard drive or computer (domain) location. It's like telling someone, "Our house is the last one on the right"—enough information to find your house when someone is already in the right place. This means you can copy or upload all the folders with your Web pages to your server, and all the pathnames will still be valid, even if your Web site is on a drive mapped to H or G instead of C. (Otherwise, the Web server might get confused, looking for a page on a C: drive that the server doesn't have access to.)

The default in StarOffice is to save all files and links with relative pathnames. To change this setting, open the Tools, Options, General dialog, and click the Save tab (shown in Figure 5.3).

Figure 5.3
Select the Save URLs Relative To options when you want your files to have relative rather than absolute pathnames.

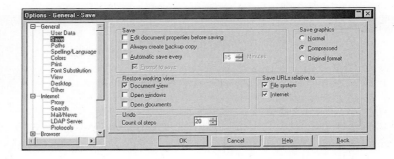

You see two options here because you can address your files in two different ways: what you might think of as a local, in-country address and an international address. File system addresses include references just to your computer (if you have a standalone system) or drives on your network (if you're on a network). Internet addresses include references to your computer's or network's *domain name*, which is the name your computer has when communicating with the outside world and makes for a more complete address.

➔ For more information on creating HTML and frame documents in StarOffice, **see** Chapter 11, "Desktop Publishing with StarOffice," **p. 415**.

TIPS FOR SAVING FILES IN FOREIGN FORMATS

StarOffice saves files in a wide range of non-native (that is, non-StarOffice) formats and does it better than most other programs. Frankly, however, its filters aren't perfect. You should be aware that, inevitably, when you create a document in StarOffice and then save it in a foreign format, you will lose some of the document's formatting and properties (including revision marks). Other aspects of formatting and styles might change as well. For example, bullet styles might change, or heading styles might not cross over properly.

Note

StarWriter is set to automatically read the first row in a table as its column headers and repeat them on subsequent pages of the table (if it breaks across pages). These repeating header rows are lost when saved in other text file formats.

Because of this possibility, it's always best to first save a document in its native StarOffice format and then save a copy in the foreign format, in case you want to still have a copy in full StarOffice-formatted glory.

Tip #73 from
Michael & Sarah

You can create Windows Help files (which require a special RTF format) in StarOffice by using this little trick. Insert the following two lines in the `install.ini` file in the `[swriter-Filters-01]` section, right after the existing lines mentioning RTF. Make sure they are each typed as a continuous line without breaks or additional spaces:

```
Rich Text Help Format=Rich Text Help
Format,application/rtf,xxxx,RichText,*.rtf,20002,WH_RTF,,Export¦Alien
```

USING FILTERS TO MANAGE FILES

Every object created in StarOffice has properties attached to it. Some properties, such as time and date of creation, are assigned by your operating system and can't be changed, at least not from within StarOffice. Some, such as filename, are required but can be changed.

Many people never bother to burrow into the intimate secrets of their folders' properties. If you want to keep your desktop free of clutter and manage your time more effectively, however, you should venture a look because, in StarOffice, you can perform some pretty great tricks by setting folder properties on certain objects. For example, you can do the following:

- Display only unread documents in a folder full of old and new versions that must be stored together
- Set your mail Inbox to automatically place links to incoming emails with the same subject header in a project folder so that all related emails can be accessed from one convenient location—without wading through your Inbox packed with 200 messages
- Automatically create backup copies of documents on a designated drive at regular intervals

First, you need to understand something about properties.

SYSTEM PROPERTIES VERSUS OBJECT PROPERTIES

If you select and right-click objects in the Explorer, you'll notice that some have two properties commands—a System Properties command and a Properties command. Another case of repetitious redundancy? Not really.

The Systems Properties command displays information managed by your operating system that's accessible in StarOffice because of its integrated desktop. Basically, StarOffice passes on this system information to you and allows you to change it from within StarOffice (which is pretty nifty, when you think about it).

PART

I

CH

5

The Properties command displays information that is totally internal to StarOffice and the objects it creates and manages. That's why if you open the StarOffice Recycle Bin, you'll see it doesn't have a Systems Properties command. We like to call this the object Properties command to distinguish it from the Systems Properties command.

Certain types of folders (shown in Table 5.1) have object properties that you can modify or set on the View and Rules tabs in their Properties dialog box. The contents of these folders can then be filtered and managed with Explorer context menu commands. (Filters are explained in more detail in the later section "Selecting What You See on Your Desktop.")

TABLE 5.1   EXPLORER OBJECTS THAT CAN HAVE FILTERS APPLIED

This Icon...	Represents This Kind of Folder...
	File folder
	POP3 mail account Inbox
	IMAP mail account Inbox
	VIM mail account Inbox
	Mail Outbox
	News account
	FTP account

Links and Subscriptions are not actual collections of objects but just pointers to objects, so they don't have the same properties as these other Explorer objects. They therefore don't have any comparable options.

Search folders are essentially filter folders that retrieve files and mail from locations you specify in the Explorer (as opposed to sort and send files and mail in the Explorer to other locations). Searches have a Properties tab called Criteria that is essentially the same as the Rules tab you find with the objects in Table 5.1.

As Table 5.1 demonstrates, all but one of the objects to which you can apply these properties are Internet-related. File folders are the exception; once again, StarOffice brings Internet concepts down to the desktop.

REVEALING HIDDEN FILE FOLDER PROPERTIES

In this next section, we focus on assigning file folder properties because this concept is more unfamiliar to most users. However, mail account Inboxes, Outboxes, news accounts, and FTP accounts have similar dialogs and use the same Rules tab commands to create filters, so the general principles discussed here apply to them as well.

Note

In this section, the term *Internet folders* refers to mail account Inboxes, Outboxes, news accounts, and FTP accounts.

We will note, where relevant, any differences in the Properties options and dialog tabs.

If you select and right-click a new file folder in the Explorer and choose the Properties command, a dialog box like the one in Figure 5.4 appears.

Figure 5.4
The Rules Active option on the View tab of the Properties dialog is checked by default in all new folders. Therefore, filtering rules you create on the Rules tab will affect the display of objects in the folder.

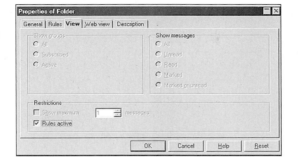

Notice that the View tab commands are grayed out and unavailable for regular file folders unless you have selected the Show, All Properties command on the folder's Explorer context menu. Once you select Show, All Properties, folders are displayed with the same properties as mail, and you can filter and sort the folders' contents in the Beamer and via filters on the Rules and View tabs. You can also mark files as read, subscribed, and/or marked.

SELECTING WHAT YOU SEE ON YOUR DESKTOP

Ever worked with someone who has a really messy desk, the kind that looks like everything might topple over with a strong sneeze? Did you wonder how anyone could live with such a desk? The answer is that your co-worker doesn't really see the mess anymore but just filters it out. Out of mind, out of sight.

In StarOffice, you can do in virtual space exactly what this imaginary co-worker does—you can filter out objects that are really there so that you see only what you want to see on your desktop. The difference is that the objects you filter out can't be seen on your desktop by anyone, even though they're there.

Tip #74 from
Michael & Sarah

If you can't find a document or file that you just know is there, try selecting the folder it's in and checking its properties. You may have set the View and/or Rules options so that it doesn't reveal itself.

You can create filters in a few different ways, depending partly on the type of folder you're working with (see Table 5.2).

Note

Don't be misled by the online Help here, which often makes it sound as though these commands can be applied only to mail and news. They can also be applied to file folders if you have selected the Show, All Properties command on the folder's context menu.

PART

I

CH

5

TABLE 5.2   FILTERING OPTIONS FOR FOLDER OBJECTS

Folder Object	Types of Filters That You Can Apply
	Show message and Show group filters and Rules.
	Show message filters and Rules.
	Show message filters and Rules.
	Show message filters and Rules.
	Show message filters and Rules.
	Show message and Show group filters and Rules.
	Show message and Show group filters and Rules.

You can manage all these objects using the same basic logic and rules, but this section focuses on managing files.

→ The topics of managing mail and news are discussed further in "Techniques for Managing Mail and News," **p. 1075**.

GROUPING AND MARKING FOLDERS AND FILES

The principles of both grouping and marking are very simple. Using these options, you can choose to display or hide files that share common properties. These properties are as follows:

- Marked or Unmarked
- Subscribed
- Read or Not Read
- Active

You assign the Marked, Subscribed, and Read properties to folders and files by using commands on the Explorer and Beamer context menus. StarOffice determines whether a file is active.

The Explorer file folder context menu is shown in Figure 5.5 with the Show submenu open, so you can see where all the commands for managing groups and marking folders (or files) are located. Some of the same options as on the Properties tabs also appear here, so you can change them on-the-fly.

New to version 5.1, you can display documents as well as folders in the Explorer so you can manage individual files from either the Explorer or Beamer.

A marked folder is one to which you have applied the Explorer context menu Marked command (Ctrl+M). It then appears with a check mark. It's just as if you put a sticky note on it, flagging it for attention.

Figure 5.5
The Explorer context menu contains most of the commands you need to manage your folders and files. Your menu may appear slightly different because some commands are linked to plug-ins (non-StarOffice programs) that you might not have on your system.

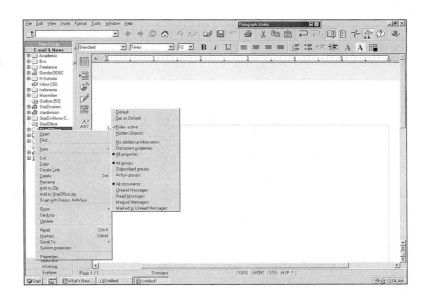

A subscribed folder has a specific meaning in connection with newsgroups. With file folders, it just means a folder to which you have applied the Explorer context menu Subscribed command.

→ For more information on newsgroups, **see** "Beyond mail–Joining Newsgroups with StarDiscussion." **p. 1068**.

Tip #75 from
Michael & Sarah

> The Subscribed, Read, and Marked commands appear only on the context menus of folders that contain files.

A read folder is one to which you have applied the Explorer context menu Read command (Ctrl+R). The idea is that you indicate you have read the folder and are finished with it.

An active folder is one that contains unread files—which, in this case, means files that you have not yet opened and closed in StarOffice. You cannot mark a file as active. Basically, it's like the Read command, but StarOffice, not you, marks it as read, based on activity within the program.

Caution

> If you read a file in another application outside the StarOffice desktop, it might not register as read when you re-enter or relaunch StarOffice.

Note that the Subscribed, Read, and Marked commands apply to entire folders, whereas the Active command is a finer-grained option. If only one item in a folder has not yet been opened, the folder is active, even though it might contain other files that have already been opened.

MARKING FILES IN THE BEAMER

You mark individual files as subscribed, read, or marked in the Beamer by using the Beamer context menu (shown in Figure 5.6). After you have marked files with the Subscribed, Read, or Marked commands, your folders will perform a finer-grained filtering.

Tip #76 from
Michael & Sarah

Once you select the Show, All Properties command, you can also mark your files in the Open and Save As dialog boxes   an even easier way to manage your files.

Figure 5.6
The Beamer document context menu is similar to the Explorer file folder context menu command but only allows you to manage files, not folders. You can print files without opening them and attach a different document template as well as mark and group them in various ways.

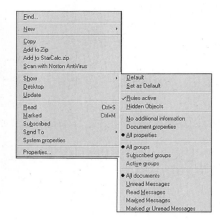

FILTERS AT WORK

Because creating filters can be confusing, we're going to step through a simple example. If you're not experienced with filtering, you might find re-creating this example useful.

We've selected a folder in the Explorer called Working (see Figure 5.7). This folder is set to show all document properties to make the View options available. We've also opened its Properties dialog, clicked the View tab, and selected Marked under the Show Messages option set.

Tip #77 from
Michael & Sarah

If you look at Figure 5.7, you'll see that the Working folder displays numbers to the right of its name (44/44). This represents the number of read files over the total number of files in the folder. Your folders display this information even if your View tab is set to Display All.

Now, we click OK to exit the dialog and go into the Beamer. The Beamer was open in Figure 5.7, and as you can see, the folder has a lot of files. Some we don't need to see or open, like our document template and regular backups of our chapters. So we're going to apply the Marked command to those files we *do* want to see (see Figure 5.8).

Figure 5.7
Create simple filters for your files by setting folder properties and then applying the Read, Marked, and Subscribed commands on the Explorer and Beamer context menus. You can also apply these commands from the Open and Save As dialog boxes or in the Beamer window.

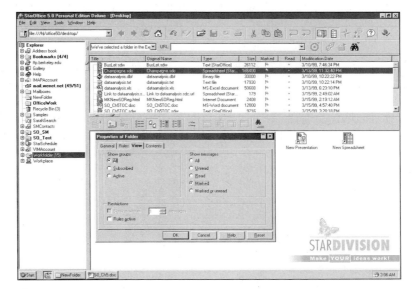

Figure 5.8
When you mark a file as Subscribed, Read, or Marked on the Beamer context menu, it will appear (or not appear) in the Beamer based on the options and rules you've set on the View and Rules tabs of its file folder's Properties dialog.

A check mark indicates a marked file

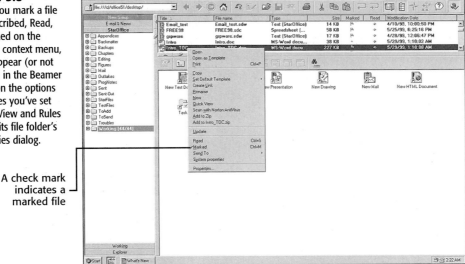

Although it's hard to see in the figure, a small check mark appears on marked files. Now, see what is displayed in the Beamer when we click Working in Figure 5.9.

Tip #78 from
Michael & Sarah

The same check mark is placed on files and folders that are marked as Subscribed, Read, or Marked, so it isn't a good visual cue to the kind of marking that has been applied. If files have been marked Read or Marked, check these fields in the Beamer. For folders, you must open the Properties dialog and look. For subscribed files, select them in the Beamer and open the context menu.

Figure 5.9
Because the Show Messages, Marked option was checked on the Properties, View tab, only the files we mark with the Marked command are displayed.

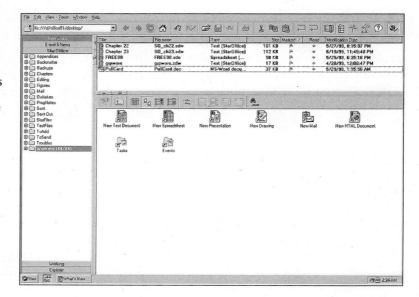

Notice that a new field, Marked, appears in the Beamer, and little flags appear to indicate that the files are marked.

Tip #79 from
Michael & Sarah

Clicking the Marked flag icon and the diamond Read icon turn the Marked and Read properties on and off.

To make unmarked files visible again, enter the Properties dialog again, and change Show Messages from Marked to All. Only then can you select them again to unmark them.

Note

To see your newly entered filtering properties at work, you might need to close the folder and then open it again, redisplaying it in the Beamer or on the desktop workspace.

This simple example just gives you a flavor of the power of these commands.

Tip #80 from
Michael & Sarah

Both files and folders can simultaneously be marked as Subscribed, Read, and Marked, so you can make objects appear selectively in different folders.

A good reason to store your files and folders in the Explorer, or create a linked group in the Explorer, instead of just creating an individual linked folder is that you can't apply filters to a linked folder. Of course, if you're using StarOffice on a network, you can apply filters to the folder on the server or host computer.

CREATING FILTERS WITH RULES

On the Rules tab, you can create complex Boolean filters that can not only filter what appears, but also perform a number of other actions on whatever objects meet the criteria you set with your rules. You can apply the following actions:

- Show
- Hide
- Mark
- Unmark
- Mark Read
- Mark Unread
- Copy
- Create Link
- Move

With this feature, you could, for example, create rules for a mail Inbox so that all incoming emails with the same subject header—say, Annual Meeting—could be moved automatically into a folder called AnnMeet.

The syntax and operation of the Rules feature is complex and is essentially the same as that used to construct searches; so for a better sense of how to create and apply rules, see the section "Retrieving Distant Files and Folders" later in this chapter.

Caution

If you are creating rules, be sure that the Rules Active option is checked on the View tab, or your rules will not take effect.

TRACKING DOCUMENTS WITH DOCUMENT PROPERTIES

Documents can't have rules and filters applied to them (it's your job to edit and filter them!), but they have their own document properties, which you set in a dialog opened by the Properties command on the Edit menu (see Figure 5.10).

PART
I
CH
5

Figure 5.10
You can check basic document properties such as character, word, paragraph, and page counts on the Statistics tab. This tab also displays the number of tables, graphics, and OLE objects in the document.

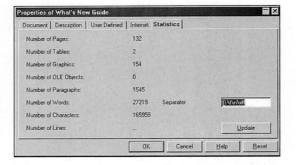

Tip #81 from
Michael & Sarah

You can have this Document Properties box appear automatically every time you use Save As by selecting the Edit Document Properties Before Saving option in the Tools, Options, General, Save dialog box.

Just as with folders, some of these properties are fixed by the system or predefined, but you can set or modify some of them. These properties can help you find the files later when you're searching for them, as well as record such often vital information as the files' author(s), history of creation and publication, current storage locations of hard copies, or previous recipients.

Tip #82 from
Michael & Sarah

Although you can't save different documents with the same filename, you can assign different documents the same title. This way, you can quickly retrieve a set of documents on the same topic—for example, a set of reports on current market conditions along with spreadsheets that contain statistics—that may be stored in different folders or drives. Conversely, you can assign different titles to files with the same name   for example if you need to distinguish between different versions of the same document.

Tip #83 from
Michael & Sarah

Set your documents to load as Web pages by using the Internet tab of the Edit, Properties dialog.

RETRIEVING DISTANT FILES AND FOLDERS

StarOffice is designed with the assumption that you'll work within the StarOffice desktop, using the Explorer as your home directory and primary storage depot for frequently used files, links, and folders. However, surely you don't want to store all your work in the Explorer. Many of your files, including your email, may be stored on a server.

Of course, you can navigate through your directory with the desktop Object bar, one folder at a time, or open the Workplace on your desktop and navigate in the same way. This slow and cumbersome method doesn't allow for quickly locating related objects that may not be in the same place.

You can retrieve files in easier ways. Using links was discussed in "Streamlining Your Desktop Navigation" in Chapter 2. Designating a folder as a desktop is another good way; the folder doesn't have to be stored in the Explorer, just visible on your desktop so that you can select it and apply the Desktop command. All the folder items will then be available on the desktop menu.

However, if you want to pull together files and folders scattered on many different servers or drives, your best method is to use the Explorer menu Find and Search commands.

UNDERSTANDING SEARCHES

The Find command, available from the main context menu, enables you to create a temporary search on-the-fly. This search retrieves whatever you select to the desktop after you finish entering your rules and search locations and click Apply. The second, available via the context menu New command, allows you to create and save a search to the Explorer as a special kind of folder. Since Find is a truncated version of Search, we will use the saved search here as our example. The methods are also the same as those you would use to create filters using the Rules tab of the folder Properties dialog (shown in Figure 5.11).

Figure 5.11
You can use the same operators and logic rules on the Search Criteria tab to search for and retrieve distant files as you can on the file folder Properties, Rules tab to filter and sort objects on your desktop.

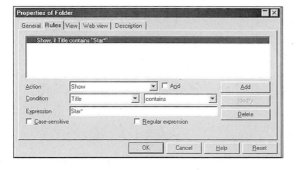

PART

I

CH

5

This saved search is a special kind of folder that gathers together links to objects on your system based on rules and locations you've specified in the Search dialog. The objects of your search appear on your desktop, but they really still live in their original locations.

The major difference between Find and Search is that with Search, you have a tab for determining the properties (or, in the case of mail and news, headers) that display. Search is therefore more useful for targeted retrieval and management of mail and news.

When your search is saved in the Explorer, double-clicking it opens its contents on your desktop, just like any other folder.

Tip #84 from
Michael & Sarah

If you want to retrieve an entire folder to your desktop, it's simpler to just create a link by navigating from the desktop to its location and then using Shift+Ctrl+drag to drag a link into the Explorer.

Saved searches do not automatically update upon opening unless you choose the command of the same name from the saved search context menu. You can also set a search to update periodically based on settings you enter in its Contents properties tab.

The steps for constructing searches are similar to those you would also take to construct filters using rules. You begin by opening a new search through the Explorer, Beamer, or desktop context menu. A four-tabbed dialog box opens (see Figure 5.12). On the General tab, you assign a name to the search. On the Location tab, you set the location(s) to be searched. On the Criteria tab, you have to define the text string or strings you are searching for. On the Description tab, you determine what information displays about your retrieved files.

Figure 5.12
Creating a saved search (opened from the New submenu) is the best way to bring files scattered over different servers or folders together into one folder.

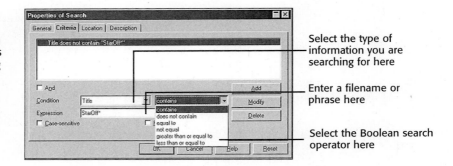

Select the type of information you are searching for here

Enter a filename or phrase here

Select the Boolean search operator here

SETTING SEARCH CRITERIA

Setting the criteria is the most complex and important part of creating a search (or constructing a filter).

Two elements define the string that you are searching for:

- The string itself. For example, if you were searching for a specific file called Report1, the string would be Report1.
- The conditions set upon that string.

The most logical way to begin is to set the conditions for your search (or filter) first, and then enter your text string.

The two types of conditions are as follows:

- The type of string for which you are searching. It usually is a specific text field or document property, such as the From field of an email or a document title.
- The Boolean operators (also known as logical operators) that define how that string will be evaluated if it is located.

Table 5.3 lists the types of strings you can search for (or filter).

TABLE 5.3   FIELDS AND PROPERTIES THAT CAN BE SEARCHED OR FILTERED

Field or Property	Searches
Blind Copy To	Address field in emails.
Copy To	Address field in emails.
Date	Creation date of the file, folder, or document. The creation date is not the same as the date last saved.
Document Count	The number of documents saved in a folder or number of words saved in a document.
Filename	Name of saved file.
Keywords	Keywords you have defined for a document using the document Properties dialog box.
Marked	Emails that have been marked with the Mark command.
Message ID	Email message ID number.
Modification Date	Date the file was last modified and saved.
Next Update	The scheduled time for the next update of the file(s).
Priority	Emails or files that have been labeled priority.
Re:	Subject field in emails.
Read	Emails that you have already read, or files or folders marked as Read.
Recipient	Recipient of the file, folder, or mail message.
References	References you have attached to an email.
Reply to	Address field in emails.
Sender	Sender of the file, folder, or message.
Size	The size of the folder or file, in kilobytes or megabytes.
Status	Current status of the file, folder, or mail.
Target URL	The target pathname, FTP, or Web address of a file.
Title	The filename of the document, folder, or Web page, or the title of a document if you have assigned one through the document Properties command. (If you have not assigned a name, the title is the same as the original name.)
To	Address field in emails.
Type	The type of file that you specify in the Expression box. (For example, you could search for all files of the type `.sdw` to locate all StarWriter text documents in the specified location.)
URL	The pathname, FTP, or Web address of a file.

PART

I

CH

5

Table 5.4 lists available Boolean operators that create the logical rules used to evaluate found strings in both filters and searches. The specific operators available depend on the condition you have selected. These Boolean logical operators should be familiar to anyone who has used a Web search engine or online library catalog.

TABLE 5.4   BOOLEAN (LOGICAL) OPERATORS USED IN SEARCH COMMAND

Name of Operator	Retrieves Files and Folders That
Contains	Contain the expression(s) you have entered. This is the default operator. Works equally well for numbers and characters.
Does not contain	Do *not* contain the expression(s) you have entered. Works equally well for numbers and characters.
Equal to	Contain a text string or strings exactly equal to the expression(s) you have entered. Best for numerical types of text strings such as dates and file sizes. Useful when you're searching for objects created on a specific date or that have specific address information of which you are certain.
Not equal to	Contain a text string *not equal* to the expression(s) you have entered. Best for numerical types of text strings such as dates and file sizes.
Newer or from	Are marked with a date equal to or more recent than the date you have entered.
Older or from	Are marked with a date equal to or older than the date you have entered.
Newer than	Are more recent than the date you have entered.
Older than	Are older than the date you have entered.
Greater than or equal to	Contain a text string *greater than or equal to* the expression(s) you have entered. Best for numerical types of text strings such as dates and file sizes. Useful when you're searching for objects created within a specific date range.
Less than or equal to	Contain a text string *less than or equal to* the expression(s) you have entered. Best for numerical types of text strings such as dates and file sizes. Useful when you're searching for objects created within a specific date range.

You can also search for two kinds of strings:

- Normal filenames and words
- Strings constructed using StarOffice's Regular Expressions

The default type is Title, which searches either for the title you may have entered in the Title field of the document properties or (if you have not assigned a title) the filename.

Figure 5.13 shows an example of a search constructed using the And check box, which strings two criteria together to target the search.

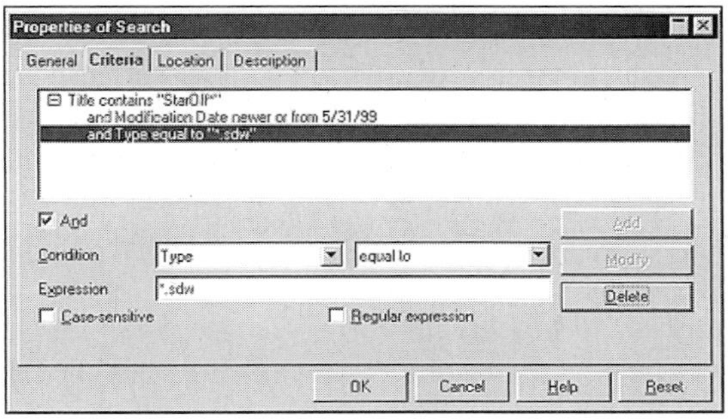

Figure 5.13
When you create string multiple criteria (rules) together using the And check box, your secondary criteria appear below the first. Click the – or + to the left of the first criteria to hide or reveal (respectively) the complete set of criteria.

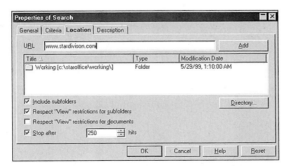

You can also just continue to add unlinked strings to your search and thus bring together a number of different items into the same folder.

You can add as many strings as you like to the search. However, keep in mind that complex searches take longer and use more system resources.

Once you have constructed your criteria, you can enter the path of the folder where you want your messages to be automatically copied or moved, or where you want links to be created. If you give an invalid path, you will see an `Invalid Target Directory` dialog in which you can then enter further information.

SELECTING LOCATIONS TO SEARCH

The Location tab should look familiar to you because it shares features with the Open and Save As dialogs (see Figure 5.14). It does have a few wrinkles you should know about, however.

Figure 5.14
Using the Location tab of a saved search, you can enter local paths or Web addresses—both are URLs, according to StarOffice logic—so you can use searches to create custom Web searches as well as retrieve files and folders.

First, you'll probably notice there's no obvious way to remove locations that you don't want anymore. Believe it or not, the method you use is to select the item in the list and press the

Delete key. Given that you can actually delete folders and files this way from the Open and Save As dialogs, you might worry that you're about to do the same here. No worries. Your folder or drive remains intact. You can also drag a location name within the dialog, but this function is pretty useless here because it creates a link to the same location.

Just as in the Beamer or in similar dialogs, you can add and subtract from the fields list displayed. To do so, place your pointer on a field name, and right-click to open the context menu. It's useful to set these fields to reflect the field types or properties you're going to search for.

Notice that you need to check Include Subfolders; this option is not selected by default.

You can type a pathname or URL directly into the URL field, or you can browse your local directories by clicking the Directory button. The Search Location box that appears (shown in Figure 5.14) has the same navigational buttons as in the Open and Save As dialogs. Its fields are managed separately from those on the Location tab.

After you've set your locations and criteria, choose OK to simultaneously save and run the search.

SEEING THE RESULTS OF YOUR SEARCH

A task window automatically opens to display the results of your search. If nothing is found, the window will be empty. After the search is created, you can manage it just like any other folder.

Because of the way StarOffice caches files in the program, you might need to select your search folder and choose Update on the Explorer context menu before you successfully see your results.

You can set the search to automatically update itself by choosing the Update on Open command on the Explorer context menu or manually update by selecting the Update command on the same menu.

SEARCHING AND FILTERING WITH REGULAR EXPRESSIONS

Not only when you're constructing searches and building filters, but in many other StarOffice dialogs, including Search and Replace from the Edit menu, you see an option called Regular Expressions.

You're surely familiar with the wildcard character (*) used in file searching in many programs and operating systems. That's one example of a regular expression, which is a set of notations you can use to search for more complex text strings. For example, you might want to search for similar words or phrases rather than exact matches. You can also use these expressions to search for hidden characteristics such as formatting codes. (The complete list of regular expressions is listed in the tearbook that appears in the front of this book.)

Being able to use regular expressions greatly expands your search, filtering, and file management capabilities. It also complexifies them, and sometimes searches and filters don't work the way you expect them to.

That a regular expression doesn't work quite as you expect is to is not such a problem with searches, although it can be frustrating when they don't work. With filters, though, where you can assign actions such as Hide and Move, you could have some unhappy results. It's always a good idea to give your filter a test run a few times before you assign actions whose results might not be immediately apparent. (For example, you could assign the action Create Link instead of Move to the same folder you intend to use to test your filter's accuracy.)

CONDUCTING MULTIPLE SEARCHES

Clicking the Multiple Search button on the desktop Object bar turns Multiple Search on and off. With this feature turned on, you can perform a multiple search in the Beamer, in the desktop Details view, or in the results of a search. Normally, in a file search (as opposed to an email search, where you can look for all kinds of fields), you can look only for filenames. With Multiple Search turned on, you can retrieve files by searching for file type, size, or modification date.

PROTECTING FILES AND FOLDERS

As we previously discussed, you can protect a file by making it read-only, either when you open it from the Open dialog or by selecting the read-only option on the General tab of the document's properties.

Because anyone who knows how to use StarOffice can easily turn off the read-only status, the safest way to protect a critical document is to assign a password. You can assign a password to a document by using the Save As command.

You cannot assign passwords to folders from within StarOffice. You can, however, make a folder read-only by choosing the appropriate option from the General tab of its Properties dialog.

PART
I

CH
5

KEEPING YOUR DESKTOP UP-TO-DATE

Keeping track of your work on a single desktop is hard enough, but when you start working with others on a network or become dependent on Web sites for up-to-the-minute information, trying to keep your files, Web references, and mail up-to-date can become truly maddening.

From the system's point of view as well, keeping files up-to-date is a challenge when lots of information is being sent and received over phone and network lines. StarOffice has a particular way of handling this challenge that affects the way your files and mailboxes are handled.

You can help stay cool and up-to-date by understanding StarOffice's Update and Subscriptions commands.

UPDATING FILES, FOLDERS, AND MAIL

To offer superior speed, StarOffice uses *memory caching*. Copies of files and objects currently in use are stored in system memory or temporary files rather than continually fetched from their original location. It's like working on or viewing a copy.

This feature enables faster program performance, but means sometimes when you're reading a Web page or sorting through your mailbox, you might not be looking at the most current version. For example, the Web site you're browsing may already have changes on the very page you're looking at, but you don't know because you're looking at a cached page.

When you update, StarOffice searches for the original object and updates the cached version from the original. This process is a bit like refreshing your monitor display.

Mail and news accounts are automatically updated each time you open them (if you are online; if you're not, you'll see a connection error message). You can also update them manually by using the Update command on the Explorer context menu.

If you want to be able to update most other objects, you need to enable Update from the Contents tab of the Explorer Properties dialog box.

If you work on a network and frequently work with files stored on network drives, it's a good idea to set this option so that you can continually refresh your working copies of those files on your local system.

> **Note**
>
> The Contents tab is visible on some objects only when you have selected the Show, All Properties command on their Explorer context menu.

On the Contents tab, you can also set any object, including mail and news folders, to update automatically at periodic intervals.

SETTING MAIL, NEWS, AND OTHER OBJECTS TO UPDATE AUTOMATICALLY

You can set folders (except links) to update automatically by selecting the Include in Update command on the folder's Properties, Contents tab.

When this command is selected, you can set an automatic update interval in minutes or hours (up to 999). For example, if you select your mail Inbox and set this number to 15 minutes, StarOffice automatically checks your email account every 15 minutes and downloads any new mail (assuming you are online).

→ For information on setting up an email account, **see** "Getting Online," **p. 85**.

→ For information on setting up your news subscriptions, **see** "Beyond Email—Joining Newsgroups with StarDiscussion," **p. 1068**.

→ For more information on email, **see** "Creating and Sending Mail," **p. 1053**.

Caution

> Set your account to update at timed intervals only if you're regularly connected to a server. If not, it's best to set it to 0. If you have your account set to update at regular intervals and are disconnected from the network for some reason, be sure to click the Online button on the function bar to go offline.

With saved searches, you have another automatic update option. You can choose Update When Open from its context menu. Choosing this option is a good idea because, otherwise, the next time you open it, you'll see the results of the last search you executed before exiting the program, even if new items match your search criteria. If you forget to update manually, you could be fooled into thinking you have everything you need on your desktop.

SETTING STORAGE OPTIONS FOR MAIL, NEWS, AND FILES

You also change the storage options for mail and news on the Contents tab of the Explorer Properties dialog. With news, you can choose to store the entire contents of messages (as opposed to just headers) locally, as well as set news of a certain age or older to be deleted automatically. Deleting messages automatically helps cut down on the clutter of old news postings. With mail, you can choose to delete all mail from the server and/or to store your mail locally. Most commercial Internet service providers (ISPs) require that you immediately download your mail from their server and store it on your own hard drive. The practices of office networks vary.

Caution

> If you choose to remove all messages from the server but not store the document contents locally, wave good-bye to all your incoming mail after you read it. Mail deleted in this way is not recoverable, unless your server has a backup.

SYNCHRONIZING MAIL AND FILES

If you've accidentally deleted mail from your local drive and it's still on the server, or your download of mail has been interrupted and incomplete, choose the Synchronize command on the Explorer context menu to reload your mail from the server. Do the same if any network file transfer between a document on your local drive and the server has been interrupted.

USING THE EXPLORER UPDATE COMMAND

After you've turned on the Update option on the Contents tab, you can manually update the object using the Update command on the Explorer context menu.

One reason it's good practice to group your work in project folders is that you can update all your local files with two clicks: select the folder, right-click, and then click Update.

KEEPING UP-TO-DATE WITH WEB SUBSCRIPTIONS

Information changes so quickly these days that keeping up is hard. StarOffice's Subscriptions command helps make it easier, at least with information posted on the Web.

Note

The Subscriptions command is not related to the Subscribed command on the Explorer context menu (linked to options on the Properties, View tab).

Subscriptions are folders in which you store bookmarks (links to Web sites). Any time you go online, StarOffice automatically checks the Web site of all bookmarks you have saved in the subscriptions file and alerts you if the pages have changed since you last visited the site.

To create a Subscriptions folder, select the Explorer icon or the folder in which you want the Subscriptions folder to be stored, right-click, and choose the New, Subscriptions command. Enter a name for the folder, choose OK, and place in it bookmarks for sites you want regularly checked.

Caution

StarOffice automatically tries to update subscriptions even when you might not be online. If you try to exit StarOffice before it can check the Web sites, it may alert you that the program is still updating subscriptions and prompt you to decide whether you really want to exit. Choose OK if you want to exit; it won't harm the subscriptions.

PROJECT PAGE: CREATING A FILTER FOR MAIL

The concept of filters originated in the world of email and newsgroups, and with good reason: Sending email and posting news has proved too easy, and we all find ourselves with a major job of sorting and filing these messages.

For this project, you'll create a filter for an email account Inbox that will sort and redirect mail based on rules that you set. You'll also set the Inbox to display only mail that hasn't yet been read, hiding the rest of the unsorted and filed mail.

Be aware that such filters work best applied to the host email directory. Translated into English, this means they work best either if you are running a POP3 account (where you download your email to your hard drive and store it there) or if you apply these rules to your mail folder on the server (where your mail is actually stored). If you don't store your mail locally, every time you go online and download your mail, you receive all your messages, including old ones, all over again. StarOffice therefore treats them as newly received messages. If you're setting Copy or Create Link as your actions, you'll end up with multiple copies and/or links to the same message.

After you select the account Inbox and open its Properties dialog, click the View tab and make sure that the Rules Active option is checked (see Figure 5.15). Otherwise, the rules you create won't be applied.

Figure 5.15
The View tab controls what appears in a folder, including determining whether filtering rules are in effect.

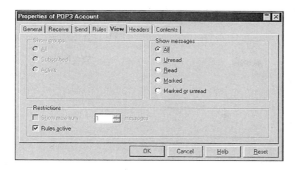

Go ahead and check the Marked and Unread options now. Checking this option applies a global filter that will hide from view all mail you've already read, except for messages that you've marked. With this option, you can mark to keep in view important messages you've already read, like directions to a party or an announcement of a meeting.

Now click the Rules tab–and the real work begins.

Let's say this mailbox subscribes to a number of email mailing lists. Mailing lists are collective email communities where one person serves as the central hub, sending and redirecting messages that come from the group. One feature of mailing lists is that they usually place a common phrase, such as the name of the list, in their subject line to identify all messages generated by the list. You can use this feature to your advantage to filter and redirect these messages.

Let's say you subscribe to a list called TECHWRITER-L. To create a filter to redirect all this mail into a folder of its own, first select Move as the action from the drop-down list. Then set the condition as Title Contains, and type TECHWRITER-L. Check Case-Sensitive as a safety measure because this header always appears in uppercase letters only. Now be sure to click Add. Otherwise, the rule will not be added to the list.

Next, click the Browse button to select the directory (folder) where this mail will be redirected. The Select Path dialog box appears (see Figure 5.16). Choose the Create New Directory button, and create a folder called TECHWR in the Office50/Explorer directory so that the folder will appear in the Explorer.

Next, create a filter to delete mail from a different mailing list that always has CUE in the title.

The Delete option is a dangerous tool, so be cautious when you're using it (although deleted objects will, as usual, be stored in the Recycle Bin until you actively delete them). Here, we'll assume you've already checked your filter and made sure it's not capturing something you might want to keep.

Figure 5.16
With Rules filters, you can select to copy, move, delete, or make links to files anywhere on your local directory structure.

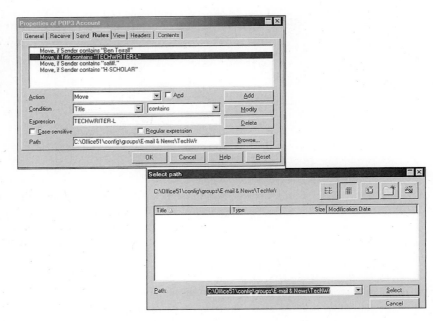

First, select Delete from the Action list. Notice that the And check box is grayed out; it becomes active only after you click Add and add your first rule to the rules list.

Enter as your condition Title and Contains, and list CUE as your expression. Again, check Case-Sensitive. No Browse button appears because deleted objects are automatically placed in the Recycle Bin. Browse appears only when you select Move, Copy, or Create Link. Now, choose Add.

Next, you'll create a link. Because your office is making the transition to using StarOffice on your network, and you're the point person for receiving support emails, you need to redirect mail to colleagues as appropriate. You can do so automatically by creating a link in another folder according to the rules you set.

After you've selected Create Link as your action, set the conditions to From and Contains (as in Figure 5.17).

Figure 5.17
The capability to auto-matically create links to specific email mes-sages based on an email's header fields is one of the most use-ful features in StarOffice's powerful filtering system.

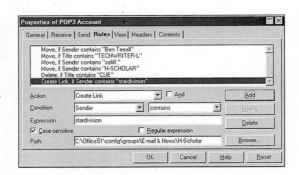

Choose Add, and then choose OK because you've finished building your filter. That's it! Now, every time you download your email, your mail will be handled according to your rules and View options. (If you store your mail locally and delete it from the server, existing mail will not be filtered.)

CREATING DOCUMENTS—STARWRITER

CREATING AND EDITING TEXT DOCUMENTS

In this chapter

GETTING STARTED WITH STARWRITER

StarWriter is more than just the word processing module of StarOffice. It supports frames, applets, and plug-ins and enables you to save and load documents from the Internet. You can also create text of varying length without once losing track of the different elements in your document. As if that weren't enough, the latest version of StarWriter also provides desktop-publishing enhancements that enable you to design professional-looking brochures and newsletters. But we're getting ahead of ourselves here. This section provides a quick overview of the various toolbars and context menus within StarWriter.

> **Note**
>
>
>
> For the most part, StarWriter looks and feels very much like other Windows applications, with a few notable exceptions that enable you to be even more productive and creative than working in MS Word or WordPerfect.

STARTING STARWRITER

You can start StarWriter by selecting File, New, Text Documents or Start, Text Documents. After you open a new text document, you have access to all common tasks and functions you might know from other word processing applications and more. The major hurdle is to get accustomed to the StarOffice way of doing everything in one place. When you do that, you'll be in charge of making your ideas work rather than managing applications.

EXPLORING THE STARWRITER WORKSPACE

When you open a new text document, the screen contains a blank document (called Untitled1) with default settings framed by handy tools, buttons, and status displays that assist you in creating a variety of simple and complex text and HTML documents, including letters, reports, newsletters, and brochures. Figure 6.1 shows the default document window and workspace, as well as the various context menus you can open by right-clicking certain areas and fields within your StarWriter window.

> **Note**
>
> You can't activate all these context menus at once. We've arranged them here to give you a quick overview of your options.

> **Tip #85 from**
> *Michael & Sarah*
>
> If you're new to StarOffice, you might want to select Tips or Extended Tips from the Help menu. After you activate these tip features and point your cursor to an icon, box, or button, you will see a little help balloon pop up describing the icon (Tips) or its function (Extended Tips).

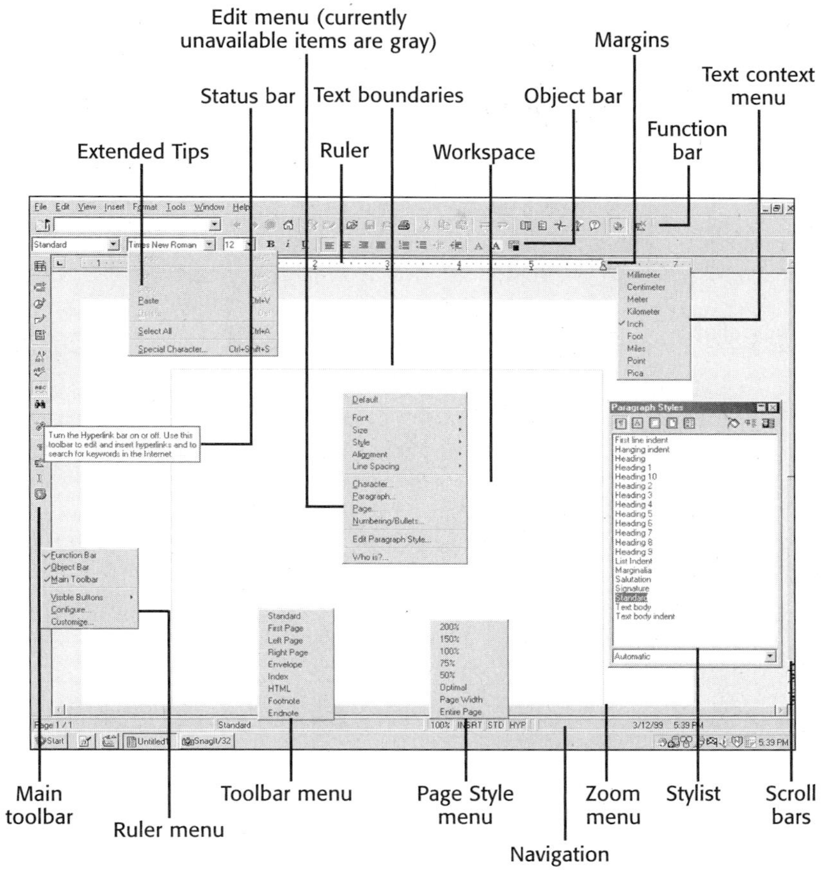

Figure 6.1
StarWriter comes with
its own set of handy
tools and shortcut
menus that enable you
to create professional-
looking documents
and Web pages on-
the-fly. Just right-click
in the areas indicated
to access these menus.

While working in your document, you can right-click anywhere in your work area to bring
up the Text context menu. This menu gives you access to the most common formatting
functions in StarWriter. From here, you can quickly change basic text elements—such as
font, size, style, alignment, and line spacing of your document—or call up dialogs to define
more advanced character, paragraph, page, and numbering/bullets functions—such as different font styles and effects, hyperlinks, macros, background, paragraph and page properties,
and numbering and bullet styles. In addition, you can edit the properties of your applied
styles—including indents and spacing, text flow, drop caps, border, and background—and
summon the Address Book (Who Is?...) to quickly insert contact information about a person
into a document or at the top of a letter.

Tip #86 from
Michael & Sarah

To undo the changes you made to a paragraph or text block, select Default from the context menu, and StarWriter reverts to the original formatting and style. However, if you applied numbering/bullets changes, edited your paragraph styles, changed the page style, or inserted contact information, you will have to revert to the original format and style manually.

USING THE TEXT OBJECT BAR

At the top of the window, you'll notice the object bar, which is known to MS Word users as the formatting bar. The text object bar contains one-click shortcuts to the most popular character and paragraph formatting features that enable you to quickly change the appearance and arrangement of your text.

Depending on the context, you may see various object bars while working on a single document. For example, if you insert a table into your document, the Text object bar will be replaced with the Table object bar as soon as you click inside a table cell. If you're inserting a numbered or bulleted list, the List object bar appears as soon as your insertion point is within the limits of the list area. If you insert an object, you'll get the corresponding object bar when you select the inserted object. In each case, StarWriter places all the necessary formatting and editing tools within a mouse click's reach.

Table 6.1 lists the various menus and icons of the Text object bar and explains their function.

TABLE 6.1   USING THE TEXT OBJECT BAR

Click This Icon	If You Want To
Standard ▼	Assign *existing* styles to your documents. Click the down arrow to select a style from a list of applied styles. The default for a new text document is Standard. You can apply additional styles by using the Stylist (see "Using the Stylist" in Chapter 8, "Using Styles and Templates").
Times New Roman ▼	Change the font and size of selected text. The default font is Times New Roman, and the size is 12 point. Your choices are limited by the number of fonts you have chosen to install on your system. Right-clicking in either box brings up the Edit shortcut menu.
B *i* U	Change the attribute style—bold, italics, underline—of a word or selected text.
▤ ▤ ▤ ▤	Change the alignment —left, center, right, justified—of a current paragraph.
1▤ ·▤	Add numbered or bulleted lists to your text.
◀▤ ▤▶	Decrease or increase the indent of a paragraph or line by the amount of the defined tab stop.

Click This Icon	If You Want To
A A ▦	Change the font color of selected text, highlight selected text, or add color to the background of the current paragraph. (Note: All three buttons give you access to floating toolbars that you can place anywhere on your desktop.)
◁	Toggle between the various object bars in StarWriter, including the Text, Table, and List object bars, provided your document contains tables, lists or other text elements (such as graphic objects, for example) that come with their own set of formatting and editing tools.

→ For more details on using these features and options, see the sections "Formatting Characters," **p. 263**, and "Formatting Paragraphs," **p. 270**.

Tip #87 from
Michael & Sarah

Right-click the object bar or main toolbar to open a context menu that enables you to customize, configure, and select your toolbars for display. You have a choice of three options: Function Bar, Object Bar, and Main Toolbar. If you select the Visible Buttons option, a submenu opens that enables you to choose which icons to show or hide on the current object bar or toolbar—a quick way to customize your toolbars.

Tip #88 from
Michael & Sarah

If you've inserted one or more tables in your document, you can click inside a table cell to gain access to the StarCalc Object bar and easily edit your table. If you want to manipulate the contents of the table cells, you can right-click the Object bar and select Text Object Bar from the context menu, or click the small arrow on the right of the bar to toggle between the two Object bars.

USING THE STARWRITER RULER

Underneath the object bar is the ruler, which enables you to set tabs, indents, and margins of the current paragraph. In addition to the horizontal ruler, you can also display a vertical ruler. Just choose Tools, Options, Text Document, Layout and select Vertical Ruler in the Windows Options portion of the dialog.

→ For more details on using the ruler, **see** "Setting and Clearing Tabs" **p. 276**.

Tip #89 from
Michael & Sarah

Double-click in the gray area of the ruler to bring up the Paragraph dialog, which enables you to change the indents, spacing, alignment, text flow, numbering, tabs, drop caps, borders, and background of the current or selected paragraphs. Right-click anywhere on the ruler, and you get a shortcut menu that enables you to change the units and system of measurement—try miles, foot, kilometer, or meter for a puzzled smile.

Using the StarWriter Main Toolbar

On the left of the document window is the Main toolbar, which enables you to insert various objects into a document and quickly access the most frequently used functions in StarWriter. Table 6.2 lists the various buttons and explains their functions.

Table 6.2   Using the Main Toolbar in StarWriter

Click Here	If You Want To	Button Name
	Insert frames, pictures, tables, other documents, footnotes, special characters, multiple text columns, index entries, or named bookmarks. Your selection is shown in the toolbar icon. A short click brings up the dialog of the last selection (default: Table Format).	Insert
	Insert fields in a text document. An extended-click opens a shortcut menu that lists Date, Time, Page Numbers, Page Count, Subject, Title, or Author fields.	Insert Field
	Insert a chart, picture, mathematical formula, floating frame, OLE object, plug-in, or applet. Yourselection is shown in the toolbar icon. A short click activates the last object used (default: Chart).	Insert Object
	Create and insert a drawing. Clicking the icon opens a floating toolbar that gives you a choice of various drawing tools and functions. Your last selection appears as the toolbar icon.	Draw
	Create a database form. Clicking this icon opens a floating toolbar with various form functions and fields. A short click activates the last used field or control, which appears on the toolbar icon.	Form
	Insert frequently used text passages such as signatures, standard phrases, or templates. A short click brings up the AutoText dialog that enables you to organize and record frequently used text passages, which you can then insert by entering a shortcut and pressing F3.	AutoText
	Check the spelling of your document.	Spelling

Click Here	If You Want To	Button Name
[ABC]	Have your spelling checked automatically as you go (default). Typos are underlined with a wavy red line. If you right-click the misspelled term, you get a context menu with suggestions for change.	Auto Spellcheck
[binoculars]	Search for and replace specific terms and phrases in your document.	Search and Replace
[pen]	Turn the hyperlink bar off (default) or on to edit and insert hyperlinks and search for keywords on the Internet.	Hyperlink Bar
[¶]	View or hide (default) the nonprinting characters in your text, such as line breaks, tab stops, paragraph marks, and spaces.	Nonprinting Characters
[image]	Switch the graphics display in your document on or off (default). In Off mode, you see empty boxes as placeholders for the graphics.	Hide Graphics
[I]	Activate the Direct Cursor feature, which enables you to place the cursor anywhere in your document and start typing (off by default).	Direct Cursor
[monitor]	Switch between online and default layout. Online mode enables you to see your document as one continuous page, regardless of length. Switch to Online mode if you're working on HTML documents.	Online Layout

USING THE STARWRITER STATUS BAR

At the bottom of the StarWriter window, you'll notice the status bar (see Figure 6.2). It provides at-a-glance information on your current document and gives you shortcuts to special functions and features.

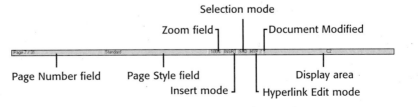

Figure 6.2
Keep an eye on the status bar. It provides details on your current document and shortcuts to common formatting and editing functions.

PART

II

CH

6

In the field on the left, you'll see the page number you're currently working on and the number of total pages of the document. Right-click this field to open a context menu that lists all previous bookmarks in the current document; select a mark to navigate to it. Double-click to turn the Navigator on and off.

→ For more details on using bookmarks, **see** "Bookmarking Your Documents" **p. 388**.

Note

You must have previously inserted bookmarks in your document to be able to access the right-click function in the Page Number field. If you didn't insert bookmarks, this function is not available.

The next field indicates the page style you are currently using (Standard, by default). Right-click to switch to another style (if multiple styles are listed). Double-click to open the Page Style dialog and edit the selected page style.

The third field from the left indicates the current scale of your document. Right-clicking opens a Zoom shortcut menu that enables you to enlarge, reduce, or optimize your view. Double-clicking opens the complete Zoom dialog.

The next three fields indicate the current Insert mode, Selection mode, and Hyperlink Edit mode. Clicking in each area cycles you through the choices.

Tip #90 from
Michael & Sarah

You can also press Insert on your keyboard to toggle between the Insert and Overwrite modes.

Table 6.3 details the various modes and their functions.

TABLE 6.3   THE INSERT, SELECTION, AND HYPERLINK MODES EXPLAINED

Display	Mode	Using This Mode, You Can
INSRT	Insert	Insert new characters at the cursor insertion point. The following text is moved to the right.
OVER	Overwrite	Replace the existing characters to the right with new ones.
STD	Standard	Click and drag to select text (default mode). Each time you click in a new place, you lose the previous selection.
EXT	Extend	Select a block of text. Click to place your cursor at the beginning and end of the section you want to select. (Press Esc to undo your selection and exit this mode.)
ADD	Additive	Select nonconsecutive blocks of text. (Press Esc to undo your selection and exit this mode.)
HYP	Hyperlink	Jump straight to the URL.
SEL	Select	Edit or change a hyperlink.

The narrow field to the right of Hyperlink Mode field, called Document Modified, indicates whether changes have occurred in your open document since you last saved it.

Tip #91 from *Michael & Sarah*	An asterisk (*) in the change field indicates that changes have occurred in your document that have not been saved yet.

The field on the right is a combined display area that, depending on the placement of your cursor, lists the current date and time or other document-related details. For example, if you have a table in your document and click in a cell, the date and time display are replaced by a cell number display. Double-click this field to bring up the Fields dialog, which enables you to insert fields at the insertion point of your cursor.

USING THE SCROLL BAR

By default, StarWriter displays a vertical and a horizontal scroll bar. The vertical scroll bar on the right side of the window enables you to move up or down in your document. If you click the Navigation icon between the double scroll arrows at the bottom right, you get a floating toolbar that enables you to select how you want to browse through your document—page by page (default), heading by heading, picture by picture, object by object, section by section, frame by frame, or note by note, depending on what elements and objects your document contains.

The horizontal scroll bar at the bottom of the window enables you to scroll left or right, depending on the current view of your document. You can quickly change your document view by right-clicking in the Zoom field of the status bar and selecting an item from the Zoom shortcut menu.

Tip #92 from *Michael & Sarah*	To move around more speedily and to save time when you're working on long documents, use the Navigation toolbar. To open it, click the Navigation icon (see Figure 6.1). You can then click the title bar, drag the toolbar to a convenient place on your desktop, and use it to move through your document. Just select a browse category, and click the blue scroll arrows to jump from category to category. (For more details on using the Navigation toolbar, **see** "Introducing the Mini Navigator," **page 374** in Chapter 10, "Working with Long Documents"). To close the Navigation toolbar, click the Close (X) button in the upper right.

If you click the scroll box and drag it up or down, a text box tells you the page number and section that is on display as you go.

MOVING AROUND YOUR DOCUMENT

In general, you have four basic options of moving around in a text document:

- **Vertical scroll bar**—Click the down or up scroll arrows to move three lines at a time. Click and drag the scroll box to quickly move down or up. Click between the scroll box and scroll arrows to move one full screen.

- **Direction keys**—Press the left-arrow and right-arrow keys on your keyboard to move the insertion point one space or character to the left or right, respectively. Pressing the up or down arrow moves it one line up or down; pressing the Page Up or Page Down key moves it one full screen up or down. Pressing End moves the insertion point to the end of the line; pressing Home moves it to the beginning of the line.

- **Keyboard shortcuts**—Press Ctrl+Home to move the insertion point to the top of a document; pressing Ctrl+End moves it to the end. Pressing Ctrl+left arrow moves it to the beginning of the previous word; pressing Ctrl+right arrow moves it to the beginning of the next word. If you press Ctrl+Page Up or Ctrl+Page Down you can switch between a header (if present) and the main text.

- **Navigator**—Use the Navigator, one of the quintessential tools in StarOffice, to jump to any desired location in your document.

Tip #93 from	If you want to quickly move among open tasks in StarOffice, press Ctrl+Tab or
Michael & Sarah	Ctrl+Shift+Tab to cycle forward and backward, respectively.

ENTERING TEXT, SPECIAL CHARACTERS, AND FORMULAS

Entering text in a StarWriter document is straightforward and not any different from other word processing applications. StarWriter differs in the additional tools you have for entering text and formulas in a document. This section describes the basic techniques of entering text and special characters, including using some special StarWriter tools: the Direct Cursor, StarMath, and AutoText.

TYPING AND INSERTING TEXT

When you open a new text document, you see a blank document (named Untitled1), a vertical blinking line (called the *insertion point*) in the upper-left corner, and the Stylist. The document itself contains a shadowed frame called *text boundaries*. Although visible onscreen, the text boundaries will not print   they are meant as a visual aid as you enter text and insert objects into your document. You can type anywhere inside the text boundaries; beyond the text boundaries is the area called *margins*. You can control the size of your margins using the Page tab in the Page Style dialog box (Format, Page). If you don't like to look at the text boundaries while typing, select View, Text Boundaries.

→ For more details on the Stylist **see** "Using the Stylist," **p. 296**.

As you type, the insertion point moves to the right. When you come to the right margin or reach the end of a line, text automatically moves to the next line (a feature commonly known as *text* or *word wrap*); you don't have to press Enter. You should press Enter only when you want to start a new paragraph or create a blank line.

Tip #94 from
Michael & Sarah

If you want to start a new line but have that line—for formatting purposes, for example—be part of the same paragraph, press Shift+Enter, and StarWriter inserts a "soft" return.

If you want to insert new text within an existing paragraph, place the I-beam pointer at the new location, click, and start typing. The following text is automatically pushed to the right as you type.

Note

If your text is not moved to the right but replaced with the new text, then you're entering text in Overwrite (OVER) mode instead of the default Insert (INSRT) mode. To see which mode is activated, look at the Insert field in the center of the status bar. If you see OVER in the field to the right of the Scale field, Overwrite is active. You can toggle between the two modes by clicking the Insert field or by pressing Insert on your keyboard.

INSERTING TEXT WITH THE DIRECT CURSOR

Like other word processing applications, StarWriter defines a paragraph as any number of letters, words, or sentences ending with a paragraph mark. Normally, you cannot type and insert text to the right of a paragraph mark within any given line or after the last paragraph mark in your document. For example, if you want to add text in the center of a blank page, you typically press Enter until you are halfway down your page and then click the Center alignment command to place your cursor in the center of that line.

To overcome this limitation, StarWriter was the first application to include the Direct Cursor feature, which enables you to insert text (as well as tables, graphics, and other objects) virtually anywhere in your document, including protected areas. Using the Direct Cursor you can click in your document and start typing. StarOffice automatically inserts the corresponding number of spaces, tabs, or lines (paragraph marks) in front of the first letter of the new text—in accordance with your defined paragraph styles (including tab and line spacing attributes).

Whether the Direct Cursor inserts tabs, tabs and spaces, or whether text appears left, center, or right-aligned is controlled by the settings in the Text Document Cursor dialog (Tools, Options, Text Documents). Your options include the following:

Paragraph alignment—Depending on whether you are closer to the left, center, or right of the document, the text you type at the Direct Cursor insertion point will align with the left margin, the center of the page, or the right margin, even after you press the Enter key. To exit this mode, press return after the last line you entered, turn off the Direct Cursor (by clicking its icon on the Main toolbar), and then click the desired alignment button on the object bar to continue typing as usual.

Left paragraph margin—This option enables you to redefine the left margin. Anything you type from the insertion point will be left aligned with regard to this new margin, even after you press return. To exit this mode, press return after the last line you entered, turn off the Direct Cursor (by clicking its icon on the Main toolbar), and then click the desired alignment button on the object bar to continue typing as usual.

Tabs (default)—With this setting you can start typing at any predefined tab stop. If you place the Direct Cursor in the center of your page or table cell, the pointer changes shape from an arrow pointing right to two arrows pointing in opposite directions. When you place text at this insertion point, it is automatically centered on the line or within the cell. Text that is entered left and right of center is left-aligned by default. Text that is placed at the right margin will be right-aligned.

Tabs and spaces—With this setting you can start typing virtually anywhere in your document. StarWriter will insert the missing number of tabs and spaces between the left margin and the insertion point.

Note

You can easily tell the alignment of the text you enter at the insertion point by keeping an eye on the Direct Cursor arrow(s). If the arrow is point right, text that is entered will be left-aligned. If the arrow is pointing left, text that is entered will be right-aligned. If you see two arrows pointing in opposite directions, text you enter is centered on the line.

Using the Color drop-down list box, you can also define a new color for the Direct Cursor.

To use the Direct Cursor, click to select the Direct Cursor icon on the Main toolbar; then click any area in your text document and begin typing.

Figure 6.3 shows a document created with the Direct Cursor.

Tip #95 from
Michael & Sarah

Be sure to double-check your AutoCorrect settings (by choosing Tools, AutoCorrect/AutoFormat). If the options Remove Blank Paragraphs or Combine Single Line Paragraphs If Length Greater Than 50 Percent on the Options tab are selected, the inserted blank tabs or lines may be automatically removed from your document when you AutoFormat (by choosing Format, AutoFormat, Format Document) from the menu bar. In this case, you have to decide which function is more important to you. You can't have your cake and eat it too—not even in StarWriter.

Tip #96 from
Michael & Sarah

Because StarOffice sets tabs in front of the first letter of the new text you type when you're in Direct Cursor mode, any changes to your default tab stops—as a result of manual or style changes—affect the placement of the text you enter in this mode.

INSERTING SPECIAL CHARACTERS AND SYMBOLS

StarWriter includes an extensive collection of up to 233 special characters for each available font, plus a set of special text and math symbols (StarBats and StarMath). You might need special characters if you're using foreign language words or currency symbols, copyright or trademark symbols, common fractions, and so on in a document. To insert a character or symbol, select Insert, Special Character from the menu bar or extended-click the Insert icon on the main toolbar and click the Character icon (seventh icon from the left) to open the

Special Character dialog. Next, click to select the character or character combination you want to insert. You can preview your selection in the Characters line at the bottom of the dialog. To redo your multiple selections, select Delete. When you're done, select OK. StarWriter automatically inserts the characters at the insertion point in your document.

Figure 6.3
This memo was created using the Direct Cursor with hidden characters visible. Notice how StarWriter inserts the corresponding number of tabs and lines (or paragraph marks).

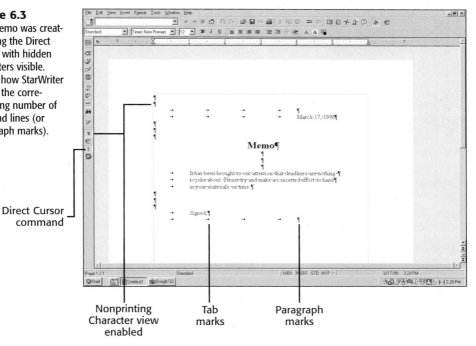

Direct Cursor command

Nonprinting Character view enabled

Tab marks

Paragraph marks

Tip #97 from
Michael & Sarah

If you frequently use the same special character or symbol, you should memorize its numeric value in the bottom right of the Special Character dialog. You can then enter the character anytime at the insertion point by pressing Alt+[*numeric value*] on the numeric keypad. (You may have to press the NumLock key first to turn on the keyboard.) If the numeric value consists of three figures, you need to insert a zero (0) in front of the figures. The same code calls up different characters in different fonts; the special character you insert reflects the font at your insertion point.

PART

II

CH

6

CREATING AND INSERTING FORMULAS WITH STARMATH

If you're working on scientific documents, chances are you need to add formulas to your text. In StarWriter, you have two options to create and insert formulas: You can work with the StarMath character set or the StarMath Formula Editor. The StarMath character set—which you can select from the Font combo box in the Special Character dialog (by choosing Insert, Special Character)—enables you to create simple formulas by providing you with the most common relational symbols and Greek letters. You can select and insert the symbols in a document in the order in which you need them. If you want to create more complex formulas, you need to work with the Formula Editor.

Note

The Formula Editor is just that—an editor, for creating mathematical formulas. It's not a calculator, nor can you generate results with the formulas you create with the Formula Editor. If you want to perform calculations, you have to work with tables or a StarCalc spreadsheet.

CREATING FORMULAS WITH THE FORMULA EDITOR

To launch the StarMath Formula Editor and start creating formulas, select Insert, Object, Formula from the menu bar or extended-click the Insert Object icon on the Main toolbar and select the Formula icon (the suspiciously mathematical looking one with the square root). When you're working in a text document, your StarWriter toolbars are replaced with the StarMath Main toolbar, your menu options change to reflect the commands available in StarMath, and an empty frame is inserted at the insertion point in your document. Your screen will look similar to Figure 6.4. If you don't see the Selection window upon launching StarMath, select View, Selection from the menu bar.

Note

You can also create formulas as standalone documents. Select File, New, Formula, and you can create and save formulas in their own file format (.smf), which you can then insert as OLE objects into other StarOffice documents.

StarMath has its own "lingo" and logic that sets somewhat of a learning curve before you can start to create formulas. In a nutshell, your basic tools and work area include the Selection and Commands windows. The Selection window is divided into two parts: mathematical categories (the top two rows) and elements within a selected category (below). You can choose from a variety of unary/binary operators, relations, set operations, functions, attributes, and brackets, as well as colors and formatting attributes for placeholders. Note that all these options are also available to you when you right-click in the Commands window.

Tip #98 from
Michael & Sarah

If you're new to StarMath, be sure to select Extended Tips from the Help menu to see brief explanations of your Selection options as you place your pointer over the various icons.

To create a formula, click to select a category from the top two rows of your Selection window; then click to select a desired element or expression within that category. Your selection appears in the Commands window with placeholders (<?>), which you can select and replace with numbers or placeholders of your own, or expand with new operators, relations, functions, or attributes from the StarMath Selection window.

Figure 6.4
The StarMath Formula Editor is shown at work in StarWriter. The Formula Editor automatically translates and inserts the contents of the Commands window as an object into your text document as you create the formula.

Refresh formula

Open Symbols dialog

Text document

Object frame with formula

Selection window

Categories

Functions

Toolbar

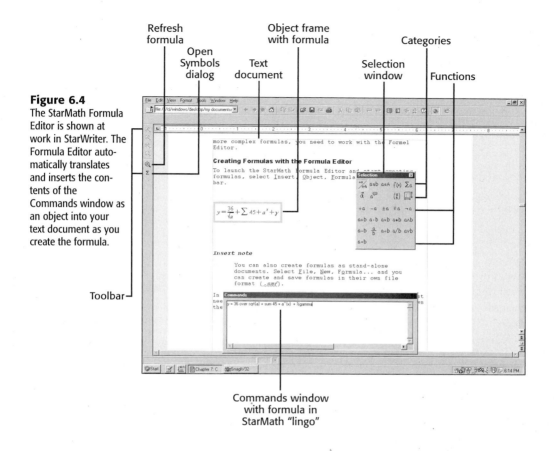

Commands window with formula in StarMath "lingo"

Tip #99 from
Michael & Sarah

If you want to include multiple formulas on several lines, you have to right-click in the Commands window and select Format, New Line. Pressing Enter does not do the trick.

If the AutoRedraw function is enabled (View, AutoRedraw), StarMath automatically updates the contents in your document as you create your formula. If this feature is not enabled, you can update your formula manually by clicking the Refresh icon on the Main toolbar (fifth button from the top) or pressing F9.

Note

The Zoom In, Zoom Out, Zoom 100%, and Show All commands—accessible via the View menu and the Main toolbar—are only available if you are creating a formula in a stand-alone document.

PART

II

CH

6

When you're finished, you can return to the familiar text window by clicking anywhere outside the Formula object box. To return to the Formula Editor, double-click the object box, or click inside the object to toggle between the Formula and Text object bar.

Note

StarOffice comes with a series of sample formulas located in the Samples, Formula folder in the Explorer that you can use or modify for your own purposes, including formulas for investment returns, annual interest rates, annuities, and other mathematical and statistical functions. You can insert these equations by selecting Tools, Import Equation and then locating the desired folder and formula.

FORMATTING YOUR FORMULA

If so inclined, you can access the Format menu and select options that enable you to change the font, font sizes, spacing, and horizontal alignment of formula elements. To change the font of a specific formula element, select Format, Fonts and click Modify in the Font Types dialog. In the Modify submenu, select the element for which you would like to define a new font. You can change the Formula fonts (Variables, Functions, Numbers, and Text) and Custom Fonts (Serif, Sans, and Fixed). After your selection, StarMath opens the Font dialog box where you can select a new font for the selected element and define its attribute as bold, italic, or bold and italic. Click OK to accept your changes. The new font appears in the drop-down list box of the respective element. If you don't like your new choice, you can always go back to the previous font by selecting it from the elements font drop-down list. Click Default if you want to save your changes as the new default setting, then click OK to return to StarMath.

To change the relative sizes of formula elements, select Format, Font Sizes and start scrolling through the spinner boxes. StarMath enables you to change the font size of text, indices, functions, operators, and limits relative to a defined Base font size. (By default, the relative size of text, functions, and operators is 100 percent, which means the size is equivalent to the defined base font size.)

If you really want to get picky, you can also adjust the spacing between formula elements right down to the spacing between the excess length of fraction bars in relation to nominators and denominators. Select Format, Spacing from the menu bar, and click Category to explore your options. Once your formula is created, you can also define its horizontal alignment by selecting Format, Alignment.

Note

StarWriter interprets and treats inserted formulas like any other inserted object. For a general introduction to working with objects in StarOffice, **see** "Working with Objects," **page 176** (Chapter 4, "Working in StarOffice"). For more details on working with Objects in StarWriter **see** "Rehearsing Objects," **page 421** (Chapter 11, "Desktop Publishing with StarOffice").

WORKING WITH SYMBOLS IN STARMATH

On occasion, you might need to add Greek characters or symbols to your formulas. StarMath comes with its own symbol and font sets that you can access through the Symbol icon on the Main toolbar. You can choose between the Greek and Special font sets.

In addition, StarMath enables you to create your own symbol set and edit existing ones. Just select Edit from the Symbols dialog, and type a new name in the Symbol Set box on the Edit Symbols dialog. Next, select the symbol you would like to include in your custom set, specify a name in the Symbol box, and select Add. You can add as many symbols as you like from the installed font sets to your custom set this way. You can also edit the name of an existing symbol by selecting the character first, selecting Modify, and then typing a name in the Symbol box. Select Add to have the symbol appear under a new name in the selected symbol set. When you're done, click OK. You can select your new or modified symbol set in the Symbol Set combo box in the Symbols dialog. To delete a custom set, go to the Edit Symbols dialog, highlight the name of the set in the Symbol Set box, and select Delete. Figure 6.5 shows the various steps involved in creating your own symbol set or editing existing ones.

Figure 6.5
StarMath enables you to create your own set of symbols for special projects.

Click to open Symbols dialog

Select Edit to edit existing symbol set or add new one

Select symbol and name it; then select Add to add the new symbol to the selected symbol set

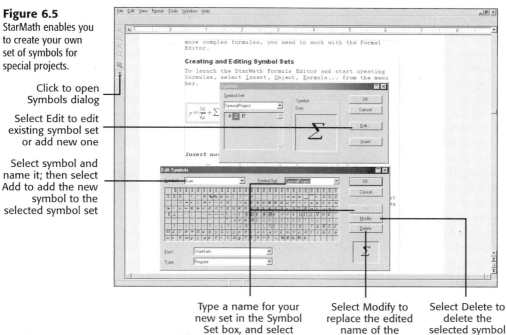

Type a name for your new set in the Symbol Set box, and select Add to add new set

Select Modify to replace the edited name of the selected character

Select Delete to delete the selected symbol

PART

II

CH

6

To insert a symbol from a chosen set, select it and click Insert. Note that if you select OK, you just close the Symbols dialog; your selection is not inserted. The name of the symbol is inserted at the insertion point in the Commands window of the Formula Editor, preceded by %. If you memorize the name of a symbol, you can also enter it directly in the Commands window, as long as you precede it by the % sign.

Note

StarMath's system of notation is pretty straightforward. After you learn the rules, you might find yourself increasingly editing a formula manually, moving elements around, combining them as new expressions by applying operators such as { and }, or inserting blank spaces between formula elements by inserting the tilde character (~).

AUTOMATING TEXT ENTRIES WITH AUTOTEXT

StarWriter comes with a series of features that accelerate text entry, including AutoText and AutoCorrect/AutoFormat. AutoText inserts various stock text passages from a list or by way of an extended click on the AutoText button on the Main toolbar. AutoCorrect/AutoFormat takes care of various common typing errors and will be discussed in the section "Correcting Spelling as You Type" later in this chapter.

The AutoText command enables you to quickly insert words, phrases, or paragraphs of text that you regularly use. You can create an AutoText entry (or text block) that includes text only, formatted text, or graphics. Some good applications for AutoText include company slogans, mission statements, logos, or copyright notices.

Tip #100 from
Michael & Sarah

To quickly identify AutoText entries, you can select Display AutoText name as you type in the AutoText dialog (choose Edit, AutoText). When the first three letters you type match the shortcut of an assigned AutoText entry, you see a balloon tip with the name of the entry pop up. If multiple names have the same first three shortcut letters, you can cycle backward and forward through the names by pressing Ctrl+Tab and Shift+Ctrl+Tab, respectively.

StarWriter comes with a set of predefined AutoText entries—including personal and business signatures, boilerplate cover and rejection letters, and standard closings—which are divided into three categories: Signature, Standard, and Template.

To insert an existing text block, you need to enter the respective shortcut and press F3. For example, if you type SY and press F3, StarWriter replaces the letters SY with Sincerely Yours.

Note

AutoText shortcuts are typically based on the first letter of each word within an assigned name, so you can easily memorize them.

To view the list of existing text blocks, select Edit, AutoText from the menu bar or press Ctrl+F3 to open the AutoText dialog. Click a category on the left to see the various text blocks saved under this category listed in the text block field on the right.

Tip #101 from
Michael & Sarah

To view a list of existing AutoText names and shortcuts, select Tools, Macro from the menu bar. In the Macro From list box, find and double-click Gimmicks to expand the Gimmicks tree. Select AutoText and then Run to start the macro that lists the existing AutoText names and shortcuts in a new text document, which you can save or print for future reference.

ADDING NEW AUTOTEXT CATEGORIES

You don't have to make do with the existing categories. StarWriter enables you to add new categories to the AutoText dialog, under which you can save your own AutoText entries or text blocks. This enables you to create smaller, and hence, more succinct, groupings of text blocks that are easier to manage. Press Ctrl+F3 to open the AutoText dialog, and select Categories. Enter a name for your new category in the Category field of the Edit Categories dialog, and select New. StarWriter adds the name to the list of existing categories, complete with the default path where it stores the AutoText entries of this new category. Select OK to close and return to the AutoText dialog; then select Close to return to your document. You can access the new category the next time you perform an extended-click on the AutoText button on the Main toolbar.

CREATING YOUR OWN AUTOTEXT ENTRIES

You can expand the existing AutoText library by adding your own entries (see Figure 6.6). Open a new text document (by choosing Start, Text Document); enter and format the text that you would like to save for future reference (for example, a standard disclaimer added to a price quote letter). Next, select the text you just entered, and press Ctrl+F3 to open the AutoText dialog. Select a category under which you want to save the new text block; then enter a descriptive name in the Name box above the text block list. If so inclined, you can also replace the suggested shortcut—based on the initial letters of each word entered (here, CSD) with another one of your choice. Next, select AutoText to save your new entry. Select New if you want to save your text block with all formatting and styles applied, or New (text only) if you want to save it as ASCII text (which is recommended for signature files used in emails, for example), or if you want the AutoText entry to take the format of the current paragraph when inserted. You can now close the AutoText dialog. Your new entry is then added to the selected category and is available when you need it.

Tip #102 from
Michael & Sarah

As your list of AutoText categories and entries grows, it will become harder and harder to memorize all shortcuts. In that case, extended-click the AutoText icon on the Main toolbar, and select the desired entry from the available list of categories and entries. As soon as you release your left mouse button, your selection is entered at the insertion point of your cursor.

PART
II

CH
6

Figure 6.6
Expand StarWriter's
existing AutoText
library by adding new
entries that are useful
to you.

Enter a name and
(custom) shortcut

Save the new AutoText entry

Enter and select text

Click to show
AutoText names
when Tips help is
active

Open a new text
document

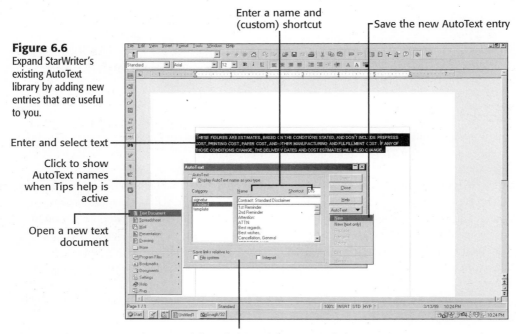

Using Save Links Relative To is recommended
when you're managing files on a network or
server

CHANGING CATEGORY PATHS

AutoText entries are automatically saved and registered under their category name in the autotext folder of the StarOffice root directory (name.bau). If you ever decide to move AutoText entries to a different folder or directory, you can assign a new path to your categories in the AutoText dialog. Press Ctrl+F3 to open the dialog, and select Path and then Add in the Select Path dialog. Find the directory that you want to add to your Paths list, and select Open. Select OK in the Select Paths dialog to confirm your selection. The new path is then added to the AutoText paths list. You can now move your category file(s) to the newly assigned path. AutoText automatically finds and recognizes the category file(s).

> **Caution**
>
> If you're on a network, you might have to select one of the Save Links Relative To options in the AutoText dialog.

EDITING EXISTING AUTOTEXT ENTRIES

Occasionally, you might have to update or change the wording of an existing AutoText entry. To do so, press Ctrl+F3 to open the AutoText dialog. Find the entry you want to edit, and select AutoText, Edit. AutoText opens the entry as a new task. When you're done applying your changes, press Ctrl+S to save your changes and close the task. Your selected entry is updated for future reference.

You can also rename or delete existing text blocks. Find the name of the text block you want to change, and then select AutoText, Rename in the AutoText dialog. In the Rename Text Block dialog, enter the new name and shortcut in the respective fields underneath the old name and shortcut. If you want to delete a text block, select AutoText, Delete and confirm your selection in the Delete AutoText alert box.

Caution

The Undo command does not undo a deletion from the AutoText dialog. If you accidentally delete a text block, you cannot recover it.

WORKING WITH THE AUTOCOMPLETION FEATURE

StarWriter also contains an autocompletion feature. Using this feature, you can store a predefined number of words of a predefined length. When you enter the first three letters, StarWriter finds the first match for you and automatically enters it into your text against a dark blue background. As you continue to type, StarWriter will find additional matches. If you see the word you're in the process of typing, press Enter and StarWriter will insert it for you. If more than one word begins with the same three characters, you can enter the key combination Ctrl+Tab to search the list of stored words from the beginning or Shift+Ctrl+Tab to search from the end of the list of familiar words.

Note that this feature is on by default and can be controlled via the Options tab in the AutoCorrect dialog (Tools, AutoCorrect/AutoFormat). If you would like to change the number of characters and words, click the Edit button and specify new numbers in the Min. Word Length and Max. Entry spinner boxes of the Automatic Word Completion dialog. If this feature is starting to annoy you, select, Tools, AutoCorrect/AutoFormat, Options and turn it off by clicking (removing the x) next to the "Auto completion min. word length 10, Max. no. of entries 500" entry.

EDITING AND SELECTING TEXT

After you're done writing, you might want to format, copy, move, or delete—in short, edit—portions or all of your document. StarWriter offers you various ways of doing all the above. This section covers basic editing and formatting techniques. For more detailed information on formatting your text documents, see Chapter 7, "Formatting Text Documents."

PART

II

CH

6

CORRECTING SPELLING AS YOU TYPE

StarOffice includes solid tools for checking and, if necessary, correcting your spelling. For example, if the AutoSpellcheck function is active, you'll notice a wavy red line underneath each misspelled word or term that is not recognized by your currently installed dictionary. To correct your misspelling, right-click the misspelled word, and select the correct term from the shortcut menu. If you can't find the term on the list of suggested replacements, yet you're sure that the term is spelled correctly, you can tell the spell checker to pass over the unrecognized term by selecting Ignore; or you can elect to add it to the apparently limited vocabulary of your installed standard dictionary by selecting Add. You can also look up AutoCorrect to see whether the term is part of a list of replacements. To turn on the AutoSpellcheck feature, click the AutoSpellcheck icon on the main toolbar ("ABC" with a wavy read underline) or select Tools, Spelling, AutoSpellcheck.

→ StarOffice enables you to check your spelling in up to three languages. For more details on the spell checker and installed dictionaries, **see** "Proofing Your Work," **p. 460**.

Tip #103 from Michael & Sarah	If you don't see any wavy red lines in your document, you're either a darned good speller or your AutoSpellcheck is disabled on your machine. To turn on this function, select the AutoSpellcheck button on the Main toolbar, or select Tools, Spelling, AutoSpellcheck. Alternately, the Don't Mark Errors option in the Auto spellchecking portion of the General Linguistics dialog may be selected (choose Tools, Options, General, Linguistics).

Beyond waving your mistakes in front of your nose, however, StarWriter also provides you with a function that can actually help you avoid making the most common mistakes: AutoCorrect/AutoFormat. If enabled, this tool automatically corrects common typing errors on-the-fly. For example, due to the layout of standard keyboards that do not reflect the logic of spelling, most people repeatedly make the same typing errors, reversing "ha" as in "ahve" or typing TWo INitial CApitals.

In addition to correcting your spelling, this tool can also take care of some basic formatting and text entry chores for you, such as replacing standard quotes with custom quotes or changing *bold* and _underline_ into **bold** and underline or replacing (c) with the copyright symbol ©. Correcting as you go saves a lot of time spellchecking later. You can toggle the various AutoCorrect options on or off, using the Options tab in the AutoCorrect dialog (Tools, AutoCorrect/AutoFormat). Table 6.4 lists the various AutoCorrect/AutoFormat configuration options you can access by selecting Tools, AutoCorrect/AutoFormat.

Tip #104 from Michael & Sarah	You can undo any individual instance of autocorrection with the standard Edit menu Undo command (Ctrl+Z).

TABLE 6.4 AutoCorrect/AutoFormat Options in StarOffice

Use This Tab	**If You Want To**
Replace	Use the standard replacement table to have a certain letter combination replaced by another (for example, .5 by 1/2). You can edit this table, add new combinations and replacements, or delete existing ones.
Exceptions	Exempt abbreviations and words with two initial capitals from AutoCorrect's attention. If you select the Automatically Add to List option on this tab, any abbreviations or words with two initial capitals for which you undo the automatic correction once are automatically recorded in the respective exception list. You can edit these tables in the same way you do the replacement table.

Use This Tab	If You Want To
Options	Turn on or off predefined AutoCorrect/AutoFormat options. Select the T column if you want to autocorrect/autoformat while typing; select the M column if you want changes applied while modifying the existing text in its entirety. Note that you can switch between these two modes by selecting Format, AutoFormat and then selecting either While Typing or Format Document. If you want to review each change individually, select Format, AutoFormat, Format Document and Review Changes. After StarWriter has autoformatted the entire document, you'll see the AutoFormat dialog where you will be asked to Accept All, Reject All or Review Changes. Click Review Changes and select which changes to accept of reject using the List tab in the new dialog.
Custom Quotes	Replace the system quotes with custom symbols.

CORRECTING TYPOS AFTER THE FACT

If you want to replace or correct text you've already typed, you can do so by switching from the Insert to the Overwrite mode. If you're working in Insert mode, press the Insert key (or click the Insert field on the status bar) to switch modes, and start typing to replace the current text. Don't forget to switch back to the Insert mode when you're done typing.

In most cases, however, you'll probably use the mouse or the direction arrows and keys on your keyboard to navigate to the location of the offensive typo and whack it by pressing Delete or Backspace.

→ For more details on proofing and correcting your spelling, **see** "Using Search and Replace," **p. 460**, and "Checking Your Spelling," **p. 464**.

SELECTING AND DELETING TEXT

After you've entered text, you might want to select it so that you can format, copy, move, or even delete it. StarWriter distinguishes between three selection modes: Standard (default), Extended, and Additive. You can tell the mode you're in by looking at the selection field on the status bar. If you're in the default Standard (STD) mode, StarWriter behaves like any other word processing application, and you can use the keyboard and mouse to type and select text. The Extended (EXT) or Additive (ADD) modes are solely selection modes that enable you to use your cursor to select continuous or non-continuous portions of text, respectively. As soon as you press the Esc key or start to type in either mode, StarWriter defaults to the Standard selection mode. You can click in the selection field to switch from Standard to Extended mode; another click switches you to the Additive mode.

Caution

After you select text, keep in mind that anything you type will replace the selected text. If you accidentally replace text, you can undo your last action by immediately selecting Edit, Undo from the menu bar or pressing Ctrl+Z.

PART

II

CH

6

SELECTING TEXT

When selecting text, you basically have three options: You can use the mouse, the keyboard, or both. Here are some practical techniques for selecting text in StarWriter in Standard mode:

- To select consecutive characters, place the insertion point at the beginning of the first character; then click and hold the left mouse button and drag through the last character.

- To select a word, double-click anywhere in the word. You can select adjacent words by holding down the mouse button after the second click and dragging through the additional words.

- To select a line, triple-click anywhere in the line. You can select additional lines by holding down the mouse button after the third click and dragging through the additional lines.

- To select a paragraph or block of text, click at the start of the desired selection, and drag to the end of the desired selection, which need not appear in the same screen view as the starting point. You can drag for pages if necessary. Note that the farther you move your pointer beyond the workspace, the faster the text scrolls.

- To select the entire document, select Edit, Select All from the menu bar, or press Ctrl+A.

Tip #105 from
Michael & Sarah

If you want to select noncontiguous text, double-click the selection field on the status bar to switch from Standard (STD) to Additive (Add) selection mode. You can now quickly click and drag repeatedly anywhere in the document to select nonconsecutive portions of text. Press the Escape key (or click the selection field) to switch back to Standard selection mode. Alternatively, you can press and hold the Ctrl key and click or drag.

You can also use the Shift key in combination with the various direction keys and shortcut keys for moving around the document (**see** "Moving Around Your Document" in this chapter) to select portions of text. For example, to select text from the insertion point to the end of a line, press Shift+End. Shift+Home selects text from the insertion point to the beginning of the line.

To deselect selected text, click once (on your selection or in the workspace of your document), or press the Esc key.

DELETING TEXT

You can delete text in several ways. You can delete one character at a time by using the Backspace and Delete keys on your keyboard. Using the Backspace key removes the text to the left of the insertion point; using the Delete key removes it to the right. Note that the remaining characters move automatically to the left when you use the Delete key.

You can also delete entire blocks of consecutive text by first selecting the text you want to delete and then pressing the Delete or Backspace keys.

COPYING AND MOVING TEXT

StarWriter makes it easy for you to copy and move existing text to a new location. The new location can be within the same document or in a different document within StarOffice or even between StarOffice and other applications. First, select the text you want to copy; then select Edit, Copy from the menu bar. If you prefer to work with buttons and shortcuts, you can also click the Copy button on the Function bar or press Ctrl+C. In Windows, StarWriter saves the selection to the clipboard, an area of memory that stores temporary information; in Linux, it is saved to the *general-purpose buffer*. Next, move your cursor to the desired location, and select Edit, Paste to insert the selection at the insertion point. Alternatively, you can also use the Paste button on the Function bar, or press Ctrl+V to paste the selection from the Clipboard (Windows) or general-purpose buffer (Linux) to the new location.

CUT-AND-PASTE EDITING

If you want to actually move, rather than copy, information from one location to another, you can do so with cut and paste. Select the text you want to cut; then select Edit, Cut from the menu bar. If you prefer to work with buttons and shortcuts, you can also click the Cut button on the Function bar or press Ctrl+X. Now move your cursor to the new location, and select Edit, Paste to insert the selection at the insertion point. Alternatively, you can use the Paste button on the Function bar or press Ctrl+V to paste the selection from the clipboard (Windows) or general-purpose buffer (Linux) to the new location.

→ For information on moving text with the Navigator, **see** "Working with Outlines," **p. 376**.

Tip #106 from *Michael & Sarah*	If you want to move an entire paragraph or consecutive paragraphs within the same document, you can place your cursor inside the paragraph and then press Ctrl+up arrow or Ctrl+down arrow to move the selected paragraph up or down, respectively.

DRAG-AND-DROP EDITING

If speed is of the essence, you'll soon find that StarWriter offers an easier way of copying and moving text from one location to another; it's called drag-and-drop editing, and it's the preferred method if you're moving or copying small amounts of text.

To move text to a new location via drag and drop, you first select and click the text you want to move, and then you drag it to the desired location by holding the left mouse button as you drag. As you drag the selection, a small rectangle appears next to the mouse pointer; the rectangle indicates that you are dragging text. After you release the button, the selected text appears in the new location.

If you want only to copy—rather than move—information to a new location, you need to press and hold the Ctrl key as you perform the drag-and-drop operation. If you release the Ctrl key before you release the mouse button, your selection is moved rather than copied.

EXPLORING YOUR BASIC FORMATTING OPTIONS

Typically, you won't be satisfied with just entering text in a document. Ideally, you will want to enhance your document by adding color, style, or graphics to your text. This section gives you a brief overview of your basic formatting options in StarWriter, all of which are available from the StarWriter object bar. For brief descriptions of these options, refer to Table 6.1.

→ For more details on how to format text documents, **see** Chapter 7, "Formatting Text Documents," **p.261**.

For the most part, changing the appearance of your text is pretty straightforward. First, you have to select the text unit (words, sentences, or paragraphs) you want to change; then you select the type of change you want to apply to the selected unit from the object bar.

StarWriter distinguishes between three levels of formatting: character, paragraph, and page. On the character level, you can change the font, size, style, or color of a selected unit of text.

> **Note**
>
> If you want to change the type style or attribute of a single word, you don't have to high-light the word first (as in MS Word). Just click the word, and then click (any combination of) the Bold, Italics, or Underline button on the object bar to apply the change(s).

On the paragraph level, you can change the alignment and indents, numbering and bullets, and background color of a selected unit of text.

Finally, on the page level, you can change the margins, layout, and background of your document. Note that these changes typically affect the entire document, not just portions of it.

Apart from formatting your text directly by choosing formatting attributes on the Text object bar, you can also work with styles and templates.

→ For more details **see** Chapter 8, "Using Styles and Templates," **p. 291**.

UNDOING, REDOING, AND REPEATING ACTIONS

Don't panic if you accidentally deleted important information. You can reverse many (though not all) mistakes by using the Undo command. If you accidentally delete an entire text block, select Edit, Undo from the menu bar (or press Ctrl+Z) before carrying out another task, and the deleted selection reappears in its original place. If you add one word too many at the end of a sentence, press Ctrl+Z and the preceding entry is deleted. Depending on how StarWriter is set up, the Edit, Undo command (or Ctrl+Z) enables you to reverse up to 100 (default: 20) previously executed commands and tasks—depending on how you configure the Undo command in StarWriter. (For more details, see Chapter 13, "Creating Spreadsheets.")

Note

A single word or space counts as a command or an insert in StarWriter. In other words, even if you type five words consecutively, you still have to select the Undo command nine times to delete the entire entry (five words plus four spaces, each of which counts as an insert).

If you decide you don't need the previously deleted and recovered information after all, you can use the Redo command by selecting Edit, Redo. In general, the Redo command reverses the last Undo command. You can also access the Undo and Redo commands on the Function bar.

Another useful (albeit not very well implemented) feature is the Repeat command, which you can use to repeat the last command or insert. To repeat a previous action, select Edit, Repeat from the menu bar.

Tip #107 from
Michael & Sarah

Unlike many other word processors, StarOffice does not provide you with an easy way to repeat an action out of the box through the Ctrl+Y keyboard combination. For example, if you press the standard Ctrl+Y shortcut in StarWriter, you activate the Style Catalog (which will be discussed in Chapter 8, "Using Styles and Templates") instead of repeating the last action. However, you do have an alternative. You can assign your own keyboard shortcut to the Repeat command. Just choose Tools, Configure and select the Keyboard tab. In the Keyboard list, select the Ctrl+Y key combination; in the Functions: Category list, select Edit; and in the Functions: Command list, select Repeat. Then click the Assign button—the Repeat command will appear next to the Ctrl+Y combination in the Keyboard list. If you ever want to remove a key combination assignment, simply select it and click Delete. For more details on assigning keyboard shortcuts, **see** "Customizing Your Keyboard Shortcuts," in Chapter 3, "Getting Ready for Work."

SAVING, CLOSING, AND OPENING DOCUMENTS

Saving is a crucial part of working with documents, and you should make it a habit to save your work regularly. Apart from protecting hours of work, saving a document also enables you to give it a unique name and save different versions of it so that you can easily keep track of it. After you've saved a document, you can continue to save changes by pressing Ctrl+S or clicking the Save button on the Function bar.

SAVING A NEW DOCUMENT

StarOffice gives you three basic ways of saving a document. You can click the Save button on the Function bar; select File, Save from the menu bar; or press Ctrl+S on your keyboard. The first time you try to save a new, previously unsaved document, StarWriter automatically opens the Save As dialog. Here, you can enter a name for your document in the File Name text box, select a directory where you want to save the file (default: ...\Office51\Explorer\ Workfolder), or create a new (sub)folder within a directory of your choice. When you're finished, select Save to return to your document.

→ When the Save As dialog is open, you can move, copy, and delete files and folders as you like. For more details on managing your files and folders, **see** "Managing Files and Folders from the Open and Save As Dialogs," **p. 192**.

Tip #108 from *Michael & Sarah*	Be sure to select the Automatic File Name Extension check box in the lower-left corner of the dialog. StarWriter saves the file with the extension corresponding to the selected file type, which is important if you exchange files across platforms or work with files in other formats. Otherwise, the others can't automatically recognize and open the file. If you like, you can also select Save with Password to protect the file from curious eyes. Just don't lose your password, or you can't reopen the file.
Caution	When you're on a network, be sure to work in Online mode (select the Online button on the Function bar). If not, you can't see the current contents on the network, only the information that has been cached on your hard drive.
Note	When you're working with frames, the Save As function is called Save Frameset As. For more details on working with frames, see Chapter 31, "Creating and Saving HTML Documents."

SAVING CHANGES TO AN EXISTING DOCUMENT

After you've saved a StarWriter document for the first time in the Save As dialog box, further saves require only a quick Ctrl+S. Practice that key combination until it's second nature to you, and you'll never have to exclaim, "I just lost an hour's work!" again.

Tip #109 from *Michael & Sarah*	You can also tell StarOffice to automatically save open documents at specified time intervals. To see if the xe "autosave function" autosave function is enabled, select Tools, Options, General, and click the Save tab to verify your save options. Look in the Save area in the upper left and, if necessary, select the Automatic Save Entry check box and a number in the Minutes spinner box to the right to have your documents automatically saved at the specified time interval.

→ For more details on customizing your save options, **see** "Setting Your Save Options," **p. 77**.

StarWriter saves the current document under the existing filename and path on your hard drive, network, or Web server.

SAVING VERSIONS OF AN EXISTING DOCUMENT

On occasion, you might need to save an existing file under a different name, file format, or version. In this case, you can select File, Save As and rename the existing file accordingly. A quicker and more convenient way is to have StarWriter save different versions of the same file, which keeps your hard drive less cluttered.

To save a file as a different version, select File, Versions and then click the Save New Version button. Enter a comment in the Insert Version Comment window for easy reference; select OK and then Close. The existing document is saved as a new version to the same file (which means your file can get rather large if you save multiple versions of an existing document). The versions are identified in the Versions dialog by the date and time they were last saved, the author of the version, and (optional) comments that the author has entered. If these comments are rather lengthy, you can select Show to read them.

To compare versions, click the Compare button to see a list of changes. You can accept or reject some or all of the changes to the original document. If the list of changes is rather long, or if various authors have contributed to the document, click the Filter tab in the Accept or Reject Changes dialog, and then select Date, Author, or Action to see a select list of changes.

Note

The Versions feature is helpful if you frequently exchange documents with other users in a workgroup environment, but it works only if you save files in the native StarWriter format. If you decide to save a document in a different file format, all changes are automatically accepted, and you can no longer track them.

Tip #110 from
Michael & Sarah

To automatically save versions of a document, select Always Save a Version on Closing in the Versions dialog.

SAVING IN DIFFERENT FILE FORMATS

Whether you're working with a brand new document or one that's been around for some time, you have the option to save it in a file format other than the standard (or *native*) one used by preference by StarWriter when you open the Save As dialog. To change the file format, select File, Save As, and then use the File Type drop-down list to select an alternative format for the document. Your alternatives are limited by the availability of filters and choices you made during the initial StarOffice installation. In addition, you can save files as HTML documents, which is discussed in the section "Saving Files in HTML Format" in Chapter 25, "Creating Web Pages with StarWriter/Web."

> **Note**
>
> Saving files in a format other than the standard format may result in loss of data and formatting. Be sure to check the results against the original before sharing documents.

→ For more details on file types and what types you save in, **see** Appendix B, **p. 1395**.

→ Installing previously uninstalled filters is covered in Appendix A, **p. 1353**.

SAVING ALL OPEN DOCUMENTS

If you're looking for a quick way to save all open documents in StarOffice, select File, Save All, and you're home free. You might be asked to confirm your save based on whether you're saving in a native or "foreign" file format. Note also that this function is available only if you have at least two tasks open.

CLOSING AND OPENING EXISTING DOCUMENTS

After you've finished and saved your document, you can close the document (or task) by selecting File, Close or right-clicking the document's task button and then selecting Close Task from the shortcut menu.

> **Note**
>
> If you're trying to close a document, or if you're trying to switch between tasks, without having saved your recent changes, an alert dialog gives you the option to save your changes before closing or switching. Also, if you're trying to save a file in a format other than the native one, you are alerted that "Saving in foreign formats may cause information loss" and are given the option to proceed or not to proceed.

To open an existing document, you can select the File Open button on the Function bar; choose File, Open from the menu bar; or press Ctrl+O. When the Open dialog is open, you can move, copy, and delete files and folders as you like. You can also open existing versions of files by selecting first the file and then the file version from the Version drop-down list.

→ For more details on managing your files and folders this way, **see** "Managing Files and Folders from the Open and Save As Dialogs," **p. 192**.

STARTING A NEW TEXT DOCUMENT

After you launch StarOffice (by choosing Start, Programs, StarOffice 5.0, StarOffice 5.0), you can start working in StarWriter by double-clicking the New Text Document icon in the work area of the StarDesktop. Alternatively, you can select File, New, Text Document from the menu bar. A blank document (called Untitled1) appears in the StarOffice workspace—framed by handy tools, buttons, and status displays, which were discussed in the previous section "The StarWriter Window and Context Menus." You can start typing at the blinking insertion point.

Instead of starting from scratch, you can save time by using a wizard that guides you step by step through the creation of a document template, or by selecting a ready-made template, which results in a document with an attractive layout that leaves it up to you to fill in the blanks.

To use the AutoPilot Wizard, select File, AutoPilot from the menu bar, and then choose letter, fax, agenda, memo, or HTML document, depending on what type of StarWriter document you want to create.

To create a new document from a template, select File, New, From Template or press Ctrl+N. You are given a choice of various templates in different categories (not all of which are text documents).

→ For more details on using templates, **see** "Working with Templates," **p. 308**.

CREATING DOCUMENTS AND TEMPLATES WITH THE AUTOPILOT

StarOffice includes a series of template wizards, which help you quickly create a professional-looking document and document template. To activate any of these wizards, select File, Autopilot, then select the AutoPilot wizard that best fits the type of document you want to create. Your options in StarWriter include Letter, Fax, Agenda, and Memo. When you complete the wizard, the document you've created is saved as a StarWriter template in the Office51\template directory, and a new document based on the template opens on your desktop so you can get right to work.

Note

You can start these wizards from the desktop or any document. At the end of the step-through, in most cases, StarOffice will automatically open the module you need to work with the created document. If it's a text document, it will appear in StarWriter; if it's a presentation, it will appear in StarImpress, and so on. However, in the case of StarBase objects (tables, forms, queries, and reports), you must first create a database in the Explorer before you can create objects with the AutoPilot.

Using these wizards is pretty straightforward. In each case, the AutoPilot wizard steps you through a series of dialogs that enable you to define the layout and content areas of the final document. All you have to do is select the desired elements from a list of options. In some instances, you may also have to enter text (for subject titles or agenda items, for example). You can preview the results of your layout choices in the window on the left of each AutoPilot dialog. Click Next to advance to the following dialog; click Back at any time to change a previous selection. At the end of the template creation process (indicated with a racing flag in the preview window), you'll be asked how you want to save the wizard-created template. The next time you want to use this template, you can load it in one easy step by selecting File, New, From Template or pressing Ctrl+N, rather than re-creating it from scratch.

→ For more details on opening existing templates, **see** "Opening Templates," **p. 313**.

PART

II

CH

6

Note

Note that you do not have to step through each individual dialog in order to create the desired document or template   you can click the Create button at any time. If you're familiar with the various steps involved in the template creation process and know the default settings the wizard applies, advance only as far as you have to make the desired changes, then click Create   in this case, the AutoPilot will create the document template for you without asking how you want to save the created document.

The Letter wizard, for example, enables you to create customized personal and business letters. Here's a sample walkthrough of what you need to do when using the AutoPilot Letter wizard:

1. Select File, AutoPilot, Letter.

2. Select the type of letter you want to create and choose a layout style (Modern, Classic, Decorative). Typically, different styles present different fonts and placement options for your logo. Click Next.

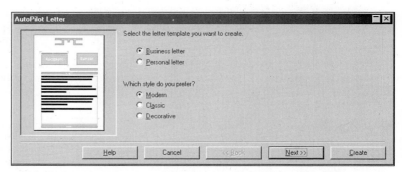

3. Select the type, size and position of the logo you would like to insert. When you select Picture (default), click the Select Picture button

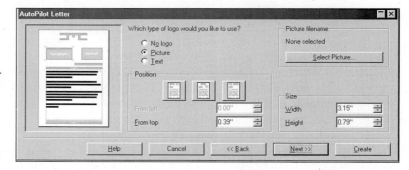

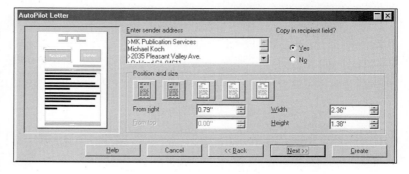

to locate the desired logo file on your system. When you select Text, you'll see the Logo Text list box instead of the Select Picture button on the right which enables you to enter the desired text for your logo. Click on the left, center, or right icon in the Position portion of the dialog to define if you want your logo left-, center, or right-aligned. In each instance, you can specify the distance of the logo from the top of the page. If you select left- or right-aligned, you can also specify the distance of the logo from the left or right page margins. Using the Size portion of the dialog, you can specify the width and height of your logo. If you don't want a logo, select No Logo and click Next.

4. Select a position and size for your return address. The AutoPilot automatically assumes that the person creating the letter is also

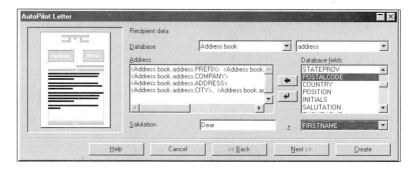

the sender; hence the AutoPilot retrieves the return address information from the user data information (Tools, Options, General, User Data) on the system on which the letter is created and fills it in the Enter Sender Address box. You can always change the sender information manually—just type the sender's company, name and address over the existing address. As with your logo, you can also define a position and size for the sender's contact information by clicking the page icons in the Position and Size portion of the dialog. You can place your return address on the top left, top right, bottom left, bottom right, or adjacent to the recipient's address. (Note that if you chose to left- or right-align your logo, you won't be able to place your return address on the top left or top right of your page.). You can also choose if you want your return address to appear as a copy above the recipient's address field (which is handy if you use envelopes with clear windows). Click Next.

5. Select the database that contains the desired address(es); then select the database fields for the recipient's address area (business letter only).

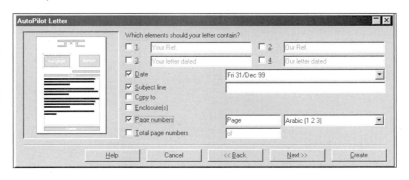

Select the desired field on the right, then click the right-pointing arrow in the middle to transfer a copy of the field to the recipient's address area. Insert spaces and punctuation between fields as needed. To force a line break, click the angled arrow before copying the field that you want in a new line. You can also type in the name and address if the letter is addressed to a single recipient, inserting spaces, punctuation and line breaks as if you were to type a letter. (Using fields is especially helpful for mail merges as detailed in "Creating Letters with Mail Merge," page xx in Chapter 9.) You can also enter a salutation (manually or via a field command). Click Next.

6. Select the elements you want to include in your letter, including up to four customized reference lines, a format for the date, and page

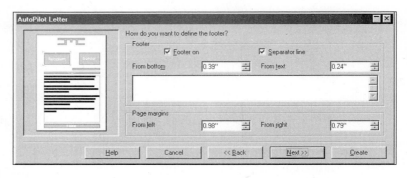

numbers (if applicable). You can enter up to 4 customized references, define a format for the letter date, enter a subject line, and define the format for your page numbers in case the letter runs longer than one page. You can even indicate the total number of pages on your letter. Click Next.

7. Define the size of the footer and margins area. You can enter text that you want to show in the footer area of your letter and add a separator

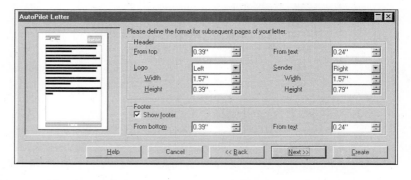

line between footer and letter text. You can also specify the left and right page margins. (Note that these margins will not affect the letter head area, only the body and footer area.) Click Next.

8. Define the format for subsequent pages, if you expect your letter to run longer than one page. Using the header portion of this dialog, you can specify the size and position of your logo or return address on subsequent pages; using the footer portion, you can specify the distance of your footer from the bottom of the page and the text, provided you decide to show the footer at all. Click Next.

9. Decide where and how you want to save both your document and the created template. You can save your template under a database field name (Document Info), or under a custom Template Filename, in which case you can enter a few explanatory words in the Info line of the dialog. If you save your template in the Office 51\template folder, you'll be able to retrieve it easily the next time you select File, New, From Template or press Ctrl+N. Click Next. You can also choose to have a filename automatically assigned to the document you're creating by choosing the Filename, Automatic option. Otherwise, your document will be opened with the usual [Untitled] name and you will need to assign a filename when you first save it.

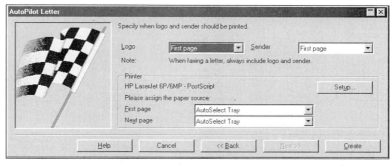

10. Specify the circumstances under which logo and sender information should be printed, and set up your printer. Click Create.

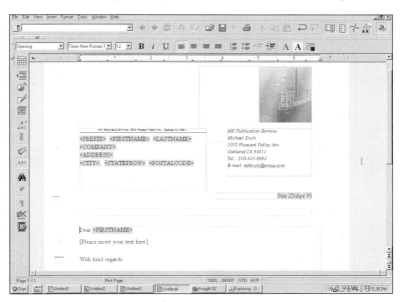

Finished! You can now proceed to write your letter, making any further changes as appropriate to this specific letter. Note that your template has already been saved; if you want to make further changes to the template, you'll need to open it from the Office51\template directory.

Tip #111 from
Michael & Sarah

> If you want to use this template for future correspondence, be sure to save any general layout changes and, if applicable, boiler text entries under the current template name. Then, "personalize" your letter with additional text entries and save it as a document (as opposed to a template) under a descriptive name.

Following this sample step-through, you can also create fax, agenda, or memo StarWriter templates in StarWriter. The Fax wizard creates a fax sheet that you can customize, similar to the Letter wizard. You can select a modern, classic, or decorative design; select a logo of varying size and placement; enter the sender's address and placeholder fields for the recipient(s); and define the elements the fax should contain. After the fax is created, you can fill in the recipient's name and address by opening your address book in the Beamer, selecting the recipient's contact info, and choosing File, Mail Merge.

→ For more details on the Address Book, **see** "Introducing the Address Book," **p. 180**.

→ For more details on the Mail Merge command, **see** "Creating Letters from Mail Merge," **p. 360**.

The Agenda wizard creates a customized agenda template that you can distribute among your associates so they arrive prepared and on time (well, at least they'll have no excuse) the next time you summon them for a meeting. You can select a modern, classic, or decorative style and logo; enter the date, time, and location of your meeting; define the elements you want included in the agenda (occasion, bring along, please prepare, and notes); select the name fields the agenda should contain; enter a list of agenda topics and assign responsibilities and duration of presentation to individual participants.

The Memo Wizard helps you create customized memos. You can choose a style (Modern, Classic, Decorative) and title (as text or as picture), the elements the Memo should contain (such as date, subject line, To and From lines, and so on), and the elements that should be placed in the header or footer area of the memo.

→ For a general introduction to the AutoPilot, **see** "Creating New Documents," **p. 132**.

Troubleshooting

The text I enter is always automatically formatted. How do I turn this off?

If you want to completely prevent StarOffice from making changes to your document formatting, select Tool, AutoCorrect/AutoFormat and deactivate all options (by removing the check mark) on the Options tab that you don't want. When done, click OK. Next, select Format, AutoFormat and deselect While Typing.

How can I get AutoCorrect to convert —> into a regular arrow ([insert arrow])? Entering the numeric value in the Replace With field in the AutoText dialog doesn't seem to work.

Open a new text document, choose Insert, Special Character, select the desired arrow from the StarBats character set and click OK. Next, select the arrow and open the AutoCorrect dialog (Tools, AutoCorrect/AutoFormat). Using the Replace tab, enter your "text" (—>) in the Replace text box; the With text box already has the desired replacement entry in number form. Be sure the Text only option is not selected, then click New, followed by OK. The next time you type —> and press space, StarWriter will insert the desired arrow.

StarWriter always crashes when I try to import a certain document.

Try pressing Ctrl+Alt+L in the Open dialog when opening a document. You'll see the Load document without layout dialog. Click OK and proceed to open the document as usual by clicking Open. StarWriter will try to open the document by ignoring any defect formatting characteristics. You can also try to copy and paste the contents of the defect document into a new document, provided StarWriter doesn't crash while you attempt to do so.

I can't find a specific file format in which I want to save my text document.

There are two options: either you didn't install all filters during the install process (in which case you have to run StarOffice Setup again and select Modify), or the particular filter only exists as import filter, not as export filter. In that case, try saving the document in another general format, such as RTF or HTML.

Why does StarWriter keep crashing on me?

Chances are your `soffice.cfg` file is corrupt. Simply delete the file from the `\Office51\config` folder. Unfortunately, you will also lose all custom settings, unless you regularly make back-up copies of your important system files. In that case, you can restore an earlier version of the `soffice.cfg` file.

When I insert special characters from the StarMath or StarBats font set or if I press the plus (+) sign, I only see a weird symbol, but not what I originally inserted.

You've just identified yourself as a Windows user. On occasion, the StarMath (`starmath.ttf`) and StarBats (`starbats.ttf`) font sets are not registered correctly with the Windows registry. Select Start, Settings, Control Panel and double-click the Font module in the Windows Control Panel. Locate and double-click StarMath and StarBats. When the font windows open, the corresponding font set will be newly registered.

Is it possible to align my formula in such a way that it looks like this:

$$25 - y = -8 + 2y$$

$$25 = 3y$$

$$4.2 = y$$

Yes, you can use the "Matrix" command (if necessary with "alignr" and "alignl"). For example:

$$\text{matrix}\{ 20 - y \ \# \ \text{“=”} \ \# \ -8 + 2y \ \#\#$$
$$\text{alignr } 25 \ \# \ \text{“=”} \ \# \ \text{alignl } 3y \ \#\#$$
$$\text{alignr } 4.2 \ \# \ \text{“=”} \ \# \ \text{alignl } p\}$$

Note that you have to put the equal sign between quotation marks, so StarMath treats it as a character rather than an operator.

When I open and then subsequently close a document, StarWriter asks me if I want to save my changes, although I didn't change a thing in the document. How come?

Could it be that you printed out a copy of the document? StarWriter interprets printing a copy as a change to the document over its previous form: it updates the statistical information that is shown in the Properties dialog (Document: Printed).

CHAPTER **7**

FORMATTING TEXT DOCUMENTS

In this chapter

UNDERSTANDING YOUR FORMATTING OPTIONS

Every new document you open in StarWriter comes with its standard (default) settings for font and font size, paragraph alignment and line spacing, and margins and paper orientation. If you want to add individuality and readability to a document, we recommend you modify these default settings by adjusting the various elements of style and presentation.

Tip #112 from
Michael & Sarah

> You can control the default font settings using the Standard Fonts option in the Tools, Options, Text Document category. Using this option, you can change the standard fonts for the Standard, Heading, List, Caption, and Index styles. If you select the Current Document Only option in the lower left, your changes will only apply to the current document; if you leave this option open, your changes will apply to all documents that use the current template and styles. For more details on templates and styles, see Chapter 8, "Using Styles and Templates."

StarWriter gives you a series of formatting options that enable you to control the appearance of your document. Using StarWriter's distinctive features and commands, you can change the look and style of individual characters and paragraphs, as well as entire pages. You can divide text into columns, assign different fonts and font sizes to sections and portions of your text, adjust the spacing between lines and paragraphs, and add color or graphics to the background of paragraphs or pages. You can apply these changes directly by selecting text and then choosing the desired formatting option from the Text context menu, Object bar, or Format menu. Or, you can streamline the formatting process by using styles, which are collections of many different formatting options that you can apply all at once to a paragraph or text selection. Style formatting (as opposed to direct formatting) is the preferred method if you're working with long documents or want to achieve a consistent look.

→ This chapter gives you a detailed overview of your direct formatting options. Style formatting is covered in detail in Chapter 8, "Using Styles and Templates" **p. 291**.

In general, your formatting options can be mapped onto a hierarchy of three levels:

- *Character* formatting governs the appearance of individual letters, numerals, symbols, and punctuation marks and is often used to make a word or group of words in a document stand out. Attributes such as font, size, color, bold, italic, underline, special font effects, and character spacing and positioning fall into this category.

- With *paragraph* formatting, you can specify the manner of settings that affect the paragraph as a whole, including alignment, indents, tab settings, line spacing, spacing before and after paragraphs, text flow, and background color. In addition, each paragraph has a style that determines the default appearance of individual characters. Although you can override these default settings by applying character formatting, the paragraph style still determines the look of the rest of the paragraph.

- *Page* formatting governs the basic layout of the entire document. Page formatting includes settings for margins and columns, headers and footers, and paper size and orientation.

Tip #113 from
Michael & Sarah

StarWriter's refined Search and Replace feature also enables you to search for and replace character attributes and text formatting options. For more details, **see** the section "Using Search and Replace," **page 460**, in Chapter 12, "Proofing and Printing Your Documents."

FORMATTING CHARACTERS

StarWriter provides many options for changing the appearance of individual characters. You can select from a variety of fonts and sizes, font effects and styles, as well as font color and background color (for highlighting portions of your text) to enhance the readability of your work. In addition, you can assign macros or a language to your text so that the spell checker recognizes the styled term(s) or phrase(s). And because StarWriter doubles as an HTML editor, you can also format selected text as hyperlinks in a document.

→ For more details on spellchecking, **see** "Checking Your Spelling," **p. 464**.

→ For more details on StarWriter as an HTML editor and how to use the Hyperlink formatting option, **see** Chapter 25, "Creating Web Pages with StarWriter/Web," **page 919**.

The full complement of character formatting options is available through the Character dialog (see Figure 7.1), which you can open by selecting Format, Character or right-clicking in your document and selecting Character from the context menu.

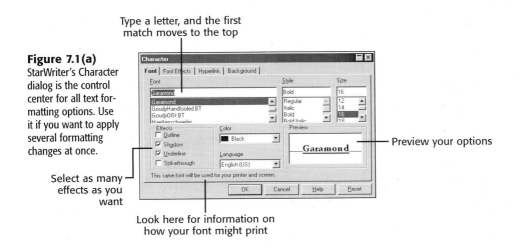

Type a letter, and the first match moves to the top

Figure 7.1(a)
StarWriter's Character dialog is the control center for all text formatting options. Use it if you want to apply several formatting changes at once.

Preview your options

Select as many effects as you want

Look here for information on how your font might print

Figure 7.1(b)

Change the spacing between characters

Kerning is available only for scalable fonts

Check if you want only individual words underlined

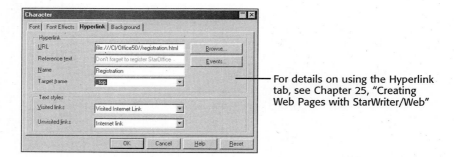

Fine-tune the superscript/subscript position

These options are available only if Underline or Strikethrough is selected on the Font tab

Figure 7.1(c)

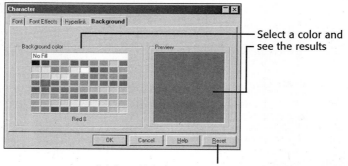

For details on using the Hyperlink tab, see Chapter 25, "Creating Web Pages with StarWriter/Web"

Figure 7.1(d)

Select a color and see the results

Click here if you want to revert to the default settings

For quick and easy formatting tasks you can also use the StarWriter context menu or the Text object bar, which supplies drop-down lists and buttons for the most frequently used character formats in documents, including font, size, style, and color. To apply any combination of the style attributes (bold, italic, or underline) to selected text, simply click the **B**, *i*, or U button or press Ctrl+B, Ctrl+I, or Ctrl+U. To add font color or highlighting, select the Font Color or Background Color button, respectively.

Table 7.1 lists the various character formatting options available in the Character dialog in StarWriter.

TABLE 7.1   CHARACTER FORMATTING AND FONT EFFECTS OPTIONS

Option	What It Does
Font	Lists the various fonts installed on your system. A font is a set of characters with a consistent, identifiable typeface such as Courier, Times New Roman, or Arial. A type font typically contains all the alphanumerics (letters and numbering), punctuation marks, special characters, and so on contained in one version of a typeface.
Style	Specifies a visual variation of a basic typeface used to create emphasis, such as regular (or normal), *italic*, **bold**, and ***bold italic.***
Size	Determines how big the text should be. Font size refers to the height of a font and is usually stated in *points*. A point is 1/72 of an inch, so a 72-point-size font can be up to an inch tall. Note that characters increase proportionally in width as they increase in height, and each font has characteristics that determine its size. (Hence, an *A* in one font may look bigger than an *A* in another font.)
Effects	Specifies appearance attributes such as ~~strikethrough~~, underline, ALL CAPS, lowercase, SMALL CAPS, Title Case, and blinking text (which can be used in combination with any other font effect).
Color	Provides a choice of 80 predefined colors that can be applied to selected text. If you have defined custom colors, using the Colors option in the Tools, Options, General category, you will have more than 80 colors available. (For more details on defining custom colors, see "Creating Custom Colors," page xx, in Chapter 3, "Getting Ready for Work.")
Spacing	Controls the amount of space that appears between characters. You can select between Standard, Expanded and Condensed, and specify a value that defines how much characters expand or condense.
Position	Controls the position of characters on an imaginary baseline, such as Super (the characters appearing above the baseline), Normal, and Sub (the characters appearing below the baseline). You can also fine-tune the relative position of the superscript and subscript relative to font size.
Hyperlink	Links selected text to specified URLs and enables you to define the text style of visited and unvisited links.
Background	Offers a choice of 80 possible colors to choose from for highlighting selected text elements.

You can format characters by first selecting the text and then applying the formatting changes. Alternatively, you can position the insertion point, select the formatting changes, and then enter the text, in which case everything you type from that point on is formatted according to your specifications until you change formatting options, press the right arrow on your keyboard (which resets the standard setting), or move the cursor to another part of the document.

CHOOSING THE RIGHT FONT FOR THE JOB

You should be aware of two points when using fonts. First, fonts are used by computers for onscreen displays and by printers for hard-copy output. In both cases, fonts are created either from bitmaps (patterns of dots) or from outlines (as defined by a set of mathematical formulas). You should note that some fonts can be used both for screen display and printing (such as TrueType fonts, an outline font format developed by Apple Computer and adopted by Microsoft Corporation); others are strictly printer fonts, and their onscreen display might vary from printed output.

Note

StarOffice will tell you if the same font will be used for your printer and screen display. Just select Character from the Text context menu or the Format menu and click the Font tab. At the bottom left of the tab, you can read if the currently selected font is a printer font, or printer and screen font.

Second, fonts are like a document's clothes: They're the first thing people see, and they convey an impression that becomes part of your document's message. Although you might often be irresistibly compelled to use many different fonts (or typefaces) in a document, it's best to refrain from cluttering your document with too many typefaces, type sizes, and effects. As a rule of thumb, follow these guidelines:

- Use a maximum of three fonts per document—one for the body text, one for headings, and one for special areas or main title.

- Select simple fonts with clean lines for the body text and headings, and reserve those cool display/effect fonts for judicious use on those occasions where you want to evoke a certain mood in the reader (for example in a title or headline). Simple fonts include serif fonts (which are characterized by small finishing strokes) for body text and sans serif fonts for headings.

- Match the type size to the importance of the message that you would like to convey. Body text typically is 10 to 12 point; indexes no smaller than 6 point; headings typically run 16, 18, or 24 point; and titles and headlines may be anywhere from 26 to 48 point.

- Avoid using italics or underling for emphasis in body text; use ordinary italics instead.

- Use restraint with visual elements, effects and colors.

Choosing the right font for a resume, invitation, or any other form of correspondence is an art. After all, there's a reason people say, "He looks good on paper." *Type* is the basic printing block of any printed page, and the font and font size you choose should enhance readability and help create an impression about the author or purpose of the document.

Note

When choosing your fonts, you should also ask yourself whether you will be sharing fonts across platforms. If you're working on the Windows platform, for example, chances are you're using True Type fonts. However, if you're sharing documents with Linux, Macintosh, or Unix users you may experience problems. For example, Mac users are more likely to work with Adobe Type formats, a different type of scalable font. When the Mac user loads your document (most likely saved as a Word 97 or Word 95 document), your fonts are likely to be replaced with new ones—what was Times New Roman or Arial on the PC may become Times or Helvetica on the Mac. As a result, text that previously fit nicely on one page now may run longer.

APPLYING CHARACTER FORMATTING

The quickest way to apply character formatting to selected text is to right-click in the workspace of your document to open the StarWriter context menu. From its submenus, you can choose the font and size you want and apply attributes such as bold, italic, underline, strikethrough, shadow, outline, superscript, and subscript. If you want to reverse your changes to the paragraph standard, select Default.

Tip #114 from
Michael & Sarah

StarWriter provides you with a quick-and-easy way for applying character formatting to individual words. Place the insertion point between two letters, and then apply the chosen character format by selecting the appropriate context menu option or by pressing its keyboard shortcut.

If you want to preview your formatting changes before applying them, change several formats at once, or make adjustments to existing ones, select Character from the StarWriter context menu (or choose Format, Character from the menu bar) to open the Character dialog. Using the Font tab, you can select a font, style, and size, and preview the results in the Preview box.

Tip #115 from
Michael & Sarah

When you're selecting fonts from the Character dialog, keep an eye on the bottom of the Font tab. StarWriter tells you if the selected font is scalable and will print just as it appears onscreen, or if it is a printer font, in which case what you see onscreen may not be what you get on paper.

The Font, Style, and Size text boxes across the top of the Font tab list the current typeface, style, and size. To select a different font, style, or size, you can either type over the existing names and numbers or select the option you want from the respective list boxes underneath. Note that fonts are listed in alphabetical order and that available styles and font sizes depend on the selected font and printer, respectively.

Tip #116 from
Michael & Sarah

You don't have to scroll through the list of Font choices if you know the name of the font or font family you're looking for. Just type the first letter of the name in the text box above the list, and the first font that matches the letter jumps to the top of the list box.

PART

II

CH

7

When you're satisfied with your selection, click OK to exit the Character dialog. If you would like to exit the dialog without accepting any changes, click Cancel. You can also always revert to the default settings without closing the dialog by clicking Reset.

ADJUSTING CHARACTER SPACING AND POSITION

If you want your printed document to look good, pay attention to the fine points of spacing between adjacent characters. The Spacing portion of the Font Effects tab provides options for varying character spacing uniformly for all characters in a selected passage (Standard, Expanded, Condensed) or by a specified amount. Because StarWriter modifies the spacing after each individual character, you can also change the spacing between two characters by selecting the first one and assigning it Expanded or Condensed attributes. In addition, you can also achieve a better letter fit by selecting Pair Kerning, which reduces the space between a pair of letters along a line of text. Note that kerning can be used only with pro-portionally spaced TrueType fonts and/or with similar scalable fonts that are larger than 12 point. As with your other formatting options, you can preview the results in the Preview box.

Note

Although using character spacing and kerning options can give your printed document a better appearance, you can't see the finer points of your formatting efforts unless you out-put your document to a 600 dpi laser printer.

Character spacing adjustments are useful when you want to achieve a particular density of type or if you want to fit a passage into a limited space (for example, if one or two lines of a one-page document spill over to the next page). Using Pair Kerning makes the most sense when used with large-size type in titles or headings. At smaller sizes, it may cause the letters to look too close together.

StarWriter also enables you to create superscripted (raised) and subscripted (lowered) text; you can do so by selecting the Super or Sub option in the Position area of the Font Effects tab. If you don't like the default formatting applied by the superscript and subscript com-mands, you can define your own and adjust the relative position and size of the raised or lowered text in relation to the current font in the Position Options area. Figure 7.2 shows various examples of character formatting with StarWriter.

ADDING IMPACT WITH ATTRIBUTES AND COLOR

StarWriter also offers a number of attributes or "special effects" that enable you to add impact and emphasis to selected characters. Using the Font and Font Effects tabs in the Character dialog, you can choose from nine effects, including outline, shadow, strikethrough, underline, all caps, lowercase, small caps, title case, and even blinking text (which is most useful for creating documents for the Web, or sending funky email with an HTML email client).

Figure 7.2
StarWriter's character formatting options enable you to make big changes without losing sight of the finer points of lettering.

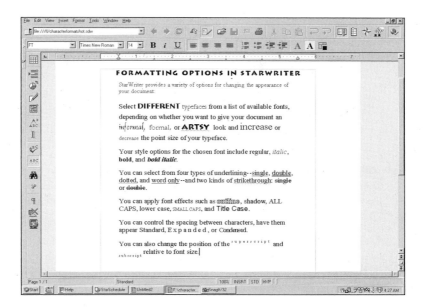

On the Font tab, you can select as many effects as you want at one time and combine them with an effect in the More Effects area on the Font Effects tab plus the blinking text effect. In addition, you can choose from three types of underlining (<u>single</u>, <u>double</u>, and <u>dotted</u>) and two types of strikethrough (~~single~~ and ~~double~~), provided you've selected Underline or Strikethrough in the Effects portion of the Font tab.

Tip #117 from *Michael & Sarah*	Because most of these effects affect the readability of your text, use them sparingly and for impact or emphasis only. Your readers will be grateful.

EXPERIMENTING WITH COLOR

Apart from using font effects, you can also make text stand out by using color—either as font color or as background (highlighting) color. The Color drop-down list on the Font tab gives you access to 80 different colors. If you know the basic color you're interested in (such as blue or green), just type the first letter or two in the box, and the first match jumps to the top of the list box. Using the Background tab, you can pick a color and preview your selection in the Preview box. To apply color to your text, you must first select the text you want to change and then select the color you want from the Character dialog.

Tip #118 from *Michael & Sarah*	If you have a color printer connected to your computer yet can't seem to get it to print your document in color, you should check the Print option on the Tools, Options, Text Document category. The Print Black option in the Contents portion of the Print tab may be selected.

Formatting with Color

 You can also use the Font Color and Highlighting buttons on the Text object bar to add color. Although applying font color and highlighting this way is faster, it may take a short time until you're fully comfortable using these buttons.

You can use either button in one of two ways: as an application tool (similar to a paint brush) or as a (floating) color palette from which to pick and choose. Sound intriguing? You bet it does. Not only is this a more time-efficient way of applying font color and highlighting, it also saves you from having to select the text you want to colorize first.

For example, a short click on either button turns your cursor into a paint bucket as soon as you move over the workspace of your document. You can then click and drag over the text you want to colorize. To turn off this function (and return to your familiar mouse pointer), you need to click the button again or press Esc.

If you want to apply a different color than the one currently associated with your "pointer brush," perform an extended-click on either button to open a floating color palette. You can pick one of the standard color choices, and then click and drag over the text you want to change as usual. The most recent color you used automatically becomes the new default color for the button. (Note that you can always tell the current color selection by looking at the *A* of the Font Color button or the highlighting behind the *A* of the Highlighting button (red and yellow are the respective defaults when you first open StarWriter).

Tip #119 from
Michael & Sarah

You can also undock the color palette by clicking its title bar and dragging it to a convenient spot on your desktop. This way, you can quickly select colors and apply them to your text. If the palette ever gets in your way or you no longer need it, click the Minimize button to reduce it to a floating title bar or click the Close (X) button, respectively.

If you select the text you want to change first, the buttons no longer double as "pointer brushes," and the text automatically changes color when you click the button or pick a color from the standard palette.

Tip #120 from
Michael & Sarah

If you want to use custom colors rather than StarOffice's standard ones, select Tools, Options, General and go to the Colors tab. Here, you can edit and name colors of your own and compare the results in the Preview box. Note, however, that once you save changes to an existing color, you won't be able to return to the original color setting (unless you reinstall StarOffice).

Formatting Paragraphs

 A paragraph is defined as a block of text ending in a paragraph mark. StarWriter places a paragraph mark in your text each time you press Enter. A paragraph mark is a hidden, nonprinting character that can be made visible on your display when you select the Nonprinting Characters On/Off button on the Main toolbar.

Paragraph formatting enables you to specify a wide range of details, including indents and spacing (between lines and paragraphs), alignment of text (left, center, right, justified) and text flow, numbering styles and options, tab settings, drop caps, and borders and shading.

To access your paragraph formatting options, select Format, Paragraph from the menu, or right-click in the StarWriter workspace and select Paragraph from the context menu. Table 7.2 lists the various character formatting options available in StarWriter.

TABLE 7.2   PARAGRAPH FORMATTING OPTIONS

Go Here	If You Want To
Indents & Spacing	Change paragraph indents and spacing between lines and paragraphs
Alignment	Adjust the alignment of your text
Text Flow	Control paragraph breaks
Numbering	Define your numbering/bullet list options
Tabs	Set precision tab stops
Drop Caps	Insert an oversized first letter ("drop capital"), or number of letters, that extends below the first line at the beginning of a paragraph
Borders	Apply borders and shading according to your specifications around the current paragraph
Background	Add a background color or graphic to the current paragraph

Tip #121 from
Michael & Sarah

Because StarWriter handles styles differently (and better) than other word processors, most notably MS Word, to move a paragraph with its formatting intact, you must select the entire paragraph through to the first letter of the following paragraph.

Note

When you combine two consecutive paragraphs that have different formats, the resulting combined paragraph retains the formatting of the first paragraph. You can combine paragraphs by pressing either Delete (if at the end of the first paragraph) or Backspace (if at the beginning of the following paragraph).

ADJUSTING INDENTS AND SPACING

A common change to paragraphs involves setting the indents and spacing between lines and paragraphs. StarWriter enables you to indent paragraphs from the left and right margins of a page, as well as adjust the indent of the first line of a paragraph in relation to that paragraph. In addition, you can adjust the amount of space between paragraphs as well as between lines within a paragraph.

SPACING BETWEEN LINES AND PARAGRAPHS

Line spacing, or *leading* (pronounced *ledding*), refers to the distance of the baseline of a line of type from the baseline of the line above it, measured in points. You should be careful that the line spacing is sufficient so that uppercase letters, *ascenders* (the top strokes of characters such as *b*, *d*, *f*, *h*, *k*, *l*, and *t*), and *descenders* (the bottom strokes of characters such as *g*, *j*, *p*, *q*, and *y*) of one line do not touch those of the line below or above.

To adjust the spacing between pairs of lines in a paragraph, right-click anywhere in a paragraph, and select Line Spacing from the StarWriter context menu. Your options include Single, 1.5 Lines, and Double. If you want more options, select Paragraph from the context menu to open the Paragraph dialog. Using the Line Spacing drop-down menu on the Indents & Spacing tab, you can now also set Proportional, At Least, Leader, and Fixed spacing as well as specify an amount for each of these options in the spinner box below. Table 7.3 explains your various line-spacing options.

Note

Line spacing is dependent on the font size. The larger the text, the larger the line spacing. General typesetting design guidelines commonly call for line spacing to be about 120 percent of the point size of the font.

Tip #122 from
Michael & Sarah

If you use varying font sizes within a given paragraph, StarWriter automatically adjusts line spacing in accordance with the largest point size. If you prefer to have the line spacing consistent throughout, select At Least and specify a value that accommodates the height of the biggest letter.

TABLE 7.3   LINE SPACING OPTIONS IN STARWRITER

Option	What It Means
Single	Default line spacing. Single spacing is usually sufficient with most text. Note also that the larger the text size, the larger the line spacing, even if you select Single.
1.5	One and a half times the default spacing.
Double	Double the default spacing.
Proportional	Proportional by 100% is the equivalent of single (default) spacing. You can adjust your spacing by going above and below this percentage.
At Least	Sets the minimum spacing that StarWriter adjusts when needed to allow for larger font sizes and graphics by the amount specified.
Leader	Adds an additional amount between the base of one line and the top of the following line by the amount specified (spacing typically is measured from base to base).
Fixed	Forces StarWriter to maintain consistent line spacing by the specified amount, regardless of the font size. (Note that the tops of characters taller than the amount specified might be cut off.)

Using the Indents & Spacing tab, you can also add extra space between the top and bottom of selected paragraphs by specifying values in the Spacing portion of the tab (see Figure 7.3). If you're working with multicolumn layouts and want to ensure that adjacent paragraphs align with their baselines, you must select the register-true option.

→ For more details on the Register-true option **see** "Aligning Text in Columns," **p. 432**.

Sets the first line indent
(here hanging) Sets the left indent Sets the right indent

Figure 7.3
On the Indents & Spacing tab, you can set numeric values for all your spacing and indenting needs and preview your changes in the area on the right—sort of. If accuracy is not an issue, you can also use the ruler to set indents.

Specify indents/hanging indents here

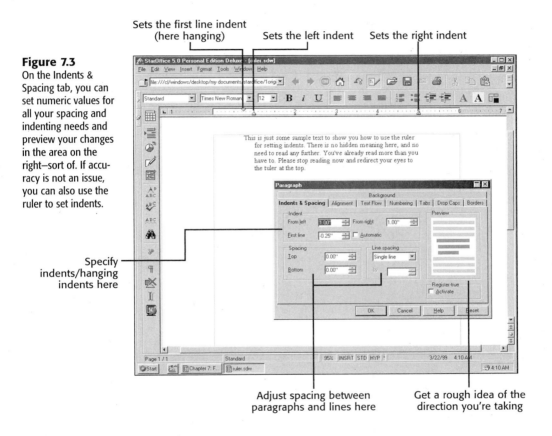

Adjust spacing between paragraphs and lines here

Get a rough idea of the direction you're taking

INDENTING PARAGRAPHS

Another common change to paragraphs involves setting indents. In the Indent portion of the Indents & Spacing tab, you can specify any additional distance from the page margin to the left or right side of a paragraph. In addition, the first line can have its own setting for the left indent. If you select Automatic, the first line is indented in relation to the font size and line spacing, independent of what has been specified in the First line box.

StarWriter also enables you to create *hanging indents*—a special type of indent in which the first line runs farther to the left than the remaining lines. To create a hanging indent, you must specify a positive value in the From Left box and a negative value in the First Line box. Note that you can create hanging indents of indented paragraphs only.

PART
II

CH
7

Tip #123 from
Michael & Sarah

If accuracy is not an issue, you can also quickly set indents with the ruler. Just click and drag the small gray triangles on the bottom left and right to adjust the left and right indents of selected paragraphs. Click and drag the triangle on the top left to adjust the indent of the first line.

If you want to quickly change the left indent, you can do so by selecting the Increase Indent and Decrease Indent buttons on the object bar. Clicking either button moves the left indent to the next tab stop in the appropriate direction.

CHANGING ALIGNMENT AND TEXT FLOW

Sometimes you might want to change the organization of paragraphs on a page to present the information in a more attractive format to the readers. In these instances, you change the alignment of paragraphs. *Alignment* refers to the placement of text on a page (or within a column) in relation to the left or right margins of the page (or column). StarWriter enables you to align individual paragraphs in one of four ways—left, right, center, and justified. Figure 7.4 shows an example of StarWriter's various paragraph formatting features at work.

Figure 7.4
StarWriter's paragraph formatting options enable you to enhance the readability and attractiveness of your document.

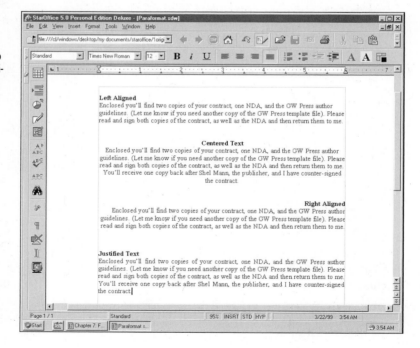

Generally, you would set the alignment of a paragraph by selecting the corresponding align button on the Text object bar; it's faster than using the Paragraph dialog. If you want to justify text, however, you have more options if you select the Paragraph dialog. Click the Alignment tab in the Paragraph dialog to specify if you want the last line of the paragraph to be left-aligned, centered, or justified. In addition, you can select to expand a single word if you choose Justify in the Last Line list box and want the only word in the last line to extend all the way across the line. Because StarWriter adjusts the spacing between the individual characters, choosing this option is advisable only if you work with narrower text columns and the word is lengthy.

Tip #124 from
Michael & Sarah

You can fool StarWriter into believing you have only one word, while in fact you have more. Just press Ctrl+spacebar to insert nonbreaking spaces between words. You can now justify, for example, the heading of a multicolumn document section.

If you really care about the look of your document, you will also learn to utilize the options on the Text Flow tab. In the Hyphenation portion of the tab, you can set hyphenation automatically or specify a minimum number of characters that is to remain at the end or beginning of a line after hyphenation is applied. In addition, you can also set the number of hyphens at the end of consecutive lines.

Note

Publishing guidelines often vary as to the number, but as a rule of thumb, don't try to have more than two hyphens consecutively, or else readers may lose the flow as their eyes try to find the right line to skip to at the end.

Turning on hyphenation is recommended when you work with justified text. If you don't select any option in this portion of the Text Flow tab, StarWriter does not hyphenate your text.

Your other text flow options work as follows:

- **Break**—Enables you to add a page or column break before or after the selected paragraph. If you select the Break, Page, and Before options, you can also select With Page Style and specify a page style and number in the respective drop-down list boxes for your new page. Select this option for major sections that should always start on a new page.

- **Don't Separate Lines**—Determines whether your paragraph will be moved in its entirety to the top of the following page or column if one or more of its lines run long. Use this option carefully because it can cause vast stretches of empty space in your document.

- **Keep with Next Paragraph**—Ensures that the selected and following paragraph will remain on the same page or in the same column. This setting is vital for most headings.

- **Orphan Control**—Moves the beginning of a paragraph to the next page or column if otherwise its beginning line(s) would be left alone at the bottom of the page. You can specify the minimum number of lines of a paragraph that are allowed at the bottom of a page or column before the paragraph in its entirety is moved to the next page. (Note that this option is not available when Don't Separate Lines is selected.)

PART
II

CH
7

■ **Widow Control**—Moves the paragraph in its entirety to a new page or column if otherwise its ending line(s) would be left alone at the top of the page. You can specify the minimum number of lines of a paragraph that are allowed at the top of a page or column before the paragraph in its entirety is moved to the next page. (Note that this option is not available when Don't Separate Lines is selected.)

SETTING AND CLEARING TABS

Tabs are useful if you want to create tables or multicolumn lists quickly. StarWriter gives you two options for setting tabs in a document. You can either use the Tabs tab in the Paragraph dialog or the ruler (provided it is turned on, of course). The easiest way to set a new tab is to use the ruler (look ahead to Figure 7.5).

Note

If you can't see the ruler in your document, your cursor may either be inside an object or table (in which case you'll temporarily "lose" your StarWriter toolbars), or the ruler view may be disabled. To show the ruler, select View, Ruler from the menu bar.

Select the paragraph you want to format; then click the little black angled icon at the left of the ruler to cycle among four types of tabs: left, right, decimal, and center. When you see the icon for the correct tab type, click the lower part of the ruler where you want your new tab to go. The same tab icon appears there, and any default tabs that may have previously existed to the left of it are removed. (When you open a new text document, StarWriter sets default center tabs at one-inch intervals, and the selected tab is an ordinary left tab.) Table 7.4 explains the various tab options.

Note

StarWriter measures tab stop positions from the left margin as set in the Page dialog, which means the actual location of your tab stops on the page change when you change the margins on your page.

TABLE 7.4   TABS IN STARWRITER

Tab Option	Entries at This Tab
Left	Extend to the right from the tab stop
Right	Extend to the left from the tab stop
Decimal	Are aligned with the specified character (such as , or . as in $1,200.50, for example)
Center	Are centered on the tab stop

To reposition a previously placed tab stop on the ruler, click and drag the tab marker to a new location. (Notice the guideline that follows the tab marker—a handy feature if you want to align a tab stop with another text element.) To remove a marker, simply click and drag it off the ruler.

The alternative to setting tabs with the ruler is the Tabs tab in the Paragraph dialog. On this tab, you can type in each tab's position with numeric precision, as well as add a symbol along which you can align entries (such as numbers) aligned with decimal tabs.

In addition, you can also assign leaders to your tabs. A leader is a string of repeated characters or dots that fill in the space between a tab stop and any text on the left. For example, if you create a table of contents and want to fill in the blank space between a heading and a page number, you can use a leader to fill in the whitespace and guide the eyes of your readers from the heading to the page number (see Figure 7.5).

Cycle through tabs   Left tab   Decimal tab   Right tab   Click to accept the new value

Figure 7.5
If you want to enter your tab stops with numeric precision, use the Tabs tab of the Paragraph dialog. If accuracy is not an issue, the ruler is by far the easiest way to set tab stops.

Enter numeric value

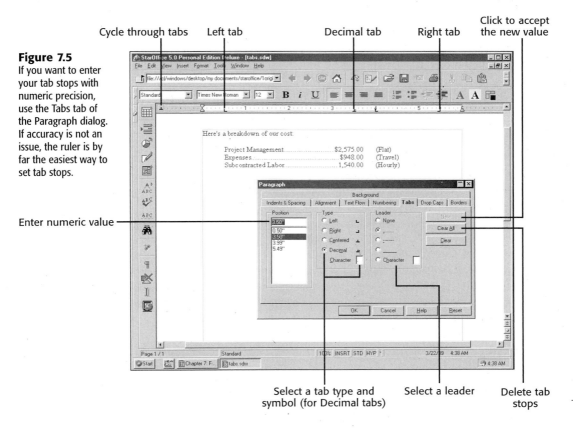

Select a tab type and symbol (for Decimal tabs)   Select a leader   Delete tab stops

Another advantage of using the Tabs tab is that if you make a mess, you can select Clear All to start all over.

Note

You can change existing tabs by selecting their position and reassign a new tab type or leader. However, you can't change the position of an existing tab without first clearing its current position and then adding a new one. (But you can drag the marker on the ruler if you exit the Paragraph dialog.)

FORMATTING DROP CAPS

Magazine and newspaper articles as well as the chapters of a novel often begin with a drop cap, a large initial letter at the start of a paragraph that drops into the line or lines of text below. Combined with other layout choices, drop caps can be an effective means to pull the readers into the text. Using the Drop Caps tab in the Paragraph dialog, you can specify drop cap settings and styles. You can specify how many letters should be dropped, how many lines they should be dropped, and how much distance appears between the drop cap and the adjacent, indented text.

Using the Contents area of the Drop Caps tab, you can also enter new text or characters that will replace the existing drop cap(s). For example, you can enter a symbol and then select a corresponding (Symbol) character style from the Text Style drop-down list. When you click OK, StarWriter places the first character in the paragraph as a shaded letter (don't worry, the shading won't print), dropping it according to the settings that you specified.

Note

The font of your drop cap is determined by the font of the paragraph and cannot be changed after it has been placed. However, you can use the Text Style drop-down list box at the bottom of the tab to select a predefined style for each drop cap—that way you'll get some variety.

ADDING BORDERS AND BACKGROUND COLOR

You might also find borders useful if you want to emphasize a particular portion of your text. Using the Borders tab of the Paragraph dialog, you can choose from various line and shadow styles, and tell the program where you want the border to appear. StarWriter provides you with a set of Presets (or samples) that you can use as building blocks for your own border design. To get a general idea of what the final border will look like, you can use the Preview area of the tab to create your borders and shading. You can add or subtract borders by clicking the little black arrows at the end of lines, specify the distance between text and borders, and change the size and colors of your lines and shadow style. Figure 7.6 shows the Borders tab settings and commands with a border under construction.

Tip #125 from
Michael & Sarah

If a plain old border without any fancy formatting or background color suffices, you can also extend-click the Insert button on the Main toolbar and select the Frame icon. Your cursor changes into a plus symbol (+), and you can quickly draw a frame around a text block of your choice.

Select a line style   Select a shadow style

Figure 7.6
Designing borders has
never been this easy.
Just click and select
until you're satisfied.

Select a Preset

Click to add or
subtract a line

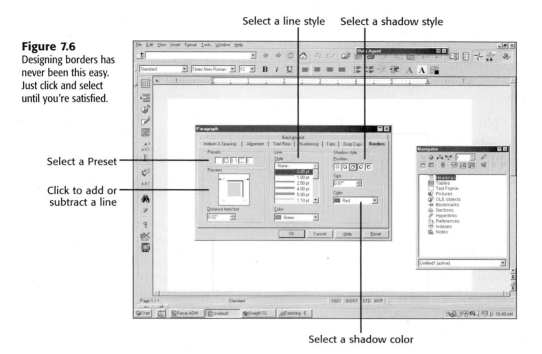

Select a shadow color

If you feel the final results are missing something, you can try adding a color or graphic to your (bordered) text.

The quickest way to add color to the background of the current or selected paragraph(s) is to click the Background Color button on the Text object bar and then select a color of your choice from the color palette. As soon as you click into a color square, the color is applied to the background of your paragraph(s). To remove a color, select the white square (or swatch).

Tip #126 from
Michael & Sarah

As with the Font Color and Highlighting buttons, you can undock the color palette by clicking its title bar and dragging it anywhere on your desktop.

Using the Background tab in the Paragraph dialog, you can not only preview the various colors first, but also select a graphic from StarOffice's vast clip art and graphics gallery or even your own archives. You need to follow these steps to add a graphic to the background of selected text:

1. Open the Paragraph dialog, and select Graphic from the As drop-down list on the Background tab. The Background tab switches from the color into the Graphic mode.

2. Click Browse to find the graphic you want to use as background on your system or on a network. You can select a graphic from the StarOffice Gallery subfolders or pick a graphic or photo of your own. Then click OK.

3. (Optional) Select Link if you want to link the graphic with the document.

4. Specify how you want the graphic to appear in the background. In the Type portion of the Background graphic tab, you can specify whether you want the graphic to show up in a certain location (Position), in which case you can click any point in the rectangular area; the graphic will appear relative to your choice in your text. Alternatively, you can select Area (which stretches the graphic across the entire background) or Tile (if you want it to appear in a pattern similar to the tiles on your bathroom wall).

5. Select OK. Or, as with all the other tabs, if you've changed your mind about your selection, click Reset, and you will lose all changes made during the current Paragraph dialog session.

If you want to remove a graphic, press Ctrl+Z or turn off the Graphic mode by selecting Color in the As box and click OK. If you want to remove a background color, select No Fill above the color palette.

Note

You can apply only one type of formatting to any given paragraph. You have to decide between color or graphic.

FORMATTING PAGES

Most of StarWriter's essential layout settings are contained in the Page dialog. Using this dialog, you can control the appearance of each page for the entire document, including printer orientation, margins, and layout. Table 7.5 lists the Page Formatting options in StarWriter.

TABLE 7.5   PAGE FORMATTING OPTIONS

Go Here	If You Want To
Organizer	Switch the current page style
Page	Set margins, paper format, and orientation, and change page layout and pagination style
Background	Add a background color or graphic to the current page
Header	Specify headers for your document
Footer	Specify footers for your document
Borders	Apply borders and shading according to your specifications
Columns	Use a multicolumn layout
Footnote	Add footnotes and separator lines to your document

Note

Unlike formatting changes in the Character and Paragraph dialog, changes in the Page Style dialog cannot be reversed after you click OK by pressing Ctrl+Z or selecting Edit, Undo. You have to reopen the dialog and make the appropriate changes manually. Thus, if you're not sure about the changes you made, hesitate for a moment before selecting OK. With the dialog box still open, you can always revert to the previous defaults by selecting Reset.

SETTING YOUR BASIC LAYOUT OPTIONS

If you want to set up only a basic layout (as in a memo or letter, for example), all you ever need is the Page tab, and perhaps the Borders tab, of the Page Style dialog. Using the Page tab, you can set the margins, size, orientation, and page numbering style of your document.

Tip #127 from
Michael & Sarah

You can also use the AutoPilot wizard to quickly set up letters, faxes, memos, or agendas. For more details **see**, "Creating Documents and Templates with the AutoPilot," **page 253**, Chapter 6, "Creating and Editing Text Documents".

In the Margins area, you can enter a numeric value to determine the distance between the top and bottom of the page and the first or last printed lines. You can also enter a numeric value to determine the distance between the left and right edges of the paper, and the left and right edges of the printed lines.

In addition, you should select a desired paper size in the Paper Format area. Your options include Letter, Legal, A2, A3, A4, A5, B4, B5, B6, C4, C5, C6, C65, DL, Tabloid, and User (defined). Looking at the Width and Height boxes, you can tell the dimension of your current selection or define your own (if you select User). In the area next to the Paper Size list box, you can also specify the orientation of your document. Text documents typically use the Portrait orientation (default). However, if your document consists of multicolumn lists, tables, or charts, you might want to consider Landscape so that your columns and cells don't end up being too narrow.

If you intend to add page numbering to your document, you can select a style from the Numbering drop-down list.

In the Page Layout area of this tab, you can select what pages of your document will be affected by the current formatting changes. Your options include All, Mirrored, Right, and Left.

Note

On Mirrored pages, you force StarWriter to mirror margins on facing pages. You use this option if you want to print on both sides of a page.

The Borders tab in the Page Style dialog has the same options as the one in the Paragraph dialog. When you apply borders and shading to pages, the border is drawn around the margins of your pages.

PART

II

CH

7

ADDING HEADERS, FOOTERS, AND FOOTNOTES

Headers and footers refer to the printed matter added at the top or bottom of every page in a document, such as document title, section title, author name, or page number. Using the Header and Footer tabs (which are virtually identical) in the Page Style dialog, you can turn the header and footer option on or off, specify the amount of spacing between the header/footer and the main part of the document, select a fixed height for the header area, and turn the AutoFit option on (default) or off. When AutoFit is on, StarWriter automatically extends the header/footer area depending on the size of the header content. This capability is helpful when you plan to experiment with different formatting options.

Note

Unlike in other word processing documents, headers/footers in StarOffice are not printed in the top and bottom margins but in the main part of the document. You never have to be afraid that your headers/footers will get cut off when you reduce the top and bottom margin settings of your page.

In addition, you can specify left and right header/footer margins, and select whether the same header content should appear on the left and right pages. If you select More, the Borders/Background dialog opens. It enables you to add borders, shading, color, or even a graphic to the header/footer.

→ Adding borders, background colors, and graphics to headers and footers is no different than adding the same to paragraphs or pages. For more details, **see** "Adding Borders and Background Color," **p. 278**.

The actual content of the header/footer has to be entered directly into the header and footer area of your document. You type and format text in headers/footers the same way you type text in the main part of the document. You can also insert fields and other objects into headers and footers as you would in the rest of the document. Natural choices for fields in header and footer areas include the Page Numbers and Page Count fields as well as Author, Title, and Date among others.

→ For more details on headers/footers and fields **see** "Working with Fields," **p. 350**, and "Adding Headers and Footers," **p. 381**.

To delete a header/footer, simply turn off the feature (by deselecting the Header/Footer on option). However, be aware that any previously entered header/footer content is irrecoverably lost when you turn off this option.

If you're working on research papers or other long documents, you might also find a need for footnotes. Using the Footnote tab, you can specify the size of the footnote area, and the position, length, weight, and spacing of a separator line that separates the footnote from the main part of the document.

→ For more details on working with footnotes, **see** "Inserting Notes, Footnotes, and Endnotes," **p. 384**.

ADDING BACKGROUND PAGE COLOR AND GRAPHICS

Adding background color or graphics to pages is no different than adding color or graphics to selected paragraphs (see the previous section "Adding Borders and Background Color"). In case your document contains both paragraph and page background formatting, you should note that any instance of paragraph-style background formatting is nontransparent and will be placed "on top" of your page background formatting.

CREATING NUMBERED AND BULLETED LISTS

Numbered and bulleted lists are, technically speaking, indented paragraphs that start with a number or symbol, hanging-indent style. You can use these lists to detail the steps involved in a procedure (numbered) or the features of a product (bulleted).

You can create numbered and bulleted lists in two main ways. You can have StarWriter number them as you type or you can select already written text and then apply numbering and bullets manually. If you want StarWriter to apply numbering as you type, all you have to do is type "1." (without quotation marks) followed by a space and then the desired text. When you press Enter, StarWriter automatically creates a numbered list for the first and all consecutive items. To exit the Numbering list mode and return to your regular body text, press Enter twice after the last numbered item.

> **Note**
>
> StarWriter's Numbering/Bullets feature also works with tables in documents.

 The quickest way to add numbering and bullets is to use the Numbering and Bullets icons on the object bar. Click either one once to switch on the command; click again to switch it off. When the command is active, it turns every consecutive line into a number or bullet when you press Enter.

If you want to convert existing text into numbered or bulleted lists, you first have to select the text; then you can apply either command.

> **Tip #128 from**
> *Michael & Sarah*
>
> You can also use automatic numbering; simply type a few words and press F12 or Shift F12 —your text automatically turns into a numbered or bulleted item, respectively. When you press Enter, every consecutive line is turned into a numbered/bulleted item as well. To exit automatic numbering, press F12/Shift+F12 again or press Enter twice after the last numbered/bullet item.

If you would like to have more variety in your numbering options, you can also select Format, Numbering/Bullets from the menu bar. The Numbering/Bullets dialog gives you a series of options for selecting the style of numbering (from the Numbering tab) or bullets

PART

II

CH

7

(from the Bullets and Pictures tabs). The Outline tab lists a series of numbering schemes. Using the Position and Customize tabs, you can adjust the Numbering alignment and the distance between numbers/bullets and text, and between borders and text (if applicable). You also can change the default indents. Using the Customize tab, you can make changes to the existing bullets, numbers, and pictures and assign new symbols.

Note

You get different instances of the Customize tab, depending on the type of numbering selected in the Numbering drop-down list on the Customize tab.

Tip #129 from
Michael & Sarah

If you're working with various levels or hierarchies of numbers and bullets, you can assign different numbers and bullets or graphics for different levels in the hierarchy. Just select the corresponding level you want to assign different numbering or bullets to, and then make your selection.

USING THE NUMBERING OBJECT BAR

After you've already created numbered or bulleted lists, you can also make changes quickly by using the Numbering object bar. Just click in the list; then click the small arrow on the right of the Text object bar to switch to the Numbering object bar (if it doesn't appear on its own). Table 7.6 lists the various icons of the Numbering object bar and their functions.

TABLE 7.6   USING THE NUMBERING OBJECT BAR

Name	Icon	Description
No Numbering		Turns off numbering or bullets for the selected paragraph
Promote		Promotes selected item(s)
Demote		Demotes selected item(s)
Promote with Subpoints		Promotes selected item(s), including its subitems
Demote with Subpoints		Demotes selected item(s), including its subitems
Paragraph without Numbering		Adds a new paragraph to the existing level
Move Up		Moves selected item(s) up
Move Down		Moves selected item(s) down
Move Up with Subpoints		Moves selected item(s), including subitem(s), up
Move Down with Subpoints		Moves selected item(s), including subitem(s), down
Restart Numbering		Restarts numbering from the selected item
Numbering/Bullets		Opens the Numbering/Bullets dialog

Tip #130 from
Michael & Sarah

If you're working with automatic Numbering/Bullets, you can turn off the function by pressing Enter twice.

GENERATING MULTILEVEL LISTS

Using the Numbering object bar, you can quickly generate multilevel lists (see Figure 7.7). To do so, follow these steps:

1. Type the list, pressing Enter after each item. You don't have to worry yet about which item is part of what level in the list hierarchy.

2. Select all items in the list.

3. Open the Numbering/Bullets dialog, make a selection, and click OK.

4. Select the item(s) you want to demote; then click the Demote button on the Numbering object bar.

Tip #131 from
Michael & Sarah

Be sure to turn off Consecutive Numbering in the All Levels portion of the Customize tab when you're working with multilevel lists.

Numbering object bar

Figure 7.7
Using the Numbering object bar enables you to quickly generate multilevel lists.

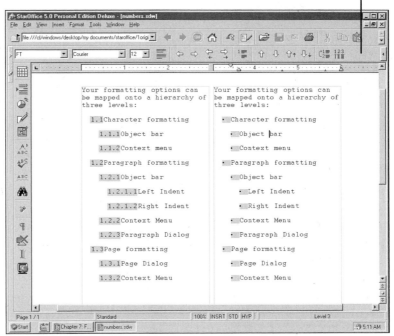

NUMBERING NONCONSECUTIVE PARAGRAPHS IN SEQUENCE

When you need to alternate numbered and unnumbered paragraphs, you have two options. When you are using automatic numbering, switch to the Numbering toolbar, select the Add a New Paragraph command to insert a new paragraph within the same level hierarchy, and continue typing. Repeat as often as needed. Press Enter when you're ready to continue with the next highest number, and the new paragraph will pick up in sequence where you left off two or more paragraphs ago.

If you've already typed your text and are now selecting and numbering paragraphs by hand, you can always restart numbering by selecting the numbering tab in the Paragraph dialog. Using the Numbering tab gives you the option to restart numbering with a specified number (as well as select a numbering or list style for the current paragraph and include the current paragraph in line numbering). Select Restart at this paragraph, and specify a number in the Start With box.

Tip #132 from
Michael & Sarah

If a numbered/bulleted list item runs two paragraphs rather than one, bring every paragraph into a numbered/bulleted list, then press Backspace at the beginning of the paragraph which shall not have a number/bullet   you'll still have a list with consecutive numbering/bullets, except that one item now consists of two paragraphs.

Tip #133 from
Michael & Sarah

Using this option, you can also start a numbering sequence with a number other than 1.

SPEEDING UP FORMATTING WITH SHORTCUTS

StarOffice has its own set of default keyboard shortcuts for the most common formatting tasks. They are easier to use when you're typing than removing your hands from the keyboard and navigating to the Format menu or object bar. Using these shortcuts toggles the formatting option on or off. Table 7.7 lists the default shortcut keys you can use for applying character and paragraph formatting.

TABLE 7.7   SHORTCUT KEYS FOR CHARACTER/PARAGRAPH FORMATTING

Format	Shortcut
Bold	Ctrl+B
Italic	Ctrl+I
Underline	Ctrl+U
Double Underline	Ctrl+D
Superscript	Ctrl+Shift+P
Single line spacing	Ctrl+1

Format	Shortcut
Double spacing	Ctrl+2
1.5 spacing	Ctrl+5
Left-aligned	Ctrl+L
Centered	Ctrl+E
Right-aligned	Ctrl+R
Justified	Ctrl+J
Manual page break	Ctrl+Enter
Nonbreaking space	Ctrl+spacebar
Autonumbering on/off	F12
Autobullets on/off	Shift+F12

Tip #134 from
Michael & Sarah

You can assign your own keyboard shortcuts if you find yourself frequently using other character formats for which no default shortcuts are available. The Keyboard tab in the Configuration dialog gives you numerous options to assign new keyboard shortcuts and reassign existing ones. For more details, see the "Customizing Keyboard Shortcuts" section in Chapter 3, "Getting Ready for Work."

USING AUTOFORMAT

StarWriter has an integrated AutoFormat command that works in conjunction with AutoCorrect to catch common typos and replace custom styles, numbering, quotation marks, and more. You can use AutoFormat while typing, or you can run AutoFormat after you've finished creating your document. To turn the AutoFormat feature on or off, select Format, AutoFormat, While Typing from the menu bar. To run AutoFormat individually after you're done typing, select Format, AutoFormat, Format Document.

New with StarOffice 5.1, you can also choose to run AutoFormat and review your changes. When you select Format, AutoFormat, Format Document and Review Changes, StarWriter formats your document and then alerts you with the AutoFormat dialog box that the formatting process is completed. You can then click Accept All or Reject All to accept or reject all autoformatting changes; or you can click Review Changes, in which case StarWriter opens the Accept or Reject AutoFormat Changes dialog.

Using the List tab of the dialog, you'll see a four-column list of changes that informs you about the type of change (Action), the author of the document (Author), the time and date when the changes were made (Date), and an explanatory comment that elaborates on the action that occured. You can now individually select each item and then click Accept or Reject, depending if you want to accept the autoformatting change or restore the original format. If the list of changes is too long, you can switch to the Filter tab of this dialog and filter the list of changes according to Date, Author (if more than one are listed), Action, or comment. When you've gone through the list, StarWriter automatically returns you to your document.

To set your AutoCorrect/AutoFormat options, select Tools, AutoCorrect/AutoFormat from the menu bar. Table 7.8 lists some common AutoFormat options that you can apply to the entire document.

TABLE 7.8   AUTOFORMAT OPTIONS IN THE AUTOCORRECT/AUTOFORMAT DIALOG

Option	Description
Use Replacement Table	Corrects common typos and automatically replaces certain letters or letter combinations with a special character or symbol (for example, type (C) to insert a copyright symbol).
Correct TWo INitial CApitals	Changes an accidentally entered second initial capital letter to a lowercase letter.
Capitalize First Letter of Every Sentence	Capitalizes the first letter after a period (which is understood to mark the end of a previous sentence).
Automatic *Bold* and _Underline_	Reformats expressions framed by an asterisk on either side in boldface and those framed by underscores with underlining. This feature is helpful when you're working with ASCII text, which doesn't contain any special formatting, and thus forces people to use another standard to create emphasis in text. As soon as you import an ASCII text file, StarWriter reformats ASCII standards for "formatting" into regular word processing standards.
Detect URL	Formats expressions that appear to be URL addresses as hyperlinks. Use it cautiously, as there is a possibility of false alarms.
Replace 1st with 1st	Applies superscript character formatting to the *st*.
Replace 1/2 with [bf:1/2]	Inserts a fraction character in place of a fraction entered from the keyboard.
Replace dashes	Replaces two hyphens (--) with an em dash.
Remove Blank Paragraphs	Does just what it says—removes blank paragraphs.
Replace Bullets With	Has AutoFormat automatically change the bullet character.
Replace Standard Quotes with Custom Quotes	Changes straight quotation marks to quotation marks that you defined on the Custom Quotes tab in the AutoCorrect dialog.

If you want to disable certain AutoFormat options, you must deselect each option in the Options tab.

Tip #135 from *Michael & Sarah*	You can also undo any individual instances of autocorrection by using the standard Edit menu Undo command (Ctrl+Z).

→ For more details on customizing AutoCorrect, **see** the section "Automating Text Entries with AutoText," **p. 240**.

TROUBLESHOOTING

Can StarWriter number the lines in normal text?

Not yet. However, there is a workaround to achieve consecutive numbering of lines—by pressing Enter at the end of every line, each line is formatted as a single paragraph. These one line paragraphs can then be continuously numbered via the Numbering icon in the Text object bar. If an existing text is to be numbered, select it as a block and activate the paragraph numbering as above. Select Format, Numbering/Bullets to define the type and format of your numbering.

How can I turn off automatic numbering?

To turn off automatic numbering, select Format, AutoFormat and select While Typing (to remove the check mark next to it). This turns off all AutoFormat functions. Alternatively, you can also select Tools, AutoCorrect/AutoFormat and go to the Options tab in the AutoCorrect dialog. Here you can individually choose which options to disable by clicking in the squares with the cross. In this case, click Apply Numbering. (Note, you may have to click Help first for the change to take effect.)

How can I insert bullets in the middle of a nubmered text without the numbering starting at 1 again?

Here's what you need to do:

1. Start the numbering.
2. In the paragraph where you want the bullets to begin, click the bullets icon on the Text object bar twice—once to turn of the numbering, twice to turn on the bullets.
3. Insert the bullets.
4. In the paragraph where you want to continue the numbering, click the Numbering icon on the object bar twice.
5. The numbering starts with "1." To assign a different number, go to Format, Nubmering/Bullets and click the Options button on the Numbering tab.
6. In the Start At box, you can enter the number with which you want to continue numbering. Click OK to confirm the settings and again to exit the dialog.

CHAPTER **8**

Using Styles and Templates

In this chapter

WORKING WITH STYLES AND TEMPLATES

It's quite possible to use StarWriter day in and day out and never learn about the flexibility of styles or about any templates other than the standard default template StarWriter uses. Do yourself a favor and become accustomed to these tools. Styles and templates can make your life much, much easier.

For example, suppose you typed up a report and painstakingly formatted headings, sections, paragraphs, and lists using the usual menu commands or object bar buttons. You present the finished document to your committee, but they don't like your formatting choices and send you back to the drawing board. If you had used styles, all you would have to do in that instance is redefine (or edit) the styles in question—which can be done in a matter of seconds—and the desired changes would take effect immediately.

Styles are the key to efficient, consistent document formatting. If you use styles, you can save time that you might otherwise spend formatting your documents, plus you have the added advantage of giving your documents an agreeable look. For example, you might routinely apply a half-inch left indent, a first-line indent, and Times New Roman font to paragraphs in a document. You can define this set of formatting attributes as a style, which you can then apply to any paragraphs in a document with a single operation.

And if you really wanted to work smarter, you would save a routinely used document as a template. When using a template, you can be certain of the consistency of elements and layout from document to document (such as a cover letter or invoice, for example), without having to re-create that type of document from scratch. As with styles, you can edit and modify templates to make quick changes if needed.

Note

All other StarOffice document types use templates as well, and some–including StarCalc, StarMath, StarMail, and StarImpress–use styles of different kinds. With StarOffice's desktop integration, the skills you learn creating styles and templates in StarWriter translate easily to these other application modules.

SO WHAT ARE STYLES AND TEMPLATES?

In a nutshell, styles and templates are tools that enable you to mold the appearance of routinely produced documents in an easy and efficient manner. A *style* is a collection of character formatting and paragraph settings that are stored under different names. Styles are saved along with the active document, but can also be copied to a specific template.

A *template* is essentially a standard document stored with the special .vor extension. Templates typically consist of a collection of styles, but can also contain any boilerplate text that you want included in each variation of a document that you create (see Figure 8.1). Templates can also include additional information such as layout, custom keyboard and toolbar assignments, and macros. In StarWriter, you can convert any document into a template by saving it as a StarWriter template file. Templates are stored in the Template folder of the StarOffice root directory.

Note

StarOffice occasionally betrays its German roots when it comes to file (as well as item and command) naming conventions. This is one such instance. "Vor" comes from "Vorlage," which is German for template.

Personal data fields (linked to User Data information)

Figure 8.1
StarOffice comes with a series of ready-made templates that you can use or tweak for your personal or business purposes.

Fields (linked to Address Book for mail merge)

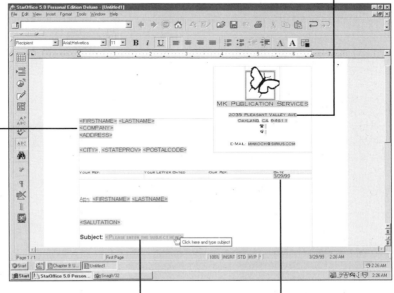

Text fields for messages   Date field (shows current date)

WHY USE STYLES AND TEMPLATES?

Since formatting can be very time-intensive, you're better off using styles when working on long and complex documents. StarOffice comes with a slew of features and ready-made styles that make formatting long documents a breeze. And if needed, you can easily add styles of your own to StarWriter's extensive catalog of built-in styles.

Besides making formatting your document easier and speedier, styles also give you an edge when revising document formats. When you change the formatting in the style, all text that is formatted with this style will automatically inherit these changes, too. For example, you may decide to add a border and shading to all paragraphs with a particular style. By modifying the definition of the style to include the border and shading, you automatically add the border and shading to all paragraphs in all documents that use that particular style.

If you want to carry consistency of document design beyond the level of styles, you'll want to make use of templates, too. Templates provide a quick way for tailoring a document and ensure that documents based on the same template share consistent common elements. You can use templates both as boilerplates and molds for routinely created documents. Out of the box, StarOffice ships with a variety of templates that you can use and modify for your own personal or business purposes.

You select a template whenever you create a new document. And since every template includes a collection of styles, it's important to understand styles before you begin working with templates.

FORMATTING WITH STYLES

Formatting refers to the act of creating and shaping the appearance of text with a word processor or desktop publishing program (DTP) and includes defining paper size, margins, fonts, effects, and indents and spacing, among many other options.

As mentioned in Chapter 7, "Formatting Text Documents," there are two kinds of formatting: direct formatting and style formatting. *Direct formatting* is what you do when you use the commands on the Format menu, keyboard shortcuts, or object bar buttons to apply attributes to a specific selection of text or a paragraph. Any formatting changes you make to your document will only be valid for the current selection. You can remove direct formatting any time by selecting the formatted text, and then choosing Default from the StarWriter shortcut menu. The selection will be reset to the standard paragraph default.

Style formatting, by contrast, relies on styles to do the formatting for you. Styles are collections of many different formatting attributes that you can apply all at once to a text, paragraph, or page selection. Style formatting dictates the format of the current selection and overrules any instance of direct formatting.

Tip #136 from
Michael & Sarah

To clean your document of any traces of direct formatting, press Ctrl+A and select Default from the StarWriter context menu.

UNDERSTANDING YOUR STYLE FORMATTING OPTIONS

StarWriter offers the following five varieties of styles:

- **Text (Character)**—Text styles control the appearance of text on the level of characters and punctuation, including font, font effects, and color. You can apply text styles to individual words or phrases for emphasis or style. Text styles will retain their attributes even if you change paragraph, numbering, frame, or page styles.

- **Paragraph**—Paragraph styles control the appearance of text on the level of, well, paragraphs. For StarWriter, a paragraph is defined as any unit of text that ends with a special symbol known as a paragraph mark. Typical paragraph formatting attributes include indents and spacing, alignment, tab settings, text flow, drop caps, borders, and background color, as well as fonts and font effects.

  Using paragraph styles, you can also define the style of the next paragraph. For example, you could specify that a heading style should always be followed by a regular or body text style. Thus, each time you press Enter after applying the heading style, the next paragraph will automatically show the attributes of the style that is defined as body text.

Tip #137 from	You can use the Applied Styles drop-down list on the left of the Text object bar to view a list
Michael & Sarah	of applied paragraph styles in the current document.

- **Numbering**—Numbering styles are, technically speaking, a special case of paragraph attributes. The reason StarWriter puts them into a class of their own is that numbering (and bullet) styles require a different set of commands and controls than ordinary paragraph styles. Numbering styles are used in lists and often involve different outline levels while still appearing as one coherent unit. Like paragraph styles, numbering styles control the appearance of units of text that end with a paragraph mark.

- **Frame**—Frame styles control the appearance of text and graphics within an invisible rectangular boundary of some type on a page. A *frame* is the graphic equivalent of a paragraph; it typically encloses an object (for example, graphic, text, or OLE object), but has no other influence on the appearance of the object attributes as such.

- **Page**—Page styles govern the overall appearance of your document. Typical page formatting attributes include paper size and orientation, margins and layout, headers and footers, and background color and graphics. Think of page styles as the ultimate reference frame that controls the overall flow and positioning of text onscreen or in print.

Note

StarOffice uses the term *frame* to refer to two different types of objects in the program:

- An invisible rectangular bounding box that surrounds pictures, OLE objects, special non-body text, and some other kinds of special objects. The Insert, Text Box or Picture or Object commands all insert this type of frame.

- A *floating frame*, which you use in conjunction with Web pages. The Insert, Floating Frame command inserts a floating frame.

APPLYING STYLES

Using styles provides an easy way to control all aspects of paragraph formatting. You can apply styles throughout your documents in a variety of ways. You can select styles from the various lists of available styles in the Stylist (press F11 or select Format, Stylist) or Style Catalog (Press Ctrl+Y or select Format, Styles & Templates, Catalog). Once you've applied styles to a document, you can also select styles from the Applied Styles drop-down list on the Text object bar. Or, you can use the Fill Format mode, which you can use to quickly format selected text.

Because StarWriter already comes with a solid selection of default styles, putting them to work is as easy as choosing the desired style from the list of available styles in the Stylist.

Tip #138 from Michael & Sarah	If you don't like the style you applied, remember you can easily undo it by pressing Ctrl+Z or selecting the Undo command on the Edit menu or function bar.

USING THE STYLIST

 The Stylist is a marvelous tool that enables you to assign styles quickly to selected text and objects. Place your cursor inside the text you want to format and double-click the desired style in the list of available styles in the Stylist. The selected text will automatically be formatted according to the attributes that have been assigned to that particular style.

Tip #139 from Michael & Sarah	You can quickly apply the same style to a number of items in your document by using the Fill Format mode. For more details see the section "Working Faster in Fill Format Mode" later in this chapter.

Using the Stylist, you can quickly format entire documents in whichever way you choose. You can also add to StarWriter's already extensive catalog of styles by formatting an object according to your desires, and then importing it into the Stylist. If so desired, you can also update existing styles with a click of the mouse and still have time left to preview the results in Page view.

Tip #140 from Michael & Sarah	Like the Navigator, the Stylist is a dockable tools window that you can open and close like the Explorer or Beamer. To dock it, press Ctrl while dragging it toward the edge where you want to dock it. To make it float again, press Ctrl while double-clicking the lower border of its title bar.

Here's a breakdown of the various buttons and lists in the Stylist (see Figure 8.2):

- **Available Styles**—A click on these buttons opens the corresponding Paragraph, Text, Frame, Page, and Numbering list of available styles. For a filtered view, use these buttons in combination with the Categories drop-down list at the bottom of the Stylist.

- **Fill Format Mode**—This feature works similarly to Microsoft Word's Format Painter. Select the desired style, click the Fill Format button, move cursor to the text you want to change, and click to apply the format changes. Fill Format is a toggle button, which means the Fill Format mode is on until you click the button again.

- **New Style by Example**—Click this button to create a new style based on the selected style in your current document. Using this function opens the Create Style dialog in which you'll be asked to enter a name for the new style.

- **Update Style**—Click this button to overwrite a selected style in the Stylist with the current or selected style in the workspace.

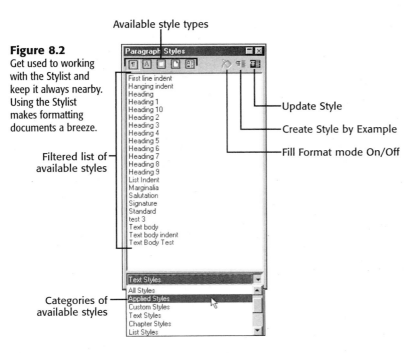

Available style types

Figure 8.2
Get used to working with the Stylist and keep it always nearby. Using the Stylist makes formatting documents a breeze.

Filtered list of available styles

Update Style

Create Style by Example

Fill Format mode On/Off

Categories of available styles

In order to keep a better overview, the Stylist also contains a list of style categories that you can access through the drop-down list at the bottom of the Stylist window. Use this list in combination with the style type buttons to filter the various lists of available styles and thus make finding a desired style easier. Note that most categories are only available when the Paragraph Style list is active, including Automatic (StarWriter takes its best guess as to what styles you may need for the current document) Text, Chapter, List, Index, Special, HTML, and Conditional Styles. When Conditional Styles is selected, StarWriter lists the styles that make most sense based on the context of the document. The following categories are shared by all types of style:

- **All Styles**—Lists all available styles for the currently selected style type.
- **Applied Styles**—Shows the styles that are used in the current document. You can also access these styles through the Applied Styles list on the object bar.
- **Custom Styles**—Lists all user-defined styles available in the current document.
- **Hierarchical**—List dependencies of available styles of selected type. You can click the plus symbol (+) to expand levels.

Tip #141 from
Michael & Sarah

Use the Hierarchical List view if you want to see interdependencies of styles. Dependent styles are listed in the Expanded Tree view.

WORKING FASTER IN FILL FORMAT MODE

 StarWriter enables you to apply the same style to a number of items in your document quickly when switching into Fill Format mode. You switch in and out of this mode by clicking the Fill Format button in the Stylist. When using Fill Format, your mouse pointer will change into a paint bucket when it's over the workspace.

To speed up common formatting tasks, turn on the Fill Format button (the one with the paint bucket) and select the desired style from the list of available styles. Next, move your cursor over your workspace, and then select and click the text you want to format. With each click, StarWriter applies the selected style in the Stylist to the selected text in the current document.

USING THE OBJECT BAR

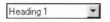 When applying styles, you can also select styles from the Applied Styles drop-down list on the Text object bar. However, as the name suggests, this list contains only those styles that you have already used in the current document. If you would like to use another style, you have to return to the Stylist.

DEFINING A STYLE

StarWriter provides two basic methods for creating or defining styles. In the first method, you create a style (almost) from scratch with the New command, which is available from the Stylist context menu or the Style Catalog (Format, Styles & Templates, Catalog).

You can also create new styles by example. In plain English, this means that you can define a style based on existing text that already has all the desired formatting. This method is easier, but you can be sure of exactly what you are getting only if you use the first method.

CREATING STYLES FROM SCRATCH

 Each new document in StarWriter comes with standard sets of predefined styles. However, you can add to the existing catalog of styles by creating styles of your own.

When creating new styles, you have two options. You can either use the Stylist (press F11 or select Format, Stylist) or you can use the Style Catalog (press Ctrl+Y or select Format, Styles & Templates, Catalog). In both instances you follow the same steps:

1. Select the list of style types to which you want to add and right-click in the list and select New from the context menu (Stylist), or click the New button (Style Catalog). Depending on which list you're adding to, you'll see the Organizer tab of the Paragraph, Text, Frame, Page or Numbering Style dialog.

2. Fill in the formalities on the Organizer tab, including Name and Category of the new style, and specify whether the new style should be based on an already existing style or followed by a different style.

3. Once the formalities are out of the way, select the desired attributes for the style using the available tabs. If you make a mistake, you can click Reset or Standard at any time to revert all changes to the default values of the current style or standard, respectively.

4. When satisfied with your choices, select OK.

Table 8.1 lists the various formatting options you have when creating a new style, divided by type. Most of these options are also available when you select the Character, Paragraph, and Page items from the Format menu; the Numbering/Bullet item from the Tools menu; or the Text Box item from the Insert menu. There is one notable exception: When creating paragraph styles, you have the option to create conditional styles.

→ For more details on these formatting options, **see** the corresponding sections on character, paragraph, page, and numbering formatting starting on **p. 261**

→ For text box formatting options, **see** "Working with Text Boxes," **p. 435**.

TABLE 8.1   STYLE FORMATTING OPTIONS BY TYPE OF STYLE

Type	Formatting Options
Paragraph	Indents & Spacing, Alignment, Text Flow, Font, Font Effects, Numbering, Tabs, Drop Caps, Background, Border, Condition
Text	Font, Font Effects, Background
Frame	Type, Options (including links), Wrap, Background, Borders, Columns, Macro
Page	Page, Background, Header, Footer, Borders, Columns, Footnotes
Numbering	Bullets, Numbering, Outline, Pictures, Options

MAKING SENSE OF THE ORGANIZER

When you create a new style, StarWriter automatically presents you with the Organizer tab of the respective style dialog (see Figure 8.3). Think of the information presented in the Organizer as a style's personal ID or fingerprint. Using the Organizer, you can assign a name to a new style (Name), determine if attribute changes should take effect immediately and globally (Automatically Update), specify the style of the paragraph that StarWriter should use when you press Enter (Next Style), base the new style on an already existing style (Based On), and select a category for the new style (Category).

Note

By default, StarWriter assigns styles you create to the Custom Styles category (where you can find them easily when you're looking for a style you created). However, you can also select a category of your own, assigning your custom styles to a category of your choice. (The options include the same categories that you can select from the Available Styles drop-down lists of the Stylist or Style Catalog.)

Figure 8.3
The Organizer tab is a style's fingerprint.

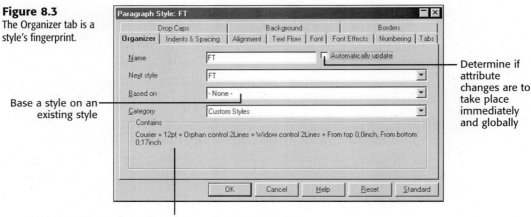

Base a style on an existing style

Determine if attribute changes are to take place immediately and globally

Get at-a-glance information about assigned style attributes

Once you've specified attributes for a style, you can review the assigned attributes in the Contains area underneath the Category list box. If you ever need a quick overview of a style's "fingerprint," look here first rather than browsing through the various tabs in the respective dialogs.

SPECIFYING THE STYLE OF THE FOLLOWING PARAGRAPH

When you're creating a new paragraph style, you have the option to specify the style of the paragraph StarWriter should use when you press Enter (Next Style). By default, this is the same style as the one you're creating; when you press Enter, StarWriter starts another paragraph of the same style. However, there may be occasions when you want a different paragraph style to follow the first one. For example, if you create a special section heading, you wouldn't want StarWriter to continue using this style after you press Enter. Instead you would want it to follow with a regular text style. In that case, you would select the style you want from the Next Style drop-down list.

Note

StarWriter's default heading styles are already set up to use Standard as the Next Style for the following paragraph.

BASING A STYLE ON ANOTHER STYLE

When creating new styles, you also have the option to base the new style on an already existing one. The style you select from the Based On drop-down list defines the formatting for the style you're creating, except for those formatting attributes that you (re)define exclusively for the new style.

Although you can save yourself some formatting time by basing a style on another style, you should be careful when using this option because it creates a chain of interdependencies that can easily wreak havoc on your screen. For example, if you base a new paragraph style

(New) on an already existing style, and then change the attributes of the existing style, you'll inadvertently make the same changes to the New style.

Tip #142 from	Basing styles on other styles comes in handy when you work on complex documents. If you use related styles and plan the hierarchy of styles based on other styles carefully, you can make sweeping changes by modifying a style or two at the bottom of the hierarchy.
Michael & Sarah	

Most built-in styles in StarWriter are based on the Standard style. Since each type (Text, Paragraph, and Page) has its own Standard, you can easily reset a formatting job gone crazy by selecting Default from the StarWriter context menu.

SETTING CONDITIONS FOR NEW PARAGRAPH STYLES

When selecting style attributes, your formatting options are virtually identical to the Character, Paragraph, Page, Numbering, and Text Box formatting options described in detail in Chapters 7 and 11 respectively, with one notable exception: You have the option to assign a condition to a paragraph style.

→ For more details on Character, Paragraph, Page, and Numbering formatting options **see** the corresponding sections, starting on **p. 261**.

→ For more details on Frame formatting options, **see** "Rehearsing Objects," **p. 421**.

Using conditions with your new paragraph styles enables you to have selected paragraphs take on different formatting depending on the context in which they appear. These contexts are predefined and include special *regions* in your document such as headers, footers, footnotes, endnotes, text boxes, outline levels, numbering levels, tables, and sections. You can define a condition only when creating a new paragraph style. You cannot add a condition to a non-conditional paragraph style. However, you can modify (add or remove) the conditions of conditional styles at any time. The number of conditions you can define is limited by the number of predefined contexts.

Here's what you need to do to create a conditional paragraph style: Using the Condition tab in the Paragraph Styles dialog (see Figure 8.4), select a predefined Context on the left (such as Header), choose a style from the Style list on the right, and click Assign. (If your list of applied styles is too long, you can filter the Styles list by selecting a category from the drop-down list below.) The selected style will appear in the Applied Styles column of the Context box. To remove a condition, select the Context that has the condition you would like to delete and click Remove.

You can now format your text with the conditional style. If the text appears in the context for which you assigned a style on the Condition tab, StarWriter will use the attributes of the assigned style. In all other instances, StarWriter will use the attributes that you defined as the new paragraph style. You can use conditional style formatting to speed up certain formatting tasks. For example, you can type up a standard business letter or memo, add text boxes, headers, and numbering levels, and then format the entire document in one swoosh by selecting Ctrl+A and assigning a previously created conditional paragraph style (for example, Business Memo). The various elements will display the attributes of the styles that have been assigned to them, while the remainder of your paragraphs will exhibit the attributes of the (conditional) Business Memo style proper.

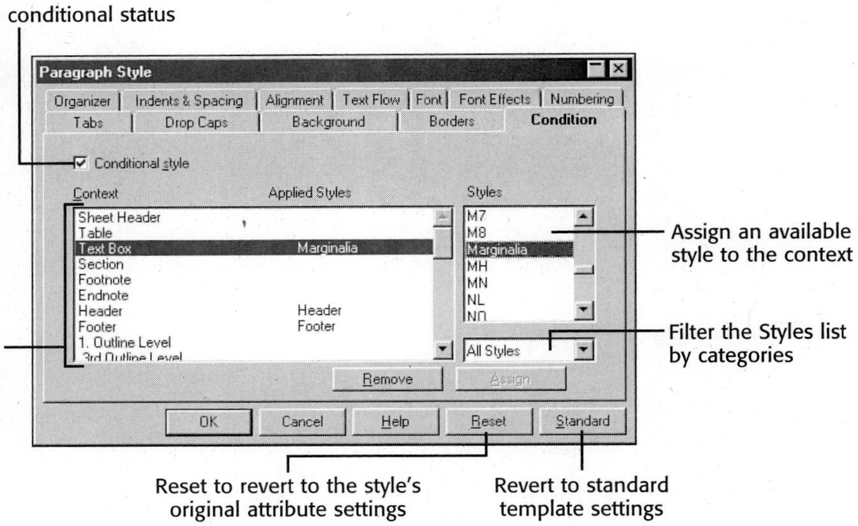

Figure 8.4
Using conditions with your new paragraph styles enables you to have selected paragraphs take on different formatting, depending on the context in which they appear.

Select to assign conditional status

Assign an available style to the context

Filter the Styles list by categories

Select a predefined context

Reset to revert to the style's original attribute settings

Revert to standard template settings

> **Note**
>
> When saving the StarWriter file (.sdw) in another format such as RTF or HTML, StarWriter will retain the formatting attributes for the assigned context styles. Note also that StarWriter's extensive list of available styles already contains a conditioned style: Text Body.

CREATING STYLES BY EXAMPLE

 The easiest way to add a new style to StarWriter's existing catalog of styles is to base it on existing text, and then click the New Style by Example button in the Stylist. StarWriter will automatically add the new style to its extensive collection. Here's how:

1. Place your cursor inside the formatted text that you would like to make the basis for a new style.

2. Select the type of the new style. For example, if the formatted text is a paragraph, click the Paragraph Styles icon; if it is a string of characters only, click the Text Styles icon, and so on. Be sure to open the right list for the type of style you want to define. StarWriter does not enable you to use a style that contains text attributes only but has been placed in the Paragraph Styles list.

3. Click the New Style by Example button. The Create Style dialog appears.

4. Enter a descriptive, yet short, name for your new style and click OK. StarWriter will create a custom style for the selection and make it available in the selected type style list.

Tip #143 from
Michael & Sarah

You can also create styles by example via drag and drop. Using this method, you first need to select the text that you would like to make the basis for a new style. Then drag and drop the selection into the main area of the Stylist. Be sure to select the correct type of style, and drop your selection below the list of available styles. Otherwise StarWriter will not be able to recognize it.

MODIFYING STYLES

StarWriter gives you two basic options for modifying existing styles. You can update a style based on changes you made to an existing style in the current document. Alternatively, you can select the Modify command from the Stylist context menu or the Style Catalog to edit and existing style.

UPDATING STYLES

 StarWriter enables you to update existing and available styles. You might want to use the Update option if you made simple attribute changes to a current selection and would like to have these changes permanently saved in the current style for future reference. You don't have to create a new style by example; you can update your existing style. Suppose you're using one of StarWriter's built-in heading styles but would like to change the style or indent attributes. Perform your changes quickly via direct formatting, and then select the correct heading style from the catalog of available styles in the Stylist and click the Update button (first button from the right). StarWriter will automatically update the stored style with the attributes of your current selection.

Note

If you selected the Automatically Update option on the Organizer tab of the updated style, all text elements that are currently formatted using this style will immediately be updated to reflect the new formatting attributes. Likewise, if you change the attributes of a text element via direct formatting, all other text elements that use the same style will be updated as well if the Automatically Update option is selected.

Caution

Be careful when using the Update button. It's easy to accidentally overwrite the attributes of an existing style with new ones. Be sure to select the style you want to update *before* clicking the Update button.

EDITING AND DELETING EXISTING STYLES

When modifying styles, you have the same two options as if you where creating new styles. You can either use the Stylist (press F11 or select Format, Stylist), or you can use the Style Catalog (press Ctrl+Y or select Format, Styles & Templates, Catalog). In both instances, you follow the same steps:

1. Select the style you want to modify, right-click in the list, and select Modify from the context menu (Stylist) or click the Modify button (Style Catalog). Depending on the type of style you want to modify, you'll see the Paragraph, Text, Frame, Page, or Numbering Style dialog.

2. Using the tabs in the respective dialogs, perform the desired modifications. If things get unwieldy, you can always click the Reset button to revert to the style's original attribute settings. Clicking Standard reverts you to the settings the style is based on.

3. When finished, click OK.

When deleting existing styles, select the style you want to delete, right-click, and select Delete from the context menu (Stylist) or click the Delete button (Style Catalog). StarWriter will ask you to confirm your decision, and then remove the style. Note that once a style has been removed, it can't be recovered.

TRANSFERRING STYLES

Each new document in StarWriter comes with standard sets of predefined styles. You can add to the existing library of styles by creating new styles, or, if you know the desired styles exist elsewhere, by transferring the styles from another document.

StarWriter gives you two options for transferring a style from another document into the current document: You can either copy the style directly or select Format, Styles & Templates, Load.

COPYING STYLES

If you only need one or two styles that you know exist in another document, copying them is the route to go. Select the text that contains the desired style, press Ctrl+C (or select Edit, Copy), switch to the current document (by clicking the button on the taskbar), place the insertion point at the location where you want to use the copied style, and press Ctrl+V (or select Edit, Paste). StarWriter inserts the copied text, complete with style attributes. You can now delete the copied text without losing the style. The copied style appears in the Applied Styles drop-down list, as well as in the in the list of available type styles of the current document.

TRANSFERRING STYLES FROM ANOTHER DOCUMENT

If you need to import more than a few styles from another document or template, select Format, Styles & Templates, Load. As with the copying method, you will only be able to use the imported styles in the current document. If you would like to include these styles for use with other documents, you have to save the current document as a template first, and then make that template the base for other documents.

Note

You can also import (read convert to StarOffice format) entire MS Word, MS Excel, and MS PowerPoint templates and documents using the AutoPilot Microsoft Import wizard. For more details see "Importing Microsoft Templates and Documents with the AutoPilot" at the end of this chapter.

When importing styles into the current document, StarWriter gives you two options: You can import styles either from an existing document or from a document template. In both cases, you start out by opening the Import Styles dialog (see Figure 8.5) by selecting Format, Styles & Templates, Load from the menu. Scanning the bottom of the Import Styles dialog, select the type of style(s) you would like to import from the selected document into the current one. Your options include: Text, Frame, Pages, and Numbering. You can choose one, two, three, or all of the above. When you select the Overwrite option, currently selected styles will be replaced by imported ones, if they carry the same name.

Caution

When you select Overwrite, StarWriter will not ask you to confirm style replacements. If you want to keep your current styles, check the selected document first for name conflicts, and don't select Overwrite.

Figure 8.5
StarWriter enables you to import styles from another document or template into the current document.

Select the file that has the desired styles

Select if styles are in a template

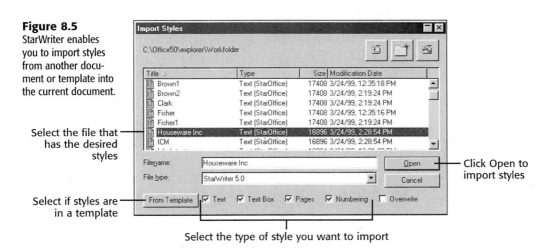

Click Open to import styles

Select the type of style you want to import

If the desired style(s) can be found in an existing document, locate the file on your system or network using one of the three directory navigation buttons, select it, and click OK to import the desired styles.

If the desired style is part of another template, select From Templates in the lower left of the Import Styles dialog, and you'll see the Load from Document Template dialog. Select a category on the left to see the available templates on the right. Select the template that contains the desired style and click OK to import the desired styles.

MANAGING STYLES WITH THE STYLE CATALOG

Welcome to Style Central! The Style Catalog is one big archive that gives you all the options you have with the Stylist, plus the added advantage of transferring applied styles from the current document to another one and vice versa.

The buttons in the Style Catalog dialog—shown in Figure 8.6—work as their names suggest, though a few comments are in order with regard to the most important option: the Organizer button.

Click the Organizer button to open the Document Templates dialog (see Figure 8.6). Don't be fooled by the deceptive simplicity of design. Using the options in this dialog, you can control the transfer of styles (and configurations) from templates to documents and vice versa, as well as from documents to documents. You can change the view in either list box by switching from Documents to Document Templates in the bottom list boxes.

Figure 8.6
The Stylist and the Style Catalog give you virtually the same options. Use the Stylist for your quick-and-easy formatting chores; use the Style Catalog if you want to transfer styles between documents.

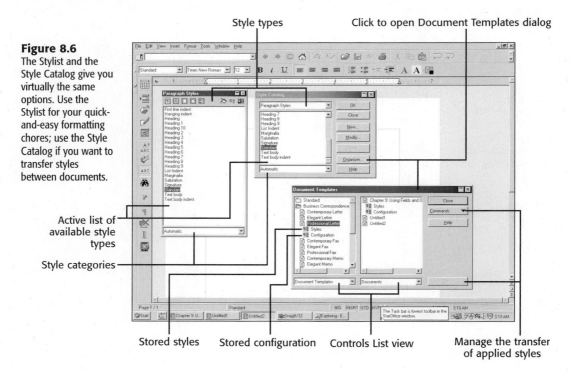

Style types

Click to open Document Templates dialog

Active list of available style types

Style categories

Stored styles   Stored configuration   Controls List view   Manage the transfer of applied styles

Tip #144 from
Michael & Sarah

By default, StarOffice templates (which may include templates you create with the AutoPilot, including imported Microsoft templates) are stored in the Templates folder of the StarOffice root directory. You can change the default path by selecting the Paths tab in the Tools, Options, General dialog.

When in Document Template view, you'll see all the contents of the StarOffice Template folder, including subfolders and templates. Double-click a folder to view its contents. Double-click a template to expose the Style and Configuration attributes (refer to Figure 8.6). Double-click either the Style or Configuration icon, and you can see a list of applied styles and custom configurations that you defined via the Tools, Configure dialog (such as toolbar or keyboard configurations).

Tip #145 from
Michael & Sarah

You can assign a particular configuration with a StarOffice document. For example, when you change the configuration of your toolbars while a text document is active, the same configuration will be available each time a text document is active. Alternatively, you can also assign a certain configuration that is only valid with a particular document, in which case you would store the configuration information with that particular document in one file. For more details, see "Configuring Templates" later in this chapter.

If you select the Templates view on the left and the Documents view on the right, you can use drag and drop to move styles and configurations from a template into a document and vice versa. If both document and template have a style or configuration of the same name, StarWriter will ask you to confirm whether you want to override the existing item with the one that you are transferring.

If you would like to expand your administrative options, click the Commands button for a series of options that include printing a list of existing styles in a document or template. Which of these commands is available depends on your current selection (Document, Document Template, or Document Template folder). Table 8.2 explains the items of the Commands submenu.

Tip #146 from
Michael & Sarah

You can have access to the same options and commands by right-clicking a document, document template, or Template folder in the List view window.

The File button enables you to bring other documents into the Organizer, so you can copy styles or configurations between StarOffice documents. (Note that this button only works with documents, not with templates.) Just select the document with which you want to exchange style and configuration information and click the File button, and you'll see the standard Open dialog. Locate and select the target file for your desired transaction, and then click Open. The new document will show up in the List view. You can now start copying information via drag and drop.

TABLE 8.2 DOCUMENT TEMPLATES ADMINISTRATIVE COMMANDS

Option	Function
New	Creates a new document template folder.
Delete	Deletes the selected Template folder or document template; you will be asked to confirm your choice.
Edit	Enables you to edit the contents of the selected document template
Import File	Enables you to import document templates; select the folder in which you want to save the imported document template first, and then select Import File. You'll see a standard Load dialog.
Export File	Enables you to export the selected document template. Select the template first, and then select Export File. You'll get the standard Save As dialog. The default path is the workplace directory specified under Tools, Options, General, Paths.
Print	Prints the attribute settings of applied styles. Double-click the document template and select Symbol, Print.
Printer Setup	Enables you to set up your current printer or select a different one.
Update	Updates the List view in the dialog.

WORKING WITH TEMPLATES

Templates are redesigned documents that contain fields, formatting, and standard layout choices. They are useful for streamlining the creation of documents you generate on a regular basis. When you need to set standards for more than just the character and paragraph formatting of your documents, you should use templates.

When you open a New Text Document in StarOffice, you get a blank document with default settings based on the Standard template. It includes a set of standard margins and no formatting. Once you begin entering text in your document, you can edit these settings and add new fields and formatting choices, if so desired.

Note

You can also set your own template to serve as the StarWriter default template, if you like. For more information, refer to the section "Changing the Default Template" later in this chapter.

→ For details on managing templates across the desktop, **see** "Managing Styles and Templates," **p. 167**.

If you find it too time-consuming to change these settings or create new ones, you can use one of many ready-made templates in StarOffice by selecting File, New, From Template from the menu bar. The New dialog that appears gives you access to various template categories that list one or more templates appropriate to a specific task (see Figure 8.7). Click a category on the left and you'll see its contents in the Templates list on the right.

Tip #147 from
Michael & Sarah

The first time you open the New template dialog, you'll see a screen with two list boxes: Categories and Templates. Select the Preview option and click More, and then you can actually preview each template you click before you open it. In addition, you can fill in descriptive keywords and slugs—such as title, subject, and commentary—a feature that comes in handy when telling templates apart, especially once you start adding your own templates to the list (some of which may vary only in minute detail).

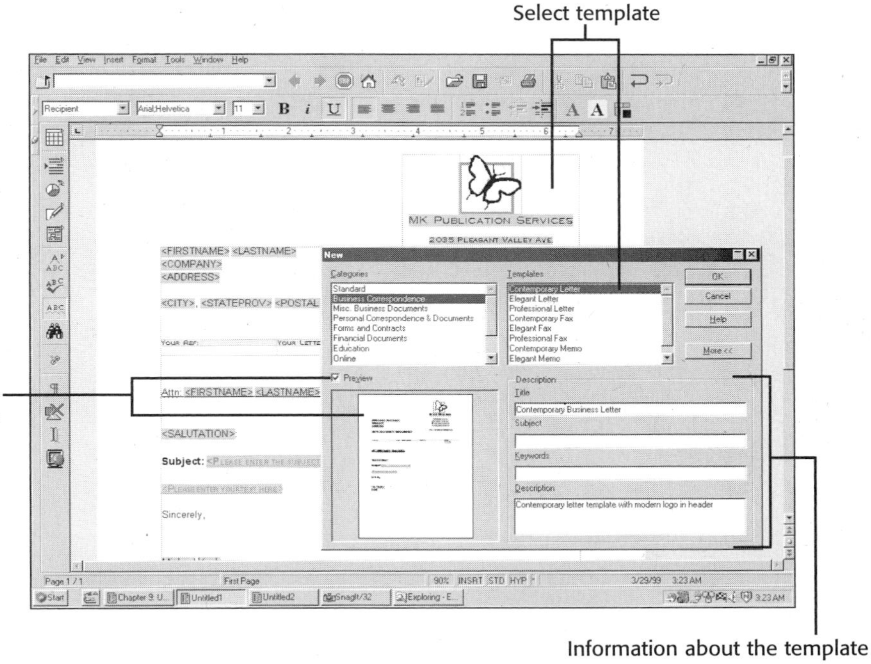

Select template

Figure 8.7
Check the Preview option and click More to get a detailed description and thumbnail view of the selected template.

Select for thumbnail preview

Information about the template

For example, if most of the documents you create are letters, you can select various templates from the Business and Personal Correspondence categories. After you have selected a template, the template controls the appearance of the document that you create. In the case of a contemporary business letter, for example, you'll find a company logo, name and address heading; name and address fields for the recipient; a date and subject line; a salutation; and closing information, leaving it up to you to fill in the blanks.

EXPLORING TEMPLATE CATEGORIES

StarOffice comes with a series of templates that you can use and modify at will. Table 8.3 lists the various categories and templates you might find helpful while working in StarWriter. The names of the templates speak for their functions.

TABLE 8.3   TEMPLATES AVAILABLE IN STAROFFICE

Category	Templates
Standard	Blank Document
Business Correspondence	Contemporary Letter
	Elegant Letter
	Professional Letter
	Contemporary Fax
	Elegant Fax
	Professional Fax
	Contemporary Memo
	Elegant Memo
	Professional Memo
Misc. Business Documents	Professional Delivery Receipt
	Professional Invoice
	Contemporary Minutes
	Elegant Minutes
	Professional Minutes
	Professional Press Release
	Report
Personal Correspondence & Documents	Formal Letter
	Personal Letter
	Résumé
	Formal Fax
	Personal Fax
	Visiting Cards
	Envelope
Education	Thesis
	Written Academic Lecture
Forms and Contracts	Notice
	Packing Note
	Receipt
	Telephone Notes
	What's New?
	Leaflet
	General Sales Contract

Category	Templates
Online	HTML Template (Standard)
	Contemporary HTML Template
	Colored HTML Template
Presentation Layouts	Maps (World, North America, Europe)
	Various backgrounds and borders
Miscellaneous	Newsletter
	Book
	Gift Certificate
	Cassette, CD, Zip (covers)

USING TEMPLATES

When using templates, you have three basic options. You can attach a new document template that comes with its own basic formatting attributes but not much else. You can load one of StarWriter's many ready-made templates and fill in the blanks. Or, you can use the AutoPilot command to create new templates on-the-fly.

The first of these three options is nothing special: the template you choose is part of your stockpile of basic document templates that you can access from the File, New menu, from the Start menu, or the desktop. Each time you open a new document, you use StarOffice's (minimalist) Standard template, which provides a basic framework for your work—literally.

LOADING AN EXISTING TEMPLATE

Things get more interesting when you load one of StarOffice's courtesy templates. To load a template, you proceed as if you were loading a new document. Select File, New, From Template from the menu bar or press Ctrl+N. In the New dialog you can select a template category; and from within that category, you can select a template of your choice. Double-click to open the template. When you first open a template, you see a series of shaded fields and placeholders in addition to what looks like a rough framework of what could become a nice-looking document. You'll notice that some of these fields can be edited, others are connected to your database and available for mail merge and so on. Double-click the shaded fields and you can enter data. In short, you don't have to worry about a thing—StarWriter has done some up front work for you already. Of course, if you want to fine-tune some rough edges, you can do so by consulting the Stylist and making the appropriate formatting and layout choices.

Tip #148 from
Michael & Sarah

Take a look at StarOffice's extensive collection of templates (Ctrl+N); you might find the one that you would like to adopt for your own personal or business use. However, note that not all templates are StarWriter templates. There are StarCalc documents as well as StarImpress presentations! Depending on the template you select, you may find yourself all of a sudden inside another module. Only the templates listed in Table 8.3 are StarWriter templates.

FLYING ON AUTOPILOT

The AutoPilot is, in principle, a template-creation wizard that assists you in turning out polished, formatted versions of the most common document types—including business letters, memos, and faxes—by walking you through a limited set of formatting and layout options. The available template wizards for StarWriter include Letter, Fax, Agenda, and Memo. (It also assists in creating StarBase database elements, importing Microsoft templates and documents, and setting up StarOffice to connect to the Internet.)

→ For more details on creating letters, faxes, agendas, and memos with the AutoPilot, **see** "Creating Documents and Templates with the AutoPilot," **p. 253**.

Using the AutoPilot is intuitive and straightforward. Select File, AutoPilot, and the type of document you want to create; then follow the onscreen instructions. StarOffice will take you, step by step, through a series of dialogs that assist you in creating a template according to your specifications. Click Next to advance through the various wizard screens; click Back if you've changed your mind about a certain choice; click Create once you've provided all the necessary information, or, if you're familiar with the AutoPilot (through repeated use), you can also select Create at any time. The AutoPilot skips the intermediate dialog boxes and uses its default settings to create the selected document template.

After you complete the entire process, StarWriter opens a blank document based on the template you created.

Note

With ordinary text documents and presentations, your custom template is automatically saved under the name you entered during the creation process, even if you do not save the document. With Web (HTML) documents, you must click the Save Template option box to save your custom template. For more details see Chapter 25, "Creating Web pages with StarWriter/Web."

The next time you select File, New, From Template (or press Ctrl+N), your template will be listed under Templates in the Standard category; double-click to open it.

Tip #149 from
Michael & Sarah

AutoPilot automates the process for the most common text (as well as presentation, table, and other) documents. You can also create templates for most other types of StarOffice documents from scratch, including presentations, spreadsheets, and drawings, but you must do so as outlined in the next section, "Creating Templates."

CREATING TEMPLATES

StarWriter comes with many built-in templates, but on occasion you might want to create a template *from scratch*—without using the AutoPilot. In those instances, you would take as your starting point an existing document that you then save as a template for future reference. Seen in that light, creating a template is indeed almost as easy as saving a document.

Follow these steps to create a new template out of an existing document:

1. Edit and format the document as desired, and delete all unnecessary content.

2. Select File, Templates. The Document Templates dialog appears.

3. In this dialog, enter a descriptive name in the New Template list box and click OK. Your new template is automatically saved in the Standard Templates folder. The next time you open the New Templates dialog, you'll see your template listed in the Templates list box.

PART

II

CH

8

Tip #150 from	If you want, you can save your templates in a separate folder or add them to an existing
Michael & Sarah	folder. Just click File, Open and locate the StarOffice Template directory (`...\Office51\Template`). Using the options in the Open dialog, you can create new folders and move existing files and folders as desired. When done, click Cancel.

OPENING AND MODIFYING AN EXISTING TEMPLATE

To modify an existing template, select File, Templates from the menu bar. In the Document Templates dialog, select the template you want to modify. If you don't see the desired template, click the category on the left to see a list of its contents on the right. Click Edit. Your template opens in StarWriter. You can now make the desired changes to the template and later save it with the Save command from the File menu, or by pressing Ctrl+S.

OPENING TEMPLATES

You can configure StarWriter to search for attached templates each time it opens a document. Typically templates are stored in the Template folder of the StarOffice root directory. When attached to a document, all the information in a template is saved with the document, including styles, configurations, and name. If configured, StarOffice will check to see if it can find the name of the template in the Template folder of the StarOffice root directory.

Tip #151 from	This search function is off by default, but you can activate it in the `soffice.ini` file. Open
Michael & Sarah	the file, go to [Common] and add `SearchTemplate=1` at the end of the listing in this category. As always, be careful when editing `.ini` files. These files control vital configuration and startup options for your program.

When opening a document that contains a changed template, StarWriter will ask you whether you want to replace the existing styles. Click Yes, and the document will be loaded together with the StarOffice template in the Template folder. All styles that are in your current document will be replaced with the styles of the new template. These changes will then be stored with your document when you save it.

If you click No, the document will be loaded as is. The styles in your Style Catalog will not be taken into account.

If StarOffice can't find a document with the name listed in the document information, it can search your system for templates with the same name, provided you edit your StarOffice .ini file in the StarOffice directory. If StarOffice can locate a template with that name, you'll be asked if you want to use it. If you select Yes, you have the option to replace the existing styles in the current document with those of the template. If StarOffice can't find any styles, you'll be asked if you want to sever the document from its styles.

CHANGING THE DEFAULT TEMPLATE

When you open a new text document, you may not be aware that this blank document is actually based on a (default) template. It comes, for example, with standard margins and a standard set of available styles that are offered no matter which document you are using. If you want StarWriter to use a different template each time you load a new text document, you can do so by creating create one for yourself. Here's how you define your own standard:

1. Define the basic layout of your page using the Page Style dialog (choose Format, Page or right-click and select Page from the StarWriter context menu).

2. Define any desired character or paragraph attributes for your document by applying available styles from the Stylist, or by creating new ones.

3. Select Save As. In the Save As dialog that appears, you can target a location for your future template, and save it as a StarWriter Template file. (Note that unless you changed the path information in the Tools, General, Options dialog, your default saving path is \Windows\Desktop\My Documents in Windows and /Office51/Workfolder in Linux.

   Alternatively, you can also select the New Folder button and create a new folder for your template (for example, My Templates) and save the current document to that folder. That way you can keep things organized.

→ For more details on managing files with the Save As dialog, **see** "Managing Files and Folders from the Open and Save As Dialogs," **p. 192**.

4. Press Ctrl+Shift+E, or click the Explorer button on the function bar to open the Explorer. (Be sure the Explorer is set to Hierarchical View; if not, right-click the Explorer group title bar and select Hierarchical View from the context menu.)

5. Click the plus sign next to the Workfolder to expand the folder tree, and select the My Templates folder.

6. Open the Beamer—by pressing Ctrl+Shift+B or clicking the Beamer button on the function bar—to look at the contents of the Workfolder.

7. Right-click your future template and select Set Default Template, Text Document from the context menu.

That's it. The next time you open a new text document via File, New, Text Document (or using any of the other methods for creating a new text document), your template will be attached to the new document.

To return to the original StarOffice template, open the Explorer (Ctrl+Shift+E) in Hierarchical View and expand the Workplace tree. Locate the StarOffice directory on your system, and select the Config, New subfolder. Next, open the Beamer (Ctrl+Shift+B), right-click _05_~Text Document, and select Reset Default from the context menu. (Note that this command appears only if you have set another document or template to serve as the default template.) Restart StarOffice. The next time you open a new text document via File, New, Text Document, it will display the attributes of the StarOffice default template.

CONFIGURING TEMPLATES

Templates are not only repositories for styles, they can also store valuable information about your desktop, including toolbars configurations and keyboard shortcuts. StarWriter enables you to define a configuration globally for all documents of the same type, or you can store configuration information "locally," with a selected document.

→ The principles for customizing are the same across StarOffice. For more details on customizing your workspace, **see** "Customizing Desktop Tools and Menus," **p. 115**.

→ If you want to get serious about customizing your StarWriter environment, take a look at "Manipulating StarWriter Documents," **page 1317**, which introduces you to using macros and StarBasic scripts to automate your work and customize your workspace.

To add configuration information to a document template, follow these steps:

1. Open an existing document to which you want to assign toolbar or menu configurations.

2. Select the desired configuration for this document from the Tools, Configure menu. Here in the Configuration dialog's Toolbars tab, you can select the toolbars you would like to have available when opening the selected document, as well as specific menu items from the Menu tab.

3. Select Save in the Configuration dialog.

4. In the Save Configuration dialog that appears, select All from the File Type drop-down list.

5. Next, locate the current document from within the Save Configuration Dialog, and then click Save. StarWriter will ask you whether you want to overwrite the existing file. Don't panic. The alert only refers to any configurations that might reside in the Files template. The actual content of your document will not change, but you will lose any existing configurations.

6. Click OK.

Your new configuration has been embedded in the desired document.

Tip #152 from
Michael & Sarah

To check on your file, select File, Templates, and click the Organizer button. Double-click your document in the Document List view. Then double-click Configuration to view a list of configurations that resides in that document's template.

The next time you open your newly configured document, StarWriter will appear according to your specifications. Load different documents and StarWriter will revert to the global Standard configuration.

Tip #153 from
Michael & Sarah

> Note that you can return to the StarWriter standard at any time by selecting Tools, Configure, and then clicking the Reset button.

MANAGING TEMPLATES MORE EFFICIENTLY

What good are the best tools if you can't access them quickly when you need them? In keeping with the company philosophy of putting everything at the tip of your fingers, StarOffice provides three basic options of where to put your templates for quick-and-easy access.

If you want to manage your templates from one central location where you can easily edit and preview them, select the File, Templates when saving new templates. Your templates will automatically be saved in the \Office51\Template folder where you can easily access them by pressing Ctrl+N (or selecting File, New, From Template).

If you want your templates to appear on your File, New menu, place them into the \Office51\Template folder, then create a link to the office51\config\new folder. To create a link, open the template folder contents in the Beamer. Next, locate and right-click the new template file and select Create Link from the context menu. Then, expand the Office51\config folder in the Explorer (in Hierarchical View) and drag the link from the Beamer to the config folder.

Tip #154 from
Michael & Sarah

> Templates are typically listed in alphabetical order; however, you can influence the order if you place numbers framed by underlines such as _01_, _02_, and so on in front of the names. The numbers will not show up on your menu, but StarOffice will recognize the order in which to display the templates.

In most cases, however, you probably won't administer the templates in the new folder, but you will attach them to documents. In that case, you can place the template in the Template folder or one of its subfolders (or create one of your own). In doing so, you guarantee that you can easily access them via the Template dialog, where you can use, open, and preview them and not end up with two different templates.

If you prefer to keep an overview of your templates, add them to your desktop (right next to the existing new document files). However, when placing templates on your desktop, be sure to create links to your Template folder, rather than placing the templates themselves. That way, you can be assured that templates are attached to new documents.

To create links to the desktop, locate and right-click the document and select Create Link from the context menu. You'll notice the Properties dialog. Select a name for the template, including a Template folder, or click the File button, and then select a template of your choice. Click OK and you'll see the new template on your desktop.

If you prefer to work with the Start menu, you can place entire template folders there. Here's what you do:

1. On your desktop, navigate to the Templates folder and locate the template or folders you want to place on the Start menu.

2. Click the plus sign (+) next to the Workplace folder in the Explorer. This enables you to navigate easily on your local drives.

3. Locate the Office51 directory, and find the \config\start folder and select it.

4. Open the Beamer and extended-click so the Start folder contents are visible in the Beamer window.

5. Ctrl+Shift+drag your template from the desktop in the Beamer. You've just placed your templates into the Start folder.

If so inclined, you can also show the template in the Explorer. In the Properties dialog of the template or link, you'll find the Show in Explorer check box. Double-click a link on the desktop and the file opens. If you don't want to work with the template directly, but want to open a new document on the basis of the template, use the context menu. There you'll find the Open from template command—select it to open a new document.

IMPORTING MICROSOFT TEMPLATES WITH THE AUTOPILOT

Would you like to use the styles and templates that you created in MS Office? No problem. StarOffice can import your MS Word, Excel, or PowerPoint documents or templates on-the-fly—the AutoPilot fly that is. Just follow these steps, and you can use MS documents in the SO environment:

1. Select File, AutoPilot, MicroSoft Import. The MS Office Import Autopilot splash screen appears, informing you that the AutoPilot will search your directories for existing MS Office documents and templates.

2. Click Continue to advance to the first (of two) AutoPilot dialog(s), shown in Figure 8.8.

3. Specify the type of MS document you want to import. Your options include Word, Excel, or PowerPoint templates and/or documents. You can also tell StarOffice which directory, including subdirectories, to search, and where the imported templates should be stored.

Tip #155 from
Michael & Sarah

By default, the AutoPilot wizard will search for Word, Excel, and PowerPoint documents and templates. If you only want to search for a particular document or template type, be sure to deselect all other import options by clicking the Word, Excel, and Powerpoint icons across the top of the wizard, and then deselecting the options you don't need—it'll speed up the import process.

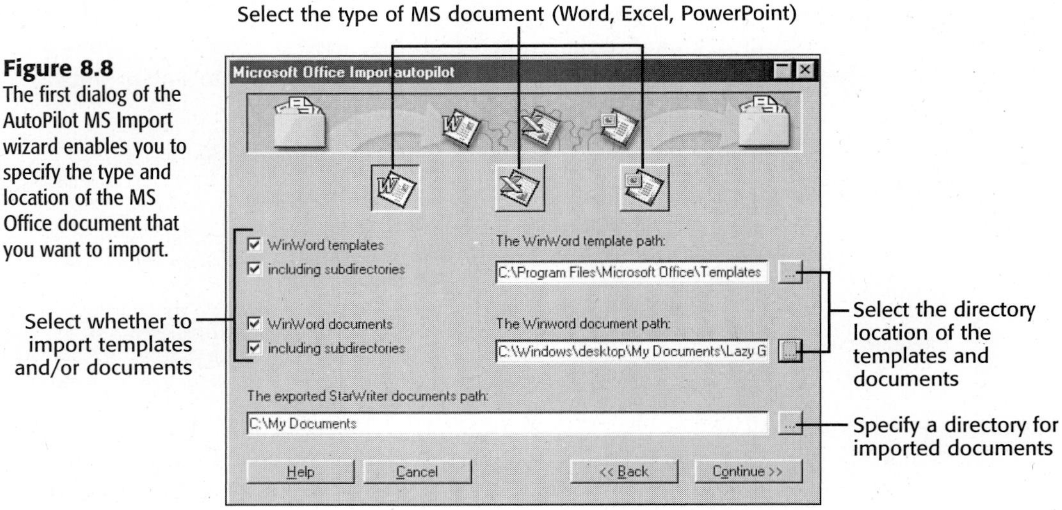

Select the type of MS document (Word, Excel, PowerPoint)

Figure 8.8
The first dialog of the AutoPilot MS Import wizard enables you to specify the type and location of the MS Office document that you want to import.

Select whether to import templates and/or documents

Select the directory location of the templates and documents

Specify a directory for imported documents

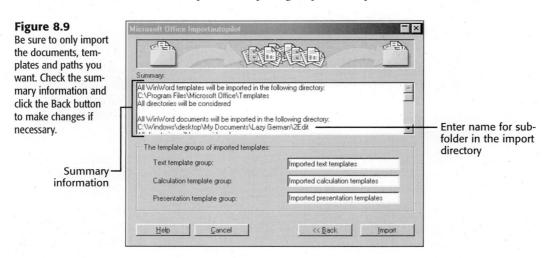

4. When finished, click Continue to advance to the second AutoPilot dialog (see Figure 8.9). Here, you can see a summary of the import tasks that will be performed, as well as enter a name for the imported template groups or accept the default name.

Figure 8.9
Be sure to only import the documents, templates and paths you want. Check the summary information and click the Back button to make changes if necessary.

Summary information

Enter name for sub-folder in the import directory

5. Click Import to start the import process. This may take a while, depending on the number of documents and templates StarOffice has to convert and import. When finished, StarOffice adds the imported template group(s) or folder(s) to the StarOffice template folder (office51\template). Your imported documents are located in the import directory you specified in the first AutoPilot dialog.

6. To access your newly created templates, select File, New, From Template. Click the desired import folder, select the template and click OK.

TROUBLESHOOTING

I assigned my own template to be the StarWriter default and then re-assigned the Standard template as you described, but nothing happens now when I try to open a new text document!

Try deleting the file named `soffice.cfg` in the `\Office51\config directory` and re-starting StarOffice. (The program generates a new configuration file if it doesn't find one on start-up.)

I've imported templates from another program, but the documents I create with them in StarWriter look funny.

There are a number of possible reasons. Have you created a font substitution table in StarOffice? If so, you may use fonts in the imported template for which you have set substitutions in that table. Check in the Font Substitution dialog that opens from the Tools, Options, General dialog. Are all the fonts you originally used still available on your system? If not, StarOffice will substitute other fonts, which may cause a variety of things to look odd. Did your templates make use of special commands (like, for example, conditional formatting) that are program specific? Not all characteristics of templates translate across programs, and you may need to re-create some of your styles and layouts in StarWriter.

Suddenly, my fonts have changed! What happened?

If you create a style based on another style—in what is called a parent and child relationship—when you change the parent style's, the fonts of all its children automatically change as well. That is the most common reason for what you describe.

I don't have all the templates you describe here.

If you downloaded your copy of StarOffice from the Internet, you only receive a limited set of templates. If you buy the Personal Deluxe Edition or Professional Edition, you get a full set of templates, samples, and fonts. If you installed off a network, it's possible that your administrator chose not to install all the templates that are included. Ask your administrator for assistance.

I want to create a style for a cover sheet where the text is centered both vertically and horizontally. How can I do this?

Insert a new text box (select Insert, Text Box). Double-click it to open the Text Box formatting dialog. Select Anchor to Page. Then, in the Position section of the dialog box, select Centered to Entire Page for both the Horizontal and Vertical positions. Select any other formatting options that you want, and click OK. Then, click the New Style By Example button in the Stylist, and name a new Frame style. There you have it! Note that your text will not be centered, just the text frame. You'll have to center the text separately, either manually by using the Center Alignment button or by creating a centered text style that you apply to the text in the box.

I'm creating a document where I need to have some pages in landscape orientation, others in portrait. I've created two separate page styles with no problem. However, when I apply my landscape page style to the desired page, all my other pages change too! How can I apply my page style to a selected page only?

You need to insert manual page breaks (Insert, Manual Break command) before and after the page to which you want to apply a new page style so StarOffice knows where to start and stop applying it.

I don't like the default Standard template and would like to make another template the default template. How do I do this?

To define your own template as the default template, display the contents of the directory containing the document templates in the Beamer (you may have to switch the Explorer to Hierarchical view, then click the folder that contains the desired template—usually Templates or one of its subfolders). Right-click the desired template and select Set Default Template from the context menu, and specify the document type. The template is now set as the default and will be used for the new document.

How can I apply a document style from an existing document to my current document?

Select Format, Styles & Templates, Load, then select the document that contains the desired styles or click From Template to locate the import styles from an existing tempalte. To apply changes to styles with the same name, click the Overwrite check box at the bottom right. Click Open.

How can I set up a document to use different layouts for different pages (for example, left- and right-hand pages)?

To use alternate page styles in your document, use the Next Style option in the organizer tab of the Page Styles dialog. Using the Stylist (press F11), assign, for example, the page style Right Page to the first page and then modify this style via the context menu to assign Left Page as the Next Style. Do the same with the Left Page style by right-clicking it in the Stylist and selecting Modify from the context menu and then Right Page as the Next Style. After these changes, your document will automatically alternate between left and right changes.

What is direct and style formatting and which is better?

Style formatting refers to Styles assigned in the Stylist. If the style is modified, it immediately affects all text in the document to which the style is applied. Direct formatting refers to modifications made by selecting text and assigning various attributes via the Format menu or the object bar. The use of styles is recommended if you want to ensure a uniform appearance in various documents. This also makes it easier to subsequently reformat individual documents.

WORKING WITH TABLES, CHARTS, AND FIELDS

In this chapter

USING TABLES IN STARWRITER

By definition, a *table* is any grouping of information arranged in (vertical) columns and (horizontal) rows. Each intersection of a row and a column is called a *cell*. In addition, tables often come with column headers across the top row, and sometimes also with row labels across the first column. (Look ahead to Figure 9.3 to see an example of a table with both column and row headings.)

Tables have long been a staple in business correspondence, including invoices and résumés. They enhance documents by presenting data and information in an organized, easy-to-follow fashion. Tables can also be compelling when used to divvy up a page into sections, so you can neatly place text adjacent to a graphic object or create a professional-looking résumé. Because StarWriter doubles as an HTML editor, you can use tables to arrange text and graphics on a page and then save the arrangement as an HTML document for Web display.

Note

Tables in HTML documents have given more than one Web designer headaches because Web browsers at times have difficulty interpreting the defining table tags as intended. As a result, a table that looks fine in Internet Explorer might look different in Netscape and vice versa. In StarWriter, tables have been optimized for online display. For more details on using tables in HTML documents, **see** "Working with Tables and Text Frames" in Chapter 26, "Enhancing HTML Documents."

Tables in StarWriter are simple to use and easy to create. Each table you insert comes with a Table Heading style for column headings and a Table Contents style for the table body. When the table runs longer than a page, StarWriter automatically repeats the column headings at the top of the new page. You can even use StarWriter tables for simple and complex calculations in text documents.

StarWriter also provides useful commands that make your life easier when you need to edit a table. For example, adding or deleting rows and columns is as easy as clicking a button on a toolbar. Less commendable, however, is StarWriter's blocky way of placing tables on a page as well as its inability to let you move rows and columns within a table. Still, if you need to present a series of related items or would like to arrange text and objects on a page, go tables!

CREATING TABLES

By default, StarWriter's table feature creates a group of cells that expands as needed to fit all your required text or graphics. Each new table you insert appears with thin borders surrounding the cells, and some basic formatting attributes that include a centered, boldfaced, and italicized Table Heading style and a regular, left-aligned Table Contents style. Of course, you can always change the default attributes of the table, as well as add some of your own, via direct or style formatting.

INSERTING A NEW TABLE

 Inserting a new table in a StarWriter document is oh-so-easy. If you can live with a completely uniform table design aligned with the left and right margins, a standard table heading row, and all the columns and rows equally spaced, use the Insert Table command on the Main toolbar (see Figure 9.1). Place the insertion point at the location in your document where you want to insert a table. Extended-click the Insert button on the Main toolbar to open the Insert tear-off toolbar, and then move your pointer over the Insert Table command (the third icon from the left). A submenu opens showing a five column by five row table grid; drag down and to the right to select the number of rows and columns for your table.

Note

You can drag down and to the right beyond the initial 5×5 grid; StarWriter automatically adds rows and columns to the preset template grid. The number of selected rows and columns is shown in the field underneath the grid.

Table command

Figure 9.1
Using the Table command from the Insert tear-off toolbar, you can quickly "draw" and insert a standard text table.

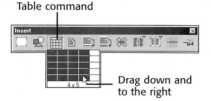

Drag down and to the right

When you release the mouse button, StarWriter inserts a standard table with a Table Heading style for each cell or column in the first row (if you have more than one row), a Table Contents style for all other cells, and a 0.05 pt border around each cell.

Tip #156 from
Michael & Sarah

Since regular tables cannot be moved easily, you may consider placing a table inside a frame or text box. To do so, first create a text box by clicking the Frame icon in the Insert tear-off window (first icon from the left), then click and drag to create a text box. Then click anywhere outside the frame to deselect it. Next, click inside the frame to place the insertion point inside. Now insert the table as described in this section. You can now move the table (inside the box) freely in your document, anchor it in a certain location, even resize the text box or have text wrap around it. For more details on text boxes or frames see "Working with Text Boxes" in Chapter 11, "Desktop Publishing with StarOffice."

USING THE AUTOFORMAT COMMAND

For more control over the initial table format and design, use the regular Insert Table command, as shown in Figure 9.2. In the Insert Table dialog, you can enter a name for your table (by default, StarWriter uses Table1, Table2, and so on), specify the number of columns and rows as well as whether you want to show table headers and borders (in the

Options portion of the dialog), and select one of 17 table styles by clicking the AutoFormat button. Click the More button in the Table AutoFormat dialog to accept or reject the various predefined AutoFormat options—including Number Format, Font, Alignment, Borders, and Patterns—that come with each table design. If you reject one or more of these options, StarWriter uses the corresponding standard table defaults. You can also rename or delete a selected table style and insert a style of your own.

Tip #157 from
Michael & Sarah

To insert a style of your own, you must first create the desired table, complete with formatting. When you're finished, select the entire table, and choose Format, AutoFormat. In the AutoFormat dialog, click the Insert button. Add a name in the Add AutoFormat dialog, and click OK. StarWriter adds the new table style to the list of available styles.

Note

If you want to change the insert table defaults, select Tools, Options, Text Documents, Insert. Using the Tables and Insert in Tables portion of the dialog you can define the Header, Border, and Numbering options for inserted tables.

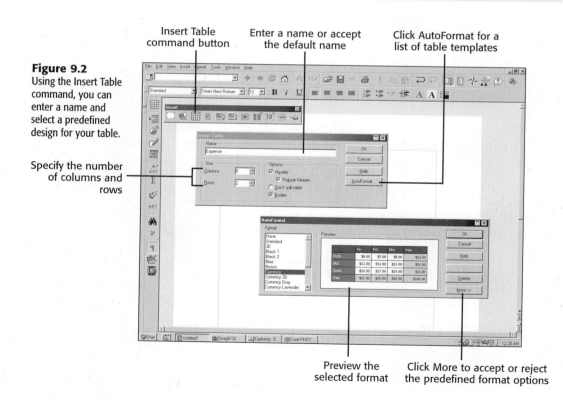

Figure 9.2
Using the Insert Table command, you can enter a name and select a predefined design for your table.

Insert Table command button

Enter a name or accept the default name

Click AutoFormat for a list of table templates

Specify the number of columns and rows

Preview the selected format

Click More to accept or reject the predefined format options

IMPORTING EXISTING TABLES

The easiest way to import an existing table from another StarWriter document is to use the copy and paste method. Simply select the desired table in its entirety, and press Ctrl+C (or select Edit, Copy). Then place the insertion point at the location where you want to insert the table, and press Ctrl+V (or select Edit, Paste). StarWriter inserts the selected table, complete with contents and formatting.

When you're importing tables from other StarOffice programs—such as StarCalc, for example—you have two options. You can import the table as an OLE object, in which case StarWriter creates and inserts an exact copy of the original table in the current document. Note that when you insert a table as an OLE object, the data in the imported table is "fixed"; it will no longer reflect any changes to the data in the original table. If you want the inserted table to reflect changes to the original table, you have to import the table contents as a dynamic data exchange (DDE) link. Inserting a table as a DDE link enables you to update the contents of the inserted table from the original table.

PART

II

CH

9

IMPORTING TABLES AS OLE OBJECTS

To import a table as an OLE object, select the desired table in the original program; then press Ctrl+C or select Copy from the selected table's context menu to copy the table to the Clipboard (Windows) or General-Purpose Buffer (Linux). Switch to the document in which you want to insert the table, and place the insertion point in the location where you want StarWriter to insert the copied table. Press Ctrl+V or select Edit, Paste to paste the table from the Clipboard (Windows) or General-Purpose Buffer (Linux) to your document. StarWriter inserts the table as a copy of the original table in the desired location. Because the copy is inserted as an OLE object, you can move, scale, and wrap text around the table object as you would with any other object.

→ For more details on sizing and formatting objects in text documents, **see** "Rehearsing Objects," **p. 421**.
→ For more details on OLE and exchanging data between StarOffice documents, **see** "Sharing Data Between Documents," **p. 171**.

IMPORTING TABLES AS DDE LINKS

If you want to update the data in the copied table of your document with the data in the original document, you have to insert the desired table with DDE links. Select the desired table in the original StarOffice program, and press Ctrl+C to copy the entire table. Then switch back to your StarWriter document, and select Edit, Paste Special. From the Selection list of the Paste Special dialog, select DDE Link and click OK. StarWriter inserts the contents of the selected table as DDE links in your current document, which means any changes you make to the original table are immediately reflected in the copied table. You can format a table with DDE links as you would any other table created in StarWriter.

Tip #158 from
Michael & Sarah

You can also drag and drop tables from one StarOffice module into another. Just make the document that contains the desired table a floating task window that is always visible. Then select the table, and click and drag the selection while pressing Ctrl (OLE Object) or Ctrl+Shift (DDE links), and drop it at the desired location in your text document.

CONVERTING TEXT TO TABLES

On occasion you might need to convert text formatted into columns with tabs. Each tab marks the beginning of a new column; each paragraph symbol marks the beginning of a new row. To convert a crude table of this kind into a regular table, select the entire text (all tabular blocks) first, and then choose the Insert Table command (via the Main toolbar or the Insert menu). StarWriter creates a standard table based on the number of tabular blocks of the text-based table, with columns of equal width that retain the original text styles, and a 0.05 pt border line around each cell. You can then format and edit the new table like any other StarWriter table.

Tip #159 from
Michael & Sarah

When you're working with text-based tables, turn on the Tabs and Paragraph marks option in the nonprinting characters section of the Tools, Options, Text Document, Contents tab, or click the Non-Printing Character button on the Main toolbar. That way, you can easily find irregularities such as missing or additional tabs between columns in a tabular block. Note that each column is separated from the following column by one tab only.

If the text-based table uses semicolons or other characters to separate items and columns, you can still convert it into a StarWriter table. Just select the table contents, and then choose Tools, Convert Text to Table. In the Convert Text to Table dialog, select the type of column separator (Semicolons or Other, in which case you have to specify the character separator), click AutoFormat to select a table style (optional), and click OK. StarWriter creates a number of rows and columns based on the number of blocks of the text-based table. Again, you can proceed to edit the new table as desired.

Tip #160 from
Michael & Sarah

StarWriter divides columns at the separator mark (tab, semicolon, paragraph, or other). If a space appears after the separator mark, this space is inserted in front of the content of each cell in the new column. To ensure the alignment of contents between cells, use the Search & Replace feature to eliminate additional spaces after the separator marks before converting the text to a table. Select the text, and then press Ctrl+F to open the Search & Replace dialog. Enter the separator (or the regular expression for tabs: \t) followed by a space in the Search For box; then enter the separator (or regular tab expression) by itself in the Replace With box. Next, mark the Current Selection Only option (if it isn't marked already), and then search and replace the current selection (or click Replace All).

Likewise, you can convert sequential paragraphs of any length into a table, in which case StarWriter will squeeze each paragraph in its turn into the next available row. (Remember, a paragraph is any unit of characters that ends with the nonprinting paragraph character; you can show and hide these characters by clicking the Non-Printing Characters button on the Main toolbar.) For example, to create a four-row table from four sequential paragraphs, select all four paragraphs (regardless of whether every paragraph mark comes with any accompanying text), and then select Convert Text to Table from the Tools menu.

CONVERTING TABLES TO TEXT

You can also convert existing tables back to text so that other programs that can't handle StarWriter's table feature can read them. To convert a table to text, select the entire table first; then choose Tools, Convert Table to Text. In the Convert Table to Text dialog, you can select the type of separator StarWriter will use to separate columns. Your options include Tabs, Semicolons, Paragraphs, and Other, so you can specify a separator character of your choice. Select the option you want; then click OK. StarWriter converts the existing table into text, inserting the selected option as a separator between text that used to be in separate columns.

PART

II

CH

9

Note

When StarWriter converts tables to text, it retains the Table Heading and Table Contents styles for the individual table elements. Table column headers are grouped together as one unit—separated by a tab, semicolon, paragraph mark, or other chosen separator—followed by the table contents.

ENTERING AND FORMATTING TEXT IN A TABLE

You can enter, edit, and format text in a table much the same way you enter, edit, and format text in a document by using the character or paragraph formatting options, applied directly or via styles, as discussed in Chapter 7, "Formatting Text Documents," and Chapter 8, "Using Styles and Templates."

ENTERING TEXT

To enter text, place the insertion point in a desired cell, and then start typing. Press Tab or Shift+Tab to move to the next or previous cell, respectively. To insert a tab within a cell, press Ctrl+Tab, and then set the tab stop as you usually do.

Note

Pressing Tab at the end of a table (the last cell in the last row) creates a new table row.

You can also use the arrow keys (left, right, up, or down) to move to adjacent cells. If a cell contains text, the left- and right-arrow keys first move one character at a time and then from cell to cell.

Finally, pressing Ctrl+Home moves the cursor in front of the text of the current cell or, if it's already at the beginning, to the first cell in the first column (or row). If this cell contains text, the cursor appears before the text. Pressing Alt+End moves it to the end of the text in the current cell or, if it's already at the end, to the last cell in the last row (or column). If this cell contains text, the cursor appears after the text.

SELECTING TEXT

To select text, drag the I-beam pointer over the text in a cell or across rows and/or columns. In larger tables, you can also quickly select an entire row or column by placing the insertion point in a cell and then selecting Row, Select or Column, Select from the Context menu. StarWriter automatically moves your cursor into the last cell of the selected row or column. To select more than one row or column at a time, you can drag the I-beam pointer across rows and columns or Shift+click in leaps and bounds until the desired columns and rows are selected. Alternatively, you can also press Ctrl+Shift in combination with the arrow, Home, and End keys on the keyboard. For example, pressing Ctrl+Shift+End selects all cells from the current cell to the end of the row and down to the end of the table. Pressing Ctrl+Shift+Home selects all cells from the current cell to the beginning of the row and up to the beginning of the table. Pressing Ctrl+Shift in combination with the left- or right-arrow keys yields similar results with the proviso that you move in increments of one cell at a time toward the beginning or end of the document. Try it! The possibilities might not be endless, but they are surprising nonetheless.

→ For more details on your general selection options, **see** "Selecting and Deleting Text," **p. 245**.

If you find yourself selecting entire columns or rows often, consider adding a Row Select and Column Select button to the Table object bar by performing these steps:

1. Select Tools, Configure. The Configuration dialog appears.

2. Click the Toolbars tab, then click Configure. The Customize Toolbars dialog appears.

3. In the Functions portion of the dialog, select Table in the Category list on the left and Select Column in the Command list on the right. You'll notice the "Select Column" icon selected in the Icons list at the top of the dialog.

4. Drag the Select Column icon to the Table object bar

5. Now choose Select Rows in the Command list. As with the Select Column icon, you see the Select Row icon selected in the Icon list at the top.

6. Drag the Select Rows icon to the Table object bar, then click the Close (X) icon to exit the Customize Toolbars dialog.

Using these steps, you can also place other commonly used commands on your toolbars.

FORMATTING TEXT

Formatting text in a table is also similar to formatting text in a document. You can apply all the direct character and paragraph formatting techniques discussed in Chapter 7,

"Formatting Text Documents," or you can change attributes via styles (which is the preferred method if you want consistency across table cells). Experiment with borders and shading to make your text stand out in individual cells such as table headers. Figure 9.3 illustrates how you can enhance a standard table via direct or style formatting, without using any other table formatting options.

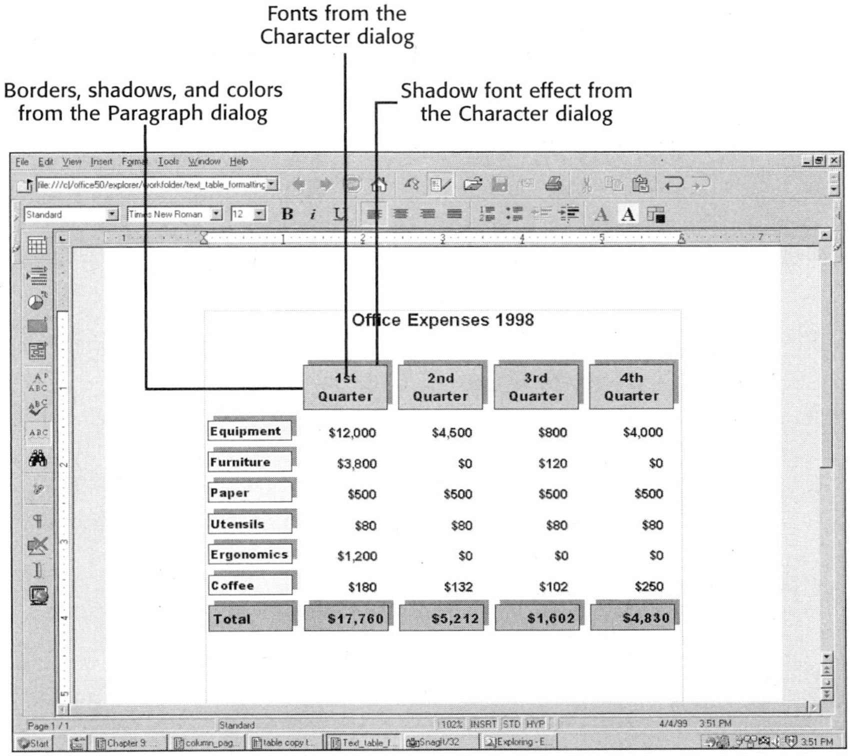

Figure 9.3
You can format text in a table much the same way as you would in a document by using direct and style formatting techniques.

Fonts from the Character dialog

Borders, shadows, and colors from the Paragraph dialog

Shadow font effect from the Character dialog

DELETING CELL CONTENTS

To zap the contents of a table, simply select the desired cell, range, row, or column, and press Delete or Backspace. StarWriter deletes the contents of the selected cell(s); the actual table cell(s), row(s), or column(s) are not deleted.

→ For details on how to delete cells, rows, or columns, **see** "Inserting and Deleting Rows and Columns," **p. 337**, later in this chapter.

FORMATTING AND EDITING TABLES

By default, StarWriter's table feature creates a group of cells that expand vertically as needed to fit all your required text or graphics. Each new table you insert appears with borders surrounding the cells and some basic formatting attributes that include a centered, bold-faced, and italicized Table Heading style and a regular, left-aligned Table Contents style. In addition, each cell is formatted for text entry. And although you can control the overall look of your table by using the AutoFormat feature, sometimes you might want to change the default attributes of a StarWriter table via the Table context menu and/or toolbar.

Note

By default, each cell in a Text table is formatted for (left-aligned) text entry. However, as soon as you enter a number into a cell, StarWriter switches the table format to the default standard for (right-aligned) number entry, which does not show zeros after the decimal point. To change the number format of individual cells or a group of cells, select Number Format from the Table context menu.

USING THE TABLE CONTEXT MENU AND OBJECT BAR

As soon as you insert a table in your document, your blinking cursor appears in the first cell at the top of the table, and the Text object bar is replaced by the Table object bar. (You can switch between the two at any time by clicking the small black triangle on the right of the respective object bar.) In typical StarOffice fashion, all the tools you need while working on a table are only a mouse click away. As long as your cursor is inside the table, you can accomplish most table formatting tasks by using the Table object bar or the Table context menu.

EXPLORING THE TABLE CONTEXT MENU

The Table context menu contains most of the commands you'll ever need when working on a table. Using the context menu, you can change character and paragraph attributes such as font, size, style, alignment, and line spacing of cell contents. If these common direct format-ting options do not meet your text formatting needs, you can also summon the Character and Paragraph dialogs. Last, but not least, you can control all major formatting aspects of the current table (from cell to row to column); choose a Number Format for the selected cell or group of cells; split the current table in two (if the table has more than two rows); and if that's not enough, you can open the Table Format dialog (Table) which puts a few more precision tools at your fingertips.

Figure 9.4 shows the Table context menu and its submenus. Most of the available functions are self-explanatory and can be derived from their names. Some, such as the Number Format and Split Table commands, are explained in "Using the Number Format" and "Splitting Tables," respectively.

Figure 9.4
Using the Table context menu, you can find most of the commands you'll ever need just a mouse click away. You can show or hide Table Boundaries if no border is applied.

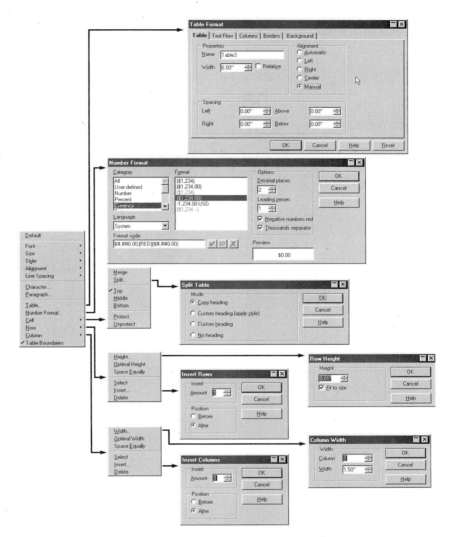

EXPLORING THE TABLE OBJECT BAR

The Table object bar is more select in its offerings, but, as always, StarOffice's power is there when you need it. Using the Table object bar, you can insert and delete rows and columns; merge cells; select a table border, line style, and background color; and open the Text Formula bar. Table 9.1 explains the various Table object bar command buttons.

TABLE 9.1 TABLE OBJECT BAR COMMANDS

Command	Result
Σ (Sum)	Opens the Text Formula bar, which enables you to perform simple and complex calculations with operators and functions.
(Modes)	Controls how keyboard changes to selected cells affect the table as a whole. The same options are available on the Table tab of the Text Document Options dialog (see "Using the Keyboard" in this chapter).
(Merge)	Merges a selected group of cells into a single one.
(Split)	Opens the Split Cells dialog, which enables you to split single cells or a group of cells horizontally or vertically into a specified number of cells.
(Optimize	Opens a floating toolbar that enables you to make adjustments to table rows and columns. Your options for a selected group of cells include assigning identical column width, spacing rows equally, and selecting optimal row heights or column widths for the selected cells.
(Insert)	Inserts a row or column below or to the right of the insertion point.
(Delete)	Deletes the row or column at the insertion point. If more than one cell is selected, it deletes the rows or columns that run through these cells.
(Borders)	Opens the Borders floating window, which enables you to select a border style for the selected cell or group of cells.
(Border style)	Opens the Border Style floating window, which enables you to select a line style for the selected cell or group of cells.
(Color)	Opens the floating Color palette, which enables you to select a back ground color for the selected cell or group of cells.

ADJUSTING ROW HEIGHT AND COLUMN WIDTH

By default, StarWriter adjusts the height of table rows according to the amount of text you place in each cell, leaving the column width fixed as it was when you created the table. Of course, you can modify the default settings at any time, using the mouse, keyboard, context menu, or Table Format dialog.

Note

The height and width of a cell are limited by the printable text area on a page. StarWriter does not allow you to insert a cell, row, or column that exceeds the text boundaries of a page—unless the table has been placed inside a text box or frame as described in the tip in section "Inserting a new Table" in this chapter.

USING THE MOUSE

The easiest way to adjust the column width is by dragging the cell boundaries. To make a column wider or narrower, drag anywhere on the column boundary. You can also drag the column markers in the horizontal ruler. StarWriter automatically changes the width of all aligned cells. Dragging the boundary of a cell that doesn't align with the ones in the row above or below changes the width of only that particular cell. Note that you can't change the row height by using the mouse.

USING THE KEYBOARD

StarWriter accommodates all kinds of computer users—especially those who prefer to keep their fingers over the keyboard rather than wrapped around a mouse. Besides, when it comes to changing the height and width of rows and columns (as well as inserting or deleting cells as detailed shortly), the convenience of using the keyboard is hard to beat.

Using the keyboard method, you can work in one of three table modes—Fixed, Fixed/Proportional, and Variable—which you can select from the Table object bar or the Effect portion of the Tools, Options, Text Document, Table dialog (look ahead to Figure 9.5). Each mode results in a different table behavior when you're adjusting the height and width of rows and columns.

For example, if you enlarge a cell in Fixed mode, the adjacent cell is reduced in width accordingly to accommodate the change. The table width itself stays the same. If you enlarge a cell in Fixed Proportional mode, all the following cells are reduced in width to accommodate the change; wider cells are reduced proportionally more than narrower ones. The overall table width, again, stays the same. In the (default) Variable mode, by contrast, the overall table width increases or decreases when you enlarge or reduce columns or cells. If the table width stretches the entirety of the printable area (between the text boundaries), and you enlarge a cell, the following cells are reduced proportionally.

To use the keyboard method, position the cursor in the row or column you want to modify, and press Alt in combination with the arrow keys on your keyboard. StarWriter adjusts the rows, columns, and/or cells incrementally as specified in the Shift portion on the Tools, Options, Text Document, and Table dialog, shown in Figure 9.5.

Note

The width of a table is limited by the text boundaries in a document. When a table borders the text boundaries to the left or right, cells or columns can no longer be shifted in the direction of the boundary; instead, StarWriter reduces them individually or proportionally. However, there is one exception: when you place a table inside a text box or frame as described in the tip in the section "Inserting a New Table" earlier in this chapter.

Specifies the amount by which rows, columns, or cells are shifted

Specifies the height and width of inserted rows and columns

Figure 9.5
The settings on the Table tab of the Text Document Options dialog control the way StarWriter modifies a table when you use the keyboard to adjust row height and column width.

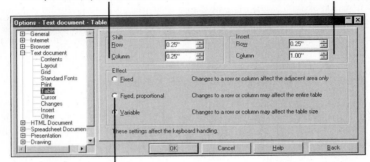

Controls how adjustments to rows and columns affect the table

Table 9.2 lists the various options for modifying row height and column width with the keyboard in the (default) Variable mode.

TABLE 9.2   ADJUSTING ROW HEIGHT AND COLUMN WIDTH WITH THE KEYBOARD

Keyboard Combination	Result
Alt+right arrow	Enlarges column width. Columns to the right are moved to the right or reduced evenly (if the table stretches to the right text boundary).
Alt+left arrow	Reduces column width. Columns to the right shift left.
Alt+down arrow	Enlarges row height.
Alt+up arrow	Reduces row height (if the current height is larger than the value specified in the Shift portion of the Table tab).
Alt+Ctrl+right arrow	Enlarges cell width. The cell to the right is reduced.
Alt+Ctrl+left arrow	Reduces cell width. The cell to the right is enlarged.
Alt+Shift+right arrow	Reduces column width. Columns to the left shift right.
Alt+Shift+left arrow	Enlarges column width. Columns to the left are moved to the left or reduced evenly (if table stretches to the left text boundary).

Keyboard Combination	Result
Alt+Shift+down arrow	Enlarges row height.
Alt+Shift+up arrow	Reduces row height (if the current height is larger than the value specified in the Shift portion of the Table tab).
Alt+Ctrl+Shift+right arrow	Reduces cell width. The cell to the left is enlarged.
Alt+Ctrl+Shift+left arrow	Enlarges cell width. The cell to the left is reduced.

Note

Pressing the Alt key in combination with the arrow keys enlarges or reduces cells starting from the lower-right corner. Pressing Alt+Shift in combination with the arrow keys also moves the left or upper corner.

USING THE CONTEXT MENU

You can also control the row height and column width more precisely by using the Row Height and Column Width dialogs, which you can open from the Row and Column submenus of the Table context menu or the Format menu on the menu bar.

In the Row Height dialog, you can specify an absolute value by using the spin box (see Figure 9.4). If Fit to Size is selected (default), the specified value in the spin box becomes the minimum height for the selected cell and row, and StarWriter automatically adjusts the row height to accommodate the largest font or graphic or the amount of text.

In the Column Width dialog, you can adjust the width of the current column or select a different one from the Column spin box (refer to Figure 9.4). Note that changes to the width of individual columns affect the column width of the adjacent cells to the left or right (if the current column is the last one).

Note

The left and right border of the table is controlled via the Spacing portion of the Table tab in the Table Format dialog and cannot be changed when you're adjusting column width via the Column Width dialog.

Tip #161 from
Michael & Sarah

You can also adjust the width and height of a selected group of cells quickly by using the Optimize command on the Table object bar. Use (from top to bottom) Space Columns Equally and Space Rows Equally to assign equal width and height to a selected group of cells; use Optimal Row Height and Optimal Column Width to better fit the contents of selected cells.

USING THE TABLE FORMAT DIALOG

If you want to change several columns at once while keeping an eye on the individual column width or adjust the columns proportionally, select the Columns tab in the Table

Format dialog (see Figure 9.6). To open the Table Format dialog, right-click with your cursor inside a table, and select Table from the context menu or select Format Table.

Figure 9.6
Using the Columns tab in the Table Format dialog, you can keep an eye on the remaining space between text boundaries and the table while adjusting all columns at once.

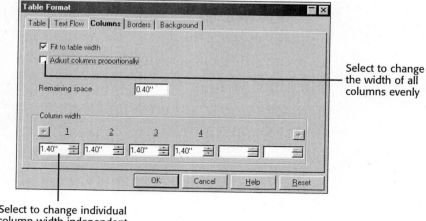

Select to change the width of all columns evenly

Select to change individual column width independent of other columns

MOVING AND POSITIONING TABLES ON A PAGE

StarWriter likes to arm-wrestle with you when it comes to positioning a table on a page. By default, the inserted table stretches from the left to the right text boundaries, regardless of the number of columns you chose for the table. Even if you manually adjust the column width so that the table no longer spans the entire width of the printable text area, you can't just select and drag the table to reposition it horizontally between the text boundaries. Instead, you have to deal with the Table Format dialog to align the table manually.

Place the insertion point inside any cell in your table, and open the Table Format dialog (via the Table context menu or choose Format, Table). Select an option in the Alignment portion of the Table tab (other than Automatic), and then inch the table with numeric precision away from the left and/or right text boundaries by using the Left and Right spin boxes in the Spacing portion of the tab (refer to Figure 9.4).

If you select Left in the Alignment portion, you can adjust the spacing between the right table and text boundaries. Center and Right enable you to adjust the spacing between the left table and text boundaries; Manual gives you the option to indent the table both from the left and right. In each instance, you increase the spacing between table and text boundaries at the expense of the overall table width.

If you want the table to stand out even more from the rest of the text, use the Above and Below boxes to increase the spacing between the top and bottom table boundaries and the surrounding text. (By default, the spacing between the text and table corresponds to the spacing between paragraphs, which you can define on the Indents and Spacing tab of the Paragraph dialog.) When you click OK to save your changes, StarWriter repositions the table according to your specifications while reducing the width of each column equally to accommodate the new table width.

Note

Unlike with graphics and other objects, you cannot wrap text around a table, nor can you move a selected text block above or below tables by using the Ctrl+up/down arrow combination. StarWriter Tables firmly plant themselves in between paragraph marks, regardless of table width, drawing an invisible line between the above and below text that cannot be crossed. When you continue to insert text above a table, you move the table one line down with each new line wrap or paragraph break.

Tip #162 from
Michael & Sarah

As mentioned before—there is one exception to this stationary stubbornness of tables—you can insert it in a frame or text box. To do so, first create a text box by clicking the Frame icon in the Insert tear-off window (first icon from the left), then click and drag to create a text box. Then click anywhere outside the frame to deselect it. Next, click inside the frame to place the insertion point inside. Now insert the table as described in this section. You can now move the table (inside the box) freely in your document, anchor it in a certain location, even resize the text box or have text wrap around it. For more details on text boxes or frames see "Working with Text Boxes" in Chapter 11, "Desktop Publishing with StarOffice."

To move an entire table to another location in the document, select the table, and click and drag the selected table to the desired location. If you press Ctrl while dragging, StarWriter creates a copy of the table at the drop location.

COPYING AND MOVING ROWS AND COLUMNS

Unfortunately, you cannot move or copy individual rows and columns within the same table unless you painstakingly cut and paste the information into newly created rows or columns and then delete the old ones.

INSERTING AND DELETING ROWS AND COLUMNS

You can insert or delete rows and columns in a StarWriter table in several different ways. For example, you can use the respective Insert buttons on the Table object bar. Using the Insert Row button inserts a row below the cell with the insertion point; using the Insert Column button inserts a column after the insertion point. If you select more than one cell in a row or column, StarWriter inserts an equal number of columns or rows.

Tip #163 from
Michael & Sarah

When you're inserting columns via the Table object bar or Table context menu, StarWriter cuts the width of the current column in half. To reassign identical width to all columns, select the Optimize button on the Table object bar, and click the Space Columns Equally command (first from the top).

Likewise, you can use the Delete Row and Delete Column buttons to delete the row or column that intersects the insertion point; if more than one cell is selected, StarWriter deletes the rows or columns that intersect the selected cells.

You can also use the Table context menu to insert or delete rows and columns. The Insert command in the Row and Column submenus opens the Insert Row and Insert Column dialogs, respectively. Using these dialogs, you can specify the number of rows or columns to insert as well as select whether the columns should be inserted before or after the current cursor position. The Delete command in the Row and Column submenus works just like the Delete buttons on the Table object bar.

Keyboard aficionados will be happy to learn that there is also a way to insert and delete columns and rows without leaving the periphery of the keyboard. First, however, you have to activate the respective Insert and Delete mode. For example, pressing Alt+Insert turns on the Insert mode. This mode is active for about three seconds. During this time, you can use the arrow keys to insert a column or row to the left or right of or above or below the current cell, respectively. Likewise, pressing Alt+Delete turns on the Delete mode, which also remains active for about three seconds. Using the arrow keys during this time deletes a row or column above or below or to the left or right of the current cell.

Note

You can control the width of the inserted column as well as the height of the inserted row via the Insert portion of the Table tab in the Text Document Options dialog.

As is the case when you're adjusting row height and column/cell width via the keyboard, your moves are controlled by the selected table mode (Fixed, Fixed/Proportional, Variable).

→ For more details on these table modes, **see** "Adjusting Row Height and Column Width," **p. 332**, earlier in this chapter.

SPLITTING AND MERGING CELLS

The easiest way to split or merge cells is to use the Split Cells and Merge Cells commands on the Table object bar. Simply select the cell or group of cells you want to split, and click the Split Cells button on the Table object bar. In the Split Cells dialog, you can select whether you want the selected cell or group of cells to split vertically or horizontally. Using the Amount spin box, you can also specify into how many cells you want to split the selected cell(s).

Note

> The default row height of split cells is controlled by the settings in the Row Height dialog. Note that the height of the remaining cells in the row automatically increases by the cumulative number of horizontally split cells.

To merge two or more cells into one, simply select the group of cells, and click the Merge button on the Table object bar.

SPLITTING TABLES

StarWriter enables you to divide a table with two or more rows into two by slicing it horizontally above the row containing the insertion point. Using the Split Table dialog (see Figure 9.4), you can even select whether to keep the current heading for the second table, assign a custom one, or go with no heading at all.

And what about splitting a table vertically? You might not find a command that will do the job for you, but there is a way, or better put, there is a trick: You have to create a false split.

Here's what you need to do to present two tables side by side in no time. Insert a new column between the columns where you want the split to occur. Remove all borders from the newly inserted column, and resize it so that it is somewhat smaller than the other columns (basically, you're creating "white space" to separate the two columns). Now, select the cells to the right, and use the Space Columns Equally option from the Optimize tear-off window (Table object bar) so that they have a more uniform look. Do the same with the cells to the left of the newly inserted column. Next, apply borders and other formatting to the remaining columns so that the two parts of the table look truly independent. Voilá, un faux couple de tables, perfectly placed next to each other.

Caution

> If you want to insert this kind of arrangement in a StarImpress document, you will see gray lines around the "empty": columns.

ADDING BORDERS AND BACKGROUNDS

To give your table a distinct look and help group and separate its contents visually, use the Border, Line Style, and Background Color buttons on the Table object bar. In each instance, you can make your selection from the corresponding tear-off windows, shown in Figure 9.7.

Tip #164 from
Michael & Sarah

Ideally, the use of borders and color should link those cells that form a unit of information (such as column or row headers) and thus set them apart from other units. In large tables, alternating the background color of rows makes it easier for the reader to interpret and read the information presented. For example, you could use a background color for every fifth row and leave the other rows without background color, or you could alternate between five rows without background color and five rows with background color. You can also look at the table designs provided in the AutoFormat dialog (which you open by choosing Insert, Table, AutoFormat).

Figure 9.7
The Table object bar provides the easiest way to add borders, lines, and color to a selected cell or group of cells.

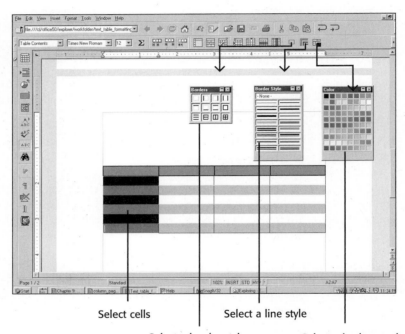

Select cells

Select a border style

Select a line style

Select a background color

To apply a border, place the insertion point in the cell where you want the line border to appear, or select a group of cells, rows, columns, or the entire table. Then select a border format, line style, or color of your choice. How StarWriter applies the border depends on the selection you make in the Borders window. Your options include, from left to right, No Border, Left Border, Right Border, Left and Right Border, Top Border, Bottom Border, Top and Bottom Border, Outside Border, Row Border, Outside and Horizontal Inside Border, Outside and Vertical Inside Border, and Outside and Inside Border. With the exception of the inside borders, all borders are applied to the outside of your selection. For example, if you select a group of 3×3 cells and apply the Outside Border format, you frame the entire group, leaving the inside blank.

Tip #165 from
Michael & Sarah

Before applying borders, you need to do some planning first. You add borders with each selection you make, which might result in overlapping border formats. Hence, it helps to start out with a clean slate. Select the entire table, and apply the No Border format; then start applying border formats as desired. If you make a mistake, you can always use the Undo command (on the function bar) to cancel your last action or press Ctrl+Z.

For example, if you want to draw a full border around your selection, select the fourth format in the second row. If you want the columns separated by a vertical line, select the third format in the third row.

If you really want to get creative, you can also use the Borders and Background Color tabs in the Table format dialog (which you open by choosing Format, Table or choosing Table from the context menu). Using the Borders tab gives you fewer preset border formats in exchange for the option of adding shading to a selected cell or group of cells.

Building a custom border format for the selected cell or group of cells is no different from building a border format using the Borders tab in the Paragraph dialog. You can choose from various line and shadow styles, and you can tell the program on which side of the object to place a border. StarOffice provides you with a set of presets (or samples) that you can use as building blocks for your own border design. You can add or remove border lines by clicking the little black arrows at the end of a line, specify the distance between text and borders, and change the size and colors of your lines and shadow style. To get a general idea of what the final border will look like, consult the Preview area when creating your borders and shading.

If you're handling many tables, you might appreciate that StarOffice gives you the freedom to give each cell and row its own background color. Using the Background tab, you can select and preview a background color for your table, as well as a graphic from StarOffice's Gallery or even your own archives. Select Graphic from the As drop-down list, and click Browse to locate the desired graphic in a directory or folder on your system or network. You can add a background color or graphic to a selected cell, row, column, or the entire table. To remove a background graphic, press Ctrl+Z, or turn off the Graphic mode by selecting Color in the As box and click OK. If you want to remove a background color, select No Fill above the color palette.

Tip #166 from
Michael & Sarah

Given the size of individual cells and rows, you should use only simple background graphics such as lines for cells and rows. Also, keep in mind the busier the background, the harder it is for the reader to focus on what is really important—the information presented in the table.

→ For more details on using the Borders and Background tabs, **see** "Adding Borders and Background Color," **p. 278**.

FORMATTING CELLS

As you learned earlier, each new table you insert in StarWriter comes with some basic formatting attributes that include a centered, boldfaced, and italicized Table Heading style and a regular, left-aligned Table Contents style, which have been defined via the Character Styles and Paragraph Styles dialogs. In addition to these text style attributes, StarWriter defines two cell attributes that affect the appearance of the contents of each cell and can be changed only via direct formatting: vertical alignment and number format.

By default, the contents of a cell are top aligned. Using the Cell submenu of the Table context menu, you can select Center or Bottom as an alternative to the default Top alignment. (You can also define the alignment attribute on the Text Flow tab of the Table Format dialog.)

StarWriter also assumes that you use its tables mostly for text entry; hence, each cell is, by default, formatted as plain old text. Using the Number Format command from the Table Context menu, you can define a different format for the selected cell(s). In the Number Format dialog, formats are divided into categories, including Number, Percent, Currency, Date, Time, Scientific, Fraction, Boolean Value, Text, and User-Defined (see Figure 9.8). To assign a different format to a selected cell or group of cells, choose a category from the list on the left; then click a format in the box on the right. If you select a regular Number, Percent, or Currency format, you can use the Options portion of the dialog to define the appearance of numbers in these categories. For example, you can specify the number of decimal places and leading zeros, and whether the number should appear in red if negative or with a thousands separator.

Select a number format

Figure 9.8
Using the Number Format dialog, you can assign an existing format for your cell or create one of your own.

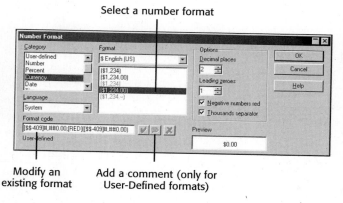

Modify an
existing format

Add a comment (only for
User-Defined formats)

When you select a number format on the right, you can see the corresponding format code in the text box at the bottom of the dialog and a brief comment that describes the selected format underneath. Using the Format Code text box, you can modify the code of a selected number format or create your own. By default, each change you make to an existing code or each code you enter is categorized as User-Defined. To be more specific, you can assign a comment to your custom code. Just click the Comment button (the one with the text balloon icon), and enter a descriptive word or two that will help you identify the format when selected. You can preview the results of your code in the rectangular box at the bottom center of the dialog. To enter the custom code in the Categories list, click the Enter button. The Delete button removes only selected user-defined formats.

PROTECTING TABLE CONTENTS

StarWriter enables you to protect a selected cell or group of cells from accidental changes. Simply select the cell(s), and choose Cell, Protect from the context menu. If you want to make changes to a protected cell, select the cell(s), and choose Cell, Unprotect from the context menu.

SORTING TABLE DATA

StarWriter may not hold a torch to StarCalc when it comes to manipulating large amounts of data, but sometimes you only need a lighter. StarWriter tables can sort numbers or text according to the contents of up to three columns or rows of your choice in ascending and descending order.

To perform a sort, follow these steps:

1. Select the columns or rows that you want to sort. For example, if you're sorting a list of contacts alphabetically by last name, select the entire table (without column heading!), and memorize the number of the last name column (counting from left to right).

   If you want to sort only a particular column, without moving the entries in the other columns, select that column only.

2. Select Tools, Sort to display the Sort dialog. In the Sort Criteria portion of the dialog, you can select a primary, secondary, and tertiary sort key. Using the Column spin boxes, you specify the number of the column that contains the sort criteria.

   For example, if you're sorting a list of contacts alphabetically by last name, and if the last name column is the second column from the left, enter 2 in the Column spin box next to the primary key. In the Key Type box, you specify whether the item to be sorted is alphanumeric (text) or numeric (numbers). Then you select whether the key should be sorted in ascending or descending order.

3. Click OK, and StarWriter rearranges the data as requested.

The Sort command works on any selected text even if it isn't neatly tucked into a StarWriter table. If you're sorting a tabular list that isn't a table, you can tell StarWriter which character indicates the separation between columns (usually a tab, but it can be any character) and then proceed to sort by columns or rows. You can even rearrange selected paragraphs in alphabetical order according to the first word in each one.

Tip #167 from
Michael & Sarah

> If you're preparing a glossary or an alphabetically arranged reference list of any kind, you don't have to worry about keeping everything in correct order as you're compiling the data. When the time comes to call the chaos to order, select the entire list, and tell the Sort command to sort the list (Column 1) of entries (most likely alphanumeric) in ascending order.

WORDSMITHING WITH NUMBERS

Although StarCalc, the number-crunching workhorse of StarOffice, is only a mouse click away, you don't have to give StarWriter a break when it comes to simple spreadsheet-type calculations and formulas. StarWriter gets by easily with a little help from the Text Formula bar, shown in Figure 9.9.

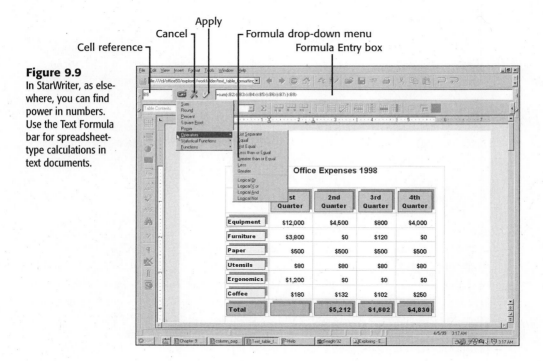

Figure 9.9
In StarWriter, as elsewhere, you can find power in numbers. Use the Text Formula bar for spreadsheet-type calculations in text documents.

Press F2 anywhere in a table or text to show the Text Formula bar. When in tables, it suffices to enter an equals sign (=) in a cell to get the same toolbar, or click the Sum symbol on the Table object bar. Press F2 again or Esc to hide the Formula toolbar.

Note

As long as the Text Formula bar is displayed, you cannot make any other changes to your table or document.

LOOKING AT THE TEXT FORMULA BAR

The Text Formula bar makes it easy for you to perform simple and complex calculations. For example, using the Formula drop-down menu, you can enter operators and functions via mouse clicks. You can also enter a formula directly into the Formula Entry box. Table 9.3 details the various functions of the Formula bar.

TABLE 9.3   THE TEXT FORMULA BAR EXPOSED

Function	What it does
Cell reference	Indicates the current cell at the insertion point
Formula	Contains a drop-down menu that enables you to select various kinds of operators and functions that you can insert in the Formula Entry box via mouse clicks
Cancel	Removes all Formula Entry box entries and closes the Formula bar
Apply	Enters the results of the formula in the Formula Entry box into table (or text) and closes the Formula bar
Formula Entry box	Provides a place for you to build the formula, either by entering the formula directly or by opening the Formula drop-down menu

➔ For more details on operators, **see** "What Is a Formula?" **p. 590**.

➔ For details on functions, **see** "Working with Functions," **p. 601**.

ADDING NUMBERS IN STARWRITER

Why would you want to add numbers in a text document? Well, say you have designed a professional-looking invoice, using all the desktop publishing power StarOffice puts at your fingertips. You created a three-column table. The first column breaks down the various services supplied; the second column breaks down the cost per item and/or hour (for example, 10 hours @ $75 per hour); the third column lists the cost for the service or item. Naturally, you want to add the various categories of the invoice before sending it off. Give your left brain a well-deserved break; StarWriter can do the math for you.

To add numbers in an invoice-style text table, follow these simple steps:

1. Insert the desired table in your document, and fill in all the cells except the ones in the third column.

2. Place the insertion point in the first cell of the third column, and press = to open the Formula bar. (The equals sign shows up in the Formula Entry box.)

3. In the Formula Entry box, insert the formula that calculates the cost for the item or service detailed in the first row (for example, 10*75). Then click the Apply button, or press Enter. StarWriter inserts the result into the current cell. Do the same for all the other rows that detail a service or item in your invoice table.

4. After detailing the cost for each service or item provided, you can add the total. Place the insertion point in the last cell of the third column (which should be empty), and click the Sum symbol on the Table object bar. StarWriter displays the Formula bar with the Sum formula for the above cells already entered in the Formula Entry box:
   ```
   =sum(<C1>¦<C2>¦....
   ```

5. Click Apply or press Enter, and StarWriter inserts the sum total in the current cell while closing the Formula bar.

6. To put the finishing touches on the invoice, select the third column, and choose Number Format from the Table context menu. In the Number Format dialog, select Currency to have your figures appear with a $ symbol.

Following these basic steps, you can add any numbers in a table and apply any desired format to the figures and final results. One advantage of adding numbers in a single text table by using the Formula bar is that you can adjust individual figures if needed; the sum is automatically updated.

StarWriter can do more than just add numbers in the same table, though. It can actually show the routinely updated numbers of text tables in the text—well, sort of. What you have to do is insert a single cell in a line by itself; then you need to add a formula to this cell that reflects the sum of the desired cells in other tables. To make this cell appear more in line with the surrounding text, you might want to avoid adding borders or any other distinctive cell formatting features. Simply center the cell contents.

To have this single cell show the sum of other table cells in your document, follow these steps:

1. Place the insertion point into the cell that is supposed to show the sum total of existing table cells, and press = or F2 to open the Formula bar.

2. Enter Sum after the = sign in the Formula Entry box.

3. One after the other, click each cell in the respective table(s) that you want to add to the sum total; after each click, press the + key. StarWriter enters something similar to the following expression into the Formula Text Entry field:

=SUM<Table2.A1>+<Table2.B1>+<Table2.A2>+<Table2.B2> and so on.

4. After you've finished selecting all cells, click Apply or press Enter. StarWriter inserts the result of your calculation at the insertion point into the currently selected cell and closes the Formula bar.

Using this method, you can add any number of cells across separate tables, using the scrollbar to locate distant tables, and show the sum total in a separate table or cell. If any of the figures in the original cells should change, simply place the insertion point in the summary cell, and press F9 to update the sum.

CALCULATING FORMULAS IN TEXT

On occasion, you might have to add the results of a formula or calculation in your text. Using the StarMath Formula Editor (discussed in Chapter 6, "Creating and Editing Text Documents"), you can insert simple and complex formulas as text objects into your document. These formulas, however, cannot be used as the basis for a calculation; they are only meant to show relations and functions. To actually show the result of a formula or calculation in your text, proceed as follows:

→ For more details on inserting formulas with StarMath, **see** "Creating and Inserting Formulas with StarMath," **p. 235**.

1. Enter the desired formula and numbers in your text document as if you were to enter the same into a calculator (for example, 25+(7*6)-4=). If you want to enter the result after the formula, also insert an equals sign after the formula.

2. Select the entire formula (without the equals sign), and press Ctrl+C.

3. Place the insertion point after the equals sign in your text (or at the place where you want the result to appear).

4. Press F2 to open the Text Formula bar, place the insertion point after the equals sign in the Formula Entry box, and press Ctrl+V to paste your copy of the calculation into the Entry box.

Note

Alternatively, you can enter the formula by hand by using the numeric keypad of your keyboard.

5. Press Enter, or click the Apply button. StarWriter inserts the result as a (Variable) field at the insertion point in your document.

Note

Calculating formulas directly in text–without using tables–does not enable you to update the results if the numbers in the calculation should change.

If your calculation is more complex, you can use the Formula command of the Formula bar to help you out in a pinch. For example, if you want to calculate the mean value of a series of numbers (25, 45, 3, 78, 98), just open the Formula bar (press F2) and select Statistical Functions, Mean from the Formula drop-down menu. The Formula Entry box now shows =mean. Next, enter your numbers, separated by the list separator (25¦45¦3¦78¦98). When you're finished, click Apply or press Enter to place the result at the insertion point in your document. To edit the formula or result, double-click the result field. In the Edit Fields: Variable dialog, you can edit the formula in the Formula box or assign a different number format to it. Alternatively, you can place the insertion point directly in front of the field and then press F2 again to edit the formula in the Formula Entry box of the Formula bar.

If your text already contains a formula, you can get the result without using the Formula bar, as follows:

1. Select the formula in the text. Note that the formula can contain only numbers, operators (+, -, *, /), and perhaps currency symbols.
2. Press Ctrl++ or select Tools, Calculate. The results of the calculation are in the Clipboard (Windows) or General-Purpose Buffer (Linux).
3. Place the cursor at the place where you want to insert the result, and press Ctrl+V or select Edit, Insert. The result is then inserted. If the formula is still selected, it is replaced with the result.

Using the Formula bar for basic as well as complex calculations in a text document is pretty straightforward, and now that you know where the various functions and operators are hiding, you can start to do some exploring yourself.

INSERTING CHARTS

 You can insert charts into StarWriter by using the Insert, Chart command (from the menu bar or the Main toolbar). Charts are useful when you want to present your data in a graphical fashion. Although you can investigate details by scrutinizing the individual values in a table or spreadsheet, a chart shows you the big picture, clarifying, for example, the way numbers change from one time period to another or from one region to another or from one person to another. In addition, charts add a splash of color to an otherwise drab-looking text report.

Chapter 18, "Analyzing and Charting Data," tells you everything you ever wanted to know about charts and more. In this section, you'll briefly examine through the mechanics of inserting charts into a StarWriter document.

→ For more details on charts, **see** "Charting Data," **p. 666**.

Charts come in various forms and shapes, including column charts, line charts, pie charts, or bar charts, to name just a few. Because a chart is a graphical representation of your data, you must have the raw data out of which you want to create a chart type before you can insert a chart into your document. Hence, the first step to creating and inserting a chart is to create a table with data and then select the desired data, complete with column and row headings (if applicable), you want to convert into a chart.

Next, you can select the Insert, Chart command (from the menu bar or from the Main toolbar) to open the AutoFormat Chart wizard, which walks you through these four steps in the chart-creation process:

PART

II

CH

9

1. You are asked to confirm whether the selected data is the desired data. Looking at the Selection portion of the first AutoFormat Chart wizard window, you see the selected range of data inserted in the Area text box, similar to this: `<Table2.A1:D5>`. Translated into English, this means that you selected everything from the first cell in the first row (`A1`) to (`:`) the fifth cell in the fourth row (`D5`) in Table2 (name of the table).

   You can leave the range as is or make changes if you believe the desired data is not represented in full. In addition, you can select First Row as Label, if the first row of your table consists of column headings that you want represented; select First Column as Label, if the first column consists of row headings. Click Next when you're done.

2. Select a chart type. You can also choose between having your data series presented as Rows or as Columns. Select Show Text Elements in the Preview area if you want to show elements such as a legend in the thumbnail preview of your chart. When you're finished, click Next.

3. Select whether you want to show gridlines emanating from the x-axis, y-axis, or both in your chart. Gridlines are applied at regular intervals and work like rulers—they provide points of reference for the reader's eyes. Click Next.

4. Select the Chart Title option if you want to include a name for your chart; if yes, you can enter a name in the adjacent text box. You can also choose whether to include a legend with your chart and whether you want to assign a name to the x-axis and y-axis. Finally, click Create.

StarWriter inserts your chart as an OLE object above the selected table. You now can move, position, and format your chart like you would any other object in StarWriter.

Note

As with StarCalc tables, you can also insert charts created with the StarChart module from StarChart—but only as OLE objects (like the StarCalc tables). For more details on OLE and exchanging data between StarOffice documents, see "Sharing Data Between Documents," in Chapter 4, "Working in StarOffice."

→ For more details on working with objects in StarWriter, **see** "Rehearsing Objects," **p. 421**.

UNDERSTANDING FIELDS

Fields are special codes hidden in your document that instruct StarWriter to perform a special task. Viewed in this light, fields are "text-producing machines" of sorts; StarWriter translates the fields' instructions into text that appears at a given location in your document. The basic difference between fields and text is that with fields, the computer inserts the information for you. One key benefit of using fields is that the resulting text is not static. Fields are dynamic: They can change to reflect the prevailing conditions at the time StarWriter performs the translation from field to text. For example, each time you insert a date or page number field in your document, you're inserting a field that StarWriter can automatically update as time goes by or as the number of pages in your document increases or decreases.

You can use fields as placeholders for certain information, or you can use them to insert references, execute a macro, or update information that routinely changes. You can also instruct fields to show or hide text or data depending on certain predefined conditions, or import data from StarCalc worksheets or Starbase databases.

Fields are most commonly used in headers and footers to insert specific document information such the author's name, filename, page numbers, and the like. Fields can also be used to gather all the headings in your document into a formatted table of contents or to create personalized form letters in mail merges.

StarOffice has dozens of fields. Some, like the page number field and current date field, are simple to understand and use. Others, like the conditioned text fields, are more complex and require a bit of a learning curve before you can use them to their full potential.

In general, all fields can be inserted into a document and updated using the same procedures, unless they are of the Fixed type. The following sections focus on the mechanics of inserting and editing fields while providing a brief field guide to the available fields in StarOffice.

WORKING WITH FIELDS

You can easily spot fields in StarOffice when you select the Field Shadings command from the View menu; each field appears against a shaded background. Some fields, such as input fields or database fields, may show a brief reference as to the name, value, or function of the field when you move your cursor over them (similar to Tips and Extended Tips). You can specify the reference text for variable, database, user-defined, and function fields in the Fields dialog.

Fields typically consist of two elements: a field name and field contents. When you select View, Fields, you can toggle between the display of field names and field contents. For example, the field name for page numbers is Page numbers; the field contents might be shown as 4/12/99 or whatever number format you defined for this particular field.

Fields can come with fixed or variable contents. If fixed, the field contents reflect the prevailing condition at the time the field was inserted; if variable, StarWriter updates the contents automatically or upon request.

You can also instruct fields to recognize certain conditions in your text and, depending on the condition, perform a different task. For example, you can define a condition for a certain mail merge field such as Company. If your address database lists the company name for a certain contact (read: if the condition is TRUE), StarWriter inserts the Company field into your document; if no company name is listed with a contact (read: if the condition is FALSE), StarWriter skips to the next defined database field and inserts it into your document. Using conditions in this way prevents you from inserting empty fields into your document that might result in a blank line between the first and last name of a contact and the contact's address in an address block.

PART

II

CH

9

Caution

Using non-static fields such as "Author" in an email or newsgroup posting can cause problems as everybody who uses StarOffice will see his own name in the posting.

→ For examples of conditional fields, **see** "Using Conditions in Mail Merges," **p. 364**, later in this chapter.

Even though most fields are used to insert variable contents into a document, some fields— such as the Placeholder, Insert Reference, Execute Macro, and Input Field fields—perform a specific function when clicked. When you move the mouse pointer over one of these field types, it changes shape into a hand, signaling that you can click the field contents to perform a function. If you click a Placeholder field, you open a dialog that enables you to insert an object, or you can start typing text, depending on the type of placeholder. If you click an Insert Reference of Execute Macro field, you are moved to the target of the reference or start of the macro, respectively. If you click an Input Field, you open a dialog that enables you to edit the contents of the field.

All fields in StarOffice are divided into six broad categories: Documents, References, Functions, Properties, Variables, and Databases. Each category has its own tab in the Fields dialog, and you can access it by selecting Insert, Fields, Other from the menu bar or the Main toolbar, or by pressing Ctrl+F2.

The Fields dialog is the central gathering place for all available fields in StarOffice. Using the various tabs, you can select both predefined and user-defined fields and field formats for each category. The basic layout of each tab is virtually the same. You have an area that lists the available field types of the category by name, another area that lists the names of fields of a selected field type (if the type consists of more than field), and an area that enables you to assign a specific format or condition to a selected field type or name.

INSERTING FIELDS

Many commands in StarWriter insert fields indirectly; for example, if you generate reference tables, such as a table of contents and indexes, or footnotes and endnotes, you are inserting fields that gather all the headings in your document to produce the table of contents with page numbers or insert reference markers, respectively.

→ For more details on creating reference tables and inserting footnotes and endnotes, **see** the corresponding sections in Chapter 10, "Working with Long Documents," **p. 369**.

You can also insert fields directly into a document by using the Insert, Fields command or pressing Ctrl+F2 to open the Fields dialog. The actual process of inserting fields is simple:

1. Place the insertion point where you want to insert the desired field.

2. Select Insert, Field form the menu bar or Main toolbar. The Fields submenu lists a small selection of the most common field types, including Date, Time, Page Numbers, Page Count, Subject, Title, and Author. Alternatively, you can also extended click the Insert Fields icon on the main toolbar for the same field options.

3. Select the desired field from the Fields submenu. StarWriter inserts the selected field using the information from the File, Properties dialog (Subject, Title, and Author), the computer system (Date, Time), or other document information (Page Number, Page Count).

   Or, for a complete listing of all available fields, select Other from the Fields submenu. Using the tabs in the Fields dialog, select the desired field and field format, and click Insert to place it in your document.

Tip #168 from
Michael & Sarah

You can leave the Fields dialog open while working on your document; just double-click the title bar to minimize the dialog when it gets in your way.

When it comes to knowing which type of field to insert, the real fun starts. The following sections provide brief reference information on all available StarOffice fields.

INSERTING DOCUMENT FIELDS

Use the fields of the Document tab if you want to insert information related to the current document, such as user data, file or template names, or date and time when the document was created. Select the field you want to insert from the Type list or Select list; using the Format list on the right, you can also choose a specific format for the field contents. Your options include the following:

- **Author**—Inserts the document author's name (Name) or initials as listed on the User Data tab in the Text Document Options dialog (which you open by choosing Tools, Options, Text Document). Note that this is a variable field; if the same document is opened on another computer, the field contents display the information that is stored on the User Data tab of that machine. Hence, you should select Fixed Content in the lower right if you want to "lock" the field content so that it doesn't change when the document is opened on someone else's computer. (As mentioned earlier, this can cause problems for recipients who use StarOffice as an email client when used in emails.)

- **Chapter**—Inserts the chapter information at the insertion point. You can choose from four format options for the field contents: Chapter Name, Chapter Number, Chapter Number and Name, or Chapter Number Without Separator. In the lower right of the Fields dialog, you can select the heading level number that is the point of reference for the Chapter field. For example, if you select one, the field shows the name and/or number of the closest level one heading above the insertion point.

- **Date**—Inserts the date at the time the field was inserted, based on the computer's system clock. You can choose between Date (fixed) and Date (Variable). Select Date (fixed) if you want to insert the current date only; select Date (variable) if you want the computer to update the field with the current date each time the document is opened. In the Format list, you can define the appearance of the date field contents; for more choices, select Additional Formats at the end of the list. Using the Number Format dialog, you can create a user-defined format for the current field. In the Offset in Days spin box, you can enter a corrective number that is added or subtracted from the currently displayed days in the field.

→ For more details on using the Number Format dialog, **see** "Formatting Cells," **p. 342**, earlier in this chapter.

- **Document Template**—Inserts the document's template name.

- **File Name**—Inserts the document's filename. Using the Format options, you can insert only the filename, the filename without extension, the path, and the path and filename (Path/File Name).

- **Page**—Inserts the page number of the current page at the insertion point. You can choose between inserting the Previous Page, Next Page, or (current) Page Numbers. In the Format list, you can select a numbering scheme for the field contents. By default, StarWriter recommends As Page Style (which lists the numbers as defined in the Page Style dialog). If you want to override the page style, the most logical choices include Arabic (1, 2, 3), Roman (i, ii, iii) and Roman (I, II, III), although you can use all the available options. Select Offset to enter a corrective factor (for example, +1 or –1) that will be added to or subtracted from the field contents in case you selected the Previous Page and Next Page fields. Note that page numbers have to be larger than zero (0), which means the numeric value –1 makes sense only with number 3 and higher when used in combination with the Previous Page field.

- **Sender**—Inserts the document's sender information as listed on the User Data tab of the Text Document Options dialog. You can select which fields to insert (Initials, First Name, Last Name, and so on). Most of this information is provided during the installation process and can be updated after the product has been registered.

- **Statistics**—Inserts statistical information on the current document. You can show the total number of pages, paragraphs, words, characters, tables, graphics, and objects in the current document. Because you're mostly interested in the number, the most logical format for this field type is Arabic (1, 2, 3).

- **Time**—Similar to the Date field type, this field inserts the time the field was inserted, based on the computer's system clock. You can choose between Time (fixed) and Time (variable). Select Time (fixed) if you want the field to reflect the time it was inserted; select Time (variable) if you want the computer to update the field with the current time each time the document is opened. In the Format list, you can select the format in which the time field will appear; for more choices, select Additional Formats at the end of the list. Using the Number Format dialog, you can create a user-defined format for the current field. In the Offset in Minutes spin box, you can enter a corrective number to the currently displayed time in the field.

INSERTING REFERENCE FIELDS

Reference fields are used for creating cross-references. You can insert references in the active document as well as between documents that are part of a master document. Reference field types include the following:

- **Set Reference**—Inserts an invisible "bookmark" at the target field for a cross-reference. The target can be located in the same document or in another document if it is part of a master document. Enter a name for the target in the Name box in the lower right of the tab, and click Insert to insert the field at the insertion point in your document as well as in the Select list of the References tab.

Note

In HTML documents, you have to insert a bookmark as a cross-reference.

- **Insert Reference**—Inserts a reference field at the insertion point in the current document. Select a target for the reference field from the Select list. Using the Format options, you can select from Page, Chapter, Reference, Above/Below, and As Page Style. Click an Insert Reference field to be whisked to the target of the reference.

Note

Once you click on a reference, you end up at the target. To get back to the originating point, you have to set another reference at the starting point.

- **Bookmarks**—When you insert bookmarks using the Insert, Bookmark command, the name of the inserted bookmark appears in the Select list. If these references are used in an HTML document, they become anchors that enable you to jump to a certain location on a page. Using the Bookmarks field, you can define anchors in HTML documents. Your (anchor) Format options include Page, Chapter, Reference, Above/Below, and As Page Style.

INSERTING FUNCTIONS FIELDS

Function fields perform a certain function; depending on the type of field, a function can be tied to a specific condition. For example, you can define fields that execute a certain macro when clicked or that hide a defined text section when a certain condition is fulfilled. For graphics, tables, and frames, you can use these fields to define placeholders that you can insert in the document if necessary. Function fields include the following:

- **Conditional Text**—Inserts one of two possible results depending on a predefined condition. In the Condition box, enter an expression that defines the condition. In the Then box, specify the text to be inserted when the condition is fulfilled; in the Else box, specify the text that appears if the condition is not fulfilled. Conditional Text fields are often used in combination with the Set Variable field of the Variables tab.

→ For more details on using conditional text fields, **see** "Using Conditions in Mail Merges," **p. 364**, later in this chapter.

- **Input Field**—Inserts form fields for text entry in the current document. Enter a reference in the Reference box. If you click Insert, you can enter the text.

- **Execute Macro**—Inserts a chosen macro directly into the document where the reader can run it by double-clicking the field contents. Click Macro to select the desired macro. In the Reference field, you can enter a brief explanation that will pop up when the reader moves the mouse pointer over the field contents.

- **Placeholder**—Inserts a placeholder at the insertion point. You can define the type of placeholder by using the Format list box. Enter a brief description in the Placeholder text box; in the Reference box, you can include a brief directive that pops up when the reader moves the mouse pointer over the field. For example, placeholder text in a document might read <Please Enter the Subject Here>; the reference might say Click here and type subject. Placeholders are useful to indicate text areas in templates that can be filled by the user. Just click placeholder text to select it, and start typing to replace the placeholder with your own text. Placeholders can also be used for tables and objects, including text boxes and graphics.

- **Hidden Text**—Marks text that remains hidden unless a certain condition is no longer fulfilled.

- **Hidden Paragraph**—Marks an entire paragraph that remains hidden unless a certain condition is no longer fulfilled.

→ For examples on working with hidden text and hidden paragraph fields, **see** "Using Conditions in Mail Merges," **p. 364**, later in this chapter.

INSERTING PROPERTIES FIELDS

The fields in this tab enable you to insert specified document information from the Properties dialog box (which you open by choosing File, Properties). Some field contents appear only if you filled in the information in the respective text boxes of the Properties dialog (Description, Document Number, Info, Keywords, Subject, Title). Others retrieve user data or insert information based on the computer's system clock (Created, Editing Time, Modified, Most Recent Print). If you select Created, Modified, or Most Recent Print, you can choose Author, Time, and Date fields. For the Time, Date, and Editing Time fields, you can define a format for the field contents. Select the Fixed Content option in the lower right of the tab if you want to lock the field contents to the information inserted at the time of its creation.

INSERTING VARIABLE FIELDS

Variable fields enable you to control the contents of your document dynamically. For example, you can control the numbering of the page variable to enable an automatic update. You can define variables individually or use one of the provided variables.

Note User-defined variables are saved only to the current document.

Variable field types include the following:

- **Set Variable**—Defines a variable that can be used in combination with conditions. In the Name box at the bottom of the tab, you can enter a descriptive name for the variable and specify a number or other identifying marker in the Value box. You can modify the value of a defined variable by using the entry field so that a variable in the document can assume different values at different places.

- **Show Variable**—Inserts the current value of a predefined variable at the insertion point. The value of the variable in the document is controlled by the Set Variable field or the previous entry field.

- **DDE Field**—Sets up dynamic data exchange (DDE) links with information in a document from another application. Enter a descriptive name for this field in the Name box; in the adjacent text box, enter the DDE statement.

- **Insert Formula**—Inserts the result of calculations that you enter in the Formula box at the bottom of the tab. Using the Format options, you can control the appearance of the field contents.

- **Input Field**—Inserts a new value for an already defined variable or user field. With a variable entry field, your newly assigned value is valid from the position you insert it until you change the value by inserting another entry field. The available Input Field variables are shown in the Select list. When you click Insert, the Input Field dialog opens; there, you can enter the new value with an additional comment.

- **Number Sequence**—Inserts automatic numbering for tables, graphics, and frames.

- **Set Page Variable**—Sets a second page numbering scheme. Select On to define the Offset reference point; select Off to cancel it.

- **Show Page Variable**—Shows the number of pages between a reference point (set via the Set Page Variable field) and the current field.

- **User Field**—Enables you to define a global variable that can be used, for example, for controlling certain functions. If no user fields are shown in the Select list, you first have to define a field name and value. Then you can click Apply to enter the name in the Select list.

INSERTING DATABASE FIELDS

Use this tab to insert database fields from a database. With the exception of the Mail Merge field, you may never use most of these fields. In the DataBase Selection box, you can select a database for which the fields are valid. Database fields include the following:

- **Any Record**—Inserts the data that is defined under Record Number in the next Merge Mail field, provided a predefined condition is fulfilled. The only records that are taken into account during the mail merge are the ones selected in the Beamer via multiple selection. This field enables you to insert the contents of several data sets on one page by inserting a field command of the type Any Database in front of the Mail Merge fields. In the Record Number box, you enter the number of the record whose content should be inserted when the criteria, listed under Condition, are met. The record number always refers to the current selection in the Beamer. For example, if you select only the last 5 records in a database that has a total of 10 records, using the Record Number 1 selects the first record of the selection; this would be the sixth record in the database example.

- **Database Name**—Inserts the name of the database that you can select in the box to the right.

- **Mail Merge Field**—Inserts the name of a database field as placeholder. The field contents are automatically inserted when you're merging the data.

- **Next Record**—Inserts the next record after the current record on the same page during a mail merge operation.

- **Record Number**—Adds the number of the currently selected record in the Beamer. Using the Format options, you can select a format for the number.

> **Note**
>
> You can link the Any Database and Next Record fields with a condition. Data is then inserted only if the condition is met. Because entering a condition is optional here, you always see True in the Condition box; therefore, the condition is, by default, always met unless you define a condition of your own.

DEFINING CONDITIONS FOR FIELDS

StarOffice enables you to instruct some fields to recognize certain conditions in your text and, depending on the condition, perform a specific task.

You can define conditions for the following functions and database field types:

- **Conditional Text**—The inserted text is dependent on a certain condition. If the condition is TRUE, Text A is inserted; if the condition is FALSE, Text B appears in its stead.

- **Hidden Text**—The inserted text is hidden if a certain condition is TRUE.

- **Hidden Paragraph**—The inserted paragraph is hidden if a certain condition is TRUE.

- **Any Record** and **Next Record**—Conditions defined for these data fields control how data is inserted into the current document.

When you're defining conditions, you can use these variables:

- User-defined variables such as Set Variable and User Field
- Predefined StarOffice variables such as CHAR (number of characters in a document), WORD (number of words), PARA (number of paragraphs), GRAF (number of graphics), TABLES (number of tables), OLE (number of OLE objects), and PAGE (total number of pages)
- Contents of database fields

Note

You can't use the variables of page numbers, chapter numbers, and so on to define a condition.

Any variable x can be incorporated into a condition, whereby x is either the name of the field you defined with a fixed value (Set Variable or User Field) or a StarOffice variable, the value of which depends on the document. Consider these examples (note that EQ or == stands for "equals," and NEQ or != stands for "not equal to"):

- x EQ 1 or x == 1—The condition is TRUE if the variable equals 1. If you want to formulate a condition that takes into consideration the total number of pages in your document, you enter Page == 1, for the condition to be true if the document contains only one page.
- X NEQ 1 or x != 1—The condition is TRUE if the variable x does not equal 1.

→ For examples of how to use conditions in a document, **see** "Using Conditions in Mail Merges," **p. 364**, later in this chapter.

VIEWING FIELD NAMES

By default, when you insert a field, you see the results of that field. For example, when you insert a date field, you see the current date; when you insert a page number field, you see the current page number, and so on. At times, however, you might want to get a concrete idea of the types of fields that are actually in a document to ensure that the fields are set up to produce the desired results. For example, a number in a field could be the result of a Page field type or a Statistics field type. You can easily toggle between a field's content and its name by using the View Fields command. Just select View, Fields (or press Ctrl+F9) to show the name of all inserted fields in the current document. Select View, Fields (or press Ctrl+F9) again to return to the (default) field contents display.

Note

Some fields might not display contents; instead, you always see their names.

UPDATING FIELDS

The important point to remember is that StarWriter does not update all fields automatically unless you close and open a document. You can update a field by selecting the text containing the field and then choosing Tools, Update, Fields or pressing F9. To update all fields in a document, simply press Ctrl+A to select the entire document, and then press F9.

Tip #169 from
Michael & Sarah

If you've previously saved your document, you can achieve the same results by pressing the Reload button on the function bar.

Note

Some fields like those used in page numbering are automatically updated whenever you print or repaginate a document (by inserting additional pages, for example, or redefining the page numbering). Others, such as fields used for conditioned or hidden text, are not updated until you select the Tools, Update, Update Fields command or press F9.

FORMATTING FIELDS

You can format a field's results just as you would ordinary text—select the field and then apply the desired attribute(s) using the character formatting options on the context menu, object bar, or Character dialog. If the field is part of a special area, such as the header/footer or footnote/endnote area, StarWriter automatically updates all fields of the same type in that area to ensure a consistent look and appearance. If the fields are in the body text, the assigned attributes are valid only for the selected field. However, if you have a page number field in the body text, this field is not affected by the attribute change(s). Note that you cannot format part of a field; it's all or nothing.

EDITING FIELDS

If you want to change the format of a given field, you have to edit it. To edit a field, place the insertion point in front of the field, and select Edit, Field from the menu bar. Alternatively, you can double-click the field. Both methods open the Edit Fields dialog. Here, you can make formatting changes to fields. If the document contains other fields of this type that are not automatically updated by the changes you make, you can use the arrows in the bottom right to jump from field to field of that type. As soon as you click the arrow to jump to another field of the same type, the changes you made to the current field are accepted. Click OK to accept the current change and exit the dialog; click Cancel to exit without saving the current change. All previous changes that were accepted by clicking the arrow keys remain in effect.

Note

When you're making changes to a field, you can't undo them by pressing Ctrl+Z or selecting the Undo command from the function bar or Edit menu. Instead, you might delete the inserted field (if you press Ctrl+Z immediately after you insert the field).

LOCKING A FIELD'S CONTENTS

Sometimes you might want to prevent the results of a field from being updated. In some instances, you can do so by selecting a Fixed field type, as in the case of the Time and Date fields. In other instances, you can lock a field by selecting the Fixed Content option in the Fields dialog. Fields that can be locked include Author, Sender, and all Properties fields.

COPYING AND MOVING FIELDS

Copying and moving fields are no different than copying and moving text from one place to another. You can use the old cut, copy, and paste method by first selecting the field(s) you want to cut or copy, pressing Ctrl+X (cut) or Ctrl+C (copy), and then placing the insertion point at the new location and pressing Ctrl+V to paste the info from the Clipboard (Windows) or General-Purpose Buffer (Linux) into your document. Alternatively, you can also use the Cut, Copy, and Paste commands in the Edit menu.

DELETING FIELDS

Deleting a field is much easier than trying to get your arms around them. Just place the insertion point in front of or after the field you want to delete, and press Delete or Backspace, respectively.

CREATING FORM LETTERS WITH MAIL MERGE

One way to take advantage of fields in your documents is to use them in mail merges to create personalized form letters or mailing labels and envelopes. Mail merges enable you to print multiple copies of a document, where certain information (such as name and address) changes with each document. The form letters you receive from businesses and solicitors are examples of applied mail merge fields.

In a nutshell, mail merges combine two kinds of documents: a main document and a data source. The main document contains the text that is identical for each printed copy of the letter. The data source, typically a database with contact information, lists the information that is specific to each copy printed. (For example, for a form letter, the data source might identify the prefix, first and last name, company, address, city, and zip code for each recipient of your form letter.) To combine the two, you need to insert fields into the main document to tell StarWriter where to find the information that is stored in the data source. These fields are referred to as *merge fields*. After you have everything in place, you can print multiple copies of the main document, based on the data contained in the data source. When you print the document, StarWriter reads the first record in the data source, inserts the field contents of that record into the main document, and prints the copy. Then it does the same for the second record, and so on, repeating this process for as many records as are contained in the data source or as you selected.

Based on this premise, a mail merge consists of three main steps: creating a data source (or mailing list), creating a letter (complete with merge fields), and merging and printing the data.

CREATING A DATA SOURCE

Creating a data source is actually easy. If you've previously used StarOffice, you're probably familiar with the Address Book. The Address Book contains all your business and personal contacts. You can look at it through a user interface by selecting Edit, Address Book from the menu bar, or you can look at it in the raw by using the Explorer and Beamer. Simply open the Explorer (by pressing Ctrl+Shift+E), click the plus sign next to Address Book, click the plus sign next to Tables, and then click Address. Now open the Beamer (by pressing Ctrl+Shift+B), and you'll see a table with a header line (Prefix, Firstname, Lastname, and so on) that identifies the data in your Address Book.

PART
II
CH
9

Typically, your Address Book contains much more information than is needed in a regular mail merge. And unless you've created multiple Address Books for different purposes (for example, personal use and business use), your Address Book probably also contains more contacts than you need. In either case, you need to create a single data source that contains only the information and contacts you need for the mail merge, such as the prefix, first and last names, company, address, city, state, and zip code. In short, you need a customized mailing list.

You need to do the following:

1. If you're working with multiple databases or Address Books and all the recipients of the form letter are already in one database, you can go to step 2. If you're working with a single database or Address Book, you first need to identify those contacts that should be the recipients of the from letter mailing. The easiest way to do so is to open the Address Book in the Beamer and to use a column (for example, the last column in the table, ID) and insert an identifier that separates business contacts from personal or other contacts (for example, \m\ and \p\ or \mail\ and \personal\). To modify the existing database, you need to click the Edit button on the Database toolbar (the pen next to paper); clicking this button disables the Read-only mode of the database, enabling you to enter the necessary data.

Tip #170 from
Michael & Sarah

In general, you should make it a habit of classifying your contacts so that you can easily identify them if needed. Another solution is to manage and maintain multiple Address Books.

---

2. In the Explorer, click the plus sign to open the Address Book tree.

3. Right-click Queries, and select New, Query, AutoPilot from the context menu.

4. In the Query AutoPilot Table Selection dialog, select the name of your Address Book database (if you have more than one Address Book) in the Table Name list, and click Next.

5. In the Query AutoPilot Field Selection dialog, use the top-center arrow (pointing to the right) to move the desired mail merge fields from the Available Fields list to the Chosen Fields list.

   Typically, the fields involved in mail merges include the prefix, first name, last name, company, address, city, and postal code fields. (When you're creating a mail merge for a letter to be distributed via email, you use the first and last name and email fields instead, for example.) If you make a mistake, you can click the single arrow pointing to the left to move a selected field back from the Chosen Fields list to the Available Fields list. Clicking the double arrows moves all fields at once.

6. When you're finished, click Next.

7. In the Query AutoPilot Filters dialog, you can separate those contacts that are recipients of the form letter mailing from those that are not. Using the Field Name drop-down list, select the field that contains the identifying parameters (in this example, ID).

8. Using the Condition drop-down list, select Like.

9. In the Value box, insert the identifying parameter *exactly* as it appears in the database table, framed by the % symbol (for example, %\m\% or %\mailing\%).

   Click Preview to see a filtered list of your contacts in the Beamer; if you want to change the selected fields, click Back.

10. If all the contacts in your address database should receive the form letter, you don't have to enter anything in this step of the Query AutoPilot process. Click Next.

11. In the AutoPilot Sort dialog, you can specify the sort order of the current query; you can use altogether four sort criteria. Note that the sort criteria consists of all available fields, not just the chosen fields for the current query. Again, you can click Preview to take a peak at the results in the Beamer and click Back to make any necessary changes.

12. Click Next when you're finished.

13. In the Query AutoPilot Complete dialog, you can enter a name for the current query in the Query Title box. Use a descriptive name, such as Business or Mailing_Biz, for example.

14. In the After Completion portion of the dialog, select the Store Query option so that you can use the results of this query—the mailing list data source—for future mail merges.

15. When you're finished, click Create.

The Query AutoPilot generates a new data source according to your specifications and saves it as a subcategory of Queries. You can see it when you click the plus sign next to Queries.

CREATING THE FORM LETTER

Now that you have created your data source, you need to create the actual form letter in StarWriter; then you need to add the merge fields. You can format the information in any way you want, as if you were formatting individual words, using the formatting options from the object bar or the context menu. Follow these steps to finish your mail merge:

1. Add any text or graphics that you want to include in your document; reserve space for the recipient's name and address. If you want to include the recipient by name in the salutation as well as in the text, you have to insert the respective first and/or last name and prefix fields as well.

2. Add the merge fields. The easiest way to add the fields to your document is to drag them from the Beamer to the location in your document. Just click the previously created data source in the Explorer to expose its content in the open Beamer. Then click, one after another, the header of the merge field you want to insert (for example, PREFIX), and drag and drop it into the desired location in your letter.

   Insert a merge field where you want each category of information to appear in printed form. Be sure to add any spaces and punctuation that you want to include between merge fields. For example, when you're placing two fields next to each other (such as the first name and last name fields), insert a space between the two, just as you would if you entered single words.

3. Add a comma and a space after the inserted City field.

4. Don't forget to insert the first and last name fields wherever you want the recipient's name to appear (for example, in the salutation, or even the actual text, depending on the content).

5. When you're finished, save your document.

MERGING THE DATA

Now comes the part where you actually merge the data with the form letter. Before you proceed, scroll once more through your document to make sure that it contains all the necessary data and merge fields.

When you're done proofing your letter, click the Mail Merge icon (stacked envelopes) on the Database toolbar (or select File, Mail Merge). Using the Records portion in the Mail Merge dialog, you can choose to output all letters at once or only selected records (that you selected in the database, for example, if you decided not to include all contacts in the mailing list), or specify a range of records starting from a certain record and ending with a certain record. (The number n you insert for the range indicates the nth record in the database, counted from the beginning.) In the Output portion, you can select Printer, Mailing (email) and File.

If you select the Printer option, you can also select Single Print Jobs, which enables you to print one letter after another, in case you have to feed your printer.

If you select the Mailing option, you have to select the email address from the list of chosen fields in the Address drop-down box. (This option works only if you selected the email field during the creation of your mailing list table.) In addition, you need to enter a subject line that identifies the content. You also have to attach the actual file by clicking the small button next to the Attachments field and then click Add in the Select Files dialog to browse for the attachment. Last, but not least, you need to select a mail format (RTF, HTML, or StarWriter document).

If you select File, you can select a path and folder where StarWriter will save all documents as files (later to be printed). You can also indicate the field name from which StarWriter should generate the individual filenames for each letter, or you can enter a name yourself (in which case, StarWriter adds numerals after the name you enter to keep the files separate).

In all three instances, you start merging the data and outputting as soon as you click OK.

USING CONDITIONS IN MAIL MERGES

Using the Conditional Text, Hidden Text, and Hidden Paragraph function fields, you can refine the final results of your mail merge by eliminating blank lines and additional spaces from the final address block.

HIDING PARAGRAPHS

For example, mail merge fields in StarOffice typically take this arrangement:

```
<PREFIX> <FIRSTNAME> <LASTNAME>
<COMPANY>
<ADDRESS>
<CITY>, <STATEPROV> <POSTALCODE>
```

As long as each record in your database lists a first and last name, company name, address, city, state, and zip code you have nothing to worry about. However, if certain records don't list a company name, StarWriter inserts a blank line or paragraph instead. To prevent the addition of this line, you can insert a Hidden Paragraph field at the beginning of the paragraph or line and assign a condition that, if met, tells StarWriter to ignore the paragraph when printing. You just need to follow these steps:

1. Using your mail merge template, place the insertion point at the beginning of the paragraph that contains the Company field.
2. Press Ctrl+F2 to open the Fields dialog, and select the Functions tab.
3. Select Hidden Paragraph, and enter COMPANY EQ "" or NOT (COMPANY) in the Condition text box; StarWriter enables you to say the same thing in different expressions.
4. Click Insert.

StarWriter then hides the paragraph (and prevents it from printing) when company information is missing (the condition is TRUE).

Tip #171 from
Michael & Sarah

> If you can still see the "hidden" paragraph, check the settings on the Contents tab of the Text Document Options dialog. At the bottom of the Non-Printing Characters portion of the tab, you can see the Hidden Paragraph option. Be sure this option is not selected.

HIDING TEXT

Apart from hiding entire paragraphs, you can also hide individual characters that throw off the alignment of your address block.

For example, if the first line of your mail merge fields takes the form

```
<PREFIX> <FIRSTNAME> <LASTNAME>
```

you end up with an extra space if the prefix for one of your records is missing. To prevent the addition of this extra space, insert a Hidden Text field in between the Prefix and First Name fields instead of a regular space. Following the same steps as in the Hidden Paragraph example, open the Fields dialog (by pressing Ctrl+F2), and select Hidden Text on the Functions tab. In the Condition text box, enter PREFIX, and in the Text box, enter a space. Then click Insert to insert the Hidden Text field between the Prefix and First Name fields in your document. When StarWriter "sees" a prefix, it inserts a space and then the first name of your contact. If no prefix is present, the paragraph begins with the first letter of your contact's first name.

DEFINING CONDITIONAL TEXT

Every letter has to have a salutation, of course—even form letters. Rather than use the standard "Dear Sir or Madam," you can personalize the salutation as in this example:

```
Dear <FIRSTNAME> <LASTNAME>,
```

As long as your mailing list lists both first and last name of each record, you won't run into any glitches. However, what if some records are listed by their last names only? In that case, inserting the prefix in combination with the last name would be more professional. Using the Conditional Text field, you can instruct StarWriter to choose between one or the other salutation—depending on the available information. Follow these steps:

1. Enter a salutation followed by the first name and last name fields.

2. Place the insertion point in front of the first name field, and open the Fields dialog (by pressing Ctrl+F2).

3. In the Functions tab, select Conditional Text.

4. In the Condition text box, enter FIRSTNAME EQ "" to indicate the condition of an absent first name.

5. If this condition is met, StarWriter is supposed to insert the prefix of the corresponding record. Hence, enter PREFIX in the Then box to insert Mr. or Ms. when the first name of the record is not present.

6. In all other instances, StarWriter is supposed to use the first name of the record, so enter FIRSTNAME in the Else box.

7. Click Insert to place the Conditional Text field in your document.

And what do you do if your records lack both a prefix and a first name? Well, short of blowing a fuse, you can always look at this (and the following) section as a practical field guide to some of StarOffice's more intriguing fields.

CREATING LABELS, LISTS, AND INVITATIONS

Mail merges are fine if you want to insert one record per page. But what if you want to insert several records on one single page, as you do when you create labels, mailing lists, or invitations? Once again, it's a field that'll make your day—in this case, the Next Record field. Insert the Next Record field between two addresses to instruct StarWriter to insert the next record right after the current record. Follow these steps to print multiple addresses on a single page:

1. Using a table, divide the page into segments of equal size. If you want to create invitations that are postcard size, you can select a landscape orientation and then divide the page into a table that spans one row and two columns. If you want to create an address list, you can use a portrait orientation with three columns and 10 or 15 rows per page.

2. Open your Address Book in the Beamer, and drag the desired address fields into the first cell of your table. Be sure to insert spaces and punctuation between fields where necessary. Format the information as desired (for example, in an address list, you probably want all the information left-aligned).

3. Place the insertion point after the last field in the cell, and open the Fields dialog (by pressing Ctrl+F2). In the Database tab, select Next Record and click Insert.

4. Copy and paste the cell contents of the first cell into all the other cells on the same page.

5. Select File, Mail Merge. In the Mail Merge dialog, select your printing option (Printer, Mailing, or File). Finally, click OK.

StarWriter generates the desired list without much ado.

Alternatively, instead of a table, you can use multiple text frames on a page to arrange the address information. If you do so, be sure to insert the Next Record field after each contact.

→ For more details on text frames, **see** "Working with Text Boxes," **p. 435**.

If you want to create mailing labels, StarWriter makes it even easier for you—with the Labels command. Just select Insert, Labels to open the Labels dialog. On the Labels tab, select a database and table and the desired database fields; then insert them into the Label Text area of the tab. In the Format portion of the tab, you can specify the brand and type of your labels and whether you feed a continuous roll of labels or sheets. Using the Format and

Options tab, you can make adjustments to the column and row sizes and how it should print. Click Setup to select your printer, and change the printer properties as needed. When you're finished, select Print to print your labels to the selected printer.

→ For more details on printing labels, **see** "Printing Labels," **p. 483**.

TROUBLESHOOTING

I don't like the way StarWriter's table feature formats numbers. Can I somehow turn it off or change it?

Unfortunately, you can't turn it off globally. However, you can control the formatting for each table individually. To do so, select the desired column or table, and then choose Number Format from the Table Context menu or the Format menu. In the category list on the left, select Text. To define your own number format, select User-Defined in the Category list, and enter your own format code in the text box at the bottom of the dialog.

How can I align the text table column headers vertically?

This option exists only in StarCalc tables (via the Cell Formatting option). The solution is to insert a StarCalc table as an OLE object. The other alternative is to use align text along an invisible line and then anchor it with the paragraph.

How can I easily select an entire table row or column?

Place the insertion point into the row or column you want to select, and right-click to choose Row, Select or Column, Select from the Table context menu.

How can I make a StarWriter table always show the latest results of a StarCalc table?

Insert the StarCalc table as a DDE link in the StarWriter document. Select the table in StarCalc, press Ctrl+C, switch to the StarWriter document, and then place the insertion point in the location where you want to insert the table. Finally, select Edit, Paste Special.

Can I use a style that enables me to format all tables in a document at once?

You can't format all tables at once. However, you can format one table after another quickly. To do so, select the first table, and format it as desired. Then select Format, AutoFormat. In the AutoFormat dialog, click the Insert button to name, and add your table to the list of table templates. Next, use the Navigator to jump from table to table to apply your own format to the current table. Simply click inside the table, choose Format, AutoFormat, and then select your table template from the Format list. Alternatively, you can also change the fonts in every table by modifying the table style in the Stylist.

I don't like the way StarWriter formats the text in my tables. Can I change it easily?

By default, StarWriter applies the Table Heading (for column heading) and Table Contents (for the rest of the table) paragraph styles to a text table. Using the Stylist, you can easily change the existing attributes. Just right-click the styles in the Stylist, and select Modify from the context menu. In the Paragraph Style dialog, you can make any desired changes to the existing attributes.

When I try to add numbers in my table, all I get is a zero sum. Why?

Check the number format of the cells that contain the numbers. If the cells are formatted as Text, you cannot use them for calculations. Select the desired cells, and then choose a number format from the Number Format dialog.

I've created a database table in StarWriter that's now too big, and I need to export it as a delimited text file into a database. How can I do this?

Select the entire table, and choose Tools, Convert Table to Text. In the Convert Table to Text dialog, select a text separator, typically a comma or tab to separate the columns. StarWriter automatically inserts a paragraph mark at the end of each row.

I want to move my StarWriter chart into a StarImpress document. What do I need to do?

A chart is inserted as an OLE object. You cannot easily move it from one document type to another. What you need to do is create a chart from scratch using the File, New, Chart command from the menu bar. For more information, see "Inserting Charts into Other Documents" in Chapter 18, "Analyzing and Charting Data."

I've inserted the Page Numbers field into my footer area, but I can't see the number; all I see are the words Page numbers. Why?

Check your View menu. If a mark appears next to Fields, you're looking at the field name rather than the field contents. Just select Fields to take off the mark, and StarWriter will display the field contents.

CHAPTER 10

WORKING WITH LONG DOCUMENTS

In this chapter

THINKING THROUGH LONG DOCUMENTS

Make no mistake. Putting together an annual report or book-length document is an ambitious undertaking. You need special organizational and document management skills that help you navigate the Scylla of losing sight of your content and Charybdis of keeping track of your changes and references. You also need good tools for creating elements such as numbered headings and captions, footnotes and endnotes, and indexes and tables of contents. StarWriter can help. Using its rich set of tools for adding these items (almost) painlessly, you can choose between two basic strategies for the overall project. You can store the entire book in a single StarWriter document; or you can store each chapter or section of the entire document in its own file, combining them all with a master document.

→ Using master documents is described in "Building Books with Master Documents," **p. 403**.

→ This chapter focuses on long documents only. If you would like to learn more about inserting graphics or multicolumn layout, refer to Chapter 11, "Desktop Publishing with StarOffice," **p. 415**.

Whichever approach you choose, you first have to get your ducks in a row. Here's what you need to do:

- **Get a clear idea of the project**—Don't just start typing in front of a blank document screen. Things can get unwieldy fast. First get a clear idea of the scope of the project you're trying to tackle, so you know what information (and tools) you might need.

- **Put together an outline**—A sound working outline provides an overview of the entire document. Chapter heads should be followed by subheads that explain the content at a greater level of detail. Be sure to include brief paragraphs that clarify the topics of your outline (for yourself and others).

- **Get organized**—Once you have a clear idea of what you want, as well as a working outline, you should create a folder for your project, so you can store all the information pertaining to it in one easy-to-find spot. If your project also includes graphics, you might want to create a graphics subfolder. And why not a memo subfolder in which you can store notes or other miscellaneous information pertaining to the project.

Note

You don't have to store everything in one place. StarOffice is quite adept at keeping track of where things are on your hard drive or network, thanks to its linking capabilities. And if you're incorporating data from a database, its ODBC or JDBC awareness will help you always stay up to date.

Here are some StarWriter features that can help with complex documents:

- **Styles and templates**—Using one template ensures consistency of appearance throughout the document and makes style changes easy.

- **Headings versus other styles**—Using StarWriter's built-in heading styles (Heading 1, Heading 2, and so on) for your chapter and section titles and headings enables you to generate a table of contents. Be sure to use the heading styles only for elements you would like to show up in a table of contents, and use different levels to assign different degrees of detail in descending order.

- **Headers and footers**—Adding headers and footers enables you to repeat information at the top or bottom of a document, such as chapter or section titles, page numbers, dates and time, author name, or any combination of those elements.

- **Footnotes/endnotes and cross references**—These are standard features if you're referencing sources or expanding on a subject or topic with suggestions for further readings, or if you want to cross-reference certain sections in a document.

- **Versions and changes**—These commands help you keep track of the history of a document as it evolves.

- **Notes and bookmarks**—Indispensable features if you want to include a note to yourself or bookmark a place in your document so you can easily return to and finish it later. Bookmarks also help you navigate quickly through your document.

→ Using the Versions, Changes, and Notes commands also is useful when developing documents in a group environment. For more details, **see** "Exchanging and Reviewing Documents," **p. 1002**.

For more details, **see** "Exchanging and Reviewing Documents," **p. 1002**.

PART
II
CH
10

INTRODUCING THE NAVIGATOR

Your biggest challenge when dealing with long and complex documents is to navigate them while keeping track of their various elements and levels of content. Although you can always use the directional keys (Home, End, Page Up, Page Down) and arrow keys on your keyboard to move around, do yourself a favor and refrain from doing so. StarWriter has a feature that makes navigating long documents a breeze. It's called the Navigator and it comes with a capable assistant, which we'll refer to as the *mini Navigator* (although the documentation introduces it as the *Navigation tool*).

Tip #172 from
Michael & Sarah

There are two old standby keyboard commands you may still find useful—Ctrl+Home takes you to the top of your document, and Ctrl+End to the end.

Using the Navigator, you can quickly spot and jump to every element and object in your document—including headings, tables, text frames, pictures, OLE objects, bookmarks, sections, hyperlinks, references, indexes, and notes—as well as look at your document in Outline view. Just double-click the selected object or element, and you will be whisked to its location in your document. The Navigator also enables you to speedily move from one page to another. Not surprisingly, you can open and close the Navigator by double-clicking in the Page Number field in the status bar. (Alternatively, you can also press F5.) To jump to a specific page, enter a number in the Page Number spin box at the top and press Enter. Your cursor will be placed at the beginning of the page. Figure 10.1 shows the Navigator at work.

Tip #173 from
Michael & Sarah

For even speedier page navigation, press Ctrl+Shift+F5, which brings up the Navigator toolbar by itself with your cursor already placed inside the spin box. All you have to do now is press Backspace to delete the current number, and then enter the new page number and press Enter. To expand the Navigator to its full size, select the Expand button (the first button on the left of the second row).

Figure 10.1
Together with its smaller cousin, the mini Navigator, the Navigator is unbeatable when it comes to navigating long documents and keeping an overview of complex document.

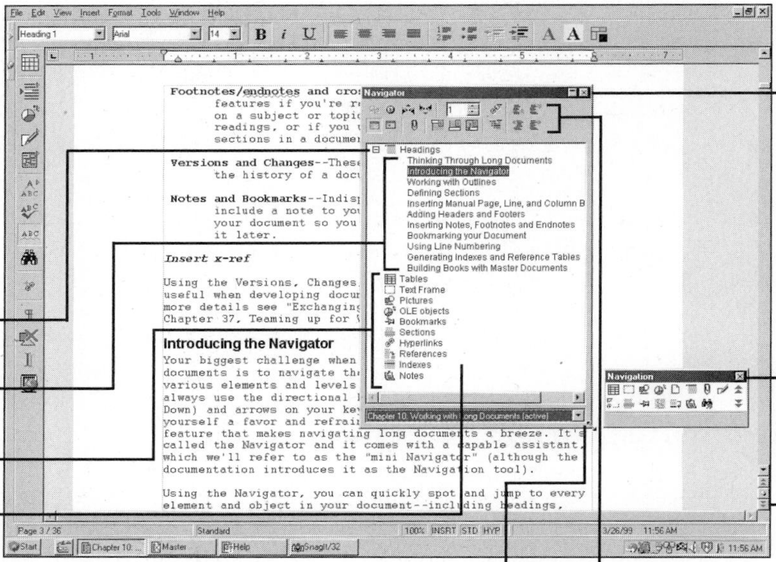

Shows all currently open tasks of the same type

An outline view (shows only Level 1 headings)

Drop-down list with all currently open documents

Navigator list box

Drag to resize Navigator window

Opens mini Navigator

Navigator commands and options

Table 10.1 lists the various Navigator commands and options.

TABLE 10.1   THE NAVIGATOR'S TOOLS AND OPTIONS

Click Here...	If You Want To...
(Toggle)	Toggle between Master Document and Normal view
(Navigation)	Choose browse objects
(Previous/Next)	Jump to previous/next object (depends on your current browse object)
1 (Page Box)	Go to a particular page; just select or enter a number, and press Enter (pressing Page Up or Page Down with the cursor inside takes you to the beginning and end of your document, respectively)

Click Here...	If You Want To...
(Drag mode)	Select a drag mode; the drag mode defines the way an object is inserted into a document when dragged from the Navigator; you can choose between Insert as Hyperlink, Insert as Link, and Insert as Copy
(List Box)	Show/hide list box or the lower part of the Navigator (only available when Navigator is not docked)
(Content view)	Toggle between complete view of all elements in the Navigator or only the selected one; note that when this icon is selected, you can shift headings in the navigator via drag and drop
(Reminder)	Set an invisible reminder at the insertion point; reminders are automatically removed when document is closed; you can set up to five reminders
(Header/footer)	Move cursor between the header/footer and text (you must have a header/footer in your document for this function to be active)
(Anchor)	Move cursor between footnote area or reference marker
(Outline Level)	Select different outline views; you can show anywhere from 1–10 levels at a time
(Move)	Move heading elements, complete with contents, closer to the beginning or end of the document; to move only the selected heading (without subheadings) press Ctrl while clicking this icon
(Promote)	Promote or demote headings, complete with subheadings, by one level; to promote only the selected heading (without sub headings) press Ctrl while clicking this icon

PART

II

CH

10

Note

The Navigator is a dockable tools window that you can open and close like the Explorer or Beamer. To dock it, press Ctrl while dragging it toward the edge where you want to dock it. To make it float again, press Ctrl while double-clicking the lower border of its title bar.

Tip #174 from
Michael & Sarah

The Open Documents drop-down list at the bottom of the Navigator lists all currently open documents. Select a document from the list to view its contents in the Navigator without having to switch to the document. Likewise, you can select the Display command from the Navigator context menu to achieve the same results. When you select the Active Window option, the view in the Navigator is adjusted automatically to reflect the contents of the new document; when you switch documents without the Active Window option selected, the contents view in the Navigator will not be adjusted to reflect the currently active window.

Using the Navigator, you can also arrange the order of your outline, as well as promote and demote individual headings. All you need to do is click the respective buttons on the Navigator toolbar and you're in business.

INTRODUCING THE MINI NAVIGATOR

If you're pressed for work space, you can also use the Navigator's smaller cousin—the mini Navigator. To open this curious little helper, click the Navigation button (second button from the left in the top row). You'll see a floating toolbar that you can drag by its title bar and drop anywhere on your desktop.

Tip #175 from
Michael & Sarah

You don't have to open the Navigator first to get to its cousin. The mini Navigator can also be opened by clicking the dot between the double arrows on the scrollbar.

The mini Navigator shows its full potential when you want to move from one object to another or continue a search that you've already started. Just select the object you would like to browse—the name of the object appears in the gray area at the bottom—then click the backward and forward arrows on the right. You'll be guided from object to object at your own speed. To deactivate the browse mode, click the Cancel button (the white square in the lower right, next to the forward arrow).

You can use this tool to scan your document quickly for tables, text frames, pictures, OLE objects, pages, headings, reminders, drawings, numbering/bullets, sections, bookmarks, selections, footnotes, notes, or continue a search in progress. And what's best is that all this power comes in a package small enough so that it can always be kept within reach at all times. Kind of like the caddy that zigs.

TARGETING OBJECTS WITH THE NAVIGATOR

Use the Navigator when you need a broader view of your entire document or a specific type of object within. A plus symbol next to a category indicates your document contains objects of this kind. If you place your pointer over a category with a plus sign, a balloon Tip will pop up telling you how many elements it contains. Click the plus symbol to expand the category tree and get a detailed view of the individual objects. Double-click an object and you'll be whisked to its place in the document.

Tip #176 from
Michael & Sarah

If you would like to edit any of the objects in your document, double-click the object to activate it, and then right-click the object in the Navigator and select Edit from the context menu. You'll get that object's Edit dialog. If the object is a table, you also have the option of removing its protected status.

SETTING TEMPORARY REMINDERS

Typically with long documents, you're constantly adding, rearranging, and deleting things. The Navigator gives you a handy tool—reminders—to mark your place within a document that you need to revisit. They're like specialized bookmarks during your current editing session. There's one caveat though: Once you set a reminder, you have to remember what it's all about. Reminders are just invisible markers with no text added. To set a reminder, place the insertion point at the appropriate location in your document, and then click the Reminder button in the Navigator. To easily find your reminders again, use the mini Navigator. Select the Reminder Browse option, and then use the backward or forward arrows to hunt down your reminders.

Note

You can use up to five reminders during one session. If you use more than five, StarWriter will automatically delete the oldest one. Reminders are valid for your current document session only. You will lose them as soon as you close your document.

USING THE NAVIGATOR FOR DRAG-AND-DROP OPERATIONS

Another nice feature of the Navigator is that you can drag and drop elements from one document into another—even if one of the documents is not open!

To drag and drop elements between two open documents, make active the document into which you want to drop the elements. Then, click the name of the inactive source document in the open document list at the bottom of the Navigator. All its elements will appear in the Navigator.

To drag and drop elements from a closed file into an open document, you must first list the file in the Beamer. Then, drag and drop the file from the Beamer into the Navigator. The Navigator will automatically update its categories to include the elements of the dragged files.

Note

The group in which the file is located must be set to Hierarchical View in order to display files in the Beamer.

Once the Navigator displays the elements of the file you want to use as your source, you can then drag and drop the newly "inherited" elements from the Navigator to a location in your current document.

The Drag Mode button determines the results of your drag-and-drop operation. Click it to open a submenu where you can select among the three different insertion modes: Insert as Hyperlink, Insert as Link, Insert as Copy. The symbol changes depending on the mode you choose. If you select Insert as Hyperlink, StarWriter inserts a hyperlink to your selected object. If you select Insert as Link, StarOffice inserts it as an OLE link. Any changes you make in the source document can be automatically updated upon opening, or can be manually updated with the Update command in the Tools menu. This is particularly useful if you insert tables in a document that are linked to a database or StarCalc worksheet.

> **Note**
>
> The Insert as Link mode is not available for graphics, existing OLE objects, references, or indexes.

Insert as Copy creates a copy of the element you dragged and dropped into your document.

> **Note**
>
> The Insert as Copy mode is not available for graphics, OLE objects, references, or indexes.

Once you've set your drag mode, all you need to do is select the element and drag it into the desired location in your active document.

WORKING WITH OUTLINES

Much of what you can do with StarWriter's tools for managing long documents depends on using the built-in heading styles. When outlining your document, be sure to assign headings from the Stylist's Paragraph Styles list to your document.

Headings signify different levels of topic development. In StarWriter, you can create up to 10 different level heads that you can easily move and arrange with the Navigator. In general, using an outline makes it easier for both you and the program to arrange headings and text, reassign level hierarchies, and move headings to new positions.

> **Tip #177 from**
> *Michael & Sarah*
>
> If you're familiar with MS Word, you know that you can print the outline of a document when you're in Outline view. Although StarWriter does not have an equivalent Outline view—it has the Navigator instead—you can still print your outline. Just select File, Send, Outline to Clipboard to copy your outline to the clipboard. Then, open a new Text document and press Ctrl+V to paste the clipboard contents into the new document. You can now print (and save) the outline of your document. If you select Send to Presentation, StarOffice will launch a new Presentation document and insert outline in Outline View so you can start structuring your slide show. You can of course also always generate a Table of Contents, which, unlike a regular outline, includes page number references.

CREATING AN OUTLINE

You create an outline by entering, formatting, and assigning headings using the Style Catalog (Ctrl+Y) or the Stylist (F11). For example, Heading 1 style is used for the broadest topics; Heading 2 is used for the subdivisions of Heading 1 topics; and so on. To view or change a style, click the I-beam mouse pointer anywhere in the paragraph and use the context menu of the Stylist or the Style Catalog to modify the existing styles or assign new ones. After creating your outline, you can easily change the hierarchy level of headings using the Navigator's Promote or Demote commands.

CHANGING AN OUTLINE VIEW

Unlike Microsoft Word, StarWriter does not provide an Outline view within your document. Instead you use the Navigator. Using the Outline Level button in the Navigator, you can expand and collapse your outline according to your specifications. If you select Level 1 from the button's submenu, for example, Navigator will list all headings that use the Heading 1 style; if you select Level 2, you will see headings that use the Heading 1 and Heading 2 style, and so on. Alternatively, you can right-click in the Navigator and select the outline level from the Outline submenu.

EDITING AN OUTLINE

You can edit an outline by adding, deleting, or rearranging headings. Unfortunately, there is no way to add or delete headings in the Navigator—you have to do it in the document. You add to an outline by typing the new heading at the location of your choice into your document, and then selecting a heading style from the list of applied styles on the Text object bar; or, if the style you're looking for has not been used yet, by selecting a new heading style from the Style Catalog or Stylist. Place your cursor in the line that contains the text of your new heading, press Ctrl+Y (Style Catalog) or F11 (Stylist), and select the heading style you're looking for. To delete a heading, select the text in your document and press Delete.

PART
II
CH
10

Things get easier if you want to rearrange the order or level hierarchy in your outline. In that case, you can use the Navigator as described in the following sections—although of course, you're rearranging not just the outline but all the accompanying text as well.

REARRANGING HEADINGS AND TEXT

You can rearrange sections in your document by selecting and moving headings in the Navigator. The easiest method is to collapse the outline to the level you want to move using the Navigator context menu (this is especially helpful if you're dealing with many levels). Next, select the heading you want to move in the Navigator's Headings list and move it up or down using the Up and Down buttons in the Navigator bar. StarWriter will follow your motions and move the selected heading(s), complete with text and objects, accordingly. Each click moves the heading and its contents above or below the adjacent ones. If you click the Navigator's Contents View button (second row, second button), you can also move headings via drag and drop.

PROMOTING AND DEMOTING HEADINGS

You can also change the level hierarchy itself by reassigning levels to selected headings. For example, you can promote a Heading 2 to a Heading 1; or you can demote a Heading 1 to a Heading 2 or lower. To do so, select the heading you want to change in the Navigator, and then click the Promote or Demote buttons. Each click promotes or demotes the selected heading by one level, complete with subheadings. If you only want to promote or demote the selected level (without promoting or demoting the subheadings), press Ctrl while clicking the Promote and Demote buttons.

Tip #178 from
Michael & Sarah

If you're inside the document and you only need to change text independently of the heading, you can also place your cursor inside the paragraph you want to move and press Ctrl+up arrow or down arrow to move the paragraph up or down. If you select several paragraphs at once, you can also move them this way.

DEFINING SECTIONS

Sections may not be everybody's cup of tea, but those who would like to hide certain text passages from curious eyes or prevent others from making changes to existing text should be aware of this feature. They are useful when creating boilerplate legal documents, for example, where you must be sure that the language cannot be easily changed. Sections can also be useful when composing Web pages because you often need to structure your document in screen chunks that are smaller than your normal printed pages in size.

Using the Insert, Section command, you can either define selected text as a section or insert a section at the current cursor position in the Insert Sections dialog (see Figure 10.2). Everything you enter to the left of the paragraph mark, including returns will then be part of that particular section. To exit that section, you have to move your cursor manually to the right of the paragraph mark at which you inserted the section. Figure 10.2 shows the Insert Sections dialog.

Figure 10.2
Use the sections if you want to hide or protect text.

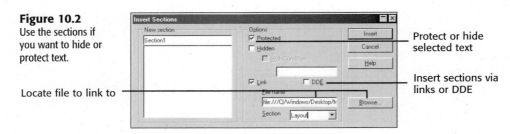

Protect or hide selected text

Insert sections via links or DDE

Locate file to link to

Here's how you handle the Sections command. Select Insert, Section. In the Insert Sections dialog that appears, you'll notice two major areas: New Section and Options. Enter a name for the section in the New Section text box. StarOffice, by default, follows the labeling scheme of Section1, Section2, and so on. Using the Options portion of the dialog, you can define the particularities of this section. If you select Protected, the contents of this section can no longer be modified or edited.

Tip #179 from
Michael & Sarah

Consider protecting finished portions of important documents so you don't accidentally make changes to them (via the Replace All command, for example), or delete them; or if you want to prevent others from making changes to your document (naturally, this only makes sense if you assign a password to this section; we'll come to that shortly).

HIDING SECTIONS WITH CONDITIONAL STATEMENTS

Select Hidden if you want to hide temporarily unpolished or unfinished passages of text from curious eyes. Once you select this option, you can also specify a condition under which the hidden text can become visible. If the condition is met (TRUE), the text will be shown; if it is not met (FALSE), it will remain hidden. *Conditions* are logical expressions, such as x eq 1 (x equals 1), whereby x is a field variable that you specify using the Variables tab of the Fields dialog (select Insert, Fields, Other).

For example, select User Field from the Type list of the Variables tab. Next, enter "show" (or another descriptive name) in the Name box and enter the numeric value 1 in the Value box. Then select Invisible underneath the Format list and click the Fields button to insert the field at the cursor position. Now, select the text that you would like to mark as a section, then open the Section dialog and select Hidden, then With Condition, and enter `"show eq 1"` (with quotation marks) as the condition. Click Insert. The inserted section disappears. If it doesn't, select Tools, Update, Update All to see the change take effect.

REVEALING HIDDEN SECTIONS

To show the section again, select Edit, Sections, select the hidden section from the Section list, then deselect the Hidden check box and click OK. If it doesn't show immediately, select Tools, Update, Update All.

If you want to make the section into normal text again, just delete it as a section from the Edit, Sections dialog box. This does not delete the text of the section, just its designation as a section.

Note

Hidden text will not print.

CREATING SECTIONS BY LINKING TO EXTERNAL FILES

You can also create a section by inserting a link either to another section in your document, another entire document, or a section of another document. (This is the manual equivalent of what you can do with drag and drop from the Navigator, with a few added twists.)

To insert a copy of a section located elsewhere in the current document as a link, click Link and select the desired section from the Section drop-down list. To link to a section in another document, select the Link check box, then click Browse to open the Insert dialog which enables you to locate another file on your system or network that contains the section(s) or information that you would like to insert. Select the desired file and click Insert to return to the Insert Sections dialog. Next, select the section you would like to insert from the Section drop-down list and click Insert. StarWriter will insert the selected section as a protected section at the insertion point. If you don't select a section, StarWriter will insert the entire document as a protected section. When you reload your document, you will be asked if you would like to update the existing links. Select Yes.

You can also choose to insert a section from your current (or another) document as a *DDE* (*Dynamic Data Exchange*) object. A DDE object, like an OLE object, is dynamically linked to its source document, so its information is updated regularly. However, unlike an OLE object, double-clicking it does not open the source application, and you can format it using all of StarWriter's tools (instead of needing to use the source application as with OLE objects). You can take advantage of DDE, for example, to insert a StarCalc table as a section, using StarWriter's superior formatting and table features to create a professional appearance. Using DDE links, you can also link to non-StarOffice documents and insert them as sections into the current document.

When you select the DDE option, you have to enter a DDE command. DDE commands typically follow this syntax:

```
<Server> <Topic> <Item>
```

Server is the DDE name of the application; *Topic* is the location where the item is saved (such as drive, path, and filename), and *Item* refers to the individual object that is being presented. For example, suppose you want to insert via DDE Section1 of the imaginary StarOffice file `abc.sdw` in `Samples folder on drive C`, the DDE command would read:

```
soffice c:\Samples\abc.sdw Section1
```

If you want to insert the contents of the first row of an MS Excel table from the imaginary file abc.xls in the Samples folder on drive C, your command would read as follows:

```
excel c:\samples\[abc.xls]Table1 d1m1
```

When you're finished, select Insert. StarWriter will insert the section for you according to your specifications. You can target your section anytime from within the Navigator. To edit a section, select Edit, Sections. The Edit Sections dialog is almost identical with the Insert Section dialog, except that it also gives you the opportunity to assign a password to the current section when you select the Password Protected option.

INSERTING MANUAL PAGE, LINE, AND COLUMN BREAKS

StarWriter enables you to insert manual page, line, and column breaks any place in a document you see fit. For example, if you don't want to split up a paragraph over two pages or columns, or if you want to reserve space for an object, adding manual page and column breaks is the solution.

Tip #180 from
Michael & Sarah

Of course you can always edit the respective page and paragraph styles if necessary. For more details see Chapter 7, "Formatting Text Documents."

Given that any occurrences of manual breaks are out of the realm of StarWriter's responsibility when it comes to formatting issues, our recommendation is to avoid page and column breaks if at all possible; they only mess up your formatting and can cause ugly holes in your document. If you insist, you can find the command under Insert, Manual Break. (Don't forget to select a style for the following page when inserting page breaks.) When you insert breaks, everything to the right of the insertion point will move to the following page or column.

Note

Of course, there are always exceptions to a rule. You may actually have to insert manual page breaks if you change your orientation from portrait to landscape and vice versa within the same document. In that case, create a second page template based on your standard page and set it to landscape orientation (or whatever change you'd like to have). Then insert a page break with that template. You may find this an acceptable solution when showing source code with long lines in the appendix of a paper.

Manual line breaks, however, are a different matter. For example, if you're working with tables and the text doesn't fit in one line, or if you want to control the awkward line length when inserting a long line of code or Web address, you might consider breaking a line manually. To insert a manual line break, place your cursor to the right of the text or character at which you would like to break the line, and then select Insert, Manual Break. In the Insert Break dialog, select the Line option (all other options will be automatically grayed out), and then click OK.

Tip #181 from
Michael & Sarah

You can also insert manual line breaks at your cursor position by pressing Shift+Enter. To view manual line breaks, switch on the Show Non-Printing Character command.

ADDING HEADERS AND FOOTERS

Headers and footers are text elements that are printed at the top or bottom of every page, respectively. They can help you keep track of versions of your document, as well as keep printed pages together and provide a professional look. You can insert fields that will add the filename of your document, page numbers, and the date and time, which will automatically adjust to reflect changes in the document. For example, if you insert the Date and Time field, each time you open the document, it will update itself based on the system clock of the computer being used.

Headers and footers are always relegated to a page style; all pages that have the same style automatically have the same header and footer. Via field commands (select Insert, Fields), you can insert variable contents (such as date or time or even chapter titles) into headers and footers.

Tip #182 from
Michael & Sarah

If you want different contents in headers and footers or different formatting for left and right pages, specify this on the Header and Footer tabs in the Page Style dialog (Format, Page).

INSERTING AND DELETING HEADERS AND FOOTERS

You have two options. You can select Insert, Header or Footer from the menu bar and select the current page style (Standard). In this case, StarWriter inserts the default header/footer for this page style into the top/bottom margin area. Or you can select the Header tab or Footer tab in the Page Style dialog (Format, Page) and select Header On or Footer On. In both cases, StarWriter will insert default headers that you can change at any time. To remove headers and footers, you have to go to the respective tab in the Page Style dialog and deselect Headers On and Footers On.

EDITING AND FORMATTING HEADERS AND FOOTER

You type and format text in headers and footers the same way you type text in a regular document. Just place your cursor into the header or footer area and start typing.

To edit and format your headers and footers, you have two options. You can do it manually by moving your mouse into the respective areas, and then applying direct formatting options. You can also do it via the Header and Footer tabs in the Page Style dialog (Format, Page). Here you can make changes to the default settings, add more spacing between the header and text area, or set a fixed height for the header/footer. You can select if the same header and footer information is supposed to be on left and right pages; and, if you click More, you open the Borders dialog where you can set a separator line for your headers or footers, depending on which tab you're using. Click between the two bottom or top horizontal corner markers in the Preview area of the Borders dialog to add a line under the header or above the footer, respectively. Using the Border/Background dialog, you can also set the distance between the separator line and text in the Distance from Text spin box; pick a line style (not too thick, keep it subtle), line color, and line shadow if desired, perhaps even a background color for the header or footer area, and click OK. Your headers and footers have just been redressed according to your specifications.

INSERTING CHAPTER AND SECTION TITLES INTO HEADERS AND FOOTERS

Here's what you need to do to add sections and chapter information in your headers and footers:

1. Use the Heading 1 style for section/chapter titles.
2. Place the cursor into the header or footer.
3. Select Insert, Fields, Other.

4. Using the Document tab, select Chapter in the Field Type box and Chapter Name in the Format box. If you prefer to format chapter titles as Heading 2, you have to specify 2 in the Level spin box if you want to insert that heading into your header/footer. (Note, if you set a value in the Level spin box that is not present in the document, StarWriter will automatically insert the next highest level number; for example if you specify 2, but there are now Heading 2 styles, StarWriter will insert Heading 1 styles).

5. Click Insert and close the Fields dialog. The chapter title has been added to your dialog box. If you want, you can change its appearance by applying any attributes you choose.

Caution

Be sure that only your chapter/section titles use the respective Heading style. The Chapter field will reflect the title of each preceding Heading 1 style. If a new title appears, the header changes automatically.

INSERTING DOCUMENT INFORMATION, DATE, AND TIME

You can use the same steps for inserting date, time, page numbers, page count, subject, title, and author name. Any other fields can be selected from the Other submenu.

Tip #183 from
Michael & Sarah

If you entered a title in the Title box on the Description tab of your document's Properties dialog (File, Properties), you can also select Title from the Insert, Fields submenu. The Title field is linked to the Title text box on the Description tab and any name it contains (such as Chapter 10, "Working with Long Documents") will be applied throughout your document if this field is inserted in a footer or header.

SWITCHING HEADER/FOOTER POSITIONING

When you use the Standard page style, headers and footers will be the same on every page. If you would like to have different headers and footers for even and odd numbers, you have to specify this in the Page Style dialog. Using the Page tab, you can select different styles for left and right pages from the Page Layout drop-down menu. If different headers and footers are not necessary, you can also select Mirrored from the same menu. StarWriter will automatically alternate between even and uneven page styles once you tell it to.

To switch headers (or footers) between left (even) and right (odd) pages, follow these steps:

1. Open the Page Style dialog (choose Format, Page or select Page form the Text context menu).

2. On the Header (or Footer) tab, deselect Same content left/right.

3. Place your cursor inside the header/footer of the first left page and insert the fields you would like to appear on every left page in the document. Do the same for the right page. If so inclined, you can also have the left header/footer be left aligned, and the right header/footer right aligned.

→ For more details on alignment, **see** "Adjusting Indents and Spacing," **p. 271**.

For more details on alignment, see "Adjusting Indents and Spacing," p. 271.

Note

If you select Same Content Left/Right Again, you'll lose the information that was entered on the left (even) page, and you'll have to re-enter it if you want to go back to different left and right headers/footers.

When you're starting from scratch, you can also set up a template for left and right. Here's how:

1. Open a new text document.
2. In the Stylist, select the Page Style button and then double-click the style First Page, which will become the first building block for your new document.
3. In the Stylist, right-click and select New from the context menu.
4. In the Page Style dialog, switch to the Organizer tab. Enter a name for your page style in the Name box (for example, Page 1).
5. From the Next Style drop-down list, select Left Page; then select Right Page as the next style for the Left Page, and then Left Page again for the next style for the Right Page. (In other words, you're telling StarWriter that after a Left Page style comes a Right Page style; and after a Right Page style comes a Left Page style.) You're all set to assign different headers and footers for your new document. And you can define different margins for your left-hand and right-hand headers and footers.

Note

Alternatively, you can also modify the existing styles: First Page, Left Page, and Right Page. In that case, you would have First Page followed (Next Style) by Left Page; Left Page followed by Right Page; and Right Page followed by Left Page. Then select First Page for your document.

INSERTING NOTES, FOOTNOTES, AND ENDNOTES

Like many office suites today, StarOffice allows you to insert notes into your documents in an intuitive, easy way, just like you might place a Post-It note on a report you place on a colleague's desk. This feature isn't unique, but combined with the power of the Navigator, it offers you an efficient way to annotate and review documents (in addition to the standard mark-up features available on the Edit menu).

To insert a note, place your cursor inside the text where you would like the note to appear, and then select Insert, Note. An Insert Note dialog box opens where you can enter your note. If you click Author, your initials (as entered in the User Data tab in the General Options dialog) and the current date and time are automatically appended. When you're finished entering the note, click OK. A small yellow rectangle appears in your document to indicate a note has been inserted. To delete a note, place your cursor inside the note and press Delete.

PART

II

CH

10

Tip #184 from
Michael & Sarah

You can move a note any time by selecting it and dragging it with your mouse to a new location.

If you have multiple notes in your document and want to review them, place your cursor inside a note and select Insert, Note. In the Edit Note dialog box you can use the backward and forward arrows to cycle through your notes while reviewing their contents. If you've found the one you're looking for, select OK and StarWriter will take you there.

You can also find notes easily with the Navigator. Just click the plus symbol next to the Notes category to expand the list. All existing notes are listed in sequence. Click a note to jump to its location. To delete a note, put your cursor on the note insertion and press Delete.

INSERTING AND MOVING FOOTNOTES AND ENDNOTES

Adding a footnote or endnote to a document couldn't be easier: Place the insertion point behind the term you want to reference, and select Insert, Footnote. The Insert Footnote dialog box appears (see Figure 10.3).

Figure 10.3
From inserting to managing, footnotes in StarWriter are easy.

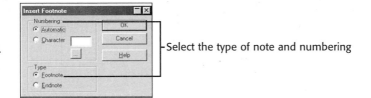

Select the type of note and numbering

You can choose between automatic numbering or a custom character display for footnotes. In the Type portion of the Insert Footnote dialog, you can define the note either as a footnote proper or as an endnote. When you select OK, StarWriter inserts a superscripted reference mark and places the insertion point into a special (default) area at the bottom of your page (Footnote) or end of document (Endnote) where you can type the footnote text. Since the reference markers are linked fields, you can click on the reference marker in the footnote/endnote area to jump back to the reference marker in the text and vice versa. (Alternatively, you can also use the Footnote button in the Navigator to toggle back and forth between the reference mark in the document and the footnote at the bottom of your page, or, in the case of an endnote, at the end of your document.)

Tip #185 from
Michael & Sarah

If your document has both footnotes and endnotes, they should probably have different numbering formats so as not to confuse the reader. In those instances, symbols (for example, *, **, ***) are often used for the footnotes and numbers for the endnotes. If you select symbols, choose Restart with each page. You can assign your symbols through the Custom-Character option in the Insert Footnote dialog. Just click the Ellipses button (…) to select a symbol from the Special Character dialog. To change the footnote page options, select Tools, Footnotes.

Tip #186 from
Michael & Sarah

Just like notes, you can move a reference marker any time by selecting it and dragging it with your mouse to a new location. StarWriter will automatically adjust the numbering order if necessary.

EDITING AND FORMATTING FOOTNOTES AND ENDNOTES

StarWriter automatically applies the Footnote or Endnote paragraph style to the note text. It applies a character style, Footnote Reference, or Endnote Reference to the reference mark. You can edit the attributes of these styles by right-clicking the respective style in the Stylist, and then selecting Modify from the context menu; or you can create your own. To control the position of the reference marker, you have to open the Character dialog (choose Format, Character) and go to the Position portion of the Font Effects tab, where you experiment with your position options.

Tip #187 from
Michael & Sarah

If you would like more distance between footnotes and endnotes, you can add an invisible white line as a bottom border to the respective Paragraph style or Region style. Place the cursor on a footnote and open the Stylist. Select Special Region Styles and right-click the style to be changed (here it's Footnote) and select Modify. Click the Borders tab and add a white, bottom line; then increase the value of distance to text and click OK and press Enter.

If you would like to change the numbering and symbols of your footnotes, select Tools, Footnotes to open the Footnote Options dialog. Choose either the Footnotes or Endnotes tab, shown in Figure 10.4.

Figure 10.4
The Footnote Options dialog enables you to define the autonumbering styles of your footnotes and endnotes.

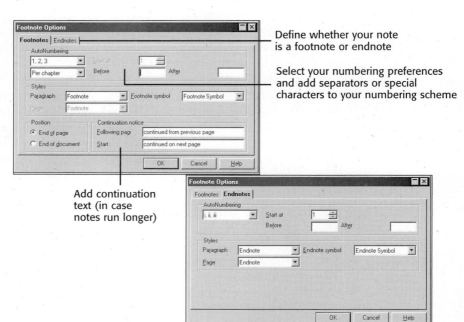

Define whether your note is a footnote or endnote

Select your numbering preferences and add separators or special characters to your numbering scheme

Add continuation text (in case notes run longer)

Using the Footnotes and Endnotes tabs, you can define the AutoNumbering style for your respective notes. If you are using both footnotes and endnotes in your document, you can also select to have your footnote numbering restart on each page (Per Page).

If you are using footnotes only, you can choose whether you want your footnote numbering to restart with each chapter (Per Chapter)—recommended when your document contains multiple chapters or when you are working with master documents—or whether you want consecutive footnote numbering from beginning to end (Per Document).

If you select Per Document, you can also select the starting number for footnotes in each new document. This is useful if you are working with multiple documents or master documents and would like to apply one style of consecutive numbering throughout.

In some instances, footnote text may be so long that it does not fit into the defined footnote area at the bottom of the page. If that happens, it is standard practice to indicate to a reader that the footnote text is a continuation from the previous page. You can use the Continuation Notice portion of the Footnotes tab to specify text that introduces a continuing footnote (for example, *continued from previous page*) or ends a footnote that runs into the next page (for example, *continued on next page*).

If you don't like StarWriter's default way of managing the footnote area, you can redefine the size of your footnote area using the Footnote tab in the Page Style dialog (choose Format, Page) (see Figure 10.5).

PART

II

CH

10

Figure 10.5
From inserting to managing, footnotes in StarWriter are easy (Insert, Footnote). The Footnote Options dialog (Tools, Footnotes) enables you to define the autonumbering styles of your footnotes and endnotes. Using the Footnote tab in the Page dialog (Format, Page), you can define the size of the footnote area.

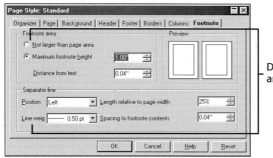

Define the size of the footnote area and add a separator line

DELETING FOOTNOTES AND ENDNOTES

To delete a footnote or endnote, place your insertion point to the right of the reference marker in the text and press Backspace. StarWriter will automatically renumber the remaining references.

PRINTING NOTES

You can choose to print notes in a number of ways through the Notes option in the Printer Options sub-dialog, shown in Figure 10.6. Just select File, Print, and select Options in the Print dialog. In the Notes portion of the Options dialog you select the desired notes printing options:

- Select None if you want to suppress your personal notes from printing altogether.

- Notes Only prints all the personal notes you inserted throughout your document.

- End of Document prints first your document, including footnotes and endnotes, and then prints your personal notes on a separate page at the end of the document.

- End of Page prints the footnotes at the end of each page together with any notes you might have added to that particular page.

Figure 10.6
You can choose to print notes by themselves, or print them in footnote or endnote positions with the complete document.

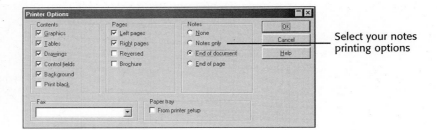

Select your notes printing options

BOOKMARKING YOUR DOCUMENT

Another neat feature for working with long documents is the Bookmark feature. Based on the same principle as the Navigator's reminder, bookmarks are better repositories for your thoughts because you can actually name and save them for future reference. Use bookmarks to flag an unfinished or unpolished place in your document so you can easily return to it later. To use this feature, place your cursor in front of the text location to be bookmarked, select Insert, Bookmark from the menu bar, and enter a descriptive name in the text box at the top of the Insert Bookmark dialog. Click OK to insert the bookmark in your document. You can easily return to your bookmarked location by expanding the Bookmark tree in the Navigator and double-clicking the respective bookmark title. To delete a bookmark, open the Insert Bookmark dialog (choose Insert, Bookmark), select the entry you would like to delete from the list, and click OK. Your bookmark will immediately be removed.

USING LINE NUMBERING

If you find yourself using StarWriter for legal documents or technical writing, you may be interested in StarWriter's Line Numbering tool. Line numbering is extremely helpful when working with long documents that are passed between two or more people, such as drafts of books or research theses. When you want to be sure that everyone is on the same page—literally—be sure to turn on the Line Numbering feature, and tell your fellows and associates to do the same.

To turn on line numbering, select Tools, Line Numbering from the menu bar. In the Line Numbering dialog that appears, select Show Line Numbers. In the View portion of this dialog, you can also control the text style, format, and position of the numbering, as well as specify by how much you would like the numbers to be offset from the left/right or inner/outer margins of your document. (Note that "inner" is left on right pages and right on left pages, and vice versa with "outer"; you can play with this feature and look at the results in File, Page View/Print Preview to determine which style suits you best.) In addition, you can determine whether you want to include blank lines in the final count. You can also add a separator symbol, such as a hyphen, to make scanning the margins even easier on the eyes of the reader. Figure 10.7 shows you an example of line numbering in documents.

Figure 10.7
Using StarWriter's Line Numbering feature ensures that everyone is "on the same page" when two or more people are looking at a document.

Specify style, format, and position

Refer to line numbers when referring to text

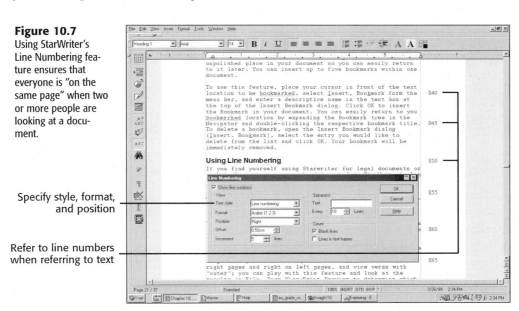

GENERATING INDEXES AND REFERENCE TABLES

StarWriter can create indexes and reference tables (such as a table of contents) instantly, with correct page numbers all perfectly in place. What really counts, though, is that these features are a great time-saver—not counting the time it takes to mark the individual index entries, of course.

The key to advanced work with the Indexes feature is to understand that the index you see in your document is a StarWriter field. As such, many formatting options can be controlled via field switches, and you can update the whole index or table at any time to bring it in sync with any changes made to the document.

Using the Indexes feature (select Insert, Indexes), you have four choices: Entry, Index, Table of Contents, and User-Defined. Of these four options, Entry is used to mark the items you want to appear in an index or reference table. The other three options are used to insert the actual index or table in your document.

Both standard and user-defined indexes differ from reference tables mainly in that a table can have up to 10 levels, each appearing in its own format, whereas indexes can only have two levels.

CREATING INDEX AND TABLE ENTRIES

The mechanical act of generating indexes and reference tables is easy. However, before StarWriter can generate indexes and tables, it has to be told what it is supposed to index and reference. That's where you come in. Based on your insider status as the creator of the document, you have to plough through your pages and identify the specific words or phrases you would like to show up in your index and table.

GENERATING A TABLE OF CONTENTS

In the case of a table of contents, it's actually quite simple. StarWriter's Insert Table of Contents command scans your document for certain heading styles. If you've used the built-in Heading 1, Heading 2, and so on styles consistently throughout to separate the various sections of your document in order of importance, StarWriter can generate a table of contents for you at the click of a mouse. All you have to do is follow these steps:

1. Position your cursor at the place where you want to insert your table of contents (usually toward the beginning of a document).

2. Select Insert, Indexes, Table of Contents. The Insert Table of Contents dialog box appears. You'll see three tabs: Index, Entries, Styles.

3. On the Index tab, enter a name for your table of contents in the Title text box. The default name is Table of Contents, but you can also name it Contents.

4. In the Create From portion of the Index tab, select Outline and specify how detailed you would like your table to be by selecting a number in the Collect Until Level box (1 will show only Heading 1 style headings, 2 will show only Heading 1 and Heading 2 styles, and so on). If you marked additional headers or paragraphs that do not use the heading styles for inclusion in the table of contents (for example, an introduction, appendix, or even brief abstracts), select the Marked Entries option.

Note

Marked Entries refers to text that you marked using the Insert, Indexes, Index Entry command. For example, if you chose a style other than a predefined heading style for your introductory text heading or if you want to include a brief introductory paragraph as abstract in your table of contents, select the text that you want to include in your reference table. Next, choose Insert, Indexes, Index Entry to open the Index Entry dialog. Select Table of Contents from the Index drop-down list and specify a level number in the Level box and click OK. Your text has been marked as a table of contents entry and can be added to your table when you select the Marked Entries option.

5. Use the Styles tab to edit and assign styles to the table of contents title and entries (see the section, "Editing and Formatting Indexes and Reference Tables" in this chapter for more details).

6. Click OK, and zap, you're looking at a standard table of contents in outline form with all the page numbers in place (see Figure 10.8).

Figure 10.8
StarOffice makes generating a standard table of contents a breeze. If you want to get fancy, you can select the Styles tab and the Outline button to assign different styles and numbering schemes to your table.

Select to assign styles to the table elements

Mark to generate table from index entries

Mark to generate table from heading styles

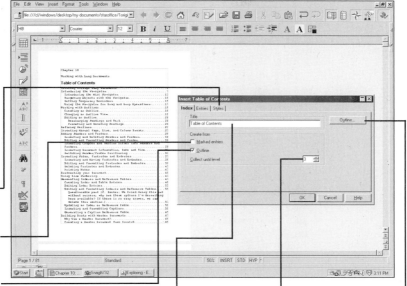

Enter title for reference table

Specify the level of detail of your reference table

Select to assign a numbering scheme to the heading styles

Tip #188 from
Michael & Sarah

If you want to get fancy, you can also edit the structure of your table, assign different paragraph styles to the table elements, as well as define a numbering scheme for the individual heading styles. Just select the Entries and Styles tabs, as well as the Outline button in the Insert Table of Contents dialog before clicking OK, and you can start digging through a number of options that we will explain to you shortly.

GENERATING AN INDEX

When it comes to indexes, however, things tend to get a bit more time-consuming for the indexer. Indexing is an art. Choosing what to index, deciding on concise index entries to refer to complex ideas, and ensuring consistency is not for the faint of heart. However, short of hiring a pro to do the work for you, you can take a crack at StarWriter's indexing feature. StarWriter actually does a pretty good job at keeping the index up to date as edits or format modifications change the documents page breaks.

In general, the mechanics involved in indexing are quite simple. You mark index entries in your documents by using the Index command:

1. First, select the word to index. (It suffices to put your cursor inside the word.)

2. Select Insert, Indexes, Entry. In the Insert Index Entry dialog that appears, select Index from the Index drop-down list (see Figure 10.9). If you want to have a multilevel index, you can enter the respective level name(s) in the 1st Key and 2nd Key list box. StarWriter will include the selected entry underneath the respective key when it generates the index. If you want to automatically index other instances of the same word in your text, select Apply to all similar texts—StarWriter will mark all similarly spelled terms for inclusion in your index. To accept your entry, select OK. If the Field Shadings option is on (View, Field Shadings), you'll see the indexed word appear against a shadowed background in your document.

Tip #189 from
Michael & Sarah

Note that once you entered a 1st or 2nd Key term, StarWriter will remember it, and you won't have to retype it. Just select the term you need from the respective drop-down list the next time you want to group a selected entry underneath either key. (Note also that you must have already entered a term in the 1st Key field, before the 2nd Key field becomes available.)

Tip #190 from
Michael & Sarah

The Apply to Similar Text option in the Index Entry dialog marks all instances of the same word; however, you should know that this option is case-sensitive. If you want to mark all terms regardless if they are lower-cased or capitalized, follow these steps: Select Edit, Search and Replace, enter the word in the Search For box, and click Search All. StarWriter will highlight all occurrences of the word in the text. Now select Insert, Index, Index Entry and proceed to define the index entry as described earlier. StarWriter will mark all selected words for inclusion in the index.

---

3. When you're done indexing your document, place your cursor on the page that is supposed to collect the index information.

4. Select Insert, Indexes, Index. The Insert Index dialog appears.

5. On the Index tab of the dialog, specify a name for your index or accept the default (Index). Using the Options portion of the Index tab, select the indexing options you want. Your options include:

   - **Combine identical entries**—Select this option if your index contains several entries by the same name on different, non-consecutive pages; StarWriter will combine them as follows: graphics 10, 24, 45 (instead of graphics 10, graphics 24, graphics 45).

   - **Combine identical entries with pp**—Select this option if your index contains several entries by the same name on consecutive pages; StarWriter will combine them as follows: graphics 10pp (instead of graphics 10, graphics 11, graphics 12). (This option is only available if Combine identical entries is selected.)

- **Case sensitive**—Select this option if you want to list index entries that are lower case or uppercase separately (for example, windows (as in screens) and Windows (as in the operating system)). This option is only available if Combine identical entries is selected.

- **Keys as separate entries**—Use this option if you want to include keys as separate entries in your index. All terms that have been assigned to a key will then be listed underneath the respective keys.

- **Alphabetical headings**—When you select this option, StarWriter automatically takes note of a change in first letters and inserts the respective letter as a heading in front of the index entries.

Figure 10.9
Indexing your document just got a whole lot easier with the Apply to similar text option.

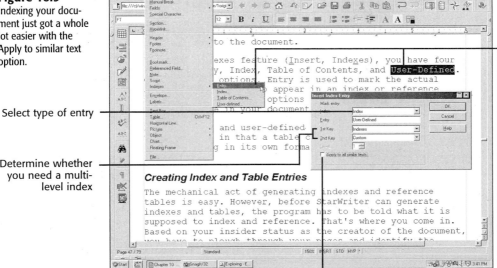

Select type of entry

Determine whether you need a multi-level index

Select if you want to automatically include similar words in the index

Select index entry

6. Use the Styles tab to edit and assign styles to the index title, separator, and entries (see the section, "Editing and Formatting Indexes and Reference Tables" in this chapter for more details).

7. Click OK. StarWriter will then generate the index according to your specifications.

Note

In many respects, StarWriter's indexing feature is somewhat limited. For example, you can't easily identify an entry as the major discussion of a particular topic, short of direct formatting it manually in the index. (One or two check boxes in the Index Entry dialog could take care of this.) Finally, you're only allowed two levels in an index, which is sufficient for most projects, but when it comes to more scientific and technical topics, three or four levels are often needed.

EDITING INDEX ENTRIES

If you would like to quickly review your indexing choices or delete index entries, you can use the Index Entry command. Place your cursor inside an entry, and then select Edit, Index Entry from the menu bar. In the Edit Index Entry dialog that appears, you can reassign an entry to a different key or delete it altogether (see Figure 10.10). Using this dialog, you can also quickly move from entry to entry by using the backward and forward buttons in the lower right of the dialog.

Figure 10.10
StarWriter enables you to edit index entries—one after another.

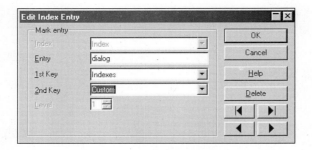

EDITING AND FORMATTING INDEXES AND REFERENCE TABLES

You can change the appearance of an index or reference table in one of two ways: you can edit and assign paragraph styles to the index and table elements before inserting the index or table by using the appropriate options from the Insert Index or Insert Table of Contents dialog; or you can modify the style(s) StarWriter applies automatically to each entry (such as Index 1/Contents 1, Index 2/Contents 2, and so on).

The fastest and most convenient way to format indexes and tables is before inserting them. Here's how:

1. Click the Styles tab in the open Insert Index or Insert Table of Contents dialog (see Figure 10.11).

2. Select a paragraph style that you would like to assign to an index or table element from the list on the left. Click the Edit button to refresh your memory about the attributes of a particular style and, if necessary, change the desired attributes.

3. Select the index or table element to which you want to assign the selected (and possibly edited) paragraph style.

4. Click the Assign button. When finished, click OK.

If you didn't change the styles of your index and table elements when generating the index or table of contents, don't despair. You can still edit the styles of the respective elements. Just select Insert, Indexes, Index or Table of Contents and go to the Styles tab in the Edit Index or Edit Table of Contents dialog, respectively. You can now make the desired changes, following the steps above. When you're finished, click OK to accept the changes.

Figure 10.11
Using the Styles tab in the Insert Table of Contents and Insert Index dialog box, you can change the appearance of the reference elements before inserting the index or table of contents.

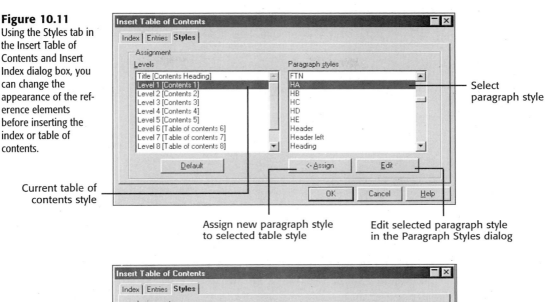

Current table of contents style

Select paragraph style

Assign new paragraph style to selected table style

Edit selected paragraph style in the Paragraph Styles dialog

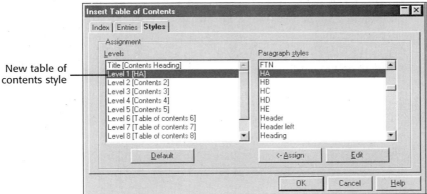

New table of contents style

PART

II

CH

10

Alternatively, you can also open the Stylist (F11), click the Paragraph Styles icon (if it isn't already selected), locate and right-click the index/contents style you would like to change, and select Modify. Using the Font and Indents and Spacing tabs in the Paragraph Styles dialog, you can make the desired formatting changes. When finished, select OK. Your changes will take effect as soon as you click the Update button in the Stylist.

CHANGING THE OUTLINE OF A TABLE OF CONTENTS

In addition to style formatting changes, you can also change the outline structure of your table of contents by using the Outline button of the Insert (or Edit) Table of Contents dialog. The Outline button opens the Outline Numbering dialog, where you can select a numbering style and position for your call-out levels, as well as separators (such as ")" or "." or even a space as in (1) Heading or 1. Heading). Using this dialog, you also can refine the outline numbering scheme.

Note

You have to select each level you want to change individually, and then perform your changes on both tabs for the changes to take effect.

Here's what you do to change the outline of your table of contents before inserting the table:

1. Click the Outline button on the Insert Table of Contents dialog. The Outline Numbering dialog appears.

2. From the Level list box, select a level number for which you want to define a numbering style. You can define a style for each level individually (1, 2, and so on), or for all levels collectively (1–10).

3. Using the options in the Numbering portion of the tab, you can define a style and format for the selected level. Your options include the following:
   - **Paragraph style**—Select a paragraph style for the selected level.
   - **Numbering style**—Select a numbering scheme for the selected level. Your options include None, capital letters (A, B, C and so on), lowercase letters (a, b, c), uppercase Roman numerals (I, II, III), lowercase Roman numerals (i, ii, iii), Arabic numerals (1, 2, 3), and alphabetical numbering (A, AA, AAA), in which case the number of the letters reflects the level number (for example, BBB refers to the second numbering of the third level).
   - **Text style**—Select a character style for the selected numbering scheme.
   - **Show sublevels**—Select the number of subordinate levels that are supposed to be included in the numbering. For example, if you call out two levels and specify "2" for Level 2 in the Show sublevels box, your outline will look like this: 1.1 Heading, 1.2 Heading, and so on for all Level 2s that are listed under the first Level 1. Likewise, if you select "3" for a second-level section, your outline will appear as 2.1.1, 2.1.2, 2.1.3 and so on.
   - **Separator**—Enter a desired separator in the Before and After text boxes. For example, if you're using an Arabic numbering scheme, you may want to include a period (.) and a space in the After box, so that the level reads: 1. Heading 1 text.
   - **Start at**—Specify the start number of the numbering scheme. If you're using an alphabetical or Roman numbering scheme, the number you enter here controls the start letter.

4. Use the options of the Position tab to define the positioning and spacing between text and number format for a selected level. You can see your changes in the Preview box. If you make a mistake during your selection, use the Default button to return to the default values of the program. Your options include the following:
   - **Level**—Select a level for which you want to define the positioning.
   - **Indent**—Use this spin box to define the distance between left paragraph indent and left margin of the numbering character. If the left paragraph indent is zero (0), the indent corresponds to the distance between the left page margin and the

numbering symbol. If you also select Relative, the value you specified in the Indent spin box will be seen relative in relation to the next higher level. Note that this option is not available for Level 1 styles.

- **Distance text**—Use this spin box to control the distance between the numbering character and the level text.

- **Minimum distance numbering <-> text**—Here you can enter the minimum distance between the numbering character and the following text. This option guarantees that you have sufficient space between numbering character and text when you opt to right-align the numbering character.

- **Numbering alignment**—Select an alignment style for your numbering character from the drop-down list. Your options include: Left, Centered, and Right. Note that your centered and right alignment options are restricted by the number specified in the Minimum distance numbering <-> text spin box.

5. Click the Format button if you want to save the current outline numbering settings. Saving your custom outline settings has the advantage that you can use them in other documents as well, not just in the current one. To save your outline settings, select Save As from the Format submenu, enter a name for the current settings in the Save As dialog, and click OK. The name will appear in the Format submenu list (which by default list Untitled 1–Untitled 9), where you can select it in order to "quickformat" existing outline numbering formats.

Note

Any changes on the Numbering and Position tabs overlap with the settings on the Indents & Spacing and Numbering tabs of the Format, Paragraph Styles dialog. Any value you enter in the Indent spin box on the Position tab will be added to the value specified in the Indents box of the Indents & Spacing tab in the Paragraph Styles dialog. Note that this behavior is new with StarOffice 5.1. If you use documents that were generated with previous versions of StarOffice, the original indents will be kept without changes.

When you're satisfied with your choices, choose OK twice, and StarWriter will generate a table of contents according to your specifications. When you look at your document, you'll notice that StarWriter inserted the numbers and separators as fields according to your specifications in front of the headings in your document.

If you want to change the outline and numbering format of your table of contents after you inserted the table, place your cursor inside the table you want to change, select Insert, Indexes, Table of Contents. The Edit Table of Contents dialog appears. Click the Outline button. Using the Numbering and Position tabs, you can make your desired changes. When you're finished, click OK to return to the Edit Table of Contents dialog. Click OK again to accept your changes.

Tip #191 from
Michael & Sarah

You can also select Automatically Update on the Organizer tab of the Paragraph Styles dialog. StarWriter will make all changes for the respective style as soon as you select OK. However, be careful that the Name box on the Organizer tab actually shows the style you want to change.

CHANGING THE ANATOMY OF YOUR INDEX AND REFERENCE TABLE ENTRIES

Every index and reference table is made up of certain standard elements. In the case of an index, these elements include the entry text, a page number, and a space between the entry and the page number. In the case of a table of contents, you may also see a chapter number before the entry text.

Using the Entries tab in the Insert Index or Insert Table of Contents dialog, you can change the structure of these entries. You can delete existing elements or add new text and hyperlinks. You can make these changes before inserting an index or table of contents, or afterwards (in which case you have to place your cursor inside the index or table you want to change and then select Insert, Indexes, Index or Table of Contents, respectively). Here's how you go about changing the structure of your reference table before inserting the index or table:

1. Select the Entries tab of the Insert Index or Insert Table of Contents dialog. On the top of the tab, you'll see the Structure list, which shows the formal breakdown of the various levels (1–10):

Index	Table of contents
<E> = entry text entry	<E#> = chapter number
<T> = tab	<ET> = entry text
<#> = page number	<T> = tab
	<#> = page number
	<LS> = begin hyperlink (optional)
	<LE> = end hyperlink (optional)

2. To change the structure of an entry, select a level entry in the Structure list. When you select a level in the Structures list, you'll see its code in the text box below. You can delete an element that you don't want to appear (such as a number (<E#>), for example); or you can add a Tab (if you'd like to increase the indent) or Hyperlink (great for online documents, if you'd like your reader to click a reference in the table of contents and then jump to that place in the document).

   When adding hyperlinks, you have to press Hyperlink before and after the part you'd like to see as a link. StarWriter than inserts the <LS> and <LE> tags, respectively. So "<LS><ET><LE><T><#>" inserts an entry followed by a tab and the page number, where the entry itself is a hyperlink that takes you to the corresponding chapter when clicked. This is not only useful when working on online-documents but also for faster navigation within regular documents. Note that the appearance of this type of hyperlink is different from the appearance of Internet hyperlinks. For example, you will not see blue, underlined text; instead, your mouse pointer will change shape when you place it over the hyperlinked text.

Add desired text anywhere between the chapter number code and the page number code. For example, if you add the word "page" before the page number code, the code for the selected level may look like this: <E#><ET><T>page <#> (notice the extra space after "page" so that the word and the number don't run into each other).

3. If you want to apply your changes to all levels, click the All Levels button.

4. Select None, or one or more of these additional options:

   - **Calculate and set tabs**—Use this option to set a tab to the very right. The position of the tab does not depend on the paper width or number of columns. The tabs in the paragraph styles are no longer valid.

   - **First tab position**—Use this option to add an additional tab to the very right. By the default, the first tab is set at .5 cm from the left, but you can also enter a different value in the spin box on the right.

   - **Left margin from paragraph style**—Select this option if you want StarOffice to calculate the tab relatively in relation to the left margin of the paragraph style. If you do not select this option, the numbering or text will always start next to the left margin. You can use this to align the table list of numbers and text.

5. When you're finished, click OK.

Tip #192 from
Michael & Sarah

By default, StarWriter does not insert a space between the chapter number (<E#>) and the entry text (<ET>). If you want a more professional-looking table of contents, insert a tab (<T>) between the chapter number and the entry text: <E#><T><ET><T><#>. In addition, add a tab or indent after the chapter number of the respective paragraph styles to have your table of contents entries line up properly.

Changing the structure of an index follows basically the same steps, although your options are more limited. If you want to change the structure before you insert the index, select the Entries tab in the Insert Index dialog. Here you can change the structure of the separator and index levels. If you want to change the structure after you inserted the index, place your cursor in the Index you want to change and select Insert, Indexes, Index from the menu and select the Entries tab in the Edit Index dialog. If you want to change the anatomy of a table of contents after you inserted the table, place the cursor in the table you want to change and select Insert, Indexes, Table of Contents. In the Edit Table of Contents dialog, select the Entries tab to make the desired changes.

UPDATING AN INDEX OR REFERENCE TABLE

The page numbers listed in the index or table of contents are valid when StarWriter first generates them, but they can get out of whack quickly once you edit your text, add additional index entries, or change any aspect of the formatting. Unfortunately, StarWriter is not equipped to deal with these changes automatically on-the-fly, so it's up to you to update your table of contents and index.

Don't panic. It's actually quite easy. Because indexes and reference tables are just fields, you can use the standard Update command, which you can find on the Tools menu. To update a specific item, table, or index, place your cursor anywhere within the index or reference table, and then select Tools, Update, Current Index (or All Indexes, if you have more than one that might be affected by the changes) to bring your indexes up to date.

INSERTING AND FORMATTING CAPTIONS

StarWriter enables you to add explanatory text or captions above or below illustrations (pictures or graphics), tables, OLE objects, and text frames. In outline, the mechanics of inserting captions are easy:

1. Select the object to which you want to assign a caption.
2. Summon the Insert, Caption command.
3. Specify your settings in the Insert Caption dialog.
4. Click OK to have your caption inserted.

Now you can edit and format the text in your caption as usual via direct formatting or style formatting.

Note

When inserting captions for graphics and OLE objects, StarWriter automatically defines the width of the caption as 100 percent and sets the height of the caption area to automatic. That way, the caption will automatically adjust itself if you decide to resize your graphic or object.

The devil, however, is in the details, if you want your captions to be consistently numbered throughout a chapter or document—for example, have graphics captions in Chapter 1 appear as Illustration 1.1, Illustration 1.2, and so on; and graphics captions in Chapter 2 appear as Illustration 2.1, Illustration 2.2, and so on. Here's an example of what you need to do to insert and number captions according to chapters:

1. Select Tools, Outline Numbering from the menu.
2. In the Outline dialog that appears, outline your document by applying the Heading 1 style to chapter titles. Then assign a numbering style (for example, 1, 2, 3) to the paragraph (heading) style.
3. Select the first object in the first chapter of your document to which you want to add a caption, and then select Insert, Caption to open the Insert Caption dialog.
4. In the Category field, select the type of object (illustration, table, or text) the caption accompanies.
5. In the Numbering box, select a numbering style for your caption (for example, Arabic (123)).

6. In the Caption box, enter a brief description of the object. You don't have to come up with an informative description right away; you can always add or change it later in the document.

Tip #193 from
Michael & Sarah

StarWriter does not automatically give you the option to add a separator (such as period or colon) after the caption number. You have to do that yourself by entering it in the Caption box, followed by a space and then the caption text.

7. In the Position box, select whether you want the caption to appear above or below the object.

8. Select OK. StarWriter inserts the caption according to your specifications. You'll notice, for example, Illustration 1, Table 1, or Text 1.

9. Next, place the insertion point in front of the number 1 in the caption, and select Edit, Fields to open the Edit Fields: Variables dialog.

10. Select the desired chapter number from the Level drop-down box of the Chapter numbering portion of the Edit Fields dialog. In the Separator box, you can add a separator symbol, for example a period (.).

11. Click OK. You'll notice the current chapter number listed in front of the caption number. You can manually insert a separator symbol (such as a period or hyphen).

12. You can now copy both fields together and paste them over the fields of the other captions in your document (which should already be inserted of course), overwriting the existing caption field. Voilà! You now have captions identified by chapter and caption number.

PART
II
CH
10

To start captions in Chapter 2 as caption 2.1, caption 2.2, and so on, you must first reset the caption numbering at the beginning of Chapter 2. You can automate this process by inserting an invisible field, which automatically resets the caption variable to zero (0) at the beginning of a new chapter, so it can restart with 1. Here's how you do it:

1. Put the insertion point at the beginning of the Chapter 2 heading, and then select Insert, Fields, Other to open the Fields dialog.

2. Using the Variables tab, select Number Sequence from the Type list, and specify the type of caption (Illustration, Table, or Text) in the Selection list.

3. Enter 0 in the Value field underneath the Selection list, and then click Insert.

4. You now have to turn the visible field into an invisible one. Again, select Insert, Fields, Other (or press Ctrl+F2) to open the Fields dialog.

5. Using the Functions tab in the Fields dialog, select Hidden Text from the Type list.

6. Next, enter False in the Condition box, and then select Insert. The field is now invisible.

7. Copy the Chapter/Caption field from the first chapter over the captions in Chapter 2. In the following chapter, you again reset the variable for your caption type (Illustration, Table, Text), and so on.

Admittedly, this might not be the easiest way to have your captions comply with publishing standards, but it sure is nice once you look at the finished results.

GENERATING A CAPTION REFERENCE TABLE OR USER-DEFINED INDEX

Generating a reference table for your captions is not much different from generating an index or table of contents. You place your cursor in your document where you want the table to appear and select Insert, Indexes, User-Defined. In the Insert Custom Index dialog that appears, enter a title for the index (for example, Figures) on the Index tab, and then select the Object check box and specify the type of object for which you would like to generate the index (Pictures, OLE Objects, Tables, Text Boxes). Click OK and StarWriter will generate your user-defined index.

Caution

Don't place your cursor in front of another index heading when generating an index—your current index will be replaced by the new one, due to the way StarWriter handles index styles. Be sure that indexes are separated by at least one non-index paragraph style.

In general, you can use the Insert, Indexes, User-Defined Index command to generate indexes that consist of any combination of the following:

- Marked entries—includes all entries that have been marked for the inclusion in a user-defined index, using the Insert, Indexes, Index Entry dialog.
- Paragraph styles—includes text that has been formatted with the selected paragraph style.
- Objects—includes the caption of the selected object in the index.

As with the Insert Index and Insert Table of Contents dialogs, you can also change the user-defined index entries and styles, using the Entries and Styles tabs of the Insert Custom Index dialog.

Tip #194 from
Michael & Sarah

You can also use the Insert Custom Index dialog to generate a table of contents out of text that has been formatted using a specified paragraph style. For example, if you want to generate a reference table of footnotes, or if you used a different paragraph style for your headings than Heading 1, Heading 2, and so on, you can select the style you used from the Paragraph Styles list on the Index tab. Click OK, and StarWriter will generate a user-defined index out of these styles.

There is one rather annoying problem with the way StarWriter generates these user-defined indexes from captions—you can't change the default names in the index. A picture or graphic will always show "Illustration" to the left of the caption number. In the index, however, it will be listed as Graphic 1, Graphic 2, and so on. Although you can rename the caption (for example, changing "Illustration" to "Figure"), the index cannot be changed. If you go ahead and change the default name anyhow, the index will revert to the default (Graphic, Table, or

Frame) each time you update it. The caption name, if changed, however, remains. A small comfort in an otherwise insufficient feature.

BUILDING BOOKS WITH MASTER DOCUMENTS

Keeping an entire long document in one file sounds simple enough. You don't have to worry about managing different files; no special steps are required to create cross-references and indexes; all the information is in one place and, most importantly, you don't have to learn about a new feature. Still, the preferred method of dealing with multi-chapter documents (100+ pages) is to break them up into smaller chunks. The bigger the document, the longer it takes to load it or send it as an attachment; and when the file gets corrupt, you'll probably lose more than just your data, so making regular backups becomes even more critical. But is the file still small enough to fit on a floppy? If you use StarWriter's Master Document feature, you don't have to worry about any of these concerns.

StarWriter's Master Document feature is designed to manage multiple separate chapter files as a single document, and it does a pretty good job.

Using the master document feature in StarWriter, you can do the following:

- Create a master document from scratch
- Combine existing documents into a master document
- Create a master document out of an existing document

However, StarWriter can only generate a master document if the contents of your new or existing document(s) are divided consistently by the same paragraph (heading) style.

If you create a master document from scratch, you may outline, for example, the main headings of your book project using the Heading 1 style, and then have StarWriter divide your outline into separate sub-documents for you. Alternatively, you can also start with a blank master document, and then insert existing files that you would like to combine into a master document. In both instances, individual elements have to be marked consistently.

PART

II

CH

10

Note

You don't have to use the built-in Heading 1 style to create a master document. The important thing is that you use one paragraph (heading) style consistently when subdividing your existing document.

If you create a master document out of an existing file, the Master Document command registers every occurrence of a designated "heading" paragraph style and divides the original document into as many sub-documents as there are headings, assuming each heading marks the start of a new chapter. You can expand your master document by importing existing documents at any time.

Using the Master Document Navigator, you can then manage the various sub-documents.

WHY USE A MASTER DOCUMENT?

Think of a master document as your document management headquarters, from within which you can move your troops without losing sight of the action. Using the Master Document feature enables you to do the following:

- **Work Smarter**—Master documents enable you to link separate files and manage them from within one location as one, while making navigation a breeze.

- **Work More Efficiently**—If stored on a network location, multiple users can work simultaneously on one master document.

- **Ensure Consistency Throughout Your Documents**—Since the styles and templates of the master document override any individual style and template definitions of its sub-documents, you don't have to worry about inconsistent formatting.

- **Give Your System a Break**—Smaller files means using less memory, and hence makes it less likely for things to go wrong.

Looking at these advantages, you should have another look at master documents and give them a try. We sure did; heck, this book was written using StarWriter's Master Document feature.

Note

As you might expect, however, master documents do not export to other word processing programs as they incorporate programming special to StarOffice. If you need to give someone else your document in a different file format, you'll need to save each individual file in the required format.

CREATING A MASTER DOCUMENT FROM SCRATCH

When working with master documents, the same preparatory rules apply as outlined earlier: Gauge the scope of your project, get your folders and files organized, and have that cup of java always within reach.

To create a new Master from scratch, select File, New, Master Document. You can also find the Master Document command on the Start, More submenu. StarWriter will open the new Master Document as a new text document (Untitled), together with the Navigator in Master Document mode. You can tell a master document by its extension: `.sgl`.

You can now enter the various elements—such as headings—or insert other documents by selecting the Insert command, and then selecting Text of File. You also can use the New Document command to add a new document. In this case, you'd first give it a name and path, and then you can write and save it. Note that text, files, or documents will always be inserted above the currently selected item. You can always move the list items to a new location via drag and drop.

Tip #195 from
Michael & Sarah

> Be sure to use the same template and styles for your sub-document as you define in the master document. Otherwise, they will be replaced by the master document "standard." Master styles overrule styles of the same name in sub-document. In general, it's a good idea to base master documents and sub-documents on the same templates and styles. That way, you only need to insert a new style in the master template and reload/refresh to make the new style available in all documents.

CREATING A MASTER DOCUMENT FROM AN EXISTING FILE

To create a new master document from an existing file, have all the important sections styled as Heading 1 (or a style of your choice), and then select File, Send, Create New Master document. The Name and Path of Master Document dialog appears, asking you to enter a name and select a working folder for your new master document file (see Figure 10.12). This dialog is basically very similar to the familiar Save As dialog, with the exception that you can click Template in the lower left opening of the Select Template dialog to select a different style by which StarWriter is supposed to "break down" your document.

Figure 10.12
Creating a master document out of an existing document is easy—as long as you divided your document consistently using the same paragraph style for the chapter or dominant heading titles. Click the Template button of the Name and path of Master Document dialog to select the template style you used for your headings or titles.

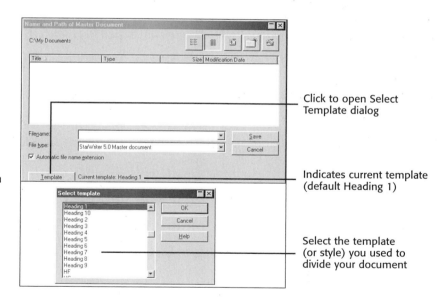

Click to open Select Template dialog

Indicates current template (default Heading 1)

Select the template (or style) you used to divide your document

When you're done, click OK and StarWriter generates your new master document, making every Heading 1 after the first one a (sub)document of its own, and giving it a numerical variant of the name you entered (*name1*, *name2*, *name3*, and so on). This may take a while, depending on the length of the original document. When StarWriter is finished, you'll be asked if you want to update links. Click yes. Voilà, you're looking at your new master, complete with Navigator in Master Document mode.

Note

Master documents in StarWriter have the extension `.sgl` so you can easily tell them apart from regular StarWriter documents. Master sub-documents have the regular StarWriter extension `.sdw`.

Tip #196 from
Michael & Sarah

Organize your text in such a way that the first heading is, for example, called "Preface" and the following ones have "Chapter" leads, such as Chapter 1, Chapter 2, and so on. This way it's easier to keep track between your actual chapters and the corresponding filenames.

SELECTING PAGE STYLES

If you want to start each sub-document on a new page, you can do so by using page styles. As an example, follow these steps:

1. Open the Stylist and select Page Styles.
2. Select and right-click Right Page and select Modify from the context menu.
3. Using the Organizer tab, select Left Page as the Next Style to the Right Page.
4. Select and right-click Left Page, choose Modify, and then select Right Page as the Next Style to the Left Page.
5. Next, switch to Paragraph Styles, right-click the Heading 1 style, and select Modify.
6. Go to the Text Flow tab and select both Break and Before, as well as With Page Style in the Options portion.
7. From the adjacent drop-down list box, select Right. StarWriter will now insert a page break in front of every Level 1 heading style in the document, and the headers will always appear on a right-hand page.

USING THE NAVIGATOR IN MASTER DOCUMENT MODE

Your Master Document Navigator comes with fewer options than your regular Navigator (see Figure 10.13). If you feel like you're missing something, select the button in the upper left to switch between Master Document and the familiar Normal mode of your Navigator. Note that when you're using the Navigator in Normal mode, your document will be read-only; but you can take advantage of all the other Navigator features you've become accustomed to, including the Open Documents drop-down list box.

If you want to work with an item listed in the Navigator document, select the item, and then click the Edit button (second from the left). If the item is a document, StarWriter will open it as a new task ready for you to work on. If it is an index, you'll be asked about the type of index. And if it is text, your cursor will be whisked to the place where you can start typing. Text and indexes are part of the Master document file; documents are files in themselves.

Switch between Master Document and Normal modes

Figure 10.13
In Master Document mode, the Navigator comes with a slightly trimmed down design, but has lost nothing of its powers of navigation. Notice the absence of the Open Documents drop-down list.

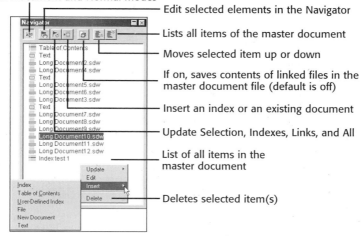

Edit selected elements in the Navigator

Lists all items of the master document

Moves selected item up or down

If on, saves contents of linked files in the master document file (default is off)

Insert an index or an existing document

Update Selection, Indexes, Links, and All

List of all items in the master document

Deletes selected item(s)

If you made any changes to your linked documents, be sure to return to the master document and select the Update command in the Navigator. Here you have the option to update the selected item(s) in the Navigator, indexes, links between documents, or all of the above.

The Insert command enables you to insert an index or existing file into the master document. Your Insert options include Index, Table of Contents, User-Defined Index, File, New Document, and Text.

If you want to insert an index or user-defined index, you'll get the Insert Index or Insert Custom Index dialogs, where you can specify a name and style for the respective indexes. If you select to insert a table of contents, StarWriter will generate it for you. To move the index or table of contents to the right location (that is, at the end and at the beginning of the Master document list, respectively), use the Up and Down buttons on the Navigator.

If you select File, you'll get the Open dialog, which enables you to track down your file. Select it, and then select Insert.

Tip #197 from
Michael & Sarah

You can also insert files into a master document via drop and drag. Using the StarOffice Explorer in hierarchical view, locate the folder of the file that you are looking for, and then drag the file from the Beamer and drop it into the Master Document Navigator. You can then use the Up and Down buttons to move the new file into the desired location. Note that the new file retains its name, so that you may not lose your system of keeping track of chapters if you insert the new chapter between two chapters that were part of the master document from the beginning (say, if you insert a file called New Chapter in between files named Chapter 1 and Chapter 2).

When you select New Document, you get the Save As dialog, where you can enter a name and select a location for your new file. After you select Insert, StarWriter opens your document for you, so you can start typing. Note that you don't have to save your sub-document files in the same folder as your master document file. Finally, if you select to insert text, your cursor will be placed inside the master document, so you can enter text. Also note that you can only enter text in that portion of the master document that has not been split up into a separate sub-document.

Select Save Contents if you want to save the contents of the individual sub-documents in your master document. Although you need twice as much space, you can work on the files even if they are not available (if they are normally stored on a network, for example). This feature is off by default and has to be activated manually.

Tip #198 from	Always use the Update command after making changes to your master document or sub-documents.
Michael & Sarah	

To change the order of things, select the Up and Down buttons. Note that when you move separate text areas next to each other, they will be combined into one. If you want to remove an entry from the Navigator list, right-click in the Navigator and select Delete.

WORKING WITH MASTER DOCUMENTS

To start working with your new master document, double-click a section in the Navigator to be transported to it or right-click a sub-document and select Edit from the context menu. Note that the inserted documents are protected areas within the master document. This means you cannot edit them from within the master document. You'll also find that your cursor will jump right over the entire section of text if you use the arrow keys to navigate through the master document. You'll have to use the scrollbar or the Page Up and Page Down keys to browse the master document, or you can temporarily switch from the Master Document Navigator mode to the Normal Navigator mode.

Your Master documents store all indexes as well as the table of contents, among some other text. Indexes and table of contents refer to the individual sub-documents. If you have edited one or more sub-documents after creating your index(es) or table of contents, select the Update command in the Navigator to bring the master document up to date.

If you want, you can save the master document, including all of its parts, as one StarWriter document. Select File, Save As, and in the File Type list box, select a "regular" StarWriter format such as StarWriter 5.0.

If you select File, Print or the Print command on the function bar, StarWriter will print all sub-documents, text, and indexes that are listed in the Master Document Navigator.

CREATING REFERENCE TABLES, INDEXES, AND CROSS-REFERENCES

It should be obvious that you must create reference tables and indexes pertaining to the entire document by inserting them into the master document. You can insert the table or index anywhere in the master document proper or in any of the subdocuments. Cross-references are inserted as fields within the single document.

To cross-reference items in subdocuments, follow these steps:

1. Start by opening the master document.
2. Double-click the chapter in which you want to insert a cross-reference.
3. Select the word that you want as target reference point.
4. Select Insert, Fields, Other to open the Fields dialog.
5. Using the References tab, select Set Reference in the Type list and enter a unique name for the target in the Name box (for example, ch1 ref1). Using a unique name is crucial to referencing across several file borders.
6. Select Insert.
7. Save and close the file and open another part of your master document.
8. Navigate to the place from which you want to cross-reference.
9. Place the cursor next to the word from which you would like to jump to the cross-reference, and then open the Fields dialog again.
10. This time, choose Insert Reference in the Type list on the References tab. The Selection box will list all available references by name.
11. Select the one you're looking for (with the exact name), and then select Insert.
12. Save and close the document.
13. Open your master document and update it.

You just created a cross-reference from point A to point B.

USING TEMPLATES FOR LONG DOCUMENTS

StarOffice comes with templates that you can use or modify to create your own long documents. Each template already contains the necessary page styles, including page styles for the title page, the table of contents, and the actual content, as well as the index.

To access these templates, select File, New, From Template or press Ctrl+N. Templates include Thesis (located in the Education category folder), Written Academic Lecture (Education), Book (Miscellaneous), and Report (Misc. Business Documents). To start working with these templates, select the desired template and click OK.

In general, there are four steps to working with these templates:

1. Open the desired template and save it as a StarWriter document.
2. Fill out the missing information of the title page by clicking the placeholder fields and inserting the necessary information.
3. Leave the second page blank for now; the second (plus) page is reserved for your table of contents.
4. Select the placeholder text of the third page and start typing. StarWriter will automatically insert new pages as your document grows.

Depending on the type of template you're working with, you may also consider the following options when working on your document:

- **Changing the page style templates**—You can change the margins or add or delete headers and footers. To change the margins, use the Page tab of the Page Styles dialog (choose Format, Page); to add or delete headers or footers, select the Header or Footer tabs in the Page Style dialog and select or deselect the Header on or Footer on options, respectively.

- **Adding numbers to your chapters or sections**—In order to keep a better overview of your chapters or sections, you may want to assign a numbering scheme to your headings. Select Tools, Outline/Numbering to open the Outline Numbering dialog box. Here you can define (and save) a numbering scheme for your chapter titles and headings. (For more details on using the Outline/Numbering dialog see "Changing the Outline of a Table of Contents" in this chapter.)

- **Inserting tables via DDE**—Most reports also present data in table form. If this data already exists in form of a StarCalc table, all you have to do is select and copy the table (press Ctrl+C) and insert it into your document using the Paste Special command (choose Edit, Paste Special and as DDE link). Using DDE links enables you to easily update the table in your document when the original data changes.

- **Inserting objects and formulas**—In some instances, you may also want to insert objects such as graphics or text boxes into your document or mathematical formulas. Inserting and working with objects is discussed in detail in "Rehearsing Objects" in Chapter 11, "Desktop Publishing with StarOffice." Working with formulas is covered in "Creating Formulas with the Formula Editor" in Chapter 6, "Creating and Editing Text Documents."

- **Inserting charts**—To insert a chart into a report or thesis, you first have to create a chart out of the original table in the original document. Select the table that forms the basis of the chart, then select Insert, Objects, Chart and follow the dialogs). When finished, select and copy the chart (press Ctrl+C) and insert it into your document using the Insert Contents command (choose Edit, Insert Contents). For more details on working with charts, see "Inserting Charts" in Chapter 9, "Working with Tables, Charts and Fields," and "Charting Data" in Chapter 19, "Preparing and Printing Reports."

- **Adding captions to tables and objects**—For easier reference, you should consider labeling your tables and objects with captions. Just choose Insert, Caption to open the Insert Caption dialog. Here you can select a category and numbering style for the inserted caption.

- **Generating an index or table of contents**—When all is said and done, place your cursor at the top of page two of your template and generate your index or table of contents as outlined in "Generating Indexes and Reference Tables" in this chapter.

- **Generating an outline for a presentation**—In the case of a business report, you may want to make the outline of your report the basis of a StarImpress presentation. In that case, simply select File, Send, Outline to Presentation. StarOffice will automatically open the Outline view of the StarImpress module which enables you to start working on a presentation document. Note that for this export to work, you must have used the built-in Heading 1, Heading 2, and so on styles. For more details on working with presentations, see Chapter 23, "Enhancing Your Presentation."

- **Using AutoText**—When you notice you're frequently using the same text blocks in various locations of a document, consider using the AutoText function which enables you to quickly insert frequently used text. The AutoText function is covered in detail in "Automating Text Entries with AutoText" in Chapter 6, "Creating and Editing Text Documents."

TROUBLESHOOTING

I want to drag and drop sections of text from the Navigator into a different document, but it doesn't work!

It sounds like you're in Content View. You can't drag and drop from the Navigator when it's in Content View. Click the Content View button (second button from the left on the bottom row of Navigator tools) so it does not look pressed in, and try again.

I try editing my outline in the Navigator but I can't!

You cannot actually edit anything in the Navigator. It's not a document; it's more like a storage center. If you want to edit your document's outline, you have two options: work directly in the document with its headings, or (if you really want a skeleton outline view), use the File, Send, Outline to Clipboard command, open a new, blank text document, paste the outline, and work in that second document to refine your outline.

I want to create a Table of Contents based on my own heading styles.

StarWriter meets you halfway on that one. You can assign any styles you like to format your generated Table of Contents on the Styles tab of the Table of Contents (TOC) dialog box. However, you can only use the built-in heading styles to generate the TOC the easy way.

If you already have assigned your own styles to the headings, you have two choices: you can reassign your headings to the default Heading 1, Heading 2 (and so on) styles (using the

Search for Styles option in the Edit, Search and Replace dialog box). Alternatively, you can highlight and mark by hand every heading in your document, and then use the Create From Marked Entries option in the Table of Contents dialog to generate your TOC. To mark a heading (or any line of text, for that matter), you must select the entire phrase you want to appear in the TOC. Then, select Insert, Indexes, Entry and choose OK.

You can see how it might be easier to just do a global styles Search and Replace and convert everything to the built-in StarOffice styles!

I try generating a table of contents, and all I see is a big heading, Table of Contents.

You either have neglected to format your headings with the built-in heading styles, or you have accidentally deselected the Outline option from the Insert, Indexes, Table of Contents dialog.

I try printing notes and footnotes together, as you and the program suggest is possible, but all I get is blank pages.

You must be running version 5.01, in which this is a known bug. Upgrade to 5.1! This bug has been fixed.

How can I assign different page numbering formats?

To assign different page numbering formats in a document you have to work with different page styles. For example, for a document consisting of a cover sheet without a page number, a table of contents with Roman numbering (i, ii, iii) and the actual text with Arabic page numbers, three types of page styles must be created.

Open the Stylist and click the Page Styles icon. Right-click in the list and select New from the context menu to open the Page Style dialog. Using the Page tab, select None from the Numbering drop-down list for the first page style; Roman numbering for the next custom style; and Arabic for the third style. After each selection, enter a descriptive name for the custom style (for example, "First Page," Front Matter," and "Body Text") in the Name box on the Organizer tab and click OK to save your choices as separate page styles. To apply a page style, simply place the insertion point on the page you want to format, then double-click the desired style in the Stylist.

For automatic page numbering, place the cursor where you want the numbering to start (typically at the top or bottom of the page), then select Insert Fields, Page Numbers to insert a page number field. Place your cursor in the first paragraph of the cover sheet, then choose Insert, Manual Break and select Page Break in the Insert Break dialog. From the Style list box, select the name of the page style that contains the Roman numbering attribute (in this example, Front Matter). Next, place the cursor on the first page after the cover sheet and select Insert, Indexes, Table of Contents to insert the table of contents. Then place the cursor below the last entry of the table of contents and select Insert, Manual Break. In the Insert Break dialog, choose Page Break and then select the name of the page style that contains the Arabic numbering attribute from the Style list box (in this example, Body Text). Then select the Change Page Number Option and be sure the number 1 appears in the spin box below (this designates 1 as the starting number for the first page of the Body Text template). Finally, place the cursor in the table of contents title of your document and choose Tools, Update, Update All (or All Indexes) to update the table of contents with the new page numbers.

How can I define different page orientations in a single document?

First you'll need to define two different page styles—one in portrait and one in landscape format. You can use the Page Style option in the Stylist to create two new styles or modify existing ones. For example, to create two new styles based on the Standard template, select New from the Stylist context menu and choose Portrait on the Page tab of the Page Styles dialog. On the Organizer tab, you can enter a name for this style (for example, Portrait). Do the same for the second template, only this time choose Landscape on the Page tab and enter a descriptive name on the Organizer tab (for example, Landscape). If the document starts out in portrait format, place your cursor on the first page and assign it the Portrait style. When you want to switch to a landscape format, select Insert, Manual Break to open the Insert Break dialog. Choose the Page Break option and select the Landscape style from the Style drop-down list. StarWriter will insert a page break with the desired page format. To return to the portrait format, follow the same steps and select the Portrait page style from the Style drop-down list.

How can I set up a document to use different layouts for different pages (for example left- and right-hand pages)?

If you want to use alternate page styles in your documents, you can apply the Next Style option on the Organizer tab in the Page Styles dialog. Using the Page Style area of the Stylist, assign the Page Style Right Page to the first page of your document and then modify this style by right-clicking its name in the Stylist and selecting Modify from the context menu. On the Organizer tab, select Left Page from the Next Style drop-down list. Do the same with the Left Page style: select Modify from the context menu and then define Right Page as the next style on the Organizer tab.

I have a document that contains two platform-specific chapters, Windows and Linux. Is it possible to show and hide the chapters depending on the context?

This may not be the most elegant solution, but you can use frames (or text boxes). Define two styles in the Stylist—one for the chapter that contains the Windows contents and one for Linux. You can then hide the inappropriate frame (or content) by deselecting the Print option in on the Options tab of the Frame Style dialog (right-click the desired Frame style and select Modify from the context menu).

If you're working with a master document, you can hide subdocuments by treating them like "sections." In that case, you can hide them using conditional fields as described in the section on Defining Sections in this chapter. Alternatively, you can also create two master documents: one that contains the chapter(s) with the Windows information and one that contains the chapter(s) with the Linux information.

How do I set up the page numbers so that the number on the first page doesn't show?

Everything in StarOffice is based on styles. If you want the first page of your document not to show a number, you have to set up a page style without a footer or header and then assign this style to your first page. Next, set up a style with a footer or header. Now, place your cursor at the very end of the first page and select Insert, Manual Break to open the Insert Break dialog. Choose the Page Break option and select the page style with the header or footer from the Style drop-down list. In the spin box below, select the starting number of the page (for example, 2). If you want a different numbering format (for example, Roman), right-click the page style that contains the header or footer in the Stylist and select Modify from the context menu. On the Page tab of the Page Styles dialog, you can select the desired format from the numbering drop-down list.

How can I change the look of my reference tables? When I generate a table of contents in StarWriter, the result looks fairly plain—without any special formatting—and the individual lines are too close together.

Changing the appearance of your reference tables is easy. Place the cursor inside the table you want to change and select Insert, Indexes, Table of Contents or Index. Using the Styles tab of the respective dialogs, you can assign different paragraph styles to the selected contents or index style. You can also click the Edit button to change the attributes of a selected paragraph style before assigning it to the contents or index style.

DESKTOP PUBLISHING WITH STAROFFICE

SETTING UP AND DESIGNING A PUBLICATION

StarWriter is not only a powerful word processor, but also a very capable desktop publishing (DTP) tool that enables you to create professional-looking newsletters, attractive brochures, and more (see Figure 11.1). Although it might not be the tool of choice for desktop publishing professionals, StarWriter is capable of some amazing strokes of page layout and graphic design. You might even say that it has more DTP power than most people ever need (which is more than other office suites can claim).

Figure 11.1
StarWriter is a very capable DTP program that enables you to create professional-looking documents—from newsletters to job ads to invitations.

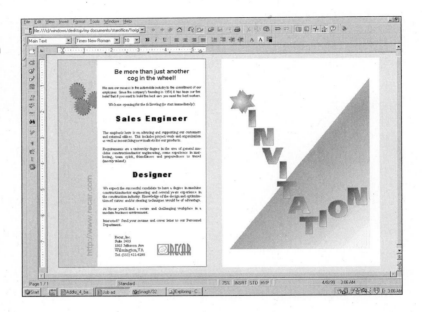

> **Note**
>
> The focus of this chapter is to provide a survey of specific tools and objects you're likely to use to make your text documents more presentable. For more details on how to manipulate, for example, graphic objects, see Part IV, "Getting Graphical—StarDraw and StarImage," which covers StarOffice's various drawing and image editing tools, or Chapter 23, "Enhancing Your Presentation."

Before you start exploring, however, you should first sketch out, on paper, how you want your publication to look. You have to make some basic design decisions about the size and shape of your publication, as well as the employment of first-rate typography and the placement of repeating elements such as headers, footers, page numbers, borders, columns, graphics, and whitespace (the creative use of space between elements).

→ For more details on placing headers, footers, and page numbers, **see** "Adding Headers and Footers,"
p. 381

First, decide on a paper format, page layout, and length that is conducive to your readers, content, and budget. For example, the U.S. standard for a small business newsletter is 8.5″ by 11″ and typically runs two or four multicolumn, portrait-oriented pages.

This size and orientation make it possible for your newsletter to be economically mailed and easily stored (in folders, for example) while still providing a format large enough for a variety of layout options.

A brochure, by contrast, involves other considerations: Will it be mailed in an envelope? Will it be on display? Should it be set apart from other brochures? How many panels should it have? The answers to these (and other) questions will determine the size and orientation of your publication, as well as help you make basic design decisions about attributes such as the width of margins, the number of columns, and so on.

To garner the attention of readers, you also have to choose the right typeface, type size, character spacing (kerning), line spacing, and alignment for the job. As any publication designer will tell you, readership drops when the wrong font, font size, or line spacing is used. Improper use of alignment and subtleties such as letter and word spacing, hyphenation, and punctuation can undermine the professionalism you hope to project in your publication.

➔ For more details on using character and paragraph formatting option, **see** Chapter 7, "Formatting Text Documents," starting on **p. 261**.

Ideally, text should be so beautiful that readers hardly notice it is there, so refrain from using too many typefaces, and make sure the copy is easy to read. As a rule of thumb, use serif typefaces, which are characterized by small finishing strokes that guide the readers' eyes from letter to letter, for body copy, and sans serif typefaces for headings and titles. Examples for common serif typefaces are Times New Roman, Garamond, New Century Schoolbook, Palatino, and Goudy; sans serif typefaces include Arial, Helvetica, Franklin Gothic, Verdana, and Avant Garde.

PART

II

CH

11

In general, setting up and designing a publication entails all the text-, paragraph-, and page-formatting options discussed in detail in Chapter 7, "Formatting Text Documents," and Chapter 8, "Using Styles and Templates." When designing a publication, you can start from scratch—using the Page Style dialog to set up the margins, layout, size, orientation (portrait or landscape), background, columns, and headers and footers of your publication—or you can use (and modify) one of StarOffice's ready-made templates by selecting File, New, From Template (Ctrl+N) and then browsing the template categories. StarWriter includes a template for brochures called Leaflet in the Forms and Contracts category, as well as templates for a newsletter, gift certificate, and zip disk, CD, and cassette covers in the Miscellaneous category.

Tip #199 from
Michael & Sarah

For inspiration, look also at the sample documents in the Text Documents folder. Just open the Explorer (Ctrl+Shift+E)—in Hierarchical view—and Beamer (Ctrl+Shift+B), click the plus (+) sign next to the Samples folder to expand the folder tree, and then click Text Documents. In the Beamer, you can see a list of sample documents, including Brochure, Flyers, IceCreamMenu, Invitation, JobAd, and LostDogNotice (no kidding!). Use any of these samples as starting points for your creative efforts; take them apart, make changes to them, and then save them as new templates. You can also import the existing styles from these sample documents, using the Import Styles dialog (select Format, Styles & Templates, Load). For more details on importing styles, see "Transferring Styles," in Chapter 8: "Using Styles and Tempaltes."

EXPLORING YOUR VIEWS AND WORKSPACE

Because StarOffice is a fully integrated office suite, you can easily insert objects such as graphics, charts, tables, and even 3D animation and video into your text. And if you have to edit an object, StarWriter puts the necessary tools for every text- or object-related task right there for you—no need to open another application. With all these tools at your fingertips, you might lose sight of the document you're working on. However, when you get accustomed to StarOffice's way of doing everything in one place, you can easily keep clutter to a minimum without sacrificing speed and efficiency.

ARRANGING YOUR WORKSPACE

The following are some tips on making the most of your workspace arrangement:

- **Use the context menus**—You can access the most common menu bar items and commands by right-clicking the text or object in your publication and then using the respective context menu. Don't navigate all the way to the menu bar, unless you can't find what you're looking for on the context menu(s); even then, you should first check the toolbars around your workspace.

- **Use the main toolbar(s) and object bars**—You can access many functions and tools from the Edit, View, Format, and Insert menus using the main toolbar(s) and object bars. Depending on your current selection—text, table or object—StarWriter replaces all or some of the main toolbar buttons with toolbar buttons of the StarImage, StarDraw, or other StarOffice modules. In addition, it whisks the right object bar for the job right in front of your eyes. You can toggle between Text and other object bars by using the small black triangle to the far right of the current object bar.

- **Use floating toolbars**—The key to working more efficiently is to have all the tools you need at your fingertips. Toolbar buttons come in two varieties: regular buttons and (what we call) "double function" buttons (the ones with the small green triangles pointing to the right). The first variety toggles a command on or off, opens a dialog, or activates a function when selected. The second variety you can click to access a single function or tool, or extended-click to open a floating toolbar or window with various options and tools that you can drag anywhere on your desktop. To select a tool, simply click the respective icon in the toolbar or window. If you no longer need it, click the Close (x) button. "Double function" buttons always show the most recently selected/used of the available functions and options.

- **Use dockable floating windows**—You can turn the Explorer and Beamer display on or off by selecting the respective button on the function bar. When they are turned on, you can minimize either display by clicking the Show/Hide arrow button on the upper left of the Explorer or the bottom left of the Beamer. Clicking the adjacent pushpin button turns the floating window display on or off. Similarly, you can use the Stylist and Navigator as dockable floating windows. Just click the Navigator or Stylist title bar, press Ctrl, and drag it toward the right side of your screen.

Tip #200 from
Michael & Sarah

You can open or close the Stylist and Navigator by pressing F11 and F5 (respectively), docked or undocked. If they're both docked (as in Figure 11.2), you can open and close them simultaneously.

Figure 11.2 shows one of many possible workspace arrangements. In this sample arrangement, the Stylist and Navigator are both docked and can be hidden at any time by clicking the Show/Hide buttons. The mini Navigator is out of harm's way yet still close enough when needed. The floating Insert functions and Color palette windows are placed for easy access, and the Explorer/Beamer arrangement enables you to drag and drop selected graphics files from the Gallery into your publication.

Tip #201 from
Michael & Sarah

You can minimize some floating windows (such as the Navigator, Stylist, Help Agent, or Search & Replace) by double-clicking the title bar. Double-click the title bar again, and they return to their regular size.

Drag and drop graphics files into your publication

Figure 11.2
Work smarter, not harder. StarWriter gives you the flexibility to arrange your own workspace as if it were your desk.

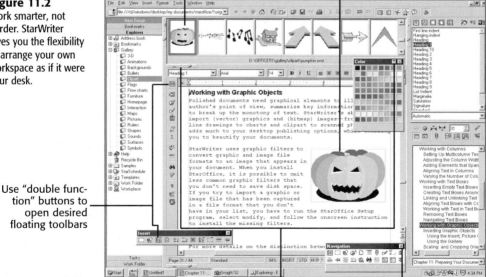

Use "double function" buttons to open desired floating toolbars

Show/Hide dockable floating windows

Close floating toolbars when no longer needed

LOOKING AT YOUR VIEWS

When working on your publication, you also might want to keep an eye on the View menu in the menu bar. Table 11.1 explains the options that help you keep a perspective on things (especially when they get cluttered).

Tip #202 from
Michael & Sarah

One of our favorite views is the Optimal view, available from the Zoom menu. When it is selected, text lines always fill the workspace, regardless of whether dockable windows are visible or hidden; StarWriter automatically squeezes or expands the workspace view so that you never lose sight of the current section you're working on. Another good one is the Page View option, which behaves virtually the same but displays the entire page; it is recommended for large screen monitors and good eyes.

TABLE 11.1   VIEWING OPTIONS IN STARWRITER

Option	What It Does
Zoom	Modifies the scale of your view; your options include 200%, 150%, 100%, 75%, 50%, Optimal (text lines fill workspace), Page Width (page borders are visible), Entire Page (shows full page), and Variable (customize view). Note that you also can open the Zoom dialog by double-clicking in the Scale field on the status bar; right-clicking in the field opens a shortcut menu with all but the Variable options.
Explorer, Beamer	If marked, Explorer and Beamer displays are turned on. If you can't see them, they may be hidden; look for a small triangle adjacent to a pushpin icon in the upper left of your screen, and click it to open the hidden Explorer or Beamer.
Toolbars	Opens a submenu from which you can select which toolbars to display. You get the same options from the toolbar shortcut menu by right-clicking any gray or empty toolbar area. The shortcut menu also gives you the option to configure or customize your toolbar options, which is explained in "Customizing Toolbars" in Chapter 3, "Getting Ready for Work."
Ruler	If marked (default), the rulers are visible. You can show both horizontal and vertical rulers by selecting the respective options on the Layout tab of the Text Document Options dialog (which you open by choosing Tools, Options, Text Document, Layout), depending on your layout needs.
Status Bar	If marked (default), the status bar is visible. Double-clicking select status bar fields gives you easy access to (from left to right) the Navigator, Page Style, and Zoom dialogs; right-clicking in the same fields opens the Bookmark (if available), Page, and Scale shortcut menus. In addition, you can activate different write and selection modes. (For more details on the status bar, see "The StarWriter Status Bar" in Chapter 6, "Creating and Editing Documents.")
Text Boundaries	If marked (default), any text boundaries in single and multicolumn layouts are visible.
Field Shadings, Fields	If marked (default), you'll see shadowed areas wherever fields (Field Shadings) or the names of fields are located.
Field	Shadings enable you to quickly spot fields in a document or template. Note that field shadings do not print.

Option	What It Does
Non-Printing Characters, Hidden Paragraphs	If marked, nonprinting characters (such as space or paragraph marks) and hidden sections are visible. Using the Non-Printing Character option enables you to easily catch double spaces and rogue paragraph marks that might cause alignment or other layout problems.
Online Layout	Shows a document as if it were an HTML page; you see one extended page, no matter how long the document.
Full Screen	Takes you into full screen view; all bars but the ruler(s) are gone. To return to normal view, click the floating Full Screen icon (which looks like a tiny monitor).

REHEARSING OBJECTS

Whether you're working with text boxes, graphics, or any other embedded objects, StarOffice always puts all the application tools you need at your fingertips. Insert or select a text box, and the Text object bar slides away to make room for the Frame object bar; insert or select a picture, and you see the Picture object bar, and so on.

Note

This section refers to objects that you can insert using the commands on the Insert menu, including Text Box, Picture, and Object. StarWriter also enables you to create and insert Draw objects via the Draw functions on the main toolbar. Draw objects are discussed in detail in Chapter 20, "Getting Sketchy with StarDraw," and Chapter 23, "Enhancing Your Presentation." For an explanation of vector graphics, see "Understanding How Computer Graphics Work" in Chapter 20, "Getting Sketchy with StarDraw."

PART

II

CH

11

In addition, objects come with their own dialog boxes and context menus, which, for the most part, provide the same basic options regardless of whether the object is a graphic, text box, or chart. Whereas the object dialog boxes consolidate a comprehensive assemblage of settings with which you can control an object's appearance in your document, object context menus share four basic commands that help you manage the object's positioning within your document: Arrange, Align, Anchor, and Wrap.

Tip #203 from
Michael & Sarah

Because all objects used in StarOffice are embedded objects, they share, with minor variations, the same basic dialog tabs: Type, Options, Wrap, Hyperlink, Borders, Background, and Macro. Get to know an object's dialog box. Its tabs enable you to control an object's overall appearance and behavior. The easiest way to access an object's dialog box is by selecting the properties command (Picture, Text Box, and so on) from the object's shortcut menu.

Note

The techniques for working with objects are virtually the same for all major StarOffice modules. Hence, much of what is said in this section refers to working with objects in general, not just in StarWriter.

→ If you just want a quick overview of working with objects across the StarDesktop, **see** "Working with Objects," **p. 176**.

USING AN OBJECT'S CONTEXT MENU AND OBJECT BAR

Using an object's context menu, you can change the positioning of the selected object in relation to other objects; align the object horizontally or vertically with respect to the left and right page borders or the paragraph layout grid, respectively; switch anchor positions; select a predefined wrapping style; and open the object dialog. Figure 11.3 illustrates the various options of the Text Box context menu, which is virtually the same for all other objects.

Figure 11.3
Using the Text Box context menus gives you quick access to the most common options for arranging and positioning boxes on a page or in a column.

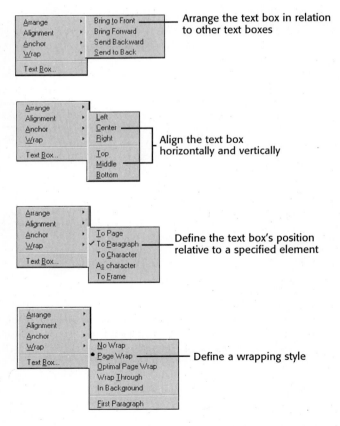

The object bar provides most of the options of the an object's context menu, plus a few extras. From a conceptual perspective, it can be divided into the following basic categories and common functions (from left to right): format attributes, wrap, horizontal positioning, vertical positioning, borders and colors, object properties dialog shortcut, arrangement, anchor, and links. Table 11.2 explains the various object bar options.

TABLE 11.2   USING THE OBJECT BAR

Use This...	If You Want To...
Attributes	Assign existing formatting attributes by styles
Wrapping	Select a style for wrapping text around a box; your options include (from left to right) None, Parallel, and Through
Horizontal	Align the text box horizontally (left, center, right) with respect to the left and right page borders
Vertical	Align the text box vertically (top, middle, bottom) with respect to the paragraph grid
Flip	Flip an object vertically and horizontally; note that this option is available only for graphic objects
Borders/colors	Assign a border, line style, line color, and background color to the text box; note that the Background Color button is not available for graphic objects
Image Editor	Starts the Image Editor (StarImage) inside a separate window, which enables you to edit inserted bitmapped graphics; note that this button is available only for graphic objects (such as horizontal lines or Gallery files)
Properties	Open the Properties dialog which enables you to edit the properties and attributes of the selected object
Arrangement	Send the object all the way to the front or back when arranged in a grouping of objects
Anchor	Switch anchoring positions
Links	Link and unlink selected text boxes; note that this button is available only for text box objects

CHANGING THE STACKING ORDER OF OBJECTS

StarWriter stacks inserted objects in an imaginary order one on top of the other. When you move objects around, you'll notice that the most recently moved object may overlap another one or may be partially covered by another object itself. Using a selected object's context menu, you can change the stacking order at any time by choosing an option on the Arrange submenu:

- **Bring to Front**—Brings the selected object all the way to the front
- **Bring Forward**—Promotes the selected object by one layer closer to the front
- **Send Backward**—Demotes the selected object by one layer closer to the back
- **Send to Back**—Moves the selected object all the way to the back

Note

Clicking the desired object in a stack of objects can be tricky, depending on the size of the invisible bounding rectangle that surrounds objects. Just remember that you can move in two directions: from the front to the back and vice versa. If the object you want to promote is buried underneath others, just demote the ones on top to achieve the same results.

Note

When working with Draw objects, you can also group objects, which means they retain their physical locations in relation to other objects in the group. For more details on grouping objects see "Arranging and Grouping Objects" in Chapter 23, "Enhancing Your Presentation."

ALIGNING OBJECTS

If you've ever tried lining up two objects with each other or with text using the mouse, you'll appreciate the ease with which you can accomplish the same task simply by right-clicking the desired objects and choosing an alignment type from the object's context menu. You can align objects horizontally (left, center, and right) and vertically (top, middle, and bottom). Note that objects are aligned based on the invisible bounding rectangle that surrounds them. If you align two or three objects together, objects are moved so that they line up with the one that's already located farthest in the selected alignment direction.

MAKING SENSE OF ANCHORS

 After you insert (or select) an object, you'll see a small gray square with an anchor symbol aligned with the first line of the paragraph to which the object is anchored, hugging the left text boundary. When you move the object, you'll notice the anchor symbol jump up or down depending on your movement. The symbol moves because StarWriter, by default, anchors every inserted object to a particular paragraph. Anchors ensure that the object will stay in place, no matter where the anchored paragraph winds up in your document after you start adding or deleting text or pages.

For regular documents, StarWriter gives you four types of anchors: Page, Paragraph, Character, and As Character. In each case, the value of the anchor is implied by its name: It enables you to keep the object anchored to its page, paragraph, or character. The As Character option keeps the object anchored within the text flow, which means the size of the object influences the spacing between characters and lines, just as if you were selecting a different point size for the typeface. Using the As Character option, you can align the object with the top, center, or bottom of the baseline. In all other instances, you can choose between horizontal (left, center, and right) and vertical (top, center, and bottom) alignment.

The type of anchor you choose depends entirely on what you want to accomplish. For example, if you want to place a logo on each page, anchor it to a page; images or charts that go with a specific segment of text should be anchored to the specific paragraph. (Remember, a paragraph is defined as any unit of characters that ends with the nonprinting paragraph symbol; hence, technically speaking, a single-line heading is not different from a paragraph stretching several lines.) When you're using a formula in your document, you might want to anchor it to a character. Use the As Character option if you want a graphic or object to remain in line with the following text; the graphic is pressed against the left text boundary, and you can move it up and down between the top, center, and bottom of the baseline alignment only.

Tip #204 from
Michael & Sarah

While you're working on a layout, anchor the images to the page; that way, you have more freedom shifting text around. You can quickly change the current anchor in the Anchor submenu of the object's context menu.

You can define anchors by right-clicking a selected object and choosing Anchor from the object context menu or the Format menu. You can also drop anchors via the Type tab of the respective object properties dialog (Pictures, Text Boxes, and so on), which you can open by double-clicking the object or choosing it from the context menu of the selected object.

Note

When you select an object's (implied) frame, you can see its anchor (a gray square with an anchor symbol) in the upper-left corner of the frame.

WRAPPING TEXT AROUND OBJECTS

One of the best ways to create visual impact in a publication is to wrap text around objects (see Figure 11.4). Using the Wrap tab in the respective object's properties dialog box, you can select alternative ways of wrapping body text around your object. In addition, you can specify the amount of space between the object and body text. Wrapping text around objects works the same for all objects, although you do have a few more options with graphic objects such as the Contour feature, which enables you to wrap text around irregularly shaped graphic objects (or polygons).

When wrapping text around objects, you have two options. You can right-click the selected object to open the respective object context menu and then select a wrapping style from the Wrap submenu. (Note that the same options are available from the Format, Wrap submenu.) Alternatively, you can use the Wrap tab that comes with each object's properties dialog. Table 11.3 explains the various common text wrapping options available from the Wrap tab in each object dialog.

Figure 11.4
Wrap text for visual impact.

Wrap right; Contour option on

No wrap

Register-true option on

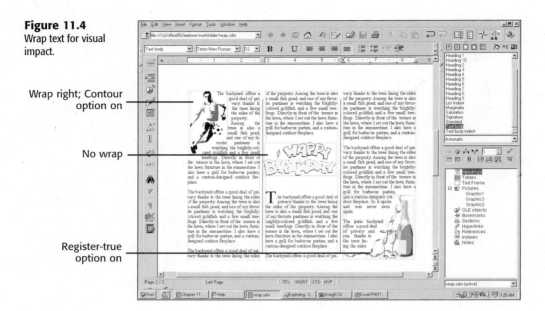

TABLE 11.3   TEXT WRAPPING OPTIONS EXPLAINED

Option	Result
None	Text flow is interrupted by the inserted object; it stops above the object and continues below, regardless of size of the object.
Left	Text wraps on the left of the object if sufficient space is available.
Right	Text wraps on the right of the object if sufficient space is available.
Parallel	Text wraps around both sides of the object if sufficient space is available.
Through	Text continues behind the object. Use this option only with transparent objects.
Optimal	Text wraps around one, both, or no side, depending on available space and the size of the object.
First Paragraph	This option starts a new paragraph underneath an object after you press Enter. The distance between paragraphs depends on the size of the object. If this option is selected, text might still wrap around the object; however, the next paragraph (for example, a heading) will not wrap, but instead will start below the object.
In Background	Text runs in the background behind the object. If this option is not selected, text may be hidden by the object. Use this option only with transparent objects (it is available only if Through is selected).
Spacing	This option controls top, bottom, right, and left spacing between the object and text.

EDITING AND FORMATTING OBJECTS

After you've imported an object into a document, you don't have to accept the way it looks onscreen. Using the Edit menu or the object's dialog box and object bar, you can redefine the appearance and attributes of a selected object, including size, spacing, position, borders, and background. In the case of graphic objects, you also have access to additional tools for manipulating imported and embedded graphics, such as the Image Map Editor (which is used to create so-called "hot spots" in HTML documents) or the Contour Editor.

RESIZING WITH SELECTION HANDLES

The quickest way to resize an object is to first click to select it, and then drag one of the eight green *sizing handles* surrounding the selected object—one in each corner and one centered between each pair of corner handles.

Click the sizing handles on the sides to resize the object in one dimension. For example, click and drag the top handle in between the corner handles to stretch or shrink the height of an object from the top; click the sizing handle on the right to stretch or squeeze the width of an object from the right, and so on. In each instance, the side opposite of the one you're dragging remains anchored.

Click one of the corner handles to resize an object in two dimensions. For example, if you click the handle in the lower-left corner of an object, you can enlarge or reduce the height and width of the object simultaneously from that corner; the handle in the opposite corner remains anchored during this operation.

Note

Press Shift while clicking and dragging the sizing handles to maintain an object's height-to-width ratio.

MOVING AND DUPLICATING OBJECTS

Sometimes you might want to move an existing object to another location in your document, or you might want to duplicate an existing object (such as a text frame) to save the steps of importing or creating it once more. StarWriter makes it easy for you to move or copy an existing object.

MOVING VIA DRAG AND DROP   Moving an inserted object to the desired location is as easy as clicking and dragging with the mouse. Simply move the mouse pointer over the object (the pointer changes into a four-directional arrow), click, wait a second, and then drag the object to the desired location. As you drag the object, a dark closed line indicates its virtual drop location. The object moves to the new location only after you release the mouse button.

Tip #205 from
Michael & Sarah

When you're moving objects, you can switch into Full Screen or Entire Page view to better scale the positioning of your object on the current page.

Tip #206 from
Michael & Sarah

To move objects with precision, be sure to select Guides in the Lines portion of the Tools, Options, Text Document, Layout dialog. When this option is selected, you can see visible guides that extend horizontally and vertically from the bounding box of an object to the horizontal and vertical rulers. This enables you to position objects more precisely on a page. If you can't see the vertical ruler, select Vertical ruler in the Window Options portion of the Tools, Options, Text Document, Layout dialog.

USING CUT, COPY, AND PASTE If you're more attached to your keyboard than your mouse, or find it cumbersome to scroll through several screens or pages while holding the left mouse button to move objects, you can use the familiar Cut, Copy, and Paste commands (from the Edit menu) or keyboard shortcuts to move or duplicate objects. Just select the object you want to move (or copy), and press Ctrl+X (or Ctrl+C) to cut (copy) the object to the Clipboard (Windows) or General-Purpose Memory Buffer (Linux). Next, select the desired location for the object (which can also be in another document, in which case you might have to open the document first); then press Ctrl+V and StarWriter inserts the object from the Clipboard (Windows) or General-Purpose Memory Buffer (Linux) above the current paragraph (in a text document), cell (spreadsheet), or in the center of the current slide (presentation).

Tip #207 from
Michael & Sarah

You can also move a selected object incrementally by points (as defined in the Subdivision spin box on the Grid tab of the Text Document Options dialog) to the top, bottom, left, or right by pressing the Alt key in combination with the respective cursor keys on the keyboard.

Tip #208 from
Michael & Sarah

The quickest way to duplicate an object is by pressing the Ctrl key while dragging it. A small rectangle with a plus sign next to the mouse pointer appears when you're copying an object this way (as opposed to an empty rectangle that appears during a simple drag-and-drop operation).

POSITIONING OBJECTS ON A PAGE

After you have inserted an object in your document, you might want to change its default position. To reposition your object, simply open its dialog from the context menu and use the Position portion of the Type tab in the object's dialog. Using the Type tab, you can specify the horizontal and vertical positioning of the object with regard to selected areas that you can specify in the drop-down lists to the right. Select Mirror on Even Pages, if you want the horizontal position of objects on even-numbered pages to mirror those on odd-numbered pages. For example, if you want to create a book or pamphlet with facing pages that are mirror images of each other in terms of their margins (which you would set in the Page dialog), check the Mirror on Even Pages option so that objects anchored to paragraphs follow suit with the page design.

Note

> Sometimes the object doesn't seem to stay where you want it. Instead, it slightly moves to the right or left or up or down. That's because the Snap to Grid option may be selected on the Grid tab in the Text Document Options dialog. Just deselect it, and you'll regain some measure of control over the placement of your object.

Adding Borders and Backgrounds

Using the Borders and Background tabs of each individual object dialog works the same as using the Borders and Background tabs in the Paragraph (Style) and Page (Style) dialogs. You can choose from various line and shadow styles and tell the program on which side of the object to place a border. StarOffice provides you with a set of presets (or samples) that you can use as building blocks for your own border design. You can add or remove border lines by clicking the little black arrows at the end of a line, specify the distance between text and borders, and change the size and colors of your lines and shadow style. To get a general idea of what the final border will look like, consult the Preview area when you're creating your borders and shading.

Using the Background tab, you can select and preview a background color for your object, as well as a graphic from StarOffice's vast clip art and graphics gallery or even your own archives. To select a background image file, select Graphic from the As drop-down list, and click Browse to locate the desired graphic in a directory or folder on your system or network. To remove a background graphic, press Ctrl+Z (immediately after inserting it) or turn off the graphic mode by selecting Color in the As box, and click OK. If you want to remove a background color, select No Fill above the color palette.

→ For more details on adding background colors and graphics, **see** "Adding Borders and Background Color," **p. 278**.

Protecting Objects

After you've spent all that time sizing, positioning, and formatting an object, it would be a shame to just lose all that work accidentally. Using the Options tab of the object's dialog, you can lock the contents, position, and size of your object. Just select the desired mode of protection in the Protect portion of the Options tab.

Note

> When you're working with text boxes, you can select Editable in Read-Only Documents, which enables you to edit the contents of a text box in write-protected documents.

WORKING WITH COLUMNS

Newsletters, brochures, and even advertisements are often divided into columns. In StarWriter, columns are an attribute of page formatting. This means you cannot alternate between single and multicolumn layout on one page or even between pages without defining a new page first or inserting a workaround in the form of multicolumn frames or multicolumn sections.

Theoretically, you can insert up to 99 columns in a StarWriter document. In practice, however, the number of columns depends on the size and orientation of your publication. As a rule of thumb, and to maintain readability, you shouldn't use more than three columns on an 8.5″ by 11″ portrait-oriented page or more than five columns on an 8.5″ by 11″ landscape-oriented page.

SETTING UP MULTICOLUMN TEXT ON A PAGE

Setting up a multicolumn layout is easy. You divide a publication (or page) into columns by using the Columns tab in the Page Style dialog, as shown in Figure 11.5. (You can access this dialog via the Text context menu, the Format menu, or by double-clicking the Page Style field on the status bar.) Since columns are attached to pages, they control the appearance of the entire page and any other pages that share the same page style (Standard, Left Page, Right Page, or HTML).

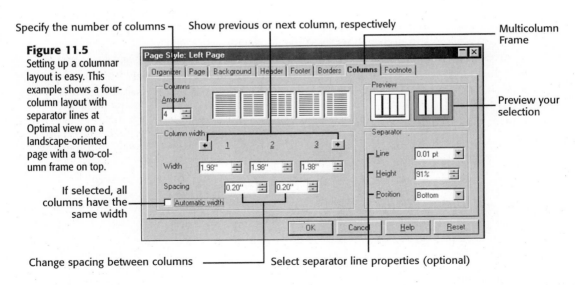

Specify the number of columns — Show previous or next column, respectively — Multicolumn Frame

Figure 11.5
Setting up a columnar layout is easy. This example shows a four-column layout with separator lines at Optimal view on a landscape-oriented page with a two-column frame on top.

Preview your selection

If selected, all columns have the same width

Change spacing between columns — Select separator line properties (optional)

Follow these steps:

1. Open the StarWriter context menu, select Page, and click the Columns tab in the Page Style dialog.

2. In the Columns portion of the tab, specify the number of columns in the Amount spin box, or select one of the presets.

3. In the Column Width portion of the tab, you can define the width of each column individually or make all columns the same width by selecting Automatic Width in the lower left of the tab. Using the Spacing spin box, you can also specify the spacing (called *gutter space*) between individual columns. The value you add in each of the two spacing boxes changes the distance between the two columns shown above each box. If you have more than three columns, you can cycle through them by using the left and right arrows above the Width boxes.

Tip #209 from
Michael & Sarah

Always insert gutter space between columns to enhance readability of your text. Also, for a neater appearance, use justified text when you're working with columns, and be sure to turn on automatic hyphenation on the Text Flow tab of the Paragraph dialog (which you open by choosing Format, Paragraph) to avoid gaps between words.

➔ For more details on hyphenation, **see** "Using Hyphenation," **p. 473**.

4. In the Separator portion of the tab, you can select a line of varying strength and length as a separator between columns. If it is less than 100 percent of the column length, decide whether to align the separator line with the top, center, or bottom of the columns. Separator lines will be placed between each pair of columns.

5. When you're finished, click OK. StarWriter then inserts the columns according to your specifications. If the View, Text Boundaries option is marked (default), you can see the fine blue outlines of columns.

PART

II

CH

11

Tip #210 from
Michael & Sarah

You can also access the Columns tab via the Insert option on the main toolbar. Extended-click the uppermost toolbar button, and click the Insert Column option (the seventh icon from the left) to open the Columns tab. Or you can extended-click the Insert Column icon to open a small submenu, where you can click and drag to the right to select the number of columns to be inserted on the current page (and all other pages that share the same page style). Note that the last option places columns of equal size (Automatic Width) at a default distance without separator line(s).

ADJUSTING THE COLUMN WIDTH AND SPACING

You can adjust the width of columns by entering new values in the Width and Spacing spin boxes underneath each column on the Columns tab of the Page Styles dialog (or Text Box dialog, if you're working with multicolumn frames), or you can drag the column markers on the horizontal ruler (a less accurate but more useful method because you can see your changes immediately). When you're using the column markers on the ruler, click and drag in the center of the marker to adjust the column width (your pointer changes into a vertical double arrow). To adjust the spacing between columns, click and drag between the column markers and the scale (your pointer changes into a horizontal double arrow).

Tip #211 from
Michael & Sarah

To change the scale of the ruler, right-click anywhere inside the ruler area, and select a different unit of measurement. Your (most useful) desktop publishing options include Inch (default), Pica, Point, Centimeter, and Millimeter. To change the unit of measurement on the Columns tab (as well as Character, Paragraph, and Page Style dialogs in general), select a new unit from the Units portion of the Layout options tab in the Text Document Options dialog (which you open by choosing Tools, Options, Text Document). Note that 1 pica equals 12 points, and 72 points equal 1 inch; 1 centimeter equals 10 millimeters, and 2.54 centimeters equal 1 inch.

ADDING ELEMENTS THAT SPAN TWO OR MORE COLUMNS

The easiest way to add a headline that spans two or more columns is to drop a text box onto your page, adjusting the width and height as desired, and then enter and format the text in the text box. For more details on how to add and work with text boxes see "Working with Text Boxes" later in this chapter. You can also create a section for elements that span the entire page or column width.

→ For more details on creating sections, **see** "Defining Sections," **p. 378**.

ALIGNING TEXT IN COLUMNS

Most publication designs are based on a *leading grid* to ensure accuracy and consistency. A leading grid determines the spacing of lines of body text in the publication. If your leading is 12 points, you'll want most of your vertically measured type and design elements, such as margins, graphics, and paragraph spacing, to be set in multiples of 12 (for example, headings might have 18 points of leading and 6 points of space before the paragraph to amount to 24 points). If your type or design elements don't meet this requirement, the leading of the following paragraphs may be off when compared to previous paragraphs. As a result, text in paragraphs that appear side by side in a multicolumn layout may no longer line up at the baseline.

Tip #212 from
Michael & Sarah

You can control the size of your layout grid and your grid options by selecting Tools, Options, Text Document, Grid. To look at the default grid in the current document, select Visible Grid. You can change the default by using X axis (horizontal) and Y axis (vertical) spin boxes in the Grid portion of this dialog. If you want to change the current grid settings symmetrically, select the Synchronize Axes check box.

StarWriter provides an attribute that enables you to prevent this misalignment from happening. It's called *Register-true* and can be applied to paragraphs or paragraph styles, as well as to pages and page styles. For example, it's common for multiline headings or inserted graphics to fall off the leading grid for baselines, which in turn throws off the baseline alignment of the following paragraph(s). When you activate the Register-true option, StarWriter adjusts the spacing between the unaligned paragraph (in this case, the heading or graphic) and the next paragraph so that the top of the subsequent paragraph falls on the grid again.

Turning on this option ensures that regular text across columns aligns with the leading grid for baselines.

To apply this attribute, go to the Indents & Spacing or Page tabs of the Paragraph (Style) and Page (Style) dialogs, respectively (see Figure 11.6), and select Activate in the Register-true portion of the respective tabs. When you're applying this attribute to a page, you can also select a reference style from a list of available styles in the current document.

Figure 11.6
Using the Register-true attribute for multicolumn layouts ensures that regular text across columns aligns with the leading grid for baselines.

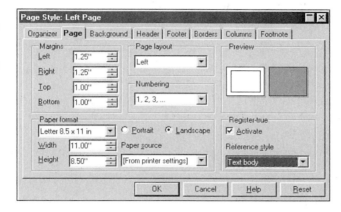

Sometimes columns do not fill evenly with text. In that case, you can use the mouse and the vertical ruler on the left to adjust the height of the column. Place the cursor in the lower part between the gray area and the scale. The pointer changes into a vertical double arrow. Click and drag up or down to adjust the height of the column until your text evenly fills both columns. Note that the more columns you use, the harder it is to fill the columns evenly.

PART

II

CH

11

Tip #213 from *Michael & Sarah*	If you can't see the vertical ruler, activate it in the Windows options portion of the Tools, Options, Text Document, Layout dialog.

Basically, you're increasing the bottom margin of the page. Because changing the margin affects all pages of the same page style, you should avoid using this option on multipage publications. The more elegant solution would be to edit your text to shorten (or lengthen) it or adjust the size of inserted objects and the spacing between (wrapped) text and objects.

Tip #214 from *Michael & Sarah*	You can also try adjusting the text flow by using the Text Flow tab in the Paragraph dialog. Select Break, Column in the Options portion of the tab to enforce column breaks before or after selected paragraphs.

VARYING THE COLUMN LAYOUT ON THE SAME PAGE

Because columns are formatted per page, you can't switch easily between different column layouts You have to start a new page style; use multicolumn frames (or text boxes; or create sections.

VARYING THE COLUMN LAYOUT WITH TEXT BOXES

Inserting and working with text boxes is covered in the next section. However, to get you started, check out this summary of the major steps involved in varying the number of columns on the same (or consecutive) page(s) by using multicolumn frames in combination with text boxes:

1. Insert a multicolumn frame at the desired place in your publication. Click the Insert icon on the main toolbar, then extended-click the Insert Frame icon (third icon from the right) on the Insert toolbar to open a small submenu that enables you to click and drag to the right to select the number of columns to be inserted in the current frame. As soon as you release the mouse button, StarWriter inserts a frame with the specified number of columns that spans the entire width of your printable area.

2. Right-click the selected frame and select Text Box from the context menu. The Text Box dialog opens.

3. Go to the Type tab, enter a size and position for the text box, and make sure the anchor is set to Paragraph.

4. Select the Wrap tab, and specify the text flow around the box.

4. Using the Columns tab, modify the width and spacing of the existing columns (if necessary), and select Automatic Width (to ensure that all columns are of equal width).

5. Click OK.

You now have a multicolumn layout inside a single column page (provided the original page is set up as a single column). Click inside the text box and first column, and start typing your text.

Tip #215 from	To frame already existing text, just select it before clicking the Insert Frame icon (or choosing Insert, Text Box). The text automatically becomes part of the multicolumn box.
Michael & Sarah	

Modifying or adding columns to text boxes is no different from modifying or adding columns to pages, and it enables you to switch columnar layout on the same page or between pages of the same style.

VARYING THE COLUMN LAYOUT WITH SECTIONS

If frames are not your cup of tea, you can also insert multicolumn sections. Just place the insertion point at the place where you want to start the new layout and select Insert, Section from the menu bar. In the Insert sections dialog that appears, click the Columns button to open the Columns dialog. Here you can define the number of columns, control column width and spacing between columns, as well as add a separator line. (Using the Columns dialog is identical to using the Columns tab of the Text Box and Page Styles dialogs.) When finished, click OK to return to the Insert Sections dialog, where you can further define your section, then click Insert to insert the section into your document.

→ For more details on working with sections, **see** "Defining Sections," **p. 378** .

→ For more details on working with sections, **see** "Defining Sections," **p. 378** .

WORKING WITH TEXT BOXES

Text boxes are the key to placing text into a freestanding container, running elements across multiple columns, and "switching" between different column layouts on one page. Typical uses for text boxes include *sidebars* and *pull quotes*, as well as headings and titles that span several columns or the entire width of the page.

StarWriter enables you to wrap text around text boxes and "flow" text from one box to another by linking text boxes on the same page or following pages. After you insert a text box into a document, you can move and resize (or scale) it as needed. Note also that text boxes are not confined by the thin shadowed text boundaries on a page (which reflect your margin settings); they can run up to the physical page borders.

Note	When you're using text boxes, you have the same options as if you're working with a regular text document. You therefore can insert graphics, use multicolumn text, and so on.

INSERTING EMPTY TEXT BOXES

StarWriter gives you two options to insert a text box. If you want more control over the type of box you want to insert, select Insert, Text Box from the menu bar. In the Text Box dialog that appears, you can specify the size, position, and anchor for your text box. Using the Columns and Wrap tabs, you can also determine the number of text columns in your box and whether the adjacent body text should be permitted to wrap around the box.

In addition, you can define hyperlinks, borders, and background color (or graphic) of the text box. If you choose this option, StarWriter inserts a text box at the insertion point.

→ For more details on anchors and defining text box properties, **see** "Rehearsing Objects," **p. 421**, earlier in this chapter.

The second option is faster. Extended-click the Insert button on the main toolbar, and select the Frames icon (the first icon from the left). Your pointer changes shape to a crosshair cursor as soon as you move it over your workspace. You can now click and drag anywhere on your page to create a text box. When done, you can double-click the text box to open the Text Box dialog and start fine-tuning your box.

Tip #216 from
Michael & Sarah

When you're creating several text boxes at once, you have to click in your document to deselect the most recently created box. Otherwise, the Insert Frame feature is unavailable.

Note

You can create text boxes inside text boxes if needed. StarWriter automatically anchors the inside box to the top paragraph mark of the outside box.

CREATING TEXT BOXES AROUND EXISTING TEXT

You can insert a text box around existing text—one or more characters, paragraphs, or the entire page—by following these steps:

1. Select the text for which you want to create a box, using your favorite method of selection.

2. Extended-click the Insert button on the main toolbar, and select the Frame icon (the first icon from the left) of the floating Insert toolbar.

Note

The Frame icon replaces the Table icon on the Insert button because the Insert button always reflects your most recent selection from the floating toolbar. To use the Frame function again, you don't have to extended-click to select it; because it's already active (just as the default Insert Table command before), a short click suffices to enter the Insert Frame (text box) drawing mode again.

3. When you move the pointer over your page, it changes shape to a crosshair. Click in the upper-left corner at the beginning of the selection, and drag a frame around the text. The text is then taken out of its regular context and placed into the frame.

Note

You can press Esc to abort the Frame function before starting to draw.

Note

If AutoHeight is not checked, any text that doesn't fit within the text box area "falls off" the bottom of the box; although it's still there, it is invisible to the eye. AutoHeight ensures that StarWriter automatically adjusts the height of the text box if you add to the existing contents. But remember that a frame can't be bigger than one page. If you insert too much text—even with AutoHeight activated—the text disappears. You can select this feature from the Properties dialog.

LINKING AND UNLINKING TEXT BOXES

StarOffice 5 has another way-cool feature: the capability to link text boxes and have text flow from one box to the next. With this feature, you can mimic newspaper-style column layouts, starting a story on page 1 of your newsletter and continuing it on page 2 in column 3. You can even move text boxes to a new location in your publication without losing the existing links. Although this feature sounds too good to be true for an office suite, one caveat still applies: If you ever want to change the order of linked boxes, you have to individually unlink and relink the boxes in the desired order.

Creating text box links is easy enough—follow these steps:

1. Make sure that the text box from which the link originates is not set to AutoHeight. You can verify the setting on the Type tab of the Text Box dialog.

2. Select the first text box, click the Text Box Link button on the Text Box toolbar (the second button from the right), and move your cursor to the second (empty) text box to which you want to link. As you move your cursor across the document page, you'll notice two symbols attached to it: a circle with a line across (similar to a no smoking sign) and a chainlink symbol. The circle indicates that you can't link to the current area; the chain link signifies that you can click here to create a text box link.

Note

The second text box in a link must be empty before you can create the link.

3. Click in the second, empty text box. You'll notice a thin black line linking the lower-right corner of the first text box with the upper-left corner of the second one. As soon as the link is created, any available text (read: text that was not visible but there) automatically flows from the first to the second text box.

Note

When you're linking frames, StarWriter automatically removes an existing AutoHeight attribute of the frame you link to. If the linked frame is the last one in a chain, you can reassign this attribute manually.

Following these steps, you can link one frame to another in a linear chain of frames. Note that it doesn't matter whether the frame with the receiving link comes before or after the frame with the originating link in your publication. All that matters is that the following conditions are met:

- The frame you link to has to be empty.
- It has to be the sole recipient of a link; if it is already the receiving link of another frame, you cannot link to it.
- It has to be part of the same document area; for example, you can't link a frame in a header with a frame in a footer.
- It cannot be a frame inside a larger frame.
- It cannot be a larger frame surrounding a smaller frame.

Note

The contents of a linked frame wrap around any frame, graphic, or other object that has been anchored inside the linked frame. Likewise, if a standalone frame anchored to a paragraph and a graphic anchored to a page overlap, the text inside the frame wraps around the graphic as specified on the Wrap tab in the Graphic dialog.

By contrast, if this same frame is part of a linked chain, the text inside the linked frame runs over or behind the same graphic—depending on the selected arrangement of the linked frame. If the graphic is anchored to a paragraph or to the linked frame, however, the text inside the linked frame wraps around the graphic.

To remove a link, select the text box from which the link originates, and click the Unlink button on the Frame object bar (the first button from the right). By doing so, you disconnect the current box from the following one (and all subsequent ones) in the chain. Your text automatically returns to the current text box, but because it can't fit there, that text "falls off" the bottom edge of the box where you can't see it.

Note

StarWriter uses a small red triangle to indicate that more text exists in the box than is visible onscreen.

ALIGNING TEXT BOXES WITH COLUMNS

The most common use for text frame links is in newspaper-style layouts. Although StarWriter does not include a command that automatically lines up text boxes with columns, there is an easy solution to this quandary. You need to do the following:

1. Insert a text box into a column, using your favorite method.
2. Select the text box, and open the Text Box dialog.

3. Select the Type tab, and click the Relative box (to the right of the Width spin box). The default unit of measurement changes to percentage. Make sure the value in the Width box is 100%—which means the width of your column uses the width of the printable area of this column.

4. Click the As Character option in the Anchor portion of the Type tab to place the text box right within the column.

5. Select OK. You've just placed a text box precisely into a column, and nobody will be able to tell the difference from looking at a printout.

WORKING WITH TEXT IN TEXT BOXES

You can edit and format text in frames just as you would in the rest of the document. You can set paragraph alignment, control the spacing between lines and paragraphs, add bullets and numbers, and apply paragraph styles. The trick is to get into the box in the first place. This is no problem when you move the cursor from the document into a text box—just click inside the box and start typing, editing, or formatting. However, if the current text box is selected, and you want to access the contents, you first have to deselect it by pressing the Esc key—your cursor is placed automatically at the beginning (upper left corner) of the text box. (Alternatively, you can also click anywhere outside the text box; then you can click inside the box and start typing. However, using the Esc key is faster.)

Note also that in a chain of linked boxes, you can enter text in consecutive boxes only when the previous box is filled. For example, text box 1 is linked with text box 2 but not filled with content yet. You cannot place your cursor in text box 2 and start typing. You first have to fill text box 1—either by adding content or empty lines (pressing Enter) or, more elegantly, by reducing the size of the box.

REMOVING TEXT BOXES

When you cut or delete a selected text box, its contents are cut or deleted as well. If it was part of a chain of linked text boxes, the box is removed without breaking the chain.

If you want to keep the contents of a text box, you have to cut and paste it into the main part of your document. To do so, select the contents, and then press Ctrl+X to cut it and Ctrl+V to paste it at the insertion point into the document.

NAVIGATING TEXT BOXES

The more text boxes you use, the harder it is to navigate them. If you want to quickly jump from box to box, use the Navigator. Expand the Text Frame tree in the viewing area by clicking the plus sign. Frames are listed by their names in the order in which they were created. Double-click a frame, and StarWriter takes you there. However, when you click a frame that is linked to another frame, the Navigator always only takes you to the originating frame.

Thus, when you're navigating linked frames, use the "mini Navigator." Select the frame icon, and use the navigational arrows to jump from frame to frame—linked or unlinked.

WORKING WITH GRAPHIC OBJECTS

Polished documents need graphic elements to illustrate the author's point of view, summarize key information, or simply to break up the monotony of text. StarWriter's capability to import (vector) graphics and (bitmap) images—from simple line drawings to charts and clip art to scanned photographs—adds much to your desktop publishing options, while enabling you to beautify your documents.

> **Note**
>
> In StarOffice terminology, drawings are vector graphics and pictures are bitmapped images (or graphics).

> **Tip #217 from**
> *Michael & Sarah*
>
> StarWriter uses graphic filters to convert graphic and image file formats to an image that appears in your document. When you install StarOffice, you can omit less common graphic filters that you don't need to save disk space. If you try to import a graphic or image file that has been captured in a file format that you don't have in your list, you have to run the StarOffice Setup program, select Modify, and follow the onscreen instructions to install the missing filters.

→ For more details on the distinction between vector graphics and bitmapped images, **see** "Understanding Computer Graphics," **p. 733.**

You can insert graphics in text areas and frames, as well as header and footer areas, or use them as backgrounds for paragraphs or pages. Like text boxes, graphic objects are not confined by the thin shadowed text boundaries that delineate the borders of your text; they can run up to the page borders. If a graphic is larger than the specified page format, StarWriter automatically scales (or resizes) it to fit the page. Using the Contour attribute, you can wrap text around an irregularly shaped graphic (or polygon).

INSERTING GRAPHIC OBJECTS

When inserting graphics into your document, you have two main options. You can either choose Insert, Picture from the menu bar, or you can use the Explorer and Beamer to preview and insert graphics via drag and drop from StarOffice's extensive Gallery of clip art files and images.

> **Note**
>
> The Pictures you insert using the Insert, Picture command are bitmapped graphics. For more details on the distinction between vector graphics and bitmapped images, see "Understanding How Computer Graphics Work" in Chapter 20, Getting Sketchy with StarDraw.

USING THE INSERT PICTURE COMMAND

When you're inserting graphics with the Insert, Picture command, you have three options: You can insert a graphic from a file, you can insert one from the Image Editor (StarImage), or you can scan an image (if you have a scanner connected to your computer). In all three instances, StarWriter places the image horizontally centered and anchored to the current paragraph. You can then reposition and/or resize the image as needed.

To insert an existing graphics file, select Insert, Picture, From File. You then see the Insert Picture dialog, which works like the Open dialog (see Figure 11.7) when it comes to locating the desired file on your hard drive or network. In addition, you can take a peek at what you're about to insert in the boxed area on the right if you select the Preview option at the bottom of the dialog. Depending on the graphic filters installed in StarOffice, you can preview (and insert) a variety of common and less common formats of bitmap and vector graphics, including JPG, PCX, GIF, EPS, PCT, BMP, WMF, and CGM.

Figure 11.7
In the Insert Picture dialog, you can preview graphics and images before inserting them, and you can assign attributes to the desired graphic object before placing it.

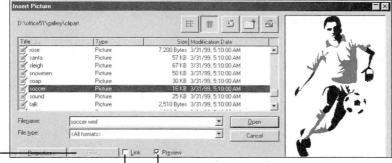

Select attributes for the graphic object

Select to link to the file (rather than embed it)⏋

⎿Select to preview files

PART
II

CH
11

Tip #218 from
Michael & Sarah

If the selected folder contains a long list of files of different formats, and you know the format you're looking for, select the format in the File Type list. This way, you can save time locating the desired file.

Select the Link option to link the graphic in your document without saving it in the document. Use this option if the source file is still a work in progress of sorts, and you want the inserted (linked) graphic to reflect any future changes in the original file; or to keep the size of your documents small (and since the graphic is not saved with the document, it also loads faster). You can update a linked file by selecting Tools, Updates, Links (or Update All).

Note

Linking files using the Link option of the Insert Picture dialog does not mean OLE linking. Double-clicking a linked picture does not edit the original file but only the copy in your document. On the other hand, linked files which are linked using OLE can be edited by double-clicking. This will open the original file in its application.

Tip #219 from
Michael & Sarah

Always link pictures by using the Link option in the Insert Picture dialog (not OLE), especial-ly when you're dealing with long documents with lots of graphics. The difference in file size can be tremendous. For example, a paper of about 120 pages with more than 50 linked graphics weighs in at about 800KB. When it's saved with the pictures in the document, it may take up to 10MB and more (depending on the size of the graphics)!

Of course, when linking files, the files need to be accessible any time you open the docu-ment. Note also that accessibility can be a problem in platform independence when paths are stored absolutely (for example, file:///c|/images/mypic.jpg)–Linux users won't be able to find the pictures. To work around this problem, always store pictures in subfolders of the document's location.

The Properties button opens the Pictures dialog, which is to graphics and images what the Character, Paragraph, and Page dialogs are to text, paragraphs, and pages. Using the Pictures dialog, you can assign a name as well as attributes to your insert, including posi-tioning, size, and the way text is supposed to wrap around it. Note that you can always change these attributes later by double-clicking the graphic. When you select Insert, Picture, From File, the default directory is \Office51\Gallery.

Tip #220 from
Michael & Sarah

To insert an existing graphics file, you can also select the Insert Picture command from the floating Insert window on the main toolbar. Just extended-click the Insert button at the top of the main toolbar, and select the Picture icon (the second from the left) to open the Insert Picture dialog.

You can also insert a graphic by selecting Insert, Picture, From Image Editor. Selecting this command opens StarImage, the image manipulation module of StarOffice. Using this com-mand, you can create a pixel image and insert it into your document. You can determine the size and number of colors, as well as select from a number of special effects and shapes when creating a pixel image. Insert the finished image by clicking its anchor.

Note

When inserting an image from the image editor, you will be asked to define the size and number of colors for your image. Select a size for the image (in pixels) and the number of colors in the New Image dialog.

→ For more details on using StarImage, **see** Chapter 21, "Creating and Modifying Images with StarImage," **p. 779**.

Finally, you can insert a picture by scanning it into StarWriter. Just select Insert, Picture, Scan. To select a scanner or open the dialog of an already selected scanner, choose Select Source or Acquire from the Scan submenu. Of course, you need to have a scanner and the accompanying software installed to take advantage of this option.

Note

Scanning with Linux is only possible on glibc-based installations using the software driver SANE. SANE has to be linked using this library.

USING THE GALLERY

The StarOffice Gallery is the place to go when you're looking for images of any kind. It holds an extensive collection of bitmap and vector graphics categorized by themes that can be expanded by adding images and categories of your own. To maximize your use of the Gallery, use the Explorer (in Hierarchical view) and Beamer. Open the Explorer (by pressing Ctrl+Shift+E) and Beamer (by pressing Ctrl+Shift+B), and click the plus (+) sign next to Gallery to expand the folder tree. Click a category (or theme), and you can see its contents in thumbnail view in the Beamer. Find the desired graphic (note that the name and path are shown at the bottom of the Beamer), click, and then drag and drop it into a document. As with the Insert, Picture command, the image will appear horizontally centered between the left and right margins of the page. If the graphic is a StarDraw object (extension .sda), however, you can place it anywhere you want—even outside the logical page.

→ For details on adding files to the Gallery, **see** "Adding New Folders and Files to the Gallery," **p. 448**.

> **Note**
>
> When you're inserting Gallery graphics by dragging and dropping from the Beamer, you don't have the option to assign attributes to the graphic object first. To select different attributes, double-click the object to access the Picture dialog, and make the desired changes.

PART

II

CH

11

Instead of using drag and drop, you can also use the picture shortcut menu in the Beamer to insert a graphic. Just right-click the desired graphic, and select Copy from the Insert submenu to embed the desired graphic in your document; select Link to link it; or select Background to insert it as a background graphic of the current paragraph or page. When you select Copy or Link, StarWriter inserts the graphic above the current paragraph.

Using the shortcut menu, you can also preview the selected graphic or delete its thumbnail display (not the original file). Although the Preview option might seem somewhat redundant at first (given the existence of thumbnail previews), it does give you a slightly bigger and less pixilated (read: better) view of the selected graphic. Using the Preview option, you can also look at animated GIFs (located in the Animations folder) and play sounds (Sounds folder).

Consider using the Preview option if you want a better idea of how your graphic looks or when you're selecting rulers or photos for your document. Note that you can also toggle between preview and regular thumbnail view by double-clicking the thumbnail.

Tip #221 from
Michael & Sarah

To maximize or minimize the preview of your graphics file, extend the Beamer by dragging its bottom part (where your pointer changes into two parallel horizontal lines).

SCALING AND CROPPING GRAPHICS

By default, StarWriter inserts objects horizontally centered above the current paragraph, often way bigger than you'd expect. You can change the size of an object by resizing (scaling) or trimming (cropping) it.

SCALING A GRAPHIC

You have two options when scaling a graphic object: the Type tab in the Pictures dialog or the mouse. If accuracy is an issue, use the Pictures dialog, which you can open by double-clicking the graphic object (or by selecting Format, Picture or by using the context menu). Using the Type tab, you can define the size and position (as well as the anchor) of the selected graphic object. In the Size portion of the tab, you can specify the absolute (default) or relative width and height of the selected graphic. Relative width and height determine a percentage of the printable area on a page. For example, a relative width of 80 percent sets the text box width at 80 percent of the width of the printable area of the page or column in which it is inserted. Select Keep Ratio to scale a graphic object proportionally (without distorting it vertically or horizontally). If you want to change a scaled graphic back to its original size, click the Original Size button.

If you prefer a quicker method of scaling the graphic, use the mouse. Select the graphic, and click and drag any of the selection handles in the corners to scale the graphic. To scale the graphic proportionally, click any selection handle, and press Shift while dragging.

CROPPING A GRAPHIC

When you insert a graphic from another program or from a file, you can crop parts of the graphic that you do not want to print by adjusting the size of the surrounding bounding box. Double-click the graphic to open the Pictures dialog. Use the measurement boxes in the Crop area to enter the amounts by which you want to crop the image. A negative measurement in the Left and Right boxes specifies how much the image should be cropped on the left and right sides; a negative measurement in the Top and Bottom boxes specifies how much the image should be cropped on the top and bottom. Select Keep Scale (default) to retain the proportional relationship between the various sides of the object after the crop and to avoid distortions. If you select Keep Size, StarWriter retains the original size of the object after the crop, which might lead to distortions.

In the Size and Scale areas of the Crop tab, you can see how your changes reduce the Width and Height of the original graphic in inches (size) and percentage (scale), depending on what you decided to keep. You can gauge your cropping choices in the Preview box on the right. To restore the size of the graphic before the start of your most recent editing session, select the Original Size button. To restore the graphic to its true original size, restore the original values in the Size boxes (the original size is displayed above the Original Size button), and reset all Crop measurements to zero.

WRAPPING TEXT AROUND GRAPHIC OBJECTS

Wrapping text around graphics works the same as wrapping text around any other object; you select a wrapping style from the context menu or from the Wrap tab in the Picture dialog. Unlike other objects, however, graphic objects have two more wrapping aces up their sleeves:

- **Contour**—Text wraps around the shape of the object. Use this option especially with polygons. (This feature is available only for graphic and 3D objects, but not when Through is selected.)

- **Only Outside**—Text wraps only around the left and/or right of the object but not "inside" (for example, if you have an open wedge in a pie chart). (This function is available only for graphic objects and only when Contour is selected.)

For best results when you're using the Contour feature, be sure to do the following:

- Select automatic hyphenation so that the wrapping text fills out all lines. You can turn automatic hyphenation on and off by using the Text Flow tab in the Paragraph dialog (which you open by choosing Format, Paragraph or by using the StarWriter context menu).

- Justify your text.

- Adjust the spacing between the graphic and text so that they don't run into each other. You can adjust the spacing to the left, right, top, and bottom of the object by using the Spacing portion of the Wrap tab in the Pictures dialog.

USING THE CONTOUR EDITOR

Although StarOffice does a pretty good job of recognizing the contour of irregularly shaped graphics, the graphic might still have a corner that you don't like; or you want to completely redefine the wrapping area of a graphic. In that case, edit the contour manually by using the Contour Editor.

To use the Contour Editor, follow these steps:

1. Select the graphic whose contour you want to edit and open its context menu.

2. Select Edit Contour from the Wrap submenu. The Contour Editor, shown in Figure 11.8, opens.

PART

II

CH

11

Figure 11.8
Use the Contour Editor to redefine the contour of irregularly shaped graphics.

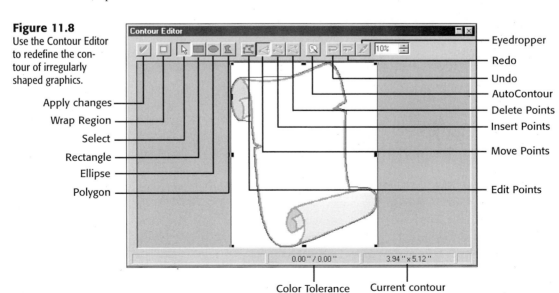

Apply changes
Wrap Region
Select
Rectangle
Ellipse
Polygon

Eyedropper
Redo
Undo
AutoContour
Delete Points
Insert Points
Move Points
Edit Points

Color Tolerance   Current contour

3. To modify the way text wraps around your object, use the tools on the Contour Editor's object bar. Here's a brief summary of your options and tools:

- **Apply**—Click this button frequently to save your changes.
- **Wrap Region**—Click here to delete the current contour and replace it with a new wrap region.
- **Select**—Use this tool to select an area of the contour that you can then individually modify.
- **Rectangle, Ellipse, Polygon**—Select these tools to define a new rectangular, elliptical, or irregularly shaped area around which your text will wrap. (Using these tools is identical to using the Rectangle, Ellipse, or Polygon tools in StarDraw (for more details, see "Using the Geometric Drawing Tools and "Using the Bézier Tools" in Chapter 20, "Getting Sketchy with StarDraw").
- **Edit Points, Move Points, Insert Points, Delete Points**—Select these tools if you want to edit the control points of freeform shapes (aka Bézier curves). Using these tools is identical to using the corresponding tools of the Bézier object bar in StarDraw (for more details see "Working with Bézier Curves" in Chapter 20).
- **AutoContour**—Click this button to automatically define a contour that you can then refine using the tools on the object bar (see Figure 11.9).

Figure 11.9
Click AutoContour and use the tools on the object bar if you want to refine the original wrap region.

Object bar

AutoContour

Defined contour (consists of numerous control points)

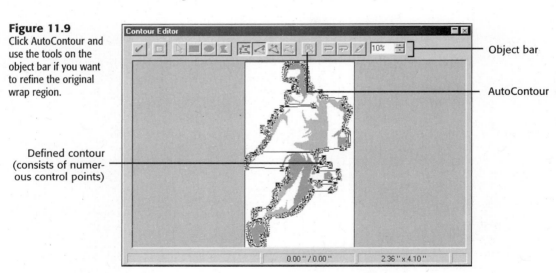

4. After each change, click the Apply button to save the changes to your wrap region. When finished, click the Close button in the upper right corner to exit the Contour Editor.

ADDING HORIZONTAL LINES AS SEPARATORS

StarOffice includes a number of horizontal lines that you can use as separators between headers and footers and the body text area or even between blocks or sections of text.

To add a horizontal line, place the insertion point at the location where you want to insert the line. Then choose Insert, Horizontal Line and select the desired line style from the Insert Horizontal Line dialog that appears and click OK.

A horizontal line is a (bitmapped) graphic object, which means you can work with it as with every other graphic object.

CREATING YOUR OWN GRAPHICS

 StarWriter also comes with its own assortment of drawing tools that you can use to create graphic objects. To access these tools, extend-click the Draw icon on the main toolbar to open the Draw Functions floating toolbar, shown in Figure 11.10.

> **Note**
>
> The drawings you create and insert using the Draw tools are vector graphics. Vector graphics differ from bitmapped graphics in crucial ways. For more details on the distinction between vector graphics and bitmapped images, see "Understanding How Computer Graphics Work" in Chapter 20.

PART
II

CH

11

Figure 11.10
StarWriter includes a minimal set of drawing tools that enables you to maximize your desktop publishing power. For example, you can use a geometric drawing tool to create a basic shape and then import a graphic background to create an interesting effect for a title page of a book or report. Notice the Draw object bar, which appears when you select an object created with the Drawing functions.

Draw object bar

Draw icon   Drawing tools

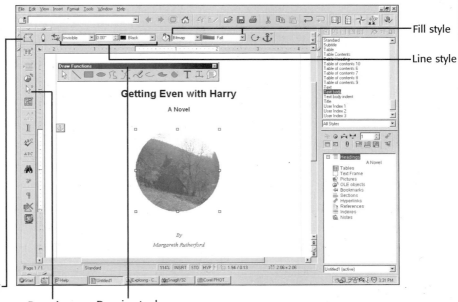

To use the drawing tools, click the desired tool, then click the place in the document where you want to create your drawing. Using these tools is identical to using the drawing tools in StarDraw and StarImpress and is discussed in detail in "Using the Basic Drawing Tools" and "Working with Bézier Curves" in Chapter 20.

Using the drawing tools enables you to enhance your document with dramatic effects. For example, to achieve the graphic effect shown in Figure 11.10, follow these steps:

1. Create a title page by entering and formatting the desired title, subtitle and author information.
2. Extend-click the Draw icon to open the Draw Functions floating toolbar.
3. Select the Ellipse tool and shift-click and drag below the subtitle to create a circle.

Note

If you use the Rectangle or Ellipse tool click and drag when using the Rectangle or Ellipse tools, you create what the name suggests—a rectangle or an ellipse, respectively. If you press Shift while dragging, you create a square or circle, respectively.

4. Right-click the selected drawing object to open its context menu and select Area. The Area dialog box appears. (Using the Area dialog is discussed in detail in "Adding Fills and Color to Your Object" in Chapter 20.)
5. Go to the Bitmaps tab and click the Import button. The Import dialog appears.
6. Double-click the photos folder, then select the autumn file and click Open. The Name dialog box appears asking you to enter a name for the external bitmapped image file.
7. Enter a custom name or leave the default one and click OK. You've just imported your new background file.
8. Go to the Area tab and be sure to deselect Tile and select AutoFit in the upper right corner of the tab.
9. Click OK. StarWriter will import the selected graphic as a "fill" for the circle. To hide the border of the circle, select Invisible from the Line Style drop-down list. That's it.

ADDING NEW FOLDERS AND FILES TO THE GALLERY

Using the Beamer to insert graphics from the StarOffice Gallery is convenient. Although StarOffice comes with an extensive collection of graphics, you can expand its archive with creations of your own or those of other people.

You can follow these steps to add a new folder and files to StarOffice:

1. Open the Explorer—in Hierarchical view—by pressing Ctrl+Shift+E, right-click Gallery, and select New Theme from the context menu.
2. In the Properties of New Theme dialog, select the General tab, and enter a name for your theme in the text box.

3. Select the Files tab, and click the Find Files button. Using the Select Path dialog, locate the folder that contains the desired files. If the folder has subfolders with additional files that you want to use as well, select the Subdirectories option in the lower left of the Select Path dialog. Click Open to return to the New Theme dialog.

4. Add the desired files from the folder you just selected to your new theme folder. You can add the desired files in one go, selecting the Add All button, or you can go through the list on the left one by one, preview the selected file, and then click the Add button if it's the one you want. If you're looking for a particular file format (such as BMP or JPG), you can use the File Type list at the top to filter the list of files by format.

5. Select OK to close the New Theme dialog and save all changes. StarOffice then adds the new folder and files to the Gallery tree. If you click the newly created folder, you see the thumbnails in the Beamer.

Note

If you place graphics files manually into a Gallery folder and then click the folder, you cannot see thumbnail previews of the newly added files because they have not been added yet to the Thumbnail database. To add them, right-click the folder, and select Update from the context menu.

Tip #222 from
Michael & Sarah

Keep an eye on the files in your Gallery subfolders. The Gallery directory not only stores graphics files, but also the data files for each theme. For example, `sg*.thm` stores the name of the folder, and `sg*.sdg` stores thumbnail data.

USING TEXT AND TYPE EFFECTIVELY

At the beginning of this chapter, we mentioned the importance of first-rate typography to garner the attention of readers. When you're working with text in a document intended for publication, you should pay close attention to the typefaces you choose for the various text elements, including headlines, subheads, headers, footers, folios (page numbers), body text, and the spacing between characters, lines, and paragraphs, as well as between headers, footers, and folios. You also should pay attention to the overall arrangement of text elements on a page.

Chapter 7, "Formatting Text Documents," and Chapter 8, "Using Styles and Templates," cover all the mechanics of direct and style character, paragraph, and page formatting. Chapter 10, "Working with Long Documents," tells you how to insert such important page layout elements as headers and footers, sections, captions and reference tables. In the following sections, we want to direct your attention to some cool attributes and features that add impact to your publication. Use them sparingly, and you will dazzle your readers; if you use them excessively, you might overwhelm if not annoy your readers.

APPLYING DROP CAPS

Newspaper and magazine articles usually begin with a single capital letter—set into a block of text and often followed by letters in small caps—that extends two or more lines below the opening line, commonly referred to as a *drop cap*. Combined with other layout choices, drop caps can be an effective means to pull the readers into the text. StarWriter makes it easy to include drop caps in your document. Just put the insertion point in the paragraph that is to be altered, and open the Paragraph dialog (from the context menu or the Format menu). Using the Drop Caps tab in the Paragraph dialog, you can control drop cap settings and style (see Figure 11.11). You can specify the number of letters to be dropped (typically one is enough), how many lines they should be dropped, and how much distance appears between the drop cap and the adjacent, indented text.

Figure 11.11
Use a drop cap, followed by half a line or so of small caps, to draw your readers' attention to the beginning of a chapter or article.

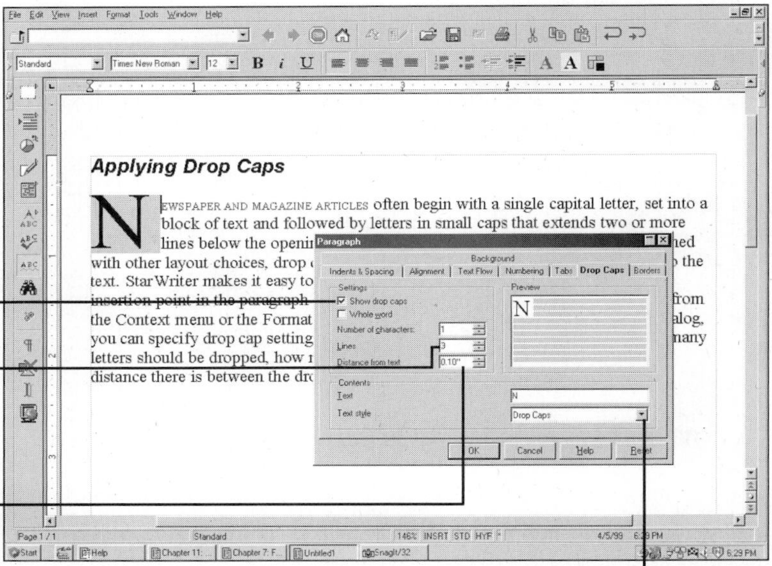

Select to show drop cap

Specify the number of drop lines

Specify the horizontal distance between drop cap and text

Select a predefined style for drop cap formatting

Using the Contents area of the Drop Caps tab, you can also enter new text for the drop cap (in case you don't want to replace the existing first letter(s) of a paragraph), and select a style from the Text Style drop-down list. When you click OK, StarWriter places the first character in the paragraph as a shaded letter, dropping it according to the settings that you specified.

Note

StarWriter inserts drop caps as unalterable fields; hence, if you select Field Shadings from the View menu, you see the shading behind the letter(s). Note also that the font of your drop cap is determined by the font of the paragraph and cannot be changed after it has been placed. However, you can assign a style to your drop cap, using the Text Style drop-down list on the Drop Caps tab *before* inserting the drop cap.

USING FONTWORK

StarWriter has a tool that enables you to do the coolest things with your text—FontWork. FontWork enables you to apply customized font effects to text (see Figure 11.12). Using FontWork, you can bend, stretch, flip, and rotate text along invisible lines and curves. To access FontWork, you must first create a text object using the Text draw function on the main toolbar and then select FontWork from the Format menu. Just follow these steps:

1. Extended-click the Draw button in the main toolbar, and then select the Text draw function (the large T icon) from the Draw Functions floating toolbar. Your mouse pointer changes to a cross as soon as you move it over the workspace.

2. Click an empty area in your document, and drag down and to the right to create a frame. Inside the frame, you'll notice a blinking insertion point. Start typing your text.

> **Caution**
>
> After creating the frame, don't click anywhere else in your document or the frame. If you do, the frame is removed.

3. After you enter your text, click anywhere in your document. The frame then disappears, leaving the text you entered behind as an object inside an invisible frame that you can select and resize and move as you would any other object.

4. With the text object selected, choose Format, FontWork to open the FontWork dialog. The spin box across the top lists various curves and line styles along which you can align your text. Just click a style, and the text object on your screen changes accordingly. Changes take effect immediately, so you can edit your effects in real-time. When you're done, click the Selection icon in the Draw Functions toolbar to switch from the draw mode back to the regular (text entry) mode, or click anywhere outside the text object boundaries to return to your document. To reselect the text object, click it.

> **Tip #223 from**
> *Michael & Sarah*
>
> Depending on the size of the text object, the boundaries of the object might extend quite a bit beyond the actual text you see onscreen, and if you selected the Wrap Through style, you cannot see it. If you want to edit text that is behind the object, you might inadvertently select a FontWork modified text object if you try to place the insertion in the vicinity of the object. In that case, just find the closest place where you can place the insertion point, and use the cursor keys to get to the desired passage. With any other wrapping style, you can see the boundaries of the text object.

You can spend an hour or more just experimenting with this cool tool. Using the first row of buttons, you can slant the text object or place it at a 90-degree angle in relation to the contour line, or you can flip it horizontally or vertically. Using the second row of buttons, you can reverse the order of letters and align the text object with regard to the selected curve or line. The spin boxes in the center enable you to specify the distance between the selected curve and the text object and between the beginning of the curve and the beginning of the object, respectively. Finally, the lower part of the dialog enables you to select shadow styles of varying colors, degrees, and distances from the individual letters of the text object.

Distance
Slants On/Off
Orientation
Text alignment

Figure 11.12
Fancy stuff, these font effects with FontWork.

Shadow color
Shadow positioning
Contours and Shadow styles
Indent

Click the Contour button (the one with the squiggly line below the center spin boxes) to show the invisible curve or line along which the text is aligned. You can manually scale and "edit" the shape of the selected line style, squeezing, extending, or inverting it, by dragging the sizing handles of the text object. If you don't like the selected style, choose another one, or click the Out button (the first button from the left below the spin box) to cancel the effect. The possibilities of what you can do with this tool are indeed numerous. All you need is a dash of creativity and a willingness to experiment. Try it—it's fun!

ROTATING TEXT

You can try yet another eye-catching trick: Place your text vertically on a page, with the baseline running parallel to the left and right margins. Here's how:

1. Extend-click the Draw button on the main toolbar, and then click the Text tool (the large T). (Note that the Text object bar changes to the Draw object bar as soon as you select the Text tool. For more details on the Draw object bar, see "Using the Draw Object Bar" in Chapter 20.)

2. Click and drag in your document to draw a rectangle. When you release the left mouse button, you see a thick, gray rectangle and a blinking cursor in the upper left corner of the document. (Note also that the Draw object bar meanwhile has given way to the Draw Text object bar.)

3. Enter the desired text. As with text documents, you can modify the font, the font style and the size of the text. Just right-click and select the attribute you want to change from the context menu, or use the options on the Object Bar. You don't have to select the text to change the attributes. Any attribute changes apply to all characters and words inside the box.

4. Click outside the box to leave the text edit mode (recognizable by the gray border). Next, you have to rotate and possible resize the text object.

Tip #224 from
Michael & Sarah

If you want to change the text or attributes after leaving the text edit mode, double-click the text to reactivate the text edit mode—you see the familiar thick, gray rectangle and the blinking cursor in the upper left corner of the document.

5. Click the text once again, the text will then be selected as an object. (You can recognize this mode by the eight control points in the rectangle surrounding the text.) You can now scale the object as usual (for example, to fit your text in one line) by clicking and dragging the selection handles.

6. Right-click the text object and select Position & Size from the context menu. In the Position & Size dialog, select the Rotation tab. Enter the desired degree by which you want to rotate the text object in the Angle spin box, or click a desired white point in the graphic option field to the right. (The red point indicates the current choice.)

7. Click OK. StarWriter rotates your text according to your specifications. To format your text, double-click the invisible text rectangle, and use the Character formatting option from the Format menu.

Using the principles and mechanics covered in this section, you can enhance your publication with many more bold, daring, and appealing effects. The final outcome is up to you and your imagination.

PREPARING DOCUMENTS FOR PRINTING

It's a long journey between creating a carefully designed document onscreen and getting a printed copy of it into the hands of customers. In a nutshell, your project must be *imaged*, as they say in publishing. Camera-ready artwork must be produced, and a print shop needs to duplicate the quantities you want. When you're preparing camera-ready copy, you have two options: You can deal with a service bureau or prepare the copy yourself.

Tip #225 from
Michael & Sarah

Before preparing final files or camera-ready copy, you should print a proof of the document to check the visual effect of the page. To save toner, you can change the printer properties to print more economical (read: lower resolution) copies. You can also select Options in the Printer dialog and prevent graphics from printing to save even more. All you're looking for is the overall design and flow of the text.

POSTSCRIPTING WITH STARWRITER

Because StarOffice is not the tool of choice for desktop publishing professionals, you will have a hard time finding a service bureau to output your raw StarOffice files. Don't despair, though; you do have an option. You can prepare a PostScript file by following this basic procedure:

1. Install a PostScript printer driver (for example, the Apple LaserWriter driver, which is part of the Windows driver database). Ask your service bureau for recommendations.

2. Open the Print dialog (by choosing File, Print), and select the name of the installed PostScript printer driver in the Name list box.

3. Select Print to File, and enter a name for the file in the text box, followed by the extension .ps (for example, mydoc.ps)

4. Click Print, and StarWriter outputs the current document as a PostScript file (by default to the \office51 root directory) that you can take to any service bureau for final output.

Note

The size of the PostScript file varies. Depending on the size and number of graphics in your document, you may need to send it out on a zip disk.

Tip #226 from
Michael & Sarah

If you don't have a PostScript printer, you can check the PS file using GhostScript. This PS interpreter displays your pages on screen and can print to almost any printer. Your Linux distribution may well have included GhostScript, as it's the standard utility used to enable Linux to print to non-PostScript printers. If not, check for Linux sites on the Web that have this handy program available for download.

USING HIGH-RESOLUTION LASER PRINTERS

As an alternative to using PostScript, you can use a high-resolution laser printer to prepare camera-ready pages yourself. The standard for print shops is 600 dots per inch (called dpi); these days, though, you can get an even higher-resolution laser printer for an affordable price. Remember, the higher the resolution, the better the final results. A print house then can take your pages and prepare film for printing your document.

Tip #227 from *Michael & Sarah*	Higher resolutions produce crisper letters, smoother background fills, and immeasurably better looking art. Also, be sure to use the best quality paper for final printouts (brightness of 90 percent or better).

ADDITIONAL CONSIDERATIONS AND TIPS

Using the features and tools discussed in this chapter, you can enhance your document with stunning text effects. Beyond these bells and whistles, however, you should not forget the finer points of desktop publishing. Here are brief summaries of additional things to watch out for when composing your publication:

- **Use white space**—White space is easily the most over-looked design element in desktop publishing. Don't think of it as wasted space. Instead, consider it as a powerful tool that adds balance and enhances readability. White space around a headline, for example, creates contrast that attracts the reader's eyes. Use white space to communicate relationships. large amounts of white space separate elements; small amounts of white space connect elements. For example, use more white space above subheads then between the subheads and the text they introduce. If you create an advertisement that will run in a newspaper or magazine, surround your advertisement with white space so it stands out from the surrounding ads and editorial content.

  In general, consider using white space surrounding pages, between columns, within and around headings, between lines and paragraphs, between letters and words, and around subheads. You can control the amount of white space at the sides of your page(s) by changing the left and right margins via the page tab of the Page Styles dialog (Select Page from the context menu or the Format menu, or modify the desired page style in the Stylist). To control the white space at the top and bottom of your page, increase the top and bottom margins (via the page tab of the Page Styles dialog) or the height of the header and footer areas (via the Header and Footer tab of the Page Styles dialog). To control the white space around headings and between lines and paragraphs, adjust the Top and Bottom Spacing spin boxes on the Indents & Spacing tab of the Paragraph Styles dialog.

PART II CH 11

Tip #228 from *Michael & Sarah*	If you use "deep" left margins, you can add emphasis to headlines and subheads by allowing them to begin to the left of the text columns. Figure 11.13 shows an example of the creative use of deep margins.

Figure 11.13
Deep margins add
emphasis to headings
and sub-headings.

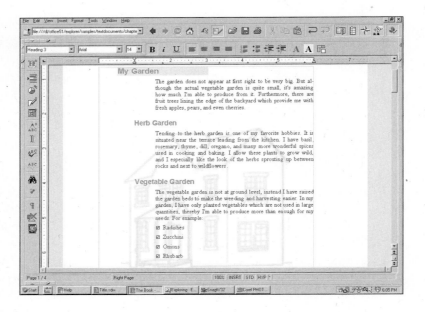

- **Adjust character spacing and kerning**—Control over letter spacing is vital to the appearance of headings and titles, and at times even in body text. StarWriter enables you to uniformly condense or expand the spacing between words and individual characters throughout a range of text via the Spacing portion of the Font Effects tab in the Character dialog (Select Character from the context menu or the Format menu, or modify the desired character style in the Stylist). Consider adjusting letter spacing to improve the appearance of your headings or body text. For example, by placing letters in headings closer together, the word shapes become more pronounced. The larger a headline, the more important it is that you control the letter spacing.

  Kerning is another one of those refinements that distinguish you as a pro if applied correctly. Kerning refers to increasing or decreasing letter spacing for individual pairs of letters and is especially important when you work with combinations of upper- and lowercase letters. As with character spacing, kerning gains in importance as the size of your headings increases. StarWriter automatically performs this function when you select Pair Kerning on the Font Effects tab of the Character dialog.

- **Avoid widows and orphans**—Widows (a word or part of a word standing alone at the bottom of a column, page, or paragraph) and orphans (a word or part of a word standing alone at the top of a column or page) project a less than professional image. Typically, widows and orphans are corrected by adding or deleting text in the respective paragraph. However, if they are short enough, you may also get rid of them by adjusting the spacing between characters and words (via the Font Effects tab in the Character dialog). Alternatively, you can also turn on the Orphan and Widow control options on the Text Flow tab of the Paragraph Styles dialog.

■ **Choose the right type**—We already mentioned the importance of choosing the right typeface at the beginning of this chapter. Apart from the right typeface, however, you should also consider the right type size. Avoid long lines of small type (as they are so common in legal disclaimers) or short lines of large type, both of which create hard-to-read text.

When using fractions or numbers, use typeset fractions and numbers rather than 1 1/2 or 1st, for example. StarWriter can automatically format your text entry when you select the respective options on the Options tab of the AutoCorrect dialog (select Tools, AutoCorrect/AutoFormat).

■ **Choose the proper alignment**—When aligning text on a page or column, you typically choose between left-aligned (ragged right) and justified. Some iconoclasts may also consider right-aligned, which can create a nice balance if used properly. For example, if your body copy is left-aligned, you could make your captions for images right-aligned.

Depending on the type of alignment you choose, you'll convey different impressions. For example, left-aligned text is generally considered friendlier and more informal (as well as easier to read), while justified text is often used to project a serious or classic image. Consider also the width of the column(s) your working with—justified text in narrow columns often creates awkward word spacing, even with automatic hyphenation turned on. One work-around in this case is to reduce the character spacing via the Font Effects tab of the Character dialog.

Also, when aligning text with objects, be sure to align the left and right margins of your text with pre-printed elements such as header or footer rules or logos.

■ **Use proper punctuation**—Knowing the difference between an em dash and an en dash is another one of those refinements that spells the difference between amateur and professional. To project a professional image through your print communication, consider using the following:

- Curly or custom quotes ("") instead of vertical foot marks or straight quotes (""); to use custom quotes in StarWriter, select Tools, AutoCorrect/AutoFormat, go to the Custom Quotes tab and click the single and double quote buttons to select a desires quote style from the special character set of the current font
- Typeset apostrophe (') instead of a typewritten inch mark (')
- em dash (—) to indicate a parenthetical phrase instead of two hyphens
- en dash (–) to indicate duration (for example, 1958–1963) instead of a single hyphen
- bullets or check boxes instead of asterisks when introducing lists (StarWriter has a huge collection of bullet styles that you can access via the Format, Numbering/Bullets dialog.)

In addition, don't use two spaces after periods (Using two spaces after a period made sense when people used typewriters or monospaced font (such as Courier).

- **Use graphic accents**—StarWriter offers an enticing variety of graphic accents, including horizontal lines (Insert, Horizontal Line), bullet styles (Format, Numbering/Bullets), and backgrounds. Use them functionally rather than decoratively. Too many graphic accents create unnecessary clutter, which projects a disorganized image. Use horizontal lines at the top and bottom of a page to frame the pgae and use them within text columns as separation device. Use shaded backgrounds to attract attention to separate text blocks.

- **Work with grids**—A grid consists of a network of non-printing horizontal and vertical lines. Grids determine the placement of text and visuals. When preparing your document, consider turning on the layout grid (select the Visible Grid option in the Tools, Options, Text Document, Grid dialog), then define your styles, including indents, margins, and column widths. Defining styles against a grid adds opportunity for creative use of white space and consistent placement of elements via styles.

- **Create templates and styles**—Templates and styles eliminate the needthe need to reinvent the wheel every time you start a new project. Templates are files containing page layouts and styles that ensure consistency throughout your document. Styles enable you to assign multiple formatting options with a single key stroke. Diligently use the existing styles and templates or create your own. (For more details see Chapter 8, "Using Styles and Templates.")

CHAPTER 12

PROOFING AND PRINTING YOUR DOCUMENTS

In this chapter

PROOFING YOUR WORK

When all is said and done, you want to proofread your work before sending it out or printing it. StarWriter has its own complement of little helpers that make proofreading easy. You can rely on the built-in Spelling, Thesaurus, and Hyphenation commands to proofread documents and supply suggestions for improvement. You can also use the Search and Replace command to help you review your text and make global changes to individual words, phrases, attributes, and formats.

Note

> In its current incarnation (version 5.1), StarOffice does not have a grammar checker, so if you have problems with your writing, including excessive use of passive verbs, pronoun errors, punctuation errors or double negatives, you're on your own.

USING SEARCH AND REPLACE

You might find in reviewing and proofing your document that it would be easier if you had a tool that could locate specific text or formatting attributes rather than you having to scan the document with your own eyes. With StarWriter's Search and Replace command, you can search for character attributes and styles, and even perform similarity searches and searches with regular expressions.

Tip #229 from
Michael & Sarah

> Using the mini-Navigator on the scrollbar, you can easily continue a search that has already been started using the Search and Replace command. Click the Repeat Search icon (binoculars) to turn on this feature, and then use the blue double arrows on the Navigation toolbar (or the scrollbar) to continue your search toward the end (forward) or beginning (backward) of the document. Note that this symbol is only available if you have previously started a search.

SEARCHING FOR TEXT

Using StarWriter's Search and Replace feature is pretty straightforward. To search for text, you select Edit, Search and Replace or press Ctrl+F. In the Search For box of the Search and Replace dialog, you enter the desired word or phrase, and then you select Search or press Enter. StarWriter finds the first occurrence of the text. You can then continue the search for subsequent occurrences by pressing Enter again. If you press Search All, StarWriter searches the entire document and then marks all occurrences of the search term—pretty nifty if you want to check how often you use certain expression, or if you want to assign the same attributes (such as italics, boldface, or underline) to a recurring word or expression.

Tip #230 from
Michael & Sarah

StarWriter keeps track of your searches. Click the down arrow next to the Search For box and you'll see a list of terms you've searched with your most recent item at the top. That way you don't have to retype a word if you want to look for it once more—just select it from the list. Note, however, that this history list cannot be longer than ten entries. StarWriter will automatically delete the oldest item to make room for a new one once the list is full.

SEARCHING FOR ATTRIBUTES AND MORE

Using the Attributes and Format buttons, as well as the Options portion of the Search and Replace dialog gives you even more choices to aid you in your search. Attributes enable you to select one or more character attributes. For example, rather than looking for any occurrence of a specific word, you could search only for instances in which you use attributes such as italics or bold with the word. All in all, you can search for up to 26 attributes, including Effects, Font Color, Kerning, Language, Character Background, Widows, Orphans, Tab Stops, Indents, Spacing, Page Style, and Keep with Next Paragraph among others.

Format enables you to narrow down your search even more. If the Attribute search is rather generic (for example Font Color or Effects), in Format you can specify the size, style, color, indent, spacing, alignment and all other attributes. Basically, you can have the same options for refining your search as you do when you define character and paragraph attributes using the Font, Font Effects, and Background tabs of the Character Style dialog (Format, Character) and the Indents and Spacing, Alignment, Text Flow of the Paragraph Styles dialog. If you don't want any attributes included in the search or replace process, click No Format.

In the Options portion of the dialog, you can also specify if you want StarWriter to search for Whole Words Only, hence a search for "form" would exclude words such as "conform;" Match Case only shows words that match cases; Backwards reverses the direction of your search; and Current Selection Only searches for only selected text (note that this option is only available when you have selected text).

You can also Search for Styles (in which case the currently applied styles in the document show up in the Search For drop-down list, while the Replace With drop-down list offers all possible styles. (If you don't see the list of currently applied styles in the Search for box, click once or twice on the down arrow of the box and the list will magically appear.) Once a style has been replaced, it will be deleted from the Search For drop-down list, as well as the list of applied styles in your document.

PART
II
CH
12

Tip #231 from
Michael & Sarah

You can always reapply accidentally deleted styles by searching for the style with which you replaced it, and then selecting the old style from the Replace With drop-down list of available styles.

Note also that once you select Search for Styles, all other search options become unavailable with the exception of Backwards.

Another search option includes Similarity Search, which enables you to search for similar expressions. You can define the conditions of this search by selecting the Ellipse button (…) to the left and entering a specified number of characters by which the word in your document is allowed to differ from the word entered in the Search For box to still count as a hit. For example, if you specified that one character in your search is allowed to be exchanged, a search for *compliment* would also yield *complement* if the term exists in the document. In general, you have the option to exchange, add, or remove a specified number of characters. You can also combine all three search options by selecting the Combine option in the Similarity Search dialog.

Tip #232 from
Michael & Sarah

You can also use the Search and Replace command to quickly select specific terms in order to apply attributes to them or mark them as index entries (using the Insert Index Entry dialog box). Simply type the word(s) in the Search For box and click Search All. StarWriter will mark all occurrences of the search term in your text. You can now format the selected words or mark them as index entries by selecting Insert, Indexes, Entry.

SEARCHING WITH REGULAR EXPRESSIONS

Search can track down essentially anything in a document. In addition to text and formatting, your potential targets include paragraph marks, tabs, or manual breaks. In long documents it's much easier to have StarWriter find them for you rather than scanning the pages yourself.

Table 12.1 shows a select list of expressions or codes you must enter in the Search For box to track down special characters. (Some of these are admittedly arcane.)

TABLE 12.1   SPECIAL CODES FOR SEARCH AND REPLACE

Code	What It Does
.	Works like a placeholder or wildcard; for example, p.t would find "pit" and "pet"
^Word	Finds the word only if it is at the beginning of a paragraph
Word$	Finds the word if it is at the end of a paragraph
*	Finds all instances of a character or string of characters to the right. For example, Peter.*home will find "Peter goes home" and "Peter is at home." (Note that the combination .* stands for any character or no character.)
\c	Finds exactly the character indicated (here c). This is helpful if you want to search for occurrences of international currency signs, for example.

Code	What It Does
\n	Finds any instance of manual line breaks (Ctrl+Enter)
\t	Finds tabs (you can also use this in the Replace With box)
\>	Finds instances of the search text when it is at the end of a word; for example, ment\> finds "management" but not "mention"
\<	Finds instances of the search text at the beginning of a word; for example, \<intro finds "introduction" but not "reintroduction"
^$	Searches for empty paragraphs
$	Searches for the end of a paragraph
^	Searches for the beginning of a paragraph
&	Enables you to combine Replace text and Search text. For example, frame in the Search for box and &work in the Replace with box yields "framework."
'hint'	Characters between single quotes will not be considered in regular expressions; if you want to include them, enter \ (for example, \'hint\').
This¦That	Finds this or that.

REPLACING TEXT

You can use the same search techniques to replace the search text with other text as well. For example, you might want to replace every occurrence of the word "allow" with the word "enable" throughout a document. Or perhaps a certain word has been underlined rather than italicized. In that instance, you would enter the (underlined) word in the Search For box of the Search and Replace dialog. Then you would select Attribute and mark the appropriate style reference in the Attribute dialog. Next, you would enter the same word in the Replace With box, and then select the appropriate style reference in the Attribute dialog. Now you can select Search or press Enter. StarWriter finds the first occurrence of the text. You can select Replace and then continue the search for subsequent occurrences by pressing Enter again; or you can select Replace All to have StarWriter search for and replace all occurrences of the specified word and attribute.

Caution

Be careful when using the Replace All button, because it may cause you to make some replacements that you don't want to make. For example, if you want to replace "fall" as in the season with "autumn" and you choose Replace All, the phrase "He falls into that category" would also get changed to "He autumns into that category". Oops!

If you do not care to make a certain replacement, select Search (or press Enter) again, and StarWriter continues the search. To exit Search and Replace, select Close or click the Close button on the title bar.

Tip #233 from
Michael & Sarah

Like so many other dialogs and toolbars in StarOffice, Search and Replace is a floating dialog box. This means you can leave it open all the time and collapse it if you need the space by double-clicking its title bar.

CHECKING YOUR SPELLING

Whether you're creating a simple business letter, a complex report, or a legal contract, the core vehicle for communicating your ideas is your text—properly chosen, spelled, and formatted. Using StarOffice, you have a knowledgeable, multilingual consultant when it comes to matters of choosing the proper spoken and written word.

StarOffice offers multiple dictionaries, enables you to create custom dictionaries, and permits you to check your spelling and usage in one, two, or three languages at a time. Your dictionaries include a hyphenation, spelling, and synonym dictionary (thesaurus) that also has definitions for each installed language. And once you understand how the program handles installed and custom dictionaries, you can get even more mileage out of its multilingual capabilities.

As with most modern word processing programs, there are two ways you can check and correct your spelling in StarOffice: manually and automatically. You can check your spelling manually by invoking the Spelling command from the Tools menu. This opens a dialog box that enables you to check the spelling in your document against the program dictionaries and your designated custom dictionaries. If you would like to have your spelling checked automatically, you have to invoke the Auto Spellcheck command.

StarWriter's Spelling command uses a main dictionary and custom dictionaries. The main dictionary is supplied with the program and cannot be changed. When you're adding new words to a dictionary—which you can do when the Spellchecker comes across a word it does not recognize, but you know is correct—you are adding them to the Standard custom dictionary that comes with StarOffice, unless you specify another one.

Auto Spellcheck uses the main dictionary and any custom dictionaries you have selected in the Custom Dictionaries portion of the Tools, Options, General, Spelling/Languages dialog, as well as a build-up list of frequently misspelled words in the AutoCorrect/Autoformat command that then are automatically corrected as you type.

Note

StarOffice distinguishes dictionaries and other *linguistic* files (such as help files or thesauruses) by country code. For example, the main spelling dictionary for the United States is called `01_spell.dat`. All main dictionaries are located in the root directory of StarOffice. Custom dictionaries are stored in the Wordbook folder of the StarOffice root directory.

CHECKING YOUR SPELLING AUTOMATICALLY

The easiest way to check your spelling in StarWriter is to turn on the Auto Spellcheck function by pressing the button on the Main toolbar or selecting Tools, Spelling, Auto Spellcheck. Auto Spellcheck checks your spelling as you type, flagging any potential misspellings with a wavy red line underneath each word. You can get help correcting your mistakes by right-clicking each word and selecting alternative spellings and suggestions, including suggestions regarding the language of the underlined word (provided StarWriter has any), from the context menu (see Figure 12.1). You can choose the desired word from the list of suggestions, select Ignore All to pass over any other occurrences of the word, or add the word to a custom dictionary of your choice.

Tip #234 from
Michael & Sarah

Some misspellings are common typos that are more a reflection of the user's typing skills rather than her language skills (such as reversing the order of certain letter combinations as in "ahve" instead of "have"). If the misspelling is a common typo, select AutoCorrect from the context menu. StarWriter automatically adds the misspelled word together with the correct spelling to the replacement table of the AutoText dialog.

Figure 12.1
Auto Spellcheck checks your spelling on-the-fly, and even provides alternative spellings and suggestions for the misspelled word.

Select AutoCorrect to avoid common typos in the future

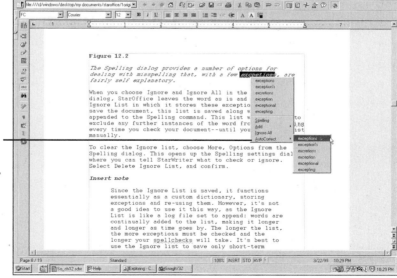

PART
II
CH
12

You can configure your Auto Spellcheck options in the Auto Spellchecking portion of the Tools, Options, General, Spelling/Language dialog box. If you select Check spelling as you type, StarWriter will flag typos, misspellings, and foreign words with a wavy red line; if you select Don't Mark Errors, you will no longer see the little wavy red lines (which may also result in a false sense of confidence on your part).

Tip #235 from
Michael & Sarah

You can also skip over any text that would otherwise earn poor marks from the Spellchecker by using the Language option in the Character Styles dialog. Just select the word(s) you want to exclude, and then choose Format, Character to open the Character dialog. Then select None from the Language drop-down list on the Font tab.

SPELLCHECKING IN MULTIPLE LANGUAGES

If you've installed one or two foreign language dictionaries in addition to the U.S. English dictionary, you can spellcheck words in multiple languages. To control how StarOffice goes about Spellchecking your work, open the Tools, Options, General, Spelling/Languages dialog. If the All Languages option in the Check Spelling portion of the dialog is not selected, StarOffice will only check your text in the language that has been attributed to it. Commonly, this is the default language, which you can set in the Default Language drop-down list of the Tools, Options, General, Spelling/Languages dialog. All other foreign (and misspelled) words will be flagged with a wavy red line. However, StarOffice may give you a helping hand and tell you what language the word or text is part of, provided you have the respective dictionary installed. All you have to do is right-click the foreign text and select StarOffice's suggestion from the bottom of the context menu. StarOffice will automatically assign it the proper language attribute, and it will recognize the text from there on out as acceptable spelling.

If you select the All Languages option, or if you assign a language to a foreign text (using the Language option on the Font tab of the Format, Character dialog), StarOffice will automatically check foreign text against the installed dictionaries. In that case, StarOffice will no longer provide suggestions on the context menu—it doesn't have to; either it recognizes the word based on the installed dictionaries, or it flags the word as unknown due to the lack of an installed dictionary.

Note

Even if the foreign word is spelled correctly, StarWriter will only recognize it if the respective language dictionary is installed. If the dictionary is not installed, but the word is spelled correctly, simply right-click the word and select Ignore from the context menu. If you catch yourself doing this with too many words, it's clearly a sign that you have the wrong language dictionaries installed. To change dictionaries, select Setup from the StarOffice directory, click Modify and follow the onscreen instructions.

USING THE SPELLING COMMAND

If you get annoyed with Auto Spellcheck's in-your-face way of telling you when you're wrong and doing things its way, turn it off and use the Spelling command after you're done typing. Using the Spelling command, you can check the spelling of a single word or of the entire document, including headers and footers, indexes, and footnotes. To check the spelling of only part of a document, you must first select the section you want to check, and then select Spelling, Check from the Tools menu (or press F7). If no selection has been made, StarWriter assumes you want to check the entire document.

Spelling starts at the insertion point and continues to the end of the document at which point StarWriter will ask you if you would like to continue the spelling check at the beginning of the document. Spelling occurs in the default language as specified in the Tools, Options, General, Spelling/Language dialog and as indicated in the Language box and title bar of the Spelling dialog. If you want spelling to occur in all installed languages, you have to check All Languages in the Check Spelling portion of the dialog.

Tip #236 from
Michael & Sarah

Note that you can also assign individual words to a language. Just select the word(s), and then open the Character dialog (Format, Character) and select the language from the drop-down list in the language potion of the Font tab.

After you select Tools, Spelling, Check, StarWriter checks all words against the main dictionary as well as any specified custom dictionary. If it finds a suspected misspelled word, the Spellchecker stops and the Spelling dialog box appears (see Figure 12.2), often showing a list of suggestions for the misspelled word in the Suggestions list. A progress indicator at the bottom of the screen gives you a relative idea of how much of your document has been checked already.

Figure 12.2
The Spelling dialog provides a number of options for dealing with misspelling that, with a few exceptions, are fairly self-explanatory.

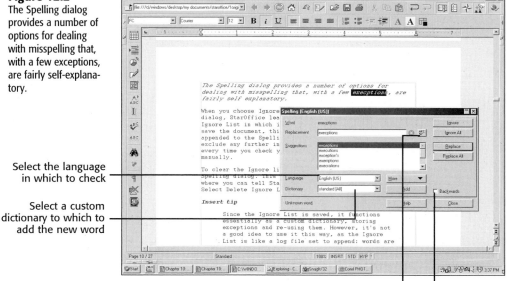

Select the language in which to check

Select a custom dictionary to which to add the new word

Select if you want to check toward the beginning of the document

Toggle suggestions on/off

The Spelling dialog provides a number of options for dealing with the suspected misspelled word, most of these are fairly self-explanatory and nothing unusual. For example, if one of the suggestions is the desired spelling, click it and select Replace (to replace the selected word) or Replace All (to replace all other instances of this word). If you know the unrecognized word is spelled correctly, select Add to include it in a custom dictionary of your choice. Close cancels the spelling check operation.

When you choose Ignore and Ignore All in the Spelling dialog, StarOffice leaves the word as is; in the case of Ignore All, the program also creates an Ignore List in which it stores these exceptions. When you save the document, this list is saved along with it and appended to the Spelling command. This list will be used to exclude any further instances of the word from spellchecking every time you check your document—until you clear the list manually.

To clear the Ignore list, choose More, Options from the Spelling dialog. This opens the Spelling Settings dialog where you can tell StarWriter what to check or ignore. Select Delete Ignore List, and confirm.

Tip #237 from
Michael & Sarah

Since the Ignore List is saved, it functions essentially as a custom dictionary, storing exceptions and re-using them. However, it's not a good idea to use it this way because the Ignore List is like a log file set to append: Words are continually added to the list, making it longer and longer as time goes by. The longer the list, the more exceptions must be checked and the longer your spellchecks will take. It's best to use the Ignore List to save only short-term exceptions (say, for example, an abbreviation of a project name), and store words of more durable use in custom dictionaries.

Choosing More also enables you to access the AutoCorrect command and the Thesaurus.

You can also manually change the word in the Replacement box and then press the Spell Word button to the right to verify the spelling or show a new list of replacement suggestions. When the word is spelled correctly, the round red icon next to the Replacement box changes into a green one with a white check mark, indicating that the word is spelled correctly. (Notice the Status area at the bottom of the Spelling dialog, it will also tell you if you spelled the word correctly.) You can now proceed with your spelling changes, adding the word to your custom dictionary and/or using the Replace or Replace All buttons.

Tip #238 from
Michael & Sarah

If you replaced the word in the Replacement box with a word from the list of suggestions, or if you manually changed the word, you can easily restore the original word by double-clicking the word in the gray area above the Replacement box. It reflects the spelling of the original word before you made any changes.

Tip #239 from
Michael & Sarah

If you want StarWriter to also check spelling in tables, headers, footers, and text boxes, turn on the Check Special Regions option in the Check Spelling portion of the Tools, Options, General, Spelling/Language dialog.

ADDING UNKNOWN WORDS TO A CUSTOM DICTIONARY

Wouldn't it be nice if you could add all correctly spelled unknown words at once to a selected dictionary? Well, you actually can. All you have to do is assign the proper command to a keyboard shortcut or icon on the function bar. Here's what you need to do:

1. Open any text document.
2. Select Tools, Configure to open the Configuration dialog.
3. If you want to create a keyboard shortcut, click the Keyboard tab.
4. In the Category box on the bottom left, select Options; in the Command box to the right, select Add Unknown Words.
5. If you want to create an icon for your function bar, select the Toolbars tab and click the Customize button. In the Customize Toolbars dialog, select Options from the Category list on the left and Add Unknown Words from the Command list to the right.
6. Select an available keyboard shortcut in the Keyboard box (for example, F6), and click the Assign button.
7. If you want to create an icon, click the Icon button on the Customize Toolbars dialog and select an icon of your choice in the Customize Buttons dialog.
8. Click OK to close the Configuration dialog.

You can now add unknown words to a selected dictionary by pressing the respective shortcut key or clicking the proper icon. If you selected an icon, click OK. Then click and drag the icon from the Customize Toolbars dialog to the function bar (or any other toolbar), and close the dialog by clicking the Close button.

You can assign or create a dictionary for these words in the Custom Dictionaries portion of the Tools, Options, General, Spelling/Language dialog.

Caution

Be aware that pressing the shortcut key or clicking the icon will add all kinds of "unknown" words to your dictionary, including misspelled words. For this reason, only use this shortcut to add after running the spellchecker (Tools, Spelling, Check). The purpose of this command is to save you time adding correctly spelled yet unknown words to your custom dictionaries.

PART

II

CH

12

Note

Using these steps, you can also assign other keyboard shortcuts or icons to StarOffice commands. Go ahead and snoop around the Keyboard and Toolbars tab options. It's easy to adapt StarOffice to your way of working—even without macros (which are discussed in Chapters 37–39).

WORKING WITH CUSTOM DICTIONARIES

As mentioned before, StarWriter checks spelling against the main dictionary, which you cannot alter. If you would like to add a word to a dictionary so StarWriter can memorize it, you'll add it to a custom dictionary. You can add words to the already existing custom dictionaries—Standard and StarDiv, a short dictionary of computer and program-specific terms— or you can create dictionaries of your own.

Note

Don't let the name deceive you. The Standard dictionary does not actually contain all the entries of the standard dictionaries installed with the program. It's a custom dictionary that the considerate folks at StarDivision created for your own personal use. It remains empty until you add words to it. And if you decide to delete it, it re-creates itself each time you run the Spellchecker again.

Tip #240 from
Michael & Sarah

If you're bouncing back and forth between projects that involve their own lingo, such as legal documents or medical reports, consider creating and using a custom dictionary that is specific to the task at hand. Working with smaller custom dictionaries speeds up the spellchecking process as StarWriter spends less time searching a smaller dictionary than a large one that contains terms for many subjects.

CREATING CUSTOM DICTIONARIES

You can create or delete custom dictionaries from within the Spelling dialog (More, Options), or in the Custom Dictionaries portion of the Tools, Options, General, Spelling/Language dialog. Select the New Dictionary button to add a new custom dictionary (see Figure 12.3), select Edit to add or remove words from existing custom dictionaries, and select Delete to remove selected custom dictionaries from the list.

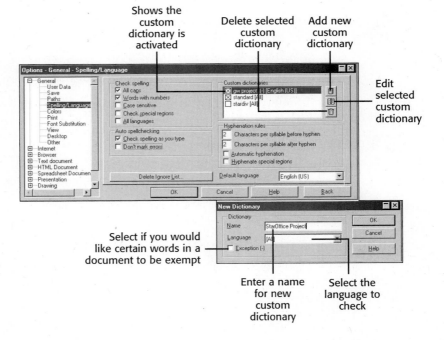

Figure 12.3
StarWriter makes it easy to create, edit, or delete custom dictionaries.

APPENDING CUSTOM DICTIONARIES TO LANGUAGES

When you create a new custom dictionary, you can choose to append it to all three installed dictionaries, a single installed dictionary, or two out of three installed dictionaries by clicking the Exception box and selecting the language you want to exclude.

A custom dictionary is used to check documents only when it is both turned on (as indicated by an X next to its name in the Custom Dictionaries box) *and* appended to the installed dictionary (or dictionaries) chosen to check that document. This gives you a lot of flexibility in handling spellchecks. For example, let's say you frequently write reports for your company's German office and use a number of specialized German technical terms that are not relevant to your English documents. You don't have to turn this custom dictionary on and off—just append it to the German dictionary only, and turn it on. It will only be checked when you have German selected as the language in the Spelling dialog.

The dictionaries to which your custom dictionary is appended are always noted in square brackets after its name.

You can change the dictionaries to which a custom dictionary is appended in the Custom Dictionaries Edit dialog box.

Generally, you will want to use the Standard custom dictionary to add words you commonly use across projects. Create separate custom dictionaries for specialized technical terms, foreign words, or other words that you're only likely to use on specific projects or in specific documents. This modular approach allows you to turn off dictionaries you don't need, which speeds up the spellchecking process.

Tip #241 from
Michael & Sarah

A useful tool for converting StarOffice custom dictionaries to conventional ASCII format (so you can edit your custom dictionaries as text documents) is available on the Internet at `http://www.wernerroth.de/staroffice` (this is for the most part a German-language site). Internet newsgroups report that it has been tested under Windows, and can be run in UNIX under Wine. Save a copy of your custom dictionary under a different name first, so you don't lose your dictionary if you encounter any problems.

In general, all dictionaries listed in the Custom Dictionaries section work in the same way: They are add-on text files that, if selected, StarOffice will check in addition to the installed program dictionaries. You can have as many custom dictionaries selected at one time as you like.

Note

Custom dictionary files are saved in the `Office51\wordbook` folder.

Tip #242 from
Michael & Sarah

Don't forget to include custom dictionaries in your regular back-up routines.

ACTIVATING AND DEACTIVATING CUSTOM DICTIONARIES

The more dictionaries StarWriter has to search, the longer it takes the program to react. If your documents cover a wide range of topics, it may make sense to keep separate custom dictionaries and only activate the ones you need. Select which custom dictionary you want activated by checking its box. You can activate or deactivate custom dictionaries from within the Spelling dialog, as shown in Figure 12.2, or in the Custom Dictionaries portion in the Tools, Options, General, Spelling/Language dialog.

Note

Unlike with Microsoft Word, there is no limit as to how many custom dictionaries can be activated simultaneously. However, remember that the more dictionaries StarWriter has to search, the longer it takes for the spellchecking operation to end.

SPELLCHECKING IN MULTIPLE LANGUAGES

Although StarOffice sets one language as the default, it's easy to check your work in multiple languages. Select the All Languages option in the Check Spelling portion of the Linguistic tab (Tools, Options, General), and StarOffice will use all three installed dictionaries when spellchecking.

Tip #243 from
Michael & Sarah

You can also change the language being used for checking a specific document by selecting it from the Language drop-down list in the Spelling dialog box.

Note

Some of the program menus—for example, the Language drop-down menu in the Spelling dialog box—give a longer list of available languages that reflect language options only available in the European editions of StarOffice (Danish, Finnish, German CH, Norwegian Bokmal, and Norwegian Nynorsk). Again, StarOffice can only check spelling of languages that are installed.

FINDING WORDS WITH THE THESAURUS

StarWriter's Thesaurus helps you find synonyms for selected words in your document and check their meaning. To use this proofing aid, you must first select a word. Then, open the Thesaurus by selecting Tools, Thesaurus, or press Ctrl+F7.

In the Word box of the Thesaurus dialog, you'll find the word that is to be replaced. The Meaning box underneath lists the various possible meanings of the selected word. Selecting a word in the Meanings list displays one or more synonyms in the Synonym box to the left. Select a synonym and it appears in the Replace box above. Click OK to accept the replacement, or click Search to find alternative meanings of the selected synonym.

Tip #244 from
Michael & Sarah

Do you feel like you're entering a linguistic labyrinth when using the Search option? Relax. Each time you click Search to expand your hunt for alternative meanings of a word, StarWriter enters the synonym you're searching in the drop-down list of the Word field. Click the down arrow next to the Word box to see a list of synonyms with the original word that started the search at the top.

If the word you're looking for is not part of the default language as specified in the General Options dialog, click Language to select another language for your current search. Note that the language Selection dialog lists all available languages in StarOffice, which is more than the languages you installed. For your search, however, you can only use installed languages.

The Thesaurus can be run independently from the Tools menu, or you can open it from within the Spelling dialog by selecting More, Thesaurus.

Tip #245 from
Michael & Sarah

You can also run the Thesaurus without first selecting a word. In that case, type the word you want to investigate in the Replace box of the Thesaurus. Then you can proceed hunting for the desired meaning by clicking the Search button.

USING HYPHENATION

Hyphenation refers to the process of hyphenating words in order to reduce the ragged appearance of a document's right margin (if left aligned) or the space between words to fill out a line (if justified).

StarWriter provides different ways to handle hyphenation. You can use hyphenation manually or automatically.

Automatic hyphenation is an attribute of paragraph formatting, which means you can turn hyphenation on or off when you create a paragraph style or make changes to an existing one. When automatic hyphenation is used, StarWriter makes its best guess as to where hyphenation should occur.

If you'd like more control over your hyphens, you have to place them manually. Manual hyphenation is more time-intensive, but it also enables you to hyphenate long words that otherwise would leave a huge space at the end of a line.

If you choose to hyphenate as you type, you can choose one of two types of hyphens: optional and non-breaking. Optional hyphens appear only if the word is at the end of a line and automatic hyphenation is turned on. To insert an optional hyphen, press Ctrl+-.

If you want to exclude a word permanently from hyphenation, you have to enter it into a custom dictionary followed by the equals sign (=). If you only want to exclude a certain occurrence of that word from hyphenation, you have to select the word and select None in the Language portion of the Font, Character dialog.

Using the Hyphenation command in the Tools menu, you can start the hyphenation operation for the current document. The Hyphenation dialog walks you word by word and hyphen by hyphen through all instances of possible hyphenation, enabling you to confirm the desired location for each hyphen or whether to leave the word without hyphens.

UNDERSTANDING DICTIONARIES IN STAROFFICE

Technically speaking, from StarOffice's point of view, dictionaries are language modules. Each module includes three .dat files—one for hyphenation, one for spelling, and one for synonyms (thesaurus)—that are identified by country code and type (for example, 01_hyph.dat, 01_spell.dat, or 01_thes.dat). For convenience sake, we'll refer to these files collectively as *dictionaries*.

In the United States, StarOffice 5.0 ships with nine available dictionaries out of the box, including U.S. English (01), U.K. English (44), German (49), French (33), Portuguese (351), Spanish (34), Dutch (31), Italian (39), Swedish (46). During the install process, you have the option to install three out of these nine available dictionaries. If you chose the default installation, your dictionaries would include U.S. English, U.K. English, and German.

Why only three? Under the terms of StarDivision's license agreement with the company that provides the dictionaries, you may only have three dictionaries in use at any one time. Therefore, the program only allows you to install three (out of nine possible) language modules and prevents the install from proceeding if you attempt to select more.

INSTALLING NEW DICTIONARIES

If you need access to a dictionary (or language) that was not installed but is available, you have to run StarOffice Setup again.

Note

The setup file is located in the StarOffice root directory (...\Office51). Windows users can also select Start, Programs, StarOffice, StarOffice Setup to rerun the installer. If you're installing it off a network, the setup file is located on your server.

Note

The setup file is located in the StarOffice bin directory (.../Office51/bin). Run the setup script from within X Window by typing ./setup at a shell prompt. If you installed the program as a network installation, the setup script is located on the server or the directory to which you installed the program files as admin.

Follow these steps to install additional dictionaries:

1. Run StarOffice Setup, either from the Programs menu (Windows) or from the directory (Linux).

2. Select Modify at the install screen. Note that Modify can install new components and uninstall existing ones. You may be asked for the original download location of StarOffice or the StarOffice CD, so have your file(s) or program CD ready.

3. Open (click +) the Optional Components branch, and then the Language Modules list.

4. Select the language you would like to install. If you already have three languages installed, you must first deselect a language module you can do without before you can select a new one.

Caution

Be careful not to deselect anything else. If you select an item and a red X appears next to its name, this item will be uninstalled from StarOffice.

5. Select Next, and follow the instructions of the installer program. The new selection of dictionaries will be available the next time you reboot your system and start up StarOffice.

Tip #246 from
Michael & Sarah

If you plan to switch back to your original dictionaries, you don't have to run StarOffice Setup again. Back up your current set of dictionaries from the StarOffice root directory before installing new ones first. (As mentioned before, dictionary files are .dat files and are identified by country code and type.) Since StarOffice only looks for the country code and dictionary type, you can switch them on-the-fly. Just make sure you never have more than three dictionaries installed at one time.

PREVIEWING DOCUMENTS

StarWriter enables you to see what your document will look like on paper before you actually print it, using the Page View/Print Preview command (File, Page View/Print Preview). Think of all the trees you can save by catching glaring layout problems or missing headers and footers and page numbers *before* looking at the printouts.

Note that you cannot edit documents in Page view, nor can you make any changes to the margins, headers, footers, or other aspects of the document. Hence the number of tools and commands you have at your disposal in Page View/Print Preview is comparatively small, but sufficient. Almost all menu commands are grayed out. All that you are left with, apart from the Function bar (if it is on), are the Page View object bar and context menu, both of which are virtually identical in the choices they offer with one exception that we're going to tell you about in the next section.

MAKING SENSE OF THE PAGE VIEW OBJECT BAR

As soon as you select the Page View/Print Preview command, StarWriter opens a new task and Page view will open to the page on which you currently have your cursor (see Figure 12.4).

Figure 12.4
Page view shows the document onscreen as it will be printed.

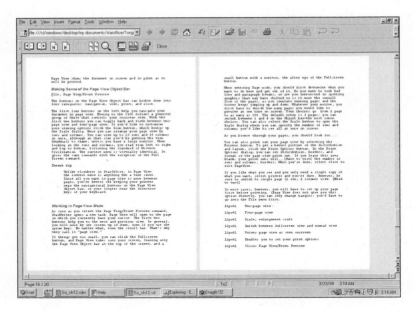

Above the viewing area, you'll notice the Page View object bar. The buttons on the Page View object bar can be broken down into four categories: Navigation, View, Print, and Close. Click the appropriate button to perform a task as outlined in Table 12.2.

TABLE 12.2   THE PAGE VIEW OBJECT BAR BUTTONS

Click This Icon…	If You Want To…
	Move to previous page view
	Move to next page view
	Move to beginning of page view
	Move to end of page view
	Show two-page view
	Show four-page view
	Scale or customize your view by rows and columns; you can view up to 10 rows and 20 columns at once
	Switch between Full-screen view and Normal view
	Print page view as seen onscreen
	Enables you to set your print options
Close	Closes Page View/Print Preview

WORKING IN PAGE VIEW MODE

When entering Page view, you should first determine what you want to accomplish. Do you want to look for bad line and paragraph breaks, object locations or graphics that may have shifted, or text that doesn't wrap around objects and graphics? Depending on what you're looking for, you might have to scale your page view session, meaning that you have to decide how many document pages you would like to preview at one time onscreen. You can look at one document page at a time, or you can look at two (default), four, or as many as 200 (which becomes more like a thumbnail view then). Page view "thinks" in rows and columns. Clicking the Scale button opens the Scale dialog where you can specify the number of rows and columns you'd like to see all at once onscreen.

When looking at the rows and columns of document pages, you read from left to right and top to bottom. The first page of your document will always appear "indented" by one page from the left in Two-page view or any larger print preview. That's because your first page is a right-hand (uneven-numbered) page, and Page view tries to present you with a layout that shows potentially facing pages so you can see what your document would look like if you decided to print it as a brochure, for example. To move between views, you can use the navigation buttons on the Page View object bar or the direction keys on your keyboard.

Tip #247 from
Michael & Sarah

Unlike elsewhere in StarOffice, in Page view the context menu is anything but a time saver. Although the context menu is virtually identical to the Page View object bar (with the exception of the Full Screen command), you're better off keeping your pointer near the navigational buttons on the Page View object bar or your fingers near the direction keys of your keyboard. After all, all you want in Page view is to move between pages.

In general, you will move by one screen up or down, even if you use the arrow keys or scrollbar. That's why they call it Page view.

If things get too small onscreen, click the Fullscreen button, and Page view takes over your screen and desktop, leaving only the Page View object bar at the top of the screen, and a small button with a monitor (the alter ego of the Fullscreen button) that you can press to return to Normal view.

You can also print your Page view by selecting the Printer button. To get a better picture of the distribution and layout, click the Print Options button. In the Print Options dialog, you can set distribution, borders, spacing, and format of the Page view print out.

If you notice anything in your document that should not be there, or if you notice that something is missing that should be there, return to your original document.

PART

II

CH

12

Tip #248 from
Michael & Sarah

You don't have to exit Page view if you're not done yet. Just click the Task button of your document and you return to it while leaving Page view open.

When you're finished previewing your document, you can either exit Page view by selecting Close on the Page View object bar (or deselecting Page View/Print Preview on the File menu). Or, if you like what you see and you only need a single copy of what you want, select the Printer button and you can print out one copy. Page view will print exactly what you see onscreen. That is, if you look at two pages at once, Page view will squeeze two document pages onto one printed page. If you would like to have one document page per printed page, be sure to select File, Print or press the Print icon on the function bar. Clicking the Print button on the Desktop function bar prints the document using the default options in the Print dialog box.

PRINTING TEXT DOCUMENTS

Any word processor lets you print a document, but with StarWriter you can choose whether you want to print all or only selected pages of a document; multiple copies of a document; include your graphics, tables,graphics, drawings, control fields, backgrounds, or notes in the printed output; print to paper or file; or use a third-party fax driver to fax the document.

You can print documents by selecting File, Print from the menu bar or by pressing Ctrl+P. Figure 12.5 gives you an at-a-glance view of your print options in StarWriter.

Figure 12.5
Any word processor lets you print a docu-ment, but StarWriter gives you more.

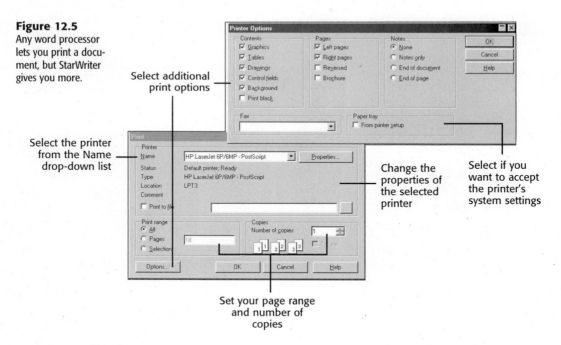

Select additional print options

Select the printer from the Name drop-down list

Change the properties of the selected printer

Select if you want to accept the printer's system settings

Set your page range and number of copies

When you print from StarWriter, you generally use the default set up in your operating system.

Note

> You must have a printer driver installed for StarWriter to be capable of printing to paper to a printer of your choice. Otherwise, StarWriter cannot access the available fonts on your system and format the pages according to your specifications.

The available options in the Print dialog include the following:

- **Printer**—Enables you to choose the default printer that you want to use by selecting it from the list of possible candidates. After making a selection, StarWriter provides you with the name and status of the printer. If you don't see your printer listed here, you first need to install it. If you select Properties, you can change the properties of the selected printer. Any changes here will be in effect for all future documents printed.

Note

> The Print dialog box also contains four comment fields underneath the Name list box that cannot be changed in this dialog: Status indicates if the selected printer is ready; Type lists the selected printer driver (in case you gave your printer a different name); Location indicates the printer port; and Comment lists any commentary you or the manufacturer included in the driver's Properties dialog.

- **Print to File**—Prints the document to a file on disk so you can take it to another computer or service bureau. To use this option, you must have a postscript printer driver installed and selected in the Printer Name drop-down list. (For more details on printing to file, see Postscripting with StarWriter in Chapter 11, Desktop Publishing with StarOffice.) As soon as you click the Print to File option, StarWriter opens the Save As dialog, where you can enter a name and extension (typically .ps) for your postscript file.

- **Page Range**—Enables you to select which portions of the document should be printed. All prints the entire document; Pages prints selected pages; and Selection Only prints selected text. Remember you can also select non-consecutive text when in additive mode.

→ For more details, **see** "Editing and Selecting Text," **p. 243.**

PART
II
CH
12

Tip #249 from
Michael & Sarah

> To print single, non-continuous pages, separate page numbers by a semicolon (;). To print a range of pages, enter the first page number followed by a hyphen (-) and the last page number. For example, 3;7;10-15;23 will cause pages 3, 7, 10 through 15, and 23 to print. If you select 4- StarWriter will print the document starting at page 4.

- **Copies**—Enables you to enter the number of copies that you want to have printed. If you print more than one copy of a document, you can also select the Collate option. When you collate copies, StarWriter prints the entire document all the way through for as many times as you've specified by the entry in the Copies box. Without the Collate option on, StarWriter would first print all needed copies of page 1, and then page 2, and so on.

- **Options**—Enables you to select what to print and what not to print in your document:
  - **Options Contents**—Controls whether you want to print the graphics, tables, graphics, drawings, control fields, or backgrounds in your document, or if the document should be printed in black (even if it is connected to a color printer).
  - **Options Pages**—Controls whether you want to print both left and right pages, reverse the print order, or print the document as a brochure.
  - **Options Notes**—Controls whether you want to exclude notes from printing, or print notes only; print the document first, then the notes (End of document option); or have the notes show up at the end of each page (End of page option).
  - **Options Fax**—Lists every installed printer and fax driver; you can choose the desired driver (just like in the Printer Name list).

Note

The Print Options dialog is identical to the Tools, Options, Text Documents, Print dialog.

Tip #250 from
Michael & Sarah

With StarWriter, you can also show several document pages on one printed page. Go to Page view and select Two-page or One-page view, or specify your desired view by entering a number of rows and columns in the Scale dialog. (Press the Scale button to open the dialog). When you select Print on the object bar, you'll get as many document pages per printed page as you see onscreen. Select Print Options to change the distribution of your document pages and orientation of your printout.

PRINTING A BROCHURE

StarWriter enables you to print your document as a brochure, which means you'll get two document pages on each side of the printed page in Landscape format. (Note that with most printers, you will have to turn the pages manually.) You can then fold and staple the printed pages and use them like a booklet.

Note

Unfortunately, the current version of StarOffice does not stop for turning the pages when printing a brochure. You can still use this option when selecting Right Pages, Left Pages, and Brochure in the Pages portion of the Print Options dialog. When StarOffice is done printing, you have to collect the pages and place the blank (back) pages facing each other; use the pages in the order in which they were printed.

To print your document as a brochure, follow these steps:

1. Open the Print dialog (File, Print) and select Properties.
2. Change the paper orientation to Landscape and click OK. (Note that, depending on how you set up your document or brochure, this step may not be necessary.)

3. Select Options in the Pages section, and select Brochure. If you have a duplex printer, you can also select Left pages and Right pages, and start printing.

4. If you don't have a duplex printer, select Left Pages and Brochure, select OK to close the Options dialog, and then choose OK again to print. StarWriter will print all left-hand (even numbered) pages. When finished, you then have to feed the printed pages upside down to the printer again.

5. Open the Print dialog again, select Right pages and Brochure in the Pages options, and start printing. StarWriter will now print the right-hand (uneven-numbered) pages. When finished, you can fold the pages along the middle.

Tip #251 from
Michael & Sarah

It's best to run a test on this option first because so much depends on your printer. For example, if your printer outputs paper with the printed side down, you may have to select the Reversed option in the Print Options dialog so that the proper front (right-hand) pages are printed on the proper back (left-hand) pages. In any case, take note of how you have to feed your printer in order to turn the pages out as desired. And don't forget to turn off the Brochure option when you're done printing, so that none of your other print jobs will be affected.

Tip #252 from
Michael & Sarah

When printing brochures, StarWriter reduces the overall size of your document proportionally to fit pages next to each other. For this reason, you should use a font size that is still readable at a reduced size.

PRINTING ENVELOPES

StarWriter also has an Envelope Printing feature that enables you to print envelopes. To print an envelope, follow these steps:

1. Open a new text document and select Insert, Envelope from the menu bar. This opens the Envelope dialog box.

2. Using the Envelope tab, you can enter the recipient by hand or by adding the desired fields from the Database field drop-down box (see Figure 12.6). Transfer fields via the left arrow button, insert spaces and punctuation between fields as necessary using the cursor and your keyboard, and press Enter to start on a new line. Fields will be entered at the insertion point. Note that StarWriter by default enters the name stored under User Data in the General Options dialog as the Sender.

3. If you want to change the size of the envelope or change the position of the sender's and recipient's address, select the Format tab and make the desired changes (see Figure 12.7). Click the Edit buttons to edit the character and or paragraph styles of the recipient and sender address information.

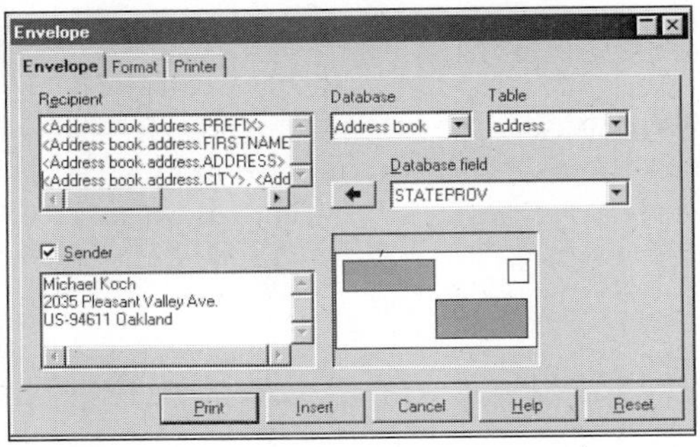

Figure 12.6
Enter the envelope's recipient from the database.

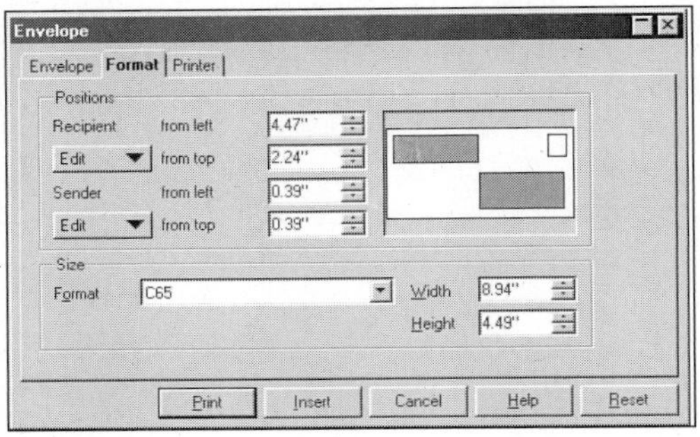

Figure 12.7
Change the format of the envelope with the Format tab.

4. Using the Printer tab, you can control the way envelopes are printed (see Figure 12.8). You can choose either a horizontal or a vertical feed method and select whether the envelopes are printed from top (face up) or bottom (face down).

Figure 12.8
Using StarWriter's envelope-printing features makes printing envelopes easy.

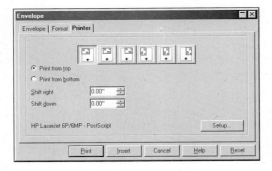

5. Select New Doc to insert the envelope into a new text document or Insert to insert it into the current document. The Beamer opens the address database, and your envelope will be inserted into a new or current text document, complete with the recipient's address (as text or database fields, depending on your input earlier). Since it is a normal text document, you can now format it as you like. For example, you can select the text boxes of the sender and recipient information and move them if necessary, or you can refine the character and paragraph formatting of the sender's and recipient's addresses.

Note

StarWriter automatically opens the default Address Book. If you would like to use a different Address Book, you must first create a new database and register it. For more details **see** "Introducing the Address Book" in Chapter 4, "Working in StarOffice."

6. Select the records you want to merge by (Shift- or Ctrl-) clicking the respective row headers in the database in the Beamer.

7. Next, select File, Mail Merge. In the Mail Merge dialog, you can select if you want to print all or only the selected records. You will also be given the option to merge to printer, email, or file.

→ For more information on the mail merge **see** "Creating Form Letters with Mail-Merge," **p. 360**.

→ For information on sending mass emailings with mail merge, **see** "Creating Mail Merges with StarMail," **p. 1062**.

Note

If you select to print to file, you can generate the filename from a database field of your choice, or you can enter a filename manually. In either case, you will be asked to save your original template first, before StarWriter generates on file per record.

Tip #253 from
Michael & Sarah

If you're only printing an envelope for one addressee, you can insert the contact information by using the new Address Book. Just select Edit Address Book to find the name of the recipient, and click the Update Fields button to replace the existing placeholder with the contact information.

8. Select OK. (Don't forget that you have to place the envelopes according to your printer's specifications on the respective printer tray first!)

Tip #254 from
Michael & Sarah

If you don't want to go through this series of steps each time you want to print an envelope, save the document as a template. You can then easily create an envelope document whenever you want.

PRINTING LABELS

Printing single address labels or entire sheets of labels follows basically the same overall steps as printing envelopes:

1. First, select Insert, Labels from the menu bar.

2. Using the Labels tab, enter the desired text or the name of the recipient (or use database fields) and select the proper format for your label.

3. In the Format portion of the Labels tab, select a predefined label format from the Brand list of manufacturers, and whether you feed a continuous roll of labels or sheets.

4. On the Format tab, you can define a custom label by specifying the exact format and position of the labels on the page.

5. On the Options tab, you can determine whether to print an entire page or sheet or only a single label. Using this tab, you can also adjust the printer setup if necessary. If you make a mistake during your labels setup, click Reset in the Labels dialog. This reverses any changes you make back to the default values when you started the application.

6. When finished, click the New Document button to create a new document named Labels1. If you want, you can edit and add to the label inscriptions. This document can be saved and printed.

7. Again, StarWriter opens the Address Book in the Beamer. Select the desired records. You can use the old standby Ctrl+click and Shift+click to make multiple selections. Just click in the header row (the little gray box on the left) next to contact(s) you want to include., Then select File, Mail Merge to print the labels. In the Mail Merge dialog, you can specify which data to merge (All or only Selected Records). Click OK.

→ To learn more advanced methods of filtering and querying your Address Book, refer to "Manipulating Table Contents," **p. 1156**. (Chapter 33, Working with Data in Tables), and "Creating a New Query with AutoPilot," **p. 1205**.

Note

The filtering and sorting tools used in the Address Book are the same as those in StarCalc.

FAXING YOUR DOCUMENTS

If you have a fax modem—and assuming you have installed the fax services and driver that come with your operating system or comparable faxing software—you can fax any document by printing it. Just choose the name of your fax software driver in the Name drop-down list of the Print dialog. As soon as you click OK, the dialog of your fax software driver opens, enabling you to enter the name and phone number of the recipient.

If you want to send a fax at a mouse click, you need to add a Fax icon to the function bar. Follow these steps:

Note

These steps assume that you have a fax modem as well as the fax services and driver that come with your operating system or comparable faxing software installed.

1. Open a text document using the familiar File, New, Text Document or Start, Text Document command.

2. Right-click the function bar and select Visible Buttons, and from the submenu that opens, select Print Fax. StarOffice adds the Print Fax icon to your function bar, right next to the Print icon. If you click the icon, you get the message: "No fax printer is configured under Tools/Options/Printing." In order to be able to fax, you first have to identify a fax driver for StarOffice.

3. Choose Tools, Options, Text Document, Print, and select the desired third-party Fax driver from the Fax drop-down menu.

4. Click OK.

You can now use the Fax button for sending faxes from within StarWriter. Clicking the Send Fax icon opens the dialog of your fax software, where you can enter the name and fax number of the recipient.

TROUBLESHOOTING

When printing, how can I make the current page option the default?

The setting to print only the current page applies to the current print job and cannot be applied globally.

How do I print more than one page of labels? I've selected a hundred records but still only one page of labels gets printed.

To print multiple pages you must use the File, Mail Merge command rather than the regular File, Print command. Once you've created a labels document with the fields from a database, click New Document in the Labels dialog. The first page of labels will be set up. From the Database Beamer (press F4), select those records you want to print and click the Mail Merge icon in the Beamer object bar. This dialog starts printing the labels documents with multiple pages. For more details on the Mail Merge function see Chapter 9, "Working with Tables, Charts, and Fields."

When I print, graphics don't appear, even though I can see them on screen.

To print graphics in text documents, choose Tools, Options, Text Documents, Print and select Graphics and Drawings in the Contents area of the Options, Text Documents, Print dialog. If your graphics still don't print, right-click the graphic(s) that don't print and choose Pictures from the context menu to open the Pictures dialog. Make sure Print is selected in the Options portion of the Options tab.

I'd like to print sideways (in landscape format). What settings do I need to change for this?

If you want to print a document in landscape format, open the Stylist (press F11, click the Stylist button on the function bar, or select Format, Stylist) and click the Page Styles icon. The current page style is highlighted. With the right mouse button, click this style and select Modify from the context menu to open the Page Styles dialog. Click the Page tab and select the Landscape option. Click OK. All pages formatted with this style will now print sideways. However, be aware that this also causes your text to reflow and your objects to reposition.

Can I print pages in reverse order in StarOffice?

Yes. If you want to print pages in reverse order once for the current document, choose File, Print to open the Print dialog and click the Option button. In the Print Options dialog that appears, select Reversed in the Pages portion of the dialog.

If you would like to set this option as a default, select Tools, Options, Text Document, Print and mark the Reversed option in the identical looking Pages portion of the Options, Text Document, Print dialog.

PART III

WORKING WITH SPREADSHEETS— STARCALC

CHAPTER 13

CREATING SPREADSHEETS

In this chapter

ORIENTING YOURSELF IN STARCALC

StarCalc offers everything users have come to expect from spreadsheet programs, including a huge number of built-in functions, tools for managing lists and databases, sophisticated formatting options, and filters for opening and saving the most popular spreadsheet and database formats. It also has a few tricks up its sleeve that reflect the StarOffice philosophy "do everything in one place."

→ For a discussion of using spreadsheets versus using relational databases and tables for keeping lists or databases, **see** "Why Create Databases with StarCalc?" **p. 620**.

The StarOffice samples include some creative uses for spreadsheets, including a biorhythm chart and a handy universal converter for American and metric measurements.

This chapter introduces you to the StarCalc workspace and the basics of creating spreadsheets in StarCalc. Experienced spreadsheet users should already be familiar with most of the introductory concepts presented here, but may benefit from skimming the chapter. Although StarCalc has many similarities to Excel and other spreadsheet programs, some of its features work in unexpected ways. (For example, AutoFill is set by default to create trend series, not to copy numbers, as in Excel.) Users new to both StarOffice and spreadsheets should read this chapter thoroughly.

When you open a new spreadsheet document with the File, New command, you see a clean worksheet with numbered rows and lettered columns, called [Untitled1], like the one shown in Figure 13.1. By default, a new spreadsheet has three worksheets, but you can add your own, up to a total of 256.

THE STRUCTURE OF A SPREADSHEET

As noted earlier, by default, a new StarCalc spreadsheet contains three *worksheets*. Each worksheet is composed of 32,000 rows and 256 columns. Rows are numbered from 1 to 32,000. Columns are designated with letters, beginning with A through Z, and continuing with AA through AZ, all the way through IV. These rows and columns define cells, which are displayed with gray borders. Data is stored in cells. To enter data, you click a cell and type. This system of labeling rows and columns enables each cell to have a unique *cell address*, or, as it is also called, *cell reference*.

The other two worksheets are visible only by their tabs. To move to another worksheet, simply click its tab. After you add additional worksheets, the set of buttons in the lower-left corner become active. These buttons enable you to navigate quickly from one end of the spreadsheet to another.

Tip #255 from
Michael & Sarah

Don't add more worksheets than you really need. The larger your spreadsheet, the longer it takes to open and the more system memory it occupies.

Sheet and named range area field   Select all   Column   Active cell

Figure 13.1
A spreadsheet is made up of columns, rows, cells, and worksheets. You can turn on and off the display of gridlines in the Tools, Options, Spreadsheet, Layout dialog box.

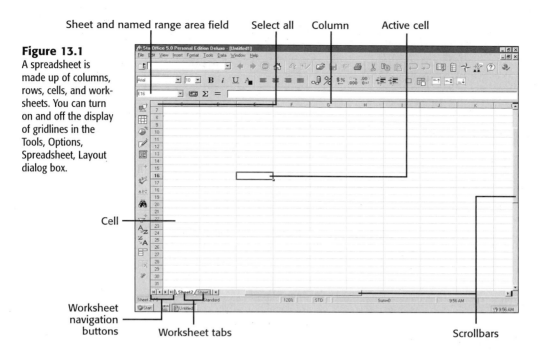

Cell

Worksheet navigation buttons

Worksheet tabs

Scrollbars

Worksheets are the basic working unit of the spreadsheet. Although they visually resemble pages of an accounting ledger, they're dynamic in ways that real pages aren't. You can link data from one part of your worksheet to another (or even from one worksheet or spreadsheet to another) with formulas and functions so that changing a number in one area automatically changes the results somewhere else.

Tip #256 from
Michael & Sarah

You can link separate spreadsheets together either with links or StarBasic buttons and scripts. For example, see the spreadsheets Movie1, Movie2, and Movie3 in the Explorer, Samples folder.

PART
III

CH
13

Two keys to making the most of this dynamic power are understanding cell addresses and learning navigational shortcuts, which are discussed in the following sections.

→ For details on navigational shortcuts in StarCalc, **see** "Navigating in StarCalc," **p. 500**.

UNDERSTANDING CELL ADDRESSES

Each cell has a unique cell reference defined by the combination of its column letter and row number. For example, Figure 13.1 shows cell E16 selected.

The selected cell's outline appears in bold, as do the row number 16 and column label E. The address also appears in the Sheet area to the far left on the Formula bar. This Sheet area also stores any named cell ranges you create.

→ For information on created cell ranges, **see** "Naming Cell Ranges for Faster Navigation," **p. 501**

Cell addresses become critically important when you begin to write formulas and work with functions, as you almost always need to refer to a cell or group of cells in a formula or function. Incorrectly entered cell references are one of the most common sources of errors in spreadsheets.

THE STARCALC WINDOW AND CONTEXT MENUS

The StarCalc window should look familiar to users of other spreadsheet programs, although it has a few unique elements as well. The main elements are identified in Figure 13.2.

Note

This figure also performs a feat that you can't, which is to show the most important StarCalc context menus all at once. When you're working, you can only have one context menu open at a time.

Column

Figure 13.2
The StarCalc context menus include a Sheet Area shortcut menu that enables you to cut and paste cell range names and cell addresses.

Row

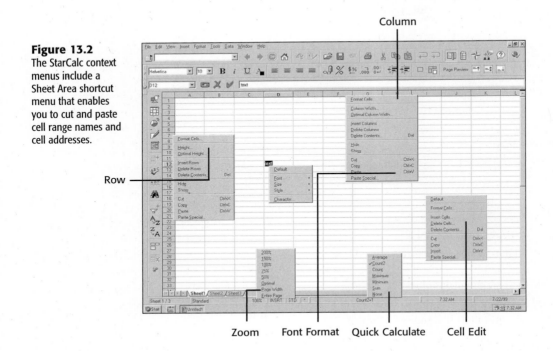

Zoom   Font Format   Quick Calculate   Cell Edit

The Cell Edit and Font Format context menus can be opened from anywhere within a worksheet area, if you have either a cell or its contents selected, respectively. The others can only be opened when your cursor is placed in the relevant area. In Figure 13.2, the Zoom, QuickCalculate, and Sheet Area context menus are placed near the areas you need to right-click. The Toolbar menu can be opened from any of the toolbars (not just the one illustrated) by clicking an empty area of the toolbar.

Tip #257 from	By turning your toolbars off, you can gain extra visibility, which can be helpful when you're
Michael & Sarah	working on a large data area or are entering data in a form and using in-cell editing.

The following sections give you a quick tour of StarCalc's tools.

THE SPREADSHEET OBJECT BAR

The Spreadsheet object bar, shown in Figure 13.3, contains buttons for the most commonly used formatting commands.

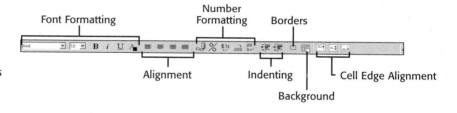

Figure 13.3
Although the object bar is common across StarOffice applications, in StarCalc it displays some tools that are unique to working with spreadsheets, such as the Number Formatting and Cell Edge Alignment tools.

Most of the buttons on the left half of the bar are probably familiar to you. On the far left is a Font drop-down menu that displays the currently applied font. Moving right, you see the Font Size drop-down menu and the Bold, Italic, and Underline buttons. Next to the Underline button is the Cell Font Color button, which opens a color palette, enabling you to apply font colors with a single click. The next four buttons set the overall alignment for cell contents (left aligned, center, right aligned, or justified). The group of five buttons in the middle of the object bar allow for quick number formatting, and from left to right display the cell contents in currency format, percentage format, standard number format, add one decimal place, and subtract one decimal place. Next to the Number Format tools are the Decrease Indent and Increase Indent tools, which increase and decrease the indents of cell contents according to the number entered in the Format, Cells, Alignment tab.

PART
III
Ch
13

Tip #258 from
Michael & Sarah

Unlike in a regular text document, you can indent cell contents until they're no longer visible in your cell. If this occurs, a small red arrow indicates that the cell has invisible contents. Click the cell, and its contents appear in the Formula bar; double-click, and its contents display to the right of the cell (reflecting the number of spaces it has been indented).

You might not immediately recognize the five buttons on the far right. The Borders button opens a floating Borders toolbar that enables you to select and apply a border style for your currently selected cell or range. The Background button opens a floating Background color palette toolbar and enables you to select and apply a background color to your currently selected cell or range. As shown in Figure 13.4, you can keep both of these floating toolbars open as you work.

Note

To apply a background color or graphic to the entire worksheet, use the Format, Page command.

Figure 13.4
You can speed up formatting by keeping the Borders and Background floating toolbars open on your workspace.

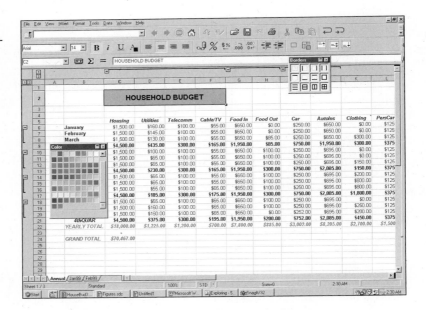

The Cell Edge Alignment buttons enable you to align your cell contents to the upper or lower edge of the cell, or to center the contents vertically.

Note

When you insert graphics or other objects into your spreadsheet, the object bar changes and displays tools relevant to manipulating the object at hand. You can click the arrow button that appears at the right of the object bar to bring the Spreadsheet object bar back into view.

THE FORMULA BAR

Unlike the other toolbars, the Formula bar (shown in Figure 13.5) is unique to StarCalc. (The Text Formula bar in StarWriter look similar but has limited functionality.)

Sheet area   Sum Function   Input field

Figure 13.5
The Formula bar is the most important toolbar in StarCalc. It contains the input field for creating and editing formulas and offers timesaving navigation and formula entry shortcuts.

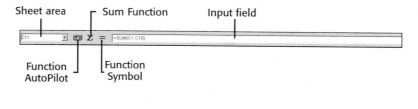

Function AutoPilot   Function Symbol

When you type data in a cell, it appears in the Formula bar Input Line, where you can see and edit it more easily. In the standard mode, data is not entered in your cell until you press Enter.

→ For more information on entering data, **see** "Entering Data," **p. 508**.

→ For more information on editing modes and editing data, **see** "Editing and Deleting Cells and Cell Contents," **p. 530**.

The Formula bar also has buttons for the Function AutoPilot, Sum, and the function symbol that must appear at the beginning of all formulas (just as in Excel, StarCalc begins formulas with an =).

On the far left of the Formula bar is the Sheet Area text box, which lists the address of the active cell and has a drop-down list with all named cell ranges (known in StarOffice as named areas). After you have created named ranges, you can click a named range on this list to jump to its location. You can also quickly jump to any single cell location by typing its cell address here and pressing Enter.

THE MAIN TOOLBAR

Just like the Object bar, the Main toolbar (shown in Figure 13.6) has a number of tools common across StarOffice applications as well as a few that are specific to StarCalc.

The top buttons on the Main toolbar open floating toolbars that you can keep open on your desktop as you work. The button that you see on the bar initially is the default tool. When you start using tools, this button changes to represent the last tool you selected. You activate the visible button with a click, and you open the complete toolbar with an extended-click.

Table 13.1 summarizes the contents of each of these floating toolbars and lists the default tools.

Figure 13.6
Clicking the top five buttons opens floating tools palettes—including one for inserting new cells, columns, and rows—that you can move anywhere on your desktop. The Grouping, Sorting, and Filtering tools on the lower part of the bar are particularly useful for working with spreadsheets.

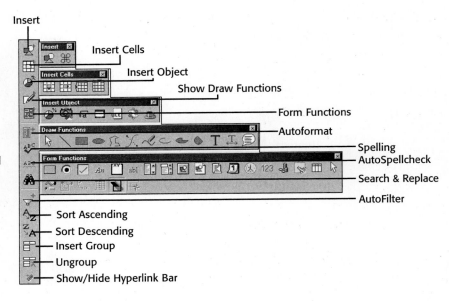

Insert

Insert Cells

Insert Object

Show Draw Functions

Form Functions

Autoformat

Spelling

AutoSpellcheck

Search & Replace

AutoFilter

Sort Ascending

Sort Descending

Insert Group

Ungroup

Show/Hide Hyperlink Bar

TABLE 13.1. STARCALC'S FLOATING TOOLBAR BUTTONS

Click This	And the Result Is This	Default Tool
▣	Opens floating toolbar for inserting graphics and special symbols.	Insert
▦	Opens floating toolbar for inserting rows, columns, and individual cells.	Insert Cells
◓	Opens floating toolbar for inserting charts, new StarImage objects, StarMath formulas, floating Web page frames, OLE objects, plug-ins, and Java applets.	Insert Chart
✎	Opens Form Functions floating toolbar with complete set of tools for building database forms.	Form Functions

Note

Although you'll find some of the same tool sets available on the Main toolbars of other application workspaces, the specific offerings on a tool set may differ.

The remaining buttons toggle specific commands or functions on and off. Table 13.2 summarizes the purposes of these buttons.

TABLE 13.2. STARCALC'S MAIN TOOLBAR TOGGLE BUTTONS

Click This	And the Result Is This
	Turns the AutoFormat feature on or off.
	Opens the Spelling dialog box.
	Automatically checks spelling and underlines spelling errors as you type.
	Opens a dialog with search and replace options.
	Turns the AutoFilter function on or off.
	Sorts selected rows, columns, or cells in ascending order.
	Sorts selected rows, columns, or cells in descending order.
	Groups selected cells.
	When applied to any one cell of a defined group, ungroups the cells.
	Turns the Hyperlink toolbar on or off.

THE STATUS BAR

Figure 13.7 identifies elements of the status bar, located at the bottom of the worksheet. The status bar gives valuable summary information about your worksheet and currently selected cell. It also, unexpectedly, contains a number of shortcuts and fly-away menus that can really speed up your work. The Date option is not turned on in the status bar shown in the figure, but the field marked as Date is where the date displays if you do.

From the left, the status bar lists your current sheet location out of the total number of sheets in the workbook, the name of the page style attached to that worksheet, and your current zoom setting. Double-clicking the page style field opens the Format, Page dialog box, where you can make a range of changes to your worksheet's format and get access to your catalog of styles. If you have multiple page styles, right-clicking moves you through the list of available styles so you can change the page's attached style. Double-clicking the Zoom area opens the Zoom dialog box, and right-clicking opens a Zoom shortcut menu.

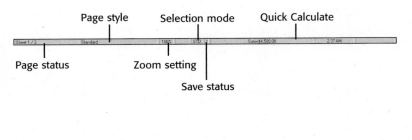

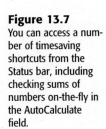

Figure 13.7
You can access a number of timesaving shortcuts from the Status bar, including checking sums of numbers on-the-fly in the AutoCalculate field.

Tip #259 from
Michael & Sarah

You can customize your status bar, including adding current data and time fields, by selecting Tools, Configure, and then choosing the Status Bar tab.

CHANGING DATA INSERTION AND SELECTION MODES

Next to the zoom setting on the status bar are two areas that display current insert and selection modes. The area on the left indicates whether you are in overwrite or insert modes in your cell. (You will only see these modes displayed when you are doing in-cell editing; this field appears blank otherwise.) The area on the right toggles between the three cell selection modes. Details of the three modes are listed in Table 13.3.

TABLE 13.3. SELECTION MODES IN STARCALC

Display	Mode	When This Mode Is Turned On...
STD	Standard	Clicking a cell clears previous selections. Dragging selects all cells included in the defined area.
EXT	Extended Selection	Clicking or dragging selects an extended area. If you click one cell in STD mode, move to a distant cell, select EXT mode, and click the second cell, the entire range is selected. Use for quick selection of large, contiguous cell ranges.
ADD	Additive Selection	Clicking a cell adds to your previous selection. Use to select noncontiguous cells.

→ For more information on selecting cells and data, **see** "Selecting Cells and Ranges," **p. 505**.

If you have made changes to your worksheet that have not yet been saved, the Save field in the Status bar displays an asterisk.

You can adjust the width of the fields by grabbing and dragging their borders.

Tip #260 from
Michael & Sarah

Changes you make to the status bar are saved with your document, so you can customize it for each individual document.

CALCULATING ON-THE-FLY

On the far right of the status bar is what we call the QuickCalculate field, which calculates on-the-fly using selected functions on the context menu. By default, QuickCalculate is set to display sums on-the-fly. To change the function applied, right-click in the QuickCalculate field, and make a selection. The available functions are Sum, Average, Count, Count2, Minimum, Maximum, and None.

To do a quick calculation, select a range of cells. The calculation instantly appears in the QuickCalculate field.

THE SCROLLBARS

The StarCalc scrollbars (shown in Figure 13.8) function like those in many other programs and don't offer any hidden tricks or shortcuts. Clicking the up, down, left, and right arrows, respectively, moves you one row up or down, and one column left or right in your worksheet. Clicking the scrollboxes moves you more quickly in the selected direction.

You can quickly and easily select large ranges of cells by using your cursor selection tools and scroll bars together. For example, click the uppermost cell in your range, then scroll to the lowermost cell and Shift+click to select the entire range.

Figure 13.8
The scrollbars allow for speedy navigation. A pop-up box displays the letter of the leftmost column or number of the topmost row to help keep you oriented.

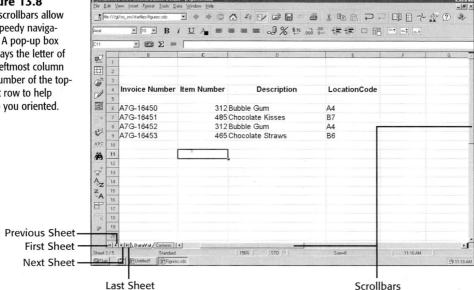

Previous Sheet
First Sheet
Next Sheet
Last Sheet
Scrollbars

NAVIGATING IN STARCALC

Spreadsheets are useful because they can contain large amounts of data. However, that also makes them difficult to navigate as well as to conceptualize, because you can't take in everything at a glance.

You can work much more efficiently in StarCalc if you learn some basic keyboard and mouse shortcuts for moving within and between worksheets. You can also benefit greatly from learning to use the Navigator, StarOffice's unique and handy "shuttle craft" for zooming around and keeping track of many different kinds of objects, including named data areas. And linking areas, worksheets, and spreadsheets together with hyperlinks (created with both the Hyperlink bar and the Navigator) can help you remember relationships between data in different locations as well as jump around quickly.

MOVING AROUND WITH KEY COMBINATIONS

Besides the obvious key functions such as the left, right, up, and down arrow keys, there are a small number of keyboard shortcuts listed in Table 13.4 that can really speed your work. The Ctrl+arrow shortcuts are particularly handy, as you can quickly move from data block to data block in your worksheet, even if your data blocks are spread far apart, and you end up in the best position for adding data to your column or row.

→ For a complete list of keyboard shortcuts in StarOffice, **see** Appendix D, Keyboard Shortcuts in StarOffice, **p. 1413**.

TABLE 13.4. KEYBOARD NAVIGATION SHORTCUTS

Pressing These Keys	Moves You Here
Ctrl+Home	Cell A1 (beginning cell) of worksheet.
Ctrl+End	Bottom-right-corner cell in your worksheet where you have data or that marks an intersection of columns and rows with data.
Ctrl+left arrow	First or last column in a row's data block, moving to the left (otherwise, to column A).
Ctrl+right arrow	First or last column in a row's data block, moving to the right (otherwise, to column IV).
Ctrl+up arrow	First or last row of the closest block, moving upward (otherwise, to row 1).
Ctrl+down arrow	First or last row of the current block or to the next block, moving downward (otherwise, to row 32,000).
Ctrl+Page Down	Next sheet.
Ctrl+Page Up	Previous sheet.
Tab	One cell to the right.
Shift+Tab	One cell to the left.

Pressing Home returns you to Column A in your current row, and pressing End takes you to the last column in which you have data in your current row. (If you have not yet entered any data, pressing End has no effect.) Page Up moves you one screen up, and Page Down one screen down.

Tip #261 from	To see a complete list of keyboard assignments in StarCalc, open the Tools, Configure dia-
Michael & Sarah	log and click the Keyboard tab. You can use this tab to edit and delete existing assignments as well as add your own.

MOVING AROUND WITH CELL ADDRESSES

Another way of quickly moving around in your worksheet is to type a cell address into the Sheet Area field and press Enter. This method has its limitations with complex spreadsheets, however, as it's hard for most people to remember cell references such as C12354. A better way is to name cell ranges.

NAMING CELL RANGES FOR FASTER NAVIGATION

You can give a name to any group of selected cells (whether they are contiguous or not) by using the Insert, Names, Define command (Ctrl+F3). You can assign the existing name of column, header, or footer to a range by using the Insert, Names, Create command.

After you've named a range—which StarCalc calls a *named area*—its name appears in a drop-down list in the Sheet area. It also appears in the Navigator (see Figure 13.9).

Figure 13.9
Both the Navigator and the Sheet Area drop-down list provide speedy selection and navigation to named ranges of cells. The Navigator also enables you to copy data and objects from one spreadsheet to another via drag and drop.

Sheet Area drop-down list

To quickly jump to the range, click on the down arrow to open the Sheet area drop-down list and click its name, or open the Area Names display in the Navigator and double-click its name.

Tip #262 from
Michael & Sarah

You can keep the Navigator open but reduce it to a small floating window by clicking the Hide/Show button to the right of the Row spin box. Alternatively, you can dock it to your desktop and hide and reveal it as you like using the Hide/Show arrow icon on its border.

Naming cell ranges after the kind of data they contain can help users get a better conceptual grasp of the spreadsheet as well as speed navigation. For example, on a spreadsheet tracking sales data, you might select and name ranges for SalesJan99, SalesFeb99, SalesMar99, and so on.

To create a list of all named ranges and their cell addresses, first position your cursor in a blank area of a worksheet. Be sure there's enough room to paste the entire list. Then, choose the Insert, Names, Paste command and choose Paste List from the Paste dialog box. All your ranges and their references are inserted as text, not as references.

MOVING AMONG WORKSHEETS

The simplest way to move between worksheets is to click their tabs. You can drag the border between the scrollbar area and the tab display to make hidden tabs display.

When you have a large number of worksheets, this method becomes inefficient. Besides the Ctrl+Page Up and Ctrl+Page Down shortcuts (which move you from worksheet to worksheet), you can also use the Navigator, which tracks sheet names (see Figure 13.9), and the Sheet Navigation buttons to the left of the worksheet tabs.

JUMPING AROUND WITH NAVIGATOR

The Navigator, which you can open by pressing F5, is one of StarOffice's most useful and unique features.

Besides tracking area names and worksheets, as already discussed, you can use Navigator to track database areas, linked areas, pictures, OLE objects, and notes. As you can see in Figure 13.10, when you have an object of one of those types in your spreadsheet, a small plus or minus sign appears in a box to the left of the object name. You can click this sign to open or close the list of objects. Click the name of an object to jump directly to the object. You can also jump to any cell by typing its cell address in the the column and row spin boxes and pressing Enter.

For navigation, it functions much like the Go To command in Excel, but you can see all your objects at once. However, it does much more than enable speedy navigation—it can also help with data selection and entry, as well as copying, linking, and hyperlinking data.

→ For more information on using the Navigator for data entry, **see** "Guarding Against Entry Errors," **p. 522**.

Tip #263 from *Michael & Sarah*	The Navigator actually makes it easier to work between two different spreadsheets in StarOffice than to work in one. By default, the objects that appear in the Navigator are those of your active spreadsheet. However, when you have multiple spreadsheets open, you can have the Navigator display the objects in a non-active, open spreadsheet by clicking its name in the drop-down menu at the bottom of the Navigator window. You can also drag a closed spreadsheet file from the Beamer into the Navigator to list its contents in the Navigator. You can then jump to the other open worksheet by clicking a worksheet name (or other object) in the Navigator list. You can also drag and drop data from the Navigator into the active spreadsheet.

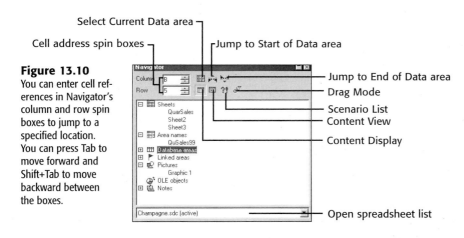

Figure 13.10
You can enter cell references in Navigator's column and row spin boxes to jump to a specified location. You can press Tab to move forward and Shift+Tab to move backward between the boxes.

 There are two additional navigational aids on the title bar: the Start of Data Area and End of Data Area buttons. Clicking one of these takes you to the beginning or end of your data block, as defined by your current cursor position.

LINKING WORKSHEETS AND SPREADSHEETS WITH HYPERLINKS

Using the Navigator and the Hyperlink toolbar, you can create hyperlinks between worksheets and even separate spreadsheets that enable you to jump directly from one to the other.

To insert a hyperlink from an area of a worksheet to an object or area listed in Navigator, first click the Drag Mode button in the Navigator title bar and select Insert as Hyperlink from the Drag Mode menu (shown in Figure 13.11).

Figure 13.11
With the Drag Mode menu, you can set drag and drop options from the Navigator.

Then, select the object you want to hyperlink and drag it where you want the hyperlink to appear. Notice that your pointer changes appearance when it moves outside the Navigator window—it now displays a small plus symbol.

 The hyperlink is highlighted in gray and written in blue to distinguish it from worksheet data. Click it, and you're where you want to be!

Tip #264 from
Michael & Sarah

If you're creating a spreadsheet that others use, hyperlinks are a simple way to guide their navigation and ensure that they're entering or analyzing data in the right order and location. You can also insert text instructions along with the hyperlinks.

Note

If you select Link mode, dragging and dropping inserts your selected range or object as a DDE link.

Tip #265 from
Michael & Sarah

To delete a hyperlink, don't try to select the contents. Click the cell and press Delete, or choose Delete from the cell context menu.

You can insert hyperlinks to objects in other spreadsheets in the same way. First, make sure the other spreadsheet is open. Then, select its name from the drop-down menu of open tasks at the bottom of the Navigator. All its objects then appear in the Navigator window. Now, select, drag, and drop the name of the object you want to jump to.

To insert a hyperlink to an entire spreadsheet, turn on the hyperlink bar by clicking the Hyperlink Bar icon in the Main toolbar. Position the cursor in the cell where you want to insert the hyperlink. Then, type the spreadsheet's complete pathname into the hyperlink bar's URL field and press Enter.

 Note that clicking a hyperlink to another spreadsheet or one of its objects has a slightly different effect than clicking a hyperlink within a single spreadsheet: It prompts you with a dialog that asks if you want to close the current task and open the linked document, or open the linked document as a new task.

SELECTING CELLS AND RANGES

Before you can enter, edit, or modify the contents of cells, you must select the cell or cells you want to change. A single selected cell is called the *active cell*, and multiple selected cells are called a *range* or *area*.

Many of the navigational aids and techniques described in the section "Navigating in StarCalc" earlier in this chapter can help you quickly select large blocks of data.

SELECTING CELLS

When selecting cells, you can select the cell's contents, the cell, or both.

Tip #266 from *Michael & Sarah*	You get a different context menu depending on whether you select a cell or its contents. If a cell is selected, right-clicking opens the cell editing and formatting context menu. If the cell contents are selected, right-clicking opens the character formatting context menu.

To select a cell, click it, and it is outlined in black. If it's empty, you can immediately begin typing to enter data. If the cell already contains data and you begin to type, all existing data is replaced by your new data.

To enter the cell to modify its contents (without deleting the contents), select the cell contents by double-clicking. An *I-beam* cursor appears, to mark your current insertion point. You can move this I-beam by using the arrow keys. Anything you type is added to the cell from your current insertion point.

Triple-clicking selects the cell contents (but not the entire cell). If you being to type, the selected text is replaced by your new entry.

Pressing Shift while clicking selects both the cell and its contents; the cell is outlined in black with an inner white border, and the cell is highlighted in black.

SELECTING CELL RANGES

The simplest way of selecting a range of cells is to click the cell that marks the beginning of the range and then drag the mouse. However, when you want to select larger blocks of data, sometimes other methods are more efficient.

Table 13.5 lists the most useful keyboard shortcuts for selecting cell ranges. They're easy to remember because they conform with shortcuts in other StarOffice applications. Generally, you use the Shift key in combination with other keys or mouse actions to select a range by clicking the first and last items in the range; you use the Ctrl key in combination with other key or mouse actions to select non-contiguous cells, rows, columns, or areas.

TABLE 13.5. SHORTCUTS FOR SELECTING CELL RANGES

Pressing This	Selects from the Active Cell to This
Shift+arrow key	Next cell selected (additive)
Shift+Ctrl+arrow key	End of data block
Shift+Ctrl+End	End of worksheet data areas
Shift+Ctrl+Home	Beginning of worksheet (cell A1)
Shift+Home	Beginning of row (does not recognize hyperlinks)
Shift+End	End of row (does not recognize hyperlinks)
Shift+Page Up	Cell in same column, one window up
Shift+Page Down	Cell in same column, one window down

Reversing the action described in Table 13.5 deselects selected cell(s) or ranges.

SELECTION MODES IN STARCALC

As you learned earlier in the chapter, there are three selection modes in StarCalc: Standard mode (STD), which is the default, Extended Selection mode (EXT), and Additive mode (ADD). You can move between these modes by clicking the Mode Status field of the status bar until the name of the mode you want is visible.

As its name suggests, Extended Selection mode lets you extend your selection quickly. Click to place your cursor at the start point of your selection. Then, turn on Extended Selection mode. Now, click in the cell that defines the endpoint of your block. Everything in between the two cells is selected. If you want to continue your selection further in the same direction, just continue to click; if you shift to another direction and click, the selected block pivots around your original cursor point accordingly.

Tip #267 from
Michael & Sarah

Using Shift+click is similar to working in Extended mode.

In Additive mode, you can select noncontiguous cells or blocks of cells. However, it's a little tricky to make your first selection because turning on Additive mode is not enough. First, either drag to select two cells (they become highlighted in black), or press Shift+Ctrl while selecting the first cell. After that, you can add selections by either dragging or clicking without pressing any keys.

Tip #268 from
Michael & Sarah

You can use Selection mode combined with the scrollbox to select a large area more easily and accurately than with dragging. (It saves wear and tear on your wrists, as well.) First, click the Selection Mode area of the status bar until EXT appears. Then, click to select the first cell of your range. Finally, move the scrollbox to the last cell in your desired range, and click to select. Voilà!

To turn off Extended Selection or Additive modes, click until STD appears on the status bar again. Clicking anywhere in the worksheet in Standard mode then deselects any selections made in Extended Selection or Additive modes.

SELECTING ROWS AND COLUMNS

To select an entire row or column, you can click its row or column header. You can also select the row or column that contains your active cell by pressing Shift+spacebar (to select the entire row) or Ctrl+spacebar (to select the entire column).

To select a contiguous block of rows or columns, click the first in the block, and then press Shift and click the last in the block. To select a noncontiguous block, press Ctrl while clicking the headers of all the rows and/or columns you want to select.

SELECTING NAMED, DATABASE, AND LINKED AREAS

When you have defined your own named areas or database areas in a spreadsheet, you can simultaneously jump to an area's location and select the area by double-clicking its name in Navigator.

You can jump to and select a named area by clicking its name in the drop-down Sheet area as well, and you can jump to and select database areas by using the Data, Select Area command.

SELECTING A WORKSHEET'S CONTENTS

There are two easy ways to select an entire worksheet's contents. One is to click the Worksheet area button. Clicking this button immediately selects the entire worksheet, as shown in Figure 13.12. Another way to select an entire worksheet's contents is to right-click a worksheet's tab to open the worksheet context menu (shown open in 13.12) and select the Move/Copy command.

Caution

Be sure you've really clicked the tab and opened the correct menu. It's very easy to right-click the cell border of the cell just above the tab and open the cell context menu instead.

Figure 13.12
Clicking the Worksheet area button (to the upper left of cell A1) selects the entire worksheet contents. The worksheet context menu Move/Copy command enables you to simultaneously select a worksheet and copy or move it elsewhere.

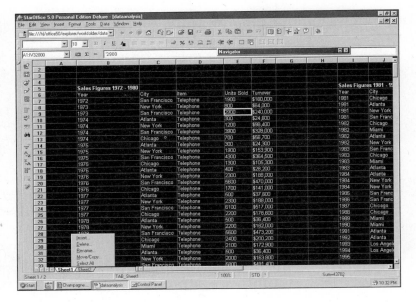

Canceling Selections

Pressing Shift+Backspace cancels your current selection in any selection mode. In Standard mode, you can also just click in another location on your worksheet. In Extended or Additive modes, you need to first change your selection mode back to Standard and then click.

Entering Data

In StarCalc, a cell can contain text, formulas and functions, or values. There are three types of values: numbers; date and time information; and the results of formulas and functions. (Formulas and functions operate on and generate values but are not themselves values.) Although you can enter the logical values TRUE and FALSE, they are not recognized as distinct types of data.

There are two modes of data entry: entering via the Formula bar input field and in-cell editing. The default mode is entering via the Formula bar.

Tip #269 from
Michael & Sarah

In-cell editing may be more convenient if you have the Formula bar turned off, or if you've designed a form or applied formatting that makes it easier to see and edit in the cell.

In-cell editing enables you to add data to existing data in a cell, and clicking and beginning to type in a cell in Formula bar mode automatically erases any existing data.

To enter data by using the Formula bar, click the cell and begin typing. Notice that your data appears simultaneously in the input field, and a red × and green check mark appear in place of the function symbol button. You can click the × to cancel your entry, or the check mark to accept it. Pressing Enter also accepts the input.

Tip #270 from
Michael & Sarah

You don't need to press Enter if you're entering a sequence of data. If you enter data in a cell and then press Tab to move one cell to the right, or press any of the arrow keys to move one cell over, the data is automatically entered.

Note

If you begin typing new data in a cell that overwrites existing data and then realize you've made an error, press Enter and immediately invoke the Undo command. If you do not press Enter first (even though you don't want to accept the new data), the program does not recover your previous data.

To turn on in-cell editing, press F2. If you've selected a cell that contains data, the cursor is placed at the end of the current data string. Enter data and press Enter to accept it, or press Esc to cancel your input.

Tip #271 from
Michael & Sarah

By default, pressing Enter moves you one cell down. You can change this default on the Tools, Options, Spreadsheet, Input tab.

You can enter up to 255 characters in a cell, which far exceeds the default width of the column. If the cells to the right of your active cell are empty, all your data displays. However, if the cells to the right contain data, a small red arrow appears in the active cell to indicate hidden text, and ### appears to indicate hidden numbers (see Figure 13.13). To widen the column to reveal hidden data, click one of its borders and drag, or double-click its right border to automatically size the column to fit your data.

Tip #272 from
Michael & Sarah

Double-clicking a cell with hidden data temporarily opens the cell for full view on your worksheet, covering (but not altering or deleting) data in adjacent cells.

ENTERING NUMBERS

Numbers are constant values containing any of the following characters:

> 1 2 3 4 5 6 7 8 9 0 _ + / . E e

You can enter numbers as integers (whole numbers, such as 245), as decimals (23.45), as fractions (35 1/4), or in scientific notation (3.79E+7). The default format for numbers is General, which displays numbers as integers. However, if you enter numbers with notations or symbols that indicate how they should be formatted, in many cases StarCalc automatically changes the cell's formatting as appropriate. For example, if you type $500.25, StarCalc automatically changes the cell's number format to Currency.

Figure 13.13
Cells can contain much more than may be visible on your worksheet at one time, but their full contents always display in the Formula bar input field.

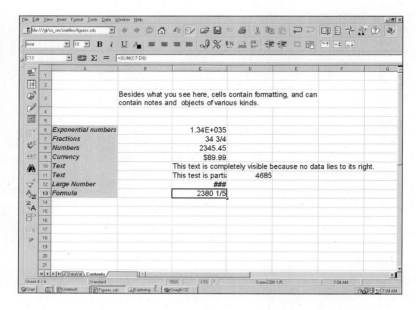

Tip #273 from
Michael & Sarah

To quickly format a number in scientific notation, place your cursor in its cell and press Shift+Ctrl+2.

The default number of decimal places is two. If you enter a number with more decimals, only the leading two numbers display, but the entire number has been stored (as you can see if you select the cell and look at the input field on the Formula bar).

To change the number formatting, right-click in the worksheet to open the context menu and select Format Cells.

→ For more information on formatting, **see** "Formatting Cells," **p. 559**.

Tip #274 from
Michael & Sarah

If you enter a number with 17 or more zeros at the end, StarCalc automatically converts the number into scientific notation.

To enter improper fractions, type the integer, a space, and the fraction. If you're entering fractions that aren't preceded by a whole number, you must enter a 0 and a space, and then the fraction. Otherwise, StarCalc interprets it as a date.

ENTERING TEXT

Text can include alphabetic characters, numbers, and symbols. To enter text, click in a cell, type the text, and press Enter or click the check box next to the formula bar input line.

If you enter numbers together with text (in a street address, for example), StarCalc automatically recognizes the numbers as text. If you enter numbers by themselves and want them to be stored as text, you must first preface them with a single quotation mark, as in the following example:

    '1499

Note

If you select a cell with numbers entered as text and choose Format, Cells, notice that the cell is still formatted as Number, General. Don't be fooled! This is the default format for all cells and recognizes text. Such entries are not treated as numbers for calculation purposes, nor do number formats affect their appearance, although you can change their format in any other way. If you want the number to appear in a different number format—for example, if you want to add leading zeros—you must manually edit the entry.

Numbers formatted as text automatically appear left-aligned so that they stand out from regular numbers (which by default align on the right).

If you right-align text items that could be confused with numbers (for example, dates or numbers you have entered as text), it's a good idea to turn on value highlighting (by choosing Ctrl+F8) so you can still visually distinguish between the two.

→ For details on applying value highlighting, **see** "Using Value Highligting," **p. 514**.

You can use all the usual functions to edit text. If you type text in cell A1 and press Return, the text is entered in cell A1, and the cursor automatically jumps to cell A2. The cell cursor always selects the active cell, in which you can make entries and changes.

If you enter text that exceeds the current column width, a small red arrow appears at the right of the cell.

Tip #275 from
Michael & Sarah

You can turn off the text overflow arrow by selecting Tools, Options, Spreadsheet, Contents dialog deselecting the Text flow option. This does not affect the appearance of text in the cell.

ENTERING DATES AND TIMES

StarCalc recognizes numbers entered in the mm/dd/yy format as dates, and all numbers entered with colons as separators (hh:mm:ss format) as times.

You'll know your date or time has been recognized correctly it is right-aligned in the cell. If it is left-aligned, StarCalc has entered it as text.

Caution

> If you enter a date in an unrecognized format and then format the cell as a date, StarCalc still does not recognize it as a date. If you want dates to have a different format, first enter them in the mm/dd/yy format and then apply your desired date formatting to their cells.

Internally StarCalc converts dates and times to serial numbers so it can make calculations involving dates and times. The serial number for dates is calculated from the base date 12/30/1899 (which is given the value 0). Time is recorded as a decimal fraction of a 24-hour day. However, StarCalc displays the date and/or time onscreen according to the date and time formats that have been applied to the cell after you have entered it in mm/dd/yy format.

Note

> StarCalc is Y2K compliant in its date handling and works with four-digit years. (Years you enter in two-digit abbreviations are converted internally into four-digit years, based on settings you enter in the Tools, Options, General, Other dialog box.

→ For more information about formatting dates and times, **see** "Formatting Cells," **p. 559**.

Tip #276 from
Michael & Sarah

> Numbers recognized as dates display in the Formula bar in mm/dd/yy format even though they appear in their cells with different formatting.

ENTERING FORMULAS

Entering formulas in StarCalc is similar to doing so in Excel: You select a cell or click the Formula bar input field and insert an =. Then, you can enter values, cell references, named areas, operators, and functions. You press Enter or click the green check mark on the Formula bar to accept the formula, or press Esc or click the red × to cancel it.

For more information on working with formulas and functions in StarCalc, see Chapter 16, "Using Formulas and Functions."

For quick and easy entry of functions, you can use the Function AutoPilot, which you open by clicking the Function AutoPilot button on the Formula bar. The AutoPilot contains all of StarCalc's functions, organized by category, including matrix, statistical, and logical functions.

SPEEDING UP DATA ENTRY WITH AUTOCOMPLETE

Oftentimes, the data you enter in a spreadsheet is repetitive in nature. For example, say you're creating an inventory list that uses only five categories to classify your stock. StarCalc assists you with such data entry—and helps keep errors to a minimum—with AutoComplete. AutoComplete recognizes patterns of words and numbers that you enter, and if you're entering a familiar pattern, after you enter the first few characters, StarCalc automatically completes the entry for you, based on the pattern of your previous entries. If the entry is indeed correct, all you need to do is press Enter. If it's not what you want, just keep typing.

Caution

Although AutoComplete is clever, don't be too hasty in accepting its conclusions. If you're typing both South and Southwest, for example, AutoComplete might recognize only South as the pattern and you might end up entering South in places where you meant Southwest.

You can turn AutoComplete off by deselecting it in the Tools, Cell Contents submenu.

GETTING A BETTER VIEW

The large size and complexity of spreadsheets sometimes make it difficult to keep everything you need in view, or to keep a sense of the overall structure of your document. The Navigator is a powerful tool for keeping a larger overview, but there are some other basic ways of improving your spreadsheet's visibility on your desktop. The following sections explain some of the ways you can tame your spreadsheets.

→ For an introduction to the Navigator in StarCalc, **see** "Jumping Around with Navigator," **p. 502**.

FREEZING HEADER ROWS OR COLUMNS

If you're keeping any kind of list or lengthy record that has either row or column headers, at some point you'll want to keep those headers in view while you're entering data deep down on your worksheet.

One way to do that is by *freezing* the header rows or columns so that they remain in place while you scroll or navigate to your new data entry point (see Figure 13.14).

To freeze rows or columns, select the first row or column *after* the block you want to freeze and choose Window, Freeze. To unfreeze, select a cell anywhere in the frozen region and deselect the Freeze command.

If you select a cell rather than rows or columns, your window is divided into quarters, with columns to the left of the cell and rows to the top—all frozen.

SPLITTING YOUR WORKSHEET WINDOW

You can also split your worksheet window into sections by using the Split command, visible on the Window menu in Figure 13.14. You cannot have your window both split and frozen at the same time, however.

When split, the new top and/or lower-left portions of the window have their own scrollbars so you can navigate independently in those sections. To unsplit a window, deselect the Split command from the Window menu.

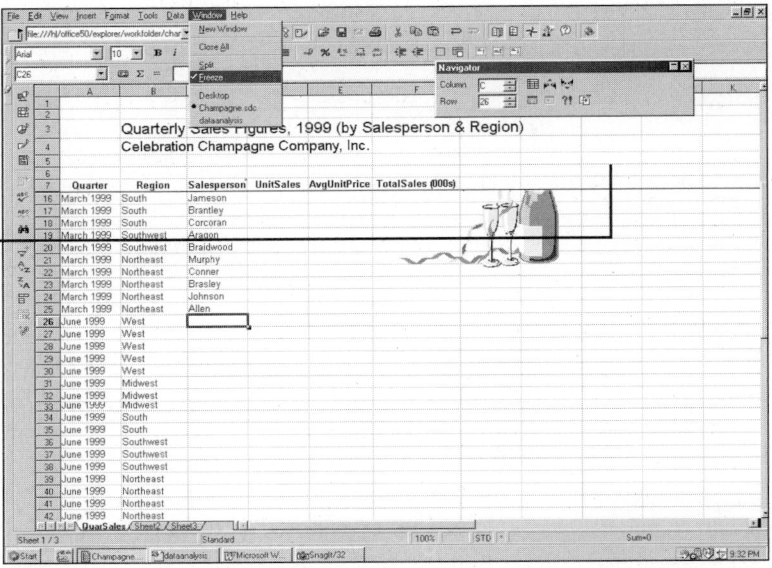

Figure 13.14
When you freeze a row or column, the last frozen row or column is bordered with a thin black line.

Frozen area

TURNING OFF COLUMN AND ROW HEADERS

If you want more onscreen display room for cells, or you are creating an onscreen form where you don't need these guides, you can turn off display of the column and row headers by selecting the View menu Column and Row Headers command. (You can also set this more lastingly using the Column/Row Headers option in the Tools, Options, SpreadsheetDocument, Layout dialog box. The column and row locations still display in pop-up notes as you scroll through your worksheet.

USING VALUE HIGHLIGHTING

By turning on value highlighting (by selecting Ctrl+F8), you can make results of formulas, numbers, dates and times, and text each display in a different color on your screen so that you can more easily distinguish cell contents. This option affects only your screen display, not printed output.

Caution

If you apply value highlighting, character color formatting you apply may not display correctly in Normal view, but only in Preview view.

You can turn on value highlighting globally for all spreadsheets, by choosing Tools, Options, Spreadsheet, and then selecting the Contents tab. Or you can turn it on for a specific document by choosing the Value Highlighting command in the View menu or pressing Ctrl+F8.

When value highlighting is on, results of formulas display in green, and numbers, dates, and times in blue. Text, which is not a value, remains in black.

USING OUTLINES

Maintaining an overview of your data is a constant challenge when working in spreadsheets. StarCalc's Outline command on the Data menu (Shift+O) can help you group your data onscreen so you can quickly view it in different ways. You can also use outlines to selectively hide and reveal groups of data and bring groups of data that are far apart, side-by-side for comparison.

Tip #277 from
Michael & Sarah

You can also create different views of your data using StarCalc's DataPilot. However, you can only temporarily add or alter data in a DataPilot table (known as a pivot table in Excel) so for some purposes, outlines may be more useful.

To create an outline, first select the data you want to group in the first section of the outline. You don't need to select an entire row or column; just select enough cells to mark off the number of rows or columns you want to group. Then, open the Data menu and choose the Outline command. A submenu appears like the one shown in Figure 13.15.

Click to hide or reveal all groups in your column or row

Figure 13.15
When you've grouped data with the Outline command, group controls appear on the left and/or top margins. You can hide or reveal the groups by clicking the plus or minus signs on the controls. Outline groups do not appear in the Navigator.

Click to hide a group

Click to reveal a group

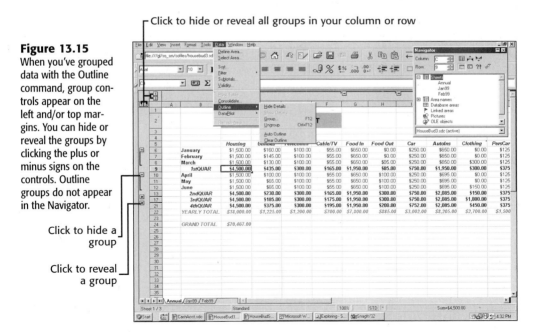

Choose Group (or press F12) to group the data. If you haven't selected an entire row or column, a dialog appears that prompts you to choose the grouping method. Select a method and click OK, and your data is grouped, with controls like those shown in Figure 13.15 on the left or top margin (depending on whether you choose to group by rows or columns, respectively). Click the small buttons marked 1 and 2 to close and open all groups in your row or column from view, or click the plus and minus signs on the control next to the group to hide or reveal that group only.

Tip #278 from *Michael & Sarah*	If you select a data area and choose Auto Outline, StarCalc groups it for you automatically.

The Hide Details and Reveal Details commands close and open selected groups, depending on where your cursor is currently located or what you have selected.

To ungroup data, place the cursor somewhere within the grouped area and either press Ctrl+F12 or choose the Ungroup command from the Data, Outline submenu.

Tip #279 from *Michael & Sarah*	When StarCalc calculates subtotals, it also creates the selected area in Outline view. However, the Subtotals command doesn't offer as much flexibility as outlines when it comes to grouping and sorting data; for example, it doesn't allow for the automatic creation of quarterly subtotals in the location shown in Figure 13.15.

Zooming In and Out

At 100% scale (which is the default), StarCalc's cells still can look pretty small onscreen. On the other hand, sometimes when you are charting data or creating a DataPilot table for analysis, you want a wider view than is normal.

Whether you want a closer view or a more distant one, you can use the Zoom command.

Tip #280 from *Michael & Sarah*	If you're visually challenged, you might find it useful to turn on the large tool icons on the StarOffice toolbars. Select Tools, Options, General, choose the View tab, and select Large Buttons. You can also increase the size of everything on your screen by increasing the Scaling ratio in the Tools, Options, General, View dialog box.

The quickest way to zoom is to right-click in the Zoom status field of your StarCalc status bar. The fly-away menu that appears lists the basic zoom options. If you want to set your own zoom scale, double-click in the same area, or choose View, Zoom to open the Zoom dialog box.

The Zoom scale you set becomes the default for all StarCalc spreadsheets you open until you change the Zoom scale again.

REPEATING AND UNDOING COMMANDS

It can be disturbing to sweat over entering data, and then apply a command that transforms your data into unrecognizable gobbledygook before your eyes. Because spreadsheets manipulate data in complex ways, sometimes, as they say, stuff happens. For those times, there is the Edit, Undo (Ctrl+Z) command. Learn this key combination. If you have any doubts about what's been done to your data, invoke Undo. The default number of undo steps is 20, but you can set this number anywhere from 0 to 100 in the Tools, Options, General, Save dialog

Note

The Undo command does not work until you've pressed Enter or clicked in a new location to complete your current action. If you know you've made an error before you complete your current action, press Esc instead of using Undo.

If you're fickle and change your mind again, you can use the Redo command, which undoes the effects of the Undo.

You'd think that the Repeat command would repeat your last action. This is only an approximation of what really happens in StarCalc, as Repeat works with only a limited set of commands. If you do a lot of routine, repetitive work such as adding columns or rows, or inputting repeating nonserial data, the Repeat command is useful and you might want to assign the command to a keyboard combination or function key. Otherwise, using it isn't really a timesaver over invoking the original command.

Tip #281 from
Michael & Sarah

To assign a command to a key, choose Tools, Configure, and then click the Keyboard tab. First, highlight the key you want to accept the assignment. Then, select the category to which the command you want to assign belongs. Browse through the category until you find the command, click to highlight it, and then click the Assign button (in the top-right corner of the tab).

→ For more information on customizing your keyboard, **see** "Customizing Desktop tools and Menus," **p. 115**.

Tip #282 from
Michael & Sarah

To find out what Repeat will actually repeat, after you've taken an action, open the Edit menu and look at the Repeat command. The action currently set to repeat displays.

PART

III

CH

13

CREATING DATA SERIES

There are three kinds of typical data entry in a spreadsheet: repeating text, dates, or numbers; trends or series of numbers that change in patterned increments; and unpatterned (though not necessarily random) data.

There isn't much that can be done about automating the input of unpatterned data. However, StarCalc has a number of fill commands for speeding data entry for the other two kinds of data.

Caution

Excel users, beware! The default setting for drag-and-drop Fill is to create a simple trend series, not to simply copy and paste data.

CREATING SIMPLE DATE AND NUMBER TREND SERIES

Nothing could be simpler than building a simple trend series in StarCalc: Just enter the first number or date in the series, select the cell, and drag the Fill handle in the lower-right corner (see Figure 13.16) in the desired direction, and your series appears. Note that your cursor changes into a cross as you grab the Fill handle.

Figure 13.16
Fill commands have different effects, depending on the type of data you're filling in.

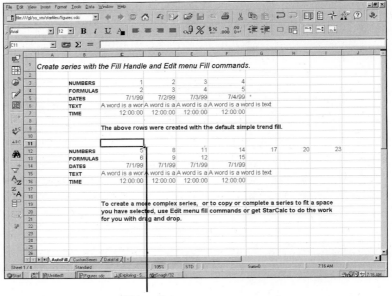

Fill handle

Fill is *directional*—that is, it increases numbers in the series if you drag to the right or down, and decreases them if you drag to the left or up.

Fill overwrites any existing cell data in cells after the first item in the series.

A few custom lists for English day and month series are included with StarCalc, so if you enter Mon (or Monday) and drag with the fill handle, the remaining days of the week are automatically completed in a repeating series. The same applies for month names.

If you want to create a series that increases (or decreases) in increments other than one, first you must enter at least two values in the series (depending on the pattern) and select those initial cells. (Be sure to select them by dragging across the middle of the cells—not the corner—or you activate Automatic Fill.) If you've selected cells properly, you can grab the automatic fill handle, and AutoCalc figures out the series pattern and complete it for you.

You can also select the initial cells and then choose the Edit, Fill, Series command. This opens the Fill Series floating dialog (see Figure 13.17).

Figure 13.17
You can extend your Fill options with Edit, Fill submenu commands and Fill Series dialog box options.

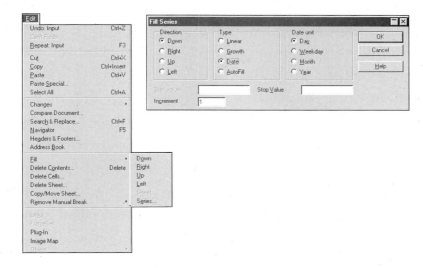

Select AutoFill and click OK to confirm and exit the dialog. Next, grab the fill handle at the end of the selected cell range and continue dragging in the desired direction. Your series is completed automatically.

> **Note**
> You must have at least two cells selected, or commands on the Fill submenu are not available.

CREATING GEOMETRIC GROWTH SERIES

To create a geometric growth series, select the range of cells you want filled. Then, select Edit, Fill, Series (which opens the dialog shown in Figure 13.17) and select Growth series. Enter the starting value in the Start value field. In the Increment field, enter the number by which you want the first value—and all subsequent values—multiplied. You can choose whether to enter a Stop Value. If you don't enter a stop value, only the cells you have selected are filled. If you enter a stop value, values continue to be generated and entered until your limit has been reached.

Caution

Be sure you don't have data in the way of a growth series because it will be overwritten.

CREATING COMPLEX DATE SERIES

By default, Fill is set to increment by one day per cell in a seven-day week. You can change this default in the dialog you get by selecting Edit, Fill, Series (refer to Figure 13.17) so that your series increases in five-day weeks, months, or years by increments you define in the Increments field. You can choose whether to set a Stop Value. If you don't choose a stop date, only the selected cells are changed, but you can drag the fill handle and continue the series after you click OK and exit the dialog.

COPYING WITH AUTOMATIC FILL

Besides aiding with number entry, Fill commands can also help automate the copying and pasting of numbers, dates, text, times, and formulas.

COPYING NUMBERS AND DATES WITH AUTOMATIC FILL

There are three ways to copy numbers and dates with fill. First, if you have at least two cells with the same data entered, you can select those cells using usual methods. Then grab the automatic fill handle and drag. Second, you can enter the value you want to copy into a single cell, and then select the range you want to fill with that value. Then, select Edit, Fill. Depending on whether you have selected rows or columns, or both, the appropriate Right, Left, Up, and Down commands are active (refer to Figure 13.17). Choose the direction in which you want your copies to be entered.

Third, you can copy a set of numbers by selecting the set and then pressing Ctrl while dragging the AutoFill handle.

COPYING TEXT AND TIMES WITH AUTOMATIC FILL

To copy text strings and times, select the cell with the desired data and drag the fill handle. You can also use the Left, Right, Up, and Down commands from the Edit, Fill menu.

COPYING FORMULAS WITH AUTOMATIC FILL

Using the Fill command to copy formulas has a different result using the Fill command with other types of data. If you use Fill commands to copy formulas with relative references, the cell references always shift by one column or row in the direction in which you are filling.

For example, if you copied the formula =SUM(A4:A5) from cell A1 into cells B1, C1, and D1 with Automatic Fill, the resulting formulas would be =SUM(B4:B5), =SUM(C4:C5), and =SUM(D4:D5), respectively. This feature makes copying formulas for reuse on other data sets extremely easy.

→ For discussion of relative versus absolute cell references, **see** "Referencing Cells in Formulas," **p. 593**.

If you don't want the cell references to change when using Fill commands, use an absolute reference.

CREATING AUTOMATIC FILL SERIES

You can also create your own custom text series that help speed entry of routine series such as names of subsidiary companies, names of employees, product categories, or budget categories.

One way to create your series is to choose Tools, Options, Spreadsheet to open the Spreadsheet Options dialog, and choose the Custom Lists tab (see Figure 13.18).

Figure 13.18
Creating your own custom lists doesn't just make data entry faster, but also prevents errors.

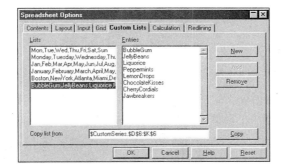

Choose New, and the Entries box becomes active, enabling you to type your list. When you start typing, the Add button becomes active and the New button turns into a Clear button. After you type a list, click Add to add it or Clear to remove the list and begin again. Now, whenever you want to enter your custom list, you can enter the first item and drag with the fill handle.

Another way to enter a custom list is to create the list on a worksheet, select the range, and then open the Spreadsheet Options dialog (refer to Figure 13.18). The Copy button is active. Choose it to add the entire list to the Entries box, and click OK to confirm the addition.

You can remove lists by highlighting the list name and choosing Remove.

Note

If you enter compound words with spaces (as in Figure 13.18), StarCalc automatically removes the spaces when saving the list because spaces can interfere with StarCalc's operations.

GUARDING AGAINST ENTRY ERRORS

Accurate data entry is critical in business and science. Data entry, unfortunately, is a tedious task for which the human animal is ill-designed.

StarCalc has a number of tools that help ensure that only the correct data is entered.

SETTING VALIDITY CRITERIA FOR CELLS

One of the most useful commands in guarding against entry errors is the Data, Validity command, which opens the Data Validation dialog box.

This command enables you to define the type of data that a cell will accept. You can also enter custom messages that offer help and deliver warning messages to the user, as well as automatically run a stop command to prevent an entry error.

First, select the range of text for which you want to set validity criteria. The Values tab enables you to determine both the type of value that can be entered and the range of permissible values. This includes limiting the length of text strings that can be entered. On the Input Help tab, you can enter and choose to display on-screen help when a user selects that cell.

By selecting options on the Error Alert tab, you can also choose to display an error message when a user tries to enter an incorrect value (see Figure 13.19), as well as invoke one of four actions: preventing the entry, displaying a warning, displaying information, or running a macro. In Figure 13.19, the Stop command has been applied.

Figure 13.19
In this example of data validation at work, users are given a customized error message to alert them that they cannot enter a number lower than 200. Erroneous data is cleared from the cell automatically after the user clicks OK.

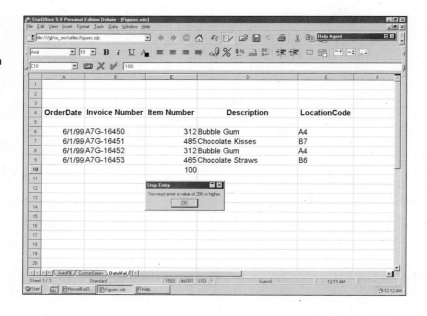

PROTECTING CELLS, SHEETS, AND DOCUMENTS

Another way of preventing entry errors is to protect cells, sheets, or documents so that only authorized users can make changes.

By default, all cells have cell protection enabled on the Format, Cells, Cell Protection tab. However, cell protection becomes active only when you have turned on protection for either a worksheet or the entire spreadsheet document.

To turn on protection, select Tools, Protect Document. Choose either the Sheet command or the Document command. A Protect Sheet or Protect Document dialog box appears, asking for a password; type a password and click OK. You are then asked to confirm the password and click OK again.

Now, anyone who tries to enter data in the protected cells receives an error message. No changes can be made until an authorized user selects a cell in the worksheet or selected range again, selects the appropriate command from the Tools, Protect Document menu, and types the password.

Tip #283 from
Michael & Sarah

The quickest way to protect a limited range of cells is as follows: Select the entire worksheet by clicking the blank box in the upper-left corner of the worksheet (at the intersection of your row and column headers). Then, select Format, Cells and deselect cell protection. This deselects cell protection for the entire worksheet. Click OK to exit. Now, select the range of cells you want to protect and repeat the same steps, but this time select cell protection. When you choose to protect the worksheet or document, only your selected range of cells on that worksheet is protected.

ENTERING DATA USING NAMED CELL RANGES

Using named cell ranges to enter cell references in formulas and functions is a good way to avoid cell reference errors. When you have a named range, all you need to do is select Insert, Names, Paste. A list of all named ranges in the spreadsheet appears. Click a name to select it, and click OK to paste it at the current cursor location.

→ For information on creating named cell ranges, **see** "Naming Cell Ranges for Faster Navigation," **p. 501**.

PART

III

CH

13

OPENING, SAVING, AND CLOSING SPREADSHEETS

Opening and saving spreadsheets in StarCalc is as easy as it should be. Besides coming equipped with creative sample spreadsheets and a number of templates for common spreadsheet uses, StarCalc also has filters to open Excel and Lotus 1-2-3 spreadsheets and a number of text and database formats. It can also save files in almost as great a variety of formats.

Note

Although StarCalc opens Lotus 1-2-3 documents, it cannot currently save in Lotus 1-2-3 formats.

OPENING NEW SPREADSHEETS

To open a new blank spreadsheet, select File, New, Spreadsheet, or select Spreadsheet from the Taskbar Start menu. This opens a new, blank worksheet onscreen and places all the StarCalc tools on the desktop. If the desktop is visible, you can also double-click the New Spreadsheet icon on the StarOffice desktop.

If you're in a hurry or want to get an idea of just what a spreadsheet can do, you can choose from a range of spreadsheet templates by choosing File, New, From Template (or pressing Ctrl+N). This opens a dialog box with templates for a number of common tasks (not all of which use spreadsheets).

Tip #284 from
Michael & Sarah

Opening a template, selecting cells, and reading their contents in the Formula input field is a good way to learn how to create new formulas and use StarCalc's built-in functions.

Table 13.6 lists the spreadsheet templates available from the Templates dialog and their category. Their names explain their functions.

TABLE 13.6. STAROFFICE SPREADSHEET TEMPLATES

Template Category	Template Name
Financial Documents	Household Budget
	Stock Portfolio
	Loan Calculation
	Car Financing
	Automobile Expenses
	Cash Book
Education	Timetables
Miscellaneous	Calendar
	Schedule

You can modify these templates any way you like and save them as your own spreadsheets.

Caution

You can also open templates by choosing File, Templates. Be careful, though! The default Save As option in the Templates dialog is set to save your document as a StarOffice template—which means you will overwrite the StarOffice template with your own document unless you assign a new name.

OPENING EXISTING SPREADSHEETS AND DATABASES

To open an existing file in StarCalc, choose File, Open and enter the file's name in the file-name input field or browse to its location and double click its name. By default, <All> is selected in the File type input field, which means StarCalc evaluates any file you try to open and determines its file format. If StarCalc recognizes the format, the file opens automatically on your desktop.

Because of StarOffice's integrated functions, you may find that if you open a file using short-cut methods like double-clicking the filename, it may open in an application other than StarCalc. For example, a conventional text file might open in StarWriter when you want to import it into StarCalc. A simple way to solve this for an individual file is to open the file via the File menu Open command rather than using shortcuts. You can then select the specific filter you want to use in the Filter drop-down list. If you want to change the file association permanently so that you can open the file using shortcuts, you can change the default StarOffice application for opening that specific file type by choosing Tools, Options, Browser and then selecting the File Types tab and making the needed changes.

StarCalc comes with filters to open files saved in the two most popular spreadsheet formats: Microsoft Excel and Lotus 1-2-3. As is the case with filters in any program, they don't work perfectly, although they do a very good job. However, as a practical precaution, you should always have a copy of the original spreadsheet safely stored before you begin, in case any unexpected transformations occur.

Tip #285 from
Michael & Sarah

StarCalc uses a different base date for date and time calculations than Excel uses. This can cause your dates to suddenly change by four years when importing or exporting in either direction. You can easily change the reference base date in StarCalc to match Excel's by choosing Tools, Options, Spreadsheet. Select the Calculation tab, and click the 01/01/04 option. Do this before you open your Excel spreadsheet in StarCalc, and you won't find time slipping away!

Note

LINUX

In its current incarnations, StarOffice does not support ODBC or Oracle connectivity on Linux. JDBC connectivity is fully implemented in version 5.1. The best way to import database files into StarCalc in version 5.0 is to save them as .csv text files before opening them in StarCalc.

→ For more information on importing databases into StarCalc, **see** "Importing and Exporting Data," **p. 636**.

SAVING SPREADSHEETS

To save a spreadsheet, click the Save button on the Function bar. The Save As dialog opens, and you can enter a filename and choose a file format. You can also choose to save the file with a password.

PROTECTING FILES WITH PASSWORDS

If you want to limit who can open your file, you can save it with a password by selecting the Save With Password option in the Save As dialog. After this option is selected, when you choose Save, you are prompted to enter a password and then confirm it. No one without your password will be able to open it—including you!

To clear a document of its password, simple save it again without the password option checked.

Note

Because this is a powerful command, StarOffice automatically clears this option every time you save a file. StarOffice does not store it as a default.

→ For information on how to protect data in spreadsheets but still enable users to open and enter data in it, **see** "Protecting Cells, Sheets, and Documents," **p. 523**.

Tip #286 from
Michael & Sarah

You can prevent accidental alterations but give people viewing access by selecting the read-only option on your spreadsheet's General tab of the Properties dialog.

ADDING DOCUMENT PROPERTIES

Spreadsheets are often complex documents shared among many people. You can prevent confusion and make sharing easier by entering basic information about the document in the document Properties dialog, which you open by choosing Edit, Properties. You can also check a document's basic statistics and systems information in this dialog.

Tip #287 from
Michael & Sarah

You can have document properties appear automatically every time you save by choosing the Edit Document Properties Before Saving option on the Tools, General, Save tab.

You can use the Internet tab in the Properties dialog if you want your file to be automatically refreshed as you work. Type in the file's complete path name (which, in StarOffice, is considered a URL)set an auto reload time (in seconds) and your spreadsheet will continually be refreshed when it's opened on your desktop.

Tip #288 from
Michael & Sarah

You can also use this field to create a slide show. Enter the URL of the next file to display. After the reload time you've specified, this next file will be loaded. In that document's Internet tab URL field, enter the name of the next file in your slide show, and so on.

SAVING VERSIONS

If you're creating a complex spreadsheet, whether it's full of formulas for calculation, a complex form with controls, or a database with a lot of data, you'll probably go through many iterations before perfecting it. You might even need input from others in your office or company. In either situation, you might want to save versions using the Versions command as well as saving in the usual way. This enables you to both keep a history of changes and to compare different versions. This might help you track sources of error or quickly find a colleague's revisions.

To save a version, select the Versions command from the File menu and choose Save New Version. You can also check the Always Save a Version on Closing option and have StarCalc automatically save a version every time you close the document.

→ For details on how to track changes with the Versions command, **see** "Tracking Changes to Spreadsheets," **p. 548**.

SAVING IN OTHER FILE FORMATS

To save in other file formats, choose File, Save As and select the file format you want from the file type drop-down list. As is always the case, when you save in foreign formats, some formatting characteristics may be lost or change. Formulas may also be affected, so it's always a good idea to save one copy in StarCalc format first, and then save in a foreign format.

Note

Although StarCalc does a good job of saving files in other formats, your macrocs don't translate. One nice byproduct is that you don't have to worry about inadvertently infecting your StarOffice files with viruses that attach themselves to Visual Basic for Application (VBA) code!

TROUBLESHOOTING

I type in a number, but all I see is ###.

Your number is longer than the cell is wide. Double-click the right column border to resize the column so it automatically fits your data.

I want to autofill a series of cells with exactly the same number, but when I grab the corner and drag, my number is increased by increments of one!

The default autofill setting in StarCalc is to create a simple trend series, in which the number 1 is added to the previous number in the series. To carry out an autofill which just copies a number into contiguous cells, press Ctrl while dragging the cell's lower right corner.

I'm trying to select a range of cells, and my data is being replaced instead.

You're probably accidentally grabbing the lower right corner of the cell, which activates the AutoFill command and automatically creates a trend series. To select, drag from the middle of cells, not their edges.

How can I use StarCalc to add a series of text data?

You can create custom lists. To create a custom list, choose Tools, Options, Spreadsheet Document, Sorted Lists. In the Sorted Lists dialog, click New and then type the list with items entered in the order you want them to appear. Click Add to add the new list. Once you have saved a custom list, simply type the first item in the list in a cell, grab the cell by the AutoFill handle, and drag. The rest of the list fills in automatically.

I want to drag part of a spreadsheet from the Navigator into another spreadsheet, but all that happens is I insert a hyperlink.

You need to change the Navigator's drag mode. The default is set to Insert as Hyperlink; you need to click the Drag Mode button (the button on the bottom row, far right of the Navigator toolbar) and select Insert as Copy.

CHAPTER 14

EDITING SPREADSHEETS

In this chapter

EDITING AND DELETING CELLS AND CELL CONTENTS

Because of the way cells store information, the process of selecting and editing cells works a bit differently than the process of selecting and editing text in a document. Understanding the cell's contents will help you select and edit more efficiently and avoid deleting valuable data.

You also have choices about where you edit cells—in the Formula bar or directly in the cell itself. Each choice has its own advantages; which choice is better depends on your task.

UNDERSTANDING CELL CONTENTS

Cells might appear blank and empty, but their emptiness is more than it appears. A cell *is* a blank space where you can enter data. However, it also contains formatting instructions that control the appearance of the cell contents. Cells can also contain different kinds of programming objects and have notes attached to them. These cell contents might not be visible on your screen or might not be visible at all times.

Cells themselves are also objects, and if you delete an entire cell, as opposed to its contents, you can throw off all the existing cell references in formulas and create errors in calculation.

Caution

Cells that appear empty can contain spaces. Spaces also might exist at the beginning or end of data in cells. Spaces can interfere with calculations in StarCalc (and other spreadsheets), so be careful to never delete cell contents by placing your cursor in a cell and pressing the spacebar.

A cell always has formatting attributes attached; all other contents must be inserted by a user. Table 14.1 lists everything a cell can contain, and Figure 14.1 displays some examples.

TABLE 14.1 WHAT A CELL CAN CONTAIN

Type of Content	Description
Character strings	Any alphanumeric characters formatted as text.
Numbers	Numbers formatted with a numbers format.
Dates and times	Dates and times formatted with dates and times formats.
Formulas	Data prefaced with an = and its results. Note that the results of a formula can be an error.
Notes	Notes inserted with the Insert Note command.
Formats	Formatting attributes of the cell.
Objects	OLE objects, applets, or plug-ins you insert by using the Insert, Object command.

> **Note**
>
> In this book, *cell contents* mean anything that can be in or attached to a cell, including formatting and objects. *Cell data* refers to text, formulas, or values you enter into a cell.

> **Caution**
>
> If you have formatted a number as text, it is not included in calculations, even if you have included its cell address in your formula.

Figure 14.1
Seeing should not be believing in a spreadsheet because a cell can have hidden contents, including formatting that changes a number into text as far as StarCalc is concerned.

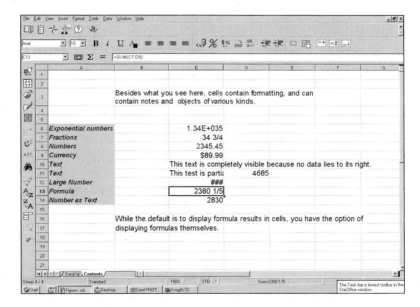

By default, formulas are not displayed in cells; their results appear instead—which means that deleting a formula can be all too easy. However, when you select a cell, its formula appears in the Formula bar. Turning on value highlighting can also flag formulas for you; results of formulas appear in green, and ordinary numbers and dates appear in blue.

Tip #289 from
Michael & Sarah

If you want to have formulas instead of their results displayed in the cells, select Formulas on the Tools, Options, Spreadsheet, Contents tab. Figure 15.1 shows a worksheet with this option turned on.

EDITING WITH THE FORMULA BAR

The advantage of editing in the Formula bar is that you can see the entire cell contents more easily than on a basic worksheet layout (see Figure 14.2).

Figure 14.2
When you start entering data into the Formula bar's Input field, the Function tool disappears and is replaced by a green check mark and a red X–Accept and Cancel, respectively. You can also cancel your input by pressing Esc.

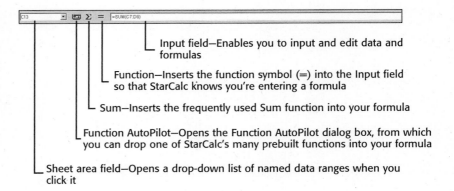

Input field—Enables you to input and edit data and formulas

Function—Inserts the function symbol (=) into the Input field so that StarCalc knows you're entering a formula

Sum—Inserts the frequently used Sum function into your formula

Function AutoPilot—Opens the Function AutoPilot dialog box, from which you can drop one of StarCalc's many prebuilt functions into your formula

Sheet area field—Opens a drop-down list of named data ranges when you click it

To overwrite an existing cell entry and enter new data in the Formula bar, select the cell and begin typing. Your data simultaneously appears in the cell and the Formula bar Input field. To change something in the middle of your entry, move your cursor over the Input field entry, and click next to the value you want to edit. The I-beam cursor flashes to indicate your editing point.

To edit an existing entry in the Formula bar, select the cell, move your pointer over the value in the Input field until it becomes the I-beam cursor, and then click where you want to edit.

 After you've made your changes, press Enter or click the green check mark to accept your changes, or press Esc or click the red X to reject them and leave the cell as is.

IN-CELL EDITING

In-cell editing is useful when you are creating or working in an online form. Forms make data entry easy through good layout, graphic design, and convenient placement of buttons and other automated features, so you don't need to look at the Input field to see what you're doing.

To edit directly in a cell, double-click it. When the I-beam cursor appears, you can move around with the arrow keys and edit as usual.

Depending on your mouse-click speed, either double-clicking twice, or triple-clicking a cell selects the entire cell contents, which are then replaced if you begin typing.

CLEARING CELL ENTRIES

The simplest way to clear a cell's contents is to place your cursor in the cell and press the Delete key. However, what is deleted depends on the settings in the Delete Contents dialog box, which opens from the cell editing and format context menu.

You can also clear a cell's data by using the Cut command (Ctrl+X), which also stores the entry in the general-purpose buffer (Linux) or on the Clipboard (Windows) for reuse.

CLEARING SELECTED ELEMENTS FROM A CELL

By default, pressing Delete is configured to delete everything in a cell except formats and objects. However, you can select the types of contents to be deleted when you press Delete. You might think of this process as the editing equivalent of conditional formatting—conditional destruction!

If you select a cell and press Delete, a Delete Contents dialog box appears (see Figure 14.3). By default, Delete All is selected, and all other choices (except Formats) are checked but grayed out. This might not seem very intuitive, but you must deselect Delete All before you can choose any of the other options.

Figure 14.3
You can choose specific cell elements for deletion after you deselect Delete All and the options are active (as they are in this dialog box). Deleting formats returns the formatting of the cell to Standard style, with General as its numbers format.

Any changes you make to the dialog box affect the action of the Delete key from that point forward, until you change the selections again. However, the dialog box appears every time you press Delete to remind you of the current selections and allow you to change them for the currently selected cell.

Note

> You can delete objects with this command only if the object's complete contents are fully visible in the cell—which usually means your cell must be enlarged.

The Delete Contents command is terrifically useful because you can guard against accidental deletion of important material but still use shortcut keys to do quick editing in your cells. Using this command is also a great way to selectively delete formatting from specific cells, leaving their contents untouched, or delete specific values without affecting formulas.

Tip #290 from
Michael & Sarah

In Search and Replace, you can't search for styles or content types *and* a specific value or text string at the same time, but you can achieve the same effect by combining the power of Search and Replace with the precision of Delete Contents. From the Delete Contents dialog box, deselect everything except the one type of data you want to delete. For example, perhaps you want to delete a date, 12/31/99, but don't want to delete that date if it's the result of a formula, or delete anything else for that matter. Leave only Date & Time selected, open Search and Replace, enter 12/31/99, and use the Delete key to delete.

Note that the Backspace key is unaffected by any changes you make to this Delete Contents dialog box; pressing Backspace still does away with all visible cell contents (but leaves notes, formats, and objects untouched).

DELETING CELLS FROM THE WORKSHEET

If you want to delete an entire cell, row, or column, select the area and right-click to open the cell context menu. Select Delete Cells. The Delete Cells dialog box opens and gives you four choices of how your worksheet can be adjusted after losing those cells: shifting the cells left or up or deleting an entire column or row (see Figure 14.4).

Figure 14.4
The Delete Cells dialog box is intended to make you think before you delete, to avoid errors in cell references.

Caution

Be careful when you're deleting cells, rows, and columns. Deleting affects all cell references on the worksheet and might generate reference errors in existing formulas, especially where you have entered absolute cell references. For more information about addressing cells in formulas, see "Absolute and Relative References," in Chapter 16, "Using Formulas and Functions."

If you delete an entire row, all rows below the deleted row shift their location and cell addresses by one increment. If you delete a column, all columns to the right of the deleted column shift their location and their cell addresses by one increment. For example, if you delete row C, cell D1 becomes cell C1.

Relative references in any formulas that refer to those cells are automatically updated throughout the spreadsheet, but where formulas rely on other formulas or their results, errors might still occur.

COPYING AND MOVING CELL DATA

Once you have a large amount of data and formulas in a spreadsheet, naturally you want to copy and move data around—not only within a worksheet or spreadsheet, but also among different spreadsheets, and perhaps even to other StarOffice document types.

StarOffice's Integrated Desktop makes copying and moving spreadsheet data easy, whether from one set of cells to another or from a worksheet into a StarWriter or StarImpress document. However, if you want to copy data between documents, be sure you understand linking versus copying data.

Caution

If you link documents (just as if you insert a graphic object as a link), you must always have the source document available in its indicated directory. Otherwise, your linked data will not update and your target document might become corrupted.

→ For an introduction to linking documents, **see** "Sharing Data Across Documents," **p. 171**.

Your three basic tools for moving data are your Edit menu Cut, Copy, Paste, and Paste Special commands; drag and drop directly between two open documents; and dragging and dropping via the Navigator. This section discusses all three. If you're new to StarOffice, it's recommended that you take the time to acquaint yourself with the Navigator. It offers a radically new way of editing and sharing data between applications that is elegant, fast, and simple.

Entering and copying data with automatic Fill commands is discussed in "Creating Data Series" in Chapter 13, "Creating Spreadsheets." You can also use conventional editing techniques to copy and move cell data in StarCalc. However, because of the special characteristics of cells, the way these commands are activated and function is somewhat different than in text documents or graphics programs.

USING CUT, COPY, AND PASTE

 You can cut, copy, and paste data in cells and the Formula bar Input field. You can also cut and paste between cells and the Input field, which can be a good way to copy formulas if you need to change or double-check them.

EFFECTS OF CUT, COPY, AND PASTE

The Cut, Copy, and Paste commands affect only cell contents, objects, and inserted graphics, not cell formatting. If you cut a formatted column label such as the one you see in cell B6 in Figure 14.5 and paste it in a cell that has only the Standard cell format applied, the result is as you see in cell B6—plain vanilla text. However, if you paste this data into a cell that has already had formatting applied, the text takes on that cell's characteristics, as it has in cells C8, D8, E8, and F8.

PART
III

CH
14

Figure 14.5
The effects of pasting cut and copied data in a spreadsheet varies in part depending on the cell formatting applied to the receiving cell.

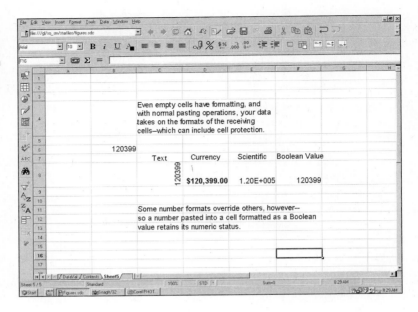

The Cut command doesn't cut cells, and Paste doesn't insert new cells but pastes over any existing data that might be in the way.

If you want to delete a cell's formatting, use the Delete Contents command (Del) on the cell context menu. If you want to delete entire cells, use the Delete Cells command.

Tip #291 from
Michael & Sarah

If you use drag and drop to move a cell range, you can see an outline of the range size while you're trying to place it, which makes it easy to place the range in a space of the right size.

COPYING AND PASTING SELECTED CELL CONTENTS

Just as you can selectively delete cell contents by using the Delete Contents command (Del), you can selectively paste cell contents with the Paste Special command. You can also perform simple mathematical operations with the pasted data.

Figure 14.6 shows the Paste Special dialog box that appears after you select some cells in StarCalc and choose the Paste Special command. You can choose the Paste Special command from the Edit menu, or from the cell, row, and column context menus.

This dialog box appears only when spreadsheet cells are in the system general-purpose buffer (Linux) or on the Clipboard (Windows). The Paste Special dialog box looks quite different when you're pasting data from other kinds of documents.

Figure 14.6
The Paste Special command gives you control over how your data is pasted and even allows you to perform calculations with your targeted data.

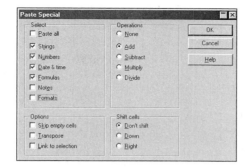

Note

Some versions of the online Help say that the StarCalc Paste Special dialog box is called Paste Contents. It's not (at least, not in the English version).

The options in the Select section should be familiar to you from the Delete Contents dialog box; the effect is the same as with Delete but the contents are added rather than deleted. (See the section "Clearing Selected Elements from a Cell" earlier in this chapter, for a description of these different options.)

The other three sets of options are unique to pasting, however.

PERFORMING ARITHMETICAL OPERATIONS WITH PASTED DATA   In the Operations section (refer to Figure 14.6), you can choose to have values in your selection added, subtracted, multiplied, or divided into values in your target area. For this option to be available, you must have selected Numbers, and you must have selected a sheet area with cells that already contain values. The values in your target area are changed accordingly.

For example, let's say prices were just raised by $1 each on every piece in your inventory list of 125 items because of a tax change. You can adjust all 125 prices in a few easy steps. First, enter 1 in a cell. Use the automatic fill handle to fill 124 more cells with the same number, and then copy the entire block of 125 cells. Choose the Paste Special Add operation, and paste the column over the column of current prices. All the prices are changed just like that—and likely with many fewer errors than if you had used other methods.

In the Options section (refer to Figure 15.6), you can make choices about how your pasted selection will be entered in its new area. If you select Skip Empty Cells, blanks in your selection do not affect your target area when you paste. Selecting this option is particularly important when you're carrying out division or multiplication operations because an empty cell is counted as a zero in calculations. This means your multiplication result is 0, and your division result is the error message #VALUE! in any cells that meet with a blank from your source.

PART

III

CH

14

TRANSPOSING ROWS AND COLUMNS If you select Transpose, the orientation of your selection is reversed: If you select a row, it is pasted as a column, and if you select a column, it is pasted as a row.

PASTING LINKED DATA If you select Link to Selection, changes you make to your source data—that is, the original location of the data you're pasting—are also made to the corresponding values in the target area.

> **Note**
>
> If you are linking your source area to your target location, and your source area contains blank cells, you should select Paste All in the Paste Special dialog box. Otherwise, later additions made to the cells will not be updated in your pasted area.

The default selection in the Shift Cells section is Don't Shift, which means existing data is overwritten or combined with your source data as you have selected. However, you can choose to have existing cells displaced either down or to the right instead of being overwritten.

CUTTING AND PASTING BETWEEN STAROFFICE DOCUMENTS

You can easily use the standard editing commands—Ctrl+C (Copy), Ctrl+X (Cut), and Ctrl+V (Paste)—to transfer data from a single cell. Just triple-click (or double-click twice) to select the data, and take off from there.

You can also use the edit shortcut keys to cut or copy a range of cells and paste it into other StarOffice documents as an OLE object. This object is no longer linked to the source area and will not be updated. Your ability to edit and manipulate this data within your target document is limited; only StarCalc commands are available for changing its layout and appearance. (Double-clicking it opens a miniature worksheet window and brings StarCalc commands and context menus on your desktop.) In this case, you'll have greater flexibility if you use the Paste Special command or drag and drop—particularly if you insert your StarCalc range as a DDE object, a concept that is explained in the section "Dragging and Dropping StarCalc Tables into Other StarOffice Documents" later in this chapter. You can find some illustrations of these different types of objects there.

DRAGGING AND DROPPING

Drag and drop is a much more flexible and powerful feature in StarOffice than you're probably used to, and StarCalc is one of the applications in which it really shines. However, it's a little tricky to select data in cells properly so that you can move or copy them with this method, and it requires good dexterity with the mouse.

An easier way to use drag and drop is to drag and drop elements from the Navigator into a worksheet location. This approach works, of course, only for those elements the Navigator tracks. The convenience and efficiency of using the Navigator is such that you should get in the habit of naming data ranges and database ranges that you frequently copy or edit—for example, a tax table—so you can use it to full advantage.

USING THE MOUSE

The marvels of automatic fill and the complexity of cell contents in StarCalc force some adjustments in drag-and-drop methods compared to how they work in StarWriter or on the desktop. However, they're still available in full force.

Having said that, we'll start by telling you that you can't use drag and drop to move a single cell or its contents. (You can, however, copy a cell's contents this way.) Cells are the bricks in the structure of the worksheet: They're what holds everything else together, particularly formulas. Because of their critical structural role, you're not allowed to move them with impunity.

The key to successful dragging and dropping in StarCalc is realizing that you must first select your cell data or cell range, and then press your mouse button while over the selected range to pick it up (so to speak). *Then* press your Ctrl or Shift+Ctrl key combination. If you try to simultaneously click your selected range and press a key, you'll end up deselecting your selection and are back at square (or cell) one.

COPYING DATA FROM A SINGLE CELL   To copy data from a single cell, triple-click (or double-click and double-click) to select it. Then move your mouse pointer over the selection, press the mouse button, and begin to drag. The pointer doesn't change from its I-beam shape into its characteristic copy shape until you're outside the cell borders. When you see the pointer, you're set and can drop your copy anywhere you want.

MOVING, COPYING, AND CREATING A LINK TO A BLOCK OF DATA   To move, copy, or create a link to a block of data with drag and drop, first select your cell range in the usual ways. Then move your pointer over the selected range, and press your mouse button. Here the methods diverge.

To move the block, drag with your mouse. A thick black outline previews the size and shape of your selection to better help you select an appropriate drop area.

To copy the block, press Ctrl until you see a small plus sign appear by the tip of the pointer. Now you can drag and drop your copy to the desired location.

To create a copy linked to the original source, press Ctrl+Shift and drag and drop it to the desired location. Your mouse pointer then displays a small arrow to indicate you're creating a link.

USING THE NAVIGATOR

To open the Navigator, click the Navigator icon. The Navigator is a really great tool. To learn to use it is to love it.

You can quickly copy and paste cell ranges and other objects in StarCalc by dragging and dropping their names from the Navigator (see Figure 14.7). You can use it to copy data within a single worksheet, between worksheets, or between spreadsheets with equal ease. As always with the Navigator, you can select the way in which you move data: as a copy (which no longer has any connection to the source document), as a link (in which case the data is copied as a DDE link), or as a hyperlink (in which case the worksheet or data area name is inserted as a clickable hyperlink that automatically opens the source document and jumps the user to the data).

Figure 14.7
The lower window of the Navigator lists all open task windows in a drop-down list. Clicking a task window name doesn't change your active task window but brings up a list of the selected task's objects so that you can easily drag data from one task into another.

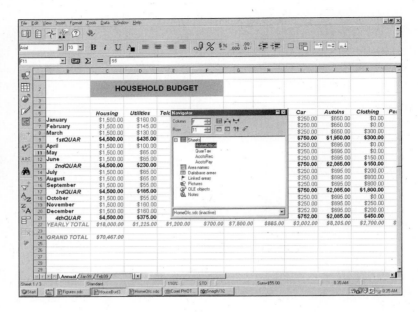

If you want to drag and drop between two spreadsheets, you don't need to have the second spreadsheet in view (although it must be open). Just select its filename from the Navigator drop-down list of open documents, and all its objects appear in the Navigator window.

The objects tracked by the Navigator in StarCalc are listed in Table 14.2.

TABLE 14.2   STARCALC OBJECTS TRACKED BY THE NAVIGATOR

Icon	Object	To Create	For More Information, See
	Worksheets	Open a new spreadsheet.	"Opening a New Spreadsheet," page xxx
	Named areas	Select the desired ranges of cells, and use the Insert, Names, Define command.	"Naming Cell Ranges for Faster Navigation," page xxx
	Database areas	Select the desired range of cells, and use the Data, Define command.	"Defining a Database Area," page xxx

Icon	Object	To Create	For More Information, See
	Linked areas	Drag and drop a selection with the Ctrl+Shift key combination, paste as a DDE object with the Paste Special command, or copy as a link from the Navigator.	"Using Cut, Copy, and Paste," page xxx "Dragging and Dropping," page xxx
	Pictures	Use the Insert Picture command to insert a picture (image or graphic).	"Using Graphics," page xxx.
	OLE objects	Use the Paste Special command to insert an object from another document type or program, or create a chart.	"Using Cut, Copy, and Paste," page xxx "Dragging and Dropping," page xxx "Charting Data," page xxx.
	Notes	Use the Insert, Note command.	"Documenting Formulas with Notes," page xxx.

Note

You cannot use the Navigator to drag and drop copies of, or links to, StarCalc objects into other StarOffice documents. You can only create hyperlinks to other StarCalc documents in this way.

When you have trackable objects in your spreadsheet, dragging and dropping works as usual in the Navigator. First, select your Drag mode (insert as hyperlink, link, or copy). Then, if necessary, click the plus sign to the left of an object category name to see the list of objects. Select the name of the object you want to insert, and drag it into your spreadsheet.

→ For more information on using the Navigator, **see** "Steering Through Your Documents with Navigator," **p. 158**.

DRAGGING AND DROPPING STARCALC TABLES INTO OTHER STAROFFICE DOCUMENTS

One of the great advantages of StarOffice's integrated approach to work is that moving data among different kinds of documents is in many cases as simple as dragging and dropping. This capability is particularly valuable in the case of spreadsheets because they often contain data critical for reports and presentations, but they offer limited formatting and presentation options compared to text documents and slide presentations.

Ctrl+Shift+dragging a selection of cells into StarWriter creates a dynamically linked table that you can edit, format, and manipulate by using StarWriter's powerful table commands (see Figure 14.8). The one limitation is that you cannot add or delete rows or columns from within StarWriter; you can only make these structural changes to the table from within StarCalc. You can, however, merge cells and make other cosmetic changes using the Table object bar that appears in StarWriter.

Note

This kind of dynamically linked object is referred to as a DDE object. DDE stands for *Dynamic Data Exchange,* which is considered a predecessor of *Object Linking and Embedding,* or *OLE*. With DDE, objects are linked via file reference but not embedded. In this case, that's a good thing because otherwise you couldn't take advantage of StarWriter's terrific table and formatting features.

Figure 14.8
Using Paste, Paste Special, and drag-and-drop commands, you can easily copy and link data from spreadsheets to other StarOffice documents. Here, you can see the same StarCalc cell range inserted as a DDE table and an OLE object.

If both files are open, any changes you make to the source spreadsheet file are automatically updated in your document as you make them in the spreadsheet. However, changes you make to StarWriter tables do not affect the original spreadsheet.

The next time you open your document, you'll be asked whether you want to update all links. Answer Yes if you want StarOffice to update the information in your table from the StarCalc source document.

If you drag and drop tables from StarCalc into StarImpress, Ctrl+Shift+drag creates what is called a *metafile*—a platform-independent graphic—whereas regular drag and drop and Ctrl+drag create copies of the data as OLE objects, just as those actions do from StarCalc to StarWriter.

Tip #293 from
Michael & Sarah

If you want to do some fancy formatting on StarCalc data that requires simple calculations, consider Ctrl+Shift+dragging it as a table into StarWriter. Pressing F2 in StarWriter opens the Text Formula bar, with which you can create and insert simple formulas to do your calculations. The available functions include Sum, Round, Percent, Power, Mean, Average, and some trigonometry functions. You can then take advantage of StarWriter's superior formatting and layout capabilities to create a much more impressive document.

Note

Pressing F2 in StarWriter doesn't work if your cursor is placed inside a table. Click somewhere outside your table, and then press F2.

Caution

Because you can change your StarCalc table in StarWriter without affecting the StarCalc source, there's a danger that someone may change data so that it no longer reflects the source document, even though you need it to. To be sure you have the most recent data, select the Tools, Update command, and choose either Update All or Update Links.

Ctrl+dragging and dragging both have the same effect: They create a copy of your data as an OLE object that is embedded in your text document but no longer dynamically linked to the source spreadsheet. You can edit and make changes to the data and formatting as with any StarCalc spreadsheet; however, you don't have access to the StarWriter command set.

INSERTING AND DELETING CELLS, ROWS, AND COLUMNS

As you make changes to your worksheets, inevitably you find that you need to insert and delete worksheet elements. Although you can do so by using commands on the Insert menu, the easiest way is to use the cell, column, and row context menus, shown in Figure 14.9.

To insert cells, rows, or columns, place your mouse pointer over a cell, row header, or column header, respectively; then right-click to open its context menu. You will see commands for inserting. If you choose Insert Rows or Insert Columns, immediately a row or column is inserted. A row is inserted above your currently selected row, whereas a column is inserted to the right of your currently selected column.

Note

The Insert Row and Insert Column commands do not work in rows or columns that you have merged with the Merge Cells command.

If you choose Insert Cells, a dialog box appears requesting that you select how the existing cells should adjust to your insertion (see Figure 14.10).

Figure 14.9
The cell, column, and row context menus offer the fastest access to editing and formatting commands.

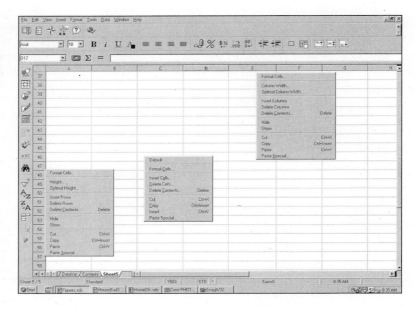

Figure 14.10
Because inserting cells can wreak havoc on your existing formulas by changing cell references, the Insert Cells dialog box prompts you to select precisely how your new cells will be inserted.

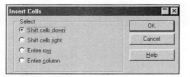

Choose your answer wisely. If you choose to shift cells right or down, you will likely interfere with formula results because the formula references are not automatically adjusted and the cell values are likely to change as cells are shifted. If you have a formula that refers to another formula that gets shifted out of position, you'll be in an even bigger pickle. However, if you choose to insert an entire row or column, cell references in formulas will be adjusted and it's less likely that your formula results will be thrown off.

Tip #294 from
Michael & Sarah

Because inserting cells can cause serious problems with formulas, if you have a complex spreadsheet, it's a good idea to save a copy of that spreadsheet under a different name before you start adding cells, just to be sure. (Even though you can use the Undo command, it's better to be safe than sorry.)

Tip #295 from
Michael & Sarah

If you want to change the orientation of a row or column—that is, make a row into a column, or a column into a row—select the row or column, choose Edit, Paste Special, and choose Transpose.

EDITING WORKSHEETS

As you start building up your spreadsheet, you can reorganize and edit your worksheets in various ways. StarCalc makes renaming, inserting, deleting, moving, and copying worksheets a snap and places all the commands you need at your fingertips with the worksheet context menu (see Figure 14.11).

Figure 14.11
Many commands on the worksheet context menu open dialog boxes that offer further options.

Insert...
Delete...
Rename...
Move/Copy...
Select All

To open it, right-click a tab—be sure your mouse pointer is far down enough because it's very easy to click a cell in the last visible row instead.

RENAMING WORKSHEETS

Worksheets in a new spreadsheet are given default names of Sheet1, Sheet2, and Sheet3.

To rename worksheets, press Alt, click the tab you want to rename, and type the new name. Alternatively, select the tab, right-click to open the sheet context menu, and choose the Rename command.

Your worksheet name can consist only of letters, numbers, and spaces, up to 49 characters long. Other symbols are reserved for formulas and functions.

It's a good idea to give worksheets short, simple names that reflect their contents. Using short names makes using the tabs as visual aids and navigational tools easier and also helps you use the Navigator effectively to maintain an overview of your spreadsheet—your sheet names become like chapter headings in a book.

INSERTING AND DELETING WORKSHEETS

To insert and delete worksheets, using the worksheet context menu is easiest, although you can find all its commands on the Insert and Edit menus as well (except Rename, which is on the Format menu). When you select the Insert command, an Insert Sheet dialog box opens enabling you to select the number and location of sheets you want to enter.

PART
III

CH
14

You can also choose to assign a name to the new sheet at that time, although you don't have to. If you enter a number larger than one, the Name box grays out because you can name only one sheet at a time.

INSERTING WORKSHEETS FROM ANOTHER SPREADSHEET

You can also insert worksheets from another spreadsheet, including spreadsheets in foreign formats, by using the Insert Sheet command. Select the From File option on the Insert Sheet dialog box, and then click Browse to navigate to the directory where the spreadsheet is stored.

Tip #296 from
Michael & Sarah

Be sure the appropriate file type is selected in the File Type box, or the spreadsheet file-names you're searching for don't appear as you browse. StarCalc 5.1 files are the default, but StarCalc can also insert pages from dBASE, Lotus, text, and Excel 95 and Excel 97 files, among others.

Click to highlight the spreadsheet's filename. When you do, a list of all the worksheets contained in the spreadsheet appears in the window (if that file format supports multiple worksheets). In some instances, depending on the file type selected, a Text Import dialog box may appear, prompting you to confirm certain settings before importing the data.

→ For more information on importing text files into StarCalc, **see** "Importing and Exporting Data," **p. 636**.

When you choose to insert worksheets from another spreadsheet, you have the option of linking the worksheets through DDE or just inserting a copy of the data. You are prompted to update the links every time you open the document. You can also manually update and manage links while a spreadsheet is still open by using the Links command on the Edit menu.

SELECTING MULTIPLE WORKSHEETS

You can use the old reliable Shift and Ctrl selection shortcuts to select multiple worksheets.

To select a continuous series of worksheets, click the first sheet's tab to select it; then press Shift while clicking the tab of the last worksheet in the series. To select a number of non-contiguous worksheets, press Ctrl while clicking each worksheet's tab. You can deselect in the same way. The tabs of selected sheets appear in white.

Tip #297 from
Michael & Sarah

If you can't see more than one tab, grab and drag the gray border between the sheet tab area and the scrollbar to make more tabs visible.

You can also select all the worksheets in your spreadsheet by choosing the Select All command on the worksheet context menu.

MOVING AND COPYING WORKSHEETS

To move or copy worksheets, first select the worksheets. Then open the context menu and select Move/Copy.

You then see a dialog box that contains a list of all currently open spreadsheets (To Document) and a list box in which all the worksheet names of the currently selected spreadsheet are listed (Insert Before). Besides listing currently open spreadsheets, the To Document list offers the choice of copying or moving your worksheet(s) to a new StarCalc document.

Select your target spreadsheet. Then select the name of the worksheet in your target before which your selected sheets will be added.

The default is to move the sheets. If you want to merely copy the sheet, be sure to check the Copy option in the lower-left corner of the dialog box.

Tip #298 from
Michael & Sarah

A quick way to move a sheet is to drag and drop its tab name at the bottom of the screen. A quick way to copy it is to use Ctrl+drag.

USING SEARCH AND REPLACE IN STARCALC

The general logic and procedures for using Search and Replace have already been discussed in the section "Using Basic Editing and Selection Tools" in Chapter 4. The table of regular expressions you can use is also listed there. However, like all StarOffice's common tools, Search and Replace in StarCalc has a few spreadsheet-specific wrinkles of its own that relate to the specific tasks at hand, as is apparent when you look at the StarCalc Search & Replace dialog box (see Figure 14.12).

Figure 14.12
By clicking the More button on the Search & Replace dialog box, you see the complete list of options that appear here. You can search or search and replace your entire spreadsheet by selecting Search in All Sheets; otherwise, the default is to search only the currently active worksheet.

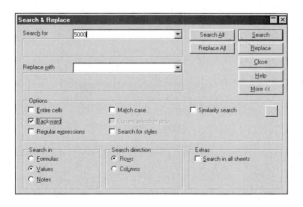

These specific differences relate, once again, to the odd sorts of things you can keep in a spreadsheet's cells. So you can choose to search and replace only in cells with formulas (extremely useful when you need to check or update cell references in formulas) or values (useful if you need to change values but want to be sure your formulas are left intact). You can also choose to search only in notes, which is another good reason to use notes to document formulas and data entry.

You can use the Search for Styles option to search for specific cell styles and, if you like, replace them for another.

Tip #299 from *Michael & Sarah*	You can use the Search for Styles feature in creative ways to make for quick navigation around your worksheet. For example, you can create specific cell styles for sales figures for specific salespeople so that you can easily track their figures even across many worksheets.
	If you select the Search for Styles option, you cannot search for anything else but the style; the Input field appears with a drop-down list of currently available cell styles, and you aren't allowed to enter anything else (unless you deselect the option).
	Note that if you do not choose the More button and open the additional options, by default all data (formulas, values, dates, and text) is searched, but notes are not. Notes are searched only if the Notes option is selected.

Tip #300 from *Michael & Sarah*	You can quickly locate specific financial targets by selecting Search in Formulas and entering the desired value. This way, you can quickly pinpoint, for example, all salespeople who have achieved sales over a certain amount or all divisions that have cost overruns of more than a certain dollar value.

Similarity searches work on numbers and dates as well as text.

SETTING SEARCH CRITERIA

In the Calculate dialog box of the Tools, Options, Spreadsheet category, you can set two aspects of how StarCalc executes Search and Replace actions. If the option Search Criteria = and <> Must Match Entire Cells is selected, Search and Replace will live up to those standards. Otherwise, only partial cell contents containing the text or numbers in question will be considered a match. This option is turned on by default in the Standard template, as is Search Column and Row Labels Automatically. The latter option is what enables StarCalc to read your row labels and column headers for what they are. (It always helps to assign different styles or formats to cells you are using as headers or labels.)

TRACKING CHANGES TO SPREADSHEETS

In version 5, StarOffice has added a revisions feature that allows you to track changes to your documents. Although this feature is by now standard in top word-processing programs, finding it in spreadsheet programs is not very common. Yet it's valuable for spreadsheets because they are often very complex documents on which many different people work.

Note

Revision marks do not translate into other programs, so they are useful only if you're working and sharing files in StarCalc format.

If you want to track changes to a spreadsheet, select the Changes, Record command on the Edit menu. When you select it, Record Changes is in effect in the document until someone deselects it, even if the document is opened and closed and opened again.

When you begin making changes to your spreadsheet, two visible changes occur. First, any cells you modify appear outlined in red to highlight them. Second, a note is automatically added to each cell you modify, complete with the time, date, author of the modification (based on system information, such as your logon name or user information in the program), and—here's the kicker—the old and new cell data (look ahead to Figure 14.13). What could be easier?

Tip #301 from
Michael & Sarah

To see the notes, slowly move your mouse pointer over modified cells. If you move too fast, StarCalc assumes you're working and want to select or navigate and so hides them from view.

You can also add your own comments to any cell by selecting the cell and then selecting the Changes, Comments command. This action opens a dialog box where you can enter a message.

After you have made changes in a document, you can select the Show command from the Changes submenu. Selecting this command opens a dialog box from which you can selectively filter and view changes in the document, such as choosing to see only changes made by a particular author.

You can also either merge your document with an earlier version (which you need to have saved under a different filename) or compare them with the Compare command, which is located just below the Changes command on the Edit menu.

To merge your document with another file, select the Changes, Merge Document command. After you browse and choose the document to be merged, you see an Accept or Reject Changes dialog box, which lists all changes made in both documents since tracking was turned on (see Figure 14.13).

This dialog box displays a number of data fields, including author name, date of modification, and nature of the modification. You can change the sort order of these fields in the same way you do in the Beamer or the Open and Save As dialog boxes—by clicking the field titles.

Figure 14.13
You can gain greater control over changes made to your spreadsheets without locking out access to the document by using the commands on the Edit, Changes submenu. You can easily review changes at a glance in the Accept or Reject Changes dialog box.

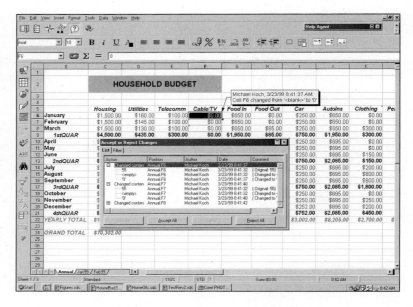

If you choose Compare from the Edit menu, you see the same dialog box, but only changes that reflect differences between the two documents appear. (That is, changes made to document1 do not appear if document2 is a later version of document1.)

This dialog box also contains a second tab that allows you to filter your view of changes, similar to the one in the Show command.

You can choose to accept or reject any or all revisions in this dialog box. It does not have a Cancel or Reset button; to exit, click the Close button in the upper-right corner or press Esc. Even if you choose to accept all changes in the document, if you select the Compare command again with the same document, all your previous changes are displayed again, unless you have made subsequent changes to the more recent document.

If you want to be able to track changes but keep a file under the same filename, you can use the Versions command on the File menu instead. It's not quite clear why Versions and Changes both exist; they seem to repeat much of each other's core functionality yet are not integrated. The Versions command doesn't offer quite as many options but does have the nice feature of enabling you to select the option Always Save Version on Closing to ensure that you keep versions as you go along.

Because that feature works better for someone working on a file individually, we suspect it's an older version of what was implemented as Changes to enable networked users working in teams to make full use of tracking. Regardless, both are useful ways of documenting your changes and offer significantly expanded possibilities beyond the Notes feature.

SETTING REDLINING (REVISIONS) OPTIONS

You can set the colors used to mark changes in the Changes dialog box of the Tools, Options, Spreadsheet category. If you choose By Author, each user's set of changes will be marked in a different color regardless of the type of change. Alternatively, you can choose a specific color to mark changes, insertions, deletions, and moved entries, regardless of the individual who has made the changes.

Note that the changes you make here have no effect on StarWriter revisions marks but affect only StarCalc.

TROUBLESHOOTING

I can't seem to drag and drop a single cell's data.

It's possible but requires a slightly different mouse movement than you may be used to. Position your cursor in the cell, and then double-click to select the cell data. Now *release the mouse button.* The data will remain selected. Grab the data and drag. This will create a copy of your data, rather than moving it. If you want to cut the data and move it somewhere else, use your Ctrl+X and Ctrl+V shortcuts, respectively.

When I try to move a block of selected data, my data just gets overwritten with different values instead!

You must be grabbing the cells by the automatic fill handle in the bottom-right corner, so StarCalc is automatically filling your selected cells with a series based on the first value. Just grab anywhere other than that corner, and you should be able to drag and drop without problem.

I've inserted a worksheet from another spreadsheet and made changes to the original spreadsheet, but the worksheet doesn't update.

When you inserted it, did you check the Link option? If you neglected to do so, your worksheet was inserted as a copy, not a link. You'll need to reinsert the sheet, making sure to choose the Link option. Alternatively, you might need to update your link. You're prompted to update every time you open and close your spreadsheet, but in the middle of a work session it may not update. To update the link manually, choose the Edit, Links command. In the dialog box that appears, click the Update button.

I've inserted a worksheet from a source spreadsheet, but I need to work on the target spreadsheet on a different machine now, and the source spreadsheet won't be available.

That will cause problems, as the linked source spreadsheet needs to be available for the target file to function properly. If it's not possible to copy the source spreadsheet to disk or network and have it available on the other machine, your only solution is to break the link between the inserted worksheet and its source spreadsheet. This means, of course, that the worksheet will no longer be updated. You cannot restore the link later; you'll need to insert the worksheet again from the source spreadsheet.

I want to drag some data from the Navigator onto a worksheet, but I keep getting hyperlinks instead of my data!

You need to change the Navigator Drag mode to either Copy or Link. Open the Drag Mode menu by extended-clicking the tool on the bottom right of the Navigator toolbar.

I can't see all the objects I'm supposed to in the Navigator.

There are a couple of buttons on the bottom row of the Navigator toolbar that change what displays in the Navigator window—the Toggle button and the Scenarios button. If one of these is on (pressed in), you won't see the full range of objects tracked by the Navigator. Be sure both of these are clicked so they don't look pressed in. If you're not sure which is the right button, turn on Tips from the Help menu; the name of the button pops up as you move your mouse over it.

CHAPTER 15

FORMATTING SPREADSHEETS

In this chapter

FORMATTING FOR DIFFERENT TYPES OF PRESENTATIONS

A standard spreadsheet, full of tiny cells densely packed with numbers and other data, might make calculation and data tracking easy, but it doesn't make for attractive or effective display. With StarCalc, you aren't stuck with the gridline format for screen display or printing. You have a wide range of formatting and style options, including the ability to create and save custom cell and page styles. Figure 15.1 shows some of what you can do in StarCalc. Note that this form could easily have been created in a word processing program, but making it in StarCalc allows this business to track catering orders and avoid double entering of critical business information.

Figure 15.1
This sample spreadsheet has more conventionally formatted cell tables on the back tabs, but it creates an attractive order form on the front page.

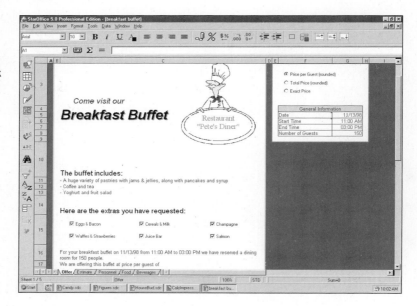

Given how easily you can move StarCalc data into StarWriter and StarImpress, however, you might consider doing your fancy formatting in one of those applications rather than in StarCalc, depending on your time constraints and the kind of final product you need.

DIRECT FORMATTING VERSUS STYLE FORMATTING

Just as with text documents, you have the choice of applying formatting directly to cells for formatting on-the-fly (which in StarOffice is called *hard formatting*) or creating styles (which StarOffice calls *soft formatting*). You can create both cell styles and page styles, the spreadsheet equivalents of paragraph and page styles in StarWriter.

Applying formatting on-the-fly is best when you're doing a one-time job or creating a spreadsheet that you don't expect to change much in the future.

Using styles is a good idea if you are creating a spreadsheet that you often change or update, use to create a variety of presentations or publish on the Web, or use as a template for other spreadsheets. With styles, you can quickly make global changes to formats and ensure stylistic consistency.

Before going wild with formatting, though, you should think about how your spreadsheet or individual worksheet will most likely be used because different types of formatting work well for different purposes.

Tip #302 from *Michael & Sarah*	Check out the sample spreadsheets in the Samples folder in the Explorer to get ideas for formatting your own spreadsheets. You can use the Paste Special command to copy and paste formats from samples into your own worksheets; or, if the samples use a non-Standard template, you can import its styles into your spreadsheet's template.

FORMATTING FOR SCREEN DISPLAY AND EASY DATA ANALYSIS

If your spreadsheet is being used for online data entry, management, and analysis, keep the following tips in mind:

- Format with monitors and weary-eyed users in mind, not the printed page or screen.

- Consider the screen size and resolution of the monitors on which StarCalc will be used, as well as the type and memory capacity of the video card(s). People might have a difficult time displaying certain formats because of hardware limitations.

- Check hardware before you create a complex spreadsheet. Very large and complex spreadsheets with lots of buttons, form elements, and other graphics can cause system crashes if a user's video card doesn't have enough RAM or is otherwise not of sufficient quality.

- Keep in mind goals of minimizing entry error, avoiding accidental deletion of valuable data and formulas, and keeping users oriented in the complex space of a worksheet—a very different set of goals than if you are preparing a printed report or slide presentation.

- If you need to export StarCalc files to be used in other programs, consider that not all formatting attributes will translate properly. Check the appearance of the exported file in the other program(s) to ensure you will achieve the effects you seek.

Tip #303 from *Michael & Sarah*	Make results stand out on a monitor display as well as in a report by applying conditional formatting, which applies a particular format to a cell only if the value falls within the parameters you specify. For more information, see "Making Results Stand Out with Conditional Formatting" later in this chapter.

If users need to do a lot of routine data entry on the spreadsheet you're creating, you might want to build a form.

FORMATTING FOR PRINTED REPORTS OR INVOICES

If you're creating a report or invoice for the printed page, keep the following tips in mind:

- Be sure that the most important information is in a larger font size and/or highlighted in some other way (in bold or given a colored background, for example).
- Don't mix too many fonts. Too many fonts confuse the eye.
- Choose graphics that match the quality of your printer. Don't choose a highly detailed color graphic if you have only a black-and-white inkjet printer.
- Leave some whitespace on your page. It gives people the visual space they need to take in your data.
- If you want to format very fancy tables, consider importing data from StarCalc into StarWriter.
- Consider using charts instead of tables to create greater visual impact.

FORMATTING FOR PRESENTATION SLIDES

If you're importing StarCalc data into StarImpress to create a presentation, keep the following tips in mind:

- Less is more. Presentations are most effective when they highlight a few key points and reinforce them with appropriate fonts, images, and charts rather than overwhelm people with data.
- Numbers don't speak for themselves. Use appropriate graphics, which can include use of background colors or images, as well as selected text and even sounds.

Although you can import data directly from a StarCalc spreadsheet, in most circumstances you'll probably want to create a chart to place on your slide rather than raw data, in which case you don't need to worry about how your data is formatted in StarCalc itself.

Tip #304 from
Michael & Sarah

You can just drag and drop table data from StarCalc onto a StarImpress slide. A StarImpress template with a blank spreadsheet is even ready and waiting. To make dragging and dropping easier, you can combine your StarCalc and StarImpress task windows by dragging one task button onto the other.

FORMATTING FOR WEB PUBLISHING

Publishing on the Web or a company intranet is a great way to make use of the valuable information stashed inside spreadsheets. With the rapid expansion of Internet commerce, spreadsheet databases are also useful for placing inventory lists and product descriptions online for shoppers.

If you're creating a spreadsheet or worksheet for publication on the Web, keep these tips in mind:

- Think presentation, not printed report. Don't put too much data on a page and, if you're saving basic spreadsheet rows and columns, make sure you've made them wide enough. You need whitespace between rows in particular so that people can easily follow rows across.

- If you're publishing for the general public rather than on a corporate intranet, don't use complicated graphics. They take a long time to download. People might become frustrated and give up.

- If you use imagemaps to create hyperlinks, consider including alternative, text-only hyperlinks as well. By doing so, you ensure that even if the user has trouble downloading graphics, he or she can still follow your links. It also aids blind and sight-impaired users who rely on programs that read the text of the site out loud to them.

If you're going to publish StarCalc worksheets on the Web, just save them as HTML files. (See Figure 15.2 for an example of a StarCalc file saved in HTML).

Figure 15.2
If you save StarCalc data in HTML, it is saved in a table format. Some of your fonts or formatting might be adjusted to match HTML conventions and limitations.

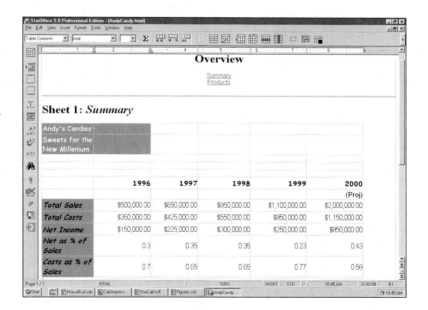

A lot of the work is done for you in this conversion process; you can then open the file in StarWriter/Web, add hyperlinks by using the hyperlink bar, and otherwise edit the material.

Tip #305 from
Michael & Sarah

Check the Tools, Options, General, Save dialog box to be sure that the option Save URLs Relative to Internet is selected. Otherwise, when you upload your files to the Web or intranet server, you need to manually edit your hyperlinks to reflect their new drive locations. (However, it's a good idea to check that your hyperlinks still work correctly after you've uploaded your files to your server, as sometimes strange things can happen in cyberspace.)

QUICK FORMATTING WITH AUTOFORMAT

If you already have a table of entered data and you just want to format it quickly for printing and presentation, then the AutoFormat command is for you. You have choices of 18 different formats. You can apply each format in full or selectively apply certain aspects of the formatting.

APPLYING EXISTING AUTOFORMATS

To open the AutoFormat dialog box, you must first select a range of cells in your spreadsheet. Then, choose the Format menu Autoformat command. The AutoFormat dialog box opens. It lists all available formats on the left and previews them on the right.

Click the More button to open a section that enables you to selectively apply portions of the format. By default, all options are selected (indicated by a black check mark in the check box). To deselect an option, click it. You immediately see the change in the Preview window.

If you find a format you like and are satisfied with all the options, click OK and your selected range is formatted before your eyes.

ADDING YOUR OWN CUSTOM FORMATS

If you have created your own custom format that you like, you can insert it into the AutoFormat dialog box using the Insert command. First, select the range of cells that have your applied formats. Then, open the AutoFormat dialog box and click Insert. You'll be prompted to enter a name for the format. Once you've entered a name, click OK. That's it! Your format is now available for application across all StarCalc spreadsheets *and* all StarWriter tables.

The StarCalc AutoFormat feature is exactly the same as the Table AutoFormat dialog used to autoformat tables in StarWriter. You can find more details about using the AutoFormat feature in Chapter 9, "Working with Tables, Charts, and Fields."

→ For additional information about using the AutoFormat, **see** "Formatting and Editing Tables," **p. 329**.

FORMATTING CELLS

By default, all cells are formatted in the Standard style. In this style, the General number format is applied, text is in Arial 10-point font, and cells have Standard horizontal and vertical alignment (which means that text is left-aligned, numbers are right-aligned, and all data is centered vertically and horizontally). The advantage of the Standard style is that cells recognize whether text or numbers are being input and place data accordingly, so you can tell the types apart.

Cells also, by default, have cell protection selected in the Protection tab of the Format, Page dialog box, but protection is activated only when you choose Tools, Protect Document to protect your worksheet or spreadsheet.

➔ For more information on protecting your work, **see** "Protecting Cells, Sheets, and Documents," **p. 523**.

➔ For more information on formatting cells to prevent them from printing, **see** "Selecting What to Print," **p.704**.

The most common tools you need for cell formatting are located right at your fingertips (or mousetips) on the object bar (see Figure 15.3).

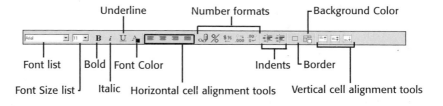

Figure 15.3
The StarCalc object bar contains the formatting tools you'll likely use most frequently.

If you open the Stylist, you see the four other predefined cell styles you can apply: Heading, Heading1, Result, and Result2. To apply a style from the Stylist, first select the cell or range you want to format, and then double-click the style name.

You can modify these predefined styles. If you do, be aware that these styles are called up internally and applied when the program carries out certain operations—for example, when subtotals are run—to format the results.

You can also create your own cell styles that then are added to the Stylist. Creating your own cell styles is discussed in the section "Creating and Applying Cell Styles with the Stylist" later in this chapter.

FORMATTING NUMBERS AND CURRENCY

By default, all cells have the General number format. This format automatically recognizes and formats the cells of numbers that you enter in StarCalc's recognized formats.

For example, if you enter 12% in a cell with General number format, StarCalc automatically recognizes that number as a percentage and applies the Percentage number format to the cell. From that moment forward, the cell will have the Percentage format until you change it.

The basic number formats are illustrated in Figure 15.4. The formats have each been applied to the same initial number, 12345, so that you can see the ways in which an existing number can be affected by applying a particular number format.

Figure 15.4
Applying number formats can make unexpected changes to a number's appearance—and in the case of time and percent styles can alter the actual number StarCalc stores as well.

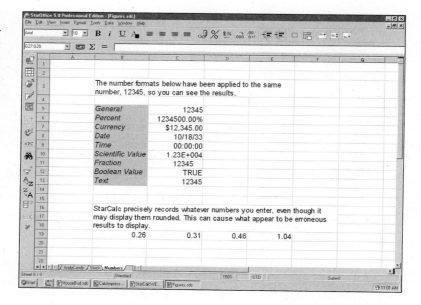

You can change number formats on the Numbers tab of the Cell Attributes dialog (which you open by choosing Format, Cells). You can also create and store your own custom number formats here.

You can apply formats to cells with existing data, or you can change the number format of any selection of blank cells. After you format blank cells, all numbers input are automatically formatted in the number style you assign (assuming you have input them correctly—for example, dates in mm/dd/yy format and times in hh:mm or hh:mm:ss format).

Within each category of number type, you also can choose a range of display options with regard to such characteristics as leading zeros, use of a thousands separator, and the display of negative numbers. For example, with currency you can choose to display negative numbers in the traditional red surrounded by brackets. You can see what your changes will look like in the Preview window. If you're not pleased, you can clear your changes by clicking the Reset button and start again, or you can cancel them and abandon the dialog altogether by clicking the Cancel button.

You can change the language assigned to any number format, which is handy if you're writing notation in a language that uses other symbol sets or numbers fonts. The default is System.

APPLYING NUMBER FORMATS WITH SHORTCUT TOOLS

 The StarCalc object bar contains shortcut tools for the most common number formatting needs; from left to right, they are the Currency, Percentage, Default (General) Number Format, Increase Decimal, and Decrease Decimal tools.

 These shortcut tools apply the current style assigned to that category in the Numbers tab of the Cell Attributes dialog (again, choose Format, Cells from the main menu to open this dialog). To change, for example, the number of decimal places that appear when you click the Percentage format tool, change the format of the Percent Category.

Tip #306 from	Regardless of the applied number formatting, when you select a numeric value, it appears
Michael & Sarah	as an integer in the Formula bar and in your cell—appearing as StarCalc actually saves it.

THE DANGERS OF FORMATTED NUMBERS

There are a few things you should particularly notice in Figure 15.4. When you apply the Percent format to an existing number, it has the effect of multiplying that number by 100 as well as adding a percent sign.

Also, when you apply the Time format to a number not already entered in the correct `hh:mm:ss` time format, the number ends up misshapen beyond recognition.

Caution	Even converting an accidentally time-formatted number back to Standard number format does not restore its original value, so be careful. If you accidentally apply the Time format to nontime values, you must re-enter your data.

There's also something important you *can't* see in this figure: You can't see any difference between the number that has been manually formatted as text and other numbers in the column. When the General number format and Standard alignment are applied to cells, text (even a number entered as text) is automatically recognized and entered as left-aligned so that it visually stands out from numeric values. However, when you apply the Text format to cells yourself, the alignment is determined by whatever the current settings may be on the Alignment tab of the Cell Attributes dialog (which you open by choosing Format, Cells).

Also, be aware that what you see on your screen does not necessarily reflect the actual number value of that cell, depending on the format you've assigned. For example, if you set your number format to display only two decimal places, but you enter the number `12.7456`, it is displayed as `12.75`. However, the actual number used in calculations is still 12.7456. This difference can cause the results of formulas to seem to be erroneous (see Figure 15.4 for an example). Always check the results of your calculations for these types of anomalies when proofing your work before printing.

Tip #307 from Michael & Sarah	You can set StarCalc to perform calculations with the rounded numbers displayed in the sheet instead of the internal values in the Calculation dialog box (which you open by choosing Tools, Options, Spreadsheet Documents).

CREATING CUSTOM NUMBER FORMATS

You can begin editing number formatting formulas right in the Format Code input field on the Numbers tab of the Cell Attributes dialog (which you open by choosing Format, Cells); see Figure 15.5. When you do so, you don't damage the program's existing formats.

Figure 15.5
You can create your own custom number formats by editing existing formats or creating your own from scratch using StarCalc's formatting codes.

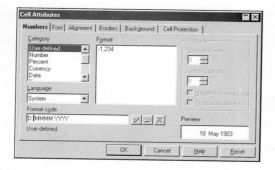

As soon as you begin altering a preset format, StarCalc starts creating a User-Defined format for you. If you click the green check mark or OK to accept your changes, the format is added both to your current category and to the User-Defined category.

The number formats are created through a formatting code. The best way to learn this code is just to browse through the preset formats and see their format codes roll by in the Format Code input field. We've included a few in Table 15.1 to get you started. The 0s in the formulas represent the number of leading zeros and the number of decimal places, respectively.

TABLE 15.1   SAMPLE STARCALC NUMBER FORMATTING CODES

Type of Format	Examples of Code	Result	Comments
Number	#,###	1248	No leading zeros or decimals in this example. The command inserts a thousands separator. The # symbol is a placeholder for any number (The number of placeholders does not place a limit on the number of digits you can enter).

Type of Format	Examples of Code	Result	Comments
	#,#00.0000	1,248.0000	Two leading zeros and four decimal places in this example.
Currency	$#,##0.00;[RED] (#,##0.00)	$1,200.00 ($1,200.00) (in red)	Note that the text color is in square brackets [ ], whereas the currency format is in regular parentheses ( ).
	¥####.00	¥ 1234.00	You don't have to use the dollar sign; you can use any symbol you like to preface currency figures. The # symbol is a placeholder for any number. (The number of placeholders does not place a limit on the number of digits you can enter).
Percent	0.00%	87.00%	StarCalc assumes you're applying the format to decimal values and always multiples by 100.
Date	M/D/YY HH:MM	12/31/99 23:59	Note that only a single M and D are required.
	NNNNMMMM DD,YYYY	Saturday, January 1, 2000	
	QQ.YY	4.Quarter.99	
Time	HH:MM AM/PM	02:00 PM	
	[HH]:MM:SS	14:00	The square brackets are translated by the program into the numeric code 8776, but this translation doesn't affect calculations.
Fraction	-1234 3/4		Space is made in the cell for fractional values even if none are entered.
	-1234 10/81		
Scientific	-1.23E+003		
	-1.23E+o3		
Text	@	Text	Anything formatted as text is ignored for purposes of calculation unless you choose otherwise.

TURNING THE DISPLAY OF ZEROS ON AND OFF

You can choose whether zeros display on your worksheets. By default, zeros are set to display. To change this setting, choose the Tools, Options command. Click the plus sign next to the Spreadsheet Documents entry, and click Contents to open the Contents dialog box. You see on the left a section labeled Display; deselect the Zero Values options to turn off the display of zeros. Select this option again to turn the display of zeros back on.

As with all other aspects of display in StarCalc, turning off the display does not delete anything: the zeros are still stored in your spreadsheet.

FORMATTING DATES AND TIMES

To change a cell or cell range's default date and/or time formats, select the cell(s) and choose Format, Cells. Then click the Numbers tab. Choose Date or Time from the Category list, and select the format you want from the list of options.

Tip #308 from
Michael & Sarah

To format a date in the default format, select the cell and press Shift+Ctrl+#.

If your system is set to display dates according to U.S. conventions, StarCalc recognizes dates entered only in the mm/dd/yy format. Dates entered in other forms are automatically formatted either as Text or as General. It's therefore best to enter your dates in mm/dd/yy format and then apply a different date formatting.

You can also apply the date formatting to blank cells, but you still must enter dates in the mm/dd/yy format. (When you enter them, they then automatically change their appearance to the formatting you chose.) If you apply a date format to a date entered before you applied date formatting, the entry does not change its appearance.

Whatever format you choose, you'll notice that just as with numbers, when you select a date, it appears in the date format StarCalc actually uses to store it, which is the mm/dd/yy format.

Tip #309 from
Michael & Sarah

StarCalc actually treats dates as integers for calculation purposes, counting a base date as zero and each subsequent day as a value one greater than the previous day. The default setting for 0 is December 31, 1899. You can change this default in the Tools, Options, Spreadsheets, Calculate dialog box.

When entering times, you should always enter them using colons as separators. Otherwise, they aren't recognized as times. Regardless of the time format applied, and with the General number style as well, you can enter times in the a.m./p.m. format, and they are recognized and formatted appropriately.

Another legacy of StarOffice's German origins, however, is that by default StarCalc is set to use a 24-hour clock instead of the common American a.m./p.m. style. Although you can change cell time formats, there doesn't seem to be any way to change the default time formatting on a global basis.

CHANGING FONT SIZES, STYLES, AND COLORS

One of the most common ways to improve the looks of your document is to change font sizes, styles, and colors. Whether for onscreen work or printed results, applying attributes such as bold and italics, changing font sizes so that headings are larger and easier to find, and judiciously applying color to make important results stand out can significantly improve the impact and readability of a document.

You have shortcut tools for the most commonly used font formatting commands right at your fingertips on the object bar. You can apply attributes to blank cells, or you can select the data you want to beautify and then click the desired tool. Using these tools is the best way to format on-the-fly. If you're creating styles or want to see a preview of the new look, use the Font tab of the Cell Attributes dialog box.

Tip #310 from
Michael & Sarah

Here's a great way to speed up your cell formatting. Choose Tools, Options, Spreadsheet. Click Entry to display the Entry dialog box, select Expand formatting, and choose OK. When you apply character formatting to data in a cell, you can now copy the formatting only to adjacent cells by selecting the cell and dragging it from the middle into surrounding blank cells. (Don't grab by the automatic fill handle, or you'll copy the entire word, not just the formatting.) Type your next entry into one of the cells to which you copied the format and press Enter, and the same formatting is applied.

CHANGING FONT AND FONT SIZE

To change your font or font size, just open the Font and Size drop-down lists on the StarCalc object bar, scroll until you find the font or font size you want to apply, and double-click (refer to Figure 15.3). Alternatively, you can apply a font or new font size through the Font tab of the Cell Attributes dialog, where you can see a preview of what it will look like before you apply it (see Figure 15.6).

Figure 15.6
The Format, Cells,
Font tab is the best
place to experiment
and create new styles
because you can com-
bine many effects at
once and preview
your results.

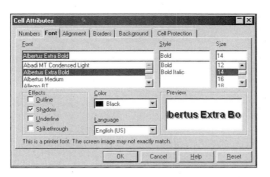

CHANGING FONT STYLE

To apply bold, italic, or underline styles, just select your cell(s) and click the corresponding tool.

Alternatively, you can change font style on the Font tab of the Cell Attributes dialog box.

CHANGING FONT COLOR

To change font color, first select the data and/or cells whose data you want to color. Then click the Font Color button, which opens a color palette. There, just click the color you want to apply.

Note that the Font Color button colors your text or numbers, not the cell background; another tool does that—the Background Color button on the far right of the object bar.

Tip #311 from
Michael & Sarah

You can make the color palette into a floating toolbar that remains open on your desktop as you work. Just click the Color Palette button and drag the palette by its title bar onto your desktop workspace.

Coloring your data can be a great way to make values you want to emphasize stand out. Coloring is equally useful for all forms of presentation (assuming you have a decent quality color printer). Keep in mind, however, that StarCalc uses color fonts in certain preset ways too, depending on options you have chosen. Specifically, in certain Currency number formats, StarCalc displays negative cash flow in red; and in Value Highlighting, it displays numeric values and dates in blue and the results of formulas in green. These preset options might be enough for your needs, and they're very easy to turn on and off. Of course, their effects are also global and give you less control over specific areas or elements of your spreadsheet. If you apply your own colors, you might want to choose colors other than blue, green, and red so that your message doesn't become confused.

APPLYING SPECIAL FONT EFFECTS

Besides being able to preview your changes on the Font tab of the Cell Attributes dialog, you can apply some additional font effects that aren't available through the object bar—outline, shadow, underline, and strikethrough.

The outline and shadow effects are best left for printed invoices or reports in which you want to make a strong visual impact, or Web pages and presentations in which you need visual excitement. They aren't the best choices for onscreen data entry. Using these effects is a simple way of introducing variety into a document that uses the same font throughout. Just be careful not to overdo it; remember that these effects essentially make your text into a graphic object, lessening its readability.

Underlining numbers can be a simple and useful way to make some numbers stand out, whereas strikethrough is traditionally used to indicate editing changes.

Note that StarCalc uses the double underline style when it creates subtotals with the Subtotals command.

CHANGING YOUR SPELLING LANGUAGE

You can change the language used in spellchecking for a selected worksheet or group of cells by choosing your new language from the Language list on the Format, Cells, Font tab. Assigning a language to your selected cells is the equivalent of assigning a language to specific words or paragraphs in StarWriter; it does not change the default settings of the document as a whole but just overrides those defaults in the case of the selected cells.

You also have the option of adjusting spelling options when you run the manual Spell command.

→ For more information on spellchecking your document, **see** "Using Common Proofing Tools," **p. 170**.

APPLYING CELL BACKGROUNDS AND BORDERS

Another way to make your data stand out is to apply background colors and borders to your cells. This way, you can make a title stand out, make the rows of a table easier to read, set off row or column headers, or set off data from notes and side material.

Tip #312 from	You can create your own custom colors using the options in the Colors dialog box. To open
Michael & Sarah	it, choose Tools, Options, click the plus sign next to General and click Colors to open the Colors dialog box.

Again, you can apply both borders and backgrounds on-the-fly by using the Border and Background Color buttons on the StarCalc object bar. Click the buttons to open palettes that you can tear off and move around your desktop. Just click a selection on a palette to apply it to your currently selected cell(s).

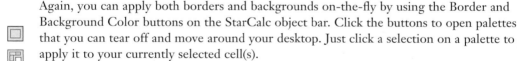

Although you can preview your background color on the Background tab of the Format, Cells dialog, doing so is not terribly useful because you just see a larger swatch of the color rather than see your data or sample data against the background. The Borders tab, however, is important because here you can change the line type being used on your borders palette, apply shadowing effects to cells, change line color, and change the preset bordering options.

Tip #313 from	Although, by default, StarCalc does not print gridlines, you don't have to apply borders
Michael & Sarah	yourself to achieve this effect. If you want gridlines to print, select Format, Page, click the Sheet tab, and select the Grid check box.

ALIGNING DATA IN CELLS

Because StarCalc, by default, differentiates between numeric and text entries, alignment works differently in StarCalc than in StarWriter. In StarWriter (as in most word processing programs), you cannot ever have a document set to *no alignment*. When you look at the alignment shortcut buttons on your toolbar in StarWriter, you'll notice that one of them is always pressed in and "on," so to speak.

In StarCalc, however, by default, all data is assigned the Standard alignment, which automatically adjusts the alignment of data in the cell based on its type. When Standard is on, you'll notice that none of your StarCalc horizontal or vertical alignment buttons appear pressed.

You can force the alignment to one of your choosing by selecting another option. Your choices are left, right, centered, or justified horizontal alignment, and top, bottom, or middle vertical alignment. When you choose one of these alignments, all cell data in the formatted cells, regardless of the type, is displayed accordingly.

Note that after you apply a left or right horizontal alignment to data, you might not be able to visually distinguish between a cell that has the Standard format applied or one that has hard right or left horizontal alignment.

Tip #314 from
Michael & Sarah

If you want your text right-aligned and have many numbers formatted as text, distinguishing them from numbers in numeric formats can become confusing. Turn on Value Highlighting (Ctrl+F8) to make your text-formatted numbers stand out; they all appear in black, whereas regular numbers appear in blue.

The quickest way to change alignment on-the-fly is to use the alignment buttons on the Function bar. The Horizontal alignment tools are grouped together between the font attributes shortcuts and the number format tools, and the vertical alignment tools are the last three tools on the right.

Note

The Vertical Top button has a bug in Version 5.0. It works as a toggle, moving your cell's alignment between Vertical Top and Vertical Bottom instead of just applying Vertical Top alignment to your cell. If you click it once and don't get the desired effect, just click it again and it should do what you want.

If you adjust your alignment through the Format, Cells, Alignment tab, you have a wider range of choices. Besides choosing your basic alignment options, you can also set an indent on left horizontal alignment and determine the distance your data will be from the gridlines—something useful when you start adjusting row and column heights and creating more variable page layouts.

WRAPPING TEXT TO FIT A CELL

If you don't want your spreadsheet text to look like one big run-on sentence, another option you have on the Alignment tab of the Cell Attributes dialog (which you open by choosing Format, Cells) is to turn on text wrapping within your selected cell(s). To do so, check the Text Flow Line Break option (look ahead to Figure 15.7). When you select it, your text is wrapped to fit the current column width.

Tip #315 from
Michael & Sarah

You can make text wrap on-the-fly by pressing Ctrl+Enter to create a manual line break. Make sure the cursor is positioned in the place you want the break to occur.

If you want your text to be wrapped but not *that* wrapped, you might also want to merge some cells so that you can create an attractive and readable text block. Look back at the lower text block in Figure 15.4 to see an example.

Text wrapping affects only data formatted as text.

→ For more information on merging cells, **see** "Merging and Centering Cells," **p. 570**.

ROTATING TEXT AND NUMBERS

On the right side of the Cell Attributes Alignment tab is a rotation wheel with which you can twirl your data around (see Figure 15.7).

Figure 15.7
The Alignment tab has some important options, including one for wrapping text in cells and another for rotating text and numbers.

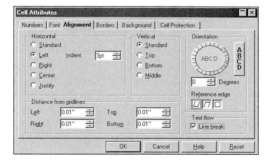

Rotating text is often very useful for labeling row and column heads, and it couldn't be simpler to do. However, the effects don't always turn out as you expect, so it's always a good idea to make a copy of your data on a blank worksheet and experiment rather than just apply rotation to your original data and perhaps mess up formatting of other data in the process.

Tip #316 from
Michael & Sarah

It's a good idea to adjust your row heights and/or column widths to the approximate size they need to be to accommodate your rotated data before you apply rotation effects because row heights do not automatically adjust. You then can see the results instantly.

When you're ready to rotate, select the cells you want to rotate. Although you can rotate blank cells so that data input later will automatically be rotated, doing so is not a good idea because proofing your data then becomes difficult.

The next step is to open the Alignment tab and either grab the dot on the rotation wheel and drag it around (the fun way), or enter the number of degrees you want to rotate your text (less fun but more precise and often faster). If you want your text to be rotated but still appear in the upright orientation, click the ABCD button that's next to the rotation wheel.

Rotation must occur around a pivot point or edge, and you're given three choices of reference edges: the top or bottom of the cell or the cell center (as if an imaginary line were drawn through the middle of the cell from left to right). Frankly, the differences in the final result seem negligible.

Rotating text is one of those tricks that a human has no trouble performing but turns out to be rather taxing of a computer's capability, and the results of the rotation option in StarCalc are far from perfect. The program seems to have some difficulty spacing fonts properly with rotated text, especially when you choose the upright text option. You might want to experiment with different fonts because some may look better after rotation than others.

Tip #317 from
Michael & Sarah

When you find a rotation angle and font that work well together, save them in a cell style so that you can apply it again in a single click. See "Creating and Applying Cell Styles with the Stylist" later in this chapter.

MERGING AND CENTERING CELLS

Often you might want to center text across columns of data. Obviously, you can't change the column width because doing so would disrupt the layout of data underneath your title. To achieve this effect, you need to merge a selected range of cells.

Note

Columns cannot be inserted into areas with merged cells. If you need to insert columns, you have to split your merged columns first.

To merge cells, select the range to be merged and choose the Merge Cells command from the Format menu. The command is available only when you have a selected range.

Choose Define from the submenu. If some cells in your selection have data that will be hidden when the merge occurs, you are prompted to decide the data's fate—to allow it to be hidden or to add it to the data in the first cell in the merged area. Make your decision and choose OK.

To split the cells again, place your cursor somewhere inside the merged area and select Format, Merge Cells, Split.

To center your cell contents, use the horizontal and vertical alignment buttons on your object bar, or make your settings on the Alignment tab of the Cell Attributes dialog.

DELETING A CELL'S STYLES

Using the Delete Contents command (Del), you can choose to delete only the formatting in a cell or range of cells. Because formatting is invisible (unless you select a cell and read its characteristics in the Cell Attributes dialog, which is quite time consuming), deletion may be the better part of valor when you're entering unknown cell territory. Deleting is also useful when you've applied hard formatting that you want to change.

→ For a more complete discussion of the Delete Contents command, **see** "Editing and Deleting Cells and Cell Contents," **p. 530**.

To delete cell formatting, select the cells in question, right-click to open the context menu, and choose Delete Contents. Make sure Delete All is deselected because only then can you choose other options. Select only Formats and then choose OK. All your formats—and nothing but your formats—are then deleted.

Tip #318 from
Michael & Sarah

If you format cells by applying styles, you can more easily delete and change formats.

RETURNING TO DEFAULT STYLE

If your hard formatting is becoming a buzzing, blooming confusion, you can revert any selection to the default Standard style by choosing the Default command from the Format menu.

FORMATTING ROWS AND COLUMNS

By default, the row height is 0.18 inch, and the column width is 0.89 inch. With the default font size of 10 points, these default row and column sizes work well for data entry because they give you enough room in a cell to see but enough cells on a page so that you can see a range of data. However, there quickly comes a time when you want or need to change the appearance of your rows and columns to suit your specific needs.

The task of managing your rows and columns can be summed up briefly in a few well-chosen words: context menus, clicking, and dragging. The Column and Row context menus, respectively, are shown in Figure 15.8.

Figure 15.8
The Column and Row context menus provide you with most of the commands you need to format columns and rows, but you can quickly resize them to fit your data by double-clicking a column's right border and a row's lower border.

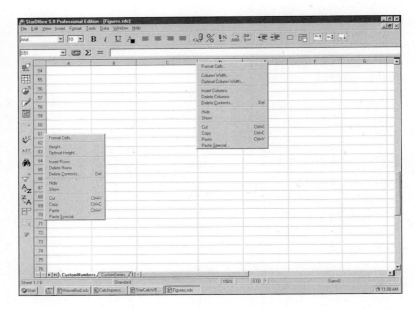

CHANGING ROW HEIGHTS AND COLUMN WIDTHS

You can change your row heights and column widths in a number of ways. The simplest but least precise way is to drag their headers with the mouse. Move your mouse pointer over the thin border between one row and another, or one column and another, until it turns into a double-facing arrow.

When the double-facing arrow pointer appears, click and drag the lower row border or right column border until the row or column reaches the desired size. As you drag, notice that a little yellow note pops up as a guide to the current measurement of your row or column.

The more precise way is to select the Height or Column Width command from the respective context menus. Selecting one of these commands opens a dialog in which you can enter a measurement in inches for your row or column. You can also choose to return a row or column to the program default sizes by clicking the Default check box in this dialog.

Although rows automatically adjust their size to accommodate the application of larger font sizes, columns do not automatically adjust to fit all your data. However, you can easily get your columns to automatically fit around existing data: Double-click the right border of the column, which is a shortcut for the Optimal Column Width command. You can use a similar shortcut to resize rows: Double-click the lower border of the row.

Note

The Guide refers you to a command that does not exist—Format, Column, AutoFit—to make a column automatically resize itself to accommodate the largest data string in it. The name of the command is really Format, Column, Optimal Width. Rows have an equivalent command, Optimal Height.

If using the shortcuts makes the job too easy for you, you can also choose the Optimal Column Width command from the column context menu. Choosing this command opens a dialog, where, once again, you can input a precise value in inches. You can also specify the amount of clearance you want between your data and the edge of the column. By default, the clearance for columns is 0.01 inch.

The equivalent menu command for rows is the Optimal Height command, which opens a similar dialog box. The default clearance for rows is 0.00 inch.

Tip #319 from *Michael & Sarah*	For resizing columns on-the-fly, press Alt together with the up- or down-arrow key to increase or decrease row height. Press Alt together with the left- or right-arrow key to increase or decrease column size.

Setting a column or row to optimal width or height is a temporary measure; if you change the size or length of data in the row or column, they do not automatically adjust again. The same is true of settings made through the Row Height and Width commands on the context menus.

The same commands are available on the Format menu, although they try to confuse you by having slightly different names—you're smarter than that.

HIDING ROWS AND COLUMNS

Seeing the data you need can be tricky with a spreadsheet. One way to improve visibility is to hide rows and columns.

Tip #320 from *Michael & Sarah*	Because hidden rows and columns don't print, you can use the Hide Row and Hide Column commands to help define the print data area.

To hide rows or columns, select the ones you want to hide and choose the Hide command from the appropriate context menu. (Remember that your cursor must be in the header area to make the context menu appear.)They disappear before your eyes, leaving a thickened black border line between the remaining rows or columns. (Alternatively, you can hide them with the Format menu Row or Column Hide commands.) To reveal them—which is the trickier part—click somewhere on this darkened black border in the header area, and choose the Reveal command. If you have difficulty, try selecting the adjacent rows or columns on either side and choosing the Reveal command again.

FORMATTING WITH GROUPS AND OUTLINES

Using the Group feature is also a good way to selectively hide rows and/or columns on a worksheet.

→ For information on using outlines, **see** "Entering Data," **p. 508**.

Using this feature can also be an excellent way to format spreadsheets that are used primarily online for data entry and viewing. When you group rows or columns, you can quickly and easily hide areas that you no longer need to see for your work and reveal them with a click when you want to see their data again.

CREATING AND APPLYING CELL STYLES WITH THE STYLIST

Many people never bother to learn about or create styles in their documents, preferring to just format as they go along. Working like this is the equivalent of using a spreadsheet but never creating formulas because it seems faster to calculate each result as you go along.

Tip #321 from	Using cell styles consistently instead of formatting on-the-fly can help you avoid errors that
Michael & Sarah	result from having hidden formatting in cells.

Using cell styles enables you to make formatting changes to your spreadsheet much more quickly. It also opens up automation possibilities for you with powerful commands such as conditional formatting. These commands can even help you navigate quickly around your spreadsheet and proof your document, just as the Search and Replace command can search for particular styles.

The five default cell styles serve as parent styles for all subsequent styles you create. Although you can modify these styles, you cannot delete them from the program.

CREATING A NEW CELL STYLE BY EXAMPLE

To create a new cell style in StarCalc, first apply formatting to existing cell data until you achieve the look you want. You can apply formats via the toolbar and keyboard shortcuts and/or through the Cell Attributes dialog (which you open by choosing Format, Cells). If you use this dialog, you can preview your work, and you also have access to a number of options that aren't available through shortcuts.

When your text appears as you like it, click the Stylist button to open the Stylist on your workspace (see Figure 15.9). Be sure that the Cells Styles button is pressed, not the Page Styles button.

Figure 15.9
You create new styles and apply and update existing styles with the Stylist.

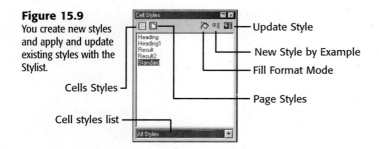

Select your formatted text, and click the New Style by Example button. You then are prompted to enter a name for your style in the Create Style dialog, which also lists the names of all the other custom cell formats you've already created in that spreadsheet. Type the name and choose OK—you're in style!

APPLYING CELL STYLES

You can choose from two different methods of applying an existing style. The first is to select a range of cells and then double-click the style name you want to apply in the Stylist list.

The second—which enables you to quickly apply formatting to noncontiguous cells—is to click the style name you want to apply and then click the Fill Format Mode button on the Stylist toolbar (the one that looks like a paint bucket).

When you move your pointer outside the Stylist, you see that your pointer changes into a paint can. Click the cell(s) you want to format until you're done, and then click the Fill Format mode tool again to turn it off.

UPDATING CELL STYLES

To update an existing cell style, select the cell that represents the updated style, and click the Update Style tool on the Stylist toolbar.

CREATING FAMILIES OF STYLES

Besides creating a new style by example, you can also create a new style by basing it on an existing style. Why do this? You might do so for a number of reasons.

One is that well-designed documents usually use a family of closely related styles. These styles apply characteristics such as color and different font weights and alignments to provide variety and make various document elements stand out or recede. Typically, though, you should use a limited number of fonts—perhaps one or two—to ensure that the document is still easy to take in with both eye and mind.

If you create a family of styles, using your initial style as a base on which to build is much faster than re-creating the entire style from scratch.

Another reason to create a new style based on an older one is that after you have built a style family this way, you can make a change to the parent style and globally change all other styles based on it. For example, say you have created a style family of 10 cell styles using the Arial font, but your business then switches to using Futura fonts. To update all 10 styles, all you need to do is change the font assigned to the parent style. All the others are automatically updated.

You can also, via the Organizer, attach your styles to other templates to make the same sets of formatting available to other spreadsheet documents.

→ For more information on using the Style Catalog and the Organizer, **see** "Managing Styles with the Style Catalog," **p. 306**.

CREATING A NEW STYLE FROM THE OLD

To create a new style from an existing cell style, select an existing style name in the Stylist, right-click to open its context menu, and choose New. You then see a tab labeled Organizer on top, with a name like Untitled1 in the Name field. Type in a name for your new style here.

Next, select the existing style on which you want to base this new one. The default parent style is Standard, but you can select any style you want from the drop-down style list.

If you're creating a style for a specific purpose—say, making low student scores stand out or highlighting top sales performers—it's good practice to name your style after its use rather than its formatting attributes. Names like LowGrade or TopSales help guide both you and others in applying the style with consistency.

Behind the Organizer tab lies the already-familiar cell format tabs, currently filled in with all the characteristics of your selected existing style. Make whatever modifications you want to the style characteristics, and choose OK when you're done.

→ For more information on the Numbers, Font, Alignment, Borders, and Background tabs, **see** "Formatting Cells," **p. 559**.

If you want to erase everything and start from scratch, you can click the Standard button, which returns the formatting on the tabs to the program default Standard cell format. The Reset button resets the tabs to reflect the styles on first opening the dialog, and Cancel exits the dialog altogether without registering the new style.

Caution

After you've created a style based on another, these styles exist in a hierarchical chain of dependence. If you delete the parent style, all its children are affected, and your document reverts to aspects of one of the preset styles.

If you try to base a style on itself or on another style that depends on it, you receive an error message stating that you cannot create such a style because it involves a recursive reference. After all, a mother cannot be granddaughter to herself.

MODIFYING AN EXISTING STYLE

If you want to modify a style you've created, select its name, right-click to open its context menu and choose Modify.

You then see a summary of all its current style characteristics in the lower portion of the Organizer tab, in the section labeled Contains.

Make the changes you want on all relevant tabs, and then choose OK. All cells currently formatted in that style are updated automatically.

MAKING RESULTS STAND OUT WITH CONDITIONAL FORMATTING

A good reason for creating cell styles, if you're not convinced already, is that they enable you to apply conditional formatting. *Conditional formatting* is formatting that is selectively applied to data in cells based on specific conditions that you set through the Conditional Formatting dialog box (see Figure 15.10). Select Format, Conditional Formatting to open this dialog.

Figure 15.10
You can apply conditional formatting directly to values, or you can write formulas that apply formatting to a range of cells that meet a specified target. When you apply it to values, you use the same kind of Boolean logic as in creating filters.

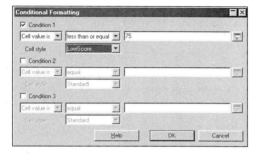

Perhaps, for example, you're preparing for a monthly staff meeting in which you'll go over staff productivity reports, and you want to highlight the outstanding performers, as measured by the number of tasks they've completed. You decide to format their names and numbers in bold and blue.

You can apply conditional formatting to the relevant cells—that is, all the cells containing data on employee productivity. Then, as you enter data and the totals are calculated, StarCalc automatically applies your formatting to the appropriate names and figures, based on your criteria. After you format the worksheet in this way, you can save it and use it as a template for future monthly reports. As employees' productivity changes, the formatting automatically changes as appropriate.

A simple example of conditional formatting is shown in Figure 15.11. Here, it's been applied to a student grade sheet. Students who have an average grade of 75 or lower at midterm are sent warning notices. Conditional formatting has been applied to the values in the column MidtermAvg (which are the results of an averaging formula) such that if the cell value is less than or equal to 75, the style LowGrade, created earlier, is automatically applied. This style highlights the number in red and places a red border around the cell.

Figure 15.11
Creating cell styles gives you the benefit of advanced automation and productivity commands such as conditional formatting, which highlights values automatically based on criteria you set. Here, a teacher's work is made easier by automatic flagging of students with low grades.

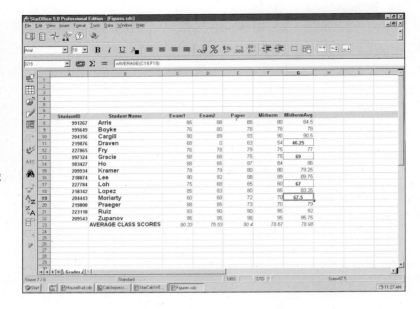

You can also choose to highlight a range of cells if together they meet criteria you spell out in a formula. For example, you can use the formula AVERAGE(C23:F23)=80 and choose cell style HIAVG to highlight all averages that result in a high midterm average. (Of course, for this particular class, the conditions would not be met!)

After you have created the cell style you want to apply, select the range of cells to which you want to apply conditional formatting. These cells can be blank and/or contain data.

Tip #322 from
Michael & Sarah

You might want to open the Stylist so that you can see all your cell style choices in one glance. You should also prepare your formula beforehand because you can't open the Function AutoPilot from within the Conditional Formatting dialog box.

Choose Format, Conditional Formatting to open the Conditional Formatting dialog box. First, choose the type of cell data you're targeting—Formula or Cell Value. Then, if your choice is Formula, type in the formula.

You can combine rules (up to three) so that you can look for both types of data—for example, choosing to format only results of a particular formula that have achieved a certain value. To add other criteria, you must click the Condition 2 or Condition 3 check box before the entry fields become active.

Note that you cannot enter text strings as conditions without writing formulas that allow for them; text entered as a value is interpreted as a 0.

CREATING STARCALC TEMPLATES

If you go to the trouble of creating your own styles, why not go all the way and create and save your own StarCalc templates?

Originally, the word *template* referred to a kind of pattern mask used by carpenters and other craftsmen to help cut out and create pieces of standard size and shape. The word was adapted in computer publishing to mean a model document that stores the tools you need to quickly and easily create a specific type of document.

In StarOffice, those tools can include styles, program options, and custom desktop configurations (for example, specific toolbar and menu configurations). You can also extend the functionality of StarCalc by creating and attaching your own macros, StarBasic scripts, and StarBasic programs. You can even substitute your own template for the default StarCalc Standard template.

Just as with customizing tools and menus, working with templates shares many commonalties across applications. Aspects of working with templates specific to StarCalc are discussed in this section, but you'll find relevant information elsewhere in this manual as well. You'll also find that what you learn here translates directly to other program modules.

→ For more tips and details on managing templates, **see** "Managing Templates," **p. 167**.

→ For more information on creating and working with macros, **see** "Creating a Macro for an Everyday Task," **p. 1242**; and "Organizing Macros in Libraries and Modules," **p. 1252**.

→ For more information on attaching macros, **see** "Assigning Macros to Events," **page 1312**, and "Surviving Everyday Tasks," **page 1316**. Many of the examples are for StarWriter, but the procedures are the same across application modules.

UNDERSTANDING STARCALC'S STANDARD TEMPLATE

Although you may not realize it, you use a template every time you open a StarCalc document. A document can't be created or opened, in fact, without a template to guide the program in laying out the page and ordering and displaying your data. By default, the StarCalc Standard template is used. The Standard template contains a number of basic styles (including the Standard cell format).

Tip #323 from
Michael & Sarah

Each module in the program has its own Standard template that's the default used to generate a new, blank document. Most of these templates are actually special StarBasic scripts, however, not just documents saved with a special suffix. This is why your Standard StarCalc spreadsheet can do fancy things like automatically recognize data as numbers, dates, or text and other such magic. The StarCalc Standard spreadsheet file is referred to as `_10_~Spreadsheet`, and its path (URL) is represented in a special way, `private:factory/scalc`. However, there is no physical file with this name. Because of the special nature of these Standard templates, you can't directly edit them. It's also best not to delete the links to these templates (found in the Office51/config/new directory and the Office51/Desktop directory, among other locations).

CREATING A TEMPLATE FROM SCRATCH

There is no AutoPilot wizard for creating a spreadsheet or spreadsheet template as there is for creating a text or presentation document. You must create a template from scratch. However, there's not much more to creating a template than creating a document. In fact, the best way to go about creating a template is to create a dummy document that can then serve to show future users what styles, tools, and commands the template offers. After creating a spreadsheet with all the cell and page styles, workspace customization features, and macros, scripts, and attached programs you want, you'll save the file as a StarCalc 5.0 or 5.1 template rather than a regular StarCalc document.

You can also use the preset spreadsheet templates and samples included with the program as models for new templates and just modify them to suit your own purposes. Look for spreadsheet templates in the Templates dialog box (look ahead to Figure 15.12); most are in the category Financial Documents. Look for spreadsheet sample documents in the Samples\Spreadsheet folder that opens from the Explorer.

To create a new document based on a spreadsheet template, use the File, New, From Template command (Ctrl+N). If you click More, the dialog box expands to give you more options and you can view a thumbnail preview of the template.

To create a new template based on one of these templates, or to modify a default template, choose the Templates command from the File menu, which opens the Templates dialog box, your template management headquarters (see Figure 15.12).

Note

To open the Templates dialog box, you must first be inside a StarOffice document; the command is not available from the StarDesktop.

Figure 15.12
The File, Templates dialog presents all templates saved in the Office51/templates folder. Double-click to open a new document based on the template, or select and choose Edit to modify it as a template. Choosing Organizer opens the Document Templates Organizer, the same one you can open from the Style Catalog (Ctrl+Y).

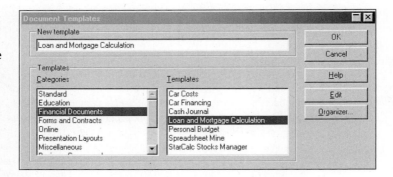

Select the Financial Documents category; you see a list of all available templates appear on the left. Select one you want to modify and save as a a template and click Edit. It opens on the desktop, and you can proceed just as if you were working in a regular StarCalc document, creating styles and making modifications as usual. When you save it, be sure to save it as a StarCalc template, not a regular file. You can assign it a new name, or overwrite the existing template. It will be available to you the next time you use the New, From Template command or open the Templates dialog.

You can preview samples and templates on your desktop without opening them. Both the Samples and Templates folders are in the Explorer. Double-click the folder you want to open on the desktop. Then, click the Preview button on the desktop object bar. Click a document, and a preview loads in the desktop preview window, as shown in Figure 15.13.

Figure 15.13
You can preview spreadsheet samples or templates on the desktop to see if any might be suitable as a basis for your own template.

Preview button

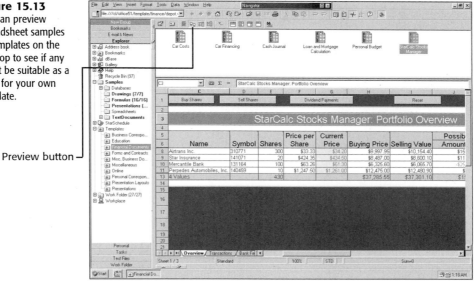

SUBSTITUTING YOUR TEMPLATE FOR THE STANDARD TEMPLATE

If you find the Standard template—the one that generates a new spreadsheet document with the File, New command—doesn't meet your needs, you can set your own template or document to serve as the default template in its place.

To set your StarCalc template file as the default Standard template, follow these steps:

1. Create and save a StarCalc document or template.

2. Open the Explorer and navigate to the folder in which you saved your template.

3. Open the Beamer.

4. Extend-click on the folder with your template to reveal its contents in the Beamer.

5. Select your template or document file in the Beamer.

6. Right-click to open the Beamer context menu, and select Set Default Template, Spreadsheet.

RESETTING THE DEFAULT TEMPLATE TO THE STANDARD TEMPLATE

You can reset your template to the Standard easily if you haven't deleted its links in the Office51/config/new folder. Other places you can find links to the Standard new spreadsheet template are the Office51/Desktop folder and the Office51/config/start folder. You can create a new link in the Office51/config/new folder if you need, by using the Create Link command in the context menu.

Assuming you already have a link to the spreadsheet Standard template in the /new folder, here are the steps to follow to reset the Standard template as the default:

1. Navigate to the Office51/config/new folder in the Explorer.

2. Extend-click to display its contents in the Beamer.

3. Select the 10_~Spreadsheet filename, with the StarCalc spreadsheet icon.

4. Right-click to open its context menu and choose the Return to Default.

CUSTOMIZING YOUR STARCALC WORKSPACE

A template is not just a place to store styles, but also to store customized settings for your work environment. Most of your spreadsheet-specific customization options are located in the Spreadsheet Documents dialog boxes opened through the Tools, Options "master dialog" box. There are numerous settings you can adjust that change your workspace appearance and can make your formatting and layout work easier. (Many of these options can also be turned on and off on the fly while working in StarCalc either through keyboard shortcuts or menu commands.) This section reviews a number of these options.

You can also customize your toolbars, menus, and the StarCalc status bar as well as attach macros and scripts. With this type of customization, you have the option of saving your settings to your active template or saving a configuration to a file that you can then either load as needed or attach to a specific template. This customization is done via the Tools, Configure dialog. The procedures for these types of customization are discussed in Chapter 3, "Getting Ready for Work."

→ For more information on customizing your desktop tools and menus, **see** "Customizing Desktop Tools and Menus," **p. 115**.

MODIFYING THE WORKSPACE APPEARANCE

You can change the appearance of your StarCalc workspace in a number of ways in the Layout dialog box of the Spreadsheet Documents options, opened by choosing Tools, Options (see Figure 15.14).

Figure 15.14
Selections in the Layout dialog box affect the layout grid of your StarCalc worksheet, which determines how you place objects and text on your printed page; and the display of other layout guides.

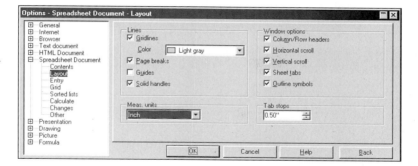

TURNING VISIBLE CELL BORDERS ON AND OFF

By default, StarCalc displays on your screen with light gray gridlines that show the borders of cells and help orient you on your worksheet. On the Lines area of the Layout options dialog box, you can turn off and on the display of these gridlines. You can also change the color used to render the lines on your monitor.

Tip #324 from
Michael & Sarah

The Gridlines option in the Spreadsheet Documents Layout dialog box affects only the workspace display on your monitor. If you want to print gridlines in your documents, check the Grid option on the Sheet tab of the Format, Page dialog box.

Note

The Gridlines option in the Layout dialog box has no relationship to the grid whose options are set in the Spreadsheet Documents Grid dialog box of the Tools, Options master dialog.

You can also turn off and on the display of page breaks, guides, and/or object's "solid handles" (the green boxes that appear on their perimeter). Turning off their display does not delete these lines and guides; it only makes them invisible while you work.

CHANGING MEASUREMENT UNITS OF YOUR GRID

If you're using U.S. system settings, by default your worksheet grid uses inches as measurement unit. You can change your units to millimeters, centimeters, points, or picas. This affects only the measurement units used to create your workspace grid. The workspace grid is normally invisible, but you can turn on its display on the Grids tab of this same dialog.

CHANGING TAB STOPS

The Tab Stops setting on the Layout options dialog box affects the tab settings in text boxes you create in StarCalc. It has no affect on the action of the tab key within your worksheet where pressing Tab key moves you one cell to the right rather than creating an indent.

CONTROLLING DISPLAY OF COLUMN AND ROW HEADERS

By default, StarCalc displays row and column headers—the numbers and letters on the left and top borders of your window, respectively—to help you navigate and determine cell references. Sometimes, however, you may want to turn these headers off. For example, if you have created a form or invoice which uses in-cell editing, you may find the headers distracting rather than useful. Deselect the Column/Row Headers option in the Window Display section of the Layout dialog box to turn off their display.

CONTROLLING DISPLAY OF SHEET TABS AND OUTLINE SYMBOLS

Sheet tabs are the projecting areas at the bottom of your worksheets that display worksheet names. You can turn off their display by deselecting the Sheet tabs option. If you turn the display of tabs off, you will not be able to open the worksheet context menu or navigate among worksheets in a spreadsheet.

By default, the Outline symbols created when you group areas, create Subtotals, or create outlines are set to display. You can turn their display off and on by deselecting and selecting the Outline Symbols option.

SETTING ENTRY AND FORMATTING OPTIONS

In the Spreadsheet Documents Entry dialog box (opened through the Tools, Options "master dialog"), you can change the effects of pressing the Enter key and adjust a potpourri of other options that affect the input of data in StarCalc.

By default, pressing Enter enters any data in a cell and/or the formula input line and moves the cursor down one row to the next cell. You can change the direction in which the cursor moves after pressing Enter by selecting another direction (up, right, or left) from the drop-down list visible in Figure 15.15.

Figure 15.15
Options in the Entry dialog box actually affect both window display and entry options. The most commonly used options are those that allow you to change the effect of pressing Enter.

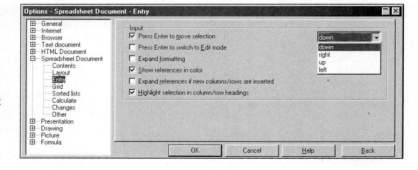

You can also make pressing Enter switch you into in-cell editing mode rather than immediately moving you to the next. If this option is selected, when you press Enter in a newly active cell, your cursor will switch to a blinking insertion cursor and you'll be in in-cell editing mode. When you've completed any data entry and press Enter (or if you just press Enter again), you'll move to the next cell as usual.

The Show references in color option works counter-intuitively. When selected (the default) cell references display in different colors when a cell with a formula is selected and the formula displays in the input line. This can be helpful when editing formulas, as it makes different references stand out more clearly. If you clear this check box, references from formulas in the Input Row will not be highlighted in color.

The Expand Formatting option is by default deselected, but is a very useful aid for fast formatting. When selected, you can copy the formatting characteristics only of a cell to its adjacent cells by selecting the cell and dragging it, from the middle of its border, into surrounding blank cells. (Don't grab by the automatic fill handle, or you'll copy the data in the cell as well, not just the formatting.) Type your next entry into one of the cells to which you copied the format and press Enter, and the same formatting will be applied.

Expand references if new columns/rows are inserted is selected by default, and you should not deselect this option except with good reason. This option, when selected, automatically adjusts all your (relative) cell references when you insert new rows and/or columns into the middle of databases or other existing data areas. This ensures that all your cell references in formulas remain accurate. If you deselect this option, your references will not be updated and it could wreak havoc with your formulas in a complex spreadsheet (which is especially nasty if you have cross-references across different worksheets or spreadsheets).

By default, row and column headers of selected rows and columns display in bold to help orient you as you make selections. You can turn this feature off by deselecting the Highlight Selection option in Row/Column Headings.

SETTING LAYOUT GRID PREFERENCES

From your point of view, your StarCalc workspace is defined by a grid of cells. From StarOffice's point of view, it's defined by an invisible grid (created in the default measurement units you've chosen) that StarOffice uses to determine the placement of objects and text. You can make this grid visible, if you like, by selecting the Visible grid option in the Spreadsheet Documents Grid dialog box (choose Tools, Options, Spreadsheet, Grid). Figure 15.16 shows the Grid tab on top of a worksheet with the grid turned on. Having the grid visible can help you positions charts and other objects when preparing your spreadsheet for printing.

Note This grid has no relationship to the Gridlines option in the Layout dialog box.

A grid is more than a useful visual aid, however. If you turn on the Snap-to-Grid option in the same section, layout becomes faster and easier. With Snap-to-Grid on, objects that you move within a certain distance (the tolerance) of the grid line automatically "snap" into place on that line, as if the line were a magnet grabbing the object's border. (This snap effect occurs even if the visible grid is turned off.) This helps you do precise layout with the somewhat imprecise movements of a mouse. Such precision is important when creating documents for professional printing output.

Figure 15.16
In the Grid dialog box, you can customize the size of your layout grid. To change the measurement units used for the grid, change the default units in the Layout dialog box first.

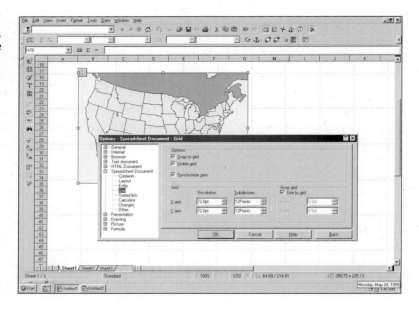

The options on the Grid portion of the dialog box enable you to determine the size of the main grid. If you select the Synchronize Axes option up above, the X and Y axes of the grid are automatically matched to each other's size. If you deselect this option, you can set independent sizes for the X and Y axes.

Normally, in desktop publishing layout programs, you have only one grid. In StarCalc, technically the main grid that you use as a visual guide and Snap grid that aligns your objects are separate, and you can determine their axes independent of one another. The Snap Grid portion of the dialog box enables you to set the size of the Snap grid. In practice, however, you don't want to make the Snap grid entirely independent of the main grid because the main grid is the one you can make visible. Otherwise, the Visible Grid option loses its usefulness—the whole point is for you to see where to place your objects.

You can, however, link the size of the Snap grid to that of the main grid (by selecting the Size to Grid option) and use the Subdivision spin boxes to fine-tune the size of the Snap grid in fixed relationship to the main grid. The Subdivision uses points, the standard measurement for type bodies, as the unit of measurement. (A point is approximately 1/72 of an inch.) This enables you to have fine control over the placement of your objects while also setting the main cells of the grid to a more reasonable size.

If you need this type of precision in your layout, your first step should be to return to the Layout dialog box of the Spreadsheet Documents options, and select Points as your standard unit of measurement for the grid. Since the subdivision units are in points, you want your main and snap grids to be set in points as well. Then, return to the Grid dialog box and follow these steps:

1. Set your X and Y axis values.

2. Select the Size to Grid option in the Snap portion of the dialog box.

3. Set the subdivision spin boxes at 0. You'll notice that the values for the snap grid X and Y axes match those you've entered for the main grid.

4. Click the up arrow in the subdivision spin boxes to set the grid subdivision to the degree of precision you desire. Note how the snap grid measurements change in relation to the changes you make in the subdivision spin boxes. The higher the number of points you enter, the more precise is your snap to grid tolerance.

5. When you have created a grid of the desired size and precision, click OK. If you have the Visible Grid option selected, you'll immediately see your grid appear.

Your subdivisions appear as small dots that create borders between the larger points of the grid. For example, in Figure 15.16, the basic grid is set to display at 72 points with synchronized axes, which creates an even appearance of square cells. The subdivision is set at 12 points, with a snap-to-grid setting of 5.5 inches.

TROUBLESHOOTING

I have some formula results that seem too low, and I can't figure out why.

You could be experiencing calculation errors for many reasons, but a common one is that you've accidentally entered numbers, dates, or times in cells formatted as text. Any data defined as text is not included in calculations. You can use the functions TIMEVALUE and DATEVALUE to cause text-formatted dates and times to be converted into serial numbers for calculation purposes, but for integers the only solution is to reformat your cells. The quickest way to do so is to select the ranges of cells involved in your calculations and choose the Default command from the Format menu, which returns all data to the default General Number format.

The results of my formula don't add up from my input.

If you've applied a format to your cells that rounds your numbers, your onscreen numbers might look off compared to the actual numbers stored in StarCalc. You have a couple of options: In the Format, Cells, Number tab, increase the number of decimal places your numbers display; or select the Precision as Shown option in the Tools, Options, Spreadsheet, Calculation dialog box, which uses your rounded display numbers for calculations.

I applied color formatting to my cells, but the color doesn't show up onscreen, or it shows up as the wrong color.

You probably have Value Highlighting turned on; this feature overrides formatted font colors. Try viewing your document in Page view; the colors should appear correctly there. If you want them to appear in your document, turn off Value Highlighting in the View menu, or in the Tools, Options, Spreadsheet, Contents dialog box.

Suddenly, my cell formats changed on me.

You may have created a family of styles and then deleted a parent style. Without the parent style to refer to for style definition, StarCalc reverts to characteristics of whichever default format serves as the "grandparent."

Alternatively, you may have accidentally deleted cell formats when using the Delete Contents command (Del). The default in the Delete Contents options list is for Formats to be deselected, but it might be turned on. Select a cell and press Del to open the Delete Contents command; then check its settings. If your styles have indeed been deleted, you need to reapply them.

CHAPTER 16

USING FORMULAS AND FUNCTIONS

In this chapter

WHAT IS A FORMULA?

A *formula* is a mathematical or logical statement that performs operations on input and calculates a result. The ability to apply formulas to data and to use the built-in formulas called *functions* is the reason that people use spreadsheets. With formulas and functions, you can automate most routine calculations as well as calculate very complex "what if?" scenarios, analyze text data in databases, and manage your spreadsheet in a variety of ways.

Of course, the trick is having the right input in the first place—but that's your job, not StarCalc's. Give it your numbers, though, and StarCalc will do them right.

You always begin a formula in StarCalc with an equals sign (=). In this as in many other matters (although not all), StarCalc's procedures for working with formulas and functions are like those in Excel, making the transition to StarCalc relatively easy. Unlike Excel, however, StarCalc arguments are separated by a semicolon (not a comma). Functions or parts within a complex formula are bracketed with parentheses.

The following is an example of one of the formulas you might use in StarCalc:

```
=SUM(C10:C20)
```

The preceding example returns the sum of all values in the cells C10, C11, C12, and so on through cell C20. The following

```
=DCOUNT(Sales;"turnover";Criteria.A3:E5)
```

returns a count of all cells in the named data area `Sales`, in the column named `turnover`, that meet the criteria you specified in the cell range that falls between cell `A3` and cell `E5` on the worksheet named `Criteria`.

After you enter a formula on your sheet, by default, the results are displayed. However, you can make formulas appear directly in their cells by choosing the Display Formulas option on the Tools, Options, Spreadsheet, Contents tab. This capability can be quite useful when you're checking and debugging formulas.

CREATING FORMULAS IN STARCALC

You can enter formulas in-cell or in the Formula bar input line. To ease your work, you can use the Function symbol tool, which is located to the immediate left of the input line. Just click it, and an = is placed at the beginning of your line. Next is the Σ symbol, which stands for `Sum`, the most commonly used function. Click to enter an = and the `Sum` function in the input line. To the left of `Sum` is the Function AutoPilot tool. Click it to open the Function AutoPilot, which lists all of StarCalc's functions and enables you to build and test formulas before you enter them into your worksheet.

Working with the Function AutoPilot is described in more detail in the section "Using the Function AutoPilot" later in this chapter. StarCalc's add-in functions are listed in Table 16.4.

Tip #325 from
Michael & Sarah

If you find it awkward to reach for the = key, you can just type your formula and press Shift+Ctrl+Enter. When you do, StarCalc automatically puts the = sign at the beginning.

ELEMENTS OF FORMULAS

The elements that a formula can contain are listed in Table 16.1.

TABLE 16.1   ELEMENTS OF A STARCALC FORMULA

Type of Element	Explanation	Example
Numeric and text values (constraints)	Numbers and text strings 12, that you directly enter into your formulas.	`Today's Date Is.`
Cell references	The equivalent of values, except instead of directly inputting values, you refer StarCalc to a cell or cells from which StarCalc takes the values.	`C12:D15`
Cell and database range names	Names you assign areas of cells in your spreadsheet. You can't use any special characters (symbols reserved by StarCalc, including operators), but otherwise you can name rangesas you like.	`Sales, WorkSheet1`
Parentheses	Markers that split your formula into meaningful segments and help define the logical order in which operations are performed.	`( )`
Arithmetic operators	Operators for the basic arithmetic functions of subtraction, addition, division, and multiplication as well as more advanced mathematical operations such as exponents.	`- + / * ^`
Comparison operators	Operators that make comparisons between two values or sets of values.	`= < > <= >= <>`
Text operator	An operator that joins together two pieces of text data.	`&`

continues

TABLE 16.1   CONTINUED

Type of Element	Explanation	Example
Reference operators	Operators that inform StarCalc how to treat an entered value or reference.	Colon (:), semicolon (;), and exclamation point (!)
Functions Sum(A1:B10)	Special types of operators.	

REFERENCE OPERATORS

Reference operators are operators that enable you to refer to cells in more complex ways than to just list a single cell address.

When you join cell references with a colon, you alert StarCalc to treat those two cells as the first and last in a range in which all values should be figured into the formula.

When you join cell references with a semicolon, you indicate that two references should be treated as one (a union). For example, a reference to C10:C12;C14 combines the values of all the cells together. Essentially, using the semicolon is a way to include noncontiguous cells in your reference, as if you were Ctrl+clicking cells to select them.

When you join two cell references with an exclamation point, you indicate that StarCalc should read the value of cells common to the two ranges, that is, values in the cell(s) that intersect.

> **Note**
>
> Excel users should pay special note to StarCalc's reference operators because two of them differ from Excel's. Where Excel uses a comma, StarCalc uses a semicolon. Where Excel uses a space to indicate an intersection, StarCalc uses an exclamation point. If you enter a comma between cell references, you receive an Error 501 (Invalid character) message. If you enter a space, you receive an Error 509 (Operator missing) message.

HOW STARCALC EVALUATES OPERATORS

If you build a formula without any parentheses, the operators are evaluated in a particular order. The order in which operators are evaluated is shown in Table 16.2 (from first to last).

TABLE 16.2   EVALUATION ORDER OF MATHEMATICAL AND LOGICAL OPERATORS IN STARCALC

Operator	Description
:	Range
!	Intersect
;	Union
-	Negation

Operator	Description
%	Percentage
^	Exponentiation
* and /	Multiplication and Division
+ and -	Addition and Subtraction
&	Text Joining
=, <, <=, >, >=, <>	Comparisons

You can determine the order in which calculations are performed, however, by using parentheses because operations are performed on values within the parentheses first. Consider these examples:

25*12+5=305

but

25(12+5)=425

COMPARISON OPERATORS

If you don't remember your comparison operators from high school, Table 16.3 refreshes your memory.

TABLE 16.3   COMPARISON OPERATORS

Operator	Description
=	Equal to
>	Greater than
<	Less than
>=	Greater than or equal to
<=	Less than or equal to
<>	Not equal to

REFERENCING CELLS IN FORMULAS

Cell addresses and references were introduced in the section "Navigating in StarCalc" in Chapter 13, "Creating Spreadsheets." We've deferred discussing cell references until this section because cell references are of greatest importance when you're building formulas.

UNDERSTANDING ABSOLUTE AND RELATIVE REFERENCES

When you create a formula, references to cells or ranges are usually based on their position relative to the cell that contains the formula. For example, in Figure 16.1, cell C19 in the row TOTALS contains a formula that reads =SUM(C11:C18), and even though three worksheets are available, each of which has a range of cells that could be identified as C11:C18, StarCalc assumes the reference is to cells in the formula's neighborhood, so to speak.

Figure 16.1
Relative referencing is useful when you want to repeat a single formula and apply it to different rows or columns of values. Absolute addressing is useful when you need to refer to a fixed value or set of values whose cell locations do not change.

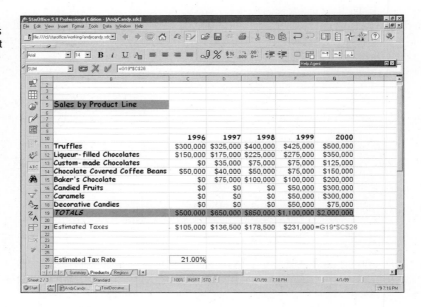

When you copy a formula that uses relative references, the references in the pasted formula update and refer to different cells, relative to the new position of the formula. For example, in Figure 16.1, the formulas for all the cells in the TOTALS row were created by using the automatic fill handle to copy the formula from C19 into the adjacent cells. Because that formula used relative references, StarCalc automatically adjusted the cell references to match the formula's new location. In cell D19, the formula now reads =SUM(D11:D18), in cell E19 it reads =SUM(E11:E18), and so on.

In many circumstances, you want to use *relative cell references* so that the references will shift as you cut and paste formulas to reuse them. In others, however, you need the same value to be used repetitively in a formula. A good example is a formula that refers to a tax table, where the range of cells containing appropriate values is fixed.

You can see an example of an absolute reference in Figure 16.1, where the totals in C19 through G19 are multiplied by the same fixed percentage to estimate taxes paid on revenues.

In StarCalc, as in Excel, an *absolute reference* is indicated with a dollar sign ($) in front of the cell address, as in $C$26. You can place an absolute reference in front of just a row reference, just a column reference, or in front of both, as in cell G19.

> **Note**
>
> The concept of absolute and relative references is similar to that of absolute and relative pathnames for files.

You can easily convert references in the Formula bar input line from relative to absolute, and vice versa, by pressing Shift+F4. The first time you press this key combination, both your row and column reference change to absolute references. The second time you press, only your row reference is marked as absolute, and the third time, only your column reference. If you press the combination once more, your references return to relative form.

ENTERING CELL REFERENCES

You can enter cell references into your StarCalc formulas in numerous ways. The simplest and usually most accurate way is to select the cell(s) you want to reference by using your mouse and to let StarCalc do the rest. You can use all the standard selection methods to mark cells and ranges, even when the Function AutoPilot is open.

→ For more information on selecting cells in StarCalc, **see** "Selecting Cells and Ranges," **p. 505**.

Note that if you click cells in succession, StarCalc replaces the previous cell reference with that of the newly active cell. To select a range, you must use the standard selection methods of dragging—Shift+click or Ctrl+click. To enter a cell reference and move on to enter another, you must manually enter a semicolon in the formula so that StarCalc knows you're moving on to the next argument in your formula.

StarCalc automatically enters cell references as relative references. Use the Shift+F4 key combination to change relative references to absolute ones.

INSERTING NAMED AREA AND DATABASE RANGES

If you prefer typing cell references directly into the input line, naming your cell and database ranges helps you avoid reference errors. Note, however, that after you begin creating and editing formulas in the Formula Input line, the drop-down area name list converts into a Function List. To enter the name, you either need to remember the exact name of your area, or use the Insert, Names, Paste command (which opens the Paste Name dialog box) to paste the name into your formula.

Alternatively, you can open the Area Names and Database Area lists in the Navigator and click the name of the area you want to reference. You then jump to its location, where you can click the first cell of the range and Shift+click the last cell to enter its reference in your formula.

> **Caution**
>
> When you're in editing mode in the Formula Input line, you continue to work in that mode until you press Enter to confirm the formula or Esc to abandon it, and every cell you click or highlight is entered as a reference in your formula.

AUTOMATIC ADDRESS AND AREA RECOGNITION

StarCalc does everything it can for you so that you can avoid entering those nasty column and row references, even if you're too lazy to create named cells and areas for yourself.

By default, StarCalc recognizes column and row text labels as headers to rows of data. You therefore can enter a column or row label name in a formula and have StarCalc automatically search below and to the right of that name in search of data. If it finds any, it assumes you want the cells included in your formula and adds their addresses behind the scenes. You can even use the usual copying methods to copy formulas created in this way.

For example, in Figure 16.2, the total in cell K4 has been created with the formula visible in the Formula input line, =SUM(January). No data range is named January, but StarCalc assumed January to refer to a column or row of data, figured it was a row, and entered the appropriate values to deliver the total.

Figure 16.2

StarCalc has brains as well as calculating brawn and automatically reads column and row header labels (such as the month names in this figure) as names of cell ranges.

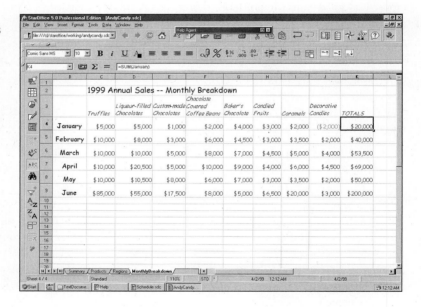

Automatic recognition works only with cell references, not with functions and formulas within a more complex formula. Also, for names to be automatically recognized, the names must consist of alphanumeric characters, and the first character must be a letter.

If you want to use nonalphanumeric characters (including spaces), enclose the names in single quotation marks ('). If a single quotation mark appears in a name, such as "Jan '97", enter a slash in front of the quote ("Jan /'97").

> **Note**
>
> Automatic recognition does not work with earlier versions of StarOffice. Earlier versions also do not recognize non-alphanumeric characters, regardless of how they are entered.

You can turn off this automatic recognition feature by deselecting the Search Column and Row Labels Automatically check box on the Calculation tab of the Spreadsheet Options dialog (which you open by choosing Tools, Options, Spreadsheet).

Besides automatically knowing to find data labeled with column and row headers, StarOffice also automatically recognizes most cell areas that are grouped together. To see how StarCalc groups your data, place your cursor in a cell in the middle of a data area, and press Ctrl+*, using the * key from the numeric keypad. The area is selected. (If StarCalc has grouped your data correctly, this is a nice shortcut for selecting a data range.)

REFERRING TO CELLS ON OTHER SHEETS (3D REFERENCES)

You can refer to cells that lie on three or more worksheets. They are called *3D references* because you're referring to cells by three dimensions—height (row), width (column), and depth (sheet).

To refer to cells on multiple sheets, add the sheet name to your reference separated from the cell reference with a period. For example, Figure 16.2 shows a spreadsheet with four sheets—Summary, Products, Regions, and Monthly Breakdown. To construct a formula that adds the value of cell F13 on the Summary sheet with cell F21 of the Products sheet, you enter the following:

```
=SUM(Summary.F13:Products.F21)
```

If you're referring to more than one cell per sheet and need to use the colon reference operator, use the semicolon to separate sheet references, as in this example:

```
=SUM(Summary,F13:F15;Products.F21:F23)
```

The same distinction between relative and absolute references applies to worksheets as it does to cells. You write absolute references in the same way, so the preceding reference made absolute would be `$Sheet.$A$1`.

Using an absolute reference for a worksheet might seem unnecessary because you cannot have two worksheets with the same name. However, because you can refer to other spreadsheets, using an absolute reference for a sheet name is a good idea if you're referring to information that is specific to that one sheet.

REFERRING TO CELLS ON OTHER SPREADSHEETS

To refer to cells in other spreadsheets, you must refer to the complete pathname of the file along with sheet and cell references. For example, the following is a formula on a spreadsheet called Annual Report that references cell D19 in the Andy's Candy spreadsheet on the Products worksheet:

```
=SUM('file:///C¦/StarOffice/Working/AndyCandy.sdc'#$Products.D19;C18)
```

Pay particular attention to the single quotation marks surrounding the file address (beginning with the word `file` and ending with the filename and its extension); and the # symbol, which, in StarOffice's URL-style file reference format, indicates a location within a file. You can use either a colon or a vertical line (pipe) after the disk drive reference.

As you can tell from the preceding rather lengthy and inelegant reference, you can easily make mistakes when referring to other spreadsheets. If you need to refer to cells in a different spreadsheet, it's therefore a good idea to have the documents open side by side so that you can select by dragging or pointing and clicking.

Tip #326 from
Michael & Sarah

The easiest way to work on documents side by side is to combine them in the same task window. To do so, open both spreadsheets, and then Ctrl+drag the task button of one spreadsheet over that of the other. To separate the documents again, reverse the action.

You can use an even easier method, however, if you've created named areas in your spreadsheets. You can simply create a link to the named areas on your second sheet by dragging and dropping them from the Navigator onto your current spreadsheet. Then you can refer the cells on your current spreadsheet that display the linked data, avoiding the trouble of inserting a complete file reference. (In fact, StarCalc maintains such a reference, but in the background, where you don't see it or need to worry about it.)

Tip #327 from
Michael & Sarah

You don't even need to have your second spreadsheet open to link its named areas to your current spreadsheet. Just open the Navigator, and drag the second spreadsheet into the Navigator from the Beamer. Be sure you set your Drag mode to Link (assuming you want your information to continually be updated), and then drag and drop the areas from the Navigator into your current spreadsheet.

When you open and close your file, you are asked whether you want to update your links. You can also update your links manually during a work session through the Edit, Links dialog box. Be aware that if you are working on both spreadsheets simultaneously, changes you make in your source data are not immediately reflected in your linked site; you need to save the spreadsheet with the changed data and then update the link in your second spreadsheet.

AVOIDING CELL REFERENCE ERRORS

The greatest danger on your worksheet lies not in the blatant errors that blare out ERROR from your cells, but those that lie hidden because you've entered values that make sense— but are not the correct values.

One of the most common (and easily avoided) sources of errors in spreadsheets comes from incorrectly entered cell references. Check out these tips for avoiding errors:

- Use your ability to name cell ranges, worksheets, and even column and row headers to full advantage. Most people can remember words more easily than numbers. Also, after you've named a range, you can select it and enter it into formulas with only one or two clicks.

- Don't type in cell references. Always use the arrow keys, mouse, Navigator, and/or Function AutoPilot to select the relevant cells and let StarCalc enter the correct references. Creating complex formulas that contain buried cell reference errors is too easy.

Tip #328 from
Michael & Sarah

If your formula generates an error and you want to try again, you can also always delete the = from the beginning of the formula to convert it to text and return later to troubleshoot the formula.

- When you want to edit formulas to update or change cell references, double-click the cell that contains a formula. The formula appears, and all its referenced cell(s) appear outlined in blue on your screen. The cursor automatically is placed in the middle of the reference to make editing easy. If you want to enter a new cell reference, just click that cell (or select the range). If you want to edit the formula directly, use your arrow keys to move back around. If you don't want to change anything, just press Enter to keep the current formula, or Esc to cancel and return to your worksheet.

- This same powerful in-cell editing tool can be a double-edged sword, however, because after you've double-clicked in a cell, every time you click somewhere else, you're entering its address as a new reference in your formula until you press Esc or Enter to leave editing mode. So pay attention!

- Be cautious when cutting, copying, or deleting cells. Sometimes you might inadvertently copy relative cell references that automatically update in ways you don't want, or delete important formulas. Some of what might strike you as annoying aspects of drag and drop and the Cut and Delete commands in StarCalc are actually great built-in safety features to prevent these kinds of errors, but they still can happen.

- If you're doing extensive editing on your worksheet, you might want to make formulas visible in-cell on the Contents tab of the Spreadsheet Options dialog box (which you open by choosing Tools, Options, Spreadsheet) so that you don't accidentally delete or move them.

- If you need to reference cells on other spreadsheets or worksheets, you can take advantage of Dynamic Data Exchange (DDE) to paste a linked copy of your data into cells on the worksheet where you're building your formula. This makes referencing these cells a snap, as all you need to do is click the cell that's right there; StarCalc takes care of the rest. Here's how to create a DDE link: Select the cell(s) with the data you want to use and choose the Copy (Ctrl+C) command. Switch back to the worksheet where you are building your formula and select the area where you want to paste your data. Then, choose Paste Special from the Edit menu. In the section named Options, select Link to Selection. In the section named Select, check the Paste All option; then click OK. Your data is pasted into the selected cell(s). The cell(s) are automatically updated if changes are made to the source data.

Tip #329 from
Michael & Sarah

If you click one of these DDE cells and look at the Formula Input line, you won't see the cell's data; instead, you'll see a reference to the source worksheet. If you want to reference this data elsewhere, you can copy and paste this reference into other formulas and be assured your reference is correct.

EDITING FORMULAS

After you've selected a cell with an existing formula, you can edit it in the Input line just as you edit any other text. However, you can use an easier way to change cell references in an existing formula: Double-click the cell with the formula to activate in-cell editing. (You can also click the cell and press F2.) A blue box appears, outlining the currently referenced cells in the formula. Your cell references also appear in different colors to make them stand out.

Tip #330 from
Michael & Sarah

Use in-cell editing frequently? You can enter in-cell editing mode by just pressing Enter, if you select Press Enter to Switch to Edit Mode in the Tools, Options, Spreadsheet, Entry dialog box.

In the Formula Input line, highlight the specific cell reference you want to replace. Now click or otherwise select the new cell(s) you want to reference. Instantly, its address appears in the place of your previous reference. Just press Enter, and your formula is done. Press Esc to exit without changes, or press Ctrl+Z to undo your changes.

Tip #331 from
Michael & Sarah

You can use Search and Replace (Ctrl+F) to quickly find formulas. Simply type an equals sign (=) in the Search box and choose Search. Continue choosing Search to cycle through all formulas on the worksheet.

RECALCULATING FORMULA RESULTS

By default, the StarCalc AutoCalculate function is turned on for all cells. This means the results of most formulas are automatically recalculated as you enter new data and/or update your formulas. The exception is formulas that contain the NOW() function because setting it to AutoCalculate would constantly engage the spreadsheet in updating and needlessly slow down your work.

To turn AutoCalculate on or off, click its name in the Tools, Cell Contents submenu.

To manually recalculate formulas with NOW() or (if AutoCalculate is turned off) all formulas, press F9.

DOCUMENTING FORMULAS WITH NOTES

 If you're building a complex spreadsheet, as you build and link formulas in different parts of your spreadsheet, you might want to document your steps and logic with notes. Taking a few moments now may save you or a colleague many minutes of head scratching later.

To insert a note, first select the cell to which you want to attach the note. Then choose Insert, Note. A small yellow square (like a sticky note) appears. Type in your note. You don't need to press Enter; when you're done, just click somewhere in your worksheet area.

By default, a small red square appears in the upper-right corner of the cell. To view the note temporarily, move your mouse pointer across the middle of the cell; the note pops up and then disappears again as you move your mouse pointer elsewhere.

PART

III

CH

16

Tip #332 from
Michael & Sarah

You can choose to print your notes along with your spreadsheet, or print your notes by themselves, using options on the Sheet tab of the Page Style dialog box (which you open by choosing Format, Page).

To show the note continuously, select the cell and choose Show Note from the cell's context menu. To hide it again, deselect Show Note.

WORKING WITH FUNCTIONS

Functions are formulas that have been built in to StarCalc through its programming. They're easier for you as well as faster to use than formulas you construct by hand. For example, using the Average function calculates more quickly than does a formula you construct with + and / arithmetic symbols (although you're not likely to notice the difference in formulas with a small number of values).

Functions also take up less room in memory and your spreadsheet. Spreadsheets can become complex and large very quickly, so it's a good idea to use functions whenever possible, except for the simplest of arithmetic operations. By using functions, you keep your spreadsheet compact and resource-lean and save room to grow without problems.

Functions accept data through *arguments*, which are entered in parentheses after the function's name. The specific arguments a function requires vary depending on the function, but the structure of your formula is always the same: Arguments are separated from one another with semicolons (;), and all your arguments are enclosed by parentheses, bracketing the arguments off from the function itself.

A typical financial function calculates monthly mortgage payments on a house. In StarCalc, you use the PMT function, which takes the arguments Rate (annual interest rate), NPER (number of payment periods), PV (the present value, or amount, of the loan), FV (ending value of the loan at completion), and type (type of loan). The FV and Type arguments are optional.

A formula built with the PMT function might look something like

=PMT(B15;120;B20)

where cell B15 contains the interest rate, 120 is the number of payments on the 10-year mortgage, and cell B20 contains the present value of the loan.

INSERTING FUNCTIONS

StarCalc can't make you a math whiz if you aren't already, but it does make the job of inserting functions into your spreadsheet as easy as can be with its Function AutoPilot.

The *Function AutoPilot* contains all 247 of StarCalc's functions organized by category, along with a brief description of each. You can create formulas here and preview the results before entering them. If you're interested in analyzing or modifying an existing formula, you can also click the Structures tab to see a graphic portrayal of the structure of your formula that lays clear the relationships between its different parts—a very useful feature when you're debugging formulas.

USING THE FUNCTION AUTOPILOT

To use the Function AutoPilot, you first should select the cell in which you want to place your formula. Then open the Function AutoPilot by clicking the Function AutoPilot tool on the Function bar or choosing Function from the Insert menu (Ctrl+F2). You then see something like Figure 16.3.

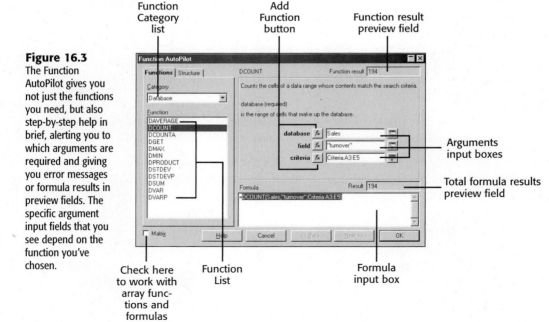

Figure 16.3
The Function AutoPilot gives you not just the functions you need, but also step-by-step help in brief, alerting you to which arguments are required and giving you error messages or formula results in preview fields. The specific argument input fields that you see depend on the function you've chosen.

Tip #333 from
Michael & Sarah

Choosing Help in the Function AutoPilot opens the Help Agent and pulls up the StarOffice Help dictionary entry on (almost) every function that you click.

The first step is to select the category of function that you want to choose from. The default is to open with All selected, which lets you browse through the entire Function List, but it's often easier to select a specific category, such as Database functions or Financial functions, where you can then see all or most of the related functions at a glance.

Tip #334 from
Michael & Sarah

Before you click in the Function List, pressing the up and down arrows moves you backward and forward through the available function categories. After you've clicked in a Function List, you can quickly jump around by typing the first letter of the function(s) you're looking for, which takes you to the first word beginning with that letter in the list. Continue pressing the letter to cycle through all entries beginning with that letter.

When you're in the Function List you want, start scrolling and you'll see a brief description of each function as it is highlighted. When you find the function you want, double-click to enter it into the Formula input box in the lower right of the AutoPilot.

Now your real work begins. To complete the function, you need to enter your arguments—which might be cell references, constant values, or even results of other functions—in the Argument input boxes. The specifics of what you need to provide depend on the function you're working with, but StarCalc always guides you with labels next to the input boxes and pointers that appear above when you click in an input box.

In Figure 16.3, for example, the Database function DCOUNT is used. You can see three arguments are possible: Database, Field, and Criteria. The fact that these three input boxes appear doesn't mean that all three are required inputs; StarCalc lets you know whether a specific argument is required when you click in its input line. In this case, StarCalc lets us know that the Database argument is required.

Enter your arguments. If you need to enter cell references, you can do so in a number of ways:

- Type in the data area, cell range name, or cell reference directly.
- Click the cell you want to enter. It appears outlined in red, and StarCalc enters its correct address automatically.
- Click and drag to select a cell range you want to enter. The Function AutoPilot temporarily is reduced in size to an input line so that you can see your entry more easily.

At any time, in fact, you can click the Minimize button next to an argument input field to reduce your window to an input line and click the Maximize button to restore it.

You don't need to press Enter or click anything; just move on to the next field. (The quickest ways to navigate through the argument input boxes are to use the up- and down-arrow keys, move your mouse and click, or press the Tab key.) The AutoPilot automatically places a semicolon (;) between arguments. If you skip a field, it enters a semicolon regardless, because even if you leave an argument blank, StarCalc needs a marker to indicate the field so that it can read your final formula correctly.

CREATING NESTED FORMULAS

If you need to create a nested formula (in which a function returns a result that another function then uses), click the Add Function button. By doing so, you then jump back to the Function List so that you can make another selection before you continue with other arguments. The result of your nested function is previewed in the upper-right corner, and the result of your total formula is previewed in the Result preview field just above the Formula input box. Pay attention to your Function result preview; it can help you spot and fix a small error before you insert it into your larger formula and make it into a big error that's more difficult to track.

Your formula can contain up to seven levels of nested functions.

Note that after you've entered the maze of nested formulas, you can't backtrack to your original formula; you can only plow ahead or cancel. If you enter a second function in error, then you just need to manually edit your formula and perhaps re-enter arguments.

After you've finished entering all your functions and arguments, check out your results. If you have an error that you don't understand, your best move, believe it or not, is just to choose OK anyway. StarCalc assesses the formula as you enter it, and if the program finds you've made an error, it alerts you and suggests a correction. Accepting StarCalc's suggestion initially is best, even though it doesn't always guess your intention correctly, because StarCalc's answer might give you clues to where you went wrong with your formula.

→ For more information on troubleshooting errors in formulas, **see** "Auditing Formulas and Functions," **p. 610**.

USING THE FUNCTION LIST

As with most things in StarOffice, a shortcut is also available for entering functions: the Function List dockable window. To open this window, choose Fields List from the Insert menu.

The Function List window like the one you see in Figure 16.4 appears, displaying a list of your most recently used functions. Clicking the arrow opens a drop-down list with the complete list of program functions organized by category. If you want to edit and preview a formula with functions, however, use the Function AutoPilot (Ctrl+F2).

Double-click a function name to insert it into your currently selected cell, or click the Insert Function button (see Figure 16.4).

Insert
Function
button

Function
List menu

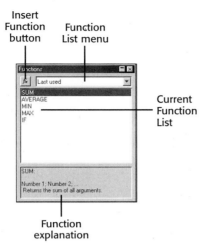

Figure 16.4
The Function List float-
ing window is like a
function Stylist; it
gives you your most
frequently used func-
tions at your finger-
tips, constantly
adjusting its display
to match your new
choices of functions.

Current
Function
List

Function
explanation

The Functions List is a dockable window, just like the Beamer and Stylist. When you open it for the first time, it is docked but unpinned on the right side of your desktop. To undock it, press Ctrl and double-click in its border. To dock it again, press Ctrl and push it against the edge where you want to dock it until you see its outline change. Then release your mouse button. If you find it hard to see your worksheet with the Function List open on your desktop, try adjusting your view with Zoom commands. Also, be sure to set your monitor to the highest resolution you can (ideally, at 1024∞768).

Figure 16.5 shows the Function List in a docked, pinned position.

Figure 16.5
You can dock the
floating Function List
to keep it by you as
you work.

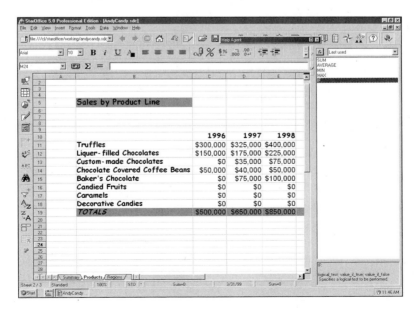

To close the Function List, click the Close button in the corner, or choose its name from the Insert menu.

Tip #335 from
Michael & Sarah

If you want to see more functions when the Function List is in its floating state, make it bigger by grabbing one of its corners until the cursor turns into a diagonal, double-headed arrow. Then drag outward until it's the size you want.

USING THE SHEET AREA SHORTCUT MENU

Normally, the Sheet Area list next to the Function AutoPilot tool contains a drop-down list of all the named areas and data ranges in your spreadsheet. After you begin entering functions and editing formulas in the input line, however, that list changes into a Functions shortcut list that records the last 10 functions you entered. To enter a recently used function into your formula, first be sure your cursor is in the input line. Then open the list and click the function name you want to enter.

FINDING HELP WITH FUNCTIONS

The StarOffice online help system contains a (nearly) complete dictionary of StarCalc functions, so you can always find a quick reminder of a function's use and arguments when you need it. There are some exceptions, however: It does not contain descriptions of logical functions—assuming that you can figure them out on your own—nor does it include descriptions of the optional add-in functions. The add-ins are listed here in Table 16.4.

Note

Some functions are referred to with slightly different names in the Online User's Guide (Help, Contents) than in the Help Agent or in the Function AutoPilot.. Also, a matrix function listed in the online User's Guide, VARIATION, is not implemented in the program.

To get help with functions within the program, you can do the following:

- Open the Function AutoPilot, and highlight a function on one of the lists of functions. A brief description appears in the dialog window.
- After you double-click to select a function, argument entry boxes appear, each labeled with the argument's name or abbreviation. Position your cursor in an argument's field to see a brief description and a notation as to whether it is optional or required.
- Click Help in the Function AutoPilot, and the Help Agent opens with information on your currently highlighted function. Click a new function to pull up its entry.
- Open the Help Contents (through the Help menu), and search by function name for the specific function you're interested in. Alternatively, search on the Text tab for the phrase *Categories and functions* to go to the table of contents page for the entire functions help file.

Tip #336 from	If you need help on how to reference cells properly, open the AutoPilot, create a dummy
Michael & Sarah	formula, and select cells to fill the formula. You can then use the way AutoPilot enters references as a model.

STARCALC'S ADD-IN FUNCTIONS

If you chose the custom installation, you had the option of installing additional StarCalc functions, called *StarCalc add-ins* by StarOffice (see Table 16.4).

If you did not install these functions during your original installation but want to install them now, find the StarOffice Setup program, double-click to run Setup, and follow the onscreen instructions for adding components. (If you didn't move it, the Setup program is located in the \Office51 directory.)

TABLE 16.4 STARCALC'S ADDITIONAL DATE, TIME, AND TEXT FUNCTIONS

Function	Argument	Description
DAYSINMONTH	Date	Returns the number of days in a month for a given date
DAYSINYEAR	Date	Returns the number of days in a year for a given date
ISLEAPYEAR	Date	Returns 1 if date is a leap year, 0 otherwise
MONTHS	Date1, Date2, Mode	Returns the number of months between two dates
ROT13	Text to be changed	Changes each alphabetical character of the text by 13 characters in the alphabet
WEEKS	Date1, Date2, Mode	Returns the number of weeks between two weeks
WEEKSINYEAR	Date1, Date2, Mode	Returns the number of weeks for a given date
YEARS	Date1, Date2, Mode	Returns the number of years between two given dates

USING DATES AND TIMES IN FORMULAS

If dates and times are formatted correctly, StarCalc can convert them into serial numbers that can be used in formulas. That can be a tricky "if," however, because StarCalc recognizes a limited number of date formats. The specific format recognized depends on your system date and time settings. If you have your system set for ordinary US time and data standards, StarCalc will recognize as dates only those input in the mm/dd/yy format.

Note

The environment variable LANGUAGE determines your system language settings. Set it on the shell level, for example, LANGUAGE=US for U.S. English, or LANGUAGE=FR for French.

Caution

If you're going to reference dates and times in your formulas, be sure you enter them in the correct format to begin with. If you input your dates in other formats, they probably will be automatically formatted as text. Even if you manually select and apply a date format to cells whose dates were entered in a nonstandard format (that is, a non-mm/dd/yy format), these cells will still not be recognized as dates that can be converted into serial numbers.

You can use the functions TIMEVALUE and DATEVALUE to convert times and dates formatted as text (respectively) into serial numbers that can be used in calculations. Using these functions might be a better solution than re-entering a lot of dates that you've just discovered aren't being recognized as numbers. For more information on these functions, you can open the Function AutoPilot and locate them in the Date and Time category, or select Contents from the Help menu, click the Search tool (the binoculars), and search by function name.

If you calculate with cell references in which at least one of the references is assigned a date or time format, StarCalc automatically determines the format it considers proper for the operation, assuming you have not applied any special formatting to the formula cell. Table 16.5 lists the initial input and the resulting formats.

TABLE 16.5   RETURNED FORMATS WITH DATE, TIME, AND NUMBER INPUT

Initial Format	Result Format
Date + Date	Number (Days)
Date + Number	Date
Date + Time	Date&Time
Date + Date&Time	Number
Time + Time	Time
Time + Number	Time
Time + Date&Time	Date&Time
Date&Time + Date&Time	Time
Date&Time + Number	Date&Time
Number + Number	Number

WORKING WITH TEXT IN FORMULAS

To enter text in a formula (including numbers or dates that you want treated as text rather than numbers), enclose it in quotation marks (" "). Otherwise, you get a #NAME? error.

If you're *concatenating* (joining together) text with other data and want to ensure that spaces are properly entered between words or phrases, enter a space at the beginning or end of your phrase (as appropriate), inside the quotation marks. For example, say you want to create a formula to combine a text phrase and a date read from cell C30 to deliver the result, "Your bill is due on 12/31/99." To achieve the proper spacing, you should enter a formula that looks like the following, with underscores indicating where your spaces should go:

```
"Your_bill_is_due_on_"&C30.
```

WORKING WITH ARRAYS AND MATRIX FUNCTIONS

An *array*, or *matrix*, is a rectangular range of numbers or formulas that StarCalc operates on as a single group. The terms *array* and *matrix* are used interchangeably in the StarOffice help system; however, the functions that act upon them are just called Matrix functions. Don't be confused by this inconsistency in usage; for your purposes, arrays and matrices are the same thing.

Some matrix formulas and functions both operate on and return results in multiple cells, whereas others operate on multiple cells but return results in a single cell. Each cell in the matrix contains the formula, not as a copy, but as a shared formula for all matrix cells.

Working with matrix formulas and functions is a highly technical and specialized mathematical skill, so we aren't going to explain them in detail here. We will just describe briefly how you can work with arrays and matrix functions and formulas in StarCalc.

You can insert a matrix formula in StarCalc in two ways: by entering it manually in the Formula bar input line or by using the Function AutoPilot.

To insert a matrix formula manually, follow these steps:

1. Select the range of cells where you want your results to appear. For example, if you want to add each of the column pairs C and D in rows 5 through 10, you select rows E5 through E10 for your results to appear.

2. Enter an equals sign (=) in the Formula bar input line.

3. Select your first input series—here, column C, rows 5 through 10—by dragging with your mouse.

4. Enter a plus sign (+), and then select your second input series (column D, rows 5 through 10).

5. When you're done, press Ctrl+Shift+Enter. Notice your formula is surrounded by curly brackets ({}) to mark it as a matrix formula.

You can also build a matrix formula with the Function AutoPilot. Again, begin by selecting the range of cells in which you want your results to appear. Then open the Function AutoPilot, and check the Matrix option at the bottom of the dialog. Select the Matrix function you want to use, and proceed to build your formula as usual. (You can also build a formula using just arithmetic operators, if you choose.) When you choose OK to enter your formula, StarCalc enters it as a matrix formula.

> **Note**
>
> StarDivision says that the maximum size of a matrix area is 128∞128 cells in 32-bit Windows and 64∞64 cells in 16-bit Windows. In our own tests, we were able create matrices of up to 1000 x 1000 on both Linux and Windows systems (although it strained the system resources)! The chief limit seems to be available RAM. Just be aware that matrix operations are very memory intensive, and you could cause a system crash if you work with a very large matrix.

Note that cells into which a matrix formula has been inserted are protected; you cannot edit or alter them individually using normal methods. (However, you can modify the attributes, change the cell background, for example.)

If you try to select a matrix cell, you get an error message.

If you need to edit your formula, you must first select the entire range that contains the matrix formula (in the example, that would be cells E5 through E10). Just as with regular formulas, the cells that formula refers to then appear outlined in blue. You can then either edit the formula directly in the input line, or open the Function AutoPilot and edit the formula in its dialog. If you edit the formula in the input line, you must press Ctrl+Shift+Enter when done; otherwise, your changes are not allowed.

You cannot convert a matrix formula to a regular formula. You can only delete all the cells containing the matrix and start again.

> **Note**
>
> StarDivision tech support personnel suggest that you can convert a matrix formula into a regular formula, but we have never successfully achieved such a conversion. The steps they offer: To convert a matrix formula into a regular formula, place your cursor somewhere in the matrix and press F2 to switch into edit mode. Then, press Enter to leave the cell. The curly braces ({}) disappear, and the formula is not an array formula any more.

AUDITING FORMULAS AND FUNCTIONS

Computers are very, very good at what they do. Unfortunately, they are also very stupid machines that do only exactly what you tell them to do. They're like four-year-olds who have discovered the power of literal interpretations of language and just won't let go. That's a good thing to remember as you embark on auditing your formulas and functions because auditing requires the same patience as does tending a four-year-old—especially when you trace that nagging error in your formulas down to a single missing semicolon.

You have a number of tools for helping you audit and correct erroneous formulas and functions in StarCalc; ranging from onscreen error messages to the Detective, which reveals the links in your chain of references, to the Structure tab of the Function AutoPilot, which lays the bare bones of your formula and arguments.

UNDERSTANDING ERROR MESSAGES

StarCalc does its best to help you as you go along, and one way of doing so is displaying error messages in the Function AutoPilot dialog and in your cell, if you've entered a formula already. For additional help with these error codes, select the cell with the error, and look at the Quick Calculate field in your status bar (which displays a cell's contents or, if you select a range of cells, calculates their value based on the function you have currently selected). When you have an error in your cell, this area displays a brief explanatory message, as you can see in Figure 16.6.

Figure 16.6
The status bar comes to your aid when your formulas have errors, displaying brief explanations of StarCalc's cryptic error codes.

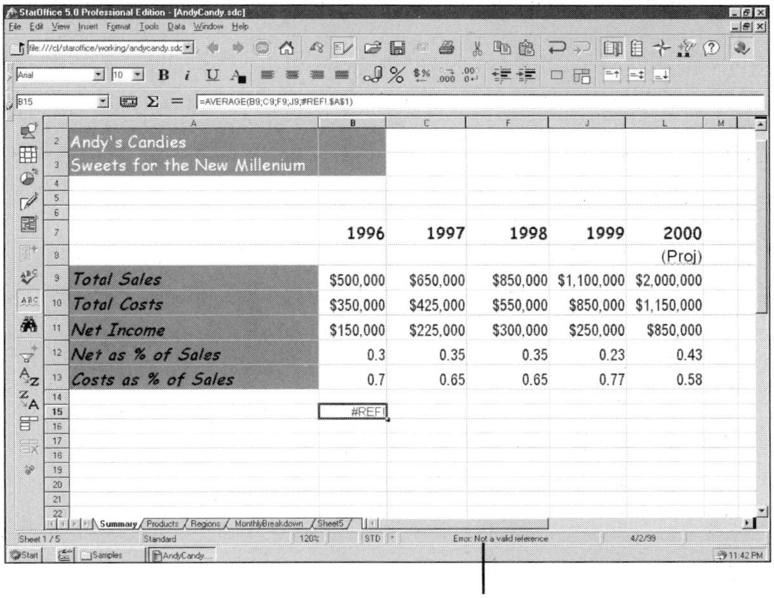

Status bar error help

The most common of StarCalc's error messages are listed in Table 16.6, along with a brief description of common causes, to help you better interpret erroneous results.

TABLE 16.6   COMMON StarCalc ERROR VALUES

Value	Meaning	Common Causes
#NAME?	Invalid name	This error is frequently caused by a failure to use the correct punctuation—for example, using a comma instead of a semicolon to separate arguments or failing to enclose text in quotation marks (" ").
#NUM?	Invalid number	The number may fall out of the acceptable range of input, or your formula may depend on a result from a function that is not forthcoming or incorrect.
#REF!	Incorrect or invalid cell reference	These errors are frequently caused by referencing cells, sheets, and/or spreadsheets that you've deleted or altered such that the references are no longer accurate. You can use the Edit, Links command to check on external links.
#VALUE?	Missing proper value	The value is not the right kind for the argument, you have failed to enter a necessary value, or the reference you've entered does not refer to a value at all (for example, it refers to text when the function requires a number).
Error 501	Invalid character	
Error 502	Invalid argument	
Error 503	Invalid floating-point operation	The formula is attempting to divide by zero (which could be caused by a blank cell or a cell with a space in it).
Error 504	Error in parameter list	The parameters are not entered correctly. This error is often caused by using incorrect punctuation to separate cell references.
Error 508	Pair missing	StarCalc is expecting further reference pairs. This error could be caused by missing punctuation that causes StarCalc to misinterpret data you have entered or by a failure to enter all necessary data.
Error 509	Operator missing	An arithmetic operator to connect two references is missing. This error could be caused by incorrect punctuation between arguments or cell references.
Error 510	Variable missing	You have failed to enter a necessary value.
Error 511	Variable missing	You have failed to enter a necessary value.
Error 518	Internal syntactical error	You have constructed arguments and/or functions improperly. You may have left out a parenthesis.
Error 522	Circular reference	You have entered a cell reference that includes the address of the formula itself. This error can easily occur if you're doing in-cell editing and accidentally click on the cell with your formula.

Tip #337 from
Michael & Sarah

If you have a number that's not being registered in a formula, check to see whether it has been accidentally formatted as text. StarCalc does not count it as a number for calculation purposes if it's been formatted as text.

StarCalc does not always give you error messages when you've entered values that are not appropriate for your chosen function. For example, the Date function requires that you enter three serial numbers, representing the year, month, and day of your date. You can enter the year as either a four-digit number or a two-digit abbreviation. If you enter it as a four-digit number, you must enter a number between 1583 and 9956. Then you must enter a number between 1 and 12 for the month and 1 and 31 for the day.

If you enter 99, 12, and 40, respectively, and choose OK, StarCalc accepts your input and returns 01/09/00; it interprets your 40 to mean 31 days plus 9. However, if you enter 9958 (or any number between 9958 and 9999), 12, and 40, StarCalc returns 12/31/99 as if nothing were wrong—which is a very fine date, but may not be the date you intended to enter.

REVIEWING COMMON SOURCES OF ERRORS IN FORMULAS

The following are some common sources of errors in formulas:

- You've entered a name or cell reference either that StarCalc doesn't recognize or that does not contain the type of value required.
- You've neglected to enter a required variable in a formula or function.
- You've left out an argument that is required for the function to return a result.
- You've entered a nested function that returns the wrong kind of value for your higher-order function.
- You've failed to use the correct punctuation in your message to StarCalc, and StarCalc doesn't understand.

That last error is usually the first possibility you should investigate, particularly because incorrect punctuation can result in a variety of error messages. The three most common punctuation errors are as follows:

- A comma (,) is used to separate cell reference or arguments instead of a semicolon (;).
- One of a pair of parentheses is missing from a nested function or function.
- Text has been entered without quotation marks (" ").

DEBUGGING WITH THE DETECTIVE

The *Detective* is a visual aid that helps you spot just where, in a trail of cell references and formula results, the dead body of your error might lie.

With the Detective, you can trace both *precedents* (values that plug in to your formula and help determine its result) and *dependents* on your formula (other formulas or values that derive from your formula's result). These commands work for any formula, regardless of whether StarCalc has returned an error value for your formula. They make proofreading your worksheet easier and ensure that you're referring to the correct data as you build your chain of formulas.

When you have a formula that returns an error value, you can also use the Trace Error and Mark Invalid Data commands to retrace the chain of arguments that resulted in the error.

To use the Detective, first select the cell that contains the formula you want to audit. Then choose Detective from the Tools menu (see Figure 16.7).

Figure 16.7
When you choose Detective from the Tools menu, you can choose to track a specific error message or just evaluate the data chain in any of your formulas by tracing a formula's precedents and dependents. In this example, the precedents of cell G21 have been traced.

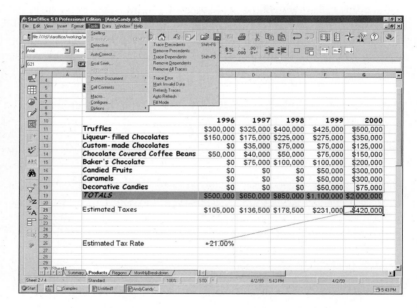

Choose Trace Precedents and Trace Dependents to draw lines from your formula to its data input and to other cells and formulas that reference its results, respectively. In Figure 16.8, the precedents and dependents on the formula in cell K9 have been traced. You can see that the first cell reference in the formula, K4, is marked with a dot as the terminus, and an arrow points ahead to formulas that are dependents.

If you have an error value in a cell (such as in cell H15 in Figure 16.8) and want to trace your error, select Trace Error. Lines are drawn to all your precedents (except those located on other sheets or spreadsheets) to aid you in tracking down your error. The cursor turns into a magnifying glass with an arrow as you move up or down your logical chains (as it does for precedents and dependents as well).

Figure 16.8
Besides helping you trace the logic of your formulas and locate the source of errors, the Detective also highlights data that doesn't meet the validation standards set for the worksheet or cell range.

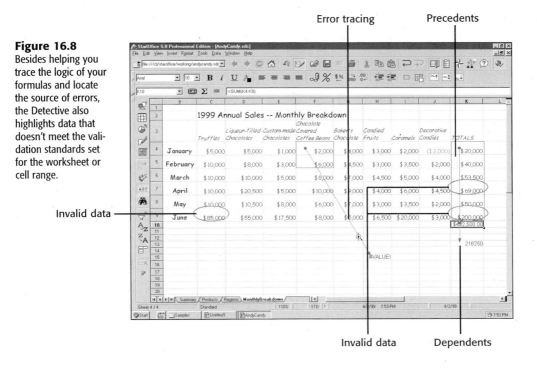

Error tracing

Precedents

Invalid data

Invalid data

Dependents

Tip #338 from
Michael & Sarah

If you want to apply the Detective to multiple cells at once, select Fill Mode from the Detective submenu. Your pointer turns into a paint can, just like the Fill Format Mode pointer of the Stylist, and you can click continually on cells to trace their precedents and dependents. Press Esc to return to normal pointer mode, or deselect Fill Mode from the Detective submenu.

If you have previously set validation rules for specific cells, worksheets, or your entire spreadsheet by using the Data, Validity command, selecting the Mark Invalid Data command circles (with nice, big, red marks) any data that is invalid—that is, falls outside your previously established parameters (refer to Figure 16.8).

As you debug your formulas and change them, select the Refresh Traces menu command to recheck and redraw lines as appropriate. (You can also turn on Auto Refresh by selecting it, which updates your lines automatically as you go.)

To remove just precedents or dependents, select Remove Precedents or Remove Dependents, respectively. To remove all traces, including error tracings and invalid data marks, choose Remove All Traces.

DEBUGGING WITH THE FUNCTION AUTOPILOT

The Detective, flashy and useful as it is, is not enough to help you analyze and correct your formulas. It can trace relationships only in two dimensions, that is, relationships on your current worksheet. It also helps you trace only errors that result from incorrect input rather than errors made in the writing of the formula itself. That's where the Structure tab of the Function AutoPilot comes in handy.

 To open the Function AutoPilot, click the Function AutoPilot button on the StarCalc Formula toolbar.

When you select a formula and open the Function AutoPilot, this tab breaks down your formula into parts and helps you pinpoint the precise area of your formula that might be causing your problems.

As you can see in Figure 16.9, the Function AutoPilot breaks your formula into sections. Each section is defined by a function or an operator and contains arguments, which might be cell references, values you enter directly, or other parameters.

Figure 16.9
The Structure tab of the Function AutoPilot uses the same hierarchical structure familiar to you from the Explorer to lay out the structure of your formula, along with color coding that marks correctly phrased entries (blue) and those that contain syntactical errors (red). Be aware, though, that blue entries might still contain other kinds of errors.

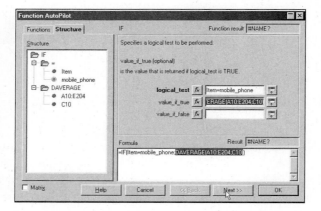

The metaphor here is to that of folders and files, with functions and operators being the equivalent of folders (they contain other things, namely arguments), and arguments, the equivalent of files. Just as with folders in the Explorer or categories in the Navigator, you can click the – sign to hide the contents of a folder and the + sign to reveal them.

What appears as an error in your cell might not record as an error on the Structure tab, and vice versa, because each is focusing on different aspects of your formula. What appear as errors on the Structure tab are *syntactical* errors in your formula—errors in phrasing or punctuation that make your formula unreadable by StarCalc, such as "sentence a this like. contains many errorserrors syntactical."

Arguments that are syntactically complete and correct are marked with blue dots, and arguments that contain errors are marked with a red bull's-eye, like that next to the item name `mobile_phone` in Figure 16.9. (This item is incorrect because it hasn't been entered in quotation marks, as text items must be, and therefore returns a `#NAME?` error.)

However, you can create a formula whose syntax is perfect but still doesn't make any sense because you're referring to things that aren't really there—as if I said that I was late for dinner because the dragon on the corner refused to let me pass. Those are the kinds of errors that the Detective helps you trace.

Tip #339 from *Michael & Sarah*	If you want to review your formulas on paper, you can print them by checking the Formulas option on the Sheet tab of the Page Style dialog (you choose Format, Page to open this dialog).

TROUBLESHOOTING

I put notes in my document, but I can't see them now.

Someone must have turned off the Note tags option on the Tools, Options, Spreadsheet, Contents tab, so the red square markers, which indicate that the cells contain notes, do not appear. Select the Note tags options, and if your notes are still there, you'll see their tags again.

StarCalc prevents me from editing my formula, telling me that protected cells can't be modified.

You might have unintentionally entered your formula as a matrix formula. Cells into which a matrix formula has been entered are protected and can't be edited by normal means. Open the Function AutoPilot and see whether the Matrix option is selected. If it is, there's a good bet that's your problem. First, deselect Matrix so that it doesn't happen again. Then you need to figure out which cells have been included in the matrix, select them as a group, and delete their contents simultaneously.

If you don't want to lose your formula, take the following action: After you've selected the entire matrix, click at the end of your formula in the Formula bar input line, highlight your formula, and press Ctrl+C to copy it. Then press Esc to leave formula editing mode. Delete the matrix by pressing Del. Then paste your formula into the cell of your choice by using Ctrl+V. (Your cell references will be incorrect, so you'll need to fix them.)

Another reason you're unable to edit is that the cells might have been protected with a password. If that's the case, you need to get the password for the worksheet or spreadsheet to get access.

I need to enter text in a formula, but StarCalc just keeps returning a `#NAME?` error.

You need to enclose your text in quotation marks (" ").

I click a cell that has an error with the Detective Fill Mode, but it doesn't do anything.

The Detective Fill Mode works only to reveal precedents and dependents, not trace errors. Select the cell again, and choose the Tools, Detective, Trace Error command.

I've changed my formulas and data, but my Detective tracing marks haven't changed.

Select Refresh Traces from the Detective submenu.

I've pasted cells from another worksheet as DDE links, but they're not updating properly and my formula has errors as a result.

When you insert a table from StarCalc into StarWriter as a DDE link, the table is protected and you can't make changes. However, when you paste cells from one StarCalc document to another, those cells are not automatically protected and you can modify or delete data just as with any other cell. If you modify the cells in any way, the DDE link is deleted. That's probably what happened to cause your errors. You will need to re-copy and paste the cell(s) in question. To avoid such errors in the future, you should protect the cells. To protect them, first select them and make sure cell protection is turned on for them in the Cell Protection tab of the Format, Cells dialog box. Then, open the Tools, Protect Document menu and select either Worksheet or Document. You will be prompted to enter a password.

CHAPTER 17

CREATING LISTS AND DATABASES WITH STARCALC

In this chapter

WHY CREATE DATABASES WITH STARCALC?

You're surely familiar with lists; lists contain rows of information in a single column that relate to a common theme or category, like a shopping list or a to do list. A *database* is a more complex list that contains two or more columns.

StarCalc has a number of powerful commands that you can use to sort, filter, and summarize data in lists and databases. If you specifically define an area as a *database area*, you can also use advanced features to sort and filter your data using StarOffice's regular expressions and copy the results to defined ranges or database areas in your spreadsheet.

→ For more information about analyzing data in databases, be sure to read Chapter 18, "Analyzing and Charting Data." **See** particularly " Advanced Analysis of Lists and Databases," **p. 646** and "Creating Subtotals," **p. 653**

Why use StarCalc to create a database when you could use a database application like StarBase?

If your data consists primarily of numbers and dates which you use in calculations, you should probably use a spreadsheet. Spreadsheets have more mathematical functions and compute much more quickly than relational databases.

However, StarBase offers much more sophisticated data sorting and filtering using a special language, SQL, as well as the option of *indexing* your file for faster and more efficient searching, whether you create a stand-alone table or a relational database

If you create a relational database in the native StarBase format (available on Windows only) your data entry is much more efficient because of the way you can link information in different tables through relationships. If you're keeping a large number of records which you use primarily to track and analyze non-numerical trends and patterns, you should probably use a relational database.

If you are preparing lists primarily for presentation, not for data manipulation (including lists of numbers), consider using a StarWriter table, or working between StarCalc and StarWriter. You can easily move table data between StarWriter and StarCalc by cutting and pasting or dragging and dropping. The table features in StarWriter allow you to quickly sort and order information in lists or databases, just as you can in StarCalc, but allow you to apply a much wider range of formatting; and you can compute simple calculations as a sum or even simple statistic figures as well.

You might also consider a relational database if you have a large numerical database—say, more than a few thousand records (rows)—that you expect to keep growing. You can always extract a limited set of data from the relational database that you then import into a spreadsheet to run more complex computational analysis. Very large databases kept in spreadsheet-style flat list databases become memory hogs and increasingly cumbersome to work with.

Frankly, however, StarBase as currently implemented does not offer the functionality and ease of use that you have come to expect from leading relational database programs, so if you need a relational database program, you might need to look outside of StarOffice.

StarBase does have its strengths, however. Where it shines is as a data manager, facilitating such data transfers as selectively importing data into a spreadsheet or creating mail merges. In fact, in this realm, StarBase is without peer and greatly facilitates working with databases in StarCalc, as is discussed in the section "Importing and Exporting Data," later in this chapter.

→ For a more detailed discussion of StarBase and its uses within StarOffice, **see** "Introducing StarBase," **p. 1086**.

One problem is that the implementation of StarBase differs on the Windows and Linux platforms. Since cross-platform portability of files and consistency in user interface and functionality are two of the program's key advantages, this is a significant limitation.

Note

One of the issues of StarBase in Windows and Linux is that the Linux version of StarBase does not support relations between tables (even if you are importing tables with relations set in another program), nor does it support OBDC.

The user interface for StarBase is also, at this writing, not as graceful and intuitive as it could be.

The program is evolving quickly, and these limitations will likely soon be addressed by StarDivision because they have been repeatedly criticized by users and reviewers . For the moment, however, you may find that StarCalc better serves your database needs.

DESIGNING A LIST OR DATABASE

The process of designing a list or database for a spreadsheet is different than that of designing a relational database, but a number of the same concepts and principles still apply.

BASIC DATABASE TERMS AND DESIGN PRINCIPLES

In a spreadsheet database, each column represents a category, or *field*. Each row in the database is a *record*.

To create a good database, you need to think carefully about how to break your data into fields and what fields to include.

In general, you want to break your information down into the smallest fields possible. This gives you the maximum flexibility in sorting and filtering your data. For example, do not make a name field that combines first and middle names, as you may want to sort people with the same first name by middle initial.

ELEMENTS OF A SPREADSHEET DATABASE

A spreadsheet database is what's called a *flat list database* because it consists of a single, potentially very long, table. It's structure is easy for people to grasp because everyone is familiar with lists. (By contrast, a relational database consists of a series of related tables that can be thought of as overlapping rather than flat. Its structure is much more complex, but it handles data more efficiently.) A flat list database requires three elements to be maximally useful:

- A data area
- A criteria range
- An extract range

→ For a more detailed discussion of relational databases, **see** "What Is a Relational Database?", **p. 1132**.

DATA AREA

A data area is where you enter your data, and includes any row or column headers you might have. If you look ahead to Figure 17.1, it shows the upper data area of a flat list database called Sales Figures, which includes the column headers and initial data entries.

CRITERIA RANGE

Advanced filters make use of complex criteria that you set to sort and filter your data. A criteria range is an area of your spreadsheet where you enter the criteria you want the advanced filter to use. When you create your advanced filter, you'll then enter the cell references of your criteria range to direct StarCalc to your filtering criteria.

EXTRACT RANGE

When you filter your data with an advanced filter, you have the option of copying your filtered results to a separate area of your spreadsheet, rather than just temporarily changing your view of the entire database. This allows you to further manipulate, format, and arrange this filtered data in ways impossible if you kept it in the original database. An extract range is an area you've set aside for StarCalc to copy your filter results.

Tip #340 from *Michael & Sarah*	Data extracted in this way from a flat database is no longer connected to the source table and will not be automatically updated if your original data changes. If you need to manipulate sorted and filtered results that are still dynamically connected to their source, use a relational database.

You might also want to create a separate extract range for StarCalc's DataPilot to summarize and organize your data in cross-tabulations. Otherwise the DataPilot automatically places its results at the end of your table, which may interfere with continuing data entry.

TIPS FOR SPREADSHEET DATABASE DESIGN

Figure 17.1 shows a list of telephone sales in U.S. cities over a period of years. The data is well organized to be made into a database, with a clear header row of field names and no other data on the worksheet, although it doesn't have a criteria range set. It doesn't seem as useful a grouping of data as it might be, however, in order to take full advantage of StarCalc's database tools.

Figure 17.1
This list of sales figures, with over 400 entries, is a simple example of a flat list database you might create in StarCalc. The surrounding cells have been formatted with a background color to help visually define the database area and indicate that nothing should be entered on either side.

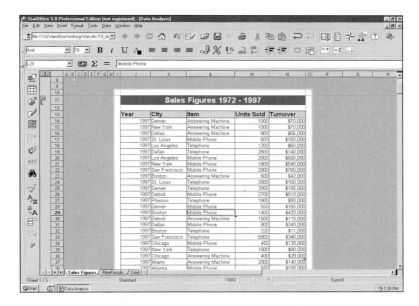

For example, it might be more useful to break down sales into quarters so you could then use filtering tools to spot seasonal sales patterns and better target efforts to control marketing costs. Sometimes your original data has been gathered without thought to what your tools can do. The design phase of your database can be a time to reconsider the kinds of data you've been collecting, or the ways that data might be broken down into fields.

However, be cautious in including fields or gathering extra data. Include only fields that have a well-defined purpose and help meet your critical goals. Otherwise, your database will become unwieldy and difficult to maintain.

Here are some other tips for designing a good database in StarCalc:

- Think before you create. Consider how you might later want to sort and filter your data.
- Eliminate fields that you'll likely never use, including fields that contain data you can calculate from other fields. For example, you don't need a subtotals field, as you can always calculate that with the Subtotals command.

- If you might export your spreadsheet database to a relational database, enter your field names without spaces or special characters. (You can use underscores (_) instead of spaces.) This matches relational database naming conventions and will save you from needing to rename your fields later.

Note

StarBase follows dBase III conventions and limits you to field names of 13 characters or fewer. Keep this in mind if you plan to swap data between the two. If you create StarCalc field names longer than 13 characters, the latter part of the name will be truncated when you import your data into StarBase or another database program.

- Place each database on its own worksheet.
- If there is other important data on the worksheet, place it above your database area. Data on the left or right may be hidden when you apply standard or advanced filters.
- Leave room at the bottom of the database for the database to expand, or for the DataPilot to place its results if you haven't set aside a specific extract range.
- Format your column headers (field names) so they stand out from your rows of data.
- Don't insert blank lines between records. (They're alright at the end of the database area.) If you want to set off areas, use backgrounds and borders instead. Blank lines or cells can create problems in sorting and filtering.
- Create cell styles that help differentiate your different types of entries—for example, a style for your header row, a style for data (or even for different types of data), and a style for filter results. You can later use Search and Replace to quickly find all instances of data in that style. Remember: You can format blank cells.
- Don't insert extra spaces at the beginning of a cell. Extra spaces affect sorting and searching and can cause calculation errors.

Tip #341 from
Michael & Sarah

If you experience problems working with your database that you think may be the result of having extra spaces, use Search and Replace to search for a space (or spaces). Don't enter anything in the Replace With box. Click Search. Don't choose Replace All right away—you should always check the results of your selection before you replace anything. If your search finds any cells with blank spaces, choose Replace or Replace All.

CREATING AND DEFINING YOUR DATABASE

To create a new database in StarCalc, begin by entering and formatting your field names at the top of the columns, like you see in the Sales Figures database (refer to 17.1). To use advanced filtering options (or to export data to a relational database), each field name must be unique. Don't leave a blank row between the field names and your data. This makes it impossible for StarCalc to recognize your fields.

Once you define your fields, you can enter data and format cells in the usual ways (refer to Chapter 13, "Creating Spreadsheets," and Chapter 15, "Formatting Spreadsheets.") When you're working with text data, you also have an additional handy method of entering data, courtesy of your context menu: the Selection List command (Ctrl+D).

To activate the Selection List command, right-click in any cell in a column of text data and choose Selection List from the context menu. You'll see a drop-down list that contains an example of every text-formatted item already in the list (except the current entry, if there is already data in the cell). To enter an item, click it. If you do a lot of repetitive data entry in a column (as with the City column in the Sales Figure database), using the selection list cuts down on entry errors and speeds data entry.

Keep in mind that if you've inserted numbers prefaced by an apostrophe ('), they are treated as text, and will appear on a selection list. (They won't be included in calculations though, as they are not considered numbers.)

PART

III

CH

17

Tip #342 from *Michael & Sarah*	If you do a lot of data entry, consider creating a custom data entry dialog box with StarBasic. It can help speed up data entry and cut down on entry errors. For more information, see Chapter 39, "Programming with StarBasic."

DEFINING A DATABASE AREA

To take advantage of StarCalc's advanced database management features, you must define your list or database as a database area.

Note	There's a bug in StarCalc's Sort Ascending toolbar command. It treats column headers as regular data. (Sort Descending works without problem.) Sort Ascending works properly if activated from the Data, Sort dialog box. However, if you want the convenience of quickly sorting using the toolbar, you should create two named database areas: one that includes column headers (which is a must for using advanced sorting and filtering options), and one that does not.

To define a database area, select the sheet or area and choose the Data, Define Area command. The Define Database Area dialog box, shown in Figure 17.2, appears.

First, type a name for your database area. You can't edit or change options until you type a name. Just as with filenames, you can't use any spaces or special characters, nor are you allowed to use numbers.

The address of your selected area appears in the Area dialog box. The address consists of the sheet name, the upper-left corner cell address, and the lower-right corner cell address. In Figure 17.2, the upper-left cell address is $B$6 and the lower-right cell address is $F$33. Because there is more than one sheet in this spreadsheet, the cell references are prefaced by the sheet name.

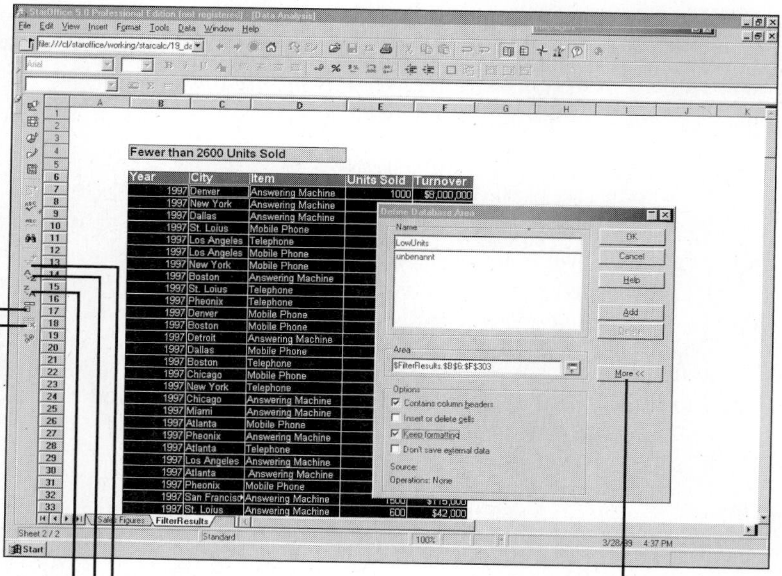

Figure 17.2
Once you've entered data, the next step is defining a database area so you can put StarCalc's database management tools to work. You can find simple tools for sorting and filtering data on the Main toolbar, with advanced tools on the Data menu.

Group
Ungroup

Sort Ascending
Sort Descending
Autofilter

Choosing More gives you additional options, which include maintaining your cell styles (formatting).

Note that the addresses use absolute references. You should always use absolute references when defining database areas.

→ For more information on absolute references and cell addressing, **see** "Referencing Cells in Formulas" **p. 593**.

You can edit the address, or delete it entirely and type in another.

Click More to see the complete list of options, as shown in Figure 17.2. The first check box, Contains Column Headers, is checked by default. This lets StarCalc know your first row is not data but field names. The other options relate to importing data from external sources and are discussed in the section "Importing and Exporting Data," later in this chapter.

After you have defined the area and chosen your options, choose Add. Confirm your addition and close the dialog box by choosing OK. Choosing Cancel exits the dialog without adding any new data areas.

Your list is now a database area. If you choose Data, Select Area, the name of your database area appears in the Data list. Clicking its name immediately selects the entire database area and jumps you there.

MODIFYING A DATABASE AREA

StarCalc automatically changes the definition of a database area if you add more rows to the middle. However, StarCalc does not automatically change the definition if you add more data to the end (unless you have included blank rows in your data area definition).

If you've defined a limited area of a worksheet as a database and find yourself adding more data to the end, you'll need to modify your defined database area. Otherwise, the new records will not be included in your sorting, filtering, and subtotaling operations.

Tip #343 from *Michael & Sarah*	Avoid needing to modify your data area by placing your database on its own sheet and selecting the entire sheet below and to the right of your header row as a database area.

To modify your database definition, first choose Data, Select Area, and click the database name to select it and jump to its location.

Next, choose the Data, Define Data command to open the Define Database Area dialog (refer to Figure 17.2). The current definition of your database appears in the Area box.

Click the cell that defines the new upper-left limit of your database area. Then, navigate to the cell that defines the new lower-right limit and select it with a Shift+click. Your modified address appears in the Area box.

A thin red border appears that marks your modified database area; and a small box appears near the lower-right cell that gives you the measurement of your database area in number of rows by number of columns.

Choose Modify to enter the new definition, and OK to confirm it and close the dialog. Cancel closes the dialog without making any changes to the current data definition.

DELETING A DATABASE DEFINITION

If you no longer want your data list to be defined as a database, you can delete its database definition. Deleting the database definition has no effect on the list data itself. However, once you delete the database definition, you can no longer apply some of the sorting, filtering, and subtotaling commands to your list (unless you redefine it as a database area).

To delete the database definition, choose the Data, Define Data command. Select the database definition you want to delete from the list, and choose Delete.

A message box appears asking for confirmation that you really want to delete. Choose Yes to confirm or Cancel to exit without making changes.

SORTING AND FILTERING DATA

You can sort and filter any area you select in a StarCalc spreadsheet, regardless of whether you define it as a database.

However, when you choose a sorting or filtering command from a cell within a defined database area, the command is automatically applied to the entire database area. This ensures that all information in a single record always stays together.

You can also only apply standard and advanced filters to database areas.

SORTING WITH THE MAIN TOOLBAR SORT BUTTONS

 You can quickly sort any list of data or defined database area by selecting its left-most column and clicking the Sort Ascending or Sort Descending button on the Main toolbar. Columns of data on either side will not be affected. You don't need to select the entire database area, just click somewhere within its area. (That's one of the advantages of defining it as a data area.)

> **Caution**
>
> There's a bug in the toolbar shortcut for the Sort Ascending command. Column headers are treated as ordinary data. However, you can Sort Ascending without problem from the Data, Sort dialog box. First, be sure to choose the option Area Contains Column Headers on the Options tab. Then, on the Criteria tab, choose Sort Ascending.

> **Note**
>
> If your sort turns out unexpectedly, immediately choose Undo (Ctrl+Z).

If there are blank cells at the top of a column or database area, StarCalc shifts sorted data up to fill these cells.

SORTING WITH THE DATA MENU SORT COMMAND

The Data, Sort command allows you to sort by three fields instead of just the one enabled by the Sort Ascending and Sort Descending buttons. You can also sort by rows instead of columns, and set other sort criteria.

CREATING A SIMPLE SORT

To sort a list, first select the list area. To sort a database area, click anywhere in the database area; or choose the Data, Select Area command and click its name in the Database Area list. Then choose Data, Sort.

> **Note**
>
> If you have selected a cell or range of cells within the database area, the Sort command will apply only to those selected cells.

The Sort dialog box, shown in Figure 17.3, opens with the Sort Criteria tab on top. By default, the left-most column of the selected list or database area is entered as the first sorting criterion.

Figure 17.3
You can do a quick sort based on the leftmost column by clicking a Sort button on the Main toolbar, or construct a more complex sort with the Data, Sort dialog shown here. On its Options tab, you can choose to sort based on custom lists you created earlier in the Tools, Options, Spreadsheet, Sorted Lists dialog box.

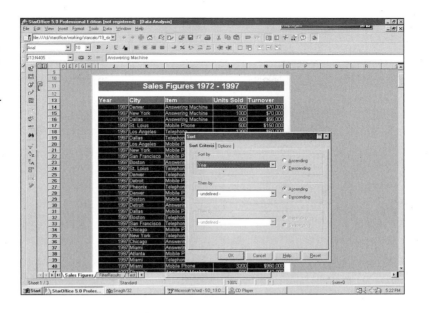

If you are sorting a list, this column will be identified by its column name (for example, Column C). If you are sorting a database area, the first row of your database area is automatically read as column headers (field names), and the column is identified by its field name (for example, Year).

Tip #344 from
Michael & Sarah

You can sort by columns (from left to right) as well as rows; choose the direction of your sort on the Options tab.

Use the drop-down menu to select a different category or column by which to sort. Choose the Ascending or Descending option to define the sort order.

To sort by additional fields, press Tab to move to the Then By box, and select the second sort field and sort order. Press Tab again if you want to refine your sort even further with a third field.

Once you have set your sort criteria, choose OK to execute the sort and close the dialog.

CREATING A COMPLEX SORT WITH OPTIONS

You can create a complex sort by using options on the Options tab of the Sort dialog, shown in Figure 17.4.

The effect of each option when it is selected is listed in Table 17.1.

Figure 17.4
With advanced sorting options, you can sort by rows or columns.

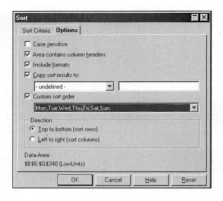

TABLE 17.1 SORT OPTIONS IN THE SORT DIALOG BOX

Option Name	Effect
Case Sensitive	Words beginning with lowercase letters are placed before those beginning with capitals.
Area Contains Column Headers	First row in the selected area is read as field names. These names appear in the Sort Criterion drop-down menus.
Include Formats	During sorting, the cell formatting characteristics are moved along with the contents of the cell.
Copy Sort Results To	Allows you to select a named cell range or defined database area, or enter a cell range address, to which the sort results will be copied.
Custom Sort Order	Allows you to sort your list or database area based on custom lists. Create your own custom lists in the Tools, Options, Spreadsheet, Sorted Lists dialog box.

Tip #345 from
Michael & Sarah

With the Copy Sort Results To option, you can quickly create a sorted copy of your database on another worksheet. It's easiest if you first define the worksheet as a named range with the Insert, Names, Define command (Ctrl+F3)—otherwise, you have to enter the cell reference manually. You must include the sheet name in the reference, for example, $SortResults.$A$1. If you're using the entire sheet, it's enough to enter the first cell reference in the range, as in this example.

Caution

Sort commands work on the entire list or database area, even if you have filtered the list so only a portion of it is visible. If you want to sort a filtered list, use the Standard or Advanced filter to copy your filtered list to a separate area of your spreadsheet.

FILTERING IN PLACE WITH AUTOFILTER

As your database grows in size, sorting alone quickly becomes insufficient for getting a grip on your data. That's where filters come in. Filters are like masks that hide the data you're not interested in and reveal the data you do want to see more clearly. They're a way to find that proverbial needle in a haystack.

The Autofilter is the filtering equivalent of the Sort Ascending and Sort Descending commands—good for finding selected data on-the-fly. It offers a limited set of filtering options and it creates the filter on top of your entire database, rather than giving you the option of copying the filtered data into a new list of its own. However, it's fast, it's simple, and it's very useful.

Figure 17.5 shows you the same Sales Figures list you've seen in Figures 17.1–17.4, transformed by application of an Autofilter that's created a select list of the top 10 numbers of units sold.

PART

III

CH

17

Tip #346 from
Michael & Sarah

If you click the small button with the minus sign on the left margin of the sheet shown in Figure 17.5, you see a list further filtered to the top five in the Units category.

Even though all you see are the selected records, the rest of the database is still there—it just has conditional cell formatting applied that makes it temporarily invisible (until you click All again in one of the filter lists, or turn off Autofilter).

Figure 17.5
Once you've turned Autofilter on, each column has a drop-down list that contains each unique entry in the list, plus a few other filtering choices. Rearrange your view in an instant by selecting a different item in a drop-down list.

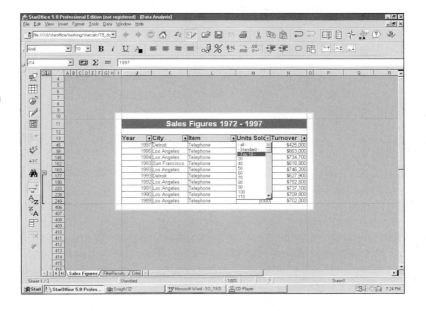

To create an Autofilter, either select the list (if it's not a defined data area) or place your cursor somewhere in your data area, and click the Autofilter button on the Main toolbar. Immediately, you'll see arrows appear to the right of each of your field names (refer to Figure 17.5). Click an arrow to open its drop-down list, and scroll in the usual way. If you want to sort by that field, click the criterion you want to apply and voilà! your results appear.

When you've created your initial filtered list, you can continue to refine it by selecting criteria from other fields with which to filter, making a smaller and smaller mask, so to speak.

If you want to start all over again—filtering from the entire database—you need to choose All in one of the drop-down lists. If that doesn't work, turn Autofilter off, and then back on again by clicking its button on the Main toolbar twice. You can also choose Data, Filter, Hide Autofilter, and then choose Autofilter again. (The Remove Filter option has no effect on the Autofilter; it removes Standard and Advanced filters.)

CREATING SELECTIVE LISTS WITH STANDARD AND ADVANCED FILTERS

Working with Standard and Advanced filters on the Data menu, you can apply types of criteria, such as logical and mathematical, that aren't available with a simple Autofilter. You can also generate new, selective lists by copying the results of your filtering operation onto a new worksheet or area.

In Figure 17.6, a Standard filter is being constructed that will pull out only records of cellular phone sales in Miami. You can see the result of the finished filter in Figure 17.7.

Figure 17.6
Choosing the More button on the Standard filter dialog opens you to its most powerful options: searching with regular expressions, saving your filter criteria for re-use, and copying your results to another area of your worksheet while leaving your original database intact.

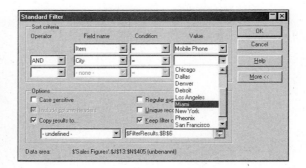

The same result could be achieved with an Autofilter in two steps (first, click Miami in the City drop-down list, and then click Cellular Phones in the Item list). However, using the Standard Filter, you can copy the result to a separate worksheet and create a table that can be reformatted easily for presentation, or saved as its own file and given to sales associates in Miami (who may not need to know the history of cellular phone sales in New Orleans).

Figure 17.7
Once you have created a copy of your filtered data, you can then sort and reformat your new table in any way you like. You can even bring it into StarWriter to really dress it up.

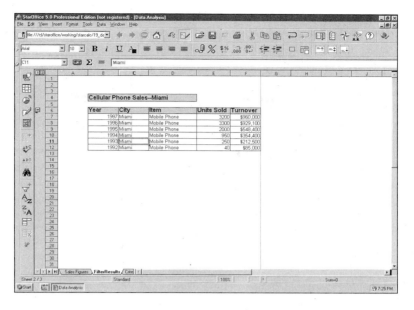

Data copied from your database in this way is no longer connected to the original source and will not be updated if the original data changes. (In this case, since the data is historical, it's not an issue, but for current data it might be.)

The Standard filter also offers filtering options not available with Autofilter, which can only filter based on the content of the tables' own fields.

The Advanced filter offers even greater power in filtering because it enables you to construct your own complex queries using Boolean logic to filter your data using as many criteria as you like.

To use an Advanced filter, you must first create a *criteria range* somewhere on your spreadsheet. This range contains the criteria your data must meet in order to survive the filtering. See Figure 17.8 for a simple example.

The first row of your range consists of your database's field names, copied exactly from your database header rows. (Just copy and paste to be sure.) While strictly speaking, you don't need to list all the fields—only those you're filtering by—it's not a bad idea to just copy and paste them all. That makes it easy for you to later add and delete criteria but still use the same range. It also guards against making errors in the header row, which is important because your filter won't work if the header rows don't match exactly those of your source database.

Figure 17.8
The criteria for an Advanced Filter can be as complex as you can make them, combining regular expressions with Boolean logic and basic arithmetical operators.

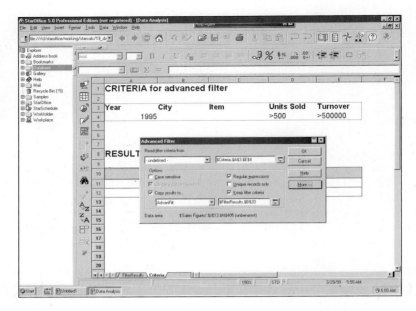

The second row is where you place your criteria. You can place criteria in any cell whose field you want to use for filtering. Just leave the others blank. If you choose More in the dialog box, and then select Regular Expressions, you can use any of the program's standard regular expressions for filtering. For example, here you could search for all 1990s sales figures by entering 199., using the period character, in the Year field. Note that a cell in StarCalc is the equivalent of a paragraph in StarWriter.

TABLE 17.2   SELECTED LIST OF REGULAR EXPRESSIONS FOR USE IN FILTERS

Expression	Description
.	Acts as a wildcard character. The search term 199. would find all years in the decade of the 1990s. You can use more than one period in a search string, in multiple locations. The period character serves the same function here as does the * symbol in DOS.
^Begin	Finds the entered word or number only if at the beginning of a cell. Special objects or contents (e.g., anchored frames, notes) are ignored.
End$	Finds the entered word or number only if at the end of a cell. Special objects or contents (e.g., anchored frames, notes) are ignored.
*	Indicates that the character placed before this symbol can appear in unlimited instances or not at all. Used together with the . (period) character, allows you to search for variations on a sentence or phrase structure. For example, "Sales figures .* have" would find "Sales figures for the month of May have risen," and "Sales figures have been promising for the second quarter." The combination .* represents unlimited or no characters. Note that this is a different meaning that the * has in DOS.

Expression	Description
[^w-z]	Excludes all instances of the specified range of characters or numbers from the filter.
have | were	Searches and filters for alternative words or numbers in the same position in a longer phrase, or in the same cell. You can string more than two words or numbers together. For example, you could use the following expression in the Year field of an advanced filter for Sales Figure database to display only sales figures for the years 1992, 1995, and 1997: 1992 | 1995 | 1997

If you want to filter against multiple conditions on one field—say you want to filter the Sales Figures list so that all records with turnover of between $100,000 and $300,000 display—use two rows or as many rows as necessary. Just be sure not to include any blank rows in your criteria range, as every record in your database turns up a positive match against a blank in StarCalc's book.

After you've created your header and criteria rows, it's a good idea to select and name your criteria range with the Insert, Names, Define (Ctrl+F3) command. This makes it easy to select it later in the Advanced Filter dialog and ensures you don't make a cell reference entry error.

However, StarCalc makes it easy to enter the correct references even if you don't do that. Once you've selected the database area to be filtered, you can navigate to where your criteria are located, even if it's on another worksheet. After you're there, you can draw a box around your criteria range (refer to Figure 17.8) and the correct cell references will be automatically entered in the cell reference entry box.

In order to make it easier to enter your cell references, you can click the Minimize button next to the cell reference entry box. This reduces the dialog to a one-line floating box that registers the cell addresses anywhere you click. In Figure 17.9, that method is being used to enter the extract range, which is just below where the criteria have been entered. (The special formatting is the result of an earlier filtering operation.)

When you have entered all the information you need about your criteria range and options, choose OK to actually run the filter. You can see the final results of this particular operation in Figure 17.10.

You can create a cascading series of filtering operations with Advanced filters, continuing to filter your filtered results with new criteria until you get just the results you want.

Figure 17.9
Once you've clicked your cell (or cells) to enter your reference, click the Maximize button on the right of the entry box to return to the full-sized dialog.

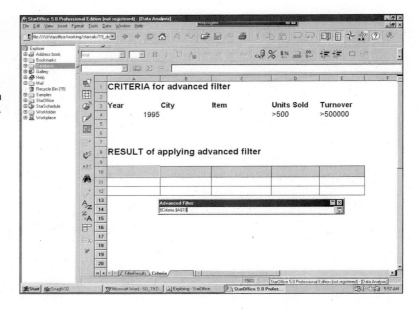

Figure 17.10
A lot of advance planning results in a very small number of results—just what you want in order to pinpoint critical data and patterns that might go unnoticed without the power of an Advanced filter.

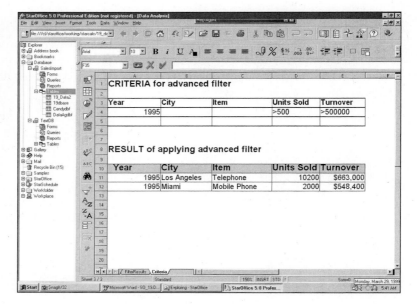

IMPORTING AND EXPORTING DATA

Databases are all about connectivity to information, and portability of data both in and out of StarCalc is an important issue to consider when deciding whether to use it as a database.

StarCalc rates a solid B at the moment, importing a large number of database and text file formats, and exporting a more selective number of the most common formats—although it does not export in MS Access format. It does not have built-in SQL functionality but under Windows (32 bit), you can connect to external DB2, DAO, Oracle, JDBC, and ODBC database servers if you have the proper drivers and database engines installed. You can also import StarCalc tables into a StarBase database and use SQL from within StarBase, if your table becomes large enough to require more robust tools.

Just as with StarBase, however, StarCalc's lack of OBDC support on Linux is a significant weakness. The good news is that according to the company, JDBC connectivity has been significantly improved in version 5.1 (although we were unable to test this independently before publication). Anything would be an improvement because the reality is that JDBC connectivity did not work in version 5.0.

Other Linux users have also reported problems connecting with Sybase databases. If you work heavily with databases and need to connect to external SQL servers, you should run tests first to be sure StarOffice can really meet your needs.

You can import data into StarCalc by the back door, so to speak, by importing database tables into a StarBase database in the Explorer, and then dragging and dropping data from that table into StarCalc. It's not exactly an intuitive process, so it is detailed for you in the section "Selectively Importing Data from the Explorer," later in this section.

PART

III

CH

17

Note

> OBDC connectivity may be coming soon to Linux as StarDivision is switching to a different third-party source for its database engine to have better access to the source code.

FILE IMPORTING OPTIONS

If you are not connecting to external data sources, you must have your database file in a format StarCalc can open.

StarCalc opens a wide range of formats, including DIF, SYLK, dBase III, and numerous text formats, including CSV files. It can also open MS Access 97 files through the back door—importing it through a StarBase table. A complete list of supported file formats is listed in Appendix B, "File Formats and Extensions."

There are two ways you can bring external data into StarCalc: You can insert the entire database into your spreadsheet, or you can create links to the database in the Explorer, open the database, and select specific records to transfer into your StarCalc spreadsheet.

IMPORTING AN ENTIRE DATABASE FILE

To import a file that has been saved in an appropriate format, choose the File, Open command and open the file as usual.

You'll be asked to select the appropriate character set for your data. Usually the IBMPC default is fine if you're opening the data on the same operating system in which it was created. The dBASE IV format uses Codepage 437 (U.S.).

Choose OK to confirm, and your file will open with the first row listing the header information for your database file (assuming your program saves this information with the file). You will likely need to adjust the column widths, and you may need to delete extraneous symbols that appeared during the import process.

Tip #347 from *Michael & Sarah*	If you imported a text file and your records were not broken up appropriately into fields, check to be sure you selected the right type of text file import filter.

Caution	If you are importing a very large file, be sure to back it up before attempting the job. It's also a good idea to close out of any other open tasks because importing a large file can cause a system crash.

SELECTIVELY IMPORTING DATA FROM THE EXPLORER

To selectively import data into StarCalc, you must first create a database in the Explorer to hold the table(s) from which you want to import.

Here, briefly, are the steps you must follow:

1. Create the folder in which you want to create your database.
2. Select the folder and right-click to open the Explorer context menu.
3. Choose New, Database. A multitabbed dialog box appears.
4. Enter a name for your new database in the text box on the General tab. You don't need to enclose the name in < >.
5. Click the Type tab.
6. Click to open the drop-down list of database types that you can import (see Figure 17.11). Note that you will only be able to import data from Oracle, ODBC, or JDBC servers if you have the correct drivers already installed on your system. Otherwise, you'll be limited to importing dBase, Text, StarBase, and MS Access 97 files.
7. Select the type of file you're importing. Your tabs will change, depending on the type of database you selected.$I~importing;data;StarCalc>
8. If you selected to import a file rather than connect to an external server, choose the Browse button (refer to Figure 17.11), locate the directory in which the database file is located, and choose OK to confirm. If you want to create a directory into which you will then move your database file, choose the Create Directory button instead and name your directory. You don't need to enter the database file name—assuming you've steered StarOffice in the right direction, your file will appear in the Explorer as described in a few steps that follow.

Figure 17.11
Once you've named your database on the General tab, you can select the type of database file or server from which you're importing.

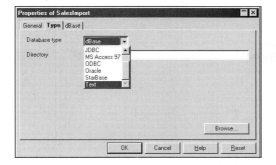

If you're connecting to an external server, follow the instructions on the tab.

If you're importing a text file, click the Text tab to bring it to the front and check the default settings for interpreting your file (see Figure 17.12).

Figure 17.12
If you're importing a text file, you can inform StarCalc if your file has a header row, adjust the way StarCalc interprets punctuation in your file, and indicate the character set used to generate your original database.

PART
III

CH
17

9. Choose OK to complete the creation of your new database and exit the dialog.

→ For a more detailed discussion of creating a database in the Explorer, **see** "Creating a New Database in the Explorer," **p. 1092**.

You should see a new database icon in the Explorer with the name you entered to the right. Click the + sign next to the database to open its elements, and then click the + sign next to the Tables folder to view your table name(s) in the Explorer. In Figure 17.13, there is more than one table of the dBase type in the folder, so multiple tables are displaying.

10. If the Beamer is not already open, click its icon on the Function bar to open it.

11. Extended-click the table you want to open in the Beamer. Once you open your table in the Beamer, you can filter and sort your records with the Beamer's filtering and sorting tools, identified in Figure 17.13. You'll recognize the sorting and filtering tools from StarCalc.

Caution

Clean up your imported table before you sort or filter because unlike in StarCalc, you can-not undo most actions in the Beamer. You will likely need to delete your column headers and possibly other stray characters in your upper rows before filtering and sorting, so there aren't any anomalous results. By default, tables are opened as read-only in the Beamer, so you'll need to click the Edit button (identified in Figure 17.13) before you can edit any records.

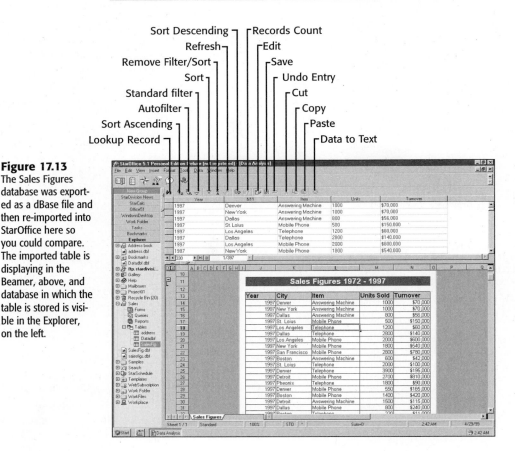

Figure 17.13
The Sales Figures database was export-ed as a dBase file and then re-imported into StarOffice here so you could compare. The imported table is displaying in the Beamer, above, and database in which the table is stored is visi-ble in the Explorer, on the left.

Once you sort and filter your data, you can drag and drop data from the Beamer into your spreadsheet.

To drag and drop records from the Beamer, first select those you want to import into StarCalc by clicking the header row to highlight them. You can use the usual Shift+click selection trick to select multiple contiguous rows, and Ctrl+click to select non-contiguous rows. Then, click and drag from the header row—not from within highlighted fields—into the open cells of your StarCalc worksheet. (You can select the entire data table in the same way you select an entire worksheet, by clicking the gray button in the upper left corner, where the column and row headers meet.)

Note that as alluring as the toolbar buttons may be, you cannot use the conventional Cut, Copy, and Paste commands to copy rows of data. Nor can you use the Copy command that appears when you right-click on a field in the Beamer—it will copy and paste exactly one field of one record. Those commands are used only for editing data in table fields.

→ For more information on dragging and dropping data from tables into spreadsheets, **see** "Manipulating Table Contents," **p. 1156**.

Even easier, you can simply click the Data to Text button (refer to Figure 17.13) on the far right of the Beamer toolbar, and all your selected rows of data will be neatly dropped into continous rows in your spreadsheet starting from your current cursor position, pushing any existing data out of the way (rather than overwriting it).

However, you can't add data into the middle of a defined database area this way—you'll end up replacing all the existing data, whether you drag and drop or position your cursor in the middle of the database and click Data to Text. (If you drag and drop, StarCalc will ask you first if you really want to replace your current data. If you use the Data to Text button, you have no such luck; your existing data will be replaced without warning.) And you can only append it successfully if you have previously defined your database area to include a large number of blank rows at the bottom. (You can see the wisdom of setting aside an entire worksheet as a database area.)

Tip #348 from
Michael & Sarah

Given that you might need to clean up your data or, at the very least, check it to be sure it imported properly, it might be wise to drag and drop it on to a clean worksheet first. That way you can append it later when you can work entirely within StarCalc.

EXPORTING DATA FROM STARCALC

You can save your StarCalc database in a number of foreign formats that enable you to transfer data to other programs, although you can save in fewer formats than you can open.

The formats you can export in are as follows:

- SYLK (Symbolic Link)
- DIF (Database Interchange Format)
- dBase
- Text-txt-csv
- Excel 97
- Excel 95
- Excel 5.0

The format you choose will, of course, depend on the program in which you want to open the file. In general, the Text-txt-csv (delimited text format) is the most flexible, as virtually any database or spreadsheet program is able to open such a file. dBase is also a very common (although not universal) database file. SYLK and DIF are also data exchange formats meant to enable transferring data between computers using different database programs but are not as widely used. If you're saving the file to give to someone else, you should always ask about the recipient's preferred file format.

To save in one of these formats, select its name from the file type drop-down list in the StarCalc Save As dialog box and proceed with the save as normal. Be sure the Automatic file extension option is selected so the appropriate extension is appended and your file can be recognized by your other application without problem.

If you save in text (CSV) format, a dialog appears listing the default field delimiter, text delimiter, and character set. You can change them if you like—just open the drop-down lists and click your alternative choice, and choose OK.

Be aware that special features including arrays, StarOffice pivot tables, and DataPilot tables will not export, and oftentimes complex formulas don't translate very well either. Results of formulas may be translated into normal integers. You should always save your file first in StarCalc format and only then in a foreign format in case of problems or data loss.

WORKING BETWEEN STARCALC AND STARBASE

Oddly enough, you can't save your StarCalc files in StarBase format, although you can save them in dBase format and work between StarBase and StarCalc in that way. The major reason to do this is because StarBase has SQL, which gives you considerably more powerful tools for sorting and filtering your data than does StarCalc. dBase files seem to import and export quite cleanly, making this a legitimate alternative.

TROUBLESHOOTING

StarCalc keeps confusing my column header with my data when it sorts and filters.

Try formatting your headers in their own special cell style. That may help StarCalc tell them apart. However, never separate your column heads from your data with an extra row, because then it will never see them as header rows.

There's a bug in the main toolbar Sort Ascending tool; if your problems occur only when using that tool, try using the Data menu Sort command instead, which also enables you to sort in ascending order, by any field you choose.

If you're using the Data menu Sort command, just make sure you've selected the Area Contains Column Headers option on the Sort dialog box Options tab. Otherwise, StarCalc doesn't know that you have column headers.

I keep clicking All in my Autofilter list, but I can't get my original database back in view.

Sometimes when you create nested filters, clicking All in one row won't do the trick. The simplest solution is to turn Autofilter off (what the program refers to as *hiding* it) by clicking its button on the Main toolbar or choosing Hide Autofilter on the Data, Filter submenu.

My criteria range doesn't seem to work at all—my data looks the same as before I ran the Advanced filter.

Check to ensure you didn't accidentally include any blank rows in your criteria range definition or reference. If you include a blank row, StarCalc assumes you want it to match every record in the database against all records in the list. That won't get your filtering very far.

When I run my Advanced filter, I keep getting an error message that it can't find a valid query in my criteria range.

Check and make sure your field names match exactly those of your database area. The usual reasons for this message is that it's looking for an exact match on header information that isn't there. Also make sure that you selected the entire critiera range and nothing but the criteria range. You should select all the field names plus the row or rows that have your criteria.

I'm trying to open a database text file in StarCalc, but it keeps opening in StarWriter instead!

You've bumped into one small downside of the integrated workspace. StarWriter is associated with text files and so when you try to open a text file, it automatically opens in StarWriter =. You need to change the file association in the Tools, Options, Browser, File Types dialog box for your type of text file from StarWriter to StarCalc. Of course, if you ever need to edit the file in a word processor, you'll need to reverse the process. A simpler option is to change the file extension of your file from *.txt to *.csv.

I've just copied some new database tables into my database directory, but they don't show up in the Explorer.

Because of the way StarOffice caches data rather than checking against original sources all the time, it's common for new objects to not register immediately in the Explorer. Right-click your tables folder and choose Update. StarOffice will check the source and refresh the Explorer display to reflect your new tables.

I can't select records in my table in the Beamer.

You're probably still in Read-only mode. Click the Edit button on the Beamer toolbar (refer to Figure 18.12).

I can't drag records from the Beamer the way you say I can.

Be sure you're grabbing and dragging from the header row, not from a field.

Is there any way to insert fields from a StarCalc spreadsheet into a StarWriter document?

Save your spreadsheet as a dBase database file. Then, create a new database in the Explorer that contains the file. Open a new text document, choose the Edit, Change Database command, and select your dBase database as your default database. Open the database in the Beamer. You can now just drag and drop your field names (column headers) from the Beamer table into your StarWriter document.

CHAPTER 18

ANALYZING AND CHARTING DATA

In this chapter

ADVANCED DATA ANALYSIS TECHNIQUES

Chapter 17, "Creating Lists and Databases with StarCalc," introduces a number of StarCalc's data sorting and filtering tools in connection with keeping lists or databases. This chapter presents StarCalc's advanced tools for data filtering and analysis. The first tool, DataPilot, is most likely to be used on lists and databases, and the discussion in this chapter builds on Chapter 17. If you're particularly interested in DataPilot, we suggest you familiarize yourself with Chapter 17 first, particularly the section "Searching, Sorting, and Filtering Lists."

The remaining tools described in this chapter—Consolidate, Subtotals, Goal Seek, Pivot Tables, and scenario-building—are used in numerically oriented data analysis, which may be appropriate for databases or for other types of data, such as budgets, financial projections, and scientific data.

Whether you're working with databases or numbers, at some point you'll surely need to view and present your results in easy-to-grasp graphic form. With StarChart, you can quickly transform StarCalc data into charts that help you and your audiences better see patterns, trends, and relationships.

ADVANCED ANALYSIS OF LISTS AND DATABASES

The limitations of creating a large database in a spreadsheet quickly become apparent when you try to take in a long database at a glance—even a simple one like that shown in Figure 18.1. For example, here much of the information is repetitive—the year of the sales figures, the city in which sales took place—and it isn't easy to get an overall picture of sales. What you need is a summary of the data that presents the same information as the table, but in compact form. In a relational database like StarBase, you would use queries and SQL to create new views of your data. In StarCalc, you use DataPilot.

Figure 18.1
As lists and databases begin to get large, you need tools like DataPilot to summarize and analyze your data.

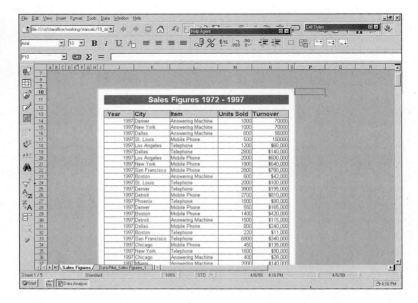

DataPilot creates what is generally called a pivot table in the United States, and if you're familiar with Excel's pivot tables, you'll find using DataPilot easy. (You might also know such tables as *cross-tabs*.)

Note

> Translation issues come up again with StarCalc's data commands. The DataPilot in StarCalc creates what we in the United States call *pivot tables*, whereas the Pivot Tables command enables you to conduct data sensitivity analyses—that is, to see how changing variables affects the results of a specified formula.

What can you do with a DataPilot table? It's equally useful for analysis and presentation. Here are some possible uses:

- Create summary tables that help with a big-picture analysis. For example, you could create a table that summarizes the data in the Sales Figures database by city and product category, creating subtotals of sales. You can also display averages and other summary statistics.

- Reorganize the data in your table to give new perspectives on the same data.

- Analyze data imported from an external source.

→ For details on how to import data from external databases into StarCalc, **see** "Importing and Exporting Data," **p. 636**.

- Filter your data in more useful ways by beginning with the DataPilot's summarized data.

- Create a summary chart from your DataPilot table. In fact, there are few better ways to quickly grasp the essence of a large amount of data than to create a chart from a DataPilot table.

Even though the DataPilot table is just a view of your data, you can enter or change its data, unlike with a pivot table in Excel. However, the table is linked to your source data, and if you select the Refresh command on the table's context menu, your DataPilot table's data is updated with the most recent data in the source database table—and you lose any changes you have made, including formatting. If you frequently use DataPilot tables for presentation, you would be smart to create styles to format them as you like. You can then update the data first and format them with styles just before printing.

CREATING DATAPILOT TABLES

The first step in creating a DataPilot table is to think about your data and choose the categories that will best analyze and summarize it. The categories that are appropriate depend entirely on the answers or information you hope to derive from it. For example, in the database in Figure 18.1, we have five categories from which to choose (the five column headings). It might seem obvious to summarize by city and item. However, if you were preparing an annual report, you might want to summarize by year to get a broad overview of sales trends over the past 25 years.

Tip #349 from
Michael & Sarah

Check your database for unintentional spaces and spelling errors before running DataPilot. DataPilot reads any variation in an entry as a separate item. For example, if you were summarizing your data by city, and Phoenix was misspelled in a number of entries as Pheonix, you would have two separate summaries, one for each spelling of the city. Likewise, if there were an extra space in front of Phoenix, it would be read as a different word than Phoenix without a space. If you turn on the AutoSpellcheck feature (on the main toolbar), it automatically flags most basic errors.

After you finish planning your table, select the data you want to analyze. (If you've already defined a database area with the Data, Define Area command, you can select the database with a click by choosing its name from Database Areas list in the Navigator, or from the Data menu Select Area dialog box.) Then, choose Data, Data Pilot, Start.

The DataPilot dialog appears (see Figure 18.2), displaying a blank table defined by three areas: a Row area to the left, a Column area to the top, and a Data area in the middle. To the right are buttons that list the fields (categories) of your database. If you click More, you see additional options for placing and defining results.

Figure 18.2
The Data Pilot dialog presents all your database categories in the form of buttons that you drag and drop to define your DataPilot table. You can choose to have DataPilot create totals for rows, columns, or both by checking options in the Result area.

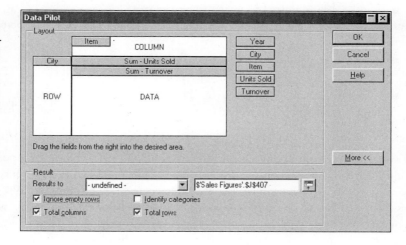

Drag the name of the field(s) that you want to define your rows into the Row area, those you want to define your columns into the Column area, and the data you want summarized into the Data area. In Figure 18.2, we've chosen to summarize the sales totals (Turnover) and units sold categories by city and item, and we've left the Year category off entirely. However, rearranging the table is as simple as rearranging the category buttons through drag and drop, so it would be easy to analyze the figures by year later. Alternatively, you can still use the Year field to sort the data in the table even if Year is not visible.

PLACING TABLES   You could just click OK at this point and let DataPilot generate your table. However, if you do this, DataPilot automatically places the results at the bottom of your current database. This might not be the best location because you might need to add data to your database later. As you add data to your database, your DataPilot table might grow in size as well. If you want to create a chart or use an advanced filter on data, you'll also want some elbow room so that you won't be disturbing your source data. The Results To drop-down list enables you to place your results on another existing worksheet, on a new worksheet created by DataPilot, or in another location on your current worksheet. (In Figure 18.2, you see the default selection, -undefined-, with the cell reference of the first blank row of the database listed.)

You can enter a cell reference just as you do with the Function AutoPilot—navigate to the area or worksheet you want to select, and either click the cell that defines the start of the area or type its reference. You can click the Minimize button to reduce the dialog to an input line and make it easier to see your entered reference, and click Maximize when you're done to return to the full dialog size.

CREATING TOTALS AND CHOOSING ANALYSIS OPTIONS   The remaining options affect how your data is analyzed, displayed, and presented by DataPilot. If you want DataPilot to create totals, choose the Total Columns and/or Total Rows options here. (Total Columns is selected by default.) If you choose Ignore Empty Rows, DataPilot ignores any blank rows in your database—this is a good safety precaution if you're planning to apply any statistical functions to your summarized data because otherwise blank cells are counted as zeros. If you choose Identify Categories, DataPilot places buttons for your categories as headers just like those in the initial DataPilot dialog to save you some steps in rearranging your data later.

Selections you make regarding row and column totals are saved and automatically applied when you use DataPilot until you change them again, but you must actively select Ignore Empty Rows and Identify Categories every time you create a DataPilot table.

When you complete your selections, click OK, and your DataPilot table is generated.

WORKING WITH DATAPILOT TABLES

Figure 18.3 shows the DataPilot table that results from the selections in Figure 18.2, after it's been reformatted for easier reading. You probably want to resize columns and rows and adjust cell formatting as well, as the DataPilot is powerful but not very graceful in the way it presents results. However, be forewarned that all your formatting will be lost when you update your data from its source database.

Figure 18.3
The DataPilot table summarizes a complex list in a compact table that can be formatted, copied, and manipulated in virtually the same ways as regular data.

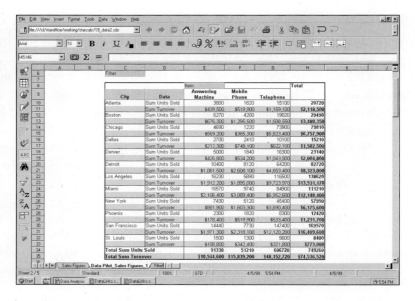

You can see that the database of 400 or so rows has been compacted into 25, with totals by both item sold (columns) and city (rows). Notice also that a standard filter is automatically placed at the top of your table to make further refining of your data just a step away.

CHANGING VIEWS   The organization of the table in Figure 18.3 facilitates comparing sales figures for different items in your database. What if you wanted to compare sales by city? If you selected the Identify Categories option, it's a snap to rearrange your view: All you need to do is drag and drop your category buttons into their new locations—the Item button into the Row area and the City button into the Column area. (The table is arranged in three sections just as in the dialog box, but it looks a little different because you don't have a blank space in the upper-left corner.)

If you didn't choose the Identify Categories option, you can still rearrange your view—just place your cursor in the table, right-click to open its context menu, and choose Start. This opens the Data Pilot dialog with a display of your current table structure and all your categories. You can add new categories as well as rearrange the categories in your current table.

As you're rearranging the buttons, your table data shifts and looks strange, but when you've moved all the category buttons to their new locations, the table sorts itself out again. You can see the result of changing the view in Figure 18.4.

Figure 18.4
If you choose the Identify Categories option, you are able to rearrange your data by just dragging and dropping buttons representing the categories you've included in your table. Otherwise, you need to open the context menu and re-enter the DataPilot dialog.

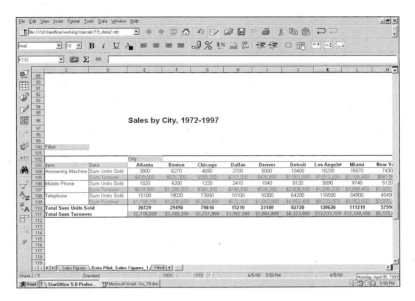

EDITING AND FORMATTING Because StarOffice caches most data and updates links only when you tell it to, you can edit your DataPilot table data in any way you want, including changing the values in totals fields. However, if you manually update your data or confirm StarCalc's desire to update links on program closing and opening, all your changes, including any formats you've applied, are lost, so this ability to change table entries is somewhat illusory.

This means you should play around with your table organization first, perfecting your analysis, before investing a lot of time in formatting your table for printing or presentation. If you want to print multiple views of the same data, you might want to create multiple tables so you can format them all at once. (However, don't save and store multiple tables—just keep one because DataPilot tables are memory intensive.)

If you find errors in the organization of your table's data, it may be due to errors in your source data that weren't apparent before—such as misspellings or spaces entered at the beginning of cells. If your data hasn't turned out as you expected, check and edit the source before you edit the DataPilot table.

PART
III

CH
18

Tip #350 from
Michael & Sarah

If you want to create a version of your DataPilot results with more stable formatting, create a new table with cell references to your DataPilot cells and format away!

SORTING AND FILTERING You can sort and outline your DataPilot table as you can any other table. With a standard filter (the type provided at the top of your DataPilot table), you can also further refine what you see, even using categories that aren't visible to filter the data that is. For example, you could use the Year category to filter the Sales Figures DataPilot table in Figures 18.3 and 18.4 so that only the sales figures for a specific year are visible. The DataPilot standard filter is preset to recognize your DataPilot table as a data area.

This preset standard filter lets you get around the fact that the category headings in a data table are special objects, not normal column or row labels. They cannot be selected as can headers. You can select them as part of the entire table, but StarCalc might not read them correctly as headers.

Tip #351 from *Michael & Sarah*	If you move your DataPilot table, you lose your standard filter. Just use the Refresh command from the context menu to bring it back.

Because of these particularities of DataPilot table column and row headers, you cannot apply advanced filters. However, using a combination of DataPilot options and a standard filter, you should be able to accomplish all you need to, given that your data is already considerably condensed and filtered.

UPDATING DATA After you perfect your table organization, clean up your source data, and complete your analysis, then you can update the table data from your source. With your cursor somewhere in the table, right-click to open its context menu and choose the Refresh command.

FORMATTING DATA When your data is ready, you can format it for final presentation. You can format your table just as you would any other StarCalc data. Keep in mind that you can copy and paste DataPilot tables into a StarWriter document as a DDE link table, an OLE object, or an HTML table to format and print your table. (However, you can't change the structure of a DDE link table—only format it.) The OLE and HTML versions are copies no longer linked to the source data, and the DDE link table remains linked to your source data. You can also copy and paste your table in RTF (Rich Text Format), which preserves your StarCalc formatting.

→ For more information on moving data between StarCalc and StarWriter, **see** "Copying and Moving Cell Data," **p. 535**.

DELETING DATAPILOT TABLES To delete a DataPilot table, place your cursor somewhere within the table, right-click to open the context menu, and choose Delete. Deleting the table has no effect on the source data.

CREATING SUBTOTALS

As you begin to accumulate financial and numeric data, you'll surely want to summarize portions of it with subtotals. Although you can always create your own subtotaling formulas, you can perform subtotaling more quickly with StarCalc's subtotals command, especially if you need to sort and group a large amount of data in a list or database.

> **Note**
>
> Version 5.0 has a major bug in it that causes subtotals to erroneously output 0 as the result. This bug has been fixed in 5.1.

You are not limited to adding data with the Sum function. You can choose from a list of functions, including functions for averaging, creating standard deviations, and counting. A complete list is given in Table 18.1, later in this chapter.

> **Note**
>
> You can also subtotal data with DataPilot tables and the Consolidate, Data command, depending on the form of your data and your needs.

Be aware that when you create subtotals, you end up adding rows to your data area—the rows in which subtotals and the grand total are recorded—and so change its structure. You can of course invoke the Undo command immediately after subtotaling to undo this, but if you work with a table for a time, there is no built-in way to delete these rows. You need to delete the rows manually. You therefore might want to work on a copy of your data to create subtotals, rather than subtotaling an entire database to which you're still actively adding data.

The first step is to select the data that you want to subtotal. If you have large databases or data areas, it's easiest if you have previously assigned them names. You can then just place your cursor anywhere within the area and select Data, Subtotals, and the area is automatically selected. Otherwise, you need to manually select the area and then select Subtotals.

The Subtotals dialog appears, like the one shown in Figure 18.5. If you have column headers in your database area, these are read and shown as category checkboxes in the left pane. Select the column whose data you want subtotaled. In this example the Turnover column contains the sales figures that need to be sorted and subtotaled.

Under the Group By label is a drop-down list of the same categories, where you can select the category with which you want to group and sort your data. After the subtotals command has done its work, your data is grouped into outlines based on your selection here, so you can choose to hide or reveal details. Next, choose the function you want used to create the subtotals.

As you can see in Figure 18.5, you can make two additional rounds of selections on the 2nd Group and 3rd Group tabs to group and subtotal your data with further refinements.

PART
III

CH
18

Figure 18.5
With the Subtotals command, you can simultaneously sort and subtotal your data, with up to three levels of grouping.

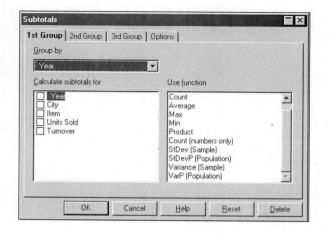

You can select the way StarCalc reads, sorts, and places your results on the Options tab. If you want to place each subtotaled group onto a separate page (to create monthly or yearly subtotal reports, for example), select Page Break Between Groups. If you choose Case Sensitive, StarCalc differentiates between lowercase and uppercase letters—so staroffice would be considered a different word than StarOffice. This affects both subtotaling and sorting of your data. Th option Pre-sort According to Groups is selected by default, and so the Sort options below are active. If you don't want StarCalc to pre-sort your data according to the groups you select, deselect this option; the Sort options will then gray out, and your work will be done. However, if you do want StarCalc to perform sorts, you can change the sort options here. By default, sorts are performed in ascending order; you can choose to have them performed in descending order instead. If you have previously created a custom list that reflects categories used in your database, you can sort your data by the ascending or descending order of that list.

When you complete your selections, click OK, and your subtotals are generated. Your results will look something like Figure 18.6, which shows a list sorted by year and city, with Sum subtotals created for the Turnover column. A grand total is generated at the bottom of your totaled columns.

Tip #352 from
Michael & Sarah

If you want to delete your subtotals rows, sort your table first to group the subtotals tows together so you can delete them in one step.

Note

Even if you choose to insert page breaks between different groups of your table, StarCalc continues to treat it as a single table.

Figure 18.6
The subtotaled data is grouped according to your selections, enabling you to hide or reveal details by clicking the minus (-) or plus (+) buttons next to the Main toolbar, respectively.

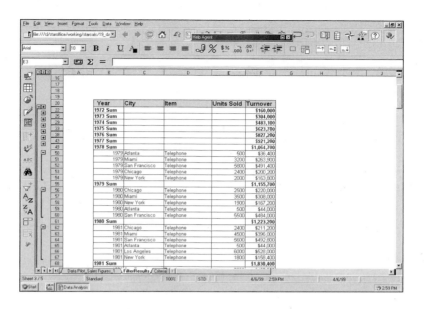

Tip #353 from
Michael & Sarah

If you don't like the appearance of StarCalc's subtotals, you can modify the Result cell style of the Standard template.

It's useful to know that StarCalc creates subtotals with a special function, SUBTOTAL. This function takes two arguments (from left to right): the number assigned by the program to the function you selected and the absolute cell references to the grouped cells to be subtotaled. The function number is the program's shorthand reference for the function. You can manually edit the formula after your subtotals have been created, changing cell references or even the function reference. Table 18.1 lists each function and matches it to its program number.

Note

If you're using verion 5.0, you can get Subtotals to work if you reveal the formula in the input line, manually delete the function number, re-insert it, and press Enter.

TABLE 18.1. FUNCTIONS AVAILABLE WITH THE SUBTOTALS AND CONSOLIDATE COMMANDS

Function	Program Code
Count	3
Minimum	5
Product	6

continues

TABLE 18.1. CONTINUED

Function	Program Code
StDev (Sample)	7
Variance (Sample)	10
Average	1
Maximum	4
Count (Numbers Only)	2
StDevP (Population)	8
VarianceP (Population)	11
Sum	9

CONSOLIDATING DATA

The Consolidate command goes beyond the simple Subtotals command and enables you to perform calculations on similar numeric data from a number of data tables or worksheets, and place your results in a new table. The tables you consolidate must share at least row labels or column headers.

Consolidating data offers some of the same advantages as creating a DataPilot table. It allows you to summarize large amounts of information, in this case located on different sheets or areas. Although they are not as flexible as DataPilot tables, they enable you to summarize and analyze numbers in more complex ways as well as perform counts on non-numeric data.

Tip #354 from
Michael & Sarah

To ensure that tables on different spreadsheets or worksheets share the same structure, you can create a template that contains an empty, formatted table with appropriate row labels and/or column headers.

Some common uses of the Consolidate command include consolidating monthly balance sheets into annual reports and consolidating budgets from different departments or divisions. You can also use it to perform simple statistical analysis on numeric data such as laboratory or field measurements or coded questionnaire results. Table 18.1 lists the available functions.

There are limitations on the type of data you can consolidate. You cannot consolidate the results of formulas, only values, and consolidation functions (with the exception of Count) are applicable only to numbers.

Tip #355 from
Michael & Sarah

If you want to consolidate the results of formulas, copy the table that contains the formulas and paste it on a new sheet using the StarCalc Paste Special command. In the Paste Special dialog box that appears, deselect Formulas. Your new table contains numbers only.

To create a consolidated table, follow these steps:

1. Select the area where you want to place your consolidated table. You can select only a single cell. StarCalc uses as much space as necessary to place your table, so be sure you've chosen an area large enough to contain the consolidated data. If you have a lot of data, it might be wisest to place your consolidated data on a separate worksheet, just to be sure no other data is accidentally overwritten.

2. Choose Data, Consolidate. The Consolidate dialog appears (see Figure 18.7).

Figure 18.7
After choosing the function you want to apply to the consolidated data, select data area names from the Source data area drop-down list, or enter cell references in the input line to its right.

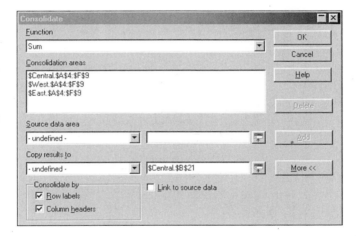

3. Select the function you want to apply.

4. Add the data areas you want to consolidate to the Consolidation areas list. This process is much easier if you have named data areas, as you can just double-click their names on the Source data area list. However, you can also enter cell references with the usual methods of clicking or manual entry.

   Select data areas plus row labels and column headers. Although cells with formulas won't be consolidated, nor will cells with text that aren't row labels or column headers, it doesn't matter if they're included in your selection—StarCalc just ignores them. Be sure you click the Add button after you enter a new reference.

Tip #356 from
Michael & Sarah

You cannot consolidate multiple spreadsheets. If you need to consolidate data from multiple spreadsheets, drag data areas or worksheets from one spreadsheet into another by using the Navigator, or use the worksheet Move/Copy command to copy worksheets into a single spreadsheet.

5. Click More.

6. Tell StarCalc how to map the table layouts of the different worksheets onto one another. If you choose row labels, you are indicating that all your tables have the same row labels. If you choose column headers, you are indicating that they have the same column headers, and if you choose both, you are indicating that they have both the same row labels and column headers. The fields do not have to be in the same order; StarCalc sorts them by name.

7. Select whether you want your consolidated table to be a copy of the data (the default) or linked to the source data.

8. Click OK to create your consolidated table.

Figure 18.8 shows the results of a simple data consolidation.

Figure 18.8
Budgets from three worksheets have been consolidated into one.

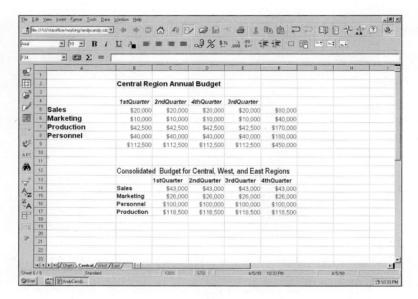

If your source areas have different arrangements of rows and/or columns, StarCalc takes it cue for the final order from the first data reference you entered.

Conducting Sensitivity Analyses

In StarCalc, the Pivot Table command doesn't actually create a pivot table. Instead, it enables you to conduct what's normally called a *sensitivity analysis* in the United States.

In a sensitivity analysis, you first create a formula that successfully calculates the result to a problem you're trying to solve, using just a single set of inputs. After building and testing your formula, you enter it into a StarCalc cell. Then you create a data table that contains values to substitute for one or two of the variables (arguments) in your formula. Finally, you use the Pivot Table command to generate an array of answers that show the results of your formula after substituting each of the values in your data table.

For example, let's say you're trying to figure out how much you need to invest each month in a particular mutual fund and you want to calculate what the 20-year returns would be on varying monthly investments.

First, you would create a formula by using the FV (Future Value) Financial function. The FV function calculates the future value of an investment based on regular payments into the investment and a constant interest rate.

Tip #357 from
Michael & Sarah

If you're not sure of the function to use, open the Function AutoPilot and browse the categories. Select the category you think best describes the topic or typical use of the function. Open that category, and browse through. Brief descriptions of the function appear in the dialog.

You assume a 12% annual return over the 20-year life of the investment, which translates into a 1% monthly return. 1% is the figure you actually plug into your formula because you are creating a formula based on monthly, not annual, payments. Your initial formula, then, would be FV(.01;240;100), where .01 is your 1% assumed monthly interest rate, 240 is the monthly equivalent of 20 years of monthly payments, and 100 is your monthly payment.

You want to enter these numbers into cells, however, and refer to cells rather than numbers. When you break up your formula into cellular components like this, StarCalc is able to substitute the values in your data table for the cell references in your formula. Therefore, the formula you would actually enter would be FV($C$7;$C$8;C6).

You can see the results of this formula in the Return on Investment row in Figure 18.9. (The result is returned as a negative number because it represents what you are owed as the investor.)

PART

III

CH

18

Figure 18.9
The first step in creating a sensitivity analysis is to build the formula. Here, the formula calculates the future value of a regular monthly investment. You test the returns on the different monthly investment amounts entered in the selected data table.

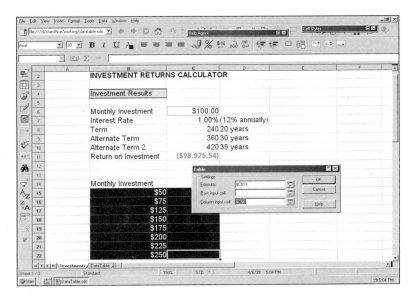

Next, you create your data table of possible monthly payments. After you complete data entry, select all the cells with the variables to be tested and their adjacent cells, where the results will appear (just as you see in Figure 18.9). Then, follows these steps:

1. Select Data, Pivot Table. (Note that the Pivot Table command is grayed out unless you've selected a range of cells.) A Table dialog appears, like the shown in Figure 18.9.

2. Click to place your cursor in the Formulas input line, and then click the cell that contains your formula to be tested. In this example, that's cell C11.

3. Enter the cell reference of the cell whose value you want to substitute with the values in your data table. In this example, that's cell C6.

4. Because your data table variables are arranged in a column, you input the reference to C6 in the Column input cell input line. You need to click in this input line to be able to enter the reference—otherwise, anything you click just overwrites your current reference in the Formulas line. When you know your cursor is in the right place, click C6.

5. Click OK.

Your results should look like column C in Figure 18.10.

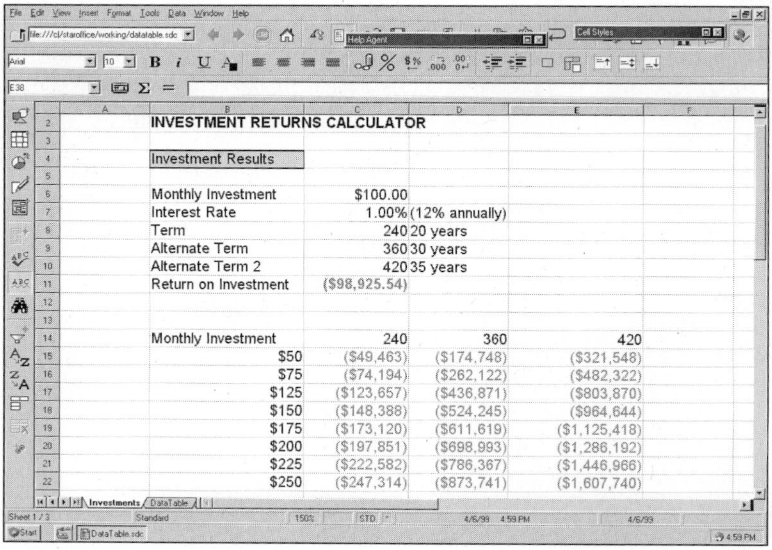

Figure 18.10
After you run the Pivot Table command, your results appear in the blank cells you selected next to your data column. You can test the results of varying the values in two values as well, in which case you get an array of answers returned, as shown here.

In order to add a second variable to your analysis and see what your investment returns would be over different time spans—say, 30 and 35 years, as well as 20—you need to construct a data matrix, like the one shown in Figure 18.10. Place your second set of variables (here, 240, 360, and 420) along the top of your data column. Then, select the entire matrix (here, cells B14 through E22) and select Pivot Table. This time, after entering the reference to your formula cell (which is still the same), you would click in the Row input cell line and click cell C8, and then click in the Column input cell input line and click cell C6. After you click OK, your table is completed in two dimensions, with results for all permutations of your two sets of variables.

The results of the Pivot Table command are not protected and can be deleted and modified like any other StarCalc data.

SOLVING SIMPLE PROBLEMS WITH GOAL SEEK

Goal Seek enables you to solve simple problems where you have a specific numeric target and want to determine the input required to achieve it.

Suppose, for example, you want to forecast your business's income for the coming year. You have a target net income you'd like to achieve, but you want to determine the level of sales you need to achieve to reach your target. That's a problem tailor-made for Goal Seek.

Figure 18.11 shows a worksheet for Andy's Candies, a candy-making business developing a 5-year forecast. Let's say that, based on existing figures for the past 3 1/2 of the business, you're going to determine a forecast for the year 2001. You know your financial target: a net income of $1,000,000 in 2001. Based on trends in chocolate prices, labor costs, and other known costs of doing business, you've projected costs to be $1,400,000. Now, you need to figure out the level of sales the business must achieve to meet that target.

Figure 18.11
In the Goal Seek dialog, you first enter the cell where your target value will be, and then enter the value you want to achieve. Finally, you indicate the variable cell whose input will be sought by Goal Seek.

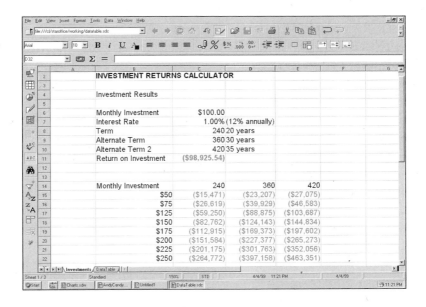

Your target cell should contain a formula, not a value, whereas your input or variable cell cannot contain a formula, but should be empty or contain a numeric value. In Figure 18.11, for example, the target cell is H11, which contains a simple formula, =H9-H10, that results in the Net Income figure. At the moment, the result in that cell is negative $1,4000,000 because you've input the project costs and the formula, doing its work, doggedly subtracts that figure from $0, the current value of H9.

If you select your target cell, when you select Tools, Goal Seek, the target cell's address already appears in the Formula cell input line because StarCalc automatically enters the reference of the current cell. Next, you input the target value. In this example, it's 1,000,000 because that's the net income target for the company. Finally, you enter the cell reference of the variable cell, which is the Total Cells cell, H9. Clicking the cell to add its reference is the easiest method.

Tip #358 from
Michael & Sarah

> If you have set StarCalc to use rounded numbers in calculations by selecting the Precision as Shown option, you should turn it off while running Goal Seek, as this may interfere with Goal Seek's ability to achieve the best possible answer.

Click OK, and StarCalc begins to calculate. Depending on the complexity of your problem, it might be a few seconds before anything happens. When StarCalc has calculated the answer, it informs you with a dialog that says "Goal Seek successful" and politely asks if you want the result (which it previews for you) inserted into the selected cell. Because the number previews for you in the dialog, you can jot it down, choose No, and run another round of Goal Seek with a different target goal.

There's a chance Goal Seek will not be successful. If that happens, you'll need to change either your target value or your formula. There might also be multiple solutions to your problem but Goal Seek finds only one possible answer.

CREATING SCENARIOS

Predicting the future is a daily part of our lives. We plan our lives today based on what we think will happen—or want to happen, or fear might happen—tomorrow. StarCalc can't predict the future, but with the Scenario Manager, it can help you build and manage alternative quantitative models of what might happen, given varying conditions.

Using the Scenario Manager (and putting in a bit more work), you can create a more sophisticated year 2001 projection for Andy's Candies than you did with Goal Seek.

To build scenarios, you first must have some type of data table, like the business projections table in the Andy's Candies example in Figure 18.11. Once again, the key to performing the analysis is to create formulas rather than just input values into cells. In this case, you want to test alternative projections of growth rates for both sales and costs. You therefore need to create a formula that uses the year 2000 figures as a baseline, multiplying those figures by growth rates for sales and costs. You then vary the growth rates in alternative scenarios so you can see what the various results would be.

Here are the steps:

1. Type in the row labels Sales in D19 and Costs in D20. These are reminders of the variables you're testing.

2. In cell E19, enter .30. That represents the 30 percent average growth rate for sales. You use this figure to create your first scenario, Current Trends.

3. In cell E20, enter .35. That represents the 35 percent average growth rate for costs, to complete the Current Trends scenario.

   Now that you have some inputs, you're ready to construct your formula.

4. In cell G9, enter the following formula: =$F$9*(1+$E$19) This projects sales for 2001 based on the projection for 2000, multiplied by the growth factor you've input in cell E19.

5. In cell G10, enter the following formula: =$F$10*(1+$E$20) This projects costs for 2001 based on the projection for 2000, multiplied by the growth factor you've input in cell E19.

   The Net Income figure is already a formula that relies on the inputs from the sales and costs items, as are the two ratios below, so you can leave those as they are. As the sales and costs projections change, so will they.

6. Select cells E19 and E20.

7. Choose Tools, Scenarios. The Scenario dialog box appears.

Note

The Scenarios command is not available unless you have selected two or more cells.

---

8. A default name is offered in the input line for the new scenario—something like New_Scenario_1. You can accept that name, but it's easier to remember what the scenario is testing if you give it a more specific name. If you want to assign your own name, type it in. In this example, call it Current Trends.

9. If you like, enter a comment in the Comment field. By default, information about the creation date, time, and author are inserted here, but you can add to that or delete that comment and type in your own. In the example in Figure 18.12, comments have been added to each scenario that briefly explain the assumptions behind the figures. This is very useful when you return to the scenarios for later review.

10. You can change the color of the border that will appear around your scenario input cells (see Figure 18.12). The default is a nice, conservative gray; to spice it up, you can click to open the drop-down list and select the color of your choice.

11. If you want your data to update immediately with your new values, select Update Scenario with Modified Sheet Values. If you don't select this option, you can update your data later by double-clicking the scenario name in Navigator.

12. If you select Copy Entire Sheet, your scenario (the inputs and the entire data table that it is connected to—in the example, cells A9:G13) are copied to another worksheet. This enables you to easily create a separate worksheet for each scenario, which is handy for creating printed reports or presentations. (Otherwise, you just switch between different scenarios on one worksheet.)

Tip #359 from
Michael & Sarah

> You can choose Copy Entire Sheet for Each Scenario. Then, cut and paste the columns with the differing results next to one another to create a composite table; you can then create a chart that makes it easy to see the different results in a glance. (This works well only for relatively simple scenarios; otherwise, your chart becomes too confusing to interpret.)

13. Click OK.

    You've created your first scenario, and an impressive-looking frame with a drop-down list (like the one in Figure 18.12) appears around the cells that contain your inputs. However, a single scenario isn't worth much and relying on it would suggest an overconfidence in your own, and StarCalc's,predictive abilities. To make the best use of this feature, you should create other scenarios.

Figure 18.12
This is the final result of creating four scenarios. Currently, TheUgly scenario is selected. Its growth assumptions–the variable inputs–are visible in cells E19 and E20. The figures in column G are the result of those inputs. You manage scenarios in Navigator; double-click a scenario name to apply it, and right-click to manage its properties and delete it.

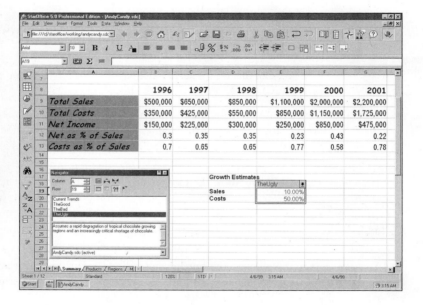

14. Select the two cells that contain your inputs. You can't do this if your text cursor is still active in one of the cells. If you're having trouble, try clicking a cell outside the scenarios input area and then selecting the input cells by clicking the first cell in the input column (or row) and dragging.

15. Choose Tools, Scenario again.

16. Type a name for the second scenario—use TheGood—enter any comments, select your options, and click OK.

    Your new name appears in the top of the scenario frame. Now, any changes you make to the values in those cells are saved to the new scenario.

17. Select cell E19, delete the existing value of .30, and enter a value of .40 for your TheGood scenario.

18. Select cell E20, delete .35, and enter .15.

You now have two scenarios. To create additional scenarios, repeat steps 14–18, substituting new growth figures and names.

Note

If you don't save your spreadsheet after creating your additional scenarios, they may not take effect when you click them in the Navigator. Save your spreadsheet and try again.

MANAGING AND APPLYING SCENARIOS

You can switch to a different scenario by opening the drop-down list and clicking the name of the scenario you want to test. Your data should update immediately. However, the main tool for applying and managing scenarios is the Navigator.

Note

If your column does not immediately update, you may have Automatic Recalculation turned off. Try pressing F9 (Recalculate) to update. Or, you can turn on Auto Calculate in the Tools, Cell Contents menu.

To reveal your list of scenarios, click the Scenarios button on the Navigator toolbar. A list appears of all the scenarios saved to your current worksheet, with a comments field below. Only the scenarios on your current worksheet appear.

EDITING SCENARIO COMMENTS

You cannot edit comments directly in the Navigator display. To change comments, select the scenario name, right-click, and choose Properties on its context menu. The Edit Scenario dialog appears, where you can edit your comments and change other properties as well.

EDITING SCENARIO INPUT VALUES

To change the input values for a specific scenario, first make its inputs visible on your worksheet by double-clicking its name in the Navigator. Then, edit the cell contents using normal StarCalc methods. As soon as you enter the new value in a cell, it is saved to your scenario.

You can also delete the values entirely, which leaves you with an empty scenario—the scenario name still exists in the Navigator, but no input values are associated with it. (It's like having a saved file with no data in it.)

DELETING SCENARIOS

A scenario is comprised of two parts: the input values (in this case, the two growth figures) and what you might call the scenario frame. You can modify and delete the input values when they are visible by using regular StarCalc editing tools (as described in the section "Editing Scenario Input Values"). If you delete the input values, you are left with an empty scenario frame, and the title of the frame indeed reads (empty). The only way to delete an entire scenario, or an empty scenario frame, is from the Navigator.

To delete a scenario, select its name, right-click, and choose Delete from its context menu.

CHARTING DATA

Charts are useful for both data analysis and data presentation. They can help you visualize correlations between different variables, compare different sets of measurements or figures, and present information so that it can be taken in at a glance.

You can chart data either by selecting data you've already entered in StarCalc (or another StarOffice table), or creating a chart with dummy data and then altering the data in a StarChart data window.

Unless you have specific reasons for creating a standalone chart (such as wanting to pass the file on to someone else or not wanting to worry about maintaining linked files), you will find it easiest to use data you've entered elsewhere. It's much easier to both create the chart and to view and update your source data.

WHAT IS A CHART?

A chart is a summary graphical representation of a quantitative data series. From StarOffice's point of view, a chart is a graphical representation of data stored in a StarOffice table—which is most likely to be a StarCalc spreadsheet, but could be a table in StarWriter or a table you create through a spreadsheet-like data entry window in StarChart. (The spreadsheet serves as the basic model for all tables created in StarOffice, so from StarOffice's point of view, all tables are spreadsheet objects. That's why you can so easily drag and drop data between StarCalc and StarWriter.)

Note You cannot create charts from a StarBase table. However, you can import data from a StarBase table into StarCalc via the Beamer, and then create a chart in StarCalc. For more information, see the section "Selectively Importing Data from the Explorer," in Chapter 17, "Creating Lists and Databases with StarCalc."

We've included discussion of StarChart in this chapter because most people are likely to make charts from within StarCalc, but you follow the same procedures and use the same tools to create a chart in all StarOffice applications.

INSERTING CHARTS IN OTHER DOCUMENTS

It might seem strange to discuss inserting charts in other documents before you've even created a chart. However, it's important that you understand possibilities for sharing charts across StarOffice documents before you invest in creating and formatting a chart in StarCalc.

A chart you create in StarCalc based on StarCalc data is an embedded object rather than a document on its own two feet. This means that you can't save it by itself, nor can you readily insert it into another StarOffice document, whether it be a spreadsheet, a text document, a presentation slide, or an HTML document.

If you intend to create a chart that you know you'll need to use in multiple documents or document types, you might want to create the chart as a standalone StarChart chart. You begin this process by choosing File, New, Chart, which gives you a prebuilt chart with dummy data that you can edit and format following the same procedures discussed throughout this section. When you've completed the chart, save it as a StarChart document. Then, open the document into which you want to insert the chart and choose Insert, Object, OLE object (*not* Insert, Chart). Select Create from File in the dialog that appears, and either enter the path and filename of your chart or browse to locate it on your drives and click to enter its name. Your chart is inserted as an OLE object that you can work with in the same ways described in this chapter.

Your alternative is to create your chart in the document from which you intend to present or print your chart, using the same Insert, Chart command or tool that you use in StarCalc. A chart you create in another document is bound by the same limitations as a StarCalc chart.

However, you can easily copy and paste data from StarCalc into StarWriter as a DDE linked object and then use that data as the basis for creating a chart in StarWriter. Just select and copy the data, and then use the Paste Special command, choosing DDE Object in the list of choices. This ensures that your chart data is still dynamically linked to the StarCalc source, which means you need to update your data only once if it changes. This is your best option if you're working with complex or extensive data that's too much trouble to create in a standalone form. You cannot create a DDE linked table in StarImpress, however, so if you want to chart data for a presentation, you need to use one of the other two methods described in this section.

→ For more information on bringing StarCalc data into StarWriter documents, **see** "Copying and Moving Cell Data," **p. 535**.

ARRANGING DATA FOR EASY CHARTING

Just as when you create a database area, sort your data, or create advanced filters, there are ways to arrange data on your worksheet to ensure that your chart turns out as it should. The key is to keep all your data together, including your column and/or row headers (if any).

Be sure not to have empty rows in data areas you're selecting for charting. You don't need to place empty rows between column headers and data—if you want to give them a gracious distance, use the Format Row Height command (on the row context menu or the Format menu) to create a custom-width row that gives you the look you want.

Don't worry about perfecting column and row headers in StarCalc before charting your data. When you create the chart, you'll have a choice of whether to include the existing column and row headers, and after your chart is created, you can modify them without affecting your source data.

CREATING CHARTS

A chart is created from some type of *data series*. If you're using existing data, you select the series you want to chart before you invoke the Insert Chart command. If you're entering data directly into StarChart, you can create a chart with dummy data and then replace it with your own data in the Chart Data data entry window.

Tip #360 from *Michael & Sarah*	If you have a complex or lengthy database, create a DataPilot table and then create a chart from that table to summarize your data.

As usual, there are a number of commands or tools you can select to begin your chart-creation process. However, whatever command you invoke, all paths lead to the chart AutoFormat wizard. This wizard steps you through a series of dialog boxes that enable you to define the type of chart you want and the elements you want to display.

UNDERSTANDING CHART TYPES

The most commonly used chart types in business are the bar, column, and line graphs, which are useful for seeing broad trends over time and making summary comparisons of different groups or variables. However, you can create a number of other chart types with StarChart as well.

 Figure 18.13 shows the Chart Type dialog box (which you open by clicking the Chart Type button on the StarChart Main toolbar), which identifies the seven basic chart types. Variants of each type display in the Variants section at the bottom of the dialog; Figure 18.13 shows the variants for the Columns chart type.

A line chart compares trends over even time intervals (or some other evenly spaced interval) plotted on the category axis. It's a good choice for representing data such as stock prices, sales revenues, or production output over time.

An area chart is similar to a line chart, but shows the continuous change over time in terms of volume. It sums the data from each individual series to create the top line of the data area.

A pie chart compares the size of different elements of a whole. A typical use of a pie chart is to represent a budget. Each piece of the pie represents one budget category, with the pie representing the entire budget. Pie charts can represent only a single data series and aren't useful for comparing data points or seeing trends or patterns.

Figure 18.13
In the Chart Type dialog, you can change the chart format or variant of an existing chart. You see these same choices in the second and third dialogs of the AutoFormat Chart Wizard.

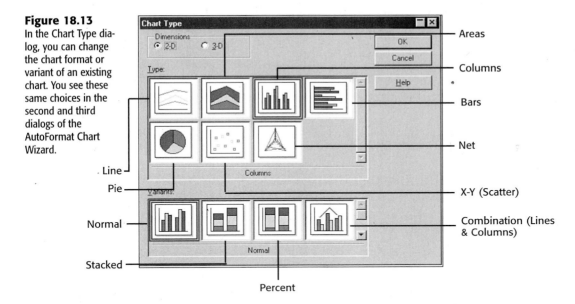

The X-Y, or scatter, chart is used to show data over uneven time intervals or from discrete X and Y measurements. It's useful in data analysis for spotting pattern clusters. For example, an X-Y chart would be a good choice if you wanted to see how age correlated with opinions about the importance of the Internet is in today's society. By plotting age along the X (category) axis and people's numerically coded responses along the Y (value) axis, you could get a quick visual take on whether there is any correlation between age and people's answers.

The net chart (also known as the radar chart) is plotted in a radically different way than the others, and because of that, can be difficult for those unfamiliar with them to interpret. With the net chart, each data series (that is, row or column of data) is plotted along its own axis, which pushes outward from the center, creating a visual effect like a spider's web or a net. The data points in the series appear along the line. The lines connect all the points in each data series.

UNDERSTANDING THE ELEMENTS OF A CHART

Figure 18.14 identifies the basic elements of a StarChart chart. Some of the elements are self-evident from the dummy labels StarChart attaches; we've attached our own labels to those that are not as apparent. A few elements are not visible but are listed in Table 18.2, which names each chart element and identifies the tool buttons and menu command(s) you can use to modify it.

PART
III

CH

18

Figure 18.14
You can choose the elements that display on your StarChart chart. Shown here is a typical bar chart with dummy data. Besides the elements you see here, you can also add percent data labels, basic statistical indicators and error bars, and additional gridlines.

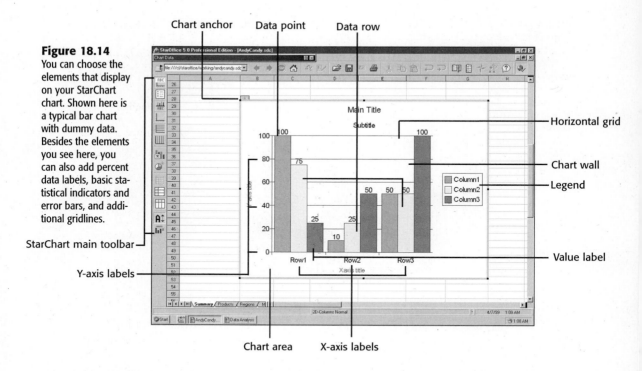

TABLE 18.2. STARCHART CHART ELEMENTS AND COMMANDS TO MODIFY THEM

Name of Element	Click to Turn	To Modify Data	To Format On/Off
Chart title		Insert, Title	Format, Title
Subtitle		Insert, Title	Format, Title
X-axis title		Insert, Title	Format, Title
Y-axis title		Insert, Title	Format, Title
Legend		Insert, Legend	Format, Legend
Vertical (Y-axis) grid		N/A	Format, Grid
Horizontal (X-axis) grid		N/A	Format, Grid
Data point		View, Data	Format, Object Properties or Format, Chart Type

Name of Element	Click to Turn	To Modify Data	To Format On/Off
Data series	⊞	View, Data	N/A
Chart area	N/A	N/A	Format, Area
Chart wall	N/A	N/A	Format, Wall
X-axis label	▢	View, Data	Double-click and format with usual text formatting tools.
Y-axis label	▢	View, Data	Double-click and format with usual textformatting tools.
Data labels	Insert, Data Labels	Insert, Data Labels	Format, Object Properties
Statistics and error indicators	Insert, Statistics	Insert, Statistics	Insert, Statistics

CREATING CHARTS WITH THE AUTOFORMAT CHART WIZARD

The AutoFormat Chart Wizard quickly takes you through the steps of creating a chart. After you've created your chart with AutoFormat, you can then modify any element of your chart that you're not satisfied with.

To create a chart from existing data, first select the entire data area, including any row and column headers.

You then have the following two choices of how to create your chart:

- You can click the Insert Object (Chart) tool on the StarCalc Main toolbar. Your cursor changes into an Insert Chart cursor like the one you see in the margin here. You can then click to draw a box that defines the area you want your chart to cover. Don't worry too much about getting the size just right —you can easily resize your chart later, after it's created. Once you've drawn the size you want and release the mouse button, the first dialog of the AutoFormat Chart wizard appears (see Figure 18.15).

Note

By default, the Insert Object (Chart) button is the visible button on the Insert Object floating toolbar. However, if you've used another tool on the toolbar, the Insert Object (Chart) tool might be hidden. To reveal it, extended-click the currently visible Insert Object tool to open the entire toolbar and then click the Insert Object (Chart) button.

- You can choose Insert, Chart, which inserts a chart of a preset size that you can then resize. The advantage of choosing this command is that you can insert your chart onto a different worksheet than your source data series.

Figure 18.15
If you've already selected a data series, its address appears in the first dialog of the AutoFormat Chart Wizard. If you just want to insert dummy data and then add your data through the View, Data data entry window, delete any address and choose Create or Next, or select a blank cell.

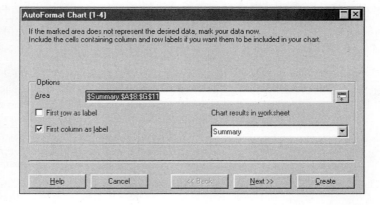

References for your selected data series appear in the Area input line of the Options area. If you want to insert different data, edit the cell references now. If you've gotten this far by choosing the Insert, Chart command, you can also choose to insert your chart onto a different worksheet than that of the data series by clicking the worksheet name from the drop-down list in the lower right of the Options area. (If you've drawn your chart area, StarCalc assumes you don't want to place it on a different sheet. You can always cut and paste the chart onto another sheet later

Sometimes, the chart AutoFormat lets you totally delete cell references identifying your data series and create a chart with dummy data; sometimes it forces you to select a cell before it proceeds. (It's a little quirky this way.) Do what you need to do, and don't worry—when the chart is created, you can add or alter your data without problem. If you don't want the chart linked to any existing data, just be sure you select a blank cell as your data area.

Tip #361 from
Michael & Sarah

Click the tab of a worksheet, and StarCalc identifies its main data area sheet and automatically enters its cell references in the Area input line.

By default, the first column is chosen as a label. If you have a row header, check First Row as Label. Otherwise, StarChart assumes that the row contains data.

Clicking Next moves you to the dialog you see in Figure 18.16, where you can select a chart type. If you want to see how your titles and labels will appear, check the Show Text Elements in Preview option. By default, your data series is assumed to be laid out in rows, but you can change it to columns. (You can change this later, with the StarChart Main toolbar, as well.)

Click Next when you've made your choices, and you can then select a variant format for your chart type and choose to have X- or Y-axis gridlines appear (see Figure 18.17). For bar charts, you have the option of choosing Overlap, which overlaps the bars rather than leaving space between them.

Figure 18.16
In the second dialog of the AutoFormat Chart Wizard, you select a chart type. If you want to create a 3D chart, complete the Autoformat Chart Wizard first, and then click the Chart Type button on the StarChart Main toolbar.

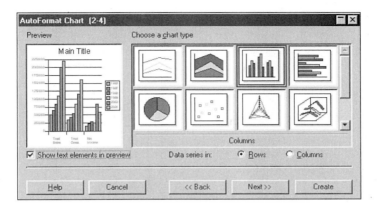

Figure 18.17
In the third dialog of AutoFormat Chart Wizard, you can choose a variant format of your chart type. The specific choices you see depend on the chart type you've chosen.

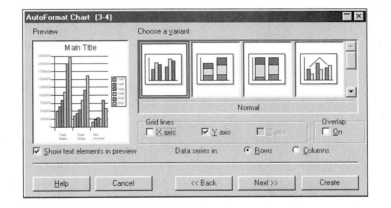

In the fourth and final AutoFormat Chart Wizard dialog (shown in Figure 18.18), you can enter a chart title and X- and Y-axis labels, as well as choose whether to display a legend.

Figure 18.18
After entering any titles in the fourth dialog of the AutoFormat Chart Wizard, choose Create, and your chart is inserted into your spreadsheet.

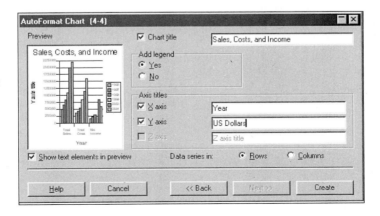

Click Create, and your chart is inserted into your spreadsheet as an OLE object.

Your completed chart should look something like the one shown in Figure 18.19. In this particular chart, the column and row headers have been used, and X- and Y-axis labels and a title have been inserted. The data points have not been labeled, but the horizontal grid is turned on.

Figure 18.19
After you've created a chart, you can modify it in virtually any way you like. Here, the chart is selected as a graphic, so the Graphics Object tool-bar displays up above and you can modify its position, size, and anchor point. If you double-click the chart, you can then modify its format and content via context menu com-mands, tools on the StarChart main tool-bar, and menu com-mands on the StarChart menus.

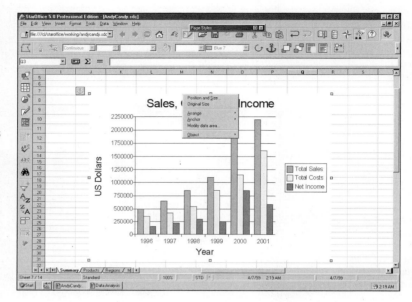

WORKING WITH STARCHART TOOLS

Although your chart is inserted into StarCalc, you use object and StarChart tools to work with it. As always in StarOffice, virtually all the commands you need are at your fingertips in context menu commands and toolbars after you have selected your chart. (You can also find most commands on menus.)

When your chart is inserted, it's already selected as a graphic object. The visible signs of this are the eight green square handles visible on each corner and border midpoint, the object anchor, and the appearance of the Object toolbar (Help identifies as the Draw Object toolbar) in place of your StarCalc object bar. You can see the graphic handles in Figure 18.19. When these handles are visible, your chart is in object mode, and you can reposition and resize it by dragging and dropping, but you can't format or edit the chart contents. If you right-click in this mode, the object context menu you see in Figure 18.19 appears.

When you click outside the chart area in a StarCalc cell, the handles and Object toolbar disappear. To reselect the chart as an object, click it.

When you double-click the chart, the StarChart Main toolbar appears, which enables you to turn off and on the display of each set of chart elements, change your chart type, and switch the reading of your data series from columns to rows and vice versa (look ahead Figure 18.20).

If you want to format an element within the chart, your first move should always be to select the object you want to modify and right-click to open its context menu. To insert or modify titles and labels, use Insert menu commands. To open the Data Entry window (if it doesn't open automatically, as it should), choose the View, Data command or click the View Data button on the Main toolbar.

MODIFYING CHARTS

You can modify a chart in two fundamental ways: You can change its position, size, and definition in the spreadsheet as a graphic object; and you can edit and format it as a chart, including adding, modifying, and deleting data.

MOVING, POSITIONING, AND RESIZING CHARTS

To change the size and/or position of a chart, you must first click to select it as an object so that the green object handles are visible around the chart's perimeter. (If these handles are already visible, you don't need to click it again.)

To move it, just click and drag anywhere on the main chart area. To resize it, grab and drag the object handles.

→ For more information on the object toolbar and working with objects in StarOffice, **see** "Working with Objects," **p. 176**.

see "Working with Objects," p. 176

Caution

Be careful. When you move or resize the entire chart, you can undo these actions with the Edit menu Undo command (Ctrl+Z). However, it's easy to accidentally move or resize individual chart elements (like the title or data series) when you intend to move the entire chart. If that happens, Ctrl+Z will not work. Instead, you need to click the Reorganize Chart button on the StarChart main toolbar. The Undo command works only for undoing changes to a chart's object properties, such as background color, line shape and color, and character formatting.

You can also resize and position your entire chart with precision by using the Position and Size command on the object context menu (shown in Figure 18.19). To open this menu, be sure the chart is in Object mode, position your cursor on the border of the chart, right-click to open the Object context menu, and choose Position and Size.

The Position and Size dialog offers some other options, including the Protect option, which prevents the position or size from being further modified. If you have converted your chart to a 3D type, this dialog also enables you to set with precision the rotation and the slant and corner radius of your data series.

If you're unhappy with any resizing changes you've made in an editing session, choose the Original Size command from the Object context menu to reset the size. (Note that it won't restore your chart to its size at initial creation—just its size when you opened the dialog and began making changes.)

MODIFYING, ADDING, AND DELETING DATA

If you've created a chart by selecting existing data, you can add or delete data to your chart in three ways:

- Change the area of your worksheet that is charted by entering new cell references in the Define Data Area dialog box.

- Change your source data in StarCalc, which instantly changes the data points in your chart.

- Edit the chart data directly, without affecting your source data, in the Chart Data window.

If you've created a chart with dummy data, the Chart Data window is where you insert and edit your data.

Normally, double-clicking to select your chart automatically opens the Chart Data dialog box. If this doesn't work, click the Chart Data button on the Main toolbar or select Insert, Chart Data. The Chart Data tools are identified in Figures 18.20a and b, as are the StarChart Main toolbar tools.

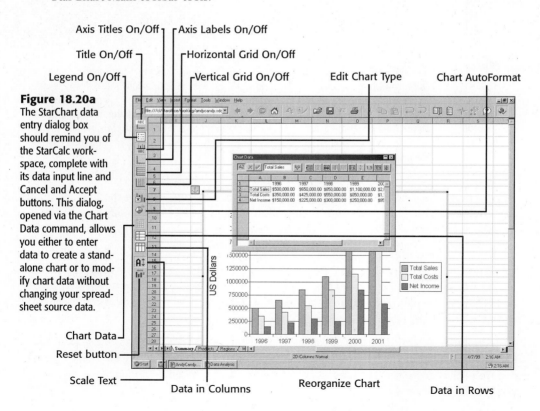

Figure 18.20a
The StarChart data entry dialog box should remind you of the StarCalc workspace, complete with its data input line and Cancel and Accept buttons. This dialog, opened via the Chart Data command, allows you either to enter data to create a stand-alone chart or to modify chart data without changing your spreadsheet source data.

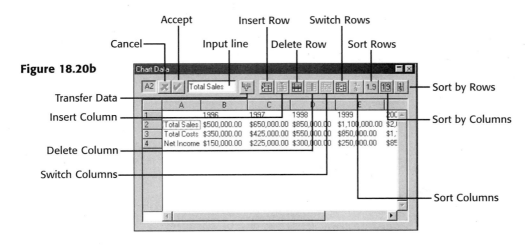

Figure 18.20b

Although this window looks just like a StarCalc worksheet, it behaves a little differently.

> **Caution**
>
> Actions you take within the Chart Data window cannot be undone with the Edit menu Undo command (Ctrl+Z), so be careful! If you're inserting data directly into a chart, be sure you have the original data written or saved somewhere else in case you accidentally delete any from StarChart.

PART
III
CH
18

Tip #362 from
Michael & Sarah

If you can't see your data clearly, you can change row heights and column widths in the usual way, by dragging their borders. These changes don't affect anything in your chart or spreadsheet.

DELETING AND INSERTING ROWS AND COLUMNS When you click a row or column header, you don't see the entire row or column highlighted. However, it is in fact selected, and you can delete the entire row or column by clicking the Delete Row or Delete Column button.

To insert rows or columns, click their respective buttons on the toolbar. A new row is inserted above the currently active row, and a new column is inserted to the left of the currently active column.

CHANGING HEADERS AND DATA POINTS To change any item of data in your chart, including row and column labels, click that item. A dotted rectangular box appears, to indicate that the item is selected, and the item also appears in the input line on the Chart Data toolbar. You can edit the item in the input line the same way you edit cell contents in the StarCalc Formula bar.

Note

> Although changes you make to external data sources affect the data in this window, changes that you make in this window do not affect your source data.

After you've made changes, click the Transfer Data button to update your chart.

SWITCHING ROWS OR COLUMNS   To switch the position of two rows, place your cursor in the row you want to move down and then click the Switch Rows button. Only if your cursor is in the last row of the series will the row move up. To switch two columns, place your cursor in the column you want to move to the right and then click the Switch Columns button. If your cursor is in the last column to the right, it will be switched with the column on the left.

ADDING AND DELETING TITLES AND LABELS

To change the text of the title, subtitle, or X-, Y-, and Z-axis labels, select Insert, Titles. The Titles dialog opens. If you want to insert a new element, select it first, and then type in the title. To change an existing title, place your cursor in the input line and edit as usual. To delete or turn off an element, deselect it. Keep in mind that you can also turn the display of titles on and off with Main toolbar tools; you don't need to delete a title to make it disappear from view.

EDITING LEGEND LABELS

To edit the names assigned to data rows or columns, open the Chart Data window by clicking the Chart Data button or choosing View, Chart Data. Then, select the row or column header being used in the legend that you want to change, and edit it in the input line. When you've completed your changes, click the Transfer Data button to update the chart.

ADDING AND DELETING AXES AND GRIDS

To change the display of axes or grids, use the Insert, Axes and Gridlines command. You can control the display of major and minor gridlines in all dimensions as well as the display of axis labels.

INSERTING DATA LABELS

Data labels, which are associated with specific data points on a chart, can help your audience read your chart data more easily.

You have four options when inserting data labels. These options are described in Table 18.3. Although you can insert them in any chart type you like, some of the options are suitable for only specific types.

TABLE 18.3 DATA LABEL OPTIONS IN STARCHART

Type of Label	Meaning	Used For
Value	The numeric value attached to the data point	All chart types
Percent	The proportion of that data point in relation to the total chart. The total pie is 100%.	Pie charts, net charts
Labels	Repeats the appropriate row or column label above the data point.	All chart types
Labels and percent	Shows both the proportion of the data point and its row or column label.	Pie charts, net charts

If you want to insert labels globally for all data points, use the Insert, Data Labels command. Options you select here affect all data points.

If you want to apply labels selectively, select the individual data group, or individual data point, and right-click to open the context menu. To select a data row, click once in the Chart Wall area (which selects the Chart Wall area). Then, click one of the data points in that data group. You can tell your selection is successful if small square boxes appear on each item of the data group. To select an individual data point in that group, click once more; object handles appear around that data point. (You cannot resize or move it, however.) Choose the Object Properties command and click the Data Labels tab. You have the same options as with the Insert command, but your choices apply only to your currently selected data point(s).

PART

III

CH

18

HIDING CHART ELEMENTS

You can instantly hide (or reveal) chart elements by using tools on the Main toolbar. Table 18.4 shows the tools and their names.

TABLE 18.4 TOOLS TO HIDE AND REVEAL CHART ELEMENTS

Click This Button	To Turn This Element On and Off
[button]	Title
[button]	Legend
[button]	Axis Titles
[button]	Axis Labels
[button]	Horizontal Grid
[button]	Vertical Grid

You can also turn most labels and titles off and on through their formatting dialogs.

FORMATTING CHARTS

Besides turning on and off the display of chart elements and editing their contents, you can also change the appearance of elements in your chart in a number of ways. Here's what you can do:

- Determine the line type of borders around the legend, chart wall, chart area, and text boxes (titles and labels).
- Insert hatching, colors, gradients, or your own bitmap file as background for the legend, chart wall, chart area, and text boxes.
- Change the color of data points and data rows (or columns).
- Change the orientation of X- and Y-axis labels and titles.
- Insert basic statistical measures and error bars.
- Change the position of any elements on your chart.
- Rotate the data series on a 3D chart.
- Change the chart type entirely.

The dialog boxes and techniques that you use to format a chart are similar to those you use to format a StarCalc worksheet, or almost anything else you might format in StarOffice, so we focus here on those elements unique to StarChart.

→ For information on rotating text, **see** "Rotating Text and Numbers," **p. 569**.

→ For more information on formatting backgrounds and borders, **see** "Applying Backgrounds and Borders," **p. 567**.

CHART FORMATTING BASICS   As always, you should begin by selecting the element you want to format by clicking it and right-clicking to open its context menu. Figure 18.21 shows a composite picture of a line chart (showing the same data as the bar chart shown in Figure 18.19) with its two basic context menus. (Note that you can have only one context menu open at a time.)

With most elements, you can take the shortcut of double-clicking, which simultaneously selects the object and opens its formatting dialog box. The one exception is a data group, which you must select by clicking one of the data points in the group. (You can tell you've selected the group successfully if a small box appears on each elementas shown in Figure 18.22). Once your data group is selected, you can then right-click to open the data group's context menu and select Object Properties to open the Data Row (or Data Column) formatting dialog.

If you've chosen to insert data labels on your data row or column, you can change their font characteristics on the Characters tab.

Figure 18.21
Commands for formatting border line types, area backgrounds, text characters, axis alignments, and chart type can all be found on the StarChart context menu. You can also change your chart type by using the Chart Type command, or redo many aspects of your chart by using the AutoFormat command.

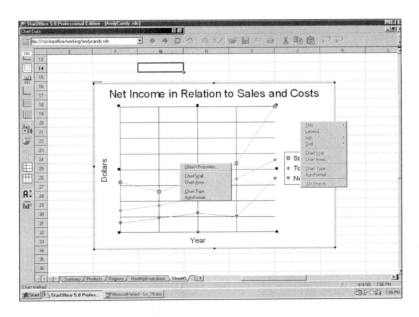

Figure 18.22
With the Data Row (or Data Column) formatting dialog, you can add error indicators, data labels, and borders, as well as change the color of line, bar, or pie pieces.

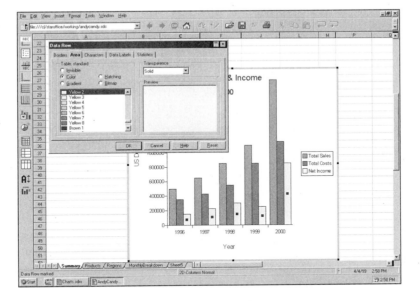

FORMATTING A CHART'S WALLS AND AREAS   You have a wide range of choices when formatting the background appearance of your chart. First, you can choose to apply a background to your entire chart area, or you can apply it to the chart wall (the area in which your data series is actually represented) only. (Actually, you can apply a background to both as well, but they overlap in the Chart Wall portion of the chart.) Choose the Chart Area or Chart Wall command, accordingly.

After you choose a command, you see the same dialog for both (see Figure 18.23). The Borders tab enables you to select whether a line borders your area or wall and choose the appearance of that line. The Area tab enables you to choose a background color or pattern to apply. The default choice is Invisible. For the Color, Gradient, and Hatching options, click to activate the scroll list, scroll to preview the backgrounds, and click OK after you've seen the background of your dreams.

For the Bitmap option, the procedure is slightly different, as is the dialog (shown in Figure 18.24).

Figure 18.23
You can change the visual impact of your data by applying a wide range of backgrounds to either the chart wall or the entire chart area.

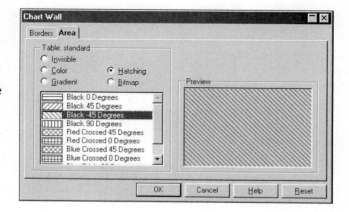

Figure 18.24
If you insert a bitmap graphic as a background, you can select how it is scaled and positioned relative to your chart background.

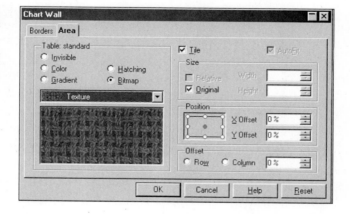

First, click the down arrow to open the drop-down list of bitmap selections. (A bitmap is also known as a *pixel graphic* or *image file*.) Only then do you see the choices. Then, scroll down the list and select the bitmap you want to use. After you select a bitmap, the commands on the right side of the dialog box become active, and you can adjust the size and positioning of the bitmap relative to the chart wall or area. You probably want to leave the Tile option checked. That option repeats the bitmap in tiled format to cover the area.

If you choose the AutoFit option, a single copy of the bitmap will be stretched to fit the selected area, and the quality is likely to be poor.

→ For more information on the nature of pixel graphics, **see** "Understanding Computer Graphics," **p. 773.**

INSERTING STATISTICAL MEASURES AND ERROR BARS   With the Insert, Statistics command, you can insert a number of statistical measures in a chart to help illustrate the validity of your data and show the mean values for each data category.

If you choose Mean Values, lines are drawn across the X-axis, representing the mean value of each data category. For example, the mean value lines for the chart in Figure 18.22 would show the mean values for sales, costs, and income over the five-year period charted.

That's not a terribly useful indicator in this instance, which points to the danger of this command—it's very easy to insert values that aren't appropriate to your data. This is particularly important with regard to the error indicators you can also add from this dialog, which are appropriate to use only if you've collected and analyzed your data using proper statistical methods.

If you select the variance and standard deviation options, StarCalc calculates those figures and changes the display according to your selections. In the case of standard deviation, StarCalc automatically adjusts the Y-axis values so that the entire range of the sample can be displayed. If you select the Percentage, Error Margin, and Constant Value options, you can input the value you want to be used.

After you select an error option, you can choose to have error indicators display to show the range of variation for each data point. Click the up and down arrows in the Error indicator box to switch between the two display options, and click the display option you want.

MAKING 2D CHARTS 3D   To convert a 2D chart into a 3D chart, select the chart and click the Type button on the StarChart Main toolbar. In the dialog that appears, click 3D in the Dimensions area. You then see samples of the five 3D chart types. Click the type you're interested in, and you see all its variants in the Variants area at the bottom of the dialog. Make selections and click OK, and your chart bursts out in three dimensions.

3D charts don't necessarily help with data analysis, but as Figure 18.25 shows, they sure pack a visual wallop. Because you can shade and apply other effects to 3D objects that go far beyond what you can apply to 2D objects, you can make your 3D chart look much more eye-grabbing and sophisticated, suitable for slide presentations, brochures and other desktop publishing, and printed matter such as annual reports where making a good impression counts more than data analysis.

PART

III

CH

18

Formatting a 3D chart is the same as formatting a 2D chart. However, you can also change its appearance by rotating the position of the data series in space. To activate the rotation cursor, extended-click somewhere on the data series. You see a pivot point appear as well. To rotate, just click and drag. If you don't like the position in which your data ends up, click the Reorganize Chart button (which doesn't reorganize your chart but resets its position)

Figure 18.25
You can show your data in all its depth by transforming it into a 3D chart.

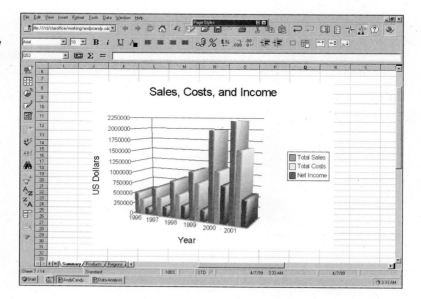

APPLYING 3D EFFECTS   If you select a 3D chart type, you can change the visual properties of the data points in the 3D Effects dialog (via the Format menu or the main chart context menu). Properties that you can change include surface appearance, shadowing, shading, illumination, textures, and material.

PRINTING CHARTS

Printing a chart from within StarCalc is no different from printing data or any other object: You first select the cells that define the chart's area and mark them as a print range. You can then preview the chart by using the Page View command. The page formatting commands, of course, do not apply to charts, as they exist on top of a StarCalc page, not on their own. If you want to make changes to a chart, you need to exit Page View mode and use StarChart tools.

TROUBLESHOOTING

I tried consolidating data from a number of worksheets, but a lot of categories were left out of the final results.

Only categories shared among your worksheets are included in the consolidated table. If you need to, create categories with empty values.

I tried to rearrange the categories in my DataPilot table, but I just ended up with a mess!

Sometimes it's confusing to rearrange headings directly on a worksheet. Use the Start command on the DataPilot table context menu instead—that opens a dialog much like the one where you created your table. It's easier to see where to drag and drop category buttons.

I need to update the data in my Data Pilot table but I can't find the update command.

Place your cursor in a cell in the DataPilot table. Right-click and choose Update. Alternatively, you can choose Data, DataPilot, Refresh. The commands do the same thing.

I want to add a subtitle to my chart, but I can't find the right command.

Choose the Insert, Titles command.

I want to change the legend text, but when I double-click, all I get is formatting commands.

You need to change the row labels or column headers to change the legend text. Open the Chart Data window by double-clicking your chart or choosing View, Chart Data, and edit your labels or headers there. Be sure to click the Transfer Data button. Your legend should update immediately.

I made some changes to my chart and saved and closed my file. When I reopened it, all my changes were gone.

You probably have a chart created from data elsewhere on your spreadsheet. When you close or open a file, StarCalc prompts you to update links. If you choose Yes, your chart data is refreshed from the source data and any changes you've made directly to the chart data are lost (although your formatting changes should be saved). If you want to edit chart data, create a standalone chart by using the File, New, Chart command.

CHAPTER **19**

PREPARING AND PRINTING REPORTS

In this chapter

OVERVIEW OF THE PREPARATION AND PRINTING PROCESS

When your data is in shape and you're ready to create a report, you need to shift your thinking from data entry and analysis to presentation of results.

In their work clothes, spreadsheets can be a dull and dense thicket of numbers or data. Using charts, already discussed in detail in Chapter 18, "Analyzing and Charting Data," is one way to transform your data into pictures that speak. Sometimes charts aren't appropriate to your data, or sometimes you want to create graphically appealing invoices, order forms, or bills that you can still use to enter and track numerical data. On these occasions, inserting drawings and images, such as company logos, clip art graphics, or photographs, can help create a more powerful report. If you're using StarOffice on Windows, you can also insert text boxes and create fancy text effects by using FontWork.

After you insert any charts or objects, your next step is to format your pages for printing or publishing on the Web or intranet. It's a good idea to save your commonly used page layouts as page styles so that you can quickly apply them again and create templates for new spreadsheets.

Then it's time to proof your work. With spreadsheets, proofing means more than just checking spelling because numbers can be incorrect and still spelled perfectly. StarCalc's Search and Replace feature enables you to quickly and easily fix nonlinguistic errors you find as well as tour your formulas for a final look. The Detective helps you snoop out errors in your formulas. You also might need to use the Recalculate command on the Tools menu to ensure that all your formula results are based on the most current data (if your spreadsheet isn't set to AutoCalculate) or use the Update command to update linked data.

Before you begin the printing process, you should set up your printer according to your operating system requirements.

Note

LINUX

StarOffice has a printer setup utility to assist in configuring your printer for StarOffice. Just click the icon on the StarOffice desktop, and follow the dialogs. However, StarOffice includes print drivers only for PostScript printers because it is the Linux (and UNIX) standard. If you have a non-PostScript printer, you need to use a utility such as GhostScript to translate the StarOffice PostScript output into PCL or whatever printer language is used by your printer. See your online manual resources or other Linux documentation for assistance.

Printed output is always composed for a specific printer, so if you compose your page before you have selected the correct printer for output, you might find that your headers and footers are not properly placed, part of your print range is cut off, or your fonts don't come out looking right.

Printing a spreadsheet usually consists of the following steps:

1. Select the area you want to print (your print range).

2. Check your headers and footers in the Format, Page dialog box.

3. On the Page tab of the same dialog, check your paper orientation, margins, paper source, page layout, page number style, and paper size.

4. On the Sheet tab of the same dialog, select your page order and print scale, and select the objects within the print range you want to print.

5. Preview your page breaks by choosing View, Page Break Preview. Adjust your page breaks as necessary by inserting manual breaks with the Insert menu's Manual Break command.

6. Preview your layout by choosing File, Page View. Make any final adjustments to the page layout through the Page View context menu.

Tip #363 from *Michael & Sarah*	While you won't find a Page Preview button on your StarCalc main or object toolbars, you can easily add one. With a StarCalc document active on your desktop, choose the View menu Toolbars, Customize command. Select View in the Functions Category list; then scroll through the display of buttons in the top part of the dialog box until you see a button with the words Page Preview on it. Click this button and drag it onto the toolbar where you would like it to be.

INSERTING DRAWINGS AND IMAGES

Sight is our dominant sense, which is why most people find it easier to make sense of information presented graphically than abstractly in text or numbers. StarOffice has excellent drawing tools that seamlessly blend with StarCalc so that you can create or insert and place pictures and images that dress up your final presentations.

StarOffice also comes with a large number of ready-to-use graphics and drawings in the multimedia Gallery (see Figure 19.1). You open the Gallery in the Explorer and preview its offerings in the Beamer. If you like what you see, you can just drag and drop the graphic into your open document (unless you want to attach it as a background, in which case you must go through the Page Style dialog box).

→ For more information on achieving top results when printing graphics, **see** "Printing Graphics," **p. 776** and "Printing Your Images," **p. 810**.

Figure 19.1
Create organizational charts by dragging and dropping prepared graphics from the Beamer into your document and drawing lines with the Line tool to connect the parts.

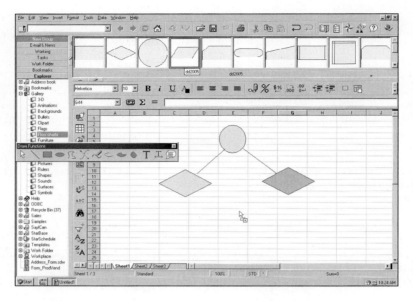

You can add your own graphics file galleries to the Gallery. You don't need to do so, however; you can import any graphics file as long as StarOffice has the right graphics filter to open and place it.

INSERTING GRAPHICS VIA THE INSERT MENU

 When working with computer graphics, you have two types of graphics files to choose from: vector graphics or bitmap graphics. Vector graphics provide high-quality, resolution-independent output suitable for professional printing. Bitmap graphics provide resolution-dependent images suitable for use online, publishing on the Web, or for editing and outputting photographs. If you're not sure which type of graphic is the best for your job, you might want to read the section "Understanding How Computer Graphics Work" in Chapter 20, "Getting Sketchy with StarDraw" before proceeding.

Regardless of the type of graphic you're using, you insert and manipulate them in the same way in your StarCalc document.

To insert an existing graphics file in StarCalc, Browse in your directories to locate the file you want to insert and choose OK. You can insert any bitmap or vector graphics files in this way (as long as you have the proper filter installed).

Tip #364 from
Michael & Sarah

Just right-click the Gallery icon in the Explorer, and choose Import to import other clip art galleries.

To create a new bitmap graphic from scratch, choose Insert, Picture, From Image Editor. You are prompted to define the color set and image size you want to create, and you are given an image workspace on which to work.

You cannot cancel the Insert, Picture From Image Editor command after you've invoked it; you just have to insert the image palette into your spreadsheet and then delete it. If you're having trouble selecting it to delete, click in the spreadsheet proper somewhere, and then click the image again. Its green sizing handles should appear, which means you can delete it by pressing the Del key.

→ For more information on working with graphic objects in documents, **see** "Rehearsing Objects," **p. 421**, and "Working with Graphic Objects," **p. 440**. Although this chapter focuses on StarWriter, the techniques for working with inserted graphic objects are the same across StarOffice modules.

THE EFFECTS OF INSERTING GRAPHICS ON THE STARCALC WORKSPACE

Inserting graphics is different from attaching them as a background through the Page Format command. When you insert a graphic with the Insert command, the graphic is inserted as a graphic object anchored to a specific point in your document. When you click the graphic, a new set of tools appropriate for working with inserted objects appears on your desktop.

WORKING WITH GRAPHICS IN STARCALC

When you insert a graphic, your Object toolbar automatically changes to reflect your new task. Your old StarCalc object bar doesn't disappear, however. You see a leftward-pointing arrow at the right end of your toolbar. Click it, and your StarCalc object bar returns to view.

To select graphic objects, you use the white pointer—the Selection tool—that is on the Draw Functions toolbar floating toolbar. You can open the Draw Functions toolbar from the main toolbar by extended-clicking its icon; grab the title bar and drag it onto your desktop to keep it open. With this tool, you can also draw a selection box around multiple graphic objects to group and move them all at once.

To reposition your graphic, click and drag it. You might see a four-headed arrow that indicates you are in moving mode, or your cursor may remain in Selection mode. Pressing Ctrl while dragging makes a copy of the graphic. (Pressing Shift+Ctrl+ dragging constrains the direction in which you copy your graphic.)

To resize a graphic, move your pointer over one of the eight square handles at the corners and edges until the pointer becomes a bi-directional arrow, and then click and drag. Pressing Shift while you're resizing constrains your resizing so that the graphic retains its original scale.

Tools on the graphics object bars enable you to rotate many of your graphics as well as position them in relation to other elements on your spreadsheet (such as sending your graphic to the back so that your data appears on top and is not covered up).

As long as you are working with the graphic, most of your StarCalc tools are unavailable. To return to the StarCalc workspace completely, just click somewhere in the worksheet outside the boundaries of the graphic.

DELETING GRAPHICS

Although a graphic is anchored to a particular cell, it really lies on top and is not part of the cell's contents.

To delete a graphic, select it so that its green handles are visible, and either press Del or choose Cut from the Edit menu (Ctrl+X). Using the Cut command, of course, retains the graphic on your clipboard or in your buffer so you can paste it elsewhere, if you like.

CREATING DRAWINGS AND TEXT WITH THE DRAWING TOOLBAR

Another way to dress up your final report is to draw your own basic shapes, text boxes, call-outs, and animated text (for use on Web pages or other online document) with the Drawing tool palette on the Main toolbar (see Figure 19.2).

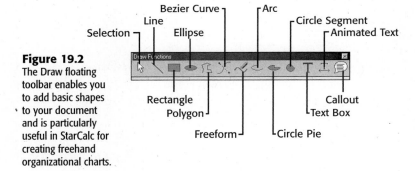

Figure 19.2
The Draw floating toolbar enables you to add basic shapes to your document and is particularly useful in StarCalc for creating freehand organizational charts.

To open the Draw palette, extended-click it. You can then tear the palette off the Main toolbar and move it anywhere on your workspace.

To use a tool, click its icon on the tool palette. Your pointer changes to indicate its new function, and it will continue to serve as that tool until you choose another one or click the same tool icon again to turn it off. When nothing is pressed, the Selection tool is turned on.

Note

If you create a text box, animated text, or a callout, FontWork becomes available on the Format menu. You can then open it to a floating toolbar on your desktop. With FontWork, you can create arcs of text and apply shadow effects and other special effects.

Tip #365 from
Michael & Sarah

Turn Extended Tips off and leave Tips on while you're working with FontWork so that you can see the names of the tools to guide your work. If Extended Tips and Tips are both on, Extended Tips suppresses Tips.

You can see some examples of what you can do in Figure 19.3.

Figure 19.3
With drawing tools, you can draw basic shapes to serve as backgrounds for clip art graphics and create callouts to label your work.

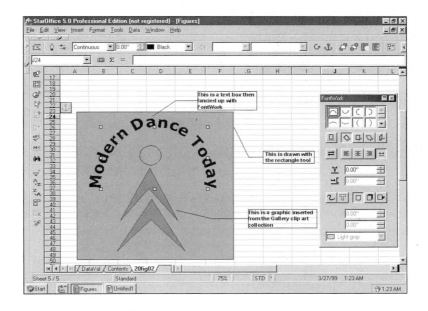

Callouts are an alternative to notes for annotating worksheets or spreadsheet forms that will be used as models; for example, if you're creating a Web site for customers, you can create a sample form and show the customers how to fill it out properly. A callout stays attached to the point where you insert it even as you move the callout around to reposition it. You can format callout text while you cannot format notes.

→ For more information on drawing tools, **see** "Using the Basic Drawing Tools," **p. 752**.

→ For more information on working with text as a graphic object, **see** "Using Text in StarDraw," **p. 773**.

FORMATTING PAGES

In StarCalc, as in StarWriter, you'll find a clear hierarchical logic to formatting, with formatting options moving from the smallest units (in StarCalc, cells) through intermediate units (rows and columns) to the largest units (pages). You might think the worksheet should be the largest unit, but because you never print an entire worksheet, what's more relevant is how you format the page that will come out of your printer.

→ To learn more details about formatting cells, rows, and columns, **see** Chapter 15, "Formatting Spreadsheets," **p. 553**. All the general formatting issues raised in that chapter are relevant when you're formatting pages. If you haven't already, you might want to read the initial section, "Formatting for Different Types of Presentation," **p. 554**.

Just as StarCalc has a default Standard cell style, it also has a default Standard page style, which sets the basic characteristics of a printed page. You can modify this style, and you can also create and save your own styles so that you can then apply them through the Stylist and use them as a basis for creating new templates. However, you cannot delete the Standard style.

FORMATTING PAGES WITH AUTOFORMAT

If you're in a hurry but still want your work to look good, a quick way to format a sheet or cell range is to use the Format, AutoFormat command. StarCalc's included formats aren't exactly burning with style, but they're decent, basic formats that give you a good head start. You can, of course, change your layout in any way you like after applying an AutoFormat.

To apply an AutoFormat, select the sheet or area you want to format and choose the command. You then see a long Format list on the left and a Preview window on the right. Scroll down the list to check out the previews until you see a format you like, and choose OK to apply it.

Unless you've deselected some of the options (as discussed in the next section on selectively applying AutoFormat styles), any existing formatting is changed to reflect the AutoFormat styles.

If you're not happy with the result, immediately press Ctrl+Z (Undo) to undo the formatting.

SELECTIVELY APPLYING AUTOFORMAT STYLES

A nice feature of AutoFormat is that you can selectively apply a particular AutoFormat style. If you choose the More button, you see an options list that contains the six elements that make up an AutoFormat style: number format, border appearance, font (type, size, and style), pattern (which means the patterned application of different background colors to make data stand out), orientation, and automatic height and row adjustment. Click an option to turn it off, and the preview of your selected format changes to show you the new look. When you're satisfied, choose OK and you're done.

Tip #366 from
Michael & Sarah

If you've already applied an appropriate number format to your cells, be sure to deselect the number format option so that yours are not overwritten.

CREATING YOUR OWN AUTOFORMAT STYLES

You can overcome StarOffice's style limitations by creating your own AutoFormat entries. Format at least a 4x4 cell range, select that range, select AutoFormat, and choose the Insert button. An Add AutoFormat dialog opens, prompting you to enter a name for your new format. Enter your name, click OK, and your style joins the AutoFormat family.

SETTING PAGE MARGINS AND OTHER PAGE LAYOUT CHARACTERISTICS

StarCalc doesn't have a page setup command, but it does have a broader page style command that offers a wide range of options for formatting and printing your page. You set page margins and a number of other page layout features on the Page tab of this dialog. You can also set your spreadsheet to fit on a single page here.

To open the Page Style dialog box, select Page from the Format menu. Click the Page tab to bring it to the front, as in Figure 19.4.

Figure 19.4
A shortcut for opening the Page Style dialog box is double-clicking the Page Style field on the StarCalc status bar.

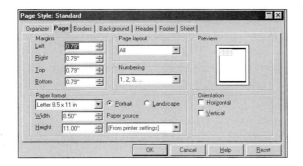

The default margins are .79 inch all the way around. You can enter new measurements directly or click the up and down arrows on the spin boxes to change the measurements in increments.

Below the Margins section is the Paper Format section, where you can select your paper size and type, orientation (landscape or portrait), and paper source. Because of StarOffice's European heritage, you have an unusually large built-in selection of paper types and sizes.

DEFINING A CUSTOM PAGE SIZE

You can also define your own page size by typing the page measurements directly in the Width and Height spin boxes on the Page tab. (Just be sure your printer can handle your paper size!) As you type in your new measurements, the page size in the preview field dynamically resizes to give you an approximate view of how your currently selected print range will fit.

This user setting is not saved in the dialog box, although it is saved along with the page. If you frequently use a custom page size for printing, you should create a page style with the correct page measurement.

CENTERING YOUR DATA ON THE PAGE

By default, your selected range is printed in the upper-left corner of the paper; it might look pretty scrunched up, depending on how much you're printing. The Orientation options on the Page tab enable you to position your data so that it's either horizontally centered, vertically centered, or both. If you're no good at directions, just watch the preview field.

CHOOSING THE NUMBERING STYLE

By default, StarCalc is set to print Arabic-style numerals as page numbers. You can change the numbering style to use Roman numerals or alphabetic characters, or you can turn numbering off altogether.

Be aware that the Page tab is like the central command post for determining page characteristics, so setting numbering to None here prevents you from adding page numbering anywhere else. For example, you cannot add page number fields to your headers or footers.

SETTING YOUR PAGES TO PRINT AS FACING PAGES

In StarCalc, you can print your sheets as facing pages, which is the way that books or pamphlets are printed. This feature is particularly nice in a spreadsheet program because spreadsheet tables are often far too long to fit comfortably on a standard US 8.5″ by 11″ page. Although you can always print in landscape orientation (sideways) to fit a wider table, being able to print on facing pages gives you another option.

Unfortunately, you can't do the sensible thing by adjusting the orientation of each page individually. Your choices, therefore, are to have the data on each page centered or have it left-aligned. (Ideally, you should be able to right-align it on the left page and left-align it on the right page.)

Tip #367 from
Michael & Sarah

If you want to create a pamphlet, be sure to leave enough room on the inner margins (called the *gutter*) to staple or bind your document. If you want to tape your two pages together, make these inner margins as small as possible.

Your choices are All (the default, which prints each page as an individual), Mirror, Left, and Right.

If you choose any of these options, immediately check your Header and Footer settings on those tabs. By default, they both have the option Same Content Left/Right selected; you should deselect this option so that your headers and footers mirror as well.

APPLYING PAGE BACKGROUNDS AND BORDERS

Just as you can apply background colors and borders to cells, you can apply them to an entire page as well. They apply to any page that shares the same page style as the one you modify.

INSERTING PAGE BORDERS

To insert borders, go to the Borders tab of the Format, Page dialog. There, you can change the line style and color of the border, choose to apply a shadow effect, and determine the distance of your border from your text.

You can choose from five preset border styles in the Presets area; just click one to apply it. If you want to create a different pattern, click the line style you want in the Line Style box, and then click the areas on your page where you want the border to appear.

The borders are drawn around your selected print range or the actual amount of data you have in a printable area (based on your current page size settings) rather than just bordering the edge of the page. They are offset by the distance you've entered in the Distance From Text spin box on the Borders tab.

After you apply borders, you see thin lines on your worksheet that show where your page breaks will occur just as if you had set a print range. However, you don't actually see your borders until you enter Page view (through the Edit menu).

INSERTING GRAPHICS AND FILLS AS PAGE BACKGROUNDS

By inserting graphics, you can give visual presence to reports or other types of documents prepared from spreadsheets. Using uniform background colors is less useful for printed reports but can improve visibility of data on Web pages (that is, worksheets saved in HTML format) or serve to create shadow backdrops for page-sized logos or fill graphics.

This option is not useful if you're formatting spreadsheets primarily for online data entry because the color you apply appears only during printing or HTML export. If you want to use color to backlight or highlight data, apply it using cell styles.

Using the Page Format command, you can easily apply a background to a spreadsheet for printing or publishing. When you apply a background to your page by using this command, your spreadsheet's screen appearance does not visibly change, but the graphic (or fill color) does appear in Page view and prints or is output with the graphic appropriately placed. The graphic and/or fill is applied to all pages that share the same page style.

To apply a background color and/or graphic to your page, choose the Format, Page command, click the Background tab, and make your selections. The Background tab is essentially the same as the one you see to apply a background graphic and/or fill to the desktop, so refer to "Changing Your Background Color and Graphic" in Chapter 3, "Getting Ready for Work" for additional help in navigating this tab.

PART
III

CH
19

Tip #368 from	Remember to check the Preview option on the Background tab and in the Browse dialog if
Michael & Sarah	you want to see what a graphic looks like before attaching it to the page.

You can insert your background graphic as one of three types: a position graphic, placed in the position you specify in the rectangular page layout box to the right of the Type Options list; an area graphic, which expands the graphic to cover your entire printable page; and tiled, which places repeating copies of the graphic in the background.

If you choose the Position option, StarCalc places the graphic in your chosen position relative to your current selected print range, so it appears no matter where from your worksheet you might be printing.

The disadvantage of inserting a graphic in this mode is that you cannot manually resize or otherwise alter the graphic you have attached to your page. The advantages are that the graphic is automatically sized to fit your defined print area, and you can quickly and easily make global changes to the background without the tedium of selecting and deleting individual graphics files.

If you want to use a background only occasionally, create a page style that contains the background. You can then apply it and change it with a single mouse click each time.

When you're ready for printing and have selected your print area, choose Page View from the File menu to see what your final printed or published output will look like. When you're in Page view, you can always choose to change your graphic background if you don't like the way it looks; you don't need to exit and return to Worksheet view. Just right-click your page to open the layout context menu, choose Page Layout, and you're back at the Background tab again.

Note When you change your background in Page view, you change the page style itself, not just the individual page you are about to print. You cannot apply direct background formatting to a page; it's all done through styles.

CREATING PAGE HEADERS AND FOOTERS

Page headers and footers are hard to do without if you're creating multipage printed reports because they help you and your readers keep track of the page order and the source of the report. StarCalc gives you an unusually wide range of options for formatting your headers and footers so that they can look great and be informative.

By default, StarCalc prints pages with the name of the worksheet as a centered header and the page number as a centered footer, in the form *Page #* (where # represents the actual page number). To change your header and footer text and/or formatting, select Format, Page and click either the Header or Footer tab (see Figure 19.5).

The process for modifying headers and footers is the same, as are the options, so we'll just refer to headers as our example here. On the main tab, you can choose to turn headers off altogether, to turn AutoFit Height off and on, and to set the spacing, height, and left and right margins of your header. The default height is 0.20 inch, with a spacing of 0.10 inch from the page edge. The margins are set at 0.00. (The defaults for footers are the same.) If AutoFit is turned off, your headers (or footers) remain the size you set here and do not adjust even if you add more text to them than can be printed in that area.

Figure 19.5
Choosing the Edit button of the Header (or Footer) tab opens a three-column box from which you can select and format the text that will print on your header (or footer).

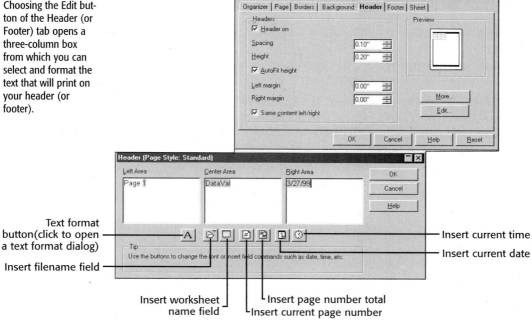

Text format button(click to open a text format dialog)

Insert filename field

Insert worksheet name field

Insert current page number

Insert page number total

Insert current time

Insert current date

If you want to print your work in a book or pamphlet style, you can choose to create different headers and footers on facing pages.

Tip #369 from
Michael & Sarah

If you intend to print on facing pages, be sure to make your inner page margin wider than your outer margin to allow enough room for binding or stapling. Change your margins on the Page tab. While you're working on this tab, be sure to select Mirror Under Layout so that your page format matches your header and footer format.

PART
III
CH
19

Choose the Edit button to open the dialog in which you can modify the content of your header. You can insert various fields using the six fields tools there (refer to Figure 19.5), or you can type directly in the edit windows. You can edit just as you would in a word processor. Your choices of fields are limited compared to those in StarWriter; you cannot, for example, insert fields that insert information from your Document Properties dialog.

Tip #370 from
Michael & Sarah

If you just want to edit your header or footer text, choose the Header/Footer command from the Edit menu.

Clicking the button with the black A opens a text formatting dialog from which you can apply the full range of text attributes to your header (or footer) text.

Choose More to open dialog tabs in which you can apply borders and color backgrounds to your header. These dialogs are just like those discussed in the previous section, "Applying Page Backgrounds and Borders." You can also refer to the section "Changing Your Background Color and Graphic" in Chapter 3 for additional help in navigating this tab.

Tip #371 from
Michael & Sarah

You can select a row and/or column to print as a horizontal and/or vertical title on every page in the Edit Print Areas dialog box, which you open by choosing Format, Print Range.

INSERTING MANUAL ROW AND COLUMN BREAKS

If you need to determine just where breaks in your data occur to ensure a decent print job, you can insert your own manual row and column breaks. Breaks are inserted to the left of a selected column and on the top of a selected row.

To insert a break, select the column or row that will mark the break. Then choose Insert, Manual Break. Only one option is available on the submenu, depending on whether you've selected a column or a row. Your break is immediately displayed with a heavy blue line.

To remove a manually inserted break, select the row or column that defines the break, and choose Remove Manual Break from the Edit menu.

Note

You cannot remove page breaks inserted by the program with the Remove Manual Break command. You can change them in the Page Break Preview viewing mode, however. See the section "Previewing Page Breaks" later in this chapter for more information.

CREATING PAGE STYLES

The section "Formatting Pages" earlier in this chapter describes how to apply page formatting directly, one attribute at a time. An easier way to format pages is to create a *page style*, which is a collection of formatting attributes saved together under one name.

StarCalc comes with two built-in page styles: Standard and Report. Although you cannot delete either of these styles, you can modify them to meet your own tastes and work needs so that every time you open a new spreadsheet, your worksheets appear as you like them. You can also create your own page styles for more specialized tasks that help you format for final printing and presentation in just a few quick steps.

Below are a few ideas as to how you might use page styles:

- Create a gridlines page style that has the Grid option turned on so that you can quickly switch between blank and gridline page formats.

- Create a page style that prints only formulas and notes so that you can quickly print an overview of a document's formulas and the process used to create them.

- Create a page style that has your company's or business's logo attached as a background graphic so that you can quickly print professional-looking reports and invoices but not waste time and printer ink printing graphics for everyday use.

- Create a page style that has a background wallpaper or tiled graphic to use when you export HTML files to be posted on the company intranet or a Web site.

To create a page style, you follow the same process for creating a cell style—or creating paragraph and page styles in StarWriter for that matter. First, apply the attributes you want to the page through direct formatting in the Format, Page dialog. Then open the Stylist. Be sure the Page Style button is pressed and page styles (not cell styles) are visible in the window. Look in the title bar to be sure.

Next, click the New Style by Example button on the Navigator toolbar. That's it!

After you've created a page style, just double-click its name in the Stylist to apply it. You can check to be sure the style has been applied by looking in the status bar the second field from the left displays the name of the currently applied page style.

You can also import styles from other documents by using the Organizer, opened from the Format menu Style Catalog (Ctrl+Y) (see Figure 19.6).

Figure 19.6
The Style Catalog is a cousin to the Stylist. It contains not only a list of all cell and page styles available in your active StarCalc document, but it also opens the Organizer (titled Document Templates), which enables you to drag and drop styles between documents and templates.

The commands available from the Style Catalog are the same as those from the Stylist context menu. Double-clicking a style name applies it to your currently selected cell or page. However, you can open the Organizer from here, which widens your style horizon considerably.

The Organizer lists all currently loaded document templates and their styles. You can copy any other StarCalc styles into your current document by dragging and dropping. You can double-click folders and then template names to see their contents. You can also load a new template into StarOffice and attach it to your open spreadsheet.

Tip #372 from
Michael & Sarah

Both cell and paragraph styles are contained under the heading Styles. Cell styles have a page icon with a paragraph mark, whereas page styles have one with a page number at the bottom. You cannot copy configurations by dragging and dropping.

Note

Although you can drag and drop styles between different types of StarOffice documents, styles from non-StarCalc documents might not work properly.

What's a little disconcerting with page styles is that often nothing visible changes on your display because many elements of pages become visible only in Page view. However, if you have your status bar turned on, you see the name of your current page style in the second field from the left. Double-clicking that field opens the Page Style dialog, in which you can modify the style. If you have the Stylist open and set to show page styles, it also highlights the page style of your current page in its styles list.

PROOFING YOUR WORK

You can check your spelling and vocabulary with the Spelling Check command (F7) and the Thesaurus, respectively; these tools are common across StarOffice. Working with these tools is discussed in "Using Common Proofing Tools" in Chapter 4, "Working in StarOffice," and from a different angle in the part on StarWriter in the section "Proofing Your Work" in Chapter 12, "Proofing and Printing Your Documents."

The following sections focus on aspects of proofing and checking your work that are unique to StarCalc.

USING SPELLING CHECK AND THESAURUS IN STARCALC

When you check your spelling, be sure you choose More on the main dialog box, and then select the options to check words with numbers and check special regions. Selecting these options helps you catch errors that aren't detected just by matching words against a common language dictionary and ensures that your headers and footers don't ruin it for the rest of your document by boasting evident mistakes.

If you use a lot of odd phrases on your spreadsheet—for example, part numbers or company-specific abbreviations or entry codes that are business-critical—consider creating a custom dictionary of these odd terms to use during spellchecking.

Although the Spelling command executes globally and checks all cells formatted as text, the Thesaurus does not. You must select the cell or range of cells you want to check against the Thesaurus first and then choose Thesaurus from the Tools menu. If your active cell or current selection is not formatted as text, the Thesaurus command is grayed out.

USING SEARCH AND REPLACE TO CORRECT MISTAKES

Search and Replace (found on the Edit menu) can help you quickly correct any errors you may have found that can't be corrected automatically—as is often the case with spreadsheets, where installed dictionaries can't do much to repair the ravages of data errors.

USING SEARCH AND REPLACE TO HELP PROOF FORMULAS

Search and Replace can help you proof in another way as well. In StarCalc, if you choose More on the main dialog, you have the option of searching in formulas only. By doing so, you get a quick tour of all your formulas before you commit their results to paper. This feature is even more powerful when used in conjunction with the Detective, StarCalc's auditing assistant.

USING THE DETECTIVE TO SNOOP OUT ERRORS IN FORMULAS

Although we recommend that you use the Detective as you go along so that little errors don't compound into big ones as you build complex spreadsheets, checking right before you print is also a good idea.

Here is a quick way to do it: Choose Fill Mode from the Tools, Detective submenu. Your pointer turns into (what is meant to represent) a paint can; the idea is that you're painting your cells with colors that trace the precedents and dependents in your formulas and marking your errors. Click cells you know or believe contain formulas, and immediately precedent or dependent formulas are indicated with dots connected through blue lines.

→ Using the Detective is discussed in detail in "Auditing Formulas and Functions," **p. 610**.

You can turn on Value Highlighting (Ctrl+F8) to make your formulas easier to spot. You can also set your cells to display formulas instead of their results in the Contents tab of the Tools, Options, Spreadsheet dialog.

If you want to change the Fill Mode setting, right-click to open its context menu, and choose the setting you want. You can also turn off the Fill Mode and clear all traces here.

PART

III

CH

19

Tip #375 from *Michael & Sarah*	Be sure to position the black stream of paint coming out of the lid in the cell you want to audit because that is what registers the cell address, not the can itself.

After you've marked all your formulas, you can navigate to them quickly by using Search and Replace, as discussed previously.

UPDATING YOUR SPREADSHEET

Many times, spreadsheets contain OLE and DDE objects and/or are connected to external databases through ODBC or JDBC. If you work with such a spreadsheet, be sure to update its links before you print your report. You can update your links from within an open spreadsheet by opening the Edit menu Links dialog box and choosing Update; if you are printing from the Explorer or Beamer, select your spreadsheet, right-click, and choose Update from the Explorer context menu.

RECALCULATING YOUR SPREADSHEET

You might need to recalculate your spreadsheet to be sure that your formula results are based on the latest and most complete data inputs. (Be sure to recalculate *after* you update any links: That's why we put this section where it is.) Even if you've been working with AutoCalculate turned on, you might want to consider running the Calculate command again, depending on the complexity of your spreadsheet and the time required.

To recalculate, press F9 or choose the Recalculate command from the Tools, Cell Contents submenu.

SELECTING WHAT TO PRINT

A worksheet contains 32,000 rows and 256 columns—many more than you could or would want to print at one time. The first step to printing your spreadsheet is selecting your *print range*, the specific area you would like to print. After you set a print range, you can then preview the page to check its layout and see page elements such as borders and backgrounds in place.

If you have not defined print ranges on any sheets in your spreadsheet, all sheet areas that contain data are printed.

SETTING A PRINT RANGE

To set your print range, select the area you want to print, and choose Add, Set, or Edit from the Format, Print Range submenu.

Set makes your current selection the new print range for that worksheet and erases all the previous print ranges you selected for that sheet. Add, however, adds your current selection to a list of any print ranges you have previously defined.

The Edit command opens the Edit Print Areas dialog you see in Figure 19.7. Using this dialog, you can edit your current ranges, add new ones, and set selected rows and columns to print as header labels on your document.

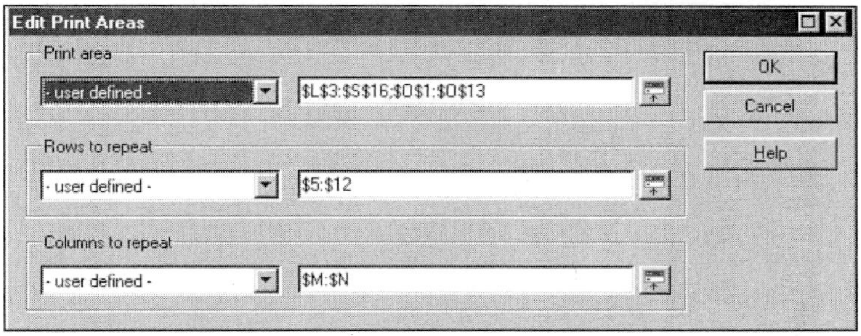

Figure 19.7
The Edit Print Areas dialog enables you to select a row and/or column to print as labels on your report.

The parts of the dialog are as follows:

- **Print Area**—User Defined lists all currently defined print ranges; ranges are separated by a semicolon. Any changes you make here affect the defined print ranges for the sheet, not just the current print job. Your other menu choices are Selection, which enters the cell reference of your current selection, and None, which clears the entry box of all entries.

  Clear erases the entire list of currently defined print ranges that you may have accumulated for that sheet and leaves you with no defined print ranges. The advantage is that nothing from this sheet previews when you enter Page view mode. When you have a large and multisheeted spreadsheet, you'll be grateful because Page view is global and previews all currently selected print ranges in your spreadsheet.

  Choosing Clear clears any entries in the Print Area portion of the Edit Print Areas dialog, but it leaves your row and column settings intact.

- **Rows to Repeat**—If you want a row to repeat as a header row on multiple pages, select User Defined. Either enter the cell reference manually, or use the method detailed in the descriptions of the Minimize/Maximize buttons.

- **Columns to Repeat**—If you want a column to repeat as a header column on multiple pages, select User Defined. Either enter the cell reference manually or use the method detailed in the following paragraph. Your other choice is None, which clears the boxes.

- **Minimize/Maximize buttons**—These buttons reduce the dialog to a single-line entry box. Click the first cell in your selection and Shift+click the last, and the correct cell references are automatically entered. Your other choice is None, which clears the boxes.

You set print ranges by the worksheet page only. You do not set them globally for an entire spreadsheet. Therefore, the commands on this dialog apply only to your current worksheet.

Note

If you are working in a new spreadsheet and have already entered data but have not set any print ranges, clicking Page View previews your current data. However, if you have already set at least one print range and click Page View, you see previews only of those areas that you have expressly defined as a printing range.

PROTECTING SELECTED CELLS FROM PRINTING

If you have activated cell protection by using the Cell Protection command on the Tools menu, you can hide your protected cells when you print. To select this option, choose Format, Cells and go to the Cell Protection tab.

→ For more information on protecting your work, **see** "Protecting Cells, Sheets, and Documents" **p. 523**.

CREATING PRINTED GRIDLINES

Unlike Excel, StarCalc, by default, does not print gridlines; it prints a blank white background just like a word processor.

To print gridlines, select the Grid option on the Sheet tab of the Format, Page dialog. These default gridlines always print as black; you cannot change their color.

Tip #376 from
Michael & Sarah

If you want to print gridlines in a different color, create a cell style with colored cell borders. Then apply it globally to all cells on the page by turning on the Stylist Fill Format mode, clicking the Sheet Selection shortcut button to select the entire sheet, and clicking once in the selected sheet with your Fill Mode pointer. Note that just clicking the Sheet Selection button is not enough; you have to click somewhere in a cell as well.

SELECTING OBJECTS TO PRINT

On the Format, Page, Sheet tab, you'll find options that enable you to control the printing of certain types of objects (see Figure 19.8).

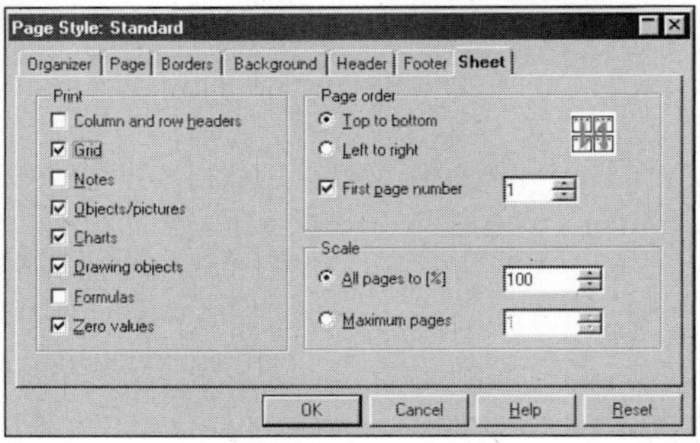

Figure 19.8
One of the final steps in getting ready to print should be checking the Sheet tab of the Page Style dialog box to ensure that you're printing only the objects and special contents that you want.

Most of these options are self-explanatory. Objects/Pictures refers to objects and pictures inserted with the Insert Objects toolbar or the Insert menu commands, and Drawing Objects refers to objects you have created with the Main toolbar drawing tools.

If you choose to print formulas, formulas—instead of their results—appear in the cells.

Caution

Formulas usually occupy more room in a cell than their results. Your columns might not be wide enough to accommodate them, which causes only the error message ### to print. If you want to print formulas, you would be wise to check your column widths first with the Tools, Options, Spreadsheet, Contents, Display Formulas option turned on.

When you enter Page view, you see previews of all currently defined print ranges in your spreadsheet; note that numbering is not consecutive but begins at 1 again for each new print range.

SELECTING PAGE ORDER AND NUMBER

You set your page order on the Sheet tab of the Page Styles dialog as well (refer to Figure 19.8). You can choose to have your worksheet printed from top to bottom or left to right. Be sure to check the Page tab of the same dialog to ensure that your page layout and data alignment selections are in accord with your page order setting. If you've chosen to print mirrored pages, for example, it makes a difference in your final product if you print top to bottom or left to right.

You can also select what number will be assigned to your first page, which allows you to print pages from multiple spreadsheets and easily combine them into one continuously pagi-nated report. Just enter the number you want to use in the spin box.

CHOOSING THE PRINT SCALE

Adjusting your print scale is much like zooming in and out of your document, except that the result is committed to paper instead of existing momentarily on a monitor.

The default print scale in StarCalc is 100 percent—data is printed at 100 percent scale, as determined partly by your font size(s) and partly by the spacing of elements on your page and the sizing of objects such as charts and graphics. You can adjust this scale anywhere in a range from 1 percent to 400 percent.

By reducing the print scale, you can fit more data on a page, but that data is also smaller in size and so may be more difficult to read. If you're going to shrink your data, you might consider setting it to 12 points.

FITTING DATA TO A SINGLE PAGE

Besides entering a precise figure yourself in the Scale spin box on the Sheet tab, you can also let StarCalc figure out the scale for you by just telling it how many pages you want to fit the data on. If you set this number to 1, you're instructing StarCalc to fit all data in the selected area onto one page.

PREVIEWING PAGE BREAKS

After you've finished formatting your page, it's time to check your page breaks. Because they're so expansive, spreadsheets rarely create output that fits on just one standard 8.5- by 11-inch page, and sometimes the way pages are formatted can make the data almost unusable as printed, so checking is important.

The Page Break Preview command on the View menu gives you a clear view of how your print range will break into page segments. When you choose the command, your display is transformed, with your printable areas outlined in thick blue borders and each page stamped with its number across its middle in gray (see Figure 19.9).

Figure 19.9
How simple can it get? Drag and drop your page break borders to redefine the page breaks of your print job. StarCalc adjusts everything automatically, changing scale and inserting manual page breaks where needed.

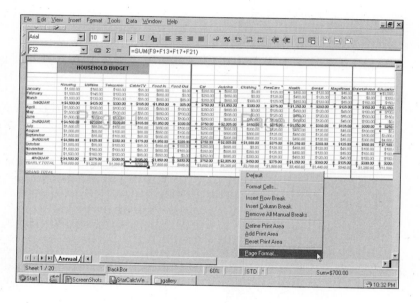

If you don't like the breaks, you can tweak your layout in a number of ways. The simplest is to use your mouse to shift the indicated print areas and page breaks by dragging the borders where you want them. If you reduce a print area so that nothing remains, the print area is deleted (not, however, your data). If you shift an automatic page break, a manual page break is inserted at the new position. You cannot move a manual page break; you must delete it completely by using the Edit menu's Remove Manual Break command.

If you shift an automatic page break down or to the right, the scale is reduced automatically, if necessary, to display the area between the previous break and the new break on an entire page. A manual page break is inserted.

You can delete a manual page break in this viewing mode by dragging the break outside the defined print area.

The context menu (which you open by right-clicking in the worksheet) gives you all the other commands you need to manage page breaks and adjust your cell and page formatting (refer to 20.9).

Note

Although Page Break view does not look like your normal worksheet view, you're still in your regular StarCalc workspace and can modify (and delete) anything on your worksheet.

To turn off Page Break view, choose the command again from the View menu.

After you've defined a print range, your page breaks also always appear on your worksheet as slightly thickened borders around your page areas.

PREVIEWING YOUR PAGE LAYOUT WITH PAGE VIEW

After you've set your page breaks, you can preview your final page layout by using the File menu's Page View command. This feature might feel a bit clunky to you at first because it doesn't work as fluidly as Excel's or Word's Page Layout views, but when you get used to it, you'll find it does all you need. The keys, once again, are to look to the context menu and toolbar.

Tip #377 from
Michael & Sarah

Page view is actually opened as a copy of your task in its own task window. You therefore can drag and drop its task button onto the task button of your document to see your layout and normal workspace views side by side.

When you enter Page view, you're in a changed world. Most of your StarCalc tools and menus are gone or unavailable, and you have only a limited set at hand. Even the Format menu is grayed out. However, you have access to the page formatting dialog via the context menu's Page Layout command and the Page Layout button on the Page View toolbar (see Figure 19.10).

The default scale and layout show you two pages side by side—not the most useful layout for spreadsheets—but you can easily zoom in and out by either clicking the toolbar buttons or right-clicking the status bar Zoom field to open the familiar Zoom shortcut menu.

Your document is read-only (even though the Edit button may appear to be pressed), so you can only look, change your view, and enter the page formatting dialog to make adjustments to the page settings before you print—and, when you're ready, print.

PART

III

CH

19

Zoom In
Last Page ┐ ┌ Zoom Out
First Page ┐ │ │ ┌ Full Screen View
Next Page ┐ │ │ │ │ ┌ Page Layout
Previous Page ┐ │ │ │ │ │ ┌ Close Page View

Figure 19.10
You can check your
layout to get a sense
of what your printed
report will look like in
Page view. In StarCalc,
unlike in StarWriter,
changes you make in
your viewing scale do
not affect your printed
output; your print
scale is determined by
your settings in the
Page Layout dialog.

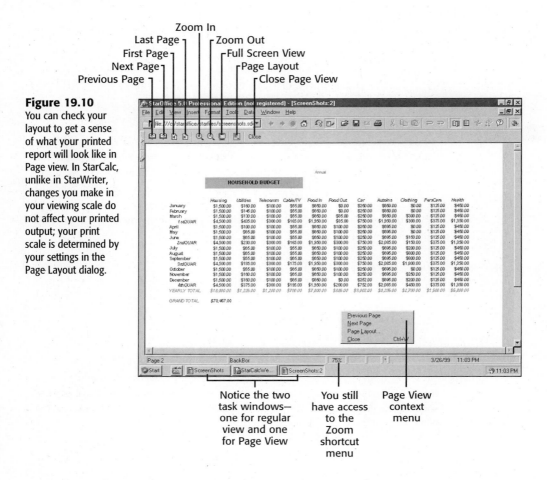

Notice the two
task windows—
one for regular
view and one
for Page View

You still
have access
to the
Zoom
shortcut
menu

Page View
context
menu

PRINTING YOUR RESULTS

Printing is the easy part, assuming that your printer is properly configured, turned on, and
full of paper. You can print directly to your printer without seeing the Print dialog box by
clicking the Print button on the function bar. Alternatively, you can choose the Print command (Ctrl+P) from the Edit menu. There, you can set various print options, such as the
number of pages and copies printed.

TROUBLESHOOTING

I keep trying to put a page number field in my footers, but StarCalc won't let me!

You probably have page numbering on the Format, Page, Page tab set to None. Set this option for the form of numbering you want, and try again.

When I try to check my layout in Page view, my pages are so tiny that I can't proof them.

Check the Sheet tab of the Format, Page dialog. See whether someone has set the scale to less than 100 percent. If so, set the scale to at least 100 percent. If you have vision problems, try setting it in the 150 to 200 percent range. Just keep in mind that changing the scale affects your printed output as well as what you see in Page view. You can always change your print scale back to 100 percent after you've finished proofing; just right-click in Page view to open the Page View context menu, and choose the Page Layout command to go back to the Sheet tab again.

How can I get the data I need to print on the same page?

Keeping everything on the same page can be accomplished in a number of ways. You can reduce the scale (that is, increase the resolution) of your output by setting the print scale at less than 100 percent on the Format, Page, Sheet tab. You can print on larger paper; StarCalc accommodates a large range of paper sizes and even allows you to define your own custom sizes. You can try printing in landscape orientation (sideways) rather than portrait (up and down). You can also try changing your row heights and/or column widths to fit more data into your printable area. And if you choose the Maximum Pages command on the Format, Page, Sheet tab and set it to 1, your print area is automatically forced to fit onto one page. This solution isn't always the best, though, because reducing the scale can reduce the readability of your document.

GETTING GRAPHICAL—STARDRAW AND STARIMAGE

CHAPTER 20

GETTING SKETCHY WITH STARDRAW

In this chapter

GETTING STARTED WITH STARDRAW

StarDraw is the vector graphics module of StarOffice. Comparable in function to CorelDraw, it sports some of the best drawing tools available in an Office suite, including sophisticated 3D modeling tools (that enable you to fuse basic shapes together to make complex ones), Bézier curves, a range of "connectors" that draw connecting lines between objects and adjust those connections as you move the objects they connect, and even the elusively simple "text on a curve."

Using StarDraw, you can create drawings of varying degrees of complexity. You can add color, text, or textures to your shapes and 3D objects; create buttons and icons for your Web pages and then export the results as an HTML file; or design a multipage interactive document. You can create organizational charts and technical drawings. In general, every object you create in StarDraw can be inserted into any other StarOffice document as a graphic object. And because StarDraw is an OLE-compliant application, you can use OLE to move images between StarDraw and other StarOffice modules.

> **Note**
>
> Technically speaking, you can do everything in StarDraw that you can do in StarImpress, except create and run a slide show. StarDraw has these capabilities because it is an extension of StarImpress. The two modules used to be one until StarOffice 5.0, when the developer decided that the available functionality for StarImpress is too complex for a single module. This chapter focuses on the mechanical aspects of using the drawing tools and working with objects. For details on working with layers and slides, refer to Chapter 22, "Getting Started with StarImpress."
>
> In general, almost everything mentioned in this chapter can also be done in StarImpress unless otherwise noted.

> **Caution**
>
> StarOffice, like other Office suites, gives you the option of installing only the modules you need. However, be aware that if you decide not to install StarImpress when installing StarDraw, you'll have problems working with StarDraw (and vice versa). Since both programs are virtually the same modules, installing one without the other can cause serious problems (for example, you won't be able to cut and paste anymore).

STARTING STARDRAW

You can launch StarDraw by selecting File, New, Drawing from the menu bar or Start, Drawing from the taskbar. Alternatively, you can click the Drawing icon in the Tasks group in the extended Explorer. After you open a new drawing document, you have access to a series of tools and functions that enable you to put a graphic spin on your imagination. As with the other StarOffice modules, the major hurdle is once again to get accustomed to the StarOffice way of doing everything in one place.

Note

The Draw tear-off window on the StarWriter main toolbar is a simplified version of the Draw toolbar. It includes the Selection tool, a small collection of basic geometric and Bézier curve drawing tools, and the Text tools.

EXPLORING THE STARDRAW WORKSPACE

After you start StarDraw, you see the StarDraw desktop and Stylist with a portrait-oriented drawing surface surrounded by the Draw object bar, toolbar, status bar, and color bar (see Figure 20.1). If you don't see the Stylist, select Format, Stylist or press F11. To minimize the Stylist, double-click the Object Styles title bar. (Working with the Stylist in StarDraw is virtually identical to using it in StarImpress and is discussed in the section "Working with Styles" in Chapter 22.

Note

One thing to be aware off when you're working in StarDraw/StarImpress: unlike in StarWriter, StarCalc, or StarImage, you don't have to worry about text or image boundaries; you can actually drag objects outside the printable area of your page or slide and onto the surrounding workspace. This capability is very useful when you are building complex graphics out of individual elements because you can place temporarily unused graphic elements and objects outside the page/slide area as if it were one convenient layout table.

Figure 20.1
StarDraw comes with a variety of tools that enable you to create stunning graphics for your presentations or desktop publishing needs. Note that the option bar is not visible by default; you have to activate it manually by right-clicking the main toolbar and then selecting Option Bar from the shortcut menu.

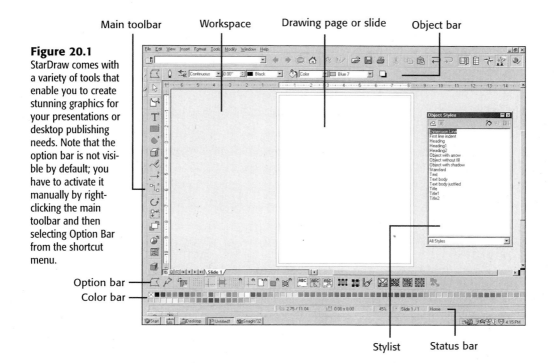

Main toolbar   Workspace   Drawing page or slide   Object bar

Option bar —
Color bar —

Stylist   Status bar

PART
IV

CH

20

USING THE MAIN TOOLBAR

The Main toolbar provides access to 15 major tools, with variations of some tucked away in handy fly-out windows that you can tear off and place anywhere on your desktop for easy access (see Figure 20.2). To select a tool, click its icon, and then use the tool by clicking or dragging with it inside the workspace. (Remember, you can draw anywhere you like. When saving your work, however, make sure it is placed within the boundaries of a slide (or page.) As in other StarOffice modules, you can extended-click icons that show a small green triangle in the upper-right corner to open a tear-off window with additional tools.

Tip #378 from
Michael & Sarah

When you click a drawing tool, it is available only for as long as you hold the left mouse button. If you want to use a drawing tool repeatedly, you have to double-click it. It then is available until you switch to another tool.

Figure 20.2
The Draw context menu and the tools of the drawing trade are shown here. To access these floating tool groups, click the respective tool icon on the main toolbar. You can than click in the title bar area of the respective group and drag the tool group window anywhere on your desktop.

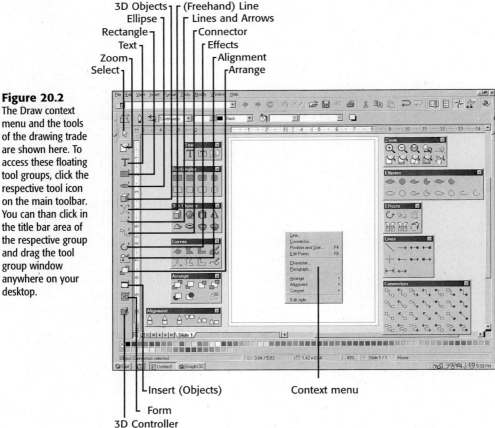

3D Objects
Ellipse
Rectangle
Text
Zoom
Select

(Freehand) Line
Lines and Arrows
Connector
Effects
Alignment
Arrange

Insert (Objects)
Form
3D Controller

Context menu

Table 20.1 explains the available icons and tools on the main toolbar.

TABLE 20.1   EXPLORING THE STARDRAW TOOLBAR

Click This Icon	If You Want To
⬚ Select	Switch from a Draw mode back to the regular Selection mode. In Selection mode, you can click any object or object group and move it within the current slide area. You can also draw a selection rectangle around a group of objects; the objects that are inside the selection rectangle are automatically selected.
⬚ Zoom	Change the view of the slide. Clicking this icon opens the Zoom tear-off window, which includes the following options (from left to right): Zoom In, Zoom Out, View 100%, Zoom Previous, Zoom Next, Zoom Page, Zoom Page Width, Optimal (all objects are shown), Object Zoom (only selected objects are shown), and Shift, which enables you to move the entire slide up and down or left and right.
⬚ Text	Add text to your graphic. Your options include regular text that can be formatted and edited as desired (Text), single-line text that corresponds to the size of the text frame (Fit Text to Size), or callout text that appears in a frame by itself and is anchored to a selected object (Callout).
⬚ Rectangle	Draw a filled or outlined rectangle or square with or without rounded corners. You can select a color for your border and background fill from the Line Color (border) and Fill Style/Color (fill) drop-down list boxes on the object bar. The thickness and shape of your border or outline can be controlled through the Line Width spin box and the Line Style drop-down list box from the object bar.
⬚ Ellipse	Draw a filled or outlined ellipse or circle, ellipse or circle segments, or ellipse or circle arcs. As with rectangles, you can select a color for your border and background fill from the Line Color (border) and Fill Style/Color (fill) drop-down list boxes on the object bar. The thickness and shape of your border, outline, or arc can be controlled through the Line Width spin box and the Line Style drop-down list box from the object bar.
⬚ 3D Objects	Draw 3D objects. Using this tool, you can draw cubes, spheres, cylinders, cones, pyramids, toruses, shells, and half-spheres.
⬚ Curves	Draw filled or unfilled curves and polygons. As with the rectangles and ellipses, you can select a color for your outline and background fill from the Line Color (Border) and Fill Style/Color (Fill) drop-down list boxes on the object bar. The thickness and shape of your border, outline, or arc can be controlled through the Line Width spin box and the Line Style drop-down list box from the object bar.
⬚ Lines	Draw a linear, hard-edged line with or without arrow, round, or square ends. To control the thickness, color, and style of your line, use the Line Width spin box and Line Color and Line Style drop-down list boxes, respectively.

PART

IV

CH

20

continues

TABLE 20.1   CONTINUED

Click This Icon	If You Want To
Connector	Connect objects with a linear or angled line. You can choose from various connectors with or without round or arrow endpoints.
Effects	Turn, flip, rotate, or distort a selected drawing. (Note that with the exception of the Rotation tool, these tools are unique to StarDraw and cannot be accessed in StarImpress.)
Alignment	Align selected objects horizontally (left, center, right) or vertically (top, middle, bottom). (Familiarize yourself with this tool if you frequently have to align several objects with each other.)
Arrange	Arrange the stacking order of a selected group of objects.
Insert	Insert a chart, formula, frame, OLE object, plug-in, applet, StarCalc table, file, slide, picture (from file or image editor) into the current slide or page.
Form	Create an interactive form.
3D Controller	Modify or edit 3D objects. Clicking this icon opens the 3D Effects window.

Note

One of the advantages of StarOffice is that you are working in a seamlessly integrated environment. In fact, StarOffice is the first office package to unite all functions for working with text, graphics, spreadsheets, slides, mathematical formulas, and databases into one common, visually slick user interface.

The modules that make up StarOffice have standardized, context-sensitive toolbars and menus and consistent commands and dialog boxes. Once you learn one application, it's easy to familiarize yourself with the others. Hence, you come across tools in one module that you may find more useful in another work environment. For example, you may find that you're more likely to use the interactive Form tool in StarWriter/Web or StarBase than in StarDraw.

Tip #379 from
Michael & Sarah

If you press Ctrl while clicking in a gray area on the toolbar, you can drag the toolbar anywhere on your desktop.

USING THE DRAW OBJECT BAR

The StarDraw object bar enables you to edit or change the existing attributes of a selected object or group of objects (see Figure 20.3).

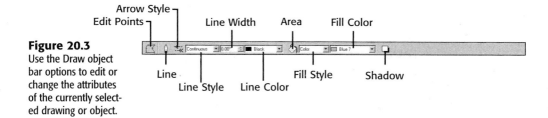

Figure 20.3
Use the Draw object bar options to edit or change the attributes of the currently selected drawing or object.

For example, using the Edit Points command, you can edit the individual control points of a Bézier curve or scale the curve of a segment, pie, or arc. If you select a polygon or Bézier curve and then click the Edit Points icon, the Draw object bar is replaced by the Bézier object bar, shown in Figure 20.27 later in this chapter.

→ For more details on the Bézier object bar, **see** "Working with Bézier Curves," **p. 767**, in this chapter.

Tip #380 from *Michael & Sarah*	If Edit Points is active when you insert or select a rectangle, square, or callout box, you see a small box at the upper-left corner of the object. If you place your cursor over the box, it changes shape to a hand symbol. You can now click and drag the box to change the amount of rounding. An outline shows a preview of the results as you go.

Clicking the Line icon opens the Line dialog box (shown in Figure 20.24 later in this chapter). Using the Line, Line Style, and Arrow Styles tabs of the Line dialog, you can edit the style, color, and width of any given line and arrow style or line ends, as well as save your changes to existing and custom line and arrow style configuration files.

Tip #381 from *Michael & Sarah*	You can access the Line icon any time you want, even when you haven't even drawn a line yet. The values you set are used as defaults for your drawings.

The Arrowhead icon gives you access to a tear-off window that consists of a table of available arrow styles that you can add to the left end and/or right end of a selected line. If you load another arrow style configuration file—using the Arrow Styles tab in the Line dialog—the arrows you see in this table may differ.

The Line Style, Line Width, and Line Color boxes enable you to quickly change the appearance of a selected line or outline of a selected shape or object. Note that if you load another line table—using the Line Styles tab in the Line dialog (see "Setting Line Style Properties" later in this chapter)—the styles you see in the Line Styles drop-down list may differ.

PART

IV

CH

20

Clicking the Area icon opens the Area dialog box, which enables you to edit the fill style, color, and shadowing of the selected object. Using the Colors tab of this dialog, you can edit existing colors, add your own RGB or CMYK custom colors, as well as save custom color palettes and load existing palettes. Using the Gradients, Hatches, and Bitmaps tabs, you can edit existing fill style schemes, as well as save your own fill style configuration files. Gradients are visual color effects that transpire around a shape or line and lead to the gradual transition between colors. Hatches are patterns of parallel or crossing lines. Bitmaps are textures.

The Fill Style/Color controls enable you to select a fill style and color from the currently loaded gradient, hatch, bitmap, and color palettes.

Finally, the Shadow icon enables you to turn the shadowing for the selected object on or off. You can define the position color and transparency of the shadow, as well as the distance between the shadow and the object on the Shadow tab of the Area dialog.

USING THE RULERS

Below the object bar and to the right of the main toolbar are the horizontal and vertical rulers, respectively. You use the white area of the rulers to gauge the height and width of the printable area of the current slide. You can change the margins of the current template by dragging between the white and gray areas of the ruler.

When you select an object on your slide, you see thin gray lines inside the white vertical and horizontal ruler areas. Dragging these lines up or down or to the left or right, you can scale an object vertically and horizontally. To change the unit of measurement of a ruler, right-click the ruler, and select a different unit from the shortcut menu.

Note

Although you have various options when changing the unit of measurement (including Meter, Kilometer, Foot, and Miles), the most useful unit for working with graphics is Inch or Centimeter. If you elect to show the underlying drawing grid (by choosing Visible Grid from the Draw context menu, or by selecting Tools, Options, Drawing, Grid and then selecting Visible Grid), you might also find Point, Pica, and Millimeter useful units. Other units of measurement (such as Meter, Kilometer, Foot, or Miles) come in handy when you change the Scale settings in the Tools, Options, Drawings, Zoom dialog. For more details see "Choosing the Right View for the Job" later in this chapter.

If you click inside the horizontal or vertical ruler and then drag toward the work area, you can "pull out" horizontal and vertical *guidelines* (or *snap lines*) that you can place anywhere in the drawing window to help you align and position elements of your graphic; as soon as the object is close enough, it snaps to the guides. You can use any number of horizontal or vertical lines. By default, guidelines are nonprintable.

Note

You can set the Snap To options on the Tools, Options, Drawing, Snap to Grid dialog box. If you find your objects aren't really snappy, check these settings.

Tip #382 from
Michael & Sarah

If you show the option bar at all times (select View, Toolbars, Option bar), you can quickly turn these snappy things on and off.

Finally, when you're editing text that you previously placed inside an object, you can use the ruler to edit or change any existing tab positions.

USING THE STATUS BAR

The StarDraw status bar provides information about the currently active slide, selection, and tool (see Figure 20.4). (If the status bar doesn't appear on your screen, check the View menu; you should see a check mark next to Status Bar.) Table 20.2 details the various status bar fields.

Figure 20.4
The StarDraw status bar provides basic information about your active slide, including the current command and selection and viewing size.

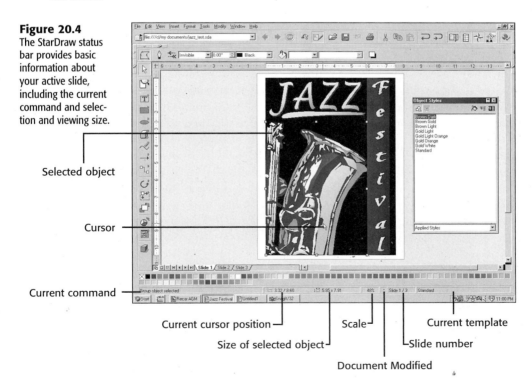

Selected object

Cursor

Current command

Current cursor position

Size of selected object

Scale

Document Modified

Slide number

Current template

TABLE 20.2	EXPLORING THE STARDRAW STATUS BAR
Field	**Displays**
Command	The currently selected menu command or tool.
Position	The current position of the cursor in inches. The unit of measurement corresponds to the currently selected ruler unit of measurement.
Selection Size	The physical size of the current selection in inches. The unit of measurement corresponds to the currently selected ruler unit of measurement.
Scale	The current view size. You can right-click in this field to select a different size from the shortcut menu; double-clicking opens the Zoom dialog box.
Document Modified	An asterisk if changes have occurred since the image was last saved.
Slide Number	The current slide number, followed by the total number of existing slides (x/y). In Layer mode, you see the name of the currently active layer (provided you've selected an object on that layer).
Template	The background template applied to the currently active slide. You can double-click to open the Slide Design dialog, which enables you to quickly switch templates (if you have more than one slide in your file) or to load a different background template. (For more details on using the Slide Design dialog, see "Working with Slides" in Chapter 22.)

USING THE COLOR BAR

The color bar lists all currently available standard and custom colors; standard colors are listed first in the order in which they appear in the color drop-down list on the object bar, followed by any custom colors in the order in which they have been defined. If you create more custom colors than fit in the available free space after the last standard color swatch, your color bar creates a new row of swatches that you can make visible by extending the bar. (To extend it, click and drag the top of the bar.)

Note

When Tips is selected in the Help menu, you can place your cursor over a color swatch to see a pop-up note that gives you the name of the color.

Using the color swatches, you can quickly change the outline, border, or fill color of a selected object. Just left-click a color swatch to change the fill color of the selected object; right-click a swatch to change the color of the outline or border of the selected object. StarDraw automatically indicates your current line or fill color selection in the Fill Style/Color and Line Color drop-down list boxes on the object bar. Note that you can also assign an "invisible" border or fill color by left- or right-clicking the first swatch in the first row. If you want to change the standard colors, define custom colors, or load another color palette, select the Colors tab in the Format, Area dialog.

Note	
	If you don't see the color bar onscreen, you can show it by selecting View, Toolbars, Color Bar.

Tip #383 from *Michael & Sarah*	
	The color bar is a dockable floating toolbar. If you press Ctrl while double-clicking a gray area of the color bar, the color bar turns into a floating window that you can resize and place anywhere on your desktop. To redock the color bar, press Ctrl, click in the title bar area of the Colors window, and drag it to the lower part of the screen.

USING THE OPTION BAR

Using the option bar is, well, optional. If you decide to use it, though, you can access handy commands that enable you to edit and position graphics and text without first having to find your way through menus and dialog boxes.

By default, the option bar is hidden from view. To use it, you can just right-click the toolbar on the right and select Option Bar from the shortcut menu. (Alternatively, you can select View, Toolbars, Option Bar from the menu bar.) The option bar appears above the color bar when you first show it. However, like the color bar, the option bar can also be used as a dockable floating toolbar that you can place anywhere on your desktop. To drag it out of its anchored position, simply press Ctrl, and click and drag in a gray area of the bar.

→ For more information about working with dockable toolbars and windows, **see** "Other Floating and Dockable Windows," **p. 58**, and "Floating Toolbars and Dialog Boxes," **p. 59**.

Table 20.3 explains the available icons and tools on the option bar.

TABLE 20.3 EXPLORING THE OPTION BAR

Click This Icon	If You Want To
Edit Points	Edit the individual control points of a Bézier curve or scale the curve of a segment, pie, or arc. (Note that this is the same icon as on the object bar.)
Edit Glue Points	Edit the glue points of an object. *Glue points* refers to the connecting points that "glue together" connectors and objects.
Rotation Mode	Activate the Rotation mode by clicking an object twice. You can then click any corner control point to rotate the object. (For more details on rotating objects see "Rotating and Skewing Objects" in this chapter.)
Show Grid	Show the predefined drawing grid.

PART

IV

Cʜ

20

continues

TABLE 20.3 CONTINUED

Click This Icon	If You Want To
placement	Display guides for easier object placement.
Display Guides	Display guides while moving an object. When this option is on, you see guides that extend from the four corners of the bounding box of an object to the rulers.
Use Grid	Use the snap to grid option. When you use this option, the contours of frames and draw objects automatically snap to the nearest gridline when you move them. (For more details on this and the following "snap to" options, see "Looking at the Draw Context Menu and Grid System" in this chapter.)
Snap to Guides	Use the Snap to Object Guides (grid points and snap lines) option when moving objects.
Snap to Page Margins	Use the Snap to Page Margins option when moving objects.
Snap to Object Border	Use the Snap to Object Border (or frame) option when moving objects.
Snap to Object Points	Use the Snap to Object Points option when moving objects.
Allow Quick Editing	Enter immediately the text edit mode when clicking text or a text object. Alternatively, you can select this option in the Tools, Options, Drawing, Other dialog. (This option is turned on by default.)
Select Text Area Only	Select a text frame only when clicking the corresponding text. When this option is turned on, you can no longer click once in the frame area to select the frame. Alternatively, you can select this option in the Tools, Options, Drawing, Other dialog.
Double-click Text to Edit	Enter the text edit mode by double-clicking a text object. (This option is turned on by default.)
Standard handles	Display the standard object (or sizing) handles.
Large Handles	Display enlarged object (or sizing) handles.
Object with Attributes	Create objects with attributes. When this option is turned on, you can draw a shape that automatically contains the attributes that you preselected using the object bar options.

Click This Icon	If You Want To
Picture Placeholders	Suppress the original graphic and show only the contour of inserted graphic objects.
(Contour Mode)	Suppress the fill color of drawing objects.
Text Placeholders	Suppress the content of text frames and show only the contour of the text box.
Line Contour Only	Show lines and borders only as thin lines.
Exit All Groups	Exit all groups. Click this icon if you've finished editing a group and would like to exit it. Note that this option is available only after you've previously entered a group using the Edit Group command.

LOOKING AT THE DRAW CONTEXT MENU AND GRID SYSTEM

Using the Draw context menu, shown in Figure 20.5, you can manage your slides and turn various visual aids on and off. Most of the available functions are self-explanatory and can be derived from their names. Some, such as the entries on the Slide submenu (Page Setup, Slide Design, Modify Slide, and Insert Slide), are perhaps more relevant when you are working in StarImpress. Others, such as the Grid options and the Insert Gridpoint/Line command, require a brief introduction into StarDraw's grid system.

Figure 20.5
Using the Draw context menu, you can show or hide your alignment aids, including snap points and snap lines and the underlying grid.

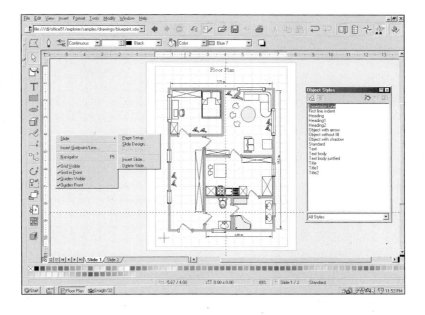

PART

IV

CH

20

Together with the ruler guidelines, StarDraw's grid system helps you align and position objects accurately. StarDraw displays the grid as a series of intersecting dotted lines spaced according to settings you specify in the Tools, Options, Drawing, Grid dialog. By showing the grid, you provide an easy and accurate way to position objects relative to one another and to the drawing page.

Tip #384 from
Michael & Sarah

You can also control the grid system via the option bar, which is hidden by default. To show the option bar, right-click on any toolbar, and select Option Bar from the shortcut menu or choose View, Toolbars, Option Bar. The option bar appears above the color bar. You can easily identify the grid-related icons; they show dots and dotted lines.

If you want your objects always to automatically line up with the grid as you move them, select the Snap to Grid option in the Tools, Options, Drawing, Grid dialog. If the Size to Grid option in the Snap Grid portion of the dialog is selected, then the snap grid coincides with the regular layout grid. (Technically, you can define two separate grids: a visual one for your general layout needs and a snap grid for special layout needs. If you want to define a separate snap grid, you have to deselect the Size to Grid option first before you can define the new snap grid.) Using the options in the Grid dialog, you can also define the horizontal and vertical distance between grid points (Resolution) as well as the number of intervals between grid points (Subdivision).

Note

You control grids the same way in StarDraw as you do in StarImpress—by selecting Tools, Options, Presentation, Snap to Grid or Grid.

Tip #385 from
Michael & Sarah

StarDraw also enables you to define other "snap to" options. For example, using the Tools, Options, Drawing, Snap to Grid dialog or the option bar, you can also control whether the contour of the object you're moving will snap to guides, page margins, object frames, or object points. If you're using the Snap to Grid dialog, you can also define the snap range (in pixels) and snap position (in degrees). If the object contour or the mouse pointer are within the snap range, the contour snaps magnetically to the nearest snap to option.

Alternatively, you can select Insert Gridpoint/Line from the context menu. The Insert Gridpoint/Line command opens the New Snap Object dialog, in which you can specify a snap point or horizontal or vertical snap line to ensure that objects automatically line up with the defined point or line as you move them. You can set any number of snap points and lines. Snap points and lines are nonprintable and are saved with your document. To show or hide any existing snap points and lines, select Guides Visible from the context menu, or click the Display Guides icon on the option bar.

Tip #386 from
Michael & Sarah

To quickly generate snap lines, click inside the horizontal or vertical ruler, and then drag toward the work area. If you press Ctrl while dragging, you can create snap points.

After you've defined a snap point or snap line using the New Snap Object dialog, you can move this point or line anywhere within your work area. For example, you can put it aside until you need it for another alignment job. You can also right-click the snap point or line to specify a new position; if you no longer need it, select Delete Snap Point/Line from the Snap context menu.

Although useful in some contexts, the "snap-to" options are not omnipotent. When you're performing any of the following actions, your movements are immune to their magnetic charm:

- Drawing in freehand mode
- Rotating and skewing graphic objects
- Positioning objects via the Position and Size dialog box

WORKING IN DIFFERENT MODES

When you look at the bottom left of your drawing window, you'll notice three icons—Slide mode (default on program start), Background mode, and Layer mode—located right next to the navigational buttons that you can use to browse through additional drawings (or slides or pages). Each mode represents a different mode of working in a presentation document. When you're in Slide mode, you can edit the individual slides of a document. In Background, you can define an identical background for all the drawings or slides in your document. When you're working in Layer mode, you can assign different layers to different objects of the current slide. Using these different modes is identical in both StarDraw and StarImrpess and is discussed in detail in the section "Understanding the Working Modes" in Chapter 22.

Note

When switching to the Background mode, StarDraw 5.1 (like StarImpress 5.1) will automatically display the current slide in a Preview window. This makes it easy to determine how changes to the background affect the overall look of the slide.

WORKING WITH MULTIPLE SLIDES

A StarDraw document can consist of more than one drawing slide or page. This is useful if you're working, for example, on various ground plans and want to collect all of them in one document (rather than saving them individually as single documents).

You can quickly add, rename, or delete slides to a drawing document by right-clicking the name tab of a slide and selecting Insert Slide, Rename Slide, or Deleting Slide from the context menu, respectively. To move between slides, simply click the name tab of the slide that you want to work on to bring it to the front. If you can't see the slide you want, click the left- and right-arrow icons in the lower left of the StarDraw workspace until the slide you want appears. (Clicking the leftmost and rightmost arrow icon reveals the first and last slide tab in your drawing document, respectively.) Alternatively, you can press the Page Up or Page Down keys to cycle through your slides one by one, or the Home or End keys to go to the first and last slide in your presentation.

PART

IV

CH

20

Tip #387 from
Michael & Sarah

To increase the number of name tabs shown onscreen, click the separator between the horizontal scrollbar at the bottom and the name tab area (your cursor changes shape to a two-headed arrow); then drag the separator to the right.

Tip #388 from
Michael & Sarah

To move quickly between slides, use the Navigator for drawings. The Navigator is useful if you want to jump to a certain slide in an extensive collection of drawings or quickly switch between open documents. Just double-click the slide you want to move to in the Navigator list box, and StarDraw displays it in the work area. To open the Navigator, press F5.

In general, when working with slides—including setting up your drawing page (or slide) using the Format, Page dialog or creating uniform background designs—you have virtually the same options in StarDraw as in StarImpress. For more details, see "Working with Slides" in Chapter 22.

SELECTING A VIEW

When you're changing views in StarDraw, you can change either the size at which a graphic appears onscreen or the display quality. If you change the size of an object, each change in view size is expressed as a zoom ratio. If you change the display quality, you are preventing certain attributes in your graphic from showing onscreen.

Note

In StarDraw 5.1 (and by extension StarImpress 5.1), the conflict with the Windows 95/98 graphics driver has been eliminated, and graphic display has been improved. Quicker graphic display has been achieved through better cache handling. All graphic editing is now completely independent from the operating system. This results in a considerable improvement of display quality. Plus, you now have bi-linear filtering instead of the "Nearest Pixel" method to scale graphic images.

USING THE ZOOM TOOLS

Changing your views in StarDraw works the same as in the other StarOffice modules. You can right-click in the Scale field on the status bar and select a preset viewing size from the shortcut menu, including 200%, 150%, 100%, 75%, 50%, Optimal, Page Width, and Entire Page. Alternatively, you can double-click in the Scale field or select View, Zoom from the menu bar to open the Zoom dialog, which in addition to the listed ratios enables you to set a custom (variable) view size for the current image.

Apart from these menu options, you can also click the Zoom icon on the Draw toolbar to open the Zoom tear-off window, which gives you an added measure of control over your view size. For example, you can click the Zoom In (+) and Zoom Out (-) icons to interactively zoom in and out of your image. To zoom in, you must first click the Zoom In tool (your mouse pointer changes shape into a magnifying glass with a crosshair) and then click the image to select a focal point around which you would like to increase the image. Each click doubles the currently selected view size up to the maximum size possible. You can also click and drag to select an area that you would like to see at optimal view (which means it fills out your workspace). To zoom out, just click the Zoom Out icon. Each click reduces the view size by half.

Note

In StarDraw, unlike StarImage, you can use a Zoom tool only once—even if you double-click the respective Zoom icon. If you want to use a tool repeatedly, you have to activate it again after each click.

To view the slide at its approximate print size, select the Zoom 100% icon.

The Zoom Previous and Zoom Next icons work similarly to the Undo and Redo commands on the Edit menu; after you've changed your views, you can use these commands to return to the previous or next view.

Tip #389 from
Michael & Sarah

You can also press Ctrl+, or Ctrl+. to execute the Zoom Previous and Zoom Next commands, respectively.

Using the Zoom Page and Zoom Page Width commands, you can show the entire page or the entire page width of your slide, respectively. Optimal shows the existing object or group of objects at its optimal (largest possible) view size. The Object Zoom icon is active only after you've selected an object. Clicking this icon displays the selected object at its largest possible size onscreen, including the invisible rectangle around the object.

Finally, you can use the Shift icon to move the draw page up or down or left or right. As soon as you release your mouse button, you can continue using the most recently used tool (provided you double-clicked it). Using the Shift icon is especially useful if you are working with enlarged objects and you want to move quickly to a new or adjacent area.

Tip #390 from
Michael & Sarah

When you're working with graphics—vector-oriented or bitmap—don't pin down your docked windows. That way, the Explorer or Beamer (or Stylist and Navigator, if docked) "glide over" the visual display when opened rather than push it aside, which causes graphics to redraw on your screen. Depending on the view size of the image and your graphic card and memory, this redrawing can be rather annoying.

PART

IV

CH

20

CHOOSING THE RIGHT VIEW FOR THE JOB

StarDraw also includes a Scale configuration option in the Tools, Options, Drawing, Zoom dialog. This option is the key to the Meter, Kilometer, Foot, and Miles units of measurement options in the ruler. For example, if you define your drawing as scaled 1:50 and use a Meter as the unit of measurement, you can draw a line of 1 cm (on screen), and it will measure 500 meter or 0.5 km. This is quite handy if you want to draw accurate ground plans or maps or other architectural or technical drawings, since it saves you the time (and inconvenience) of having to come up with a conversion scale yourself. You'll be able to draw a line of 10 feet and it will only be a few inches on your screen or paper.

Using the Options Drawing Zoom dialog, you can also manually change the width and height of the original plan or object—the scale will adjust automatically, and your current page dimensions are shown in the gray area between the Scale drop-down list and the Original and Width and Height spin boxes. To quickly change the units of measurements, right-click anywhere in the ruler and select the desired unit of measurement.

CHANGING THE DISPLAY QUALITY

Selecting a different display quality enables you to avoid looking at the screaming colors your boss wants you to draw or to get a better idea what your colorful results may look like when they are output to a black-and-white laser printer.

Tip #391 from
Michael & Sarah

Professional drawing packages use the Display Quality feature to boost the performance of the software. Since display quality is video and system memory dependent, display selections can affect the screen refresh speed and performance. For example, choosing a less memory-intensive display enables those users with complex images and slower computers to save time when working with graphics. If you want a performance gain in StarDraw, select the Use Background Cache option in the Tools, Options, Drawing, Other dialog while you're working with graphics or graphic intensive presentations. When this option is turned on, StarOffice keeps background objects in the memory.

You can specify the display quality of elements in your work area by selecting View, Display Quality. Your options include the following:

- **Color**—You can see all fills and objects.
- **Grayscale**—All colors are converted to grayscales.
- **Black and White**—Any colors, grayscales, or fills are hidden. Two-dimensional graphics turn into outlined shapes; three-dimensional graphics resemble wire-frame illustrations.

Tip #392 from
Michael & Sarah

If you feel uncomfortable working in grayscale or black-and-white views, you can always select View, Preview. When you do so, a small Preview window opens above the extended Explorer; there, you can watch the effects of your changes in real-time.

LOOKING AT PREVIEW

Another welcome viewing feature is the floating Preview window. Using the Preview window, you can track changes to the graphic you're working on in real-time, as well as see what the graphic would look like if it were inserted into a presentation.

Note

> A subtle but crucial difference between working in StarDraw and working in StarImpress is the orientation of the slides (or pages) you're working on. StarDraw opens to portrait-oriented slides; StarImpress, by contrast, uses landscape-oriented slides by default, reflecting the height-to-width dimensions of a monitor.

Because the Preview window floats, you can place it anywhere on your desktop. If it gets in the way, you can double-click its title bar to temporarily minimize it. Double-click again to return it to its original size.

To use the Preview window while you're working in StarDraw, select View, Preview from the menu bar. You can adjust the display quality of your Preview window by selecting View, Preview Mode. Your options include Color (default), Grayscale, and Black and White.

UNDERSTANDING COMPUTER GRAPHICS

Computer graphics fall into two main categories: *vector graphics*, which are created in drawing programs such as StarDraw, or *bitmapped images*, which are created in paint or photo-editing programs such as StarImage. You need to understand the difference between the two if you want to create, edit, and import graphic and image files in StarOffice. For example, some file formats support only bitmapped images and others only vector graphics. Depending on the format you choose, you will be limited by what you can do with each file. Graphic formats also affect the size of files and the filters and effects you can apply to them.

→ For more details on graphics file formats in StarOffice, **see** Appendix B, "File Formats and Extensions," **p. 1395**.

The following sections present the basic concepts of a vector-based program such as StarDraw and outline the differences between vector graphics and bitmapped images such as the ones you work with in StarImage.

WHAT IS A VECTOR GRAPHIC?

Vector graphics, also known as *object-oriented* or *draw images*, are made of lines and curves defined by mathematical objects called *vectors*. Vectors describe graphics according to their geometric characteristics. For example, a donut in a vector graphic is made up of a mathematical definition of a circle drawn with a certain radius, set at a specific location, and filled with a specific color. Because each object is a self-contained entity, you can move, resize, or change the color of the donut without losing the quality of the graphic (see Figure 20.6). These characteristics make a vector-based program such as StarDraw ideal for illustration and 3D modeling, where the design process often requires individual objects to be created and manipulated.

PART

IV

CH

20

Figure 20.6
When working with vector graphics, you can change the size or color of an image without losing its original clarity and crispness.

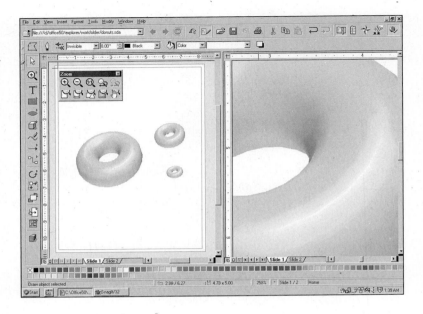

WHAT IS A BITMAP IMAGE?

Bitmap images, also called *raster images*, are made up of a collection of small, individually colored squares, known as pixels. Unlike vector graphics (where the image is a composite of objects such as rectangles or circles), bitmapped images are "mapped" directly from corresponding bits within the computer's memory (hence, the name). Thus, when you're working with bitmapped images, you edit pixels rather than objects or shapes.

Bitmaps can represent subtle gradations of shades and color. Hence, they are the most popular electronic medium for continuous-tone images such as photographs or images created in painting programs.

Unlike vector graphics, however, bitmaps are resolution dependent. *Resolution* (the number of pixels per inch) is an umbrella term that refers to the amount of detail and information an image file contains, as well as the level of detail an input, output, or display device is capable of producing. For example, a donut in a bitmapped image is made up of a fixed number of pixels, with each pixel part of a mosaic that gives the appearance of a donut. When you look at the image from a greater distance, the color and shape appear continuous and smooth. However, when you zoom in, you can see the individual squares that make up the total image (see Figure 20.7). You can see them because increasing the size of a bitmap has the effect of increasing individual pixels, making lines and shapes appear jagged.

Figure 20.7
Bitmapped images appear jagged and lose detail if they are scaled onscreen or if they are printed at a higher resolution than they were created for.

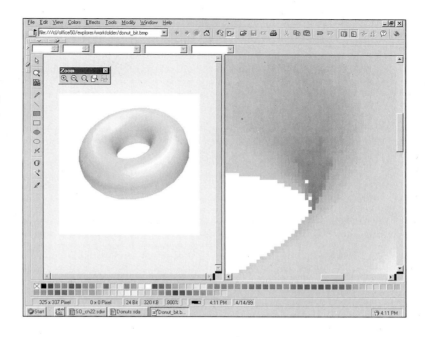

KNOWING WHEN TO USE STARDRAW AND STARIMAGE

Drawing programs and painting programs each have their strengths and weaknesses. The strength of a painting program is that it offers an extremely straightforward approach to creating images; its core painting tools are as easy to use as a pencil. The downside of a painting program is that it limits your resolution options. Whether you print a bitmap file to a 300 dpi laser printer or a 1270 dpi imagesetter, the file prints at the resolution you set when you created the image, unless the printer resolution is lower than the image resolution. Hence, working with painting programs requires some planning.

A drawing program, by contrast, creates a graphic out of mathematically defined lines and shapes that can be scaled to any size and printed on any output device at any resolution without losing their original clarity or detail. The drawing program sends the math to the printer driver, and the printer driver renders the math to paper.

Thanks to their specialized methods, drawing programs and painting programs fulfill distinct and divergent purposes. Drawing programs such as StarDraw are best suited to creating more stylized artwork such as the following:

- Traditional logos and text effects that require crisp and smooth edges
- Business graphics such as charts and other visual representations that reflect data or show how things work

PART

IV

CH

20

- Architectural plans, product designs, or other precise line drawings (note that the Gallery folder includes many clip art files that you can use for architectural and product designs)
- Brochures, flyers, and other single-page documents that mingle artwork, logos, and standardized text
- Poster art and high-contrast graphics that heighten the appearance of reality

By contrast, painting programs such as StarImage are best suited to creating and editing the following kinds of artwork:

- Scanned photos and other realistic artwork that relies on the play between naturalistic highlights, midranges, and shadows
- Impressionistic-type artwork and other images created for purely personal or aesthetic purposes
- Special effects that require the use of filters and color enhancements you simply can't achieve in a drawing program
- Nearly any graphic or photograph you intend to post on the World Wide Web

When you've stepped this far into the virtual space of StarOffice, you'll soon realize that StarDraw and StarImage are the final cogs in the mighty wheel of StarOffice modules used to create impressive documents and presentations that are guaranteed to garner the attention of your readers.

Working with Graphic Objects

StarDraw (as well as StarImpress) works its magic by looking at artwork in terms of mathematically defined objects. Each line, shape, or text element you introduce in your drawing is an object. When you combine these objects into a drawing, you are constructing (rather than drawing) a graphic because you actually build lines and shapes point by point and then stack them on top of each other to create the final graphic. Because StarDraw defines lines, shapes, and text as mathematical equations, you can edit each object independently. The following sections cover the various ways you can manipulate the components of each object-oriented drawing, individually or as a group.

Selecting an Object

Selecting objects is one of the most basic tasks in StarDraw. If you want to select an object, StarDraw must be in the regular Selection mode. You can tell which mode you're in by looking at the Draw main toolbar. When the Select icon (the one with the white arrow) is pressed in, you're in Selection mode; if it is not pressed in, you're most likely in Draw mode.

Tip #393 from
Michael & Sarah

> You can always tell whether you're in Draw mode. Your mouse pointer changes shape to a symbol that corresponds to the selected drawing tool.

A selection can consist of a single object or a group of objects. To select a filled, single object, click anywhere inside the drawing object; to select an outlined, single object, you have to click the outline or border of the object. If you want to select more than one object, press the Shift key while selecting objects. If you want to select multiple objects that are in close proximity, click in a corner outside the grouping, and drag a selection rectangle around the objects; a dotted box appears around the selected area. As soon as you release the mouse button, the dotted box disappears, and the objects that were located inside the parameters of the box are selected. If the objects have been grouped or combined using the Group or Combine command, you can click anywhere inside the group to select the grouped or combined unit.

Tip #394 from
Michael & Sarah

> Turning off Double-Click Text to Edit in the option bar (the button that shows the letters *ABC* and the hand) makes selecting groups even easier.

When you select an object or group of objects, it appears in the drawing window with eight green sizing handles around it—four in each corner and one between each corner pair—identifying the object's bounding box.

To deselect an object or group of objects, just click anywhere on your workspace, outside the object or group of objects.

Moving and Copying Objects

You can move any object or group of objects by selecting the object or objects and then dragging it or them to the desired location. As you click and drag your object or group of objects, the mouse pointer changes shape to a four-directional arrow. To move more than one object at a time, draw a selection rectangle around the objects you want to move, and then click and drag any object of the group to move all objects at once; the objects maintain their position in relation to each other as you move the group.

Tip #395 from
Michael & Sarah

> To move your objects with more precision, select Grid Visible from the Draw context menu. Then select the object or group of objects, and use the arrow keys to move your selection.

To move an object numerically by the numbers, select and right-click the object, and then choose Position and Size from the context menu. Using the Position tab of the resulting dialog, you can specify new horizontal and vertical values for the X and Y coordinates of the base point of your object. The base point is indicated with a red dot in the Graphic Option field on the right. Here, you can also define a new base point by clicking one of the sur-

PART

IV

CH

20

rounding white points. To prevent your object from being repositioned by dragging with the mouse, select the Protect option.

When you're moving objects in other modules, you can make a copy of the object by holding the Ctrl key while dragging. You can do the same in StarDraw after you've made a minor adjustment to the default settings. Open the Tools, Options, Drawing, Other dialog, select Copy When Moved in the Other portion of the dialog, and click OK to return to your drawing. You can now make a copy of your selection by pressing Ctrl while dragging.

If you need more than one copy of an object, you can use the familiar copy-and-paste routine: Select the desired object, press Ctrl+C (Edit, Copy) and then Ctrl+V (Edit, Paste). StarDraw pastes a copy on top of the original object. You can then drag the copy to its new location. You can press Ctrl+V for as many times as you need copies; all copies appear stacked on top of each other, and you can drag one after another to its new location.

If you want to move a copy to a new slide or page, make a copy of the selected object first; then open the new slide or page, and press Ctrl+V. StarDraw inserts the copy at the same coordinates as in the original slide.

DUPLICATING OBJECTS

Duplicating objects is similar to copying objects. When you create a duplicate of an object, StarDraw places the duplicate on top of the original. The first time you use the Duplicate command, StarDraw offsets the duplicate by .20 inch down and to the right of the original object. You can change the amount of the offset in the Duplicate dialog box, shown in Figure 20.8. Using the Duplicate command, you can try out effects on the duplicate object without risking your original. If you don't like the results, you can simply delete the duplicate. Or you can create a duplicate of a line of text or other object, give it a different color than the original, and place it slightly off the original to create a cool shadowing effect.

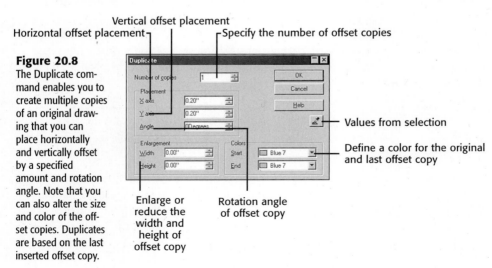

Figure 20.8
The Duplicate command enables you to create multiple copies of an original drawing that you can place horizontally and vertically offset by a specified amount and rotation angle. Note that you can also alter the size and color of the offset copies. Duplicates are based on the last inserted offset copy.

Horizontal offset placement
Vertical offset placement
Specify the number of offset copies
Values from selection
Define a color for the original and last offset copy
Enlarge or reduce the width and height of offset copy
Rotation angle of offset copy

You can also use the Duplicate feature to create and place repeating patterns. For example, if you need to place horizontal lines half an inch apart on a business form, you can specify 0 inch for the horizontal placement and .5 inch for the vertical placement of duplicate objects and then specify the number of copies. After you draw a single line, the Duplicate command places successive duplicates precisely half an inch apart on the drawing page. Or you can create cool visual effects by rotating the repeating patterns. Figure 20.9 shows two possible applications of the Duplicate feature.

Figure 20.9
Two sample applications of the Duplicate command: In the example at the top, the y-axis value is 0.5 inch; all other values are zero. In the example below, we generated 38 offset duplicates. We used -0.10 for the x-axis value and 5 degrees for the rotation angle. For the Start color, we used Blue 7; the End color is Yellow.

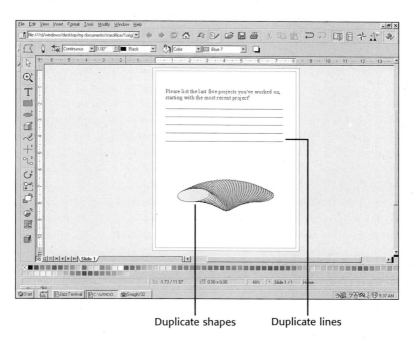

Duplicate shapes   Duplicate lines

To duplicate an object, first select the object, and then choose Edit, Duplicate. Using the x-axis and y-axis spin boxes in the Placement portion of the Duplicate dialog box, you can specify the amount by which you want to offset the duplicate copy. Enter positive values if you want to offset the object to the right (x-axis) and down (y-axis); negative values offset the copy to the left and up, respectively. Using the Angle spin box, you can also specify an angle by which the duplicate will be rotated around its center.

In the Enlargement area of the Duplicate dialog, you can specify whether you want the offset copy to be larger or smaller than the original. Positive values in the Width and Height spin boxes result in a larger copy; negative values result in a smaller one.

In the Colors portion of the dialog, you can define colors for the first object and last object. If you select the same color in the Start and End spin boxes, duplicates may differ only in terms of size and placement. If you select different colors in the Start and End boxes, the first object shows the color listed in the Start box, and the last object shows the color in the End box. If you're creating multiple copies, the color will gradually transition from the first to the last object based on median values.

Clicking the Values from Selection icon (underneath the Cancel button) enters the width and height and color of a selected object into the x-axis and y-axis and Start color spin boxes. Using this option, you can create a series of diagonally placed repeating objects (see Figure 20.10).

Figure 20.10
The Value from Selection option enables you to create a series of repeating shapes of the same object(s).

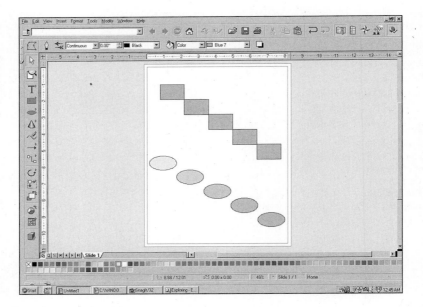

RESIZING OBJECTS HORIZONTALLY, VERTICALLY, AND PROPORTIONALLY

Each two-dimensional object is surrounded by invisible rectangular bounding boxes that define the dimensions of the shape of the objects when you select it. (Note that if the object is a square or rectangle, these boxes coincide with the outline of the object.) To resize (or scale) objects, click the Select tool to switch from a Draw mode into the regular Selection mode; then click the object you want to scale. You see eight selection handles—one in each corner and one centered between each corner pair. Dragging a handle on either center side enlarges or reduces the width of an object; dragging a handle on the center top or bottom scales the height of an object. Dragging any of the corner handles scales both the width and height of the object. If you press Shift while dragging any of the handles, you scale the object proportionally.

If you want to size or stretch an object with numeric precision, select and right-click the object you want to scale, and choose Position and Size from the context menu. Using the Size tab of the Position and Size dialog box, you can specify a new number in the Width and Height spin boxes (see Figure 20.11). If you want to adjust the width and height of the selected object proportionally, select Match. If you want to "lock" the size of your object so that it cannot be changed by dragging with the mouse, select the Protect option. Using the Graphic Option field on the right, you can also click a white point to specify a base point in relation to which the object will be sized. The current base point is shown as a red dot.

Specify the width and height of the object

Figure 20.11
Using the Size tab of the Position and Size dialog, you can scale an object with numeric precision.

Click to scale the object proportionally

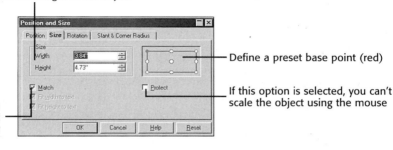

Define a preset base point (red)

If this option is selected, you can't scale the object using the mouse

ROTATING AND SKEWING OBJECTS

Rotating or skewing an object is as simple as scaling it. Just click the Effects icon on the Draw toolbar, and select the Rotate icon (circular arrow) from the Effects floating toolbar. Then click the object that you want to rotate. As soon as you click the object, you see eight red handles surrounding your object—four round corner handles and four rhombus-shaped ones between each pair of corner handles. In the center of the selected object is the pivot point.

Note

At any one time, you can have only one pivot point per slide or page. This has the advantage that you can rotate multiple objects around the same rotation point. If you double-click an object, the pivot point is moved to its center.

Tip #396 from
Michael & Sarah

When the object is already selected, you can also click to switch to the Rotation mode; click again, and you're back in Selection mode. However, this is only possible if the Rotation Mode After Clicking Object button (third button from the right) on the option bar is on. For more details on the option bar, see "Using the Option" bar in this chapter.

PART
IV
CH
20

ROTATING AN OBJECT

To rotate an object, click and drag the round corner handles clockwise or counterclockwise. You can also click and drag inside the frame of a 3D object for a different rotation effect. As you rotate the object, an outlined bounding box appears, and the Command field of the status bar shows the current rotation angle. When you release the mouse button, the rotation is finished, and the object appears at a new angle (see Figure 20.12).

Tip #397 from
Michael & Sarah

Pressing the Ctrl key while you're dragging creates a copy of the original object and then rotates or skews the copy (provided the Copy When Moved option is selected in the Tools, Options, Drawing, Other dialog). Pressing the Shift key while you're dragging forces the rotation to increments of 15 degrees. If you want, you can change this constraint value by selecting When Rotating in the Snap Position portion of the Tools, Option, Drawing, Snap to Grid dialog and specifying a new value in the accompanying spin box.

Figure 20.12
Drag the round (rotation) handles to rotate an object clockwise or counterclockwise. When you click a rotation handle, your cursor changes shape into a circular double arrow.

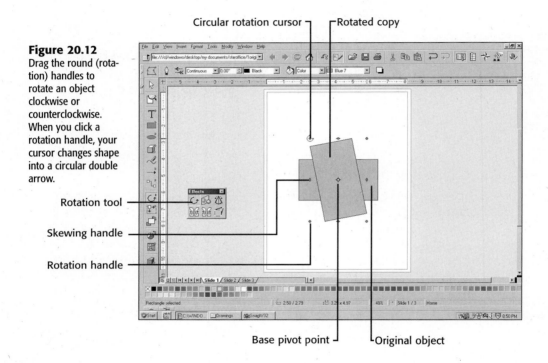

Circular rotation cursor — ┌Rotated copy

Rotation tool

Skewing handle

Rotation handle

Base pivot point ┘ └Original object

SKEWING AN OBJECT

When you skew (or slant) a selected object, you slant it horizontally or vertically. The result can make objects appear to recede from the viewer, giving especially two-dimensional objects the appearance of depth. You can skew only polygons and Bézier curves. If the object you want to skew is neither one, the program asks whether you want to convert it to a curve or polygon.

To skew an object, click and drag the rhombus-shaped skewing handles clockwise or counterclockwise. Similar to when you're rotating an object, you can see an outlined, skewed bounding box as well as the slant angle in the Command field in the status bar while you're dragging the object. When you release the mouse button, the object appears slanted at a new angle, as shown in Figure 20.13.

Tip #398 from
Michael & Sarah

Whether you're rotating or skewing an object, you can click and drag the base rotation (or anchor) point anywhere on your drawing surface. As you rotate your object, it moves in a circle around the new pivot point location. Changing the pivot point, you can create some really great effects.

Figure 20.13
Drag the rhombus-shaped (skewing) handles to skew an object clockwise or counterclockwise. When you click a skewing handle, your cursor changes shape into two parallel arrows pointing in opposite directions.

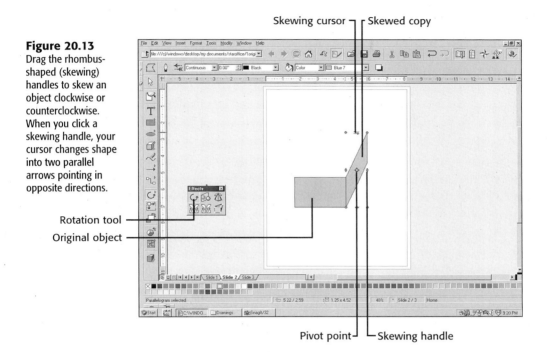

Skewing cursor ⎤ ⎡ Skewed copy

Rotation tool

Original object

Pivot point ⎦ ⎣ Skewing handle

ROTATING AND SKEWING AN OBJECT WITH PRECISION

Instead of rotating or skewing your object interactively, you can also achieve the same effect with much more precision by defining a pivot point and rotation or slant angle in the Position and Size dialog box, shown in Figure 20.14.

Using the Rotation tab of the Position and Size dialog, you can specify the rotation angle as well as how you want an object to rotate. By default, StarDraw rotates objects around the center of rotation. However, using the Position X and Position Y spin boxes, you can specify new coordinates for the pivot point.

Using the Slant & Corner Radius tab, you can define the angle by which to slant the object, as well as a corner radius for the object to round the corners of a rectangle or square.

PART
IV

CH
20

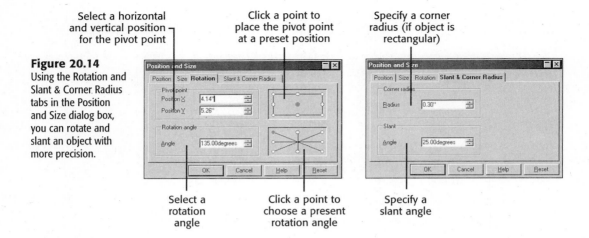

Figure 20.14
Using the Rotation and Slant & Corner Radius tabs in the Position and Size dialog box, you can rotate and slant an object with more precision.

Select a horizontal and vertical position for the pivot point

Click a point to place the pivot point at a preset position

Specify a corner radius (if object is rectangular)

Select a rotation angle

Click a point to choose a present rotation angle

Specify a slant angle

DISTORTING AND CURVING OBJECTS

While we're at it, we may as well point out three more effects that you can apply to text and other objects: the Set in Circle (Perspective), Set in Circle (Slant), and Distort effects (see Figure 22.15 for examples). Applying these effects is as easy as applying the Rotation effect. You click the Effects icon on the Draw toolbar and select the desired icon from the Effects floating toolbar. Then you click the object that you want to set on a curve or distort. As soon as you click the object, you see eight green handles surrounding your object. In the case of the Distort tool, you see four square corner handles and four rhombus-shaped ones between each pair of corner handles (Distort); in the case of the Set on Curve tools, you see eight square handles. To achieve the desired effect, just click a handle, and drag it into a new position.

MORPHING OBJECTS

Morphing is another trick that is part of StarDraw's magic repertoire. *Morphing* refers to the transition by shape of one object to another so that it appears that one transforms into the other. You can morph two separate, selected objects by choosing Edit, Morphing from the menu bar. In the Morphing dialog box, you can specify the number of increments (or steps) for the morphing effect. If you want to retain object attributes such as line and fill color, select the Fade Object Attributes option. This way, you achieve a gradual transition from one attribute to another if both objects have different attributes. To maintain the direction of your rotation, select the Same Orientation options; otherwise, morphing occurs in opposite directions. Figure 20.16 shows two sample applications of the Morphing command, one with and one without the Same Orientation option selected. (Note that the Morphing tool is only available in StarDraw, not in StarImpress.)

Figure 20.15
More magic tricks up
the StarDraw sleeve:
using the Effects tools,
you can set objects on
a curve or distort
them.

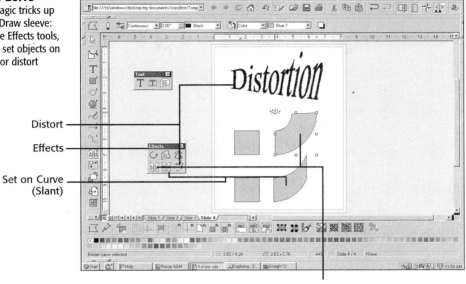

Distort

Effects

Set on Curve
(Slant)

Set on Curve
(Perspective)

Figure 20.16
Using the Morphing
dialog, you can
achieve cool transi-
tional effects. The
object on the top
right has been mor-
phed with the Same
Rotation option
selected; the one on
the bottom left has
been morphed with-
out this option
selected.

Select to gradually
fade attributes from
first to second object

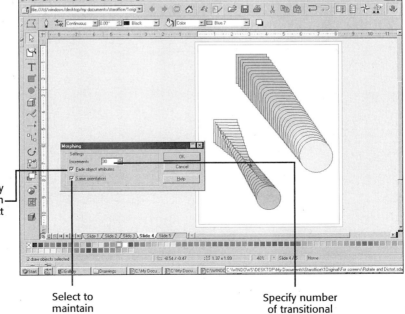

Select to
maintain
direction of
rotation

Specify number
of transitional
shapes

MIRRORING OBJECTS

By mirroring objects, you can reverse their appearance by flipping the objects. For example, using the Modify, Flip command, you can mirror an object or text string horizontally or vertically so that it appears reversed or upside down, respectively. Alternatively, you can also select the Flip tool from the Effects floating toolbar to mirror objects and text in relation to a mirror axis. For example, to achieve the effect shown in Figure 20.17, follow these steps:

1. Select the Text tool (large T), click the drawing surface, and enter the desired text.

2. Format the text as needed by using the Format, Character dialog. (In the example, we chose the Outline font effect, Times New Roman, 24-point type size, and Turquoise as the font color.)

3. Convert the text into a graphic object by selecting Modify, Convert, Convert to Curve. (This step is necessary because you can use StarDraw's Effects tools only on vector-based objects.)

4. Select the text object, and then choose the Flip tool from the Effects floating toolbar. You see a black line with two crosshair-like circles at both ends cutting vertically through the middle of the text object. Your mouse pointer changes shape into a hand with a pointing finger when the pointer is above the crosshair circle.

5. Click and drag the top end of the line, and align it with the lower-right corner of the bounding box of the text object. Then click and drag the bottom end of the line, and align it with the bottom-left corner of the bounding box. You have now created an axis along which you can mirror the text object.

6. Click the lower-left corner handle of your text object, and drag it across the axis. StarDraw creates a mirrored copy of the original object.

7. You can now select each object individually and apply different attributes to it. In our example, we chose a Bitmap area fill for the object at the top and a light blue color for the mirrored object on the bottom.

Of course, you can also mirror (or flip) objects to create symmetrical shapes (and ease your workload). Figure 20.18, for example, shows a polygon with layered color effects that has been mirrored along a vertical axis to create the body of an ocean liner. After the polygon is flipped, each half was assigned slightly different color attributes to create a more natural, three-dimensional effect. You can look at this figure (ship.sda) in the Samples, Drawings folder of StarOffice (which is located in the Explorer group).

ARRANGING, GROUPING, AND COMBINING OBJECTS

Arranging objects in relationship to one another is one of the key advantages of using a vector program such as StarDraw for creating drawings. StarDraw enables you to arrange the stacking order of overlapping objects, as well as to group objects, which means they retain their physical locations in relation to other objects in the group. When objects are grouped, you can move and transform them as a unit, or you can select individual objects within the group to edit.

Figure 20.17
Using the Flip tool on the Effects floating toolbar, you can create cool mirroring effects.

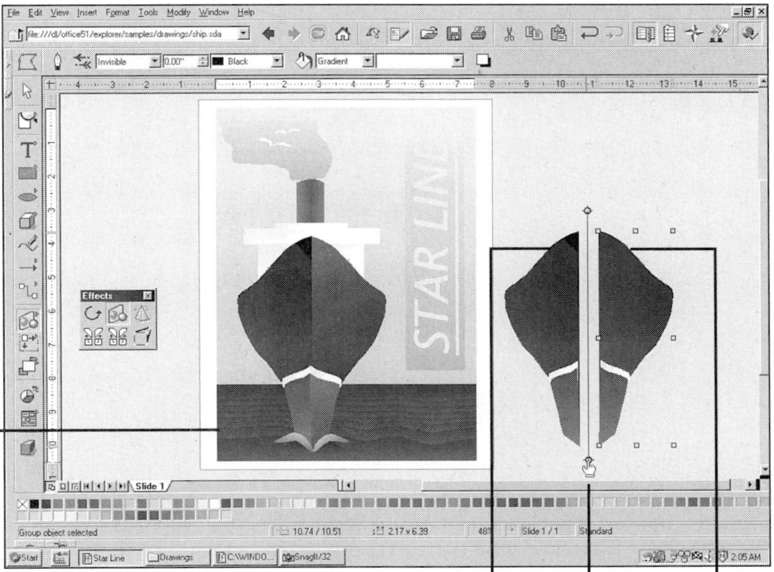

Original text

Effects icon and floating toolbar

Flip tool

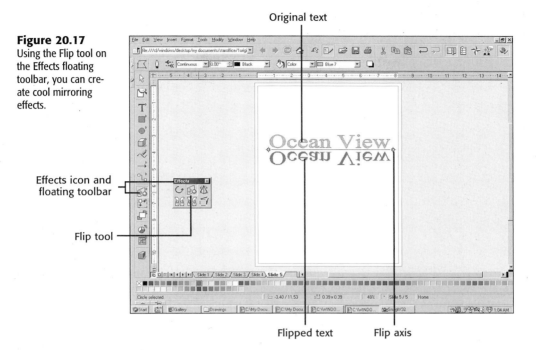

Flipped text   Flip axis

Figure 20.18
The body of the ocean liner in this example was created by interactively flipping a polygon along a vertical axis. The two separate halves were then moved closer together to give the illusion of one solid shape.

Original drawing

Left side of   Mirrored right
the ship body   side of the body

Mirror axis

ARRANGING OBJECTS

To change the stacking order of objects (or arrange objects), select an object in the stack of objects; then choose Modify, Arrange or click the Arrange icon on the main toolbar. Both the Arrange submenu and the Arrange floating toolbar give you the following options:

- **Bring to Front**—Moves the selected objects all the way to the front (top) of the stack of objects. The keyboard shortcut is Ctrl+Shift++.

- **Bring Forward**—Moves the selected objects one "layer" closer to the front (top) of the stack of objects. The keyboard shortcut is Ctrl++.

- **Send Backward**—Moves the selected objects one "layer" closer to the back (bottom) of the stack of objects. The keyboard shortcut is Ctrl+-.

- **Send to Back**—Moves the selected objects all the way to the back (bottom) of the stack of objects. The keyboard shortcut is Ctrl+Shift+-.

- **In Front of Object**—Positions the selected object(s) in front of another object. To use this command, you first have to select the objects you want to move to the front. Next, select the In Front of Object command, and then click the object that will be moved behind the selected object(s).

- **Behind Object**—Positions the selected object(s) behind another object. To use this command, you first have to select the objects you want to move to the back. Next, select the Behind Object command, and then click the object that will be moved in front of the selected object(s).

- **Reverse**—Reverses the stacking order of selected objects.

> **Note**
>
> You can also change the stacking order of more than one object at once by clicking the Shift key while selecting your objects. That way, you can move the objects as a group.

Figure 20.19 shows various possibilities of arranging three objects in relation to each other.

USING THE GROUP AND UNGROUP COMMANDS

Groups consist of a selection of two or more objects. You can use the Group command to create an ordered array of selected objects. The resulting group of objects behaves as a single unit. When you move the group, each object maintains its spatial relationship to the other objects within the group; when you apply other transformations on them (such as changing color or line attributes and the like), each object in the group is transformed. Grouping objects is useful when you want to apply formatting or other actions such as resizing all the objects in a group. It's also useful when you've finished work in one area of your graphic and you want to protect the individual elements against changes. You can have as many objects in a group as you like.

To group objects, you must first select the objects you want to group by using the Select tool and drawing a selection rectangle around the objects. Then select Modify, Group from the menu bar, or press Ctrl+Shift+G.

Figure 20.19
StarDraw enables you to do what you can only dream of in StarImage: change the stacking order of your drawings.

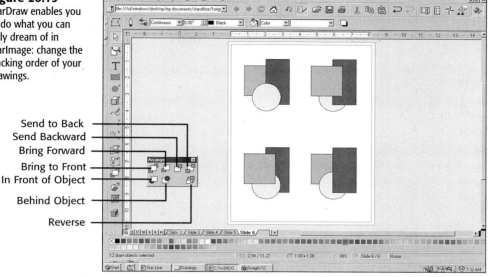

Send to Back
Send Backward
Bring Forward
Bring to Front
In Front of Object
Behind Object
Reverse

Tip #399 from
Michael & Sarah

You can also create a nest of groups or groups within a group or groups. Simply select the first group of objects, and group them by selecting Modify, Group from the menu bar. Then select this group and the next group of objects, and choose Modify, Group again and so on. Note that nested groups require more memory than individual objects do to refresh and display them.

To separate an existing group into its individual objects, simply select the group you want to ungroup, and then select Modify, Ungroup or press Alt+Ctrl+Shift+G. If the group you want to break down contains a group within a group, the nested group continues to exist as a group until you select it and choose Modify, Ungroup again.

Note

StarDraw does not contain a command that enables you to ungroup all selected groups, including nested groups, at once.

Also, you cannot edit a group using the Bézier edit options. If you want to edit the control points of a Bézier object, you first have to ungroup the group or select Edit Group to enter the group.

Editing Groups

StarDraw also enables you to edit the individual objects within a group without ungrouping them. To edit a single object within a group, select the group of objects, and then choose Modify, Edit Group or press F3. You can then select the objects in your group individually and modify them as desired. When you're finished applying your changes, select Modify, Exit Group, or press Ctrl+F3. StarDraw then "locks" all objects into a single unit again. If you want to edit a nested group, you have to select the nested group and choose Modify, Edit Group again.

COMBINING OBJECTS

Combining objects is similar to grouping objects, except that the objects might not retain their original attributes. For example, if you change the attribute of one or more objects after they are created and then combine the objects using the Combine command, each object assumes the attributes of the object that was created first. Note also that overlapping areas between objects that are stacked on top of each other are "knocked out." Figure 20.20 shows an example of three combined objects, two of which—the circle and the vertical rectangle—have been changed after their original creation: We stretched the elongated rectangle vertically and assigned a different fill color to it; we also changed the line width of the circle and added a fill color to it.

Figure 20.20
Using the Alignment floating toolbar, you can quickly align objects horizontally (left column) and vertically (right column).

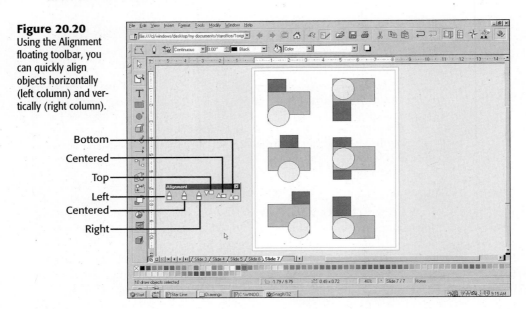

To combine objects, select the objects you want to combine, and then choose Modify, Combine or press Ctrl+Shift+K. Using the Modify, Split command (Alt+Ctrl+Shift+K), you can separate a combined object group into individual objects; each object retains the attributes of the combined group.

> **Note**
>
> When you combine or split objects, the existing objects are turned into Bézier curves. When you click the Edit Points icon on the Draw object bar and select a combined object, the Draw object bar is replaced by the Bézier object bar. You can now edit the combined or split object as you would any other Bézier object or curve.

ALIGNING OBJECTS

Similar to StarWriter, StarDraw enables you to align your objects horizontally and vertically in relation to the left/right and top/bottom margins of your drawing page. To align one or more objects, select the object(s) you want to align, click the Alignment icon on the main toolbar, and then choose the desired alignment option from the Alignment floating toolbar or select the desired option from the Modify, Alignment submenu. If the objects are part of a group, you can change only the overall alignment of the group; individual objects within the group are not aligned.

Your horizontal alignment options include the following:

- **Left**—Objects are aligned with their left sides along the leftmost side of the bounding box.
- **Centered**—Objects are aligned horizontally along their center points.
- **Bottom**—Objects are aligned with their right sides along the side of the bounding box that is closest to the right margin.

Your vertical alignment options include the following:

- **Top**—Objects are aligned with their top sides along the side of the bounding box that is closest to the top margin.
- **Centered**—Objects are aligned vertically along their center points.
- **Bottom**—Objects are aligned with their bottom sides along the side of the bounding box that is closest to the bottom margin.

If you apply the Alignment command to a single object, you align it exactly with the right or left (top or bottom) margin of your page or center it horizontally (vertically) between the left and right (top and bottom) margins, depending on your alignment choice. If you left/top or right/bottom align it, the left/top or right/bottom border of the object or bounding box nudges the respective margins. If you center align it, the center point of the object is placed horizontally or vertically between the left and right or top and bottom margins, respectively.

Figure 20.21 shows your various alignment options at a glance.

DELETING OBJECTS

Getting rid of stuff is always easier than building it. Simply select the object you want to delete, and press the Delete key.

PART

IV

CH

20

Figure 20.21
Similar in function to the Group command, the Combine command does unite separate objects into one unit; however, if you change the attributes of individual objects, these attributes are lost after you use the Combine command, and the objects assume the attributes of the first-drawn object.

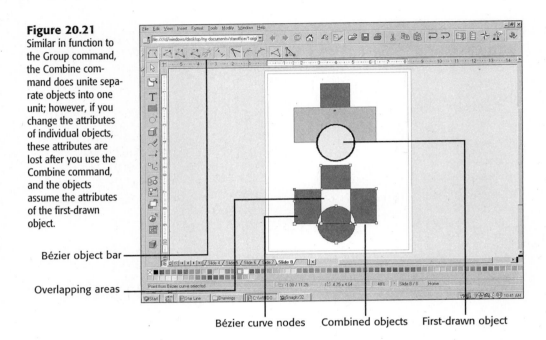

Bézier object bar

Overlapping areas

Bézier curve nodes   Combined objects   First-drawn object

USING THE BASIC DRAWING TOOLS

StarDraw offers a finite number of tools that enable you to create an infinite variety of objects. Using these drawing tools, you can draw geometric shapes and freeform shapes with equal ease. The final result may be as "simple" as a construction blueprint for your next apartment (refer to Figure 20.5) or as complex as a jazzy festival poster (refer to Figure 20.4).

Tip #400 from
Michael & Sarah

If you want to cancel the current drawing process, just press Esc at any time.

USING THE GEOMETRIC DRAWING TOOLS

StarDraw comes with two sets of tools for drawing two-dimensional geometric shapes: the Rectangle and the Ellipse tools. In addition, you can also draw a variety of curves and three-dimensional objects by using the Curves and 3D Objects tool sets.

Tip #401 from
Michael & Sarah

As you are creating your drawing object, keep an eye on the Selection field on the status bar; it informs you about the size of the current rectangle.

WORKING WITH THE RECTANGLE TOOL

 Working with the Rectangle tool enables you to create outlined and filled rectangles and squares with or without rounded corners.

Tip #402 from Michael & Sarah	You can also round the corners of a selected rectangle after the fact by clicking the Edit Points icon on the object bar. The moment you click the Edit Points icon, the green sizing handles of your rectangle turn into blue nodes. When you move your mouse pointer over the larger corner node (which indicates the original starting point of your rectangle), it changes shape into a hand. To round the corners of your rectangle, click and drag this corner node toward the center of your rectangle. As you drag, you round all four corners of your rectangle equally. Release your mouse button when the rounded corners are the desired shape.

To draw a filled or outlined rectangle or square, click the respective tool in the Rectangles floating toolbar. Then click in a location in the slide draw area, and drag diagonally to the desired size. As you drag, you'll notice the outline of a small rectangle or square in the lower-right corner of your pointer. When you release your mouse button, you see your shape complete with selection handles.

Tip #403 from Michael & Sarah	If you press the Shift key while drawing the rectangle, you can draw a square as well as flip the object along the vertical line that cuts through your starting point by dragging with the mouse. If you press the Alt key while drawing the rectangle, the beginning point of your drag becomes the center point of your rectangle.

WORKING WITH THE ELLIPSE TOOL

 Working with the Ellipse tool enables you to create ellipses, circles, arcs, and segments. You can edit these shapes by using the Edit Points command on the object bar or the Object context menu. Each shape is surrounded by an invisible rectangular bounding box, which defines the dimensions of the shape.

Drawing an ellipse or circle is similar to drawing a rectangle or square. Select the desired tool from the Ellipses floating toolbar, click in a starting location on the drawing slide, and then drag the mouse pointer diagonally away from the starting point. As you drag, you'll notice the outline of an ellipse or circle in the lower-left corner of your crosshair cursor.

Drawing a filled/outlined ellipse or circle pie/segment or arc involves a few more steps:

1. Select the respective tool. Then click in a starting location on the drawing slide, and drag diagonally away from the starting point. As you drag, you'll notice the outline of the selected tool in the lower-right corner of your crosshair pointer.

2. When the shape is the desired size, release the mouse button. You then see a closed circular or elliptical shape.

3. Move the pointer toward the center of your shape. You then see the radius of the shape—a straight line that runs from the center of your shape in the direction of your pointer and stops at the boundary of the ellipse, circle, or arc. When you move your pointer, the line follows your movement.

4. Click once to define a starting point for your pie, segment, or arc.

5. Move your pointer in a circular motion around the center point—clockwise or counter-clockwise—to define the shape or outline of a pie or segment.

6. To finish your pie, segment, or arc, click again when the shape or outline is the desired size. Your object appears surrounded by the familiar eight sizing handles.

CREATING 3D OBJECTS

 As the French Impressionist painter Paul Cézanne once said, "everything in nature can be looked at in terms of cylinders, cones, and spheres." Drawing 3D objects is just as simple as drawing rectangles and ellipses. Click the respective tool in the 3D Objects floating toolbar, click in a location in the slide draw area, and then drag diagonally to the desired size. When you let go of your mouse button, you see your 3D shape complete with selection handles.

Note

StarOffice comes with a sophisticated 3D engine that supports the OpenGL standard. OpenGL represents a 3D graphics language, initially developed by Silicon Graphics Inc. (SGI). Note that two dialects of this language are commonly used: Microsoft OpenGL, developed for the use in Windows NT and supported by Windows 95b and Windows 98, and Cosmo OpenGL made by SGI. The latter represents an independent graphics language for all platforms and all kind of computers, and can even be used on machines without special 3D graphics hardware.

Although using the 3D Objects tools is pretty straightforward, you should be aware of the following options. If you press the Shift key while using the Cube or Sphere tools, you get a perfectly shaped cube or sphere; otherwise, the final result is a rectangular solid (or cuboid) or elliptical solid, respectively. Likewise, pressing the Shift key while using the Torus, Shell, and Half-Sphere tools guarantees that you draw a perfectly shaped torus, shell, or half-sphere.

Note

If you select Continuous from the Line Style drop-down list on the object bar, you can see the longitudinal and latitudinal lines that define most 3D forms.

Tip #404 from
Michael & Sarah

By the default, the Pyramid tool creates a pyramid with four base corners. If you want a pyramid with three base corners, click the 3D Controller tool on the main toolbar, click the Geometry button (second from the left), and enter 3 in the Segments, Horizontal spin box. For more details on the using the 3D controller, see "Creating 3D Effects" in this chapter.

Figure 20.22 shows the various 3D shapes you can create using the 3D tools.

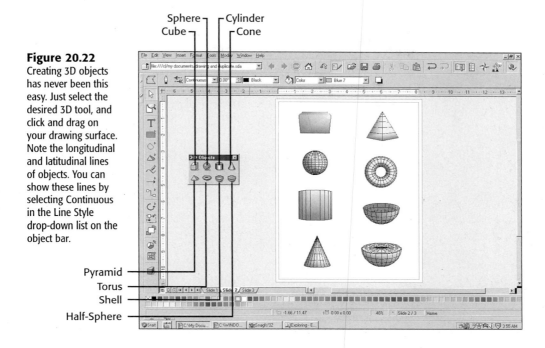

Figure 20.22
Creating 3D objects has never been this easy. Just select the desired 3D tool, and click and drag on your drawing surface. Note the longitudinal and latitudinal lines of objects. You can show these lines by selecting Continuous in the Line Style drop-down list on the object bar.

MERGING 3D OBJECTS Never say StarOffice doesn't have enough options. As if the capability to create 3D effects weren't enough, you can also easily combine 3D objects by following these steps:

1. Draw the first desired 3D object (for example, a cube).

2. Draw a second 3D object (for example, a sphere), but make it somewhat bigger than the first one.

3. Select the second object (sphere), and press Ctrl+X.

4. Select the first object (cube), and press F3. This way, you virtually step inside the first object.

5. Press Ctrl+V to paste the second object inside the first one. To return to your drawing surface, press Ctrl+F3.

CONVERTING 2D OBJECTS TO 3D OBJECTS StarDraw also enables you to convert 2D objects into 3D objects, allowing groups of vector and bitmapped images to be converted directly. During the conversion process, the 2D depth orientation (foreground and background) is used as information in case more than one object is converted. This is done to

PART
IV

CH

20

create a group consisting of various 3D objects with different depth. During the conversion, the visibility of the 2D presentation is preserved. To convert 2D drawings, bitmaps, and metafiles into 3D objects, use the commands on the Modify, Convert submenu. The following are your options:

- **Convert to 3D**—This command transforms the two-dimensional object into a three-dimensional extrusion. The object is "pulled" into a third dimension perpendicular to its two-dimensional surface. You can rotate the new object freely, using the Rotate tool in the effects window. If the original drawing consists of more than one element, or if you select more than one drawing to be converted into 3D, StarDraw converts all elements or drawings as one 3D group. To modify individual elements of this group, open the group's context menu, and select Edit Group or press F3. (You can also choose Modify, Edit Group, although using the keyboard shortcut or context menu is faster.)

Note

Technically, you can convert virtually every 2D object into a 3D object. You can even convert groups, as long as they contain objects that can be converted. Bitmaps are placed on a rectangle as texture and then converted into 3D. Metafiles are split into groups of polygons and then converted. Draw objects with text (for example, a rectangle with text) show the text in 3D after they're converted.

- **Convert to 3D Rotation Object**—This command "rotates" the object via a 360-degree turn into a third dimension. If you turn the object a little before converting it, the results are even more dramatic. Using this command is most meaningful if you want to convert a freeline drawing (or Bézier) object instantaneously into a 3D rotation object. (For more details on Bézier objects and tools, see "Working with Bézier Curves" in this chapter.)

The actual process of converting 2D objects into 3D objects takes two simple steps. First, you select the drawing (or group of drawings) that you want to convert, and then you select the respective command from the Modify, Convert submenu.

 When you're converting a 2D drawing into a 3D rotation object, you can also use the 3D Rotation Object tool on the Effects toolbar. Using this tool does not instantly convert the 2D object into a 3D rotation object. Instead, you have the option to adjust the rotation axis and hence the look of the final image first, and then perform the actual rotation. Follow these steps:

1. Select the object, and then extended-click the Effects icon on the main toolbar to open the Effects floating toolbar.

2. Select the 3D Rotation Object tool (the third icon in the upper row). As soon as you click the tool, you see a rotation axis running vertically through the left-hand border of the invisible rectangular bounding box, and the object is mirrored along this axis.

3. Click the endpoints of the rotation axis to change its position. Or, to convert the object immediately, click in one of the three selection handles along the rotation axis, and drag it slightly to the right to create the 3D rotation object.

CREATING 3D EFFECTS   Another strength of StarDraw is its capability to create stunning 3D effects. When you're creating 3D effects, you basically assign 3D attributes to an existing 3D object. Using the 3D Effects toolbar, you can change the geometry material properties, illumination, and textures for selected 3D objects. As with every other object in StarDraw (as well as StarImpress), the 3D object you create and enhance in StarDraw can be used in text, spreadsheet, and presentation documents as well. Creating 3D effects is discussed in detail in Chapter 23, "Enhancing Your Presentation."

→ For more details on 3D effects, **see** "Creating 3D Effects," **p. 875**.

DRAWING LINES, ARROWS, AND CONNECTORS

 StarDraw enables you do draw a variety of hard-edged lines (with or without arrows and starting points) and connectors. You can use them in graphs to indicate relationships and directions between elements. When you're drawing arrows and connectors, your starting point resembles the left end of the icon; your endpoint resembles the right end of the icon.

Select the desired tool, click in a start location, and drag in the desired direction. As you drag, you see a line/connector symbol in the lower right of your cursor position. After you release the mouse button, the line becomes the desired object.

→ For more details on Connectors, **see** "Working with Flow Charts and Connectors," **p. 870**.

> **Note**
>
> Connectors typically connect to the center of one side of an object's invisible bounding rectangle. The point of connection, also known as a *glue point*, appears as red. If you want to edit the glue point, click the Edit Glue Point icon on the option bar. (For more details on the option bar, see "Using the Option Bar" in this chapter. For more details on editing points, see "Editing Curves with the Bézier Object Bar, also in this chapter.)

To edit the line properties of a selected line, select the line whose attributes you want to modify, and then select a different attribute from the object bar. For some heavy-duty line attribute editing, right-click the selected line and choose Line from the context menu, or click the Line icon on the Draw object bar to open the Line dialog (which is discussed in detail in "Setting Line Style Properties" in this chapter).

All the tools in the Lines toolbar are self-explanatory and intuitive to use; basically, you get what you see. The only two that stand out somewhat from the lot are the Line (45 degree) and the Dimension Line tools. The Line (45 degree) tool enables you to draw lines at a 45-degree angle. Use this tool if you want to quickly draw perpendicular lines or lines that are crossing each other at a 45-degree angle.

USING THE DIMENSION LINE TOOL

The Dimension Line tool is great for architectural drawings or construction drawings in which you want to indicate the dimension or length of a space or object. When you draw a dimension line close to an object, press the Ctrl key while using this tool, and you can line up the beginning and end of your line exactly with the width or height of the nearest object. You can edit the attributes of a selected dimension line in the Dimensioning dialog (which you open by selecting Format, Dimensions), shown in Figure 20.23 (together with examples of 45-degree and dimension lines). Your options include the following:

- **Line Distance**—Controls the distance between the line and the object.
- **Guide Overhang**—Controls how far the length of the guides extend above (in the case of a horizontal line orientation) or to the right (in the case of a vertical line orientation) of the dimension line.
- **Guide Distance**—Controls the distance between the guides and the object.
- **Left Guide/Right Guide**—Controls the length of the left and right guides, respectively.

Figure 20.23
The Line (45-degree) and Dimension Line tools are handy additions that make your life easier when you're working on construction or architectural drawings.

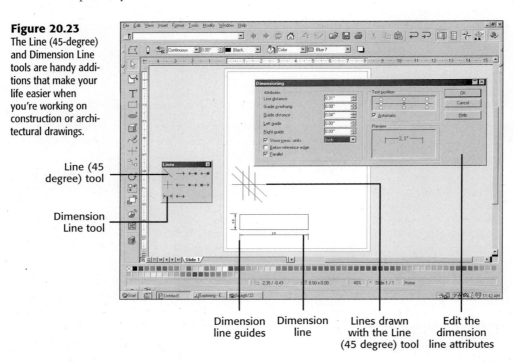

Line (45 degree) tool

Dimension Line tool

Dimension line guides   Dimension line   Lines drawn with the Line (45 degree) tool   Edit the dimension line attributes

In addition, you can define the appearance and position of the unit text and line in relation to the object. To give your audience an idea of the measurement of an object, select the Show Measurement Units option, and choose a unit from the drop-down list to the right. Select Automatic if you want StarDraw to use the current unit as defined by the rulers. You can also select a unit of your choice if you want to indicate real-life dimensions. If you select the Below Reference Edge option, you turn the dimension line by 180 degrees. Using the Parallel option enables you to show the measurement text parallel to the dimension line and object, and deselecting Parallel enables you to show the text perpendicular to the line and object.

> **Note**
>
> If you ever wondered why you can choose Meter or Foot as a unit of measurement for your rulers throughout StarOffice, here's the reason. So much in StarOffice comes out of one single data source, it makes the suite a "lean and mean" program compared to the bloatware of its competitors. Having the option to customize the unit of measurement you want to show above a dimension line, for example, also results in what at first glance seems to be an odd choice for a ruler unit of measurement. Of course, in StarDraw, there is also another practical dimension to this wealth of units of measurement as discussed in the section "Choosing the Right View for the Job" earlier in this chapter.

Finally, you can use the Text Position portion of the Dimensioning dialog to define a position of your measurement text. Click a white dot in the graphic option field to define a new position for your text (a red dot indicates its current position). Select Automatic to have StarDraw define the best placement for you. As with many dialogs of this nature, you can preview your choices in the Preview window.

SETTING LINE STYLE PROPERTIES

When you draw a line (or shape for that matter), StarDraw uses the values currently displayed in the various boxes on the object bar to define the line style (or in the case of a shape, border style), width, and color. If you want to change the values for a certain line (border), you can do so interactively before using the drawing tool (by defining new values in the object bar) or after the using the tool (by selecting the tool and then assigning new attributes using the object bar or color bar options).

If you really want to get creative, use the Line dialog (see Figure 20.24). To open it, first select the line whose attributes you want to modify. Then right-click and choose Line from the context menu, or click the Line icon on the object bar. Using the left portion of the Line tab, you can select a predefined line style, color, width, and transparency value for a selected line; using the right portion, you can select a predefined arrow style and width for either end of the line. Selecting the Centered option positions the middle of the arrow symbol at the end of a selected line, which means the line will be extended (otherwise, the length of the selected line will be maintained). If you select the Synchronize option, both arrow endings will have the same settings. The types of line styles and arrow styles that are available depend on the currently available line and arrow table that you can load using the Line Styles and Arrow Styles tabs.

Using the Line Styles and Arrow Styles tabs of the Line dialog, you can modify and save the attributes of a given line and arrow end style, as well as load different line and arrow end tables. To add or save a new arrow style to an existing or custom Arrow table, you must first create and select an arrow in your drawing. Note that any naming and other changes you make in the Line dialog using the Add and Modify buttons will take effect immediately, and will remain in effect even if you press the Cancel button of the Line dialog.

Indicates currently loaded
Line and Arrow tables

Figure 20.24
Using the three tabs of
the Line dialog box,
you can edit the attrib-
utes of a given line
and line end, as well
as create, save, and
load line and arrow
tables.

Select predefined arrow
ends, and assign width
and position

Select to have both
ends the same

Modify an existing name

Add and name your
custom line style to
the current Line table

Select predefined
line styles and
assign color, width,
and transparency
attributes

Preview your
current selection
and attribute
assignment

Define the type and attributes
of a given line style

Open an existing Line table

Save changes to an existing
or custom Line table

Delete the currently
selected line style

Add a selected arrow style
to the current arrow table

Click to replace the current
name of an arrow style with
a new name

Open an existing
Line table

Save changes to an
existing or custom
Line table

Delete the currently
shown arrow style

Restore the attribute values that were in effect
before you started your editing session

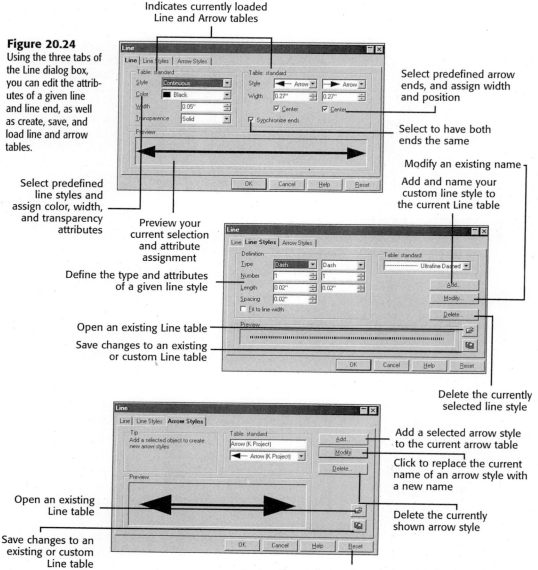

Note

Line and arrow style tables (or configuration files) are saved in the Office51\config folder. Line style configuration files have the extension .sod; arrow style configuration files
have the extension .soe. Currently loaded configuration files are listed at the top of each
Line dialog box tab (for example, Table: standard).

ADDING FILLS AND COLOR TO YOUR OBJECTS

The quickest way to add fill style or color to a selected object is to use the Fill Style/Color drop-down lists on the object bar. For an added measure of control, you can also use the Area tab of the Area dialog box. Just select Area from the Draw context menu or the Format menu, or click the Area button on the object bar.

Using the Area tab, you can control the fill style or color for the surface of a selected object.

> **Note**
>
> The Area tab of the Area dialog is identical to the Background of the Format, Page dialog.

Your options include the following:

- **Invisible**—Using this option renders the existing object fill invisible. If you want to make an invisible fill visible once again, you have to switch to another fill style and then select a fill color, gradient, and so on. If you select only a new fill style (without selecting an attribute), the fill remains invisible.

- **Color**—This option enables you to select a fill color from the currently loaded color palette. Using this option, you can also specify the transparency of the selected color: Solid (100%), 75%, 50%, 25%, and Transparent.

- **Gradient**—Gradients are visual color effects that transpire around a shape and lead to the gradual transition between colors. Select this option if you want to fill your object with an intriguing color scheme. When you select Gradients, you can specify the "bandwidth" of the gradient by entering a number in the Increments spin box. Alternatively, you can also select Automatically, in which case the program selects a default number that has the color transition appear as smooth as possible.

- **Hatching**—Choosing this option enables you to add a fill style that consists of patterns of unicolored parallel or crossing lines.

- **Bitmap**—Use this option if you want to add a bitmapped texture fill of your choice to the surface of your object. You can select the texture from the drop-down list. In addition, you can define whether you want the bitmap to display in tiled format (Tile) or fill the entire area (AutoFit). You can also define the size, position, and offset of the selected bitmap. For example, in the Size portion of this dialog, you have the option to retain the original size of the bitmap (Original), define a relative size of the bitmap in relation to the surface area, or enter an absolute value for the width an height of the bitmap. Using the options in the Position portion, you can select where in relation to the surface area you want to place your bitmap. (The current position is indicated through the red dot in the graphic box.) Using the Offset portion, you can shift the rows or columns of pixels in the selected bitmap.

PART
IV

CH
20

Note
> The fill color of a selected object is always shown in the Fill Color drop-down list on the object bar, even if the color is not part of the current color palette. To add the fill color of a selected object to the color palette, click the Add button. The program then adds the color to your current palette so that you can use it for other objects.

Using the Shadow tab of the Area dialog, you can control whether the selected area should have a shadow. If you want to add a shadow, you can specify the position of the shadow (by clicking a white dot in the graphic field; the current position is indicated by a red dot) and its distance from the fill surface; you also can select a shadow color and color intensity.

CREATING CUSTOM COLORS

Using the Colors tab of the Area dialog, you can edit the existing color palette, add your own RGB or CMYK custom colors, delete existing ones, as well as save custom color palettes and load existing palettes.

Note
> Changes to the default (Standard) color palette are irreversible and permanent. As long as you are simply adding new colors, you won't run into problems. However, after you delete or modify an existing color, the original color is lost for good—unless you create a backup copy of the standard color file (standard.soc) or save the changes as a new, custom color file. In general, any changes you make to the default or custom palettes in the Area and Line dialogs are saved immediately. You just need to click the Save button on the respective tabs if you want to save the settings under a different name.

→ For more details on RGB and CMYK colors, **see** "Understanding Color Models and Modes," **p. 796**.

To edit your existing color palette (or create a new one), follow these steps:

1. Click a color on the color palette on the left to form the base for your mixing.
2. Select RGB or CMYK in the Color sample drop-down list box, and then change the percent value for the individual colors (Red, Green, and Blue or Cyan, Yellow, Magenta, and Black).
3. Keep an eye on the Preview area in the lower right. The lower window shows your results, whereas the upper window shows the original base color before you applied changes.
4. When you're satisfied with your choice, label the color by typing a name in the Name text box, and then click the Add button. The color is immediately added to the currently loaded color palette but does not appear on the palette until you click its name in this menu. Alternatively, you can also choose to replace the existing palette color (the one you picked as the base for your new color) with your custom color by clicking the Replace button.

If you prefer to edit colors by selecting absolute values from the color spectrum rather than adding a percent value in the respective spin boxes, click the Edit button to open the Color dialog. The color window on the left displays a blended range between four colors. You can use it to create and mix colors from the RGB, CMYK, or HSB (hue, saturation, and brightness/luminance) color models. The window on the right displays the entire color spectrum. Use the left- and right-pointing arrows at the bottom of the windows to define your custom color and change the color display in either window.

For example, select a color square in the left window, and click the right-pointing arrow to place the small selection square in the left window in an area that matches closely the selected square on the right. You can also select an area in the color, click in one of the four corners of the window on the right, and then click the left-pointing arrow to introduce a new color to your color blender. Double-click a square in the window on the right to select and preview a custom color scheme. (Of course, you an always edit the color values with numeric precision by entering new numbers in the respective spin boxes.) Click OK to accept the color and return to the Colors tab, where you can add the new custom color to the existing palette or replace an existing color with the new one.

As with the line and arrow style tables, you save your custom colors to an existing (Standard) or custom color palette or load a different palette using the Save Color List and Open Color List buttons.

Tip #405 from	When you're working on a special project that requires only a certain number of standard
Michael & Sarah	or custom colors, delete the colors you don't need, create new ones you do need, and then click the Save Color List to open the Save As dialog. Enter a descriptive name for your custom palette in the Filename box, and click Save to save the palette in the Office51\config folder. Color palettes are saved with the .soc extension.

The Reset button returns all colors to the values they had before you made changes in your current session. Cancel cancels all changes and exits the dialog.

Figure 20.25 illustrates the various steps involved when creating and editing custom colors.

Tip #406 from	When you're working with colors, make a mental note of two files in the Office51\config
Michael & Sarah	folder: cmyk.soc and web.soc. Each palette contains colors that have been optimized for print and Web publishing, respectively. For an overview of these palettes, open the StarDraw sample document, ColorProfile, which is located in the Offiec51\Examples\Samples\Drawings folder.

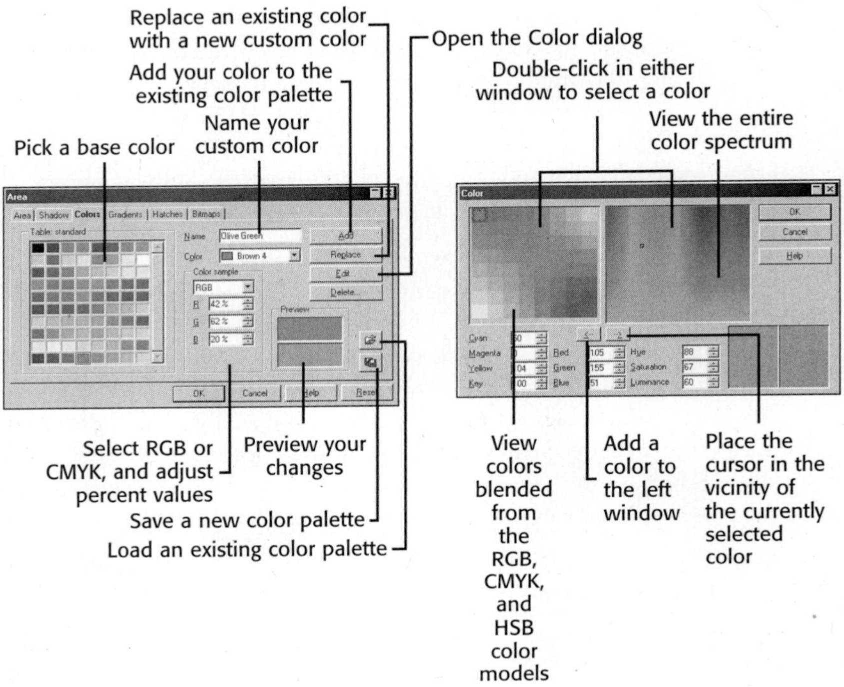

Figure 20.25
Use the Colors tab of the Area dialog (which you open by choosing Format, Area) to create and edit custom colors for your drawings and presentations.

Replace an existing color with a new custom color

Add your color to the existing color palette

Name your custom color

Pick a base color

Open the Color dialog

Double-click in either window to select a color

View the entire color spectrum

Select RGB or CMYK, and adjust percent values

Preview your changes

Save a new color palette

Load an existing color palette

View colors blended from the RGB, CMYK, and HSB color models

Add a color to the left window

Place the cursor in the vicinity of the currently selected color

CREATING CUSTOM GRADIENT, HATCHES, AND BITMAPS

Using the Gradients, Hatches, and Bitmaps tabs, you can edit an existing fill style. In broad strokes, creating custom styles basically follows the same general steps:

1. Select an existing fill style on which you want to base your custom style.

2. Make the necessary modifications.

3. When you're finished, click the Add button to assign a name to your custom style and add it to the current gradient table. Or you can select Modify, and enter a name for the existing style that you want to replace with the new one.

4. Save your own fill style table files and load existing ones by using the Load and Save buttons at the bottom right of each tab. You can switch between existing tables by opening them using the Load button above the Save button. Note that for each style, you can load only one table at any one time.

Note

Like the line and arrow style tables, Gradient, Hatches, and Bitmaps table files (or palettes) are saved in the `Office51\config` folder. Gradient palettes have the extension `.sog`; hatches palettes have the extensions `.soh`; and palettes files have the extension, you guessed it, `.sob`. Color palettes have the extension `.soc`.

If you make a mistake or want to restore the original attributes of a style that has not yet been added to the fill style table, click the Reset button. The program restores the style attributes that existed when you opened the Area dialog.

CREATING CUSTOM GRADIENTS   Click the Gradients tab to modify existing gradients and add new ones to your gradient table (see Figure 20.26). To create a custom gradient, follow these steps:

1. Select a gradient from the Table list.

2. Define the type and appearance of your custom gradient using the options to the left of the Table list. Your options include the following:

    - **Type**—Use this drop-down list to select one of six gradient styles for your fill: Linear, Axial, Radial, Ellipsoid, Square, or Rectangular.

    - **Center X/Center Y**—Use these spin boxes to enter a percent value that defines the distance between the left/top border of the area to the center of the second color. A value of 0% places the center at the left/top border; 100% places it at the right/bottom value. Note that these options are available only when you select Radial, Ellipsoid, Square, or Rectangular from the Type drop-down list.

    - **Angle**—In this box, you can enter the angle of the linear, axial, ellipsoid, square, and rectangular gradient type.

    - **Border**—Use this box to enter the amount of space the first color takes up in relation to the gradient. A value of 0% means the gradient is most prominent; 100% basically suppresses the gradient; the first color becomes the fill color.

3. Select a start (From) and end (To) color for your gradient from the Color portion of the Gradient tab. Using the spin boxes to the left of the From and To drop-down lists, you can specify the intensity of the color (at 100% the color appears solid; at 0% it appears nonexistent or black).

CREATING CUSTOM HATCHES   Compared to creating gradients, creating custom hatches doesn't exactly exhaust your creativity and imagination. But then, what do you expect from a bunch of crossing or parallel lines. Your options are as follows when you're creating custom hatches using the Hatches tab of the Area dialog:

- **Spacing**—Here, you can control the distance between two parallel lines.

- **Angle**—Use this box to specify an angle at which the hatch lines cross. Alternatively, you can also click the graphical option field below the Angel spin box to define an angle (in 45-degree increments). The current angle is shown in red.

- **Line type**—Select one of three line types from the drop-down list: Single, Crossed, or Triple.

- **Line color**—Select a color for your line from the existing color palette.

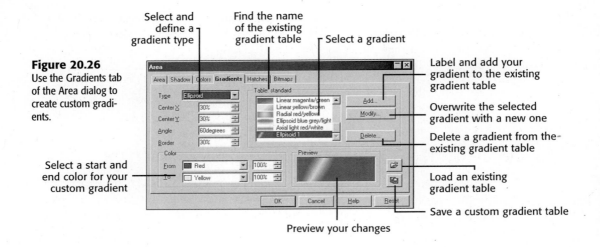

Figure 20.26
Use the Gradients tab of the Area dialog to create custom gradients.

(Figure callouts:) Select and define a gradient type · Find the name of the existing gradient table · Select a gradient · Label and add your gradient to the existing gradient table · Overwrite the selected gradient with a new one · Delete a gradient from the existing gradient table · Select a start and end color for your custom gradient · Load an existing gradient table · Preview your changes · Save a custom gradient table

CREATING CUSTOM BITMAPS In terms of taxing your creativity, creating custom bitmaps is halfway between creating custom gradients and creating custom hatches. When you create custom gradients or hatches, you first select an existing style, and then you modify it as needed by changing various attributes. In the case of custom bitmaps, however, you first have to create a bitmap before you can modify it, and even then you can modify only two attributes: foreground and background colors.

Tip #407 from
Michael & Sarah

The existing bitmaps—Orange, Wallpaper, Texture, and Chocolate—cannot be modified (and the pattern you create in this dialog will look nothing nearly as intriguing as the existing bitmaps). However, if you click the Import button in this dialog, you can import any bitmap you want. Note also that you can even map scanned photographs onto any object, including 3D-objects. You can drag and drop a picture from the gallery. If you press Ctrl+Shift, the picture become the selected object's background.

In a nutshell, to create a custom bitmap, select the desired foreground, and then create a pattern in the Pixel Editor by clicking the individual squares. When your pattern is finished, select a background; the program immediately colors the remaining (blank) squares in the color you selected. Note that you can use only one color for your foreground pattern.

USING THE EYEDROPPER

When you're working with bitmaps and metafile graphics in StarDraw/StarImpress, you can also use the Eyedropper tool to sample up to four colors from an image and then have them replaced by a color of your choice.

To use this tool, select Tools, Eyedropper from the menu bar to open the Eyedropper dialog. Click the Eyedropper icon in the upper-left corner of the Eyedropper dialog box, and move the mouse pointer over your image. The color at the current pointer position shows up in the box to the left of the Eyedropper icon. If you click at any point, a check mark appears in the first Color Source check box, and the color sample appears in the Source Color box. You can then select a color from the Replace With drop-down list.

→ For more details on the Eyedropper tool, **see** "Using the Eyedropper," **p. 795**.

WORKING WITH BÉZIER CURVES

Basic drawing tools, such as the line, rectangle, and ellipse tools, enable you to create regular geometric shapes that can provide the basis for more complex shapes. Some jobs, however, may require you to create a shape that does not closely resemble a basic geometric shape. For those jobs, StarDraw/StarImpress provides a set of tools that give you the freedom to create absolutely any line or shape you need to begin or complete an illustration.

UNDERSTANDING BÉZIER CURVES

The magic word that is associated with these tools, and the underlying structure of the object they create, is Bézier. As the story goes, a French mathematician named Pierre Bézier developed a method to describe any curve using points that are not on the curve itself but define tangents to that curve. Handles along the curve act as levers. As a curve passes from one point to another, it is magnetically attracted to control handles. One handle tells the curve how to enter the point; the other tells it how to exit the point. Still following? No? Then have a quick look at Figure 20.27.

For better or worse, these so-called Bézier curves are at the heart of StarDraw's Curves tools (as well as those of the PostScript page-description language—but that would be another chapter). And don't worry if you don't fully understand the world of Bézier things. You don't need to know the math behind these curves; however, you have to be able to identify the elements we're talking about in order to be able to edit Bézier curves.

USING THE BÉZIER TOOLS

 StarDraw/StarImpress offers altogether eight tools for drawing Bézier curves and polygons. You can access these tools by clicking the Lines icon on the main toolbar and selecting the desired tool from the Curves floating toolbar. The upper row consists of tools that enable you to create filled shapes, including (from left to right) the Curve, filled; Polygon, filled; Polygon (45°), filled; and Freeform Line tools. The bottom row consists of basically the same tools except without the fill: Curve, Polygon, Polygon (45°), and Freeform Curve.

Figure 20.27
According to the French mathematician Pierre Bézier, irregular curves can be broken down into a series of points, and each point is controlled by handles. Notice the Bézier object bar at the top of the workspace.

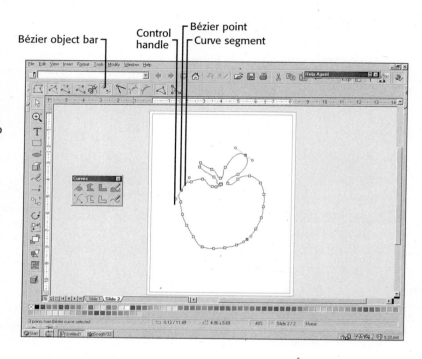

As with the other tools, as soon as you select a Bézier tool, your regular cursor changes shape into a crosshair-like pointer when over a drawing surface, and the shape of the selected tool appears in miniature form in the lower-right corner of your cursor. When you're using a tool, the command field on the status bar informs you about each and every move you make (in the case of the Curve, filled and Curve tools, it even indicates the coordinates of your points and the angle of the respective line segments in relation to the point of origin).

When you're using these tools, you create a shape or line out of individual, connected points. Depending on the tool and how you use it, you can create the following points:

- **Symmetrical points**—Symmetrical points sport two symmetrical Bézier control handles. The curve segment that passes through a point has the same curvature to the left and right.

- **Smooth points**—Smooth points also show two control handles; however, in contrast to symmetrical points, the curve segment that passes through a smooth point is curved differently to the left and right of the point.

- **Corner points**—A corner point represents the corner between two straight lines. The points you create when using the Polygon tools are corner points. However, you can also create corner points with the Curve tools when you define points by clicking only (rather than clicking and dragging), in which case the program inserts a straight line segment between two points. Note that corner points have only one control handle—the one that tells the curve how to exit the point.

Only the Curve tools enable you to create all three point types; the Polygon tools and Freeform tools create line segments and shapes that consist of corner and smooth points, respectively (the starting and endpoints of the Freeform tools are defined as corner points). However, using the tools on the Bézier object bar, you can change the identity of the points of an object created with the Curve tools. You can convert a symmetrical point into a smooth or corner point and vice versa, which, of course, changes the curve dramatically. (Note that if you convert the corner points of a polygon, however, you change the object into a curve.)

Using the tools on the Curves toolbar is pretty straightforward. First, you select the desired tool. Then you click on your drawing surface and drag ever so slightly in one direction to define a starting point and direction for the first segment of your curve or line segment. (Note that if you only click without dragging, you switch from the Draw mode back to the Select mode.) After you've defined a starting point, the following are your options of how to proceed depending on the tool you're using:

- If you're using the Curve tools, you can continue to drag and click to define a second point, and then drag and click to define a third point, and so on. Alternatively, you can just move your pointer to a new location and then click to define a new point. When you choose the second method, each click defines a corner point, and the connecting line between two points becomes a straight one. Otherwise, you create symmetrical or smooth points, depending on your movement.

  If you press Shift while dragging or moving to a new location, the program creates a linear segment that appears in multiples of 45-degree angles with regard to the current point. If you press the Alt key, the program creates a linear connection between the point you last clicked (endpoint) and the point you first clicked (starting point). You can then use the same tool to create a new curve, which the program combines with the first curve. Using this function, you can create a bigger shape and then create a smaller shape inside the bigger one. The smaller shape is subtracted from the bigger shape, punching out a hole in the middle, so to speak.

- If you're using the Polygon tools, you can create additional line segments and shapes by clicking the desired locations on your drawing surface; the program automatically creates a straight line segment that connects the previous point with the newly created one. (Note that using the Polygon (45°) tools defines a filled or unfilled polygon in which the angles consist of multiples of 45 degrees.)

- If you're using the Freeform tools, you drag the mouse pointer (without releasing the mouse button) to create the curve or shape you desire. Both Freeform tools enable you to draw lines and curves that drag the movement of your mouse pointer on the drawing page. Depending on the steadiness of your hand, the results can vary from a smooth flowing curve to one that is rough and requires varying degrees of editing (as does the curve in Figure 20.27, which was created with the Freeform Curve tool.) If you press Shift while dragging, you can force the program to draw a "reasonable" straight line— reasonably straight because it appears to get slightly out of whack as soon as you release the Shift key and draw a curve. However, you can always edit it later by using the Bézier object bar, as described later in this chapter.

To exit the curve drawing mode, double-click when you're creating the last point. If you use any of the tools with fills or the Polygon (45°) tool, the program closes the curve by creating a linear segment that runs from the endpoint (the point you created last) to the starting point of your curve. You can now continue to work with other tools.

Tip #408 from *Michael & Sarah*	Using the object bar, you can assign the same attributes to the lines and fills of your (irregular) Bézier objects as to the regular drawing objects, including gradients, hatches, or bitmaps.

EDITING CURVES WITH THE BÉZIER OBJECT BAR

You can edit points that appear as small rectangles. If you want to edit an existing curve, click the Select tool, and then click an element of the curve you want to edit to select the curve in its entirety. Next, click the Edit Points icon on the object bar (or the option bar if it is visible) to show the various control points of your curve as blue squares. If the selected object has been created with the Curve or Freeform tools, click the point you want to edit, and you can see its two support lines with control points at the end. Note that corner points have only one support line that becomes visible when you click and drag a point. Note that you can move the lines. When you do, the points change position accordingly, as does the curve to the left and right of the points.

Note	Of course, you can also edit the curve along more conventional lines, changing the line width and color and, in the case of filled curves, even the fill color. To change these attributes, use the commands on the object bar, the context menu, or in the Format and Modify menus.

Using the Bézier object bar, you can also change the type of a selected point. For example, you can change points into other points: Corner, Smooth, or Symmetrical just by clicking the respective icon on the Bézier object bar.

Table 20.4 explains the functions of various Bézier icons.

TABLE 20.4   USING THE BÉZIER OBJECT BAR

Click This Icon	If You Want To
Edit Points	Toggle the Bézier mode on or off. When in Bézier mode, you can select and modify the individual nodes of Bézier objects.
Move	Move individual nodes of an object to a new position. The curve to the left and right of the node follow your movement. (If you click and drag the curve between two nodes, you move the entire object without modifying its shape.)

Click This Icon	If You Want To
Insert Points	Insert a smooth or symmetric node in a Bézier object. To insert a new node, click the curve between two nodes. Using this mode, you can also move a node (similar to the Move mode). If you're slightly off the curve, StarDraw automatically adjusts the curve by guessing the coordinates of the inserted node.
	If you want to insert a corner node, you first have to insert a smooth or symmetric node and then convert it into a corner point by using the Set Corner Point command.
Delete Points	Delete one or more selected nodes. To select more than one node, press Shift while selecting each node individually. Alternatively, you can use the Delete key to zap selected nodes.
Split	Split a curve at or between the selected point or points.
To Curve	Convert a curve into a line and vice versa. If necessary, round points are converted to corner points and vice versa.
Set Corner Point	Convert the selected node(s) into a corner point(s). Corner points consist of two independent handles. The curve does not pass smoothly through the node but consists of a corner.
Smooth	Convert a corner point or a symmetrical node into a smooth node.
Symmetric	Convert a smooth or corner node into a symmetrical node.
Close	Close the current line. The end node is connected with the start node (which is differentiated through a larger square than the other nodes).
Eliminate Points	Mark the selected node(s) for deletion. Use this option if the node(s) is located on a line. When you then convert the curve into a line, the marked nodes are removed. You can define the angle at which points will be eliminated by using the Snap Position portion of the Tools, Options, Drawing dialog.

CONVERTING BITMAPS (AND OTHER OBJECTS) INTO VECTORS

Using StarDraw (or StarImpress), you can also easily convert bitmapped images (or other objects) into vector or line art, giving them the same advantages (and disadvantages) of vector graphics that have been created from scratch. When converting bitmapped images to vector or line art, StarOffice creates a separate "working" file for editing the new vector art. During the conversion process, you can define the following vectorization parameters:

- You can set the maximum number of layers for the new file.

- Using the Point Reduction method, you can define the number of objects or polygons used to create the artwork, thereby designating each bitmapped layer or color as an outline or a solid object creating the different pieces of the art. Polygons smaller than the defined number of pixels will not be created.

- You can add a background fill, in case the single-color layers are not aligned. This option consists of single rectangle objects that vary in size and create a mosaic of objects or polygons in the background where you can then define the separate layers.

After you've converted the objects, you can easily modify and edit them.

Just do the following to convert a bitmapped image into a vector graphic:

1. Select the bitmapped image that you want to convert to a vector graphic.

2. Select Modify, Convert, Convert to Polygon. (In StarImpress, you can find this command on the context menu.) The Convert to Polygon dialog appears.

3. In the Settings portion of the dialog, you can define the parameters for the conversion process. Your options include the following:

   - **Number of Colors**—Indicate the maximum number of colors that you want to have in the converted metafile. StarDraw allows a maximum of 32 colors.

   - **Point Reduction**—Define the environment of the polygons that will be shown. For example, if you select 0 pixels, StarDraw generates all polygons. If you select a number "x," polygons that are surrounded by a rectangle with fewer than "x" are not generated.

   - **Fill Holes**—Select if you want StarDraw to automatically fill any existing holes between color transitions using tiles.

   - **Tile Size**—Define the size of the tiles that will be used to fill the background holes between color transitions.

   Click the Preview button to preview the vectorized image before performing the actual conversion.

4. When you're finished, click OK. StarOffice then converts the selected bitmap into a vector graphic metafile. This process might take awhile; you can track the progress of the conversion process by looking at the Progress indicator at the bottom of the dialog.

Note

Convert to Polygon changes the object into a polygon that you can then split into its basic components by using the Modify, Split command. Or you can edit the object like a Bézier curve, adding and deleting points and so on. If you select this option, the dialog appears.

Convert to Curve instantly changes the object into a Bézier curve. As a Bézier curve, the object can be edited using the Edit Points command on the object bar.

USING TEXT IN STARDRAW

More so than StarWriter, StarDraw enables you to create text that has impact. You can add regular text to filled shapes, or you can use the Text tools to create text objects. In both instances, you can edit and format the text as you would in a text document. However, when you convert existing text into curves, StarDraw treats your text as individual objects to which you can apply the same infinite variety of effects that you can use for drawing objects. The finished result can then be imported into your text documents and HTML documents, as well as incorporated in presentations. However, you will no longer be able to change the font or style of the converted text.

TRANSFORMING TEXT TO 3D

If you want to transform text into a 3D object, follow these steps:

1. Extend-click the Text icon on the main toolbar to open the Text floating toolbar, and select the Fit to Size text tool (the second tool from the left).

2. Click and drag in your work area to create a rectangle. When you release the mouse button, you see a blinking cursor in the center of the frame.

3. Start typing your text.

4. When you're finished, click anywhere outside the frame, or press the Escape button to exit the text entry mode.

Click the text again, and select Modify, Convert, Convert to 3D from the menu bar. StarDraw converts your text into a 3D object that you can then rotate or scale as desired (see Figure 20.28).

→ For more examples of 3D effects in StarOffice, **see** "Creating 3D Effects," **p. 875**.

Note
Windows users can also create numerous text effects with the FontWork module. For more details, see "Creating Special Effects with FontWork (Windows Only)" in Chapter 23.

PART
IV
CH
20

ADDING TEXT TO DRAWINGS

You can add text to filled rectangles, squares, ellipses, and circles that you created using the drawing tools in StarDraw. Just double-click the drawing object to which you want to add text to enter the text entry mode. A blinking cursor appears in the center of the object. Start typing to enter your text. Click outside the object to leave the text entry mode.

When you're in text entry mode, the Draw object bar is replaced with the StarDraw Text object bar, enabling you to modify the attributes of the text you enter. Alternatively, you can change attributes via the context menu or the Character and Paragraph dialogs (which you open by selecting Format, Character or Format, Paragraph, respectively). Note that you don't have to select the text to change its attributes. Any attribute changes apply to all characters and words within the parameters of the object.

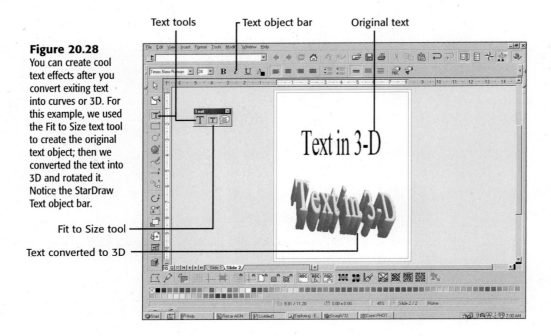

Figure 20.28
You can create cool text effects after you convert exiting text into curves or 3D. For this example, we used the Fit to Size text tool to create the original text object; then we converted the text into 3D and rotated it. Notice the StarDraw Text object bar.

→ For more details on using the Text object bar, **see** "Working with Text," **p. 838**.

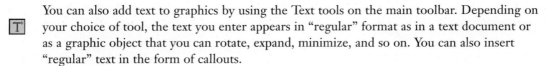

Tip #409 from
Michael & Sarah

For quick and consistent formatting choices, use the default object styles in the Stylist (press F11), or create your own.

You can also add text to graphics by using the Text tools on the main toolbar. Depending on your choice of tool, the text you enter appears in "regular" format as in a text document or as a graphic object that you can rotate, expand, minimize, and so on. You can also insert "regular" text in the form of callouts.

→ For more details on using the Text tools, **see** "Using the Text Tools," **p. 843**.

WORKING WITH STYLES

Using styles provides an easy way to control all aspects of object formatting. You can apply styles throughout your drawing documents in one of three ways. You can select object styles from the list of available styles in the Stylist (press F11 or select Format, Stylist to open); you can go straight to the styles master archive, the Style Catalog (press Ctrl+Y or select Format, Styles & Templates, Catalog to open), or you can use the Fill Format mode, which you can use to quickly format selected objects with predefined attributes. Using styles in

StarDraw is identical to using styles in StarImpress and is discussed in detail in Chapter 22, "Getting Started with StarImpress."

→ For more details on using styles, **see** "Working with Styles," **p. 859**.

SAVING AND CLOSING A GRAPHIC

You save a drawing document in StarDraw the same way you save a file in other StarOffice programs—by selecting File, Save. If you have not saved the document before, the Save As dialog box opens, where you are prompted to enter a name for your presentation document. If you have already given the drawing a name, it is saved under that name.

→ For more details on saving files, **see** "Managing Files and Folders from the Open and Save As Dialogs," **p. 192**.

After you've finished and saved your document, you can close the document (or task) by selecting File, Close, or right-clicking the document's task button and then selecting Close Task from the shortcut menu. Alternatively, you can click the Close (X) button in the upper right of the task window.

EXPORTING A GRAPHIC

Exporting a slide or object in StarDraw is virtually the same as saving a bitmapped image or graphic in another file format. You select the file or object you want to export; then you choose File, Export from the menu bar. In the Export dialog (which is identical to the Save As dialog) that appears, enter a name and location for the file to be saved and select the desired (non-native) file format from the File type list box. Your options include BMP, EPS, GIF, JPG, MET, PCT, PBM, PNG, PGM, PPM, RAS, SVM, TIF, WMF, and XPM file formats.

→ For more details on graphics file formats in StarOffice, **see** "Importing and Exporting Graphics File Formats," **p. 1400**.

Note	Depending on the file format you choose, you may be asked to provide additional information in subsequent dialog boxes. For more details on the various file format-saving options, see "Saving and Closing Files" in Chapter 21, "Creating and Modifying Images with StarImage."

Tip #410 from *Michael & Sarah*	If you export an entire slide, it is printed in full-page size. To export only certain objects, select them and check the Selection box in the Export dialog. This way, you can ensure that you don't export too much of the white margins.

SAVING A GRAPHIC FOR THE WORLD WIDE WEB

StarDraw, like StarImpress, comes armed with an HTML Export Wizard that enables you to output your graphics as presentation-quality Web pages for use on the Internet or an

PART

IV

CH

20

intranet. Using the HTML Export Wizard is the same in StarImpress as in StarDraw and is covered in detail in Chapter 24, "Previewing and Presenting Your Presentation."

→ For more details on the HTML Export Wizard, **see** "Exporting a Presentation, Slide, or Object," **p. 909**.

OPENING AN EXISTING GRAPHIC

If you want to open an existing image stored on disk, choose File, Open or press Ctrl+O to display the Open dialog box. The Open dialog box behaves just like the ones in the other StarOffice modules, with three navigational buttons in the upper-right corner and the possibility to open a file as read-only. Use the navigational buttons to locate the desired file on your hard drive or network, and double-click it. The File Type list contains the names or extensions of the file formats that StarOffice can open. If you know the extension or file format of the desired file, select it in the File Type list. This capability is useful when the selected folder contains numerous files with different formats and you want to quickly locate the desired file or file format.

→ For a complete list of graphics file formats that StarOffice can import (and export), **see** "Importing and Exporting Graphics File Formats," **p. 1400**.

Alternatively, you can also use the Explorer in combination with the Beamer to open or drag and drop files into your drawing document. When the Explorer is set to Hierarchical view—right-click the Explorer title bar and select Hierarchical from the context menu—you can click any folder in the Explorer or your Workplace and show it's contents in the Beamer. If you select a Gallery theme, you can see thumbnail previews of the theme folder's contents in the Beamer.

→ For more details on using the Gallery, **see** "Inserting Graphic Objects," **p. 440**.

Tip #411 from
Michael & Sarah

If you can't open an image that has been saved to one of these formats, chances are you didn't install the respective filter during the installation process. To install additional conversion filters for StarOffice, you need to run the StarOffice setup program again. Choose Modify, and follow the onscreen instructions. Then select the missing filter.

PRINTING GRAPHICS

Printing drawing documents, including preparing graphics for commercial printing, is identical to printing presentation documents in StarImpress and is discussed in detail in Chapter 24, "Previewing and Presenting Your Presentation."

→ For more details on printing graphics, **see** "Printing Your Presentation," **p. 906**.

Note

Because drawing documents consist of vector graphics, they can be printed optimally in any resolution supported by your printer or imagesetter. For more details on vector graphics, see "Understanding Computer Graphics" in Chapter 20.

ADDITIONAL TIPS FOR DRAWING DOCUMENTS

A thorough elucidation of everything that StarDraw has to offer would require a book by itself. The following list provides additional tips for working in StarDraw:

- **Don't delete objects; make them invisible**—You've spent a lot of time creating a drawing, and then you discover that you really don't need certain (or all) parts of it. Instead of deleting the object, use the Line and Fill Style/Color list boxes in the object bar to change its line and fill attributes to Invisible. That way, you can always come back to it if needed.

- **Use the entire workspace**—Remember that you can move your objects outside the slide or page. You can leave them there until you need it again. Or you can use the area for concept sketches.

- **Use the arrow keys when moving objects**—If you want to move an object only a few pixels in one direction, select the object, and then use the arrow keys.

- **Use the Alt key to select hidden objects**—If you want to select an object that is hidden underneath a stack of other objects, you don't have to rearrange the stacking order to get to the hidden object. Instead, select the topmost object, press the Alt key, and then "click through" the stack. Each click selects the following object. If you use Shift+Alt+click, you can cycle through the stack in reverse order.

- **Change views quickly with the plus (+) and minus (-) keys**—If you want to quickly zoom in or out of a graphic object, use the plus (+) and minus (-) keys on the numeric keypad to incrementally zoom in or out. (Press the Num Lock key to turn on the numeric keypad.) Use the multiplication symbol/key (*) to show the drawing at the 1:1 ratio.

- **Don't scan large images in StarDraw/StarImpress/StarImage**—If you're planning to scan images that are larger than 10MB, 20MB, or more, you might experience problems because of lack of resources.

- **Use separate color palettes for different jobs**—Consider creating and saving different color palettes for different jobs. That way, there will be no confusion as to which color to use. To save or load color palettes, go to the Colors tab of the Area dialog. (The same applies for hatches, bitmaps, and gradients, as well as line and arrow styles.

PART

IV

CH

20

TROUBLESHOOTING

Can I work with a bitmapped image in StarDraw/StarImpress?

StarDraw enables you to import bitmaps into your illustrations and to export bitmaps you create. However, your options of what you can do with a bitmapped graphic in StarDraw/StarImpress are limited to changing the position, size, color resolution, and alignment of the object in relation to other existing objects or its use as an object's background. However, if you convert a bitmapped image to a curve, you can shape and modify it like any other vector object in StarDraw/StarImpress.

What's the easiest way to move a graphic from the Gallery into my drawing document?

If the desired file is in the Gallery, select the Theme folder in which it is located in the Explorer group, and drag and drop the graphic from the Beamer into the open StarDraw workspace. For you to be able to drag and drop files from the Gallery theme folders into your StarDraw/StarImpress document in StarOffice 5.1, the Explorer group must be in Hierarchical view. To switch to the Hierarchical view, right-click the Explorer group header, and select Hierarchical from the context menu.

Can I work with a StarDraw file in StarImage?

You can open vector-based StarDraw illustrations directly in StarImage. StarImage automatically creates a bitmapped version of the original when you open the StarDraw illustration.

My printer doesn't seem to print transparent graphics.

Some printer drivers have problems printing graphics with transparent attributes. Because StarOffice treats the transparent attribute as a color, try replacing it with the color white.

Is it possible to save part of my drawing as a separate file?

If you want to save part of your drawing, select the object(s) that you want to save. Then choose File, Print from the menu. In the Print dialog that appears, click the Selection option in the Print Range portion of the dialog. For more details on your other printing options, see "Printing Your Presentation" in Chapter 24.

My StarDraw and StarImpress documents are growing bigger and bigger.

If you've tried several different page layouts using Page Styles, be sure to activate Remove Unused Master Pages from the Slide Design dialog.

Can I somehow put my own drawings into the Gallery?

Yes, just create your own theme within the Gallery. Open your drawing and theme. Then simply drag and drop all your objects into the Beamer. For more details on adding graphics to the Gallery, see "Using the Gallery" in Chapter 11, "Desktop Publishing with StarOffice."

CHAPTER 21

CREATING AND MODIFYING IMAGES WITH STARIMAGE

In this chapter

GETTING STARTED WITH STARIMAGE

StarImage is the image-editing module of StarOffice. Comparable in function to MS Paint, StarImage enables you to alter photographs and other scanned images by applying special effects and adjusting the color balance. Similarly to StarDraw, StarImage provides a small but colorful variety of tools that enable you to create images from scratch, or polish scanned photos before printing or inserting them in another document.

As an image editor, StarImage falls into the larger software category of painting programs. In a painting program, you draw a line, and the application converts it to tiny square dots called *pixels*. The painting itself is called a *bitmapped image*.

→ For more details on bitmapped images, **see** "Understanding Computer Graphics," **p. 773**.

STARTING STARIMAGE

You can start StarImage by selecting File, New, Image or Start, More, Image. StarImage welcomes you with the New Image dialog, shown in Figure 21.1.

Figure 21.1
When starting StarImage, you first have to define the size and number of colors of the image you want to create.

StarImage automatically assumes that you want to create an image from scratch. So before you can start working in StarImage, you have to define the physical dimensions or size (in pixels) of the image you want to create and specify the number of colors that can appear in your image. Think of it as creating a digital window or surface for your creative efforts. Click OK to accept the default settings (256 pixels by 256 pixels, and 256 colors), or enter the desired width and height in the spinner boxes, and select the number of colors. Your color options include 2, 16, 256, and 16 million colors.

After you click OK, StarImage creates a borderless window with a transparent background that is x pixels wide and y pixels high (where x and y correspond to the numbers you specified in the Width and Height spinner boxes). Inside this window, you can paint to your heart's content, using the tools and special effects filters that StarImage provides.

Note

If you defined 2 as the number of colors that can appear in your image and you use a painting tool in a color other than black or white, StarImage alerts you that the use of this tool increases the color depth of your image. StarImage does the same if you selected 16 and try to paint in a color that is not part of the basic 16-color palette.

Tip #412 from
Michael & Sarah

In earlier versions of StarOffice, you could only create one image per document. Since StarOffice 5.1, you can add a new "canvas" to an existing image document, just like you add a new slide to a drawing or presentation document—by clicking in the gray area to the right of the right-most image tab. Alternately, you can also right-click the Image tab and select Insert Image from the context menu. To delete an image, open the Image tab context menu and select Remove Image.

EXPLORING THE STARIMAGE WORKSPACE

After you start StarImage—via the File menu or Start Menu—you see the StarImage desktop, surrounded by the Image object bar, the main toolbar, the status bar, and the color bar (see Figure 21.2).

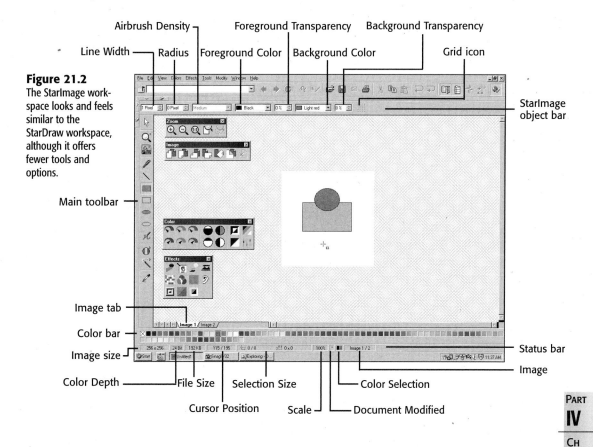

Figure 21.2
The StarImage workspace looks and feels similar to the StarDraw workspace, although it offers fewer tools and options.

USING THE STARIMAGE MAIN TOOLBAR

The main toolbar offers 13 major tools, with variations of some tucked away in handy fly-out windows that you can tear off and place on your desktop for easy access (see Figure 21.2). To select a tool, click its icon, and then use the tool by clicking or dragging

PART
IV
CH
21

with it inside the defined window of your image. As in other StarOffice modules, you can extended-click icons that show a small green triangle in the upper-right corner to open a tear-off window with additional tools.

Tip #413 from *Michael & Sarah*	When you click a tool, it is available only for as long as you hold the left mouse button. If you want to use a painting tool repeatedly, you have to double-click it. It is then available until you switch to another tool.

Table 21.1 describes the icons and tools available on the main toolbar.

TABLE 21.1 USING THE STARIMAGE MAIN TOOLBAR

Click This Icon	If You Want to...
	Switch from Draw mode back to the regular Selection mode. When in Selection mode, you can click and drag in the image window to define an area that can be modified independently of the rest of the image.
	Change the view of the image. Clicking this icon opens the Zoom tear-off window, which includes the following options (from left to right): Zoom In, Zoom Out, View 100%, Page Size, and Optimal, which shows all elements of the current selection at maximum size.
	Transform the shape of your selection. Clicking this icon opens the Image tear-off window, which includes the following options (from left to right): Flip Horizontally, Flip Vertically, Rotate 90 Degrees (to the) Left, Rotate 90 Degrees (to the) Right, User-Defined Rotation, Re-Size, and Crop.
	Paint hard-edged lines of varying thicknesses. Clicking this icon opens the Pens tear-off window, which includes the following options (from left to right): Round Pen, Square Pen, Vertical Pen, Horizontal Pen, Diagonal Pen (Left), Diagonal Pen (Right). You can set the thickness of your strokes, in pixels, in the Line Width spinner box on the object bar.
	Paint a straight, hard-edged line. You can define the thickness of the line in the Line Width spinner box on the object bar.
	Paint a filled rectangle. You can select a color for your border and background fill color from the Foreground Color (Border) and Background Color (Fill) spinner boxes on the object bar. You can also round the corners of the rectangle by specifying a value larger than 0 pixels in the Radius spinner box on the object bar.
	Paint an outlined rectangle. You can round the corners of a rectangle and select a different outline color by defining a value larger than 0 pixels in the Radius spinner box and selecting a color from the Foreground Color drop-down list box on the object bar, respectively.

Click This Icon	If You Want to...
▢	Paint a filled ellipse. You can select a color for the border and background fill color from the Foreground Color (border) and Background Color (fill) spinner boxes on the object bar.
⬭	Paint an outlined ellipse. Select a color for the outline from the Foreground color box on the object bar.
✐	Spray diffused strokes of color that blend into the image—like graffiti artists do. You can set the density of this tool in the Airbrush Density box on the Image object bar. The options include Low, Medium, and High.
◖	Control the RGB color, brightness, and contrast of an image or a selection. Clicking this icon opens the Color tear-off window, which includes the following color control options (from left to right): reducing and increasing the red, green and blue values; reducing and increasing the brightness and contrast; inverting the color scheme; changing the color to black and white; grayscaling; and opening the RGB Values controller dialog.
◥	Apply special effects to an image or a selection. Clicking this icon opens the Effects tear-off window, which includes the following filter effects options (from left to right): Charcoal Sketch, Poster, Solarization, Smooth, Mosaic, Pop-Art, Tile, Remove Noise, Relief, Aging, and Definition.
⚲	Lift (or select) a color from an image and replace it with another one.

USING THE STARIMAGE OBJECT BAR

More humble in its offerings than the Draw object bar, the Image object bar (refer to Figure 21.2) provides a series of attributes that control the thickness, shape, and color of the various paint tools on the main toolbar.

For example, Line Width defines, in pixels, the thickness of the Round Pen, Square Pen, and Line tools, as well as any borders around rectangles and ellipses. If you select the Horizontal, Vertical, and Diagonal Pens, the currently displayed line width applies if you stray from the linear path of the currently selected pen tool.

When using the Rectangle tools, you can round all four corners of a rectangle by specifying a pixel size in the Radius spin box.

The Airbrush Density list box, as the name suggests, enables you to define the density of the Airbrush tool, from low to medium to high.

The color controls enable you to change the colors with which you paint. The Foreground Color box defines the color of the current painting tool, as well as the borders or outline of rectangles and ellipses. The Background Color box specifies the current fill color if you're painting filled rectangles or ellipses. The Foreground and Background Transparency spin boxes enable you to create screened shades (or tints) of a color. StarImage enables you to create tints in 1-percent increments.

Note The Image object bar always displays the most recently used line width, radius, airbrush density, and foreground and background color. If you want to switch to another value, you have to do so before continuing to paint with a new tool.

The Grid icon enables you to show and hide the grid of an image area. Using the Grid is helpful when you want to align different paintings or lines with each other. (Unlike in StarDraw or StarImpress, you can not customize the grid in StarImage—what you see is what you get. When using the object bar, you have to make your selection(s) in the object bar after you choose a tool but before you start to paint. When your paint tool touches the digital surface of your image, you cannot change its attributes anymore.

Note Sadly, the current version of StarImage does not come with an Eraser tool. So if you make a mistake, you have to press Ctrl+Z immediately to undo the last action. Pressing Ctrl+Z (or using the Undo command) removes only the most recent action; if you drew a complex shape, you remove the shape in its entirety, not just the last few pixels. You cannot undo steps beyond the most recent one.

USING THE STATUS BAR AND COLOR BAR

The StarImage status bar provides information about the currently active image, selection, and tool. (If the status bar doesn't appear onscreen, open the View menu—there should be a check mark next to Status Bar for it to be visible.) Table 21.2 details the various status bar fields.

TABLE 21.2 INTERPRETING THE STARIMAGE STATUS BAR

Field	What It Displays
Image Size	The physical size of an image, in pixels.
Color Depth	The bit depth of an image, which is the size of each pixel in memory. A black-and-white image takes up 1 bit per pixel; a 16-color or 16-grayscale uses 4 bits; a 256-color or 256-grayscale demands 16 bits; and a 16-million-color image consumes 24 bits.
File Size	The file size of the current image in the computer's memory. StarImage calculates this value by multiplying the height and width of the image, in pixels, by the bit depth of the image.
Cursor Position	The current position of the cursor on the painting grid.
Selection Size	The physical size of the current selection, in pixels.
Scale	The current view size; you can right-click in this field to select a different size from the shortcut menu; double-clicking opens the Zoom dialog box.

Field	What It Displays
Document Modified	An asterisk if changes have occurred since the image was last saved.
Color Selection	Two overlapping bars that indicate the current foreground and background color selection.
Image	The current image you're working on and the total number of images in the current document (for example, 2/3).

The color bar in StarImage works the same as in StarDraw. Colors are listed in the order in which they appear in the color lists on the object bar; any custom colors you have defined are listed at the end of the standard StarOffice list. When you select the Pen, Line, or Airbrush tools, you can click any color square to select a color (Foreground Color) for the respective lines or strokes you want to paint. When using the Rectangle and Ellipse tools, clicking a color square assigns a fill color (Background Color); right-clicking a color square selects the color of the outline or border (Foreground Color). (Remember to select attributes (such as colors) *before* clicking with the cursor on your canvas. Once a bitmapped painting has been finished, you can no longer change its attributes.)

Note If you don't see the color bar onscreen, you can show it by selecting View, Toolbars, Color Bar.

UNDERSTANDING HOW BITMAPS WORK

As mentioned in Chapter 20, "Getting Sketchy with StarDraw," computer images come in two fundamental types: vector images and bitmapped images. Bitmapped images are made up of individual dots (pixels) arranged in a grid x pixels wide by y pixels high and z pixels deep (where z is known as *pixel depth* and determines the number of possible colors for each pixel). Unlike vector images, bitmapped images have fixed dimensions; their file sizes go up as the size and resolution of the image increase. The screen image that shows up onscreen is one large bitmap, updated continuously. When working with bitmaps, you have to be aware of the interrelationship of color depth and resolution and the file size and physical size of the image as it defines and limits what you can do with a bitmap.

COLOR DEPTH AND FILE SIZE

Bitmaps are formed by a rectangular grid of a fixed number of small squares, known as *pixels*. Each pixel is assigned a specific location and contains data that describes whether it is black, white, or a level of color. The number of colors in a bitmapped image determines the file size of the image. More bits per pixel means more colors. For example, a 24-bit (16 million) color image is much larger than the same image saved as an 8-bit (256) color image.

> **Note**
>
> Because each pixel contains a set number of colors that form a color palette, increasing or reducing the color depth results in changes to the existing color palette and look of the image. When you increase or reduce the color depth, the file uses combinations of the existing colors to create a new palette that simulates the original color of the image.

When you're creating image files for other StarOffice documents or the Web, the image file size becomes an issue because it not only affects the size of the document and your hard drive space, but also the time it takes to download the image and display it onscreen. For most StarOffice jobs, 8-bit color images suffice.

> **Note**
>
> The number of colors your system displays depends on your graphics card and the amount of video RAM installed.

IMAGE SIZE AND RESOLUTION

When looked at from a distance, the color and shape of a bitmapped image appear continuous and smooth. However, when you zoom in, you can see the individual pixels that make up the total image (as shown in Figure 20.7 in Chapter 20). That's because increasing the size or physical dimensions of a bitmap increases the size of individual pixels, making lines and shapes appear jagged.

When you change the physical size of bitmaps, you are in fact changing its resolution. Resolution refers to the number of pixels per linear inch. For example, if the resolution of an image is 72 pixels per inch (ppi), you get 5,184 pixels per square inch (72 pixels wide ∞ 72 pixels tall = 5,184 pixels). Because bitmapped images are formed by a rectangular grid of a fixed number of small squares, increasing the size of an image reduces the number of pixels per inch (and hence the resolution). In contrast, reducing the size of a bitmap increases the number of pixels per inch (and hence also increases the resolution of an image).

Why should you care about this? If you change the physical dimensions of an image or if you print an image at a resolution other than the one in which it was created, you sacrifice the level of detail and quality of the image.

If you care about the quality of bitmaps (and you should), avoid scaling bitmapped images manually, using the sizing handles as you do with other objects, *after* inserting them in text documents, spreadsheets, or presentations. Always scale, rotate, or crop bitmapped images in StarImage, as both resolution and scaling settings are saved with the image. Changing bitmaps in anything else but an image-editing program only leads to distortions and the loss of detail and information an image file contains.

VIEW SIZE AND ONSCREEN RESOLUTION

Regardless of the resolution and scaling values, StarImage displays each pixel onscreen according to the zoom ratio. For example, if the zoom ratio is 100%, each image pixel takes up a single screen pixel. Although the zoom ratio has no effect on printer output, it affects the quality of a screen presentation or display. Hence, when creating onscreen presentations in StarImpress, for example, you always want the image size to fit inside the prospective monitor at the 100% zoom ratio.

Note

> Most monitors are capable of displaying different resolutions, depending on the graphic card installed on the computer system. Thus, a 640∞480 pixel image may shrink or grow on onscreen.

USING VIEWS EFFECTIVELY

You can change the *view*—that is, the size at which an image appears on screen—so that you can either see more of an image or concentrate on individual pixels. Each change in view size is expressed as a *zoom ratio*. When you first open an image, StarImage displays it at 100% zoom ratio. If the image is larger than the current screen size, you can use the scrollbar to scroll to the bottom or top of the image.

Changing views in StarImage works the same as in the other StarOffice modules. You can right-click in the Scale field on the status bar and select a viewing size from the shortcut menu, including 200%, 150%, 100%, 75%, 50%, Optimal, Page Width, and Entire Page. Alternately, you can double-click in the Scale field or select View, Zoom from the menu bar to open the Zoom dialog, which also enables you to set a custom (variable) view size for the current image.

 Besides these menu options, you can also click the Zoom icon on the Main toolbar to open the Zoom tear-off window, which gives you an added measure of control over the view size. For example, you can click the Zoom In (+) and Zoom Out (-) icons to incrementally zoom in and out of an image. To zoom in, first click the Zoom In tool (your mouse pointer changes into a magnifying glass with a crosshair), and then click the image to select a focal point around which you want to increase the image. Each click doubles the currently selected view size, up to the maximum size possible. If you want to use the Zoom In tool more than once in a row, you need to double-click the Zoom In icon.

To zoom out, click the Zoom Out icon. Each click reduces the view size by half, down to the minimum size, 10%. When you want to return to the original size, click the View 100% (1:1) icon.

Tip #414 from
Michael & Sarah

> To view the image at its approximate print size, select the View 100% icon. When using StarImage with the integrated desktop active, your work area approximates the landscape view of a printed page.

If you can't see the entire image in View 100% view, click the Page Size view. The Optimal icon is only active after you've selected parts of your image; click it to show the selection at its optimal (largest possible) view size.

Tip #415 from *Michael & Sarah*	When working with images—vector-oriented or bitmapped images—don't pin down docked windows. That way, the Explorer or Beamer (or Stylist and Navigator, if docked) can "glide over" the visual display when opened rather than push it aside, which causes graphics to redraw onscreen. Depending on the view size of the image and your graphic card and memory, this can be rather annoying.

CREATING A NEW IMAGE

Apart from polishing scans and applying effects to existing images, StarImage also enables you to create new images from scratch with its limited but colorful set of painting tools, which include the Pen, Line, Rectangle, Ellipse, and Airbrush tools.

Tip #416 from *Michael & Sarah*	If you mess up something in the course of painting your image, stop and press Ctrl+Z or click the Undo icon on the function bar.

USING THE PEN AND LINE TOOLS

You can use the Pen and Line tools to create freehand lines and straight lines. For each tool, you can set the thickness in the Line Width spinner box of the object bar, and a color in the Foreground and Background Color spinner boxes. Click each tool to use it once; double-click to use it repeatedly until you select another tool or click the Select icon.

USING THE PENS

Using the Pen tools, you can paint hard-edged lines of varying thickness that come in six varieties:

- **Round Pen and Square Pen**—Use these pens if you want to paint strokes that start and end with round or square corners.

- **Vertical Pen and Horizontal Pen**—Using these pens, you can paint a 1-pixel-thick perpendicular line. If you stray from the vertical or horizontal orientation, the thickness of the line is controlled by the pixel amount specified in the Line Width box.

- **Diagonal Pen (Left) and Diagonal Pen (Right)**—Using these pens, you can paint 1-pixel-thick diagonals at a 45-degree angle to the bottom of the screen. If you stray from the diagonal path, the thickness of the line is controlled by the pixel amount specified in the Line Width box.

Tip #417 from *Michael & Sarah*	Click the Grid icon on the object bar to show the grid of your image area when using the Vertical, Horizontal, and Diagonal Pens—your mouse movement is much steadier if your eyes have a reference point to guide your hand.

To select a Pen, click the Pen icon on the main toolbar to open the Pens tear-off window, and then click or double-click the desired pen and start painting in the image area.

Figure 21.3
In this figure, six lines are painted in black with the round, square, horizontal, vertical, and diagonal pens and the line tool. Notice how the thickness changes when you stray from the predefined path of the vertical, horizontal, and diagonal pens.

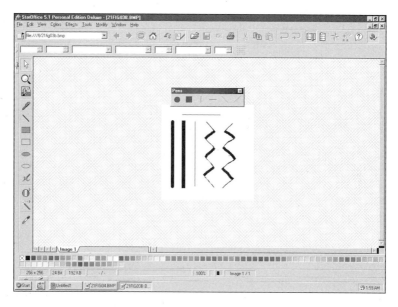

SWITCHING COLORS WHILE PAINTING

StarImage enables you to switch colors while using the Pen tools. The colors are controlled by the Foreground Color and Background Color boxes on the object bar.

To switch colors while using the Pen tools, left-click in the image and drag to paint with the selected foreground color while holding the left mouse button. At the point where you want to switch to the background color, right-click and continue to drag without interruption. When you want to switch back to the foreground color, hold still at the point where you want to switch, release both mouse buttons, and then left-click again and continue to drag. Note that you can use this technique only when you've double-clicked the selected Pen tool.

USING THE LINE TOOL

If you think using the Pen tools is easy, try painting a straight line of any substantial length using the vertical, horizontal, and diagonal pens—it's a challenge, especially after a night on the town. Trust me! That's why the considerate folks at StarDivision threw in the Line tool.

Using the Line tool is, well, pretty straightforward. After selecting the tool, drag with it inside the image area to create a line. Note that you cannot switch colors when using the Line tool. When you right-click while painting the line, StarImage starts the line all over at the point where you right-clicked.

PART

IV

CH

21

USING THE RECTANGLE AND ELLIPSE TOOLS

The Rectangle and Ellipse tools are identical in both StarImage and StarDraw. Select the desired tool—filled or not—and click and drag in the image area to paint an outlined or filled rectangle or ellipse. The color, shape, and outline of the final result are controlled by the options in the object bar. The outline and fill colors are controlled by the Foreground and Background Color boxes, respectively. The thickness of the outline is controlled by the Line Width box. And when painting a rectangle, you can also elect to round off its corners by specifying a pixel value in the Radius spinner.

USING THE AIRBRUSH TOOL

The Airbrush tool paints a translucent line as it applies a series of colored dollops, and it continues to apply these as long as you hold the mouse button, whether you drag the mouse or not. Figure 21.4 shows the dark glob of paint that results from pressing the mouse button while holding the mouse motionless at the end of the drag. Using the Airbrush tool, you can apply the same technique as with the Pen tools to switch colors. As with the other painting tools, the colors are controlled by the Foreground Color and Background Color boxes on the object bar, and the thickness of the spray path is set in the Line Width box. In addition, you can select the concentration of the colored dollops in the Airbrush Density box.

Figure 21.4
The Airbrush tool simulates graffiti-style painting. Notice the dark glob at the end of the line where the Airbrush tool was held in place for a few moments.

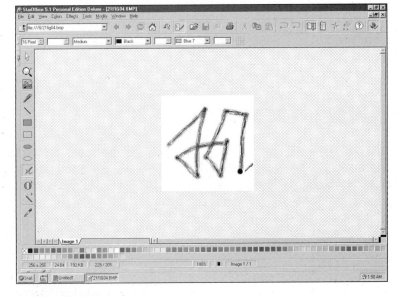

IMPORTING A SCANNED IMAGE

You can import photographs and other artwork into StarImage and modify or polish the resulting bitmap by using the Scan command.

To scan an image into StarImage, select File, Scan, Select Source to identify the scanner connected to your computer. Then choose File, Scan, Acquire. If your scanner is on and communicating properly with your operating system, this command starts the scanning process. If the software necessary for your scanner is installed, you see its dialog box. To ensure a high-quality scan, you should predetermine the scanning resolution and dynamic range your image requires, using the controls of your scanner's software.

When the scan is finished, the image appears in the open StarImage document. You can now apply special effects or adjust the brightness, contrast, and color as described in the section "*Selecting and Editing Colors*," earlier in this chapter, or save it in the appropriate folder as a new addition to the Gallery.

OPENING AN EXISTING IMAGE

If you want to open an existing image stored on disk, choose File, Open or press Ctrl+O to display the Open dialog box. The Open dialog box behaves just like the ones in the other StarOffice modules, with three navigational buttons in the upper right and the option to open a file as read-only. The File Type list contains the names or extensions of the file formats that StarOffice can open. If you know the extension or file format of the desired file, you can select it in the File Type list in order to prevent any other files from showing up in the file list. Use the navigational buttons to locate the desired file on your hard drive or network, and double-click it to open in StarImage.

Alternately, you can use the Explorer to locate and select the folder that contains the file you're looking for, and then open the file by double-clicking it in the Beamer. If the document already contains an image or a window, it is replaced by the new image, unless you create a new image canvas first (by right-clicking the Image tab at the bottom of the work area and selecting Insert Image) or press Ctrl while double-clicking (in which case StarOffice opens a new StarImage task).

If the desired file is in the Gallery, select the Theme folder in which it is located in the Explorer (in Hierarchical view), and drag and drop it from the Beamer to the open StarImage document. Any existing image in the current document is replaced with the new one. If you want to keep the original, you have to save the current document under a different name.

StarOffice comes with a series of filters that enable you to open or import various pixel file formats, including BMP, GIF, JPG, PCX, PNG, TIF, PCT, PSD, PBM, PGM, PPM, RAS, TGA, and XPM.

→ For a detailed listing of graphic file formats, **see** "Importing and Exporting Graphic File Formats," **p. 1400**.

Tip #418 from
Michael & Sarah

If you can't open an image that has been saved to one of these formats, chances are you didn't install the needed filter during the installation process. To install additional conversion filters for StarOffice, you need to run the StarOffice setup program again. Choose Modify, and follow the onscreen instructions, and then select the missing filter.

SELECTING AND DUPLICATING AN EXISTING IMAGE

When working in StarImage, you can easily copy all or part of an existing file into a new StarImage document or into any other StarOffice document. With the existing image document open, select Edit, Copy from the menu bar or press Ctrl+C. Then switch to the document into which you want to copy the image and select Edit, Paste from the menu bar or press Ctrl+V. The new image is inserted as a Picture object (with a transparent background) at the insertion point of the target document.

Note

Because bitmapped images are resolution dependent, you should not alter their size or shape after inserting them into other StarOffice documents such as StarWriter, StarCalc, StarImpress, or even StarDraw. Any changes would result in loss of detail and quality. Always scale or edit bitmapped images in StarImage.

StarImage also gives you the option to copy and paste part of an image. To copy part of an image, you must first define the area you want to copy. Use the Select tool (the topmost icon on the Main toolbar) and click in the upper-left corner of the desired selection. Then drag down and to the right to draw a selection rectangle around the area you want copy. Next, proceed with the familiar Copy and Paste command options to insert the image as a Picture object in the desired StarOffice document or copy it into a new StarImage document.

Note

When copying an existing image into a new StarImage document, the size and number of colors of the copied image override the size and number of colors you have defined for the new StarImage document. That's because StarImage saves the scale and resolution information of an image with the original document.

MODIFYING AN EXISTING IMAGE

The options for modifying or transforming an existing image are limited to changing its pixel dimensions and orientation, removing colors, and applying special effects filters. Applying special effects filters is covered in its own section later in this chapter. In this section, we focus on scaling an image, changing its orientation, and cropping it by using the Flip, Rotate, Modify Size, and Crop commands.

FLIPPING AND ROTATING AN IMAGE

You can transform an existing image by using the Flip and Rotate commands from the Modify menu or the Image tear-off window, or by pressing the respective keyboard shortcuts. Using these commands, you can flip an image horizontally (F2) or vertically (Shift+F2), or you can rotate it in 90-degree angles clockwise (F3) and counterclockwise (Shift+F3).

To flip or rotate an entire image, click the correct icon in the Image tear-off window or select the needed command from the Modify menu. If you click the User-Defined Rotation icon in the Image window (the fifth icon from the left), you can rotate an image in 45-degree increments.

> **Note**
>
> The user-defined rotation angle can be modified in the Image Options dialog box. For more details, see the section "Customizing StarImage," later in this chapter.

You can also define your own rotation angle by selecting Modify, Rotate, Free Rotation and specifying an angle in the Free Rotation Angle dialog box. Using the spin box, you can specify any angle between 0 degrees and 360 degrees; indicate in the Orientation portion of that dialog whether you want to rotate your image to the left (default) or to the right. When you're finished, click OK, and StarImage rotates your image according to your specifications. Note that the free rotation angle has to be redefined after each use.

> **Tip #419 from**
> *Michael & Sarah*
>
> StarImage may not shine that brightly when it comes to image-editing options, but at times it can catch you by surprise. Try this: Use the Select tool to draw a selection rectangle, and then select the Flip Horizontal command or the Flip Vertical command. StarImage flips the contents of the selection rectangle, leaving everything outside that rectangle as is.

MODIFYING THE SIZE OF AN IMAGE

After you scanned or imported an image into StarImage, you might want to adjust its size. The Modify Size command enables you to change the pixel dimensions, print dimensions, and (to a certain extent) the resolution of your image.

> **Note**
>
> Keep in mind that changing the size (or pixel dimensions) of an image affects not only the size of an image onscreen but also its image quality and its printed characteristics.

To change the size of an image, select Modify, Modify Size or click the Resize icon in the Image window. Using the Modify Size dialog box, shown in Figure 21.5, you can increase or decrease the Width and Height of the image by specifying a new pixel, inch, or percentage value in the respective spinner boxes. Select the Scale option if you want to resize your image proportionally. If you are increasing the size of the current image, select the Interpolation option.

> **Note**
>
> Remember that increasing the size of a bitmapped image increases the size of each pixel, creating gaps between and within pixels. When you interpolate an image while increasing its size, you are telling the program to add new pixel information based on weighted averages of the color values of existing pixels. As a result, your image looks less blocky at the larger size, although interpolation can make your image look slightly more blurry or out of focus.

Tip #420 from
Michael & Sarah

You can avoid the need for interpolation by scanning the image at a high resolution.

Figure 21.5
The Modify Size dialog enables you to change the width and height of your image with numeric precision, as well as interpolate your image when enlarging it.

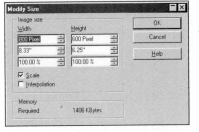

While scaling an image, keep an eye on the Memory portion of the Modify Size dialog. This portion shows the file size of the image in the computer's memory after you apply the desired changes.

CROPPING IMAGES

Another way of changing the pixel dimension of an image is to crop it, which means to clip away pixels around a selected area without changing the remaining pixels. Cropping enables you to focus on an element in your image, as shown in Figure 21.6.

Figure 21.6
Cropping an image enables you to clean up the background junk of an image and focus on the essential foreground image.

Cropping an image involves two steps. First, you have to use the Select tool to select the area you want to crop, and then you can click the Crop command on the Image tear-off window or select Modify, Crop from the menu bar. StarImage removes everything outside the selection area, leaving you with what you determined to be the essential part of the image. If you don't like the results, select the Undo command on the function bar or press Ctrl+Z immediately after you cropped the image to return it to its original size.

Using the Eyedropper Tool

The Eyedropper tool enables you to sample colors from an image and then have them replaced by a color of your choice.

Although this tool is great for single-color backgrounds (such as fills), it can create surprising results when used on photographs or other scanned artwork. For example, most bitmaps have palettes of 256 colors or more. With that many colors available, you'll rarely find large areas of all one color. Because you use the Eyedropper tool to replace one color with another color, the new color may show up in unexpected areas of your image, giving your image a freckled appearance.

To use the Eyedropper tool, follow these steps:

1. Click the Eyedropper icon on the Main Toolbar or select Modify, Eyedropper.

2. Click the Eyedropper icon in the upper left corner of the Eyedropper dialog box—the mouse pointer changes into an eyedropper—and move with the mouse pointer over the image. The color at the current pointer position shows up in the box to the left of the Eyedropper icon.

3. Click to select a color that you want to replace. As soon as you click, you can no longer sample colors from your image. If this is your first selection, a check mark appears in the Color Source check box, and the color sample appears in the Source Color box.

4. Select the color with which you want to replace the currently selected one from the Replace With drop-down list. (Note that Transparent is also considered a color.) Reduce or increase the Tolerance Level if you want to exclude or include similar colors within a certain range.

5. Click Replace to replace the sampled color with the new one, or, if you want to sample more colors, click the next Color Source check box, reactivate the Eyedropper, and select another color to be replaced from your image. You can select and replace up to four colors this way. If your image contains transparent areas, you can remove them by selecting the Transparency option.

Selecting and Editing Colors

Regardless of whether you want to create images for print or for the Web, color is a prime concern. Computer monitors, printers, scanners, and other pieces of electronic publishing equipment all perceive and reproduce colors somewhat differently. Certain types of equipment can reproduce a broader range of colors than others. A color printer, for example, does not produce as many colors a monitor. Hence, the colors you get when you print your document may not match the colors you see on your monitor. When working with color, you need to be aware of the difference between monitor and printed publication. You'll be surprised to learn that identifying and defining a color is at times surprisingly non-subjective.

| Tip #421 from | Most of the Color commands can also be applied to selections of an image. |
| Michael & Sarah | |

UNDERSTANDING COLOR MODELS AND MODES

When it comes to nature, color perception is certainly in the eye of the beholder. Objects appear to be certain colors because of their ability to reflect, absorb, or transmit light, which we perceive as color. In the realm of commercial printing or Web publishing, however, these vague distinctions won't do. Every device used to create a color document or an image—be it a scanner, color monitor, or color printer—interprets and manipulates color in different ways.

For example, your computer's monitor produces colors by combining red, green, and blue signals, which means that the millions of colors that your monitor produces can all be described as varying proportions of red, green, and blue light, which we perceive as different colors.

When the colors you see on your monitor are reproduced on paper, however, they are using ink instead of light. The most common method of reproducing color images on paper is by combining cyan, yellow, magenta, and black inks. These inks produce color by reflecting certain colors and absorbing others.

Because there are so many different variations of color, a precise method for defining each color is required. StarImage (as does all of StarOffice) bases its color modes on the following three established models for describing and reproducing color:

- **HSB**—This model is based on the human perception of color and describes three fundamental characteristics of color: hue, saturation, and brightness (HSB). Hue is the wavelength of light reflected from or transmitted through an object (commonly identified as orange, pink, or green). Saturation refers to the vividness or dullness of the hue. Brightness indicates the darkness or lightness of a hue.

- **RGB**—The RGB model is based on the theory that a large percentage of the visible spectrum can be represented by mixing red, green, and blue (RGB) colored light in various proportions and intensities. Where the colors overlap, they create cyan, magenta, and yellow. Where they combine, they create white; hence red, green, and blue are also called *additive colors*. Using the RGB model, StarImage's RGB mode assigns an intensity value to each pixel ranging from -100% (black) to +100% (white).

- **CYMK**—In the world of light, red, blue, and green reign supreme. But in the world of pigments, the (process) colors are cyan, magenta, yellow, and black (CYMK). The CYMK model is based on the light-absorbing quality of ink printed on paper. As white light strikes translucent ink, part of the spectrum is absorbed and part is reflected back to your eyes. StarImage enables you to edit colors in the CYMK mode, using the Tools, Options, General Colors dialog.

As a rule of thumb, choose to work with RGB colors when you're creating documents that will be output on a slide printer or distributed over the Internet or office network, where people will view them on their computer monitors. Use CYMK colors when your document is printing to a commercial printing press or to any color printer.

Unfortunately, the current version of StarImage makes it awkward to convert RGB colors into CYMK colors—you have to go to the Color Sample portion of the Tools, Options, General Colors dialog and convert each existing color manually into a CYMK color.

Hence, if you want to prepare color images for print in StarImage, save in a common printer format (such as TIF) and let the people at a service bureau worry about separating the RGB colors into CYMK colors. If you're only printing to your inkjet printer at home, the results should be just fine. If you're producing images for the Web or a presentation, you'll be home free because everyone will look at these through a monitor anyway.

Note

Unlike StarImage, StarDraw and StarImpress allow you to switch color palettes. When you're working on a drawing or presentation for onscreen display, you can work with the default Standard (RGB) color palette. When the drawing or presentation is intended for print or Web publishing, you can relatively easily switch to the CYMK and Web palette, respectively. For more details, **see** "Adding Fills and Custom Colors" in Chapter 20, "Getting Sketchy with StarDraw."

SELECTING COLORS

Like every other StarOffice module, StarImage enables you to choose a color from an existing palette or create your own color using the General Colors Options dialog. StarImage provides four locations from which you can select and control the colors of your image: the Colors menu, the object bar, the Colors icon on the Main toolbar, and the color bar.

The foreground color indicates the color you apply when you use the Pen, Line, and Airbrush tools. When you paint rectangles and ellipses—filled or not—the foreground color applies to the border around these shapes.

The background color indicates the fill color you apply when you use the Filled Rectangle and Filled Ellipse tools. Right-clicking enables you to switch from foreground color to background color with some tools, such as the Pen, Line and Airbrush tools.

In addition to the existing colors, you can also define your own RGB or CYMK color schemes by using the Tools, Options, General Colors dialog.

ADJUSTING RGB COLOR VALUES

A computer monitor uses the additive RGB color model: It transmits varying proportions of red, green, and blue light, which we perceive as different colors. Using the Red, Green, and Blue sliders in the RGB Values dialog box (which you open by selecting Colors, RGB Colors), you can add or subtract red, green, or blue from the image onscreen. If you combine 100% of red, green, and blue, you perceive the color as white. If you combine 0% of red, green, and blue, you perceive the color as black.

You can combine varying intensities of red, green, and blue to simulate the range of colors found in nature. Red, green, and blue are called the *additive primaries*.

ADJUSTING BRIGHTNESS AND CONTRAST

The Brightness & Contrast dialog box (which you open by selecting Colors, Brightness/Contrast) enables you to increase or decrease the brightness and contrast of image tones. You should use this command sparingly because it's a true color correction command that can lead to undesired and dull results.

> **Note**
>
> When working with contrast and gray tones, you would normally adjust the gamma of your monitor for better results onscreen. Increasing the gamma increases the contrast for shadows and midtones (although it also decreases the contrast for highlights). Although StarImage includes a command for adjusting the gamma correction factor, in its present incarnation this command is virtually useless since it lacks a crucial feature—a visual box that enables you to properly match the gamma against a surrounding test area. If you're a tinkerer, you can still use it by selecting Colors, Gamma Correction from the menu bar. The desired gamma is usually 1.0, although it can be anywhere from 0.5 to 2.

CONVERTING AND INVERTING IMAGES

With StarImage, you can convert a color image to a grayscale image, which means you replace the various color values with variations of gray. To convert an image to grayscale, select Colors, Convert to Grayscales. In the Grayscale dialog box that appears, you can select the number of shades of gray you want the new image to display, or you can convert the image into straight black and white.

You can also convert a color image to a black-and-white image by selecting the Black and White option in the Convert to Grayscale dialog. If you choose the Black and White option, you can also specify a threshold value for color conversion. The default value is 50%, which means that StarImage discards all color information that is above 50% of a certain color value, and converts it into black.

> **Note**
>
> When choosing the Black and White conversion option, you can only convert an entire image, not part of an image.

When you click OK, StarImage converts the image into a grayscale or black-and-white image, depending on your settings.

Tip #422 from
Michael & Sarah

If you want to print on a black and white printer it might be a good idea to convert images to grayscale in StarImage first—using the 16 Grayscale or 256 Grayscale option from the Colors, Modify Depth submenu or the Grayscale dialog (select Colors, Grayscale)—rather than to let the printer driver decide what is black and what is white.

When you select the Colors, Invert command, StarImage converts every color in your image to its exact opposite, just as in a photographic negative: Black becomes white, and white becomes black. You are telling StarImage to change the primary additives in an image into their complementary subtractive colors. You can also click the Grayscale icon in the Colors tear-off window.

Tip #423 from
Michael & Sarah

You can convert a scanned negative into a positive using the Invert command.

USING THE COLORS TEAR-OFF WINDOW

The Colors tear-off window, shown in Figure 21.7, provides the same color adjustment and manipulation options as the Colors menu, except for the Gamma Correction command. Using the window's various icons, you can adjust the RGB values in a bitmap, the brightness and contrast of an image, convert an image into a grayscale or black and white image, invert the colors, or open the RGB Values controller dialog. However, if you click a icon (with the exception of the RGB Colors icon in the lower right), you are adjusting the RGB values, brightness, contrast, and so on in increments as defined in the Picture Colors Options dialog box (which you can open by selecting Tools, Options).

Decrease Green   Decrease Blue   Decrease Brightness   Decrease contrast

Figure 21.7
The Colors floating tool window is your one-stop access to the most common color controls. Keep it handy when editing colors.

Decrease Red
Increase Red
Increase Green
Increase Blue
Increase Brightness
Increase contrast

Convert to Black & White

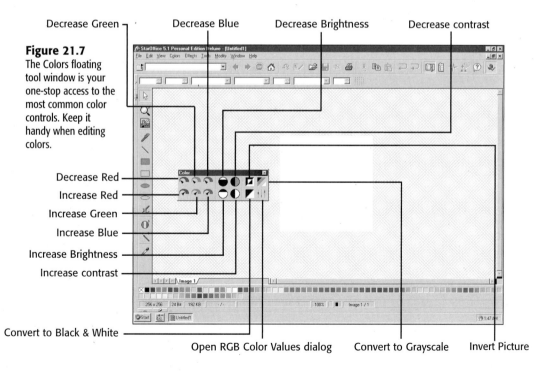

Open RGB Color Values dialog   Convert to Grayscale   Invert Picture

PART
IV
CH
21

APPLYING FILTER EFFECTS

Filters enable you to apply automated effects to an image. You can access StarImage's effects filters by choosing the commands from the Effects menu or by clicking the Effects icon on the Main Toolbar, which opens the Effects tear-off window.

> **Note**
>
> Most of the filter commands in the Effects tear-off window are controlled by settings in the Picture Effects Options dialog. If you want more control over the effect applied, you can use the Effects menu commands and specify settings in the respective dialog boxes.

Although not officially categorized that way, the effects filters fall into two large camps: destructive filters and corrective filters. Corrective filters include the Smooth, Remove Noise, and Definition filters, which can be used to modify or clean up scanned images. Destructive filters produce cool dramatic effects, but ultimately distort the image. Destructive filters include the Charcoal Sketch, Poster, Solarization, Mosaic, Pop-Art, Tile, Relief, and Aging.

When you choose a filter command, StarImage applies the filter to the selected portion of the image. If no portion of the image is selected, StarImage applies the filter to the entire image.

DESTRUCTIVE FILTERS

The following are destructive filters:

- **Charcoal Sketch**—As its name implies, this effect turns the original image into a charcoal sketch by redrawing the outlines of the image in black while suppressing all other colors (see Figure 21.8).

Figure 21.8
Charcoal Sketch.

■ **Mosaic**—This effect groups individual pixels into larger rectangles of the same color. The larger these rectangles, the less detail is retained in the image. Using the Mosaic dialog box (Effects, Mosaic), you can also define the resolution of the image as Low, Medium, or High). (see Figure 21.9).

Figure 21.9
Mosaic.

■ **Relief**—This effect converts the image into a relief. During the conversion process, you will be asked to define a virtual light source that will define the outline and shadows of the image (see Figure 21.10).

Figure 21.10
Relief.

PART

IV

CH

21

■ **Poster**—This effect reduces the number of colors in the image (see Figure 21.11).

Figure 21.11
Poster.

■ **Pop Art**—Reminiscent of the art of Andy Warhol, this effect completely changes the character of the image by reducing the overall number of colors and distorting the remaining ones (see Figure 21.12).

Figure 21.12
Pop-Art.

- **Aging**—Similar to what happens when you let photos sit in a drawer or on a shelf for decades, this effect artificially ages the image in seconds. During this conversion, all colors are moved closer to grays and browns on the color spectrum. Use the Aging dialog box to define the degree of the aging process—the higher the percentage, the older the image appears (see Figure 21.13).

Figure 21.13
Aging.

- **Solarization**—Similar to what happens when you expose a photograph, this effect inverts and distorts the colors of the image (see Figure 21.14).

Figure 21.14
Solarization.

■ **Tile**—Somewhat similar in appearance to the Mosaic effect, this effect breaks the image down into tiles of equal color (see Figure 21.15).

Figure 21.15
Tile.

CORRECTIVE FILTERS

The following are corrective filters:

■ **Definition**—This effect increases the contrast between adjacent pixels, which results in a higher degree of crispness (see Figure 21.16).

Figure 21.16
Definition.

- **Smooth**—This effect smoothes the transition between high-contrast colors which results in an overall softer image (see Figure 21.17).

Figure 21.17
Smooth.

- **Remove Noise**—This effect is useful for cleaning up bad scanning results; rogue pixels that cause harsh color transitions are removed or modified (see Figure 21.18).

Figure 21.18
Remove Noise.

PART

IV

CH

21

SAVING AND CLOSING IMAGES

As you create or edit an image, remember to save it frequently. If the image has already been saved, use the Save command or press Ctrl+S to save the file under its current name. If you are saving an image for the first time, click the Save icon on the function bar or select File, Save or File Save As. In all three instances, you open the Save As dialog, which enables you to name and save an image to a location of your choice.

> **Note**
>
> Unlike other StarOffice modules, StarImage does not give you the option to annotate your file. Using the File, Properties command opens a humble Properties dialog that only enables you to enter a name for the current image (provided that it hasn't been saved already) and determine whether the image should be read-only.

CHOOSING A COLOR DEPTH

Color depth (also called bit depth) refers to the number of colors that can be supported in a file. A 1-bit file supports two colors (typically black and white), a 2-bit file supports 4 colors, a 4-bit file supports 16 colors, an 8-bit file supports 256 colors, and a 24-bit file supports 16 million colors. StarImage also supports 4-bit and 8-bit grayscales, which translates into 16 and 256 increments of black and white, respectively. The higher the color depth supported by a file, the more space the file takes up on your hard drive.

When you save or export a file to the BMP file format, StarImage asks you to specify a color depth. If you have only a few colors in your original image, saving to a higher color depth (for example, 8 bit to 16 bit) produces an image whose colors are very similar to those of the original image. However, if your original image has many colors, and you convert it to a lower color depth (for example, 16 bit to 8 bit), the file creates a palette of colors and uses combinations of these colors to simulate the original color in the image. The colors in the palette depend on the colors in the original image.

When deciding on a file format to which you want to save your image, be sure to consider any color limitations.

CHOOSING A FILE FORMAT

Saving files in StarImage is no different from saving files in any other StarOffice application. Unlike StarDraw, however, StarImage does not have a native file format. Instead, you have to choose a file format to which you want to save your image from the Save As File Type drop-down list box. The file format options are BMP, GIF, JPG, PBM, PNG, PGM, PPM, RAS, TIF, and XPM.

Of these files, the most common ones you would probably use are BMP, GIF, JPG and TIF. TIF is the most widely supported image printing format across both the Macintosh and the PC platforms. The portable bitmap (PBM), portable grayscale map (PGM), and portable pixel map (PPM) formats were originally developed for use with email.

When you save in the PBM, PGM, and PPM formats, StarImage asks you to specify whether you want to save the image information raw (which results in a plain binary file stripped of all extraneous information) or as text.

The GIF, JPG, and PNG formats have special significance for Web publishing and are discussed a bit later in this chapter.

SAVING IMAGES TO BMP FORMAT

BMP is the native format for Microsoft Paint (included with Windows). StarImage supports BMP images with up to 16 million colors (24-bit color images). To preserve hard disk space, you can also use Run-Length Encoding (RLE) when saving in the BMP format. RLE is a *lossless* compression scheme that has been developed for the BMP format.

> **Note**
>
> When compressing images to save disk space, computer graphics experts distinguish between lossless and lossy compression methods. *Lossless* means that an image's size is reduced without losing any data and the file looks exactly like the image or graphic you created; *lossy* means that the size of an image is reduced at the expense of some pictorial information.

When you save an image in BMP format, StarImage displays the BMP Options dialog box, shown in Figure 21.19. In the Color Resolution portion of the dialog, you can specify the color depth at which you want to save the image. The options include Original, which saves the image as is; 1-bit Threshold Value, which saves all colors above a predefined threshold as black; 1-bit Dithered, which simulates shades of gray in a black-and-white image; 4-bit Grayscale and 4-bit Color Palette; 8-bit Grayscale (which looks like traditional black-and-white photography) and 8-bit Color Palette; and 24-bit True Colors. With the exception of Original, all the resolutions give you the option to select RLE encoding.

Figure 21.19
When saving a file to BMP format, StarImage gives you the option to change the current color depth of the image and compress the file via RLE.

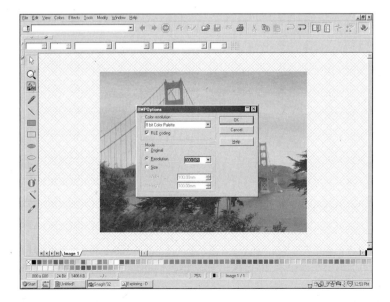

PART

IV

CH

21

SAVING IMAGES FOR THE WORLD WIDE WEB

GIF, JPG, and PNG are the file formats of choice when you're saving files for use on the World Wide Web. GIF supports only 256 colors, so it's better for high-contrast artwork and text. (Note that you must first reduce the number of colors to 256 or fewer when saving an existing 24-bit image in the GIF format by selecting Colors, Modify Color Depth, 256 Colors.) JPG applies lossy compression (which means it sacrifices image quality to save disk space), so it's better for photographs and other continuous-tone images. PNG, which is essentially a 24-bit version of GIF, is designed for small full-color images you don't want to compress.

Note
Regardless of the resolution of an image, Web browsers display one image pixel for every screen pixel. All that counts therefore is the pixel measurement of the image.

SAVING IMAGES TO GIF FORMAT

GIF was developed as a cross-platform graphics standard and is supported by all graphical Internet browsers. It is an extremely popular format that supports a maximum of 8 bits per pixel (256 colors) and uses LZW (Lempel-Ziv-Welch), a lossless compression scheme that enables you to save space on disk without sacrificing any data in the image. Saving files to GIF format enables you to store custom palettes (provided that you created custom colors) with your image and offers several advanced graphic options, including transparent backgrounds, image interlacing, and animation. Also, because GIF images use 256 or fewer colors, there is limited compression required, which means GIFs display fairly quickly onscreen. The GIF format supports the use of image maps and is an ideal choice for smaller pictures (100∞100 pixels or less).

When you're saving in GIF format, StarImage opens the GIF Options dialog, shown in Figure 21.20. Select the Interlaced option if you want Web browsers to display the image in incremental passes; select Save Transparent if you want the background of drawing objects to be saved as transparent.

Note
Selecting both Interlaced and Save Transparent can cause problems with some browsers.

SAVING IMAGES TO JPEG FORMAT

When it comes to saving photographic images, no format results in smaller file sizes than JPEG. JPEG was developed as a compression scheme specifically for computer graphics. Because it supports up to 16.7 million colors, it's an excellent choice for photographs and scanned images. JPEG files support lossy compression, providing high-quality images with a high level of compression. You can choose the display quality from high-quality to very low-quality reproductions—the higher the image quality, the larger the file size. JPEG files require some decompression time when displaying onscreen. Like GIF images, JPEG images support the use of image maps.

Figure 21.20
When saving images to GIF format you can choose between Interlace and Save Transparent, which enables you to remove a one-color background from a bitmap picture so the foreground artwork stands out.

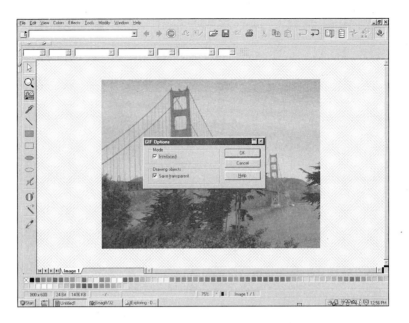

When you save an image in JPG format, StarImage displays the JPEG Options dialog box, shown in Figure 21.21. You use the Quality portion of the dialog to specify the amount of compression applied to an image. Lower values mean smaller file sizes, but also mean you are sacrificing image detail. StarImage does not follow the standard compression settings of other image-editing application, which enable you to set the value on a scale from 1 to 10, with 3 (or Medium) being the recommended setting for Web graphics. Instead, you can select a value from 0 to 100. The default setting is 75, which is slightly above what Web experts say is the best setting for Web graphics, but still yields reasonable results.

Figure 21.21
When saving files to the JPEG format, you can define the compression range in the Quality portion of the dialog—higher numbers mean less compression and larger file sizes.

PART

IV

CH

21

SAVING IMAGES TO PNG FORMAT   PNG is the new kid on the block among file formats. Developed as an alternative to GIF, PNG can handle 24-bit color images and better. The wired crowd considers PNG likely to replace GIF within the next few years. For the time being, however, your Internet browser may require that you install a plug-in filter that supports this new format. A PNG file is typically larger than a JPG or GIF file because it does not include JPEG's lossy compression, and it can contain more colors than a GIF image. Hence, it should only be used for small images, such as buttons or thumbnails, with fine details that you don't want to lose in a compression scheme. As with the GIF and JPEG formats, PNG supports full transparency.

When you save a PNG file, StarImage displays the PNG Options dialog, shown in Figure 21.22. Similar to JPEG file saves, you can select a compression factor, but for PNG it is from 0 to 9, with 9 providing the best possible quality for the image (and least compression); and as with GIF files, you are given the Interlaced option.

Figure 21.22
Saving files to PNG format has the advantage of saving files with more colors in a less compressed format than you get with either GIF or JPEG.

PRINTING YOUR IMAGES

You can print images to any black-and-white or color printing device that is connected to your computer by using the Print icon on the function bar. If you have more than one printing device connected to your computer, or if you want to print multiple copies of an image, choose File, Print, select the desired printer in the Name drop-down list box, and specify the number of copies in the Copies portion of the Print dialog box. If you have a PostScript printer driver installed, you can also print the image to file and send it to a service bureau for color processing and printing.

→ For more details on PostScript printing, **see** "PostScripting with StarWriter," **p. 454**.

Tip #424 from
Michael & Sarah

When you're printing graphics, the current version of StarImage does not automatically ask you if you want to adjust the printer orientation. In order not to have your image cut off, keep an eye on the Size field on the status bar; if the image is wider than it is high, be sure to change the paper orientation via the Properties button in the Print dialog from Portrait to Landscape.

EMAILING YOUR IMAGES

If you have an email account, you can email an image from StarImage by selecting File, Document As Email. In the Send Mail dialog box, you can specify whether you want to send the image file as an attachment or as mail content (in which case the recipient must also have access to a StarMail client in order to view the image). Click OK and follow the usual steps of composing and sending an email.

→ For more details on StarMail and sending file attachments via email, **see** "Handling Attachments," **p. 1061**.

Note

Originally designed to handle sequences of ordinary text, email systems must take special measures to send file attachments. Files attached or inserted in an email message must be encoded in ordinary text characters for the trip, and then decoded and converted back into files on the recipient's computer. StarMail and other email programs handle encoding and decoding automatically. The only concern is to ensure that the software at the sending and receiving ends use the same encoding formats.

CUSTOMIZING STARIMAGE

Every StarOffice module gives you access to a few core settings so that you can modify it to suit your personal needs. StarImage is no different.

SETTING THE COLOR CONTROLS

To customize the use of various StarImage commands on the main toolbar, select Tools, Options. In the Options dialog that appears, click the plus sign next to Picture and select Colors. Using the Picture Color Options dialog you can set the following preferences:

- **RGB values**—Using the Red, Green, and Blue proportion spin boxes, you can specify a percentage by which you add or subtract the red, green, and blue color values when you click the respective Add and Reduce icons in the Colors tear-off window. The default value is 10%, but you can set your preferences anywhere from 1% to 100%.

- **Grayscale**—In this portion of the Colors tab, you can define the number of grayscale values when using the Grayscale icon in the Colors tear-off window in the Main toolbar to convert the current color image into grayscales. The default value is 256; the other options are 4, 8, 16, 32, 64, and 128.

PART
IV
CH
21

- **Poster Colors**—Using the Numbers spinner box, you can set the number of colors that appear in an image when you apply the Poster effects filter. The default value is 16, but you can set the number of colors anywhere from 1 to 64.

- **Brightness & Contrast**—In this area, you can specify the percentage by which you add or subtract the Brightness and Contrast values when clicking the respective icons in the Colors tear-off window. The default is 10%, but you can set values anywhere from 1% to 100%.

- **Rotation**—In this section, you can set the angle by which an image is rotated to the left or right when you use the User-Define Rotation icon in the Image tear-off window. Note that you can set different values for left and right rotations; just select the To the Left option and specify an angle, and then click the To the Right option to define an angle for that option. The default value is 45 degrees, but you can go as low as 0 degrees or as high as 360 degrees (which, of course, are not very useful).

- **Black & White**—Using this portion of the Colors tab, you set a Threshold value for the number of colors that will be turned into black when you convert a color image into a black-and-white image. The default value is 50, but you can select any number from 1 to 100.

SETTING THE EFFECT DEFAULTS

Using the Picture Effects Options dialog, you can control the settings for the following Effects filters:

- **Mosaic**—Use the X Tile and Y Tile spinner boxes to set the width and height of individual mosaics in pixels. The default setting is 4 pixels, but you can go as low as 1 pixel or as high as 999. Note that you can set the size of the individual mosaics proportionally by selecting the same pixel value in each box, or disproportionately by choosing different numbers. Using the Definition drop-down list box, you can define the contrast between individual mosaics. The default setting is Medium, and the other options are Low and High.

- **Solarization**—In this area, you can set a threshold value for the degree of brightness solarization filter effect. Pixels that are above this threshold value are inverted. If you select the Invert option, pixels that fall below the threshold value are inverted. The default value is 10, and you can go as low as 0 and as high as 100.

- **Tile**—Similar to the Mosaic effect, you can use the X Tile and Y Tile spinner boxes to define the width and height of the individual tiles in pixels. The default size is 4 pixels. The lowest possible setting is 1 pixel; the highest possible setting is 999 pixels.

- **Definition**—Use the Degree drop-down list to set the contour for this filter effect. The default value is Medium; the other values are Low and High.

- **Aging**—In the Intensity spinner box, you can define the degree of the aging process from 0% to 100%. The default setting is 10%.

PROJECT: MAKE THE MOST OF STARIMAGE

Ultimately, your imagination determines what you do with StarImage. To get you started, though, here are a few ideas for making the most of StarImage:

- Put some finishing touches on a beautiful vista or product shot, save it in a common format (for example, BMP or JPEG), and then import the image (by choosing Insert Picture, From File) for use as an eye-catching background inside a StarImpress presentation.

- After scanning and adjusting an image in StarImpress, import the image (by choosing Insert, From File) into a newsletter or brochure created in StarWriter.

- Capture an onscreen image (by pressing the Print Screen key or using a third-party screen capture program such as SnagIt), and then open the screenshot, crop the part of the screen you need, and save it in a custom Gallery folder. Next, drag the image into a StarDraw document, annotate the screenshot using arrows and callouts, and print it from the drawing program or place it in a StarImpress presentation or StarWriter document.

- Apply a special effects filter to a favorite image, save it as a BMP file, place it into the Windows root directory, and then use it as wallpaper (by choosing Control Panel, Display).

- Start a drawing in StarDraw, export it as a pixel format file, open it in StarImpress and apply StarImage's unique tools to add textures, tones, and effects that are impossible to create in a vector-based drawing program such as StarDraw.

- Snap a photo with a digital camera and correct the brightness and contrast in StarImage.

- Adjust the color values of an image and reduce its size and then save it as a GIF or JPG file for Web display.

If you're serious about computer graphics, you might want to upgrade to a product such as Adobe Photoshop, Corel PhotoPaint, or GIMP (www.gimp.org). But for general use and to enhance your StarOffice documents and Web pages, StarImage will do the job.

PRESENTING RESULTS—STARIMPRESS

CHAPTER 22

GETTING STARTED WITH STARIMPRESS

In this chapter

EXPLORING THE STARIMPRESS ENVIRONMENT

StarImpress is the presentation module of StarOffice, and you can say indeed that it's impressive. For one thing, it's hard to beat the intelligent user interface that StarImpress has for switching between views and layout modes and entering content. In addition, StarImpress provides an assortment of aids that help you create professional-looking presentations in no time, including the AutoPilot Presentation Wizard, numerous AutoLayout templates, guides for aligning text and objects, grids for positioning text and objects on a slide or page, and tools that enable you to animate the elements on your slides and to assign special transition effects. The final result can be presented as an onscreen slide show or exported as an HTML document with frames, navigation icons, and hyperlinks.

EXPLORING THE MASTER VIEWS

StarImpress makes it easy for you to create your presentation by providing five master views: Drawing, Outline, Slide Sort, Notes, and Handout. Each view gives you a different way of looking at and working with your presentation. You can open each view by clicking the corresponding button above the vertical scrollbar on the right side of the screen or by selecting the appropriate command from the View, Master View submenu.

CREATING SLIDES IN DRAWING VIEW

The Drawing View, shown in Figure 22.1, is the most important view in StarImpress. In this view, you can create the slides for your presentation, insert new slides and objects such as graphics and charts, and modify the appearance of an existing slide.

When you're in Drawing View, StarImpress looks virtually identical to StarDraw. You have access to the same visual aids, including grids, snap lines and snap points, as well as all the tools you know from StarDraw, plus the Effects, Interaction, Animation, and Slide Show icons at the bottom of the main toolbar and the Presentation Box On/Off button on the object bar. The Effects icon opens the Effects floating dialog box in which you can assign transitions between slides, text effects, and attributes for the individual effects; you also can arrange the order of the effects. The Interaction icon opens the Interaction dialog in which you can control how an object behaves if it is clicked during a presentation. The Animation icon opens the Animation floating dialog box, which enables you to animate grouped objects and bitmapped images. Finally, the Presentation Box On/Off icon on the object bar shows/hides the Presentation Box—a floating window that gives you one-click access to the most useful commands and dialog boxes for working with slides (including Insert Slide and Modify Slide Layout).

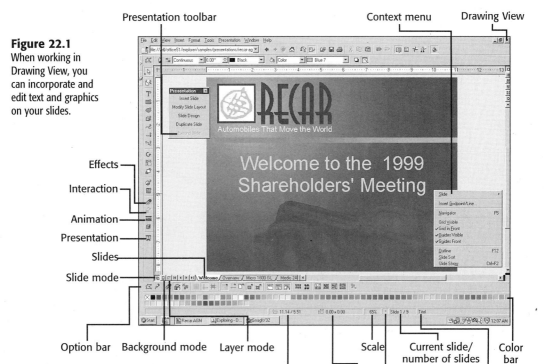

Figure 22.1
When working in Drawing View, you can incorporate and edit text and graphics on your slides.

Presentation toolbar

Context menu

Drawing View

Effects

Interaction

Animation

Presentation

Slides

Slide mode

Option bar   Background mode   Layer mode

Scale   Current slide/
number of slides   Color
bar

Current cursor   Selection size   Document   Template
position   modified

Note

The Effects icon on the main toolbar in StarImpress opens the Effects dialog box, which enables you to create various presentation effects. By contrast, the Effects icon on the main toolbar in StarDraw opens the Effects floating toolbar, which contains various tools that enable you to manipulate graphic objects. Of these tools, you'll find only the Rotation tool in StarImpress (on the main toolbar).

At the lower-left corner of the presentation window, you'll notice the Slide, Background, and Layer mode buttons. Using these buttons, you can control whether you want to work on the surface, background, or different layers of the current slide.

ORGANIZING CONTENT IN OUTLINE VIEW

The Outline View, shown in Figure 22.2, helps you develop and organize the content of your presentation. Using this view, which is comparable in function to the Outline View in the Navigator, you can create the skeleton of your presentation and move and format the headings and other information by using the buttons on the object bar. Using your outline, StarImpress creates slides that you can then embellish with graphic objects and effects.

→ For more details on working in Outline View, **see** "Editing in Outline View," **p. 839**.

Tip #425 from
Michael & Sarah

When you're working in Outline View, be sure to display the Preview window (by selecting View, Preview). In the Preview window, you can track the changes you make to a slide in real-time.

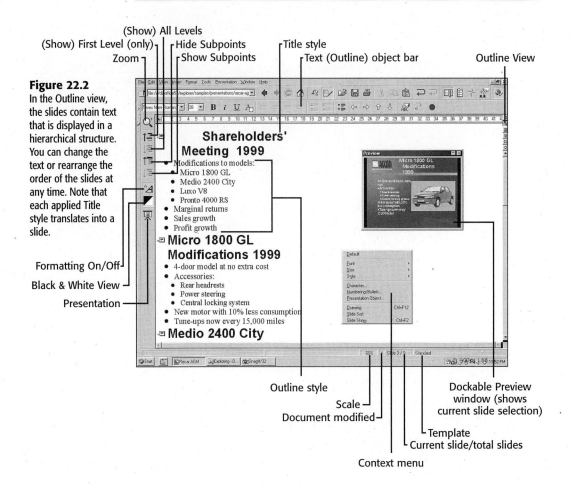

(Show) First Level (only)
(Show) All Levels
Zoom
Hide Subpoints
Show Subpoints
Title style
Text (Outline) object bar
Outline View

Figure 22.2
In the Outline view, the slides contain text that is displayed in a hierarchical structure. You can change the text or rearrange the order of the slides at any time. Note that each applied Title style translates into a slide.

Formatting On/Off
Black & White View
Presentation

Outline style
Scale
Document modified
Context menu
Current slide/total slides
Template
Dockable Preview window (shows current slide selection)

ARRANGING YOUR SLIDES IN SLIDE SORT VIEW

When you're in Slide Sort View, you can see thumbnail previews of all the slides in your presentation so that you can check their layout and sequence (see Figure 22.3). This view is best for arranging and ordering slides, adding transitions between slides, and setting the timing for the transitions and onscreen display.

→ For more details on arranging slides in Slide Sort view, **see** "Rearranging Slides," **p. 854**.

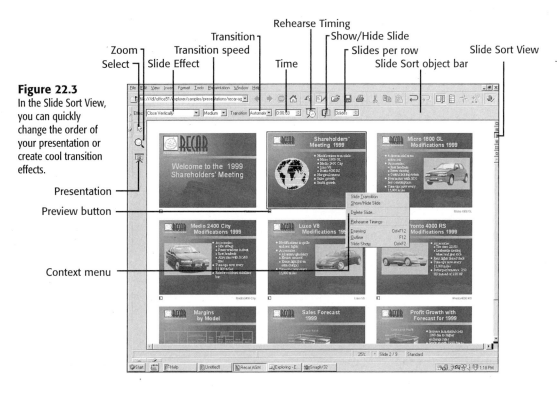

Figure 22.3
In the Slide Sort View, you can quickly change the order of your presentation or create cool transition effects.

ADDING SPEAKER NOTES IN NOTES VIEW

In the Notes View, shown in Figure 22.4, you can add text or graphics to each individual slide. These notes do not show during the presentation of your slide show. However, you can use this view to jot down ideas for your slide presentation, including transitions, or simply to enter speaker's notes that you can then print and use during your presentation. Note that in this view, you have access to the same tools and bars as in Drawing View.

→ For more details on adding speaker's notes to your presentation, **see** "Creating Speaker Notes," **p. 845**.

PREPARING AUDIENCE HANDOUTS IN HANDOUT VIEW

Comparable in function to the Page View/Print Preview in StarWriter, the Handout View enables you to print a set number of consecutive slides on one page (see Figure 22.5).

You can change the number of slides printed per page as well as the layout by clicking Modify Slide Layout in the Presentation Box or selecting Slide, Modify Slide from the context menu. Alternately, you can also select Format, Modify from the menu bar. Using the Modify Slide dialog that appears, you can choose from five predesigned layouts for your handouts.

Figure 22.4
Use the Notes View to create notes for the presenter. Just click the placeholder text, and then start typing your own.

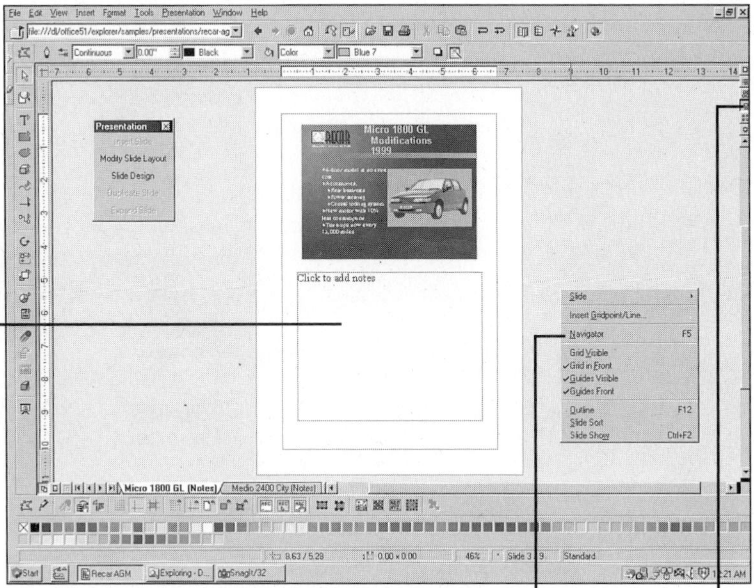

Add text or graphics

Context menu Notes View

Figure 22.5
Use the Handout View to create print-outs of your presentation for your audience.

Click to modify the number of slides per page

Context menu Handout View

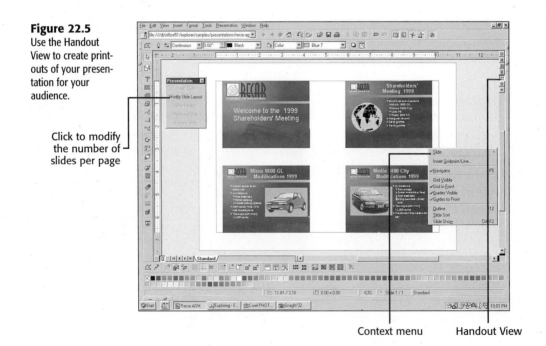

When you're in Handout View, you have access to the same tools as in Drawing view and Notes View. Having these tools available is useful because you can design different handouts and then use the available drawing and text tools to create additional art or titles for the slides, including inserting Date and Time fields (by selecting Insert, Fields), as well as Author information and Page numbers. Note that you cannot switch designs within the current presentation.

UNDERSTANDING THE WORKING MODES

When you look at the bottom left of your drawing window, you'll notice three icons: Slide mode (default on program start), Background mode, and Layer mode (see Figure 22.6). Each mode represents a different mode of working in a presentation document.

> **Note**
>
> StarImpress always remembers the last mode that was active when a document was saved. If the document is in Background mode after you open it, you should switch to Slide mode using the respective icon at the lower left of the document window.

> **Note**
>
> When you're in Drawing View, you can access all three of these modes–Slide mode, Background mode, and Layer mode. When you're in Notes View, you can access only the Slide and Background modes. For all other views, these modes are irrelevant.

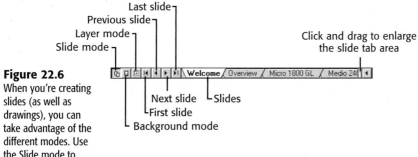

Figure 22.6
When you're creating slides (as well as drawings), you can take advantage of the different modes. Use the Slide mode to create individual slides; use the Background mode to create unified back-grounds for your slides; toggle on the Layers mode to cre-ate different transpar-ent layers.

WORKING IN SLIDE MODE

In Slide mode, you can use the various drawing, effects, and text tools in StarImpress to create and edit the foreground elements of the individual slides of a presentation. Any changes you make apply to the current slide only, regardless of whether the current slide shares a slide design (or layout template) with other slides.

→ For more details on using the drawing and text tools, **see** Chapter 20, "Getting Sketchy with StarDraw," **p. 715**.

WORKING IN BACKGROUND MODE

When you're in Background mode, you can define a unified background for the current slide design (or layout). If you're using more than one slide design in your presentation, you can edit each design individually by clicking the name tab of the design you want to edit. For example, if you've created one design for the title (or opening) page of your presentation (naming it, for example, Title) and one design for all the other slides (naming them Standard), you'll see two tabs when switching to Background mode: one for your title slide (Title) and one for all the other slides (Standard).

To switch to Background mode, click the Background mode button in the lower left in the Drawing View, Notes View, or Handouts View. Alternatively, you can choose View, Background from the menu bar and then select Drawing, Notes, or Handouts from the Background submenu to quickly switch to the desired mode. If you select Title, you can edit the background of the title slide.

→ For more details on changing the background design, **see** "Changing the Slide (Background) Design," **p. 856**.

When you're working in Background mode, you have access to the same tools as in Drawing mode. However, you cannot apply animated effects to objects that have been inserted in Background mode. But you can insert sounds. Any changes you make in Background mode are applied to every slide that shares the same template.

WORKING WITH LAYERS

Working with layers is similar to working with multiple overlapping overhead transparencies; each transparency contains different pieces of information that, when placed in a stack with the others, blend together to create one coherent set underneath the light of the projector. Layers, too, combine to create a complex graphic out of individual pieces of information. For example, if you want to draw the floor plan of a house, you can create a layer that contains only the walls and doors and windows, called Ground Plan. Another layer, called Electric, can show the electrical wiring of the house. A third layer, called Plumbing, can show the pipes, and so on. Because each layer is transparent, you can see all layers at once.

When you're working in Layer mode, you can assign different layers to different objects of the current slide. Because layers are transparent, there is no limit to the number of layers you can use. And if you don't want to show the object(s) on a particular layer, you either can make the object invisible (by changing its attributes on the object bar), or you can hide the entire layer (by Shift+clicking the layer's name tab).

To give you a head start, StarImpress and StarDraw documents come with the following default layers:

- **Layout**—This layer manages objects you create in the regular work area (in Drawing view).
- **Controls**—This layer manages all control fields, as well as interactive objects.
- **Dimension Lines**—This layer manages the dimension lines.

> **Note**
>
> These three default layers exist so that you can easily hide dimension lines and controls without having to switch layers while drawing.

CREATING NEW LAYERS   To create a new layer, follow these steps:

1. Select the slide to which you want to add a layer or insert a new one.
2. Click the Layer Mode button.
3. Insert a new layer by clicking in the gray area after the last layer (for example, Dimension Lines), or select Insert, Layer from the menu bar. The Insert Layer dialog appears. (By default, the Visible and Printable check boxes in the Options portion are marked; don't change them at this point.)
4. Enter a descriptive name for the new layer in the Name text box, and click OK.
5. Click the tab of the new layer, and start drawing.

> **Note**
>
> The layers you insert appear on all existing as well as future slides of your presentation or drawing document. However, the object you insert on a particular layer shows only on the layer of the slide that was active when you inserted the layer.

MODIFYING AN EXISTING LAYER   If you want to modify an existing layer—for example, hide it, prevent it from printing, or protect it against changes—follow these steps:

1. Select the slide whose layers you want to change, and then activate the Layer mode.
2. Click the name tab of the layer you want to modify to bring it to the front.
3. Right-click the tab of the now active layer, and select Modify from the context menu. The Modify Layer dialog appears.
4. Make the desired choices. Your options include the following:
    - **Visible**—Controls whether the layer will be hidden from view or shown. This option is useful if you're using complex graphical elements that you would like to temporarily hide while working on your presentation (or drawing).

- **Printable**—Determines whether the layer will be printed. You can use this option, for example, in drawing documents to insert notes relating to a graphic or slide. (Remember that, unlike StarImpress, StarDraw does not have a Notes view or feature.) While you're working on the graphic, you can make the layer invisible.
- **Lock**—Protects the layer against further changes.

5. When you're finished, click OK.

Tip #426 from
Michael & Sarah

If you only want to make a layer invisible, you can Shift+click the name tab of the respective layer. When a layer is marked as invisible, its name appears in blue on the name tab. To make the layer visible again, Shift+click the name tab again.

If you want to rename a layer, follow steps 1 and 2 shown here, right-click the name tab of the layer you want to rename, and then select Rename Layer from the context menu. The program automatically highlights the name in the tab, so you can type a new name over it.

To delete a layer, select Delete Layer from the Layer context menu. An alert box pops up, asking you to confirm whether you want to delete the selected layer. Click Yes to delete it.

Note

You cannot rename or delete the default layers (Layout, Controls, and Dimension Lines). However, you can insert objects on these layers, and you can lock, hide, or prevent them from printing by selecting the respective options in the Modify Layer dialog.

MOVING OBJECTS BETWEEN LAYERS   You can't easily copy objects from one layer to another. Using the familiar cut-and-paste routine only reinserts the object in the old layer. Stumped? Don't be. The solution is to drag the object from one layer to another. Here's what you need to do:

1. Navigate to the slide that contains the layer with the object that you want to move, and activate the Layer mode.
2. Click the name tab of the layer that contains the object that you want to move to bring it to the front.
3. Select the object that you want to move, click the object again, and wait a second before dragging the object from the current layer to the name tab of the new layer.
4. Drag the selected object from the active layer to the name tab of the layer to which you want to move it, and release the mouse button. (As you drag, you see a rectangle in the lower-right corner of your pointer, which indicates that the object is being moved.) The object is being inserted in the same position at the new location.

Tip #427 from _Michael & Sarah_	To move an object from a custom (new) layer in Slide A to a layer in Slide B, you have to select the object and then cut it (press Ctrl+X). Next, go to the other slide and insert it. Now you can move it to the appropriate layer following the steps above.

SELECTING A VIEW

When you're changing views in StarImpress, as in StarDraw, you can change either the size at which the slides (and by extension their contents) appear onscreen or the display quality. If you change the size of a slide, each change in view size is expressed as a zoom ratio. If you change the display quality, you prevent certain attributes in your graphic from appearing onscreen.

TAKING STOCK OF THE ZOOM TOOLS

Changing your views in StarImpress works the same as in the other StarOffice modules. You can right-click in the Scale field on the status bar and select a preset viewing size from the shortcut menu, including 200%, 150%, 100%, 75%, 50%, Optimal, Page Width, and Entire Page. Alternatively, you can double-click in the Scale field or select View, Zoom from the menu bar to open the Zoom dialog, which in addition to the listed ratios enables you to set a custom (variable) view size for the current image.

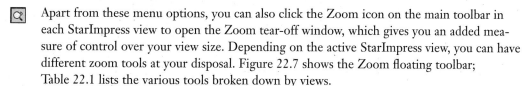 Apart from these menu options, you can also click the Zoom icon on the main toolbar in each StarImpress view to open the Zoom tear-off window, which gives you an added measure of control over your view size. Depending on the active StarImpress view, you can have different zoom tools at your disposal. Figure 22.7 shows the Zoom floating toolbar; Table 22.1 lists the various tools broken down by views.

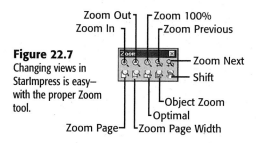

Figure 22.7
Changing views in StarImpress is easy—with the proper Zoom tool.

TABLE 22.1   AVAILABLE ZOOM TOOLS IN STARIMPRESS

Tool	Drawing View	Outline View	Slide Sort View	Notes View	Handout View
Zoom In	✓	✓	✓	✓	✓
Zoom Out	✓	✓	✓	✓	✓
Zoom 100%	✓	✓	✓	✓	✓
Zoom Previous	✓	✓	✓	✓	✓
Zoom Next	✓	✓	✓	✓	✓
Zoom Page	✓		✓	✓	✓
Zoom Page Width	✓			✓	✓
Optimal	✓			✓	✓
Object Zoom	✓			✓	✓
Shift	✓			✓	✓

CHANGING THE DISPLAY QUALITY

Like StarDraw, StarImpress gives you various options for changing the display quality of your presentation.

By selecting a display quality, you can adjust the way elements are displayed in your work area. Because display quality is video- and system memory-dependent, display selections you make affect the screen refresh speed and performance of StarDraw itself. Choosing a less memory-intensive display enables users with complex images and slower computers to save time when working with graphics. With regard to StarImpress, choosing a grayscale over a color display also gives you the option to see what a slide show might look like on a monochrome display. Note that the display quality you choose does not affect the quality of your printed or saved image; it affects only your screen display.

You can specify the display quality by selecting View, Display Quality. Your options include the following:

- **Color**—You can see all fills and objects.
- **Grayscale**—All colors are converted to grayscales.
- **Black and White**—Any colors, grayscales, or fills are hidden. Two-dimensional graphics turn into outlined shapes; three-dimensional graphics resemble wire-frame illustrations.

Note

If you feel uncomfortable working in grayscale or black-and-white views, you can always select View, Preview. By doing so, you open a small Preview window above the extended Explorer where you can watch the effects of your changes in real-time.

WORKING WITH PREVIEW

Like StarDraw, StarImpress enables you to preview the current slide inside a small floating window called the Preview window. The Preview window always presents the currently selected slide. If you make changes to a slide, you can track your changes in real-time by looking at the Preview window.

As a floating window, the Preview window can be placed anywhere on your desktop. If it gets in the way, you can double-click its title bar to temporarily minimize it. Double-click again to return it to its original size.

By default, you see the Preview window when switching to Outline view or working in Background mode. However, you can use the Preview window in all views. If you don't see the Preview window, select View, Preview from the menu bar. Just as you can do with the display quality of your monitor, you can adjust the display quality of your Preview window by selecting View, Preview Mode. Your options include Color (default), Grayscale, and Black and White.

PLANNING YOUR PRESENTATION

As with every complex document you create, spending a little time up front saves a lot of headaches later on. As you are planning your presentation, you should consider these questions:

- **What is your message?**   Always start by identifying the core ideas you want to communicate to your audience; jot them down on a piece of paper, and organize the facts that will support your ideas. That way, you can think about the text, images, or sounds you need to get the message across.

- **Who is your audience?**   Your audience is the single-most important element in planning your presentation. If you don't know whether you're creating a presentation for techies or trekkies, you can't decide on the amount of factual details or fictitious lore you have to present, not to mention whether your tone is supposed to be serious or not.

- **What is your medium?**   If you plan to present your work on an overhead projector, you won't be incorporating multimedia elements such as animation or sound effects. However, if you're fortunate enough to project your work on a multimonitor screen, you can cram so much more information and effects into your presentation than you could if you had to rely on your trusty ol' laptop.

- **Where does the presentation take place?**   You should always inquire about the size of the room and the lighting conditions. The larger the room, the larger the type and images you use (which means the less information you can squeeze into one slide).

In general, subscribe to the old adage, KISS—Keep It Simple, Stupid. Given the options you have at your fingertips when creating a StarImpress presentation, you should always remember that less is more. Depending on the conditions under which you give your presentations, you might easily overwhelm audiences with too many gimmicks. You can design slides with rich detail and sounds and animation. In the end, however, the result may be the same as if you had created a letter or résumé with 20 different fonts—the message is lost, and what is left is a flash in the pan. When designing your presentation, focus on the essentials—the content—that you want to bring across.

→ For more details on the various "gimmicks" and effects that you can insert into a presentation, **see** Chapter 23, "Enhancing Your Presentation," starting on **p. 865**.

This said, check out this list of the elements you can include in your presentation:

- **Drawings**—Import drawings (or vector graphics) created in StarDraw, or create new ones on-the-fly by using the drawing tools in StarImpress. (When you're working in Drawing view, you have access to the same drawing tools that you have access to in StarDraw.)

- **Images**—Import bitmapped images from the Gallery.

- **Text**—Using the Text tools on the main toolbar, you can create frames with regular text or anchored text, as well as callouts. You can also convert text into Bézier curves and 3D and then apply 3D effects for additional impact. Slide titles and outline headings are assigned via predefined styles and templates.

- **Background designs**—Use the StarOffice default layout templates (located in the `Office51\Template\layout` folder), or create your own using the drawing tools and effects options in StarImpress. Backgrounds should consist of unalterable elements such as logos that are supposed to appear at the same location throughout all slides.

- **Animations**—Animate text and objects to create visual interest or explain complex relations visually.

- **Sounds and video**—Enhance your presentation with sound and video clips.

- **Transitions**—Use transition effects between slides. StarImpress includes around 40 effects that you can apply to entire slides or to individual objects on slides.

- **Objects**—StarImpress supports OLE linking and embedded objects. You can insert charts, formulas, frames, OLE objects, plug-ins, Java applets, StarCalc spreadsheets, files, and graphics.

STARTING A NEW PRESENTATION

StarImpress offers a variety of ways to create a new presentation. You can start with an empty document that contains no color or style enhancements; you can open and modify an existing presentation or document; you can base your presentation on an existing template or predefined layout; or you can solicit the help of the AutoPilot Presentation Wizard, which steps you through the process of creating a framework for all the above by asking you to respond to a series of questions presented in consecutive dialog boxes.

WORKING WITH THE AUTOPILOT

By far the easiest way to create a new presentation in StarImpress is by soliciting the help of the AutoPilot Presentation Wizard. The AutoPilot Wizard walks you step-by-step through the creation of a framework for a presentation document. By default, StarImpress opens the AutoPilot automatically when you click the Presentation icon in the Tasks group of the extended Explorer, or select File, New, Presentation or Start, New, Presentation. You can also start the wizard by selecting File, AutoPilot, Presentation.

Note

To prevent the AutoPilot Presentation Wizard from showing each time you start a presentation, select Do Not Show This Dialog Again in the lower right on the first dialog of the AutoPilot Wizard. The next time you select File, New Presentation or click the Presentation icon, StarImpress will open to an empty, landscape-oriented slide. To reinstate the AutoPilot at startup, select Start with AutoPilots in the Tools, Options, Presentations, Other dialog.

To create a presentation using the AutoPilot Wizard, follow these steps:

1. Click the Presentation icon in the Tasks group, or select File, AutoPilot, Presentation.

2. Using the first AutoPilot Presentation Wizard dialog, you can select the type of presentation you want to create. Depending on your selection, you see three different variations of this dialog. Your options are as follows:

   • **Empty Presentation**—Not much to do here but click the Next button to advance to the next AutoPilot dialog, or click the Create button and then create a presentation based on a predefined layout (using the Modify Slide dialog) or from scratch (see Figure 22.8).

Figure 22.8
Empty Presentation.

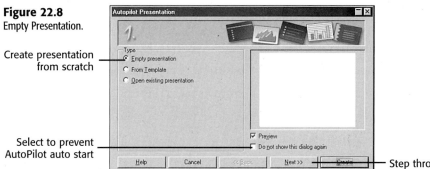

Create presentation from scratch

Select to prevent AutoPilot auto start

Step through AutoPilot

   • **From Template**—Choose a template from the list of available presentation templates (see Figure 22.9). If the template you're looking for is not listed, select a different category from the drop-down list box above the template list. By default, StarImpress includes presentation templates in the Presentations and

Education categories. (The Presentation Layouts category includes only various background designs for your slide.) You can preview each template in the Preview window on the right if the Preview option is selected. (For a complete list of available StarImpress templates, see "Using an Existing Template" in this chapter.) After you've made your selection, click Next.

Figure 22.9
From Template.

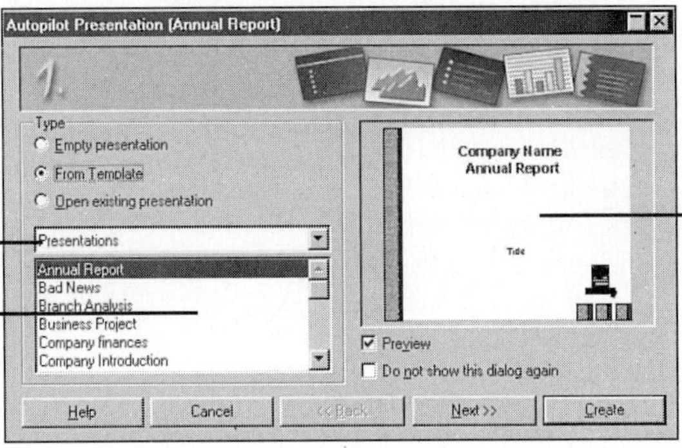

Select a template category

Choose a template

Preview selected template or document

- **Open Existing Presentation**—Select the desired presentation from the list of available presentations in your Workfolder (the default is `C:\My Documents` on the Windows platform and `C:/Work Folder` on Linux). Then click the Create button to open it (see Figure 22.10). If the presentation you're looking for is not listed in the box on the lower left of the dialog, select Other Position and click Create. This action opens the Open dialog in which you can locate the desired presentation document on your local hard drive or network. Note that you exit the AutoPilot as soon as you click the Create button. (Note also that this option may not be available if you don't have an existing presentation in your default Workfolder.)

Tip #428 from
Michael & Sarah

You can change your designated Workfolder in the Paths dialog box, which you open via the Tools, Options "master dialog."

Figure 22.10
Open Existing
Presentation.

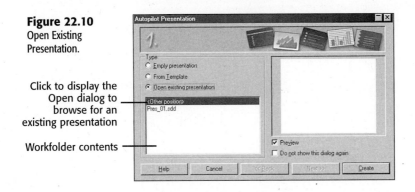

Click to display the Open dialog to browse for an existing presentation

Workfolder contents

3. In the second AutoPilot dialog, you can choose a background design (or layout) for your empty or template-based presentation (see Figure 22.11). Select a category from the drop-down list to see a list of available background templates in the box below. Again, you can preview your selection in the window on the right. Using this dialog, you can also specify the output medium for your presentation. StarImpress enables you to create presentations for onscreen display (Screen), overhead projections (Overhead), slide shows (Slide), or old-fashioned handouts (Paper). The final dimensions, margins, and orientation of your presentation depend on your selection. Click Next to accept the new settings and move to the following dialog.

Figure 22.11
Choose a background design or layout here.

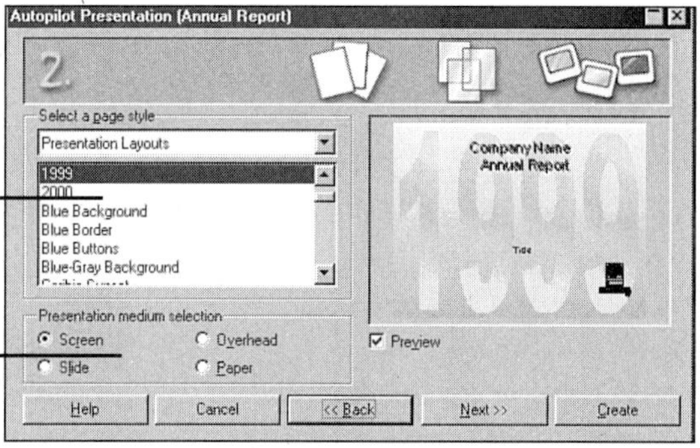

Select background

Select medium for your presentation

4. Use the third AutoPilot dialog to specify the type and speed of transition effect you want between slides. In the Presentation Type Selection portion of the dialog, you can choose between the Default presentation (which means the transitions are controlled manually, per mouse click or keyboard) and Automatically (which repeatedly shows all slides with fixed time lapses until someone presses the Escape key). If you select Automatically, you can use the Duration of Page spin box to determine the time each slide is shown onscreen before the next slide displays. In the Duration of Pause spin box, you can set a time limit for the duration between presentations. If the Show Logo check box is marked, the Created with StarOffice logo is displayed on the pause page.

Note

If your output medium is a 35mm slide, overhead transparency, or paper, the settings in the third AutoPilot dialog are irrelevant.

If you chose to create an Empty Presentation, this is as far as the wizard will take you. Click the Create button to start working on your presentation. If you're basing your presentation on an existing template, click Next (see Figure 22.12).

5. In the fourth AutoPilot dialog, you can enter additional text that will appear on the title page of your presentation, including your name or the name of your company, the focus of your presentation, and any further ideas you want the audience to think about (see Figure 22.13). If you're creating a presentation based on an existing template, you might not need to fill in the second and third text boxes.

Figure 22.12
Specify the type and
speed of the transition
you want here.

Define the
transition effect

Define the time
lapses between
slides

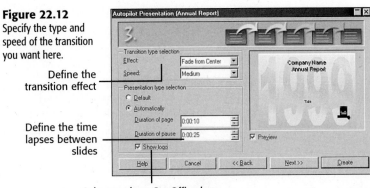

Select to show StarOffice logo
during the pause page

Figure 22.13
Enter additional text
here.

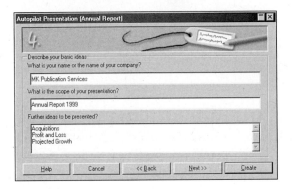

6. In the fifth and final wizard dialog, you can choose the slides or pages of the existing template that you want to appear in your presentation (see Figure 22.14). The Choose Your Pages list on the left contains all slides that are currently selected. If you want to remove some slides from your presentation, click the page icon with the green check mark next to the name. The check mark then disappears, which means that the slide has been removed from your presentation. Click again, and the slide is added to your presentation page. If you check the Create Summary check box, the AutoPilot Wizard creates a new slide that lists the names and titles of all currently present slides. (Note that creating such a slide is not necessary when you're basing your presentation on an existing template because most templates already have such a slide.)

7. Click Create. The AutoPilot Presentation Wizard generates the presentation document according to your specifications. You can then add the desired content, save it, and present or print it.

Figure 22.14
Choose slides or pages for the existing template here.

Click to remove slide

Click to expand

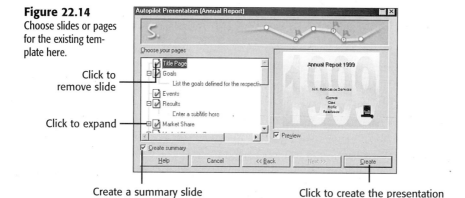

Create a summary slide

Click to create the presentation

USING AN EXISTING DOCUMENT

You don't have to use the AutoPilot when you're basing your presentation on an existing document or template. In fact, if you want to use an existing document as the base for your presentation, you're better off to select File, Open and then use the Open dialog to locate the presentation document on your hard drive or network.

Tip #429 from
Michael & Sarah

To find your existing presentation documents faster, you can select StarImpress 5.0 or 4.0 in the File Type list of the Open dialog, depending on the version of StarImpress that created the document. That way, you see only StarImpress documents listed in the folders of the Open dialog.

StarOffice includes five sample presentations that demonstrate the versatility of StarImpress:

- **Chess**—An animated chess presentation. It consists of one slide, based on the Standard template, and animation effects. Press Ctrl+F12 or click the Presentation icon on the main toolbar to start the game.

- **Holiday Pictures**—A slide show presentation, literally. It comes with 16 slides and controls at the bottom of each slide; the pictures are from the Gallery Photo theme.

- **Orgchart**—Organizational chart that uses text boxes and connectors, the standard template, and hotspots that you can click to be transported to related areas (like hyperlinks).

- **Recar-agm**—Presentation for a shareholders' meeting that demonstrates various transition and text animation effects.

- **ThreeDimensions**—A sample presentation of 3D graphics (created in StarOffice) with "bottom to top" fade effect and filmstrip template.

You can find these sample presentations in the `Office51\Explorer\Samples\Presentations` folder. Just select File, Open and locate the folder and files using the Open dialog box. Alternatively, you can click the Samples icon in the Explorer group to open the folder contents in the desktop area and then double-click the Presentations folder to show its contents.

USING AN EXISTING TEMPLATE

The advantage of using a template is that it already contains slides with content guidelines that you can follow to quickly build a presentation for your business needs. StarImpress provides one standard (general) presentation template and a total of 20 complete custom presentation templates that you can use as the starting point for creating your own presentations. You can find templates for an Annual Report, Bad News, Branch Analysis, Business Project, Company Finances, Company Introduction, Concept, Exchange of Ideas, Introduction of New Product, Marketing Plan, New Employee Introduction, Product/Service Information, Project Report, Scientific Presentation, Selling Presentation, Staff Assembly, Standard, Strategy Recommendation, Team Motivation, Technical Report, and Training.

To create a presentation using one of StarOffice's ready-made presentation templates, follow these steps:

1. Select File, New, From Template from the menu bar, or press Ctrl+N to open the New dialog.

2. Select Education (Scientific Presentation) or Presentations (all other templates) in the Categories list on the left to see a list of available presentation templates in the Templates box on the right.

Tip #430 from
Michael & Sarah

When you're browsing through the templates, select the Preview option in the lower left of the New dialog, and click the More button. You can then see a thumbnail preview and summary information (see Figure 22.19 later in this chapter) of each selected template design and layout in the Preview window.

---

3. Select the desired template, and click OK to open it as a new task in StarImpress.

When you first open a complete template, you see placeholder text on each individual slide that is part of the presentation (see Figure 22.15). This text is meant to give you an idea of what content to include on a particular slide. Click the existing text to select each item that you see (titles, outlines, or text) within the slide, and type the desired replacement text while you're in Drawing View. You can use the Navigator or the Previous Slide and Next Slide buttons at the lower-left side of the presentation window to move among the various slides of your presentation. To work on a slide, click its name tab to bring the slide to the front.

→ For more details on working with slides, including adding and deleting slides, **see** "Working with Slides," **p. 846**.

Figure 22.15
When you're working with complete templates, you'll notice that each slide contains text in the form of suggestions that you can modify by clicking the existing text while in Drawing mode. Note that the Draw object bar is pushed aside by the Text object bar as soon as you click the existing text.

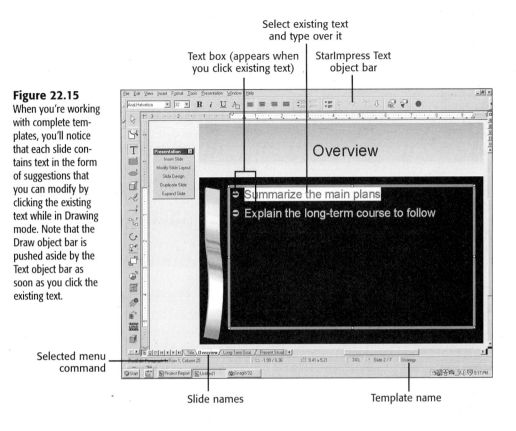

Select existing text and type over it

Text box (appears when you click existing text)

StarImpress Text object bar

Selected menu command

Slide names

Template name

After you've finished adding the desired text to the slides of your presentation, you can save it by selecting File, Save or pressing Ctrl+S. When you're finished with your presentation, select File, Close.

→ For more details and options on saving your presentation, **see** "Saving and Closing Presentations," **p. 861**.

USING AN EXISTING PRESENTATION LAYOUT

If you're looking only for a presentation background design rather than a complete presentation, browse through the Presentation Layouts category of the New dialog. StarOffice comes with 40 colorful presentation background designs (or layouts) for "serious" and "casual" business presentations, some of which are also suitable for black-and-white print.

To create a presentation based on an existing presentation background design, follow these steps:

1. Select File, New, From Template, or press Ctrl+N to open the New dialog.

2. Select the Presentation Layouts category, and then select the desired design in the Templates list box.

3. Click OK. StarOffice launches a new StarImpress task and opens to the Modify Slide dialog.

4. Choose a layout for the first slide of your presentation.

5. Click OK.

As with presentations that are based on complete templates, you see a slide that contains predefined text that you can replace with your own.

STARTING FROM SCRATCH

Starting a presentation from scratch certainly gives you the most creative freedom but also requires a certain familiarity with the program. Still, if you're up for the challenge, click the Presentation icon in the Tasks group, or select File, New, Presentation or Start, Presentation.

If you haven't previously disabled the auto-start feature of the AutoPilot Presentation Wizard, you'll see the first dialog of the AutoPilot. To prevent this dialog from showing in the future, select Do Not Show This Dialog Again in the lower right on the first dialog of the AutoPilot Wizard. Next, select the Empty Presentation option, and then click the Create button. In the Modify Slide dialog that appears, select a predefined layout, or click Cancel to really start from scratch. Selecting a layout has the advantage that your slide will already come with entry boxes for text and graphics. StarImpress provides templates that are useful for the creation of slides that contain predominantly text, as well as slides that consist of charts and graphics. All you have to do is click the placeholder text and enter your own text or import your own graphic.

Tip #431 from
Michael & Sarah

For a very rudimentary example of starting a presentation from scratch, go to the StarOffice online help and search for Presentation. Select "Presentation, create a" from the search results and double-click A Simple Presentation in the desired topic list box at the bottom of the Search dialog.

WORKING WITH TEXT

With your chosen page layout onscreen, replacing or editing existing text elements is as simple as clicking and typing in the work area that contains the text elements you want to change. The following sections cover the basics of editing text in Outline view and Drawing view, using the Text tools, creating speaker notes, and importing outlines from a StarWriter document.

Note

Don't forget to use the StarOffice proofing aids—spelling checker and thesaurus—after editing or adding new text. Nothing is more embarrassing than having a typo at 60-point size on a multimonitor display. For more details on using the various proofing aids in StarOffice, see "Proofing Your Work" in Chapter 12, "Proofing and Printing Your Documents."

Editing in Outline View

Outline View, shown in Figure 22.16, is excellent for editing text. You can see all slide titles at a glance, complete with titles and subtitles. Using the Position icons on the object bar, you can change the current slide order, as well as demote or promote individual subtitles. Looking at the Preview window, you can track your changes in real-time. To switch quickly to Outline view when you're in StarImpress, press F12 or click the Outline icon above the vertical scrollbar. (If you like detours, you can also select View, Master View, Outline from the menu bar.)

PART

V

CH

22

Tip #432 from
Michael & Sarah

In the Preview window, you can see what the slide looks like, including the text, background, and background object. If you don't see the Preview window, select View, Preview. Note also that you can dock the Preview window if you press Ctrl and drag the window to the left side of your screen.

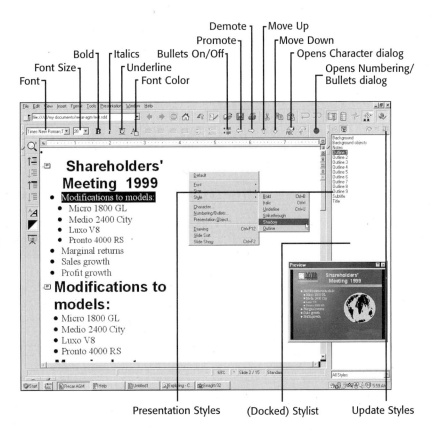

Figure 22.16
Use the tools and options on the Text object bar and main toolbar to edit text in Outline View. Note that while you're working in Outline View, you don't have access to the full complement of tools; the icons that are grayed out are not available.

When you're in Outline View, you can edit text simply by clicking it and moving the cursor to the area that you want to change. Use the Delete key to remove characters to the right of the cursor; use the Backspace key to delete characters to the left of the cursor.

To enter text in Outline View, place the insertion point immediately after the slide icon on the left. The first line is always a Title line (or slide). Press Enter to move to the next line, which again is a Title line. To change the level hierarchy, use the Promote and Demote buttons on the object bar.

CHANGING ATTRIBUTES VIA DIRECT FORMATTING

In addition, you can use various tools and options on the Outline Text object bar to change the attributes—including font, size, style, and color—of selected text. Alternatively, you can also select a different font, size, and style from the Outline View context menu. Just right-click anywhere in your work area, and select the desired font, size and/or style from the corresponding submenus. If you want to change several attributes at once, select Character from the context menu, or click the Character button (refer to Figure 22.16) on the object bar to open the Character dialog box. Using the Font and Font Effects tabs in the dialog, you can change the font, font size, font effects, style, size, color, spacing (between characters), and position (superscript, subscript, or normal) of selected text.

→ For more details on direct formatting, **see** "Understanding Your Formatting Options," **p. 262**.

CHANGING ATTRIBUTES VIA THE STARIMPRESS STYLIST

As always when you're making attribute changes, you should consult the Stylist (refer to Figure 22.16). Similar to the Stylist in StarWriter, the StarImpress Stylist is a marvelous tool that enables you to quickly change the appearance of existing text. Just select and right-click the presentation style you want to change in the Stylist; then choose Modify from the context menu. In the dialog box that appears, you can change basic font and paragraph attributes, including font, size, style, color, indents, and spacing between paragraphs and lines. When you're finished, click OK. StarImpress automatically applies the changes to all elements that have been formatted with the modified style.

Note

When you're working in Outline View, you have access only to the Presentation styles in the Stylist. And you can only modify (not add new or delete existing) styles. Of the available styles, the ones you'll find applied in Outline view include the Title, Subtitle, or Outline 1, Outline 2, Outline 3, and so on.

Tip #433 from
Michael & Sarah

If you change the attributes of a text element—for example, the title of a slide—using direct formatting, you can quickly apply these changes to all other elements that have been formatted with the same style. Just select the style you want to change in the Stylist (for example, Title), and then click the Update Style button to overwrite the current attributes of the selected style with the new ones in the workspace.

CHANGING HIERARCHIES, LEVELS, AND BULLETS

If you want to turn an Outline 1 item into a Title item or an Outline 2 item, you can do so quickly by using the Promote and Demote buttons. Just select the item you want to change, and click the respective button on the object bar; each click promotes or demotes the selected item by one level. Alternately, you can demote any title by pressing the Tab key; press Shift+Tab to promote, for example, an Outline 1 item to a Title (which is the equivalent of inserting a new slide).

Similarly, you can move an item up or down (without changing the level hierarchy) by using the Move Up and Move Down buttons (refer to Figure 22.16). Click the Bullets On/Off icon if you want to show or hide bullets in front of selected list items. You can also assign different bullet styles. Just click the Numbering Symbols icon, and select a new bullet style from the options in the Numbering/Bullets dialog box that appears.

→ For more details on using the Numbering/Bullets dialog, **see** "Creating Numbered and Bulleted Lists," **p. 283**.

Note

Promoting, demoting, and moving items in Outline View are virtually identical to promoting, demoting, and moving items in the StarWriter Navigator. For more details, see "Working with Outlines" in Chapter 10, "Working with Long Documents."

CHANGING VIEWS IN OUTLINE VIEW

In general, you can use the tools and options on the object bar or the context menu to make actual changes to the structure and appearance of your slide content. Use the icons on the main toolbar on the left to change the view and onscreen display of your outline (refer to Figure 22.16). Your options include the following:

- **Zoom**—Use the Zoom tools to zoom in or out of your outline.
- **First Level**—Click this icon to display only the titles of your slides.
- **All Levels**—Click this icon to display all levels hidden with the previous command.
- **Hide Subpoints**—Click this icon to collapse your outline view so that it shows only First Level and Outline 1 elements.
- **Show Subpoints**—Click here if you want to expand a collapsed outline to show all levels, points, and subpoints.
- **Formatting On/Off**—Use this button to toggle between a styled view of your outline (with all formatting intact) or a plain view of your outline (all text—regardless of level or hierarchy—appears in the default font and font size).
- **Black & White View**—Click here if your presentation consists of dark backgrounds and you're using a light-colored font to make the text stand out against the dark background. StarImpress automatically converts the light font color into black, so you can easily see and work with the text in Outline view.

> **Note**
>
> Any changes you make using the tools on the main toolbar affect only the onscreen display in Outline view. The actual appearance of the slides is not affected by these view changes.

EDITING IN DRAWING VIEW

When you're editing in Drawing View, you have access to all the options on the object bar you know from the Outline View (with the exception of the Promote, Demote, Move Up, and Move Down buttons), as well as some additional options you get only in Drawing view. Figure 22.17 shows the tools and options that you get only when you're working on text in Drawing view.

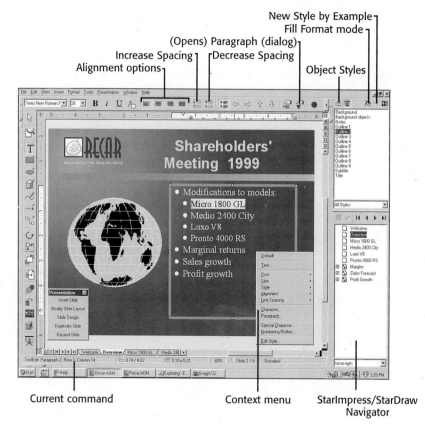

Figure 22.17
When you're working on text in Drawing view, you have access to a larger complement of tools and options than when you're working in Outline view.

To edit text in Drawing View, first click the text you want to edit. You then see a thick gray border—a text box—surrounding the existing text. Using the tools and options on the object bar and context menu, you can then add or delete selected text, redefine its attributes, or change its alignment (by using the alignment buttons) and location (by moving the entire text box via drag and drop, or by using the Move Up and Move Down buttons on the object bar).

If you want to make several attribute changes to selected text in one fell swoop, click the Character or Paragraph icons, or select Character or Paragraph from the context menu. In the Character dialog that appears, you change the fonts and font effects, respectively. Use the Paragraph dialog to change the indents and line spacing of individual paragraphs, the spacing between paragraphs, the alignment of selected paragraphs, or the tab positions.

→ For more details on the Font and Font Effects options in the Character dialog, **see** "Formatting Characters," **p. 263**.

→ For more details on the Indents & Spacing, Alignment, and Tab options in the Paragraph dialog, **see** "Formatting Paragraphs," **p. 270**.

> **Note**
>
> When you're modifying an existing Presentation style in the Stylist, you can assign only basic font and indent and spacing attributes to a selected style. To change the alignment or tabs of selected text, you have to apply direct formatting—via the object bar or the Paragraph dialog.

Using the object styles in the Stylist, you can add new styles or modify existing ones for existing text objects, as well as modify the existing presentation styles.

→ For more details on using the Stylist, **see** "Applying Styles," **p. 295**.

> **Tip #434 from**
> *Michael & Sarah*
>
> When you're working on text in Drawing View, you can also use the Stylist's Fill Format mode to quickly format selected text. Just select the desired presentation style, click the Fill Format button, move the cursor to the text you want to change, and click to apply the format changes. Fill Format is a toggle button, which means the Fill Format mode is on until you click the button again.

USING THE TEXT TOOLS

If you're creating a presentation from scratch, or if you want to add additional text to a slide (or drawing), use the Text tools on the main toolbar. You can access these tools in Drawing View, Notes View, and Handout View. Depending on your choice of tool, the text you enter appears in "regular" format as in a text document or as a graphic object that you can rotate, expand, minimize, and so on. You can also insert "regular" text in the form of a callout.

To use the Text tools, follow these steps:

1. Extended-click the Text icon on the main toolbar to open the Text floating toolbar. Your options include the following (from left to right):

    - **Text**—Use this tool when you want to add a larger amount of text using the default formatting (as if you were entering text in a text document).

    - **Fit Size to Frame**—Use this tool if you want to be able to easily scale the text.

    - **Legend**—Use this tool if you want to add a callout to a graphic object or other slide element.

2. Select the desired tool, and click and drag in your work area to draw a text frame (or container) for your text. If you use the Text tool, you see a thick, gray frame with eight selection handles and a blinking cursor at the upper left inside the frame as soon as you release your mouse button.

   If you use the Fit to Size tool, you see eight sizing handles, demarcating an invisible text box, and a blinking cursor in the middle of the box as soon as you release your mouse button.

   If you use the Callout tool, you can click and drag from the point where the arrow should point to the point where the legend should appear. Note that you don't enter automatically into the text entry mode when you release the mouse button. You first have to click the control point between the connector line and the text box to enter the text entry mode.

> **Note**
>
> In all three instances, the Draw object bar gives way to the Text object bar as soon as you release the mouse button.

3. Start typing the desired text. If you use the Text tool, the text you enter appears on a single line. When your cursor reaches the end of a line (read the right margin of the box), text automatically wraps to the next line.

   If you use the Fit to Size tool, the text you enter fills the entire text box, even expanding the box in length if the text you enter is longer than the original box.

   If you use the Callout tool, the text is entered on a single line but does not wrap when it reaches the right border of the box. Instead, the box expands to accommodate the text (similar to the Fit to Size Tool). If you want to continue your text in a new line, press Enter.

4. When you're finished, click outside the box to leave the text edit mode.

If you want to change the attributes of your text, click it to re-enter the text edit mode. Using the object bar, context menu, and Stylist, you can modify the font, size, style, and color of selected text as desired.

To move a text box, first click the text to select the box; then click its border (your cursor changes shape into a four-directional arrow) and drag it to its new location.

You can also scale the text box by clicking and dragging the sizing handles of the text box. If the box was created using the Text tool, scaling it results in longer or shorter lines of text, whereby the text automatically wraps at the end of a line. (Note also that the text box expands in height if space is needed.) If you scale the Fit to Size text box, the text automatically adjusts in height and length to fit inside the box.

To scale a text box, click and drag the top handle in between the corner handles to stretch or shrink the height of an object from the top; click the sizing handle on the right to stretch or squeeze the width of an object from the right, and so on. In each instance, the side opposite of the one you're dragging remains anchored. Click one of the corner handles to reduce an object in two dimensions. For example, if you click the handle in the lower-left corner of an object, you can enlarge or reduce the height and width of the object simultaneously from that corner; the handle in the opposite corner remains anchored during this operation. If you press Shift while clicking and dragging one of the sizing handles, the box maintains its height-to-width ratio while scaling.

Tip #435 from *Michael & Sarah*	If you have difficulty selecting a text box, check the Presentation settings in the Tools, Options, Presentation, Other dialog. If the Allow Quick Editing option is selected, and you click directly in the text of a text object, you immediately enter the edit mode (which can make it hard for you to select your text box). Click the Only Text Area Selectable option if you want to select a text frame only when clicking the corresponding text. Alternately, you can also control the editing options via the option bar. For more details, see "Using the Option Bar," page xxx. (Chapter 20, Getting Sketchy with StarDraw)

CREATING SPEAKER'S NOTES

StarImpress also enables you to annotate slides with notes that help you during your presentation. You can print the notes and use them during a presentation to recall the points that you want to make for each slide. Creating speaker's notes is explained in detail in Chapter 24, "Previewing and Presenting Your Presentation".

→ For more details on creating speaker's notes, **see** "Adding Speaker's Notes and Audience Handouts," **p. 903**.

IMPORTING OUTLINES FROM STARWRITER

StarWriter contains a multitude of useful tools that enhance your productivity and work-flow. One of these tools—the Outline to Presentation command—is easy to overlook, hidden as it is in the File, Send submenu.

For example, suppose you've already created a business report or other text document in StarWriter and would like to use its outline as the foundation for a StarImpress presentation. Each Heading 1 element represents a slide; the corresponding Heading 2, Heading 3, and so on elements represent the list items (or content) of the respective slide.

→ For more details on outlines and heading styles, **see** "Working with Outlines," **p. 376**.

Note	You can create a presentation from an outline in StarWriter only if you used the standard heading styles (Heading 1, Heading 2, Heading 3, and so on). It is irrelevant if you've changed the attributes of the individual heading styles. What matters is the name of the style.

Instead of retyping the outline as it appears in the StarWriter Navigator in Outline view in StarImpress, select File, Send, Outline to Presentation from the menu bar. StarOffice automatically creates a new presentation document based on your existing outline and opens it in Outline view in StarImpress. Each Heading 1 element is converted into a slide (the title of the slide is the same as the Heading 1 text); each Heading 2 element is now a top-level point on the corresponding slide; each Heading 3 element is a subpoint, and so on. You can now fine-tune the existing outline, using the tools and features in Outline view and Slide Sort view.

If you would like more flexibility when creating a foundation for a new presentation, or if you would like to include the first paragraph after each heading in your presentation outline, follow these steps:

1. Select File, Send, AutoAbstract to Presentation.

2. In the Create AutoAbstract dialog that appears, specify the number of outline levels you want to include in your presentation, as well as the number of paragraphs (referred to as subpoints) per heading (or level). For example, if you want to make each Heading 1, Heading 2, and Heading 3 element a slide, select 3 in the Included Outline Levels box. If you want to list the first two paragraphs after each heading element as the content points of your slide, select 2 in the Subpoints Per Level box.

3. When you're finished, click OK.

As with the File, Send, Outline to Presentation command, StarOffice automatically creates a new presentation document and opens it in Outline view in StarImpress.

WORKING WITH SLIDES

Most likely, you'll be doing most of your work in Drawing View. In Drawing View, you can see every slide pretty much as it will appear in your presentation. However, on some occasions you might want to switch views to rearrange the order of your slides or create speaker's notes to individual slides. Depending on the active view, your options of working with slides may change. Table 22.2 lists your various options when working with slides, broken down by views.

TABLE 22.2   WORKING WITH SLIDES IN DIFFERENT VIEWS

Option	Drawing View	Outline View	Slide Sort View	Notes View	Handout View
Inserting slides	✓		✓		
Modifying slide layout	✓			✓	✓
Changing slide design	✓			✓	
Duplicating slides	✓				
Expanding slides	✓	✓			
Deleting slides	✓		✓		

Option	Drawing View	Outline View	Slide Sort View	Notes View	Handout View
Rearranging slides			✓		
Renaming slides	✓				
Creating summary slides	✓	✓			
Hiding slides			✓		
Inserting copies	✓		✓		
Adding notes				✓	
Creating slide transitions			✓		
Creating handouts					✓

SETTING UP YOUR SLIDE (PAGE)

In StarImpress, as in other StarOffice modules, you use page formatting to control the appearance of each page (or slide) for the entire presentation document. Page formatting controls such settings as page margins, paper format, orientation, and background. To change the page attributes, select Format, Page from the menu bar; then use the Page and Background tabs to make the desired changes.

Changing the attributes on the Page tab is fairly straightforward. You use the spin boxes in the Margins portion of the tab to adjust the size of the page margins. In the Paper Format portion of the tab, you can change the predefined paper format, width, height, and orientation of the page. In the Options portion of the dialog, you can define whether to retain the order of drawing elements if the paper format is modified. Your options include Fill Entire Page and Fit to Size.

Using the Background tab, you can assign a background color, gradient, hatching, or bitmap to your page, or you can use an invisible background. The list of available colors, gradients, hatchings, and bitmaps depends on the currently installed palette. For example, if you see standard after Table in the upper-left part of the tab, that means that the Standard (default) palette of the currently selected background option is installed. You can change the palettes and even define your own by using the Area dialog (which you open by selecting Format, Area).

→ For more details on palettes and using the Area dialog options, **see** "Adding Fills and Color to Your Objects," **p. 761**.

Note Page formatting is view dependent. When you select Format, Page, you change only the page format for the currently active view.

INSERTING SLIDES

As you build your presentations in StarImpress, you naturally want to make changes to the presentation by inserting, deleting, or copying slides. When you add a slide to an existing presentation, you have two options. You can insert the slide in between existing slides, or you can add a slide at the end of the current presentation.

> **Note**
>
> You can insert slides only when you're in Drawing View.

For example, if you want to insert a new slide between Slide A and Slide B in Drawing View, follow these steps:

1. Right-click the name tab of Slide A, and select Insert from the context menu. The Insert Slide dialog appears (see Figure 22.18). Alternatively, you can also click the name tab of Slide A to bring it to the front and then click the Insert Slide option in the Presentation Box, or you can select Insert, Slide from the menu bar. (If you can't see the Presentation Box, click the Presentation Box icon on the object bar.)

Click to open the Insert Slide dialog

Enter a name for the new slide

Figure 22.18
Inserting slides to existing presentations is as easy as selecting the Insert Slide command from the Presentation Box or the context menu of the adjacent slide.

Select a predefined layout

Selected slide

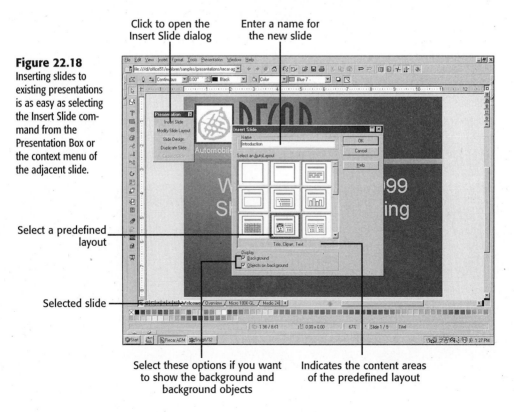

Select these options if you want to show the background and background objects

Indicates the content areas of the predefined layout

2. Enter a descriptive name for the new slide in the Name text box. (If you don't enter a name, StarImpress assigns a generic name that identifies the numeric place of the slide in the presentation—for example, Slide 5.)

3. Select the desired layout in the Select an AutoLayout list box. Your predefined layout options include slides that already contain areas in which you can easily insert text, objects, and clip art. You identify the content areas of a layout by looking in the text bar at the bottom of the Select an AutoLayout list box.

4. In the Display portion of the dialog, select the Background and Objects on Background options if you want to display the background or objects in the work area, respectively. By default, StarImpress inserts the background and background objects of the slide you selected (in this example, Slide A).

Tip #436 from
Michael & Sarah

Working with graphics is always memory intensive, and switching between slides causes graphics to redraw on your screen. Depending on the view size of the image as well as your graphic card and installed memory, having the graphics redrawn can be rather annoying. If you have a lower-end computer and/or not enough memory (for example, less than 64MB), you might be better off hiding backgrounds or background objects in the work area; doing so will save you a little time.

5. Click OK. StarImpress inserts the new slides to the right of Slide A. You can now enter the desired content as usual.

Note

In general, StarImpress always inserts new slides to the right of the selected slide. If you want to insert a slide in front of the first slide, you have to rearrange the order of the slides after inserting the new slide. For more details, see "Rearranging Slides" later in this chapter.

If you want to add a slide at the end of an existing presentation, select the name tab of the last slide, and click in the gray area after the last slide. StarImpress automatically inserts a slide with a generic name based on the layout and background of the last slide.

Note

If you don't select the last slide first, StarImpress inserts a slide to the left of the currently selected slide in your presentation.

INSERTING SLIDES FROM ANOTHER PRESENTATION

You can also add slides from a previous presentation to your current presentation. This way, you can avoid taking the time to create an entirely new presentation when you already have slides that you can use from an old presentation.

To insert slides from another presentation quickly, follow these steps:

1. Open the old presentation document that contains the slide you want to import.

2. Open the new presentation document into which you want to import the slide.

3. Switch to Drawing view, and open the Navigator (press F5) if it isn't open already.

4. In the Navigator list box, double-click the slide after which you want to insert the slide from the old presentation document to select it.

5. Select the old presentation document from the Documents list box at the bottom of the Navigator.

6. Click the Drag Mode button in the upper right of the Navigator, and make sure that Insert as Copy is selected. Then click and drag the desired slide from the Navigator list box to the current presentation document, and release the mouse button. StarImpress inserts the slide right after the one you selected in step 4.

Note

If the presentation already has a slide with the same name as the one you want to insert, the Name dialog appears. Enter a different name in the text box and click OK, or click Cancel to cancel the operation.

Alternatively, you can also use the following steps to insert objects from a drawing or presentation document into another presentation document:

1. Open the presentation containing the slide you want to copy.

2. Activate the Slide Sort View (by clicking the third button from the top above the horizontal scrollbar).

3. Select the desired slide by clicking it (a thick border appears around the slide), and press Ctrl+C or select Edit, Copy.

4. Open (or switch to) the presentation into which you want to insert the copied slide.

5. Select the slide after which you want to insert the copied slide, and then press Ctrl+V or select Edit, Paste. StarImpress inserts the copied slide following the one you selected in step 5.

Tip #437 from
Michael & Sarah

If the background of the inserted slide does not match the background of the other slides, double-click the inserted slide to open it in Drawing view. Then select Insert, Slide Design, or click the Slide Design button in the Presentation Box. Alternatively, right-click and then select Slide Design from the context menu. In the Slide Design dialog that appears, select the desired background, and then click OK.

INSERTING SLIDES AND OBJECTS FROM STARDRAW

Did you create some cool graphics in StarDraw that you would like to insert in their entirety in your StarImpress presentation? No problem. Inserting slides from StarDraw in your current presentation is similar to inserting slides from a previous StarImpress presentation. Just follow these steps:

1. Open the StarDraw document that contains the slide you want to import.

2. Open the StarImpress presentation document into which you want to import the slide.

3. Switch to Drawing View, and open the Navigator (press F5) if it isn't open already.

4. In the Navigator list box, double-click the slide after which you want to insert the slide from the StarDraw document to select it.

5. Select the StarDraw document from the Documents list box at the bottom of the Navigator.

6. Click the Drag Mode button in the upper right of the Navigator, and make sure that Insert as Copy is selected. Then click and drag the desired slide from the Navigator list box to the current StarImpress presentation, and release the mouse button. (While dragging, you'll notice the "copy indicator cursor"—a small plus sign in the lower-right corner of your cursor.)

> **Note**
>
> If the presentation already has a slide with the same name as the one you want to insert, the Name dialog appears. Enter a different name in the text box and click OK, or click Cancel to cancel the operation.

7. An alert box appears, asking you to confirm whether you want to adjust the orientation (or format) of the copied slide (or page). (By default, slides in StarDraw are portrait-oriented. Slides in StarImpress, by contrast, are landscape-oriented.)

    Click Yes if you want StarImpress to automatically adjust the orientation of the inserted slide. Note that the inserted objects may appear squeezed (in height) and stretched (in width) as StarImpress tries to fit the entire information into one slide.

    Click No if you want to keep the orientation of the original slide. Instead of adjusting the orientation of the original StarDraw object page, StarImpress inserts a portrait-oriented copy of the drawing object in its entirety. You can then modify the copy as needed to fit it on your landscape-oriented slide. (For example, you can reduce the object in size or crop it as desired.)

    Click Cancel if you want to cancel the operation.

Depending on your selection, StarImpress inserts the StarDraw slide at the location of your choice. You can then continue to modify or edit the slide as usual.

DELETING SLIDES

Deleting a slide in StarImpress is safe and simple and can be performed in Drawing view, Outline view, and Slide Sort view. Just follow these steps to remove an unwanted slide:

1. Navigate to the slide that you want to delete.

2. Depending on the view you're in, you have the following options:

- **In Drawing View:** Right-click the name tab of the slide you want to delete, and select Delete Slide from the context menu. Alternatively, you can also right-click in the slide area and select Slide, Delete Slide from the context menu or choose Edit, Delete Slide from the menu bar.

- **In Outline View:** Place the insertion point or your cursor between the Slide icon and the first letter of your slide title, and press the Backspace key.

- **In Slide Sort View:** Right-click the selected slide, and choose Delete Slide from the context menu or select Edit, Delete Slide from the menu bar. Note that you can delete more than one slide at once when in Slide Sort view. Just Shift+click to select the slides you want to delete.

In each instance, an alert box pop ups asking you to confirm whether you want to delete the selected slide(s).

3. Click Yes, and StarImpress removes the unwanted slide from your presentation.

If you delete a slide by accident, press Ctrl+Z or click the Undo button on the function bar to bring back the slide.

MOVING BETWEEN SLIDES

When you have more than one slide in a presentation, you must be able to move easily among the slides so that you can quickly work on all of them. How you move among the slides depends on the view that you are in at the time.

Tip #438 from
Michael & Sarah

To move quickly between slides, use the Navigator for presentations. The Navigator is useful if you want to jump to a certain slide in an extensive presentation or quickly switch between open documents. Just double-click the slide you want to move to in the Navigator list box, and StarImpress (or StarDraw, depending on the module you're in) displays it in the work area. The Navigator is available in Drawing View, Notes View, and Handout View, as well as during presentations. To open the Navigator, press F5. For more details on the Navigator for presentations, see "Navigating Extensive Presentations" in Chapter 24, "Previewing and Presenting Your Presentation."

For example, when you're in Drawing or Notes View, you see a series of tabs (with generic or custom names) at the bottom of the StarImpress workspace. Each tab represents a slide. Click the name tab of a slide you want to edit to bring it to the front. Click the left- and right-arrow icons in the lower left of the StarImpress workspace until the slide you want appears. (Clicking the leftmost and rightmost arrow icon reveals the first and last slide tab in your presentation document, respectively.) Alternatively, you can press the Page Up or Page Down keys to cycle through your slides one by one, or the Home or End keys to go to the first and last slide in your presentation.

Tip #439 from
Michael & Sarah

To increase the number of name tabs shown onscreen, click the separator between the horizontal scrollbar at the bottom and the name tab area (your cursor changes shape to a two-headed arrow); then drag the separator to the right.

When you're in Outline View, use the scrollbar to move to the slide you want to change. Click inside the text to perform the desired text changes. (Clicking the slide icon to the left of the slide's title selects the text of the entire slide.) If the Preview option is on (select View, Preview to turn it on), you can see the slide you're currently working on in the Preview window.

When you're in Slide Sort View, click the slide you want to work on (use the scrollbar to move to the desired slide if necessary). A border appears around the slide. If you double-click the slide, StarImpress opens the slide in Drawing View, where you can edit the slide.

COPYING, DUPLICATING, AND EXPANDING SLIDES

You copy slides in StarImpress just like you copy items in other StarOffice modules—by using the Copy and Paste commands from the Edit menu or by pressing Ctrl+C and Ctrl+V, respectively. You can copy slides in Slide Sort View by following these steps:

1. Select the slide you want to copy; then choose Edit, Copy or press Ctrl+C.

2. Navigate to the location where you want to insert the copied slide. By default, StarImpress inserts slides to the left of the selected slide.

3. Select Edit, Paste or press Ctrl+V to insert the slide to the left of the selected slide.

DUPLICATING SLIDES

If you're looking for a quick way to add slides to an existing presentation, use the Duplicate Slide command. Duplicating slides is virtually identical to copying files—you create an exact copy of an existing slide (and by extension slide design). You can create duplicate copies of a slide in Drawing view. To do so, just select the slide you want to duplicate by clicking its name tab, and then select Insert, Duplicate Slide from the menu bar or click the Duplicate Slide button on the Presentation Box. StarImpress immediately inserts a duplicate to the left of the original slide.

Tip #440 from
Michael & Sarah

If you want to quickly insert one or more slides with identical layout and design, use the Duplicate command. Then edit the content as needed.

EXPANDING SLIDES

Another time-saver is the Expand Slide command. Using the Expand Slide command, you can quickly create additional slides from the outline of the selected slide.

Note You can only expand slides that consist of two or more Outline 1 elements.

For example, suppose you created a presentation in Outline view, diligently applying the Outline 1, Outline 2, and so on presentation styles. You switch to Drawing View to put on some finishing design touches to the background design, and then, after proofing the final order of slides, you discover that each Outline 1 style (or top-level point) on one particular slide easily deserves its own slide. Instead of editing the slide in question manually in Outline View or inserting slides and then cutting and pasting the existing text, you can let StarImpress do the job:

1. Switch to Drawing View or Slide Sort View.

Note You can also expand slides in Outline View. However, when you're expanding slides in Outline view, you can't use the Undo command should you suddenly change your mind about creating additional slides.

2. Select the slide you want to expand.

3. Select Insert, Expand Slide from the menu bar, or click the Expand Slide button on the Presentation Box. StarImpress automatically splits the selected slide into as many slides as there are top-level (Outline 1) points. Each Outline 1 style element is converted into the Title element of a new slide; all other elements are promoted accordingly (Outline 2 style elements become Outline 1 style elements and so on). Note also that all new slides consist of the same layout and background design as the original slide.

4. Decide whether you want to keep the original slide. After StarImpress creates the new slides, an alert box pops up, asking whether you want to delete the selected slide(s). If the original slide contains a graphic (foreground) element that you want to keep, select No. (You can always hide the selected slide from view or copy the graphic to another location or file later and then delete the slide.) If the original slide contains only text elements, click Yes—there's no reason to keep it.

REARRANGING SLIDES

From time to time, you will need to change the order in which the slides appear in your presentation. You can quickly rearrange the order of slides in both Slide Sort View and Outline View.

When you're in Slide Sort View, you can change the sequence of the slides simply by clicking and dragging your slide to another position to the left or the right. As you drag your slide, you'll notice a thick black bar that appears to jump from slide to slide. Think of it as an oversize insertion point; the bar indicates the location where your slide is inserted when you release the mouse button.

| Tip #441 from *Michael & Sarah* | If possible, decide on the final order of slides before you assign transition effects. When you move slides to a new location, you have to redefine your transition effects because transitions are assigned between adjacent slides. |

Rearranging the order of your slides in Outline View is somewhat trickier. Click the Slide icon on the left, and drag it up or down to its new location. As you drag the icon up or down, you'll notice a thin black line that jumps from one text line to another. The line indicates where the slide contents will be inserted when you release the mouse button. To insert the selected slide in its new location, be sure the line appears right above a slide icon before you release the mouse button. Otherwise, you will insert the selected slide inside another slide, splitting its content in two. Everything above the inserted slide is still part of the original slide; everything below it becomes part of the content of the dropped slide.

Note

Clicking the Slide icon automatically selects the entire text of the current slide. However, don't assume you can use the familiar cut-and-paste shortcuts to move slides in Outline View. When you cut and paste, you move only the content (text) of the slide, not the slide itself.

MODIFYING THE SLIDE LAYOUT

Layout defines which elements of your presentation are inserted in which order. When you insert a slide, StarImpress asks you to decide on a layout. You can choose from 20 layouts. You can also change the slide layout after you have created a slide. You can modify the slide layout in Drawing, Notes, and Handout Views. To change a slide layout, follow these steps:

1. Click the Modify Slide Layout button on the Presentation Box, or select Slide, Modify Layout from the context menu in the Drawing, Notes, or Handout Views. The Modify Slide dialog appears.

2. In the Select an AutoLayout list box, choose the layout you want to apply to the selected slide. Your options include Title Only; Title and Text; Title and Object; or Title, Text and Object layouts. (Remember that the layout you choose determines the styles you have available.)

3. In the Display portion of the dialog, select whether you want to show the background or background objects in the work area of your presentation document. By default, StarImpress displays the background and background objects of the slide you want to modify.

4. Click OK. StarImpress applies the new layout to the selected slide. You can then edit the content and adjust the objects as needed.

CHANGING THE SLIDE (BACKGROUND) DESIGN

Use the Slide Design dialog to change the background of your presentation. The changes you make affect all slides that share the same template. You can change the background design of a slide in Drawing View and Notes View.

To change the background design of your presentation, follow these steps:

1. Click the Slide Design button on the Presentation Box, or select Slide, Slide Design from the context menu to open the Slide Design dialog.

2. Select the desired design from the Select a Slide Layout list box. If you can't see the design you want, click the Load button to import a design template from the Load Slide Layout dialog. The Slide Layout dialog is identical to the New (Template) dialog. To locate the desired slide design, click Presentation Layouts in the Categories list. Then select the desired design in the Templates list on the right, and click OK. StarImpress imports the selected template and shows it as a thumbnail in the Select a Slide Layout list box.

Caution

If you create custom background designs, be sure to save them to the templates folder (`Office51\Templates` by default); otherwise, you cannot load them in StarImpress using the Slide Design dialog. Note that you can assign a different path to your templates folder by using the Tools, Options, General, Paths dialog. Simply select Document Templates in the Default list, and then click the Edit button. In the Edit Paths dialog that appears, click the Add button to open the Select Path dialog. Use this dialog to navigate to the desired path. When finished, click Select, and then click OK twice to return to your document.

3. (Optional) Select Exchange Background Page if you want to replace the background page for all slides in the document with the new design. If you don't select this option, the new background will only apply to the current slide. Using the Exchange background page check box gives you the flexibility to define different backgrounds for individual slides.

4. (Optional) Select Remove Unused Master Pages if you want the program to remove all unassigned background designs.

5. Click OK.

StarImpress replaces the current background design with the new one you selected. If you select the Exchange Background Page check box, StarImpress replaces the background of all slides that share the same template. Otherwise, it exchanges only the design of the selected slide. To modify the new background design, switch to Background mode.

Note

As with fonts and formatting, less is more. A good presentation distinguishes itself through consistency. Use different backgrounds only if absolutely necessary or for a particular effect.

RENAMING SLIDES

When you're inserting, adding, or modifying slides, you can enter a descriptive name for the new slide in the Name text box of the Insert Slide or Modify Slide dialog box. If you want to rename slides quickly, right-click the name tab of the slide you want to rename, and select Rename Slide from the context menu. StarImpress instantaneously highlights the current name in the name tab. Just start typing your new name for the slide. When you're finished, click anywhere in the slide or work area, or press Enter to exit the text entry mode.

> **Note**
>
> The name tabs of your slides automatically adjust to accommodate the length of the name you enter. However, when you're working with slides, it's best to keep the names (and by extension tab size) at a manageable length. For example, *Profit Growth* is preferable to *Profit Growth with Forecast for 1999*.

CREATING A SUMMARY SLIDE

A summary slide is to a presentation what a table of contents is to a text document: It lists the titles of all slides in the current presentation in the order in which they appear. Similar to StarWriter, which scans your text document for a certain heading style when creating a table of contents, StarImpress scans your presentation document for instances of the Title style and presents them in bulleted list form on the summary slide.

However, there are two caveats. Unlike a table of contents in StarWriter, the information of a summary slide cannot be updated. If you change the title of a slide or expand a slide, after generating a summary slide, you first have to delete the existing summary slide before you can create a new one. Also, StarImpress does not automatically scan your presentation from beginning to end. You have to define a starting point for the scanning operation first by selecting a slide (defining a starting point, so to speak). StarImpress then scans your presentation document from the selected slide to the last slide for instances of the Title style.

You can create summary slides in Drawing View by following these steps:

1. Click the name tab of the first slide in your presentation that you want to appear at the top of the list on your summary slide.

2. Select Insert, Summary Slide from the menu bar. StarImpress generates the desired summary slide, using the background of the selected slide, and appends it to the end of your presentation.

3. Click the text box at the top of the slide to add a title (for example, `Shareholder's Meeting Summary`).

4. Right-click the name tab of the summary slide, select Rename from the context menu, and enter a descriptive name for the slide (for example, `Summary`).

Summary slides can be modified and edited using the same methods and tools you use for the other slides in a presentation. You can incorporate them in your presentation (even move them to another location), assign transition effects, or hide them from onscreen display.

> **Note**
>
> Unfortunately there is no easy way to update a summary slide after you've made changes to your presentation–short of creating a new one.

SHOWING/HIDING SLIDES

Hiding slides is another powerful feature of StarImpress. Use this feature if you want to temporarily hide slides without actually deleting them from your presentation. For example, you can use this feature if you want to give similar presentations to different groups but modify the content to fit each group, or if you want to exclude certain slides (such as the Summary Slide, for example) from a test run.

> **Tip #442 from**
> *Michael & Sarah*
>
> If you want to give similar presentations to several different groups, you're better off using the Custom Slide Show feature. For more details, see "Setting Up and Running Custom Slide Shows" in Chapter 24, "Previewing and Presenting Your Presentation."

To hide (or show hidden) slides, you have to be in Slide Sort view. You can prevent certain slides from showing in your slide show without deleting them. Just right-click the slide you want to hide, and select Show/Hide Slide from the context menu or click the Show/Hide button on the object bar. A shadowed background behind the name of the selected slide indicates that StarImpress will skip this slide during your slide show.

> **Note**
>
> When you're printing your presentation (as a handout, an outline, or notes), you can choose whether to print hidden pages. Just click the Options button in the Print dialog (which you open by selecting File, Print), and select the Hidden pages check box in the Print portion of the Print Options dialog.

WORKING WITH OBJECTS

In StarImpress, the basic component that you use to create a slide is an object. An object can be the box where you enter text, a picture inserted from another source, or a graphic created with the drawing tools in StarImpress (or StarDraw). You can have as many objects as you want in a slide—both in the foreground as well as in the background.

Working with objects in StarImpress is identical to working with objects in StarDraw or StarWriter and is covered in detail in Chapter 20, "Getting Sketchy with StarDraw" and Chapter 11, "Desktop Publishing with StarOffice."

→ For more details on working with objects, **see** "Working with Graphic Objects," **p. 736** and "Rehearsing Objects," **p. 421**.

WORKING WITH STYLES

StarImpress enables you to manage a series presentation and object styles via the Style Catalog and Stylist. Depending on the type of style, presentation and object styles contain font, font size, style, indents and spacing, alignment, background line, fill, numbering and/or shadow formatting settings that are stored under different names. As with text and other documents, these styles are saved along with the active document but can also be copied to a specific template. Using the Stylist or the Style Catalog, you can quickly add new styles or modify existing ones.

> **Note**
>
> Note that any modifications are valid only for those slides that use this design in the current document.

As with text documents, using the Stylist enables you to quickly format objects in whichever way you choose. You can use the Fill Format mode to quickly apply the same style to different objects. You can use the New Style by Example button to create a new style based on the selected style in your current slide. Using this function opens the Create Style dialog in which you are asked to enter a name for the new style. Finally, you can use the Update Styles button, and you can quickly modify an existing style in the Stylist with the click of a mouse.

To assign a style to an object, select the object you want to format, and double-click the desired style in the list of available object styles in the Stylist. The selected object is automatically formatted according to the attributes that have been assigned to that particular style. This capability is helpful if you want to create custom colors and elements for selected drawing areas and the like.

When working with presentation styles, things are slightly different in that you cannot assign styles as you do in StarWriter by placing your cursor inside the text and then double-clicking the desired style in the Stylist. All presentation styles in StarImpress are predefined and controlled by the slide layout you choose. For example, the Outline 1 through Outline 9 styles enable you to give your slides a hierarchical overview of all the titles and topics. Technically, you can have up to nine outline levels, plus a title level. However, if you choose a layout that does not have room for an outline, the outline functions are not available. For example, if you choose a Title Only layout, you have access only to the Title and Subtitle styles.

If you choose a Title, Text layout, you can structure your text using the Title and Outline 1 through Outline 9 styles by performing these steps:

1. Open a new presentation document, and select the Title, Text slide layout from the Modify Slide dialog.

> **Note**
> Remember, the slide layout you choose determines the styles and number of levels of your content.

2. Activate the Outline View by pressing F12 or clicking the Outline icon above the vertical scrollbar on the right. You then see a blinking cursor to the right of the small Slide 1 icon.

3. Enter the desired text—for example, Welcome. This text will be the title for Slide 1, the opening slide of your presentation.

4. Press Enter. The cursor moves to the next line, and a small icon appears to its left. Enter a title for the second slide—for example, Overview.

5. Press Enter again. To enter the first list item of the Overview, you have to make this line subordinate to the previous line. Press the Tab key, and then enter your text. In the Text, Title layout, the text in this line is styled as Outline 1, which means it will appear below the Overview title on the same slide.

> **Note**
> Alternatively, you can enter your text and then press the Tab key. StarImpress alerts you that you are about to delete Slide 3. Click OK to delete the slide and turn your text into a Slide 2 (Overview) subtitle.

6. Continue to enter additional titles (insert new slides) or list items. You can demote any title by pressing the Tab key; press Shift+Tab to promote an Outline 1 item to a Title (which is the equivalent of inserting a new slide).

The levels you create by following these steps automatically contain the Title, Outline 1, Outline 2, and so on presentation styles. To modify these styles, right-click the style you want to change in the Stylist, and select Modify from the context menu. For example, if you modify the Title style, you can change the font, font size and color, and indents and spacing of the selected style in the Title dialog.

Using the Stylist and Style Catalog in StarImpress (and StarDraw) is virtually the same as using them in StarWriter and is covered in detail in Chapter 8, "Using Styles and Templates."

→ For more details on using the Stylist and Style Catalog, **see** "Using the Stylist," **p. 296**, and "Managing Styles with the Style Catalog," **p. 306**.

> **Note**
> The availability of presentation styles is controlled by the design template. With presentation styles, unlike object styles, you cannot assign them by selecting an object and then double-clicking a desired style in the Stylist's list box of available styles. Instead, you can modify only the existing styles.

SAVING AND CLOSING PRESENTATIONS

You save a presentation in StarImpress the same way you save a file in other StarOffice programs—by selecting File, Save. If you have not saved the presentation before, the Save As dialog box opens. There, you are prompted to enter a name for your presentation document. If you have already given the presentation a name, it is saved under that name.

Using the Save As dialog (which you open by choosing File, Save As), you can also perform other tasks. You can change the name of an existing file (to save another version or make a copy, for example) by entering a new name in the Filename text box. You can save your file in the native StarImpress format as a document (with the .sdd extension) or template (with the .vor extension). You can also save your files as StarDraw or MS PowerPoint 97 documents or templates.

To protect your presentation document from prying eyes, select the Save with Password option in the lower left of the Save As dialog before clicking the Save button. You then are prompted to enter a password twice—first in the Enter Password dialog and then in the Confirm Password dialog. Click OK after each entry. The next time you (or someone else) open the file, you are prompted to enter the assigned password before you get access to the presentation.

Finally, you can save your file in a directory of your choice and manage your files and folders from within the Save As dialog.

→ For more details, **see** "Managing Files and Folders from the Open and Save As Dialogs," **p. 192**.

After you've finished and saved your document, you can close the document (or task) by selecting File, Close or right-clicking the document's task button and then selecting Close Task from the shortcut menu. Alternatively, you can also click the Close (X) button in the upper right of the task window.

SAVING DIFFERENT VERSIONS OF A PRESENTATION

StarImpress also enables you to save different versions of a presentation document to the same file. This way, you can keep track of the evolution of a presentation, especially if you're working together with others on a single document. To save a file as a different version, select File, Versions, and then click the Save New Version button. Enter a comment in the Insert Version Comment window for easy reference, click OK, and then click Close. The current presentation document is then saved as a new version to the same file.

→ For more details on saving and working with versions of a document, **see** "Working with Versions," **p. 1007**.

SAVING SUMMARY INFORMATION WITH YOUR FILES

As with all StarOffice documents, you can include summary information with the presentations you save. Summary information includes the title of your document (which may be different than the filename), a brief description of the subject, keywords that you associate with the document, and comments that you feel are needed. You can enter summary information on the Description tab of the Properties dialog (which you open by choosing File, Properties), shown in Figure 22.19.

Tip #443 from
Michael & Sarah

If you enter the title and keywords that you associate with your document on the Description tab of the Properties dialog, you can quickly find documents and templates by using the Find, Search command from the Start menu (in Windows). For more details on using the Find command, see "Retrieving Distant Files and Folders" in Chapter 5, "Managing Folders, Files, and Mail." You can also reveal these properties in the Open and Save As dialog boxes to help sort and manage your saved presentations. For more details, see "Managing Files and Folders from the Open and Save As Dialogs," also in Chapter 5.

Figure 22.19
You can view the summary information of a document by selecting File, Properties.

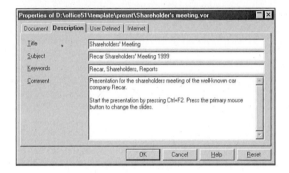

If the document has been saved as a template, you can also view the summary information by selecting File, New, From Template or pressing Ctrl+N and then clicking the More button (see Figure 22.20).

Figure 22.20
You can also view the summary information by choosing File, New, From Template.

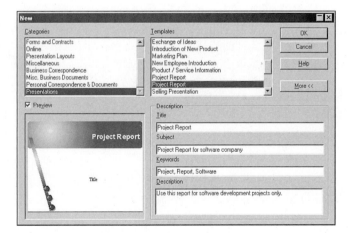

OPENING AN EXISTING OR NEW PRESENTATION

You open an existing presentation in StarImpress the same way that you open a file in other StarOffice documents—by clicking the File Open button on the function bar; selecting File, Open from the menu bar; or pressing Ctrl+O. When the Open dialog is open, you can move, copy, and delete files and folders as you like. You can also open existing versions of files, by selecting first the file and then the file version from the Version drop-down list. If you select the Read-Only option in the lower left of the dialog box, you can open the document as write-protected, which means you cannot make any changes to the opened document.

→ For more details on managing your files and folders this way, **see** "Managing Files and Folders from the Open and Save As Dialogs," **p.192**.

CHAPTER 23

ENHANCING YOUR PRESENTATION

In this chapter

CHANGING FONTS, FONT STYLES, AND COLORS

The easiest way to enhance your presentation is by formatting your text with the proper font, style, and color. Text formatting works in StarImpress as it does elsewhere in StarOffice. You can use the options on the object bar, or you can modify the presentation styles in the Stylist. Just select the text that you want to modify, and then choose your favorite formatting option. If you want a consistent look throughout your presentation, you can modify the respective styles in the Stylist. If you just want to sprinkle some color here and there or change the style of text, you can use the object bar. If you're looking for more options, you can also use the Character dialog (which you open by selecting Format, Character) to add font effects.

→ For more details on working with text in presentation documents, **see** "Working with Text," **p. 838**.

→ For details on text formatting options, **see** "Understanding Your Formatting Options," **p. 261**.

More specifically, you can add emphasis by changing the style of your font from regular to bold, italic, or underline via the object bar. Or you can use the Outline and Shadow options on the Font tab of the Character dialog or the respective style properties dialog. If used properly and in good measure, shadowing and outlining are extremely effective techniques in making certain words or phrases stand out. Shadowing adds a drop shadow behind your text to emphasize it (which is useful in headings). Outlining adds a line around your letters—leaving the inside white. You can also add superscript or subscript to your text by selecting the respective option on the Font Effects tab in the Character dialog.

WORKING WITH LISTS AND COLUMNS

When you're creating your presentations, columns and bulleted lists are perhaps the most important enhancement for your presentation slides. Putting columns and bulleted lists into your slides is easy; it's just another formatting and layout feature.

CREATING BULLETED AND NUMBERED LISTS

You can define bullets and numbers in Drawing view (when in Text Edit mode) and Outline view. Just click the Numbering Symbols icon on the object bar, or select Format, Numbering/Bullets from the object bar to open the Numbering/Bullets dialog.

The Numbering/Bullets dialog gives you a series of options for enhancing the style of numbering (from the Numbering tab) or bullets (from the Bullets and Pictures tabs). For example, the Bullets tab contains plain old variations of black-and-white bullets (most of them are more suitable for black-and-white print rather than for colorful presentations). The Pictures tab (shown in Figure 23.1) contains a variety of flashy bullets that enable you to add spunk to your presentations (and Web pages).

Note

If the text area has no provision for numbered lists (such as the Title area, for example), you don't see the Numbering and Outline tabs in the Numbering/Bullets dialog.

Figure 23.1
You can enhance your bulleted lists with bullet styles from the Pictures tab.

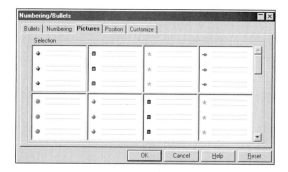

Using the Position and Customize tabs, you can adjust the numbering alignment and the distance between numbers/bullets and text and between borders and text (if applicable), as well as change the default indents. Using the Customize tab, you can make changes to the existing bullets, numbers, and pictures, and you can assign new symbols (see Figure 23.2). You can choose a format for your numbers and bullets from the Numbering drop-down list. Then you can select a picture from a file or from the Bullets theme folder in the Gallery (which is available only if a picture style has been selected), specify the width and height of the bullet (picture), and select an alignment style of the bullet or number.

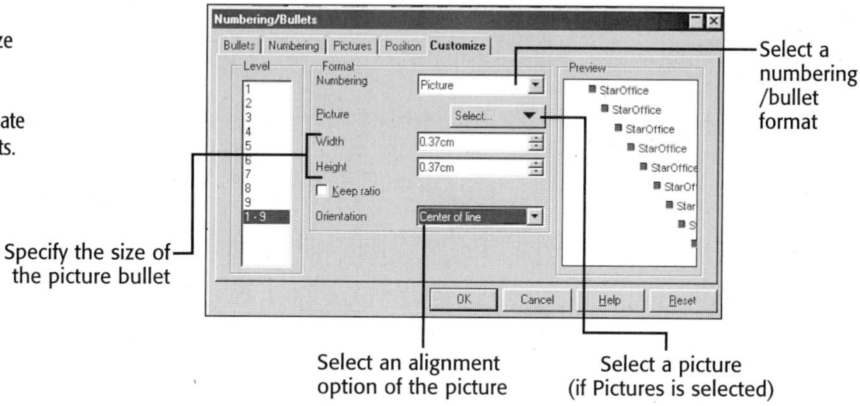

Figure 23.2
Using the Customize tab in the Numbering/Bullets dialog, you can create custom bulleted lists.

Select a numbering /bullet format

Specify the size of the picture bullet

Select an alignment option of the picture

Select a picture (if Pictures is selected)

Note

You see different instances of the Customize tab, depending on the type of numbering and bullets selected in the Numbering drop-down list or on the individual Bullets and Numbering tabs.

Tip #444 from
Michael & Sarah

If you're working with various levels or hierarchies of numbers and bullets, you can assign different numbers and bullets/pictures for different levels in the hierarchy. Just select the corresponding level you want to assign different numbering/bullets to, and then make your selection.

Technically, in a text box, you can create up to 10 indent levels. In reality, however, you would run out of space on a landscape-oriented slide if you were to go any lower than level 3 bullets. Even if you adjust the indent space (using the Position tab in the Numbering/Bullets dialog), things get crowded fast.

CREATING COLUMNS

Splitting your text in columns also makes it easier to read. Most people have an easier time reading shorter lines of text, and using columns is a good way to make them narrower. If you have a large amount of textual information to get across in your presentations, you can take advantage of columns to make the information easier to comprehend.

If you want to add columns in your slide, you have two options. You can change your existing one-column layout to a two-column layout by selecting a different layout as described in the section "Modifying the Slide Layout" in Chapter 22, "Getting Started with StarImpress." (Note that the Modify Slide dialog contains a "Title, 2 Columns Text" template.) Alternatively, you can change the existing layout manually.

Changing the layout manually is the same as scaling and copying an existing text box. Just select and resize the existing text box to the desired width by clicking the sizing handles on the sides to resize the object in one dimension. For example, click and drag the top handle in between the corner handles to stretch or shrink the height of an object from the top; click the sizing handle on the right to stretch or squeeze the width of an object from the right, and so on. In each instance, the side opposite of the one you're dragging remains anchored.

Click one of the corner handles to reduce an object in two dimensions. For example, if you click the handle in the lower-left corner of an object, you can enlarge or reduce the height and width of the object simultaneously from that corner; the handle in the opposite corner remains anchored during this operation.

Next, press Ctrl+C and then Ctrl+V to create a copy of the existing box on top of the original box. Now drag the copy to its new position. Finally, arrange and align both text boxes using the grid or guides.

ENHANCING THE BACKGROUND DESIGN

Another way to enhance your presentation is to modify the background design. When you're modifying the existing background, you have two options: You can change the slide design as described in Chapter 22, or you can manually change the objects and attributes of the existing background. All objects (rectangles, lines, or text) introduced in this view appears as background on every slide (or page) that shares that particular slide design.

→ For more details on changing the slide design, **see** "Changing the Slide Background Design," **p. 856**.

CHANGING THE PAGE BACKGROUND DESIGN

To change the background page style, follow these steps:

1. Open the document whose background you want to change, and click the Background Mode icon in the lower left of the document window.

2. Select Format, Page, or right-click and select Slide, Page Setup from the context menu. The Page Setup dialog appears.

3. Click the Background tab to bring it to the front; then select the type of background in the Table portion of the tab. Your options include the following:

   - **Color**—Click this option if you want to assign a unicolored background. (Note that your color options depend on the currently loaded color palette.) Use the Transparence drop-down list box to change the tint of the currently selected color (Solid, 25%, 50%, 75%, and Transparent).

   - **Gradient**—Use this option if you want to assign a gradient area fill to your background. Use the Increments portion of this option to specify the increment resolution of colors for the gradient fill. The types of gradients available depend on the currently loaded palette.

   - **Hatching**—This option enables you to apply a pattern fill from the currently loaded palette of hatches.

   - **Bitmap**—Use this option if you want to fill the background with a bitmapped texture pattern from the currently loaded bitmap palette. If you select AutoFit, the bitmap fills the entire background. If you select Tile, the texture is displayed in tiled format; you can specify the size and position of the tiles in the Size, Position, and Offset portions of this option.

> **Note**
>
> The selection of available colors, gradients, hatchings, and bitmaps depends on the currently loaded palettes. To learn more about switching palettes or defining your custom area fills, see "Adding Fills and Color to Your Objects" in Chapter 20, "Getting Sketchy with StarDraw." Note also that a busy background may make it hard for your audience to read the text of the slide.

4. When you're finished, click OK. StarOffice automatically applies the new background attributes to all slides that share same background (slide) design template. If you make a mistake, click the Reset button before clicking OK to revert all changes back to the original background (before the current attribute editing session).

5. Click the Slide Mode button to exit the Background mode.

Tip #445 from
Michael & Sarah

Instead of changing the entire background, you can also change the background of individual background objects by using the Area dialog. Just select the object, and then choose Format, Area from the menu bar or Area from the selected object's context menu. For more details on using the Area dialog, see "Adding Fills and Color to Your Objects" in Chapter 20.

MODIFYING THE BACKGROUND STYLE

If you want to save your changes as a style element so that you can consistently apply it to other background designs within the same document, follow these steps:

1. Open the Stylist by pressing F11 or by clicking the Stylist icon on the function bar. (Alternatively, you can select Format, Stylist from the menu bar.)

2. Click the Presentation Styles icon to see a list of available styles.

3. Right-click the Background style, and select Modify from the context menu. The Background dialog appears, displaying the Fill tab.

4. Select the desired background color. The color you choose will apply for all slides using this style. Click OK.

Note

Note that this modification is valid only for the current presentation document. If you want to make permanent changes, you have to save them to a Presentation template.

Likewise, you can modify the Background object's style in the Stylist. Using the Background Objects dialog, you can edit the Line, Fill, Shadow, Font, and Indents and Spacing attributes of this style.

→ For more details on working with the Stylist, **see** "Applying Styles," **p. 295**.

ADDING GRAPHICS, CHARTS, AND OLE OBJECTS

Because StarImpress presentations typically rely so heavily on graphic elements, be sure to draw on the information presented in Chapter 20 to supplement the StarImpress-specific options covered here. You can draw shapes (line art) or insert clip art, shapes, pictures, maps, and flowchart elements from the respective Gallery theme folders or any other directory that holds the desired graphic files and clip art. When you're working with flowchart elements, you can also take advantage of the Connectors menu on the main toolbar.

Tip #446 from
Michael & Sarah

StarOffice's Gallery contains tons of stuff—some of it useful, some of it comical. Still, if you're stuck for ideas, the Gallery is a fun place to rummage. To get there, set the Explorer group to Hierarchical view (by right-clicking the Explorer title bar and selecting Hierarchical from the context menu). Next, expand the Gallery theme folder tree by clicking the plus symbol next to the Gallery item. Then open the Beamer (by pressing Shift+Ctrl+B or clicking the Beamer icon on the function bar). Finally, select each theme folder, and use the Beamer to browse through thumbnail views of its content.

WORKING WITH FLOWCHARTS AND CONNECTORS

One Gallery theme is dedicated to flowchart shapes. They are useful if you want to present a structural organization visually. You can insert these elements from the Beamer via drag and drop into your presentation document.

To create relations between these shapes, you have to use connectors. StarImpress (and StarDraw) includes a menu with 28 connectors—each suited for different purposes and different designs. Just click the Connectors icon on the main toolbar to open the Connectors tear-off window, shown in Figure 23.3.

PART

V

CH

23

Figure 23.3
StarImpress includes an impressive collection of connectors—straight or curved, with or without ends—the choice is yours.

As with the other basic drawing tools (see Chapter 20), using the connectors is pretty straightforward. You select the desired tool; then you click and drag from one object to another to create a connecting line between the two. As you drag, you see a connector symbol in the lower right of your cursor position. After you release the mouse button, the line becomes the desired object.

Note that connectors typically connect to the center of one of the sides of the flowchart shape. The point of connection, also known as a *glue point*, appears as red. When you move the object, the connector automatically moves with it—pretty convenient when you're creating a flowchart yet still have to move the shapes around. If you want the connecting line to connect to a different side of the shape, simply click and drag the end of the connector to the new side; it automatically gravitates toward the center of the new side.

If you want to edit the connector, you can do so by selecting the connector you want to modify and then choosing Format, Connector from the menu bar. In the Connector dialog that appears (see Figure 23.4), you can adjust the line skew (available only if you're using a

Line or Curved Connector) and horizontal and vertical line spacing. You can even switch the type of connector (your options include Standard, Line, Straight, or Curved Connectors). You can preview your changes in the Preview window.

Tip #447 from
Michael & Sarah

Note that unlike other Preview windows, this one enables you to zoom in and out of the selected view by left-clicking and right-clicking, respectively.

In addition, you can change the line style, width, and color of a selected connector by using the respective boxes on the object bar or by selecting Format, Line from the menu bar.

Figure 23.4
You can use the Connector dialog to edit the skew and spacing of selected connectors.

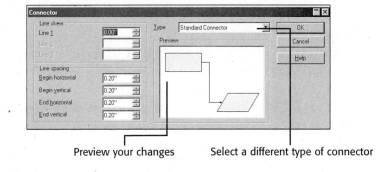

Preview your changes   Select a different type of connector

Tip #448 from
Michael & Sarah

You can also edit Connectors by editing the glue points. Just click the Edit Glue Points icon on the option bar (which you open by selecting View, Toolbars, Option Bar) to open the Edit Glue Points object bar. Using the options on this object bar, you can modify the glue points and size of selected connectors by clicking and dragging. Turn on the Extended Tips for brief explanations of each option.

Entering text inside the flowchart shapes is the same as entering text in a text box or frame. Just double-click the shape, and you see a blinking cursor centered inside the shape, at which point you can start typing. To exit the Text Entry mode, click anywhere outside the shape.

INSERTING OLE OBJECTS

Inserting OLE objects provides another way of enhancing a document. You can drag and drop data directly from StarCalc or text from StarWriter into StarImpress; that data or text then becomes an OLE object within your slide. Alternatively, you can select Insert, Object, OLE Object from the menu bar and then select the object type from the Insert OLE Object dialog. Or you can copy selected data or text and paste it into StarImpress using Paste or Paste Special. (Paste Special gives you a range of other options as well, including pasting your data as plain text and as a DDE link.) You can insert StarChart charts, StarMath formulas, and StarDraw and StarImage graphics files this way, as well as many non-StarOffice types of files. The advantage of using OLE is that double-clicking on your OLE object opens the source application (for example, StarWriter or StarCalc), enabling you to edit your data in ways you can't when using StarImpress.

→ For more details on OLE and exchanging data between StarOffice documents, **see** "Sharing Data Between Documents," **p. 171**.

For more details on OLE and exchanging data between StarOffice documents, **see** "Sharing Data Between Documents," **p. 171**.

> **Note**
>
> For an example of inserted OLE objects, look at the Recar-amg presentation document (located in the `Explorer\Samples\Presentations` folder). More specifically, check out the "Margins by Model" and "Sales Forecast 1999" slides.

CREATING SPECIAL EFFECTS WITH FONTWORK

You can also enhance a presentation by using FontWork, a StarOffice program that enables you to have your text take on a variety of shapes. Using FontWork, you can bend, stretch, flip, and rotate text along invisible lines and curves. To open FontWork, select Format, FontWork from the menu bar. To apply FontWork effects, select the text to which you want to apply FontWork. Usually, clicking inside the text box suffices; FontWork effects apply to the entire text inside a box. Figure 23.5 shows the FontWork controls window and a custom font effect.

> **Note**
>
> The FontWork controls window is a floating window that can remain open while you're working on your presentation (or drawing). If it gets in the way, double-click the title bar to minimize it; double-click again to restore it to its original size.

You can spend an hour or more just experimenting with this effects tool. Use the spin box at the top of the FontWork window to choose a layout or shape for the selected text. Using the first row of buttons, you can slant the text object or place it at a 90-degree angle in relation to the contour line, or you can flip it horizontally or vertically. Using the second row of buttons, you can reverse the order of letters, as well as align the text object with regard to the selected curve or line. The spin boxes in the center enable you to specify the distance between the selected curve and the text object, and between the beginning of the curve and the beginning of the object, respectively. The lower part of the dialog enables you to select shadow styles of varying colors, degrees, and distances from the individual letters of the text object.

Click the Contour button (the one with the squiggly line below the center spin boxes) to show the invisible curve or line along which the text is aligned. Click the Text Contour button (the one with the dotted T) to add a contour to the individual letters of your text.

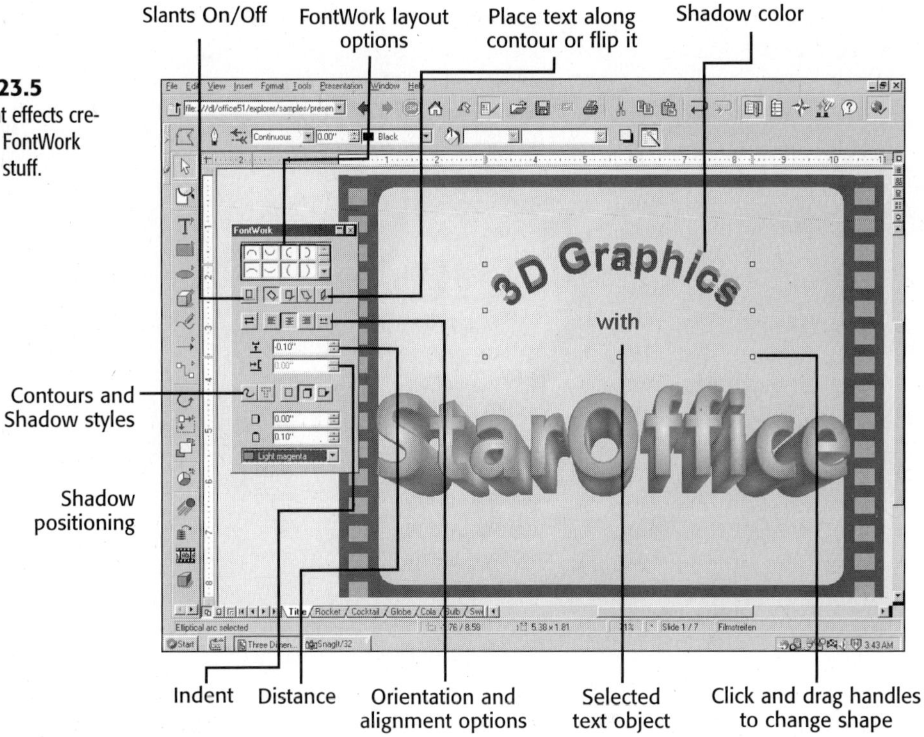

Slants On/Off
FontWork layout options
Place text along contour or flip it
Shadow color
Contours and Shadow styles
Shadow positioning
3D Graphics
with
StarOffice
Indent
Distance
Orientation and alignment options
Selected text object
Click and drag handles to change shape

Figure 23.5
These font effects created with FontWork are fancy stuff.

Note

WINDOWS

Fonts in windows are optimized to appear at their best without additional contours.

You can manually bend, scale, or "edit" the shape of the selected line style—squeezing, extending, or inverting it—by dragging the sizing handles of the text object. Alternatively, you can click the Edit Points icon on the object bar to change the shape of the curve. If you don't like the selected style, choose another one, or click the Off button (the first button from the left below the top spin box) to cancel the effect. The possibilities of what you can do with this tool are indeed numerous. All it takes is a dash of creativity and a willingness to experiment. Try it; it's fun!

Tip #449 from
Michael & Sarah

If you're new to FontWork, it is a good idea to turn on the Extended Tips option (by selecting Help, Extended Tips). That way, you can quickly tell what the effects of a particular button are by resting your cursor over a button.

If you use FontWork a lot, you can add a FontWork icon to the main toolbar by following these steps:

1. Select Tools, Configure to open the Configuration dialog.

2. Click the Toolbars tab to bring it to the front, and then click Configure. The Customize Toolbars dialog appears.

3. In the Functions portion of this dialog, select Format in the Category list on the left and FontWork in the Command list on the right. Notice the FontWork option selected in the Icons list at the top of the dialog.

4. (Optional) Click the Icons button to select an icon for the FontWork command from the Customize Buttons dialog. (Note that most of the icons listed in the Customize Buttons dialog have already been assigned to commands. So if you select an icon, don't pick one that is already on the StarImpress main toolbar—to avoid confusion.) Click OK to exit the Customize Buttons dialog. StarOffice has already assigned the icon you selected to the FontWork command.

5. Drag the FontWork icon to the main toolbar; then click the Close (X) button to exit the Customize Toolbars dialog.

Using these steps, you can also place other commonly used commands on your toolbars.

CREATING 3D EFFECTS

Another strength of StarImpress (and StarDraw) is the capability to create stunning 3D effects. When creating 3D effects, you basically assign 3D attributes to an existing 3D object. Using the 3D Effects controls window, you can change the geometry, shading, illumination, textures, and material properties of selected 3D objects. You can apply these effects to 3D objects, as well as 2D objects that have been converted to 3D. As with every other object you create in StarImpress or StarDraw, you can also insert these custom 3D objects in text and spreadsheet documents.

To access the 3D Effects controls, click the 3D Controller icon on the main toolbar, or select Format, 3D Effects from the menu bar. The 3D Controller is available in Drawing view, Notes view, and Handout view.

Note

The 3D Effects controls window is a floating window that can remain open while you're working on your presentation (or drawing). If it gets in your way, double-click the title bar to minimize it; double-click again to restore it to its original size.

Tip #450 from
Michael & Sarah

As with FontWork, when you're new to the 3D Effects controller, you might want to turn on the Extended Tips option (by selecting Help, Extended Tips). That way, you can quickly tell what the effects of a particular button are by resting your cursor over the button.

Working with the 3D Effects controller is pretty straightforward, and, as with the FontWork tool, the sheer number of effects that you can achieve is overwhelming. To start experimenting, follow these steps:

1. Click the 3D Controller icon on the main toolbar, or select Format, 3D Effects. The 3D Effects window opens to the Favorites view, as shown in Figure 23.6.

Figure 23.6
Using the 3D Effects controller, you can change the attributes of selected 3D objects on-the-fly.

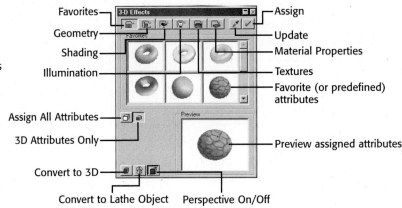

2. Select the 3D object whose attributes you want to change. If the only existing object is a 2D object, you can quickly convert it into a 3D object by using the Convert to 3D or Convert to 3D Rotation (or Lathe) Object, respectively (refer to Figure 23.6).

> **Note**
>
> When you're converting 2D objects into 3D objects, you can select several individual 2D objects at once and then convert them into one 3D object. However, to convert a 2D group, you first have to ungroup the objects before you can convert them.

3. Define the desired attributes. When you're defining attributes for a selected 3D object, you can start by selecting an effect from the list of Favorites (kind of like assigning styles via the Stylist). The donuts assign illumination effects, the spheres assign textures, and the letters (a.k.a. *Extrude* objects) assign various 3D effects. You can control the attributes you want to assign to a selected object by using the 3D Attributes Only and Assign All Attributes buttons.

> **Note**
>
> Favorites contain combined attributes of 3D objects that you can assign with the click of a mouse to other objects. Click a Favorite once to select and preview it in the Preview area. Double-click a Favorite to assign it immediately to the selected 3D object. Note also that Favorites are identical to the contents of the 3D theme folder in the Gallery. If you add new graphics into that folder, they appear as well.

Alternatively, you can also start from scratch by working your way through the various 3D effects options, including geometry, shading, illumination, textures, and material properties of selected 3D objects.

Tip #451 from
Michael & Sarah

For brief descriptions of the various controller buttons, refer to the StarOffice online help. Search for `3D Effects` and display StarChart. Then click the 3D Effects hyperlink.

4. Check the Preview area in the lower right of the 3D Effects controller window to get an idea of the changes you want to make. (Note that the Preview area does not represent a thumbnail preview of the selected object but only a stylized example of the modifications you make.) If you selected more than one option in the 3D Effects dialog, click the Update button so that the Preview area reflects all selected options.

Tip #452 from
Michael & Sarah

To get an even better idea of the applied changes, use the Perspective On/Off button at the bottom of the 3D Effects dialog. This button toggles the perspective view in the Preview area on or off.

5. When you're finished, click the Assign icon in the upper right of the 3-Effects Controller toolbar to assign the attributes in the controller to the selected object.

INCORPORATING INTERACTIVE CONTROLS

You can make your StarOffice presentations come alive by adding interactive controls. To insert action buttons, you choose the desired button in the Interaction theme folder in the Gallery. Unfortunately, the available buttons don't have descriptive names, but their symbols speak for themselves, clueing you in as to the button's function: First, Back, Stop, Next, or Last. When these buttons are inserted (via drag and drop) in your presentation (or online) document, they take you to the first, next, or last slide in the presentation—automatically, without your having to do any additional programming! Alternatively, you can draw your own buttons or elements by using the drawing tools on the main toolbar.

→ For more details on editing text, **see** "Working with Text," **p. 838**.

→ For more details on using the drawing tools, **see** Chapter 20, "Getting Sketchy with StarDraw," **p. 715**.

StarOffice includes a sample presentation called Orgchart (located in the `Samples/Presentations` folder in the Explorer group) that demonstrates the possibilities of creating an interactive presentation. You can use (and modify) this presentation for your own purposes, or you can create one from scratch.

The Orgchart sample document, shown in Figure 23.7, provides a flowchart-like diagram of a company structure. If you click the dark gray "hotspot" in the lower-right corner of each box, you advance to a new slide and, by extension, department structure, whereby the current department is indicated in the upper-right corner of the slide. To return to the opening page, click the red arrow in the lower-left corner of the slide.

Figure 23.7
The Orgchart document is a good example of an interactive StarImpress presentation.

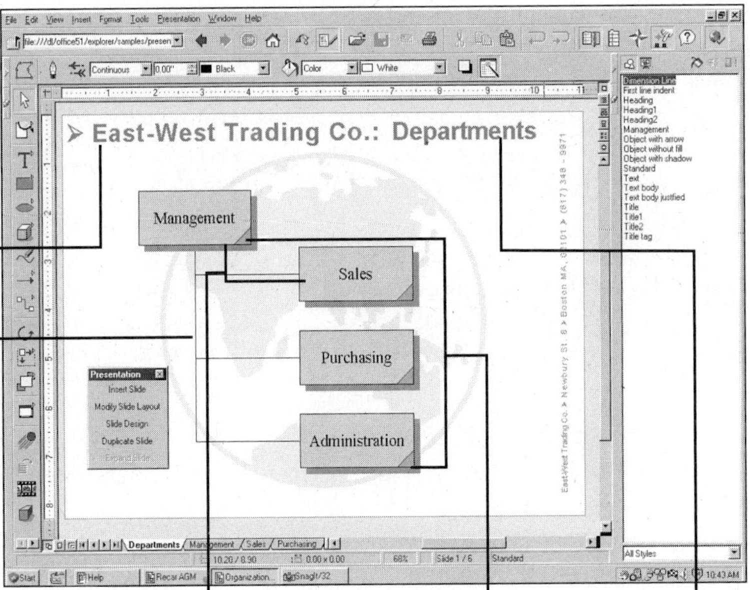

Company name and address (part of background)

Connectors

Flowchart elements

Hotspot (click to change slides)

Department name (part of foreground)

In general, you can use these interactive elements, buttons, or hotspots (or whatever you want to call them) not only to link to slides, but also to include sounds and links to Web pages or other files in the presentation.

To add an interactive element to your presentation, perform the following steps:

1. Navigate to the slide in which you want to add the element.

2. Select the object to which you want to add an interactive component. (Note that as soon as you select an object, the Interaction icon on the main toolbar becomes available.)

3. Click the Interaction icon on the main toolbar, or select Presentation, Interaction from the menu bar. (Note that this option is available only if you've selected an object.) The Interaction dialog then appears (see Figure 23.8).

4. Use the Interaction dialog to define the behavior of the element (or button). Just select a behavior in the Action at Mouse Click drop-down list box. Depending on the behavior you select, the dialog box may change. For example, if you select Go to Next Slide, what needs to happen is obvious and you don't have to do anything else. By contrast, if you select Go to Page or Object, Go to Document, or Play Sound, you have to select the proper target from the list of available slides or objects, or browse for the desired document or sound file.

5. When you're finished, click OK.

Figure 23.8
The Interaction dialog is your control center for assigning actions to mouse clicks.

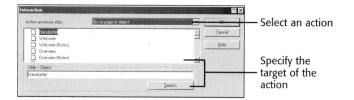

Select an action

Specify the target of the action

PART

V

CH

23

Note

The hotspots or buttons in the Orgchart document were created as separate triangles (refer to Figure 23.7). Next, an action was assigned to each triangle. Each triangle was then placed and grouped in the lower corner of the respective text box.

To edit interactive elements, Alt+click the element, and then select Interaction from the context menu. The familiar Interaction dialog appears, enabling you to make the desired changes.

ADDING SOUND TO PRESENTATIONS

When you want to enhance a presentation, sound can also be an effective tool. However, as with any special effect (or font for that matter), you should use it sparingly and only when it actually clarifies your presentation. Using sound just because you can is at best annoying and at worst a superb means of obfuscating your point.

You can add sound to your presentation by assigning it to an interactive element (see the preceding section) via the Interaction dialog by following these steps:

1. Select the element to which you want to assign a sound.

2. Click the Interaction icon on the main toolbar, or select Presentation, Interaction from the menu bar to open the Interaction dialog.

3. In the Action at Mouse Click drop-down list, select Play Sound.

4. Click the Browse button at the bottom of the dialog. As soon as you click the button, the Open dialog appears, enabling you to navigate to the location of the desired sound file.

Tip #453 from
Michael & Sarah

The StarOffice Gallery contains a theme folder chock full of sound files. From the Open dialog, just click the Sounds folder. You can preview the sounds in advance by double-clicking the various files in the Beamer.

5. Select the file and click Open. StarOffice inserts the selected sound file in the Sounds text box at the bottom of the dialog.

6. Click OK to assign the sound file to the interactive elements. If you click the element, you can hear the sound.

Tip #454 from
Michael & Sarah

Note that you can also add sound to other effects by using the Effects tool on the main toolbar. For more details, see "Creating Object Effects" and "Adding Sound and Color Effects" later in this chapter.

Tip #455 from
Michael & Sarah

Under Linux, StarOffice uses rplay to play sounds. If you don't have it installed (which also means if you don't have the rplay daemon running), you will hear nothing.

ANIMATING OBJECTS AND TEXT

Both StarDraw and StarImpress sport some of the best drawing tools available in an Office suite. Using StarImpress, you can add animation effects that enable you to enliven an otherwise "static" presentation.

CREATING ANIMATED GIFS

StarImpress includes an Animation tool that enables you to create animated GIF files. An animated GIF consists of a sequence of pixel (or bitmapped) images that, when presented, produce the illusion of a moving image.

Note

The Gallery comes with a theme folder called Animations that contains animated GIFs created with the StarOffice drawing and effects tools and assembled with the Animation tool. To use them, simply click and drag them into your document.

Before you can create an animated GIF file, you need to create all the individual images that will contribute to the illusion of a moving image. Depending on the amount of detail you want, creating these images can be rather time intensive. For the following steps, I opted to create a stylized example of individual images (using the Morphing command) in StarDraw that I then imported into StarImpress to combine them into one animated GIF file.

Note

The following example uses both StarDraw and StarImpress because the Morphing command is available only in StarDraw, whereas the Animation tool is available only in StarImrpess. If you already have a series of images that you would like to turn into a GIF file, you can skip steps 1 through 6 and start with step 7.

To create and edit animated GIFs, follow these steps:

1. Select File, New, Drawing to open a new drawing document.

2. Use the Rectangle and Ellipse drawing tools to create a simple drawing (for example, a filled red square) in the upper-left corner and another one (for example, a filled green circle) in the lower-right corner. (Remember to press Shift while using the Rectangle and Ellipse tool to create a square or circle, respectively. For more details on using these drawing tools, see "Using the Basic Drawing Tools" in Chapter 20.)

3. Select both objects (press Shift+click), and then choose Edit, Morphing from the menu bar to open the Morphing dialog.

4. In the Increments spin box, select 8. Also, be sure the Fade Object Attributes check box is selected.

5. Click OK. StarDraw creates a grouped object (consisting of 10 images) in which the square gradually morphs into the circle in eight increments or steps (see Figure 23.9).

PART

V

CH

23

Figure 23.9
Before you can create an animated GIF file, you first have to create a sequence of individual images. In this example, I used the Morphing command to create a sequence of images.

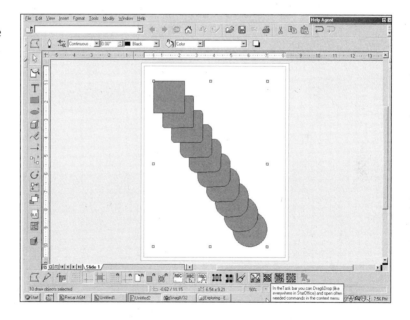

Next, you have to decide whether the animated GIF file should encompass the entire space of your slide, toppling from the upper-left corner to the lower-right corner. If so, leave the group as is. If you want the animated object to be centered and change only its form and color without moving across the screen, you have to ungroup the objects by selecting Ungroup from the context menu or by pressing Alt+Ctrl+Shift+G. (Alternatively, you can select Edit, Object, Ungroup from the menu bar.) For this example, select the Ungroup option.

6. Press Ctrl+C to copy the individual images, open a new presentation document (or switch to the document in which you want to insert an animation), and press Ctrl+V to paste the images into the desired slide.

7. Click the Animation icon on the main toolbar, or select Presentation, Animation to open the Animation dialog (see Figure 23.10).

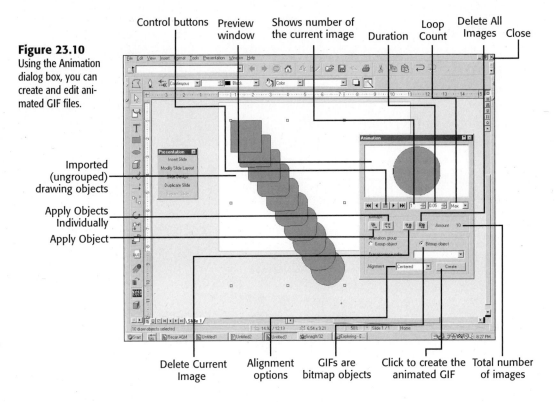

Figure 23.10
Using the Animation dialog box, you can create and edit animated GIF files.

8. Select the Bitmap Object in the Animation group portion of the dialog. (Remember that GIF images are bitmapped images.) Then click the Apply Objects Individually icon. StarOffice collects the individual images and stacks them in the order in which they appear (overlapping from top left to bottom right): The original red square becomes image 10 (the image on the top), and the circle becomes image 1 (the one at the bottom). Next, you need to specify the amount of time you want each image in the sequence to be shown.

Note

As with so many other dialogs and tool windows in StarOffice, the Animation dialog is a floating window that you can leave open while you're working in StarImpress. If it gets in your way, simply double-click the title bar to minimize it; double-click again to restore it to its original size.

9. Ensure that image 10 (the top one) is the current image. Then change the setting in the Duration spin box (for example, 0.05). Click the down arrow of the Current Image spin box so that image 9 appears, and then set the same duration for image 9. Repeat this step for images 8 through 1.

10. When you're finished, click Create to insert the finished animation in your slide. The animated bitmapped object appears in the center of the slide, provided you chose the Centered option in the Alignment drop-down list of the Animation dialog (refer to Figure 23.10).

You can now drag the object anywhere on your slide. To exit the Selection mode, click anywhere outside the animated object. As soon as you exit the Selection mode, the GIF image starts to loop endlessly.

PART

V

CH

23

SAVING AND OPENING ANIMATED GIFS

Now that you've created an animated GIF file, you need to save it, of course, for future use. To save it, you just need to do the following:

1. Select the animated object that you want to save. (The object stops moving as soon as you select it.)

2. Select File, Export from the menu bar to open the Export dialog box.

3. Enter a name for the file in the Filename text box.

4. From the File Type drop-down list, select GIF (Graphics Interchange Format); then click the Selection option in the lower left of the dialog (because you want to export only the animated object, not the entire slide).

5. Select the location where you want to save the animated GIF file, and then click Save. The GIF Options dialog appears, enabling you to save the object interlaced and transparent. Leave the settings at their default, and click OK. (For more details on saving GIF files, see "Saving and Closing Images" in Chapter 21, "Creating and Modifying Images with StarImage.")

Tip #456 from
Michael & Sarah

If you want to access or preview the object via the Gallery, save it in the Animation theme folder (Office51\Gallery\www-anim). You can then update the folder contents via the Gallery content menu as described in the section "Adding New Folders and Files to the Gallery" in Chapter 11, "Desktop Publishing with StarOffice."

---

6. Click OK.

Theoretically, you can insert animated GIF files in your documents like any other graphic file by selecting Insert, Picture, From File. If you've saved the animated GIF file in a Gallery theme folder, you can simply drag it via the Beamer from the folder into the document. In practice, however, GIF files are most effective when employed in World Wide Web or in presentation documents.

→ For more details on exporting a presentation document as an HTML file, **see** "Saving Presentations for the World Wide Web," **p. 910**.

Note

If you want to display the contents of the Gallery folder in the Beamer, the Explorer group must be in Hierarchical view. (To change the view, select Hierarchical from the context menu.) Then, when you select a Gallery theme folder in the Explorer group, you can see thumbnail previews of its contents in the open Beamer.

EDITING ANIMATED GIFs

If you want to edit the individual images of an animated GIF file after you've saved the file, you can do so in the Animation dialog by following these steps:

1. Open the animated object file in StarImpress.

2. Click the Animation icon on the main toolbar, or select Presentation, Animation from the menu bar to open the Animation dialog.

3. Import the objects into the Animation dialog by selecting Apply Objects Individually.

4. Delete all individual images except for the one that you want to edit by using the Current Image spin box and the Delete Current Image button (refer to Figure 23.10).

5. When you're finished, click Create. You can now edit the image in StarImpress (on the slide).

Note

Remember that the current image is a bitmapped image. To edit it, you have to select it and then choose Image, Edit from the context menu. StarImpress opens the image inside a small window with all the image editing tools of StarImage at your disposal.

6. After you edit the image, delete the contents in the window of the Animation dialog, and import the entire animation into the window by selecting it and then clicking the Apply Objects Individually button (refer to Figure 23.10).

7. Switch to the image you modified in the animation window by using the Current Image spin box.

8. Select the edited image (in the slide), and then click the Apply Object button in the Animation dialog (refer to Figure 23.10). StarImpress inserts the edited image right after the original image.

9. Return to the original image by using the Current Image spin box. Then click the Delete Current Image button to delete it (because it is the old version of the image).

10. Click Create, and then export the new animated GIF as described in the section "Saving and Opening Animated GIFs" earlier in this chapter.

CREATING ANIMATED OBJECTS

Apart from creating animated GIF files, you also can animate individual objects and text within a slide by using the Effects tool, shown in Figure 23.11. The effects you assign can be triggered by slide transitions or controlled by mouse clicks.

Figure 23.11
Using the Effects tool, you can animate objects and text within an individual slide.

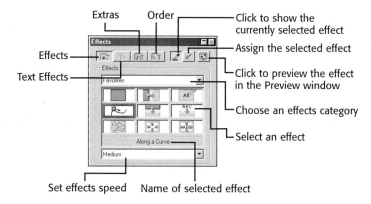

CREATING OBJECT EFFECTS

Using the Effects tool, you can animate individual objects in your presentation document. The number of effects seems infinite and invites for experimentation. To start experimenting, follow these steps:

1. In Drawing view, select the object to which you want to assign an effect.

2. Click the Effects icon on the main toolbar, or select Presentation, Effects from the menu bar to open the Effects dialog. (Notice that the Text Effects option is grayed out because it is unavailable.)

3. Select an effects category from the drop-down list on the top, and then choose the desired effect from the options below the drop-down list. You can see a brief description of the effect (refer to Figure 23.11).

4. Choose a speed for the selected effect in the drop-down list at the bottom of the dialog.

5. When you're finished, click the Assign icon. If you want, you can also preview the effect by clicking the Preview button and then clicking in the Preview window that appears.

One special effect that StarOffice offers is the option to have an object (such as a 3D cube or a sphere, for example) move along a predefined line or curve (for example, from the upper left to the lower right of an object). You can create this effect as follows:

1. Using the StarOffice tools, create an object, or select the object that you want to move.

2. Draw a freehand curve along which you want to move the object using the Freeform Line tool available from the Curves tear-off window on the main toolbar.

3. Select both the object and the curve.

4. Click the Effects icon on the main toolbar to open the Effects dialog.

5. Select Favorites from the Effects drop-down list, and then select the Along a Curve effect.

6. Click the Assign icon. You can also click the Preview icon to sneak a peek at the effect in the Preview window that appears.

Note

If you're not satisfied with your curve, select and edit it by using the Edit Points option on the object bar. For more details on editing (Bézier) curves, see "Editing Curves with the Bézier Object Bar" in Chapter 20.

Tip #457 from
Michael & Sarah

The more points the curve has, the slower the object movement. Hence, by adding additional points, you can modify the speed of this effect.

CREATING ANIMATED TEXT EFFECTS

StarImpress also enables you to fiddle with text animation effects in a seemingly infinite number of permutations. For example, you can have text "drop down" from the top of the slide, fade in from the left or right side of the slide, or slowly assemble out of a series of pixels—to name but a few of the many options. The quick way to experiment with these transition effects is to follow these steps:

1. In Drawing view, select the text to which you want to assign an effect.

2. Click the Effects icon on the main toolbar, or select Presentation, Effect from the menu bar to open the Effects controller window.

3. Click the Text Effects icon on the Effects window toolbar (the second icon from the left), and then select an effects category from the drop-down list at the top (for example, Uncover). As soon as you select a category, you see various options listed below the Text Effects drop-down list.

4. Select the desired effect (for example, Uncover From Top). You can tell the behavior of the selected effect by looking at the title bar underneath.

5. Select the effect speed from the drop-down list at the bottom. Your options include Slow, Medium, and Fast.

6. When you're finished, click the Assign icon (see Figure 23.12). You can also click the Preview button in the Effects window to open the Preview window. Here, you can click the text area to preview the effect.

Figure 23.12
You can use the Text Effects icon on the Effects dialog to create interesting text effects.

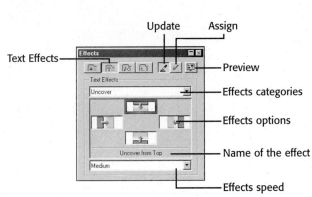

> **Note**
>
> When you're working with text only, you can use both the Effects and Text Effects options in the Effects dialog. However, if you're using both text and other objects, you can assign each one a different effect if desired.

ADDING SOUND AND COLOR EFFECTS

Using the Effects dialog, you also can assign additional attributes to an object or text effect. For example, you can have an object disappear after the effect, or you can have an image fade in from the left and at the same time play the sound file Applause by following these steps:

1. Follow steps 1 through 4 from the preceding section, and then click the Extras button in the Effects dialog.

2. Click the Browse icon in the lower right of the dialog, and navigate to the folder that contains the desired sound file (see Figure 23.13). (Note that StarOffice comes with a collection of sound files located in the Gallery, Sounds theme folder.)

Figure 23.13
Using the Extras portion of the Effects dialog, you can assign additional sound or color effects to a specified text or object effect.

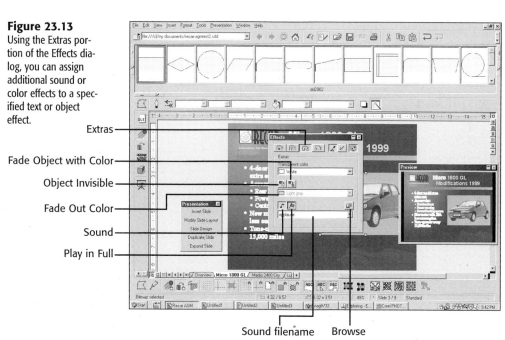

3. Select the desired sound file. Then click the Sound or Play in Full buttons, depending on whether you want to hear the sound only through the slide transition or for the entirety of the effect, respectively.

> **Note**
>
> StarOffice supports these sound file formats: .au/.snd (SUN/NeXT Audio), .wav (MS-Windows Audio), .voc (Creative Labs (=Soundblaster) Audio), .aiff (SGI/Apple Audio), and .iff (Amiga Audio).

4. (Optional) If you want, you can also control further aspects of the selected effect by using the Object Invisible and Fade Object with Color buttons (refer to Figure 23.13). For example, if you want the object to disappear after the effect, select the Object Invisible button. If you want the object to change color after the effect, select the Fade Object with Color button, and then choose the desired color in the drop-down list below. If you really want to get fancy, you can opt to have a certain color in the object appear as transparent by selecting the color in the Transparent Color drop-down list. However, note that this effect works only if the object color that you would like to render "invisible" exists in the currently loaded color palette.

5. When you're finished, click the Assign icon. If you want, you can also preview the effect by clicking the Preview button and then clicking in the Preview window that appears.

> **Note**
>
> Depending on the settings in the Slide Show settings dialog (which you open by choosing Presentation, Presentation Settings), you might have to click to advance to the next slide. If Change Slides Manually is selected in the Slide Show dialog, each object effect on a slide counts as a "slide change," which means you can view each effect individually. For more details on setting your presentation settings, see "Setting Your Slide Show Preferences" in Chapter 24, "Previewing and Presenting Your Presentation."

PUTTING THE EFFECTS IN ORDER

If you assigned a series of effects to various objects within a slide, you can click the Order option in the Effects dialog. Here, you find a list of the objects to which effects have been assigned, in the order in which they have been assigned. If you want, you can change the order at any time via drag and drop. Dragging and dropping does not affect the placement of the objects on the slide.

CREATING SLIDE TRANSITION EFFECTS

Last but not least, you can enhance your presentation by adding slide transition effects that are bound to garner the attention of your audience. For example, you can have your slides roll in and out, dissolve, or wipe in and out—to name but a few effects.

> **Note**
>
> In StarImpress, you create transitions in both Drawing view and Slide Sort view. When you're in Slide Sort view, you have two options for assigning transition effects: You can choose an effect for the selected slide from the Effects drop-down list box on the object bar, in which case the effect is assigned automatically. Or, if you want more control over the effect attributes, you can access the Slide Transition window by selecting Presentation, Slide Transition from the menu bar. In Drawing view, you have to select Presentation, Slide Transition to assign slide transitions.

To create a captivating transition between slides, follow these steps:

1. Switch to Slide Sort view by clicking the Slide Sort View icon above the vertical scroll-bar (the fourth icon above the scroll arrow) or by selecting View, Master View, Slide Sort. Your slides appear consecutively (from left to right, from top to bottom); depending on the number of slides in your presentation, you might have to scroll up or down to see all of them. Alternatively, you can adjust your view by zooming out.

2. Select a slide, and then choose Presentation, Slide Transition to open the Slide Transition dialog (see Figure 23.14). Using this dialog is similar to using the Effects dialog.

Figure 23.14
Using the Slide Transition dialog, you can assign a series of visual and sound transition effects.

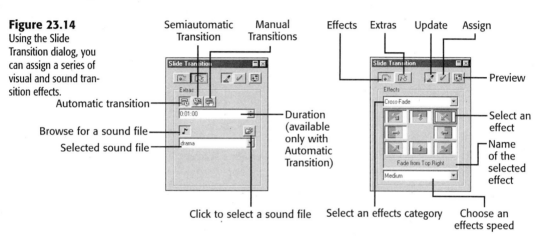

3. From the drop-down list box at the top, select the desired transition effects category that you want to apply to the selected slide (which means the effect appears *before* the slide is fully revealed onscreen). Then select the desired effect in the area below. When you click an effect, you can see a description at the bottom of the area.

4. From the drop-down list at the bottom of the dialog, select a transition speed. Your options include Slow, Medium, and Fast.

5. When you're finished, click the Assign icon.

After you've assigned a transition effect, you see a small Start button on the left below the respective slide. When you click it, you can see a preview of the transition effect.

Tip #458 from
Michael & Sarah

As with every other work in progress, don't forget to regularly save your work. Apart from saving to safeguard against data loss, you can always close a document without saving the changes you don't like and then reload the document to see the changes you last saved and liked. For an extra measure of security, you can also switch on the automatic backup feature by selecting Automatic Save Every X Mintues in the Tools, Options, General, Save dialog (whereby "X" stands for a value you define).

> **Note**
>
> Apart from using slide transitions, you can also add animated objects and text to your presentation document. These effects can occur within a slide or during a slide transition. For more details, see the section "Animating Objects and Text" earlier in this chapter.

As with everything else in StarOffice, the options are overwhelming. So that you don't overwhelm your audience, try to refrain from adding too many different transition effects; instead, stick with a couple of similar (or complementary) effects. Here, as with the other effects options (or fonts), less is more. For a good example of what you can do with transition effects, look at the Recar-agm sample presentation (located in the `Explorer\Samples\Presentations` folder).

> **Tip #459 from**
> *Michael & Sarah*
>
> If the Change Slides Manually option is selected in the Slide Show dialog (which you open by selecting Presentation, Presentation Settings), a mouse click brings up the next slide. If the slide contains additional effects, a mouse click starts the effect. If the slide contains two or more effects, each mouse click starts the next effect. Only after all effects have been revealed can you advance to the next slide by clicking the mouse. If you want to bypass the effects and move to the next slide immediately, use the right-arrow key. This feature is helpful if you want to fade in individual lines of text, for example. So rather than reveal all text at once, you can show one line of text, comment on it, reveal the next one, comment on it, and so on. Naturally, this method is useful only if you control your slide show manually.
>
> If you want to run quickly through your slides, use the right-arrow key; it takes you to the next slide immediately.

CREATING AUTOMATIC TRANSITIONS

If you want your presentation to run automatically, select all slides in Slide Sort view, and then select Automatic from the Transition drop-down list on the object bar. Because many slides contain different amounts of content and detail, you can select a duration for each selected slide in the Time spin box on the object bar or in the Duration box under the Extras option of the Slide Transition dialog. (To open this dialog, select Presentation, Slide Transition.)

CREATING TIMED TRANSITIONS

Note that you can also rehearse the timing for each slide by clicking the Rehearse Timing icon on the object bar. Each click advances you to the next slide, and StarImpress automatically records the timing for each slide.

→ For more details on the Rehearse Timing function, **see** "Timing Your Presentation," **p. 894.**

CHAPTER 24

PREVIEWING AND PRESENTING YOUR PRESENTATION

In this chapter

PREVIEWING A PRESENTATION

After you have created all your StarImpress slides, you will want to prepare your work for presentation. In StarImpress, you have several options for presenting your work, including printing presentations, creating speaker's notes and audience handouts, running slide shows, and exporting the presentation as a series of HTML pages for Web publishing.

You can also print the slides in color or have them exposed on a high-resolution imagesetter. You also can transfer them fully or partially to other applications. When printing a presentation, you have the option of either printing directly or printing to a file for later high-resolution output.

However, before you even consider any of these options, you should first run through the following checklist for better presentations:

■ **Check your spelling**—The last thing you want is to have a typo appear on a large-screen monitor. Always check your spelling after finishing text entry. When in StarImpress, you have access to the same proofing tools as in StarWriter, including AutoCorrect. (For more details, see "Proofing Your Work" in Chapter 11, "Desktop Publishing with StarOffice.")

Note

> Because StarOffice does not come with a grammar checker, you (or "another pair of eyes") should also read through your text one more time, to make sure there are no glaring grammatical errors.

■ **Check the order of your slides**—You should always run through a presentation one more time before showing it to make sure that all slides are in the order in which they're supposed to appear. (For more details on how to rearrange the order of your slides, see "Working with Slides" in Chapter 22, "Getting Started with StarImpress.")

■ **Check the timing of your slides**—Don't spend too much time on a single slide. If a slide stays onscreen for any extended amount of time (say five minutes or more), rethink your content. For example, you could break the slide in question into additional slides using the Expand Slide command. Your audience is more likely to stay with you if you break up the big chunks of information into two or three separate slides. (For more details on using the Expand Slide command, see "Working with Slides" in Chapter 22, "Getting Started with StarImpress.")

■ **Preview your presentation in Live mode**—Rehearse your presentation one last time with the Navigator visible and in Live mode. Working in Live mode enables you to catch (and edit) any inconsistencies or errors that you normally might miss, and gives you the advantage of making corrections on-the-fly. (For more details on using the Navigator and working in Live mode, see "Navigating Extensive Presentations" in this chapter.)

■ **Test your presentation**—Always test your presentation on the hardware that you plan to use (well) before the audience starts flocking in. Regardless of whether the presentation ran fine on your computer at work or all the other sites, you don't have any guarantee that the hardware you're using at the new site is correctly set up or will behave as well as the rest.

■ **Add a "blank" slide**—Add a slide with an attractive background or your company's logo at the end of your presentation. That way, your audience has an attractive slide to look at as opposed to getting stuck with a black screen or being dumped back into a StarImpress master view.

PRODUCING ONSCREEN SLIDE SHOWS

Slide shows are at the heart of StarImpress because you can create professional-looking slide shows without a great deal of hassle. StarOffice's only failing—and perhaps a deciding factor for laptop-toting executives—is the fact that in its current incarnation, it doesn't come with a standalone presentations player. You need to have the entire StarOffice program (currently some 127MB) installed on the machine you want to use for the presentation.

STARTING AND EXITING PRESENTATIONS

You can start your slide show in any master view by clicking either one of the two Presentation icons—one above the vertical scrollbar or the other on the main toolbar (by default the last icon in each master view)—or by pressing Ctrl+F2. The presentation runs automatically in standard full-screen mode or according to the preset views and options that you defined in the Slide Show dialog box box (which you open by choosing Presentation, Presentation Settings).

→ For more details on changing the presentation settings, **see** "Setting Your Slide Show Preferences,"
p. 901.

After a minute, or if you click once, the second slide is displayed (preceded by the defined transition effect). After the last slide, you see a black screen, which means that the presentation is over. At that point, you can click with your mouse to exit the slide show.

Note also that you don't have to run a slide show all the way through; you can end the presentation at any time by pressing the Esc key.

RUNNING A STANDARD PRESENTATION

Starting a presentation is one thing; running it is another. With StarImpress, you have the option of running a slide show manually or automatically.

RUNNING A SLIDE SHOW MANUALLY

Running a show manually has the advantage that a speaker can control when to advance to the next slide or return to a previous slide. To run a show manually, select Presentation, Presentation Settings from the menu bar. In the Options portion of the Slide Show dialog box that appears, select Change Slides Manually. Click OK to accept the settings.

Now, when you run your slide show, you can advance to the next slide by clicking with your mouse, or by pressing the spacebar, Enter, Page Down, or the right-arrow key. Right-click, or press Page Up or the left-arrow key, to return to the previous slide. Press Home to return to the opening slide or End to advance to the last slide. If you press Esc, you exit the Slide Show mode and return to the StarImpress workspace.

Tip #460 from	If you select the Mouse Pointer Visible and Mouse Point as Pen options in the Slide Show
Michael & Sarah	dialog box, you can draw attention to certain elements on the current display by clicking and dragging to draw a line or circle. For example, you can put a check mark after each point covered. (Using this option is a bit tricky and may require some practice because the lines you draw may at times extend diagonally from the upper-left corner to your current click point.)

RUNNING A SLIDE SHOW AUTOMATICALLY

StarImpress also enables you to run your slide show automatically, which means slides change automatically at predefined time intervals—with or without a speaker present. (For example, using this option, you can prepare a presentation and then have it show all day long at a trade show for passers-by.) To set up a presentation for automatic display, select Presentation, Presentation Settings. In the Type portion of the Slide Show dialog box that appears, select Auto. In the spin box, you can set a time for the duration of the pause between the end of a show and the start of the next run. If you select the Show Logo option, the *Created with StarOffice* logo appears onscreen between shows. To stop an automatic slide show, press Esc.

Tip #461 from	If you select Navigator Visible in the Options portion of the Slide Show dialog box (which
Michael & Sarah	you open by clicking Presentation, Presentation Settings), you can switch into Live mode while the presentation is running. By doing so, you can make final editorial adjustments to your slides while rehearsing for the big moment. For more details on using the Navigator, see "Navigating Extensive Presentations" later in this chapter.

The onscreen duration for each slide can be set manually via the option bar or with the help of the Rehearse Timings command, which is discussed in detail in the next section.

TIMING YOUR PRESENTATION

When you're producing a slide show, one of the most important decisions you make is to decide how long a slide will be displayed onscreen. Some slides contain more information than others, and hence deserve more time onscreen than others. In addition, a speaker may present accompanying text during the show; it would be embarrassing if the next slide appeared before the speaker had a chance to finish his or her sentence.

You can set the timing for each slide individually via the object by using a stop watch (or estimating the amount of time) for any given slide and then specifying the time in the Transition Time box on the object bar. A much more elegant and faster way is to employ the Rehearse Timings feature.

Rehearse Timings enables you to rehearse your slide show in real-time while defining the time each slide will be shown onscreen. To easily set the timing for each slide individually, you can follow these steps:

1. With your presentation open, switch to Slide Sort View. (Theoretically, you can set the timing in any master view. However, if you want to make changes to the settings or try transition effects, working in Slide Sort View is more convenient.)

2. Click the Rehearse Timings button on the object bar, or select Presentation, Rehearse Timings from the menu bar. Your display then changes to the Slide Show mode, and you can see a small timer in the lower-left corner of your display. (Note that the timer starts running immediately, so don't stall, but hurry on to the next step.)

3. Read the content of the slide at normal speed, or read aloud the accompanying text for the first slide. When you're finished, click the timer to advance to the next slide.

4. Repeat step 3 for each slide until you've reached the end of your presentation. When you click the timer after reading the content or accompanying text for your last slide, StarImpress automatically exits the Slide Show mode and returns to the Slide Sort View.

If you want to review the duration for any given slide, select the slide and then look at the object bar. You'll notice Automatic in the Transition list box and a time in the spin box to the right. If you want, you can add or subtract seconds to the current onscreen display time by clicking the up- or down-arrow keys on the spin box, respectively.

NAVIGATING EXTENSIVE PRESENTATIONS

Just like the Navigator in StarWriter and StarCalc, the Navigator for presentations is an indispensable tool if you want to move quickly between slides in a long document or copy slides between open documents. Using the Navigator, you can also quickly spot and jump to every element and object in your document—including tables, charts, or other embedded objects. Plus, you can use the Navigator in three (out of five) master views as well as during a presentation, which enables you to edit the current slide show in Live mode. Figure 24.1 shows the Navigator for presentation during a test run of a custom slide show.

PART

V

CH

24

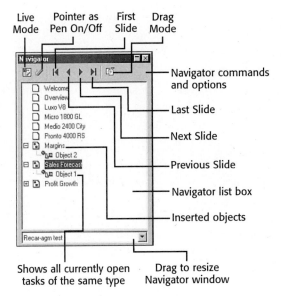

Figure 24.1
Albeit not as tool-heavy as the Navigator for text documents, the Navigator for presentations is unbeatable when it comes to navigating extensive presentations and the contents lists of open documents of the same type.

You can open the Navigator for presentations in Drawing View, Notes View, and Handout View by pressing F5 or selecting Edit, Navigator. As in the other StarOffice modules, the Navigator is a floating tools window that you can place anywhere on your desktop, minimize by double-clicking the title bar, or dock by pressing Ctrl while dragging it to the left or right side of your screen.

> **Note**
>
> You can also open the Navigator during a slide show by pressing F5.

Table 24.1 lists the various Navigator commands and options for presentation documents.

TABLE 24.1 USING THE NAVIGATOR FOR PRESENTATIONS

Click Here...	If You Want To...
Live mode	Toggle the Live mode on or off during a presentation. When the Live mode is on, you can edit slides from inside the Slide Show mode. (Note that you can switch to Live mode if the Pointer icon is selected. Note also that this option only works in Slide Show mode.)
Pointer	Draw attention to an item on a slide during a slide show. When you click this icon, your mouse pointer changes into a pen that you can use to underline or circle items on the current slide. (Note that this option is not available when you're in Live mode. Note also that this option only works in Slide Show mode.)
First/Previous Slide	Jump to the first or previous slide, respectively.

Click Here...	If You Want To...
▶ ▶| Next/Last Slide	Jump to the last or next slide, respectively.
🔲 Drag mode	Select a Drag mode when inserting slides or objects. You can drag slides and objects from the Navigator list box and insert them as hyperlinks, links, or copies in the current slide. Using this option in combination with the Open Documents list box at the bottom of the Navigator is a powerful tool to quickly insert slides and objects from other open documents into the current presentation. (For more details see, "Inserting Slides" in Chapter 22, "Getting Started with StarImpress.")
Recar-agm test ▼ Open Documents	List existing slides and objects in other open presentations (and drawings) in the Navigator list box so that you can drag and drop objects from them into your active presentation.

WHY EDIT IN LIVE MODE?

Editing in Live mode enables you to preview your presentation and edit your slides from inside the Slide Show mode. When you're in Live mode, you can do the following:

- Select and move objects
- Insert new objects and drawings (be sure to open the necessary floating tool windows in Drawing View)
- Use the Slide context menu to modify the existing slide design
- Use the Object context menu to edit the attributes and style of foreground objects
- Adjust the existing slide and interactive effects

In the case of embedded OLE objects (such as tables and charts, for example), you can also double-click an inserted object to edit it inside a window with all the tools of the module that originally created it at your disposal. After you've finished your edits, click outside the window to return to the Live mode of your show.

GETTING READY TO PREVIEW AND EDIT IN LIVE MODE

To be able to edit in Slide Show mode without problems, you should select the following options in the Options portion of the Slide Show dialog box (which you open by choosing Presentation, Presentation Settings):

- Change Slides Manually
- Mouse Pointer Visible
- Navigator Visible
- Animations Allowed

PREVIEWING AND EDITING IN LIVE MODE

For you to be able to preview and edit in Slide Show mode, the Navigator must be visible and the Live Mode icon must be activated (pressed).

To start previewing and editing your presentation in Live mode, follow these steps:

1. Press Ctrl+F2, or click the Presentation icon in any master view to start the slide show.

2. Click the Live Mode icon on the Navigator toolbar. As soon as you click the icon, you see all floating toolbars that are currently open in the StarImpress master view.

3. Use the available tools and context menus to make the desired changes. Use Navigator to advance through your slides.

4. When you're finished, turn off the Live mode, and press Esc to exit the Slide Show mode. (You cannot exit the slide show while you're in Live mode.)

Caution

When you're editing in Live mode, make sure the Change Slide on Mouse Click option is not selected in the Slide Show dialog box (which you open by selecting Presentation, Presentation Settings). Otherwise, each time you try to select an object, you advance to the next slide.

SETTING UP AND RUNNING CUSTOM SLIDE SHOWS

Picture this: You want to present revenue data and forecasts to each department in a company. Chances are that you would want to show the Sales department a more detailed analysis than the employees in Product Development, who probably are satisfied with more general numbers. If you want to give similar presentations to different groups but modify the content to fit each group, you have two options. You can exclude the unwanted slides by collectively selecting them (via Shift+click) in Slide Sort View and then choosing Show/Hide from the context menu—a rather laborious undertaking, especially because you have to hide or unhide slides each time before you start a presentation. Alternatively, you can create a custom slide show.

CREATING A CUSTOM SLIDE SHOW

Custom slide shows are basically variations on the same presentation. Using this feature, you can make on-the-fly adjustments to a presentation or make a presentation more adaptable to the circumstances. For example, what once was three presentations on the same topic directed at different audiences with some slides in common can now become one presentation with several ways of running the show. Each custom presentation is saved with the document. This way, you either can show all slides in your presentation document, or you can select a predefined custom slide show from the Custom Slide Shows dialog box. Figure 24.2 shows the Custom Slide Shows and Define Custom Slide Show dialogs.

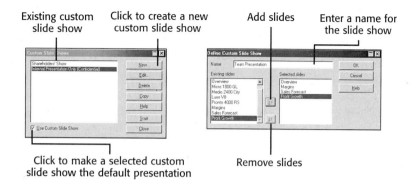

Existing custom slide show | Click to create a new custom slide show | Add slides | Enter a name for the slide show

Figure 24.2
Using the Custom Slide Show feature, you can give the same presentation with variations to different audiences.

Click to make a selected custom slide show the default presentation | Remove slides

To prepare a custom slide show, follow these steps:

1. Select Presentation, Custom Slide Show from the menu bar.
2. In the Custom Slide Shows dialog box that appears, click New. The Define Custom Slide Show dialog box then appears.
3. Enter a name for your presentation in the Name text box.
4. Select a slide you want to show in your slide show in the Existing Slides list box, and then click the arrow pointing to the right. The slide is then inserted in the Selected Slides list box on the right. Repeat this step for as many slides as you want to show. All slides that appear in the Selected Slides list will be shown in your custom slide show.

Tip #462 from
Michael & Sarah

You can change the order of your slides by dragging and dropping selected slides above or below their current location in the Selected Slides list box in the Define Custom Slide Show dialog box.

---

5. When you're finished, click OK to return to the Custom Slide Shows dialog box. The name of your new custom slide show appears in the list box (below any previously created slide shows).
6. Click Close to return to the StarImpress interface.

EDITING CUSTOM SLIDE SHOWS

Making changes to an existing custom slide show is similar to creating one:

1. Select Presentation, Custom Slide Show to open the Custom Slide Shows dialog box.
2. Select the slide show you want to edit from the list of existing shows, and then click Edit. The familiar Define Custom Slide Show dialog box appears.
3. Using the right-pointing (add) and left-pointing (remove) arrows in the middle of the dialog box, you can add selected slides from the Existing Slides list box to the custom slide show selection or remove selected slides from the custom show.
4. When you're finished, click OK to return to the Custom Slide Shows dialog box, where you can preview your edited show by clicking Start.

Tip #463 from *Michael & Sarah*	If you want to keep a copy of your original custom slide show before making any changes, click Copy in the Custom Slide Shows dialog box. StarImpress immediately creates a copy of your original, even placing (Copy1) in parentheses so that you can easily recognize it. Now you can either edit the original or the copy. Creating a copy is also great if you want to base a new custom slide show on an existing one; that way, you don't have to start from scratch when putting together your show. You can rename custom slide shows by clicking Edit and entering a new name in the text box.

To delete a custom slide show, click the Delete button in the Custom Slide Shows dialog box.

RUNNING A CUSTOM SLIDE SHOW

To run your custom slide show, follow these steps:

1. Select Presentation, Custom Slide Shows from the menu bar.

2. In the Custom Slide Shows dialog box that appears, select the desired show, and then click Start.

3. After you've run through all your slides, click to end your presentation.

Tip #464 from *Michael & Sarah*	If you select the Use Custom Slide Show option at the bottom left of the Custom Slide Shows dialog box, you can automatically start the currently selected custom show the next time you click the Start Slide Show button on the main toolbar or press Ctrl+F2.

CREATING A TOOLBAR SHORTCUT TO YOUR CUSTOM SLIDE SHOWS

If you want to quickly access the Custom Slide Shows dialog box, you can also create a shortcut icon that enables you to switch between custom presentations almost instantaneously. You can create this shortcut on the function bar or any other toolbar in StarImpress.

Note	Because toolbars keep changing as you switch views in StarImpress, it makes more sense to place the shortcut on the function bar, which is always visible, provided it is selected in the View, Toolbars submenu. Theoretically, however, you can place the shortcut on any toolbar.

To assign a shortcut to your Custom Slide Shows dialog box, follow these steps:

1. Select Tools, Options, Configure. The Configuration dialog box appears.

2. Click the Toolbars tab to bring it to the front, and then click Customize.

3. In the Customize Toolbars dialog box that appears, select Options in the Category list on the left and Custom Slide Show in the Command list on the right. As soon as you select the command, the command options above the list boxes change, and you see Custom Slide Show (as text) selected.

4. (Optional) Click the Icons button, select an icon from the list of icons, and enter a name in the Function text box or accept the default (Custom Slide Show).

5. Click OK. The icon replaces Custom Slide Show on the Customize Toolbars dialog box.

6. Click and drag the icon from the dialog box to the function bar (or any other toolbar in the current view).

7. Click the Close button (X) on the dialog box. That's it.

Note

You can use the same method to assign shortcuts to other commands and then drag the selected icon on the desired toolbar. Just pick a category on the left and a command on the right. Technically, you can create shortcuts for virtually every command in StarOffice. However, be sure to first open the context menus of the available toolbars and select Visible Buttons; some shortcuts may already exist but need to be selected in the list of available shortcuts (or buttons).

→ For more information about configuring your toolbars, menus, and other desktop settings, **see** "Customizing Your Desktop," **p. 112**.

PART
V

CH
24

SETTING YOUR SLIDE SHOW PREFERENCES

When you press Ctrl+F2 or click the Presentation icon in any master view, you typically start a presentation in standard full-screen mode. If you want to have more control over the way the presentation is shown, you can fine-tune your slide show by selecting Presentation, Presentation Settings just before you run your show. In the Slide Show dialog box that appears, you can make final adjustments to your presentation (see Figure 24.3).

Figure 24.3
Fine-tune your presentation via the Slide Show dialog box.

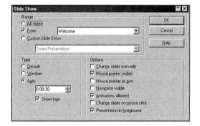

For example, in the Range portion of the Slide Show dialog box, you can define which slides to present. Your options include the following:

■ **All Slides**—Select this option if you want to show all slides in the current presentation document.

■ **From**—Select this option if you want to define the starting point of your presentation. Just select the slide with which you want to open the presentation from the drop-down list box (which lists all the existing slides in order). Your show will run from the selected slide to the end.

- **Custom Slide Show**—Select this option if you want to set the presentation details for an existing custom slide show. If you have more than one custom show saved, you can select the desired show from the drop-down list box.

Using the following options in the Type portion of the dialog box, you can specify how you want to present your show:

- **Default**—Use this option if you want to run the predefined range of your show full screen from beginning to end. To advance from one slide to the next, press the spacebar or Enter. At the end, a black screen asks you to click (with your mouse) to end the presentation. Alternatively, you can also press any key.

- **Window**—Select this option if you want to show your slide show inside the current document window. If you inserted your presentation inside a frame (for example, in a text document), the presentation will run inside that frame.

> **Caution**
>
> If you modify your presentation document in another master view, you might experience inconsistencies between both views. For example, if you delete an object from the document, the object may still show up in the presentation because the bitmaps for the presentation were calculated and cached beforehand.

- **Auto**—Select this option if you want to run the predefined range of your slide show in a looping manner. All you have to do is press Ctrl+F2 or click one of the Presentation icons in any master view to start the show; StarImpress will automatically show one slide after another. The onscreen duration for each slide can be set manually via the option bar or via the Rehearse Timings command. In the spin box, you can set a time for the duration of the pause between the end of a show and the start of the next run. If you select the Show Logo option, the *Created with StarOffice* logo appears onscreen between shows. To stop an automatic slide show, press Esc.

> **Tip #465 from**
> *Michael & Sarah*
>
> You can define the onscreen duration for each slide during your setup of the slide transitions by using the Transition options on the object bar.

Finally, in the Options portion of the Slide Show dialog box, you can fine-tune your onscreen presentation. Your options include the following:

- **Change Slides Manually**—This option enables you to press Enter or the right-arrow key to advance to the next slide. Click the left mouse button to show each animation effect for each individual slide. Press the left-arrow key to return to the previous slide.

Note

If there are additional effects on a slide, a mouse-click starts the effect. If there are two or more effects on a slide, each mouse-click starts the next effect. Only after all effects have been revealed will you be able to advance to the next slide via mouse-click. If you want to bypass the effects and move to the next slide immediately, use the right arrow key.

- **Mouse Point Visible**—Use this option if you created an interactive slide show. The mouse pointer will be visible, enabling your audience to click interactive elements and thus control the presentation of your show. Note that you can still click with the left mouse button outside an interactive element to advance to the next slide.

- **Mouse Pointer as Pen**—This cool feature enables you to use your pointer as a pen during a presentation to draw attention to certain elements on the current display. To use the pointer as a pen, click the area you want to mark, and drag with your mouse to underline or circle the desired area. (Note that your marks are not saved with the document. Note also that you cannot change the color or line width of the pen.)

- **Navigator Visible**—Use this option to show the Navigator for presentations during your slide show. Using the Navigator is especially helpful if you want to quickly jump to a certain slide in an extensive presentation. (For more details, see "Navigating Extensive Presentations" in this chapter.)

- **Animations Allowed**—Use this option to show inserted animations in their entirety. If your presentation includes animated objects or effects, and this option is not selected, you see only the first frame of an animated GIF file or plain text (without animation effect).

- **Change Slides on Mouse Click**—This option enables you to advance to the next slide by clicking the background of the current slide.

- **Presentation in Foreground**—Select this option if you want the presentation always to run in the foreground. Use this option if the computer that runs your slide show comes with automated system services that otherwise could interrupt a presentation. Note that this option is not available when you're showing your presentation in a window or text frame.

PART

V

CH

24

ADDING SPEAKER'S NOTES AND AUDIENCE HANDOUTS

In StarImpress, you can add two items to your presentation that help improve the presentation: speaker's notes and audience handouts. Each of the slides has a companion notes page that includes a small version of the slide and room for typed notes. You can print the notes and use them to recall the points that you want to make for each slide.

To create speaker's notes, switch to Notes View (by using the third button above the vertical scrollbar), and select the slide to which you want to add notes. You can use the directional buttons in the lower left of the Notes View to navigate to the desired slide(s), or you can click the desired slide in the Navigator (by pressing F5). After you've located the slide you want to annotate, click in the box below the graphic, and start typing your notes.

Tip #466 from
Michael & Sarah

You can use the same tools in Notes View as in Drawing View. So, if you really want to get fancy, you can even create drawings and other mnemonic hints that help you look even better during your presentation.

In addition, you can also print audience handouts. Audience handouts make it easy for the audience to follow your presentation and give the audience members something to take with them after the presentation is over.

To create audience handouts, follow these simple steps:

1. Switch to Handout View (by clicking the second button above the horizontal scrollbar). By default, you see four slides on one landscape-oriented page.

Tip #467 from
Michael & Sarah

While in Handout View, you're working in Background mode. This means that any layout changes you make apply to all pages in your presentation.

2. To change the number of slides per page, select Modify Slide Layout from the Presentation box, or choose Slide, Modify Slide from the context menu. The Modify Slide dialog box appears (see Figure 24.4).

Figure 24.4
Use the Modify Slide dialog box to select a handout layout template. Note that all other options are unavailable (grayed out).

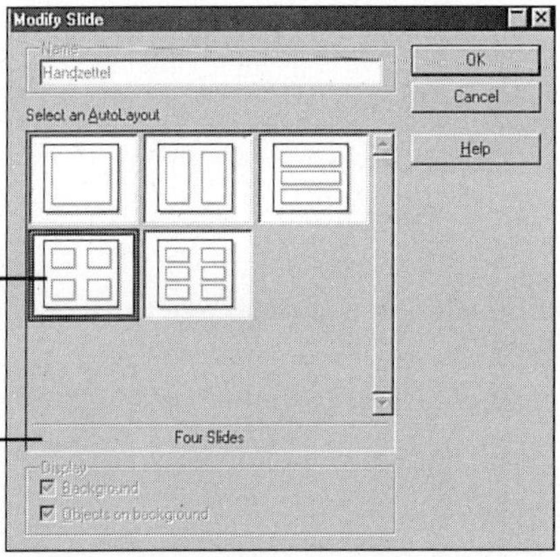

Selected layout—

Number of slides—

3. Select the desired handout layout template from the Select an AutoLayout box. Your options include one, two, three, four, or six slides per page.

4. Click OK. Depending on your choice of template, StarImpress inserts one, two, three, four, or six slides on the current page.

All you have at this point is a general handout with thumbnail-size representations of your slides. If you want, you can enhance the look of your handout with the following items:

- **Fields**—Using the Insert, Fields command, you can add fixed and variable date and time, author, page number, and filename fields. By default, fields are inserted in the center of your page (in 24-point Times New Roman). You can click and drag them anywhere on your handout. If so inclined, you can also change the font type and size by double-clicking the field box, triple-clicking the field text to select it, and then selecting the desired field. For clarification, you can also add *Author:* or *Presented by:* in front of the Author field name or */12* after the page number field to indicate the total number of pages.

- **Text**—Using the text tools on the main toolbar, you can add a title to your handout. Just click the desired tool, and drag a frame in an open area of your handout; then enter and format the desired text. You can place the frame anywhere within the printable area of your handout. (For more information on adding text with the Text tools, see "Using the Text Tools" in Chapter 22.)

- **Pictures**—Using the Insert, Picture command, you can also insert a company logo.

PART

V

CH

24

> **Note**
>
> Any change in Handout View is reflected on every handout page of a presentation because you're working in Background mode while in Handout View.

> **Tip #468 from**
> *Michael & Sarah*
>
> When you're inserting additional information, you might have to shift the mini slides on your page. Just click the slide you want to move, and then drag it into its new position. To move more than one slide at once, press Shift while selecting the slides, and then drag them collectively. To move slides more precisely, activate the Show Guides While Moving option on the option bar.

Figure 24.5 shows an example of how to enhance a standard handout with additional information.

> **Note**
>
> If your page layout does not match the print area, you see an alert box that asks you to choose one of the following options: Fit to Page (reduces the image proportionally to make it fit on your page), Posterize (in theory, print the image to several pages; in practice, it doesn't work very well), and Crop (crops those parts of the slide that go beyond the printable area).

Figure 24.5
You can enhance the look of your handout by adding text and date and author fields (among others).

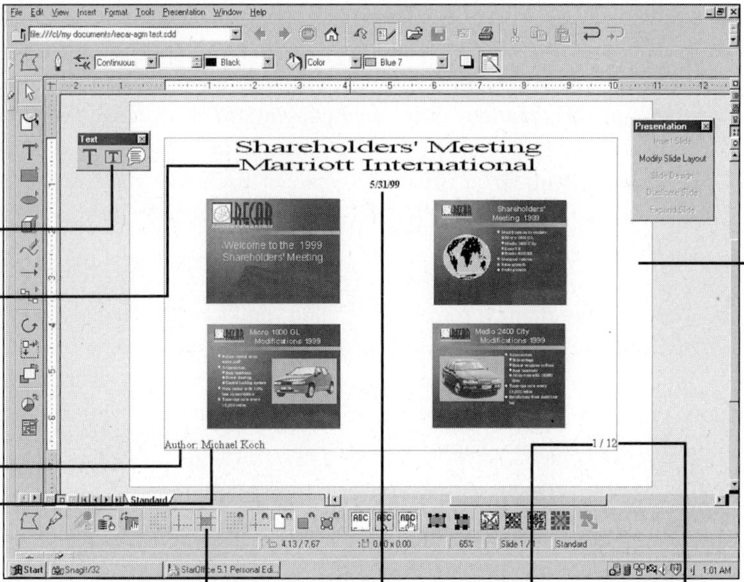

Fit to Size

Text added with the Fit to Size text tool

Author field

Author text added

Show Guides While Moving

Inserted Date field

Page numbers field

Text added

Page margins

PRINTING YOUR PRESENTATION

StarImpress enables you to print slides (in black and white or color), outlines, speaker's notes, and audience handouts. You can print all these items on paper or on overhead transparencies. Note that you can also save slides to a file or ship them to an outside service bureau for high-resolution imagesetting and printing.

The printing process is pretty much the same as in other StarOffice modules, regardless of whether you are printing outlines, notes, or handouts. You open the presentation; select File, Print or press Ctrl+P; identify your printer; specify the range of slides to be printed; choose the number of copies; and then click OK to start the printing process.

→ For a general overview of setting up your printer and printing in StarOffice, **see** "Sending and Printing Documents," **p. 184**.

→ For more details on printing documents, **see** "Printing Text Documents," **p. 478**.

Note

When you're printing via the Print dialog box, you can choose whether you want to print all slides (All), a range of slides (Pages), or only the current selection (Selection). The Selection option is available only if you have selected an object or objects on a slide.

Alternatively, you can also click the Print icon on the function bar, in which case you tell the program to print one copy of the presentation immediately according to the printer default settings, without a dialog box. If you've selected a certain area, a dialog box opens, asking you to confirm whether you want to print the whole text or only the selected area.

> **Note**
>
> Because presentation documents consist of vector graphics, they can be printed optimally in any resolution supported by your printer or imagesetter. For more details on vector graphics, see the section "Understanding Computer Graphics" in Chapter 20, "Getting Sketchy with StarDraw."

PRINTING PARTS OF YOUR PRESENTATION

Don't be too quick to print by clicking the Print button on the function bar or by immediately clicking OK in the Print dialog box. Because StarImpress has so many options for what you can print and how you can print it, you might not get what you want by fast-clicking. For example, when you print from the Print dialog box or click the Print button on the function bar, StarImpress outputs pages only in accordance with the settings in the Tools, Options, Presentation, Print dialog box.

PART

V

CH

24

> **Note**
>
> Unless you changed the default settings, StarImpress prints all slides of your presentation when you click the Print icon on the function bar or click OK in the Print dialog box without adjusting your printing options.

If you want to print certain parts of your presentation (such as speaker's notes or audience handouts), you first have to tell StarImpress which parts to print by following these steps:

1. Select File, Print, and click the Options button on the Print dialog box.

2. Using the Printer Options dialog box that appears, you can specify the parts and quality of the elements you want to print. Your options include the following:

    - **Contents**—Controls whether you want to print the drawings (or slides), notes, handouts, and/or outline of your presentation, or if the document should be printed in black (even if it is connected to a color printer).

> **Note**
>
> When you're printing from StarDraw, the Contents option is not available because you can create and print drawings only in that module.

    - **Page options**—Controls whether you want to print the pages as Standard (pages will not be scaled when printed), Fit to Page (the size of all page elements will be proportionally scaled to fill out the dimensions of the printed page), Tile Panes (pages will be tiled when printed), or as Brochure, in which case you can choose between printing the front side and back side of the brochure.

> **Note**
>
> When you select the Brochure option, you should first decide whether you want to print on the front or on both the front and back of a page. If you want to print only the front of a page, select both Front Side and Back Side. If you want to print on both the front and back, select first Front Side and then start the printing process. Turn the paper in your printer, and then print again, this time selecting the Back Side option in the Printer Options dialog box. Fold the pages in the middle—voilà, your presentation.

- **Print**—Controls which elements will be inserted into the page margins at the time of printing. Your options include Page Name, Date, and Time. In addition, you can specify whether you want to print those pages that you marked as hidden from your presentation. Note also that the options Page Name, Date, and Time are not available if you selected Brochure in the Page Options portion of the dialog box.

- **Quality**—Controls whether you want to print in color (Default), as shades of gray (Grayscale), or as pure black and white (Black & White), in which case a black shadow will appear as white inside a black frame, for example.

If you have a printer with several paper trays, and you want to use the tray defined in the printer settings for your printouts, select From Printer Setup in the lower right of the Options dialog box.

> **Note**
>
> The Printer Options dialog box is identical to the Tools, Options, Presentation, Print dialog box. However, the settings you choose in the Printer Options dialog box are valid only for the current print run and session. If you want to save your settings as defaults for all presentation documents, you have to do so in the Tools, Options, Presentation, Print dialog box.

> **Caution**
>
> When you're printing audience handouts, be careful when entering numbers in the Pages text box in the Print Range portion of the Print dialog box. The numbers you enter refer to the numbers of individual slides, not the number of handout pages.

PREPARING SLIDES AND GRAPHICS FOR HIGH-RESOLUTION PRINTING

When you're working on presentations or drawings (as well as text documents) that you want to print on a commercial printing press, you have to think in terms of what colors can be reproduced with ink on paper, not what colors you see on your monitor. Your monitor reproduces colors using the RGB color model; printing presses, by contrast, work with the CYMK color model. When you intend to send your slides or graphics to a service bureau for high-resolution color output and printing, be sure to work with CYMK colors.

→ For more details on the CYMK colors, **see** "Understanding Color Models and Modes," **p. 796**.

StarOffice includes a standard CYMK color palette; however, you can also create your CYMK custom color schemes by using the Colors tab in the Area dialog box (which you open by selecting Format, Area). Note that the CYMK color palette is not available by default. You first have to load it in order to be able to use it. To load the default CYMK color palette, follow these steps:

1. Open the Area dialog box (by clicking the Area icon on the Draw object bar or selecting Format, Area from the menu bar).
2. Click the Colors tab to bring it to the front.
3. Click the Open button. The Open dialog then appears.
4. Select CYMK from the list of files, and click Open. You can now assign CYMK colors to your current document.

PART

V

CH

24

Tip #469 from
Michael & Sarah

Using the Colors tab, you can also define your own CYMK custom colors. For more details, see "Creating Custom Colors" in Chapter 20.

If you have a PostScript printer driver installed, you can then print the image to a file and send it off to a service bureau for color processing and high-resolution output. Just select the PostScript printer driver from the Name drop-down list box in the Print dialog box (which you open by choosing File, Print); then select the Print to File check box. When the Save As dialog box opens, enter a name (with a .ps extension) for the file, and click Save.

→ For more details on PostScript printing, **see** "PostScripting with StarWriter," **p. 454**.

Note

The generated PostScript does not contain any transparency effects you might have applied to some objects. If you want to keep the transparency effects, you have to export the object in question as a bitmap and print that one instead.

EXPORTING A PRESENTATION, SLIDE, OR OBJECT

StarImpress enables you to export individual slides or selected objects of your presentation in another file format, so you can edit it in another program or insert it as a graphic in another document.

Exporting a slide or object to file is virtually the same as saving a bitmapped image or graphic in another file format. You select the file or object you want to export; then you choose File, Export from the menu bar. In the Export dialog box (which is identical to the Save As dialog box) that appears, you enter a name and location for the file to be saved and then select the desired (non-native) file format from the File Type list box. As is the case in StarImage or StarDraw, your options include BMP, EPS, GIF, JPG, MET, PCT, PBM, PNG, PGM, PPM, RAS, SVM, TIF, WMF, and XPM.

→ For more details on graphics file formats in StarOffice, **see** "Importing and Exporting Graphic File Formats," **p. 1400**.

Note	Depending on the file format you choose, you might be asked to provide additional information in subsequent dialog box boxes. For more details on the various file format-saving options, see the section "Saving and Closing Files" in Chapter 21, "Creating and Modifying Images with StarImage."

Tip #470 from *Michael & Sarah*	If you export an entire slide, it is printed in full-page size. To export only certain objects, select them and check the Selection box in the Export dialog box to ensure that you don't export too much of the white margins.

SAVING PRESENTATIONS FOR THE WORLD WIDE WEB

StarImpress comes armed with an HTML Export Wizard that enables you to create presentation-quality Web pages for use with the Internet or intranet. Using the HTML Export Wizard, you can define whether the Internet presentation will have frames, whether users will navigate the presentation using graphic buttons or text links, and whether the original StarImpress presentation should be made available for download. Each final HTML page contains one presentation slide as a JPG graphic. If so inclined, you can edit these pages in StarWriter, adding headings and additional hyperlinks, for example.

To export a presentation in HTML format, follow these steps:

1. Open the presentation you want to save as an HTML file, and select File, Export from the menu bar.

2. Enter a name in the Filename text box, and then select HTML from the File Type drop-down list.

3. Select a location to which you want to save the file, or accept the default location.

4. Click Save. The first of five HTML Export Wizard dialogs appears.

Note	Using the HTML Export Wizard is just as intuitive as using the AutoPilot Wizard, which is described in "Creating Documents and Templates with the AutoPilot" in Chapter 6, "Creating and Editing Text Documents." You step through a series of dialogs that enable you to define the layout and content areas of the final HTML document. All you have to do is select the desired elements from a list of options. Click Next to advance to the following dialog; click Back at any time to change a previous selection.

5. In the first dialog of the HTML Export Wizard, shown in Figure 24.6, you can select a design for the HTML file from the following options:

- **New Design**—Select this option if you want to define a new design.
- **Existing Design**—Select this option if you want to use an existing design for your presentation. When you select this option, you can choose a design from the Existing Design list box.

Figure 24.6
In the first HTML Export Wizard dialog box, you specify whether you want to create a new design or use an existing one.

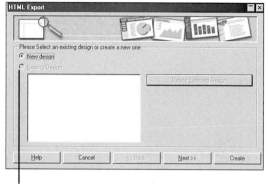

Available only if you've previously exported a presentation to an HTML file

Note

If this is the first presentation you're exporting as an HTML file, the Existing Design option is not available.

6. When you're finished, click Next to advance to the second HTML Export Wizard dialog box, shown in Figure 24.7.

Figure 24.7
In the second HTML Export Wizard dialog box, you define a basic design for the previous design choice, as well as select an image format and screen resolution.

Select an HTML design

Preview your selection

Select to create an additional title page

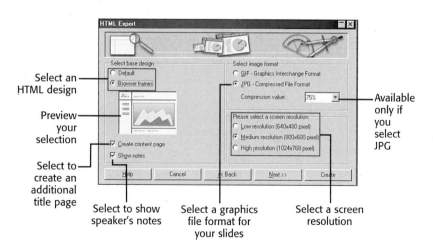

Available only if you select JPG

Select to show speaker's notes

Select a graphics file format for your slides

Select a screen resolution

7. Define a base design, and then select an image format and screen resolution. When you're selecting a design, you can choose between a standard (Default) HTML design, which uses vanilla HTML, or Browser Frames, in which case the exported slides will appear in a main frame while a margin frame contains the table of contents with hyperlinks. In addition, you can choose whether you want an additional title page for your HTML document (Create Content Page) or whether you want to show the speaker's notes you created in Notes View (Show Notes). (Note that the speaker's notes option is available only when you're exporting a StarImpress document, not a StarDraw document.)

8. Select a graphics file format. Select GIF if you want to export your slides in a lossless file format with a maximum of 256 colors. Select JPG if you want to export your files in a lossy file format that can contain more than 256 colors. When you select JPG, you can also specify a compression value in the drop-down list. Choosing 100% provides the best possible quality but also results in the largest file size; choosing 25% results in the smallest possible file size but also in an image of lesser quality. (For more details on GIF and JPG files, see "Saving Images for the World Wide Web" in Chapter 21, "Creating and Modifying Images with StarImage.")

9. Select a screen resolution. Depending on the resolution you choose, your graphic will be reduced up to 80 percent in size when displayed onscreen. The higher the resolution, the smaller your graphic appears onscreen.

10. When you're finished, click Next to advance to the third HTML Export Wizard dialog box (see Figure 24.8).

Figure 24.8
In the third HTML Export Wizard dialog box, you enter the information that you want to appear on the title page.

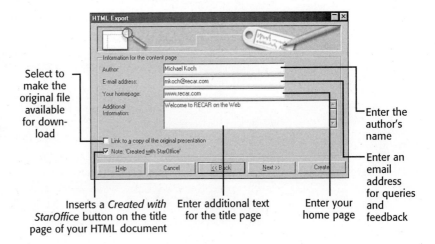

Select to make the original file available for download

Enter the author's name

Enter an email address for queries and feedback

Inserts a *Created with StarOffice* button on the title page of your HTML document

Enter additional text for the title page

Enter your home page

11. Enter the information that you want to appear on the title page of the HTML presentation document. Note that this dialog box is available only if you selected Create Content Page on the second HTML Export Wizard dialog box.

12. When you're finished, click Next to advance to the fourth HTML Export Wizard dialog, shown in Figure 24.9.

Figure 24.9
In the fourth HTML Export Wizard dialog box, you select a button style for the interactive buttons of your HTML document.

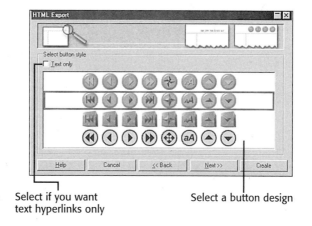

Select if you want text hyperlinks only

Select a button design

13. Select a button style for the graphical user interface of your presentation document. If you select the Text Only check box, the HTML Export Wizard inserts only text-based hyperlinks for your HTML document.

14. Click Next to advance to the fifth and final HTML Export Wizard dialog box (see Figure 24.10).

Figure 24.10
In the fifth HTML Export Wizard dialog box, you select a color scheme for your exported document. You cannot change any other text formatting attributes.

 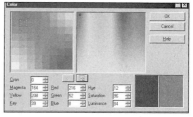

Click to define custom colors

15. Define a color scheme for the text and background of the HTML document. You can use the colors from the original template (Apply Color Scheme from Document), leave the use of colors to the readers' browsers (Use Browser Color), or create a custom color scheme (User-Defined Color Scheme). If you select User-Defined Color Scheme, you can click the Text, Hyperlink, Active Link, Visited Link, and Background buttons to open a color dialog box in which you can define a color scheme for each element.

Note

Creating custom colors with the Color dialog box is identical to creating custom colors with the Edit, Color dialog box that you can access via the Colors tab of the Area dialog box (which you open by selecting Format, Area). For more details, see "Creating Custom Colors" in Chapter 20.

16. When you're finished, click Create. The Name HTML Design dialog box appears, giving you the option to name and save the exported design.

17. Enter a name, and click Save if you want to use (or modify) the new design in the future. The Export HTML Wizard generates the desired HTML document and saves the elements and files of the document in the location you specified in the Export dialog box. Figure 24.11 shows the final presentation saved as an HTML file.

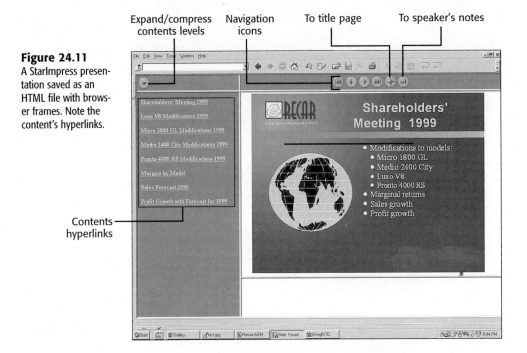

Figure 24.11
A StarImpress presentation saved as an HTML file with browser frames. Note the content's hyperlinks.

To look at the exported document, press Ctrl+P or click the Open icon on the function bar, locate the directory in which you saved it, and then select the filename under which you saved the document.

> **Note**
>
> Several files in the directory belong to the documents. To find the start page of the HTML document, you need to select the name under which you saved the document.

SENDING A PRESENTATION AS EMAIL

You can also send your presentation as email from within StarImpress by using StarMail. To send a presentation via StarMail, select File, Send, Document as E-mail. In the Send Mail dialog box that appears, you can select whether you want to send the document as a whole as an attachment (Attach) or as the body of an email (As Mail Content), only the selected object(s) (Use Selection), or not at all (Do Not Use). Choose the desired option, and then click OK. StarOffice automatically opens a StarMail document with your document (or selection) attached (or inserted). Proceed to fill in the recipient, subject line, and a brief message; then click the Send button on the object bar.

→ For more details on using email, **see** "Creating and Sending Mail," **p. 1053**.

Note

If the document you want to send as an attachment has not been saved yet, you are asked to save it first and then attach it.

You can also send the document as AutoMail, in which case you can select a name first before opening an email document. Just select File, Send, AutoMail. An alert box asks you to specify a recipient from the Address Book. Click OK, select the recipient in the Address Book that appears, and then click the AutoMail button.

PART

V

CH

24

PART VI

SPREADING THE WORD—StarOffice ON THE WEB AND AT WORK

CHAPTER 25

GETTING STARTED WITH STARWRITER/WEB

In this chapter

STAROFFICE AND THE NET

StarOffice is meant to be used with the Internet. Fully integrated and Web-aware, the suite adopts Internet-born conventions into its interface. For example, the function bar at the top of the StarOffice window includes the familiar Back, Forward, Stop, and Home buttons seen on practically every Web browser, as well as a drop-down list box for entering Internet addresses (or URLs) and file paths on your hard drive (which are automatically converted to standard URL notation).

StarOffice also integrates a large number of Internet functions and features such as email, news, and Web browsing, as well as an Address Book that searches on Internet directories like Bigfoot, WhoWhere and Switchboard. Using StarOffice, you can also perform a number of net-related tasks as you work with your documents. For example, you can easily insert hyperlinks that enable you to jump between StarOffice (and other) documents or to documents on an intranet or the World Wide Web. You can also save text and spreadsheets as HTML files, and by using the HTML Export Wizard, you can quickly save complex drawing and presentation documents in HTML format—ready for inclusion on corporate intranet or web sites and without your ever having to write one line of HTML code. Finally, using the built-in Web Page AutoPilot Wizard, you can create professional web pages on-the-fly that you can then fine-tune in StarWriter/Web, an easy-to-use visual (WYSIWYG) Web page editor that also enables you to edit HTML source code.

→ For more details on StarOffice as an email client and news reader, **see** Chapter 29, "Communicating with StarMail and StarDiscussion," **p. 1045**.

→ For details on using StarOffice as a browser, **see** "Surfing the Web with StarOffice," **p. 924** in this chapter.

→ For details on hyperlinks, **see** "Working with Hyperlinks," **p. 936** in this chapter.

To accomplish most of the tasks described in this chapter, you obviously need to be connected to a network. This can be a dial-up connection to the Internet by means of a commercial Internet service provider (such as Earthlink, Netcom, AT&T or a host of others). Your connection can also be a direct connection through your organization's local area network (LAN).

ABOUT THE INTERNET AND INTRANETS

In case some readers feel more comfortable with text and spreadsheet documents than with intranets and the Internet, a few explanations of terms may be in order. (If you're intimately familiar with the Internet, intranets and the World Wide Web, you may want to skip this section.) The *Internet* is a global collection of computers connected to one another over fast telephone lines and microwaves and accessible to the public by means of various connections in offices and in homes. The Internet grew out of a military research project that came into public use in the 1970s and originally linked university and government computers in the United States. Since its inception, the Internet has grown to encompass thousands of computers spread throughout dozens of nations. Any PC user with an Internet connection (either by means of a phone line or a direct hookup) can connect to the Internet and gain access to the volumes of information located there (as well as to the frenzied commercial activity that evolved with the introduction of the Internet's most well-known offspring, the World Wide Web).

Note

Of course, it was the World Wide Web that brought the Internet to the attention of the general public. Using graphical software such as browsers and files stored in Hypertext Markup Language (HTML), the Web added two crucial elements to the Internet. First, it gave users direct, onscreen access to multimedia documents containing formatted text, graphics, and more recently, sound and video. Second, it provided hypertext links (or *hyperlinks*) that enable users to traverse Internet documents by selecting highlighted items (text or graphic objects) and thereby moving to other, linked documents that may feature additional text, images, sounds, animations, and/or movies.

By contrast, an *intranet* is a private network of computers that is available only to the members of a specific organization. Intranets make use of Internet technology—including servers, network connections, and browser software—to enable members of an organization to share information. Intranets are very popular with corporations or government agencies because they let employees share work-related information in a confidential manner. An intranet is based on the same network protocols used by the Internet. If connected to the Internet, intranets give users seamless access to all the resources on both the intranet and the World Wide Web.

PART

VI

CH

25

UNDERSTANDING INTERNET SERVICES AND PROTOCOLS

Because the Internet connects computers of all types running many different operating systems and application programs, platform-independent standards had to be developed to make Internet communications possible. A *protocol* is the term for a standard governing the way software programs interact. The most common and often talked about protocols include:

- **TCP/IP (Transmission Control Protocol/Internet Protocol)**—This low-level protocol enables computers connected on the Internet to communicate with each other intelligibly. Other Internet protocols such as HTTP and FTP build on and require TCP/IP.

Note

Networks usually are looked at as stacks of layers: higher levels are based on lower levels. TCP and IP are low-level protocols on top of which others are built. There's no FTP, HTTP, or POP3 without TCP/IP.

- **FTP (File Transfer Protocol)**—As the name implies, this protocol enables you to download files from a computer on the Internet to your own and, if you have privileges to do so, to transfer files from your machine to the other computer. Public FTP sites allow anyone to log on as an "anonymous" user, although they usually require your email address as a password. StarOffice includes special features for working with files on FTP sites, as described in Chapter 27, "Publishing Your Work on the Web."

- **HTTP (Hypertext Transfer Protocol)**—This protocol sets Internet standards for displaying and hyperlinking multimedia documents on the World Wide Web.
- **POP3 (Post Office Protocol 3)**—This protocol is used to fetch email from your mail server.
- **SMTP (Simple Mail Transfer Protocol)**—As the name implies, SMTP transfers your messages to mail servers.
- **IMAP (Internet Message Access Protocol)**—The usual POP3/SMTP pair is somewhat limited in its management capabilities. IMAP additionally allows you to keep and organize your messages on the server in a way similar to how you organize your files. You can sort your messages into folders or even store them back from your local computer to the IMAP server.

Other Internet services, each based on its own protocol, include Telnet, which lets you run programs on another computer, and Gopher, an Internet search tool that presents the item in a text format that can be viewed with Web browsers or other search interfaces.

UNDERSTANDING INTERNET ADDRESSES

Each document on the Internet has a unique address, commonly known as the *Internet address* and less commonly known by the official name of *URL*, or *Uniform Resource Locator*. The URL's function is to provide a standard method for finding anything on the Internet— from Web pages to newsgroups to the smallest graphic on the most esoteric of pages.

A URL commonly consists of the following parts:

- The service or method that must be used to access the site, followed by a colon and two forward slashes (for example, `http://` or `ftp://`).
- The name or numerical Internet address of the server providing the resource (for example, `mcp.com`, `teamstaroffice.org`, or `205.134.233.1`).

Note

Each computer on the Internet has a unique numerical address in the form shown here. Because you might forget such numbers but easily remember names, most computers are given names. Domain Name Service (DNS) servers on the Internet translate the literal addresses into their numerical counterparts.

- The directory path of the resource preceded by a forward slash. Depending on where the resource is located on the server, you might see no path (indicating that the resource is in the public root of the server), a single folder name (for example, `/help`), or a number of folders and subfolders (for example, `/help/starwriter`).
- The filename of the resource preceded by a forward slash (for example, `/index.html`).
- The named anchor in an HTML document (for example, `#FAQ`).

The following are some real-world sample URLs:

http://www.stardivision.com/freeoffice

http://www.gwpress.com/html/j10.htm#Cheats

http://www.aetv.com

ftp://ncsa.uiuc.edu

Other common access methods and services include news: (which connects to a specified Usenet group) and mailto: (which opens an email form with the recipient's address already filled in).

Note

Addresses like these can be stored in StarOffice documents and displayed as hyperlinks. For more details, see the section "Inserting Hyperlinks" in this chapter.

ABOUT THE WEB AND HTML

The World Wide Web, or Web for short, is a global, seamless environment in which all information (text, images, audio, video, computational services) that is accessible from the Internet can be accessed in a consistent and simple way by using a standard set of naming and access conventions. All you need is an Internet connection and a Web browser software that enables you to view the information on your computer at home or at work.

The Web gives users access to a vast array of documents that are connected to each other by means of *hyperlinks* (hypertext or hypermedia links), which are electronic connections that link related pieces of information in order to allow a user easy access to them. Each Web document with its corresponding text and hyperlinks is written in Hypertext Markup Language (HTML) and is assigned an online address called a Uniform Resource Locator (URL).

HTML is a text-based language that uses special codes or instructions called *tags*, which are placed into the body of a simple ASCII text file. Files containing these tags are called HTML files, naturally enough, and are identified by the .htm or .html extension. When a Web browser such as the StarOffice browser, Microsoft Internet Explorer, or Netscape Navigator opens an HTML file, it translates the tags and other information the file contains into a formatted document on your screen. Each Web page you open with your browser corresponds to a single HTML file.

Most HTML tags are paired, enclosing the information that the tag relates to. As a simple example, in the sequence <B>HTML</B>, the paired tag for bold type encloses the word HTML and tells your browser to display that word in bold.

The HTML language includes scores of different tags. The cornucopia of HTML tags encompasses a wide range of functionality. Some govern the appearance of elements on Web pages, making a word bold, displaying a table, or telling the browser to display a specific graphical image. Some tags control placement of text and graphics. Other tags define links to other HTML files (pages) or other sites. Form-related tags define Web page fields that can be filled out by the reader, allowing your pages to receive, store, and analyze various types of information. Still other tags activate other programs to perform functions such as returning information from a database. You can even use tags to play sound files in the background or display video clips.

Regardless of the computer operating system someone is using, whether Windows 3.1, Windows 95/98, Windows NT, Macintosh, UNIX, or OS/2, a given Web page appears basically the same. Thus, you can create and publish a single HTML document on the Web, knowing that tens of millions can view it and that every user sees what you designed (or tagged) as you designed it. (There are exceptions, but this is the theory and intention of the Web's designers and of the HTML language. In reality, Web surfers use different computers, browsers, and connections, all of which control the way an HTML page appears onscreen.)

CONFIGURING STAROFFICE FOR THE NET

To take advantage of all that StarOffice has to offer, you need to connect your desktop to the outside world. Although you can choose to run third-party mail, news, FTP, and browser applications, StarOffice has good built-in Internet programs. The advantages of StarOffice's total Internet integration are particularly great when you're running StarOffice on a network. If you run StarOffice all the time and remain online, you can do everything right from your desktop—automatically download new email from your server, browse the Web, send a draft document as email to a colleague, not to mention synchronize your schedule with colleagues on a common StarSchedule calendar. Configuring StarOffice for the Net is explained in detail in Chapter 3, "Getting Ready for Work."

→ For more details on configuring StarOffice for the Internet, **see** "Getting Online," **p. 85.**

→ For more details on StarOffice on a network, **see** "Networking with StarOffice," **p. 996.**

→ For more details on StarSchedule, **see** "Getting Organized with StarSchedule," **p. 1020.**

SURFING THE WEB WITH STAROFFICE

StarOffice has a built-in browser fully integrated with the program's file searching and file management tools. If you're connected to the Internet, you can just type or paste the Internet address or URL of the Web page you want to view into the Load URL box on the function bar, press Enter, and voilà! The Web page appears on your desktop, where you can view it, email it, print it, or save it (complete with graphics) like any other StarOffice document. You can also copy and paste parts of the document into other StarOffice documents. If you click the Edit File icon on the function bar, you can even edit the retrieved document and then save it as an HTML document. Pretty cool!

→ For details on editing HTML documents, **see** "Editing HTML Files in StarWriter/Web," **p. 952** in this chapter.

Tip #471 from
Michael & Sarah

If your network connection appears to be working for your system but not in StarOffice, make sure that the Internet button on the function bar is in Online mode (pressed).

Feature-wise, the StarOffice browser stacks up quite well against Netscape Navigator and Microsoft Internet Explorer. You can define a wide range of browser characteristics, including the size of your caches and how cookies and security are handled. If you installed the Java RunTime environment, the browser also works with Java applets and JavaScript.

→ For more details on setting your cache size and browser options, **see** "Fine-Tuning Your Browser," **p. 105**.

USING THE FUNCTION BAR

Your two most important toolbars while browsing the Web are the function bar and the hyperlink bar, shown in Figure 25.1. (If you can't **see** the hyperlink bar, select View, Toolbars, Hyperlink Bar.)

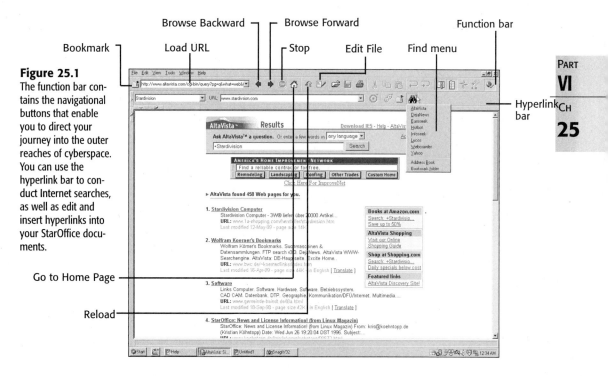

Figure 25.1
The function bar contains the navigational buttons that enable you to direct your journey into the outer reaches of cyberspace. You can use the hyperlink bar to conduct Internet searches, as well as edit and insert hyperlinks into your StarOffice documents.

Given the importance of Web access these days, and the fact that you can use many of the function bar's buttons with ordinary (that is, non-Web) documents, the following list describes each relevant button. Their basic functions are easy to grasp, but little secrets aplenty can be found. Working left to right, the Web-related buttons on the function bar are as follows:

- **Bookmark**—This icon enables you to create a bookmark for the currently displayed Web page or file path in the Bookmarks folder in the Explorer group or even any other folder you want. (For more details on using this icon, **see** "Bookmarking Your Favorite Web Sites and Pages" in this chapter.)

- **Load URL**—This box shows the Internet address (URL) or path of the current document and provides a drop-down history list of (up to 100) previously viewed URLs or documents. You can use this box to enter Internet addresses or URLs (for example, www.stardivision.com) or file and folder paths on your hard drive (for example, c:\Office51 or c:/data/accounts.sdc). When you press Enter, the Stop icon lights up red—this means that your page, file, or folder is being loaded—and StarOffice opens the desired Web page, file, or folder in your desktop work area. (File paths are automatically converted to standard URL notation. For example, the sample presentation document recar-agm.sdd, located in the c:\office51\explorer\samples\presentations folder appears in the URL box as

  file:///c¦/office51/explorer/samples/presentations/recar-agm.sdd)

Note

Documents in the history list might not be available if your network or Internet connections have changed since you viewed a document. Note also that if you select a URL from the history list, StarOffice closes the current task while opening the selected Web address or file. If you want to keep your current task open, press Ctrl while selecting the URL.

Tip #472 from
Michael & Sarah

You can also use the Load URL box to start an Internet search engine. Just enter a question mark (?), followed by the search term, and press Enter. For more details on searching the Web, **see** the next section, "Finding Web Sites."

- **Browse Backward and Browse Forward**—The two arrow buttons to the right of the Load URL drop-down list box work just like their counterparts in a browser, jumping to the next or previous document of those you've accessed via hyperlinks. The Back button takes you to the last document you viewed, whereas the Forward button reverses directions and is available only if you've already gone backward. If you extended-click, you can see a list of documents that you've accessed consecutively via hyperlinks. To quickly return to an already visited document (or link), extended-click the Back or Forward buttons, and then select the desired file from the list.

- **Stop Browse**—Use this button to terminate an attempt to retrieve a document from a Web site. If the loading process takes too long, chances are the connection is hanging, so click Stop and try loading the desired page again by pressing Enter. If several objects are being loaded at once, you can press Ctrl+Stop to stop all processes; an extended-click on the icon then opens a list of all current loading processes. Select the one you want to load.

- **Go to Home Page**—This button takes you directly to the Web page or document you've designated as your start (or home) page. Your start page is supposed to be the one you use as a home base, from which you venture out into the wilds of the Web, and to which you return when you get tangled up after pursuing one too many links. (For more details on selecting a home page, see "Setting Your Own Home Page" in this chapter.)

- **Refresh Current Page**—When the document you're viewing is stored on the Web, clicking this button retrieves the most current version of the document from the server. If the document is instead an ordinary one stored on your disk, the button enables you to discard recent changes and load the last saved version of the document stored on disk (an alert box asks you to confirm that you want to discard the changes). (When you're working with frames, this button has additional functionality. For more details, see "Using Frames and Framesets" in Chapter 27.)

ENTERING URLs WITH AUTOCOMPLETE

The StarOffice AutoComplete feature (previously only available in StarCalc and StarWriter) has been considerably improved and is now also available for the Open and Save As dialog boxes, as well as the Load URL list box on the function bar. Simply type the first three letters of a word, and an AutoComplete tip appears, showing a matching entry from the URL history list in its entirety. To accept the highlighted choice, press Enter. To cycle through the list of choices from the URL history list, use the Up and Down Arrow keys to cycle through the URL history list. Likewise, if you enter a letter (or two), you can use the Up and Down Arrow keys to cycle through the existing files and folders that start with the given letter or letter combination.

AutoComplete also simplifies the entry of complete paths. For example, if you enter c:\any-directory\ and press the End key, you can use the arrow keys to scan the subordinate directory and document structure.

Note that AutoComplete not only supports the FILE protocol, but also the FTP and HTTP protocols, as well as mail or news server URL addresses. The cursor keys can activate already existing URLs from the history list.

You can use AutoComplete to scan the existing directories; in all other instances, StarOffice will use the history list as the basis for the AutoComplete feature.

If your cursor is in the Load URL drop-down box and AutoComplete is active, then the history drop-down list will only show potential AutoComplete entries that you can accept. Only when you turn off the AutoComplete feature (by pressing the Esc key) will you be able to see the history list in its entirety again.

Note that the selection drop-down list can stay open while AutoComplete is active; just press Alt+Down Arrow to open the list. The current content always depends on the AutoComplete entry. This option has been implemented consistently throughout StarOffice and is also available in the Open and Save As dialog boxes.

FINDING WEB SITES

Looking for a specific Web site? StarOffice gives you one-click access to the most popular search engines on the Web, including Yahoo!, AltaVista, Hotbot, Lycos, Webcrawler, Infoseek, and even the news archive DejaNews. Just type the keyword or name of the company or organization whose site you want to find into the URL Name box on the hyperlink bar, click the Find icon, and select your favorite search engine from the drop-down menu (refer to Figure 25.1). The search engine then finds all pages that contain the name, and the StarOffice browser displays the search results in its window. Note that you can also perform multiple word searches. For example, you can enter the following:

- `Star + Division`—Finds all pages that contain *Star* and *Division*
- `Star, Division`—Finds all pages that contain *Star* or *Division*
- `Star Division`—Finds all pages that contain *Star Division*

Note

Not all search engines support searches with Boolean operators (and, or). Note also that some search engines are case sensitive.

SEARCHING WITH THE FUNCTION BAR   Alternatively, you can use the Load URL box on the function bar for Internet searches. Just enter a question mark (?) followed by the search term, and press Enter. StarOffice connects to the search engine you used for your last Internet search. If you haven't used a search engine during your current StarOffice session, StarOffice selects the search engine that appears at the top of the Find drop-down menu.

Tip #473 from
Michael & Sarah

The order in which the search engines appear on the Find drop-down menu is controlled by the `srcheng.ini` file, which is located in the `Office51/config` folder. To customize the drop-down menu (and bring your favorite search engine to the top), open the `srcheng.ini` file, and rearrange the order in which the search engines appear. As always, when you're fiddling with configuration files, be sure to make a backup copy before you start editing the file.

ADDING A NEW SEARCH ENGINE TO THE FIND MENU   If you can't find your favorite search engine in the Find menu, or if you would like to edit the standard configuration of the existing search engines, open the Options Internet Search dialog (by selecting Tools, Options, Internet, Search), and add the desired search engine or make the desired changes.

Note

Before you can add a new search engine, you need the URL for a given search type. To find one, go to the Web site of the search engine of your choice. Then perform three types of keyword searches with two words: one with the AND operator, one with the OR operator, and one without any operator. After you press Enter, copy the URL search string for each search type from the URL box in the function bar into a blank document for future reference.

To add a new search engine to the list of existing ones, follow these steps:

1. Enter the name of the new engine in the Name text box. (You might have to type over an existing name.) As soon as you make one change in the Name box, the Add and Modify buttons light up.

2. Select the type of search you want to conduct. This step is important if you want to be able to perform multiple word searches. Your options include And, Or, and Exact.

3. For the selected search type, enter the search prefix and suffix in the Prefix and Suffix boxes, respectively. Just split the search string URL you copied earlier at the appropriate place. Where to split? Look at the prefixes and suffixes of the existing search engines; although it's impossible to give you the exact string, you'll be able to recognize a pattern.

4. Enter the separator in the Separator box; this is the character or string of characters that the search engine uses to separate words in a multiple word search. (Again, you can easily identify it by looking at the separators of the existing search engines.)

5. From the Case Match drop-down list, select the case for your search term. Your options include None (in which case the term remains as is), Upper (lowercase terms are converted into uppercase terms), or Lower (uppercase terms are converted to lowercase terms).

6. Repeat steps 2 through 5 for the other two search types. (Note that you have to enter all three parameters—And, Or, Exact—or else the entry won't work.)

7. When you're finished, click Add.

To modify the configuration of an existing search engine, select the desired search engine from the list on the right, and click the information that you want to change. When you're finished, click Modify to accept your changes.

If you want to delete an existing search engine, select the name, and then click Delete.

BOOKMARKING YOUR FAVORITE WEB PAGES

As you spend more and more time on the Web, you'll likely develop a list of favorite places that you visit again and again. The quickest way to return to these places is to save them as bookmarks in the Explorer group.

A *bookmark* is a placeholder you ask your browser to mark for you so that you can easily return to the same spot on the Web later. By default, StarOffice comes with a standard set of Internet bookmarks that are located in the Bookmarks folder in the Explorer group.

Note

Bookmarks are managed from the Internet Explorer. When you install StarOffice on a system that already has Internet Explorer, the program tries to locate any existing bookmarks you have and automatically places them in the Bookmarks folder. If you have bookmarks that don't make the cut, you can create a link to them in the Bookmarks folder or somewhere else in the Explorer so that you have all you need at your fingertips.

PART
VI
CH
25

Note

Linux users can easily import existing Netscape bookmarks by following the directions in the section "Importing Bookmarks" in this chapter.

ADDING NEW BOOKMARKS   To bookmark or add the URL of a Web page or site to your existing Bookmarks folder, simply click the Bookmark icon to the left of the Load URL list box on the function bar (your pointer changes shape into a hand), and drag it into the desired Bookmarks subfolder. If the Bookmarks folder is collapsed, just rest your pointer over the plus (+) symbol next to the Bookmarks folder icon to expand the folder tree. Do the same for any further subfolders in the folder tree. When you've located the folder in which you want to store your bookmark, release the mouse button to drop the link.

To quickly return to a favorite place, click the folder in the Explorer group (in Hierarchical view), and double-click the desired link in the open Beamer.

MANAGING YOUR BOOKMARKS FOLDER   You can add new folders or delete existing ones via the context menu. To add a folder, right-click the Bookmarks item in the Explorer, and select Folder from the New submenu. Enter a name for the new folder in the dialog box that appears, and then click OK. StarOffice makes the new folder a subfolder of the Bookmarks folder. Following the same method, you can also create additional sub-subfolders and so on.

To delete a folder, right-click the folder, and select Delete from the context menu.

IMPORTING NETSCAPE NAVIGATOR AND INTERNET EXPLORER BOOKMARKS   StarOffice makes it easy for you to import any existing bookmarks you have, so you don't have to give up or re-create your existing list of favorites when switching to StarOffice.

For example, Netscape keeps its bookmarks in a file called `Bookmark.htm`, which is located in the `Netscape\Program\Defaults` directory or in your user directory. If you've been using Netscape Communicator and would like to import your bookmarks into StarOffice, following these steps:

1. Open the StarOffice Explorer, right-click the StarOffice Explorer title bar, and select Hierarchical from the context menu.
2. Click the plus symbol next to Workplace to expand the Workplace folder tree.
3. Locate the directory in which you installed StarOffice (Office51) and expand the Office51 folder tree.
4. Select the Bookmark folder, then open the Beamer (by pressing Ctrl+Shift+B).
5. In the Beamer, double-click Import Netscape Bookmarks. The Import Bookmarks dialog appears.
6. Locate and select the `Bookmark.htm` file (usually located in the `Netscape\Program\Defaults` directory, then click Open.

All the bookmarks contained in this file are added to your StarOffice directory.

> **Note**
>
> When you're importing Netscape bookmarks using Linux, you should bear in mind two important points. First, the file is stored in the hidden directory ~/.netscape, which is not shown in StarOffice's File dialog. Second, StarOffice shows only *.htm, but the file has the .html extension. You therefore might need to enter the path ~/.netscape/bookmark.html manually.

Microsoft keeps its bookmarks as links in a folder on your hard drive. If Internet Explorer was installed on your system prior to your installation of StarOffice, the Bookmarks folder in the StarOffice Explorer automatically establishes a link to the IE bookmarks (or Favorites) folder on your system. If you installed Internet Explorer after installing StarOffice, you have to open the Workplace item in the StarOffice Explorer group, navigate to the Favorites folder, and then drag the folder on the New Group field of your StarOffice Explorer. StarOffice automatically creates a link in the StarOffice Explorer group to the Favorites folder on your system.

SETTING YOUR OWN HOME PAGE

Your home page is supposed to be the one you use as a home base, from which you venture out into the wilds of the Web, and to which you return when you get tangled up after pursuing one too many links. As with any full-featured browser, the StarOffice browser has an icon that instantly takes you to the page designated as your home page when you click it; it's called Go to Home Page (refer to Figure 25.1).

Your default home page in StarOffice is the main StarDivision page at www.stardivision.com. If you want, you can easily specify another Web page or document that StarOffice jumps to when you click the Go to Home Page button. The key step is to start by opening the page you want to jump to with that button. Then select the URL (just click in the Load URL list box) and copy (press Ctrl+C) the URL. Next, open the Tools, Options, Browser, Other dialog, and paste (press Ctrl+V) the copied URL in the Homepage URL text box. You might have to select any existing entry first to overwrite it with your copied URL.

> **Note**
>
> The home page you set in the Tools, Options, Browser, Other dialog affects only the StarOffice browser. If you're using Internet Explorer as an external browser with StarOffice, you can define the home page settings by clicking the Settings button in the Tools, Options, Browser, External Browser dialog and then changing the URL on the General tab of the Internet Properties dialog that appears.

PART

VI

CH

25

Tip #474 from
Michael & Sarah

You can designate a folder or document as your start page. Clicking the Go to Home Page button opens the document in its home application, whether or not that application is currently running. You therefore can create a custom home page with links to your favorite sites arranged in one document rather than hidden away in your Bookmarks folder(s). In short, you can create your own gateway to the Internet this way. For more details on inserting hyperlinks, see the section "Working with Hyperlinks" in this chapter.

BROWSING FULL SCREEN IN STAROFFICE

As you can do with other documents, you can enjoy the benefit of a larger view by switching between regular and Full Screen view while browsing the Web. Just select View, Full Screen, or press Ctrl+Shift+J. To return to your regular view, click the Full Screen icon on the floating toolbar.

While you're in Full Screen view, however, you see only the floating toolbar/icon that enables you to switch back into the regular desktop view when you click it. What you're missing are the navigational controls that enable you to return to previous or next pages or enter a new URL on-the-fly. Don't despair. You can browse in Full Screen view and still have access to the navigational controls of the function bar. All you have to do is enhance the floating toolbar with additional tools and icons by following these steps:

1. Switch to Full Screen view by selecting View, Full Screen or by pressing Ctrl+Shift+J.

2. Dock the floating toolbar that contains the lonely Full Screen icon; Ctrl+click the blue title bar, and drag it to the top or bottom of your screen.

3. Open the toolbar's context menu (by right-clicking), and select Customize. The Customize Toolbars dialog appears.

4. Be sure Application is selected in the Categories list box on the left. Then click the Load URL icon in the Icons portion of the dialog, and drag it to the toolbar.

5. Select Navigate in the Category list box, and then drag the Back, Forward, and Stop icons to the toolbar. If you want, you can also drag the Home Page icon to the toolbar.

6. Select Explorer in the Category list box, and then drag the Insert Bookmark icon from the Icons portion of the dialog to the toolbar. (If you don't recognize it, select Insert Bookmark in the Command list box; the correct icon appears pressed in the Icons list.)

7. Continue to locate and drag other icons that you would like to have on your custom toolbar.

8. When you're finished, close the Customize Toolbars dialog by clicking the Close (X) button in the upper right corner.

You can now browse the Web in Full Screen view, using your custom toolbar. You can leave this toolbar docked, or you can undock it by Ctrl+clicking in a gray area on the toolbar and dragging it toward the center of the screen (see Figure 25.2). To return to your regular desktop view, click the Full Screen icon.

Tip #475 from
Michael & Sarah

When you first create your custom toolbar, StarOffice places the various navigation icons underneath the Load URL list box. If you drag in the lower-right corner of your toolbar, you can force StarOffice to arrange all icons in one slim row; doing so gives you more screen real estate, which is why you went Full Screen to begin with, isn't it?

Note

Your custom toolbar is saved even after you close StarOffice. If you want to cancel your custom changes, select Tools, Configure, Toolbars and click Reset. To save your configuration permanently, click Save and enter a name in the Save As dialog. That way, you can easily reload your configuration should you accidentally "reset" it or change it otherwise.

Figure 25.2
You can browse the Web in Full Screen view with your custom toolbar.

Custom toolbar

DOWNLOADING AND SAVING FILES FROM THE WEB

If you want to save a Web page, you can select File, Save As. StarOffice automatically downloads the HTML document with graphics to a folder of your choice.

DOWNLOADING FILES FROM THE WEB   Thanks to StarOffice's multithreading capabilities, you can download files in the background while still continuing to browse the Web or do whatever else you were doing. (You can trace the progress in the Download Task.)

To download files from the Internet, click the hyperlink that leads to the desired file. If the file type is registered with StarOffice, the suite downloads the file according to the settings in the Options Browser File Types dialog. For example, if the link leads to a ZIP file or other file type, StarOffice automatically downloads the compressed archive to the default download directory. If the link leads to a StarOffice document, the program automatically opens the document in its module; you can then decide whether you want to save it to your hard drive. If the link leads to a sound file, StarOffice uses the designated plug-in to play the file.

Note

Before StarOffice downloads a target, it checks whether the file or program already exists on your system. If so, an alert box pops up, asking you to confirm whether you want to download the file or program again. Yes or No, the choice is yours.

Tip #476 from
Michael & Sarah

By default, StarOffice stores downloads from the Internet in the `Office51\download` folder. If you want to designate a different folder for your Internet downloads, choose Tools, Options, General, Paths. Next, select Download Path from the path list, click the Edit button, navigate to a new path using the Select Path dialog box, and then click Select. That's it!

If you prefer to open files later, you have to Shift+click the hyperlink that leads to the desired file. StarOffice opens the Select Filter dialog, with the StarDownload filter selected. Click OK to download the file to your default download directory.

Note that you can customize how StarOffice should handle downloading files from the Internet in the Options Browser File Types dialog. Just select Tools, Options, Browser from the menu bar, click the plus sign next to Browser, and then select File Types. In the File Types list box, you can see all currently registered types with extensions. Each type comes with its own settings that you can see when you select a type in the list and then look at the text boxes and drop-down list boxes below. For example, if you select a StarWriter document, you see the document's Mime Type (`application/vnd.starwriter.writer`), Clipboard ID (StarWriter 5.0), and Extension (`*.sdw`). The Open With box lists the application that has been assigned to open files with the extension `*.sdw`. The Filter box indicates the filter that has been assigned to that file type. If you select StarDownload (`*dnl`), StarOffice automatically picks the correct filter for this type of file during the download and then opens the document in the module listed in the Open With box.

Tip #477 from
Michael & Sarah

Many Web pages feature information for download in the Portable Document Format (PDF). You can view this information with the Adobe Acrobat Reader software, which is available for free from the Adobe Web site (`www.adobe.com`). To install and register Acrobat Reader with StarOffice and the StarOffice browser, create a folder called `plugins` in the Office 51 directory, then copy the Acrobat plugin (nppdf32.dll) from the Acrobat\Browser folder into that folder. Next, open the Options, Browser, File Types dialog and enter `application/pdf` in the Type box; leave the Clipboard ID box blank; enter `*.pdf` in the Extension box; select `PlugIn` from the Open With list and `Adobe Acrobat (PlugIn)` from the Filter list.

If you want to delete an existing file type, simply select the unwanted type in the list, and click Delete. Note that you can delete only file types you have added yourself or types that have been added by other applications during the installation process. You cannot delete native StarOffice file types.

Note

The changes you make in the Options Browser File Types dialog apply only to the StarOffice browser. If you're using an external browser with StarOffice, you have to change the settings of that browser.

SAVING WEB PAGES TO YOUR HARD DRIVE   Web pages consists of a series of items and objects, including links, lists, forms, and graphics. If you wanted to save a single object, say a graphic, you can right-click the object and select Save Picture As from the context menu. In the Save As dialog that appears you can select the path and folder where you want to save the file. If you want to save a Web page in its entirety to your hard drive, follow these steps:

1. Be sure you are online, then enter the URL of the desired page in the Load URL box on the function bar to open the page.
2. Copy the URL from the Load URL box (select and press Ctrl+C), select File, Open from the menu bar, then paste the copied URL in the Filename text box.
3. In the File Type list, select HTML (StarWriter).
4. Click OK. StarOffice will open the desired page.
5. Click the Edit File icon on the function bar to switch into Edit mode.
6. Select Edit, Links from the menu bar. The Edit Links dialog appears.
7. Select all existing links with the mouse (click the first link, then scroll to the last link, press Shift and click the last link).
8. Click the Break Link button. (If you can't see the button, you either selected a frameset part or didn't choose the HTML (StarWriter) file type in the Open dialog.) A dialog box appears, asking you to confirm whether you want to break the selected links. Click Yes, then close the Edit Links dialog.
9. Select File, Save As from the menu bar. In the Save As dialog that appears, select the file type and path where you want to save the document, then click OK.

If you save the page as an HTML document, the graphic files continue to be linked to the HTML document; however, instead existing on a Web server, the files are now located in the same folder where you saved the HTML document. Note also that StarOffice will automatically assign new names to the graphic files.

If you save the page as a StarWriter document, StarOffice will embed the graphics in the saved document.

PART

VI

CH

25

USING EXTERNAL BROWSERS WITH STAROFFICE

If the StarOffice browser doesn't cut it for you—for whatever reason and there are a few—you can also use an external browser. Windows users, for example, may prefer to use Internet Explorer 4 or 5. If so, choose Tools, Options, Browser, External Browser from the menu bar, and select the option Use Internet Explorer as External Web Browser. Using this same dialog, you can also control the Internet Explorer settings by clicking the Settings button. Using the Addresses portion of the same dialog, you can specify domains that will continue to be opened by the StarOffice browser. Just type a URL (complete with protocol) into the text box, and click the Add button. To delete a designated domain, select it and click Delete.

> **Note**
>
> If you use Internet Explorer as an external browser in StarOffice, you will find some IE commands in your StarOffice menus while surfing the Web.

> **Note**
>
> At the time of writing, StarOffice only supports MS Internet Explorer using Windows as an external browser. Star Division is working on providing the equivalent support for Netscape Communicator in a future upgrade.

WORKING WITH HYPERLINKS

Hyperlinks are the Web. Without hyperlinks, the World Wide Web would not exist. Hyperlinks enable you to easily navigate from one file to another stored on your computer, on your company's local area network or intranet, or on the Internet. Using hyperlinks, you can even jump to specific locations in a target document or Web page, including target destinations within the current document or Web page.

Hyperlinks are typically used to enable a user to explore a topic in greater depth. Clicking a hyperlink leads to a more complete description or explanation, or to a page or document on a related topic. Using StarOffice, you can insert hyperlinks in both Web pages created with StarOffice as well as ordinary documents; you don't have to save the files as HTML documents or Web pages. In fact, when inserting hyperlinks in ordinary StarOffice documents, you have the option of inserting the link as text or button (see "Inserting Hyperlinks" in this section). Note also that hyperlinks can reference any document type. For instance, you can create a report in StarWriter, inserting one link to a StarCalc spreadsheet, one to a graphics file, and another to a public Web location. A hyperlink can also double as a live email address; when you click it, StarOffice automatically opens a new message in StarMail with the address referred to in the link already entered in the To[SMPT] box.

USING HYPERLINKS

A hyperlink's visible hot spot in a StarOffice document can be any text or image. When the link is added to the text or graphics, passing the mouse pointer over the link changes it to a pointing finger, figuratively pointing to another location. If Help Tips are turned on, a box containing the address or filename of the destination appears when you hold the mouse pointer over the link for a second or two.

To open or *follow* a hyperlink, you click the link. Clicking the hyperlink starts the application program associated with the address or file, which then opens the item. If the link points to a downloadable file or program, you can click that item to show it in a preassigned program or Shift+click it to retrieve the target and save it to your hard disk or server.

Note

Hyperlinks can jump to and activate any document or image file accessible on your system, your network, or the Internet. The only requirements are that the application that opens that file type is present on your system and that the file type is associated with that application. (If there's no application installed on your system or associated with a given file type, you still can download the file.)

INSERTING HYPERLINKS

When you're inserting hyperlinks in a StarOffice document, you have two basic options: You can insert a link automatically, or you can insert a link manually, using the Hyperlink bar, the Character dialog, or Drag&Drop.

INSERTING HYPERLINKS AUTOMATICALLY WHILE TYPING

By default, StarOffice automatically converts URLs and email addresses into hyperlinks as you type them in your documents. All you have to do is make sure that the address you type includes the proper Internet protocol or service. For example, Internet URLs should start with `http://www.` or `www.`, followed by the domain name and any existing paths. Likewise, email addresses are converted into "mailto" links as soon as they are entered in their entirety. The following is a list of acceptable sample entries, all of which would be inserted as hyperlinks when entered as text in a StarOffice document:

→ For more details URLs, **see** "Understanding Internet Addresses," **p. 922**.

```
http://www.mycompany.com/
```

```
www.mycompany.com
```

```
me@mycompany.com
```

```
mailto:me@mycompany.com
```

Tip #478 from
Michael & Sarah

To turn automatic hyperlinks on or off, open the AutoCorrect dialog box (by selecting Tools, AutoCorrect/AutoFormat), and check or clear the boxes labeled Detect URL on the Options tab. If you see an X in the Detect URL check boxes, the function is turned on.

INSERTING HYPERLINKS MANUALLY

Sometimes you want to link a certain word or phrase to a URL, or you want to hide the URL behind the facade of text. In this case, you can insert the link manually, using the hyperlink bar or the Character dialog.

USING THE HYPERLINK BAR   Your most important tool when inserting hyperlinks manually is the hyperlink bar (see Figure 25.3). Despite its importance, the hyperlink bar is not shown by default, nor can you quickly display it by right-clicking any visible toolbar and then selecting it from the shortcut menu that appears. Instead, you have to select View, Toolbars, Hyperlink Bar from the menu bar to show it.

Figure 25.3
You can use the hyperlink bar for Internet searches and for editing and inserting hyperlinks in your documents.

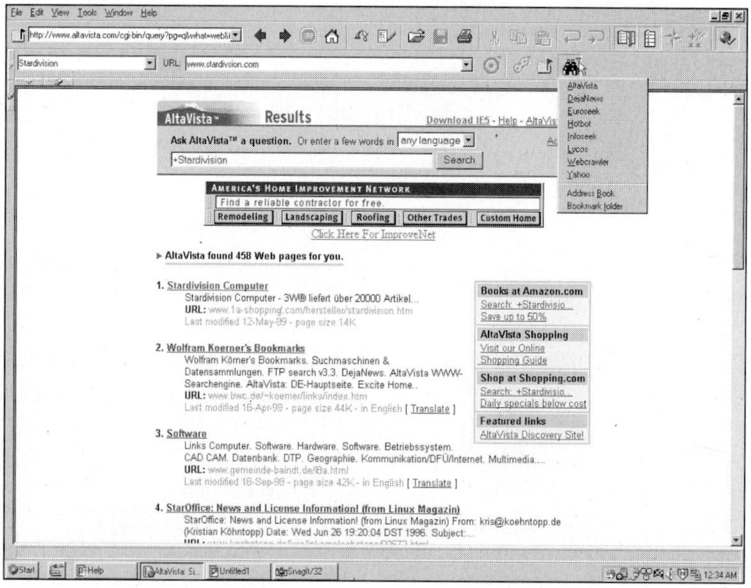

URL Name

Internet URLs

Target Frame

Hyperlink

Link

Find menu

The buttons on the hyperlink bar include the following:

- **URL Name**—Use this list box to assign a name to the Internet URL or a file path that is currently displayed in the adjacent URL list box. This name will be inserted into your document.

- **Internet URL**—Here, you can enter a URL manually. Alternatively, you can drag a file from the Beamer into the box, in which case the program automatically creates an absolute URL for the selected file and shows the existing filename in the URL Name box. Using the Hyperlink button, you can then insert the link at the insertion point in the current document.

- **Target Frame**—Use this button to open a drop-down menu and select the target frame of the currently displayed URL. Your options include Top, Parent, Blank, and Self. If you're editing a frameset, the list also contains the frames defined. (For more details on frames and linking to frames, see "Using Frames and Framesets" in Chapter 26, "Enhancing Your HTML Documents.")

- **Hyperlink**—Click here to insert a hyperlink to the currently displayed URL at the insertion point in the current document. When inserting hyperlinks in ordinary StarOffice documents, you have two options: You can click to insert the hyperlink as text, or you can extended-click and select Insert as Button from the drop-down menu to insert a graphic as a hyperlink. Note that the Hyperlink icon is available only if you entered a URL in the Internet URL box. Note also that the inserted button doesn't work with HTML documents. If you've entered a name in the URL Name box, the URL will be "hidden" behind this name.

- **Link**—Click here to save the currently displayed URL in the Internet URL box as a bookmark in the Bookmarks folder in the Explorer group.

- **Find**—Click to open a drop-down menu from which you can select a search engine for Internet searches or search the Address Book or Bookmarks folder for URLs. You can enter the search text (or name) in the URL Name box and then select the desired search engine or object. (You can define the type of search in the Tools, Options, Internet, Search dialog. For more details on searches see "Finding Web Sites" in this chapter.)

PART

VI

CH

25

To insert a link in a document, start by placing the insertion point in the location where you want to insert the link, then type the name of the link in the URL Name text box, enter (or drag or copy) the URL in the Internet URL box, and click the Hyperlink icon to insert the hyperlink at the insertion point.

To turn existing text into a hyperlink, select the text that you want the user to click. (Note that the selected text appears in the URL Name text box on the Hyperlink bar.) next, click the Internet URL text box and enter the URL to which you want to link the selected text. To finish, press Enter or click the Hyperlink icon. The selected text is now a hyperlink and appears underlined and in color.

USING THE PROPERTIES DIALOG BOX   In StarOffice, you can convert any existing text or image (or other object) into a hyperlink, using the Character and Picture dialog boxes, respectively.

To manually link a word or phrase to a URL or Web page using the Character dialog box, follow these steps:

1. Select the text (or graphic or table cell) from which you want to link to another location.

2. Choose Format, Character to open the Character dialog box.

3. Click the Hyperlink tab.

4. In the URL text box, enter the URL to which you want to link or click the Browse button to insert an absolute link to a document on your PC or network. (Be careful when using absolute links. For more details, see the sections on "Working with Relative and Absolute Links" and "Planning Your Site and Managing Your Files" in this chapter.)

5. (Optional) Click the Events button to assign an event or existing (StarBasic, JavaScript, or StarScript) macro to certain mouse actions, using the Assign Macro dialog box. (For more details on macros and StarBasic, see Part VIII, "Automating Your Work—StarBasic.")

6. (Optional) If you're working with frames, select the target from the Target Frame drop-down list. Your options include Blank, Parent, Self, and Top. (For more details on frames and linking to frames, see "Using Frames and Framesets" in Chapter 26, "Enhancing HTML Documents.")

7. Select a text style for the visited and unvisited hyperlinks in the Text Styles portion of the dialog (usually Visited Internet Link and Unvisited Internet Link, respectively; but you can choose whichever style you want).

8. Click OK to close the dialog box and return to the current document.

Alternatively, you can use the hyperlink bar to insert your hyperlinks.

To link an image to a URL or Web page using the Character dialog box, follow these steps:

1. Select and right-click the image and select Picture from the context menu, or choose Format, Picture from the menu bar to open the Picture dialog box.

2. In the URL text box, enter the URL to which you want to link or click the Browse button to insert an absolute link to a file on your PC or on a network server. (For more details, see the sections on " Working with Relative and Absolute Links " and "Planning Your Site and Managing Your Files" in this chapter.)

3. (Optional) If you're working with frames, select the target from the Target Frame drop-down list. Your options include Blank, Parent, Self, and Top. (For more details on frames and linking to frames, see "Using Frames and Framesets" in Chapter 26.)

4. Click OK to close the dialog box and return to the current document.

Likewise, you can assign hyperlinks to any other object by using that object's properties dialog, selecting the Hyperlink tab, and then inserting the desired URL.

INSERTING HYPERLINKS VIA DRAG&DROP You can also drag links (such as Bookmarks) from the open Beamer to the Internet URL box of the hyperlink bar, add a name for the link in the URL Name box, and then click the Hyperlink button to insert the link as text (or as a button, if it's not an HTML document) at the insertion point of the current document. Or you can drag links from the Beamer directly to the current document, but then they appear as URLs, not hidden behind special names. Note that you can also insert Hyperlinks via Drag&Drop from the Navigator. To do so, click the Drag Mode icon on the Navigator bar, and select Insert as Hyperlink from the drop-down menu. Now you can easily create a hyperlink to any item listed in the Navigator, including headings, tables, pictures, OLE objects, references, and indexes. These items can be part of the same document, or they can be part of another document of the same type. You can switch between open documents of the same type by using the Documents Open list box at the bottom of the Navigator.

Tip #479 from
Michael & Sarah

When working with text documents and you're dragging a hyperlink, you can also use the Beamer as a temporary repository for the link. Just Alt+click the link you want to use, and drag it in the open Beamer. From there, you can drag it to an open document at a later point.

INSERTING LINKS IN TABLE AND PRESENTATION DOCUMENTS

The easiest way to insert hyperlinks in a table or presentation document is to type the URL directly into a cell or text box, respectively. If you want to hide the URL behind a name, you have to use the hyperlink bar. Simply enter the desired name and URL in the URL Name box and URL Internet box, respectively; then click the Hyperlink icon to insert the link at the insertion point (table document) or in the center of the slide (presentation document). In the case of a presentation document, you can then click and drag the link in its box to a desired location on the slide.

Note

By default, StarOffice inserts the link as button into a presentation document. If you prefer to use text links, you have to extended click the Hyperlink icon to open the drop-down menu and then select As Text. To move text links, Alt+click and drag the link in its box to a desired location on the slide.

USING ANCHORS TO JUMP TO SPECIFIC LOCATIONS IN DOCUMENTS

Although many links only take you to the beginning of a document of Web page, you can define hyperlinks that jump to specific places within a given document. You can create hyperlinks to particular places in the current document or in any other document. These locations can be StarWriter bookmarks, StarCalc cells, StarImpress slides, or bookmarks in Web pages.

To create these well-aimed links, you first have to insert a bookmark by selecting Insert, Bookmark (text document), name the cell Or range of cells by choosing Insert, Names, Define (StarCalc), or assign a name to the slide (StarImpress) you want to jump to.

→ For more details on bookmarks, **see** "Bookmarking Your Document," **p. 388**.

→ For more details on slides, **see** "Working with Slides," **p. 846**.

Next, enter # followed by the name of the bookmark or cell in the Internet URL box on the hyperlink bar (for example, #anchor). If you want to jump to a certain place in another document, enter the URL of the file followed by the anchor's name (which can be the name of a bookmark, cell, or slide if you want to link to a presentation document)—for example:

```
C:\Office51\help.htm#test
```

```
C:\Office51\explorer\samples\presentations\recar-agm.sdd#Overview
```

Finally, place the cursor in your document where you want to insert the link, and then click the Hyperlink icon if you want to insert the link as text or extended-click the Hyperlink icon and select As Button from the drop-down menu to insert the link as a standard button (only for ordinary StarOffice documents). You can change the attributes of the text link or inserted button using the Properties Button dialog as described in the section "Editing and Removing Hyperlinks" later in this chapter.

Snatching Links off the Internet

If you come across an interesting or relevant link on the Web that you would like to use in a document, Alt+click the link, and drag it to the hyperlink bar. You can then give the link a name and insert it in a document as described earlier.

Editing and Removing Hyperlinks

To change the text a hyperlink displays, you have to be careful not to click the hyperlink because clicking activates it. Instead, Alt+click the hyperlink. Now you can use standard editing commands to make your changes.

If you want to edit the URL itself, Alt+click the hyperlink. The hyperlink and its name are automatically shown in the hyperlink bar. Here, you can modify the hyperlink. When you're finished, press Enter to accept the changes. Alternatively, you can also change the URL in the Character dialog box. Just select Format, Character from the menu bar, click the Hyperlink tab, and then enter the desired URL in the URL text box or click browse to locate the file you want to link to.

To change the color, font, and style of the hyperlink, use the respective text styles in the Stylist. For example, to change the attributes of a link, right-click Internet Link in the Stylist, and select Modify from the context menu. You can then edit the attributes as desired. Likewise, if you want to change, for example, the color of a visited link, modify the Visited Internet Link text style in the Stylist.

If the hyperlink is an inserted button, click the outermost corner of the button to select it. Then right-click and select Control from the context menu. In the Properties Button dialog that appears, you can change the attributes of the selected button, including name (Label), link (URL), color, and so on (see Figure 25.4).

Note

Looking at the available options in the Properties Button dialog seems overwhelming at first, but the options are all fairly self-explanatory and consistent with the other options of the same name in StarOffice. However, you should note that you cannot only change the attributes of the button, but also assign events to certain mouse and keyboard actions. Note also that these buttons in many ways behave like other objects. You can change the placement and size of the button via the Position and Size dialog box (by selecting Position and Size from the button's context menu) or by dragging the sizing handles. In a text document, you can anchor the button to a character, paragraph or page; in table document, you can anchor it to a cell or page. For more details on working with objects, see "Rehearsing Objects" in Chapter 11, "Desktop Publishing with StarOffice."

Figure 25.4
Use the Properties: Button dialog to change the general attributes of a hyperlink button or assign events (or macros) to certain mouse and keyboard actions.

If you want to edit a hyperlinked object (for example, a graphic), Alt+click the object to select it without activating the hyperlink. You can resize the object, move it around, or right-click the object to open the object's context menu which gives you various formatting, alignment, and other choices.

→ For more details on working with objects, **see** Rehearsing Objects," **p. 421**.

If you want to remove the link, not the text, select the entire hyperlink (all characters), and then choose Default from the context menu or select Format, Default from the menu bar. The familiar hyperlink underline and color disappear, and the hyperlink contents change back to ordinary text or graphics.

WORKING WITH RELATIVE AND ABSOLUTE LINKS

When you create a hyperlink, you have to distinguish between relative and absolute links. Relative links leave off the protocol and server segments of the URL but retain the path and filename. Absolute links specify the type of protocol, the domain name, the path, and the filename. The general implications of these choices are discussed in the "Planning Your Site and Managing Your Files" section in this chapter.

You should specify an absolute location when inserting a hyperlink to another Web site or Internet location. On the other hand, you should usually specify a relative path for hyperlinks to other pages for the site you're developing. You should do so because you move the pages to a different computer, the Web server, after they're complete. The exception would be if the computer you use to build the Web pages and the Web server computer are the same machine. In that case, you can use either type of path specification for the pages you create. Note that you can create relative links only when the file that contains the link and the file that is being linked to are on the same drive.

NAVIGATING AMONG HYPERLINKED DOCUMENTS

When you click a hyperlink in a document, StarOffice takes you to the target immediately, without opening a new task. You can open any number of (previously saved) StarOffice documents via successive hyperlinks. To navigate between StarOffice documents you've jumped to via hyperlinks, use the Backward and Forward buttons on the function bar. If you prefer to open a document as a new task, Ctrl+click the hyperlink.

To quickly navigate between hyperlinks in the current document, expand the Hyperlinks item in the open Navigator (press F5), and then double-click the desired hyperlink. StarOffice places the insertion point of your cursor at the beginning of the hyperlink.

Note

Each time you open a link, StarOffice creates a cached image of the retrieved document, which is saved in the Office51\store folder.

PLANNING YOUR SITE AND MANAGING YOUR FILES

Web sites are far more than collections of HTML documents. Every image—from the smallest navigation button to the largest image map—is a separate file that must be uploaded with your HTML page. And if you add any additional elements, such as background sound, digital video, or a Java applet, their files must be transferred as well. To preview your Web documents locally and view them properly on the Internet, you have to organize your material in a specific manner.

Note

Because each Web site varies in size and complexity, the following remarks are meant only to get you thinking of ways to organize and keep track of your site. Unfortunately, the site management feature of StarOffice is virtually nonexistent. If you're working with more complex sites, you might want to look into a commercial program to help you manage your site.

Each time you're developing or working with a Web site of more than several pages, you must do some careful planning to avoid confusion as the site grows. It's a good idea to map out your site in a logical, structured manner, much like an organizational chart. One way to approach this task is to set up a logical directory structure on your hard drive or network and then duplicate that structure on your Web server. For example, say that you have a site with pages under the headings About Us, Personnel, Products, Employment Opportunities, and Feedback. You might set up a file structure on your hard disk consisting of a main folder called "web" (for example, `c:\web`), with subfolders named for each of these headings (for example, `c:\web\about`, `c:\web\person`, `c:\web\prod`, and so on) and perhaps another subfolder for images (`c:\web\images`) and one for multimedia files (`c:\web\media`).

As you create your pages, save them in the appropriate folders. For example, place the start page (often called `start.htm` or `index.htm`) into the web root folder (`c:\web`), and place the images, sound, or video files you'll be using in the images and multimedia folders, respectively. When the option Save URLs Relative to File System is selected in the Options General Save dialog (which you open by selecting Tools, Options, General, Save), StarOffice automatically saves all links as (site root) relative addresses (for example, `IMG SRC="images/mypic01.jpg"`). When the document is on the Web server, StarOffice looks for the linked item in the same relative location on the server as it was found on your hard drive.

For example, say you include in an HTML document a picture stored in the `\images` subfolder on your hard drive (subordinate to the folder of the Web page you're creating). After you transfer the page to the server, it looks for the image in the `\images` subfolder of the server's hard drive (subordinate to the folder the Web page is in on the server). Therefore, you must be sure to create the same folders in the same relative locations on the Web server as on your hard disk and to copy the referenced files into the proper folders.

The opposite of relative addressing is absolute addressing, which you generally do when you are linking to a Web page on another server. If you save links to your own pages as absolute addresses (that is, the option Save URLs Relative to File System is deselected), you cannot see the linked image (or other file) on the HTML page stored on the Web server because the full URL (for example, `IMG SRC="file:///c¦/web/images/mypic01.jpg"`) is saved to the file. Of course, this location is nowhere to be found on the Web server, it's on your hard drive.

If you're dealing with only a dozen or fewer pages, you can copy the items to the document folder; then the image, sound, or video files are copied to the same folder that the Web page you're creating is in. This option—you may call it "document-relative addressing"—makes it easier to ensure that all files are loaded on the Web server correctly but does not allow you to organize your image, sound, and video files into separate subfolders (which soon creates problems when you want to expand your site because you're bound to lose the overview).

PART

VI

CH

25

Because these options come into play when you create HTML documents and publish your documents to the Web server, you can find related information in the sections "Working with Hyperlinks" in this chapter and "Preparing Your Work for the Web" in Chapter 27.

Note

> Even before you start organizing your site, you need to address the all-important issues of message, audience, and budget. In this regard, designing a Web publication is no different from designing a publication for print: you need a message (or concept) worth communicating, a target audience, a logical organization, and a defined level of detail. You also need to consider your available resources. Creating Web pages translates into a combination of development time, materials (such as custom graphics or stock photos), and ongoing maintenance.

CREATING WEB PAGES IN STAROFFICE

StarWriter/Web is a natural as a visual Web page editor. A close cousin to StarOffice's word processing module, it masters equally well text editing, layout, and design, and is sophisticated enough to handle frames, tables, and forms in a WYSIWYG (What You See Is What You Get) development environment. In addition, it doubles as an HTML editor, so if you like to tweak the source code or need to add pixel-fine adjustments, you can toggle back and forth between two different views of the page you're working on—WYSIWYG and HTML source code. Any changes you make in one take effect in the other the moment you toggle back.

Note

> This section assumes that you are already familiar with the basic commands and features of StarWriter, including editing and formatting text documents and inserting tables. If you would like to brush up on your StarWriter basics, refer to Chapters 6 and 7 and Chapters 9 through 11.

STARTING A NEW HTML DOCUMENT IN STARWRITER/WEB

Starting a new Web page in StarOffice is easy. You can either create a new HTML document, or you can convert an existing text, spreadsheet, drawing, or presentation document to HTML for Web display. When creating a new HTML document, you have three options. You can use the Web Page Wizard, base your document on an existing template, or start a document from scratch. In each instance, StarOffice opens the new document in the StarWriter/Web module, which, with a few notable exceptions, resembles the default StarWriter interface. For example, the StarWriter/Web object bar lacks the Justify icon because no equivalent HTML tag is available for this function. The main toolbar is modified with the addition of such Web-related features as the Insert Header, Insert Footer, Text Animation, Print Layout On/Off, and Show HTML Source icons, in exchange for the Draw, Insert Objects, and Direct Cursor icons. In general, StarWriter/Web gives you access to the same menu commands as StarWriter with the exception of those that lack an equivalent in the world of HTML. (For example, you won't find the Insert, Manual Break command because each HTML document is one continuous page. To "turn a page," the reader would have to jump to another document.) Figure 25.5 shows the standard StarWriter/Web interface.

Figure 25.5
You create Web pages with the StarWriter/Web module, which looks similar to the StarWriter interface.

Insert Header
Insert Footer
Text Animation

Picture
Print Layout On/Off
Show HTML Source

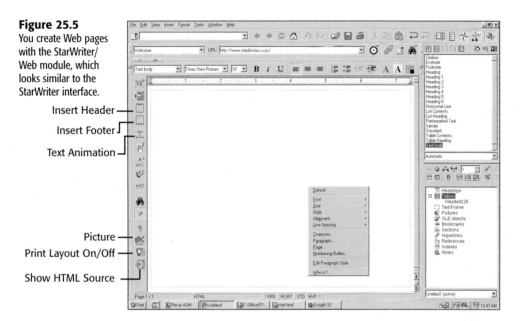

As with other StarOffice documents, when you're working on an HTML document, you have instant access to all the menus and tools you need to create these documents. Although you can theoretically do everything in StarWriter/Web that you can do in StarWriter, the menus and dialogs contain only those options that can be meaningfully translated into HTML code.

USING THE WEB PAGE AUTOPILOT WIZARD

By far the easiest way to start a new HTML document is to use the Web Page Wizard. It includes a selection of templates (which you can supplement with your own designs) from which you can choose a type and style for your new Web page.

To begin, choose File, AutoPilot, Web Page. The StarWriter/Web module opens to a new HTML document template, and the Web Page AutoPilot: Template dialog appears, asking you what type of Web page you want. You have a number of choices, from a simple Basic document to a more complex Survey Questionnaire and Registration Form. You can see what each page looks like by highlighting the selection and watching the page change in the background. (You might have to move the dialog box to get a better view.) Because you're going to be modifying the page with your own information, don't worry if you don't find exactly what you want among the available selections. Just find and select (highlight) the type of page that most closely matches how you envision your final result, and then click the Style button to switch to the Web Page AutoPilot Style dialog.

Now, select the visual style that most pleases you. As you select different styles, the background page changes accordingly. Depending on the style you choose, your fonts, style, color, background, bullets, and horizontal lines may change. After you've made your selection, click Complete. At this point, you can modify the HTML file the wizard has created by using the same tools you know from text documents and then save it as a template.

Note

If you want to save your document as a template, select the Create Template option (which is available on either AutoPilot dialog).

Tip #480 from
Michael & Sarah

You can always save your document as a template later. To do so, just select File, Templates from the menu bar, enter a name for the template in the Document templates dialog, select a category under which you want to store it (in this case Online), and click OK.

BASING NEW WEB PAGES ON A TEMPLATE

If you think less is more, you can also start out with one of three existing HTML templates by following these steps:

1. Select File, New From Template, or press Ctrl+N. The New template dialog appears.

2. Click the More button to expand the New dialog box; then click the Preview check box if it isn't selected already.

3. In the Categories list on the left, select Online.

4. Select a template in the Templates list on the right. If the Preview option is selected, you can see a thumbnail preview of the selected template. By default, you have three templates to choose from:

    - **Colored HTML Template**—Uses a sans serif font (Arial), colored text and heading, and a blue background.

    - **Contemporary HTML Template**—Same as Colored HTML Template, only without the color.

    - **Standard Template**—Uses a serif font (Times New Roman) and black text and heading.

5. Click OK to open the selected template and close the dialog.

You can now treat the document as you do any other document in StarWriter. You can enter and format text, insert and position objects, and use or modify the predefined HTML text, paragraph, and numbering styles in the Stylist. When you're finished, you can save the document as a regular HTML file or as an HTML template that you can place in the Online templates folder. StarOffice will try its best to preserve or approximate the existing text, objects, and formatting when converting your document.

CREATING WEB PAGES FROM SCRATCH

To start an HTML document from scratch, select File, New, HTML Document from the menu bar, or select Start, More, HTML Document. StarOffice opens a blank HTML document in StarWriter/Web, complete with standard HTML character and paragraph styles that enable you to quickly and consistently format the content of your Web page.

→ For more details on the StarOffice HTML styles, **see** "StarOffice as HTML Authoring Tool," **p. 957** in this chapter.

PREVIEWING AN EXISTING TEXT DOCUMENT AS A WEB PAGE

Wouldn't it be nice to see what an existing text document looks like in HTML before converting it to an HTML document? Just click the Online Layout button on the main toolbar (or select View, Online Layout from the menu bar), and StarWriter shows your document as if it were an HTML document.

Note

Unfortunately, the Online Layout preview option is available only in StarWriter.

When you're working in Online Layout view, your current page style is (temporarily) replaced with the standard HTML page template, giving you a rough idea about how the text and objects on your page are going to shift after exporting the current document into HTML. Regardless of the number of (text) pages in the document, in Online Layout view, your document consists of one continuous ("Web") page because there are no "page breaks" on the Internet.

Tip #481 from
Michael & Sarah

If the document appears too long for one Web page, you may want to split it up into two and insert hyperlinks, for example at the end of each document (read: the bottom of each Web page). This way, the reader can click the link when she reaches the bottom of the page to advance to the next page or return to the previous page. The links could be text-based and read "Next" or "Previous," respectively; or they could be icons such as a right-pointing arrow (Next) or left-pointing arrow (Previous) which you can import from the Homepage theme folder in the StarOffice Gallery or create your own.

→ For more details on hyperlinks, **see** "Working with Hyperlinks," **p. 936**.

Note

While you're in Online Layout view, you can see only one window per task or open document. If you open new windows within a given task, StarOffice closes the inactive windows when you switch to Online Layout view.

Note also that while you're in Online Layout view, the vertical scrollbar is invisible; StarWriter automatically adjusts the line length (or page width) when you change the Zoom ratio or scale of your document (or when you open or close docked tools such as the Explorer, Stylist, Navigator, or any other currently docked toolbar). Your Zoom options include absolute values (such as 200%, 150%, 100%, 75%, 50%, or any variable percentage you enter); the Optimal, Page Width, and Entire Page options are not available (nor is the Page View/Print Preview option—after all, you're already previewing the document in Online Layout view). Use the Zoom options to figure out the best view of your page, and write down the (approximate) width of the page by noting the measurement on the vertical ruler at the top of your viewing area. This way, you have an idea of how to tweak the converted document (page) later for optimal onscreen display.

Note

> Of course, many other factors influence onscreen display—most notably screen resolution, which depends on monitor size and user preferences. So, all you can do by playing with the Zoom ratio is take a wild guess.

Finally, keep in mind that Online Layout view is not really an HTML document preview. You cannot see whether the inserted elements or objects in the current document will translate well into HTML because StarWriter does not simulate an HTML conversion process. All you see is an Online Layout that helps you guesstimate the look of your page in terms of length and width.

CONVERTING AN EXISTING DOCUMENT TO A WEB PAGE

StarOffice gives you the option to convert existing text, spreadsheet, drawing, and presentation documents into HTML documents. Depending on the type of document, you can either directly save the document as an HTML document (StarWriter and StarCalc) or you can export it as an HTML Document (StarDraw and StarImpress).

Note

> Although StarOffice will attempt to preserve the format and style of the existing document during the conversion process, unless you create a document in StarWriter/Web, you will invariably lose some (visual and style) information when converting an existing document into an HTML document. Also, depending on the document, you may have to edit the results for formatting, style, and positioning of elements and objects. Note also that when you save a StarOffice document as an HTML file, the suite stores each graphic as a separate file. For more details on graphics in HTML documents see the section "Working with Graphics and Charts" in Chapter 26.

CONVERTING AN EXISTING TEXT DOCUMENT When converting a text document, you have two options: you can select File, Save As and then select HTML (StarWriter) from the File Type drop-down list in the Save As dialog, or you can choose File, Send, Create HTML Document. If you select the Create HTML Document option, the Name and Path of the HTML Document dialog box opens. Using this dialog, you can assign a name to the

HTML document and automatically split the document based on templates by clicking the Template button in the lower left of the dialog. In the Select Template dialog that appears, select the style element by which you want to split the document. For example, if your document consists of Heading 1 and heading 2 styles and you select Heading 1 as the template, after the conversion, you will have one document that lists all Heading 1 styles as hyperlinks. Click a link and you will be whisked to the contents that pertain to that heading style. If you select Heading 2 as your template, the first document you see will have all Heading 1s styles and accompanying text, and all Heading 2 styles will appear as hyperlinks. Other template options include: Footer left, Footer right, Frame contents, Header, Header left, Header right, Headings 1 through 4, Table of Contents, and Text Body.

After you've selected the desired template, click OK to return to the Name and Path of the HTML Document dialog, then click Save to save the document(s). During the conversion process, StarOffice will automatically assign names to the additional documents based on your original name choice. For example, if you saved the document as mydoc, StarOffice will name the hyperlinked document files mydoc1, mydoc2, and so on.

CONVERTING AN EXISTING SPREADSHEET DOCUMENT   Converting any part of a StarCalc spreadsheet as is as easy as saving the document in HTML format using the File, Save As command. Just select HTML (StarCalc) from the File Type drop-down list in the Save As dialog that appears and click Save.

CONVERTING AN EXISTING DRAWING OR PRESENTATION DOCUMENT   StarDraw and StarImpress come armed with an HMTL Export wizard that enables you to create quality web pages for use with the Internet or intranet. Using the HTML Export wizard, you can define whether the presentation will have frames, whether users will navigate the presentation using graphic buttons or text links, and whether the original StarDraw or StarImpress presentation should be made available for download. Each final HTML page contains one presentation slide as a JPG graphic. If so inclined, you can edit these pages in StarWriter, adding headings and additional hyperlinks, for example. Exporting presentation and drawing documents is discussed in detail in the section "Saving Presentations for the World Wide Web" in Chapter 24, "Previewing and Presenting Your Presentation."

CUSTOMIZING HTML EXPORT

StarOffice supports the HTML 3.2 standard and includes some proprietary additions that are recognized when you load pages using the StarOffice browser without "disturbing" other browsers. (The same is true for Microsoft Internet Explorer and Netscape Navigator.) Partially, these additions will be recognized by other browsers as well, but just in case, you can use the Export portion in the Tools, Options, Browser, HTML dialog to define which browser you prefer to create your pages.

→ For more details on StarOffice and HTML tags **see** "StarOffice as an HTML Authoring Tool," **p. 957** in this chapter.

The following are your options:

- **HTML 3.2**—For best compatibility, choose this option. (For more details on this standard, see `http://www.w3.org/TR/REC-html32.html`.) However, note that Netscape Navigator and Internet Explorer enhancements are not included (such as multicolumn text, animated text, blinking text, and floating frames). Also, HTML 3.2 does not support any print layouts.

- **MS Internet Explorer 4.0**—Includes, for example, the `<MARQUEE>` tag for animated text, plus you can use floating frames and regular or tiled background graphics for tables. These features can currently be read only by Microsoft Internet Explorer and StarOffice.

- **Netscape Navigator 3.0**—Exports empty text frames with the `<SPACER>` tag and multicolumn text frames with the `<MULTICOL>` tag. (Note that StarOffice can read these tags, too.)

- **Netscape Navigator 4.0**—Exports table column (`<TABLECOL>`) tags and style sheets.

- **StarWriter**—Exports all tags that are known to StarWriter/Web, in addition to the HTML 3.2 tags. If your readers mostly use StarWriter as their standard browser (for example, on an intranet), you definitely should choose this option. It enables you to export tags for paragraph borders and drop caps and print layouts. Note that this option can also read all the above.

To include unknown tags in an HTML document, use notes. For example, every note that begins with `HTML:` and ends with > is interpreted as HTML code. (Note that `HTML:` is not exported; it's only important to use during coding.)

EDITING HTML FILES IN STARWRITER/WEB

Now that you've created a new HTML file, with or without a wizard, or have saved an existing StarOffice document as an HTML document, you're ready to edit the file until it's exactly the way you want it. Even though your options when creating and editing HTML documents are somewhat limited when compared to print publications, you can still do plenty of things to create an attractive home page or intranet page once you've familiarized yourself with HTML layout options and aids (such as grids and lines), graphic file formats, image maps and some plug-in and (often browser-dependent) effects options.

→ For more details on creating enhanced Web pages, **see** Chapter 26 "Enhancing HTML Documents," starting on **p. 965**.

→ For more details on layout grids and visual layout aids, **see** "Rehearsing Objects," **p. 421**.

Tip #482 from
Michael & Sarah

One trick when publishing Web pages is to work with tables. Tables enable you to arrange graphic and text elements nicely on a page. For example, if you want to have two-column text, use a two-column table. If you want a graphic to be scaled automatically, place it in a table cell. There have been many books written on how to create attractive Web pages. For more details on working with tables **see** "Working with Tables and Text Frames," **p. xxx** (Chapter 26).

Editing text in StarWriter/Web is as easy and virtually the same as editing text in StarWriter. You don't even have to worry about inserting objects or applying attributes that don't translate into HTML because StarWriter/Web provides only the tools and functions that are applicable to Web publishing.

Before you begin, make sure that you're in HTML editing mode. The Edit File button on the function bar should be pressed, and the main toolbar should appear on the left. If you're not in this mode, click the Edit File button on the function bar. At any point during your editing session, if you want to see what your Web page looks like in a browser, click the Edit File button again to exit the edit mode.

You can use a good part of the direct and style formatting options that you know from text documents. When your cursor is in a text block, you have the Text object bar at your disposal. Move the cursor to a table or insert a table, and you see the Table object bar, and so on. Each time you click on a link, you are whisked away to the proper location.

Note

Note that the HTML editing mode is not synonymous with Online Layout view. Designed primarily for reading documents on the screen, Online Layout view is available with StarWriter documents you're working with. In this view, text is wrapped to the window size, ignoring paragraph formatting.

PART

VI

CH

25

FORMATTING TEXT

HTML is designed to be a universal cross-platform language, usable by computers with different graphic and text display capabilities. As a result, rather than describing text in a traditional word processor manner—specifying the font, style, and size—HTML uses text formatting tags for the browser to interpret according to the system it's running on. For example, to display a large heading, rather than specify 24-point Times Roman bold, StarWriter/Web applies the <H1> tag to the headline instead to produce the same result (assuming the browser's default font is Times Roman).

CHANGING FONT SIZE   Because Web pages have to appear on many different kinds of systems, they don't handle fonts in the same way as regular documents. Instead of having specific fonts embedded in them, they refer to font sizes that range from Size 1 (smallest) to

Size 7 (largest), with 3 being the default. Using the Options Browser HTML dialog (which you open by selecting Tools, Options, Browser, HTML), you can set the font size StarOffice assigns to each of these sizes and thus determine how large the type of a Web page is onscreen. The maximum font size is 50 points.

Tip #483 from	For quick font changes, add the Increase Font and Decrease Font buttons to the object bar by right-clicking on the object bar and selecting the buttons from the Visible Buttons sub-menu. Using these buttons, you can quickly change the size of a selected block of text. StarWriter/Web adds the SIZE attribute to the <FONT> tag, creating a result such as <FONT SIZE=5>.
Michael & Sarah	

CHANGING OTHER CHARACTER ATTRIBUTES   You can click the Bold, Italic, and Underline buttons to apply those options to any selected text. Clicking these buttons encloses the text within the <B>...</B>, <I>...<I/>, and <U>...</U> HTML tags, respectively.

SELECTING FONT COLOR   You can use the Font Color button on the object bar to apply a new color to text that you have selected. Be sure that the color can be easily seen against whatever background color or pattern you have chosen.

→ For more details on backgrounds and background color, **see** "Choosing a Background Color or Image," **p. 966**.

SPECIFYING PARTICULAR FONTS   In HTML, the <FONT> tag (see Table 25.1 for details on the Heading 1 style) enables you to select a typeface, style, and size for a selected block of type. Choose fonts wisely. If users of your Web page don't have the font you specify, another font (or the browser's default font) is substituted for it, and the result may be different from what you had in mind. If your page will be viewed by a general audience, then choosing any font other than Arial/Helvetica or Times New Roman is almost certain to produce unexpected results, and even Arial/Helvetica and Times New Roman may be displayed incorrectly by some browsers. On the other hand, if you are publishing to your company's intranet, you might have more flexibility in choosing fonts, particularly if all your users have similar systems.

ALIGNING AND INDENTING TEXT   Use the Left, Centered, or Right buttons to align selected text, images, tables, and forms. Clicking these buttons adds the ALIGN=Left or Center or Right attribute to the <P> paragraph tag. Use the Increase and Decrease Indent buttons on the object bar to move selected text, images, tables, and forms left and right. Although no HTML tag is available for indenting or tabbing, this function adds a margin attribute to the respective tag, creating, for example, <P Style="margin-bottom: .79in"> to force the browser to create an indent from the left margin.

Caution

Note this tag is not exported when the Export settings in the Options Browser HTML dialog show Netscape Navigator 3.0 or HTML 3.2. In general, older browsers will not recognize this tag and hence not display the page as intended.

CREATING STANDARD NUMBERED AND BULLETED LISTS   You can create two types of lists in an HTML document: an ordered or numbered list (<OL>), or an unordered or bulleted list (<UL>). To begin either one, place your cursor where you want the list to begin; then click the appropriate list button (numbered or bulleted) on your object bar. The first number or bullet is then shown. Type the first item on your list, press Enter, type the next item, and so on, until you are finished. Press Enter after the last item, and then press the Backspace key to exit the numbered or bulleted list mode, or click the respective icon on the object bar.

INSERTING MORE INTERESTING BULLETS AND NUMBERS   If you don't like StarWriter/Web's standard bullets, you can easily replace them with slick graphical bullets that you can pull from the Numbering dialog. You add bullets the same way you do in ordinary StarOffice documents: Choose Format, Numbering/Bullets; select the style of bullet you like from the Pictures tab; and then click OK. StarWriter/Web creates a new paragraph marked with the same bullet each time you press Enter. (The graphical bullets are actually .gif image files that are copied into the folder for your Web page when you insert them into the page.) Numbered lists work as they do in regular documents—the numbers are plain text characters—but outline-style numbered lists aren't available.

OPENING AND EDITING A PAGE FROM THE WEB

After you've loaded a page from the Internet, you can edit it as desired. Just click the Edit icon on the function bar. You can then edit the document, add text, delete text, and change the font color or font. Then you can save the page by selecting File, Save As. You can't click Save when editing unless you have access to the Web server that contains the page.

SAVING AND PRINTING HTML DOCUMENTS

Saving and printing your HTML document is virtually identical to saving and printing text documents. When saving a document, you have three basic options. You can click the Save button on the Function bar, select File, Save from the Menu bar, or press Ctrl+S on your keyboard. The first time you try to save a new, previously unsaved document, StarWriter automatically opens the Save As dialog. Here you can enter a name for your document in the File name text box, select a directory where you want to save the file, or create a new (sub)folder within a directory of your choice. When you're finished, select Save to return to your document. (Be sure you're really saving the document in the HTML (StarWriter) format.)

PART
VI

CH
25

Tip #484 from
Michael & Sarah

When creating your HTML document, be sure to select File, Properties from the menu bar and fill in the information in the Properties dialog appears. For example, StarWriter/Web uses the information you provide on the Description tab to generate Meta tags that help search engines locate your page on the Web as well as identify your page in a browser. The information you provide in the Title text box appears in the title bar of the browser; Subject, Keyword, and Comment text provides summary information about your Web page for search engines.

When printing a document, you can choose whether you want to print the entire document or only a selection; multiple copies of a document; include your graphics, tables, control fields, background, or notes; print to paper or file; or use a third-party fax driver to fax the document.

By default, StarOffice includes graphics and tables when printing HTML documents and prints all text in black, while ignoring the background. This guarantees that you can read the information of an HTML document regardless of background and font color when printed to a black and white printer. If you have a color printer, you can also include the background when outputting the HTML document. Simply select File, Print to open the Print dialog, then click the Options button in the lower left of the dialog. In the Printer Options dialog that appears, you can set the desired print options for the contents, pages, and notes of the HTML document.

Tip #485 from
Michael & Sarah

HTML pages are of varying length. However, you can fit only so much on one printed page. So that you don't lose a line of text or image when you're printing, click the Print Layout On/Off icon on the main toolbar in StarWriter/Web. The Page Number field on the Status bar indicates the number of printed pages. Note that if you want to print pages from the Internet, you first have to switch into edit mode (click the Edit File icon on the function bar) before you can turn the Print Layout function on.

When you're printing with the Print Layout function on, StarOffice automatically inserts header and footer areas in your document. The header area lists the title and URL of the printed HTML document, as well as the date and time when it was printed; the footer area lists the total number of pages printed.

The contents of the header and footer areas are predefined in the HTML document template. You can change these settings for the current document (via direct formatting). If you want your changes to be permanent, select File, Templates. In the Document Templates dialog that appears, select Online in the Categories list on the left and the desired template in the Templates list on the right. Next, click the Edit button, then click the Print Layout icon on the main toolbar. You can now change the selected template as desired. To save your changes, select File, Save As from the menu bar.

When you're printing framesets, you might run into some problems. A frameset is nothing but an empty page that has been divided into several frames. Each frame contains its own document. Only the document that is selected will be printed.

When you're printing pages, a great deal depends on the printer setup and the user's browser. Page breaks, fonts and font sizes, and other characteristics may vary depending on your individual setup.

STAROFFICE AS AN HTML AUTHORING TOOL

Although you don't need to know the nuts and bolts of HTML coding to create Web pages in StarWriter/Web, it's a good idea to be at least familiar with the concept of HTML, as well as StarOffice's HTML tag options and the structure of a Web page.

THE STRUCTURE OF AN HTML PAGE

An HTML page is a set of instructions suggesting to your browser how to display the enclosed text and images. The browser knows what kind of page it is handling based on the tag that opens the page (<HTML>) and the tag that closes it (</HTML>). The page itself is divided into two primary sections: the <HEAD> and the <BODY>. Information relating to the entire document goes in the <HEAD> section, such as the title, description, or keywords. The actual content of the Web page is found in the <BODY> section. All text and references to graphics, animations, Java applets, and other elements of the page are found between the opening <BODY> and the closing </BODY> tags. When you start a new HTML document in StarOffice, the following basic format is already laid out for you:

```
<HTML>
<HEAD>
    <TITLE></TITLE>
    <META NAME="GENERATOR" CONTENT="StarOffice/5.1 (Win32)">
</HEAD>
<BODY>
<P><BR><BR>
</P>
</BODY>
</HTML
```

HTML AND BROWSER COMPATIBILITY

HTML is a dynamic and rapidly evolving language. New tags are added to the language by Microsoft and Netscape with each new version of their browsers, adding features that allow for increasingly sophisticated Web sites. The downside of this progress is that older versions of browsers are unable to interpret the new commands and hence display pages differently than newer ones. Not only are some newer features such as table formatting not going to display correctly on older browser versions, but the look of text may vary from one version of the browser to another. The width of the browser window also affects column widths and how text lines wrap (move from line to line). To make the whole process even more complicated, many browsers let individual users set their own preferred fonts and sizes.

Note

Having users control the visual appearance of a Web page is fully in keeping with the original intentions of the creators of the Web and its software. If you go back in the history of HTML, you will see that today's use of HTML is mostly beyond the original intention. HTML was intended as a tool to describe a document's structure, but not its visual appearance. This second part was left to the user or, more precisely, browser. The creator only defined the various items such as a header, standard text, and so on. Then it was up to the reader if he wanted to read/print it using Times or Helvetica or whatever font he preferred. In short, having the option to select one's own fonts is one of the basic features a browser always offered—much to the dismay of Web designers.

What this all means is that Web page font sizes are going to change, columns are going to shift, and text may appear in different fonts depending on the equipment being used to cruise the Internet. That means your documents probably won't look exactly like what you create in StarOffice, even after you tweak their HTML source code when those documents are on the Web.

These discrepancies are unavoidable. Our advice is this: Don't spend too much of your time fine-tuning type sizes and column placements, or editing or changing newer tags in your HTML documents only to accommodate the lowest common denominator of browsers. This manual and tedious process should be undertaken only by someone who is reasonably knowledgeable in HTML. Instead, you should focus on the organization of your content and making your arrangements simple so that your document can survive the trip to the Web.

After all, given that browsers are either free or very inexpensive, someone who chooses not to update his or her browser is probably only marginally interested in what you or any other site has to offer. However, if you feel the need to accommodate these people (who, make no mistake, number in the millions), then you can use StarWriter/Web (or any other plain text editor) to edit the HTML code of your Web page however you want. If you're interested in learning more about the HTML language, you can find dozens of books on the subject. Of course, the Web itself is an excellent resource for this information. Type ?HTML or W3C in the Load URL box on the function bar, and press Enter to have your favorite search engine dig up listings for the overseer of the HTML language, the World Wide Web Consortium (W3 Consortium or W3C), along with many other sites that offer specifications, training, tips, and other information about HTML.

Note

Notice that this section doesn't mention anything about graphic images changing in appearance depending on where they're viewed. Pictures also can look different from browser to browser and platform to platform, although the difference is usually confined to varying color hues. Because Web graphics are bitmapped images—made up of a predefined, fixed series of dots—the likelihood of your browser making your images look any different than they do in StarWriter or StarImage (or any other desktop publishing [DTP] or image editing application) is practically impossible. For more details on graphics and Web publishing, see "Inserting Graphics and Images" in Chapter 26.

EDITING HTML CODE IN STARWRITER/WEB

If you're using StarOffice as your authoring tool, you should know that the program insists on breaking long lines of HTML code at about 70 columns with hard returns. They don't show up when you view the page in a browser, of course, but if you like to edit the source, you might find yourself stuck with this infuriating feature that you can't switch off. You should also note that StarOffice is quite temperamental when it comes to converting "hand-coded" HTML—it just drops tags it does not know, replaces others and reformats quite a lot. Therefore you should only use it as an HTML authoring tool if absolutely necessary; it can really mess up your text. It's real strength is as a WYSIWYG editor.

The HTML pages produced by StarOffice include many of the latest HTML tags, designed for viewing with up-to-date browsers. In most cases, you can view pages containing the newer tags with older Web browsers, but they may look significantly different. If you are publishing your pages on the Internet, be aware that a small percentage of your audience has browsers that are so out of date that your pages will not display the way you intended. (The same could hold true on your intranet, but there you're likely to have some knowledge of and control over the situation.) The degree of difference is proportional to the age of the browser and the quantity and type of new tags on your page.

Note

In the Options Browser HTML dialog (which you open by selecting Tools, Options, Browser), you can determine how HTML pages are imported and exported from StarOffice; you also can determine the displayed font sizes of Web pages. The export settings affect the appearance of HTML documents you create in StarWriter/Web as well as documents you export in HTML format. Using the Options HTML Document Source Text dialog, you can define different colors for the source text items.

PART
VI

CH
25

In addition, StarWriter/Web exports proprietary StarOffice tags. Proprietary tags include special regions such as headers and footers and field commands such as author and (edit) date of the document. If other browsers don't recognize these tags, they are ignored, and only the text that appears between the tags is displayed. For example, a header created in StarWriter/Web is shown only once at the top when viewed with Netscape Navigator. By contrast, if you use the StarOffice browser, the header is a "true" header that retains its header status when the HTML document is saved as a StarOffice document.

Tip #486 from
Michael & Sarah

StarOffice's proprietary tags allow for some automation in creating HTML files. Say you want the date of your last change in the footer of every page. In this case, you can insert the Date field via the Fields dialog box. Simply select Insert, Fields, Other to open the Fields dialog, then click the Properties tab and select Modified in the Type list on the left and Date in the Select field in the middle. (If you want, you can also select a desired format in the Format box on the right.) This way, your footer always shows the date of the last change with any browser, but it is updated whenever you save your file.

In StarWriter/Web's HTML editing mode, the Stylist offers a variety of paragraph and text styles corresponding to HTML text formatting tags, as shown in Table 25.1. The best way to get a feel for how these tags modify the appearance of your text is to try them. Just apply them to some selected (highlighted) text, and click the Web Page Preview button.

Note

Remember that you can modify certain attributes of styles by right-clicking the style in the Stylist and then choosing Modify from the context menu. (For more details on working with the Styles and the Stylist, see Chapter 8, "Using Styles and Templates.")

TABLE 25.1   COMMON HTML STYLES IN STAROFFICE

SO Style/Command	HTML Tag	Browser Display
(Page property)	`<HTML>...</HTML>`	Invisible.
(Page property)	`<BODY>...</BODY>`	Invisible.
(Page property)	`<head> ...</head>`	Invisible. Browsers read heads to find out how to render the page (for example, which character set to use—Western or Chinese); search engine spiders glean a brief summary of the page (if added) from header information.
(Page property)	`<title>...</title>`	Invisible. The text you enter here appears in the browser's title bar when your page is viewed; it's also considered an indexing clue by search engines. This property (like many of the following) can be set by using the File, Properties dialog.
(Page property)	`<meta>...</meta>`	Invisible. The text you enter here conveys summary information about the content of a Web page; like the TITLE tag, this tag appears within the HEAD section. These tags contain the values from the File, Properties, Description dialog.
Heading 1	`<H1>...</H1>`	Very, very large, bold.
Heading 2	`<H2>...</H2>`	Very large, bold.
Heading 3	`<H3>...</H3>`	Large, bold.
Heading 4	`<H4>...</H4>`	Bold.
Heading 5	`<H5>...</H5>`	Small, bold.
Heading 6	`<H6>...</H6>`	Very small, bold.
Sender	`<address>...</address>`	Italicized text.

SO Style/Command	HTML Tag	Browser Display
(Text) Table	`<table ...>...</table>`	Table (visible only if cell border attributes are applied).
Bold	`<B>...</B>`	Bold text.
Italics	`<I>...</I>`	Italicized text.
Underline	`<U>...</U>`	Underlined text.
Bullets	`<ul><li>...</li><ul>`	Bulleted list items.
Numbering	`<ol><li>... </li><ol>`	Numbered list items.
Subscript	`<sub>...</sub>`	Text as subscript.
Superscript	`<super>...</super>`	Text as superscript.
Insert, Note	`<!—note text —>`	Invisible.
Insert, Section	`<DIV ID="Section name"> ...</div>`	Invisible.

Table 25.2 lists the proprietary StarOffice HTML paragraph tags.

TABLE 25.2   HTML PARAGRAPH STYLES

SO Style	HTML Style	What It Does
Citation	`<BLOCKQUOTE>... </BLOCKQUOTE>`	Blocks an indented text passage that can be used for quotes.
	`<DT x>...</ DT x>` `<DD x>...</DD x>` `(x = 1 - 3)`	Formats glossaries. For example, `DT1` labels the first-level subject in a glossary; `DD1` is applied to the accompanying text, and so on.
Horizontal Line	`<HR>`	Inserts a horizontal line that stretches across the width of the page.
Preformatted Text	`<PRE>...</PRE>`	Formats text in monospaced Courier font. You can use this style, for example, with unnumbered lists that are set apart from the rest of the text by an indent.

Table 25.3 lists StarOffice's logical text styles. Logical styles are contextual rather than explicit. You choose a logical style when you want to ensure that the meaning, rather than a specific look, is conveyed. Logical styles are becoming increasingly important as more browsers (such as the StarOffice browser) accept Cascading Style Sheets. With style sheets, you can easily make the text within your `<CODE>` tags blue, and the variables (`<VAR>`) green.

TABLE 25.3 HTML TEXT STYLES IN STAROFFICE

Text Style	Meaning
<ABBREV>	Abbreviation; identifies an abbreviation so that it can be treated specially in audio browsers
<ACRONYM>	Acronym; identifies an abbreviation so that it can be treated specially in audio browsers
<AU>	Author; identifies the author
<BLINK>	Blinks the contents (not well liked); this tag was introduced with MSIE and is not supported by Netscape Navigator
<CITE>	Citations, titles, and references; usually shown in italics
<CODE>	Code; shows programming code
<DEL>	Deleted text; text marked as deleted
<DFN>	Defining instance; marks the introduction of a new term
<EM>	Emphasis; depicted usually as underlined italicized text
<INS>	Inserted text; text marked as inserted
<KBD>	Keyboard text; what a user is expected to type in response to program output (for example, Courier)
<LANG>	Language
<PERSON>	Person; identifies personal names (virtually obsolete tag)
<Q>	Quote
<SAMP>	Sample; a sequence of literal characters
<STRONG>	Strong emphasis; usually rendered as bold text
<TT>	Teletype; displayed with a monospaced font such as Courier
<VAR>	Variable; used to distinguish variables from other programming code

In addition, StarWriter/Web uses the Internet Link and Visited Internet Link text styles, which format (by default) underlined characters in blue and red, respectively.

To edit HTML source code in StarWriter/Web, follow these steps:

1. Open the latest version of the HTML document that you want to edit, and be sure that you are in Edit mode (the Edit, File button on the function bar is active).

2. Click the Show HTML Source icon on the main toolbar or select View, HTML Source from the menu bar. StarWriter/Web opens in HTML editing mode; you can see different colored text. For example, comments appear in green, keywords appear in red, the actual code appears in blue. (You can customize the appearance of these various text elements by selecting Tools, Options, HTML Document, Source Text from the menu bar.)

3. Start editing the code. (Note that you can only use ASCII text; you can't use special characters.)

4. When finished, click the Show HTML Source icon again to see the results of your edits. When you like what you see, save the document.

PROJECT: CREATING A HOME PAGE—FAST!

Usually, when you're creating a home page, you have to proceed as follows:

1. Create a directory structure.

2. Create the HTML pages in StarOffice.

3. Create or locate the graphic elements that you want to include in your home page.

4. Convert the graphics or images into GIF or JPEG files.

5. Insert the graphic elements into your HTML document.

6. Test the appearance and navigation of the page(s) by looking at the document(s) through a variety of Web browsers.

7. Upload the pages to the Web server of your Internet service provider.

Each of these steps involves a series of subordinate steps. Sounds like a lot of work, doesn't it? However, for a faster way—if you just want to put up a quick résumé-style or "Hello World" home page—just follow these steps:

1. Open a new online document by selecting File, New, HTML Document from the menu bar.

2. Enter the text, and format it as desired.

3. Insert the graphics. It doesn't matter where they are located on your system. You can insert them by dragging and dropping them from the Beamer (select the theme folder in the Gallery) or by selecting Insert, Picture from the menu bar.

4. Save the online document locally as an HTML file. All links to graphics are shown as absolute in the HTML source code (click the Show HTML Source button on the main toolbar).

5. Choose Tools, Options, Browser, HTML. Then select Copy Local Graphics to Internet in the Export portion of the resulting dialog.

6. Connect to the Internet.

7. Select File, Save As from the menu bar to open the Save As dialog.

8. In the Filename text box, enter the complete URL of the Internet service provider that hosts your Web pages (for example,
   `http://www.myprovider.com/myname/homepages/index.htm`).

9. Click Save.

StarOffice converts all linked and/or embedded graphics in the current document to the GIF format. Links appear with relative paths. Then StarOffice uploads the document, together with all necessary graphics, to the indicated path.

Usually, when you're creating a home page, you have to proceed as follows:

1. Create a directory structure.
2. Create the HTML pages in StarOffice.
3. Create or locate the graphic elements that you want to include in your home page.
4. Convert the graphics or images into GIF or JPEG files.
5. Insert the graphic elements into your HTML document.
6. Test the appearance and navigation of the page(s) by looking at the document(s) through a variety of Web browsers.
7. Upload the pages to the Web server of your Internet service provider.

Each of these steps involves a series of subordinate steps. Sounds like a lot of work, doesn't it? However, for a faster way—if you just want to put up a quick resume-style or "Hello World" home page—just follow these steps:

1. Open a new online document by selecting File, New, HTML Document from the menu bar.
2. Enter the text, and format it as desired.
3. Insert the graphics. It doesn't matter where they are located on your system. You can insert them by dragging and dropping them from the Beamer (select the theme folder in the Gallery) or by selecting Insert, Picture from the menu bar.
4. Save the online document locally as an HTML file. All links to graphics are shown as absolute in the HTML source code (click the Show HTML Source button on the main toolbar).
5. Choose Tools, Options, Browser, HTML. Then select Copy Local Graphics to Internet in the Export portion of the resulting dialog.
6. Connect to the Internet.
7. Select File, Save As from the menu bar to open the Save As dialog.
8. In the Filename text box, enter the complete URL of the Internet service provider that hosts your Web pages (for example,
   `http://www.myprovider.com/myname/homepages/index.htm`).
9. Click Save.

StarOffice converts all linked and/or embedded graphics in the current document to the GIF format. Links appear with relative paths. Then StarOffice uploads the document, together with all necessary graphics, to the indicated path.

CHAPTER 26

ENHANCING HTML DOCUMENTS

In this chapter

WORKING WITH ATTRIBUTES

Even if your Web page does not contain a single image, you can still enhance its appearance with these simple, browser-independent tricks:

- Use different-sized headings.
- Apply different styles (bold, italics, or underline).
- Use different fonts and background colors.
- Insert tables to increase your layout options (see the section on "Working with Tables and Text Frames" in this chapter).

They are just a few of the many options that you can explore.

Note

Changing attributes in StarWriter/Web is virtually the same as changing attributes in StarWriter. For more details, see Chapters 6 through 8 and the section Editing HTML Files in StarWriter/Web in Chapter 25.

CHOOSING A BACKGROUND COLOR OR IMAGE

Most browsers let the user select a default color for the background and text of a Web page. To override the default background, you can specify a background color or image.

If you set your HTML export to MS Internet Explorer 4 or StarWriter (by selecting Tools, Options, Browser, HTML), you can also specify a background color for a selected area (text block or paragraph). Simply place the cursor in the paragraph to which you want to assign a background and click the Background Color button on the object bar to open a floating color palette. Select the desired color—StarOffice applies the color as soon as you select a color swatch. Note, however, that background paragraph colors can only be seen by users who browse with the StarOffice browser or IE4 or later.

Tip #487 from
Michael & Sarah

To quickly apply a background color to a certain area, place your cursor in a blank line and select a color. StarOffice assigns the selected color to the entire length of the (single-)line (paragraph. Now press Enter—each following line will have the same color.

To specify a background color for the entire page, select Format, Page to open the Page Style: HTML dialog. Next, click the Background tab, select the desired color swatch (you can sneak a preview of the color in the Preview window on the right), and then click OK. StarOffice assigns the selected color to the entire background.

If you want to refine your Web page with a background image, start by following these steps:

1. Select Page from the StarWriter/Web context menu, or choose Format, Page to open the Page Style: HTML dialog.

2. Click the Background tab, and then choose Graphic from the As drop-down list. The appearance of the Background tab changes from background color swatches to two new control areas (see Figure 26.1).

Figure 26.1
You can add a background texture or pattern by using the Page Style: HTML dialog box.

3. Click the Browse button to locate

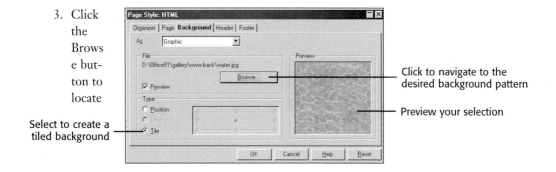

Select to create a tiled background

Click to navigate to the desired background pattern

Preview your selection

a background image. The Search Graphic dialog opens.

4. Double-click the www-back folder to open its contents in the list box; then click the desired background pattern or texture. Next, select the Preview option on the left of the dialog box to preview the selected file in the window on the right.

Note

The images in the www-back folder have been optimized for Web display. If you want to choose an image of your own, be sure it is fit for Web display in terms of size (less than 30KB). Otherwise, the page may take too long to download. For more information on images and the Web, see "Working with Graphics and Charts" in this chapter.

PART
VI

CH
26

5. When you've found the desired image, click Open to open the image and close the Search Graphic dialog. If the Preview option in the File portion of the Page Style: HTML dialog is selected, you see the image in the Preview area. Also, make sure the Tile option is selected in the Type portion of the dialog. This option ensures that the rectangular computer image you selected is repeated in a pattern, like tiles on a floor. (If you select Position, the image appears only in a certain area of your background, and you can define that area by clicking one of the white dots in the interactive area to the right. Note that options other than "Tile" are only available if you set HTML export to StarWriter, MS Internet Explorer 4.0, or Netscape Navigator 4.0 in the

Options Browser HTML dialog box. (For more details on HTML export, see "Customizing HTML Export" in Chapter 25, "Getting Started with StarWriter/Web.")

6. Click OK to accept your choice of background pattern or texture.

Note

Be careful not to make a poor background choice; your text should be easy to read. If your page includes more than a paragraph or two of text, a light-colored, smooth background goes a long way toward ensuring that the text will be read. A black background often makes for a dramatic look, but it's likely a poor choice if you've included too much copy for visitors to read. Just test it yourself and, if necessary, simplify.

Tip #488 from
Michael & Sarah

You can create your own bitmapped patterns and insert them as tiles by using the Bitmaps tab of the Area dialog in StarDraw or StarImpress. For more details, see "Creating Custom Gradient, Hatches, and Bitmaps" in Chapter 20, "Getting Sketchy with StarDraw." Or you can collect backgrounds from the Web—while browsing, just right-click the page that contains the background you like and select Save Background from the context menu.

WORKING WITH GRAPHICS AND CHARTS

Few Web sites consist entirely of words. Most contain visuals or Web graphics—photographs, illustrations, and charts. If used well, Web graphics can contribute considerably to your Web page or pages, creating a mood and helping visitors navigate the site. However, as with all Web design (or presentation) effects, too much of a good thing can be toxic. Cheesy clip art or images that are too big detract from the message you try to convey and, worse, slow the download time of the page or pages because visuals are separate graphic files that are downloaded independently of the text. The larger and more complex the visual, or the more colors it contains, the longer it takes to download.

Currently, only two graphics file formats are fully supported by browsers: GIF and JPEG. A third one, the PNG graphics format, is experiencing a limited but growing acceptance. StarWriter/Web not only enables you to use GIF, JPEG, or PNG files in your Web pages, but also to use clip art, charts, and drawings, which are automatically converted into GIF files when you save your page as an HTML file.

Tip #489 from
Michael & Sarah

When you're inserting graphics, be sure to use the GIF or JPEG format. Although other formats, such as TIFF or BMP, are automatically converted into GIF files when you save the online document as an HTML file (also inserting the proper HTML tags in the source code), converting images beforehand has the advantage of giving you more control over the conversion process. For more details on saving images for the Web, see "Choosing a File Format" in Chapter 21, "Creating and Modifying Images with StarImage."

Note

When you're creating pages and graphics, remember that not every computer user has a large screen monitor or high-end graphics card. While professional designers usually have machines that can display 24-bit images, many consumer machines have 8-bit color, which means they can display only 256 colors at a time. When you're creating your images, try to stick to a size of 800×600 pixels (or smaller) and 256 colors or less (for GIFs) or 24 bit (for JPEGs). Use only 16-bit colors for scanned photos and the like.

Note also that graphics can be anchored only to the left or right side of the page. If you want the graphic to appear in a certain area, you have to insert it in a table cell. To define the position for an inserted graphic, select Alignment from the context menu, or choose Format, Alignment from the menu bar.

Tip #490 from
Michael & Sarah

StarOffice gives you the option to insert pictures and anchor them to a character. Select and right-click the inserted or linked image and choose Picture from the context menu. Using the Type box of the Picture properties dialog, select Character from the Anchor to drop-down list. This option won't allow you to wrap text around your image; however, some Web page builders like it to feature beautiful pictures on an otherwise sparse page.

PREPARING AND INSERTING A WEB GRAPHIC

To insert a graphic into an online document, perform these steps:

1. Open the graphic that you want to include on your Web page in StarImage, and export it as a JPEG or GIF file—depending on the size and function of the graphic—to the graphics folder of your Web page directory.

2. Close StarImage, and switch to (or open) the online document in which you want to insert the graphic.

3. Place the insertion point at the place where you want to insert the graphic.

4. Select Insert, Picture to open the Insert Picture dialog.

5. Navigate to the folder that contains the desired Web graphic, select it, and then click the Properties button at the bottom left of the Insert Picture dialog box. Click the Preview option to sneak a peak of the selected file in the Preview window on the right of the dialog.

Note

If you click the Properties button on the bottom left of the Insert Picture dialog, you can access the Pictures properties dialog. Here, you can define text wrap, hyperlinks, borders, and other image attributes. However, you can also access this dialog later via the image's context menu or the menu bar.

6. Click Open.

StarOffice inserts the graphic at the location of the insertion point into the current document. If you want to edit the graphic after inserting it—for example, to change the size or color depth—it is best to do so in the program that created it.

ADDING HYPERLINKS TO WEB GRAPHICS

Sometimes you might want to add a hyperlink to an inserted graphic so that the user can click it and then be whisked away to another location of your page, site, or the Internet. To add a hyperlink to an embedded graphic, follow these steps:

1. Select the image to which you want to add a hyperlink.

2. Right-click the image and select Picture from the context menu, choose Format, Picture from the menu bar, or simply double-click the graphic.

3. Click the Hyperlink tab of the Pictures dialog to bring it to the fore; then click the Browse button to locate the document that you want to link with this file. Alternatively, you can also enter a Web URL to which you want the user to connect when clicking the graphic or a bookmark anchor within the same document. (For more details on adding bookmarks as anchors, see "Using Anchors to Jump to Specific Locations in Documents" in Chapter 25, "Getting Started with StarWriter/Web.")

> **Note**
>
> In the case of image maps (see "Using Image Maps" in this chapter), the URL and Frame options are defined directly in the image map. Hence, instead of filling out these boxes, you need to specify if it is server-side (Server) or client-side (Client) image map.

4. In the Name box, enter a name that you want to show in a pop-up box when the user rests the mouse pointer over the link.

5. If you're working with frames, select the target frame in which you want to open the target when the image is clicked. (For more details on frames, see "Working with Frames and Framesets" in this chapter.)

6. Click the Type tab, and select whether to anchor the graphic with the character or the paragraph. (For more information on anchors, see "Working with Objects" in Chapter 11, "Desktop Publishing with StarOffice.")

> **Tip #491 from**
> *Michael & Sarah*
>
> Note that you can also define a border for the image by using the Borders tab of the Pictures dialog. Defining borders for images in this dialog works like defining object borders in other StarOffice documents. For more details, see "Adding Borders and Background Color" in Chapter 7, "Formatting Text Documents."

ADDING SOUND AND VIDEO TO WEB PAGES

You can insert sound files, MIDI music files, or even AVI and MOV videos to your Web pages by selecting Insert, Object, Plug-in from the menu bar to open the Insert Plug-In dialog. In this dialog, you can click the Browse button to navigate to the media file you want to insert, select it, and then click OK.

> **Note**
>
> In the Options field of the Insert Plug-In dialog, you can add the parameters that are supposed to be taken over during the conversion process into an HTML document. Unless you know the exact parameters of the plug-in object, leave this box blank.

Keep in mind that the user must have the proper software to play back sounds and videos. Note also that you can insert the files as hyperlinks so that the user can download the files to his or her computer and play them back later.

StarOffice for Windows is compatible with most plug-ins that are offered for Netscape Navigator and Microsoft Internet Explorer. The program automatically searches for and recognizes the available plug-ins when launched. As a result, StarOffice recognizes any plug-in updates of the external Netscape or Microsoft browser.

If you don't have Netscape Navigator or MS Internet Explorer, the Installer of the new plug-in asks you for a location. In this case, select the Plugins folder in the StarOffice directory (Office51\Plugins). (Note that you may have to create this folder if it doesn't exist already.)

If you want to see which plug-ins are currently registered with StarOffice, select Tools, Options, Browser, File Types. Scrolling through the File Types list, you can see which application opens which file type by matching up the extensions with the application.

WORKING WITH TABLES AND TEXT FRAMES

PART
VI
CH
26

Tables are the key to good-looking Web sites. By using tables, you can carefully control the vertical and horizontal placement of text and graphic images when you're creating Web pages using WYSIAWYG (What You See Is Almost What You Get) HTML editors such as StarWriter/Web. In fact, tables are the basic tool for Web page design.

INSERTING TABLES

Inserting a new table in a StarWriter document is oh-so-easy. If you can live with a completely uniform table design aligned with the left and right margins, a standard table heading row, and all the columns and rows equally spaced, use the Insert Table icon on the main toolbar. Place the insertion point at the location in your document where you want to insert a table. Extended-click the Insert button on the main toolbar to open the Insert tear-off toolbar, and then move your pointer over the Table command (the third icon from the right). A submenu opens showing a 5×5 (columns and rows, respectively) table grid. Drag down and to the right to select the number of rows and columns for your table.

Note

You can drag down and to the right beyond the initial 5×5 grid. StarWriter automatically adds rows and columns to the preset template grid. The number of selected rows and columns is shown in the field underneath the grid.

When you release the mouse button, StarWriter inserts a standard table with a Table Heading style for each cell or column in the first row (if you have more than one row), a Table Contents style for all other cells, and a 0.05 pt border around each cell.

Note

Remember that StarOffice enables you to assign a background color or pattern or texture to individual table cells. Simply place the cursor in the cell to which you want to assign a background attribute, right-click and select Paragraph from the context menu. Using the Background tab, you can select a desired color or texture for the selected cell.

When you're inserting a table into an HTML document, you can define the table width as absolute or relative, depending on whether you want the table to change size if the user changes the size of the browser window. For example, if you define the width and height of a table as absolute, the table does not adjust in size when the user enlarges or reduces the browser window; instead, the user gets a vertical or horizontal scrollbar in order to be able to see the entire table. By contrast, if you select Relative, the table size adjusts itself proportionally with changes in the size of the browser window. (Of course, using relative widths can lead to visually unpleasing results if you put images and text in different sizes and amounts into the table, or overload some cells with lots of text or a huge image.)

You define this setting in the Properties portion of the Table Format dialog.

INSERTING TEXT FRAMES

To insert a text frame, place the insertion point at the location in your document where you want to insert the frame. Extended-click the Insert button on the main toolbar to open the Insert tear-off toolbar, and then click the Frame icon (the first icon from the right).

Note

When you're inserting text frames in online documents, you are limited by the HTML frame tags. This means you can anchor a frame only to the left or right side of a page. The frame, complete with its contents, is automatically linked as a JPEG file to the online document. If you want to resize the frame, you have to do so before exporting the document. If you selected the Netscape Navigator option in the Tools, Options, Browser, HTML dialog, you can export the frame with the respective Netscape-compatible HTML tags. For example, a multicolumn frame receives the <MULTICOL> tag; an empty frame receives the <SPACER> tag. (You can use empty frames as placeholders in an HTML document.) However, since these tags can only be interpreted by Netscape browsers, users who use other browsers will not be able to view the page as intended.

USING FRAMES AND FRAMESETS

Frames are dividers that separate the Web browser's viewing window into sections. Each section contains a separate Web page, enabling you to show more than one document (or page) at a time. A separate document, the *frameset*, defines the layout of the frames themselves.

By dividing the screen into two or more frames, you can simplify navigation for all your site's visitors. For example, your Web site's navigation bar, containing the links to major topics, can always appear along the top or left side of the screen. The actual content, by contrast, can appear in the frame to the left or underneath the navigation frame(s), not unlike the work area on the StarOffice desktop, which is framed by the extended Explorer to the left and the Beamer (and various toolbars) on the top. (For an example of the use of frames, visit the StarDivision Web site at `www.stardivision.com`.)

> **Note**
>
> StarOffice also enables you to insert floating frames that are not integrated into the frameset. However, this feature can only be displayed by the StarOffice browser and by MS Internet Explorer 4 or later. Hence, if you're not sure which browsers your users have, you should avoid these features. If your pages are intended for your company's intranet, you typically have more control over the use of browsers. For example, if the company is using the StarOffice browser for its intranet, you can use whatever features you like—within moderation of course, so as not to lose the most important point of your page: the message or information.

Table 26.1 describes the elements of the Frameset object bar.

TABLE 26.1   USING THE FRAMESET OBJECT BAR

Click This Button...	If You Want To...
Edit Frameset	Toggle the Frameset Edit mode on and off.
Home Name	Enter a name for the active frame.
file:///C|/My Documents/outline.htm Contents	Enter the Content file for the current frame.
Split Frame Horizontal	Split the current frame horizontally. The frame is split into two equally sized frames.
Split Frame Vertical	Split the current frame vertically. The frame is split into two equally sized frames.

PART
VI
CH
26

continues

TABLE 26.1   CONTINUED

Click This Button...	If You Want To...
Split Frameset Horizontal	Insert a new horizontal frame under the current frame.
Split Frameset Vertical	Insert a new vertical frame under the current frame.
Frame Properties	Open the Floating Frame dialog. Using this dialog, you can assign content files to each frame, as well as define the properties of each frame.
Frameset Spacing	Increase the spacing between individual frames. Note that this option is available only if the spacing was not inherited from a previous frameset.
HTML Source	See (and edit) the HTML source code.

CREATING A FRAMESET

To include frames in an online document, perform the following steps:

1. Select File, New FrameSet. You then see a blank frameset (actually one frame) that is surrounded by a dark blue border, indicating that the current frame is active. Across the top is the Frameset object bar. (Note that all commands necessary to edit a frameset are also available on the context menu of the currently active frame.)

2. Using the Split Frame Vertical and Split Frame Horizontal buttons on the object bar, you can divide the current frameset into separate frames. For example, if you want to divide the frameset into three frames, first select Split Frame Vertical, click the frame to the right, and then select Split Frame Horizontal. To adjust the size of the individual frames, just click the dividing border, and drag it with your mouse. The result is shown in Figure 26.2. (If you make a mistake while creating your frameset, click the Undo button on the function bar to cancel your recent step(s).)

Note

You can control whether the selected frame has a border by using the Properties tab of the Floating Frame dialog box. To open this dialog box, click the Frame Properties icon on the object bar.

3. Click the Frame Properties icon on the object bar, or select Properties from the context menu of the currently active frame to open the Floating Frame dialog box. In this dialog box, you can edit the properties of the currently active frame.

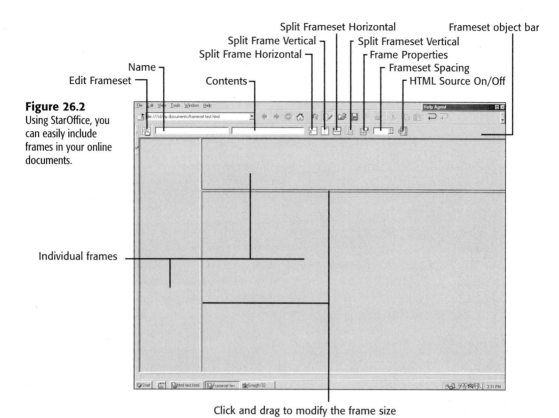

Figure 26.2
Using StarOffice, you can easily include frames in your online documents.

Split Frameset Horizontal
Split Frame Vertical ￢
Split Frame Horizontal ￢
Frameset object bar
Split Frameset Vertical
Frame Properties
Name ￢
Frameset Spacing
Edit Frameset ￢
Contents ￢
HTML Source On/Off

Individual frames

Click and drag to modify the frame size

4. Use the Properties tab to add content to the current frameset (see Figure 26.3). Start by entering a name for the selected frame. This name appears when the user rests the mouse pointer over the frame. Click the ellipse (...) button to navigate to the previously prepared HTML document that you want to occupy the space of this frame. Your other options include the following:

- **Scroll Bar**—Here, you can select whether you want to show a scrollbar (by clicking On or Off) or if you want to leave it to the browser to blend in a scrollbar automatically if necessary (by clicking Automatic).

- **Border**—Here, you can define whether you want to show the standard frame border or not (by clicking On or Off). If the current frame was created out of a previous frame, you can also select Inherited to take over the previous settings.

- **Distance from Contents**—Here, you can specify the horizontal (Width) or vertical (Height) distance between frame and content or accept the Default settings.

Figure 26.3
On the Properties tab, you can specify the content of the active frame.

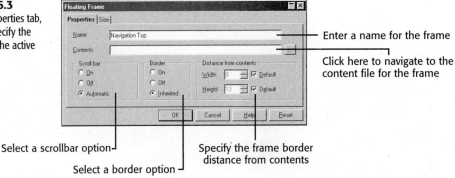

Enter a name for the frame

Click here to navigate to the content file for the frame

Select a scrollbar option

Select a border option

Specify the frame border distance from contents

5. Using the Size tab, you can define the width and height of the active frame in relation to the other frames (see Figure 26.4). Select the Pixels option to define an absolute value for the frame. Choose Percent if you want to specify a size relative to the overall frameset. Mark the Relative option if you want this particular frame to share the rest of the available frame space with other frames whose size has been specified as relative. If you select the Resizable option, you give the viewer of the page the option to change the size of the frame if so inclined.

Tip #492 from
Michael & Sarah

To change the space (or border) between frames, use the Frameset Spacing spin box on the object bar.

Figure 26.4
You can use the Size tab to define the width and height of the active frame.

6. When you're finished, click OK to accept your changes. Repeat steps 3 through 5 for all the other frames.

SAVING A FRAMESET

Saving a frameset works like saving any other document in StarOffice, with the proviso that the Save and Save As commands in the File menu have been replaced by the Save Frameset and Save Frameset As commands, respectively. You can click the Save button on the

Function bar; select File, Save Frameset from the menu bar; or press Ctrl+S on your keyboard. The first time you try to save a new, previously unsaved frameset document, StarWriter automatically opens the Save As dialog. In this dialog, you can enter a name for your document in the Filename text box, choose HTML (FrameSet) from the File Type drop-down list, and then select a directory where you want to save the file or create a new (sub)folder within a directory of your choice. When you're finished, select Save to return to your document.

Editing Framesets

When you're editing framesets, you have to distinguish between editing the actual frameset document (which contains the information on the individual frames and the content inside the frames) and editing the content of the individual frames.

If the current window is a frameset, Ctrl+click the Edit File icon on the function bar (twice, if necessary, but don't double-click) to bring up the Frameset object bar. You then can use this object bar to edit the current set. (Note that the Edit Frameset icon is pressed, which means you are in the Frameset Edit mode.)

If you want to edit the content of a particular frame, click inside the frame that contains the content that you want to edit, and then click the Edit File icon on the function bar. StarWriter/Web opens the document within the frame so that you can edit and modify it as desired. When you're finished, simply save the edited document by clicking the Save icon on the function bar.

Note

If you load a frameset from the Internet, StarOffice alerts you that the documents are read-only. You can still modify them and then save them as copies in a location of your choice by selecting File, Save As from the menu bar. If you have access to the Web server that contains the online documents, you can also save the changes directly to the server by clicking the Save button on the function bar. For more details on saving and uploading HTML files, see "Updating HTML Files Online" in Chapter 27, "Publishing Your Work on the Web."

PART

VI

CH

26

If you want to edit the contents of a frameset, you first have to save the set, reload it, and then click the Edit File icon on the function bar. At this point, you can click the frame whose content you want to edit.

Defining a Target Frame

To be prepared for the time when a user clicks a link inside a frame, you have to define a target frame in which the target will be opened. Although you can give each frame individual names, you can also use the StarOffice default names. This way, you can quickly define in which frame the content is supposed to appear.

You define target frames for hyperlinks by using the Target Frame icon on the hyperlink bar or by using the Frame drop-down list on the Hyperlink tab of the selected object's Properties dialog box. The following are your options:

- **_self**—Makes the link load in its own window.
- **_blank**—Opens the target in a new browser window that appears in front of the previous one.
- **_parent**—Opens the target in a frame that is one level up in the frame hierarchy. If no parent frame is available, the target is opened in the same frame.
- **_top**—Blows away all frames and takes you to the intended URL in a clean browser window. If none exists, the target is opened in the same frame.

USING IMAGEMAPS

Instead of including individual buttons, icons, and text links to the remaining pages of a Web site, many Home pages use an image map.

An *imagemap* is just a regular image that contains several invisible hyperlinks. Unlike a regular linked image, which leads to only one destination, an imagemap can lead to several. Visitors to your Web page activate the different hyperlinks by clicking different places (or hotspots) inside the image. Depending on the link, your visitors are then taken to another page in the Web site or to a location on the Internet. While image maps look impressive and provide visual orientation, they may also result in an increase in downloading time for your visitors. Also, when you add new links or pages to your site, you may have to completely redo your image map.

Tip #493 from
Michael & Sarah

When you're adding an image to a Web page, consider adding a list of matching text hyperlinks as well. Visitors who browse the Web with their browser's image-loading function turned off cannot see both regular images and imagemaps; therefore, they must rely on the text hyperlinks so that they can move around.

EXPLORING THE IMAGE MAP EDITOR

StarOffice comes with a nifty tool—the Image Map Editor, shown in Figure 26.5—that enables you to turn regular images into imagemaps by drawing hotspots on the images of your choice using basic drawing tools.

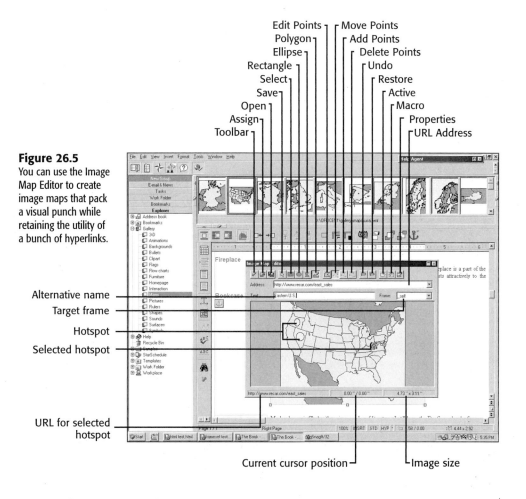

Figure 26.5
You can use the Image Map Editor to create image maps that pack a visual punch while retaining the utility of a bunch of hyperlinks.

Table 26.2 describes the elements of the Image Map Editor toolbar.

TABLE 26.2 USING THE IMAGE MAP EDITOR TOOLBAR

Click This Button...	If You Want To...
✓ Apply	Apply the changes you made to the embedded graphic. It's good practice to click Apply after each individual change you make.
📂 Open	Open a previously saved imagemap file.
📋 Save	Save your imagemap to a file.

continues

TABLE 26.2 CONTINUED

Click This Button...	If You Want To...
Select	Switch to the Select mode, which enables you to select existing imagemap objects.
Rectangle	Define a rectangular hotspot in your imagemap. To draw a rectangle, click and drag in the desired area of your image. If you press Shift while dragging, you can draw a square.
Ellipse	Define an elliptical hotspot in your imagemap. To draw an ellipse, click and drag in the desired area of your image. If you press Shift while dragging, you can draw a circle.
Polygon	Define a hotspot in the shape of a polygon. To draw a polygon, click and drag in the desired area. If you press Shift while clicking, you can limit the angles of the polygon to multiples of 45 degrees.
Freeform Polygon	Draw a freeform line that defines the hotspot. To draw a freeform shape, click and drag in the desired area. When you release the mouse button, the polygon closes automatically.
Edit Points	Edit the nodes or control points of the polygons or Bézier curves. (Note that this option is available only if you used the Polygon or Freeform Polygon drawing tool.)
Move Points, Add Points, Delete Points	Move, add, or delete selected points in a polygon.
Undo	Undo the last action or change.
Restore	Restore the last change that you canceled using the Undo button.
Active	Change the selected hotspot from active to inactive. Normally, you don't need this button when creating your imagemap. However, it does come in handy when you're updating an imagemap or temporarily suspending a link, and so on.
Macro	Assign a macro or script to the currently selected hotspot.

Click This Button...	If You Want To...
![icon] Properties	Open the Description dialog of a selected hotspot. The URL text box, Alternative Text box, and Frame drop-down list options work the same as the Address, Name (Text), and Frame boxes in the Image Map Editor. The only additional text box in this dialog is the Name box, which enables you to specify a name for the selected area of the image. Note that this name is for your own reference only and does not appear in the graphic. When you rest the mouse pointer over an imagemap hotspot, you see a pop-up text box that contains the name that is listed in the Text box in the Image Map Editor and the Alternative Text box in the Description dialog.

CREATING IMAGEMAPS

Creating an imagemap is straightforward; all you need is a graphic and the StarOffice Image Map Editor. To create an imagemap, follow these steps:

1. Select the graphic or image that you want to convert into an imagemap.

Tip #494 from
Michael & Sarah

You don't want to turn just any old image into an imagemap. Because hotspots are invisible to visitors to your page, the image you choose should clearly indicate where to click—either with the help of a visual metaphor or with text labels on the image.

2. Select Edit, Image Map to open the Image Map Editor.

3. Using the drawing tools (Rectangle, Ellipse, Polygon, Freeform Polygon) define the area(s) for the hotspot(s) in the image.

4. Click the Properties button to open the Description dialog. In this dialog, you can enter the URL and an alternative name for the target, as well as select a target frame in which the target will be opened when clicked. Alternatively, you can enter the same information in the Address, Name (Text), and Frame boxes in the Image Map Editor (refer to Figure 26.5).

Note

If you don't add an alternative name for the target, the browser displays the URL when the user rests the mouse pointer over the hotspot.

5. After each change, click the Apply icon to safeguard against data loss.

6. When you're finished, close the Image Map Editor.

Note

The Image Map Editor is a floating window that you can leave open and place anywhere on your desktop while working.

PART

VI

CH

26

Tip #495 from
Michael & Sarah

You can also use imagemaps in a document to lead users to other StarOffice documents, or you can create an "imagemap" reference table or table of contents.

INSERTING A SCROLLING TEXT MARQUEE

A *marquee* is a rectangular banner that contains scrolling text. You can use marquees to highlight announcements or other important information on your Web page. Unfortunately, marquees are supported only by the StarOffice browser and Microsoft Internet Explorer; other browsers show (part of) the text only as static text.

Note

Of course, you can include scrolling banners in other ways. For example, you can add a banner by inserting into your page a Java applet, which is a special mini-program written in the Java programming language.

To insert a marquee, follow these steps:

1. Click the Text Animation icon on the main toolbar, and then click and drag to draw a rectangle in your online document.

Note

The Options dialog must show a browser that supports the marquee.

2. Enter the desired text inside the text box.

3. Open the Text dialog box by selecting Text from the object's context menu or by selecting Format Text from the menu bar.

4. Click the Text Animation tab, and then select an effect from the drop-down list box in the Effects portion of the tab. Your options include No Effect, Blink, Scroll Through, Scroll Back and Forth, and Scroll In.

Note

The direction (and presumably many of the other options) cannot be saved with HTML files. According to one German HTML source (http://www.teamone.de/selfhtml) only scrolling and "bouncing" sideways is possible. The other options only exist with the native StarOffice format.

5. Fine-tune your text animation by using the following options:

   - **Start Inside**—Select this option if you want the text to be visible at the start of the effect. (Note that this option is not available if you select Scroll In from the Effects drop-down list.)

   - **Stop Inside**—Select this option if you want the text to be visible at the end of the effect.

- **Count**—In this area, you can specify the number of times that the text effect will take place. If you select Continuous, the animation appears as an endless loop.
- **Delay**—Here, you can define the speed of the effect in milliseconds. If you select Automatic, the program adjusts the speed of the repetition automatically.

6. When you're finished, click OK. To see the animation effect, click anywhere outside the marquee box.

ADDING FORMS

Another way to enhance your Web page is to use interactive forms. When your page uses forms, Web visitors fill in fields, either by entering information or selecting an item from a list. After the visitors complete the form, they click a button to submit the information.

StarOffice not only comes with the built-in capability to create forms, it also includes templates that already contain forms and that you can edit as desired.

Working with forms is virtually identical across all major StarOffice modules and is discussed in detail in Chapter 34, "Creating Forms for Easy Data Entry."

PLAYING BY THE RULES

The following tips will help you improve your HTML documents:

- Use graphics sparingly; consider using two smaller graphics instead of a big one. This way, you can reduce the download time of Web pages for surfers with slower connections.
- Watch the size of your image. Although imagemaps are rather sophisticated, they can result in longer download times, depending on the size of the map. Hence, you should always provide text links in addition to your imagemap.
- Make navigation within a document easier by providing internal links and anchors (bookmarks), which enable the users to quickly browse through the available information.
- Use gimmicks (such as the scrolling text marquee) and frames sparingly. You don't want to distract the visitors from the actual content of the site.
- Be sure your Web page(s) appear the same (or at least close) in different browsers. As you learned in Chapter 25, "Getting Started with StarWriter/Web," not all browsers support all HTML tags—which means not all functions and features that work in StarOffice also come out in Netscape Navigator or Microsoft Internet Explorer.
- Be careful when you're using graphics, Java applets, and other items that you may have gleaned from the Web. Ask the original owner (from the source where you got them) if you can use them, or else you might be in copyright violation.

PART
VI

CH
26

- Remember that other computer users may have slower connections and smaller monitors than you do. Remembering this fact should influence the size of graphics and the width of the pages that you create.

- Features such as horizontal scrolling are nice and encourage the users to interact. However, you should keep an eye on the width of your page and the size of your images. Horizontal scrolling considerably disturbs concentration.

- Keep an eye on the structure and organization of the content of your page(s). Here, as in print publishing, it pays to sketch out an outline as well as a directory structure for the contents of your Web page(s).

- Concentrate on creating smaller documents that load faster than longer documents. If you can't avoid using longer documents, alert your visitors to this fact with a small note at the top of your page (for example, `Due the nature of this document, you may experience a longer download time than usual. Please be patient.`).

- Be sure that the contrast between the font color and the background color or texture of your document is strong. It also pays to work with the Stylist to ensure that the same elements (lists, headings, and so on) are formatted consistently.

- Be sure to test your site offline to locate broken (or dead) links in advance.

- Stick with one way of labeling your files. Windows-based servers don't distinguish between caps and lowercase letters; UNIX-based servers do. To be on the safe side, use only lowercase letters when naming your files.

- Encourage feedback. You don't have to create an interactive form. All you need is a "mailto:" link that leads to your email.

CHAPTER 27

PUBLISHING YOUR WORK ON THE WEB

In this chapter

PREPARING YOUR WORK FOR THE WEB

Creating Web pages is one thing; making sure that they actually appear as you intended is another. As a rule of thumb, you should always test your pages on your own machine prior to publishing them on the Web. Just collect all your files, and locate the start or home page (or any other HTML file you want to test) by double-clicking it in the Beamer or on your desktop. StarOffice automatically opens the page in the StarOffice browser (or the default browser). You then can click through the various links to test them. If all files have been saved in paths relative to each other, you should be able to browse through all links (except for external ones that target other Internet sites).

One of the most difficult aspects of creating, testing, and transferring your Web pages relates to making sure that all the links remain intact. Remember that most Web pages refer to a number of elements besides the HTML file—most commonly image files for photos, illustrations, charts, tables, slides, buttons, lines, and so on. The pages also might have sound and video files and other objects that you've specified. In most cases, your pages have links to other Web pages. All these files must be on the Web server or must point to a location that the Web server has access to. They must also be in the exact location specified in the Web page (.htm or .html file) that you've created, whether that location is absolute or relative to the page being viewed. If they are not located where you expect them to be, you have what's called a *broken link*, where an image doesn't appear, another page doesn't open, or something else that was expected doesn't take place.

For sites with a dozen files or fewer, a simple solution exists. You can just put all your files in the same subdirectory. That way, your links are simple—you need to specify only the filename—and when you're transferring files, subdirectory structures between machines match up.

For more complex sites, you can upload or publish an entire folder and its subfolders rather than try to determine what elements each Web page includes and whether they match the files in the folders. This is particularly true in StarImpress-created Web pages, where numerous items are created and added to your folder, such as navigation buttons and the slide images themselves. It is also true with Web pages you create in StarWriter/Web, and especially if you use the Web Page Wizard or insert charts, bullets, lines, or backgrounds. These elements are all converted to renamed GIF files and placed in the folder where you save your Web page file.

If you specified the use of a relative path for an image or other file when creating a page, then you must upload that file to the exact relative location on the Web server that you specified. If the relative path specified is a subfolder of your Web pages folder on your hard drive, then the link should remain intact and work correctly.

→ For more information on relative and absolute links, **see** "Planning Your Site and Managing Your Files," **p. 944**.

Caution

If you're a Windows user (Linux users know this fact already), remember that many Internet Service Providers (ISPs) and businesses use UNIX/Linux-based Web servers. UNIX/Linux-based systems are case sensitive when it comes to reading filenames. For example, if your link refers to a file called `background.gif`, but the file you upload is called `Background.gif`, you will get a broken link–which means the desired background will not be displayed.

SAVING AND TESTING YOUR WEB PAGE

Always test your pages on your local machine before uploading them to the Web server by following these steps:

1. Close all other open StarOffice documents.

2. Switch to Offline mode (click the Offline icon on the function bar to disable it).

3. Select File, Open and locate the start or opening page of your site (for example, start.html or index.html or whatever name you gave it). You may have to select HTML in the File Type drop-down list to see the file.

4. Click all links on your page to see if they connect as desired (if you've inserted an absolute link to another Web page that is not part of your site, you will get a connection error message, since you are working offline).

5. If possible, look at your page with different Web browsers. As mentioned in the sections "StarOffice and the Net" and StarOffice as an HTML Authoring Tool" in Chapter 25, "Getting Started with StarWriter/Web," HTML tags are browser dependent. In other words, what you say may not be what you want when you look at the same page through different browsers.

6. When all works fine, you're ready to upload the files and folder(s) to your Web server (see the section "Publishing via FTP" in this chapter).

Tip #496 from
Michael & Sarah

As soon as you've transferred your files from your development machine to the host server, be sure to log on to the site as a normal user. See whether the site works. Test all links to make sure that they go where they're intended to go. Nothing is more embarrassing than a promising link that is broken. Make sure that you can easily move around on each page and between pages. Also, try accessing from a computer with a slow modem connection or a larger or smaller monitor to see how usable it is.

Tip #497 from
Michael & Sarah

If you want to know how many people visit your page(s), or if you want to announce to your visitor that she is the "xth visitor" to this site, consider installing a Web counter. For details go to `http://www.digits.com`.

PART

VI

CH

27

GETTING READY TO PUBLISH

Whether you're creating a personal or topical page that a few friends and/or co-workers see, or whether you're creating a site for a business or intranet, the actual process of publishing your Web pages involves two basic steps. First, you need to get Web server space; then you need to transfer your files from your local machine to the server.

GETTING WEB SERVER SPACE

A *Web server* is a computer that is connected to the Web and running special software that allows it to provide information to Web users. Only if you create your own Web server or place your files on someone else's server can your site really become part of the Web. If you're creating pages for your company's intranet or Web site, chances are server space already exists, and all you need to do is connect to the server and upload the files. If you're publishing your own Web site, however, you need to choose a server space provider that gives you reasonable pricing and support and room to grow.

Tip #498 from *Michael & Sarah*	Most Internet service providers and online services automatically provide server space for their client's home pages. This space can range anywhere from 2MB to 8MB or more. If you want room to grow or establish a business site, however, you should investigate other options with your ISP. Alternatively, you can host your site with your own Web server.

TRANSFERRING FILES ACROSS THE INTERNET

Loading files over the Internet in StarOffice is easy if you know the URL (address) or can browse to it. You may never realize how powerful this capability is until you see a Web page you would like to edit and find yourself able to switch StarOffice into Edit mode with a single click of the mouse. Suddenly, your "Web browser" has a blinking cursor in the text and new palettes of buttons for changing font attributes and inserting objects. Nice stuff.

To save your changes (or upload HTML files) to a destination on the Internet (rather than on your computer's hard drive), however, you first need to establish a service for transferring files between your local machine and the Web server or host. In short, you need an FTP account.

PUBLISHING VIA FTP

FTP, or File Transfer Protocol, is an Internet service for transferring files between different machines. FTP made the Internet popular even before the World Wide Web caught on. Dozens of FTP programs are in use for Windows, Macintosh, and UNIX, and each has its own pluses and minuses. As a StarOffice user, however, you don't have to worry about downloading third-party FTP software before transferring your files to a Web server. All you have to do is set up an FTP account in StarOffice.

Setting Up an FTP Account

The process and principles of creating an FTP account are pretty much the same as creating a mail account, regardless of its type. Before you create your FTP account, you need to know the following:

- The name or IP address of the FTP server
- The name of the FTP account (if required)
- The username and password for the FTP account
- The start directory

> **Note**
>
> There is a problem when your computer is connected to the Internet through a proxy server. You will only be able to connect in so-called HTML view, which does not allow file upload. There's no tree view of your server.

After you have all your FTP account information at your fingertips, follow these steps:

1. Select the group and/or folder where you plan to store your account.
2. Right-click to open the extended Explorer context menu.
3. From the New submenu, select FTP Account. The Properties of FTP Account dialog opens to the Server tab.
4. Enter your FTP server name (without the preceding `ftp://`), username, and password, as shown in Figure 27.1. You also can fill in FTP account information (if required by the FTP server) and the start directory (the initial path that opens when you connect). If the FTP server requires you to log in with a username and password, you can enter them as well in the respective text boxes or in the Server text box (for example, `ftp://user:password@host:port/dateiname`).

> **Note**
>
> Don't click the Log In as Anonymous check box. Typically, if you log in as *anonymous*, you only have read-only rights when connecting to an FTP server.

Tip #499 from
Michael & Sarah

If possible, specify a path in the Start Directory text box. This way, you save yourself a double-click when locating the directory of your site.

5. Click the General tab, and enter a name for the account. If you don't assign a name, StarOffice automatically names it after your FTP server.

Figure 27.1

Before you can transfer files across the Internet, you first have to create an FTP account.

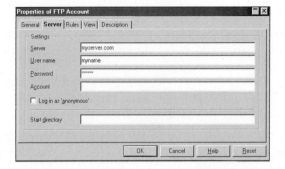

Note

Using the Rules and View tabs of the Properties of FTP Account dialog, you can create filters that control the type of information that will be displayed subordinate to the current FTP account in the Explorer group. Using these tabs is identical to using the Rules and View tabs of your mail or news accounts and is discussed in detail in the section "Using Filters to Manage Files" in Chapter 5, "Managing Files, Folders, and Mail," and the section "Techniques for Managing Mail and News" in Chapter 29, "Communicating with StarMail and StarDiscussion." However, most of the functions on these tabs are more appropriate for mail and news accounts than for FTP accounts.

6. Click the Description tab to select the amount of detail you want to see on the desktop when opening an FTP account or folder, or when clicking the Properties icon on the Desktop object bar. (If you defined a display style for an item, select the Apply Styles/Templates if Existing check box.) As with the Rules and Views tab, most of the options here are more relevant to mail and news accounts than to an FTP account. In this case, select Date, Read, Marked, Size, and Title.

7. Click OK to confirm your entries. Clicking Reset returns the settings to the way they were on opening the dialog and leaves the dialog open. Clicking Cancel returns the settings to their original state and closes the dialog.

You are now the proud owner of an FTP account, which enables you to transfer files via drag and drop from the StarOffice desktop. You can also load a file directly from an FTP site, start editing it, and know that StarOffice will save it back to the same place.

Note

If you only want to download files from a public FTP server, you don't have to create an FTP account in StarOffice. Just enter the ftp server address in the Load URL box on the function bar (for example, `ftp://ftp.ncsa.uiuc.edu/`) and press Enter.

If you frequently access a particular server, you can also create a simple link in a StarOffice Explorer group. For example, right-click the desired group and select New, Link from the context menu. In the Properties of Link dialog that appears enter the complete URL of the FTP server on the General tab. However, when connecting to the ftp server, you may be required to enter your email address as password, or click the Log In as Anonymous check box.

LOADING FILES FROM A WEB SERVER OR FTP SITE

To load a file from an FTP site, double-click the FTP account item in the Explorer group (or in whichever group you created it). StarOffice connects to the FTP server, updates the contents of the account, and then opens it on your desktop, displaying the current files and folders on the Web server. (Remember that you only need those FTP entries if you want to manage and upload files. If you just want to download files from a public software collection, for example, or a patch for an application, simply enter the URL of the ftp server in the URL field, or create a simple link to the ftp server by right-clicking in a StarOffice Explorer group, selecting New, Link from the context menu, and then entering the complete URL on the General tab of the dialog that appears.)

> **Note**
>
> If you open your FTP account when you're not connected to your ISP or network, you might get a `Connection Failure` error message, or you may be prompted with your system's dial-up networking dialog; the program seems unpredictable this way. If you receive the connection error message, you can just dial up your ISP manually and then open your FTP account. If you are connected but are not in Online mode, the program sends you a message and asks whether you want to go online. When you are connected and online, StarOffice logs in to your FTP server.

TRANSFERRING FILES VIA FTP

Transferring files with StarOffice from your local machine to a Web server is a simple matter of dragging and dropping.

> **Note**
>
> The following steps assume that you are working with the StarOffice Explorer in Hierarchical view. To switch views in the Explorer group(s), right-click the title bar of the Explorer group, and then select Hierarchical from the context menu.

To transfer files from your development machine to a Web server, follow these simple steps:

1. Double-click to open the FTP account that connects to the Web server. Depending on whether you specified an initial path on the Server tab of the Properties of FTP account dialog, you will see the entire server directory or the specified folder.

2. Navigate to the folder that contains your Web directory or folders.

3. Open the Workplace item (located in the Explorer group), and navigate to the folder that contains the files and subfolders for your Web site. You now have two options (see Figure 27.2):

   - If you want to move individual files, open the Beamer (by clicking the Beamer icon on the function bar or by pressing Ctrl+Shift+B) to show the contents of the selected Workplace folder; then click and drag the selected file(s) to the FTP desktop area.

PART

VI

CH

27

■ If you want to move a folder (including subfolders), select the folder in the Explorer, and then drag and drop it on the FTP desktop area.

As soon as you release the mouse button, the selected files or folder is uploaded to the Web server.

Figure 27.2

Transferring files from your system to a Web server is a simple matter of drag and drop. You can drag and drop individual files (from the Beamer) or an entire folder (from the Explorer) to the desktop.

FTP account

Beamer with HTML files in the selected folder

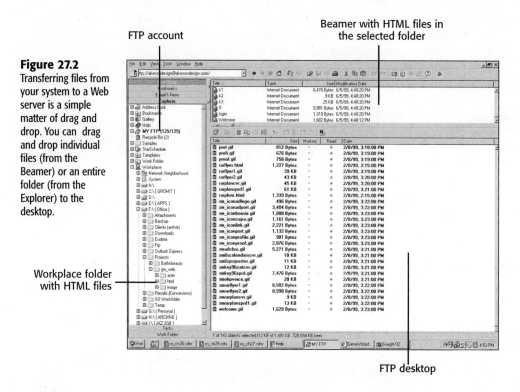

Workplace folder with HTML files

FTP desktop

Be careful when you're dragging files or folders to the FTP desktop. If you release the mouse button over an existing folder, you will drop the selected files or folder into that folder. Also, if your desktop area is full with files and folders, you might have to drag the selected files or folders to the bottom of the desktop area to be able to drop them. StarOffice automatically scrolls down to make room (whitespace) for them.

UPDATING HTML FILES ONLINE

If you only want to update an existing Web page by entering new text or deleting old text, you don't have to use FTP to transfer your files to a Web server. If you have direct access to the Web server that hosts the HTML documents, you can just load the page you want to update in the StarOffice browser, perform the desired changes, and save them to the server.

To update HTML files online, follow these steps:

1. Open the page you want to update in the StarOffice browser by entering the URL in the Load URL box on the function bar, and press Enter. The StarOffice browser loads the page as read-only.

2. After StarOffice has retrieved the page in its entirety, click the Edit File button on the function bar. StarOffice reloads the page, this time around in Edit mode.

Note If the page consists of a frameset, you first have to click the part of the frame that you want to edit. Then you can press Ctrl and click the Edit File icon.

3. Modify the page (or frame) as desired.

4. When you're finished, click Save on the function bar to save the changes to the server of your ISP. The User Name and Password Required dialog appears.

5. Enter your username and password. If you want the program to remember your username and password in the future, select the Remember Password option in the lower right of the dialog.

6. Click OK to save your changes directly to the server.

Note If you've added additional graphics, and if they are located on your system relative to the folder that contains the HTML documents and subfolders (and mimics the folder tree on the server), be sure to select the Copy Local Graphics to Internet option in the Export portion of the Options Browser HTML dialog (which you open by selecting Tools, Options, Browser).

PROJECT: PUTTING YOUR PAGES TO WORK

As soon as you've transferred your files from your development machine to the host server, be sure to log on to the site as a normal user. To see if the site works, test all links to make sure that they go where they're intended to go. Nothing is more embarrassing than a promising link that is broken. Make sure that you can easily move around on each page and between pages. Also, try accessing the page(s) from a computer with a slow modem connection or a larger or smaller monitor to see how usable it is. Are images or logos cut off? Do you have to scroll to get to the vital information?

Also, note your reactions as if you were a new user. Is there anything confusing about the way the information is presented?

TEAMING UP AT WORK

NETWORKING WITH STAROFFICE

StarOffice is designed with today's networked world in mind—whether you're a single user connecting via an Internet service provider (ISP) or an organization with a local area network (LAN) or intranet. It's using StarOffice on a LAN or intranet, however, that fully exploits the power and efficiency of the integrated desktop. This chapter explores features that are particularly useful or specifically designed for use on a network.

INSTALLING STAROFFICE ON A NETWORK

You can load any version of StarOffice for use on a network (or by multiple users on a single machine), using the /net installation option. Once you have installed the program using the /net option, each user then runs the setup program to create an individual installation on his or her client machine. In a workgroup setting, StarOffice can be installed locally on each user's individual workstation or on a network server for shared access.

If you work in a large organization, you should probably purchase StarOffice Application Server, a version of StarOffice that is specifically designed for running StarOffice on an office network. The StarOffice Application Server uses a specialized protocol that controls the load on the server, network, and client and determines which tasks should be run on which computer. This protocol redistributes the CPU load in a way that enables you to effectively use older computers on your network. Most files are stored on the server, and most tasks are executed there as well. For the user, this process occurs unnoticed, giving the impression that the computer is much faster than it actually is. Updating and supporting StarOffice are also more convenient this way.

→ For details on installing StarOffice using the /net option, **see** "Installing StarOffice for Multiple Users or On a Network," **p. 1376**, and "Individual Installation from a Server," **p. 1377**.

WORKING WITH DOCUMENTS ON YOUR NETWORK

Opening, saving, and closing documents on a network are no different than when you use StarOffice as a single user. However, some of StarOffice's special features can make working with documents on a network faster and easier. The following sections offer tips for making the most of these features.

MANAGING FILE SHARING WITH DOCUMENT PROPERTIES

The File menu's Properties command is designed with network users in mind. Although the Properties dialog can also be used by single users, it does help network users keep track of shared documents.

The Document tab of the Properties dialog records important system-assigned information, such as the file's storage location, the date the file was last modified, and the date it was last printed, so you can quickly find out when the file was last used.

On the Description and User Defined tabs, you can enter your own title, keywords, and other terms to speed search and retrieval for documents. (See the next section, "Speeding Network Navigation with Saved Searches," for more information.)

On the Internet tab, you can set documents that have hyperlinks and are used as Web pages. This tab is discussed in "Sharing Documents via HTML" later in this chapter.

Tip #500 from
Michael & Sarah

If you want to encourage everyone in your organization to use the Properties dialog, select the Edit Document Properties Before Saving option on the Tools, Options, General, Save tab. By selecting this option, you make the Properties dialog automatically appear when a user initially saves the file with the Save As command.

SPEEDING NETWORK NAVIGATION WITH SAVED SEARCHES

If you need to work on documents stored in different volumes or on different servers, the most efficient way to locate your documents is to create a saved search in the Explorer and apply rules that bring together links to everything you need. This method makes updating and synchronizing files a snap because you can update and/or synchronize all the files in your search at once.

Note

You can use saved searches like you use the Briefcase on the Windows desktop.

If you check the Regular Expressions option, you can use any of StarOffice's supported regular expressions; regular expressions enable you to cast a broad net for files rather than have to enter complete filenames.

Note

StarOffice uses the standard UNIX set of regular expressions, in which a period (.) stands for any single character, rather than the question mark symbol (?) with which Windows and DOS users are likely familiar.

Using a saved search requires some advanced planning in your organization because you must ensure that everyone working on the documents assigns titles or other document properties (such as keywords) that make creating search rules easy. You must also ensure that files are not moved or the directory structure changed without team members being notified.

If you set your search to Update on Open via its context menu, StarOffice automatically updates existing files and adds new matches. However, old matches are not deleted. You can also manually update at any time by selecting the Update command from the same context menu.

Tip #501 from
Michael & Sarah

If you update a file system folder twice within three seconds, the contents are completely reloaded and system information updated (including file size and date) instead of merely updating the number of files.

If you choose the Synchronize command from the Explorer context menu, your saved search will be matched and refreshed against your target directories and/or volumes. This means old matches files that you had saved in your cache but that were subsequently deleted from the system are deleted.

RELOADING DOCUMENTS

You typically choose File, Reload to reload Web pages that have not loaded properly or that have expired from your cache or changed since you browsed last time. However, you can also use this command to reload any document on your system, whether a Web page from your company intranet or a regular document file. If you have problems with a document you open from the network, you should try reloading it by choosing File, Reload.

Tip #502 from
Michael & Sarah

If you're reloading a frameset document and want to reload just one specific frame, press Ctrl while executing the Reload command.

Note that you also can use the Reload shortcut tool on the function bar.

SHARING DOCUMENTS VIA HTML

More and more companies are creating internal Web sites and posting internal data on a local Web site. Because of this increased use of the Web for internal work as well as external communication, saving documents as HTML files is becoming increasingly important when when sharing information in the business world.

StarOffice's total integration makes working between your desktop and a company intranet Web site extremely easy because you experience no difference between your locally stored documents and documents you access from the company's server (or external Web servers, for that matter). You can not only view Web documents on your desktop, but also edit them, save them as HTML files, and mail them from your desktop. The StarOffice File menu also includes a special command that enables you to save any text, spreadsheet, drawing and presentation document directly to your intranet server as an HTML document.

Note

When exporting documents as HTML files, you may lose some certain document properties. HTML is a special description language that makes it possible to show information using a Web browser. There are plenty of properties that only exist, for example, in the StarWriter file format and that you will lose once you export your file to HTML! For more details on HTML and StarOffice, see the section "About HTML—The Language of the Web" in Chapter 25, "Getting Started with StarWriter/Web."

SAVING DOCUMENTS FOR POSTING ON AN INTRANET If you want to save documents for posting on an intranet or Web server, do not save your file by selecting HTML as your file type in the Save As dialog box. Instead, use the command made specifically for this purpose— File, Send, Create HTML Document (for text documents) or File, Export (for drawing and presentation documents).

Tip #503 from	StarOffice also can handle cascading style sheets. You can determine how StarOffice
Michael & Sarah	document formatting attributes are exported as style sheets by setting your HTML export options on the Tools, Options, Internet, HTML tab. If you choose either the Microsoft Internet Explorer 4.0 or StarWriter options, most formatting is exported as style sheets. These style sheets are ignored unless the reader is viewing the page with MS Internet Explorer or StarOffice (respectively), but they create a cleaner, better formatted document when read in the intended application. If you export as Netscape Navigator 4, you can use Dynamic HTML, which makes it possible to layer objects on a page in three dimensions.

For example, when you choose File, Send, Create HTML Document, a dialog opens prompting you for a name and storage location. If you want to post your documents to the company intranet, it's simplest just to save them to the appropriate network volume.

After you click OK, a set of hyperlinked files is created based on the Level 1 headings in your document, with the top-level document a master document that lists any text before the first Level 1 heading in the document and all the Level 1 headings as hyperlinks. The generated files are named yourfilename.html, yourfilename2.html, yourfilename3.html, and so on. The HTML format used is the format you specified for HTML export on the Tools, Options, Internet, HTML tab. (If you use the normal Save As command, your only choice for export format is HTML [StarWriter], and the entire document is saved as a whole, just as if you had saved in regular StarWriter format.) You therefore can save your document to your network server and instantly create a Web site that anyone on the network can read and edit on his or her StarOffice desktop.

After the documents are generated, you can, of course, open and edit them as you like.

Note	If you use another browser as your default browser, double-clicking the filename(s) automatically opens the file(s) in that browser. Checking how the file looks in your browser is a good idea because HTML files can appear different in different browsers.

SETTING DOCUMENT PROPERTIES OF FILES POSTED TO THE WEB If you save documents that are posted as Web pages, you can use the Internet tab of the File, Properties dialog to set the file to automatically reload at a time interval you specify. You can also determine the default target frame for all hyperlinks of the active document, if this setting is not already defined in the hyperlink itself. If you link multiple documents with each other, you can also create self-running presentations.

To take advantage of this functionality, select the Auto Reload Every check box, and specify a number in the Seconds spin box to have the selected document reload automatically after the specified time interval. In the URL field, enter the complete URL of the following document. Finally, select a target frame for all hyperlinks in the current document from the Frame drop-down list. Your options include the following:

- **_self**—The following document will be reloaded in the same frame.
- **_blank**—The following document will be created in a new, blank frame.
- **_parent**—The following document will be created in a superordinate frame; if none exists, it will be created in the same frame.
- **_top**—The following document will be created in the frame that is the highest in the frame hierarchy; if none exists, it will be created in the same frame.

SHARING TEXT DOCUMENTS WITH OTHERS   If you want to save a document to exchange with others outside the company who don't have StarOffice, one option is to save the document as an HTML file using the standard Save As command. The advantage of using this format as opposed to saving in a format such as Word or WordPerfect is that graphics files and certain other formats may translate better into HTML. Remember, however, HTML is optimized to show information on the Web. It is not optimized to share documents that are intended for print. If you want to get your message across, you can also save documents in the good ol' Rich Text Format (RTF)—still the only truly independent file format for text documents.

SHARING DOCUMENTS VIA EMAIL

Besides sharing your documents by saving files to a common server and posting them on your company intranet, you can also email copies of documents (or Web pages that you are currently viewing) from your desktop. You don't even need to have the document open, as long as the document file is visible on your desktop or in the Beamer.

If the document is open on the desktop, you choose File, Send, Document as Email. If the file is closed, you select the file and choose File, Document as Email.

You have the option of sending the document as an attachment (in which case it will be sent in the file format in which it is currently saved) or including the text of the document in an email message.

→ For more information on sending email, **see** "Creating and Sending Mail," **p. 1053**.

MAPPING NETWORK DRIVES WITH GROUPS

Navigating on a big network is time consuming if you always start from your current location on your local drive. Although you can map (or link) your network drives by opening the Workplace icon in the Explorer, you can navigate more efficiently by using the new Groups feature in the Explorer. You can easily create a group, for example, that links to a particular volume or even a subdirectory of a volume that you frequently access. Once your group is created, all you need to do is click to open the group, and everything is right there.

To create a new group, click the New Group button in the Explorer. Then, click the Bookmark tab in the dialog that appears. Click the Directory button to navigate to the volume you want to access, select the volume with your mouse, and click Select. Finally, click OK, and your new group appears in the Explorer.

SECURING DOCUMENTS AND DATABASES

When you're working on a network, security is always a concern. StarOffice includes a number of security features that help you guard the integrity of your documents and databases. These features are discussed throughout this book in the context of their specific applications. Table 28.1 simply provides an overview of the available commands and directs you to the appropriate sections elsewhere.

TABLE 28.1   STAROFFICE'S SECURITY FEATURES

Feature	Location	For More Information, See...
Protect a saved file with a password	File, Save As dialog box	"Protecting Files and Folders," page 213
Protect specific cells or sections of a spreadsheet	Tools, Protect Document in combination with the Cell Protection tab of the Format, Cell Format dialog box	"Guarding Against Entry Errors," page 522
Protect a StarBase relational database with a password	Properties dialog, Administration tab (to set ODBC access) and StarBase tab (to set passwords for restricting local access)	"Securing Your Database," page 1146
Determine a client computer's level of network access from within StarOffice and turn on the Java Security Checks option	Tools, Options, Browser, Other tab	"Fine-Tuning Your Browser," page 105
Add to or edit the list of site certificates accepted for Web security	Tools, Options, Browser, Site Certificates	"Fine-Tuning Your Browser," page 105

PART

VI

CH

28

EXCHANGING AND REVIEWING DOCUMENTS

StarOffice not only enables you to share documents within a workgroup setting, but it also provides tools and functionality that enable you and your team members to work together on documents. To varying degrees, StarWriter, StarCalc, StarImpress, and StarDraw provide specific features that assist your group in keeping track of who changed what in a document.

> **Note**
>
> You don't need to be on a network to take advantage of these features; they are equally valid for document exchanges via email or disks. However, these features are native to the StarOffice environment, which means they do not translate if you export your documents into another format (such as Microsoft Word or Microsoft Excel).

For example, most major StarOffice modules enable you and your team to save different versions of the document to the same file. Each version is identified by the time and day it was saved and by whom it was saved.

In addition, StarWriter and StarCalc enable authors and reviewers to insert notes to selected text and cells. You can see these comments by holding the mouse pointer over the text or cell in question. Using the Edit, Changes command options(revision marks or redlining feature), you can also show additions and deletions made by each reviewer in a different color, and then compare or merge the different versions of the same document. Finally, both StarWriter and StarCalc enable you to protect text or cell contents so that multiple users can work on the same document without accidentally deleting valuable information.

> **Note**
>
> Revision marks or redlining functions are lost when you save a StarOffice document in a non-StarOffice format or if you import a redlined Microsoft document.

StarWriter also offers the Line Numbering feature, which makes it easy for people looking at long documents to always be on the same page and line.

REVIEWING DOCUMENTS

When you are working with other members of your team on a document, it helps to know who is responsible for what changes to the original document. Both StarWriter and StarCalc have three different commands that help you work together on documents:

- **Edit, Changes, Record**—Enables you to track changes during the editing process.
- **File, Versions**—Enables you to save and compare different versions of the same document in one file.
- **Edit, Compare**—Enables you to compare your original document to newer versions of the document and decide whether to accept or reject the changes.

Note

> Only one person at a time can edit documents stored on a network server, although others can open read-only copies of the document.

TRACKING CHANGES

To track changes in either StarWriter or StarCalc, select Edit, Changes, Record from the menu bar. By doing so, you turn on tracking. As you enter changes, the program records them using a predefined attribute and color that varies from author to author.

The tracking changes feature works as follows: As Author A, you send the first draft to your colleagues, B and C, for commentaries and tips. Within the text, your colleagues can mark up the text. You get the document back. You view the document with the Edit, Changes, Show command turned on, and then accept or reject the changes via the Accept or Reject dialog box that also opens from the Edit, Changes menu. As long as everyone involved in this chain is working with StarOffice, you're safe.

Note

> Some types of changes are not recorded. For example, tab changes are not recorded. However, any changes made to text (additions and deletions) and most common formatting changes are recorded.

When you make changes to a text document, the text you add or delete appears in a predefined color underlined or marked as strikethrough, respectively. If you rest your mouse pointer over a changed text element, you see a pop-up balloon that informs you about the type, author, date, and time of the change. If Extended Tips is selected from the Help menu, you also see any (optional) commentaries that may have been added.

Tip #504 from
Michael & Sarah

> If you truly want to annotate a document, select Insert, Note from the menu bar, then add your commentary in the Text area of the Insert Note dialog. The Note feature provides more space for longer commentaries; each author can identify herself by clicking the Author button in the Insert Notes dialog and then adding the desired text in the dialog; and you can use the Navigator to quickly jump from note to note. For more details on using this feature, see "Adding Notes, Footnotes, and Endnotes" in Chapter 10, "Working with Long Documents."

Likewise, when you're making changes to a Table document, you see a border around the cell that has changed. When your mouse pointer rests over the changed cell, you see the same type of information that you get when you do the same in a text document.

To stop recording your changes, select Edit, Changes, Record again. The check mark disappears, and you can hand the document back to the person who sent it to you.

SETTING TRACKING ATTRIBUTES

By default, each author (or, more precisely, the computer the author is working on) has his or her own color and attribute that indicate the nature of the change. In the case of text documents, the default attribute is underline for additions, strikethrough for deletions, and bold for a changed attribute. In the case of spreadsheet documents, changes to cell contents, deletions, insertions, or moved entries are indicated by a predefined color. When you're working in either StarWriter or StarCalc, you can accept the program's default setting, or you can define your own attributes and color for the changes.

To change the settings for tracking changes in a text document, select Tools, Options, Text Document, Changes. In the Text Display portion of the Changes dialog, you can define different attributes and colors for changes that involve the addition, deletion, or change of an attribute. For example, when the Insert option is selected, you can select a different attribute from the Attributes drop-down list that will be associated whenever you add text to the document with the Record feature active. If you don't like the (default) underline attribute, you can select another attribute from the list, including double underline, caps, or small caps. (You can also select None, but choosing that option would defeat the purpose of tracking changes, of course.) In the Color box, you can specify a color that will be associated with this particular change, regardless of who performs the change. If you keep the (default) By Author setting, additions appear in different colors, depending on who inserted the text and on what computer.

Note

Basically, the By Author setting identifies the author of the document based on the user data of the computer on which the changes are made. If the same author works on the same document but on two different computers that are not linked on a network,, StarOffice may record the user as two different authors. One advantage of doing a network installation and running StarOffice from the server is that an individual has access to his or her personal configuration files from any computer on the network (based on his or her login name).

Likewise, you can assign attributes and color to the other tracking options: Delete (the default is strikethrough) and Changed Attribute (the default is bold). You can preview your settings in the small preview window on the right.

If your document already contains "colored" elements, such as hyperlinks or color fonts, it's harder to see the recorded changes. Hence, you have the option in a text document to indicate changes by using additional markers—for example, a red line running in the margin next to the line(s) in which the change occurred. In the Lines Changed portion of the Changes dialog, you can define where you want the marks to appear, as well as assign a color to a selected mark. Use the Mark box to indicate where you want your marks to appear—by choosing Left Margin, Right Margin, Outward Margin (the default), or Inward Margin—and then pick a color from the Color drop-down list. If you don't want any margin markers, select None.

When you're working in a spreadsheet document, you are limited to tracking changes by color only. Using the Tools, Options, Spreadsheet Document, Changes dialog, you can select a color for a certain type of change from the respective drop-down list. As with text documents, the color you attribute to a particular change is used whenever this change occurs, regardless of who performed the change in the document. If you leave the settings on By Author, changes appear in different colors, depending on the computer on which the change was performed.

ADDING A COMMENTARY TO YOUR CHANGES

You can add a commentary to each change by placing the insertion point within the changed element and selecting Edit, Changes, Comment. (This function is available only when you place your cursor inside the changed area.) You can also see the commentary in the list under Edit, Changes, Accept, or Reject in that dialog. Alternately, you can also select Insert, Note from the menu bar, which has the additional advantage that various authors can quickly append the existing note with an identifying marker; plus you can quickly browse all existing notes with the help of the navigator. A comment, by contrast, cannot be appended nor easily searched out.

→ For more details on working with notes, **see** "Adding Notes, Footnotes, and Endnotes," **p. 384**.

Tip #505 from *Michael & Sarah*	If a document has a lot of changes, it may get cumbersome to read text and still get the meaning. In that case, select Edit, Changes, Show to remove the check mark next to the Show command. Although changes are still recorded, you do not see them onscreen or in print.

MERGING CHANGES

Authors do not always mark up the same copy of the document. Often, it is more efficient to send a copy to each contributor, in which case you end up with an original document and as many marked-up copies as you sent out.

It's important that all copies sent to you differ only in terms of changes and deletions; all "normal" text has to be identical (that is, all changes must have been made with the Record feature turned on).

To combine several copies with the original document, follow these steps:

1. Open the original document.
2. Select Edit, Changes, Merge Document.
3. In the Insert dialog that appears, select the copy or copies of the original document.
4. Click Insert. After the documents are merged, you can see all changes marked in the original document.

FINALIZING YOUR DOCUMENT

When you get back a document in which other authors have made changes, you can accept or reject the changes step-by-step or all at once. (If you have distributed more than one copy, you first have to merge the document before you can perform this operation.) To review the changes, select Edit, Changes, Accept or Reject. You then see the Accept or Reject dialog.

When you select a change in the list in the dialog, the change is shown in the document. You can then decide whether you want to add or reject the change. If one of the other authors corrected a change made by someone who also made a change to your original, the changes are shown in hierarchical order, with a plus sign next to the change that you can click.

If the list of changes is too long, you can switch to the Filter tab and look at the changes of only one particular individual, for example, or only the changes over the last few days. Or you can restrict the list view based on the specific action that was executed.

With text documents, you see the not-yet-accepted changes in the list. Accepted changes are removed from the list and appear in your text without additional marks.

With table documents, all accepted changes in a list can be combined under one entry, so you can continue to see which changes have been accepted.

Caution	You lose your list of changes as soon as you turn off the Record command on the Edit, Changes menu.

Tip #506 from *Michael & Sarah*	If you use the Record and Accept or Reject features a lot, consider adding buttons for each function to the object bar. To do so, select Tools, Configure, and then click the Toolbars tab. Next, click Customize, and then select Edit in the Categories list and the respective command in the Command list. Finally, select an icon, and drag it to the object bar.

➔ For more information on customizing toolbars, **see** "Customizing Desktop Tools and Menus," **p. 115**.

COMPARING FILES

If someone circulates an edited copy of a document but has not used the tracking changes feature, you can still compare two versions of the file by using the Compare command.

Tip #507 from *Michael & Sarah*	You can also use the Versions function to compare configuration files before and after the installation of new software. In that case, you might have to choose Edit, Compare to open the Insert dialog and then choose File Type Text.

Follow these steps to compare files:

1. Open your original document.
2. Select Edit, Compare Document.
3. In the Insert dialog that appears, select the copy of the document that you want to compare.
4. Click Insert.

StarOffice combines both versions of the document. All text that appears in the original document but not in the copy is marked as inserted, and text that is in the copy but not in the original is marked as deleted in the original.

You can now review the inserted text and the deletions. If you accept the inserted text, the respective text remains in your document; if you accept deletions, the respective text that is in the copy is not accepted in the document.

Don't forget to save your document when you're done.

Caution

Once you have accepted the changes to a document and then save it, you will not be able to undo all the changes. If you want to keep the document that contains all the changes, for tracking purposes or for the record, save a version beforehand.

WORKING WITH VERSIONS

When you're sharing and exchanging documents with others, you can also keep track of changes by saving different versions of the same document. Even though you can maintain multiple versions of a document by using the File, Save As command (and storing each version under a separate name in a separate file), StarOffice provides you with a less cumbersome (and more elegant) way of keeping track of different versions of an original document. Using the Versions command, you can store multiple versions of a given document created in StarWriter, StarCalc, StarDraw, StarImpress, StarChart, or StarMath in one big file.

The procedure for saving multiple versions of one document is the same in all StarOffice modules. First, you have to save the original file by using the Save As command. Then you select File, Versions to open the Versioning dialog, shown in Figure 28.1. You use this dialog to save and manage your versions.

Note

If you save a file with Versions using the Save As command, the versions information is not saved.

Figure 28.1

The Versioning dialog provides an elegant way of saving different versions of one document in one file.

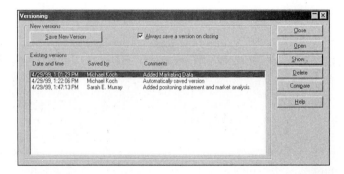

To save a new version of an existing document, click the Save New Version button in the upper left of the Versioning dialog, and (optionally) add a descriptive comment about the nature of the version change in the resulting Insert Version Comment dialog. After you click OK, the current version of your document appears in the Existing Versions list box, where it is identified by the date and time it was saved, the author of the version, and any (optional) comments the author added for clarification. Click the Show button to reveal any hidden text.

You can have StarWriter automatically save a new version each time the document is closed by selecting the Always Save a Version on Closing option in the Versions dialog. Upon the document's closing, you are asked whether you want to save a new version of the document. Note that you can't add your own comments to versions saved automatically.

Saving versions of a document with the Versions command is a good way to handle revisions made by multiple authors, especially when you want an audit trail. At the end of the reviewing process, you can manage the different versions of your document using the Versioning dialog. Click Open to open a selected version as a new, read-only document that you can review but not edit.

Click Compare if you want to compare different versions to the original document. When you click this button, you see the Accept or Reject Changes dialog, which lists any changes and highlights them in color in the document. Using the List tab of this dialog, you can accept or reject some or all of the changes listed. If the list of changes is particularly long, or if various authors have contributed to the document, click the Filter tab, and select Date, Author, or Action to see a select list of changes on the List tab. (Note that the Compare command on the Versioning dialog is available only if you have more than one version of a document.)

To delete a version you no longer need, select it in the Versioning dialog box, and click Delete. The next time you save the document, the version will be deleted for good.

Note

The Versions feature is helpful if you frequently exchange documents with other users in a workgroup environment, but it works only if you save files in the native StarWriter format. If you decide to save a document in a different file format, all changes are automatically accepted, and you can no longer track them.

Tip #508 from
Michael & Sarah

You can also save separately a selected version of your document that you want to share with others. Open the document that contains various versions, and select File, Versions. In the Versioning dialog, select the version that you want to send out, and click Open. Now, select File, Save As to save the read-only version as a separate file. Before sending out the file, you either can select the Always Save a Version on Closing option in the Versioning dialog or select Edit, Changes, Record or both to ensure that any changes by the reviewer will be properly recorded.

Note

At the time of this writing, StarDivision is working on a synchronization feature that will enable you to compare and update the files in two folders or on two drives. One folder can be on your laptop, the other on your network or your desktop. Assume you want duplicate folders and files on your laptop. You can then work with those files in those folders, delete some files, and add new ones. When you're back in the office or continue to work on your other machine, you can then update the files on your network or desktop with the most recent versions on the laptop. Comparable to (yet more powerful than) the Windows Briefcase, this feature is slated for release with the next upgrade of StarOffice and will make updated files and folders a breeze.

USING LINE NUMBERING

If you find yourself using StarWriter for legal documents or technical writing, you might be interested in using StarWriter's Line Numbering tool. Line numbering is extremely helpful when you're working with long documents that are passed between two or more people, such as drafts of books or research theses. When you want to be sure that everyone is on the same page—literally—be sure to turn on the Line Numbering feature and tell your associates to do the same.

To turn on line numbering, select Tools, Line Numbering from the menu bar. In the Line Numbering dialog, select Show Line Numbers. In the View portion of this dialog, you can also control the text style, format, and position of the numbering, as well as specify by how much you would like the numbers to be offset from the left/right or inner/outer margins of your document. (Note that "inner" is left on right pages and right on left pages, and vice versa with "outer." You can play with this feature and look at the results by choosing File, Page View/Print Preview to determine which style suits you best.)

In addition, you can determine whether you want to include blank lines in the final count. You can also add a separator symbol, such as a hyphen, to make scanning the margins even easier on the eyes of the reader.

HIDING AND PROTECTING TEXT WITH SECTIONS

If you want to hide certain text passages from curious eyes or prevent others from making changes to existing text, use the Insert, Section command. (Sections can also be useful when you're composing Web pages because you often need to structure your document in screen chunks that are smaller than your normal printed pages in size.) Using this command, you can protect finished portions of important documents so that you don't accidentally make changes to them (via the Replace All command, for example) or delete them, or you can use it if you want to prevent others from making changes to your document. (Naturally, using this command makes sense only if you assign a password to this section; you'll learn about that shortly).

To hide or protect a section, select Insert, Section. In the Insert Sections dialog, you'll notice two major areas: New Section and Options. Enter a name for the section in the New Section text box. StarOffice, by default, follows the labeling scheme of Section1, Section2, and so on. Using the Options portion of the dialog, you can define the particularities of this section. If you select Protected, the contents of this section can no longer be modified or edited.

Select Hidden if you want to hide temporarily unpolished or unfinished passages of text from curious eyes. When you select this option, you can also specify a condition under which the hidden text can become visible. If the condition is met (TRUE), the text will be shown; if it is not met (FALSE), it will remain hidden. Conditions are logical expressions, such as x eq 1 ("x equals 1"), whereby x is a field variable that you specify when you choose Insert Fields, Other.

→ For more details on conditions and fields, **see** "Understanding Fields," **p. 349**, and "Working with Fields," **p. 350**.

When you're exchanging documents with others, you should also assign a password to the section. Select the section you want to password-protect, and then choose Edit, Sections to open the Edit Sections dialog box. In the Section list, select the section you want to protect (provided you have more than one), and then click the Password Protected option. When the Enter Password dialog appears, enter a personal password of at least five characters in length (you can mix letters and numbers), and then click OK. At that point, the Confirm Password dialog appears. Enter the password again, and click OK to return to the Edit Sections dialog. Make a note of your password, and place it in a secure place.

SHARING DATA ACROSS A NETWORK

StarBase, the StarOffice database module, is one of the key components of StarOffice's desktop integration. Its primary function, in fact, is not to create databases but to make the sharing of data both between applications and within a pool of StarOffice users extremely easy. No other Office suite on the market today offers comparable data integration.

→ For an introduction to StarBase and its role in the integrated desktop, **see** "Using StarBase as a Data Manager," **p. 1087**.

These databases can be in native StarBase format (Windows only) or StarBase's implementation of dBASE, or they can be front ends for client/server databases. On both Linux and Windows platforms, StarBase can connect via JDBC; on Windows, it can also connect via ODBC as well as connect with Microsoft Access databases. On both platforms, it can also import text databases as read-only tables—a security feature for use on networks, enabling a central database administrator to maintain control of data. (If you need to edit text-only databases, you can import them as .txt or .csv files into StarCalc.)

→ For more information on creating your own database tables in StarBase, **see** Chapter 31, "Creating Standalone Database Tables," **p. 1117**, and Chapter 32, "Creating Tables with Relations," **p. 1131**.

→ For more information on using StarBase as a front end for client/server databases, **see** "Understanding StarBase's Import and Export Options," **p. 1088**, and "Orienting Yourself in StarBase," **p. 1091**.

→ For more information on working with text databases in StarCalc, **see** "Importing and Exporting Data," **p. 636**.

All you need to do is to create a database and store it on a server. After users have created a database shell in the Explorer, they can then open the individual database elements on their client machine (directly or as links). Using native SQL or StarBase's graphical queries, users can sort and filter data in various ways and drag and drop data or merge fields from the Beamer into open documents.

StarOffice also offers incredible flexibility in creating forms. You can create forms within a StarBase database but also as standalone StarWriter and StarCalc documents. (You can create a form as a StarImpress document as well, but we're not sure why anyone would want to.) This means a database administrator can create and distribute forms to users without needing to give users direct access to the database file or data tables.

The Address Book contact manager in the Explorer is a StarBase dBASE database. It serves as a good example of how StarOffice's integrated desktop makes exchanging and importing data over a network a snap. The next section, "Using the Address Book," therefore takes up the baton in discussing the use of StarBase databases on a network.

USING THE ADDRESS BOOK

The Address Book is StarOffice's built-in contact manager—a StarBase dBASE database fully integrated across all StarOffice applications, including StarSchedule. This complete integration makes pooling and sharing contact data across a network extremely easy, and use of the dBASE format ensures that your contact data transfers easily to other programs.

The ideal way to use the Address Book on a network is to store a single business contact table in the Address Book database on a network server. Users then create a link to that table in their local Address Book database. Users can keep their personal contacts in separate tables saved in their individual Address Book databases on their client machines.

If, as often happens, the boundaries between the personal and the business begin to blur, users can easily append data from personal tables to the central business contact table in seconds via drag and drop—as long as their personal tables have the same structure as does the central business contacts table.

The Address Book dialog box (which you open from the Edit menu) provides a global mask that enables users to enter, extract, and manipulate data easily into any table currently designated as their default Address Book.

PART
VI

CH

28

Users can also bring Address Book data into their documents with commands integrated across the desktop, including AutoMail and Who Is?. They also can use the Insert, Fields command and drag and drop from the Beamer. These features are fully discussed elsewhere; this section focuses on those aspects of the Address Book most relevant for project planning with StarSchedule and sharing data across a network.

→ For details on creating form letters using the Database Address Book, **see** "Creating Form Letters with Mail Merge," **p. 360**.

→ For details on creating email merges with the Database Address Book, **see** "Creating Mail Merges with StarMail," **p. 1062**.

→ For more information on working with fields in StarWriter documents, **see** Chapter 9 **p. 321**. For more information on working with database fields, **see** "Selectively Inserting Data with Fields," **p. 1201**.

→ For details on dragging and dropping data from the Beamer into documents, **see** "Moving Data Into Documents," **p. 1160**.

UNDERSTANDING THE ADDRESS BOOK DATABASE

You should understand a few important aspects of the Address Book database from the get-go so that you can take maximal advantage of its features.

The Address Book that appears in the Explorer is a dBASE database like any other you might create in StarOffice. It comes with one table, called *address*, already created with some dummy data inserted. You can create your own forms, queries, and reports to work with your data. Its tables can be imported by any database or spreadsheet program with a dBASE III filter and its data imported by any program with the proper ODBC driver.

However, a number of special hard-coded Address Book commands and an Address Book dialog box can work some special magic with Address Book data inside StarOffice. These commands enable you to create form letters in minutes, look up a client's name from inside a letter, and send a colleague a Web page while you're browsing without skipping a beat.

CHANGING YOUR DEFAULT ADDRESS BOOK

Does this mean that in order to have access to all the Address Book's feature, you must use StarDivision's Address Book as your contact manager, even if you don't like the structure of the address table, or you already have great gobs of data stored in another contact manager? Not really.

After you have registered a table in a database in the Explorer, you can designate any table you like (not just those in dBASE format) to serve as your default Address Book by simply selecting it and applying the Address Book command from the Explorer's context menu.

> **Note**
>
> You can see and select a table only when the Explorer is set to Hierarchical view. To set the Explorer to this view, right-click the Explorer group title bar, and select Hierarchical from the context menu.

The principle is the same as designating a folder as a desktop. The table you designate is now the table searched whenever you use commands such as Who Is?, AutoMail, AutoBrowse, or Mail Merge.

→ For information on creating a database in the Explorer, **see** "Orienting Yourself in StarBase," **p. 1091**.

If you're working in a large business or organization, you're likely to be concerned with data portability and perhaps incorporation of your contact table into a relational database. If that's the case, you're better advised to create a table in your client/server RDBMS (Relational Database Management System) that users then designate as their default Address Book because StarBase is not designed to be a fully robust RDBMS. (In fact, it can't create relations on the Linux platform.) However, it is a superior front end for giving users easy access to data on a network and is a great way to bring that contact data onto users' desktops.

THE EFFECTS OF CHANGING YOUR DEFAULT ADDRESS BOOK

When you want to change your default Address Book, you must consider one caveat. Because the Address Book dialog box is hard-coded to the structure of the default StarOffice address table, the dialog box is useful to you only if the table you designate as your Address Book shares the structure of the address table exactly. If you use a contact table that has a different structure and want the convenience of such a dialog box, you need to create your own by using StarBasic.

Tip #509 from *Michael & Sarah*	A simpler alternative to programming a dialog box is to create a custom form from StarBase. Just select the Forms icon in the StarBase database that contains your address table (or a link to it), right-click, and choose New. You can take the easy way out by creating a form with the AutoPilot, or if you're knowledgeable about form controls, you can create a form from scratch as a StarCalc or StarWriter document.

Because of the special integration of the default address table and Address Book database into StarOffice, keeping an intact copy of them is a good idea, even if you're not currently using them as your default contact manager.

COPYING THE ADDRESS TABLE'S STRUCTURE

If you're using StarOffice on a multiuser installation and want to use the default StarOffice address table, you'll likely want to create copies of the table's structure so that users can create personal contact tables.

Note	Be sure you have the Explorer set to Hierarchical view. Otherwise, you can't open your database to see the Tables element (which, in turn, opens to reveal the address table).

Using drag and drop in the Explorer, you can create such a copy in two simple steps:

1. Select the address table in the Tables element of the Address Book database in the Explorer.

2. Drag the address table onto the Tables icon.

 As you drag the table onto the Tables icon, your pointer changes into the copy pointer, showing a document in gray outline and a second document with a plus symbol layered on top. When you see that pointer, release the mouse button, and a Copy Table dialog like the one in Figure 28.2 appears.

Figure 28.2
The Copy Table dialog box appears when you drag a copy of a table onto the Tables icon of any Explorer database. In this dialog, you can combine data in tables or copy the structure of an existing table.

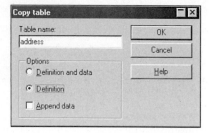

First, you must enter a new table name because you cannot create a copy that has the same name as the original table. You might want to call your copy `Personal`, for example, if you're creating a table for your personal contacts. Next, choose Definition in the Options section to inform StarOffice you want to create only a copy of the table's structure, not to copy any existing data or append that data to another table in the same database. Click OK, and a copy of the table appears in the Tables section of the database.

Note

You can copy a table structure only within or between StarOffice databases.

ADDING AND REMOVING CONTACTS WITH THE ADDRESS BOOK DIALOG

The advantage of using the default address table or another table that uses the same structure is that you can use the Address Book dialog box to work with contacts. This dialog box has been significantly improved in StarOffice version 5.1. Not only have some annoying bugs been fixed, but better functionality has been added, including an AutoInvite feature that integrates the Address Book even more tightly into StarSchedule.

Note

In database terminology, a person's complete contact information is called a **record**. The terms **contact** and **record** are used interchangeably in this chapter.

Open the Address Book dialog by choosing the Edit menu's Address Book command. When the dialog box appears, you see its title along with the total number of records you currently have in the table. You can see in Figure 28.3, for example, that the underlying contact table has a total of 38 records.

Figure 28.3
The Address Book dialog box makes adding, locating, and deleting contacts easy.

Minimize — Close

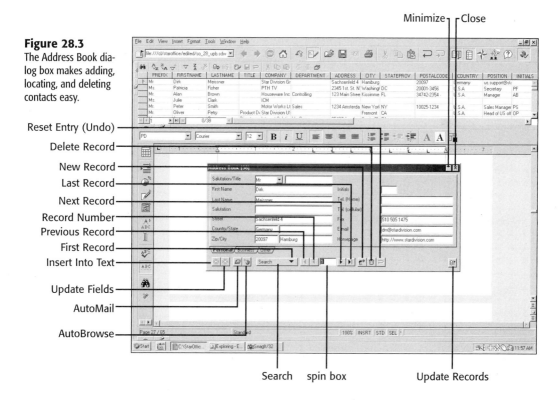

Reset Entry (Undo)
Delete Record
New Record
Last Record
Next Record
Record Number
Previous Record
First Record
Insert Into Text

Update Fields
AutoMail
AutoBrowse

Search   spin box   Update Records

ADDING RECORDS

To add a new record to your table, click the New button on the toolbar at the bottom of the Address Book dialog box. Next, click in a field to make it active, and start typing to add new data.

NAVIGATING IN THE ADDRESS BOOK DIALOG BOX

Within the Address Book dialog, you can press Tab to move forward one field at a time and Shift+Tab to move backward one field at a time.

To move between records, use the navigation buttons at the bottom of the dialog (refer to Figure 28.3). Alternatively, if you know the record number you are seeking, you can enter it into the Record Number spin box and press Enter.

SAVING NEW CONTACT INFORMATION

Your new Address Book data is automatically saved either when you click to move to another record or when you click the Update Records button.

PART
VI

CH

28

DELETING CONTACTS

To delete a record from your table, first make it visible in the Address Book dialog box. Then click the Delete button. The entire record is deleted from the underlying table.

> **Caution**
>
> After you delete a record from a table via the Address Book dialog, it's gone forever. The Reset button does not restore the record.

WORKING WITH THE ADDRESS BOOK DIALOG ON THE DESKTOP

Because the Address Book is a floating dialog box, you can keep it open on your desktop. If you do so, you can reduce it to a floating title bar by double-clicking the title bar or clicking the Minimize button in the upper-right corner. You can even continue working in your documents with it open.

BROWSING THE WEB WITH AUTOBROWSE

If you have an entry in the Homepage text box of the currently visible contact and are online, you can click the AutoBrowse button and shoot directly to the Web site in question.

SENDING MAIL WITH AUTOMAIL

From the Address Book dialog box, AutoMail works similarly to AutoBrowse. (You can also access AutoMail by choosing File, Send, but you activate it slightly differently.) If you have a currently visible contact that has an entry in the Email field, and you click the AutoMail button, a Send Mail dialog box appears. You're given the option of mailing the currently active document on your desktop as an attachment, using it as the text of an email message, or not using it at all and just opening a blank mail composition window. After you make your selection, you go to StarMail and can send your email as usual.

> **Note**
>
> You must first create an Outbox in the Explorer before you can send email.

→ For details on creating an Outbox, **see** "Getting Online," **p. 85**.
→ For details on working in StarMail, **see** Chapter 29, "Communicating with StarMail and StarDiscussion," **p. 1045**.

SEARCHING FOR CONTACTS

You can retrieve contact information from within documents in numerous ways. However, you can also always retrieve contact data by opening the Edit menu's Address Book dialog box and using the Search button.

When you click the Search button, you have the choice of searching either your current default Address Book table or any of the Internet directories that you previously set through the Tools, Options, Internet, LDAP Server dialog box. You must first choose one of these alternatives before you can begin your search.

Note

If you're searching an LDAP directory, make sure that you're connected to your network or ISP and that the Online button on the StarOffice function bar is pressed in.

After you've selected your directory, just enter your search terms into the appropriate fields of the dialog box, and click Start. If your contact is found, the information appears in the dialog box. If not, you're informed that no matching records were found.

Note

You cannot search the user-defined fields in this dialog box. To search those fields, open your underlying Address Book table in the Beamer, and use the Lookup Record tool.

If multiple matches are found, they are all available; just use the record navigation buttons to move to the next and previous records found in the search.

When you've found the contact information you want, you can add it to your documents by clicking the Insert into Text button in the Address Book dialog box.

ADDING CONTACT INFORMATION TO DOCUMENTS

You can easily add contact information to documents from the Address Book dialog box. You can insert the results of a search, or you can insert selected fields from your entire Address Book table.

When you click the Insert into Text button, a Database Columns dialog box appears. This dialog gives you three options for inserting your contact information—as a table, as fields, or as text. After you select your option, a range of choices specific to that option appears.

INSERTING YOUR CONTACTS AS FIELDS OR TEXT   With both the Fields and Text option in the Database Columns dialog box, you're given a list of your current Address Book's fields. Select the fields that represent the data you want inserted, and click the right arrow to move them into the box on the right side of the dialog. Insert spaces and punctuation as appropriate between the fields. You can then select the paragraph style that will apply to your fields or text from the drop-down list on the bottom right of the dialog box. If you leave the style set to the default None, your inserted fields or text will take on the formatting of the paragraph into which it is inserted. When finished, click OK.

INSERTING YOUR CONTACTS AS A TABLE   If you choose to insert your information as a table, you also begin by selecting the fields you want to include and moving them to the right selection box in the Database Columns dialog box. If you click the double-headed arrow, all the fields are moved over at once. Clicking the single-headed arrow moves only the currently selected field(s). You can choose whether you want table headings applied. If you choose Empty, space for table headings is included but left blank for you to fill in. The Properties button opens the Table Properties dialog box and allows you to define your table's properties beforehand, and the AutoFormat button opens the table AutoFormat dialog, where you can determine its appearance. When finished, click OK.

Tip #510 from *Michael & Sarah*	A quick and easy way to create and print a list of contacts is to insert a table of your contacts into a StarWriter document and print it. This approach is much faster than creating a report in StarBase!

CREATING GROUPS

On the Other tab of the Address Book dialog, you'll notice text boxes for four user-defined fields. These fields are included in the address table to enable you to code your contacts for easy sorting and tracking—in essence, to create groups of contacts. For example, you might want to use ALTFIELD1 to code some contacts as existing customers with an X and others as leads with an L. You could then use the table sorting and filtering commands to easily extract a list of only leads to use for creating a mass mailing seeking new customers. (The sorting and filtering commands are available when you open your table in the Beamer or on the desktop.) You could also create a query that would achieve the same result that you could save and use over and over again.

These fields are particularly useful when people are pooling together contact information into one large table—as long as everyone applies the codes consistently.

You can change the names of these fields in the underlying table by opening the table in Table Design view and editing the field names. However, changes you make to the table's field names are not reflected in the dialog box; you'll continue to see the default field names of UserDefined1, and so on.

→ For details on editing tables in Design view, **see** "Creating and Modifying Tables in Design View," **p. 1122**.

WORKING WITH YOUR ADDRESS TABLE IN THE BEAMER

Another way of working with your address table data is to open the table in the Beamer. You use this view when you're using the address table in StarSchedule.

OPENING YOUR ADDRESS TABLE IN STARSCHEDULE

From within StarSchedule, you open the Address Book in the Beamer by clicking the Address Book button on the toolbar.

OPENING YOUR ADDRESS TABLE FROM THE DESKTOP

From the desktop, you can open a table in the Beamer only when the Explorer is set to display in Hierarchical view. (To open this view, right-click the title bar of the Explorer group, and select Hierarchical from the context menu.)

To open your address table in the Beamer, first open the Beamer. Then select your table in the Explorer, and extended-click it. The address table then opens in the Beamer, along with a range of table management tools, including sorting and filtering buttons and a Mail Merge button.

The Address Book is also set as your current default database and can therefore be opened by pressing the F4 key if you don't have a document open that contains fields from another database.

INSERTING CONTACT RECORDS FROM THE BEAMER

You can insert merge fields into your document by dragging and dropping field names from the top of the table columns onto your document. If you click and drag from the Select All button—the gray button in the upper-left corner that marks the intersection of the column and row heads—or from any row header, you can also open the same Insert Database Columns dialog that appears when you click the Insert into Text button in the Address Book dialog.

You can insert data from any individual field by selecting and then dragging and dropping it into your document.

Note

Make sure the Edit button is pressed on the Beamer toolbar. Otherwise, you cannot select and drag data from individual fields.

Working with the address table in the Beamer is just like working with data in any other table, a topic that is discussed thoroughly in Chapter 33, "Working with Tables."

You can open any address table in the Beamer, whether or not it is currently selected as the default Address Book, as long as the file or a link to it is registered in an Explorer database.

APPENDING DATA TO TABLES

If you're using the Address Book with multiple users (or even if you're just maintaining multiple tables for your own use), you'll probably find yourself needing to append contact data from one table to another.

You can use the same drag-and-drop method to append data to the address table that you use to copy the table's structure. The table whose data you're appending must have the same structure as that of the address table. It must also have the same name (which means it cannot initially be stored in the same database as the target address table).

Tip #511 from
Michael & Sarah

If you have a table—called, say, Personal—with data you want to append that is stored in the same database as your address table, start by creating a second database. Copy the Personal table into the second database. Rename the table address, and then drag and drop it onto the Tables icon of the Address Book.

To append a table's data, open both the database that contains that table and the database with the target address table in the Explorer. Then select and drag the table whose data you want to append onto the Tables icon of the Address Book database, releasing the mouse button when the copy pointer appears. Choose Append Data in the Options list, and then click OK. That's it! Your data from the second table is added to the first.

However, don't move too fast. There is a major flaw with this command: Unless you have first indexed the tables and set a specific field to require unique values, duplicates are added along with new data, without distinction.

Even if you index your tables, your ability to set data validity rules through your table index is limited because you can select only one field to serve as your index field. For example, if you choose the Last Name field as your indexing field on both tables and then merge their data with the Append option, it would (perhaps appropriately) ignore a second listing for Alan Brown but also ignore a contact record for Julie Brown. You also would need to immediately undefine this field as requiring a unique value after appending your data. Otherwise, you would never be able to have more than one person with the same last name in your Address Book table. (Not being able to keep these names might cause some family problems!) Setting an index is thus only a crude filter when you're appending data.

GETTING ORGANIZED WITH STARSCHEDULE

StarSchedule is easy to overlook, hidden as it is rather modestly away in the Explorer and the time display in the taskbar icon tray (just double-click the time display to open it quickly). However, working in tandem with StarMail and the Address Book, StarSchedule is a robust scheduling and task management tool that you can use alone or as part of a workgroup environment.

As you would expect, StarSchedule does a good job of the basics. It keeps track of events and to-do lists, enabling you to combine both, together with your Database Address Book, into a single screen. In addition, it features an impressive reminder system that not only supports the usual "pop-up" dialog alerts (with or without sound), but also sends email reminders to you at a prescribed time (up to two weeks before an appointment or event)—a welcome feature when you're on the road or dividing your time between two or more computers.

Note

The reminder feature still needs some improvements. For example, at this point, there is no option that allows you to inform all participants. A workaround is to have your system administrator create an appropriate mailing list. Then you only have to send the reminder to that particular mailing list. Note also that you can specify the email server on the StarSchedule tree in the extended Explorer under, for example, My Computer\Administrator.

Because StarSchedule is designed to be used on a network (although it can be used as a standalone application, too), the following sections begin by detailing how to configure

StarSchedule for network use. Individual users might want to jump ahead to the section "Getting Started with StarSchedule," later in this chapter which introduces the StarSchedule windows, views, and tools.

CONFIGURING STARSCHEDULE ON A NETWORK

The computer that administers the calendar for other users is called the StarSchedule server. This server must have StarOffice running, and the administrator must have assigned access rights for the individual users. You either can use one person's workstation as the server or use a true network server.

Note

A separate executable, new to version 5.1, is available for StarSchedule, so you can run it on your server without running the rest of StarOffice. You therefore can save system resources.

This section assumes StarOffice has already been installed on a network by a network administrator or other knowledgeable IT professional.

→ For more details on installing a StarSchedule server on a network, **see** Appendix A, "Installing StarOffice," **p. 1353**.

When StarSchedule is run on a network, all users can access the events and tasks that have been entered on the server. You can set access rights, using the access rights settings of the task, or events that the other users are allowed to see. If an appointment or task is listed as "public," all users can access it. If it is listed as "confidential," general users see only the start and end times of the event. If it is listed as "private," only those users you have designated as Designates can read, edit, delete, or add to your calendar.

ESTABLISHING A COMMON STARSCHEDULE SERVER

One of the strengths of StarSchedule is that you can turn your computer into a server for additional users. (If you have administrative rights on other computers or servers, you can also add new users to those servers from your computer.)

CONFIGURING A WORKSTATION AS A STARSCHEDULE SERVER For multiple users to share a schedule, StarOffice (or the new StarSchedule server) must continually run on that computer, and StarSchedule must be open.

Say, for example, that on a local area network (LAN), user Robin's computer (RC) is designated as the server for StarSchedule. Users Robin, Leslie, and Bart all want to access the common schedule. The client machine *RC* also doubles as Robin's workstation.

To enable Robin's computer to function as the StarSchedule server, you must first right-click the StarSchedule icon in the Explorer of Robin's workstation and select Properties from the context menu. Then, on the Settings tab, select the option Start StarSchedule at the Same Time StarOffice Is Started. Setting this option ensures that StarSchedule is always running on Robin's machine whenever StarOffice is open. However, if Robin shuts down the computer or closes StarOffice, the other users can no longer share the schedule.

PART

VI

CH

28

ADDING ADDITIONAL USERS TO A SERVER

Note

The following steps assume you are displaying the Explorer in Hierarchical view, not either of the symbols views. If you're working with either of the symbol views, you need to open StarSchedule and then its subcomponents in turn on the desktop. Frankly, working this way is very inefficient; it's best to work in Hierarchical view.

To make your computer a server for additional users, follow these steps:

1. On the computer that will serve as the client, click the plus sign next to the StarSchedule icon in the Explorer, and then click the plus sign next to Server. You then see My Computer as the (default) StarSchedule server.

2. Right-click the Servers icon and select Properties from the context menu.

3. In the Server Connection Properties dialog that appears, click the Settings tab, and then select Sharing. Leave the Port setting as is unless your administrator assigns you a different one.

   Now you have to add the names of all users you want to have access to your computer. Only administrators are allowed to add or delete users. As the Default User on your computer, you are automatically assigned administrator privileges. When you add new users, you can give them administrator rights also (by choosing New User, User, Administrator).

4. Right-click My Computer (or another server name if one exists), and select New User from the context menu. The New User dialog box appears.

5. Enter a name for that user in the General tab. This name will appear in the Explorer group.

6. In the Users tab, enter a login name and password for that particular user (or ask the user about his or her preferences).

7. Click the Add button to add one or more designates from a list of other users on the server or network—users who can access even private data.

8. Using the Settings tab, you can create and manage a list of categories for events and tasks, as well as set your standard working hours. If you want to automatically send reminders of events or tasks, click the Send Reminders option. To be notified within a specified time frame before the event takes place, click the check box below the Set Reminders check box, and select a time from the drop-down list to the left.

   In the drop-down list below, you can also specify whether to show events as private (in which case only you and your designates can see them), confidential (everyone can see the start and end times only), or public (all details are displayed).

   To add a category, click the New button, enter a name for the category in the New category dialog, and click OK. The name then appears in the Categories list.

Note

You can always change these entries later by selecting Properties from the user's context menu.

9. Repeat steps 4 through 7 for each additional user. After you finish adding the other users, your computer becomes a StarSchedule server. The other users can now use your computer as a remote server. However, unless the Default User has been assigned a login name and password, every user can make changes to the schedule.

10. To prevent others from making changes to a schedule component, right-click the default username and select Properties from the context menu. Using the Settings tab, enter a login name and password. By doing so, you ensure that schedules can be changed only by entering this name and password.

Caution

So you don't have to enter a login name and password yourself, right-click the My Computer name and select Properties. On the Settings tab, enter the same login name and password that you entered under Default User.

Depending on your operating system, you might be asked to reboot your computer for the new settings to take effect.

SELECTING A REMOTE SERVER FROM A CLIENT MACHINE

After a machine has been set up as a StarSchedule server, other users who want access to the schedule should launch StarOffice on their machines. Then, to connect with the designated server, you need to create a new connection.

To establish a new connection, follow these steps:

1. In the Explorer group, click the plus sign next to StarSchedule to open its subordinate entries: Servers, Events, and Tasks.

2. Right-click the Servers icon, and choose New Connection from the context menu.

3. On the General tab of the New Connection dialog that appears, enter the name for your new server connection. This name will appear in the Servers list in the Explorer; you can assign it any name you like—for example, Baxter Project.

4. On the Settings tab, enter the server name and port number. (Following the example begun in the preceding section, this would be the name and port number of Robin's computer.) Enter the user ID and password you've been assigned by the StarSchedule administrator. Adding them enables you to gain access to the server. Click OK when you're done.

3. When you see a new entry under Servers (for example, Baxter Project), click the plus sign next to the name to see a list with the schedules of all users on this server.

DEFINING A NEW EVENT/TASK VIEW ON A NETWORK

After you have selected a server and established new users, you can define a new event or task view that will show, for example, the events of a particular user—let's say Bart—with a few mouse clicks. Here's how:

1. Open the StarSchedule context menu in the Explorer group.

2. Select New Event View.

3. In the New Event dialog that appears, enter a name for the new event view—for example, Bart's Events.

4. On the Data tab of the New Event dialog, specify the server connection (in the previous example, Baxter Project).

5. From the User drop-down list, select the user whose events you want to see—in this example Bart's Events.

6. Using the View Options tab, select the Layout and Filters for the selected event. Click the Modify button to change settings, colors, columns, sort criteria, or group. You might want to select a filter that shows only those events and tasks that are relevant for the participants of "Baxter Project."

GETTING STARTED WITH STARSCHEDULE

After you've configured StarSchedule properly for network use, you can work within it in essentially the same way. However, single users can start StarSchedule with a shortcut that's not available to network users.

STARTING STARSCHEDULE FROM THE TASKBAR

If you're running StarOffice on a standalone computer, you can start StarSchedule by double-clicking the time display in the taskbar. StarSchedule opens in Events view to the current day (look ahead to Figure 28.4). This shortcut opens the default My Computer StarSchedule.

STARTING STARSCHEDULE FROM THE EXPLORER

When you're using StarSchedule on a network or with multiple calendars at once, you must launch StarSchedule from the Explorer. If you're a single user, you can also choose to start StarSchedule from here, although you can skip the step of selecting your server because you have only one available to you, My Computer.

Begin by clicking the StarSchedule element in the Explorer group to reveal its three elements:

- **Server**—Lists the StarSchedule server that manages your schedule and tasks. (If you're running StarSchedule locally, your default server is My Computer.)

- **Events**—Offers a complete day, week, workweek, or month-based scheduling and appointment tracking system that enables you to manage your appointments and tasks from within one window.

- **Tasks**—Provides a to-do list that you can use for business or personal tasks. You can use the Tasks component of StarSchedule to prioritize your to-do items as well as assign tasks to others.

SELECTING YOUR NETWORK STARSCHEDULE SERVER

If you're working with multiple servers and schedules, you first need to select the server you want to access. (Single users can skip this procedure.) To do so, just follow these steps:

1. Make sure you're in the Explorer in Hierarchical view and that StarSchedule is open, revealing the Server, Events, and Tasks icons.
2. Click the plus sign next to the Server icon to reveal your server choices.
3. Double-click the desired server.
4. Double-click the Events or Tasks icon to open the respective StarSchedule component on your desktop and start getting organized.

ORIENTING YOURSELF IN EVENTS VIEW

The StarSchedule Events view window can be divided into three sections: appointments, calendar, and tasks. Most of the tools you need for your work are on the Events object bar, which runs across the top of the StarSchedule workspace (see Figure 28.4).

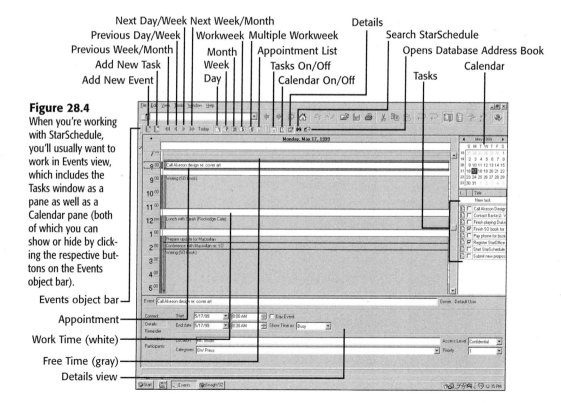

Figure 28.4
When you're working with StarSchedule, you'll usually want to work in Events view, which includes the Tasks window as a pane as well as a Calendar pane (both of which you can show or hide by clicking the respective buttons on the Events object bar).

PART
VI

CH
28

Tip #512 from
Michael & Sarah

You can drag events to your desktop as reminders. Double-clicking the event opens StarSchedule, and the event is shown.

Note

When you first open StarSchedule, you see two tasks in the Event and Task view: Register StarOffice and Start StarSchedule at the Same Time StarOffice Is Started.

Tip #513 from
Michael & Sarah

If you're new to StarSchedule, right-click anywhere in the Events or Tasks view to familiarize yourself with the various context menus. In StarSchedule—as in the rest of StarOffice—the quickest and easiest way to get things done is via the context menus or with drag and drop.

SETTING WORKWEEK PREFERENCES

By default, StarSchedule assumes your workweek lasts from Monday to Friday, and a workday lasts from 8 a.m. to 5 p.m. Your workday hours are shown in white; your free time appears in gray. If you're an independent contractor or part of a startup company, you'll soon realize that this schedule is idealistic, to say the least. Luckily, you can adjust the workdays and hours in your schedule (which will make you painfully aware that "After Hours" was nothing more than the title of a 1980s Martin Scorcese movie).

To customize your workweek, follow these steps:

1. Switch to Workweek view by clicking the Workweek icon (8th icon from the right) on the Events object bar.

2. Right-click anywhere in the schedule, and select Workweek from the context menu to open the Workweek dialog box.

3. Click in each check box to select or deselect the day that you want to make part of your workweek.

4. When you're finished, click OK.

StarSchedule immediately adjusts your schedule to reflect these changes.

Tip #514 from
Michael & Sarah

When you add Saturday or (yikes) Sunday to your workweek, StarSchedule shows the hours of both days as free time (gray background). To mark your work hours (white background) for either day, click and drag (in Day, Week, or Workweek view) to select the working hours for that particular day. Then right-click in the highlighted area, and select Background, Mark as Working Hours from the context menu. Likewise, you can "convert" working hours into free time by selecting Background, Mark as Free Time from the context menu.

You can control the start and end time of your workday in the User Properties dialog:

1. Right-click the current user (for example, Default User), and select Properties from the context menu to open the User Properties dialog.

2. Go to the Settings tab, and click Set Working Hours. The Working Hours dialog then appears.

3. Using the spin boxes underneath the workdays, you can set the work hours for each day individually, or you can click the All check box in the upper left of the dialog and change the start and end times collectively.

Note

Even if you designate Saturday or Sunday as a workday, you can control only the hours for Monday through Friday in the Working Hours dialog.

4. When you're finished, click OK twice to return to StarSchedule or your desktop.

Tip #515 from
Michael & Sarah

As part of its international orientation, StarSchedule, by default, does not list national holidays. However, you can easily import holidays by selecting File, Import Holidays the first time you start StarSchedule. In the Add Holidays to Calendar dialog that appears, select the year for which you want to add holidays, and click Create. Repeat for each year for which you want to add holidays. Holidays are shown on the calendar in boldface. If you can't see them, right-click the Calendar title bar, and select Show Events from the context menu.

VIEWING YOUR SCHEDULED ACTIVITIES

When you're in Events view, you can view the days and move around in many ways. You can view your appointments and events by day, week, month, workweek, or multiple workweeks. To switch views, click the respective button on the Events object bar (refer to Figure 28.4).

In addition, you can also create a list of your appointments by clicking the Appointment List button on the Events object bar.

In each view, you can use the arrow keys on your keyboard to move between the hours of the day (Day, Week, and Workweek views) or between the different days (Month and Multiple Workweek views).

Note

If you're using a mouse with a wheel, you can scroll through the hours and days in Day and Month view by turning the wheel. If you press the Shift key while turning the wheel, you can cycle from Day to Week to Month to Workweek to Multiple Workweek view and Appointment List View. If you press the Ctrl key while turning the wheel, you can change the time scale from 60 Minutes to 5 Minutes when in Day, Week, and Workweek view.

Alternatively, you can also click or drag in the calendar to select a particular day or certain number of consecutive days and have them displayed in the Event overview section.

HIDING DAYS AND WEEKS FROM VIEW   If you want, you can hide certain days from the weekly or monthly view. Just right-click the column header of the day you want to hide, and select Hide Day from the context menu. To show the day again, right-click the Column header to the left or right of the hidden day, and select Show Day from the context menu. If you want to hide an entire week, switch to Month view, open the context menu of a day that is part of the week you want to hide, and then select Weeks, Hide Selected Week from the context menu.

SHOWING WEEKENDS   To change the way weekends are displayed in your calendar, open the context menu and select Week Begins On Monday or Sunday. In Month view, if you click the column heads, you should see the Weekend option, where you can choose how you want to show weekends: Hidden, Normal, Compress Horizontally, or Compress Vertically.

Tip #516 from
Michael & Sarah

Click a day in the calendar, and then Shift+click the adjacent day. As you add more days, your event views change. If you Ctrl+Shift+click selected days, you can remove those days from view. Select Week or Workweek view, and drag across days in calendar; your Event view changes to reflect the selected days as soon as you release the mouse.

GROUPING AND SORTING EVENTS AND TASKS

When you want to have an at-a-glance view of your various activities or tasks, consider using the Group By and Sort By commands. Using these commands, you can easily create a grouping of your activities or to-dos for next week, or sort your schedule and tasks by category or priority.

To group or sort your scheduled activities or tasks, follow these steps:

1. (Events only) Click the Appointment List icon on the Events object bar to show all your activities in list form.

2. Right-click anywhere in the Events area to open the context menu, and select Group By or Sort By to open the Group Events or Event Sort Order dialogs, respectively.

3. Using the drop-down lists in the Group Events and Event Sort Order dialogs, you can define up to four different criteria by which to group or sort your activities in ascending or descending order, respectively.

4. Click OK to accept your settings.

To change the columns that appear in list view, open the context menu and select Column Selection. Then use the Add or Remove buttons to shift columns between the Available columns and Displayed columns list boxes in the Displayed Columns dialog that appears.

USING EVENTS

In the Events default setting, an overview of appointments for the current date appears. To the right, a monthly calendar and tasks list are displayed. Use the icons on the object bar or the commands in the View menu to view your appointments, tasks, or the calendar. You can adjust the division of the three main areas by dragging the separator with your mouse.

Note

Appointments are synchronized with the various views. If you select an appointment in any view and switch to a different view, you'll notice that the appointment is selected. In addition, the calendar highlights the day, week, and workweek that correspond to the selected appointment.

SETTING UP APPOINTMENTS AND EVENTS

Setting appointments and events in StarSchedule is as easy as selecting a day and time and entering a description for the appointment. Just follow these steps:

1. Double-click the Events icon in the Explorer (in Hierarchical view) to open the Events view window. (Alternatively, you can also click the StarSchedule icon and then click the Events icon on the desktop.)

2. Go to the monthly calendar section in the upper right, and click the day for which you want to enter the appointment. If necessary, use the arrow icons in the Calendar title bar to locate the month in which the appointment is supposed to take place. Clicking the left arrow displays the previous month; clicking the right arrow shows the next month. (If you can't see the calendar, click its icon on the object bar.)

3. If you're viewing events by the day, week, or workweek, click and drag to select the start and end time for the appointment or event; then begin typing to enter the text to be displayed for the new appointment (for example, Conference call with StarDivision). If you're viewing events by the month or workweeks, double-click the desired day to switch to the text input mode.

Tip #517 from
Michael & Sarah

By default, all appointments entered in Month or Workweeks view start at the beginning of the workday (usually 8:00 a.m.) and last for one hour. To adjust the start and end time of the activity without leaving the current view, simply drag the event up and down; a pop-up box tells you the current start and end time as you drag. To change the duration of the event, move the cursor over the start or end border of the appointment (it will change shape into a double arrow), then click and adjust the duration as desired. While keeping the Alt key pressed, you can drag to the 5-minutes grid.

4. To end the text input mode and automatically save your appointment, click anywhere outside the appointment block, or press Enter to open the Details view at the bottom of the Event overview. (Note that the Details button on the object bar has to be active for the Details view to open.)

5. Using the Details section of the Event overview, you can enter additional information for the selected appointment or event by clicking one of the buttons on the left. In each case, you get a different Events Details view. Your options include the following:

- **Content**—Click this button to enter a more detailed description of the appointment or event, or create links to related documents, emails, or other files that are relevant to the selected appointment or event. (This option is explained in detail in "Creating a 'Folder' for Your Events" later in this chapter.)

- **Details**—Use this option to create a more detailed profile of the selected event, including location (where the event takes place); category (one of the defaults or a custom one you enter); and priority (from 1 to 5, whereby 1 is the highest and 5 is the lowest). In addition, you can define how the time interval for the appointment will be displayed (Free, Busy, Tentative, Out of Office—in each case a different color will be used for the display), as well as modify the start and end dates and times of the appointment or event. Last but not least, you can use the Access Level drop-down list to control the access rights for the current event (important if your schedule is located on a network or publicly accessible server). If an appointment or task is listed as "public," all users can access it; if it is listed as "confidential," general users see only the start and end times of the event; if it is listed as "private," only those users you have identified as Designates can read or modify your schedule.

- **Reminder**—Here, you can select whether you want to be reminded of the event via a dialog box or email. (This option is explained in detail in "Setting Reminder Alerts" later in this chapter.)

- **Recurrences**—Click here to define an appointment as a recurring (daily, weekly, monthly, or annual) event. (This option is explained in detail in "Scheduling a Recurring Activity" in this chapter.)

- **Participants**—Use this option to create a list of participants in the event. In the day/time box on the right, you can enter time changes for a meeting. (For more details, see "Keeping Track of Whom You're Meeting" in this chapter.)

6. When you're finished, click anywhere outside the current event to accept your changes or modifications.

CREATING A "FOLDER" FOR YOUR EVENTS

Wouldn't it be nice if you could store all information (such as design documents, charts, calculations, emails, and so on) pertaining to a particular event in one spot? With StarSchedule, you can create links to related documents, emails, or other files that are relevant to the selected appointment or event. Just drag the relevant document to the defined appointment or the

Also Refer To box, and release the mouse button. StarSchedule automatically places the link in the Also Refer To list in the Details, Contents view.

For example, if you've come across an email or news posting that is relevant for an appointment or event, you can simply drag the message from the mail document to the StarSchedule button in the taskbar and, keeping the mouse button pressed, wait a second until StarSchedule pops up. Then drag the message to the defined appointment, and release the mouse button.

SETTING REMINDER ALERTS

One of the neat features in StarSchedule is its reminder option. You can have a message flash onscreen with a little ditty or other sound to remind you of your appointment. If you're out of the office or temporarily using another computer, you can remind yourself of an appointment by having StarSchedule send you an email reminder. You can set the alarm to go off up to two weeks in advance or only minutes before the appointment. Just follow these steps if you never want to miss an appointment again:

1. Select the event you want to be reminded of (or enter a new one).

2. Open the Details view by clicking the Details button on the object bar or by selecting View, Details. You then see the Details view pane at the bottom of the Events view window. (If necessary, you can pull up or down the separator line between the Detail view and the Events window.)

3. Click the Reminder option, and select the type of reminder—Dialog or Email.

   If you want to be reminded of your appointment by a pop-up dialog box, select Dialog. If you want to be reminded of your appointment ahead of time, you can also click the Display Dialog check box and select how much time in advance you want to be notified (from minutes to hours to days) from the Before event list box. If you think the pop-up dialog alone won't get your attention, select the Play Sound check box, which enables you to choose between the default alert sound or a sound from the Gallery's Sound theme folder.

   If you select Email, you can also specify how much time before the event you want StarSchedule to send the email. You can have the program send the email to your regular email address by selecting Use Sender Address from the Outbox Settings, or you can enter an email address manually. After you make your selection, you'll see a small alarm clock symbol next to the event.

Note

If you want to take advantage of the reminder feature, you have to run StarSchedule continually in the background (and preferably start the module at the same time StarOffice is started). When you set your first reminder, StarOffice checks whether StarSchedule is currently configured to start automatically. If not, you see the Service Configuration dialog. Click Yes if you want to activate StarSchedule automatically when StarOffice is started; the program makes all the necessary adjustments for you. Alternatively, you can change this setting manually. Just right-click the StarSchedule item in the Explorer and select Properties from the context menu. Then go to the Settings tab, select Start StarSchedule at the Same Time StarOffice Is Started, and click OK.

PART

VI

CH

28

SCHEDULING A RECURRING ACTIVITY

Some events happen at frequent intervals: For example, every year, you have to file taxes by April 15; every month or week, you might have to attend a certain meeting at the same day and time. Other events happen with irregular frequency; for example, you might have a meeting every day at 9:00 a.m. except for one Friday, when the meeting is scheduled for 10 a.m. In both scenarios, StarSchedule enables you to define an appointment as a recurring event, so you have to enter it only once.

Follow these steps to enter appointments that happen with regular or irregular frequency:

1. Enter the event for the desired time period. (For example, drag the mouse from 9 to 10, enter the text that describes the event, and press Enter to open the Details view.)

2. Click the Recurrence option, and select the frequency of the activity. In general, you can specify the frequency for as often as daily or as rarely as once per year. Your options include the following:

   - **Daily**—Specify the number of days between each occurrence of the activity, whether the activity happens only every weekday, and the date on which the activity is to end.

   - **Weekly**—Specify the number of weeks between each occurrence of the activity, the day of the week that the activity is to be repeated, and the date on which the activity is to end.

   - **Monthly**—Specify the number of months between each occurrence of the activity, the day of the week that the activity is to be repeated, and the date on which the activity is to end.

   - **Yearly**—Specify the day of the month that the activity is to be repeated each year and the date on which the activity is to end.

   For this example, select Daily, and then select Every Weekday.

3. Click the End Recurrence By list box arrow to open a calendar view. Here, you can select the last day of the recurring event to be marked in your schedule. Of course, you can also enter a date manually (for example, 7/8/99). Click in the schedule to enter the recurring appointments.

> **Note**
>
> All recurrences are entered automatically. To control your entry, switch to monthly view. Recurring events are marked with two arrows chasing each other in a circle.

> **Tip #518 from**
> *Michael & Sarah*
>
> Instead of entering an end date under Recurrence, you can also select the Events monthly view, right-click the last day of the recurring event, and select Set as Last Event for Recurrence from the context menu.

4. So far, the event has been marked as occurring every day at the same time. However, for this example, the appointment will happen at a different time on a certain day. Right-click the day and event in question, and select Separate from Recurrence from the context menu. Then drag the event to its new time slot.

Note

> Separating the event that differs from all others in the series is important; otherwise, the recurrence will be valid for this event on that particular day and all the other days (for example, every Friday). Only if you separate the event from the recurrences first is it valid only on that particular day.

KEEPING TRACK OF WHOM YOU'RE MEETING

StarSchedule makes it easy to keep track of whom you're meeting or the people who are involved in a certain event or task.

You can drag the name of a participant from your Database Address Book and drop it on the event or task, or in the Participant's box (if the Details, Participants view is open). StarSchedule lists the name and email address in the Participants field. (Alternatively, you can enter a name directly in the list box field, or you can select the name from the drop-down list and press Enter.) Click the State box to the right of the email, and select one of four options to indicate the status of the participant's involvement in the event or task (Confirmed, Tentative Confirm, Refused, Canceled).

USING TASKS

The Tasks component of StarSchedule provides a to-do list that helps you organize and keep track of your business and personal tasks (see Figure 28.5). And because tasks are time-related, you can view and enter them not only in Tasks view, but also in the Events view of StarSchedule.

Tip #519 from
Michael & Sarah

> The context menu in the task window offers several additional commands to set the display or define properties for the current task. Depending on whether you open the context menu in a task, in a column header, or in a blank area, different commands appear.

CREATING A TO-DO LIST

When creating a to-do (or task) list, you have two options: You can enter your tasks in the Tasks view portion of StarSchedule, or you can enter them in Events view.

When you're in Events view, click the New Task icon on the Events object bar, or click in the New Task box below the Tasks title bar; then start typing the text for your task.

Entering tasks in Tasks view is similar to entering them in Events view, although you have a few more options for filling in task-related data, including the Due Date, Priority, and

Status of the task. To get started, click the New Task icon on the Tasks object bar, or click in the Title of the New Task box; then start typing your task text. Next, click the Due Date, Priority, and Status list boxes, and select the task-related information from the drop-down lists. When you're finished, click anywhere in the Tasks area. StarSchedule automatically adds the text to the list of existing tasks.

Figure 28.5
Use the Tasks compo-
nent of StarSchedule
when you want to
focus on organizing
your task list.

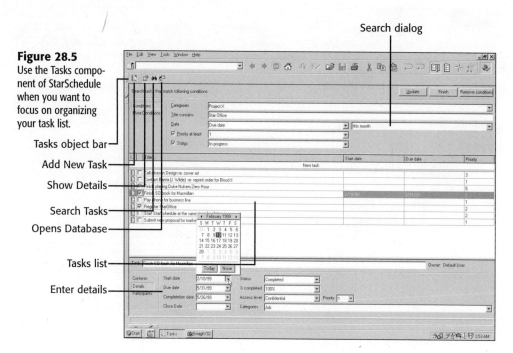

Tasks object bar
Add New Task
Show Details
Search Tasks
Opens Database
Tasks list
Enter details
Search dialog

When you're entering task text, StarSchedule automatically opens the Tasks Details view. As in the Events Details view, you can enter additional information for the current task by clicking one of the buttons on the left in the Details section. In each case, you get a different Tasks Details view. The following are your options:

- **Contents**—Click this button to enter a more detailed description of the task, or create links to related documents, emails, or other files that are relevant to the selected task. To create links, simply drag a document or message to the task or the Also Refer To list box.

- **Details**—Here, you can enter a start date, due date, completion date, and close date for the current task, as well as indicate the current status of the task and the percentage already completed. As with appointments, you can also control the access rights for the current tasks and assign a category to the task (which is important if you want to take advantage of StarSchedule's powerful search and filtering options).

- **Participants**—Use this option to keep track of people involved in a task. You can drag the name of a participant from your Database Address Book and drop it on the task or in the Participant's box (if the Details, Participants view is open). StarSchedule lists the name and email address in the Participants field. In addition, you can specify a participant's status (Confirmed, Tentative Confirm, Refused, Canceled) from the State drop-down list.

You can use tasks to prioritize your to-do items. When your task list gets overly long, you can easily search it by setting custom search conditions.

ASSIGNING TASKS TO OTHERS

Using StarSchedule, you can easily assign a task to others by sending the other person email using these steps:

1. Right-click the task (in Tasks or Events view) that you want to assign to one of your associates, and select Send Event as Email from the context menu. StarOffice automatically opens a StarMail document that contains all the necessary information on that particular task (see Figure 28.6).

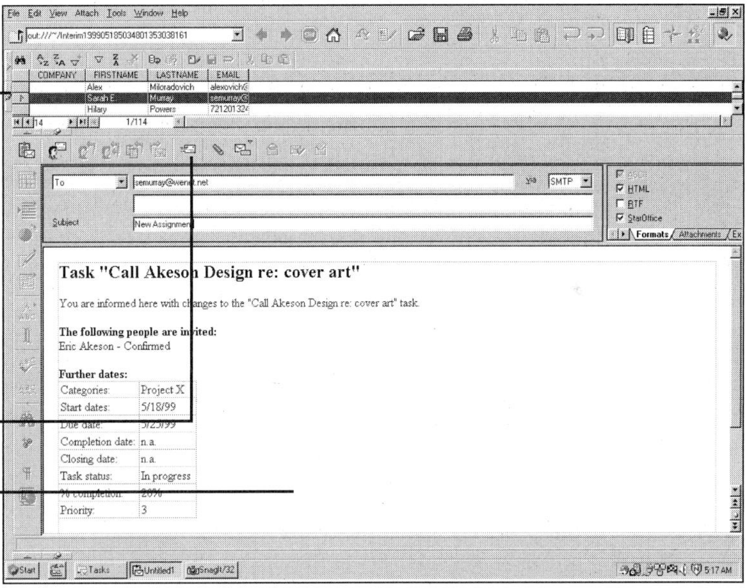

Figure 28.6
Assigning tasks to others on your team has never been this easy: just right-click the task you want to delegate, and select Send Event as Email from the context menu. StarSchedule automatically creates a mail document.

Address Book

Click to send email

Task details

2. Click the Address Book icon on the object bar to open the Database Address Book; then drag the contact to whom you want to assign a task to the To box.

3. Enter a reference to the task in the Subject box.

4. Click the Send button on the Mail object bar to send off the email.

→ For more details on using StarMail, **see** "Creating and Sending Mail," **p. 1053**.

PART

VI

CH

28

EDITING EVENTS AND TASKS

To edit an event or task, you first have to open it. Opening an event or task is the equivalent of opening its Details view. You can open events from the Events component of StarSchedule, and you can open tasks from the Events or Tasks components of StarSchedule.

To open an appointment or event, right-click the event you want to edit, and select Open from the context menu.

To open a task, right-click the desired task in Tasks view or in the Tasks list in Events view, and select Open from the context menu.

In both instances, StarSchedule opens the Details view of the selected event or task. You can then edit your event or task entry using the respective Details views. Any changes you make are saved immediately to StarSchedule.

Tip #520 from *Michael & Sarah*	To quickly modify the start or end time for an appointment, use the mouse to shift the upper or lower border of the desired event.

Tip #521 from *Michael & Sarah*	To quickly move from one appointment or task to the next or previous one, press the Tab key or Shift+Tab, respectively. In Events view, the next appointment is selected, and you can directly enter your text. In Tasks view, you can move from one column to the next within a task and then to the next task to make the desired changes (using the up- and down-arrow keys to cycle through your options in the Task drop-down lists). Press Esc to exit the text input mode. If you then press Delete, the appointment or task is deleted.

MOVING AND COPYING EVENTS

If you want to move an appointment to a different time, simply drag it to the desired time scale in the appointment overview.

To copy an appointment, drag it to the desired time scale while pressing the Ctrl key. A plus sign next to the mouse pointer indicates that the appointment will be copied when you release the mouse button.

You can also drag an appointment and drop it on the desired day in the calendar. StarSchedule automatically inserts it at the defined time to that day's events.

CONVERTING TASKS AND EVENTS

StarSchedule enables you to convert tasks into events and vice versa when you're in Events view. To convert a task into an event, click the page icon on the left side of the task, and drag it from the task area to the desired day and time scale in the event area. By dragging the upper and lower margin, you can correct the start and end times (press the Alt key while dragging to change the time in five-minute increments). StarSchedule registers the task as an event, and you can see a link to the original in the Also Refer To list box of the Details, Contents view.

Likewise, you can convert an event or appointment into a task by dragging the appointment into the Tasks area. Just release the mouse button when you have the mouse cursor over a free area or on the title bar, and the appointment is copied as a task.

DELETING EVENTS AND TASKS

To delete an event or task, right-click the event or task you want to remove in the Events or Tasks view of StarSchedule, and select Delete from the context menu.

SEARCHING STARSCHEDULE

If you use StarSchedule on a regular basis to keep track of your activities and to-do items, sooner or later you will find a use for its powerful Search feature. For example, you can search events and tasks by categories, priorities, dates, descriptions, access levels, and more.

Tip #522 from
Michael & Sarah

To make the most of the Search feature, be sure to fill in the Details dialogs (Contents, Details, Reminder, Recurrence, and Participants) of your individual events or tasks. The more information you provide, the narrower (and hence more useful) your search results.

To use this feature, click the Search button on the Events or Tasks object bar. When you're in List view, the search is executed following the criteria you specify in the Conditions and More Conditions portions of the Search view (refer to Figure 28.5). All appointments or tasks that correspond to the current filter and search conditions are displayed; the rest of them are hidden.

If you start a search from a Day, Week, or Month view, the Search feature searches all appointments that satisfy the criteria set in the current filter. The search results in these views appear highlighted as you scroll upward and downward with your scroll arrow. You also can see other appointments that follow the corresponding filter.

USING FILTERS AND STYLES

Using the Filter and Layout commands, you can select what you want to show in your Events or Tasks view. For example, you can filter appointments and events by category to show only the appointments or tasks that belong to a selected category. Furthermore, you can define certain styles that control how the information is displayed. You can combine filters and styles any which way you like; plus, you can save each combination as a view with a separate name so that you can easily find it again. The combination view is listed in the Explorer under the StarSchedule element.

You can save your personal settings at any time and reload them again later. This capability enables you to use various layouts, filter settings, and styles.

To create custom filters or layouts, open the context menu (in Events or Tasks view) and select Current Filter, Define Filter or Current Layout, Define Layout, respectively.

PART

VI

CH

28

Note

Using the filter setting, you can print your tasks and/or events anytime you like. You can see this filter setting on your screen. For example, if you want to print your "office" events, just create an office filter to display only the office events, and click the Print icon on the function bar.

WORKING WITH EVENT AND TASK CATEGORIES

To take full advantage of the filtering capabilities of StarSchedule, you should always assign a category to an appointment or task. Using categories enables you to cut to the chase in a full schedule and show only those appointments that belong to a specified category. You can assign categories in the Details view. To do so, just click the Details button, and select a category from the Categories drop-down list.

ADDING NEW CATEGORIES   If none of the existing categories describe the selected event, you can create a new one by following these steps:

1. In the Explorer group (set to Hierarchical view), click the plus sign next to StarSchedule; then click the plus sign next to Server and then My Computer.
2. Right-click the name Default User, and select Properties from the context menu.
3. On the Settings tab of the User Properties dialog that appears, click the New button. In the resulting New Category dialog, enter a new category name, and click OK.

StarOffice immediately adds the new category to the Categories for Events and Tasks list, which controls the existing categories in the Categories drop-down list in the Details view.

COLOR-CODING EVENTS AND CATEGORIES   Each event has a colored bar that appears at the left of the Event area. The bar marks the hours corresponding to the event or appointment; the color shows the activity as Free (white), Tentative (dark green), Busy (blue), or Out of Office (red), depending on the setting in the Show Time As drop-down list in the Details, Details view. That way, you always have an overview of your appointments and can see at a glance how much free time you still have.

By default, each category in StarSchedule has been assigned a color, so you can easily recognize the event as belonging to a certain category (for example, Personal is yellow, Job is green, and so on). Colors appear as thin, vertical strips to the left of the appointment text. You can accept StarSchedule's default color assignments, or you can create your own.

To assign a color to a particular activity, open the Events context menu (by right-clicking in a free area of the schedule), and select Event Colors. In the Event Colors dialog that appears, you can assign a color to an existing category by selecting the category in the Categories list and then clicking a color swatch in the Colors palette.

FILTERING VIEWS

To filter all but certain events and tasks, you have two options: You can use a temporary filter, or you can define a filter that you save under a separate name so that you can use it again in the future. You can do both using almost identical dialogs: Event Filters and Task Filter.

For example, to show only events that are part of the category Ideas, you have to do the following:

1. Right-click in the Events view to open the context menu, and select Define Filter from the Current Filter submenu. (You can also use View, Define Events Filter; however, the context menu is faster.)

2. In the Event Filters dialog that appears, select the Settings tab. Here, you can select a filter condition and click OK if you want only a temporary filter that is not saved under a special name.

If you want a filter that you can save for future use, follow these steps:

1. Open the context menu, and select Define Filter from the Current Filter submenu.

2. Select the Selection tab.

3. Click the New button to open the Create New Filter dialog.

4. Enter a name for the desired filter. If you have previously created filters, you can choose whether to create the new filter as a copy of an existing filter (Create as Copy option) and select the name of the filter you want to base the new one on from the list. All you have to do then is make the desired changes and save them, rather than create a filter from scratch (kind of like basing a new style created in the Stylist on an existing style).

5. Click OK to return to the Event Filters dialog. Notice the Selection Enabled in This View Only option in the lower left of the Selection tab. If you select this option, the newly defined filter will be available only in the context menu of the current view. As soon as you select a different view from the Explorer, the filter will no longer be available. That way, you can separate your personal events from the business events.

6. Go to the Settings tab, and select the category Ideas from the Events Assigned drop-down list.

7. Click OK.

Now you see only those events that correspond to the filter conditions. If you want to cancel this filter view, you can do so by right-clicking in the Events view window and selecting Filter Off from the Current Filter submenu.

USING DIFFERENT LAYOUT VIEWS

Working with styles is similar to working with filters. You also have the option to decide whether you want to use a temporary style (without a name) or whether you want to define a style that you can call up anytime by name.

Perhaps you want to design a style that shows events in as little a space as possible. Right-click to open the Events View context menu, and select Current Layout, Define Layout (you can also select View, Define Event Layout). The Event Layout: Default Layout dialog opens. Following the same procedure as described earlier with filters, you can define a new layout using the Selection tab and then define its properties using the Settings tab.

Using the Settings tab, you can define a Day and Week view (including a time scale) and a Monthly view. If you select the Autosize Day Event Display Area, the contents of the Day view are proportionally compressed if you compress the entire Events view window (for example, by dragging the divider between the Events view and the calendar on the right to the left). If this option is not selected, the Events view has a fixed width. If necessary, a horizontal scrollbar is added.

IMPORTING AND EXPORTING DATA

If you've been using other electronic organizers before and would like to consolidate your appointments and task lists into one spot, you can switch to StarOffice as your Personal Information Manager (PIM) without missing a beat—well, okay, perhaps missing a few. You can directly import Microsoft Outlook 97 and vCalendar PIM events and tasks, or indirectly import any PIM files exported as text files (.prn, .txt, or .csv) or dBASE files by choosing File, Import when you're in Events or Tasks view.

Likewise, you can export your StarSchedule data as Netscape Calendar- and Microsoft Outlook 98-compatible vCalendar events and tasks by choosing File, Export.

→ For more information on importing data into StarOffice, **see** "Importing and Exporting Data," **p. 636** and **p. 1085**.

LINKING STARSCHEDULE WITH PALMPILOT

If you have a 3COM US Robotics PalmPilot II or later and chose the PalmPilot add-in during installation, you can synchronize data with StarSchedule as well.

Note

To link data between StarSchedule and your PalmPilot, you must have the 3COM PalmPilot software installed on your system.

StarDivision has created the StarSchedule PalmPilot Link to enable you to link data between your PalmPilot and your desktop StarSchedule database. If you installed your PalmPilot software prior to the installation of StarOffice, the StarOffice setup program recognizes it and installs the PalmPilot add-in module automatically. Otherwise, you have to run Setup again and select Modify to add the PalmPilot add-in. (You can find the PalmPilot add-in listed in the StarSchedule module.)

After the PalmPilot add-in is installed, you have to configure the PalmPilot software for use with StarSchedule as follows:

1. Click the PalmPilot HotSync Manager icon, and select Custom from the shortcut menu. The Custom dialog appears.

2. Select the conduit for events (calendar), and click the Change button. The Change HotSync Action dialog appears.

3. Select the Do Nothing and Set as Default options, and then click OK.

4. Repeat steps 2 and 3 for the conduits tasks (to-dos) and addresses (contacts).

5. Click Done to return to your desktop.

6. Open the Palm Install Tool to install StarSync on your system. (The Palm Install Tool can be found in the PalmPilot folder of your Programs menu.) The Palm Install Tool dialog appears.

7. Click the Add button. The Open dialog then appears.

8. Locate the `Office51\Palmpilot` folder, select `starsync.prc`, and click Open.

9. Click Done to close the Palm Install Tool dialog.

10. Launch StarOffice and click the HotSync button on the PalmPilot cradle. (Be sure the PalmPilot sits in the cradle.) This step ensures that StarSync is installed on the PalmPilot.

You can now link data between StarSchedule and your PalmPilot. Just be sure to start StarOffice before pressing the HotSync button on the PalmPilot cradle.

Tip #523 from
Michael & Sarah

To modify your StarSync options, click the HotSync icon, and select Custom from the shortcut menu. In the Custom dialog that appears, select StarSync and click the Change button to open the StarSync Setup dialog. Here, you can control the details of your StarSchedule and PalmPilot data exchange.

BACKING UP SCHEDULES

All important StarSchedule information is saved in two files: `schedule.cal` (located in the `Office51\Store` folder) and `schedule.cfg` (located in the `Office51\Config` folder). The file `schedule.cal` contains your saved events and tasks, and `schedule.cfg` contains all configuration information regarding server connections, views, filters, layout, and so on. Be sure to include these files in your regular backup routine.

Note

The appointments and tasks are automatically saved in StarSchedule as soon as you enter them.

PRINTING APPOINTMENTS AND TASKS

Printing appointments and tasks is not much different from printing other StarOffice documents. You select File, Print or click the Print icon on the function bar to start the printing process. Where StarSchedule differs is that it provides print templates.

If you click the Print icon, StarSchedule uses the print template that corresponds to the current view. For example, if you're in Day view, StarSchedule prints a day view of the events schedule; if you're in Week view, it uses the print form Week overview, and so on.

PART
VI

CH
28

If you prefer to use another print template, select File, Print and click the Options button to open the Print Form dialog, shown in Figure 28.7. Choose the desired print form from the list of available forms, or use the buttons on the right to edit an existing form or template or create a new one. Next, specify the print range; then click OK twice to print your schedule or task list.

Note

When you're printing for the first time in StarSchedule, the print templates must be calculated. You can then be sure that the defaults in your operating system (language, date format, and so on) will be considered. Because the process might take awhile, please have some patience when printing for the first time.

Figure 28.7
Use the Print Form dialog to select a default template or create a custom one when you're printing your scheduled activities and tasks.

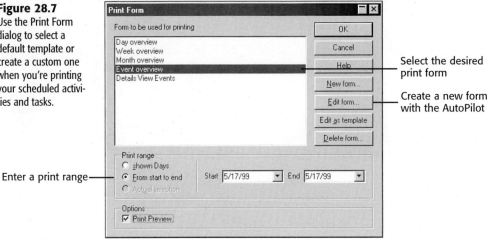

Select the desired print form

Create a new form with the AutoPilot

Enter a print range

Note

The events in your events calendar, defined as day events, are separately marked when printing them and do not contain any time information. If, for a certain event, you entered a location, it is also printed.

TROUBLESHOOTING

Is it possible to import contacts from Outlook 98 into StarOffice?

Yes. Export the addresses in CSV format, then import them into StarCalc. Arrange the columns according to the SO standard (take the existing address book as your model). Finally, copy and paste the date into a `.dbf` file.

How can I add or delete categories in StarSchedule?

Open the Explorer group. Expand the StarSchedule folder tree, then click the plus symbol (+) next to Data Source, and finally click the plus symbol next to My Computer. Now right-click Default User to open the context menu. Select Properties, then click the Settings tab in the User Properties dialog that appears. To add categories, click the New button. To delete categories, select the unwanted item and click the Delete button.

The Outlook calendar always lists events in bold. Why can't StarOffice do the same?

StarOffice can do the same, but not by default. You have to make a minor adjustment. Right-click in the Calendar window in Even view, than select Show Events. All days that have events will now appear in bold.

Is it possible to print certain events and tasks?

Yes. Select the days on which the events take place in the Calendar area of the Event view, then choose File, Print from the menu bar. In the Print dialog that appears, click OK to print immediately, or click the Options button and select a desired print form first.

CHAPTER 29

COMMUNICATING WITH STARMAIL AND STARDISCUSSION

In this chapter

ORIENTING YOURSELF IN STARMAIL AND STARDISCUSSION

StarMail is StarOffice's built-in email program. It has three components that work hand-in-hand and share common tools:

- The StarMail composition window
- The email account Inbox(es)
- The email account Outbox

You compose and send new mail from the StarMail composition window. You read and reply to incoming email in an account Inbox in the Explorer, and you manage copies of sent mail in the Outbox.

Note

What we call email and news *accounts* throughout this book are usually referred to in the StarOffice Help as email and news *servers*.

StarDiscussion is StarOffice's news reader. A *news reader* is a program designed to read Usenet newsgroups. Newsgroups are a distinct type of Internet communication that uses a different protocol—called NNTP (Network News Transfer Protocol—than email does. Although you set up and manage a news account differently versus an email account, you read and write news and email in the same way.

We discuss StarDiscussion in more depth in the section "Beyond Mail: Joining Newsgroups with StarDiscussion," later in this chapter. However, we introduce it together with StarMail because they share common tools and desktop organization. They also share the same Outbox—all news postings, as well as all outgoing emails, are saved in and routed through the Outbox.

Note

StarOffice does not have its own dial-up networking program. To use the features described in this chapter, you must have a properly configured modem and dial-up or network connection. When you are physically connected to your network, click the Online button on the function bar to activate StarOffice's connection to your network.

This chapter assumes that you have already configured your Internet connection from within StarOffice, as well as created an email account Inbox and Outbox in the Explorer. If you haven't done so, you should refer to Chapter 3, "Getting Ready for Work," and set up your Internet and email accounts before continuing.

→ For information on setting up your email account inbox and Outbox, **see** "Getting Online," **p. 85**.

After you've set up your email account Inbox and Outbox, you can read and reply to emails on your desktop. You can also compose new email messages by using the File, New, Mail command as well as send Web pages and documents as email directly from your desktop.

INTRODUCTION TO COMMON TOOLS

Each of the four desktop windows that you use to manage mail and news has its own unique tools, but they also share common tools on the object bar across the top of their windows. Table 29.1 describes each of them.

PART

VI

CH

29

Note

Only in StarDiscussion are all the tools active.

TABLE 29.1 OBJECT BAR TOOLS IN STARMAIL AND STARDISCUSSION

Name	Function
Properties	Reveals the properties of the selected email or news message. In the case of sent messages, it shows a recipient list.
Details	Changes the layout to display messages in list form with details.
Icons	Changes the layout to display messages as icons.
Message	Turns the display of message contents on and off.
Headers	Turns the display of message headers on and off.
Layout 1	Displays contents in the selected format.
Layout 2	Displays contents in the selected format.
Layout 3	Displays contents in the selected format.
Layout 4	Displays contents in the selected format.
New Message	Opens the StarMail composition window.
Reply	Opens a StarMail composition window addressed to the sender of the message or posting that is currently open. Automatically quotes the contents of the original message.
Reply to All	Opens a StarMail composition window with the addresses of all recipients of the currently open message or posting. Automatically quotes message contents.
Post Reply	Posts a reply to a newsgroup. Active only in StarDiscussion.
Forward	Opens a StarMail composition window with a copy of the currently selected email or posting, ready for addressing.
Mark Thread Read	Marks a news discussion thread or email message thread as read.
Mark Thread Unread	Marks a news discussion thread or email message thread as unread. A green diamond appears in the Read column.
Read	Marks an email message as read. A small gray diamond appears in the Read column.

continues

TABLE 29.1   OBJECT BAR TOOLS IN STARMAIL AND STARDISCUSSION

Name	Function
Marked	Applies a mark to a message, posting, or folder. A flag displays in the Marked column.
Next Unread Message	Moves you to the next unread message.
Previous Unread Message	Moves you to the previous unread message.
Next Messag	Moves you to the next message.
Previous Message	Moves you to the previous message.
Delete	Deletes the message or folder and stores it in the Recycle Bin.

Tip #524 from
Michael & Sarah

You can add a button to save a draft email to the function bar or the StarMail composition toolbar. Choose the View menu Toolbars, Customize command. Click the Explorer category and you'll find the button for Save Draft (of email). Just drag the icon and drop it onto the toolbar.

ORIENTING YOURSELF IN THE INBOX, OUTBOX, AND NEWS WINDOWS

The account Inbox, Outbox, and StarDiscussion news reader windows are variants of the same window. They share exactly the same Object bar, but some tools are always grayed out in the Outbox and Inbox toolbars because they are relevant only to news.

The commonalties are apparent in Figures 29.1, 29.2, and 29.3, which show an open Outbox, account Inbox, and StarDiscussion window, respectively.

Each window is divided into four panes. The default layout is the layout shown in Figures 29.1 through 29.3. Selected message information is displayed in a list in the top pane (sender, subject, date, and status information); complete header information (the technical stuff) is displayed in the middle-left pane; information on the format of the received message and any attachments are displayed in the middle-right pane; and the text of the currently selected message is displayed on the bottom.

Note

In some versions of the online Help, discussions of managing news and mail suggest that you can manage your Inbox and Outbox messages in the Beamer. This is an error—it should refer to the Header pane of the news and mail windows. The Beamer and the Header pane do function in very similar ways, however.

You can modify the display of fields in the Header pane just as you do in the Beamer: Open the header context menu and use the Insert and Remove commands, and click on the column field names. You can turn off and on the display of headers and messages and change the layout style with tools in the object bar.

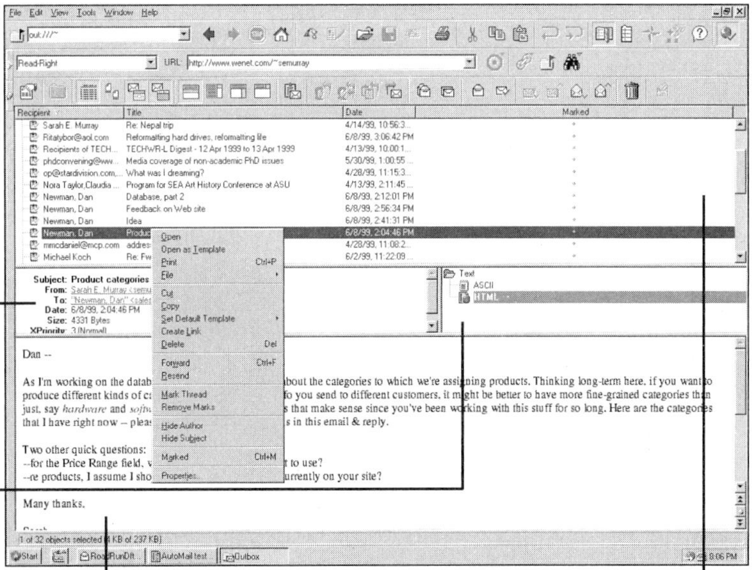

Figure 29.1
Right-clicking in each pane opens context menus and sub-menus, most of which are common across the Outbox, Inboxes, and StarDiscussion, with minor variations. You see the Outbox message context menu here, opened by selecting a message and right-clicking.

Header information

Attachments

Text of currently selected message

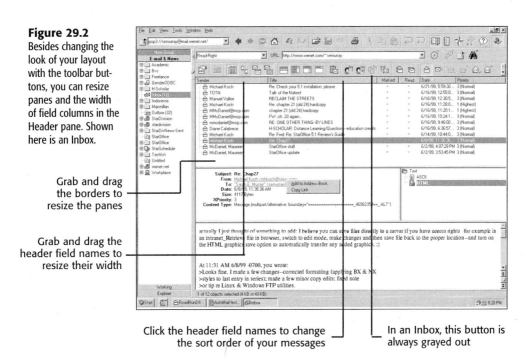

Message information. Click a message to display its contents below

Figure 29.2
Besides changing the look of your layout with the toolbar buttons, you can resize panes and the width of field columns in the Header pane. Shown here is an Inbox.

Grab and drag the borders to resize the panes

Grab and drag the header field names to resize their width

Click the header field names to change the sort order of your messages

In an Inbox, this button is always grayed out

Figure 29.3
The news posting context menu is similar to the email message context menu but has commands specific to posting newsgroup replies. Notice that only in StarDiscussion are all the toolbar buttons active.

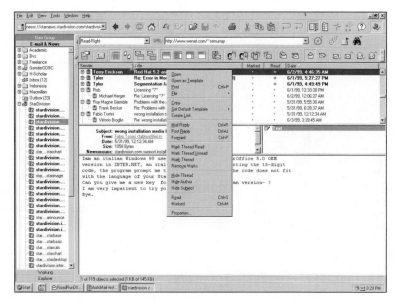

→ For more information on using StarDiscussion, **see** "Beyond Mail: Joining Newsgroups with StarDiscussion," **p. 1068**.

USING INBOXES

To download and read new email, you need to be connected to your network or ISP and have the StarOffice Online button on the function bar pressed. Then, double-click the Inbox icon in the Explorer. Your account Inbox opens on the desktop.

> **Note**
>
> If your account inbox is set to Update on Open on its Explorer context menu, you might receive an error message ("connection failure") if you are not online and connected when you open your Inbox. However, your Inbox will still open on your desktop. If you have selected to save messages locally, your previously downloaded messages will be available for reading. If you store your messages on your server, you might see only message headers. Alternately, your Inbox might be entirely empty if no headers have been held in cache.

By default, your Inbox is set to Update on Open, which means it connects with the specified server, searches for new mail, and downloads either the headers or the entire message contents to your computer (depending on the properties you assigned your Inbox during setup). If you have the Explorer open, your account Inbox name appears there in bold if you have new or unread messages. You also see some numbers next to its name, like those in Figure 29.2. The number on the left is the total number of unread messages, and the number on the right is the total number of message headers or messages currently stored in your Inbox.

Tip #525 from *Michael & Sarah*	If you store messages locally and frequently respond to mail offline, either deselect Update on Open and update your mail manually with the Explorer menu Update command when you're ready; or make sure the Online button on the function bar is set to Off (does not look pressed in).

To read a message, click its message header in the Header pane. To reply, forward, or create a new message click the appropriate button on the object bar. A StarMail composition window opens where you can type your message.

Tip #526 from *Michael & Sarah*	You can click an email address in the Header Details pane to open a new composition addressed to that recipient.

USING THE OUTBOX

You are allowed to have only one Outbox. This is because the Outbox does more than save your sent messages and news postings—it keeps track of all your outgoing email and newsgroup traffic. The Outbox is also where your mail merge email documents are sent and saved after completing a mail merge if you are not online at the time. (To send them, select the Outbox in the Explorer and choose the Update command from its context menu.)

To read the contents of the Outbox, double-click its icon in the Explorer. When your Outbox is open, you can read, mark, print, and export files with context menu commands and compose new mail by clicking the New Mail tool.

Tip #527 from *Michael & Sarah*	If you've sent a message in multiple formats, you can see how the message appears to recipients in a specific format by double-clicking its icon (HTML, RTF, StarOffice) in the Attachments pane. The message displays in the selected format in the Message Contents pane.

ORIENTING YOURSELF IN THE STARMAIL COMPOSITION WINDOW

When you choose File, New, Mail or click the New Mail tool on the Outbox and Inbox bars, the StarMail composition window opens. This window offers what should be a familiar selection of text tools for formatting and editing. The basics of entering, editing, and formatting text and objects are the same as those for any text document in StarWriter. However, because email is created to be sent over the Internet, not printed to paper, the choices of file formats are different: You can send messages only in HTML, RTF, and StarOffice formats, in addition to the default ASCII text.

Caution	Recipients of your mail might not be able to open and read mail in non-ASCII formats. Before choosing one of the other formats, read the section "Choosing Email File Formats," later in this chapter.

Figure 29.4 shows the StarMail composition window as it appears when you select File, New, Mail or double-click the New Mail icon on the StarOffice desktop. These are the same tools, minus a few, that you find on the Inbox, Outbox, and StarDiscussion object bars. Details on these tools are given in Table 29.1 earlier in this chapter. The Show Address Book command on the StarMail toolbar (not visible in Figure 29.4) has been clicked to open the address table in the Beamer in its specially filtered email form, enabling you to easily address your mail by dragging and dropping records.

The window is divided into three panes:

- The Email Header pane, where you address your mail and enter a subject line.
- The Options pane, with three tabs where you select the email format, attach files, and set the priority of a message.
- The Composition pane, where you write an email message.

When you open the StarMail composition window, most tools are grayed out. When you click in the Header window, the relevant tools on the StarMail object bar become active. When you click in the Composition window, the main toolbar on the left becomes active, as it is in Figure 29.5, and you have a range of common desktop text tools at your fingertips. The Text object bar also appears in place of the StarMail object bar. The StarMail object bar is still available—just click the button with the black arrow on the far right of the text object bar.

Figure 29.4
The key to using the StarMail composition window is realizing that the available tools change depending on whether your cursor is in the Email Header pane or the Composition pane. If you want to have the StarMail object bar always visible, click the button with the black arrow on the right side of the Text object bar.

Composition pane

Enter the recipient's address and press Enter

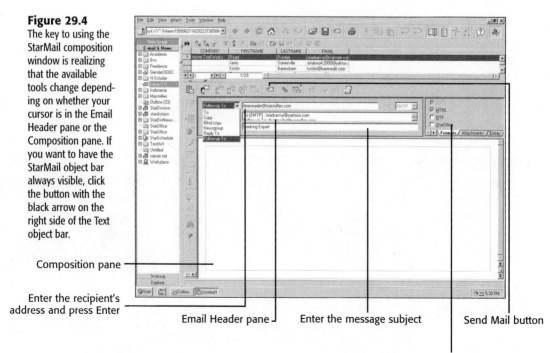

Email Header pane ⌐   Enter the message subject   Send Mail button

Options pane, where you select any additional formats, add attachments, and set the message priority

Figure 29.5
When you begin typing in the StarMail composition window, standard StarOffice text tools like tables and the Navigator become available.

Click here to select your sending options (To, Copy, Blind Copy)

Type addresses of recipients here; press Enter to add the address to the address list below

If you're sending email from a second account, select the correct outgoing mail protocol (SMTP, VIM, or NNTP for a news posting) here

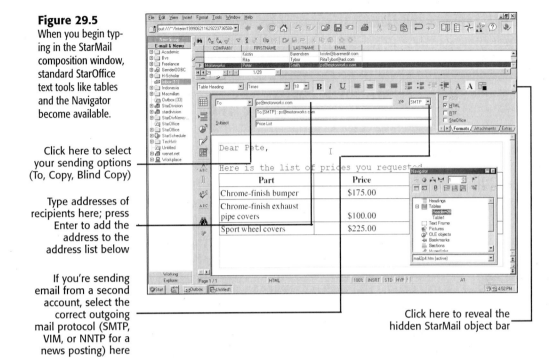

PART
VI
CH
29

Click here to reveal the hidden StarMail object bar

Take a look at the status bar—it offers you the same fields and shortcuts as in StarWriter. The one difference: with email, you don't apply a page style to your message. The page style field (second from the left) indicates instead the email format that you're currently using to create and view your message.

CREATING AND SENDING MAIL

As long as your physical Internet connection is working properly, creating and sending email messages is easy, especially if you're already familiar with StarWriter's tools. However, there are a few aspects of working with email documents that require elaboration.

CHOOSING EMAIL FILE FORMATS

The mechanical process of choosing an email file format couldn't be easier in StarOffice: Just click the option(s) you want in the Options pane of the composition window. You can select as many of the three as you like. However, there are a number of factors you should consider before choosing to send email in an additional format.

UNDERSTANDING ASCII FORMAT

Email was one of the first uses of the Internet and remains the most popular. Every day, millions of email messages are sent across telephone lines and uploaded via satellite. This huge exchange of electronic letters happens across a wide range of computers, from old dinosaur machines that are considered virtual museum pieces to the latest out-of-the box, bells-and-whistles–bedecked models.

You never need to worry about the compatibility of the computer on the other end because email messages are sent in the most basic, standard, universal computer file format: ASCII (pronounced "ask-key"). ASCII stands for American Standard Code for Information Interchange and refers to a standard character set—that is, set of letters, numbers, and symbols—that virtually every computer is able to recognize. ASCII files have no program code or specialized instructions; they are just strings of characters.

ASCII's simplicity ensure that it can be read universally but limits users' options in creating messages. You cannot insert pictures or other objects, which by definition must be text only. You can't even insert things like tables (which are actually complex graphic objects) or apply boldface or italics. In short, you can't shape the look of your message.

As the Internet has grown and developed, software companies have created programs that allow people to create and read email messages that enable fancier formatting. This has greatly expanded what you can do with a simple email message. However, many people still use email programs that can handle only ASCII messages—and you can't be sure what type of program your recipient might be using.

THE EFFECTS OF CHOOSING ADDITIONAL FORMATS

The solution that most programs, including StarOffice, offer is that they allow you to send a message in multiple formats.

In StarOffice, email messages are always composed in ASCII, but you have the option of creating them in HTML, RTF, and/or StarOffice format as well. Nothing changes in the way you compose your message. Instead, StarOffice does some trickery with your message behind the scenes. It makes a copy of the basic ASCII message, applies the appropriate formatting, and appends it to the end of the ASCII message. When your recipient gets the message, if his or her system can handle the more sophisticated format, that's what he or she sees; otherwise, the plain vanilla ASCII message opens.

Tip #528 from
Michael & Sarah

> StarOffice has a set of built-in styles especially for HTML documents; just open the Stylist and choose HTML styles from the style drop-down list.

Because formatting code requires a lot of space in addition to the text of the message itself, HTML, RTF, and StarOffice files are much larger than an ASCII-only message. Therefore, the more formats you choose, the bigger your message file—and the more likely it is to get stuck in the craw of someone's bad ISP connection or clog up someone's mailbox with unwanted bytes of non-information. It wouldn't be so bad if there weren't a good chance that the other person won't be able to see all your fancy formatting anyway!

You should therefore consider carefully whether you want to send a message in any format other than basic ASCII. If you know recipients on the other end are likely to have the right program, don't hesitate to take advantage of the greater document creation possibilities offered by other formats. If you have doubts, or if you are sending a mass-mailing, you should send messages in ASCII-only format. In fact, if you participate in newsgroups, email listserve discussions, or other public exchanges that use email, it's considered impolite to use anything else.

StarOffice, however, is a very permissive program, and it allows you to create fantastically formatted emails even if you have deselected all formatting options except ASCII. Only when you go to send the email does StarOffice present you with a warning that all your formatting is about to be lost. If you choose to send it anyway, the text only will be extracted (which can look pretty funny if you have tables in your composition).

HTML EXPORT OPTIONS

If you're composing messages in HTML, you might want to select Tools, Options, Browser, HTML tab. On this tab, you can select the specific type of HTML format in which your file will be exported: Netscape, Microsoft Internet Explorer, or StarOffice.

SETTING MESSAGE OPTIONS

If you click the Extras tab in the options window, you can set the priority of your message by selecting one of five options from the drop-down list   highest, high, normal, low, and lowest (although we doubt anyone ever uses *lowest*). You can also set your email to automatically trigger a confirmation that your message has been received at its intended address.

ADDING SIGNATURES

In most email programs, you can attach a text signature to your email by creating a signature file that is then referenced by the email program. In StarOffice, you add a signature with AutoText.

StarOffice includes four pre-formatted signatures that include your user data. These signatures are saved in the AutoText file `signatur.bau` in the `Office51/Autotext` directory. Click the Signature button on the StarMail object bar, and a menu with the four choices opens. Click the type of signature you want, and it's placed at the end of your email.

The formats of these signatures are not very attractive, and you will likely want to create your own. It's easy to do so. You have two options:

- You can replace the existing signature files. You can replace as many of the four preformatted signatures as you like; however, you cannot add new signatures to the signature category.

- You can create your own AutoText entries that are not saved in the signature AutoText category.

If you choose the latter option, you won't be able to use the Signature button on the StarMail object bar to insert signatures; you instead need to type a keyboard shortcut and press Enter.

In this section, we'll just review replacing existing signature files.

→ For more information about working with AutoText, **see** "Automating Text Entries with AutoText," **p. 240**.

To create a new signature, type and format your signature in any StarMail or StarWriter document as you want it to appear. (Keep in mind that people receiving ASCII-only mail won't be able to read fancy formatting and fonts.) Then, follow these steps:

1. Select the entire signature.

2. Choose Edit, AutoText (or press Ctrl+F3). The AutoText dialog appears.

3. If it's not selected already, select the Signature category.

4. Select the AutoText signature you want to replace. Notice the shortcut that appears when you select the file—SIG1, SIG2, SIG3, or SIG4. You can modify this shortcut. After you've completed your modifications and closed the dialog, anytime you type the shortcut and press Enter, your signature is inserted automatically.

5. Click the AutoText button and choose Replace. Your selected text replaces the existing signature.

6. Click Close.

Now, when you click the Signature icon and select the AutoText file with that name, your new signature appears, rather than the preformatted signature.

Note

The default signatures use the Sender field to insert your user data (name, phone number, and so on). If you send an email with one of these default signatures to other StarOffice users, they will see their *own* user data instead of yours as if they were sending emails to themselves. To avoid this, create a signature that uses text instead of fields.

RECORDING AND RETRIEVING EMAIL ADDRESSES

StarOffice's integrated Address Book makes it easy to both store and retrieve email addresses—and the Address Book dialog makes it easy to retrieve them from Internet directories as well.

ADDING ADDRESSES TO THE ADDRESS BOOK

To add an address to the Address Book, first make sure the Header Details pane is visible in your Inbox, Outbox, or news reader windows. Email addresses are highlighted in bright blue and underlined. Then, move the mouse over the address you want to add, and right-click. Select Add to Address Book—and that's it! StarOffice displays a message when the address has been added successfully.

If for some reason you are unable to add an address this way, you can enter it manually via the Address Book dialog, or in your address book table in the Beamer.

With the Copy Link command, you can copy the email address to the Clipboard in the complete URL format (that is, `mailto:somebody@somewhere.com`) and then paste it into a document.

ADDRESSING EMAILS FROM THE ADDRESS BOOK

To retrieve single addresses, you have three options:

- You can open the *address* table in the Beamer and drag and drop the address.
- You can use the Address Book dialog to locate an address and then insert it by clicking the AutoMail button.
- You can start typing the name or email address of the recipient into the address field. StarOffice automatically completes it if it can find a corresponding entry in the Address Book. This AutoComplete feature recognizes names in the *last name, first name* format.

→ To learn about addressing an email message to a large number of people, **see** "Creating Mail Merges with StarMail," **p. 1062**.

DRAGGING AND DROPPING FROM THE BEAMER

If you click the Address Book icon on the StarMail object bar, the currently assigned address book table opens in the Beamer in a specially filtered form—only the first and last name, company, and email address of each contact is displayed. (If the email field of contact is blank, the contact is not shown.)

When the address table is open, scroll to find the address you want to enter. Click the row header of the record that contains the person's email address to highlight the entire row. To create a distribution list, select multiple records by using the standard Ctrl+click and

Shift+click selection shortcuts Then, drag the record(s) and drop it(them) into the address list box in the middle of the Email Header pane. You don't have to press Enter; any addresses you drop are automatically registered.(You can also drag and drop addresses as text into your document, if you want to send a contact someone else's email address, for example.)

USING THE AUTOMAIL BUTTON

If you open the Address Book dialog, you can use a feature called AutoMail. You can also search for an address that you don't know via an Internet LDAP directory, the Web's version of phone books.

The simplest way to open the Address Book dialog is to select a name in an email message, right-click, and select Who Is? from the context menu. The dialog opens on your desktop (although unfortunately not at the entry for the person whose name you've highlighted).

Next, click Search to open the Address Book Search menu. The Search menu lists the designated Address Book as one database to be searched, and also lists any LDAP Web directories that you have specified during setup (look ahead to Figure 29.6).

Tip #529 from	
Michael & Sarah	You can add more LDAP directories to this menu by selecting Tools, Options, Internet, and then adding their names in the LDAP dialog box.

Click the database you want to search. The Search button changes into two buttons: a Start button and an End button. Enter the term for which you want to search (for example, a person's last name or a company name). Click Start to start the search. If StarOffice finds a match, the contact's information is displayed on the desktop.

To enter the person's address in the header of an email message, click the AutoMail button. You can continue to search for additional names until you're done. To exit the Address Book dialog, click the Close button in the upper-right corner.

SAVING COPIES OF EMAIL

All copies of mail you send are automatically saved in the Outbox. However, you can also save drafts or copies of your emails just as you would save any other document with the File, Save As command.

You have two file formats to choose from: StarMessage 5.0 and StarMessage Document. StarMessage 5.0 files have an .sdm extension, and StarMessage document files have an .smd extension. You can reopen these files as you would any other StarOffice file.

Tip #530 from
Michael & Sarah

StarMessage files contain header and formatting information as well as text, but in a pinch, you can open them in a text editor to retrieve your text if you aren't able to open StarOffice.

If you want to send a document that you also need to save to file, keep in mind that you can email a document directly. Creating your message as a StarWriter document rather than a StarMessage file gives you more flexibility in swapping the file with others.

MAILING DOCUMENTS AND WEB PAGES FROM THE DESKTOP

Using commands from the File, Send menu, you can send text documents and Web pages (which are HTML documents) as email messages directly from your desktop.

The Send, AutoMail command enables you to quickly address and send an entire document to a single person, whereas the Send, Document as E-Mail command can be used to send an entire document or just a selected portion of it.

While browsing the Web, you can use the File menu Document as E-Mail command to send Web pages. AutoMail is not available.

The procedure is very similar for creating all three types of mailings. Here are the steps for creating an AutoMail document:

1. Create the document you want to use and have it open on your desktop.
2. Select the first or last name of the person to whom you want to send the letter.
3. Select File, Send, AutoMail.

StarOffice automatically searches the Address Book. If it locates the person's email address, a dialog like the one in Figure 29.6 appears.

Caution

If you select spaces before or after the last name, or select the entire name, StarOffice will not recognize the name, even if it is entered in your Address Book.

If you have no name selected, or if that name does not appear in the designated Address Book, StarOffice asks if you want to enter the information directly in the Address Book. If you choose Yes, the Address Book dialog box opens with your highlighted name already entered.

Figure 29.6
Select your recipient's last name and then select File, Send, AutoMail to send non-StarMail documents from your desktop in a few quick steps.

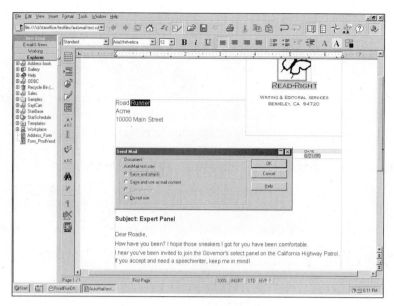

With AutoMail and Web pages, you have three sending options:

- Send your document as an attachment. If you choose this option, a blank StarMail composition window opens after you click OK, with the document already attached. The message is already addressed to your selected name. If the document is a Web page, it's attached as an HTML document.

- Use the contents as the basis for a new email message addressed to the selected name. If you choose this option, your document is be re-created in email form.

- Open a blank new StarMail composition window.

When you choose Send Document as E-Mail with a regular document, the fourth option—Use Selection—is active. If you select this option, the currently selected text is used as the contents of an email message.

After you make your selection and click OK, the mail composition window appears, and you can proceed as usual.

Be aware that file format issues rear their heads when using these nifty features with regular documents. If you have created a complex document in StarWriter, complete with graphics or text boxes, tables, and so on, it might not translate very well into the text of an email message. For example, the letter displayed in Figure 29.6 is built from a complex AutoPilot template that would work fine as an attached document, but not as the text of an email message. StarOffice automatically creates a message in StarWriter format to try to accommodate the complexity—but it still might not translate well, and your recipient might not be able to read it in the intended format. (It might also be a very big file to send via the Internet.)

If you have a fancy letter or document (such as a spreadsheet or graphics-heavy document), it is best to send it as an attachment, unless you know your recipient can open it in StarOffice format. The same is true of a Web document (although many people today have email programs that can read HTML documents.)

If your document is a new document that has not yet been saved, the Send Mail dialog options prompt you to save the file as you send it (refer to Figure 29.6). If you choose this option, your document is saved in in StarWriter format.

If you intend to send your attachmentin a non-StarOffice format, save it as a file in the intended format first, before invoking the AutoMail or Document as E-Mail commands.

HANDLING ATTACHMENTS

Attachments are files sent along with email messages. Email messages cannot handle large quantities of text, so long documents are sent as an attached file. Email messages also can't contain the complex formatting and programming instructions that most graphics, images, or spreadsheet files do, so these need to be sent as attached files as well.

Emailing someone a file as an attachment is similar to handing it to the person on a disk; if that person doesn't have the same application on their system, or a special plug-in program that enables him or her to open files in many different formats, he or she might not be able to open and read your attachment. Similarly, your ability to open and read attachments that someone else sends you depends on the programs you have loaded on your system and registered as plug-ins in StarOffice.

Tip #531 from	You can add and manage plug-ins in StarOffice by choosing Tools, Options, Browser, and
Michael & Sarah	then clicking File Types to open the File Types dialog box.

ATTACHING FILES TO EMAIL MESSAGES

To attach a file to a StarMail message, click the Attachments tab in the Options pane. Then click the Attach button. (Alternatively, right-click on the Attachments tabs and select Attach File.) An Open dialog appears; navigate to the file's location, select it, and click Open.

Tip #532 from	The most intuitive and easiest way to attach a file is to drag and drop it from the Beamer
Michael & Sarah	or Explorer.
	You can tell that a file is attached successfully if you see the file listed on the Attachments tab. When you mail the message, the file (actually, a copy of the file) is sent with it.

SAVING AND OPENING ATTACHED FILES

If you receive an attachment, click the Attachment tab in the options window, select the attachment, and right-click to see the full list of options for managing the attachment.

You can save the file to disk, separately from the email message by choosing the Save As command. You can also drag the attachment to any folder or group in the Explorer, or copy and paste it in the Beamer.

To open the document, click Open.

If you don't have the correct program to open the document, you receive an error message.

If the document opens but not in your program of choice, you need to edit the links between that type of file and its associated program by selecting Tools, Options, Browser, and then editing the associations in the File Types dialog box. For example, if the document is in a particular .txt format that you want to open in StarCalc, not StarWriter, you might need to change the file association so that StarOffice knows to always open that file type with StarCalc.

→ For more information on working with plug-ins and changing your file types, **see** "Fine-Tuning Your Browser," **p. 105**.

CREATING MAIL MERGES WITH STARMAIL

If you are using the Address Book to save contact information that includes email addresses, you can create mail merge documents—individually addressed copies of the same message—that are sent via email rather than being printed. Alternatively, you can send a single message to multiple people in the more conventional way. It's extremely easy to do either. There are two types of email mail merges you can create. The first is to simply send an ordinary email message to a large number of people. This type of mail merge is carried out from a StarMail composition window, in combination with some special tools that appear on the Beamer toolbar.

The second type of mail merge is to create a complex form letter using merge fields that you send via email rather than printing and sending via conventional mail. This type of mail merge is carried out from a StarWriter document, using the Mail Merge command.

SENDING EMAIL TO SINGLE DISTRIBUTION LISTS

Because you use StarBase databases as your data sources for contact information across the StarDesktop, you don't need to create separate mailing lists for different people to whom you want to send mail. You can select your list from your existing contact database.

The simplest way to send a single email to multiple people is to follow these steps:

1. Open a new mail message.
2. Click the Show Address Book icon on the StarMail composition toolbar.

3. Select multiple records using the Ctrl+click or Shift+click shortcuts.

4. Drag and drop your selections into the middle text box of the Header pane, between the To box and the Subject box.

5. Compose your message and send as usual.

This trick works only when you are in the StarMail composition window and open the Address Book in its specially filtered form using the Show Address Book tool.

The advantage of this method is that you generate only a single message. The drawback is that each recipient sees the entire distribution list. If you want to conceal your distribution list or create a more personalized email for each recipient, you can use the Mail Merge command.

Note

You can select all records in a table or query by clicking the gray rectangle in the upper left corner of the table, where the column and row headers meet. Don't use this shortcut when inserting email addresses as described here; you can't drop your email addresses if you've selected them in this way. Use the Shift+click shortcut instead: Click the first record; then scroll to the end of the table, press Shift+click and select the last record.

Selecting records by hand can be time consuming and tedious if you have a large contact list. You may therefore want to filter your table so that only those people you want to receive the mail appear when you open the table in the Beamer.

You might be able to accomplish this with the simple sorting and filtering tools in the Beamer. If your Address Book is large and unwieldy and you need to filter it in more complex ways, you need to create a query that achieves your result.

If you will be drawing names from a large database of contact names, building a distribution list requires some forethought. You need to create some type of code or other ID system to enable efficient sorting and filtering in your Address Book database.

→ For the basics of working with the Address Book, **see** "Using the Address Book," **p. 1011**.

→ For an introduction to sorting and filtering, **see** "Sorting and Filtering Data," **p. 627**.

→ For information on creating queries in StarBase, **see** "Creating a New Query with AutoPilot," **p. 1205** and "Creating a Query from Scratch," **page 1210**.

SENDING PERSONALIZED EMAIL TO DISTRIBUTION LISTS

When you have your Address Book in proper shape or have created the query you want to use, follow these steps to create a personalized mass emailing:

1. Open a new StarMail composition window and compose your email message.

2. If you're using your entire Address Book, click the Show Address Book tool in the StarMail composition window. (It's on the object bar, at the top.) Only the company, first name, last name, and email fields display.

Or, if you're using a query, open it in the Beamer by clicking it in the Explorer. (Make sure the Beamer is open first.)

3. Sort and filter your address table or query as necessary so that only the people you want to email appear when you open the table in the Beamer. (For example, if you want to send your email to everyone with an email address in your address table, you might want to sort it so records without email address do not show in the Beamer.)

Or, you can chose to insert the addresses of only certain record numbers in the mail merge dialog that you'll encounter in the next steps.

Note   You cannot drag and drop a merge field into the Header pane of an email message.

4. Click the Mail Merge button on the Beamer object bar.

Note   This button only appears after you open the table or query in the Beamer and then click in the StarMail window.

5. The Mail Merge dialog appears. In the Output section, click Mailing. The Address Field drop-down list becomes active. The email field is automatically selected, but you can select any other field from that same table to serve as your addressing field instead.

6. Set the other mailing options, enter a subject line, and add any attachments. If you want to send the email to only certain record numbers rather than your entire Beamer table, enter those record numbers.

7. Click OK.

That's it! Your email messages are generated in the same way print form letters are, with each person being addressed individually. The messages are stored in the Outbox. If you aren't online when you generate the mailing, you need to select the Outbox, right-click, and select Update when you go online again to mail them.

Creating Email Form Letters

The first step of creating an email form letter is to create a StarWriter (not a StarMail) document with merge fields. Creating form letters is described in detail in the section "Creating Form Letters with Mail Merge" in Chapter 9, "Working with Tables, Charts, and Fields," so we won't describe that process in detail here. In brief, you type your text as desired and use the Insert, Fields command (or press Ctrl+F2) to insert mail merge fields from the Database tab. You can insert fields from as many databases as you like.

After you have created your letter and it's ready to send, you have two choices: You can either follow the same steps as given in the previous section for sending a personalized email to a distribution list, or you can select File, Mail Merge. Whichever method you choose, you see a Mail Merge dialog like the one in Figure 29.7.

> **Note**
>
> If you don't have any mail merge fields inserted in your document, choosing the Mail Merge command opens your address table in the Beamer along with the Mail Merge dialog box.

Figure 29.7
Creating email form letters is as simple as one, two, three— create your StarWriter document with mail merge fields, open the Mail Merge dialog, and enter your selections in the Output portion of the dialog.

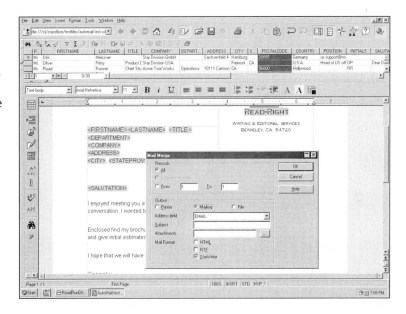

Just as you would with a StarMail message, click Mailing as your output. In the Address Field input line, open the drop-down list, and select the field in your current database (that is, the database displaying in the Beamer) that contains email addresses. Enter your mail message subject and the pathnames of any attachments. Choose any additional formats in which you want to send your mail, and click OK.

The final step is a little confusing—it's a bit of a magician's misdirection trick. You're prompted with a Save As dialog. You may be wondering why you are being prompted to save to a file when you just want to send an email mailing. Actually, you're just being prompted to save a copy of your original message for record-keeping purposes; the fields are converted to simple text field names to remind you of what you inserted. At the same time, the mailing is actually being generated and either sent through your Outbox or (if you're offline) stored in your Outbox until you log on again.

INSERTING HYPERLINKS

One of the advantages of sending mail in HTML, RTF, or StarOffice formats is that you can take advantage of StarOffice's hyperlink tools.

If you're sending someone a reference to a Web site or other Internet URL in your email and it's formatted as a hyperlink, your recipient can just click the hyperlink and jump directly to the site you're recommending (if he or she is still online). This is convenient for the recipient, who doesn't have to copy and paste or type the URL into the browser input line.

It's easy to insert hyperlinks in StarOffice documents, including email messages. You have two choices:

- Turn on automatic URL recognition in AutoCorrect/AutoFormat
- Use the Hyperlink toolbar

The first option is the simplest; the second allows you to create more sophisticated emails that might be appropriate for a mass-mailing for a business or organization.

Tip #533 from
Michael & Sarah

> You can jump from hyperlink to hyperlink and easily get an overview of all your hyperlinks with the Navigator.

When automatic URL recognition is turned on, StarOffice automatically applies a hyperlink format to any word it identifies as a URL, after you have typed it and pressed either the spacebar or Enter. This feature can be annoying if you're typing text references to URLs that you want to format and edit as regular text, but it comes in handy when you're working with emails (and Web documents).

To turn on automatic URL recognition, choose Tools, AutoCorrect/AutoFormat,dialog and click the Options tab. Scroll until you see Automatic URL Recognition and select the I (input) option in the second column. After you click OK, this option is turned on. The next time you type a word such as www.stardivision.com that StarOffice recognizes as an Internet address it automatically formats it as a hyperlink.

Tip #534 from
Michael & Sarah

> To change the color and/or other character formatting of your hyperlinks, modify the Internet Link and Visited Internet Link text styles via the Stylist or in the Format menu Character dialog box.

Using the Hyperlink toolbar enables you to assign a URL to a piece of text that is not a URL. This is a necessary tool when creating HTML documents for a Web site but can also be nice for creating sophisticated email mailings.

To enter hyperlinks with the Hyperlink toolbar, first turn it on by choosing View, Toolbars, Hyperlink Bar.

Type your message as usual. Then, select the first word or phrase that you want to turn into a hyperlink. Notice in Figure 29.8 that when you select a phrase, it appears in a drop-down box on the toolbar. Next, type the URL that you want associated with that phrase in the URL input line to the right of that drop-down box. When you're done typing or pasting the URL, press Enter or click the Hyperlink tool, and your phrase is magically transformed into a hyperlink.

Figure 29.8
Using the Hyperlink toolbar, you can create a sophisticated hyperlink document as your mail message. Combine that with the power of email mail merges to create a professional and effective email marketing campaign for an Internet site in no time!

Your selected text appears in the URL Name text box.

Enter the URL in the Internet URL text box.

After you enter your hyperlinks, you can manage and edit them with the Hyperlink toolbar.

→ For more information on using the Hyperlink toolbar, **see** "Working with Hyperlinks," **p. 936.**

MANAGING MULTIPLE MAIL ACCOUNTS

Although you can only create one Outbox in StarOffice, you can both send and receive mail from multiple email accounts. However, there isn't a convenient interface like Netscape or Eudora's profile managers to manage your different accounts. Without a wizard or dialog box to guide you, it's a little tricky to figure it out. In this section, we lay the process bare for you.

First, you must create a second account inbox in the Explorer. Here's a brief review of that process:

1. Select the Explorer icon or the folder where you want your account Inbox stored.

2. Right-click to open the Explorer context menu, and choose New.

3. Choose the type of email account you want to create—POP3, IMAP, or VIM.

4. Enter an Explorer name for the account on the General tab.

5. Click the Send tab to bring the Send tab to the top.

6. Click User Defined Settings in both the Private (mail) and Public (news) sections of the tab, if these options aren't already selected.

   This is the key to routing outgoing mail through this second account. When this option is selected, you are overriding the default Outbox settings that guide the routing of your outgoing mail, and telling StarOffice to use the settings in this mail account when this account is active (and you take other actions, described later in this section).

7. Click the User-Defined Settings button, which opens a new dialog with SMTP and NNTP tabs.

8. Enter the desired sending information for your second account.

9. Click the Receive tab to bring it to the top and enter the name of your incoming mail server for this account, and (if you choose) your user name and password. This enables you to receive mail from this account into this Inbox.

10. Click OK.

Your new account Inbox is created in the Explorer.

Tip #535 from
Michael & Sarah

By default, the return address in the Sender field is taken from your user data. To change this information, delete the existing information and input your other address. The program does not accept special characters, including the @ symbol, unless it is enclosed in < >, so enter a complete address in this way: `Loretta Lopez <lopez@isp.com>`.

After you have set your Inbox to refer to your user-defined settings instead of the default (Outbox) settings, you can create a new mail message by clicking the New Mail icon on StarMail's object bar (which means you must have this second account Inbox open on your desktop at the time) or by selecting New, Message from the account's context menu.

After you compose a new message, click the Send tool as usual. Your outgoing mail is then routed according to the settings of the currently active Inbox, not from your Outbox or Internet dialog settings. However, a copy of the message is still stored in the same old Outbox.

Note

If you edit a message stored in your Outbox, it is routed according to the settings of this Outbox, even though it was originally sent using different settings.

BEYOND MAIL: JOINING NEWSGROUPS WITH STARDISCUSSION

StarDiscussion is a *news reader* and is StarMail's companion program, completing your suite of Internet communication programs. With StarDiscussion, you can subscribe to Internet *newsgroups*.

A newsgroup is a specialized form of email that allows a group of people to participate in a communal email discussion. Newsgroup messages are not sent from one individual to another, but are *posted* back to the newsgroup, which is a kind of bulletin board. That is to say, everyone's posted message is "pinned" to the same central location so that anyone who chooses can read the message.

> **Note**
>
> True newsgroups are maintained on a special server called a *news server;* many people also participate in a lesser version of newsgroups called a *listserve,* in which an individual serves as the mediator rather than postings being automatically handled by a news server. Listserve messages are sent by ordinary email and involve a different subscription process.

As you might imagine, newsgroups can get overwhelming because of the volume of postings they generate. Some order is kept on the bulletin board itself by organizing discussions in *threads*, which, just as the name suggests, are messages tied together with a common theme or (more precisely) subject heading. If you are a regular reader of newsgroups, however, you must face the individual problem of how to maintain order on your own computer.

Most people chose to download only newsgroup *headers*, which list the sender, date, time, and subject of the message, and read messages online, leaving messages stored on their LAN or ISP's server. If you choose to download the contents of newsgroups, you should become familiar with using *filters* because otherwise you'll soon find your hard drive overflowing with the buzzing, blooming words of wisdom of your fellow Netizens.

→ For more information on creating filters, **see** "Creating a Filter for Mail," **p. 216.**

There are two types of newsgroups, public and private. Most ISPs serve as the conduit for a selected number of public newsgroups that they make available to their customers by subscription. Subscribing doesn't cost anything; you just need to sort through the list of newsgroups that your ISP carries and select those you want to read You don't need to know the originating server addresses of each individual newsgroup to which you might want to subscribe because everything is routed through your ISP's news server.

If you want to connect to a private news server, you must find and create an account with its address. A typical way of finding out a news server address is from a company's Web site; many computer companies, including StarDivision, maintain news servers in order to answer customer questions more efficiently. The StarDivision newsgroups are the most useful source of troubleshooting information and deeper insight into the program's functioning.

CREATING NEWS ACCOUNTS

The process of creating a news account Inbox is very similar to that for creating an email account Inbox. However, it's best to be online and connected when you do it so that you can select your subscriptions right away.

After you have dialed your ISP and are connected to your network, be sure the function bar Online button is pressed. Then, select New, News from the context menu.

A tabbed Properties dialog like the one in Figure 29.9 appears. This dialog should look familiar because, except for the title, it's exactly the same as the email dialog. The General tab appears on top; enter the name you'd like this news account to have in the Explorer. Then, click the Receive tab.

Figure 29.9
Creating a news account is similar to creating an email account Inbox—until you get to the Subscribe tab, which is where you select the newsgroups you want to join.

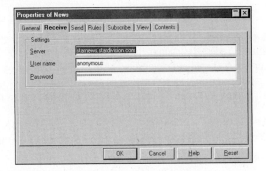

Just as with your mail account, the information you entered in the Tools, Options, Internet dialog box will have been entered already as the default.

If you're going to check out the newsgroups offered by your ISP, you can leave these settings as is, assuming that they correctly reflect your account information.

If you want to connect to a specific news server directly, you have to take a more active role. First, type the name of the news server. You might have seen the long form of a server name, which would look something like this:

```
news://starnews.stardivision.com/stardivision.com.support.stardesktop
```

You cannot use any special characters in your addresssuch as / symbols—these are reserved for the computer, so you get an error message if you try. Just enter the middle chunk, which is the main server address, as shown in Figure 29.9.

Next, you need to log on. You don't have a personal account, so your personal logon name won't mean a thing here. Fortunately, you don't need any for most news servers. Try first leaving these fields blank. If you're prompted to enter a user name and password, try *anonymous* as your user name and your email address as your password.

After you enter this information, click the Subscribe tab. If you are online, a list loads all the newsgroups currently available for subscription on your news server, like the one in Figure 29.9. If you're connecting directly to an individual server such as StarDivision's, the list should appear almost immediately. If you're connecting to your ISP's server, it might take a few minutes, as the list from your ISP is probably thousands of newsgroups long. (You can actually see the number being totaled up just underneath the All button.)

Scroll down the list and click the check box next to each group to which you want to subscribe. Generally, the titles of newsgroups are descriptive of their contents. There are certain conventions for naming them that mirror some of the World Wide Web conventions; for example, newsgroups are prefaced by abbreviations that indicate the broad category in which the newsgroup falls. For example, groups prefaced with soc deal with social and cultural issues, and those prefaced with alt deal with alternative lifestyles. There are also multitudes of groups that address issues specific to Linux and Windows users.

| Tip #536 from | Type a word or phrase into the Filter text box to pull up a list of only those newsgroups |
| *Michael & Sarah* | with that word or phrase in the title. |

SETTING NEWS STORAGE OPTIONS

After you select your subscriptions, you should take a look at the Contents tab. The options here should be familiar from working with email accounts and file folders, but they take on new meaning with news accounts.

Newsgroups are set by default, like email, to automatically update when opened. However, you can choose to have StarOffice update at a time that you specify as well. This is not advisable. News takes up a lot of bandwidth and memory, and you don't want your system resources constantly being redirected to downloading news, unless you're in the business of running a news server.

However, the storage options are useful. The Remove Messages from Server option is relevant only to email and is unavailable for newsgroups, but you can select to save newsgroup postings to your local drive. If you do, the option below becomes active, allowing you to set a time limit on the news postings that are retained on your system. You can set a time limit of anywhere from 0 to 999 days. Postings older than the period you select are deleted automatically. If you choose to download news postings, it's a good idea to select this option—although you would likely want to set it considerably lower than 999!

SETTING VIEWING RESTRICTIONS

Clicking the View tab brings up a range of viewing options particularly relevant to newsgroups.

News is hierarchically structured, from the bottom up, in postings (messages); threads, which are groups of messages that share a common subject; and groups, which are newsgroups that each have a unique news server address and topic. The Show Groups selection enables you to determine what groups display.

If you click Subscribed (which is the default when a news account is created), all subscribed newsgroups display in the Explorer. If you choose All, the entire list of newsgroups available on that server displays. If you chose Active, only subscribed newsgroups with new postings display.

Caution

Do not set your news account to Show All. This could lead to a catastrophic download of thousands of news group headers (and postings, if you've chosen to save postings to your hard drive). This would cause StarOffice to crash, as the Explorer can handle only about 8,000 elements.

You can set the maximum number of message headers that are shown in the opened newsgroup by clicking the Show Maximum option and entering a number in the associated spinner box. Limiting the number of headers you see in your box at one time can reduce the risk of being overwhelmed with the volume of postings and speeds your browsing and reading of high-volume newsgroups considerably. If you're storing contents locally, it also limits the number of messages that are downloaded—a good idea if you don't want your hard drive flooded.

If you click Rules Active, you turn on any filtering rules you have set on the Rules tab. Creating filters is almost essential if you're going to download news onto your local drive.

The Show Messages options set filters for your news based on marks you assign through toolbars on the StarDiscussion desktop—the same tools you see in StarMail. These tools are identified in "Orienting Yourself in StarMail and StarDiscussion" at the beginning of this chapter. (Particularly, refer to Table 29.1.)

→ To learn more about using rules to create filters, **see** "Using Filters to Manage Files," **p. 197**.

→ For more advanced discussion of filters, **see** "Techniques for Managing Mail and News," **p. 1075**.

After you finish making selections, click OK, and your news account is created in the Explorer.

DOWNLOADING NEWS

Because news, just like email, is received and possibly (depending on your configuration selections) stored on your server, not your local machine, you need to connect first to your ISP or network in order to get fresh news. News accounts are by default set to update automatically when you click them to open. If you're planning to work with news offline, make sure you have deactivated the Online button on the function bar. Otherwise, when you open your account, StarOffice tries and is unable to contact the server. You might receive an error message, or StarOffice might prompt you to connect by giving you a dial-up networking dialog box.

When you're online, click the plus sign next to your news account icon. A list of newsgroups similar to the one in Figure 29.10 opens.

Newsgroups with unread messages appear in bold. If you open the Explorer to a great enough width, you also see the number of unread messages over the total number in the group.

Figure 29.10
To load recent news, click the plus sign next to your news account's icon in the Explorer. Double-click a group's icon to open it and read your news.

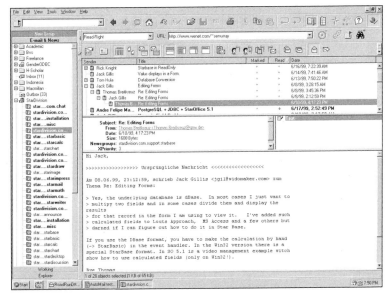

READING AND RESPONDING TO NEWSGROUP POSTINGS

After you open a newsgroup in the Explorer, click a title to open its contents in the StarDiscussion window.

Tip #537 from	The news posting of the currently selected header displays automatically if you select
Michael & Sarah	AutoLoad in the Tools, Options, Internet, Mail/News dialog.

The window is the same as the StarMail account Inbox window, except the Post Reply tool is active here.

NAVIGATING THE NEWS

Many messages in the newsgroup window have a small plus sign next to them, just like objects in the Explorer. This indicates that someone has responded to the original poster of the message, thus beginning a discussion thread. There can be multiple strands to the thread.

You can move through a thread by pressing the spacebar. Each time you press the spacebar, you are moved to the next unread message in the thread. When you come to the end of a thread, pressing the spacebar moves you to the next thread. When you come to the end of a newsgroup, pressing the spacebar takes you to your next newsgroup subscription with unread postings (if there is one).

Tip #538 from	To open all the headers of an entire thread at once, select the initial header in the thread and press Ctrl++. Be sure to use the + key on your numeric keypad, not the + on the main keyboard.
Michael & Sarah	

If you want to return to unread messages, you need to navigate with the up and down arrow keys or your mouse.

RESPONDING TO NEWSGROUP POSTINGS

Different newsgroups operate according to different standards. Some are unmoderated groups, where any message you send is automatically added to the newsgroup. Others are run by a moderator, who reads and selects the messages that appear. In either case, most newsgroups have a set of rules of conduct. Sometimes they are formally written and posted on the server. More often, they are communicated indirectly through the style and subjects of people's communication.

If you're new to newsgroups—that is, you're a *newbie*, as the slang goes—it's considered polite to just hang out for a while, reading postings and getting a sense of the group before venturing to post a question or response.

Tip #539 from	Open the Bookmarks, Internet folder in the Explorer—there's a link to a site that maintains a dictionary of acronyms, abbreviations, and terms commonly used in email and newsgroup postings. If you're online, just double-click and go.
Michael & Sarah	

When you're ready to respond to a posting, you can respond either directly to the individual concerned (as people's email addresses are included) or by posting your response to the entire newsgroup. If you want to share your message with the entire group—make it news rather than mail—you use the Post Reply button. If you want to reply to the person individually, click Reply on the newsgroup object bar (or press Ctrl+R).

WORKING OFFLINE

Although StarOffice by default assumes that you want to work in Online mode when you're reading mail and news, you might want to read and reply to news and mail offline. In fact, if you're connecting via an ISP, this is the preferred method as it can save you expensive connection charges and keep the phone line free for other users.

If you want to work offline, there are a number of settings you should adjust to enable and maximize working offline:

- Select Store Contents Locally on the Contents tab. You must select this in order to read incoming mail and news offline.
- Select the Include in Update option on the Contents tab of the Properties dialog.

- If you are downloading news, set the automatic delete function (which is labeled Not if Older Than) for a reasonable number of days. This ensures that stale news is automatically deleted from your hard drive. Otherwise, your drive can quickly become overwhelmed with old news.

- Deselect Update on Open from the box's context menu.

TECHNIQUES FOR MANAGING MAIL AND NEWS

Chapter 5, "Managing Files, Folders, and Mail," introduces issues of managing mail on your desktop in conjunction with discussing the StarDesktop. StarOffice treats your local system as part of a larger networked universe, applying naming and management conventions developed originally for mail and news to other desktop objects such as files and folders. It therefore made sense to introduce the topic during that discussion. However, there are a number of issues specific to managing mail and news that we address in this section.

UPDATING AND SYNCHRONIZING ACCOUNTS

You gain access to both mail and news through a remote computer, often called a server. Every time you want to check new mail or news, your computer must contact the server. If you save mail or news locally, the message headers and contents are downloaded across your connection; if you just read the mail and news from the server, just the headers are downloaded and stored in the program's cache.

→ For more information on the basics of updating Internet accounts, **see** "Keeping Your Desktop Up-to-Date," **p. 213**.

UNDERSTANDING UPDATING OPTIONS

By default, Update on Opening is selected on an account's context menu. If you want to use the Update command to manually contact your server and download new messages, you must select the Include in Update option on the Contents tab of the Properties dialog. If you don't, nothing happens when you click Update.

After you select the Include in Update option, you also have the option of setting StarOffice to update an account at a time interval you specify, anywhere from 0 minutes to 999 hours.

Tip #540 from *Michael & Sarah*	If you have the New Mail icon displayed in the icon tray, right-clicking opens an Update shortcut menu.

When you begin updating by either opening your account or clicking Update, StarOffice seeks the server and starts to load. You'll see information about the load's progress in your status bar, and a loading icon in the icon tray.

The number of messages to download can be huge, in the hundreds or thousands, and it can take a long time. If you want to interrupt the loading process, click the Stop button on the function bar.

UNDERSTANDING SYNCHRONIZATION

Because StarOffice saves headers it its cache, when you reopen a mail or news account, you might not be seeing the most recent mail or news; you might be seeing cached headers (and perhaps contents).

If you download headers only, these headers might represent objects that no longer exist on the originating server. When you connect with your server and try to open these (non-existent) objects, you get error messages. There might be other incongruities between the data StarOffice has in its cache and the data stored on your serve—sometimes, for example, a download is interrupted and the files are corrupted.

To bring StarOffice's cache back into alignment with the server's contents, use the context menu Synchronize command (or press Ctrl+Y). If you synchronize a news account, the list of newsgroups is updated to match the current list on the server. All header information is reloaded from the server, any messages no longer on the server are deleted, and message contents are reloaded from the server according to the properties defined for the newsgroup. (Messages you have filtered out are ignored.) If you synchronize a POP3 mail account, your entire account is reloaded (rather than just new messages being downloaded).

> **Caution**
>
> If you have copies of news messages that were later deleted from the server and you synchronize, these messages are deleted from your hard drive (if they are still stored in your news account box) unless you have marked them. Marked messages remain on your hard drive until you delete them with the Delete command or remove the mark and then execute the Synchronize function. Mail is not affected.

SELECTING, MOVING, AND DELETING FILES

Working with files in the account box header panes is much like working with them in the Beamer. You can use all the standard selection methods—click the first in a range, then Shift+click the last to select a continuous range of messages, or Ctrl+click to make multiple noncontiguous selections. You can then drag and drop individual messages or groups of messages into other folders. Messages moved in this way remain in StarMessage format, but selecting them no longer brings up the Export command on the context menu—they're now treated like any other file in a folder because the Export command is a special property of the account boxes.

To export news postings, right-click and select File, Export.

To delete selected messages, click the Delete tool on the If you store the contents of mail and/or news locally, these deleted messages are stored in the Recycle Bin and can be restored by using the Restore command.

Caution	If you have news accounts, beware—if you re-create a newsgroup, all your deleted news is restored to that folder, so empty your Recycle Bin (or just remove those selected news files) first.

Sometimes—perhaps due to the way it handles caching and memory operations—StarOffice balks when you try to delete files. If you have this problem, try exiting your account and updating and synchronizing. Then reopen and try again. If that doesn't work, close out of StarOffice, reopen, and try again.

MARKING AND UNMARKING MESSAGES

Marked files here refers to messages that are specially flagged with a marker and messages that are marked as read or unread.

Applying a mark to a message is as simple as clicking in the Marked column next to the message's title in the Header pane. A flag icon appears, waving, to alert you that the message is marked. You can also apply marks via the message's context menu, or click the appropriate button in the mail and news Object bars.

To remove a mark, click again in the same location, or choose the Mark command again.

Tip #541 from Michael & Sarah	Marking files saves them from death by synchronization. Otherwise, when you synchronize, messages that have been deleted from your server are also deleted from your account box.

StarOffice automatically marks an email message as read when you open it on your desktop. It automatically marks news as read either when you select a news posting header and then move on, or after you have double-clicked to open it on your desktop. With news, this means that if you use the spacebar or arrow keys to navigate down the headers list, every header you move by is marked as read, even if you have not opened it.

You can manually re-mark messages as unread (or mark unread files as read) by clicking in the Read column in the Headers pane. You can also apply the Mark as Unread command in the message's context menu or click the appropriate tool on the object bar.

Tip #542 from Michael & Sarah	With mail account inboxes or newsgroups from a news account, you can also mark an entire inbox or newsgroup by selecting its icon in the Explorer and choosing the Mark or Read commands, respectively, from its context menu.

You can also choose to mark an entire news posting or email message thread as read or unread. What that means for news should be clear enough, but you may wonder just what an email thread might be. Every email, when generated and sent over the Internet, has a unique message ID. If you post a reply to a message, your reply quotes—that is, makes a *reference* to—the header information, including the ID number, of the original message in *its* header. (You can actually see this header information in the Header Details pane.)

When you mark an email thread as read, you're informing StarOffice that you've read all messages that contain that header ID or a reference to it.

HIDING AND REVEALING MARKED FILES

The various marking commands give you visual cues that help while reading mail or news. However, their greatest usefulness is in helping to filter what displays on your desktop.

Using options on the View tab of each account box's Properties (or shortcuts for some on your account context menus in the Explorer), you can choose to selectively hide and reveal messages.

→ For more information on these options for newsgroups, **see** "Setting Viewing Restrictions," **p. 1071**.

→ For more information on mail filters, **see** "Creating Filters for Mail," **p. 216** and "Using Filters to Manage Files," **p. 197**.

You can also filter mail and news messages by using Hide commands on the Header pane context menu.

Choose Hide Thread, Hide Author, or Hide Subject, and StarOffice instantly hides all the relevant messages. That's easy enough to do—but how do you undo it? Because the messages no longer appear in the pane, you can't select them. The short answer is that you should look on the Rules tab of the Properties dialog for the relevant account.

The long answer is that when you select one of these commands, StarOffice automatically creates rules on the Rules tab of the Properties dialog for the Inbox that filter the selected messages based on the criteria you've indicated.

If you select Mark Thread as Read for a mail message, for example, StarOffice creates a rule that looks something like this:

```
Hide, if References contains "<v03110700b33bccea4758@[128.32.209.215]>"
```

Depending on the header information and the number of relevant messages, StarOffice might create multiple rules to accomplish your one simple command.

If you want to reveal these messages again, you must manually delete the applicable rules by selecting them individually and clicking the Delete button or by turning off the rules for this newsgroup by deselecting the Rules Active option on the View tab.

REDUCING VISIBLE AND INVISIBLE CLUTTER

The basics of using filters to manage email are discussed in the sections "Using Filters to Manage Files," and "Creating a Filter for Mail," in Chapter 5, "Managing Folders, Files, and Mail." This section goes beyond those basics to discuss advanced aspects of mail and news management.

Email and news, as wonderful as they are, also generate an extremely large volume of stuff streaming across your desktop. Some of this mail is invaluable and much of it is useful, but some of it is just junk that you'd rather never see. If you store your mail and news locally, this clutter can take up a lot of room on your hard drive.

The invisible part of the clutter is the portions of mail and news that StarOffice stores in a cache, behind the scenes. Also, a lot of extra space can exist in mail and news files that you export or save to your local drive, making for cumbersome files that hog disk space.

COMPACTING NEWS AND MAIL ACCOUNTS

Downloaded mail and news files can be filled with all kinds of transmission information that you don't care about but that still takes up a lot of space. That's why your files can sometimes be amazingly big, even when the message seems small. Mail and news accounts can be compressed and internally reorganized so that they take up less space.

To compact a news or mail account, select the account in the Explorer and choose File, Reorganize. This command can be applied only to an entire account box, not to individual files. If you plan to export files, reorganize their parent account box first.

EXPLORING RULES FOR NEWS

Rules are introduced in Chapter 5 in the context of managing file folders as well as mail. With newsgroups, rules have some special features.

In a single news account, you are likely to have many newsgroups. You might want to apply different filters to different groups. It's easy to do so on the Properties tab of each newsgroup; any settings you make add to the the settings found on the Properties tab of the parent news account. If the rules for the parent account conflict with any you have created for the individual newsgroups, the parent's rules win. For example, if you have created a rule for the parent account to hide postings by a particular author, and also have a rule in a speicfic newsgroup to display only postings by this author, nothing by this author will display.

GLOBALLY RESETTING RULES

The Set as Standard command (available only for news accounts) on the View submenu of the Explorer context menu enables you to globally reset the rules that apply to newsgroups within a specific news account. Choosing this command resets the display properties of all the newsgroups to the properties of their parent news accounts. This applies to all properties defined under Show Groups, Show Messages, and Restrictions, as well as to rules.

The Standard command, by contrast, resets the display properties of any selected Explorer object (including email account Inboxes and newsgroups) to the StarOffice program default—which means all rules are cleared from the Rules tab.

UNDERSTANDING AND MANAGING THE OUTBOX

Although you can have multiple account Inboxes, technically, you can have only one Outbox. You can actually create as many Outbox-like objects as you want in the Explorer. However, no matter how you try, you cannot create Outboxes that have different Internet settings on their Send tabs. If you try to do this, the settings of your most currently created account overwrite the settings in any existing Outboxes you have created.

This inflexibility comes for a good reason: StarOffice uses the Outbox to track all your outgoing mail and news postings, as well as store copies of it. It's a centralized archive of all your mail and news activity.

You can, however, create different views of your Outbox by making new Outboxes in the Explorer and setting the View and Show tabs to construct different filters for each outbox. You can also use filters to copy, move, or create links to outgoing mail to different folders and locations, or to delete it.

> **Note**
>
> All incoming and outgoing mail and news files are saved in the Office51/Store folder.

Be aware that when you move a mail message outside the Outbox, certain commands such as Export and Reorganize are not available. If you want to export a file, or reorganize it as part of the Outbox, you must move it back to the Outbox first.

Importing and Exporting Files

You can import .mbx (mailbox) files from Microsoft Outlook Express into a POP3 account as well as import StarOffice .mbx files. You can export mail and news messages in StarOffice's .mbx ASCII format only.

> **Tip #543 from**
> *Michael & Sarah*
>
> Be sure to use the context menu Reorganize command on your account boxes before exporting either mail or news files so that they take up less disk space.

Importing Mail and News from Outlook Express

After you have a POP3 account Inbox created in the Explorer, select it and right-click to open its context menu. Choose File, Import. Select Microsoft Outlook Express as the file type, and navigate to the location of your Outlook Express .mbx file. Select the file, click it open, and the mailbox file is imported into your current account Inbox.

You can import an outgoing mail file into your Outbox in the same way.

> **Caution**
>
> If you have Netscape Navigator installed (even if you just use Navigator for your browser), your Outlook mailbox file will be corrupted on import. If you're setting up a new system, this is easy to take care of: Just don't load Netscape until after you import your Outlook files. If you already have Netscape on your system, there's no way around it but to de-install. If you save your Netscape user folder (which contains your personal bookmarks and other customized information), along with program address books, de-installing and then re-installing should not damage your current setup and does not take that long to do.

EXPORTING FILES

To export files from your account box, select in the Headers pane all the headers of files you want to export. You can use the standard selection methods. Then, right-click and select the Export command. You are prompted to assign a directory and name. All selected files are exported into one appended file.

Alternately, you can select an entire account box in the Explorer, right-click, and select File, Export. The entire contents of the mailbox or new account are exported—as filtered by your view and rules options. This means you can easily selectively export only those messages you care to save.

Mail and news messages are exported as .mbx (mailbox) text files that should be readable by any text processing program as well as most mail readers.

TROUBLESHOOTING

I've set up my news account, but nothing displays in the Explorer when I click the icon's plus sign.

One possibility is that you have not yet subscribed to any groups, so there's nothing to show. If that's the case, first get online. Then, select the news account icon in the Explorer, right-click, and select Properties to open the Properties dialog. Click the Subscribe tab. A list of available newsgroups appears. Scroll through this list and select the newsgroups that you want to join. Click OK, and the headers of postings to your selected newsgroups should appear in your news folder when you click the plus sign.

Another possibility is that you've set your viewing options to display only acitve newsgroups. If there are no new messages, you might not see any groups display.

I created an email mail merge when I was offline, and now I can't find my messages. They're not in the directory I selected with the Save As command.

They're not saved in the directory you chose with the Save As command—only a file copy of your original email is. They're saved in the Outbox. Double-click to open the Outbox on your desktop, and you should see them there—marked with a red symbol to the left to indicate that they have not yet been mailed. To send them, select the Outbox icon in the Explorer, right-click to open the context menu, and choose Update.

All my message headers disappeared in my Outbox, and I can't get them back again!

You may have inadvertently chosen the Hide Author command from the Header pane context menu. Because you're the author of all your outgoing emails, StarMail is hiding all your messages. To clear this, close the Outbox, select its icon in the Explorer, and open the context menu. Click the Rules tab. A rule has been entered automatically to hide all messages with you as author. Delete this rule and exit the Properties dialog. When you reopen the Outbox, you should see all your messages again.

I use Linux, and my IMAP email account doesn't work.

Multiple problems have been reported with IMAP for Linux 5.0 that the company says are fixed in version 5.1. If you're running 5.0, your best solution is probably to upgrade.

I double-click on a message header in my Inbox, but only a blank window opens.

You probably have a stale header in your inbox—that is, a header to a message that has since been deleted from your mail server and therefore refers to a message that no longer exists. You're out of luck, unless the mail server has backup files with your message. If it's been deleted from the server and you haven't saved a copy locally, it's gone for good.

I try but can't delete headers and messages from my News account window.

Check your news account properties. If you do not have the Contents tab set to store your contents locally, your news headers are downloaded from your news server every time you connect. You may therefore be seeing the return of messages you believe you deleted—but you didn't really delete them, because you can't delete news from the network news server. However, you can manage the display of headers by using the Show commands on your news account context menu, or by setting viewing properties and filters on the View and Rules tabs of the Properties dialog.

I can't open any attachments.

Check the Tools, Options, Internet, Other dialog box. Make sure Enable Plug-Ins is checked.

Next, check the File Types tab. Are your plug-ins visible in the drop-down menu there? Are they associated with the correct file types? If not, configure this tab properly.

Another possibility is that you don't have the correct program to open a particular file. There are a number of good programs that open email attachments in various file formats. On Linux, you might have some included in your original system installation that you just don't know about—check your system program documentation (for example, your Red Hat or Caldera installation guide). On the Windows side, there are a number of programs you can purchase in stores or via the Web, such as Attachments Plus, NetZip, and KeyView.

A third possibility is that the file is either zipped or compressed and must be unzipped or decompressed before it can be opened. On the Linux side, the tar program zips and unzips files, and uuencode and uudecode programs encode and unencode them. On the Windows/DOS side, PKZip and WinZip are two commonly used programs to zip and unzip.

You can also try saving your files locally and opening them through the File menu Open dialog box.

I can't see the entire rule that StarOffice has created on the Rules tab, and I can't resize the dialog box.

It's true that you can't resize dialog boxes. But just slowly hover your mouse over the rule in question, and a note will pop up that displays the rule in full.

WORKING WITH DATABASES—StarBase

CHAPTER 30

WORKING WITH DATABASES IN STARBASE

In this chapter

INTRODUCING STARBASE

StarBase is StarOffice's database module. It was originally implemented into StarOffice as a database shell to facilitate data importing and exporting into StarWriter and StarCalc documents, both directly and through SQL. In version 4.0, it was developed to create and manage the Address Book, the dBASE database that handles mail merges in StarWriter and StarMail.

> **Note**
>
> *SQL*, which stands for *Structured Query Language*, is discussed in the section "What Is a Query?" in Chapter 35, "Getting Answers with Queries and Fields." dBASE is one of the most commonly used file formats for databases. These and other terms relating to databases can be found in Appendix G, "Glossary," as well as being defined in context throughout this part on StarBase.

In version 5.0 for 32-bit Windows, StarBase grew even further from its simple origins into a sophisticated relational database program. If you're an individual user on Windows who wants to create and manage a large, sophisticated, text-oriented database and you don't much care about sharing data, this StarBase format will serve you well. If you're a business user with more complex needs, it's a more open question. StarBase has all the basic features you would expect of a relational database (primary keys, indexing, drag-and-drop relations, good development tools), along with some unique and quite nice StarOffice features. Most notable are the form-building tools and Form Navigator, which make creating custom forms in StarBase quite simple. You can also create forms as standalone documents, using the same tools, in StarWriter, StarCalc, or StarImpress, making data input and maintenance really easy and flexible. Printing and formatting professional-quality forms are also made extremely easy by this powerful integration across the StarOffice modules.

StarBase has also been significantly improved in versions 5.01 and 5.1, with many bug fixes that go a long way towards fulfilling StarBase's promise as a different kind of database.

Compared to MS Access, StarBase is limited in its importing capability (although it handles ODBC imports). More significantly, even though the StarBase format is based on dBASE III, it's a proprietary format that you can't import directly into Excel, Access, or other databases even though they may have a dBASE filter or dBASE III ODBC driver. One option is that you can create a database shell in the Explorer for an external database and then drag and drop tables from a StarBase format database into an ODBC, JDBC, Access, dBASE, or text database. You would then need to set relations between your tables again in the database into which you had copied the tables.

→ For details on copying tables from one database to another, **see** "Copying, Appending, and Importing Tables," **p. 1164**.

Objects you create in dBASE III format import quite nicely into other databases, but you can't create relations, which is essential for any serious business database.

On the Linux platform, StarBase is not yet a functional relational database, although all those grayed-out tools in the interface may fool you. Don't be fooled. Relations, primary keys, indexes, and the ability to work with files in native StarBase format are not yet implemented. ODBC is limited, although improving, and problems have been reported with Oracle connectivity. Although you can import relational databases into StarBase if they're in the right format, your relations will be lost. If you're a Linux database developer looking for a robust program to run your company's core database, or even just a hacker wanting to learn about relational databases, you must look further or wait for upgrades that will expand StarBase's functionality.

Because of these limitations, most users will likely use StarBase as a "data manager" rather than a full-fledged relational database management system (RDBMS). The focus of this chapter on StarBase is therefore on using StarBase as a data manager; only in Chapter 32, "Creating Tables with Relations," is using StarBase as a relational database discussed in detail.

PART

VII

CH

30

Note

In early 1999, StarDivision switched to a different third-party provider for its database engine because of the company's desire to have greater access to the source code. This change suggests StarDivision is seriously committed to improving StarBase, so if you need a more robust RDBMS, keep your eyes open for upcoming versions.

USING STARBASE AS A DATA MANAGER

StarBase can be used as a data manager in three primary ways:

- You can use it as the front end for SQL client/server databases that you access via ODBC, Oracle, or JDBC (Windows); or via ODBC and JDBC (Linux). If your ODBC driver supports relations, then you can import relations.

Note

Users have experienced significant problems with JDBC connectivity in version 5.0 on Linux. The company says they have been fixed in version 5.1, so users who need to access external data sources should get the upgrade. However, we were not able to do extensive testing ourselves before the release of this book.

- You can use StarBase as the conduit for importing data into StarCalc and StarWriter documents.

→ Importing tables from an existing database and entering the table data into StarCalc are described in "Selectively Importing Data from the Explorer," **p. 638**.

→ Using database fields is introduced in "Working with Fields," **p. 350**. Creating mail merges from a database is discussed in "Creating Form Letters with Mail Merge," **p. 360** and "Creating Mail Merges with StarMail," **p. 1062**. Creating a single text document like a catalog using database fields is discussed in "Selectively Inserting Data with Fields," **p. 1219**.

- You can create tables without relations in either StarBase or dBASE III format and then filter them in complex ways with SQL queries, manage them with forms, and print them with reports.

Tip #544 from
Michael & Sarah

> If you use StarBase to create unrelated tables, you may be better off creating your database in dBASE III format because doing so enables you to import your data more easily into many other database and spreadsheet applications.

If you approach StarBase as a relational database, you can easily feel frustrated with its current limitations. However, if you approach it as a data manager, you can learn to love it as a database program that's uniquely and sleekly integrated across the entire StarOffice suite. Here's some of what you can do with StarBase:

- Open a table or query in the Beamer, and drag and drop data rows into StarOffice documents. By doing so, you can selectively import data into StarCalc, StarWriter, StarMail, StarWriter/Web, and StarImpress.

- Insert records from multiple database tables (not just the Address Book) into form letters. By inserting records, you can carry out such tasks as automatically generating personalized letters to customers, which include specific details of each person's order, or creating thank you letters to contributors, which mention the amount of each person's contribution.

- Manage contacts and addressing with the Address Book and its associated special commands—AutoBrowse, AutoMail, and Who Is?.

- Create email and document mail merges with any tables that contain address information.

→ For a discussion of creating mail merges with a StarWriter document, **see** "Creating Form Letters with Mail Merge," **p. 360**.

→ For a discussion of creating mail merges with StarMail document, **see** "Creating Mail Merges with StarMail," **p. 1062**.

- Create queries, forms, and reports to manage data entry and extraction from client/server databases.

- Create a catalog or other complex text with database fields that draw information from database tables.

UNDERSTANDING STARBASE'S IMPORT AND EXPORT OPTIONS

Table 30.1 shows the various options available for importing and exporting data and indicates the platforms on which they're available.

> **Note**
>
> To import MS Access files, you must have the correct ODBC driver installed, along with the Data Access Object (DAO) engine and the Microsoft Jet Engine. The engines are part of MS Access 97 or Microsoft development tool packs.

TABLE 30.1 STARBASE IMPORT AND EXPORT OPTIONS

Application	Windows Import	Export	Linux Import	Export
MS Access 97	x	x		
DB2	X			
dBASE III	x	x	x	x
Text-text-CSV	x		x	
StarBase	x	x		
Oracle	x (Version 7.3 & higher)	x		
JDBC	x	x	x	x
ODBC	x	x		

We've already discussed some of the strengths and limitations of the StarBase and dBASE III file formats in the introductory section. It's important that you understand the possibilities of working in different formats before you invest a lot of work creating a database in StarBase, so we also include Table 30.2, which briefly compares your full range of import and export options.

TABLE 30.2 COMPARISON OF IMPORT AND EXPORT OPTIONS IN STARBASE

File Format	Comments
Text-*.txt-*.csv (text delimited)	Import in read-only format. However, you can import any text-delimited file into StarCalc and save in *.csv or dBASE format if you want to modify and save your table(s). If you want to create a text-delimited database, use StarCalc.
DB2	Import. You cannot change the structure of tables; you can only add and delete data.
MS Access	Serve as a front end for MS Access 97 databases. Requires that you have the DAO and Jet Database Engine installed. You can change the structure of tables as well as add and delete data.
StarBase	Create, manage, and save a fully relational database. You can exchange the complete database only with other StarOffice users; you can move tables into other non-StarBase format databases via drag and drop.

continues

TABLE 30.2 CONTINUED

File Format	Comments
Oracle	Serve as a front end for Oracle) databases, with the proper drivers installed. (Windows only.)
ODBC	Serve as a front end for ODBC databases, with the proper drivers installed. Relations can be maintained, depending on your driver. JDBC Serve as a front end for JDBC databases, with the proper drivers installed.
dBASE III	The only format other than StarBase in which you can create tables, but it does not support relations. You can also import data from existing dBASE databases. Your tables can be opened in other databases or spreadsheets that have the proper filters or ODBC drivers.

Your ability to export individual StarBase objects is limited. You can save forms and reports as master documents and HTML documents; other than that, objects can be accessed only through ODBC and JDBC drivers.

Note that if you have the proper ODBC driver installed, you might be able to import data from dBASE III, DB2, MS Access, and text-delimited databases through ODBC links rather than directly import the database into StarBase. If you want to add and modify data in text-delimited databases, you must import them via ODBC because the StarBase text-delimited database opens text tables in read-only format.

Tip #545 from
Michael & Sarah

If you're a Linux user longing for good ODBC support for StarOffice, take heart as there are developers working on this. Check out `http://genix.net/unixODBC/unixODBC.html`, the home site of a project to develop the UNIX ODBC driver. One team member is working specifically on improving ODBC drivers that work with StarBase. The iODBC and PGSQLODBC library projects are also working on this.

With MS Access 97 databases, you'll find two key differences between the options. You can alter table design if you import via the MS Access 97 type. This capability might represent more of a danger than a blessing, given that tampering with the table design could lead to serious data loss or corruption of your relations if you then need to reopen the table in Access. Related to that point, relations are not maintained when you import via the MS Access 97 type. Instead, your primary key is converted into an index named primary key. Your ODBC connection, on the other hand, maintains relations if your driver supports them. In terms of data handling, the two options are similar because your tables remain in *.mdb format. However, the long and the short of it is that if you import via ODBC, you have greater database security.

With dBASE III tables, the tables themselves are actually imported into StarBase. If you do not want to import your tables but simply want to connect to a dBASE database located on a server, connect via ODBC instead. The virtues of linking rather than importing are two-fold: greater database security and centralized storage of data. If you have multiple users, you should take these considerations seriously.

ELEMENTS OF A STARBASE DATABASE

Even though it doesn't offer anything near MS Access's power, StarBase is similar in many ways to MS Access in its structure and logic. A database in StarBase consists of four different types of objects that exist in a hierarchical relationship:

- Tables
- Queries
- Forms
- Reports

Tables are the root objects of a database, the objects that fundamentally structure the information that is stored in the database. Forms, queries, and reports are all built on tables. Tables consist of fields and records, sometimes also called columns and rows. A *field* is a category of information, whereas a *record* is a complete set of fields on the topic of the table.

A *query* is a structured question posed to a table that sorts and filters the table's data into a more useful form. Using queries, you can filter your data in much more sophisticated ways than are possible in a spreadsheet. StarBase enables you to create queries through drag and drop in its graphical query builder or write SQL statements.

A *form* is a graphical interface for entering, editing, and viewing data in a table or query. In StarOffice, you can create forms either inside a StarBase database or from within the StarWriter, StarCalc, and StarImpress application modules.

A *report* is polished output from a table that presents some of its information in a form suitable for human appreciation rather than computer manipulation and storage. A report can be built on a query or a table and can be formatted in ways that a table or query cannot.

A relational database consists of a fifth element, namely, relations. *Relations* are the relationships constructed between tables that define how information can be linked and exchanged between the tables. If relations are not set properly, the information stored in a relational database may go to waste, be corrupted, or fail to be filtered and sorted properly.

All these objects are linked together in a database file. Although you can locate individual files that are part of the database, you can't open them as individual files but must always open them through the database shell you create in the Explorer.

ORIENTING YOURSELF IN STARBASE

StarBase follows a different logic than the other StarOffice modules because databases are different kinds of animals than StarOffice documents. A database is not an individual document, but a container for a group of database objects. It's therefore more like a folder, which is why you begin by creating a database in the Explorer.

After you've created your database, you must either import or create database objects. You can then open these objects on your desktop or (in the case of queries and tables) in the Beamer and work with them in various ways. Each type of object has its own set of tools, some of which overlap with other StarBase objects or StarOffice document types, some of which may be unique to that object type. These tools are introduced in the section "The StarBase Toolbars and Context Menus" later in this chapter.

CREATING A NEW DATABASE IN THE EXPLORER

StarBase databases are created through the Explorer context menu or the File menu New, Database command. They have their own special icon, a hand with a stack of records on it, like the one in the margin here.

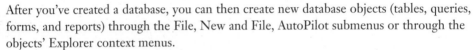

Note

Prior to version 5.1, you could only create databases in the Explorer via the context menu. New in 5.1, you can create databases via the File, New menu.

After you've created a database, you can then create new database objects (tables, queries, forms, and reports) through the File, New and File, AutoPilot submenus or through the objects' Explorer context menus.

To create a new database, start by creating a folder to contain it. Or, if you like, you can simply create and store it in the root level of the Explorer, where it will always be close at hand. Then follow these steps:

1. Select either the Explorer icon or the folder where you want your database to be stored.
2. Right-click to open the Explorer context menu, or open the File menu.
3. Choose New, Database. A multitabbed dialog box appears.
4. Enter a name for your new database in the text box on the General tab. You don't need to enclose the name in brackets (<>).
5. Click the Type tab, and choose the type of database you want to create.

The types of databases you can create are listed earlier in this chapter in Table 30.1. The variety in that table boils down to one key distinction: some you can use only to import and manipulate data from external databases (ODBC, DB2, JDBC, Access 97, and Text), while others you can use to create your own data sources from within StarBase as well as import from without (dBASE and, for Windows users, StarBase).

The choices you see on the Type tab and the other tabs you see will depend on the type of database you choose to create. The options for each are described briefly in the following sections.

CREATING AN ODBC DATABASE (WINDOWS ONLY)

You must carry out two steps to create an ODBC database in StarBase: Create a database shell in the Explorer to import and hold your database objects; and identify your external data source. The dialog boxes you use to identify your data source are not StarOffice dialog boxes but Microsoft ODBC administration dialogs you open while in the process of creating your StarBase shell.

If you choose ODBC, first enter a name for your new database on the General tab. Then, click the Browse button to open the Choose Data Source dialog. You see a list of all currently installed ODBC drivers on your system..

PART

VII

CH

30

Next, click Organize to open the ODBC Administrator dialog box. From here you can select your data source   the directory where your tables are stored. You can also add ODBC drivers that you don't already have installed. Figure 30.1 shows the StarOffice database creation dialog in the upper left, along with the Data Source and Administrator dialogs. The Data Source window in this example lists ODBC drivers that come as part of the basic options pack with MS Access 97 because this system has MS Access as well as StarOffice.

Figure 30.1
To create an ODBC database, you must specify the ODBC driver you're using and select your data source.

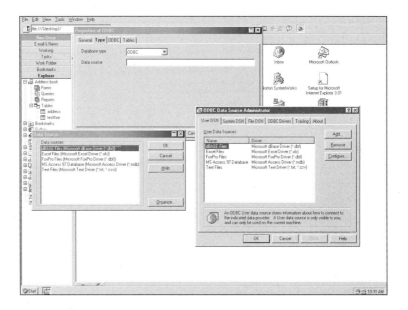

Tip #546 from
Michael & Sarah

Installing ODBC drivers is part of a custom installation in MS Office. If you have the MS Office suite but do not have any ODBC drivers currently installed, run your MS Office setup again to install them.

Note

In Figure 30.1, ODBC drivers are installed for text and MS Access 97 files, database types that you can directly create a shell for in StarBase as well. The virtues of creating links versus importing an entire database are discussed earlier in this chapter in "Understanding StarBase's Import and Export Options."

SELECTING A DATA SOURCE

After you click Organize in the Data Source dialog, the ODBC Data Source Administrator dialog box opens. (Note that this dialog box and others that open from it are part of a Microsoft program, so if you have further questions or problems, refer to your Microsoft documentation.) Make sure the correct type of data source is highlighted on the User DSN tab. Then, click Configure. You will see a Setup dialog box like that shown in Figure 30.2.

Note

If you store your text or .dbf tables in the same directory as your database shell, you do not need to select your data source as described in this section as the ODBC Administrator looks there by default.

Figure 30.2
You begin your selection of your data source from the ODBC Data Source Administrator dialog box. Click Configure to open the setup dialog box. Deselect Use Current Directory so you can navigate to your tables.

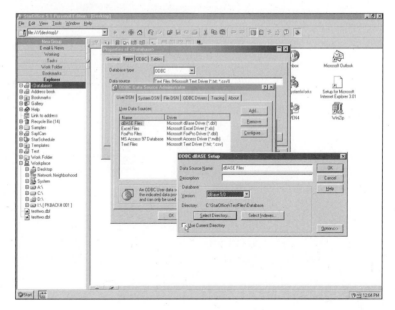

You must first deselect Use Current Directory by clicking in the check box (refer to Figure 30.2). Otherwise, the buttons that open your navigational tools remain grayed out and unavailable. (The current directory is the directory in which you have placed your StarBase database. For example, if you create your database in the Explorer, your current directory would be Office51\explorer.)

Then, click the Select Directory button. The Select Directory dialog box appears (see Figure 30.3). Extensions that match the data type you have selected appear in the File Name box on the left. On the right is a directory window showing your current location. Navigate to the directory where your tables are stored, select it, and choose OK. If you need to, select another drive in the Drives list, or click the Network button to select a volume on your network.

Figure 30.3
From the Select Directory dialog box, you can navigate on your local system or network drives to the home of your data source.

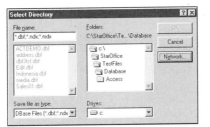

Note

If you are importing a dBASE database, you have the option of importing your index tables. Choose Select Indexes and follow the same steps as given for the Select Directory option.

Back in the ODBC setup dialog, you can enter a description for this ODBC connection, if you like. Then, choose the Options button and select the options you need to import your data correctly. These options vary depending on your database type but enable you to do such things as identify the character set used in creating your text database and determine how empty records are handled.

When you're done entering settings, click OK to exit the ODBC Setup dialog. You return to the ODBC Data Source Administrator dialog box, your work completed; click OK here as well to return to the Properties of ODBC dialog. The data type you selected should appear in the Data Source text box.

ENTERING ODBC ACCESS INFORMATION

Next, click the ODBC tab. Enter the username and password you use to gain access to the data source (if any). If any driver options exist, enter them in the appropriate input line. Select the character set used in the data source from the drop-down list. If you're not sure, choose the IBMPC set, a generic set that will usually suffice. You may not need to select this information if you have already done so in the ODBC Administration dialog box.

SELECTING YOUR TABLES OR DATABASE

For the final step, click the Tables tab. What happens next depends on the type of database you have selected.

If you have selected text or .dbf databases (dBASE or FoxPro), you will see a list of tables in the directory you selected earlier as your data source.

If you have selected any other type of database, clicking the Tables tab opens a selection dialog box that's similar to the Select Directory dialog box shown earlier in Figure 30.3. In the pane on the right, navigate to the directory in which your data source is located and select the directory. Depending on your database type, you may have other options such as to open your database in read-only form or set exclusive rights. Select any options now and click OK. (If you need to navigate on your network, click the Network button.) Once your selection is complete, a list of all the tables in your database appears on the Tables tab.

By default, all tables are selected for display as indicated by an X next to their names. If you don't want a table to appear in the database, click the checkbox to the left of its name. If you don't see any tables listed, that means you have not properly specified a data source. You're now finished creating your ODBC connection. Click OK, and your database is created in your selected group.

Note that if you have a non-text or .dbf database, every time you double-click the database icon in the Explorer to open your database, you will again see a Select Database dialog like the one in Figure 30.3 and will need to select the directory where your data source is stored.

Click the plus signs next to your database objects for that database to see a list of all your database objects. Double-click an object to open it on the desktop, just as with any other file; with tables and queries, you can also open them in the Beamer with an extended-click (if the Beamer is open). When you click the Edit button on the function bar, you can add and delete records.

Note that although you can open and view your table in design view, you cannot make any changes to your table structure. You can, of course, create and modify queries, reports, and forms based on your ODBC table(s) as you like.

CREATING AN ORACLE DATABASE

If you choose Oracle as your type, you must enter as your data source name the name created using the Oracle Tools Net8 Assistant/Easy Config. Next, click the Oracle tab, enter your username and password, enter any relevant driver options, and select the character set of the database. Choose OK, and your database is created in the Explorer.

Note

> The StarBase Oracle driver works with versions 7.3 and higher.

Double-click your database icon to begin work. You then are prompted to identify the directory in which your data source is located; your tables and other objects should then appear in the Explorer.

CREATING A TEXT DATABASE

Although you can access text databases via an ODBC driver (with the proper drivers installed), this section focuses on creating the Text type StarBase database.

→ To import a text-based database using ODBC drivers, follow the steps in "Creating an ODBC Database," **p. 1093**.

After you select Text as your type, click Browse. Navigate to the directory where you want to import text files, and choose OK or click Create New Directory. Next, click the Text tab, and select the delimiters that have been used to create the file, the file extension (*.txt, *.sdf, or *.csv), and the character set used to create the table(s). The most common delimiters for columns are commas (offered as the default choice) and tabs. If you're not sure which delimiters have been used, you might want to make a copy of the table and experiment with different options. If you're not sure of the character set, IBMPC is a good default choice; again, if your import doesn't look as expected, try again choosing a different character set.

If you already have text tables in the designated directory, you can now click the Tables tab to see a checklist of all available tables. You can deselect any that you don't want to use at the moment. If you haven't yet copied any tables into your designated directory, you can select your tables later by right-clicking your database icon, opening its properties, and returning to the Tables tab.

When you have tables selected, click the plus sign next to the Table objects icon in the Explorer to see the list. Double-click a table to open it on the desktop, or open the Beamer and extended-click to open it in the Beamer.

PART

VII

Сн

30

> **Note**
>
> Text databases are read-only, so you cannot make any changes to their tables or add or delete data.

CREATING A DB2 DATABASE

After you select DB2 as your database type, enter the pathname and filename of your DB2 data source. Then click the DB2 tab, and enter your username and password (if any), enter any relevant driver options, and select the appropriate character set. Choose OK, and your database is created in the Explorer.

CREATING A DBASE DATABASE

After you select dBASE as your database type, you need to indicate the directory where your database is or will be stored. If you don't know its full pathname or if you want to create a new directory, click Browse, and either navigate to your existing directory or create a new one in your desired location. When the correct directory path is selected, choose OK.

If you're importing a dBASE database, click the dBASE tab. Select the character set of the existing database from the drop-down list. If your tables use long table names, select Long Table Names; otherwise, they will be truncated on import. If you want to display inactive records, select Show Inactive Records.

If your tables have indexes and you want to select which indexes will import, click the Indexes tab. In the dialog that appears, you can select the tables from your database that have indexes and determine which indexes will be imported with the table. If you want to dissociate an index from a table, select it and click the right arrow to move it into the window labeled Free Indexes; if you want to attach a dissociated index to a table, select it and click the left arrow to move it into the window labeled Table Indexes. After you've completed your selections, choose OK to return to the main dialog.

Choose OK, and your dBASE database is created in the Explorer. Click the plus sign next to the database icon to open the list of database objects.

If you're importing existing data, plus signs should appear next to the object icons to indicate that they have contents. Click to reveal the object names, and double-click to open an object on the desktop.

If you're creating a database from scratch, your database will be empty because you haven't created any objects yet. Select and right-click the icon representing the type of object you want to create, and select New from its context menu to get started.

CREATING A STARBASE DATABASE

You also can select StarBase as your database type. Assuming you want to create a StarBase database from scratch, the next step is to click the button New Data Source. This action opens the familiar Save As dialog. Navigate to the directory where you want to store your database, enter a filename, and click Save. The complete path for your newly created file then appears in the Database file input line. You now can click the Administration tab and enter a username and password, if you want to control access to the database. You can later modify these values by reopening the Database Properties dialog from the database's context menu. Choose OK, and your database is created in the Explorer.

Note

Your export options are limited with a StarBase format database. You will find this format most useful for working within StarOffice. For more information, see the section "Understanding StarBase's Import and Export Options" earlier in this chapter.

Because you aren't accessing an existing data source and haven't yet created any database objects, your database is empty. To create tables, click the plus sign next to the database icon to reveal the database objects icons, select the Tables icon, and right-click to open its context menu. Select New, Table, and you can choose to create a table using the AutoPilot wizard or create it from scratch in the design View window.

→ For more information on creating tables in a StarBase-format database, **see** Chapter 31, "Creating Standalone Database Tables," **p. 1117**, and Chapter 32, "Creating Tables with Relations," **p. 1131**.

CREATING NEW DATABASE OBJECTS

After you've created a database in the Explorer, the routine is the same regardless of the type: To create a new object, select an icon for that object type in your database (for example, table), right-click, select New, and follow your menu selections.

You can also create new objects via the File, AutoPilot command, but you have a wider range of choices on the Explorer context menus.

THE STARBASE TOOLBARS AND CONTEXT MENUS

Unlike other StarOffice applications, StarBase makes virtually no use of menu bar menus. All the commands you use to manage objects are found either on database and database object context menus, or on the object and function bars. You can open tables and queries in the Beamer as well as on the desktop, and when you do, you see the same tools (in miniature) on the Beamer toolbar as you see on the object bars for tables and queries.

Table 30.3 lists all StarBase context menu commands and offers a brief description of each. Note that this table consolidates commands that appear on a number of different menus, and the specific commands you see depend on the object you've selected. Selecting the database icon, the object icons (tables, queries, forms, and reports), and the individual object icons (for a specific table, query, form, or report) each opens a different context menu.

Note

If you have saved a form as a regular document, outside of a database, right-clicking will not call up the database context menu. To open such a form in design view, open it as a regular document, open the Forms floating toolbar from the main toolbar, and click the Design Mode tool.

TABLE 30.3   DATABASE CONTEXT MENU COMMANDS AND THEIR USES

Use This Command...	To Do This...
New	Create a new database object.
Update	Update your data from your data source or refresh StarOffice's cache.
SQL	Open an SQL dialog in which you can enter and execute an SQL query.
Address Book	Designate the selected table as the default Address Book for StarOffice. This table opens in the Beamer when you press F4 or choose View, Current Database (unless you change your current database assignment).
Import vCard	Import a *.vcf address file. (Designated Address Book only.)
Export vCard	Export a *.vcf address file. (Designated Address Book only.)
Open	Open the selected object on the desktop.
Create Link	Create a link to the database or object on the desktop. You can also create links by Ctrl+Shift+dragging.
Table Design	Open a table in design view. Available for dBASE and StarBase format databases only.
Query Design	Open a query in graphical design view.
Enter SQL Statement	Open a query in SQL view.

continues

TABLE 30.3 CONTINUED

Use This Command...	To Do This...
Form Design	Open a form in design view.
Report Design	Open a report in design view.
Delete	Delete the selected object or database.
Rename	Rename the selected object or database.
Properties	View and/or change an object or database's properties.
Compress	Compact a table.

Because database objects are highly structured and interdependent, you should not go about changing their structure lightly. To guard against accidental or unknown changes, you work with database objects differently than you do with documents. For ordinary viewing and data management, you open objects in desktop view or in the Beamer. For changing an object's structure or conditions, layout, and design, you open objects in design view. You'll find different tools available in each view.

DESKTOP VIEW TOOLS AND MENUS

Figures 30.4 through 30.6 show an open table, form, and report (respectively) on the desktop in desktop view and identify the tools used for each. In desktop view, tables and queries are essentially the same object from your perspective, with all the same tools, so here the image of the table desktop view stands for both. The filtering and sorting tools you see are the same as those in StarCalc and on the main toolbar.

The use of tools and menus is discussed in detail in each of the chapters on the respective type of object; here, we just give a brief description and overview.

Note

> Despite what the table and query record editing menu may look like, it does not allow you to cut, copy, and paste data records, only data record numbers. These commands are useful when you are inserting database fields into documents and need to specify specific record numbers.

→ For more information, **see** "Selectively Inserting Data with Fields," **p. 1219**.

TABLE AND QUERY DESKTOP VIEWS

By default, tables in desktop view are opened as read-only because users most frequently open tables only to view data and enter data as text and/or merge fields into documents. If you want to insert data into tables, click the Edit button.

As you might tell from Figure 30.4, the table and query windows share some features with the StarCalc window. The table is divided into rows and columns. You can adjust the width of a column by double-clicking the right border (which automatically sizes it to fit the current data) or dragging its border to the desired size. You cannot resize rows manually; you must use the Row Height command from the row context menu. Row height is otherwise automatically set in relation to the current data display font size.

Tip #547 from
Michael & Sarah

You can more easily enter and manage data in queries and forms than directly in a table, especially as the table becomes very large.

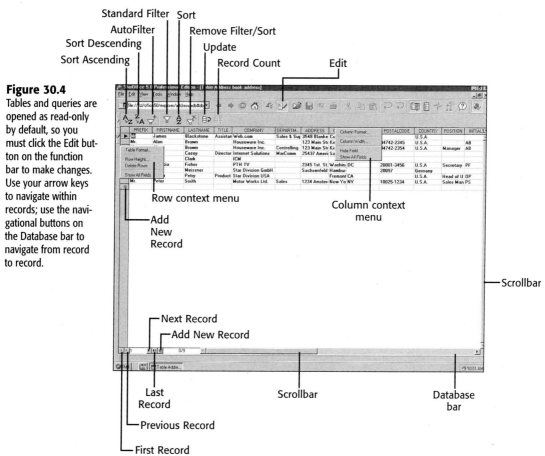

Figure 30.4
Tables and queries are opened as read-only by default, so you must click the Edit button on the function bar to make changes. Use your arrow keys to navigate within records; use the navigational buttons on the Database bar to navigate from record to record.

If you use StarBase primarily to manage your address book and create mail merges, you may find the basic sorting and filtering tools on the table toolbar enough for your needs. However, if you use your database for more intensive data management, you will likely work most frequently with queries. Queries enable you to get down and dirty with your data—sorting and filtering, as well as adding and deleting in more selective views than you can achieve with the original table. In desktop view, a query and its tools are just the same as those for a table because queries, in StarBase, are just a special kind of table. Only in design view do their differences become apparent.

→ For information on working with tables, **see** Chapter 33, "Working with Data in Tables"," **p. 1149**.

FORM DESKTOP VIEW

Forms and reports are both more document-like than are tables and queries, which is reflected both in their toolsets and how you work with them. For example, forms have an active status bar and, just as with text or spreadsheet documents, right-clicking or double-clicking often opens shortcut menus or dialogs. The composite picture of a form open in desktop view in Figure 30.5 shows the Navigator open. You can open it by double-clicking in the Current Page field. You open the Page Style and Zoom shortcut menus by right-clicking in the Page Style and Zoom fields, respectively. Different tools pop up from the status bar, however, when you're in Form Design view.

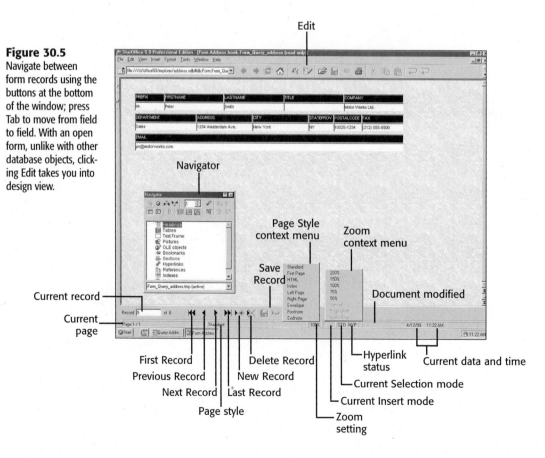

Figure 30.5
Navigate between form records using the buttons at the bottom of the window; press Tab to move from field to field. With an open form, unlike with other database objects, clicking Edit takes you into design view.

REPORT DESKTOP VIEW

Reports are documents generated from tables and queries, which means that you cannot directly edit any data that appears in a report. To change the data that appears, you must filter your data with queries or with fields you insert (in design view) that establish conditions for the display of data. The desktop viewing mode is therefore useful largely to check the design and check the results of your queries and fields before printing.

Reports are generated by creating a table for each record, and just as in text documents, the Navigator tracks these tables (as you can see in Figure 30.6). You can jump from record to record by clicking its table number in the Navigator.

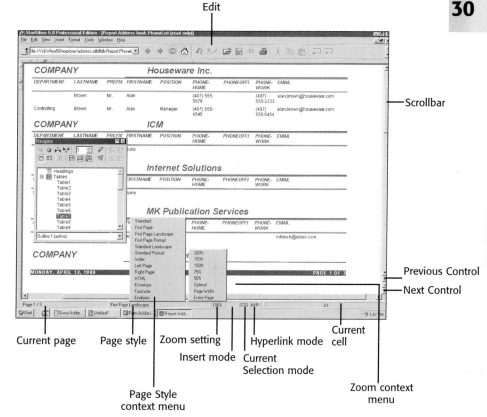

Figure 30.6
You can't do much with reports in desktop view; it's similar to Page View mode in documents. Note that the Edit button is unavailable; to make changes, you must exit and reopen the report in design view from the Explorer context menu.

DESIGN VIEW TOOLS AND MENUS

Because you can create every type of StarBase object with the AutoPilot, if your needs are simple, you may never need to muck around with design views. However, it's more likely that you will want either to create an object from scratch or modify an AutoPilot creation to better suit your own needs and tastes. To do so, you need to select the object in the Explorer and open it in design view.

TABLE DESIGN VIEW

Table Design view is available only for dBASE and StarBase databases because only in these two types can you create tables. All other types of databases are only front ends for viewing and manipulating imported data with queries, forms, and reports.

Your table design tools are basic you can see those for managing rows in the context menu in Figure 30.7. Open this context menu by placing your cursor in the row header and right-clicking. Within individual cells of the Field Name and Description columns, you can use the standard Backspace and Delete keys to delete field names one character or selected field at a time, and the standard editing shortcut keys (Ctrl+C, Ctrl+V, Ctrl+X) to cut, copy, or paste a selected field. Right-click when your cursor is in a cell to open a cell context menu that gives you these commands and a few more. Use the arrow keys to move around in the table. Ctrl+Z or the Edit menu Undo command will reverse your edit field and record edits. Note, however, that you cannot use the editing shortcuts of Ctrl+C, Ctrl+V, and Ctrl+X to edit complete records; you must use the commands on the row context menu.

Figure 30.7
Designing a table is more brain than brawn, so the tools you need besides yourself are few. The record editing context menu has most of the commands you need, along with the Format dialog that allows you to change your field types through a sneaky backdoor method.

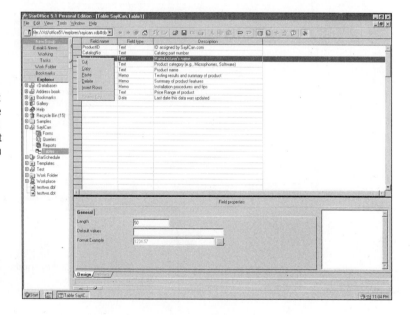

After you've entered field names, clicking in the Field Type column brings up a drop-down list of field types.

Note two other elements of the window in particular: the Indexes tab at the bottom and the Format button at the bottom right. Clicking Indexes takes you to a second columnar work-sheet, where you can create or modify indexes. (Indexes define the searching and sorting order for a table and can speed table operations considerably.)

→ For more information on indexing tables, **see** "Indexing Tables for Faster Searching," **p. 1143**.

Clicking Format opens a formatting dialog box with two tabs: Numbers and Align. These tabs are the same as the Numbers and Align tabs in the StarCalc Cell Format dialog, although only a select number of the Align commands are available in StarBase. With these commands, you can determine the appearance and system characteristics of the data in your currently selected field. Just as in StarCalc, these commands can have powerful effects on your data, sometimes causing data loss, so don't apply them before you understand the implications of using them.

→ For more information on number formats and alignment commands, **see** "Formatting Cells," **p. 559**.

Applying formats may seem a strange thing to do to data in a table; usually, formatting is associated only with forms and reports because a table cannot be printed by itself. The reason for this command is that when you import tables, the field type StarBase assigns sometimes may not match your data. (A common reason is that you have exported a database from a spreadsheet program that doesn't allow you to determine field types.) You should be extremely cautious about changing the field type of any field with existing data because changing it might result in the loss of all data in that field. Using the Format command is a way of changing your data type by the backdoor so that it appears in your table, reports, and forms as you expect.

> **Note**
>
> The Primary Key command is grayed out in dBASE databases, like the one shown in Figure 30.7, because you only create relations and set primary keys in StarBase-type databases.

QUERY DESIGN VIEW

In Query Design view, the difference between queries and tables comes clear. The query design window, rather than giving you tools for defining and formatting fields, gives you tools to create filtered and sorted views of your table data by constructing queries.

The underlying language of queries in StarBase is ANSI 1989 Level 2 SQL. However, you can create queries without knowing anything about SQL by using the drag-and-drop window that appears when you initially open a query in design view (see Figure 30.8). If you prefer to create queries by directly entering SQL statements or need to edit a query created by drag-and-drop, click the SQL tab at the bottom to see your query in SQL.

> **Note**
>
> For most StarBase databases, you can construct only single table queries. Only with StarBase relational databases or ODBC imported databases that have maintained their relations can you create a query from multiple tables.

Click Add
Table to select
a data source

Execute Query ⌐   ⌐Remove Filter/Sort   Table fields window

Figure 30.8
After you've selected a
table as the basis for
your query, you can
drag and drop field
names from the table
field window to the
query grid below,
select a sort order,
turn display of the
field on or off, and
enter criteria for filtering by typing in the
appropriate
columns(s) in the
Criteria row.

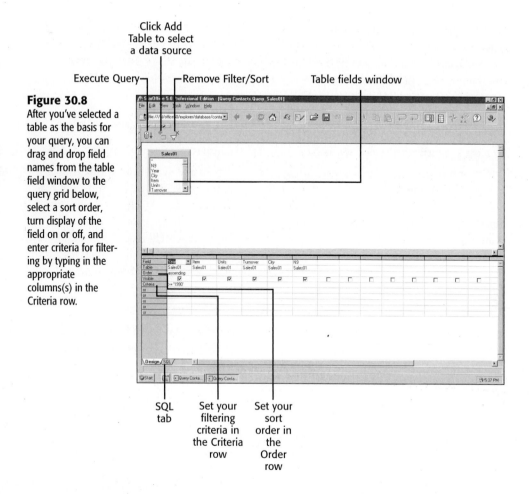

SQL   Set your   Set your
tab   filtering   sort
          criteria in   order in
          the Criteria   the
          row   Order
                        row

FORM DESIGN VIEW

A form is a special type of document in StarOffice rather than a separate type of object. In
fact, you can create forms from a StarWriter, StarCalc, or StarImpress task window and save
them as documents separate from your database, or you can save a form you create within
StarBase as a separate document as well.

Tip #548 from *Michael & Sarah*	You can export forms as HTML or Master documents by choosing File, Send.

If you create a form using the Form AutoPilot, your form is created as a text document.
Form input fields, which are automatically inserted, are linked to the database fields with
which they're associated. (These input fields are called *controls* in database terminology.) The
net result is a text document with special characteristics.

From the perspective of your form design view tools, you have a large selection of the same text editing and formatting commands you have in StarWriter. You can enter, edit, and format text in and around your form fields just as you would in any StarWriter document. (For an example, see the text in Figure 30.9.) The status bar also has a similar set of fields (although you can add a Cell field that's special to forms).

Figure 30.9
After you've clicked in the document outside the form fields, you can enter and edit text just as in a StarWriter document, although certain special commands are unavailable.

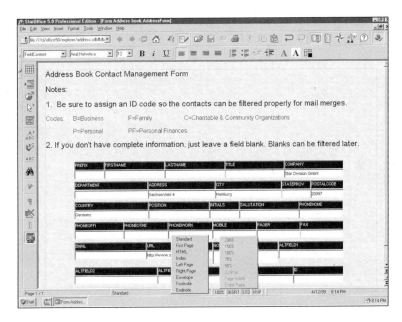

StarWriter commands that involve tables, fields, and formulas are unavailable; otherwise, everything else is free game.

Within your form controls, however, it's a different matter. These controls have special characteristics, and you can't select or format text in them as you can on the rest of your form. After you click in a control, a special Form object bar, like the one shown in Figure 30.10, appears on your desktop. Some of these tools are the same as those found on the Draw object bar and other graphics-related toolbars because form controls are graphic objects that can be positioned, resized, anchored, grouped, and ungrouped like any other object. Others are special to forms. These tools are identified in Figure 30.10; their function is detailed in Table 30.4.

A notable tool is the Form Navigator, sibling to the regular Navigator. It tracks all the controls in your form and allows you to see them all in overview as well as jump from one to another by clicking their names. You can also set the tab order of your form and manage groups from the Form Navigator.

Figure 30.10
When you click inside a form control, the Form object bar appears with commands for editing form controls, changing their position, and grouping and ungrouping them. You can keep an overview of your form with the Form Navigator, opened from the object bar.

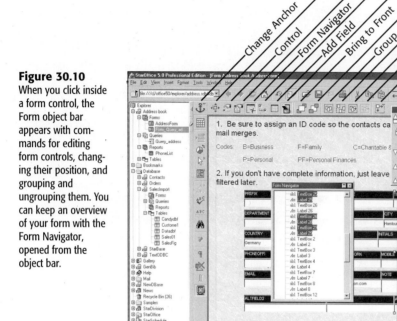

Alignment
floating toolbar

TABLE 30.4   FORM OBJECT BAR COMMANDS

Click This Tool...	To Do This...
Change Anchor	Change the anchoring from paragraph to character or page.
Position and Size control.	Open a dialog that enables you to precisely position and size your
Control	Open the Properties dialog of the selected control(s) where you can assign formatting and other characteristics.
Form properties.	Open the Form properties box, where you can edit general form
Form Navigator	Open the Form Navigator.

Click This Tool...	To Do This...
Tab Order	Determine the order in which pressing the Tab key moves you through the controls.
Add Field	Open a floating window that lists all the database fields of your underlying table(s). You can then drag and drop new fields onto your form.
Design Mode	Close design mode and return to desktop view (Input mode).
Bring to Front	Bring the selected control or group to the front of all other graphic objects.
Send to Back	Send the selected control or group to the back of all other graphic objects.
Group	Group together the selected objects and treat them as a single unit for certain purposes.
Ungroup	Ungroup a group.
Edit Group	Change the membership of controls in a group.
Exit Group	Take out of Edit mode the member of the group that you're currently modifying.
Alignment	Open the Alignment floating toolbar that enables you to set the alignment of form objects in relation to the page.

REPORT DESIGN VIEW

Just like a form, a report is essentially a document. It's structured with tables, and each cell of the table is associated with a field in your table or query. When you open the report in desktop view, a field merge is carried out (much like what happens in mail merge), and a document is freshly generated following the formatting and layout you have given the report in design view. However, just as with forms you create within StarBase, you cannot save a report as a document separate from the larger database.

The tools for working with text and tables are presented and thoroughly discussed in earlier chapters on StarWriter, so I won't rehash them again here.

→ Issues specific to creating reports are discussed in Chapter 36, "Creating and Printing Reports," **p. 1225**.
→ For more information about formatting, **see** Chapter 7, "Formatting Text Documents," **p. 261**, and (if you're still hungry for more) Chapter 8, Using Styles and Templates," **p. 291**.
→ For tools, tricks, and tips of working with tables, **see** Chapter 9, "Working with Tables, Charts, and Fields," **p. 321**.

The fact that we must send you scurrying back to sections on StarWriter points to the tight integration of StarBase into StarOffice. You don't need to learn a whole new set of tools and commands to work with reports; you need only refine the skills you've already developed working with table documents.

PLANNING AND DESIGNING YOUR DATABASE

As with many tasks that use computers as tools, the most important part of the database design process happens between people—at least it should because the only good database is the one that meets its users needs. The only way to determine those needs is to ask and do research. Whether you're planning to use StarBase to create a front end for a client/server database or create a database from scratch, you should set aside enough time to plan and design your database on paper before you ever set hand to mouse.

CREATING A FRONT-END DATABASE

If you are planning to use StarBase primarily as a front end for working with client/server databases, most of the serious heavy lifting of creating a database has already been completed, and much of your design will be shaped by the existing database tables. However, you still need to consider a number of factors before embarking on creating queries, forms, and reports in StarBase. These factors include the following:

- Does your ODBC driver support relations? Will users be able to construct the types of queries they need to work with data?

- Who exactly will be using StarBase for data import, and what specific data does each user need to view, add, and/or modify?

- Do individuals need the ability to create their own queries, reports, and/or forms, or just use these objects to work with data?

Tip #549 from
Michael & Sarah

If users only need to work with data, you might be wiser to store some or all database objects on a central server where they can easily be maintained and updated by a small number of people.

CREATING A DATABASE FROM THE TABLES UP

If you are creating a database from scratch, the issues are considerably more complex. Planning and designing your database are the most important parts of creating your database, in fact, and you should take some time with them before you start creating tables. This point is dramatically true in the case of a relational database, whose data can be totally corrupted if the tables and relations are improperly constructed. However, it's important as well in the case of single-table (flat list) databases.

The first issue to consider seriously with a single-table database is whether you're better off creating it in StarBase or StarCalc. The chief value of a single-table database in StarBase is the additional power and flexibility you have in creating queries, forms, and reports. This power is considerable. However, you do pay a price. Part of the price is greater complexity in creating and maintaining objects. Another part is a higher learning curve for users because even though the concepts used in StarBase are similar to those in StarCalc, the tools are less intuitive and more complex to learn, particularly in the case of building queries.

Using queries, forms, and reports is easy, but designing them is not. If you are going to create a single-table database in StarBase that will have multiple users, your best approach is to have a single person or team design and produce all the database objects, and train others just to use them.

Another issue to consider is the type of data you're collecting. If you're collecting primarily text data, StarBase should be your choice, hands-down. If you're collecting a mix of financial or numerical and text data, you should consider which program will offer the appropriate calculating power. StarBase reports are essentially text documents, and you have access to the Text Formula bar and its small but robust menu of mathematical and statistical functions. A Sum function is available, but no subtotals command. If you want to take a look at your possibilities, press F2 and click the Function tool to open the Text Formula bar functions menu. You cannot create calculated fields directly in StarBase, although (in theory) you can write SQL statements that create calculated fields. (In practice, StarBase's implementation of SQL is very buggy.)

After you've settled on using StarBase, the issues shift to those of database design. Although we use databases in our own work, we are not database design theorists, nor do we have the space in this book to delve into the subject very deeply. Our focus here is in presenting you the tools StarBase offers for working with data and constructing simple databases. However, we want to introduce some of the basic issues so that you don't begin your work in the dark. In the following paragraphs, we discuss some generic issues of database design common to single table and relational table databases. We'll touch on some additional design issues specific to relational database design in Chapter 32, "Creating Tables with Relations." That chapter is worth reading even if you're only beginning with a single-table database because at some point you might want to build a relational database upon that initial table. Your ability to do so will depend on your initial thoughtfulness in dividing your data into fields and considering future relational possibilities:

- What is the nature of the data you are collecting, and to what uses do you currently put it?

- What kind of information do you regularly need to extract?

- Who will enter data into the database, and how much time can be committed to data input and maintenance? You want to ensure that maintaining the database is not onerously time consuming because if it is, it will not be used.

- Who needs to have access to the database? Do you need to have multiple copies of the database tables, or can people access them from a common machine or central server?

- If you do need to have multiple copies of tables, how will the integrity of the table structure be ensured? This factor is important because you will need to combine and consolidate data from the multiple tables. If the table structure is altered in someone's copy, ensuring the integrity could be difficult to achieve and make database maintenance a real headache.

Tip #550 from
Michael & Sarah

With StarBase-type tables, you can set various access options in the table properties as well as set passwords. If you need to protect the structural integrity of tables, this format might be a better choice than dBASE.

After you have answered some of the issues in the preceding list, you need to get out your pencil and paper and start planning your table fields. The following are some important design principles:

- Break down your data into its smallest meaningful constituent parts.

- Plan for ways in which you might later need to track, sort, and filter your data. This step might lead you to create special indexing or ID fields. For example, in the Address table of the StarOffice Address Book, there is an ID field. Using this field, you can keep all your contacts in one big table and create a code that breaks them down into categories. You enter the code into the ID field—say, B for business, P for personal—and you can then later filter your contacts with a query so that only business contacts are included in a mail merge mailing you create to promote your business.

- In counterpoint to the preceding principle, only include the fields you need and will use. Don't include fields that you can create with other commands; for example, don't create totals fields when you can create totals in reports by using the Sum function.

- Plan for the possibility of duplicate data. Duplicate data can be of two kinds: truly the same data being entered twice or data that shares some of the same characteristics but is actually different, such as records of two employees who have the same name. Relational databases have built-in methods to prevent you from entering truly duplicate data (although it can still be a problem if the design is poor), but single-table databases do not. Will it matter to your database results if duplicate data appears in a single-table database? If it will, how can you guard against it? If guarding against it is important, you might need to invest in a programmer or macro wizard who can work with StarBasic to create the database you need.

The preceding is just a brief introduction to what has become a serious academic subject. Several other Macmillan/Que titles delve quite deeply into the theory of sound database design (see Que's *Special Edition Using Microsoft Access 2000* by Roger Jennings). If you are planning to create your own database, we strongly suggest that you investigate one of these books or go to your local library and nose around because quite a few books have been published on the subject. If this is too much for you to take on, then you should consider hiring a professional to at least advise you, if not actually develop your database. After you have designed your database, altering its structure without serious loss or corruption of data is almost impossible—so doing the job right from the beginning is worthwhile.

MAINTAINING A DATABASE

Whether it's research data on annual pollen counts in Canadian provinces over the past 30 years or records of recent customer-buying patterns of your business, a database is usually difficult to create, quite large, and something you don't want to become damaged or lost. Just like you brush your teeth every night (don't you?), you should get in the habit of performing basic maintenance on your database to ensure its continued good health and performance. Some additional aspects of maintenance relevant to relational databases are discussed in "Securing Your Database" in Chapter 32, "Creating Tables with Relations."

PART

VII

CH

30

BACKING UP

The most elementary and all-too-easily neglected aspect of maintenance is regularly backing up your database. Standalone databases, especially relational databases, are often very big files, and the bigger they are, the more subject they are to data corruption and loss. And, of course, the more work you lose if they crash. Even databases that just serve as a front end for client/server databases can contain a lot of valuable work in custom-made queries and reports. You should therefore back up your database regularly. If you're creating a stand-alone database in StarBase, you should ideally back it up every time you use it.

Because StarBase is an integrated program within StarOffice, no special backup command is available from within StarBase. You can copy databases by dragging and dropping, and at minimum you should create a backup folder just for your database(s) and make regular back-up copies. If you're an individual user, consider investing in a zip drive and disks and setting aside a single zip disk just for backing up your database. If you work for a small business or organization, you should invest in a backup program that automatically creates regular, timed backups of all your critical data, not just your database files. Such backup programs often require that you purchase a special tape drive that can hold a large volume of data without problem.

COMPRESSING

Because database tables record data sequentially as you enter it, rather than in logical order, gaps can develop as you delete and rearrange data or delete rows, just as when you erase someone's name from the first entry in your Address Book, a blank space results. Over time, these blanks can build up and slow down your searching procedures. They can also lead to various other database errors that you don't want. Compressing your database (what some other databases call *compacting*) removes these blanks and keeps your database structure compact and well organized.

You compress all tables in a database at the same time; you cannot compress only one at a time. To compress, select the Table Objects icon and right-click; then choose Compress from its context menu.

There's always a danger, when you compress, that compressing itself will damage your file in some way. The program therefore prompts you to save your database before it proceeds with compressing; the idea is that you should save it to a backup directory or save it under a different name so that you can recover your data in case of problems. If you have recently deleted records or changed the table design, the program also alerts you that these deletions are about to become really permanent and asks for your permission to continue. If you choose OK, StarBase proceeds to compress.

Note

Don't be scared off from compressing because of the cautions we mention here. Compressing your database is an important part of maintaining your database in good working order and should be done regularly.

UPDATING

If you're using StarBase as a front end for a client/server database, data from the source database tables is imported when you initially open your database in the Explorer and held in cache. It is not automatically updated while you are working.

Tip #551 from
Michael & Sarah

Reports are generated from table data (either directly or filtered through queries) at the time you create or open them. It's therefore a good idea to update your tables and/or queries before generating a report to be sure that it includes all relevant data. If you have generated a report on your desktop and then add new data to an underlying table, you should close out of the report and then reopen it so that the data is updated.

If you're using StarBase to create your own table or tables, your data tables are generally updated as you work, but depending on your RAM usage at the time, a time lag may still occur between entering or modifying data in a form or query and having that data appear in your table(s).

You therefore need to periodically update as you work to ensure you're seeing the most current data. You can find update commands both on the Explorer context menus for tables and on table and query toolbars in desktop view. Updating is as simple as clicking the Update button or menu command.

Tip #552 from
Michael & Sarah

You can cause the Update command to run automatically by associating it with a program event that you either set in the object's Properties dialog or determine through a macro or StarBasic script.

TROUBLESHOOTING

I want to create a StarBase database from scratch, but when I try to enter a filename for my new database, I keep getting this error message: `The specified filename or directory does not exist.`

You need to save your new database to a file first by clicking the New Data Source button, navigating to the directory where you want your database saved, entering a name, and clicking Save. You'll recognize the dialog; it's essentially the same as the Save As dialog, and you navigate in the same ways.

The name you assign your database in the New Data Source dialog is the filename with which it's saved to disk. Your new, blank database doesn't actually exist until you save it to disk; only then can you assign it a name to be used in the Explorer. The same logic is at work here as when you save a document under one filename but assign it a different title in its Properties dialog.

I successfully created a StarBase database that shows up in the Explorer, but when I click or right-click Tables, I get this message: `Error reading data from database, it was not possible to make a connection....`

We can think of two possibilities:

- You didn't actually create a new database; you just created a shell for a database in the Explorer. If you didn't assign a name to your database and just accepted the default <Database> name, this is surely your problem.

  Right-click the database icon, and open its Properties. Then click the Type tab, and click the New Data Source button. You then see a dialog just like the Save As dialog. That's no accident; what you're about to do is save yourself a new, blank database file to disk. Assign a name and click Save. Now, back on the Type tab, type in the name by which you want this database to appear in the Explorer in the Database file input line. Choose OK when you're done. Now you should be able to right-click the Tables icon and create a new table from the context menu that appears.

- You moved the files that made up your database to another directory. StarBase, like the good computer program it is, is searching for files exactly where you told it to look—and getting confused.

  Select your database, right-click, choose Properties, click the Type tab, and click Browse. Now navigate to the new directory where your database file is located, select the file, and choose Open.

I want to export my Address Book contacts but can't find an export command anywhere.

You cannot export files from StarBase. You have four options. If you have the right ODBC (or JDBC) drivers, you can connect to your Address Book as an external data source from the application into which you want to import your data. If your database or spreadsheet program has a filter for dBASE III database files, you might be able to open your database directly as is, without any changes. Alternatively, you can import the Address Book data into

StarCalc and save the file as a *.txt-*.csv-delimited text file or a *.dbf dBASE III database file. You should then be able to import that file directly into the contact manager, spreadsheet, or database of your choice, assuming they have the right filters. The *.csv and *.dbf formats are very common, so it's likely that between the two of them you can transport your data. The fourth alternative is to create a database shell in the Explorer for the database into which you want to import your address book tables. Then, drag and drop your address table(s) onto the Tables icon of the new database shell.

CHAPTER 31

CREATING STANDALONE DATABASE TABLES

In this chapter

UNDERSTANDING OPTIONS FOR CREATING TABLES

Although for many users StarBase's main purpose is to bring external data into StarOffice documents, you can also use it to create your own database tables. This chapter addresses creating standalone tables—that is, tables that are part of a flat-list database. You can create only standalone tables in dBASE III format; you can create both standalone and relational tables in StarBase format. Because indexes have the greatest importance in relational databases, creating an index is discussed in Chapter 32, "Creating Tables with Relations." Indexes are very useful for a large flat-list database as well, so if you expect to be creating a table with thousands of records, you should consider indexing your table.

→ For information about creating relations between tables, **see** "Preparing a Table for Relations," **p. 1137** and "Creating Relationships between Tables,"**p. 1139**.

→ For information about indexing, **see** "Indexing Tables for Faster Searching," **p. 1143**.

Note
Your ability to modify data tables that you import from external sources is limited. Although that's not surprising in the case of client/server imports, you might be surprised that you cannot modify text tables either. (You can if you import them into StarCalc.)

CREATING TABLES BY USING AUTOPILOT

In a phrase that you will hear throughout Part VII, "Working with Databases—StarBase," the easiest way to create a table is by using AutoPilot.

The StarBase AutoPilot includes a number of prebuilt tables for business and personal use to choose from that serve many common needs. You might not need all the fields included, but you can choose the ones you want during the creation process. You can also easily modify a table after it is created. Table 31.1 lists these table templates by name.

TABLE 31.1. STARBASE'S AUTOPILOT TABLE TEMPLATES

Table Category	Table Name
Business	Assets
	Contacts
	Customers
	Deliveries
	Employees
	EmployeesAndTasks
	Events

Table Category	Table Name
	Expenses
	Guests
	Invoices
	MailingList
	Orders
	Payments
	Products
	Reservations
	ServiceRecords
	Students
	Suppliers
	Tasks
	Transactions
Personal	Accounts
	Addresses
	BookCollection
	HouseholdInventory
	MusicCollection
	PhotoCollection
	Recipes
	VideoCollection
	WineList

If you're an experienced hand at databases, you may just want to jump into designing your own. If you're new to databases, or just want a quick way to examine the structure of a typical StarBase table, flying on AutoPilot is a good place to start.

To begin, select File, AutoPilot, Table or click the Table icon in your database in the Explorer and choose New, AutoPilot from its context menu. The Table Type dialog appears, with two drop-down lists and a list box (see Figure 31.1).

The Database drop-down list lists all the databases you currently have in the Explorer. If you have not yet created a database of your own, only the Address Book (a dBASE III database) is listed.

Figure 31.1
To create a table, you must first select the database in which it will reside.

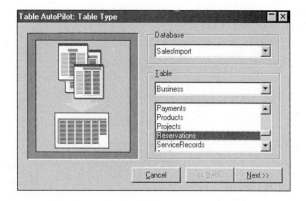

Select the database in which your table will reside. Then, in the Table drop-down list, select the category of table you want to create: Business or Personal. (If you click Personal, be patient, as it takes the list a few seconds to load.) The list box at the bottom of the dialog displays all the available tables for that category. Browse the list and make your selection. If you're not sure by its title if a table is the appropriate choice, just select it anyway. In the next dialog, you'll be able to see a list of fields and select the ones you want. When you've made your selections, click Next. The Field Selection dialog appears (see Figure 31.2).

Figure 31.2
To select the fields you want in your table, select a field name from the window on the left and click the right arrow to move it to the window on the right. To move the entire list at once, click the double-headed arrow.

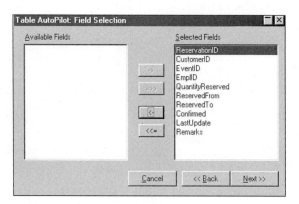

You'll see a list of available fields on the left side of the dialog. The field names are usually self-explanatory. Note that some of the field names will be truncated when the table is actually created because there is a 10-character limit on the length of field names.

If you find that the table doesn't meet your needs, you can always click Back and select another table from the list. Select the fields you want included in your table by moving them into the Selected Fields window, and click Next. The Customization dialog appears (see Figure 31.3).

Figure 31.3
In the Customization dialog, you can modify the names of your selected fields as well as the name of the table.

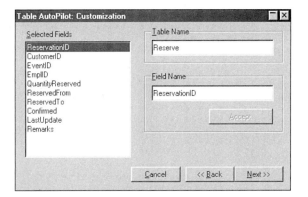

If you want to rename any of the fields, select it and type in a new name in the Field Name input box. When you input a new name, the Accept button becomes active; to enter your new name, click the Accept button. You can modify as many field names as you like—just keep in mind the 10-character limit. You can also change the default table name in the Table Name input box. When you're done, click Next (or click Cancel to abandon the table and return to the desktop). A Create Table dialog appears, like the one in Figure 31.4.

Figure 31.4
When creating your table, you can choose to have the table opened in Edit mode (Insert Data in Table) or read-only mode (Show Table), or be placed in the Explorer without being opened at all.

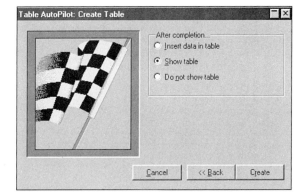

Select one of the three options for viewing the table after its creation, and click Create to start the process. If opened in Edit mode, your table will look something like the one in Figure 31.5.

If you're content with the table design, you can immediately begin entering data. To move through your fields from left to right, press the Tab key. To move backward, use the left arrow key or Shift+Tab. Data is recorded as soon as you exit the field in which you've entered it; you don't need to execute a Save command as you do with documents. StarBase also prompts you before you close the table to confirm that you want to save any new or modified data.

If you want to modify your table structure, you need to close out of either Edit mode or Read-Only mode and open the table in Design view from the Explorer.

Figure 31.5
You can tell your table is in Edit mode because the Edit mode button on the function bar is pressed in, there are gray borders around your table fields, and the table navigation buttons at the bottom of the window are active.

Edit mode

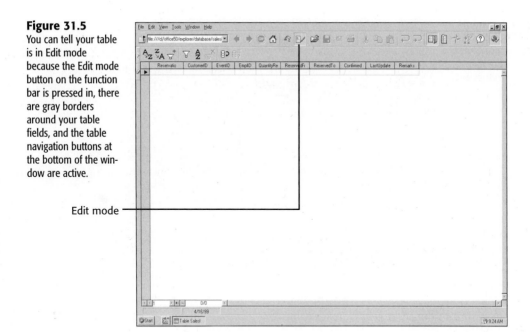

CREATING AND MODIFYING TABLES IN DESIGN VIEW

You need to be in Design view when you create or modify a table. The processes are very similar, so we discuss them together here, using the Reservations table created with the AutoPilot as an example.

> **Note**
>
> You can open any table you have registered in a database in theExplorer in design view to see its structure, even though you might not be able to modify the table in StarBase.

> **Tip #553 from**
> *Michael & Sarah*
>
> If you're creating a table, it's a good idea to have your table mapped out on a piece of paper before you sit down at the computer–this should have been part of your initial database design. Although you can improvise at the keyboard, this often results in a table that's inadequate for your needs.

To create a new table from scratch, open the database in which you want to create the table and select the Table object icon. Right-click to open the context menu, and select New, Table, Table Design.

To modify the design of an existing table, select the table in the Explorer, right-click and select Table Design.

Caution

Be extremely cautious about modifying the field types of imported tables that contain data, as this may result in data loss or corruption. If you have an imported table with data, only attempt modifications on a *copy* of that table. You can then compare the original and the copy to see the effects of your changes. If StarBase has changed numeric, currency, or date fields into text type fields as part of the import process, don't change the field type back again; open the Format dialog and apply number formats of the correct type.

Your table will look something like the one in Figure 31.6, although of course if you're creating a new table from scratch, there won't yet be any field names entered.

Figure 31.6
In Table Design view, you can add, modify, format, and delete fields as well as create an index for your table.

You can remind yourself of a field's use or meaning by adding a description here

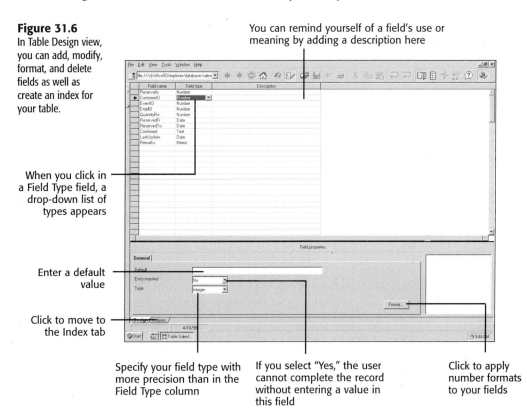

When you click in a Field Type field, a drop-down list of types appears

Enter a default value

Click to move to the Index tab

Specify your field type with more precision than in the Field Type column

If you select "Yes," the user cannot complete the record without entering a value in this field

Click to apply number formats to your fields

SETTING FIELD TYPES AND PROPERTIES

The first step in creating a table is to enter field names. In the example in Figure 31.6, field names have been created already by the AutoPilot, but entering them yourself is as simple as clicking in the field and typing. As mentioned earlier, there is a 10-character limit on field names. If you try to enter a longer name, you'll get an error message. If you just click OK, StarBase will automatically chop off any excess characters.

Every field in a database must have a unique name, so you'll also get an error message if you try to enter the same field name a second time. If you need to create fields that have similar data, you'll have to distinguish them in some way. A common way is to add a number (for example, Author1, Author2). If you find yourself frequently needing to enter fields with the same name, consider your design and make sure that you can't combine those fields into one and sort and filter the data later.

More difficult is selecting the proper field type for your field. The field type you select determines the types of data that can be entered into that field as well as the kinds of calculations and other operations that can be carried out with data from that field. Many of these field types should be familiar to StarCalc users, as they match many of StarCalc's number formats. All the available field types are described in Table 31.2.

TABLE 31.2. FIELD TYPES IN StarBASE TABLES

Field Type	Use and Comments
Text	Any alphanumeric data that you do not want to use in numeric calculations. A text field can accept up to 255 characters. If you want to limit the number of characters that can be entered, use the Text (Limited) field.
Number	Any numeric data that you want to use in calculations. You can also enter numbers as text, but text fields cannot be used in most calculations. For monetary values, use currency fields.
	You can further specify your number type in the drop-down list at the bottom of the design window as Byte, SmallInt, Integer, Single [digit], Double [digit]. The type you choose restricts entry options; for example, if you chose the Double subtype, users will not be allowed to enter numbers of more than two digits.
Date/time	Date and time values stored in a special fixed format. You can set its appearance with the Formats dialog. Numeric calculations can be performed on this field type.
Date	Date values. You can set its appearance with the Formats dialog. Numeric calculations can be performed on this field type.
Time	Time values. You can set its appearance with the Formats dialog. Numeric calculations can be performed on this field type.
Yes/No	Boolean value (Yes is TRUE, No is FALSE).
Currency	Monetary values. A special fixed format with four decimal places to prevent rounding errors when making monetary calculations. Numeric calculations can be performed on this field type.
Memo	Notes and reminders. A memo field can accept text of up to 64,000 characters, unlike other text fields, but it cannot be indexed, so it should not be used for storing core table data.
Counter	A new number StarOffice automatically generates every time a new record is created. The series begins with 1.0, Assigning a counter is useful if you want to ensure that every record has a unique identifier.
Image	A bitmap image. Use an image field if you want to include photos or other types of bitmap graphics.

Field Type	Use and Comments
Text (fixed)	A text input field of limited length. You set the number of characters that can be entered.
Decimal	A numeric field that accepts and returns decimal values. You set the number of decimal places the field accepts and displays.

Note   In StarBase, data is stored in variable-length records rather than fixed-length character fields, and all trailing characters are removed. This helps keep database files compact.

One of the principles of good table design is that each field contains data of only one type. This is particularly important when you're working with relational databases, but is still applied to standalone tables. Keep in mind that if you change your data type later, you might end up losing some data or affecting calculated fields on queries, forms, or reports. If you have created a table with AutoPilot, the ideal time to modify the field types is just after you've created it, not a few months later, after you've already entered data.

To select or change a field type, click in the Field Type cell of the field whose type you want to set. After you click, an arrow appears. Click the arrow to open a drop-down list of types. Scroll to locate the type you want to apply, and click its name.

When you click the type's name, notice that some of the options at the bottom of the table design window (on the General tab) may have changed. This is because some fields enable you to specify the characteristics of the field in greater detail. With the Text and Text (limited) types, you can enter the maximum number of characters the field will accept. (The program's limit is 255 characters.) With the Decimal type, you can set the number of decimals the field will accept. With the Number type, as mentioned in Table 31.2, you can specify the numeric subtype. If you know the subtype, it's a good idea to enter it rather than just leave the field set at Integer (even though that will work), as it makes calculation faster.

If you want to require that a field have a value entered before a record is accepted and saved in the database, choose Yes in the Entry Required drop-down list.

You can also enter a default value for the field. This value will automatically appear in the field every time a new record is created. It can then be deleted, overwritten, modified, or left as is. If there is a value that is the most common entry for a field, entering it here can be a time saver and can prevent typing errors.

APPLYING FIELD FORMATS

Setting the field type determines how StarBase internally stores and manipulates your data. Choosing the field formats affects the way your data looks in its table and *also* affects how StarOffice treats your data in calculations. For example, if you apply a text format to a date, you can't use that date in date calculations.

→ For more information on number formats and how they affect data, **see** "Formatting Cells" **p. 559**.

Each field type is by default assigned a format that StarOffice considers appropriate for its type. To examine or change this format, click the Format button at the bottom-right of the Design view window. A Field Format dialog, like the one in Figure 31.7, appears. This dialog should look familiar to StarCalc users, as the tabs are the same as those in the StarCalc Numbers Format dialog.

Figure 31.7
Choosing a number format in this dialog determines how your data will display in your table, queries, forms, and reports. Be careful in applying a format because it can affect how your data is interpreted and stored by StarOffice.

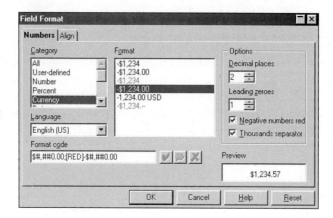

The dialog will open, displaying the format currently assigned to that field. To see other formats, scroll in the Category and Format lists. When a format is selected, the code used to generate the format displays in the Format Code input field. Studying the format codes here will enable you to create your own custom number formats. A preview of what the format will look like appears in the Preview box.

If you click in the Format Codes box and start making modifications, the three buttons on the left become active. If you click the green check mark button (Add), your new custom format is entered in the Custom Formats category and is applied to your current selection. If you click the Comments button, a new input field appears just below the Format Codes input field. By default, the comment is User-defined, but you can delete this and enter your own comment for the format—such as a name or a reminder of its use. You can enter a comment that's up to 255 characters in length.

Tip #554 from
Michael & Sarah

You can apply the font and font size of your choice to your entire table when in Edit or Read-Only modes by using the Row context menu. This does not affect the format of the individual fields (cells), only the display of table data. If you enter data directly in tables, enlarging the font size will make entry much easier!

When you find the format you want to apply, select its name in the Format list and click OK. If you've started to create or apply a different format and change your mind, clicking Reset restores the initial value the format had when you opened the dialog, and clicking Cancel cancels the action entirely and returns you to your table.

Click the Alignment tab to set the alignment of data in your table cell. Only the Horizontal alignment options are available. If you frequently enter data directly in your table rather than using a form, you might find it helpful to change the alignment here.

When inserting database fields into documents, in certain instances you can choose to have the database formatting you set here applied to your data. Otherwise, the formats you assign to data in reports determine the appearance of your final products.

→ For more information on formatting reports and changing report templates, **see** "Modifying Reports," **p. 1230**.

SAVING YOUR TABLE AND EXITING DESIGN VIEW

After you have entered new fields, set the field types and options, and applied field formats, you're done with the basic work of creating your table. If you want to get more serious about table design and efficiency, you might want to create an index.

→ For more information on creating indexes, **see** "Indexing Tables for Faster Searching," **p. 1143**.

All that remains is for you to to save your table and exit. You can select Save from the File menu, or just click the Close button in the upper-right corner of the table.

If you've created a new table from scratch and chose the Save command, you will be prompted with a Save As dialog. Enter a name for the table. You're limited to names of eight characters. You also can't use any special characters or spaces in your names. (If you want to separate words, you can use an underscore [_].) If you try to save with a name longer than eight characters or you use forbidden characters, you will receive an error message. After you have successfully saved, exit by clicking the Close button or choosing File, Exit.

If you skip choosing Save and just click the Close button, you will be prompted with a dialog that asks if you want to save. If you click Yes, the same Save As naming dialog appears.

Note

The character limits reflect standards imposed by the dBASE III database format rather than StarOffice-specific options. These limits help enable portability of data across many different types of computers and operating systems.

If you make modifications to an existing table (as opposed to just taking a peek at its bones, so to speak), you are prompted with a Save Table Design dialog which warns you that altering your design might result in loss of data (see Figure 31.8). This dire warning is given because changing your field types and formats, as explained earlier, can indeed cause loss of data. If you know you want to proceed with your changes, ignore the dire tone and choose Yes. Note that there is no Save As option for tables, so you can't save this modified table under a different name. Your only choice is to click Yes or No. If you already have data in your table and are unsure, you should click No, copy the table you want to modify, and make your modifications on the copy. You can then observe the effects that your changes have on stored data and decide whether the changes will work.

PART

VII

CH

31

Figure 31.8
Every time you alter your table design, StarBase warns you that saving your altered table could result in data loss. If you're confident of your changes, ignore the dire warning and plunge ahead; if you are unsure, click No.

Once you have created tables, you are ready to enter and manipulate data.

→ For details on working with data in tables, **see** Chapter 33, "Working with Data in Tables," **p. 1149**.

TROUBLESHOOTING

I need to change some aspects of my table design, but even though I'm in Design view, StarBase won't let me edit anything and the Edit button is grayed out.

You probably had the table opened in editable form to add data, and then opened it in Design view. When you do that, StarBase doesn't switch views, but actually opens a second instance of the table. When you have two instances of the table open, you cannot edit either one. Close all open instances of your table and try again.

Sometimes even if you've closed other instances, StarBase doesn't update properly. First try selecting the database that contains the table, right-clicking to open its context menu, and selecting Update. If this doesn't work, close StarOffice altogether and reopen it, and then try to open and edit your table.

Keep in mind that you can create and edit tables only in dBASE III and StarBase formats.

I can't find the Table Design command anywhere.

When in doubt, look for a context menu. To find the table design commands, open the Explorer. Click the plus sign next to your database icon. This will reveal four object icons—Reports, Forms, Queries, and Tables. To create a new table, select the Table icon or any existing table, right-click, and choose New, Table, Table Design. To modify an existing table, right-click and choose Table Design.

I can't seem to successfully create the Boolean data type in my StarBase table.

This is a known bug in version 5.01 (the filter update of version 5.0) when you're working with tables in a StarBase-format database. We don't know of any workaround—other than upgrading to 5.1 (or regrading to 5.0)—or running simultaneous installations of both 5.0 and 5.01.

I don't want to create a table. I want to import one, but I can't find an Import command anywhere.

You import a table through a database. You can use the Address Book dBASE III database as your import shell, or you can create a new database by using the File, New, Database command. If the table you want to import is not in dBASE format, you will have to create a separate database shell of the approriate format (ODBC, JDBC, Text, MS Access, or DB2). You can then drag and drop tables from that database shell onto the Tables icon of the StarBase database into which you want to import your data.

If you use the Address Book, you'll need to put a copy of your table in the Address Book directory. Then, select the Address Book icon in the Explorer, right-click, and choose Properties. Click the Tables tab. Your table should appear (if it's a dBASE III type data table). Click in the checkbox next to its name to select it. Click OK to exit. Now, in the Explorer, click the plus sign next to the Tables icon in the Address Book. You should see your table listed there. Double-click it to open it to view or enter data. Right-click to find the commands to open it in Table Design view.

If you create a new database, specify the table or database you want to import as your data source.

I want to assign a primary key to my table but the Primary Key command is grayed out.

You can assign primary keys only to tables created in the StarBase native format. An alternative for dBASE tables is to click the Indexes tab and set a field to be an index that requires a unique value in every field.

CHAPTER 32

CREATING TABLES WITH RELATIONS

In this chapter

USING STARBASE AS A RELATIONAL DATABASE

In the 32 bit Windows version of StarOffice, you can create a relational database in the native StarBase format. Tables with relations form the foundation of a relational database. This chapter introduces some basic relational database concepts and describes the steps for creating relational tables in StarBase.

Even if you don't want to create a relational database yourself, understanding the principles of a relational database can still be helpful if you work with client/server databases and need to use SQL to extract data, or if you are creating a single-table database that might be the seed for a relational database.

StarOffice can connect with relational databases via ODBC and JDBC, both of which have been much improved in version 5.1. Maintaining relations on import into StarOffice depends on your ODBC or JDBC driver. You can also connect with Oracle databases on a Windows NT system.

Note

> You cannot set relations between databases you create in dBASE format in StarBase. For example, the Address Book is a dBASE database, and you cannot create relations between its tables or create a query that combines fields from multiple tables.

WHAT IS A RELATIONAL DATABASE?

In Chapter 17, "Creating Lists and Databases with StarCalc," we mention some reasons you might use a database such as StarBase over a spreadsheet program such as StarCalc to manage your data. However, we did not define or explain relational databases there. Simply put, a *relational database* is a group of data tables that are linked together—related—by sharing common fields (categories). Built on top of these tables are other elements—reports, queries, and forms—that enable you to sort, filter, manipulate, and present the data in those tables in flexible ways.

→ For a discussion of creating databases with a spreadsheet, **see** "Why Create Databases with StarCalc?," **p. 620**.

When you create a large database from a single table, you often find that you must enter the same data twice. For example, if you have a single table in which you record customer sales, you find yourself repeatedly entering a customer's name and other contact information each time that customer makes another transaction. Entering this information over and over again wastes entry time, increases the risks of entry errors (say, a typo in the customer's name), and makes your table larger and slower without adding value.

The goals of good relational database design are to minimize repetitious data entry and maximize efficient storage and retrieval of data by breaking down data into smaller tables that can be logically related to one another, rather than storing all your data in one large table.

A typical use of a relational database is to track and link inventory, invoices, and customer orders. Figure 32.1 shows the structure of two tables in such a database, a Customers table and an Orders table. As you can see, these tables share a single common field—the CustomerID field. Because they share this field, a *relation* can be created between them. The relation is indicated by the line that connects the two windows.

Figure 32.1
Two tables were created with the AutoPilot, which contains a number of templates for the quick creation of common database tables for both business and personal uses. Lists of their fields are shown here in the Relations window, where a relation has been drawn between the CustomerID field in the Customers table and the CustomerID field in the Deliveries table.

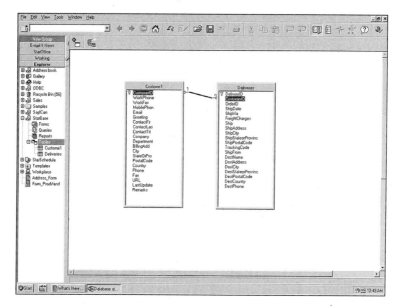

With this structure, you need to enter customer information only once into the database in the Customers table. You then create queries and forms that link the Customers table with the Orders and Invoice tables. Whenever you create a new invoice, you need enter data from only one common field—often a special ID number, such as the CustomerID and OrderID fields shown in Figure 32.1—to call up all the relevant information on that customer and drop it into your invoice and order forms and tables.

In contrast, Figure 32.2 shows a typical flat list database.

Figure 32.2
This Sales Figures flat list database has a simple design and is easy to maintain, but it is limited in the number of fields and records it can comfortably handle. In this database, for example, it would be difficult to store information about individual sales associates' productivity, track sales patterns, or record customer profiles, all typical tasks handled in a relational database.

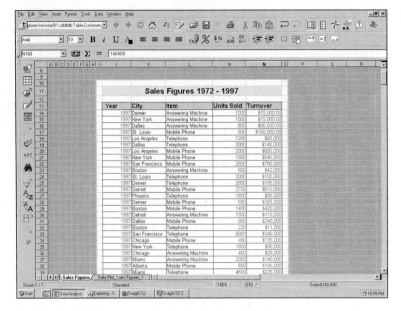

WHY USE A RELATIONAL DATABASE?

You might use a relational database for a number of reasons:

- Repetitive entry is minimized.

- Data validation rules prevent duplicate data from being entered, helping ensure data integrity.

- Searching and retrieving are considerably faster using linked tables rather than one massive table.

- Relational databases can handle very large amounts of data, much more than a spreadsheet can comfortably handle.

However, if you're new to relational databases, you should also be aware that if you don't design your relational database properly, over time your data can become corrupted and unusable. If you are creating a database just for personal use or are hacking around and don't care about preserving your data, it doesn't matter. If you intend to enter data that you want to preserve, however, you should become acquainted with sound relational database design. Although we introduce some of the principles of relational database design in this chapter, serious consideration of that topic is outside the scope of this book, so you should consult other manuals and references. The focus here is alerting you to database design issues that require further consideration and explaining the basics of creating and linking tables in the StarBase relational database format.

ELEMENTS OF A RELATIONAL DATABASE

The four basic types of StarBase objects—tables, queries, forms, and reports—were introduced and discussed in Chapter 30, "Working with Databases in StarBase." These objects are elements of all types of databases. However, relational databases have some elements not found in flat list databases. Also, an element you can create in some flat list databases—indexes—takes on a new importance in relational databases.

→ For a definition of flat list databases and an introduction to general database terms and design principles, **see** "Designing a List or Database," **p. 621**.

→ For a discussion of creating tables for a flat list database, **see** "Creating a Database from the Tables Up," **p. 1110**.

This section discusses each of these elements and introduces basic concepts of relational database design. Creating each of these elements for StarBase tables is discussed in subsequent sections in this chapter.

RELATIONS

Often people see relational databases as comprising only the four basic object types, just like flat list databases. However, something is missing in this picture—as if someone described a family as consisting of an adult, another adult, a child, and another child. What defines a family is its relationships—that a man and woman are husband and wife, father and mother to two children who are siblings. In the same way, the relations you create between tables are a fundamental part of relational databases. Designing relations between tables is a critical component of your database design.

PART

VII

CH

32

You can create these three types of relationships:

- One-to-one (often written as 1 to 1)
- One-to-many (often written as 1 to n)
- Many-to-one (often written as n to 1)

One-to-one relationships are often used only in multiuser situations in which tables might be split up for access or security reasons. In a single-user system, you can usually move the fields from one table to another—or create a unified table that doesn't split the data apart in the first place.

One-to-many relationships are the core of a relational database management system (RDBMS). A typical one-to-many relationship is that between a customer and transactions, because one customer has many transactions. The ability to construct a one-to-many relationship is what makes relational databases so much more efficient than a flat list database.

Many-to-one relationships are the glass-half-full side of one-to-many relationships; the difference is one of perspective. If you have a transactions table that records invoices, that table is in a many-to-one relationship with the customer table.

CONSTRAINTS

Constraints are rules you set that determine what values can be entered into a table. They are the equivalent of data validation rules in StarCalc.

By applying constraints to a table field, you can prevent invalid data from being entered and help maintain the integrity of your data. Constraints take on particular importance in relational databases, where you must prevent the entry of invalid data in the fields that define relations and link tables. StarBase has a more limited capability to assign constraints than some other relational databases; you can set constraints only by setting field properties that limit the type or length of data that can be entered in a field.

PRIMARY KEYS AND FOREIGN KEYS

In a relational database, every table must have a *primary key* assigned. A primary key uniquely identifies one record from another, just like your Social Security number (at least, ideally) identifies you uniquely as a U.S. taxpayer.

The easiest type of primary key to assign is a type of number field called a *counter*. A counter field automatically generates a unique integer for every new record you enter into a table.

→ For more information about field types in StarBase tables, **see** "Setting Field Types and Properties," **p. 1123**.

A frequently used alternative is to choose a method for creating an ID number made up of a more meaningful combination of letters and/or numbers—for example, an invoice number ID that combines the last two digits of the current year and an invoice number. Many pizza delivery businesses now keep track of customers with databases and use telephone numbers as unique identifiers; that's why they begin by asking for your number (even though you're already on the line)! However, you can assign any field or combination of fields you want to be a table's primary key, as long as the value will be unique for every record.

> **Note**
>
> If you enter duplicate information into a primary key field, StarBase rejects the new data and generates an error message.

Although, generally speaking, you want to have as few fields as possible define your primary key, sometimes you need to combine fields to create a unique identifier.

The primary key is indeed the key to creating a relational database because you link tables together via primary key fields. For example, looking again at the customer and order management database shown in Figure 32.1, the Customers table has the CustomerID field as its primary key. The Orders table also has a CustomerID field set to exactly the same properties as the CustomerID field in the Customers table. The CustomerID field links the two tables together. (Note that it is not a primary key in the Orders table.) In the Orders table, the CustomerID field is referred to as a *foreign key*, which indicates its status as the linking field that is the primary key of another table.

You can create a StarBase table without assigning a primary key. However, you cannot create relations between tables that do not yet have primary keys assigned.

PREPARING TABLES FOR RELATIONS

The basics of creating and modifying a table in StarBase—which are the same for flat list and relational tables—are covered in Chapter 31, "Creating Standalone Database Tables." The following sections describe those aspects of creating tables that relate specifically to creating tables in a relational database.

UNDERSTANDING DATA NORMALIZATION

The steps you execute for creating a table with relations are quite simple. (Basically, you just need to open the tables in relations view and draw a link between them, or select the appropriate fields in the Relations dialog box.) Designing good tables is not that easy. That's the problem with all these wonderful desktop database programs—they make it seem so easy to create what are, in fact, complex data storage and management systems.

The key to creating well-designed tables in a relational database is the process known as *database normalization*. This is the process of breaking your data apart into tables, eliminating redundant fields, and determining those fields that enable you to construct relations between them (such as a customer or invoice ID field).

You should always begin this process by designing your tables on paper, writing down the fields for each. That way, you can easily check whether you're repeating data from one table to another—for example, if your tables are designed so that you must enter a customer's address and phone number in more than one place.

You should also consider what fields should be set as your primary keys. Keep in mind that a primary key must have a unique value for each record. Also, keep in mind that you will likely enter a primary key into many other tables as a foreign key. What will happen to data in your source table if you delete records in another table where your source's primary key is a foreign key?

For example, in the case of the Customers and Orders tables, an order being deleted should have no effect on the Customers table because no data from the Orders table is stored there. However, if a customer's information is deleted from the Customers table, this deletion might well cause an error in the Orders table if that customer places an order. Based on the relationship created between the two tables, the Orders table looks for that customer information in the Customers table based on a customer ID that no longer exists—and therefore reports an error. Enough of these types of errors can crash or permanently corrupt a database.

You can't avoid these data dependencies; they're what make relational databases function. You just need to be aware of them from the get-go so that you assign the proper kinds of data validity rules to your tables and protect your database and/or database elements appropriately. (Ensuring you don't have these kinds of problems with your data is called *maintaining referential integrity*.) You also need to be aware of them because after you set your primary keys and begin installing foreign keys in other tables, StarBase limits your ability to restructure your tables in order to protect the integrity of your data. For example, you are not allowed to de-designate a field as a primary key if it has already been used as a foreign key in another table.

SETTING A PRIMARY KEY

To set a primary key, you must first open a table in Table Design view by selecting the table in the Explorer, right-clicking, and choosing the Table Design command.

Your table should look something like that in Figure 32.3.

Figure 32.3
To set a primary key, you must open a table in Design view.

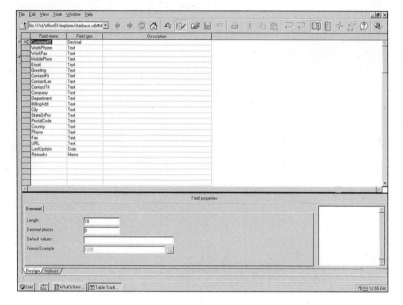

No special toolbar is available for working with StarBase tables; all the commands you need are accessible through the function bar and context menus. Make sure the Edit button is clicked so that it appears pressed. Otherwise, your table is in read-only mode, and you can't make any changes. To set a single field as a primary key, click the row header next to that field, right-click to open the context menu, and select the Primary Key command (the last command on the menu). A check mark appears beside the command to indicate you've applied it. When you close the menu, a small key icon appears in the row header next to the field name, like the one next to the CustomerID field in Figure 32.3.

To set multiple fields as primary keys, select the fields using either the Shift+click or Ctrl+click selection methods, and apply the Primary Key command in the same way as for a single field. Key icons appear next to each field that makes up part of the primary key.

Tip #555 from
Michael & Sarah

Make note of the field type of your primary key field(s), both in the Field Type column and on the Field Properties tab at the bottom. When you create other tables that use that primary key as a foreign key, you need to assign exactly the same properties to the foreign key field(s) as the primary field. Otherwise, you can't construct relations between the tables.

Note

In StarBase, you cannot create a table that has a field of the same name as another table but is of a different type; it gives you an error message. This safety feature prevents the creation of primary keys that have the same name.

CREATING RELATIONSHIPS BETWEEN TABLES

When you have tables with primary keys, you can begin to create relationships between tables. You should have already completed your paper and pencil planning and normalized your data, as mentioned in the section "Preparing Tables for Relations" earlier in this chapter.

The tables you relate must share a common field, and that field must have exactly the same properties set in both tables. You use this field to link the tables together.

Tip #556 from
Michael & Sarah

Typically, you frequently enter primary key data (such as a customer ID number) into multiple tables. It's easy to create a master list of customer primary keys in StarBase using drag and drop. Just open the table with your primary key field in the Beamer, click the gray rectangle in the upper left corner (just beneath the Find Record (binoculars) icon, and immediately drag into an open StarWriter document. In the dialog that opens, you can choose to insert data as a table, fields, or text. Select the option you want, click your primary key field and any other identifying fields that you want for your list, click the right arrow to select those fields, and click OK.

PART

VII

CH

32

Note

To open your database and see your tables as described in this section, you must have your Explorer group set to Hierarchical view.

CREATING TABLE JOINS VIA DRAG AND DROP

After you have your table relations sorted out, open your StarBase database in the Explorer so that the Tables icon is visible. Select the icon, right-click, and choose Relations from the context menu. A screen like the one in Figure 32.4 appears on your desktop, except your screen will be empty.

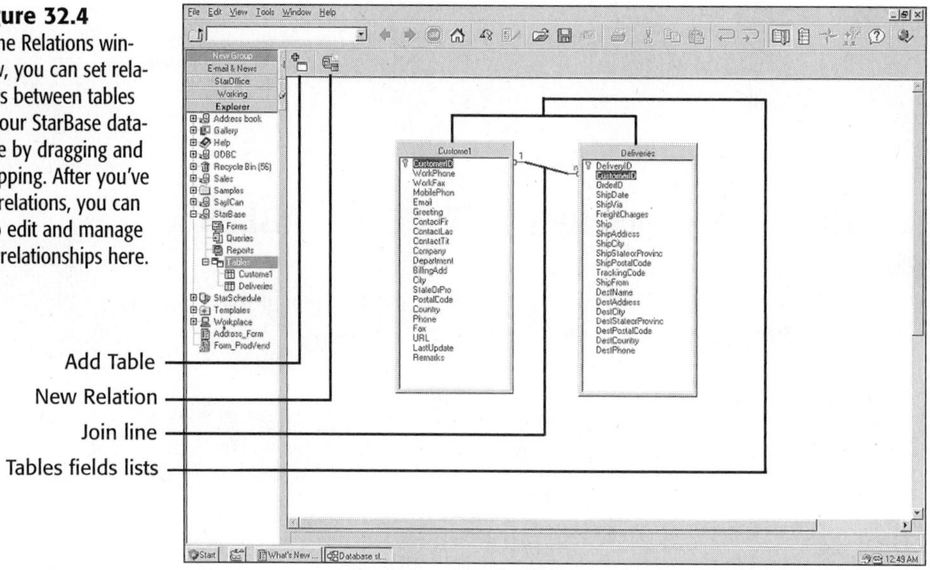

Figure 32.4
In the Relations window, you can set relations between tables in your StarBase database by dragging and dropping. After you've set relations, you can also edit and manage the relationships here.

Add Table
New Relation
Join line
Tables fields lists

Click the Add Table button (refer to Figure 32.4) on the (sparsely populated) Relations object bar. The Add Tables dialog then appears (see Figure 32.5). The list of tables you see depends on the tables you've created in or copied to your database. Note that only tables contained within that specific StarBase database are listed.

Figure 32.5
The Add Tables dialog lists all the tables you have stored in your StarBase database. To add a table to the Relations window, click its name and choose Add.

Select the tables among which you want to create relations, and click Add. Tables fields lists (like the ones shown in Figure 32.4) appear. You can resize these lists by grabbing their borders and dragging if you find them too small to see all the fields easily.

When all your tables fields lists are open, simply drag the field name you want to initiate the relation onto the field name that is the foreign key in the other table, and drop it. A *join line* appears (again, refer to Figure 32.4). This line identifies the type of relation created—in this case, a one-to-many (1 to *n*) relationship between the CustomerID field in the Customers table and the CustomerID field in the Deliveries table (because each customer ID exists in only one instance in the Customers table but [you hope!] occurs many times in the Delivery table).

New to version 5.1, you can also create relations through the Relations dialog box, which you open by clicking the New Relation button on the toolbar.

Tip #557 from *Michael & Sarah*	If you are connecting to external client/server databases, you can now create a full range of relations in queries and tables in SQL with the commands Inner Join, Left Join, Right Join, and Full Join.

MANAGING YOUR RELATIONSHIPS

After you've created your relationships, you manage them in the Relations window also. Double-click the join line to open the Relations dialog box, or click the Relations button on the Relations window toolbar (see Figure 32.6).

Tip #558 from *Michael & Sarah*	If you open the Relations dialog by clicking the toolbar button, you can choose fields from any table in your currently active database, not just those visible in the Relations window.

Figure 32.6
Using the Relations dialog, you can determine how changes to a primary key affect linked foreign keys in other tables and thus manage the referential integrity of your data.

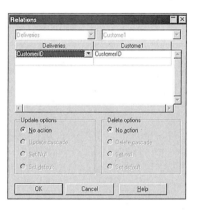

On the top of this dialog are list boxes that display the tables and the respective key fields that constitute the join. In this example, it's the CustomerID field.

Beneath the list boxes are two sets of options: a set of Update Options and a set of Delete Options. These options control what happens to the associated foreign key fields if you make changes to your primary key. Each of these options is detailed in Table 32.1.

TABLE 32.1   OPTIONS FOR MANAGING RELATIONS BETWEEN PRIMARY AND FOREIGN KEYS

Type of Option	Option	Result
Update Options	No Action	Changes made to a primary key do not affect related foreign key fields.
	Cascading Update	All foreign key fields are updated if the value of the related primary key is modified.
	Set Null	Modifying the primary key results in all related foreign key fields being set to IS NULL. IS NULL means that the field is empty.
	Set Default	Selecting this option enables you to assign a default value to all foreign key fields when the corresponding primary key is modified.
Delete Options	No Action	Deleting a primary key has no effect on its related foreign key fields.
	Cascading Delete	Deleting a primary key results in all related foreign key fields being deleted as well.
	Set Null	Deleting the primary key results in all related foreign key fields being assigned the value IS NULL. IS NULL means that the field is empty.
	Set Default	Selecting this option enables you to assign a default value to all foreign key fields when the corresponding primary key is deleted.

Caution

You should be very careful about the options you set in the Relations dialog because they fundamentally affect the structure and functioning of your database. Be sure to save backup copies of all your tables before you make any changes to these options.

DELETING A RELATIONSHIP

After you've joined tables together, you usually create queries, forms, and reports that combine data from these tables; that's the whole point of having a relational database. If you delete a relationship between tables that have queries, forms, and reports built on them, StarBase automatically deletes all those objects if they're saved within StarBase. For that reason, you should be very sure you want to delete the relationship before you do so because it cannot be undone. (Forms created and saved outside StarBase are not deleted, but of course any bound controls that refer to, say, a query created on top of the related tables are affected.)

To delete a relationship, open the Relations window for the database on your desktop. Then, click to select a table fields list that's part of the relation you want to sever. Its name appears in bold in the title bar to indicate it is the current list. Then, press the Delete key. The list disappears, as does the join line.

Alternatively, you can place your cursor on the title bar of either list and right-click to open its context menu. Select the Delete command, and the list is deleted along with the join. (Note that deleting the list does not delete the underlying table.)

INDEXING TABLES FOR FASTER SEARCHING

An index is an internal table that speeds database searching and retrieval by sorting the table as you go along based on a field that you specify. The indexed field is not fully sorted, but *pointers* to data are stored at certain key points, rather like sign posts that point the way toward a final destination. New sign posts can be added and old ones taken down as the landscape changes, but the end destination (sorted and easy-to-find data) remains the same.

Tables that you assign primary keys to are automatically indexed based on the primary key field. However, you can also assign other fields to serve as index fields in addition to the primary key field(s). If you frequently sort your table or search in it by fields that are not your primary key, it's a good idea to index them to speed sorting and searching. For example, in the Customers table, the primary key is a customer ID number that's not very useful for looking up a customer's contact information. You'll probably more frequently sort by and search in the last name field, so indexing this field would be a good idea.

Don't assign more fields to be indexes than you really use or need, however, because indexing also takes time and system resources. If you index all your fields, you're missing the point; you should select only a few frequently used fields to serve as your indexes.

You can also assign an index to a dBASE table in StarBase. This process is similar in some ways to assigning a primary key to a table in a relational database. Unlike with a StarBase table, only one field can be indexed per table. If you like, you can set that field to accept only unique values, which means that it functions like a primary key, helping ensure that only valid data, without any duplicates, is entered in the table.

PART

VII

CH

32

Tip #559 from
Michael & Sarah

You can import indexes along with dBASE tables from existing databases, if you use the database type dBASE.

WHY USE INDEXING?

When you enter data in a table on an ongoing basis, you don't usually enter it in any logical order; you enter it as it comes to you. For example, customers don't usually have the consideration to arrive on your doorstep in strictly alphabetical order, so you might find yourself adding a new record for a Mr. Zanzibar just after records for a Ms. Mumford and a Mrs. Appleton.

When your table is small, entering data this way normally isn't a problem. When you need to organize your records in a more useful way, you just sort them (alphabetically in ascending or descending order, for example). With just a few records, sorting doesn't take much time or many computer resources. However, as your table grows larger, sorting the jumble your stored records have become takes longer and longer. Setting an index is an intermediate step, between storing everything in a jumble and storing your data in a sorted form that must then be re-sorted every time you append data.

Tip #560 from
Michael & Sarah

The disadvantage of using indexing is that there are limits on the number of characters—200—that you can enter into a field that can be indexed. Keep this limitation in mind as you set the Length field property for text fields in your tables.

SETTING INDEXES

To set an index, your table must first be open in Design view. Next, follow these steps:

1. Click the Indexes tab.

   If you've made any changes to your table structure, StarOffice asks whether you really want to save the changes before it allows you to move to the Indexes tab. Choose OK if you want to save your changes or No if you don't. Either way, the Indexes tab comes to the top (see Figure 32.7). (If you choose Cancel, your move to the Indexes tab is canceled, and you remain on the table's Design tab.)

Figure 32.7
The first step in setting an index on the Indexes tab is to select a field from the drop-down list that appears when you click a cell in the Index Field column.

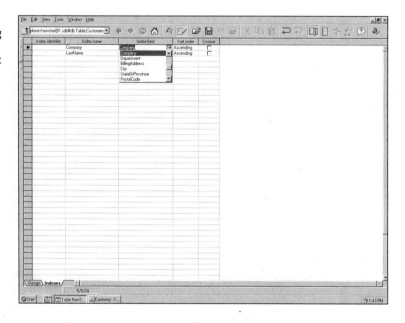

2. This step is a little counterintuitive, but the first action you must take is to click in the Index Field column in the middle of the indexes sheet to make the drop-down fields list appear.

3. Click the list arrow to open the list, which displays all the fields in your table.

4. Scroll until you find the field you want to index, and click its name to select it.

Note

You cannot index a primary key field. Primary key fields are automatically indexed by StarBase and cannot have another index set on them.

5. Assign an index name. After you've assigned a name, the sort order of Ascending is assigned by default, and a check box appears in the Unique field.

6. You can change the sort order to descending by clicking the Sort Order cell, opening the drop-down list that appears, and clicking Descending.

7. If you want that field to admit only unique values, click the check box in the Unique field.

After you've checked this option, StarBase serves as your watchdog for data integrity and prevents users from entering duplicate data in that field. Be careful what you wish for because you might get it: Don't set a field such as LastName to Unique because you then can never have two customers with the same last name!

Note

StarBase doesn't let you set a foreign key to Unique. You don't need to worry anyway; the foreign key's uniqueness is assured by its status as primary key in the parent table (as long as the two tables are joined).

PART

VII

CH

32

MODIFYING RELATIONAL TABLES

You must be careful in making any modifications to the table structure of tables in a relational database, especially to primary key fields. Changes you make might have an effect on many tables besides the one you're modifying, and have the potential to corrupt your database and delete existing data.

Although you're relatively free to make changes to your tables after they've been created (using the same techniques as with a standalone table), StarBase has a number of built-in alarm messages that warn you your modifications might affect your data. It also actively prevents you from deleting or making changes to primary and foreign key fields that define the relational structure of your database.

→ For more information on modifying tables, **see** "Creating and Modifying Tables in Design View," **p. 1122**.

SECURING YOUR DATABASE

A relational database is the result of a great deal of time and work, whether to input data or create the table structure and relations. Because your database can become corrupted and potentially unusable or suffer serious data loss if someone without proper training begins fooling with your design and data, it's a good idea to prevent unauthorized people from gaining access—or even just prevent your curious kid from exploring.

You can limit users' access to your StarBase database by using commands on the Administration and StarBase tabs of its Explorer Properties dialog box.

> **Note**
>
> You can set passwords and access rights only when all elements in the database are closed.

The Administration tab determines how users can gain access if they're connecting to your database as an external data source via ODBC (see Figure 32.8).

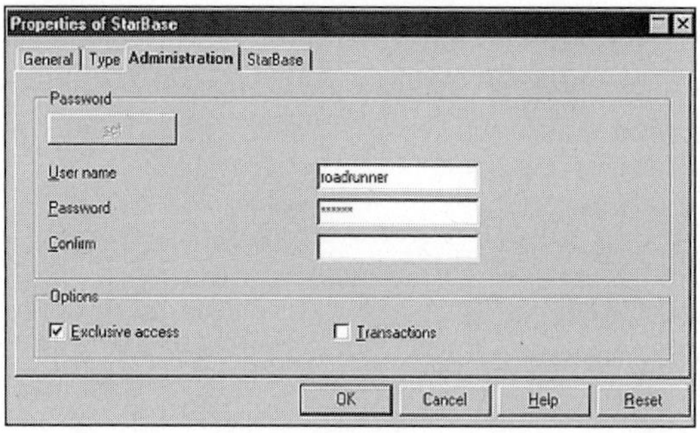

Figure 32.8
Using the Administration tab of the StarBase database properties, you can secure your database with a password.

Click Set to activate the User Name and Password text entry boxes. Type your username and password. Then confirm the password by typing it again in the Confirm box.

If you want to lock out all others and have exclusive access to the database, choose the Exclusive Access option. Then choose OK.

If the Transactions option is checked, all changes you make in a database table in Edit mode will be restored with the Edit menu Undo function. If the Transactions option is not selected, only the last action will be restored when you choose Undo.

Using the StarBase tab, you can limit local access to your database; that is, someone else using your machine cannot open it unless he or she knows the password.

Enter your username and password in the appropriate text boxes, and choose OK. The next time you want to open the database, you'll need to open the Properties dialog and enter your username and password before you can open the database in the Explorer. Your access rights continue for the length of your current session; when you exit StarOffice, your rights expire, and you'll need to log on again the next time you open the program and want to work with the database.

If an unauthorized person clicks the database in the Explorer, a generic error message saying that the database could not be opened is displayed.

TROUBLESHOOTING

I select the row with the field I want to set as primary key, but when I open the context menu, there's no Primary Key command to be seen!

Are you sure your table has been created in StarBase format rather than dBASE format? You can set a primary key only in StarBase tables (or databases you've imported via ODBC, JDBC, or the Access Import filter, if you have the appropriate drivers). Select the table in the Explorer, right-click, and open the table's properties to check what its database format is.

I want to index a field in my table, but after I select it in the Index Field column and assign its properties, when I click on Design to switch views or the Close button to close the table, the program just hangs and I can't go anywhere.

You're probably trying to set your primary key field (or one of your primary key fields) as an indexed field. Primary key fields are automatically indexed by StarBase, so you can't assign them again on the Indexes tab—that's double-dipping! If you try, StarBase doesn't let you leave Indexes view because it can't save what you've done. Delete the row in which you've created your new index, and you should be fine.

I can't do anything in my table at all.

This problem is the vanilla ice cream of problems with StarBase   everybody's favorite. You might have this problem for two reasons. To edit your table, you must be in Design view, Edit mode. Make sure you're in the proper view and that the Edit button on the function bar is pressed. The other possibility is that you've opened your table both in regular view (using the context menu's Open command or by double-clicking the table in the Explorer) and Design view. In this case, the Edit button is grayed out and unavailable in Design view. You can see why; you're not allowed to alter the structure of a table you have open in another copy. Exit the other copy of the table, and try again.

I can't find the Relations command on the Explorer context menu.

First, make sure you're looking for it in a database created in the StarBase format (which is available only on Windows). Second, be sure you're selecting the Tables icon, not an individual table stored under the Tables icon.

CHAPTER 33

WORKING WITH DATA IN TABLES

In this chapter

MODIFYING YOUR TABLES

After you have created your tables, you might need to add, edit, delete, and modify data, as well as move your data from tables into your StarOffice documents. You also might need to move data between tables. You can create forms for entering and editing data in your tables, if you prefer. However, you always work with tables (or queries, which are special views of your tables) when moving data into your documents, so it's good to be familiar with techniques for editing directly in tables. StarBase also has some drag-and-drop tricks up its sleeve that can speed and ease your work. Given all the tools you have for working with data in tables, you can accomplish many routine tasks without ever creating a query.

Working in StarBase has been made much easier in version 5.1 with the addition of small but significant improvements in drag-and-drop editing, navigation, and shortcuts.

DISPLAYING AND OPENING TABLES

Whether your tables are part of a relational or flat database, you work with individual tables and their data in the same way. You can also apply the techniques you learn for tables to queries.

WAYS OF VIEWING TABLES

You can open tables in either the Beamer or on your desktop. The Beamer view is designed particularly for you to move data or form fields from your table into an open document. You can also drag and drop hyperlinks to table fields and databases into HTML documents. You can add and delete data in this view, but you cannot alter your table's structure or set indexes.

You can work in either of two desktop views: Data Entry mode or Table Design. Data Entry mode is the easiest view in which to add data to your table. In Table Design view, you can alter your table's structure or properties. Note that this chapter does not describe table design so does not address using Table Design view.

→ For information on designing tables, **see** Chapter 31, "Creating Standalone Database Tables," **p. 1117**, and Chapter 32, "Creating Tables with Relations," **p. 1131**.

OPENING TABLES

To work with tables, you need the Explorer open and visible on your desktop. You then can open your database and click the plus sign (+) to display your list of available tables.

To open a table in the Beamer, first open the Beamer by clicking the Beamer icon on the function bar or pressing Ctrl+Shift+B. Then click the table you want to view.

To open a table on your desktop in Data Entry mode, select the table and double-click, or right-click and choose Open from the context menu. Your table should look something like the table in Figure 33.1.

Tip #561 from
Michael & Sarah

You can make your table data easier to see by changing and/or enlarging the font. To do so, click a row header, right-click to open the table context menu, and choose Table Format. In the resulting dialog box, you can select and change the size of any installed font.

Figure 33.1
If you like to have an overview of your table when entering and editing data, open it on your desktop by using its context menu's Open command. You'll find a similar set of tools as on the Beamer toolbar.

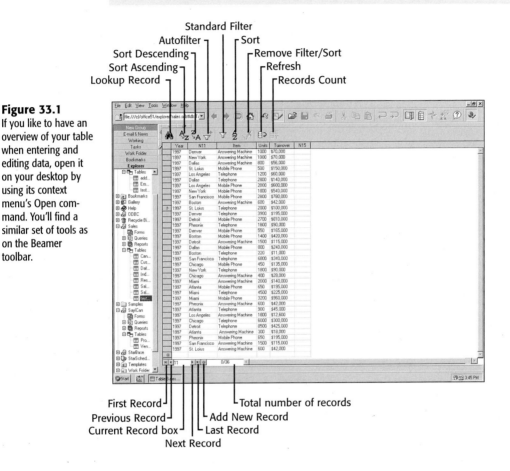

ORIENTING YOURSELF IN TABLES

Even though you navigate in StarBase tables in some similar ways, they are a different animal than other kinds of tables in StarOffice. To maintain data integrity and offer the greatest power in data management, database tables are highly structured objects, and you are comparatively limited in the ways you can work with them. However, the Beamer offers some special tools that make moving data from table to document a snap.

INTRODUCING BEAMER TOOLS

When you have a table open in the Beamer, the first nine tools on the left of the Beamer toolbar match exactly those on the Table object bar when you have a table open in Data Entry mode (refer to Figure 33.1). The remaining tools are found in relation to tables only when they are open in the Beamer. Some of these Beamer tools appear only when a specific type of document is open or something specific in the table is selected.

Note Menu commands never apply to the Beamer; this includes Undo. You can undo alterations of individual fields by pressing Ctrl+Z or data entry of a new but unsaved record by clicking the Undo Data Entry button. Other than that, all deletions or alterations of data are permanent.

Table 33.1 lists these special Beamer tools and describes their functions.

TABLE 33.1   BEAMER TABLE TOOLS

Tool	Name	Description
	Edit Data	Switches table (or query) between Read-only and Edit modes
	Save Current Record	Saves the current record
	Undo Data Entry	Undoes data in the current record if your cursor is still in the record and it has not yet been saved. Note that your data is saved as soon as you move to another record
	Cut	Cuts data in the current field
	Copy	Copies data in the current field
	Paste	Pastes data on the Clipboard or in the buffer into the current field
	Data to Text	Instantly inserts the selected record(s) into the current spreadsheet or text document as text; text takes on the formatting of the paragraph or cell where inserted (StarCalc and StarWriter documents only)
	Data to	If you have fields already inserted into your document, instantly inserts data into those fields from the record(s) you have selected in the Beamer. (StarWriter and StarMail documents only)
	Mail Merge	Opens the Mail Merge dialog box from which you carry out print, email, and print to file mail merges (StarWriter documents only; for StarMail documents, use the Mail Merge command on the File menu)

NAVIGATING IN TABLES

You have a number of methods for navigating your tables on the desktop and in the Beamer view. Some, like keyboard shortcuts, are more useful for local navigation. Others, like the vertical and horizontal scrollbars and the navigational buttons at the bottom of the table, help in both local and long-distance navigation. You can, of course, always use the mouse as well. Learn your options because the Navigator is not available in StarBase.

Your current location is always marked on the row header with a small indented arrow, and your current record number is visible at the bottom of your table. The box to the right of the Add New Data button shows the current number of selected records over the total number of records in the table. If you are editing a record, a small pencil icon appears to the left on the header row.

Table 33.2 lists the keyboard navigational shortcuts.

TABLE 33.2   NAVIGATIONAL SHORTCUTS IN StarBase TABLES

Keyboard Shortcut	Description
Tab	Moves the cursor forward through fields one at a time
Shift+Tab	Moves the cursor backward through fields one at a time
Left arrow	Moves the cursor backward one character at a time
Right arrow	Moves the cursor forward one character at a time
Up arrow	Moves the cursor up one column
Down arrow	Moves the cursor down one column
Home	Moves the cursor to the beginning of your current record
End	Moves the cursor to the end of the current record
Page Up	Moves your view one screen up but does not move the cursor
Page Down	Moves your view one screen down but does not move your cursor

PART

VII

CH

33

Note that as you move from field to field by using either the Tab and Shift+Tab keys or arrow keys, any data in your new field is highlighted as a block. If you navigate by using the arrow keys and press the arrow key a second time, the data is deselected, and you can move one character at a time.

At the bottom of your table is a navigation scrollbar (refer to Figure 33.1). If you know a record's number (or approximate number), you can enter it in the Current Record box and press Enter to zip to that location. Click the First Record button to return to the top of your table, and click the Last Record button to move to the end (which is the place you must be to enter new records). The Previous and Next Record buttons work just as their names suggest. Your cursor moves as you click, and data in the field where your cursor is located is highlighted.

ADJUSTING COLUMN WIDTHS AND ROW HEIGHTS

Just as in StarCalc, you can automatically adjust columns to their optimal width by double-clicking their right border.

> **Note**
>
> StarBase does not always adjust to the truly optimal width for the entire table; but only for the currently visible records.

Right-click in the column and row headers to open context menus with Column Width and Row Height commands, respectively. Each command opens a dialog box in which you can enter a precise width for your column or row.

The Default option, if checked, returns the width or height to its program default value.

ENTERING, EDITING, AND FORMATTING TABLE DATA

You enter and edit table data much like you do in StarCalc or StarWriter tables. In these tables, unlike in some databases, you can enter data with spaces and basic punctuation marks. Remember that the number of characters you can enter is determined by field properties set in the table's design.

ADDING AND EDITING DATA

To add new data to your tables, click or navigate to the appropriate field, and begin to type. You can use all your standard editing keys—Backspace or Del to delete backward one character at a time and right- and left-arrow keys to move one character to the right or left. The Ctrl+C, Ctrl+X, and Ctrl+V editing shortcuts work as well but apply to only one field at a time.

Right-click to open the field's context menu, and you'll find an editing shortcut menu with your Cut, Copy, Paste, and Delete commands, along with Undo (Ctrl+Z) and Select All (Ctrl+A). Another important editing tool is the Esc key. Pressing Esc cancels changes being made to the current field. Note that Select All does not select an entire record, just one field's contents.

Tip #562 from
Michael & Sarah

Recording foreign names that require special characters? Keep your customers and contacts happy by inserting the correct characters with the Special Characters command. Press Ctrl+Shift+S, or right-click in your field and select Special Characters. Your available character sets depend on your installed fonts.

SELECTING MULTIPLE RECORDS

To select a contiguous block of records in your table, select the first record in the series by clicking in its row header, press the Shift key, and select the last record in the series. (You can also select the first record, press Shift, and press the up- or down-arrow key.)

To select a noncontiguous block of records, use the standard Ctrl+click technique, also clicking on the row header.

After you have selected these records, you can drag and drop them as text into any open document.

Note that these tricks don't work on columns or data in individual fields, only on complete records.

DELETING RECORDS

Whereas entering and editing text are similar to working in StarWriter documents, deleting records from a table is a different matter. If you select an entire record (or series of records) and delete it (or them), you cannot undo this action with the Undo command; your data is gone forever, so be very careful when you delete in this way. (Don't forget to conduct regular backups of your database because accidents happen.)

If you delete data from a single field, however, you can undo by using the standard Undo (Ctrl+Z) shortcut.

> **Note**
>
> If you have your table open on your desktop you can also undo deletes of data from a single field with the Edit menu Undo command—even though it's buggy and says Can't Undo! (This doesn't work if you have your table open in the Beamer, however.)

HIDING AND REVEALING FIELDS

Sometimes, you only want to view or add data to a selected set of fields. You can choose to hide those fields that you don't need to see so your view isn't unnecessarily cluttered.

To hide a field in your table, place your cursor on its column header, right-click, and choose Hide Field.

You cannot selectively reveal fields. To reveal all fields, place your cursor on a column or row header, right-click, and choose Show All Fields from the context menu.

FORMATTING TABLE DATA

An unusual feature of StarBase tables and queries is that you can format the appearance of your data. Although you don't have the full range of tools you enjoy in StarWriter or StarCalc, you can determine the font, font size, number format, and alignment of your data. These selections affect only the display of your data; you assign formatting attributes to data that you drag and drop into documents at the time you enter your data. Formatting choices you make to queries apply only to that query, not to its associated table data.

> **Note**
>
> The Insert Database Columns and the StarWriter Fields dialog box contain a Format From Database option for assigning the database format to entered data. This option works only with numeric and date/time values when they are entered as tables.

ALIGNING YOUR DATA

To set your data's horizontal alignment, place your cursor on a column header, right-click, and choose Column Format. The Field Format dialog box appears with two tabs: Numbers and Align. Click Align and choose one of the following alignment options: Standard, Left, Right, Center, or Justify.

ASSIGNING NUMBER FORMATS

To set your data's number format, place your cursor on a column header, right-click, and choose Column Format. Then click the Numbers tab. Your choices are the same as you have when formatting numbers in StarCalc; for more information, refer to Chapter 15, "Formatting Spreadsheets."

→ For details on choosing and creating number formats, **see** "Formatting Numbers and Currency," **p. 559**, and "Formatting Dates and Times," **p. 564**.

CHANGING THE DEFAULT FONT

To change the font characteristics of your table data, place your cursor on a row header, right-click, and choose Table Format. You can set the font type, style, size, color, and language; you can also apply basic effects such as shadowing and underlining. Make your selections, and click OK to confirm and exit. Click Reset to return to the font assignments that your data had at the time you opened the dialog box, or click Cancel to cancel all changes and exit immediately to the desktop.

> **Caution**
>
> You cannot undo font characteristic assignments, and you cannot set the default font again automatically. If you want to experiment with fonts, you might want to save a copy of your table and experiment on the copy.

MANIPULATING TABLE CONTENTS

StarBase lets you do some unusual and amazing things with drag and drop in your tables. These drag-and-drop features are one of the reasons StarBase is a superior tool for data management, because transferring data between tables or between a table and your documents couldn't be easier.

To take full advantage of these features, you will likely want to edit, sort, and filter your data first to order it as you want. If you're familiar with StarCalc's sorting and filtering tools, you have a head start because StarBase's tools work in essentially the same way.

SORTING AND FILTERING DATA

If you want to do sophisticated extraction and sorting of data, create queries using the Query AutoPilot or SQL. For more basic tasks, however, you have sorting and filtering tools at your fingertips on the Table or Beamer toolbar.

SORTING BY A SINGLE FIELD

You can sort your data in ascending or descending order by one field only with the Sort Ascending and Sort Descending buttons. Place your cursor in the field by which you want to sort, and then click the appropriate button. When you sort in ascending order, records with blanks in that field are placed first, which makes sorting a handy way to find incomplete records.

SORTING BY MULTIPLE FIELDS

To sort by multiple fields, click the Sort button. Clicking this button opens a Sort dialog box in which you can sort by up to three fields in any combination of ascending or descending order.

USING THE AUTOFILTER

The Autofilter brings to view all records that have the same data as your currently selected field. For example, say you want to see the contact information for everyone in a specific company. A simple method is to place your cursor in a field that has the desired company name, and click Autofilter. Only records that share that company name appear.

The Autofilter is most effective if you have designed your tables with ID fields that enable you to code and sort your data according to your own custom groupings.

Using your Autofilter in this way makes it a breeze to create a form letter targeted at a specific group. If you have opened your table in the Beamer, you can then just drag and drop the field names from the tops of the columns into your letter or email.

→ For more information on creating form letters and mail merges in StarWriter, **see** "Creating Form Letters with Mail Merge," **p. 360**.

→ For more information on creating mail merges in StarMail, **see** Chapter 29, "Communicating with StarMail and StarDiscussion," **p. 1045**.

Undo your Autofilter by clicking the Undo Filter/Sort button on the toolbar.

USING THE STANDARD FILTER

If you want to filter your data in more complex ways, use the Standard Filter. This filter is the same as the Standard Filter in StarCalc (without the options for copying and pasting the resulting data in a new location); it enables you to set up to three conditions for filtering.

When you click the Filter button, the Filter dialog box appears (see Figure 33.2). Automatically, the currently active field is selected as your field in the first filter statement, the condition is set to Equals (=), and its data (if any) is entered as the value.

PART

VII

CH

33

The Like and Not Like operators appear to be buggy in 5.1 and do not always work as promised.

Figure 33.2
You can filter your data in sophisticated ways without building a query by using the Standard Filter.

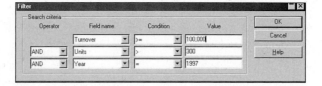

When you use the Standard Filter, you can choose from a number of comparative operators, listed in Table 33.3, to filter your data. The Null and Not Null operators are useful for locating or filtering incomplete records, respectively.

TABLE 33.3   COMPARATIVE OPERATORS FOR FILTERING DATA

Symbol or Term	Meaning
=	Equals
<>	Does not equal
<	Less than
<=	Less than or equal to
>	Greater than
>=	Greater than or equal to likeSearches for phrases or parts of phrases; for example, if you select the Field "name," the Condition "like," and enter "*a*" as your Value, you will find all names containing an a; if you enter 'm*er' as your value, you will find meier as well as mayer-not like
	Searches for records that do not contain the entered substring; if you select the Field "name," the Condition "not like," and enter "*a*" as your Value, you will find all names except those that contain the letter a.
null	Field is blank
not null	Field is not blank

UNDOING SORTS AND FILTERS

To undo the sort and return the records to their original order, click the Undo Filter/Sort button on the toolbar.

LOOKING UP RECORDS

New to version 5.1 is a Lookup tool that enables you to search your table for a specific record. To use it, click the Lookup Record button on the toolbar. A Data Record Search dialog box opens; it is essentially a truncated Search & Replace dialog.

By default, data in your current field is entered in the Text box, and Single Field is selected as the Where to Search option. Make changes as appropriate.

You can set your search order, choosing to begin your search From Bottom or Search Backwards. You can also set your search position within the field, determining whether it searches for phrases or whole words. Your choices are to search Anywhere in Field, Beginning of Field, End of Field, and Entire Field.

If you choose Placeholder Expressions, you can search for partial matches using the asterisk (*) and question mark (?) symbols, following standard file searching conventions. An asterisk is a wildcard, standing for an unlimited number of letters in its position; a question mark is a wildcard for a single character. If you choose Regular Expressions, you can use the same list of regular expressions available in Search & Replace and in many other StarOffice dialog boxes. If you choose Similarity Search, you can search for complex partial matches based on rules you set. To set your rules, click the button with ellipses to the right of the option. If you choose As Is, your search will be case sensitive. If you choose Apply Field Format, Search & Replace will search for the string as it is formatted for display, not as it is saved by StarOffice. This option is useful for numbers and dates, which are typically stored in formats different than those you might choose to display them in.

> **Note**
>
> The asterisk has a different meaning when used as a placeholder or used in a regular expression. If you use as asterisk as a placeholder, the asterisk is like a wildcard; it stands for any character in any number. For example, *mag** would find *magi*, *magic*, and *magician*. If you use as asterisk in a regular expression, the asterisk stands for an unlimited number of the characters just before the asterisk. For example, *89** would retrieve *89*, *899*, *8999*, and so on.

Once you've set your conditions, click Search. If a record is found, you should jump to that location with the data selected. Look in the State section at the bottom of the Data Record Search dialog box to see the record number or numbers found that match your criteria (see Figure 33.3).

> **Note**
>
> When you are working with tables in the Beamer, sometimes your cursor is not moved properly to the search item's location. If that's the case, note the record number in the State section of the Data Record Search dialog box, and enter it in the table navigation area at the bottom of the table to jump there.

Figure 33.3
The larger your data tables become, the more you'll appreciate the power of the Lookup Record search feature for StarBase tables and queries.

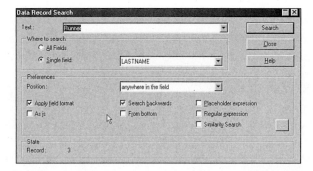

After you've completed all your searching, click Close to return to your table or query.

→ For a list of regular expressions, **see** "Using Regular Expressions," **p. 153**.

MOVING DATA INTO TEXT DOCUMENTS

When you become accustomed to the ease with which you can move data from your tables (and queries) into your documents in StarOffice, you'll never want to return to the awkward methods of other Office suites.

The simplest way to move data from a StarBase table or query into your document is to drag and drop it from the Beamer. The effects of dragging and dropping, however, vary from document type to document type. You can insert all visible data, or you can insert selected records.

→ For information on inserting table data using database fields in StarWriter documents, **see** "Selectively Inserting Data with Fields," **p. 1219**.

INSERTING TABLES, FIELDS, AND TEXT LISTS IN TEXT DOCUMENTS

You can create a table or text list of data, or insert database fields into a text document, in seconds by using drag and drop. Table and text data are inserted as copies, whereas fields are updateable, so you can present the most current data in your selected records.

Note

We experienced problems updating fields using the Update fields command (F9). To update successfully, you should open the table or query with the updated data in the Beamer, select all the records by clicking the gray rectangle beneath the Lookup Records tool, and click the Data to Fields button on the Beamer toolbar.

INSERTING ALL VISIBLE DATA

To insert all visible data in your documents, follow these steps:

1. Open your table or query in the Beamer.

2. Filter and sort your data so that it appears in the Beamer in the order you want it to appear in your StarWriter document.

3. Click the gray rectangle that marks the intersection of the row and column headers, just below the Lookup Record tool on the Beamer toolbar. This button selects all visible data in your table or query. Don't release your mouse button, but immediately begin to drag the data into your document.

4. An Insert Database Columns dialog box like the one in Figure 33.4 appears. Choose whether you want to insert your data as a table, fields, or ordinary text. The default choice is as a table, as you can see in Figure 33.4. If you choose to insert your data as fields or text, you see a dialog like the one in Figure 33.5.

Figure 33.4
The Insert Database Columns dialog box appears when you drag data from a table open in the Beamer into a text document. You can insert your data as a table, updateable fields, or ordinary text; here, the Table option is selected.

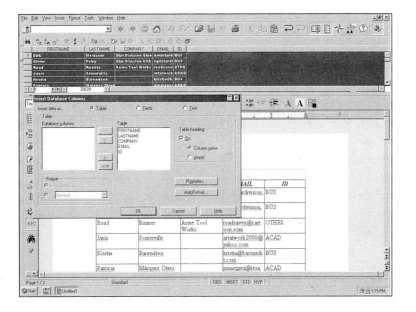

Figure 33.5
When you select the Fields or Text options, you can apply any existing paragraph styles from the drop-down list to preformat your data.

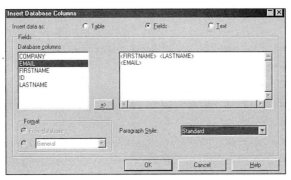

5. Select the fields (database columns) you want to import into your document, and move them into the pane on the right by clicking the single-headed arrow. In the case of tables, you can move all fields at once by clicking the double-headed arrow.

   In the case of fields and text, enter line breaks by pressing Enter as appropriate to line up your data as you like.

6. Apply any desired formatting attributes to your data. If you've selected Table as your option, you can click the Properties button to open the standard table formatting dialog box, or click AutoFormat to browse among the available AutoFormats. You can also determine your table heading style in the Table Heading option box. If you've chosen to insert your data as fields or text, you can apply a paragraph style from the drop-down list.

7. Choose OK, and your data is instantly inserted. The table in the background of Figure 33.4 was inserted in this way.

INSERTING SELECTED RECORDS

If you want to insert only selected records, use the regular Ctrl+click and Shift+click selection shortcuts to make your selections. Then you can drag and drop from the row header into your document. The same Insert Database Columns dialog box appears as in inserting all your table data; follow the steps detailed in the preceding section to complete your data import.

INSERTING MAIL MERGE FIELDS INTO TEXT DOCUMENTS

You can insert mail merge fields into your text documents by simply dragging a table or query column header into your document and dropping it there. Creating mail merges is discussed thoroughly elsewhere, so that information is not repeated here.

→ For information on creating form letters with mail merge, **see** "Creating Form Letters with Mail Merge," **p. 360**.

→ For information on creating email merges in StarMail, **see** "Creating Mail Merges with StarMail," **p. 1062** .

CREATING HYPERLINKS TO DATABASES IN HTML DOCUMENTS

You cannot drag and drop tables or text from the Beamer into an HTML document. When you drag and drop any or all records, a hyperlink is created to the query or table in question. Clicking this hyperlink closes the current HTML document and opens the selected query or table on the desktop or in the user's browser.

You can drag and drop data from individual fields, just as with other types of documents.

Tip #563 from
Michael & Sarah

If you want to publish your data on the Web as an HTML page, just insert the data you want into a StarWriter document and save it in HTML format.

INSERTING DATABASE DATA INTO SPREADSHEETS

You can quickly import a database table (or query) from StarBase into StarCalc via drag and drop. Just follow these steps:

1. Open your table or query in the Beamer.

2. Filter and sort your data so that it appears in the Beamer in the order you want it to appear in your StarCalc document. (Of course, you can always sort and filter your list later in StarCalc as well.)

3. Click the gray rectangle that marks the intersection of the row and column headers, just below the Lookup Record tool on the Beamer toolbar. This button selects all visible data in your table or query. Don't release your mouse button, but immediately begin to drag the data into your spreadsheet.

   Or you can use the standard Ctrl+click and Shift+click shortcuts to select the individual records you want to insert. When your selections are complete, drag from the row header into your spreadsheet.

4. Drag to position your pointer in the cell that you want to be the first field of the first record in your database, and release.

Your data is automatically inserted as a copy, with column headers that match the field names of the original table or query, and your data takes on the formatting attributes of the cells into which they're inserted.

Note that this data is not linked to your database and is not updateable.

CREATING MULTITABLE FORMS ON-THE-FLY VIA DRAG AND DROP

When you drag and drop column headers into text documents, you get mail merge fields; when you do the same in spreadsheet or presentation documents, you get form controls. Press Ctrl+Shift when dragging and dropping column headers into StarWriter documents, and you also get form controls. This way of creating a form is even quicker than using the Form AutoPilot.

What's even more awesome is that you can drag and drop fields from any tables or queries you can open in the Beamer into your document. This way, you can create multitable forms without hassling with subforms or manual assignments of data sources. (Your tables are handled independently, though, and are not in a true form/subform relationship. This limitation doesn't matter if you're using dBASE or text databases. Since you cannot create relations in these database formats, you cannot create true form/subform relationships anyway.)

→ For more information on working with forms, **see** Chapter 34, "Creating Forms for Easy Data Entry," **p. 1169**.

PART
VII

CH
33

COPYING, APPENDING, AND IMPORTING TABLES

You can both copy tables and append data to them through drag and drop in the Explorer. This is the easiest way to import data into a database, as you can drag and drop a table between databases of different types—for example, dragging a text format table into a StarBase format database. You can easily combine data from tables that have the same structure in just a few steps. You can also use your existing tables as templates for new tables without needing to do anything more than move your mouse, select an option, and enter a new name for your table.

COPYING TABLE DATA VIA DRAG AND DROP

You can use either of two methods of copying tables via drag and drop; one is executed from the Explorer, another from the desktop.

COPYING A TABLE'S STRUCTURE IN THE EXPLORER

Creating a well-organized table or query is a lot of work. You might find that you want to use the structure of an existing table as a template for another. You cannot formally save a table as a template, but you can achieve the same effect using drag and drop in the Explorer.

This procedure is very easy. First, open the Explorer to the group that contains the database with the table. Then open the database to reveal all its table objects. If you want to place the copied table structure in a different database, open that database as well. If it isn't in the same Explorer group, open it on the desktop so that the Tables object icon is visible.

Select the table whose structure you want to copy, and drag it to the Tables icon of the receiving database. When your mouse pointer is over the Tables icon, release the mouse button. You then see a Copy Table dialog box like the one in Figure 33.6.

Figure 33.6
When you drag and drop a table onto the StarBase Tables icon, you can copy a table or query's data or structure, or append data to an existing table with the same structure.

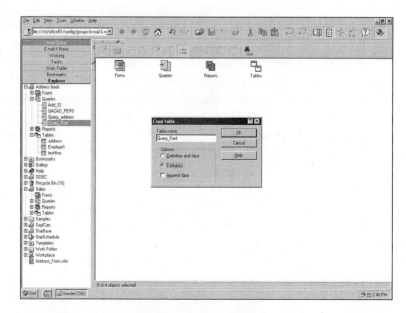

To copy the table's structure only, select the Definition option and click OK. If necessary, you can enter a new name.

COPYING OR APPENDING TABLE DATA IN THE EXPLORER

If you want to copy or append table data in the Explorer, use the same steps described in the preceding section to open the Copy Table dialog box. To create a complete copy of your table, data and all, choose the Definition and Data option.

To append the table's data to another table, select the Append Data option. Note that this option works only if the two tables share an identical structure. If they do not, try using the method described in the following section, "Moving Data Between Tables on the Desktop."

You can find detailed steps for appending data to a table in the section on working with the address book in Chapter 28, "Teaming Up at Work."

→ For more information about appending data to tables, **see** "Appending Data to Tables," **p. 1019**.

MOVING DATA BETWEEN TABLES ON THE DESKTOP

You can make copies of data in individual fields or entire records by selecting the field or record and dragging and dropping your selection. This capability is useful for copying data within a single table because sometimes you want to copy, say, one contact's phone number or company name and drop it into another record. However, it is really useful when you want to transfer data from one table to another—especially when the tables share some but not all fields.

This trick works only if the tables have common fields. Be careful to ascertain that they also have common data types, including similar limits on characters and formats. If not, you could lose or corrupt some or all of your imported data.

PART
VII
CH
33

Tip #564 from
Michael & Sarah

This method can be a useful way to combine Address Books from two different programs. Just be sure to check your data types and clean up your tables before importing in this way.

You can follow these steps:

1. Open the two tables and/or queries with which you want to work on your desktop.

2. To make dragging and dropping between them possible, make both tables into floating task windows, similar to those in Figure 33.4. Alternatively, open one table on the desktop and another in the Beamer.

3. Select all data in the table by clicking the gray rectangle that marks the intersection of the row and column headers, just below the Lookup Record tool on the Beamer toolbar. This button selects all visible data in your table or query. Don't release your mouse button, but immediately begin to drag the data onto the second table (or query).

Or you can select specific records to transfer by using the standard Ctrl+click and Shift+click methods of making multiple selections and drag from the row header onto the second table (or query).

4. If your source table has fields not found in the receiving table, a Drag Info dialog box appears (see Figure 33.7). It lists all the unique fields in the source table—at least, it should. Sometimes it seems to offer only an incomplete list. The data from these unique fields will be lost on appending, as only data from fields identical to those in the receiving table will be copied. If, on examining this list, you do not want to complete the import, click the Close button in the upper-right corner of the dialog box. If you want to proceed, click OK. Your data is automatically appended.

Figure 33.7
You can copy data from one table (or query) to another through drag and drop if they have fields in common. The Drag Info dialog box informs you of any fields unique to your source table or query; this data will not be copied.

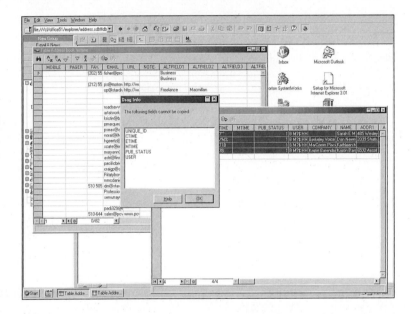

Caution

The method described here can be dangerous for appending data to a relational database because you have the potential to combine incompatible data types and import duplicate records—which could corrupt your database. Be sure to take appropriate measures to clean up your data before you import.

Tip #565 from
Michael & Sarah

You can use this method to copy data from a text database (which is read-only in StarBase) into a table in a dBASE, StarBase, or other format so that you can modify the data.

TROUBLESHOOTING

I'm searching for a phrase or string that I know exists in my table, but the Lookup Records command is not finding it.

One common reason for this problem is that you haven't set your search settings correctly in the Data Record Search dialog box. Make sure that either the correct field is selected in the Single Field option text box, or that All Fields is selected. In the Preferences section, make sure that the correct position is selected from the Position drop-down list. (Note that Anywhere in Field is different from Entire Field. Anywhere in Field finds the string if it is only a part of the data in the field; but Entire Field returns a match only if the string is the entire amount of data in the field.) If you are using wildcard characters of any sort, be sure that you have chosen the appropriate option, either Placeholder or Regular Expression.

Another common reason for this problem is that you've accidentally entered spaces before or after the string for which you are searching, either in the Data Record Search dialog box, or in your original database entry. If the dialog is set to search for an exact match in such a case, you'll come up empty.

I have a text database table that I need to edit. Is there any way I can do this in StarBase?

You cannot edit or modify tables in a text format database; this format is useful for viewing and transferring data only. However, you do have a few other options if you need to edit a text data table in StarOffice. 1) If you have a text ODBC driver that enables you to edit your table, you can create an OBDC database. 2) You can open the text table in StarCalc and save it in dBASE format. You can then create a dBASE format StarBase database, select your dBASE format table, and edit it to your heart's content. 3) You can drag and drop a copy of the text table into a StarBase format or dBASE format database in the Explorer.

I've opened a table in StarBase or dBASE format and StarOffice won't let me edit it, even though I have clicked the Edit button.

This is buggy behavior that crops up from time to time. First, try closing the table and reopening it. If that doesn't work, try closing out of the program and restarting it. If that doesn't work, well, try rebooting your system.

My text database table is imported with the incorrect separators and my data is all a jumble!

Open the Explorer and right-click the database icon of your text database to open its context menu. Choose Properties and click the Text tab in the Properties of Text dialog box that opens. You can select the correct separators, file extension and character set to match your text database file.

*I'm using criteria with the * as a wildcard, just like I do in Microsoft Access, but it doesn't seem to be working.*

StarBase, like most databases, uses the standard SQL expression, %, instead of the asterisk to serve as a wildcard.

CHAPTER **34**

CREATING FORMS FOR EASY DATA ENTRY

In this chapter

USING FORMS

Forms are a user interface for gathering data and entering it into tables. That's the computer's point of view, anyway. From a human perspective, your forms structure the way people interact with your database and your organization. Well-designed forms project a more professional image and can be an important part of an organization's brand and image development. They can help ensure that you get accurate, valid, and pertinent information that adds value and helps keep your organization on top. Forms are therefore more than just pretty dressing on top of your tables; they are a critical component of good database *and* good organizational design.

Tip #566 from
Michael & Sarah

You may have used read-only forms in other programs to display information people need to make decisions (rather than to enter or modify data). Because you can quickly display tables and queries in the Beamer—and then drag and drop data into your documents from there—you might find it more efficient to design queries for this purpose unless you also need to embed charts or other documents into your form or are creating a display-only form for use on a company intranet. Tables and queries display much faster than forms and offer the same lookup, sorting, and filtering tools.

You can structure user interaction through form design in a number of ways. You can incorporate multiple tables and/or queries into one form, either as independent forms or in parent-subform relationships. (You can create true subforms only in a relational database.) You can create custom tab orders that define the order in which users enter data, regardless of the field order in the underlying table(s). You can also create multiple-choice selections for fields that give a set of allowable values, helping to reduce entry errors and maintain data integrity. Because forms are documents (text, spreadsheet, or presentation), you can also include pictures and text that give instructions or hyperlinks that enable the user to jump to other information. You can even create command buttons that run macros and scripts when clicked by the user.

Forms are most useful when used online and directly linked to an underlying data table or query so that no further data input is required. However, you can also print forms and use them offline. You can use the same StarOffice form-building tools discussed in this chapter regardless.

Because forms are typically connected to underlying data tables and queries, they are more complex than a basic StarOffice document even though in many ways you work with forms just like you work with any other document. If you're new to forms, you should read the section "What Is a Form?" later in the chapter for an introduction to the structure and composition of forms.

If you plan to create a form for publishing on the Web, be sure to refer to Chapter 27, "Publishing Your Work on the Web" as well. Although this chapter makes reference to issues specific to Web publishing, Chapter 27 takes a more in-depth look at designing documents for the Web.

FORMS AND DATABASE INTEGRATION IN STAROFFICE

A form you create with the Form AutoPilot is actually a StarWriter document, and you can save it separately from your database as such by choosing File, Save As. You can also create forms from scratch in StarCalc, StarWriter, and StarImpress. You then can link them to StarBase tables in the form's Properties sheet by specifying a table, query, or SQL statement as the data source.

Your ability to create your form in any of the three major modules gives you great flexibility in formatting, printing, presenting, and exporting your form, without losing integration with your StarBase data table. Not to mention that creating forms is all about creating a user-friendly interface for entering data—and what could be more friendly than entering data into a familiar text document or spreadsheet? (Using a presentation format for forms seems frankly inefficient in most cases, although it might be useful for creating a graphics-intensive printed form because StarImpress has superior drawing tools.)

Note

Unlike Microsoft Office, StarOffice does not use form fields. If you want to automate routine business tasks such as preparing a quote letter or a contract, you can choose from three methods: You can create an AutoText entry and simply call the text from AutoText when you need it; you can create an unbound text box in a form and enter the text; or you can place the text in a Memo field in a database table and insert it as a bound control into a StarWriter document using the Forms toolbar. The latter two methods are slightly more cumbersome but enable easier centralized control.

Because you work with forms within the standard modules, you have the same powerful tools at your disposal as elsewhere, such as Search and Replace; character, paragraph, and page styling; and spellchecking. However, some commands that are not relevant to forms are unavailable.

DESIGNING FORMS

Without a moment's thought or planning, you can create a form lickety-split with the StarOffice AutoPilot. However, you're not likely to create a superior form that way. What is a superior form? Much like a well-designed table, a superior form does not have extraneous fields, organizes its data logically so that it can be easily understood by those using it, and enables users to input the data they need in a way that makes them feel more at ease.

PART
VII
CH
34

Tip #567 from
Michael & Sarah

If you have created an initial draft of your form with the AutoPilot, you can use the Versions command on the File menu when you're in the design phase to keep track of different versions. (Forms created from scratch cannot be saved as versions.)

If you're creating a form for personal use only, your job will prove easy, as long as you can please yourself!

If you're designing a form for multiple users in an office, however, you really should talk to those who will use the form and give them input into your design. Forms are often a critical path in determining office workflow, so your design could make the difference between a frustrated team and a productive one.

If you're designing a form for use on the World Wide Web, you might consider creating a trial version and posting it on your company intranet or personal Web site. Invite co-workers or friends to test it and give their feedback before you go fully live. This testing phase gives you a chance to improve your design as well as ensure that the scripts that process the data are working properly.

The following are some other questions and issues to keep in mind when you're designing your form:

- **Will this form be used online, on the World Wide Web, in paper form, or some combination?** If you're designing a form for use both online and offline, keep in mind that offline users can't check for additional information elsewhere in the database, so be sure that they have all the information and guidance they need on the form itself. If you use combo lists or list boxes that give users multiple choices online, don't create them as drop-down lists because they then are not formatted in a way that will print.

  If you're designing a form for Web use, you either should avoid graphics or use low-resolution bitmap graphics that are easy to download and display. These graphics aren't appropriate for printed versions, so you need to create another version for print, if one is needed.

- **Who are the primary users of this form—customers, regular employees, volunteers, students?** Determining who uses the form is critical in determining how the form should look and what kinds of graphics it should incorporate, as well as what types of information you need to include. For example, if a form is being used in-house for data entry, processing speed is more important than appearance, and you probably don't want to use graphics. Also, you can count on employees being able to ask questions if they don't understand something or the data is incorrect or incomplete in some way. If your form will be used by, say, volunteers who work for short periods of time, the form should be as self-explanatory as possible so that they don't need to ask others for assistance. If your form will be used on the Web, you need to consider the entire site design. Make sure the form includes links to other pages as appropriate so that the users can find any additional information they may need.

- **What fields do you need on the form?** Some fields in tables are used for internal management purposes only, such as linking tables in a relational database, and may not be needed by those entering or viewing data.

- **Do you need this form to be a separate file or associated with a specific database?** StarOffice gives you the option of creating a form as a standalone document or creating it from within a database with which it then remains associated. (You can still save a copy of a form separate from the database as well.) If you need to distribute the form widely or post it on a Web site, you need to save it as a separate file, although you might still want to save a copy within a specific database. See the section "Creating a New Form from Scratch" for more information.

WHAT IS A FORM?

In the world of databases, a *form* is a structured document with *labels* and data entry fields called *input fields*. The labels are like column headers in a table identifying data categories, and the input fields are the yawning blank spaces that accept the data. Typically, the input fields are linked to underlying tables and queries, known as the *data source*.

> **Note**
>
> Because the English translation is erratic, StarOffice does not always use standard U.S. English computing terms. To confuse you even further, it sometimes uses different terms for the same tool in Tool Tips and online help. Such discrepancies are noted throughout the chapter.

FORM CONTROLS

A form is made up of *controls*. Every object on a form—a label, an input field, a logo decorating an invoice—is a control. The three basic types of controls are as follows:

- **Bound control**—This type of control is bound to a table or query field. The data you enter into a bound control updates the field in the underlying table or query.

- **Unbound control**—This type of control can accept and retain a value but does not update any table fields. For example, a form label is an unbound control. You can enter text that's retained in the control, but it doesn't affect anything outside the form.

- **Calculated control**—This type of control is based on an expression such as a mathematical function or an SQL statement. Like a StarCalc cell with a formula in it, the field does not contain a value but the result of combining or acting upon values stored elsewhere.

StarOffice doesn't offer much built-in power in the way of calculated controls, one of its major limitations. In StarBase format (Windows only), it offers built-in SUM and AVERAGE functions. To create other calculated expressions, you must write and save a native SQL file and specify it as the data source for your form—and because the implementation of SQL is rather buggy, it isn't guaranteed always to work. Your other alternative is to write macros and StarBasic scripts that work with your data.

The upshot of this information is that StarBase forms are easy to work with; without the power of calculations, however, their usefulness is limited in business applications. StarDivision continues to improve the implementation of StarBase, and users can only hope that improvements will be made to forms in the near future.

→ For information on working with controls, **see** "Adding Controls," **p. 1187**.

FORM PROPERTIES

Just like every other object in StarOffice, a form has *properties*. Properties define the appearance and functioning of the object. With many objects, editing or modifying their properties is a matter of choice; for example, many people never feel the need to use the Properties dialog (opened from the Edit menu) to save their documents with keywords or change the color of their desktop. With forms, however, in many instances, you need to work directly with the Form Properties sheet to achieve your desired result. If the idea of mucking about with a form's Properties sheet is not appealing, and you need only a simple form, the AutoPilot can serve your needs. If you want to modify your form, create subforms, or create a form from scratch, however, you need to enter the world of form properties.

→ For more information about working with form properties, **see** "Assigning and Editing Form Properties," **p. 1184**.

FLYING ON AUTOPILOT

The simplest way to create a form is to use the AutoPilot templates. If you're a single user or a small organization creating forms to make data entry easier, using these templates is usually the best way to start. After you've created a form by using the AutoPilot, you can then easily change its appearance and structure in Design mode.

Note
> You can create only simple text box controls using the AutoPilot. If you want to create combo or list boxes, option groups, or other more sophisticated controls, you must create them manally in form Design mode.

To create a form by using the AutoPilot, select File, AutoPilot, Form. (Alternatively, you can select the Form object icon in your database in the Explorer and select New, Form, AutoPilot.)

Tip #568 from
Michael & Sarah
> If you begin your form from a database in the Explorer rather than the File, New command, you're one step ahead of the game because you've already selected your data source.

SELECTING YOUR DATA SOURCE

If you begin by choosing the File, New command, the Form AutoPilot opens with a Select Data Source window from which you can select a database as the basis for your form. You can click the drop-down list to see a complete list of available databases and then click to select the database you want. You can assign only one database per form. Click Next to move to the next screen.

Tip #569 from
Michael & Sarah
> Although you can select only a single table or query as the basis for your form, you can modify your form later to address multiple data sources. You also can create independent forms within the same form document or forms linked as parent forms to subform(s).

The next screen is the first dialog box you see if you start a form directly from a database in the Explorer—the Table Selection dialog (see Figure 34.1). It lists all the tables and queries in your selected database. In this case, you have only one table to choose from, the address table.

Figure 34.1
The first step in creating your form is to select the table to which the form is attached.

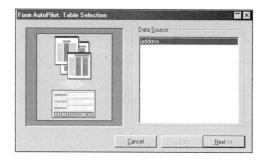

SELECTING YOUR FORM FIELDS

Click Next in the Table Selection dialog box to get to the Field Selection dialog box (see Figure 34.2).

Figure 34.2
You can select any fields from the chosen table or query that you want to appear on your form.

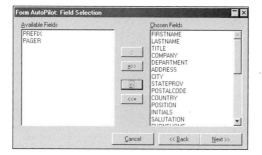

All the fields available in your selected table or query appear in the Available Fields list on the left. Select the fields you want, and click the right-facing single-headed arrow to move their names into the Chosen Fields list. You can use the usual Ctrl+click and Ctrl+Shift selection shortcuts to make noncontiguous and contiguous multiple selections, respectively. To select all the fields at once, click the right-facing double-headed arrow. To deselect a field or fields, reverse the process, using the left-facing arrows.

Tip #570 from
Michael & Sarah

Fields you add to the Chosen Fields list are automatically added to the bottom. You can't rearrange the field order in the Chosen Fields list itself; you determine the order by using your multiple selection tools in the Available Fields list to move fields over a portion at a time.

The order of fields in the Chosen Fields list determines the initial organization and tab order of the form. You can later change the tab order as well as reorganize the layout manually.

When you're satisfied with your selections, click Next to move to the Field Alignment dialog box (see Figure 34.3).

Figure 34.3
The AutoPilot does the tedious work of aligning entry boxes for you, giving you a choice of four basic layouts: Horizontal columns (previewed here), Vertical columns, Optimized, or Tabular form.

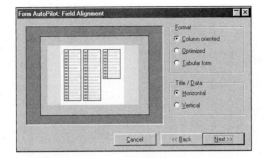

CHOOSING YOUR FORM DESIGN

As you step your way through the AutoPilot, you can also click Back to take a step backward to adjust your selections or Cancel to exit the AutoPilot without creating a form at all.

Note You can add fields to your form later if necessary.

In the Field Alignment dialog, you make the first of two selections relating to the final appearance of your form. Here, you choose the arrangement of your selected fields and their accompanying field labels. You have four choices of alignment:

- Horizontal columns (Column Orientated, Horizontal)
- Vertical columns (Column Orientated, Vertical)
- Optimized
- Tabular form

The Horizontal and Vertical column layouts place your field labels to the left and on top of your data cells, respectively, in a neat columnar layout. In the Optimized layout, StarOffice assesses the number of fields in relation to the space on the form and creates a "best fit" arrangement for the space without using fixed-size columns or table cells. In the Tabular Form layout, borders are placed around your fields to give your form a conventional table appearance. Despite the fact that one choice is called Tabular Form, all four layouts end up looking like tables—although you can rearrange the fields later to create a more flowing design.

Select your preferred layout, and click Next to move to the Styles dialog box (see Figure 34.4).

The AutoPilot gives you a small number of preformatted styles to choose from. Each style previews to the left as you select it. Note that the preview shows the form tools at the bottom of the desktop as part of your form when you work online; however, these tools do not print. Select the style you want, and click Next to move to the Create Form dialog.

Figure 34.4
When you're selecting form styles, keep in mind that some styles redraw on the screen faster than others. Choose a style that matches the resources of your system(s) as well as looks attractive.

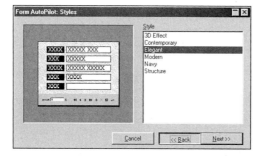

Tip #571 from
Michael & Sarah

When you're choosing background colors, consider whether the form will be printed or used only online. Also, consider whether any users might have visual handicaps that make certain color combinations more visible than others.

NAMING AND SAVING YOUR FORM

The final AutoPilot dialog box displays the form's automatically assigned name, which is *Form_data_source_name*, where *data_source_name* is the name of the table or query on which your form is based. If you change this name, make sure you assign a name that really describes what the form does. Also, make sure you include the name of the main form (or an abbreviation) in the name of any subforms so that the relationship is clear.

You can create the form immediately or simply store it. Creating the form can take a few minutes; the process is similar to creating a report because the layout is created and links are built to the underlying table and/or query. Your form is displayed in Read-only view—the view for data entry. If you want to check and tweak the design, choose Store Only, and then open the form in Design mode from your database. It's faster.

Make your selection, and click Create to complete the process. Your completed form should look something like the one in Figure 34.5.

Forms in Data Entry mode are automatically opened in Online view because it's assumed that your form will be used online. To change to Design mode, click the Edit button on the function bar.

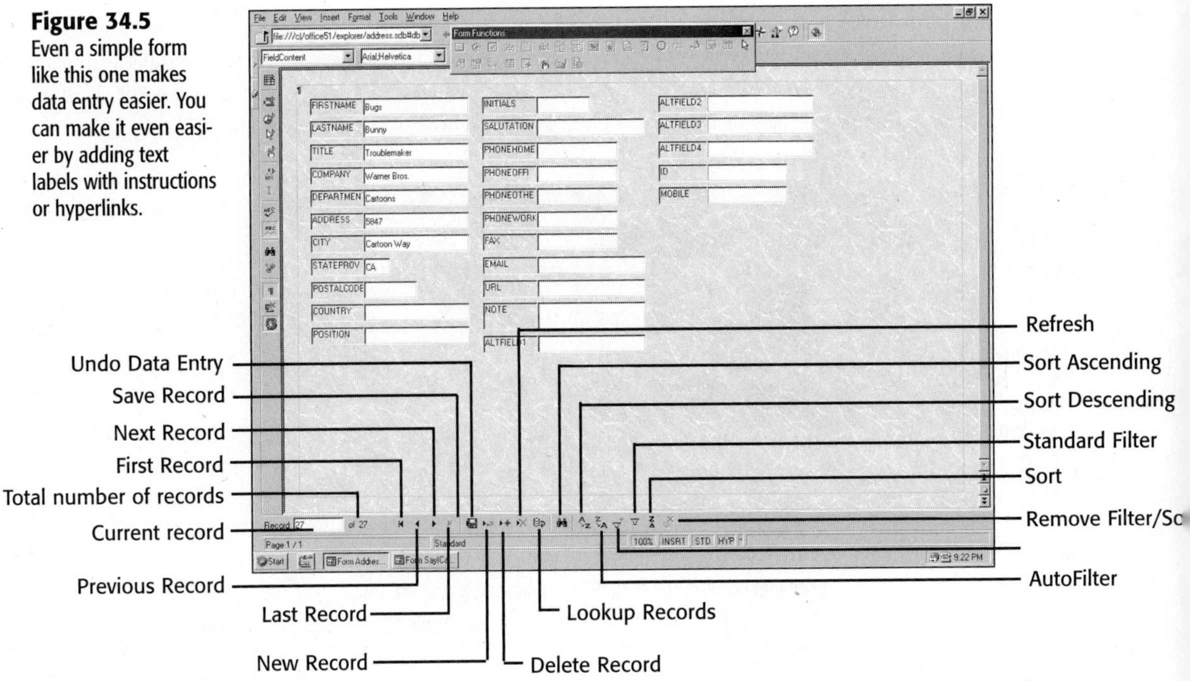

Figure 34.5
Even a simple form like this one makes data entry easier. You can make it even easier by adding text labels with instructions or hyperlinks.

NAVIGATING IN DATA ENTRY MODE

Although forms have their own special Form Navigator, you use it to navigate forms in Design mode only. In Data Entry mode, you use your Tab key to move between fields in a single record, and you use the form navigation buttons on the Form toolbar at the bottom of your window (refer to Figure 34.5) to move between records

→ For information on changing the tab order in your form, **see** "Setting the Tab Order," **p. 1194**.

Alternatively, you can jump from record to record by entering a specific record number in the Current Record text box and pressing Enter. You also have tools here for saving records, beginning a new record, and sorting and filtering your records.

ENTERING, SAVING, AND UNDOING RECORDS

To enter new data in an existing record, just place your cursor there or tab to the empty field, and begin typing.

To begin a new record, click the New Record button on the Form toolbar to create a blank record on the form. Type your data, pressing Tab to move from field to field.

After you have entered your data, clicking any button to move to another record automatically saves your record to the database. While you are still in the record, however, you can undo your data entry by clicking the Undo Data Entry button. To save your record, you can click Save Record—an action that's really necessary only if you are entering the last record before closing a session because your records are automatically saved as you navigate around.

SORTING AND FILTERING RECORDS

You can sort records based on the field in which your cursor is currently located by using the Sort Ascending and Sort Descending buttons on the Form toolbar.

To perform a more complex sort based on up to three fields, use the Sort button, and enter your conditions in the Sort dialog box that opens.

To display only records that share data in the same field, place your cursor in the field, and click AutoFilter. To construct a more complex filter that enables you to sort by up to three criteria, click the Standard Filter button. That filter remains assigned to that button until you enter new criteria.

The procedures for creating sorts and filters are the same as for tables and queries in StarBase and databases in StarCalc.

→ For information using StarOffice's sorting and filtering tools, **see** "Sorting and Filtering Data," **p. 627**, "Constructing Queries in StarBase," **p. 1202** and "Manipulating Table Contents," **p. 1156**.

Note that records without entries in the sort fields are always placed first.

To undo a sort or filter and return the records to their original entry order, click the Undo Filter/Sort button.

BUILDING AND MODIFYING FORMS

When you create a form by using the AutoPilot, you select the fields you want on it, and StarOffice creates all labels and input fields that you need. However, what if you need to alter your form or you need to add a subform? Or what if you want to create a paper form that is not bound to an underlying table? You then need to work in Form Design mode.

CREATING A NEW FORM FROM SCRATCH

You have two options for creating a new form from scratch. You can begin your form from the context menu of a database in the extended Explorer, or you can create a new text, presentation, or spreadsheet document in the usual way and use the Forms toolbar to create your form.

CREATING A FORM ASSOCIATED WITH A DATABASE

To start a new form from a database, open your database in the Explorer, and select the Forms icon. Right-click to open its context menu, and choose New, Form. From the submenu that appears, choose the document type you want to use as the basis for your form. A blank document and the Form floating toolbar open on your desktop.

If you start a new form from the database context menu, your form is saved in the Forms section of your database and remains associated with the database. Just as with other database objects saved in this way, you cannot separate your form from the database file. However, you can save it as a separate document by using the Save As command. This method gives you the most flexibility in storing your forms.

Caution

Theoretically, you should be able to save a copy of a form associated with a database, and then reassign the form to another data source in the form's Form Properties sheet. However, when we tried this, the data source reassignment did not work—and we accidentally entered data into the wrong table. Here's a workaround: When the form you want to reuse is open, click the Edit button to enter form Design mode. Open the Form Functions floating toolbar from the Form main toolbar and click the Selection tool (the white arrow). Then, follow these steps:

1. Hold your mouse button down and draw a marqee box around everything on the form you want to reuse.
2. Choose Edit, Copy (Ctrl+C).
3. Open a new, blank document (text, spreadsheet, or presentation).
4. Choose Edit, Paste (Ctrl+V).
5. Choose File, Save As, and save the form in the usual way.
6. Open the new form and enter Design Mode.
7. Open the Form Functions floating toolbar and click the Form Properties tool.
8. On the Data tab, change the Database and Data Source properties to reflect the form's new table assignment.

CREATING A STANDALONE FORM

To create a standalone form, open a new document in the usual way, and open the Form floating toolbar on the Main toolbar.

If you create a form from a document, you must save it as a standalone document by using the Save As command. You can store it in any directory you choose. You cannot open it from within your database, but you can create a link to it in the group in which your database is stored. This method is most appropriate for creating paper forms that will not be associated with a database at all and HTML forms that will be posted on a Web site.

Tip #572 from
Michael & Sarah

If you create a standalone form that is associated with a database, be sure your form name reflects the relationship so that it's clear they belong together.

ORIENTING YOUR PAGE

The blank document looks like any other document of that type, but certain tools are grayed out and unavailable on the menus.

If you're creating a form in StarWriter, it's a good idea to immediately select Format, Page and change your page orientation from portrait to landscape. That way, you get more screen real estate to use without needing to scroll. You should also switch to Online Layout view, if you are not already in it. This view also gives you a wider viewing area and is the way online users will experience your form.

In StarCalc, you might want to can use the View menu Pagebreaks Preview command to check where your natural page breaks are before you begin laying out your form if you intend to create a printed copy.

OPENING AN EXISTING FORM IN DESIGN MODE

To open an existing form in Design mode, open your database in the Explorer. Select your form, right-click, and choose Form Design.

SWITCHING FROM DATA ENTRY MODE TO DESIGN MODE

If you already have a form open in Data Entry mode and you want to switch to Design mode, click the Edit button on the function bar. Then open the Form Functions floating toolbar, and click the Design Mode button. When you're done editing the form, you can return to Data Entry mode by clicking either of those buttons.

> **Note**
>
> You should close all Properties sheets and the Form Navigator before switching back to Data Entry mode. Sometimes they don't close automatically, as they should, and you can't close these tools in Data Entry mode.

WORKING IN DESIGN MODE

When you're working in Design mode, you generally are doing one of four tasks:

- Drawing new controls with the Form Functions toolbar tools
- Resizing, grouping, and moving controls to achieve the layout you desire by using the mouse, context menus, and tools on the Form object bar
- Editing form and control properties on their Properties sheets
- Adding text, data, graphics, and OLE objects to your document with standard document commands

PART

VII

CH

34

Form controls are kinds of objects. You can resize, move, and delete them just as you can other objects (such as OLE objects and pictures, for example).

Whenever you do not have form controls selected—that is, for tasks that involve adding text and other objects outside your control fields—you are really just working in an ordinary document. All the same methods and tools apply as if you were creating an ordinary text document, spreadsheet, or presentation, including for such tasks as inserting graphics, creating page breaks, and previewing and printing your form. Don't forget that you can use the standard available tools, such as spellchecking and formatting commands, although they apply only to text you add outside the form controls.

The possibilities for forms are endless, beyond the scope of this book to explore fully. The following sections guide you through editing your form's properties and creating two of the more advanced types of controls—a combo list and a command button—to give you the basic tools you need to experiment on your own.

ASSIGNING AND EDITING FORM PROPERTIES

If you have created a form using the AutoPilot, a number of form properties have already been assigned, including the most important form properties—database, type of data source, and data source, which determine the table or other data source to which the form is linked. However, you might want to edit the form's existing properties or assign sort orders or filters.

If you are creating a form from scratch, the first step is to assign the database, data source type, and data source in the form's Properties sheet. Only then can you begin entering controls efficiently. (If you are creating a paper form that will not be connected to a database, you don't need to worry about form properties at this point. All these properties relate to the functioning of the form online as connected to a database.)

 To open a form's Properties sheet, open the Form Functions floating toolbar from the Main toolbar, and click the Form Properties tool.

If you already have controls in your document, you can also select any control, right-click, and choose Form from the context menu, or click the Form Properties button on the object bar.

Note

If the Form Properties icon is not active on the toolbar, click the Design Mode tool once to switch to Data Entry mode and once again to switch back to Design mode.

Your form's Properties sheet should look something like the one shown in Figure 34.6. Notice the title of the Properties sheet states that it is the *Form Properties* sheet—that's a useful guide because as you move to work on control properties, the sheet you use remains the same; only the title and contents change.

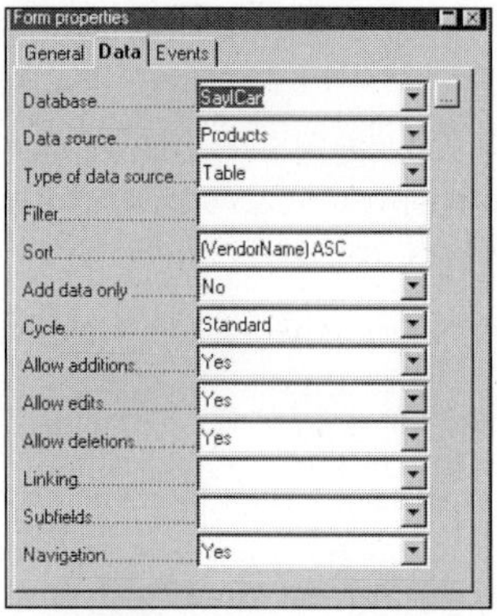

Figure 34.6
You specify the database to which your form is attached on the Form Properties sheet; you also can set parent-subform relationships and set the tab order.

Form properties	
General **Data** Events	
Database	SaylCart
Data source	Products
Type of data source	Table
Filter	
Sort	(VendorName) ASC
Add data only	No
Cycle	Standard
Allow additions	Yes
Allow edits	Yes
Allow deletions	Yes
Linking	
Subfields	
Navigation	Yes

This form is attached to a database named SayICan, specifically to a table named Products. A custom sort order has been entered in the Sort field, but no other changes have been made to the default form properties.

Notice that the Form Properties sheet has three tabs:

- The General tab has properties relevant to posting HTML forms to an intranet or Web site.
- The Data tab has properties relevant to setting your data source and sets the most general properties of the form's online behavior.
- The Events tab lists a series of form events to which you can attach macros or scripts.

To enter a property, simply click in the text box and begin typing, or (if an arrow appears) open the drop-down list and make your selection. If a text box has a button with ellipses next to it, clicking the button opens an Open dialog box.

Table 34.1 gives a summary description of the form properties on the Data tab, which contains the most essential properties.

TABLE 34.1   FORM PROPERTIES

Property	Function
Database	Select the database to which your form should be attached. Click the button with ellipses (...) to open the Open dialog box where you can navigate to the database's directory, and click to select the database.
Data Source	Select the table, query, or other data source that will underlie the form. The data source can be an existing table or query or an SQL statement saved as a file. Before you select a data source, you must first set the Data Source Type property. If your data source is a table or query, you should select your database first as well.
Type of Data Source	Indicate whether your data source will be an existing database table (Table) or query (Query) or your form will be generated by an SQL statement (SQL).
Filter	Enter filter criteria directly. Your filtering criteria should follow SQL rules without using the WHERE clause. For example, to display all records with the company name ACME, enter Company = Acme. You can also combine conditions, for example, Company = ACME OR Company = MEAC; this way, all records that meet those two conditions will be displayed. You can filter on-the-fly by using the filters on the Form toolbar; this filter is permanently attached to the form (until you delete it) and runs every time you open the form.

continues

TABLE 34.1   CONTINUED

Property	Function
Sort	Enter sort criteria directly. Specify the sort conditions following SQL rules without using the ORDER BY clause. For example, if you want all fields of a database to be sorted on the Last Name field in ascending order and on salary level in descending order, enter (LastName) ASC, (Salary) DESC (where LastName and Salary are the names of fields in the database table). You can sort on-the-fly using tools on the Form toolbar; this sort order is permanently attached to the form (until you delete it) and runs every time you open the form.
Add Data Only	Determine whether data can be added (Yes) or not (No).
Cycle	Determine whether pressing the Tab key moves you through all fields of the current page successively (Standard or Current Page), all fields of the entire form successively (All Records), or within the same field (Active Record) between different records. Note that the Tab Order property on the Control Properties sheet determines the specific tab order for controls in a form.
Allow Additions	Determine whether the form should permit the addition of new data (Yes) or not (No).
Allow Edits	Determine whether the form should permit editing of data (Yes) or not (No).
Allow Deletions	Determine whether the form should permit deletions of data (Yes) or not (No).
Linking	If you are creating a subform, specify the data field on the parent form that forms the link to the subform—in other words, specify the field that is the foreign key to the subform. (In the online help, this command is identified as Linked From.)
Subfields	If you are creating a subform, specify the field (variable) from the parent form in which you can enter values. If a subform is based on an existing query, enter the variable you defined in the query. If you create a form with an SQL statement listed in the Data Source field, enter the variable in the statement that you want to use. You can freely choose the name of the variable. (In the online help, this property is identified as Link After.)
Navigation	Decide whether the navigation functions in the form list can be used in the lower margin of the form (Yes) or not (No).

INTRODUCING THE FORM FUNCTIONS FLOATING TOOLBAR

With the exception of the Selection tool, the tools on the top of the Form Functions floating toolbar all create controls (see Figure 34.7). The tools on the bottom open and close the Properties sheets of controls and the form and control the environment of Form Design mode.

Figure 34.7
The Form Functions floating toolbar, opened from the Main toolbar, contains tools for drawing and editing form controls.

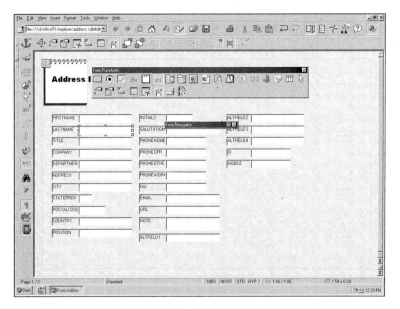

To create your form, you draw controls on your document by using tools from the Form Functions floating toolbar. You then assign each control to a specific table field (if applicable) and edit the control's other properties.

> **Note**
>
> Some of the tools on the bottom of the toolbar are repeated on the Form object bar.

The tools and their functions are listed in Table 34.2.

> **Note**
>
> Many of the tools are listed in the online help with a different name than they are assigned through Tool Tips. If a different name is used in online help, it is listed in parentheses after the button's function.

TABLE 34.2   FORM FUNCTIONS FLOATING TOOLBAR TOOLS AND THEIR FUNCTIONS

Tool Button	Tool Name	Function
	Push Button	Creates an unbound control, a gray button that you attach to a macro or script on the Events tab of the control's Properties sheet. When you click the button, the command is executed. You also can attach a graphic. (Button)
	Option Button	Also known as a radio button. Creates a bound control. You use option buttons when you have a list of exclusive options from which a user must make a single choice. (Option Field)

continues

TABLE 34.2 CONTINUED

Tool Button	Tool Name	Function
☑	Checkbox	Creates a bound control for a yes/no field. (Mark Field)
An	Label	Creates an unbound control. It is used to create form labels. (Fixed Text)
xy	Group Box	Creates an unbound frame that groups a series of option buttons. After you create the box, the options AutoPilot starts and guides you through selecting existing option buttons to place in the group. (Group Frames)
abl	Text Box	Creates a bound control that enables the user to input values through the keyboard. (Input Field)
	List Box	Creates a bound control that offers a list of choices from which the user must select one. The user cannot enter new data.
	Combo Box	Creates a bound control. The combo box combines a preset list of choices with an input field in which the user can also input new data. (Combination Fields)
	Image Button	Creates an unbound control, a transparent button that is meant to be displayed with a graphic. Just as with the Push button, you attach a macro or script on the Events tab of the control's Properties sheet.
	Image Control	Creates a bound control, a button that displays with a graphic and is tied to an underlying data field but also can have a macro or script attached. (Graphic Control Field)
	File Selection	Creates a button that opens a dialog box that enables the user to select a file (as in an Open dialog box).
	Date Field	Creates a control for entering date information.
	Time Field	Creates a control for entering time information.
123	Numeric Field	Creates a control for entering numerical information.
	Currency Field	Creates a control for entering currency values.
	Pattern Field	Creates a control that enables you to place a mask over the input field.
	Table Control	Creates a table within your form that replicates the original table or query to which your form is bound as an OLE object.
	Selection Tool	In Design mode, Enables you to select form objects to edit them.

Tool Button	Tool Name	Function
	Control Properties	When a specific control is selected in Design mode, enables you to assign properties to that control, including background color and font, printing characteristics (turning it on or off for printing), borders, and whether it accepts input that extends beyond the visible text entry box.
	Form Properties	Lists the properties of the entire form. Enables you to select the data source for your form. You also edit or create other form properties here, including filters and sort orders, relations to subforms or parent forms, and assignments of macros or StarBasic code to specific events.
	Tab Order	Enables you to determine the order in which a user cycles through the form's fields when pressing the Tab key. Note that the response of the Tab key is determined at a higher level by the `Cycle` property on the Form Properties sheet as well.
	Add Field	Opens a floating window that lists all fields in your data source. You can add a field to your form by dragging and dropping. You must first choose your database and your data source in the Form Properties dialog box.
	Form Navigator	Opens the Form Navigator, which enables you to cruise through your form control by control.
	Design Mode On/Off	Turns Design mode on and off. When Design mode is off, no other tools are available.
	Design Mode	Seems to be a bug and has no discernible function.
	AutoPilots On/Off	Turns on or off the AutoPilots that are automatically started on creating a table control field or a group box.

ADDING CONTROLS

After you set your basic form properties, you can add form controls. Although each control has some unique properties, you add them to your form and edit them in the same ways.

You can add controls by drawing them using the tools on the Form Functions floating toolbar, or by opening the Add Field field list and dragging and dropping field names onto your document. If you drag and drop field names from the field list, your field is automatically entered as a Text Box control.

DRAWING CONTROLS FREEHAND

To add a control by drawing, click the tool you want to use, move your cursor to the area where you want the control to appear, and draw. When the control is the size you want it, release the mouse button.

In most cases, when you're done drawing, your tool continues to be active until you click another tool or another control. If you click another tool, that tool becomes active. If you click an existing control, the Selection tool becomes active.

DRAGGING AND DROPPING CONTROLS FROM THE FIELD LIST

You can open the field list by clicking the Field List button on the Form Functions floating toolbar. The field list lists all the fields in your source table or query or those generated by your SQL statement. Select a field name, and drag and drop it where you want it. Your text box or other input field is automatically given and grouped with a label.

GROUPING LABELS

Unlike controls created with the AutoPilot or from the fields list, forms you draw freehand do not have labels already attached. To create a label, you need to draw a label control by using the Label tool. You can then keep the label and its associated control together by selecting both of them and grouping them with the Group command on the Format menu. Use Shift+click to make multiple selections, or click and draw a marquee (a box with a dotted line) around them. After you have grouped a series of controls, clicking one selects them all. You can edit or ungroup a group by using the commands the Ungroup or Group commands on the Format menu.

Tip #573 from *Michael & Sarah*	If you want to create a Text Box control with a label already grouped, copy and paste a control created by the AutoPilot, and change its properties. Alternatively, you can drag and drop a field from the Fields list.

DEFAULT CONTROL NAMES

Controls are assigned default names that indicate the types of controls they are and the sequence in which they were created. For example, the first four controls on the address form you created earlier using the AutoPilot are named TextField1, Label1, TextField2, and Label2. The sequence in which they were created reveals the initial tab sequence of the form, so you might want to glance through before changing any names to make sure they are sequential.

INTRODUCING THE FORM NAVIGATOR

When you have controls in your document, you can open the Form Navigator. The Form Navigator, shown on the left in Figure 34.8, is a specialized counterpart to the regular Navigator. It tracks only controls and enables you to quickly navigate your form in Design mode. (You can use the regular Navigator to track other objects in your form, such as graphics, notes, or links.)

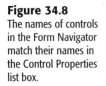

Figure 34.8
The names of controls in the Form Navigator match their names in the Control Properties list box.

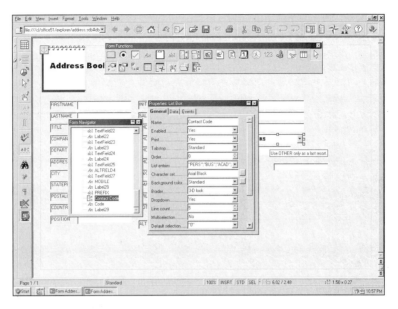

Notice that the name of the object in the Form Navigator matches the name assigned to it in the Name property of the Control Properties sheet. This name is used for internal tracking purposes—yours and the program's—only. It does not appear as a label. For a one-off form, particularly a one-page form in which you can easily see all the controls, renaming all the controls in your form from their vague defaults is probably not worthwhile. For a long multipart form, a form you intend to use repeatedly, or a form you use as a template, however, taking the time to rename is worthwhile because having familiar names makes using the Form Navigator much easier.

To simultaneously move your cursor to a control and select it, click its name in the Form Navigator.

DELETING CONTROLS

To delete a control from the Form Navigator, select its name, right-click, and choose Delete from the context menu.

RENAMING CONTROLS

To rename a control in the Form Navigator, select its name, right-click, and choose Rename from the context menu. Renaming a control in the Form Navigator has the same effect as altering the name directly in the Name property of the Control Properties sheet.

Tip #574 from
Michael & Sarah

If you're renaming a long series of controls, it's actually more efficient to rename them by opening the Properties sheet, clicking each control in succession (which cycles through their properties on the Properties sheet), and changing their names in the Name property.

OPENING PROPERTIES SHEETS

To open a control's Properties sheet, select its name, right-click, and choose Properties from the context menu. To open the Form Properties sheet, choose Form from the context menu.

When you have grouped controls together, you can select an individual field only by clicking its name in the Form Navigator list; you cannot select it by clicking it with the mouse. Clicking with the mouse selects the entire group. (This feature enables you to format grouped controls easily.)

INTRODUCING THE FORM OBJECT BAR

As usual in StarOffice, your tools metamorphose before your eyes as you work, changing as your tasks change. When you select form controls, a special Form object bar appears (see Figure 34.9). It uses some familiar object positioning and sizing tools but also has a few form-specific tools that give you visual guides to make layout easier. We highly recommend that you turn on Guides When Moving when you're working on your form's layout.

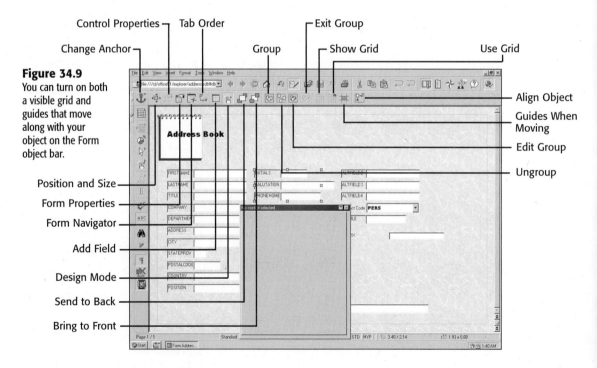

Figure 34.9
You can turn on both a visible grid and guides that move along with your object on the Form object bar.

REARRANGING FORM LAYOUT

Form controls are special types of objects. Just as with other StarOffice objects, they are inserted into your document in an invisible bounding box that you can resize and format using either the mouse or (with greater precision) the dialog boxes that open from their context menus. You can also use the Form object bar for positioning and grouping objects and changing their anchor points.

Because the techniques for working with objects are discussed elsewhere in detail, the following sections mention only a few issues specific to forms.

→ For a general introduction to working with objects in StarOffice, **see** "Working with Objects," **p. 176**. (Chapter 4, "Working in StarOffice")

→ For details on working with objects, **see** "Rehearsing Objects," **p. 421**. Although this chapter addresses desktop publishing in StarOffice, methods of working with objects are the same across StarOffice modules.

DEFAULT CONTROL ANCHOR POINTS

By default, form controls are anchored to paragraphs. In most cases, you won't want to anchor a control to a character; however, you might want to anchor a control to the page because doing so gives you the widest range in positioning it.

To change a control's anchor point, select the control, right-click, and choose Anchor. Then choose Character, Paragraph, or Page from the submenu.

MAKING MULTIPLE SELECTIONS

If you want to select more than one control at a time, the simplest method is to hold down your mouse button, draw a dotted box around the controls you want to select, and release the button.

Sometimes controls you don't want to include are too close to those you do. In these cases, press Shift while clicking each control you want to select.

Remember that if you have previously grouped any controls, you can no longer select them individually by using the mouse. You need to edit the group or ungroup it beforehand to make individual selections.

GROUPING AND UNGROUPING CONTROLS

After you have arranged a series of controls in the relations you want, it's a good idea to group them so that your layout remains intact. When you group a series of objects, they behave as a single object as far as your selecting and moving them with the mouse is concerned. (You can still select them individually by using the Form Navigator.)

To group a series of controls, first select the entire group. Then open the Format menu, and choose Group.

To edit a group, select the group, open the Format menu, and choose Edit. Then click the control(s) you want to remove from the group. When you're done, click anywhere outside a control.

To ungroup a group, select the group, and choose Format, Ungroup.

PART

VII

CH

34

Note   Controls created by the AutoPilot are automatically grouped with their labels.

ADDING FORM HEADERS AND FOOTERS

Unlike some programs, StarOffice does not have special header and footer sections for forms, nor can you use the Header and Footer commands in StarWriter. If you want to create a header or footer area, just draw your lines freehand using the Draw floating toolbar tools or the regular Draw tools in StarImpress. Alternatively, you can insert one of the many lines included in the Gallery just for this purpose by using the Insert, Picture command.

OPENING A CONTROL'S PROPERTIES SHEET

You edit and format a control through its Control Properties sheet.

When you select controls created with the AutoPilot or from the field list, the Control Properties tool remains grayed out and unavailable because these controls are automatically grouped, and this button is not available to multiselections. To open the Control Properties sheet, you must open the Form Navigator, select a specific control name, right-click, and select Properties from the context menu.

Tip #575 from	The most efficient way of working when you're editing controls that are grouped is to keep both the Form Navigator and the Control Properties sheet open on your desktop. As you click the name of a control in the Navigator list, its properties are displayed.
Michael & Sarah	

You can open the Properties sheet of hand-drawn controls in the same way; you can also click to select the control (so that its green object handles are visible) and then click the Control Properties tool in the Form Functions floating toolbar. After you open the Properties sheet, you can click another hand-drawn control, and its properties are displayed. If you select a grouped control, however, the Properties sheet appears blank, and the title says, "No control selected." You have to click that control's name in the Navigator before its properties are displayed.

Tip #576 from	After you've created controls that you like, you can save time if you save them together in a document and use them as a "library" of controls that you copy and paste into new forms. You then only need to copy and paste a control into a new form and reassign the field name in its Control Properties sheet.
Michael & Sarah	

UNDERSTANDING CONTROL PROPERTIES

The Control Properties sheet has the same three tabs as the Form Properties sheet, but here the General tab is the most important. The Data tab has only two properties: the field assignment and a property that enables you to determine how an empty field should be treated. (Certain types of controls, like Yes/No controls, only have the field assignment property.) The Events tab contains a series of events from which you can choose to associate a macro or script with the control.

Some of the general properties you can set include the display font and font size of your data—a boon for people with visual challenges or anyone who wants to create a snazzy and easy-to-read Web site—and the specific tab order within a record.

Other properties vary depending on the specific type of control. If you create a combo list or list box, you enter your list items here. If you create a button, you can associate a macro or script with your button here so that a specific action—clicking a mouse or pressing the Tab key—triggers the macro or script. You will see examples of both in sections later in this chapter. With currency, data/time, and numeric data types, you format your data here.

Table 34.3 lists the control field properties on the General tab that are shared across controls (although no one type of control has all these properties.)

TABLE 34.3   GENERAL CONTROL FIELD PROPERTIES

Property	Description
Name	Changes the internal name of the control used by the Navigator and other program tools.
Label	Changes the name used by its associated label on the form.
Enabled	When Yes, makes the control active. If set to No, the control is grayed out and unavailable.
Read-Only	When Yes, opens the form in Read-only mode. All editing tools are grayed out and unavailable.
Print	When Yes, makes the control visible during printing.
Tabstop	Sets the tab properties to the standard settings, turns tabbing off, or turns it on and uses settings from the Order property.
Order	Determines the tab order.
Character Set	Determines the font and font size of displayed data or labels. By default, this field is empty. Click the button with ellipses (...) on the right to open a font selection dialog box. After you choose a new font, you cannot return to the default setting automatically. (The default font is 10-point Arial and can be reset manually.)
Default Value	Sets a default value for the input field. The user can accept the default without change, edit it, or delete and overwrite it.
Background Color	Sets the background color of the control. Be careful not to set a color that makes the data more difficult to see. Also, keep in mind that redrawing color on the screen takes time and system resources.
Border	Sets the appearance of the border surrounding the control.
Multiselection	Places an arrow in a text box to turn it into a drop-down list.
Tag	Enables you to enter an HTML tag that relates to the form.
Help Text	Enables you to enter help text that pops up as a user moves the mouse pointer over the control field.
Help URL	Enables you to enter a URL that a user can click to jump to another page that offers assistance with the form.

NAMING A CONTROL

To change a control's name (which makes it easier to track in the Form Navigator), select it, open its Control Properties sheet, and enter a new name.

To change its label, you must select the label itself and change its properties. Make sure you change the property called Label and not the one called Name.

SETTING THE TAB ORDER

The most efficient way of moving through a form is pressing the Tab key. As you work on a form's layout, you might find that the default tab order no longer works well. No problem; you can change the tab order by making changes to the Form and/or Control Properties sheets.

Open the Form Properties sheet to choose from the four Cycle options:

- Standard, the default, in which a user cycles through the fields on a single page but pressing Tab does not move to the next record
- All Records, in which a user cycles through all records in the database one field at a time
- Active Record, in which a user cycles through all entries in the current record (similar to Standard)
- Current Page, in which a user cycles through entries on the current page, which may or may not represent a complete record

Select a control, and open its Control Properties sheet. You need to set two properties here. First is the Tabstop property. By default, it is set to Standard. If set to No, the control is skipped when the user presses the Tab key. If set to Yes, the control is accessed by Tab with reference to the tab order set in the property field below. If some controls are set to Standard and some to Yes, pressing Tab cycles through those set to Standard first and those set to Yes according to the tab order afterward.

PUTTING HELP ONSCREEN

You can add pop-up help notes that appear when the user moves the mouse pointer over a control. To do so, select the control that "needs help," so to speak, and open its Control Properties sheet. Then scroll down to the Help Text property, and type your text there. Keep it short so that your user can take it in at a glance.

If your user might require more help than a brief note can provide, you can add a Help URL that enables your user to click a hyperlink that jumps him or her to another page.

CREATING A COMBO LIST OR LIST BOX

When you create a form by using AutoPilot, it creates a standard "vanilla" form, using text boxes or their numerical equivalents as controls for each field. However, part of the power and usefulness of forms lies in their capacity to limit users' input choices and thus guard data integrity and speed data entry by providing lists of common answers.

WHAT ARE COMBO LISTS AND LIST BOXES?

You use combo lists and list boxes to present a menu of choices to the user. With list boxes, the user must select one of the items on the list. With a combo box, the user can select an item on the list or type new data in the text box. Both types of controls are now commonplace on Web questionnaires and registration forms.

The following section takes you through creating a combo list, but the procedures are exactly the same for creating a list box.

DRAWING A COMBO LIST

 Select the Combo List tool from the Form Functions floating toolbar. Before you draw, decide whether you want your entire list to be visible to the user or whether you want your control to have a drop-down list instead. (You will set this property in a moment.) If you plan to print the form, make the entire list visible. Draw your combo list accordingly. It will look like a white rectangle with a border in the upper section.

SETTING THE COMBO LIST'S BASIC PROPERTIES

To set the combo box's basic properties, select the combo box, right-click, and choose Properties. Then follow these steps:

1. Change the name to reflect the underlying field name or the function of the box.
2. Scroll down to Dropdown. The default is set to No, which means all selections on the list are displayed. If you want only a single item at a time to appear and the rest to appear on a drop-down list, select Yes as its property.
3. Just below, check the AutoComplete property. The default is Yes, which means the StarOffice AutoComplete function is turned on. This function anticipates the typist's word and completes it automatically. If you don't like this feature, select No.
4. If you want to change the background color, click the drop-down list in the Background property and choose another, or click the ellipses and mix your own custom color.
5. If you want to change the border, open the Border drop-down list, and choose one of the three options.
6. If you want to change the font, put your cursor in the Character Set property field, click the ellipses, and choose your font and font size from the dialog box that opens.

CREATING THE LIST

Now that you've done the basics, it's time to create your list entries. With your Control Properties sheet still open, follow these steps:

1. Check the Line Count property. This property sets the number of items that are displayed in the drop-down list (regardless of the total number of items on the list). The default is five, but you can adjust this number as appropriate. Make sure it's set to at least two.

2. Navigate to the List Entries property. Click the drop-down arrow, place your cursor in the box, and type your first list entry. Don't use any punctuation unless it is a part of your list. Press Shift+Enter to move to the second line, and type your second entry. Continue until the list is completed. When you click somewhere outside the List Entries properties, StarOffice automatically formats the items to match SQL conventions, surrounded by quotation marks and separated by semicolons.

3. Click the Data tab, and place your cursor in Type of List Contents. This is the equivalent of the Data Source Type property on the Form Properties sheet. Select the type of object that will receive and process this input. Your choices are Table, Query, SQL Query, SQL Native Query, and Table Fields.

4. Open the drop-down list in the List Content property, and select the table or query that will receive your data.

5. Open the drop-down list in the Field Name property, and select the field with which your combo box will be bound.

If you choose a regular list, you should see your list appear immediately on your form after step 2. If you choose a drop-down list, you need to click the Design Mode button on the Form Functions floating toolbar to turn off Design mode. Then click in your combo box to try it out. If the list is not formatted correctly, return to Design mode and its Control Properties sheet to edit it.

If you want, you can set a default value; it will always be the value that either appears in the text box or is selected on the list when the user opens it.

CREATING A COMMAND BUTTON

You might want to create a command button on your form for many reasons. One likely reason these days is that if you're creating a form for use on the Web, you must create at least one command button that people click to submit the form to your database.

StarOffice doesn't have a Submit script in the macro library—you need to write one yourself that contains the appropriate URLs—but when you have your macro in hand, just follow the steps given in the following section.

DRAWING THE BUTTON

The first step is to draw your button. You have three choices of buttons: a plain text button (Push Button), a button that uses a clip art graphics file to decorate it (Image Button), and a button that uses a bitmap file to decorate it (Image Control). If you choose to create a button with an illustration, you need to enter the path name (URL) of the graphics or image file in the button's Properties sheet after it's created. Keep in mind that fancy buttons look prettier but take longer to draw and download. If you're looking for rapid data processing, use a plain text button. If you use a picture, consider using a bitmap image, which is lower resolution and thus a smaller file than a comparable graphics file.

Click the button tool of your choice and draw. Right-click the button when you're done to open its Control Properties sheet.

SETTING THE BUTTON'S PROPERTIES AND ASSIGNING A MACRO

Setting a button's properties is similar to assigning properties to other controls. To set your button's properties, follow these steps:

1. In the case of a button, its label is bound to its face rather than being separate, as with text boxes or similar input fields. Change the label to reflect its function; for example, enter Submit.

2. Change the name, if you like, to make tracking easier with the Form Navigator.

3. Go to Button Type, and open the drop-down list. Push is the default type of button, which runs a command sequence on pushing the button. Reset resets values in the controls. Submit sends the data back to the server, and URL jumps the user to a location defined by the address you enter in the URL property below.

4. If you want to change the button's appearance, choose the background color and/or character set properties, and make the appropriate changes. You can also add a graphic if you want.

5. Click the Events tab, and review the list of events. Decide what event you want to trigger the submission of the form. The most likely candidate, of course, is Mouse Pressed. Place your cursor in the selected field, and click the button with ellipses next to it.

6. The Assign Macro dialog box opens (see Figure 34.10). Your event is already selected in the Event list in the upper left. Click the plus signs in the Macros list on the lower left to open the modules. The macros available for assignment are listed on the right.

Figure 34.10
When you select your event and click the button with ellipses, you enter the Assign Macro dialog; there, you can choose from your entire library of StarOffice macros and scripts. You can also assign JavaScripts.

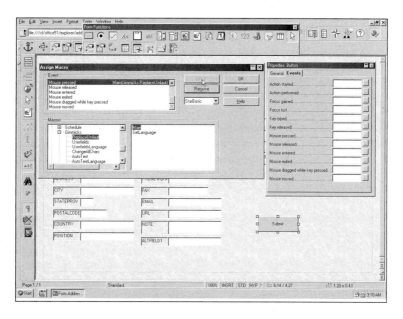

PART

VII

CH

34

7. Select the macro you want to assign. (If you want to assign JavaScript or StarScript instead of StarBasic, make sure you select the appropriate type in the drop-down list to the right of the Event list.)

8. Click Assign. (It's grayed out in Figure 34.10 because the assignment has been completed.) You then see the name of the macro appear in the event list next to your selected event.

9. Click OK, which returns you to the Properties sheet. The name of your macro or script file is entered into your event property.

All you need to do is finish making any assignments relevant to publishing your form on the Web, such as the Tag property and the target frame for the form. You need to exit Design mode to test it.

PRINTING FORMS

Because a form is just a special type of document, printing a form uses the same commands and logic as printing a text document, HTML document, spreadsheet, or presentation.

If you are preparing a form for printing and it is also used online, be sure to print a sample first to check that the colors and fonts work in a printed version. The design requirements for a good online form and a good paper form are quite different, so you might need to tweak your design.

Be sure also to use the Print Preview features to see where your page breaks lie so that you can ensure your form doesn't break across crucial controls.

→ For information on printing text documents, **see** "Previewing Documents," **p. 475** and "Printing Text Documents," **p. 478**.

→ For information on printing spreadsheet documents, **see** "Previewing Your Page Layout with Page View," **p. 709**, "Selecting Objects to Print," **p. 706**, and "Printing Your Results," **p. 710**.

TROUBLESHOOTING

How can I create a subform?

You can create a subform only in a relational database, so you must have a database saved in StarBase native format (Windows only) or be connected to an ODBC or JDBC RDBMS. If you are not working with a relational database, you can achieve a similar effect by combining two documents into the same form. You can do so in a variety of ways, including copying and pasting a document into another as a DDE link or (in StarWriter) inserting a document file into another document as a section. If you insert one form into another by dragging and dropping it as a section, turn off Online view; using this view makes it easier to place the section precisely. Beware that if you then delete such a section, it can wreak serious havoc with your form layout.

I need to print my form, but I can't see where my page breaks.

By default, forms are opened in Online view because it's assumed most forms will be used online. Because pages have no meaning online, page breaks don't appear. To turn off Online view, click the Online tool on the Main toolbar so that it doesn't look pressed in anymore. To set page breaks, use the regular technique appropriate for that document type. For more information, see the chapters on printing StarWriter, StarCalc, and StarImpress documents.

I click on my control and open its Control Properties sheet, but I can't find any field list or other properties you described. I just see a tab named General.

Is the title of your Properties sheet Properties: Multiselection? If so, you have more than one control selected. StarOffice shows you only the most general properties shared across objects in that instance. You can easily select multiple controls if you have created controls with the AutoPilot or by dragging and dropping field names from the Fields list because labels are automatically grouped with the input fields. This means when you click one with your mouse, you select them all. You can ungroup the label and its associated field, but the simplest solution is to open the Form Navigator and select the name of the specific control you want to edit in the Navigator list. (You can tell which is selected because its green object handles become visible.) Right-click and select Control from the context menu. The controls remain grouped.

I can't use the navigation tools on the bottom of my form; they're all grayed out.

Check the Data tab of your Form Properties sheet. Chances are someone has changed the Navigation property to No or Parent when it should be set to Yes.

The Versions command is grayed out in my form's File menu.

The Versions command is available only when you're creating forms with the AutoPilot.

I opened my form, but I don't have a main toolbar. How can I edit my form's properties?

You opened the form in Read-Only Data Entry mode. If you click the Edit button on the function bar, your main toolbar appears. If your Form Functions floating toolbar is not already open, open it. Then click the Design Mode button (the only active button) to enter Form Design mode.

When I try to open my form by selecting its name from the history list at the bottom of the File menu, I get a message that my form doesn't exist.

You must have saved your form as part of your database rather than as a stand-alone form. A form saved as part of a database doesn't have an independent existence. It is created as a temporary file when you open it. Once you close the form, this temporary file is deleted, so technically the form doesn't exist anymore—although the memory of its existence remains on the history list.

CHAPTER 35

GETTING ANSWERS WITH QUERIES AND FIELDS

In this chapter

WHAT IS A QUERY?

You usually enter data in tables in a relatively random way. For example, you add contact names to your Address Book as you meet new people (which usually isn't in alphabetical order)! Your table design structures your data to some extent, but you still enter it in an order very different from the way you want to retrieve it. You also might need to combine data that is in more than one table, or you might not want to see all the fields in your records at once. StarBase's basic sorting and filtering tools enable you to limit the data you view to some extent, but they are temporary and not very powerful. To get the most out of your database, you can use queries. A *query* is a structured question that you pose to your database to extract a limited set of information that you can save and use again.

Queries are useful for a number of tasks:

- You can quickly organize and summarize your data in a variety of ways.

- You can limit the number of fields that are displayed in a single table to make data entry easier or more efficient.

- You can create and save queries as SQL statements that you attach to forms as their data source.

- You can create calculated fields such as sums, averages, and percentages.

- You can bring to your desktop only the specific data you need for a complex task—for example, a mail merge for a form letter that targets customers who have not made a purchase in the last six months.

- You can produce a report with only the information you want by building it on top of a query.

CONSTRUCTING QUERIES IN STARBASE

You have two methods for constructing queries in StarBase: You can create a graphical query using the Query AutoPilot and/or the Query Design view, or you can construct queries directly in Structured Query Language (SQL). Although these methods overlap, they are not equivalent, and you are likely to use them to accomplish different tasks.

The following sections introduce both methods, but the chapter as a whole focuses on creating and modifying graphical queries in StarBase because SQL is not a StarOffice-specific language. StarBase's implementation of SQL is also, in our experience, very buggy and unstable, so you have a better chance of creating a successful query using the graphical query method. (The chapter does present some information on StarOffice's specific implementation of SQL and gives you some tips about using it.) If you are creating databases for personal use within StarOffice, you are not likely to need to learn SQL in detail. If you are creating or working extensively with databases for an office or organization and don't already know SQL, you should consider learning it because it is the industry standard for creating, maintaining, and retrieving data from relational databases.

Tip #577 from
Michael & Sarah

If you want to delve more deeply into SQL, you can find some great free resources on the Web. You might start with Jim Hoffman's excellent tutorial at
http://www.geocities.com/ResearchTriangle/Node/9672/sqltut.html.

INTRODUCING GRAPHICAL QUERIES

Graphical queries are most useful for working with StarBase and dBASE format databases that you have created in StarOffice. You create a graphical query by using the Query AutoPilot or the context menu's New, Query, Query Design command. Graphical queries are easy to create and manipulate because you don't need to master the somewhat arcane language of SQL, although you do need to learn StarBase's language for writing criteria to filter your data.

You can create a graphical query by using the AutoPilot, or you can create one from scratch by using the Query Design window. As you can see from Figure 35.1, the graphical Query Design window consists of a grid. You drag and drop table field names onto this grid and then enter various criteria to build your query. You can run your query from this window, and the results appear in the Beamer.

Figure 35.1
If you want to create a query from scratch or modify an AutoPilot-built query, you open it in Query Design view.

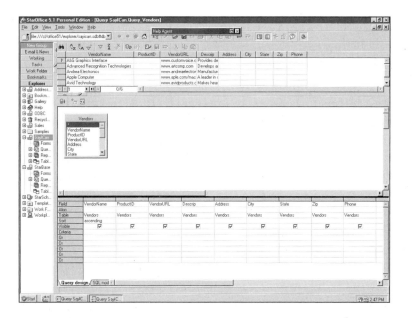

The AutoPilot and graphical query builder actually generate an SQL statement behind the scenes as you work, so you can use these methods in combination with direct editing of SQL statements (see Figure 35.2). Often the fastest way to work—and to learn the basics of SQL statements—is to create a query with the AutoPilot and then edit and extend the SQL statements manually. This method is particularly useful if you are creating a SQL statement to serve as the data source for a form.

Figure 35.2
After you've created a query using the graphical method, you can click into SQL mode to reveal the wizard behind the curtain, the plain text SQL statements that make your query run.

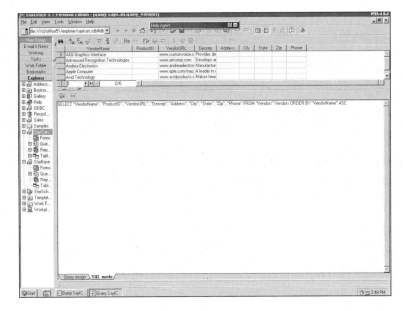

INTRODUCING SQL

SQL (often pronounced *sequel* or *seekel* but more properly called *ess cue ell*) is a platform-independent standard database language used for querying and manipulating databases. (You can actually create a database with SQL as well as construct queries.) The general SQL standard is overseen by the American National Standards Institute (ANSI), and any Relational Database Management System (RDBMS) using SQL must support the basic ANSI SQL command set. Most modern databases support and make use of SQL. Most programs also "extend" the SQL language to add functionality, but these extensions can also add to user confusion because they are not standardized and frequently are poorly documented in the program—as is unfortunately the case with StarBase.

> **Note**
>
> According to StarDivision, StarOffice supports MS-SQL and works with ANSI 1992 Level 2 SQL, with extensions.

SQL is an application language, not a programming language. A programming language, such as StarBasic or C++, enables a programmer to write a detailed procedure that specifies how a task will be carried out by the computer. SQL is non-procedural, which means that you don't tell SQL how to do anything. You just tell it what you want, and SQL figures out how to fulfill your request in the most efficient way. The advantage of using this type of language from the user perspective is that SQL resembles ordinary spoken English and everyday logic much more than does, say, StarBasic.

UNDERSTANDING SQL IN STARBASE

StarBase enables you to use SQL in two different ways. You can write *native SQL* statements that StarBase sends directly to an external data source (like an Oracle or Microsoft SQL Server database). Native SQL is the pure ANSI 1992 SQL without any extensions. StarBase itself cannot execute native SQL statements; it just passes them on to a database server that can. StarBase also implements internally a version of SQL92 that it uses to create and execute queries in StarBase format databases. The internally implemented version of SQL offers a reduced set of commands compared to native SQL, so your ability to construct queries in StarBase is somewhat limited.

Text and dBASE format databases (neither of which are relational database formats in StarBase) support only the most basic set of SQL commands that enable you to select, sort, and filter data. One result is that you cannot create calculated field in dBASE tables, a significant limitation.

> **Caution**
>
> If you open a query in design view, click the SQL Mode tab, and enter a query that contains native SQL terms that are not implemented in StarBase, you won't be able to return to StarBase's graphical query mode in that query nor will you be able to execute the query in a StarBase, dBASE or text format database.

For example, the StarBase native format (Windows only) has its own set of functions including SUM and AVERAGE and does not support ANSI SQL SUM and AVG commands. This means it doesn't recognize the SQL words if you use them in a SQL query.

AVOIDING SQL RESERVED WORDS

SQL command words are *reserved* by the program, which means that you can't assign them to your own objects (such as field or table names) or use them for anything except issuing SQL commands.

> **Note**
>
> SQL is not a case sensitive language. However, SQL syntax is conventionally represented in uppercase to distinguish it from the data.

CREATING A NEW QUERY WITH AUTOPILOT

The simplest way to create a new query is to use the Query AutoPilot. After you have created your query, you can then open it in Design view to modify it. You create a query from scratch from the same Design view window.

In this section, you'll create a simple query for your Address Book that's a mask for entering contact codes. Data entry for these codes in the complete address table is awkward and inefficient because you have to navigate from one end of a long table (where the name fields are) to the other (where the ID fields are). By creating this query, you will be able to see the key information on a single screen and make managing your Address Book easier.

> **Note**
>
> Even if you are working with a StarBase format relational database, you can select only one table as the basis for a query in the AutoPilot. If you want to create a query that joins two tables, you need to modify your AutoPilot table or create a table from scratch in Query Design view. You should make sure you set your tables' primary keys and relations before attempting to create a joined query.

To create a query with the AutoPilot, open the File menu, and choose AutoPilot, Query. The Table Selection dialog then opens (see Figure 35.3). It contains buttons familiar to you from other AutoPilots and dialog boxes. For example, the Next button moves you forward one screen, the Back button moves you back one screen, and the Cancel button cancels your selections and returns you to the desktop.

Figure 35.3
Your first step in creating a query is selecting the database and table you want to query.

Select the database you want to query from the Database drop-down list.

> **Note**
>
> The database list includes databases not only in the Explorer group, but also in any other group you have created and in any other directory where you have browsed and a .sdb (StarOffice database) file exists.

After you have selected a database, all its tables appear in the Data Source list below. Select the table you want to serve as the basis for this query, and click Next to advance to the Field Selection dialog box (see Figure 35.4).

Select the fields you want to include on your query from the list of available fields on the left. You can make multiple selections using the standard Ctrl+click and Shift+click shortcuts. Move your selections over to the Chosen Fields pane by clicking the single-headed arrow button. Click the double-headed arrow button if you want to move all the table's fields into the Chosen Fields list. After you've completed your selections, click Next to advance to the Filter dialog box (see Figure 35.5).

Figure 35.4
In this dialog, you select the fields you want to appear in your final query. You can still filter and sort your data by fields that you do not include among your chosen fields.

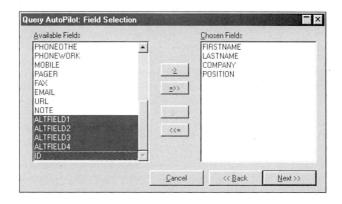

Figure 35.5
In the Query AutoPilot Filter dialog box, you can create a filter with up to five conditions and preview its results in the Beamer before moving on.

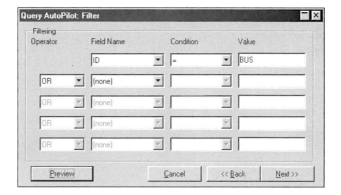

CREATING FILTERS WITH QUERY CRITERIA

Using the Filter dialog, you can create a complex filter with up to five conditions. A really nice feature is that you can click the Preview button in the lower left to preview the results of your choices before moving on, so you can adjust your filter if you don't like the results. Note that creating a filter is the same as setting criteria in Query Design view.

If you want to apply a filter, select the field which you want to filter for your first statement. You can select any field in your underlying table, even if you are excluding it from your query. Next, click the Condition drop-down list, and select an operator from the list. Table 35.1 lists all the available operators; they are the same operators you use in the Criteria field of queries in Design view.

TABLE 35.1   CONDITIONAL OPERATORS FOR QUERY FILTERS

Operator	Description
=	Equals your entered value, which can be any alphanumeric string.
<>	Does not equal your entered value, which can be any alphanumeric string.
>	Greater than your entered value.

continues

TABLE 35.1 CONTINUED

Operator	Description
<	Less than your entered value.
>=	Greater than or equal to your entered value.
<=	Less than or equal to your entered value.
Empty	Null fields; the Value field is unavailable.
Not Empty	Not null fields; the Value field is unavailable.
Like	Like the letter(s) or number(s) you have entered in the Value field; for filtering based on partial words or numbers.
Not Like	Not like the letter(s) or number(s) you have entered in the Value field.

After you select your operator, you can insert a value in the Value field (if relevant).

You can use wildcard characters (called *placeholders* in SQL) in your values when you choose the Like and Not Like operators. The SQL wildcard is a percent sign (%); however, you can also use the conventional file system placeholder—the asterisk (*)—which StarBase automatically converts into the percent sign.

> **Note**
>
> If you use the asterisk and your Like and Not Like statements don't work properly, try rewriting them using the percent sign instead. StarBase might not have converted the asterisk correctly.

Table 35.2 shows some examples of typical criteria statements you might create with wildcard characters to filter your Address Book.

TABLE 35.2 SAMPLE CRITERIA STATEMENTS WITH WILDCARD CHARACTERS

Field Name	Condition	Value	Result
ZipCode	LIKE	94%	Returns all records with zip codes beginning with the digits 94
LastName	LIKE	B%	Returns all records with last names beginning with B
URL	LIKE	%org	Returns all Web addresses ending with .org

If you want to add further criteria, you can select either the OR or AND operator and continue with the next statement. OR statements make the holes in your filter bigger, so to speak, whereas AND statements make them smaller because records must meet all conditions linked with AND to be returned.

After you have entered all your criteria, you can click the Preview button to see the results in the Beamer (refer to Figure 35.5).

When you're satisfied with your filter, click Next to proceed to the Sort dialog box (see Figure 35.6).

Figure 35.6
You can sort by any fields in your underlying table, even those you have not selected for your query.

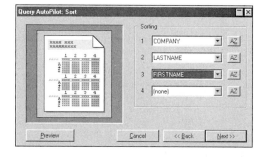

SORTING YOUR DATA

Your sorting options are similar to those you have with the Beamer Sort tool, except that you can sort by four fields here instead of three.

In the Sort dialog, select the fields by which you want to sort, and click the button to the right of the field names to select an ascending (AZ) or descending (ZA) sort.

After you've made your selections, you can click Preview to preview your sort results. If you're not happy with the results, you can click Back and change your settings.

Click Next to move to the final dialog box, the Complete dialog (look ahead to Figure 35.7).

COMPLETING YOUR QUERY

StarBase automatically assigns a name to your query based on the table on which it's based. You can see, for example, the default name `Query_address` assigned to the address table in Figure 35.7.

Figure 35.7
StarBase assigns a name to your query automatically based on standard database naming conventions.

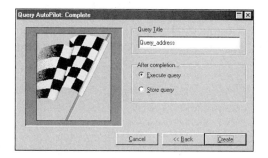

Naming a query in this way follows standard database conventions, which emphasize naming your objects as simply and clearly as possible. You will find it's much easier to keep track of your objects when their names make the relations between different objects apparent and precisely reflect their theme. Note that if you didn't preface this query with the identifier Query, it could not be named after the address table. Just as with files, no two database objects can have the exact same name. If you're worried about the name's length, you can abbreviate Query to qy.

You can choose to execute your query immediately or store the query in your database. You can see results of the query you created previously in Figure 35.8; the address table has been reduced to a few key fields that aid in assigning and managing the codes you insert to help sort and filter your contacts.

Tip #578 from
Michael & Sarah

You can double-click the query column headers to optimize the width of your columns so that you can see all your data.

Figure 35.8
Your completed query looks just like a table—and is in fact just a special view of your table. You can further filter and sort your query results by using the standard tools on the Query toolbar.

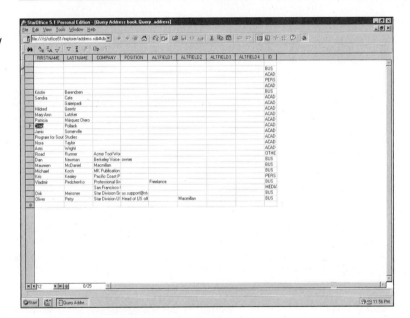

CREATING A QUERY FROM SCRATCH

The logic of creating a query from scratch is the same as creating a query with the AutoPilot. However, the interface is different and somewhat more forbidding because you have no guide pointing to signposts and keeping you on the right road. Creating queries with the AutoPilot a few times may give you a head start in the process.

SELECTING YOUR TABLE(S)

To create a query from scratch, select the Query icon in the database you're working with, right-click to open its context menu, and choose New, Query, Query Design.

A Query Design window opens along with an Add Tables dialog box (see Figure 35.9). In this dialog, select the table you want to use as the basis for your query, and choose Add. If you're working with an ODBC or JDBC client/server database that supports relations or a Microsoft Access or a StarBase format database (Windows only), you can add more than one table. If you're working with a standard dBASE III database such as the Address Book or an imported text database, you can select only one table.

Run Query   Add Table   Clear Query

Figure 35.9
The first step in creating a query in Design view is to select your table.

Address table field list

SQL Mode tab

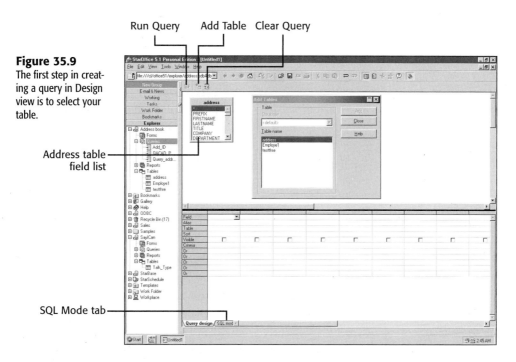

A floating list of the table's fields appears in the upper part of the Design view workspace like the one you see in Figure 35.9.

After you select your table(s), click Close to close the Add Tables dialog.

CREATING A MULTITABLE QUERY

Relational databases are powerful because you can combine data from multiple tables. In SQL, the commands that create relations between tables are called *joins*, and creating relations is called *joining tables*. If you're using StarBase to connect to an external database or are working with a StarBase format relational database (Windows only), you can use these join commands to create multitable queries.

PART
VII

CH
35

Note

If you want to create a query that draws on two or more tables, you must work in Query Design view.

WINDOWS

If you want to create a query that extracts data from more than one table, you must first create joins between the tables. You can create joins only between tables that already have primary keys set. Note that you can do set primary keys only in databases in the native StarBase format (Windows only). If you're working with ODBC, JDBC, or Access databases, you need to set primary keys in the parent applications.

→ For details on setting primary keys, **see** "Preparing Tables for Relations," **p. 1137**.

→ For details on creating joins between tables, **see** "Creating Relationships Between Tables," **p. 1139**.

ORIENTING YOURSELF IN THE DESIGN VIEW WORKSPACE

The Query Design view workspace is relatively barren of visible tools because your work takes place largely in the grid in the lower part of your screen (refer to Figure 35.9).

In the grid, you'll find a Row context menu if you right-click in the header row (see Figure 35.10). Drop-down lists appear in some of the cells, such as the Field and Sort cells, if you click in them. (Refer to Figure 35.9, where you can see such a drop-down list in the first Field cell.) If you right-click in cells without drop-down lists, you see a Cell context menu with the basic editing commands.

Caution

Note that Undo (Ctrl+Z) works only one step back in Query Design view.

Figure 35.10
The Query Design context menu holds the key to filtering out duplicate records with the Distinct Values command.

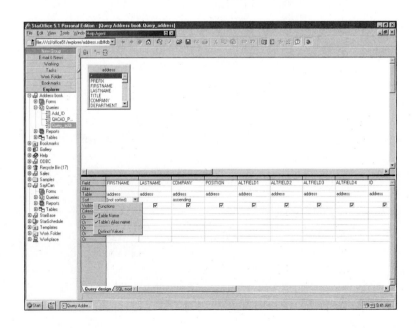

The three tools on the Query object bar are Run Query, Add Table, and Clear Query. Run Query and Add Table are both grayed out in Figure 35.9. Run Query is grayed out because no query exists to run yet. Add Table is grayed out because you have already selected one table, and the Address Book database does not support relations. Well, you might say, if no query exists, then why is the Clear Query button active? Clicking the Clear Query button now would delete the address table field list; you would then be able to click the Add Table button and start again.

Another feature to notice in this window is the SQL Mode tab at the bottom. After you create your graphical query, you can click this tab to reveal SQL's backstage chatter that actually does the work of executing your query.

The row headers on the left indicate the components you have at your disposal to construct your query, some of which correspond to options in the AutoPilot Wizard and some of which are available only in Query Design view. Some components (such as Functions) are visible only after you open the Row header context menu and select them.

Table 35.3 lists the components of a Query Design query.

TABLE 35.3   COMPONENTS OF A QUERY IN QUERY DESIGN VIEW

Use This Row...	To Do This...
Field	Select a field to be included in your query.
Alias	Assign an alias (substitute name) to the selected field. This capability can be useful if your field name is long or difficult to understand. The names of calculated fields you create with SQL statements also appear here.
Table	Select the table from which the field is drawn. If you are working with text or dBASE databases, or ODBC/JDBC databases that do not support relations, you have only one table from which to choose.
Sort	Sort your query by the selected field in ascending or descending order.
Visible	Make the field visible or invisible in the resulting query. The check box must be empty for the field to be hidden.
Functions	Perform a calculation on your selected field to create a calculated field.
Criteria	Create expressions that will be used to filter your query.
Or	Extend your filter with additional criteria expressions.

You can adjust the size of the two panes as you can other windows in StarOffice by dragging the border between them, and you can navigate within each pane by using the scrollbars.

ADDING FIELDS

Now that you have selected your table, you need to select the fields you want to appear in your query. You do so by simply dragging and dropping field names from the Field names list. Just drop the name onto any cell in the grid; if you drop it on a column header, it does not work. StarBase automatically places your field in the leftmost empty column. It does not allow empty columns between data, so you must add your fields in the order you want to see them.

If you are working on a single-table query, alternatively, you can click in the Field names list and select a field from the drop-down list. If you are creating a multitable query, you need to specify which table you are referring to in each row before you can select fields from the drop-down list.

Just as when you use the AutoPilot, you can still filter and sort by fields that you don't choose to appear. However, because you can also choose to hide fields, you can add a field that you want to use only as a filtering or sorting mechanism, which can make it easier to see what you're doing.

Tip #579 from
Michael & Sarah

By dragging and dropping the asterisk symbol (*) at the top of the Field name list, you enter your entire table into the Field cell.

After you've added your fields, you're ready to go to serious work building your query.

BUILDING AND MODIFYING QUERIES

The processes for building a new query and modifying an existing one are the same; you just have a head start with an existing query. To open an existing query in Design view, select the query in its Explorer database, right-click, and choose Query Design.

The steps for completing or modifying your query in the design grid once your fields are selected are as follows:

- Determine the sort order of your query, if any, in the Sort field.
- Enter criteria statements in the Criteria and Or fields to filter your query.
- Choose the Distinct Values command from the context menu if you want to exclude duplicate records.
- Deselect any fields that you want to hide in your final query results.

To specify a sort order, click Sort underneath the field name by which you want to sort, and choose Ascending or Descending. (To remove a sort, click None on this list.)

To specify criteria for a field in the design grid, enter an expression in the Criteria cell for that field. An expression consists of two parts: an *operator* and a *value*. The operator tells StarBase how to evaluate and treat the value you enter. The value tells StarBase what to look for.

You can enter simple expressions such as a company name, for example, if you want to pull up only records of contacts at a specific company in your Address Book. You can also use the list of operators in Table 35.1 to construct more complex criteria, as well as use the same types of expressions listed in Table 35.2 for values in LIKE and NOT LIKE expressions. Your values can be dates, numbers, and/or text strings, depending on your chosen operator.

A typical use of criteria in a query is to filter addresses so that only zip codes from a certain area appear to prepare for a mail merge. You enter LIKE 94%, for example, to create criteria that selects only those addresses with zip codes beginning with the number 94.

> You cannot use the BETWEEN criteria in dBASE format databases.

When you press Enter or click in another cell, StarBase automatically adds the correct punctuation and symbols—an equals sign as your operator and apostrophe marks around your work to indicate that it is data, not a command. It's best to let StarBase take care of the punctuation so that you can avoid entry errors.

Note Remember that StarBase is case sensitive and make sure that the values you specify in criteria match the case of the values in the underlying table or tables

ELIMINATING DUPLICATE RECORDS AND RECORDS WITH EMPTY FIELDS

To eliminate duplicate records in your query results, open the Row header context menu by placing your cursor on the row header and right-clicking; then choose Distinct Values.

To eliminate records with empty fields, click in the Criteria cell underneath that field name, type NOT EMPTY, and press Enter. This criteria statement filters the entire table of any record with a null value in that field.

CREATING CALCULATED FIELDS

If you want to create updateable calculated fields in StarBase, you can choose from two methods: using the built-in functions or writing a SQL statement that creates a calculated field.

The StarBase native format has a small number of built-in functions that become available when you open the Row header context menu (right-click) and select Functions. This action adds a row named Function to your query grid. If you click in a cell in the row, a drop-down list appears. You can open this list to select a function. Available functions are SUM, COUNT, and AVERAGE. (You can also return the MAXIMUM and MINIMUM values and GROUP fields together.)

Note You can add this row in databases of any format, but the functions don't work in dBASE or text databases. They work only in StarBase format databases.

For more details on working in SQL mode, see the section "Editing in SQL Mode" later in this section.

HIDING FIELDS

To hide a field in your query result, deselect the check box in the Visible field.

EDITING IN SQL MODE

When you click the SQL Mode tab at the bottom of the Query Design window, you enter the world of SQL, which is, unlike the query design grid you left behind, a structureless white screen with nothing but long unbroken lines of text (see Figure 35.11).

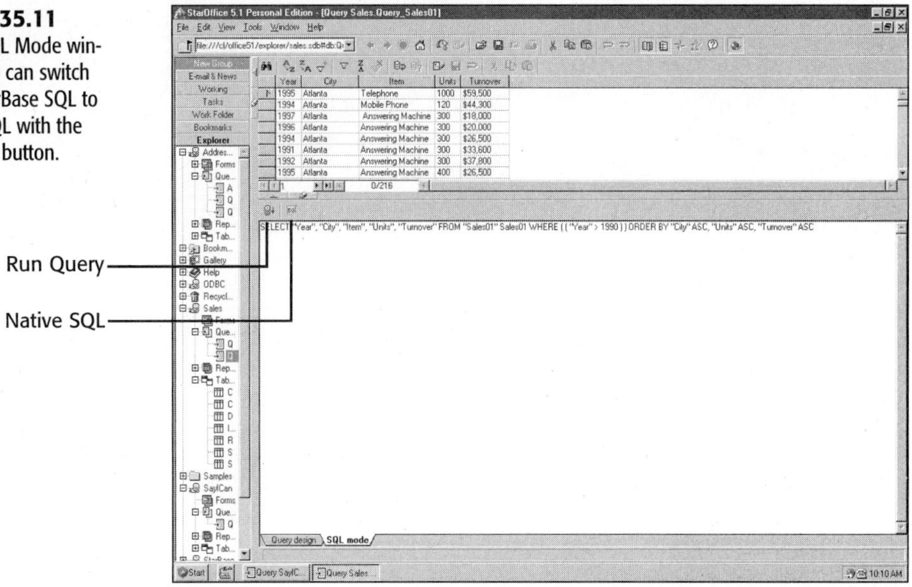

Figure 35.11
In the SQL Mode window, you can switch from StarBase SQL to native SQL with the click of a button.

Run Query

Native SQL

Notice the two buttons on the SQL Mode toolbar. The button on the left executes your query; the button on the right switches you into Native SQL mode. Be aware that if you switch to Native SQL mode and begin editing, you might not be able to return to graphical Query Design mode because native SQL implements some SQL commands differently than StarBase, and StarBase lacks some SQL commands altogether.

Note

If you switch to native SQL, save your query, and exit, the next time you select your query in the Explorer and right-click, the Design View command will be grayed out and unavailable. You must choose the Enter SQL Statement command to open your query, which opens only in SQL mode.

Tip #580 from
Michael & Sarah

Because SQL is read by computer programs that don't care whether SQL statements are easy to scan with human eyes, StarOffice generates its SQL statements in long lines. While you're working in SQL mode, you can break up existing lines and enter new lines by themselves if doing so makes it easier for you to work. However, after you run the query, StarOffice erases any breaks or spaces and returns it to "normal" SQL view.

You can edit text in this window just as you can in a database table: Use your Backspace and Delete keys to delete, and your standard editing shortcuts to cut, copy, and paste. If you right-click, you pull up the same context menu you find in tables; you can even insert special characters although adding characters is more dangerous than useful when you're writing SQL statements! You can also undo editing commands by using Undo (Ctrl+Z)—although it undoes only one step backward. Don't rely on this tool in a lazy way, or you might regret it!

EXAMINING A TYPICAL SQL STATEMENT

You can learn some SQL basics by examining a typical SQL statement generated by StarBase when you create a graphical query. This simple query merely selects a limited set of fields from a larger table and sorts them in alphabetical order by one of those fields:

```
SELECT "ProductID", "Product", "CatalogNo", "PriceRan", "Category"
    FROM "Talk_Type" Talk_Type
    ORDER BY "Product" ASC
```

The SELECT command, one of the most frequently used SQL commands, selects the columns identified by the field names that come after it. Notice that the field names are surrounded by quotation marks ("), and each field name is followed by a comma and a single space until the last field in the chain. A space but no comma appears between the final field and the next command, FROM. (Here, the statement is broken artificially into lines to make it easier to read.) When you enter a SQL statement yourself, you must be sure you enter the punctuation correctly, or your statement may not run.

The FROM command specifies the table that is the source of your fields, whereas the ORDER BY command specifies that the resulting query should be sorted by the Product field in ascending (ASC) order.

CREATING CALCULATED FIELDS WITH SQL

Although StarBase has a few built-in functions, you can't perform many calculations with them. If you want to create a calculated field to perform calculations other than SUM or AVERAGE in a StarBase format database, you must write a SQL statement. You can attach these SQL statements to your forms as well (which is the only way you can create a calculated field on a form in StarBase).

> **Note**
> You cannot create calculated fields in a dBASE or text format database.

The following SQL statement is a simple example of such a statement applied to a StarBase format table that lists invoice information for small company. The table has fields for price of an item and the number of units of that item purchased. To complete the invoice, you obviously would want to create a subtotals field that multiplies the price by the number of units:

```
SELECT "Price", "Units", "Price" * "Units" AS "Subtotal" FROM "Invoice" Invoice
```
The AS command is used to created a field that does not exist in the original table but is the result of an expression. The field appears when you run your query but the data in it isn't stored; only the expression is stored, and the results are calculated every time you open or run the query. The FROM command indicates the database in which the table is stored.

Here's a more complex series of examples taken from a database that tracks employees' salaries and personnel information. This example shows you a range of arithmetical functions at work.

The database has a table for employee salaries (Salaries), among others). If you wanted to calculate a payroll tax on employees' salaries, you could write an expression like this:

```
SELECT DISTINCT "PersNo", "Name", "Income", "Income" * 0.015 AS "Tax"
FROM "Salaries"
```

The statement generated a query that displays a complete list of employees by personnel number (PersNo), name, and income, and creates a calculated field, Tax, that is the result of multiplying the value in the Income field by 0.015 (since the payroll tax is 1.5 percent of income.) The SELECT DISTINCT command ensures that you are selecting only unique records, that is, a single instance of the PersNo field.

If you wanted to calculate the estimated federal taxes for each employee to assist them with tax planning, you would need to create queries that could sort people by income bracket. One method is to use the WHERE clause, as in the following example:

```
SELECT DISTINCT "PersNo", "Name", "Income", "Income" * .25 AS "EstTax"
FROM "Salaries"
WHERE "Income" < 30000
```

If departments have separate accounting systems, you might want to add up the payroll tax by department. To do this, you can use the SUM expression:

```
SELECT DISTINCT "Department", SUM( "Income" * 0.15 ) AS "DepTax"
FROM "Salaries"
GROUP BY "Department"
```

The GROUP BY clause, just as its name suggests, sorts and groups the data in the table by department, lining up the data so SUM can do its work.

To calculate the average income by department, you can use the AVG (average) expression, as in the following example:

```
SELECT DISTINCT AVG( "Income" ), "Department"
FROM "Salaries" Salaries
GROUP BY "Department"
```

You can also create complex expressions that use more than one arithmetical operator. For example, if you had employees who wanted $200 in additional withholding taken from their salaries, beyond their estimated tax, you could modify the expression used earlier to calculate the estimated tax like this:

```
SELECT DISTINCT "PersNo", "Name", "Income", "Income" * .25 + 200 AS "EstTax"
```

You can also use the subtraction (-) and division (/) operators in the same ways as you see the multiplication (*) and addition (+) operators used.

SAVING YOUR QUERY

To save your query, click the Save icon in the function bar, or choose the Save As command from the File menu. If you choose the Save As command, you are prompted to enter a name for the query in a dialog box. As you learned earlier in the section on creating a query with the AutoPilot, using the standard naming conventions is good practice. Naming the query involves using some variation of the word *Query* as the beginning of the name, followed by an underscore, and then the name of the table on which your query is based—for example, Qry_Address.

If you want to save your query as a native SQL query, you must be in Query Design mode. Once in Query Design mode, click the Query Mode tab. Then, click the native SQL button that appears and save your query as usual with the File menu Save or Save As command. If you are creating a mix of native and non-native queries, you might want to note that a query is native SQL in its name, for example, naming it *NatQry_Orders*. Remember that once you've converted a query to native SQL you cannot edit it in graphical query mode. (You can always copy the SQL statement and paste it into the Query Mode window of a new query, as long as the statement contain only SQL expressions that StarBase recognizes.)

If you don't save your query yourself, StarOffice prompts you to save when you exit.

SELECTIVELY INSERTING DATA WITH FIELDS

Fields are special codes hidden in your document that instruct StarOffice to insert data in place of the field when you complete a mail merge or generate the document. One key benefit of using fields is that the resulting text is not static; fields are dynamic. They can be updated to reflect the most current information at the time StarOffice translates from fields to text.

Fields are extensively discussed in Chapter 9, "Working with Tables, Charts, and Fields," in the context of using StarWriter because text documents make the most use of fields, many of which are specific to text documents and have nothing to do with databases. However, some fields—specifically the database fields used in conjunction with mail merge fields—are designed to extract data from databases to insert into text documents and are therefore more appropriate to discuss in connection with working with databases.

→ For a general introduction to fields and details on using the entire range of fields in StarWriter, **see** "Understanding Fields," **p. 349**, and "Working with Fields," **p. 350**.

Normally, in a mail merge, you generate multiple documents—that is, a group of letters, each of which is addressed to a different person. Using the special database field codes combined with mail merge fields (but not the Mail Merge dialog box), you can create a single document that extracts data from your database, such as a catalog. Using database fields in this way is a powerful alternative to creating reports because you have a lot more flexibility in how you position and format your inserted data.

GETTING READY TO MERGE

The field commands discussed here work by identifying records by their number in the Beamer table or query you open while you're working and inserting them in sequential order. Therefore, the first step in creating a catalog or other merged document from your database is to prepare a query that contains only the data you want to include in your final document, arranged in the order in which you want it to appear. (To achieve the desired ordering, you might need to create a field especially for this task and code your records.) For example, if you were creating a catalog, you might filter to exclude products that you no longer carry or are out of stock, and then sort by category and then by product name.

When your query is ready, open it in the Beamer. Then open a StarWriter document. This document will become your catalog. You might want to prepare your text to receive your database fields; for example, you could insert your catalog information in tables, if you want, or you might want to insert plain (non-field) text. You can also do some initial formatting, applying background graphics, formatting your page, and so on, although you won't want to do final formatting until after you have inserted your fields.

> **Note**
>
> If you are working with a relational database, you can insert data from multiple tables by basing it on a multiple table query.

INSERTING DATABASE FIELDS

With your table or query open in the Beamer and your StarWriter document open on your desktop, you are now ready to insert your database fields. Just follow these steps:

1. Open the Fields dialog box by choosing Insert, Fields, Other or pressing Ctrl+F2 (see Figure 35.12).

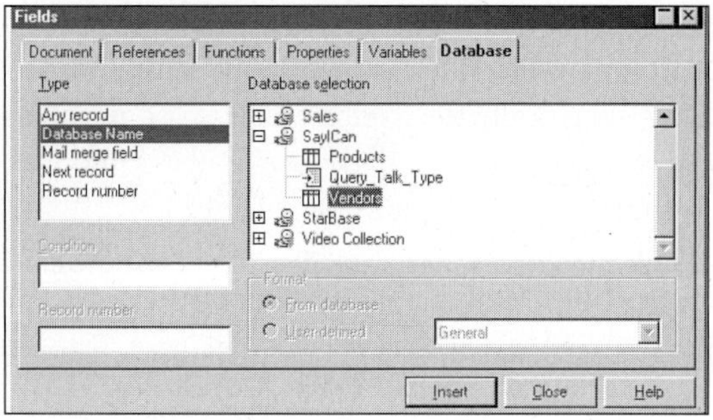

Figure 35.12
You can insert both ordinary mail merge fields and database fields from the Fields dialog box.

2. Click the Database tab to bring it to the top.

3. In the Type field list on the left, select Any Record.

4. Select the table or query whose data you want to insert on the right.

5. Leave the condition set at TRUE. In the Record Number text box, type the number 1. This means your catalog will begin by inserting the first record (record number 1) that appears in your table or query in the Beamer into the first field. (You can start at any record number you like, of course.)

4. Click Insert to insert the Any Record field into your document. Your document should look something like Figure 35.13. If you don't see the field names as they appear here, press Ctrl+F9 to toggle between the field names and the field contents.

Caution

You can keep the Fields dialog open while you work. If it's blocking your view, click the Minimize button in the upper-right corner to hide it.

Figure 35.13
The first step in creating a merged document is inserting a database field to indicate your data source and the Any Record command associated with a table. These fields will not be visible in your final document.

Note

If you neglect to enter a number in the Record Number field, your data insertion will result in blank fields.

7. Reposition your cursor within your StarWriter document if necessary. (The field is inserted at your cursor location.) The Any Record field you inserted previously is the only control field and doesn't result in text after the merge so don't fuss about positioning it, but the mail merge fields you are about to insert will produce text, so position them appropriately. Note that the fields take on the format of the paragraph into which they're inserted.

8. Choose the Mail Merge Field option in the Type list in the Fields dialog. When you do, you see plus signs (+) appear to the left of the databases listed in the Database Selection window. Click the plus sign next to your selected table or query to open a list of its fields.

Tip #581 from
Michael & Sarah

If you prefer, you can insert your mail merge fields by dragging and dropping the appropriate column headings from the Beamer into your document instead of using the Fields dialog box. You must insert the other fields by using the dialog box, however.

---

9. Select the first field you want to insert, and click Insert.

10. Select any additional fields you want to insert, and click Insert to complete your first catalog entry.

11. Press Enter to start a new line, or otherwise position your cursor as you want to begin your second catalog entry.

12. In the Fields dialog, select the Next Record field type and the same table or query. Make sure the condition is TRUE. Click Insert.

13. Select the Mail Merge Field type again, open the list of available fields, and insert the same fields in your document as you did in steps 6 and 7.

14. Repeat steps 11 and 12 until you have made as many entries as you have records in your database.

Note

Don't just copy and paste the fields. Insert them via the Fields dialog box or the merge will not work properly.

Tip #582 from
Michael & Sarah

You can create macros or StarBasic scripts to execute these kinds of routine, repetitive tasks.

---

15. After you have entered all your fields, click Close to exit the Fields dialog box.

16. Press Ctrl+F9 to see the contents of your document. Make sure that all your fields are inserted appropriately.

17. Save your document.

18. Finish adding text and formatting your document as required.

19. Print your document to the printer or a file. Make sure you still have field code names turned off and field contents turned on (see step 13).

Note

If you insert new records into your table, you need to insert additional StarWriter fields into your document; your document does not automatically add new records. If you change the context of existing records, you can update your StarWriter fields by opening the source table or query in the Beamer, selecting the entire table or query, and clicking the Data to Fields tool. The easiest way to select the entire table or query is to click the gray button that marks the intersection of the row and column headers, just beneath the Lookup Records button on the Beamer toolbar.

Tip #583 from
Michael & Sarah

If you want to avoid blank fields from your database from translating into blank printed lines in your StarWriter document, try this trick. Insert the Hidden Paragraph field at the beginning of your line. Add a condition "not(fieldname)." This prevents StarWriter from printing records that contain no information in that field. Note that you still see the empty lines in both normal view and print preview. However, the blank paragraphs will not be printed.

TROUBLESHOOTING

I want to create a query based on two StarBase tables, but I can't assign a primary key to my tables! They open in Read-only view with the Edit button unavailable.

Select your database, right-click, and choose Properties. In the Properties dialog box, click the Administration tab to see whether the option Exclusive Access is selected. (It's the default.) If it is, deselect it and choose OK. Now see whether you can edit your tables.

You might also try closing StarOffice, rebooting, and trying again.

If you're still unable to edit, your database may be corrupt. Try copying your tables into another database and opening them from there. (Make sure it is also a StarBase database if you already have relations set, or you will lose your relations.)

I tried to open my query but got an error dialog box telling me that it could not resolve my field name (see Figure 35.14).

This error dialog signals that you have renamed or deleted a field in the table underlying your query, so StarBase can't find the field and data indicated in your query. You should open the query either in Design mode or SQL mode (whichever you feel more comfortable using), and immediately correct the field assignments in the query so that they match the new structure of your table. Otherwise, you risk corrupting the file and losing it entirely.

I'm using a Microsoft Access database, but sometimes I can't change Boolean values or some other types of values.

Try connecting to your database using ODBC. StarOffice has some bugs that make it handle these values differently.

I created a query, but my colleagues can't find my query in the database.

You are probably using StarBase to connect to an external data source (an OBBC, JDBC, or SQL server database). StarOffice doesn't save any queries (or forms or reports) to the external data source; it saves them to a StarOffice database file. If you want to share your queries or other database elements with your colleagues, you must give them copies of your .sdb file. (Of course, they must have StarOffice available to open the .sdb file in StarBase.)

Figure 35.14

Because queries are built on the foundations of tables, changes to their underlying tables can generate errors and even corrupt the query files.

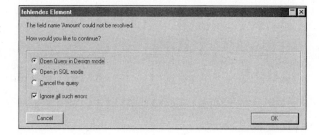

CHAPTER 36

CREATING AND PRINTING REPORTS

In this chapter

CREATING A NEW REPORT

With StarBase's total integration into the StarOffice desktop, you have many creative ways to extract data from tables and queries. Chapters on StarWriter and StarMail explore using the Address Book database to address email and letters, and using database fields and mail merge to create form letters and mass emailings. Chapter 35, "Getting Answers with Queries and Fields," discusses using database fields to create a document like a catalog that draws information from a database. However, there are still other ways to extract data from your StarBase database in presentable form. This chapter explores creating more traditional database reports, where you directly generate and print the contents of a table or query.

UNDERSTANDING REPORT OPTIONS

There are two methods of creating a report:

- Using the AutoPilot report wizard
- Dragging and dropping your data from the Beamer into a StarWriter, StarCalc, or an HTML document

When you create a report with the AutoPilot, you have a selection of preset formats that you can later modify in any way you want. Your data is inserted into a table that you manipulate and format like a table in StarWriter   in fact, your StarBase report is just another kind of text document in StarOffice. The big difference is that your StarBase report is linked to your source data in your StarBase table(s) and is updated each time you open it to reflect the latest data. (You can also update your report manually from the desktop.) New to version 5.1, you can save your StarBase report in a variety of document types   but you lose the links to the database and your report can no longer be updated.

Working with StarBase report tables can feel limiting sometimes, but you're not really limited in how you can create reports, as you have another alternative in report design   you can drag and drop data into the standard StarOffice document types. Among other things, you can import your data as fields into StarWriter, so you can (in theory) create an updateable report template (although the Update function for fields appears to be seriously broken in the initial release of version 5.1). You can use either the StarWriter Text Formula bar or the StarCalc Formula bar to insert functions and create subtotals. You also have the same wide range of export options. However, as you should already be familiar with the essentials of creating documents in StarWriter, StarWriter/Web, and StarCalc, the bulk of this chapter addresses creating and modifying reports using the StarBase AutoPilot. Only the final section details using the Beamer and drag-and-drop to insert StarBase data into non-StarBase documents.

FLYING ON AUTOPILOT

Start a new report by selecting File, AutoPilot, Report or New, Report from the Table object context menu in your database in the Explorer.

If you don't already have a database selected in the Explorer, the first dialog presents you with a drop-down list of all your databases, above a list of table names from the currently selected database. Select your desired database first, and then select the table from which you want to create a report.

If you start by selecting Table New, Report, you see the Table Selection dialog, like the one in Figure 36.1, listing all the tables and queries in your selected database.

Note

If you're working with a StarBase database or an ODBC database where relations are maintained, you can create reports that draw together data from multiple tables.

Figure 36.1
The first step in creating your report is selecting the table that will provide its data.

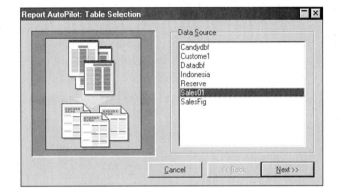

After you select your table, click Next. In the following dialog—the Field Selection dialog shown in Figure 36.2—you choose the fields you want to appear in your report by selecting them and clicking the arrow to move them into the window labeled Chosen Fields.

Figure 36.2
To select all fields at once, click the double-headed arrow. To move fields one at a time or in selected groups, select using the usual selection techniques and click the single-headed arrow.

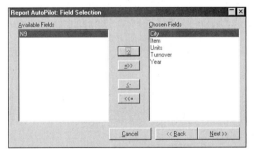

Click Next. The Outline dialog appears, allowing you to select the fields by which you want to group your data (see Figure 36.3). You don't have to choose any fields, in which case your data appears as a simple list. If you chose to group, your data appears in a more complex format, with your group fields as headers for the main data.

Tip #584 from
Michael & Sarah

In the following dialog, you can choose to sort your data—but you can't sort by any field you're already using as a group header.

Figure 36.3

In this example, where a long sales report is being created, it's a good idea to group the data so it is easier to read. Here, it is grouped first by year and then by city.

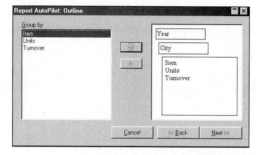

Click Next to move to the dialog where you can determine a simple sort order for your data—the Sort Options dialog (see Figure 36.4). You can sort by as many as four fields, each in ascending or descending order.

Figure 36.4

You can choose sort fields from the drop-down lists or leave them all set at None.

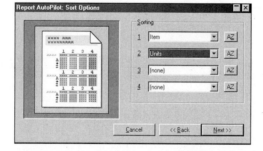

The Style Selection dialog shows you nearing your goal—here you can begin making formatting choices (see Figure 36.5). The default page orientation is landscape, as this is assumed to be the best layout for tables, but you can change it to portrait. Click any of the layout options to see a rough preview of it in the preview section to the left.

Figure 36.5

You can choose from six preset looks for your report—but you can always modify your report format later by opening it in design view.

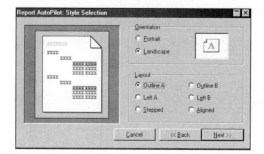

The Format Style dialog, shown in Figure 36.6, enables you to complete your formatting choices by choosing the page style you prefer. Again, you can select a Style to see its preview to the left.

Tip #585 from
Michael & Sarah

For a more lasting design solution, you can customize any or all of the four report template wizards. To open a wizard, choose File, Open and navigate to the Office51\templates\wizard directory. (You won't find this directory if you use the program shortcuts to the Templates folders—StarOffice tries to save you from dangerous meddling by making it tricky to get to the wizard directory from within StarOffice. Just navigate in the conventional way.) The report wizards are listed by their document titles Compact, Professional, Professional Compact, and Standard.

Open the template you want to modify, make your changes, and change the report title on the File, Properties dialog Description tab. This gives it a unique name for the AutoPilot menu. The default templates are named rpst01.vor rpst04.vor. Modify your filename as appropriate for example, naming it rpst05 and save it. It appears on your AutoPilot menu the next time you use it.

Figure 36.6
Choosing your page style is the last step before naming and creating your report.

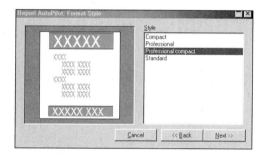

After you click Next, you'll see the final AutoPilot dialog, waving a racing flag so you know you're almost done. By default, the name of your table (or query) has been inserted as the report name, but you can change it. (Note that a report name is not restricted in length as are names of tables and queries.) You also need to select whether you want see the report immediately or just save it in the Explorer without opening.

Tip #586 from
Michael & Sarah

If your underlying table has a lot of data, it can take a long time to generate the report. If you're not going to print the report right away, or if you just want to check its design, you should select Store Report.

Click Create, and StarOffice takes it from there. Your finished report should look something like the report in Figure 36.7, which shows part of a fairly long and complex sales report. This report is based on a database table used initially as an example in Chapters 18 and 19 on working with databases in StarCalc. It was exported as a `*.dbf` file from StarCalc and then imported into StarBase.

Figure 36.7
Your completed report should look something like this. Note how the data has been grouped by the Year and City fields, which are given formats that make them serve as headings for the data.

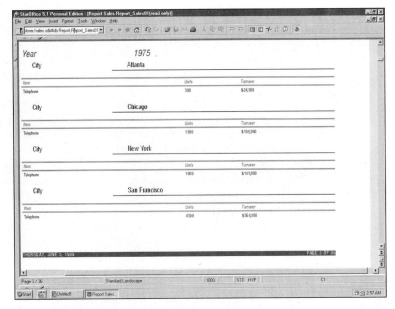

As you can see, the grouping you can accomplish with a table and the grouping function itself are limited. If you want to group your data in more of a summary form, you need to create a query that groups your data the way you want it. Even if you're a whiz at SQL, you might find that StarCalc's Data Pilot makes summarizing your data easier and that it presents your data in a more appealing graphic format.

If you choose to generate your report, it opens in Read-Only view. That's why you don't see many tools visible in Figure 36.7—editing and formatting tools are unavailable. You cannot activate design view from inside a read-only report, but must open the report in design view from the Explorer. You can have both views open at once.

Be sure to check the report's layout before printing because StarBase doesn't necessarily keep group headers together with their data. If you're using the default AutoPilot templates, it's likely that you will need to adjust the styles so that the headers will automatically stay together with the following data.

Tip #587 from
Michael & Sarah

Select the Keep With Next Paragraph option in the paragraph styles of the headers in the report templates to ensure a header always remains together with its data.

MODIFYING REPORTS

To modify your report layout and formatting, select it in the Explorer, right-click, and select Report Design. You see a much reduced document—just a single table with the report name and field names inserted where appropriate. For example, the report design for the 36-page report shown in Figure 36.7 becomes just the tiny 1-page document you see in Figure 36.8.

Figure 36.8
Editing and formatting your StarBase report requires no learning curve at all if you're already familiar with StarWriter tables and formatting commands.

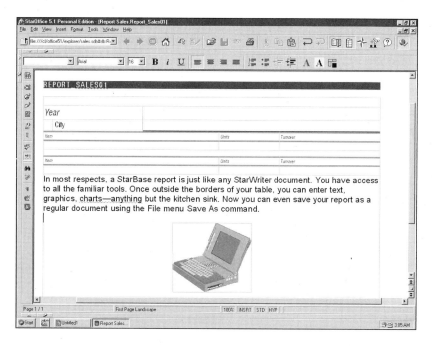

You can now format your report much as you would a StarWriter document with a table. You can also insert text or objects outside the borders of the table, or add backgrounds and other graphics effects to your page.

There are a few differences, however, between working with tables in StarWriter and in a StarBase report. You cannot alter the structure of the table. If you find that the structure really just doesn't do, you need to create a new report. The formatting is achieved by applying special styles. If you need to change the text flow characteristics, for example, so that your pages break properly, you need to select the cell you need to change, open the Stylist, and choose the All Styles option. That should flush out the style you need to change. (As noted in an earlier tip, you can also edit the report wizard templates to create your own styles.)

Caution

Although technically you are able to remove any part of your data table (that is, the Delete commands work), this action does not delete the field(s) and causes an error message the next time you open your report. The report still opens, but the data is not generated properly.

Tip #588 from
Michael & Sarah

If you keep your report open simultaneously in read-only view and design view, you can see the effect of your formatting changes as you go along. As you make changes, switch back to read-only view and click the Reload button on the Function bar.

Given that you cannot delete or rearrange any of your table fields, though, you might feel that your style is cramped. Because of their close links with the underlying table, reports are somewhat stiff and rigid in their handling. Don't fret, though, as you have a powerful alternative, outlined in this chapter's last section: importing your data into "normal" StarOffice documents.

PREVIEWING AND PRINTING REPORTS

You can choose File, Page View/Print Preview to preview your report. Again, it's the same as working with a StarWriter document. It's a good idea to check your document in this view before printing to ensure that the data breaks properly across pages—you can use the multipage layouts to good advantage.

→ For more information about using Page View mode, **see** "Previewing Documents," **p. 475**.

CREATING REPORTS WITH OTHER STAROFFICE DOCUMENTS

Getting your data from StarBase into a StarCalc document is as simple as dragging and dropping from the Beamer. Each field is inserted into a column, and each record into a row.

Getting your data into a text document or an HTML document is almost as simple, but there's a dialog box to navigate along the way. You can choose to insert your data as text, as a table, or as fields.

After you've inserted your data, you're outside StarBase's realm and back into the world of ordinary StarOffice documents.

To drag and drop data into a StarCalc document, follow the first five steps given here. To bring data into a StarWriter document, follow the complete sequence of steps:

1. Prepare your StarBase table or query so that it has all the information you want to import. Don't worry too much about filtering your data, as you will be able to select both the records and fields you import later on as well.

2. Open your table or query in the Beamer.

3. Apply any sorting or filtering commands as necessary. (For example, you might want to perform an alphabetical sort, or create a filter that filters out records with null values in a specific field.)

4. Open the document you want to use to create your report. You can use an existing document or create a new one.

5. If you want to import all the data into your document, click the gray rectangle that marks the upper-left corner of the table or query in the Beamer—located where the column and row headers intersect (see Figure 36.9). (This is the same place you click in a StarCalc spreadsheet to select all on a worksheet.) All the data in your table or query is selected. Don't let go of the mouse button, but just drag immediately from that rectangle into your open document.

Figure 36.9
The ability to drag and drop selected data from the Beamer into a StarWriter or StarCalc document as a table, text, or fields gives you incredible flexibility in creating reports from StarBase data.

Click here to select all the visible data in your table or query

Click a row header to select a record

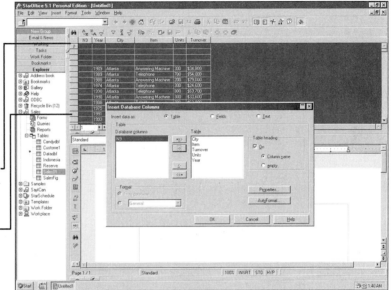

Or, alternately, if you only want to import selected records, select those records by using the standard Shift+click and Ctrl+click methods. Drag from one of the row headers into your open document.

6. An Insert Database Columns dialog box like the one in Figure 36.9 appears. At the top, you have three choices for inserting your data: as a table, as fields, or as text. Click your selection.

Note

Note that the Tools menu Update function does not seem to work in the initial release of version 5.1 which makes the Fields option useless.

7. Depending on the option you choose, different formatting options will appear.

If you choose the Table option (refer to Figure 36.9), you can insert your field names as column headings; leave room for headings that you might supply later (Empty); or leave column headers off by deselecting On. Click the Properties button to set the properties of your table manually, or click the AutoFormat button to choose from StarOffice's preset table formats.

→ For more information on formatting tables, **see** "Formatting and Editing Tables," **p. 329**.

> If you choose the Fields or Text options, you can choose a paragraph style to apply from the drop-down list of currently loaded styles.

→ For more information on creating paragraph formats, **see** "Defining a Style," **p. 298**.

8. Select the database columns (fields) that you want to insert in the window on the left, and move them into the window on the right by using the arrow buttons.

9. Click OK.

That's it! Your data is inserted, and you're ready to print or continue editing your document.

Tip #589 from *Michael & Sarah*	If you've inserted your data as fields and want to see what your printed report will look like, you can press Ctrl+F9 to toggle your fields between displaying the field names and displaying actual data; or you can choose the Page Preview command.

TROUBLESHOOTING

I've opened my table in the Beamer to move data into a document, but I can't select data in fields.

You can't select because the table is in read-only mode. However, you can still drag and drop the field contents as usual.

I've tried moving data in the way you suggest, but I manage to move only one field of data at a time!

You must be trying to select or move a row from within a field, not from the row header. You must both select and drag from the row header or the gray rectangle that marks the upper-left corner of the table or query in the Beamer.

I try to open my StarBase report, but I just get an error message. The report opens, but all I get is an empty table.

If you've deleted or modified any fields in your StarBase report, you will get error messages and your report will not generate properly. You cannot change your fields after you've created a report. Create another report in StarBase, or import your data selectively into a StarOffice text or spreadsheet document by using the methods described in "Creating Reports with Other StarOffice Documents."

I've tried to create a new report, but I only get an error message about missing objects.

Open the Tools menu Options "master dialog" box and ensure that your path settings for the file types AutoPilots, BASIC, and Document templates are the program default settings. AutoPilots are programmed using StarBasic and StarOne. Therefore, StarOffice depends on the AutoPilots, BASIC, and document templates paths to locate the program code and data it needs to run the AutoPilots. When you are in the Paths dialog box, select each file type and click the Default button. This automatically returns each path to its default setting. Their path settings should be Office51\config\wizard; Office51\basic; and Office51\Template, respectively.

When I get to the Format Style page of the report, there are no styles offered.

Again, check the path settings for the Document templates file type. If an AutoPilot can't find the appropriate templates in the StarOffice Template directory, it won't be able to create a report.

0

Automating Your Work—StarBasic

CHAPTER 37

FAMILIARIZING YOURSELF WITH STARBASIC

In this chapter

by Werner Roth

INTRODUCING STARBASIC

StarOffice is so easy to customize that you may not even find it necessary to go beyond the basic set of tools and commands provided on the desktop. Using a macro language like StarBasic may sound complicated and may seem to be a job for the sort of person who likes to tinker, however this is not true. Even if you've never dealt with macros or programming languages before, using StarBasic to speed up your daily work is not as complicated as it may appear. Simply record a series of keystrokes and StarOffice will replay them by running a macro. You won't even find it necessary to look at your macro; it will run in the background. By improving your everyday work you can delve deeper into StarBasic, step by step, allowing you to become a StarBasic programmer just by completing everyday tasks. You never know, you may even end up programming an entire application using StarBasic within a couple of months.

WHAT IS STARBASIC?

Like many other office suites, StarOffice is fitted with a macro program and programming language called StarBasic. The people of Star Division designed StarBasic following the same principles found in Microsoft's Visual Basic for Applications (VBA). Hence, StarBasic is based upon the programming structure of VBA. If you're familiar with VBA of Microsoft Office you should feel comfortable using StarBasic. Through learning the paradigms of StarOffice you are exposed to its object hierarchy structure. For example, you can port your Word macros to StarWriter macros.

Note

Although compatible with VBA, StarBasic macros and modules can't be used directly in Microsoft Office because they refer to StarOffice objects, not MS Office objects. You therefore need to edit any macros you import or export. For more information, see the section "Do I Have to Deal with Objects?" later in this chapter.

You can control almost all of StarOffice's functions by using StarBasic. You can execute tasks that usually require a series of repetitive mouse clicks or keyboard entries with a StarBasic program. You can also build your own converter to convert files received from another department into a StarOffice file, for example, or define your own function for a spreadsheet. With StarBasic, you can even create an entire application with a proper user interface. In addition, StarBasic applications port directly across platforms, so you can develop a program on Linux, say, and port it directly to StarOffice on Windows.

More than just a macro recorder, StarBasic is outfitted with a complete Integrated Development Environment (IDE). Although you can, of course, use it to assay, edit, or delete your recorded macros, with the IDE you can go to the next level and develop entire StarBasic projects for your company or organization.

What Is StarOne?

Star Division launched StarOne as an Application Programming Interface (API) for StarOffice. StarOne is designed for use within StarOffice as well as to control StarOffice from within other applications. The StarOne interface is intended to be all-purpose. In future versions of StarOffice, it will be possible to reuse StarOffice components to paint text on the screen or use a complete StarOffice program just by dropping a StarOne-Object on a form in your Java Development Software.

StarOne, however, is still in its early stages of development. The first version of StarOne was included in StarOffice 5.0 as an internal interface to StarOffice. Although it has been improved in version 5.1, StarOne remains an inferior cousin to StarBasic.

Why Use StarBasic?

Have you ever felt frustrated with having to repeat the same sequence of keystrokes over and over again? Or needing to format thousands of tables so they all look the same? It's only natural that you should because performing these tasks manually, over and over again, is monotonous work. Well, you don't need to feel frustrated any more. Instead, you can easily create a small StarBasic *macro* (or *routine*) to do the work for you.

Don't feel daunted by the mention of programming languages and creating applications. You don't need to be a programmer or even an experienced StarOffice user to take advantage of StarBasic. You can easily create macros by using the StarBasic macro recorder without any knowledge of programming.

If you need to create more complex routines than possible with the macro recorder alone, you can learn StarBasic programming techniques on-the-fly by recording macros and then dissecting them in the StarBasic development environment.

> **Note**
>
> StarBasic's language is documented in the online Help system. However, navigating that system is not so easy. For tips, refer to the section "Troubleshooting the Online Help System" later in this chapter.

If you're new to creating macros and programming, you might find it difficult to imagine just what you can do with StarBasic. Look to the following few ideas to give you a taste of its power and spark your imagination:

- Group a string of commands into one; for example, take a plain text file with a verbose address list and copy just the name, telephone number, and email address to a new StarCalc sheet.
- Assign a style to a keyboard shortcut.
- Cycle through all like objects in a text document to reformat them. For example, scale all graphics in a document down to 32 percent of the size of the original.

- Enhance the functionality of your word processor; for example, count the number of words in a selected text area.

- Create a template to enhance the work of your colleagues. For example, you can create a standard memo template for your company. Every time someone uses this template, a StarBasic dialog asks for the necessary information and saves it to the network drive.

CREATING A MACRO FOR AN EVERYDAY TASK

The best way to understand how to create macros in StarBasic is to step through an example of automating a common everyday task. Say you want to copy a list of filenames stored in a directory on your hard drive and comment on all these files in the list. You'll therefore want to create a table with three columns. The first column is for the filename, the second for the file date, and the third for your comments.

This may sound like a lot of humdrum work or a complicated macro program—one that deals with the filing system of your computer. However, you can create a macro that carries out all the aspects of this task. An easy and fast solution in such a situation is often the combination of both manual and automated work.

Here is the solution at a glance:

1. Create the file list by using the `dir` command in DOS.
2. Reformat the list with a recorded macro.
3. Create a table by choosing Tools, Convert Text to Table.
4. Copy this table to your document.

Your operating system can create file lists in plain text format. Therefore, you can work with the `dir` command of a Windows or OS/2 system. If you are using a UNIX or Linux system, no doubt `ls` will be quite familiar to you. For this example, the Windows system is used. There aren't any major differences in the solution of this task if you're on a Linux system.

CREATING A FILE LIST

Open a DOS window by selecting Start, Programs, Command Prompt. Change, if necessary, the directory to the one that contains the files you want to comment (for example, `c:\Documents`).

The DOS command `DIR *.sdw` gives you a list of all the StarWriter documents in this directory. To write this list to a file called `temp.txt`, you need to type `DIR *.sdw >temp.txt`. DOS then creates the text file and saves it in the same directory.

Close the DOS window, and open the `temp.txt` file in StarOffice. StarOffice opens this file in the Text Editor (see Figure 37.1).

Figure 37.1
You can copy a DOS or Linux file listing to a StarWriter document with ease, but as you can see in this figure, you still have to do some cleaning up, which you can automate with StarBasic.

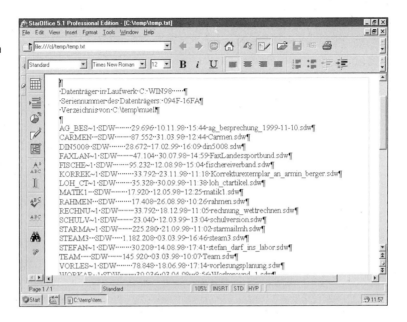

RECORDING A MACRO

As you can see, every file of this folder is given its own row. For this example, say you want only the name (in long format) and the file date from each file, separated by tabs. You could manually go from row to row, cut out all the other information, and change the order of the name and the date. However, this task is tedious, time-consuming, and boring.

Instead, you can record the keystrokes of the changes to one line with the macro recorder and then run this macro on each line.

The key to recording macros efficiently is to think through the steps you need to take, and when and where you will begin and end your recording. In this case, you place your cursor at the beginning of the line you're going to reformat, start the macro recorder, carefully reformat, jump to the beginning of the next line, and stop recording.

Place the cursor at the beginning of the first line of the filename list—where you want your automated action to begin. Then choose Tools, Macro to open the Macro dialog box (see Figure 37.2). Type a name for your macro in the Macro Name text box. If the name does not already exist, the Record button is enabled. Choose Record to start recording the macro. Note that the Record button appears grayed out until you enter an acceptable name.

Notice that a little toolbar with one dark red button appears in the upper-left corner of the StarOffice window. Later, you'll use this button to stop the macro recording.

Figure 37.2
In the Macro dialog, you record new macros as well as assign and organize existing macros.

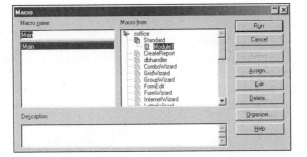

Make sure the cursor is still at the beginning of the line, hold down the Shift key and the right-arrow key, and highlight the text until you come to the beginning of the date. Press the Delete button. Move the cursor with the right-arrow key until you are past the date. Once again, use the Shift and right-arrow keys to highlight the time column situated between the date and the filename. Delete this selection as well. Press the Tab key. Now jump to the end of the line by using the End key on your keyboard. Press the Tab key again. Go to the next line by using the down-arrow key. Finally, jump to the beginning of this line by pressing the Home key.

You're done! Stop recording the macro by clicking the Record Stop button.

Note

Be aware of the file or file type for which your macro was designed. The preceding macro was recorded for a specially formatted text document (in the example, `temp.txt`). For you to be able to execute this macro, this particular text document must be active, and the cursor must be placed at the beginning of the line. Otherwise, you can be sure that some parts of your text will be destroyed. Even if the macro is written with all text documents in mind, be sure that StarWriter is your active program. Trying to activate a macro in the wrong StarOffice program is a common mistake. The StarBasic IDE can still be active, even after you've closed the text document it was designed for.

Tip #590 from
Werner Roth

Before trying out a recorded macro, it's a good idea to save the file.

You should give your macro a test run. The cursor should still be positioned at the beginning of the next row. To start the macro, choose Tools, Macro, and then choose the macro `temp` from the list box. Click the Run button. The second row is then reformatted before your eyes. If not, click the Reload button on the function bar to reverse the changes and take a closer look at your macro.

EDITING A MACRO

To edit a macro, choose Tools, Macro; when the Macro dialog appears, click the Edit button. The StarBasic IDE window then appears, displaying the macro program you see in Figure 37.3.

Figure 37.3
The actions you record in your macro are automatically translated by StarOffice into the StarBasic code you see here.

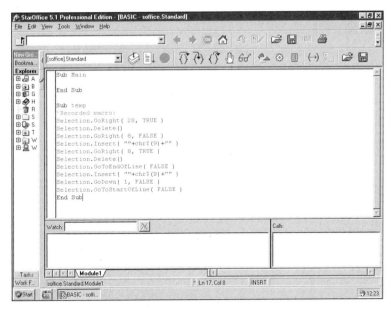

Don't worry if your code is functioning perfectly but looks slightly different from the code shown here. Different keystrokes can produce different macro code that yields the same result.

Return to your `temp.txt` document by either closing the StarBasic IDE or by selecting the `temp.txt` file from the StarOffice taskbar.

ASSIGNING A KEYBOARD SHORTCUT

You can reformat the entire file by repeating the same steps—select Tools, Macro; choose the macro `temp` from the list box; and then choose the Run button for every single line in your file. However, you can use a much quicker way to accomplish the same task—assign a keyboard shortcut to the macro.

Tip #591 from
Werner Roth

Keyboard shortcuts are assigned to the StarOffice program that is active, so be sure that the correct program is active (in this example, StarWriter). The shortcut keystrokes you create change the keyboard configuration of the StarWriter program. This means the shortcut is available in every document.

Caution

Be careful! If the StarBasic IDE window is your current active program, you will assign the keyboard shortcut to the StarBasic editor. This is a common mistake.

Open the Macro dialog by choosing Tools, Macro. Then select the macro `temp`, and click the Assign button. The Configuration dialog appears. Select the keyboard combination Ctrl+T in the Keyboard list box. The corresponding macro should already be selected. As you can see, the macro `temp` is located in Category "StarOffice BASIC Macros" in Standard.Module1, and the name of the Command is `temp`. Click the Assign button. The macro's name should now appear next to the keyboard shortcut Ctrl+T. Accept the assignment by clicking the OK button.

Note

A common mistake in dialogs such as these is to select all the elements you need and simply choose OK. However, choosing OK doesn't complete the assignment. Be sure to choose the Assign button.

Close the Configuration and Macro dialog boxes, and place the cursor at the beginning of the next row in your file list. Press Ctrl+T to run the macro. Now apply the macro to every line by repetitively pressing Ctrl+T. Afterward, your text should look something like this:

```
10.11.98→ag_besprechung_1999-11-10.sdw→
31.03.98→Carmen.sdw→
17.02.99→din5008.sdw→
30.07.98→FaxLandessportbund.sdw→
12.08.98→fischereiverband.sdw→
23.11.98→Korrekturexemplar_an_armin_berger.sdw→
30.09.98→loh_ctartikel.sdw→
12.05.98→matik1.sdw→
26.08.98→rahmen.sdw→
18.12.98→rechnung_wettrechnen.sdw→
12.03.99→schulversion.sdw→
21.09.98→starmailmh.sdw→
03.03.99→steam3.sdw→
14.08.98→stefan_darf_ins_labor.sdw→
03.03.98→Team.sdw→
18.06.98→vorlesungsplanung.sdw→
03.04.98→Workaround_1.sdw→
```

To place the new list in a table, highlight all the rows, and then select Tools, Convert Text to Table. A dialog appears asking you to confirm that separation is with tabs. Choose OK, and StarOffice produces a table ready for your comments.

After you've created this macro, you might want to try picking up another file from somewhere and trying to reformat it—for example, the output of a DOS-based accounting program or the results of an Internet search in HTML format.

Tip #592 from
Werner Roth

If you assign a keyboard shortcut to a macro and then replace the macro with a new one of the same name, the keyboard shortcut is automatically reassigned to the new macro.

> **Note**
>
> Always use the keyboard when you're recording manipulations of text. A selection made with the mouse is not recognized. Use your mouse only to select drop-down lists such as Insert, Special Character, and icons on the toolbars.

> **Note**
>
> Be careful when you use the End key in a macro. You might have a paragraph longer than the one you perform the keystrokes on. The End key brings you only to the end of the line, not to the end of the paragraph.

A Short Trip through the StarBasic IDE

Our first macro gave you an initial glance at the StarBasic *Integrated Development Environment* (*IDE*). There was no need to use the IDE for recording and playing macros. In the coming steps, we'll design our own macros. Therefore, we'll need this programming environment. Take a look at this section to gain an overview of the IDE and, if you want to know what a particular element is used for, this section acts as a good reference.

The StarBasic IDE is powerful enough to use in creating large macro applications. However, in your initial steps as a StarBasic macro programmer, you'll mainly work with the Macro Editor and the Run button. The following sections give you a tour of the basic tools you need to create and edit macros.

Main Window

After you select Tools, Macro and then click the Edit button, the StarBasic IDE task window appears. Just as with any other StarOffice task, you can easily switch from the IDE to another open task by using the StarOffice taskbar.

Figure 37.4 provides an overview of the IDE tools. At the top, you see the familiar StarOffice function bar; below it is the StarBasic Macro object bar. The main window pane is the Basic Editor. Below it are two additional panes one to observe variables and one to see function calls, known as the *Function Call stack*. At the bottom of the window are a navigation bar, a status bar, and the usual StarOffice taskbar.

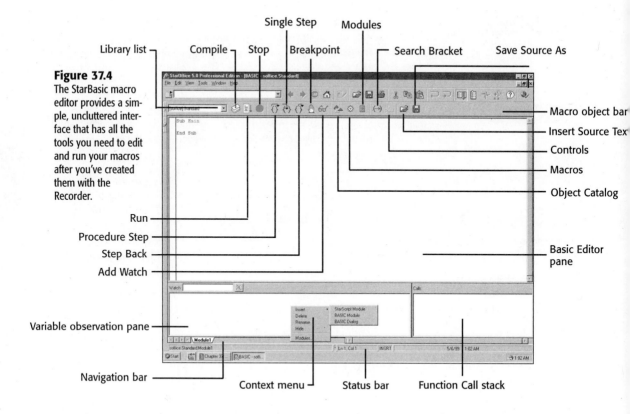

Figure 37.4
The StarBasic macro editor provides a simple, uncluttered interface that has all the tools you need to edit and run your macros after you've created them with the Recorder.

EXPLORING THE MACRO OBJECT BAR

For the beginner, a detailed explanation of all the functions shown in Figure 37.4 would result in information overload. Furthermore, to cycle through all the functions in order of their arrangement in the window would be ineffective. Instead, each function will be explained in context.

Use the brief overview of the Macro bar, shown in Table 37.1, to become familiar with any elements you find interesting at this point in time. You can always refer to this table again after exploring StarBasic more deeply.

TABLE 37.1 EXPLORING THE MACRO OBJECT BAR

Icon	Explained
[soffice].Standard Library list	The Library drop-down list gives you quick access to all currently available StarBasic libraries. StarBasic macros are organized hierarchically in libraries and then modules. (You should store a complete project in a library.) You'll love using this drop-down list when you work with different projects.

Icon	Explained
Compile, Run, and Stop	You use the Compile, Run, and Stop buttons to interact with the program. Compile checks whether your program's syntax is correct. Stop breaks or stops a program, which is particularly useful if you're stuck in an infinite loop. The button you will use the most is Run. If you select Run, the uppermost macro in the active module is started. Notice that if the IDE is open, the macro taskbar appears in all open tasks, allowing its use in every document. For example, if you write a macro for a specific text document, you can switch to the document and start your macro by using the Run button.
Procedure Step, Single Step, Step Back, Breakpoint, and Add Watch	You use this group of buttons—Procedure Step, Single Step, Step Back, Breakpoint, and Add Watch— to debug a program. These commands enable you to cycle through a program line by line, stop the executing at a critical point, and watch the scope and values of the variables you are using.
Object Catalog, Macros, and Modules	The Object Catalog, Macros, and Modules buttons enable you to organize your macros, dialogs, modules, and libraries. Object Catalog opens a window to navigate through your modules and dialogs. A click on the Module button opens the Macro Organizer in which you can add, delete, move, copy, and rename modules, dialogs, and libraries. You'll learn more about these tools in "Organizing Macros in Libraries and Modules". The Macro button opens the Macro dialog, shown in Figure 37.3.
Search Bracket	You use the Search Bracket button to control the nesting of parentheses in an arithmetical expression such a ` (((2+4)*6)/(4-5)) `. Place the cursor in front of the bracket you want to check. Search Bracket selects the text until it reaches the corresponding bracket.
Controls	The Controls button opens a toolbar (Controls) with a dialog box control field. Controls is enabled only in Dialog view.
Insert Source Text, and Save Source As	The Insert Source Text and Save Source As buttons handle program code as plain text files. Note that to save your actual module or dialog, you should use the Save button on the function bar.

Underneath the macro bar is the Basic Editor pane. This window is described in detail in Chapter 38, "Understanding StarBasic Structures and Statements." Situated under the Basic Editor are two windows used for debugging: the Watch window and Call Stack window.

In the *Watch window,* you can observe the values of variables step-by-step during the program's execution. To observe a variable, highlight it in the Editor window, and then click the Add Watch button in the macro bar. Alternatively, you can type its name in the text box in the Watch window.

The *Call Stack window* enables you to see the call hierarchy of your subprocedures or functions. For example, if a subprocedure called DropErrorMessage is active and called by Sub Main, the Call Stack window displays 0:DropErrorMessage and 1:Main.

Introducing the Basic Editor

The Basic Editor is the built-in programming editor. If you are used to working with StarWriter, you shouldn't find it difficult to use the Basic Editor. You can type, copy, delete, and drag and drop text as you would in StarWriter (or other StarOffice modules, for that matter). You can even drag and drop text from a StarBasic program to a StarWriter document and vice versa.

The main difference between writing in StarWriter and writing in the Basic Editor is the format of the text. Because a macro is a set of instructions, it must be written in a structured way. It is not possible to format text yourself in the Basic Editor because it automatically applies syntax highlighting as follows:

- Basic keywords such as control structures appear in blue.
- Expressions such as variables and subprocedure names appear in green.
- Values such as strings or numbers appear in red; unfinished string lines are dark red.
- Remarks are gray.

Like all traditional programming editors, the Basic Editor uses a monospaced font. Using this font is important to give structure to your program.

You might be able to follow the flow of a small 20-line program without the need for indentation. However, when you're dealing with bigger projects, indenting decision blocks or subprocedures is important.

Because a macro without its dialog representation is purely ASCII text, you can import text files or save the macro as a plain text file. Use the Insert Source Text and Save Source As buttons on the Macro object bar to export or import source code. The standard file extension for StarBasic source files is .bas.

Running a Macro from within the IDE

In the section "Creating a Macro for an Everyday Task" in this chapter, you recorded a macro and ran it recursively to reformat text. The next natural step after doing that is to then open your macro in the IDE editor to clean up and enhance the Basic code.

The following sections should provide you with ideas and the knowledge of how to improve a recorded macro or write your own macro from scratch. You may find everyday problems will take you deeper into StarBasic. As you continue to see recorded macros you'll gradually become more and more familiar with StarBasic objects. Hopefully this will encourage you to adapt a macro to fit to a more general or more complicated task. Clearly, it's also a good idea to gain knowledge of StarBasic by reading the following chapters. Programming your own macro will be the focus in the following sections.

If you have entered additional source code or written a complete program, you can check the code syntax by clicking the Compile button on the Macro object bar. However, this method checks only the structure and syntax of your code. Even after successfully compiling a program, you can still have errors (known as *runtime errors*) in your code.

Take a look at the two small macro programs here:

```
Sub Main
    dim result as integer
    result = 1/0
End Sub
```

In the preceding example, if you click Compile, an error is detected in line 3 because division by zero is not possible. However, a slight variation of the code hides this error from the Compiler. Create an integer variable a, and substitute a for 0:

```
Sub Main
    dim result as integer, a as integer
    a = 0
    result = 1/a
End Sub
```

The Compiler now accepts the code but expels a division-by-zero error at runtime.

After you've added and compiled your code, you can run your macro to test it. To start your macro program in the Macro dialog, choose Tools, Macro to open the Macro dialog, and click the Run button. This action starts the uppermost macro in the active module. Remember to make sure you're in the right program.

Tip #593 from
Werner Roth

Using the Run button on the Macro toolbar is quite easy. However, it always starts the uppermost macro in the module. Starting this macro isn't appropriate for testing subprocedures. The solution is to leave the uppermost subprocedure of a module empty, except the single subprocedure call of the macro you want to test.

In most cases, Compile and Run are the only two buttons you need to tweak your macro. However, if you can't find an error, or if you don't understand why your program is behaving strangely, use the IDE runtime functions (Procedure Step, Single Step, Step Back, Breakpoint, and Add Watch) to execute your program step-by-step.

Figure 37.5 shows the IDE in Debug mode after five clicks of the Single Step button. All the variables used have been added to the Watch window so that you can observe their values. If you discover the error while stepping through your program, you can stop the Single Step process by clicking the Stop button.

Figure 37.5
After you've opened your macro in the StarBasic editor, you can debug your macro code by running it with the buttons on the Macro object bar. Here, the Watch window is being used to check for errors in the macro variables.

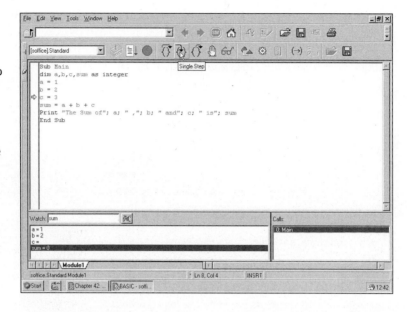

Tip #594 from
Werner Roth

Be conservative with the number of variables you place in the Watch window. If you want to know the value of a variable not in the Watch window, simply hold the mouse cursor over its expression in the editing window. A tool tip showing the current value will appear. This handy function operates during the entire step-by-step execution of the program.

ORGANIZING MACROS IN LIBRARIES AND MODULES

In Figure 37.5, you see the path `soffice.Standard.Module1` displayed in the status bar at the bottom of the window. The following sections explain just what that path means.

WHAT IS A LIBRARY?

StarBasic organizes macros into libraries. A *library* is a collection of macro source code and StarBasic dialogs. Typically, a library contains a complete application written in StarBasic. Consider a calculator, for example. It is an entire application made up of different components that are all stored in the same library—that is, a main form to input the numbers and operators, an error dialog, macro source code for the control of the dialogs, and source code to perform the calculations.

A library can belong either to StarOffice or to a document. StarOffice comes with a set of standard libraries used for database functions, wizards, and so on. The default template files also come with macros, mainly used to fill in the current date into a newly created document.

You can find a standard library in StarOffice and in every StarOffice document. After installation, the standard library in StarOffice is dependent on a module called Module1 and an empty subprocedure called Main. Module1 is the default storage space for all recorded macros. Of course, if you wish, you can choose another module and even another library in which to store your macros.

The StarOffice standard library is stored in the file C:\Office51\basic\soffice.sbl. You can save this library by clicking the Save button on the function bar or by selecting File, Save when the IDE is active. StarOffice also saves its libraries whenever you exit the program.

All libraries for a document are saved within the document. Hence, you save a document and its libraries together. Clicking the Save button in the IDE has the same effect as clicking the button to save the document.

PART
VIII
CH
37

Note

Understanding the link between saving a document and saving a StarBasic library is important because you cannot reverse changes in a StarOffice library except by using the Undo command on the Edit menu. If you tinker with a library in a document and don't want to keep your changes, you should simply close it without saving. But remember, all changes in StarOffice libraries are saved on exiting StarOffice. Therefore, keeping a backup of the libraries is essential—especially the standard library C:\Office51\basic\soffice.sbl.

LOOKING AT A SAMPLE LIBRARY

You saw the hierarchical structure of libraries and modules earlier when you opened the Macro dialog (refer to Figure 37.3). The Objects catalog window also gives you a good overview of all the libraries, modules, and dialogs you have available (see Figure 37.6). Open it by clicking the Object Catalog button on the Macro object bar.

Figure 37.6
Using the Objects catalog you can access all the StarBasic libraries, modules, and macros.

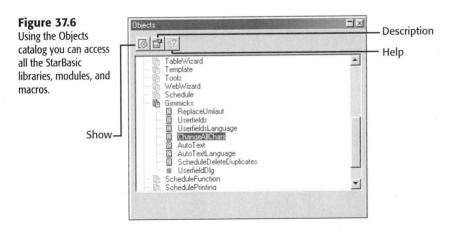

Use the scrollbar to scroll to the library Gimmicks. Double-click Gimmicks to expand to the next level containing all its modules and dialogs. Double-click a module to show all its subprocedures and functions. To open a module, select it and click the Show button at the top-left corner of the Objects catalog floating dialog box.

What Is a Module?

In an earlier example, we mentioned a complete calculator application is stored in its own library. The calculator consists of a main dialog, an error dialog, source code for the control of the dialogs, and source code for the calculations. You don't want the code for each of these components to be rattling around together in the same container, however. Therefore, each of these components is stored in its own *module*. The modules for the calculator's source codes and dialogs are displayed on the tabs shown in Figure 37.7.

Figure 37.7
When you open a StarBasic-library, individual modules are placed on separate tabs. You can navigate among them by clicking the tab names.

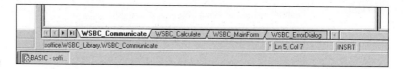

It's normal to divide your source code into different modules to separate code used for different tasks. In the calculator example, one module is used for the communication of the dialogs and the other for the arithmetical part of the application.

Note that a module can hold only 64Kb of source code. If you need more space, divide your code into two modules.

To call a subprocedure or function in another module, simply type its name. StarBasic searches through all modules in the same library. If two subprocedures have the same name, only situated within different modules of the library, StarBasic calls the first subprocedure. Be sure to give the correct path for your desired subprocedure:

```
ModuleName.NameOfTheSub_procedure
```

Clearly, a better solution is not to use the same name for different subprocedures.

If you want to call a subprocedure that is located in a different library than the one in which you are currently located, you just need to add the library name to the path:

```
LibraryName.ModuleName.NameOfTheSub_procedure
```

The exception is that if you want to call a subprocedure out of the standard library, you don't use a library name. In fact, the standard library doesn't have a name. Just think of it as the default library. Also, due to its special status, the macros contained in standard library are available even when you're in another library. Therefore, if you want to access something in the standard library, you can call it by using the subprocedure name. However, doing so is not considered good programming style.

As you can see, using the same names for different modules and subprocedures is a recipe for disaster. An easy way of getting around these difficulties is to think of a short acronym for each project—for example, *WSBC* for *Werner's StarBasic Calculator*. Then use this acronym as a prefix for all modules, subs, and functions of this project. You can see the results of applying this method of naming in Figure 37.7.

CREATING LIBRARIES, MODULES, AND DIALOGS

To create a new library for a project, click the Modules button on the Macro toolbar. After the Macro Organizer window opens (see Figure 37.8), click the Libraries tab to access your library list.

Figure 37.8
Use the Macro Organizer to add, move, delete or create StarBasic modules and libraries.

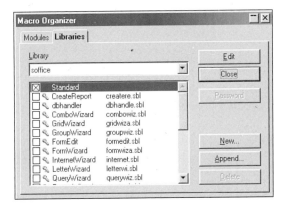

In the drop-down list box, select the area in which you want to organize the libraries. (Selecting this area is something like selecting the parent of the libraries.) For this example, select soffice, meaning all libraries that belong directly to your StarOffice installation; furthermore, you can select all open documents and templates.

The check box before a library name indicates whether the library is activated. You cannot use a function from a deactivated library; however, you can activate a library manually. Cast your mind back to the Macro dialog (refer to Figure 37.3) where you can see a list of all libraries and modules. The deactivated libraries are shown in gray, and the activated libraries are in black.

If the second column in the Libraries list displays a key, it means the library is password-protected. As you can see, all the libraries that come with StarOffice, except Gimmicks, are password-protected. Setting a password enables you to create a complete StarBasic application to share with others without letting the source code out of your hands.

You can password-protect your library with the Password button. You need to activate your library to enable the button. If you want to call a subprocedure that is deactivated or password-protected from within an application, you need to load the library first. Look in the help system for the method Application.LoadLibrary("NAME").

To rename a library, select it, wait a second, and click it again—just like Windows Explorer. Alternatively, press F2.

Caution

You are denied permission to change the name of the standard library of StarOffice or a document. We strongly recommend not to delete or change the name of any library delivered with StarOffice.

Tip #595 from
Werner Roth

Older versions of StarOffice (including StarOffice 5.0) require you to use the Alt key plus a mouse click to rename an item. This method is still accessible in some fringes of the application. So, if you can't figure out how to change a name, you might want to try Alt+click.

ADDING A LIBRARY

Make sure you're still in the Macro Organizer. To add a new library, click the New button. You then are asked to assign a name and indicate whether this library is to be given its own file (in the Attach File check box). Checking the Attach File box is a good idea; StarBasic then stores your library in the folder `C:\Office51\Basic` with the extension `.sbl`. Otherwise, the new library is stored together with the standard library in the file `C:\Office51\basic\soffice.sbl`.

The Append button that you can see in Figure 37.8 is used to import a library from a StarBasic library file (`.sbl`), a StarOffice document, or a StarOffice template document. Use this import function to distribute a StarBasic library to your friends. Copy the corresponding `.sbl` file from the `C:\Office51\Basic` folder, or save the library to a document. For example, you can create a StarWriter document named `aMacroForYou.sdw`. Type in the instructions on how to import a library. Then close the document. Open the Macro Organizer, and select the Libraries tab. Select the library that you want to send to your friend. Click the Append button. You then need to select the file to which the library will be appended; in this case, select the file `aMacroForYou`. A dialog then appears with the library to append to the document; finally, choose OK.

CREATING A MODULE

To create and organize modules and dialogs, select the Modules tab in the Macro Organizer. You then see the options for adding new modules and dialogs, as shown in Figure 37.9.

Always start the search for your libraries owned by StarOffice or documents from the bottom of the list. You also can create modules from the Module tab on the StarBasic IDE (refer to Figure 37.4).

Note

If you are given the option to create a StarScript or BASIC module, always choose BASIC. StarScript is StarOffice's version of JavaScript, which is not covered in this book.

Figure 37.9
You start new dialog boxes as well as new modules from the Modules tab of the Macro Organizer.

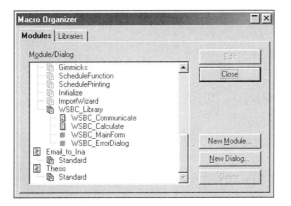

The Macro Organizer is more powerful than it appears. It enables you to drag and drop modules between libraries—even between libraries of StarOffice and other documents.

To open the next level of a library to view its modules and dialogs, double-click the library name. Repeat the double-click to close it. To drag and drop modules from one library to another, select the module, hold the left mouse button, and drag it to the destination. You can even copy modules by performing the usual trick of pressing the Ctrl key while dragging.

Caution

Be careful when you're dragging and dropping. This method has the potential to destroy complete StarBasic applications. You cannot undo your movements; you would have to drag modules or dialogs back to the original location.

ACCESSING YOUR MODULES AND SOURCE CODE

To begin to develop a StarBasic application, you first need to open the StarBasic IDE. Select Tools, Macro to open the Macro dialog; then select the module you want from the Macro From list box. To view the modules of a library, double-click the library name. If the library was previously deactivated, it is now active. (Naturally, if the library is password-protected, you have to enter the proper password.) Select the module of your choice. All the subprocedures and functions of this module appear in the left list box. Choose one and click Edit to open the IDE.

Note

After you've entered the correct password, you have free access to this library for the entire StarOffice session. After exiting and restarting StarOffice, you need to reenter the password.

You can access all the modules and dialogs of the current library from within the Basic IDE. To do so, simply click the tabs located at the bottom of the IDE window (refer to Figure 37.7).

To change libraries while you're working in the IDE, click the Library drop-down list on the Macro object bar (see Figure 37.10). This list is useful if you want to equip a macro library in a document or template with a couple of your ordinary macros stored in the StarOffice standard library. This involves a lot of switching between the Starbasic library in your document and the StarOffice standard library.

Figure 37.10

The Library drop-down list enables you to jump between your libraries.

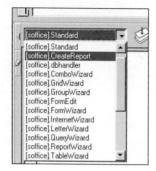

Simply select a macro from the nested list, click the left mouse button, and drag it into your source code in the Basic Editing pane. You can see the InsertURL macros being dragged in Figure 37.11.

Figure 37.11

You can drag and drop across the StarOffice desktop. You can even add a macro to a Basic routine by dragging and dropping from the Object Library organizer.

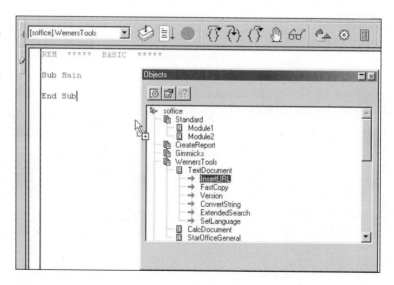

Granted, the Basic IDE lacks the Navigator available in StarWriter, StarCalc, or other StarOffice programs. However, the Objects catalog enables you to navigate and load your modules as well as easily access subprocedures and functions of a module or element, or access properties and methods of a dialog (refer to Figure 37.6).

STARBASIC PROGRAMMING FROM SCRATCH

You can record macros to manipulate documents in many ways. You can use them to reformat text, cut and paste objects, search and replace strings, export the document—the list is endless. Sometimes, however, you might require a little more than the macro recorder can offer. Take gathering information, for example. Imagine that you want to record the number of characters in a document. You can get this information by selecting File, Properties and then choosing the Statistics tab in the Properties window. But try to record this process. All you end up with is an empty macro.

The following sections probe deeper into StarBasic with the use of an example. While programming a subprocedure, you'll learn about the essential elements of a StarBasic program.

CREATING A STATISTICS PROGRAM

Open the StarBasic IDE by selecting Tools, Macro. Type Statistics in the Macro Name text box, and click the New button. The StarBasic IDE appears with the opening and closing statements of a subprocedure Statistics inserted:

```
Sub Statistics

End Sub
```

Type the following source code between these statements to produce what's called a *statement block*. This block makes the Statistic program functional.

If you choose to type in the code yourself, you can ignore the lines with an apostrophe (') in front of them. They are just comment lines inserted to document and explain the program. (Any line prefaced with an apostrophe (') is ignored when running the macro.)

> **Note**
>
> Don't double up on the opening and closing statements of the statement block, or else your program won't run.

Run the following macro from within a StarWriter document by selecting Tools, Macro, choosing the subprocedure Statistics in the Macro dialog that appears, and clicking the Run button:

```
 1 Sub Statistics
 2    'This subprocedure shows statistical information
 3    'about a Text document
 4
 5    'Define variables to store the statistical information
 6    dim NumberOfChars as long, NumberOfLines as long
 7    dim NumberOfGraphics as integer, NumberOfTables as integer
 8
 9    'Check if a text document is active
10    IF ActiveModule.Name <> "StarWriter" THEN
11       'If not drop an error-message and leave this subprocedure
12       MsgBox("This program is only available in text documents.",0+16,"Error")
13       EXIT SUB
```

```
14    ENDIF
15
16    'Collect the information
17    NumberOfChars    = ActiveWindow.GetCharCount(2)
18    NumberOfLines    = ActiveWindow.GetLineCount( FALSE )
19    NumberOfGraphics = ActiveWindow.Graphics.Count
20    NumberOfTables   = ActiveWindow.Tables.Count
21
22    'Display the information in a message box
23    MsgBox( "Number of Chars: "    & NumberOfChars    & chr(13) &_
24            "Number of Lines: "    & NumberOfLines    & chr(13) &_
25            "Number of Graphics: " & NumberOfGraphics & chr(13) &_
26            "Number of Tables: "   & NumberOfTables   & chr(13) ,_
27            0+64, "Statistical Information about this Document")
28 End Sub
```

It should produce a message box like the one shown in Figure 37.12.

Figure 37.12
All that programming work—and here's the net result, a message box that informs you of your document's statistics.

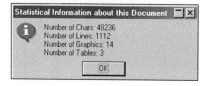

> Statistical Information about this Document
>
> Number of Chars: 48236
> Number of Lines: 1112
> Number of Graphics: 14
> Number of Tables: 3
>
> [OK]

If running the macro produces a message box with the warning This program is only available in text documents, no text document was active when running the macro. You also get this error message if you run the macro in the StarBasic IDE.

The following is a breakdown of the Statistics program:

- Lines 1 and 28 are the code that actually construct the program; they are like a frame that informs StarOffice "a subprocedure begins/ends here." The statement Sub, followed by a statement block, and the statement End Sub define a subprocedure. In this example, the subprocedure is a complete StarBasic program. However, the typical purpose of a subprocedure is to perform one function of the many functions in a program.

- Lines 2 and 3 are comments describing what the program does. A good practice is to describe, at the beginning of a subprocedure, the function of the procedure and the data it uses. Every line beginning with the apostrophe (') is ignored by the StarBasic interpreter. Think of these lines as hints for humans.

- Lines 6 and 7 define four variables used to store the statistical information the program gathers. A *variable* is an exclusive location for data of a special type. NumberOfChars and NumberOfLines are variables of type long to hold integer values larger than 32,767. NumberOfGraphics and NumberOfTables are variables of type integer, used to store smaller numbers. You can call your variables anything you want—for example, Fred. However, to make a comprehensible program, it's best if the variable name corresponds to the task it is designed for.

- Lines 10 to 14 are part of what's known as a *decision block*. If the currently active document is not a text document, the macro is not functional. If you were to run the macro from within a spreadsheet or a StarBasic IDE, it would not be able to access the statistical information. Hence, the program would throw a runtime error. To prevent this problem, the program needs to check whether the active program is StarWriter. If not, it throws its own error. To implement this check, the StarBasic condition statement `If...Then...Endif` is used. Other control statements are available in StarBasic, such as extended decision statements, loop statements and exiting-control statements.

- Lines 16 to 20 assign different values to the variables. To understand this process, look at the line `NumberOfChars = ActiveWindow.GetCharCount(2)`. `GetCharCount` is a method belonging to StarWriter that counts the number of characters in the current paragraph or in an entire document. The argument 2 in the parentheses means "count the characters in the document". By attaching the method (with the use of the period) to the object, `ActiveWindow` (the text document window), you ask the program to execute this method upon this object. As you can see, different methods belong to a text document. They can be called through various objects from StarOffice's object hierarchy. You've already seen other StarOffice objects in the introductory macro—for example, `Selection.Delete()`. Communication between a StarOffice document and a macro program is based on objects. You will often deal with objects and the StarOffice object hierarchy when working with macros.

- Lines 22 to 27 are part of one command to open a Message Box dialog. Notice that a Message Box command also appears in line 12; however, it is just one line of code. Because the second message needs to display so much information, it uses five lines chained by the underline character. You could write such a command in one line, but it would be difficult to follow. Dividing the code into five lines is more readable (and it is the only way to print the code in a book such as this).

UNDERSTANDING THE BASIC CONCEPTS OF A STARBASIC PROGRAM

As you saw in the Statistics example in the preceding section, a StarBasic program is a collection of commands. A macro program is usually a single subprocedure. Within a subprocedure, there can be a myriad of single commands, control statements, function calls, and subprocedure calls.

In StarBasic, commands are divided by lines. It's standard practice to use one line to record one command. Conversely, if a command line is too long to read effortlessly, you can interrupt the command and continue it on the next line. You need to add an underscore character (_) at the end to signal that the line is broken (as shown in the example). You also can put more than one command in one line; just divide the commands with a colon. However, writing commands this way makes for a cluttered program and goes against the conventions of StarBasic. The only exception to the rule is the initialization of variables, where the use of the colon is appropriate:

```
dim a as integer, b as integer, c as integer
a = 0 : b = 0 : c = 0
```

StarBasic is not case sensitive; an expression can be in lowercase or uppercase. If you call a variable NumberOfChars, for example, you can type numberofchars or NUMBERofCHARS, and the interpreter will recognize it. You can even type the StarBasic keywords in uppercase or lowercase.

StarBasic is also quite compliant with the use or disuse of parentheses. Take a close look at the following example:

```
Sub Main
   'Parentheses are not needed for the following line:
   ShowTheName "Scott", "Peter"
   'The same command only with brackets:
   ShowTheName("Scott", "Peter")

   'In the line below the command SumArgs requires the use of brackets.
   'Otherwise, StarBasic doesn't know which arguments belong to
   'MsgBox and which to SumArgs
   MsgBox SumArgs( 10, 20)
   'Notice that we used the MsgBox run-time function without brackets!
End Sub

Sub ShowTheName( Lastname as string, FirstName as string)
   MsgBox FirstName & " " & Lastname, 64, "Your Name here"
End Sub

Function SumArgs( a as integer, b as integer) as integer
   SumArgs = a + b
End Function
```

Notice that the arguments a and b of the function SumArgs are in parentheses. Using them is essential if you want to assign their result to the function. To avoid having to deal with the differences, simply put arguments in parentheses at all times.

DO I HAVE TO DEAL WITH OBJECTS?

The preceding sections contain a lot of references to StarOffice objects. At this point, you might be wondering what exactly objects are and whether you really need to know anything about them to work in StarBasic. The following sections explain what StarOffice objects are.

WHAT ARE STAROFFICE OBJECTS?

All functions and attributes of StarOffice are represented in an object hierarchy. With the use of the mouse, the usual way to format a character is to select Format and then Character, and the Character dialog then appears. However, if you want to open the same dialog from within a StarBasic program, you can enter the following command line:

```
ActiveWindow.Font.FontDialog()
```

Hence, you call the method FontDialog() belonging to the object Font, where Font is a property of ActiveWindow. ActiveWindow is the object referring to the actual document windows. You use this method of the Font object to open a dialog.

Take a look at an attribute for StarWriter text. The following command line underlines any text selected within a document:

```
ActiveWindow.Font.Underline = 1
```

The attribute draws a single line under a selected portion of text—just like clicking the Underline button in the object bar. The difference, however, is that this command draws the line under the text, regardless of whether it was already underlined. This command changes the value of a particular StarOffice property.

As you've already seen, you access a method or an object property by its name. Methods and properties are separated by periods. It's interesting to look back at the examples that have already been analyzed. They are jam-packed with StarOffice objects. If they still sound like gibberish to you, don't panic. Familiarizing yourself with the objects in StarOffice is not difficult, and besides, you don't need to learn all their names. The important thing is to get acquainted with their structure.

Objects are the means of communication between the StarBasic program and StarOffice. If you want to manipulate text, fill out a form automatically, or make an automatic calculation in a spreadsheet, the things you need are represented by StarOffice objects. All the attributes—the color, the font, and even the value—are properties of a StarOffice object.

Your programs will be bursting with methods and properties of StarOffice objects. The potential is at hand to manipulate the complete StarOffice suite. You can even shut down StarOffice with a macro by using this code:

```
Sub CloseStarOffice
    Application.Quit()
End Sub
```

StarOffice documents are loaded with different functions and attributes. The major difficulty with all this potential is knowing where to start. In most cases, it's easiest to find methods and properties for your application with the use of the macro recorder. It generates code with complete references to the modules used and properties changed. Even if they prove to be of no use to your task, at least you have a starting point for a StarBasic Help system search.

The three major avenues for finding reserved StarOffice objects for your programs are as follows:

- Record manipulations that you would like your manually written macro to address to a temporary macro, and examine its code.
- Find the suitable object with the StarBasic Help system. Given that the structure and contents of the Help system can be a little tricky, the next section covers its use.
- Pinch code from others. Well, not pinch as such; people on the Internet call this code *open source*. Take a look at the programs of others. StarOffice itself comes with a couple of code examples. In addition, you can check out the Gimmicks library and find plenty of code snippets in the Help system.

Again, you're not required to memorize an enormous number of objects. Simply learn about the StarBasic programming structure, its statements, and expressions. The structure is compatible with Microsoft's VBA (used in Word 97 and Excel 97). Unfortunately (although with good reason), the object hierarchy of StarOffice is not equivalent to that of Microsoft Office. If you've used both Word and StarWriter, it's obvious that the programs are different! Because they have different paradigms of usage, they also have different functions and attributes and, therefore, different objects to deal with.

> **Note**
>
> Becoming a StarBasic programmer generally means that you're familiar with Microsoft Visual Basic in the sense of application structure and use cases. However, using StarBasic, you can gain little knowledge on the objects used in Microsoft Office. Although the StarBasic and VBA languages are compatible, the objects differ. This means a StarBasic program needs to be rewritten to incorporate it into MS Office.

APPEARANCE OF STAROFFICE OBJECTS

Most of the time, you can find several ways to access one object. For example, instead of using

```
ActiveWindow.Font.FontDialog()
```

you could use

```
[letter_to_mom:1].Font.FontDialog()
```

provided `letter_to_mom` is the active document. Another option is to use `Selection.Font.FontDialog()`.

Keep in mind, however, the differences in the behavior of each command:

- `ActiveWindow.Font.FontDialog()` and `Selection.Font.FontDialog()` are functional only if the macro is started from a text document, and the text cursor must be placed in between text. These commands work in every text document.

- `[letter_to_mom:1].Font.FontDialog()` refers directly to a document with the name `letter_to_mom`. Therefore, this particular text document needs to be open. Again, the text cursor must be placed in between text.

As you can see, you can refer to a method or property in several ways, some of them depending on the context. The macro recorder always generates code closest to the context in which you recorded it. If you want to use a recorded macro for general purposes, you first need to ensure that the references are not direct.

Learn more about the StarOffice object hierarchy in Chapter 39, "Programming with StarBasic."

TROUBLESHOOTING THE ONLINE HELP SYSTEM

You can find almost everything you need to know about StarBasic in the Help system. Alas, its structure is not the most convenient; familiarizing yourself with it can be quite a challenge. This section provides a few tips on how to find the appropriate information without losing too much time.

The StarOffice Help system is organized into different blocks, one for each program. If you select Help and then Contents in a StarWriter document, a StarWriter-specific help window appears. Click the pair of binoculars in the object bar to perform an indexed search of the Help system.

To open a help file of a specific StarOffice program, open the Help system located in the Help tree of the Explorer (as shown in Figure 37.13).

Figure 37.13
An easier way into the rather convoluted StarBasic Help system is via the StarOffice Help links found in the Explorer.

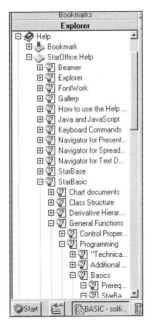

From within the search dialog of the StarBasic Help, you can find what you need via the Index or Text tabs. However, the help system poses two key problems. Due to the various appearances of StarBasic objects, a search by index is often unsuccessful. You then need to select the Text tab and launch a full text search. This method generally poses no problem; in fact, it works too well. It usually produces a superabundant list that may take you hours to decipher. Adding to the congestion are the lengthy examples StarBasic help uses to illustrate a command. On the positive side, the StarBasic help includes the StarOne API, where you can find equal names for similar objects.

When you're in the Basic Editor environment, you can open the Help Agent by pressing the F1 key. After the Help Agent appears, if you place the cursor into an object or command within your program, the Help Agent then extracts a context-sensitive explanation from the Help system. As StarOne files occur within the StarBasic help files, the Help Agent might display the wrong topic. Nevertheless, the Help Agent is very handy and quite usable in its current state.

Use the binoculars on the Help Agent toolbar to search the StarBasic help files. If you find what you're looking for, don't forget to click the Stop button. Otherwise, the Help Agent continues moving through the contents as you perform other actions.

If you find information regarding a method or property and want to get an overview of all the methods or properties of its parent object, as luck would have it, in most instances no link is available. To get around this problem, follow the Help tree in the StarOffice Explorer (refer to Figure 37.13). When you arrive at the properties and methods listing, you should be able to choose the object by using its first letter. If this method is unsuccessful, examine the sample code of the property or method you want to explore. Fortunately, the examples are quite explicit and deal with virtually all properties and methods of the referring object. The drawback, however, is that you can't flip to the explanation of the object from within the sample code by clicking a hyperlink. You therefore need to return to your help files and conduct a manual search.

If you use the text search function to look for a property, omit the parentheses. For example, you should enter `FontDialog()` as `FontDialog`. Don't conduct nested searches to look for part of an object structure (for example, `Font.FontDialog()`); your search will not produce results–even if you look for a common object property such as `Name`. Use an asterisk to search for substrings; you can place an asterisk in front of your expression, behind it, or on both sides (for example, `*Font`, `Dialog*` or `*ontDialo*`).

Tip #596 from
Werner Roth

In a regular help window or from the Help Agent, in theory you can use Ctrl+C to copy code snippets or other items. However, this method doesn't always function perfectly. A more reliable method is to select the text, right-click, and choose Copy from the context menu.

Becoming accustomed to using the StarBasic branch of the Help tree is a good idea. It helps you to find the methods you need from within the StarOffice object hierarchy (giving you an idea of the path you need to specify). You can discover anything outstanding by recording a macro and launching a search on the code generated. The code snippets in the Help system usually provide pragmatic introductory examples on how to use an object in a program. In addition, you can gain a good overview of the properties and methods belonging to this object.

Tip #597 from
Werner Roth

You can also find the StarBasic object hierarchy by searching for Class Structure in the Help system.

CHAPTER 38

UNDERSTANDING STARBASIC STRUCTURES AND STATEMENTS

by Werner Roth

In this chapter

ENTERING THE WORLD OF STARBASIC

Chapter 37, "Familiarizing Yourself with StarBasic," introduced you to the automated way of creating mini-programs in StarBasic—using the macro recorder. Using the macro recorder is a way for you to program without any knowledge of StarBasic structures. When you get bitten by the bug to debug and improve your macros or even create your own dialog boxes or other applications, you need to delve more deeply into creating programs the hands-on way—by entering StarBasic code directly in the StarBasic editor window. This chapter, along with Chapter 39, "Programming with StarBasic," gives you a basic introduction to this kind of direct programming with StarBasic.

It's far beyond the scope of this book to give a complete introduction to StarBasic, not to mention programming. Doing so would require an entire book of its own. Instead, these chapters introduce you to some of the more interesting features of the StarBasic language and structure, and give you enough information and sample program code to launch your own investigations into the world of StarBasic. This chapter focuses on StarBasic structures; teaching you how a macro program is designed in general, as well as the way a macro program controls your StarOffice document. The following chapter brings you in contact with macros that use some common StarOffice objects for everyday tasks.

To learn more about the many functions, commands, and objects that are not discussed, check out the StarBasic help system. You can pull up the StarBasic glossary by searching the Help for `general functions` and `runtime functions`. You'll also find different categories for global tasks. You can locate control statements by following the link `controlling program execution`.

Although the StarBasic glossary is complete, it's also pretty cryptic unless you are already an experienced programmer. Fortunately, StarBasic uses the same programming structures as Visual Basic for Applications, the well-known Microsoft programming language. This means that you can easily find out more about statements and flow of data in StarBasic programs by investigating some of the many fine books available on Visual Basic for Applications.

Note

If you are familiar with Microsoft Visual Basic you'll see that it uses the same statements as StarBasic. You can familiarize yourself with these Basic dialects by looking at the code that is generated by Visual Basic. However, be careful—Visual Basic is more powerful than Visual Basic for Applications and StarBasic when dealing with objects. Furthermore, a lot of commands used by StarBasic are out of the StarOffice Object hierarchy. As this hierarchy was designed by Star Division you will not find it in Visual Basic or Visual Basic for Applications. For more information about Visual Basic, check out Que's *Using Visual Basic* or *Special Edition Using Visual Basic*.

INTRODUCTION TO PROGRAMMING

Chapter 37 introduced you to some of principles of programming in StarBasic. We created a program with the macro recorder as well as another program from scratch. Creating a StarBasic macro is usually a combination of these two ways. As StarBasic macros are generally very small programs for small tasks, it's not necessary to know common programming techniques. This section introduces you to the basic concepts of programming. If you're already familiar with programming you might want to skip ahead to the section "Introduction to Runtime Functions."

WHAT IS A PROGRAM?

A StarBasic program is simply a set of instructions in StarBasic language. To adapt your program to different situations, you can use control statements to adapt your program. Chapter 37 also introduced you to StarOffice objects, which are commands that tell StarOffice to perform certain actions controlled by a StarBasic program. Think about performing a task in a StarWriter document using the mouse. As a human being, you typically have to invoke a series of actions. It's not possible to tell StarOffice to carry out these actions with a single sentence in natural language such as: "Please, reformat the document; I forgot to assign the paragraph styles!" Unfortunately, computers are unable to reason as humans do. As they take every command literally, you need to state your instructions very explicitly and in a logical order. As you would guess StarBasic programs are no exception; they too consist of a series of individual instructions written in StarBasic or, let's say, StarOffice language.

→ For more details on the StarBasic language, control statements, and objects, **see** Chapter 37, "Familiarizing Yourself with StarBasic," starting on **p. 1239**.

PART

VIII

CH

38

ELEMENTS OF A PROGRAM

The set of instructions that make up a program is called *code*. A single instruction consists of a StarBasic *command* and its *arguments*.

StarBasic has a whole set of special commands that are called statements. Some of these statements include the following:

- If
- Loop
- Function
- Sub
- End
- Do
- Else

All StarBasic statements are reserved words. "Reserved" means that you can't use these words in any other way in your code statements because StarBasic always interprets these words as commands.

Although an instruction can consist of just a single StarBasic command, more frequently a StarBasic term is modified by arguments. These arguments enable you to construct commands so that the computer can interact with a user and perhaps data stored in the computer. A command with arguments has a special *syntax*; that is, it requires that the arguments be placed in a certain order and demarcated with specific symbols (such as commas or semicolons).

> **Caution**
>
> Be sure to pay attention to the syntax and symbols used in the examples in this chapter. You must follow them exactly; otherwise, you will get an error and need to check what's wrong.

If you've worked with spreadsheet functions, this concept of a command and its arguments is already familiar to you. A spreadsheet function like SUM is essentially a command; you then enter an argument's data such as cell references and alphanumeric values (*variables*) that enable the function to calculate and return an answer.

Variables are an essential component of Basic programs. Variables store numeric values, strings, or objects at runtime. Variables can be read by the program, or the contents can be modified. Variables are sometimes called *operands* if they are being operated upon or changed in some way by the program.

To summarize these points, if you want to write a program, you write a series of commands that are modified with arguments. These commands make up your code, and your code makes up your program. Don't concern yourself too much in the beginning with writing code; the macro recorder will generate perfect working code for you. This enables you to "get into" programming by becoming familiar with the generated code.

ORGANIZING YOUR PROGRAM

If you're creating a large program, the common practice is to break up your large program into a series of smaller *subprograms* that *call* one another. These smaller subprograms are called *subprocedures* and *functions* in StarBasic. Breaking up your program like this makes it easier to test and debug because you can test each portion separately. You were introduced to subroutines in Chapter 37 because a macro is a subroutine.

As you also learned in Chapter 37, StarOffice gives you two other hierarchical levels of objects for storing StarBasic code: *modules* and *libraries*.

PLANNING THE DESIGN OF YOUR PROGRAM

If you want to create a large program using StarBasic you should design it first. Giving a cursory thought and then immediately writing code often generates horrible buggy programs. If you're just writing these ordinary small macro programs, it's important to properly design them as well. Luckily, however, in this case a sheet of paper, a pencil, and bit of joy in your heart will suffice.

Programmers call creating a new program *developing a program*. The six common steps in developing a StarBasic program are as follows:

1. Jot down what your program should do. Divide it into single tasks and solve them separately. Use a pencil for this "design" process. Draw the elements of your programs on a sheet of paper and write their tasks beside them.

2. If your program uses dialogs (as shown in Chapter 39), design the look of the program on the screen (that is, the *user interface*) as well as on a sheet of paper.

3. Write instructions in StarBasic to create the interface and make the program do what you want.

4. Run your program to see whether it works.

5. Fix any errors (bugs).

6. Keep repeating steps 4 and 5 until your program runs properly (or until you can't stand it anymore, whichever comes first).

The most important parts of the process are those that don't take place at the computer: defining what you want your program to do and deciding how the interface should look. The two go hand-in-hand because if you aren't clear about what the program should do, you can't create an interface that makes sense to the user.

The catch-22 here is that it can be difficult to define what you want your program to do until you understand enough of the language to see what's possible. That's why it's a good idea to begin by creating and tweaking macros. That's also why this chapter and the next give you a number of examples of subroutines that perform common tasks or use common commands.

DOCUMENTING YOUR WORK

The one important command in programming that is the same in all computer languages is this: Document your work!

CREATING COMMENTS

To document your work, you enter *comments* (also known as *remarks*). You precede a comment with an apostrophe, which tells StarBasic to ignore the text that follows rather than interpret it as programming language.

You can place an apostrophe at the beginning of a line to define the complete line as a comment or place it beside a command line, as shown here:

```
Sub CalculateSomething
    [...]
    'This a commented line
    a = 42 'This a commented assignment
    [...]
End Sub
```

If you've had experience with another Basic language, you may be familiar with the Rem statement. (Rem stands for *remark*.) You can use this statement in StarBasic as well.

Commenting your code is extremely important. When creating, testing, and running your program at the time of development, you might not see the need for commenting. However, explaining and documenting your code properly will make it maintainable. You'll be surprised how quickly your programs become foreign to you. Even the best programmers forget how they designed their program and the various problems they solved while developing it. And, of course, if you're creating your programs for a group of users or passing your code on to others, they won't understand your code without your explanations.

WHAT SHOULD YOU DOCUMENT?

You should comment the structure of your program with complete sentences. What is this method for? What is the task of this subprocedure? What does this public variable contain? Comment every major block of code. Explain its task, its data, and its design.

Acknowledge all problems you solved in a block of code. Perhaps a StarOffice object initially appeared to be good for a task, but it failed under usage. Or perhaps you had to circumvent a problem. You should also use lines to separate your blocks of code to make them more readable, just as you might separate a chapter into sections.

Use representative names for your variables to avoid the need to comment a single line. Avoid commenting something that is self-explanatory, like this line:

```
a = 42 'Here we assign the value 42 to a variable named a
```

A comment should not belabor the obvious but should provide insight into the purpose of the code. An example of a good comment is as follows:

```
'IntLinesAlreadyPrinted controls the lines printed on a page.
'On the first page the header is fixed 42 lines.
IntLinesAlreadyPrinted = 42
```

As shown in the previous example, use names for your variables that explain what they are doing, their type and even where they came from and who created them. The size of the project will determine just how much self documentation a variable name should provide. For example, the name of the actual module could be a handy bit of information in large projects, however, it's just a lot of senseless typing in a small macro that may last one day. You can be sure that anything you program in StarBasic will be a small task. Therefore, find a suitable variable name that describes its task and attach an abbreviation of your variable's data type to the front of it. Hence, `IntLinesAlreadyPrinted` is an integer and the variable `StrCustomerID` should be a string (this is called *Hungarian notation*).

INTRODUCTION TO RUNTIME FUNCTIONS

StarBasic has a number of built-in functions called *runtime functions*. This section introduces three of these functions: `Print`, `MsgBox`, and `InputBox`.

The `Print` statement doesn't actually print something to a printer but just displays ("prints") given data in a dialog. The data can be a string or a numeric expression. To separate the data, use a semicolon; use a comma to place a tab between them. The following is an example of the `Print` command; its result appears in Figure 38.1:

```
Sub PrintHelloWorld
    Print("Hello World!", 42)
    Print("Hello World!"; 42)
End Sub
```

Figure 38.1
The `Print` statement defines a dialog box like the one you see here.

The `Print` statement is appropriate only for a limited range of tasks, however. If the user were to choose the Cancel button, your StarBasic macro would "break" or stop immediately. Although the `Print` command has a limited usefulness in creating a program, it's useful for evaluation purposes—kind of a "poor man's debugger."

The `MsgBox` command, on the other hand, enables you to create a dialog box that gives the user more options and information. (`MsgBox` stands for *message box*.) Its syntax is

```
MsgBox(Text [, Type [, Dialogtitle ] ])
```

where `Text` and `Dialogtitle` are strings, and `Type` is an integer. The simplest way to invoke the `MsgBox` command is as follows:

```
Sub PrintHelloWorld
   MsgBox("Hello World!")
End Sub
```

The argument `Type` allows you to specify the elements and look of your dialog box. (Here, you can pull out your interface design doodles.) You simply add the appropriate code for the buttons, icons, and default button. Table 38.1 lists the code numbers associated with different elements.

TABLE 38.1   CODE NUMBERS FOR DIALOG BOX BUTTONS

Buttons		Icons		Default Button	
0	OK	16	Stop	0	First
1	OK and Cancel	32	Question	256	Second
2	Retry and Cancel	48	Exclamation	512	Third
3	Yes, No, and Cancel	64	Information		
4	Yes and No				
5	Retry and Cancel				

The *default button* is the button that is highlighted when you open the dialog and is activated if you press Enter (unless you click or move the cursor elsewhere). This button is also said to have the *focus*.

If you want to display a dialog with the buttons OK and Cancel and an exclamation mark, placing the focus on the Cancel button, you use the type-code 1+48+256. Although you could just enter the sum of these numbers, doing so isn't good programming style. StarBasic is clever enough to recognize that 1+48+256 equals 305, and leaving the code numbers as is allows other programmers to visualize the style of the dialog just from the source code.

The result of the following is shown in Figure 38.2:

```
Sub ImportantHelloWorld
    MsgBox("Hello World!", 1+48+256, "Important")
End Sub
```

Figure 38.2
The MsgBox com-
mand creates more
complex dialogs than
the Print statement,
enabling a user to
choose from a num-
ber of options.

When a button on a message box is pressed by a user, it returns a specific numerically coded value that enables the program to interpret the button's meaning. As a result, the program can respond to the user. Table 38.2 shows the values returned by the different buttons.

TABLE 38.2   BUTTON RESULT CODES

Button	Result
OK	1
Cancel	2
Retry	4
Yes	6
No	7

If you want to interact with the user as well as perform operations on entered data, neither the Print nor MsgBox commands will do. For this kind of task, you use the InputBox command.

The complete syntax for the InputBox command is

```
InputBox( Msg [, Title [, Default_Value [, x_pos,y_pos]]])
```

where the message box returns the number of the button (the button result codes) and the input box returns the string entered by the user; that is, it enables the user to enter data into the computer. (If the dialog is canceled, it returns an empty string.) Consider this example (see Figure 38.3):

```
Sub EnterTheName
    StrName = InputBox ("Enter your Name:", "Authentication", "Guest")
End Sub
```

Figure 38.3
This input dialog displays the password Guest as a default, but the user can enter a different password as well.

After the user clicks the OK button, the name entered will be stored in the variable StrName. The default value (which you entered in the code) is Guest.

If you don't specify a position, the input box is centered in the StarOffice window. Otherwise, you're required to set the screen position in *twips*, which is a screen-independent unit of measurement used in programming. For further information on twips take a look in the StarBasic Glossary.

Tip #598 from
Werner Roth

The result of InputBox is always a string. If you want to work with numeric values, you need to use the runtime function Val, which converts a string to an integer. Alternatively, you can simply pass the result of the InputBox function to a variable of numeric data type. StarBasic automatically "casts" or converts the result to a numeric value.

WORKING WITH VARIABLES AND OPERANDS

Variables and *operands* are needed to control you program. Their values could be given from within the program or input by the user. Variables and operands are used to make your program more generic (meaning that they fit into various situations). This section shows you how to use them.

DECLARING A VARIABLE

StarBasic makes it simple to deal with variables. You can declare variables without giving them a type, just by assigning a value. This type of declaration is known as an *implicit declaration*. However, declaring variables this way isn't necessarily the best programming practice, so this section introduces some other ways of handling variables as well.

To familiarize yourself with StarBasic variables, you can work with the runtime function TypeName(), as shown here. The argument of TypeName() is a variable, and the function returns the type of variable.

```
Sub Main
   MyVariable = 1
   print(TypeName(MyVariable)) 'Result is "Integer"
End Sub
```

Here, you declare an integer variable called MyVariable initialized with the number 1.

With the `Dim` statement, you can explicitly declare a variable. The following is the same program with the `Dim` statement instead:

```
Sub Main
    Dim MyVariable as Integer
    MyVariable = 1
    print(TypeName(MyVariable)) 'Result is "Integer"
End Sub
```

Why use `Dim`? The first reason is to make your code more readable; the second is to make it more stable. If a variable is not explicitly declared, its type is a so-called *variant*. This means the variable can be converted to any type just by assigning a value:

```
Sub Main
    NextOne = 1
    print NextOne, TypeName(NextOne) 'Result is "1 Integer"
    NextOne = "A"
    print NextOne, TypeName(NextOne) 'Result is "A String"
End Sub
```

Using the *variant* mechanism in your programs is not a good idea. An example of such a misuse is to recycle a temporary variable—in other words, to use it one time to store characters and the next time to calculate numbers. Using this type of temporary value doesn't improve the performance or lower the memory usage; you succeed only in getting yourself quite confused.

Implicitly declaring variables can cause major hiccups in your program. For instance, say you declare a variable `StrFirstName As String` (using the `Dim` statement). Later in the program, you refer to this variable again but accidentally make a typo (for example, `StrFirsttName`); by doing so, you automatically declare a new variable. To avoid this situation, StarBasic offers the `Option Explicit` statement. You use this statement at the beginning of a module, as shown here, to control the declaration of variables:

```
Option Explicit

Sub Main
    Dim StrFirstName As String
    StrFirsttName = "Rachel" 'Run-time error: Variable not defined
    print StrFirstName
End Sub
```

Tip #599 from
Werner Roth

For compatibility reasons, you can still declare a variable by adding a *type declaration character*, such as $ for a string and % for an integer value. However, this format of declaring variables was used in previous Basic dialects and is outdated.

VARIABLE DATA TYPES

You can use a number of data types as StarBasic variables. Table 38.3 lists them all and explains their uses.

TABLE 38.3   DATA TYPES AVAILABLE IN STARBASIC

Type	Explanation
Boolean	Boolean variables store the logical values True and False. They are used to control conditions; for example, they can control the result of a dialog box.
Currency	Currency is a numeric type used to store numeric values as monetary amounts without the need for entering currency characters. They are stored as 64-bit numbers; you can use them to calculate with high precision.
Date	Variables of the type Date are used to calculate time and date values. You can use a number of formats to assign a date to a variable, such as myvar = "10/31/1999" or myvar = "10.31.1999".
Double	Double is a type for floating-point values of high precision. Its range is from about 4.9×10^{-324} to 1.8×10^{308}. Use Single (described further down) if you don't require double precision.
Integer	Integer is the type normally used to store numeric values. It works with integer values between –32,768 and 32,767. Use numeric values only if you need to do calculations with them. Otherwise, using a string is safer. Remember that a customer number may contain leading zeros, such as "007". If you store this number as an integer, the leading zeros are eliminated:
| | ```
Sub ShowCustomerID
    Dim IntCustomerNumber As Integer
    IntCustomerNumber = 007
    Print IntCustomerNumber
'The result is "7" not "007"
End Sub
``` |
Long	Long is a long integer type and deals with numbers between –2,147,483,648 and 2,147,483,647. Use Long where a user can input a number. If you use this data type, the program can check the range of the number without causing an overflow error.
Object	Object variables are needed to store references to StarOffice objects such as documents. You can attach a single document by using a variable.
Single	Single is used to store floating-point values of single precision. The range for a single variable is about 1.4×10^{-45} to 3.4×10^{38}. For higher precision, use Double.
String	A String variable stores characters. It's useful for storing customer names, text selected in a StarWriter document, and many other kinds of data. One string variable can hold a maximum of 64,000 characters. You will use the String variable regularly.
Variant	Variant can contain different types of data. It can be substituted for all the data types mentioned here. (Doing so is not a good idea, however; you can save time and memory by using a definite data type.) The best use for a Variant type is the assignment of unknown data. After the data has been assigned, you can then examine it.

PART

VIII

CH

38
```

VALID NAMES FOR EXPRESSIONS

The maximum length of a StarBasic variable name is 255 characters. A variable name must begin with a letter. Valid characters for variables are *A* to *Z*, *a* to *z*, and the underscore (_) ; even the space character is allowed, although you need to enclose the name in brackets. The following snippet of code gives you examples of different variable names:

```
Sub TestSomeNames                      ' declare some variables containing
    dim HelloWorldPhrase as string     '   upper- and lowercase characters,
    dim StartAtColumn_42 as boolean   '   characters and numbers,
    dim Weight_in_Tons as single       '   underscore, and
    dim [Your Age] as integer          '   space (between brackets)

    HelloWorldPhrase = "Hello World!"
    StartAtColumn_42 = True
    Weight_in_Tons = 16
    [Your Age] = 42
End Sub
```

As mentioned previously, StarBasic generally ignores the case of letters in the statements. Hence, you're unable to declare a new variable just by changing the case of a pre-existing one. A variable cannot have the same name as any StarBasic reserved word. The following example gives you some forbidden names for expressions and how to correct them:

```
Sub TestSomeMore
    dim True as boolean          'Error already defined constant
    dim sub as integer           'Error Sub is a StarBasic keyword
    dim BoolIsTrue as boolean     'Allowed
    dim int_sub_counter as integer   'Allowed
End Sub
```

If you want to call a subprocedure whose name has a space in it, you need to enclose it in brackets. The same is true for StarBasic libraries or modules. It's probably easier to refrain from using spaces in item names. Instead, you could use the underscore or capital letters. Let's call two subprocedures from other libraries:

```
Sub CallASubprocedure
    'Call a procedure of another library
    LibraryName.ModuleName.NameOfTheSubprocedure
    'Call a procedure of another library with spaces in their names.
    [library name].[module name].[name of the subprocedure]
End Sub
```

ARRAYS

Arrays store a list of elements of the same type. For each element of an array to be treated and accessed as a single variable, each array element is given its own index. You use the `dim` statement to declare an array.

For example, the line

```
Dim Items(5) As String
```

declares an array called `Items` that has six elements of the type `string` (StarBasic begins counting at zero). They are called `Items(0)`, `Items(1)`, and so on to `Items(5)`. You can use them like ordinary variables:

```
Items(0) = "Gem"
Items(1) = "Magic flute"
```

The advantage of having six array elements instead of six normal variables is that you can address them by their index in the parentheses. This means you can cycle through the elements with a little loop and an index counter. By default, the index of an array begins at zero. To alter this number, you can explicitly designate the upper and lower bounds when declaring the following:

```
Dim Numbers(1 to 5) As Integer
```

In this example, the lowest index is 1 and the highest index is 5. (Now the array has only five elements.) If you need more than one dimension, simply assign a new set of bounds separated by a comma when declaring:

```
Sub MoreDimensions
    Dim Matrix(5,5) As Double
    Dim Element3d(-10 to 10, -10 to 10,-10 to 10) As Integer
    Matrix(0,0) = 34.67
    Element3d(-10, 0, 5) = 34
End Sub
```

CONSTANTS

Constants are similar to variables; however, they keep their value throughout the existence of the program and can't be changed at runtime. The syntax to declare a constant is as follows:

```
Const <ConstantName> = <Value>
```

A constant does not require a data type because the data type is made obvious by the value. When you declare a constant, the compiler performs an internal search through the program for the `<ConstantName>`. Every time the compiler finds the name in the program, it replaces that name with its `<Value>`. From a technical point of view, constants aren't necessary. However, they help you make your code more readable and flexible.

The following example shows how constants help document a program. You can use constants for physical values, mathematical constants, measures, or factors, as you see here:

```
Sub Convert
    Const Meter2Feet = 3.2809
    Const SpeedOfLight = 299792458
    Const Minute2Hour = 1/60
    '[...]
    'More constants and declarations here
    '[...]
    Dim IntMinutes As Integer, IntHours As Integer
    IntMinutes = InputBox("Number of minutes Amount of minutes", _
                        "Minutes to Hours")
    'Calculate the conversion simply by multiplying it by the factor
    IntHours = IntMinutes * Minute2Hour
    MsgBox("This took us " & IntHours & " hours!", 48, "Information")
End Sub
```

The next example shows how to use constants to make your program more flexible. Say you need to make some conversions with a grid of 10 by 15 elements. As always, it's best not to waste memory (especially when using arrays). Therefore, you should declare a two-dimensional array for the elements of the grid, sized 10 by 15. What if one day you need a larger grid? In that case, you can simply change the values of the constants `MaxGridColumns` and `MinGridRows`:

```
Sub TheGrid
   Const MaxGridColumns = 10
   Const MinGridRows    = 15
   Dim GridCells( 1 To MaxGridColumns, 1 To MinGridRows) As Integer
   [...]
   'Assign values to the GridCells array
   For i = 1 To MaxGridColumns
      For j = 1 To MinGridRows
         [...]
         ' Do something with GridCells(i,j) here
         [...]
      Next j
   Next i
End Sub
```

Making your programs as flexible as possible is a good idea. However, when you're changing constant values to adapt a program, don't neglect the rest of the code. By means of testing, make sure the new values are compatible with the rest of the program. Now and again, a programmer could insert an actual value in code instead of the constant's name. A year later, another programmer might come along with the good intention of adapting the program to current needs; the second programmer needs to change only the values of the constants. What do you know? A small disaster results!

LIFETIME AND SCOPE OF A VARIABLE

When you're declaring a variable, StarBasic saves the value in memory so that every time the variable name appears in your program, StarBasic recognizes it. The life of your variable begins on declaration, but when does it end? An additional question is, Who has access to the variable? Once it is declared, is it accessible by everyone? Take a look at the following example:

```
'It's important to use explicit declarations of variables,
'otherwise StarBasic will declare its value on use and replace
'it with an empty string or zero. You won't receive an error message
'when trying to access a variable whose lifetime is over.
'The following line must be at the top of the module!
Option Explicit

Sub SetPhrase
   Dim StrLocalPhrase As String
   StrLocalPhrase = "Hello World!"
   'Call the subprocedure PrintPhrase
   PrintPhrase
End Sub
```

```
Sub PrintPhrase
   Print(StrLocalPhrase)   'Error variable not defined!
End Sub
```

In the preceding (incomplete) program, a variable LocalPhrase is declared in the procedure SetPhrase. From the sub SetPhrase, you call the sub PrintPhrase. Ideally, the PrintPhrase sub should print "Hello World". However, because the variable LocalPhrase does not belong to PrintPhrase, it fails to recognize the variable and throws the runtime error Variable not defined!.

A variable's lifetime is normally within its subprocedure. The technical term for this is that it is a *local variable*; in other words, it begins upon declaration and ends at the End Sub statement. Because LocalPhrase is a local variable, the PrintPhrase command can't see it; it's as if that variable lives in another country.

The fact that variables live, by default, only as long as their subprocedure is running enables you to use identical variable names in different subprocedures. This approach is quite common, particularly as a counter, typically named i or j, in a for loop.

However, what if you want to share a variable with another subprocedure? The following example solves that problem:

PART
VIII
CH
38

```
Option Explicit
Dim StrGlobalPhrase As String

Sub SetPhrase
   StrGlobalPhrase = "Hello World!"
   'Call the Subprocedure PrintPhrase
   PrintPhrase
End Sub

Sub PrintPhrase
   Print(StrGlobalPhrase)   'This prints "Hello World!"
End Sub
```

> **Note**
>
> Use argument lists to pass information to subprocedures. Operating with global variables, as in the PrintPhrase example, is not recommended. It can cause drastic side effects. For example, if a programmer fails to recognize an interaction with a global variable and adds a third subprocedure, it could have dire consequences. Use global variables for global information—that is, the name of the working folder or the choice of language if your program is multilingual.

```
Option Explicit

Sub SetPhrase
   Dim StrMyPhrase As String
   StrMyPhrase = "Hello World!"
   'Call the Subprocedure PrintPhrase
   PrintPhrase(StrMyPhrase)
End Sub
```

```
Sub PrintPhrase(StrSomePhrase As String)
    Print(StrSomePhrase)   'This prints "Hello World!"
End Sub
```

Now take the time to test the preceding program. The message "Hello World!" should then appear on your screen. As you can see, the variable GlobalPhrase is declared outside all subs at the beginning of the module. Declaring it this way gives all subs and functions of the module access to the variable. Such a variable has the entire module as its scope and is called a *module level* or *private variable*.

Note

You can also use the statement Private instead of Dim when declaring a module level variable. Similarly, you can replace the statement Global with Public.

Likewise, if you need a constant in more than one subprocedure or function of your module, place the declaration outside all subs at the beginning of the module.

The statement Global declares a variable to be within the scope of all StarBasic libraries. In the event that you need a variable in different modules of a project, declare it as follows:

```
Global <Variable name> As <Data type>
```

This statement makes the variable accessible in every subprocedure or function that exists.

Note

Avoid overuse of module level or global variables. They can cause drastic side effects. Imagine every subprocedure being able to change a variable's value. Static variables are more suitable in some situations.

Earlier, you learned that the lifetime of a local variable ends with its subprocedure. This presents a problem if you need a variable for only one procedure, but the procedure repeats itself a number of times during the lifetime of the complete program.

The following example shows such a subprocedure. In this case, the subprocedure allows only three executions in one StarOffice session. (It's like a limited shareware version.) In such a case, you must somehow keep track of how many times the subprocedure is called so that you know when the limit of three is reached.

If you declare the variable IntCallsUntilNow with the Dim statement at the beginning of a subprocedure, its lifetime would end when the subprocedure ends. Following this logic, its life would begin again when the subprocedure is called again. Because the compiler always initiates an integer variable with the value zero, every time the subprocedure begins, IntCallsUntilNow will be assigned the value zero. Subsequently, if IntCallsUntilNow is declared as a global variable that's visible to other subprocedures, these subprocedures would reset the value to zero and the supposed "limited" subprocedure would start again.

If you declare the variable as *static*, its lifetime is the complete program, yet it is assigned the limited scope of the subprocedure FindTheSolution. On the first call of the subprocedure, Static declares the variable. In the following calls, the Static statement is ignored:

```
Sub FindTheSolution
    'IntCallsUntilNow is initialized with zero.
    'After the first call IntCallsUntilNow is equal to zero
    'and will be incremented by 1
    Static IntCallsUntilNow As Integer
    'Every call will increment IntCallsUntilNow
    'IntCallsUntilNow will not forget its value because it's a static variable
    IntCallsUntilNow = IntCallsUntilNow + 1

    If IntCallsUntilNow >= 3 Then
        MsgBox("Your Permit only allows 3 calls per session. Buy a bigger one.",_
               16,"Permit Restrictions")
        Exit Sub
    Endif
    [...]
    'The useful code is placed here!
End Sub
```

WORKING WITH ARITHMETIC OPERATORS

Instructions in StarBasic can consist of more than just commands and variables; they can also incorporate *arithmetic operators*, which instruct StarBasic about how to manipulate certain types of data.

In StarBasic, the equals sign (=) is used to assign a value to a variable or a property. The second most commonly used arithmetic operator, the plus sign (+), is used to add two values. A complete list of StarBasic's arithmetic operators is given in Table 38.4.

TABLE 38.4 ARITHMETIC OPERATORS IN STARBASIC

Operator	Name	Example	Value
+	Addition	a = 1 + 2	3
-	Subtraction	a = 1 - 2	-1
*	Multiplication	a = 2 * 3	6
/	Division	a = 12 / 6	2
^	Power	a = 2^3	8
mod	Modulus	a = 13 mod 6	1

You can use the arithmetic operators shown in Table 38.4 with variables of the types `integer` and `floating-point`. Odd but true, you can even use the modulus operator with floating-point values. Modulus is the integer remainder of a division operation.

StarBasic evaluates expressions containing more than one operator according to the *Operator Precedence Hierarchy*. Expressions in parentheses are evaluated first. The precedence of operators corresponds with the rules of BODMAS (having a flashback to elementary school?):

Brackets

Of

Division

Multiplication & Modulus

Addition

Subtraction

Division, multiplication, and modulus are of equal precedence and unlike normal mathematics are read right to left. Addition and subtraction are also of equal precedence and are also read right to left.

The following are some examples of these principles at work in StarBasic:

```
Sub TestArithmetic
    Print 2 + 3 * 4 'the result is 14
    Print 3 * 4 + 2 'the result is 14
    Print (2 + 3) * 4 'the result is 20
    'The next two lines produce different results, because Division,
    'Multiplication, and Modulus are of equal precedence.
    'So the associativity rule "right to left" is used.
    Print 8 mod 2 * 3 'the result is 2
    Print 3 * 8 mod 2 'the result is 0
End Sub
```

Concatenation Operator

StarBasic has a special concatenation operator (&) for strings. You can use it to join strings and other data together. You also can use the + operator to produce the same result, but doing so could become confusing, as you can see in the following example:

```
Sub PrintAmount
    Dim SingleItem1 As Single, SingleItem2 As Single, SingleAmount As Single
    Dim StrLastName As String, StrCustomerID As String
    SingleItem1 = 12.45
    SingleItem2 = 24.89
    SingleAmount = SingleItem1 + SingleItem2
    StrLastName = "Deckart"
    StrCustomerID ="00789"
    'The "&" operator will put the data together, the result is:
    'Amount of Order Deckart Id: 00789 is $37.34
    print "Amount of Order " & StrLastName & " Id: " & StrCustomerID & _
        " is $" & SingleAmount
    'When concatenating strings together the result is:
    'Amount is $12.4524.89
    print "Amount is $" + SingleItem1 + SingleItem2
    'When the parentheses have the higher precedence the result is:
    'Amount is $37.34
    print "Amount is $" + (SingleItem1 + SingleItem2)
End Sub
```

Confusing, isn't it? The best solution is to always use the & operator and avoid getting into trouble with +.

Relational and Equality Operators

You use relational and equality operators in condition and loop statements to make decisions. The result of a Boolean expression is True or False. StarBasic internally represents this result as -1 for True and 0 for False. In fact, every value other than 0 represents True.

TABLE 38.5   RELATIONAL AND EQUALITY OPERATORS IN STARBASIC

Operator	Name	Example	Value
=	Equal to	1 = 1	True
>	Greater than	1 > 2	False
<	Less than	1 < 2	True
>=	Greater than or equal to	1 >= 2	False
<=	Less than or equal to	1 <= 2	True
<>	Not equal to	1 <> 1	False

With the use of logical operators, you can combine Boolean expressions.

LOGICAL OPERATORS

If you want to test whether a numeric variable is between two values, the expression 1 < Value < 10 is invalid. You need to perform two separate checks: first, whether the value is greater than 1, and second, whether the value is less than 10. By using logical operators, you can combine these two results together so that they can be evaluated, as shown in this example:

```
Sub CompareIntValues
    Dim IntValue As Integer
    IntValue = 5
    'the result is -1, that's the internal value for true,
    'recognizable by the interpreter.
    Print( (1 < IntValue) and (IntValue < 10) )
End Sub
```

Table 38.6 lists these logical operators.

TABLE 38.6   LOGICAL OPERATORS IN STARBASIC

Operator	Name	Example	Value
and	Combination	True and True	True
or	Disjunction	True or False	True
not	Inversion	Not True	False
xor	Exclusive-Or Combination	True xor True	False
imp	Implication	True imp False	False
eqv	Equivalence	True eqv False	False

You can even abandon the parentheses in the expression (1 < Value) and (Value < 10); you don't need to add spaces around the characters either. However, brackets and spaces make your code more readable and reliable. Similarly, in most cases and, or, and not will be enough.

PART
VIII

CH
38

Table 38.7 presents three examples of using logical expressions to evaluate returned values.

TABLE 38.7   EXAMPLES OF LOGICAL EXPRESSIONS

Expression	Explanation
Value1 and Value2	Is True if Value1 and Value2 are True. In all other cases, the result of this expression is False.
Value1 or Value2	Is True if at least one or both values are True. This expression is False only if Value1 and Value2 are False.
not Value1	Negates the value of the expression. So, if Value1 is True, the expression is False and vice versa.

WORKING WITH PROCEDURES AND FUNCTIONS

As you learned at the beginning of this chapter, a StarBasic program usually consists of a number of subprocedures and functions strung together. Because every StarBasic program consists of at least one subprocedure or function, you can start any subprocedure or function (usually in a module) independently by choosing Tools and then Macro. You have to take care, though, because clicking the Run button in the macro bar starts the very first macro in the opened StarBasic module. This observation leads into the discussion of the typical usage of StarBasic programs.

THE ORGANIZATION OF SUBPROCEDURES AND FUNCTIONS

The importance of organizing your program into subprocedures and functions was described earlier in the chapter. This section delves more deeply into the reasons and methods for structuring programs in this way.

It's quite common for a user to collect many small subprocedures and functions in a module that don't interact with each other. For example, if you've created a number of different macros to automate formatting a StarCalc worksheet, they are all stored together even though they don't call one another. On the other hand, a user may have only a few StarBasic applications that are organized in modules or libraries; in other words, a module or a complete library is an entire application.

The Main subprocedure stands at the top of every module and plays a big role in regulating the other subprocedures and functions of the module. That's why StarBasic places an empty subprocedure called Main at the top of each module.

There's no technical difference between a subprocedure that is the main program and a subprocedure that's called by the main program. However, a subprocedure called by a main program may not be functional if not called in its proper context. Therefore, invoking all subprocedures listed in the Macro dialog (which you open by choosing Tools, Macro) is not a good idea, not even to test them if you don't know what they do.

The following example demonstrates how you might divide a program into different sub-procedures in relation to the Main subprocedure:

```
Sub MainProgram
    SolveTask1
    Do While MyFunction(Value) < 10
       SolveTask2(Value)
    Loop
    SolveTask3
End Sub

Sub SolveTask1
    <Statement block>
End Sub

Sub SolveTask2(Value)
    'Work with argument "Value"
    <Statement block>
End Sub

Sub SolveTask3
    <Statement block>
End Sub

Function MyFunction(Value)
    'Work with argument "Value"
    <Statement block>
     MyFunction = <Statement>
End Function
```

PART

VIII

CH

38

In this program, the MainProgram procedure calls all the other subprocedures and functions. The main task is split into the subs: SolveTask1, SolveTask2, and SolveTask3. SolveTask1 and SolveTask3 are called only once; they are only generic terms for their statement block to structure the program. SolveTask2 is called many times in the loop. Furthermore, it works in cooperation with MainProgram by passing it an argument. The self-defined function MyFunction takes an argument and determines when the loop will end.

Here, you can see how the problem is divided into three pieces and controls the program by a function. You could write the same program all in one subprocedure. However, look at the Main sub; it depends on seven command lines. Separated in different subprocedures, the code is clearer and better for debugging purposes. Writing it this way, you can section off one piece of code and check its performance.

STARTING WITH ARGUMENT LISTS

To pass information from one subprocedure to another, you use argument lists. In this section, you'll program a subprocedure to print a calculated value and use an argument list in the process:

```
Sub CalculateSomething
    Dim IntTheResult As Integer
    [...]
    'Calculate something and assign it to variable TheResult
    [...]
```

```
    'Call the subprocedure PrintOneResult
    PrintOneResult(IntTheResult)
End Sub

Sub PrintOneResult(IntOneResult as integer)
    MsgBox("The result is: " & IntOneResult, 64, "Your Result")
End Sub
```

The result of the calculations in the Main subprocedure are passed to PrintOneResult by an integer argument. Therefore, PrintOneResult is a generic subprocedure to display any integer value to the screen. The Print(PrintOneResult) subprocedure is called with the statement PrintOneResult(TheResult). The PrintOneResult sub is defined as Sub PrintOneResult(OneResult as integer). This means you can pass any integer value to PrintOneResult independent of the name of the variable. Notice that the two arguments have different names—IntTheResult and IntOneResult. Alternatively, you can call the subprocedure by using the line PrintOneResult(42).

If you need more than one argument in your subprocedure, separate them with commas:

```
Sub PrintOneResult(IntOneResult As Integer, StrMsgBoxTitle As String)
    MsgBox("The result is: " & IntOneResult,64, StrMsgBoxTitle)
End Sub
```

You are required to call this version of the sub with two arguments—the result and a title for the message box—as in this example:

```
PrintOneResult(IntTheResult, "Result of CalculateSomething")
```

USER-DEFINED FUNCTIONS

StarBasic includes a runtime function called sqr() to calculate the square root of a given argument. Typically, you pass the result of this function to a variable. An example of sqr() is as follows:

```
DoubleASquareRoot = sqr(9)
```

Hence, the value of the variable DoubleASquareRoot is now 3.

You can also create your own functions, known as *user-defined functions*. Here, you create the mathematical function Power as a user-defined StarBasic function:

```
Function Power(DoubleTheBase As Double, DoubleThePower As Double) As Double
    Power = DoubleTheBase^DoubleThePower
End Function
```

The arguments of the Power function are two floating-point values, passing the base and the power to the function. Managing the argument list of a function is the same as shown for a subprocedure. The primary difference is the return value. Your user-defined function returns a floating-point value. A function automatically declares a variable within its bounds as a type function. This variable is assigned the result of the calculations in the function. In the preceding example, this variable is called Power. You must have at least one assignment to the result variable (Power). Variables in a function can be used just like normal variables; that is, they can be assigned values more than once.

To call a user-defined function, you use the same statement as you use for the runtime function sqr(). As shown here, in respective order, you can assign its result to a variable or use your function in a complete calculation:

```
AVariable = Power(3,2) 'this results 9
BVariable = (AVariable - Power(AVariable,2))/2 'this means (9 - 9^2) / 2 = - 36
```

The syntax of a function statement is as follows:

```
Function <Name>[(<VarName> [As <data type>][, <other arguments here>]]) [As <data
type>]
    <Statement block>
    <Name> = <SomeValue>
End Function
```

The data type of your function is declared with the last [As <data type>] statement. Declaring a data type is optional, but not specifying a data type of the result means that the compiler will automatically nominate type variant, StarBasic's all-purpose data type. General use of this data type can get you into trouble; one little slip-up when you're assigning the return value can render your function kaput. As you can see below, it's not always necessary to give a function arguments; it can be useful not to. The following function returns the version number of a StarBasic program:

```
Function Version as string
    Version = "1.0 Beta"
End Function
```

To display the version number to the screen, call it like this:

```
Print Version()
```

There's no need to use the brackets. However, it's useful as a reminder that Version() is a function, not a variable.

In the everyday life of a programmer, you use functions not only to calculate things, but you also use them instead of subprocedures with the advantage of using the return value for program control. The following code tries to open a file with a function. The function returns True when the action is successful and False when a problem occurs—for example, if you get the File Not Found message:

```
Sub Main
    [...]
    If OpenAFile("c:\temp\user.dat") then
        'Continue with your actions
    Else
        'Do some error handling here
    Endif
End Sub

Function OpenAFile(FileName As String) As Boolean
    'If all went well OpenAFile = True
    'in the case the action failed OpenAFile = False
End Function
```

PART

VIII

CH

38

You can even call a function in the same way you would call a subprocedure. You don't need to assign the result to anything; you can simply start the command line with the function call (as with a subprocedure).

CALL BY WHAT?

The argument list declares variables to be used in the subprocedure. The classic use is to pass information to a subprocedure, not back from one. However, consider the following experiment:

```
Sub CallByReference
    Dim a As Integer
    a = 42
    MsgBox("a = " & a, 64, "First message box")
    TheSubroutine(a)
    MsgBox("a = " & a, 64, "Second message box")
End Sub

Sub TheSubroutine(JustAValue As Integer)
    JustAValue = 34
End Sub
```

The first message box shows a is 42; after executing the subprocedure TheSubroutine, the second message box shows a is 34. The variable a is not touched between both message boxes; just a call of a subprocedure occurs between them. What happened? The variable a is passed to TheSubroutine by reference, meaning that the variable JustAValue is in fact a reference to the variable a. Every manipulation to JustAValue is also performed on the argument.

In StarBasic, you can use another way besides calling by reference to pass arguments to a subprocedure or function. This method is called *calling by value*. When you call by value, you make a copy of the variable passed as an argument, and manipulations are performed on the copy; the original value remains unchanged. The command you use to declare a call by value argument is ByVal. The declaration for the example would look like this:

```
Sub TheSubroutine(ByVal JustAValue as integer)
```

Using call by reference arguments to pass information back from a subprocedure to the calling program is not ideal. You should use functions instead wherever possible. This approach is recommended so that readers of the source code can distinguish between arguments that are modified and those that are not. The next example calculates the cube of the value stored in the variable DoubleTheValue (3, if you recall) and passes it to the variable DoubleTheResult to demonstrate this point. This feat is accomplished by using a subprocedure with two arguments:

```
Sub CubeWithSub
    Dim DoubleTheResult As Double, DoubleTheValue As Double
    DoubleTheValue = 3
    Cube(DoubleTheResult, DoubleTheValue)
    MsgBox("The cube of " & DoubleTheValue & " is " & DoubleTheResult,_
           64, "Cube")
End Sub
```

```
Sub Cube(DoubleResult As Double, ByVal DoubleValue As Double)
    DoubleResult = DoubleValue^3
End Sub
```

`DoubleTheResult` is call by reference, and `DoubleTheValue` is call by value. However, this outcome is not readily noticeable by looking at the subprocedure call: `Cube(DoubleTheResult, DoubleTheValue)`. A better solution is to pass the result back by a function:

```
Sub CubeWithFunction
    Dim DoubleTheResult As Double, DoubleTheValue As Double
    DoubleTheValue = 3
    DoubleTheResult = Cube(DoubleTheValue)
    MsgBox("The cube of " & DoubleTheValue & " is " & DoubleTheResult,_
        64, "Cube")
End Sub

Function Cube(ByVal DoubleValue as double) as Double
    Cube = DoubleValue^3
End Function
```

The amendment to the program makes the situation a lot clearer. `DoubleTheResult = Cube(DoubleTheValue)` means no changes are made to the variable `DoubleTheValue`. Because the core StarBasic language doesn't have any user-defined objects, it's not possible, in any case, to avoid communication with call by reference variables. When you use different calling methods, properly commenting the subprocedure calls is important:

```
CalculateSumOfVectors(Rx, Ry, Ax, Ay, Bx, By)
'                      ^^  ^^                     call by reference
'                              ^^  ^^  ^^  ^^ call by value
```

OPTIONAL ARGUMENTS

In some cases, leaving out an argument is convenient. Think about the `MsgBox` command. Its syntax is as follows:

```
MsgBox Text [,Type [,Dialogtitle]]
```

You can call `MsgBox` with just one argument:

```
MsgBox( "I am the Text")
```

The message box appears in standard type, with no icon, and with the standard dialog title `soffice`. If you call it with two arguments, such as

```
MsgBox( "I am the Text", 32)
```

the type `32` represents a question—an icon with a question mark—but the dialog title remains `soffice`. Finally, if you use three arguments, as shown here, no default values are used:

```
MsgBox( "I am the Text", 32, "I am the Title")
```

In the next example, you create your own dialog that shows the amount of a bill. The standard currency is the dollar; it would be more convenient not to need to pass the string `"$"` to the `print` subprocedure. At the same time, it would be good if the program were flexible enough to show amounts in foreign currencies. To achieve this result, you can use an optional argument by placing the keyword optional before the declaration in the argument list:

```
Sub CalculateTheAmount
    'Print the amount on the screen with the default currency
    '"The amount is $ 33.45" will be the result
    PrintTheAmount(33.45)
    'Print the amount on the screen with a specified currency
    '"The amount is DM 33.45" will be the result
    PrintTheAmount(33.45, "DM")
End Sub

Sub PrintTheAmount(SingleAmount As Single, optional StrCurrency As String)
    'If sCurrency is not of the type string (8) there was no second argument
    'So assign StrCurrency the default currency dollar.
    If VarType(StrCurrency) <> 8 then StrCurrency = "$"
    MsgBox("The amount is " & StrCurrency & " " & SingleAmount,64, "Yep")
End Sub
```

The subprocedure called PrintTheAmount(33.45, "DM") is the same old routine. All arguments are given, making all variables in PrintTheAmount valid. However, the call PrintTheAmount(33.45) is a little more complicated. The second argument, StrCurrency, is not given, and in turn the variable is not valid. Using an invalid variable name in the MsgBox statement would cause an error. Therefore, you first need to check whether an argument was given. You check the data type by using the runtime functions VarType() or TypeName(). If sCurrency was not originally given a string, you need to assign one to it. You also can use an If...Then...Else...Endif statement to check whether an argument was given.

Table 38.8 gives a list of values used by the functions VarType() and TypeName().

TABLE 38.8   VALUES USED BY VarType() AND TypeName()

VarType()	TypeName()	**Explanation**
0	Empty	Variable is not defined
1	Null	No valid data
2	Integer	Fundamental data type
3	Long	Fundamental data type
4	Single	Fundamental data type
5	Double	Fundamental data type
6	Date	Fundamental data type
7	String	Fundamental data type
8	Object	Fundamental data type
8	Error	Argument not passed
10	Boolean	Fundamental data type
11	Variant	Fundamental data type

WORKING WITH CONTROL STATEMENTS

Control statements control the flow of your program. You need decision, loop, and exiting statements to control the flow of your program. In the following sections, you will formulate decisions by using the Boolean expressions mentioned previously.

DECISION STATEMENTS

You often need to use different decision statements for different cases. If the condition can have only a yes or no answer (in other words, if the answer can be only True or False), you use the If statement. The Select Case statement is often used to execute different code blocks, depending on the value of an enumeration variable.

If...Then...Else...Endif

The syntax for an If...Then...Endif block is as follows:

```
If <Condition> Then
    <Statement block>
Endif
```

If the condition results in True, the *Statement block* is executed. Otherwise, the program continues at the next command line after Endif, as shown here:

```
Sub UseMyDocuments
    Dim BoolError As Boolean
    [...]
    'Call an own function
    BoolError = CheckDocumentExists("c:\Office51\work\actual.sdw")
    'Check other stuff and assign it to Error
    [...]
    If BoolError Then
        MsgBox("Can't find the Documents needed.",16,"Error")
    Endif
    [...]
End Sub
```

Tip #600 from
Werner Roth

If the *Statement block* consists of only one command line, you can put this command into the same line as the If statement. The syntax is If <Condition> Then <Statement>. In this case, you don't need an Endif.

If you have a condition that is True, you want to execute one particular piece of code, and if the condition is False, a different piece of code, you can use the If...Then...Else...Endif statement:

```
If <Condition> Then
    <Statement block No. 1>
Else
    <Statement block No. 2>
Endif
```

Here, *Statement block No. 1* is executed if the condition results in True; otherwise, *Statement block No. 2* is executed. Now consider this example:

```
Sub PrintAddress
    [...]
    If StrGender = "female" Then
        StrSalutation = "Mrs."
    Else
        StrSalutation = "Mr."
    Endif
    [...]
End Sub
```

Because assignments such as the preceding example are quite common for administration purposes, StarBasic offers the IIF statement, shown here:

```
IIF( <Condition>, <Expression No. 1>, <Expression No. 2> )
```

The IIF is actually a function that returns *Expression No. 1* if the condition is True and *Expression No. 2* in all other cases. The If...Then...Else...Endif example can now be shrunken into a single line:

```
StrSalutation = IIf( StrGender = "female", "Mrs.", "Mr." )
```

Select Case

If you want to execute different statement blocks depending on the value of a variable or function, you can nest If statements. Therefore, you can use repetitive Elseif statements to cover a number of conditions.

Take a look at the following example. The StarBasic function called GetGUIType fetches the current graphic user interface (GUI). It returns a numeric value referring to the particular GUI because GUIs are given numeric values. (You can find out more about GetGUIType in the StarBasic help system.) Thus, if you want to create operating system-specific code, you can do so like this:

```
Sub InitializeForOS
    If GetGUIType() = 1 Then
        'Do something Windows specific here
    ElseIf GetGUIType() = 2 Then
        'Do something OS/2 specific here
    ElseIf GetGUIType() = 3 Then
        'Do something Macintosh specific here
    ElseIf GetGUIType() = 4 Then
        'Do something Motif specific here
    ElseIf GetGUIType() = 5 Then
        'Do something Open Window specific here
    Else
        MsgBox("Cannot recognize your Operating System", 16, "Error")
    Endif
End Sub
```

Because the decision depends on the value of a variable that comes from the result of one function, you can use the `Select Case` statement instead:

```
Sub InitializeForOS
    Select Case GetGUIType()
    Case 1
        'Do something Windows specific here
    Case 2
        'Do something OS/2 specific here
    Case 3
        'Do something Macintosh specific here
    Case 4
        'Do something Motif specific here
    Case 5
        'Do something Open Window specific here
    Case Else
        MsgBox("Cannot recognize your Operating System", 16, "Error")
    End Select
End Sub
```

The `Select Case` line specifies the condition. You then compare the result with each `Case` statement. The statement block belonging to the first `Case` statement found `True` is executed. The `Case Else` statement, used as the final `Case` statement, executes the code if it fails to find a match. After executing one statement block, all the other `Case` statements are passed, and the program resumes at the `End Select` statement.

The syntax for the `Select Case` statement is as follows:

```
Select Case <Condition>
    Case <Expression No. 1>
        <Statement block No. 1>
    [Case <Expression No. 2>]
        <Statement block No. 2>
    [...]
    [Case Else]
        <Last statement block>
End Select
```

`Select Case` accepts any condition that has an absolute value. Even floating-point numbers or strings are valid. The expressions in the `Case` statements should cover possible results of the given condition. The following are some possible expressions:

```
'If a case statement is valid for different values
'you can separate them with commas
Case 1,5,7
'The statement block will be executed if the condition is less than 10
'Use the Is operator.
Case Is < 10
'The condition expression must be between 5 and 15
Case 5 To 15
'Or you can combine them all!
Case Is < 10, 2, 5 To 15
```

Most people don't think to use Select Case with string conditions. The following is an example of a navigational program in a text document. Naturally, it would be nicer if the program jumped to the desired text section rather than just displayed the page number in a message box:

```
Sub DictionarySearch
  Dim StrWord As String
  'Ask for the word to look for in a user defined function
  StrWord = AskForWordInDictionary()
  'Lower case the given string
  StrWord = LCase(StrWord)
  Select Case StrWord
    Case "abacus" To "cycle"
      MsgBox("Check page 23 for words within " _
          & """abacus"" to ""cycle""", 64, "Information")
    Case "damage" To "fuzzy"
      MsgBox("Check page 24 for words within " _
          & """damage"" to ""fuzzy""", 64, "Information")
    [...]
    'Go through the rest of the alphabet using additional Case statements
    [...]
    Case Else
      MsgBox("Your word was not found in our dictionary", 16, "Error")
  End Select
End Sub
```

LOOP STATEMENTS

You use loop statements to execute blocks of code repetitively. A common use of loops is to allow a user to re-enter data after an invalid entry or to work with arrays.

Tip #601 from
Werner Roth

Sometimes when you're writing or testing a program with loop structures, you might get "stuck" in a loop; that is, the loop never terminates. This is known as an *infinite loop*. You should be able to terminate the loop by clicking the Stop button on the macro bar. In some cases, however, you cannot stop an infinite loop; for example, when the loop exhausts resources with each cycle, and thus, you must kill the complete StarOffice session. Therefore, make sure you save all documents before testing programs with loop statements; don't forget to click the Save button in the StarBasic IDE either.

Do...Loop

The Do...Loop statement is the most flexible loop command offered by StarBasic. You can check the condition before the loop starts or after the first execution of the statement block. Furthermore, you can use two condition statements: while and until.

Four basic constructions are available for these two condition statements. Take a look at their syntax here:

Until	While
Do Until <condition>	Do while <condition>
<Statement block>	<Statement block>

Until	While
Loop	Loop
Do	Do
<Statement block>	<Statement block>
Loop Until <condition>	Loop while <condition>

If the condition is controlled before entering the loop (as in the top two constructs), the *Statement block* may not be executed in a case in which the condition is False.

In some cases, the condition may depend on the value given to the variable inside the block. This means that the loop must be entered in order to initialize the variable. A perfect example is the handling of a password dialog. The user has to enter a password; then the password validity must be checked. If the password is invalid, the input password dialog has to appear again for the user to reenter his or her password. The following simple code fragment shows the password example:

PART

VIII

CH

38

```
Sub AskForPassWord
   Dim StrPassWord As String
   Do
      'Get the password from an InputBox dialog and send it
      'to the variable StrPassWord
      StrPassWord = InputBox("Enter the valid Password!","Login")
   'Check the Password with a given string, exit the loop when
   'correct password is the given.
   Loop Until StrPassWord = "Segafredo"
End Sub
```

Sometimes a loop should be entered only when the condition is valid; otherwise, some commands within the *Statement block* would cause an error. The next example opens a text file, reads through the lines of this file, and assigns each line to a string variable. Because this example makes sense only if the text file is not empty, you first need to check whether the file contains data:

```
Sub ScanTempFile
   Dim IntFileNumber As Integer
   Dim StrOneLine As String
   'Obtain a free file number belonging to the low-level.
   'For file handling stuff in StarBasic look up "FreeFile" in
   'the help system
   IntFileNumber = FreeFile()
   'Low-level open the text "text.txt" file in folder c:\temp
   Open "c:\temp\temp.txt" for Input Access Read As #IntFileNumber
   'Read each line until the end of the file is reached
   Do Until Eof(#IntFileNumber)
      'Assign a line of the file to a string variable
      Line Input #IntFileNumber, StrOneLine
      '[...]
      'Do something with the string StrOneLine here
      '[...]
   Loop
   'finished with the low-level stuff, give the file back to operating system
   Close #IntFileNumber
End Sub
```

The difference between while and until is the way in which they evaluate the condition statement. The until statement continues executing the loop as long as the condition is False. The while statement loops as long as the condition is True and stops only on the condition becoming False. For this next example, think about transporting a group of people in nine-seater vans. The following program requests the number of passengers of one van. It's likely that not all seats in this van will be needed:

```
Sub GetAllPassengers
    'Store all passengers in an array
    Dim StrArrPassengers( 1 To 9 ) As String
    'Indexcounter for this array
    Dim IntPIndex As Integer, IntVanNumber As Integer
    IntVanNumber = InputBox("Enter number of the actual van.",_
                          "Enter van number")

    'Let's perform the loop. IntPIndex starts with 0, it will
    'be increased before the input.
    IntPIndex = 0
    Do
        IntPIndex = IntPIndex + 1
        'Assign the input value of a passenger number n to the
        'array element number n
        'When there was no input or the input box was canceled
        'the result is an empty string.
        StrArrPassengers(IntPIndex) = InputBox("Enter the next passenger " &_
                    "or leave blank to finish.", "Passenger " & IntPIndex &_
                    " in Van " & IntVanNumber)
    'Perform the loop as long as there are seats in the van
    'and as long as the passenger's name is not empty.
    Loop While (IntPIndex < 9) and (StrArrPassengers(IntPIndex) <> "")
    '[...]
    'Go on and work with this array
End Sub
```

As you've already learned, you can use four basic constructions for the Do...Loop statements. There is still one remaining construction, but it is seldom used. You can jump out of a loop at any time by using the command Exit Do. Using this command as a single command line doesn't make any sense, so in the following example, it is used within an If statement:

```
Do
    <Statement block>
    if <condition> then Exit Do
    <Statement block>
Loop
```

Normally, using Exit Do in this way is not good programming practice. Finding the condition for the ending of the loop hidden in between all the other statements surrounding it can be difficult. It's a better idea to work with an extra loop condition, that is manually set to false.

For...Next

For...Next loops are often needed to work with arrays because they are designed to cycle through indexes. You can use For...Next loops to initialize, copy, or compare arrays. Another, more complex use of For...Next loops is as mathematical calculations made by iterations.

The following example copies an array of 101 elements to another array by assigning the elements one by one using a For...Next loop:

```
Sub CopyTwoArrays
   Dim StrFirstArray(100) As String, StrSecondArray(100) As String
   Dim i As Integer
   'Assign indexes to 101 elements here
   StrFirstArray(0) = "ID3453536"
   StrFirstArray(1) = "ID3452566"
   '[...]
   'Now cycle through with the index i counting from 0 to 100
   For i = 0 to 100
      'In the first round i will be 0, then 1, then 2, and so on...until 100
      StrSecondArray(i) = StrFirstArray(i)
   'Next i means loop back to the for statement with the counter i
   Next i
   MsgBox("Array successfully copied",48,"Complete")
End Sub
```

The For...Next statement is particularly well suited for cycling through a defined number of elements. For example, imagine that you're interested in each character of a string of defined length. The next example will be a little more mathematical, but don't panic, it's just to demonstrate how to calculate a value step-by-step.

To calculate the factorial of a number (denoted with !) you have to multiply all the numbers from 1 to the value, accumulating the result as you go. For example, the factorial of 4 is 4!=1*2*3*4=24. You can handle this task by using a For...Next loop as follows:

```
Sub CalculateTheFactorial
   Dim i As Integer, fac As Integer
   Dim LongTheResult As Long
   fac = InputBox("Enter the value for factorial","Hello Eric")
   LongTheResult = 1
   For i = 1 to fac
      LongTheResult = LongTheResult * i
   Next i
   MsgBox("The result: " & fac & "! = " & LongTheResult,64,"The Result")
End Sub
```

Because you cannot calculate such a large number of multiplications within one command, you have to do it step-by-step. Now you can test the preceding macro with the value 4 to see the results (see Table 38.9).

TABLE 38.9   ANALYSIS OF A StarBasic LOOP COMMAND

Step	i	Calculation	TheResult
1 Loop starts	1	LongTheResult = 1 * 1	1
2	2	LongTheResult = 1 * 2	2
3	3	LongTheResult = 2 * 3	6
4 Loop ends	4	LongTheResult = 6 * 4	24
After the Loop	5		24

What you do in the end is calculate four single multiplications one after the other instead of one big one; this concept is known as *iteration*. With this technique, you can solve a lot of calculations. Imagine the ease of calculating a bill whose individual item prices are stored in an array.

Note

You can test this macro only with the values from 1 to 12, with 12! equaling 479,001,600. The maximum value for the data type long is 2,147,483,647, and because 13! equals 6,227,020,800, it causes an overflow. To calculate numbers higher than 12, you can declare LongTheResult as a double, but then the results are no longer exact to the least digit.

If you take a closer look at the syntax of the For...Next statement, you might discover that it offers a little extra feature not previously mentioned. You are able to specify the amount the counter will be increased (or even decreased) on each iteration. By default, the counter is increased by 1:

```
For <counter> = <Start value> To <End value> Step <size of step>
   <Statement block>
Next [<counter>]
```

Just as you can do in the Do...Loop statement, you can use the Exit For statement to jump out of a For...Next loop. However, employing this concept in a For...Next loop is not recommended; it defeats the purpose of the loop. If you don't need to cycle through a specific number of elements in your program, use a Do...Loop or While...Wend statement instead.

Using the name of the counter with the Next statement is not compulsory; however, when you're using nested For...Next loops, using this statement gives you a better overview. The next program uses nested For...Next loops to transpose the first sheet of a StarCalc spreadsheet (*transposing* means to change columns to rows and vice versa):

```
Sub TransposeSpreadsheet
   Dim IntMaxRow As Integer, IntMaxCol As Integer
   Dim i As Integer, j As Integer

   'Input the number of columns and rows to be transposed
   'We start at column 1 and row 1
```

```
   IntMaxCol = InputBox("Enter the number of columns to transpose!",_
                    "Transposer(TM)")
   IntMaxRow = InputBox("Enter the number of rows to transpose!",_
                    "Transposer(TM)")

   'Declare a 2-dimensional array to save the values out of the spreadsheet
   'we have to overwrite them with columns to rows and vice versa
   Dim DoubleArrSaveMatrix(IntMaxCol, IntMaxRow) As Double

   'Save the entries to the array and delete them afterwards
   'Cycle through all columns
   For i = 1 to IntMaxCol
      'For each column cycle through all rows
      For j = 1 to IntMaxRow
         DoubleArrSaveMatrix(i,j) = ActiveDocument.Cells(i,j,1).Value
         'We have to delete the old entries for transposing
         'different numbers of rows and columns.
         ActiveDocument.Cells(i,j,1).Clear( "SVDFN" )
      Next j
   Next i

   'Put everything back only in the other order i.e. columns to rows
   For i = 1 to IntMaxCol
      For j = 1 to IntMaxRow
         'DoubleArrSaveMatrix(i,j) is assigned to Cells(j,i);
         'that's the transposing!
         ActiveDocument.Cells(j,i,1).Insert(DoubleArrSaveMatrix(i,j))
      Next j
   Next i
End Sub
```

Note

This macro is not designed for general use. First, a spreadsheet has to be the active document when running the macro. Second, parts of your table can't be transposed. Third, you must use `Sheet1`. Fourth, all the values have to be numeric; all other data will be lost. This macro is just an example to demonstrate nesting `For...Next` loops. You could easily improve this macro, but it serves, in its current form, to illustrate the concept of a general transposing program.

While...Wend

Because the third loop statement, `While...Wend`, can be easily replaced by a `Do...Loop` statement, there's no real need to use them. The syntax of a `While...Wend` loop is as follows:

```
While <condition>
   <Statement block>
Wend
```

You can replace this loop with the following:

```
Do While <condition>
   <Statement block>
Loop
```

The advantage here is that Do...Loop statements can be unconditionally canceled by Exit Do (which is not possible in While...Wend statements).

JUMPS TO CONTROL YOUR PROGRAM

Earlier Basic dialects lacked the capability to control the program flow, except for the commands Goto and GoSub, which enabled the program to jump to labels and back. So, these labels are outdated. However, StarBasic needs jumps for error handling. Jumping remains an attractive way to handle the input of users or to react in error situations.

Goto, GoSub, AND LABELS

Goto allows you to jump to a defined label within a subprocedure. A *label* is an expression with a name of your choice, followed by a colon. The next example simply adds numbers given by an input box dialog:

```
Sub CalculateTheSumWithGotos
    Dim DoubleTheResult As Double, DoubleNextValue As Double
    'We add all numbers entered to TheResult so it needs to be
    'initialized with zero
    DoubleTheResult = 0
    'This is the first label. We will jump to it to get the next value
    'from the user
    InputOneValue:
        DoubleNextValue = InputBox("Input a value to be added. " &_
                          "Zero to stop!", "Calculating a sum")
        'If no input is given jump to the label at the end of the program
        If DoubleNextValue = 0 Then Goto EndLabel
        'The next line is only calculated if there was no jump to the end
        DoubleTheResult = DoubleTheResult + DoubleNextValue
        'Unconditional Goto the label InputOneValue.
        'We jumped out of this loop with the if statement above.
    Goto InputOneValue
    'We jump out of the loop to show the result on the screen
    EndLabel:
        MsgBox("The sum of all these numbers is: " & DoubleTheResult,_
               64, "Finished")
End Sub
```

You can jump to nearly every place in your subprocedure with the use of Gotos and labels. However, doing so makes the code more difficult to read and poorly structured. Writing such code produces what programmers call "spaghetti programs." (It's not a compliment.)

StarBasic offers a second statement for jumping to labels: GoSub. In earlier versions of Basic, it was used as a kind of subprocedure because, at the time, Basic was not a very structured programming language:

```
Sub StructureOfGoSubs
    [...]
    GoSub SubProcedureLabel
    [...]
    GoSub SubProcedureLabel
    [...]
```

```
   SubProcedureLabel:
       'Place an often used subprocedure in this statement block!.
    'Return jumps back to the GoSub that called it.
    Return
End Sub
```

Because the StarBasic language includes many modern techniques, you don't need `Goto` and `GoSub` anymore. You can easily rewrite the first example without any `Gotos`, as shown here:

```
Sub CalculateTheSumWithDoLoop
   Dim DoubleTheResult As Double, DoubleNextValue As Double
   DoubleTheResult = 0
   Do
      DoubleNextValue = InputBox("Input a value to be added. " &_
                        "Zero for end!","Calculating a sum")
      DoubleTheResult = DoubleTheResult + DoubleNextValue
   Loop Until DoubleNextValue = 0
   MsgBox("The sum of all these numbers is: " & DoubleTheResult, 64, "Finished")
End Sub
```

Using `Goto` and `GoSub` statements instead of subprocedures, functions, and control statements will lead you into chaos. Using them is a good way to make you the undisputed expert on your program, however, because you will be the only one who can possibly understand the code.

Note

Don't jump in or out of control statement blocks such as `If...Then...Endif` or `Do...Loop`. Doing so causes errors or confuses your program.

Tip #602 from
Werner Roth

You can also substitute the `On...GoSub` or the `On...Goto` instructions with the `Select Case` statement, if you're familiar with it.

Exit Sub **AND** Exit Function

In the section on loop statements, you learned about canceling the execution of a loop by the StarBasic statements *Exit Do* or *Exit For* with respect to the type of loop (Do or For). You can also end a subprocedure or function on any line you want by using `Exit Sub` or `Exit Function`. Frequent use of these statements is not appropriate for well-structured programs. These statements are easily overlooked at a quick glance of a program. However, in some cases, `Exit Sub` and `Exit Function` are very useful. It's a good idea to make a note of any `Exit` commands used in the head of your program, though, to remind yourself or alert others so that they're not overlooked. Take a look at the transposing example again:

```
Sub TransposeSpreadsheet
   'Warn the reader of your code here
   'Attention there is one Exit Sub after the check
   'for the right StarOffice program
   [...]
   If ActiveModule.Name <> "StarCalc" Then
```

```
        'Throw an error-message if the active document is not a spreadsheet
        MsgBox("This program is only available in spreadsheets.",16,"Error")
        'Exit the subprocedure TransposeSpreadsheet
        'The program will continue after the call of this subprocedure.
        Exit Sub
    Endif
    [...]
    'Perform the transposing here
End Sub
```

As shown in this example, checking whether the execution of a subprocedure is valid or even necessary is a good use of Exit Sub and Exit Function. Without the use of the Exit Sub statement in the preceding example, you would have had to put the main code of this sub into the Else statement block of an If statement. In other examples, you could avoid using nested If statements by using Exit Sub. It's important, however, to always consider whether an Exit Sub is really required to solve your problem.

Error Handling

StarBasic offers a powerful option to control errors in programs. The On...Error statement gives you the freedom to perform actions and handle possible errors afterward. This concept is known as *catching an error*, and it allows you to catch the error and do something with it instead of simply producing a runtime error thrown by StarBasic.

The basic concept is to tell a subprocedure what to do in case of an error by using On Error Goto <Label>. The label is followed by code to handle the error. The following example calculates the square root of a given value. The error you expect to receive is incorrect input—for example, the user inputs a negative value. Naturally, in this instance, the square root is not defined. In the following case, the program gives the user another chance to input a value:

```
Sub CalculateSquareRoot
    'If an error occurs jump to the label ErrorLabel.
    'There is the code to handle all errors
    On Local Error Goto ErrorLabel
    Dim DoubleTheResult As Double, DoubleValue As Double
    'We need the following label to restart the action
    'if the first value was wrong
    StartInput:
    DoubleValue = InputBox("Input a numerical value greater than or " &_
                "equal to zero", "Calculating the square root")
    'Calculate the square root of the given value,
    'with the built in StarBasic function sqr()
    'This is the line where an error will be thrown when DoubleValue is negative.
    DoubleTheResult = sqr(DoubleValue)
    'If all went well, show the result
    MsgBox("The square root of " & DoubleValue & " is " & DoubleTheResult,_
        64, "Finished")
    'Here we have to use the Exit Sub statement. Otherwise the program runs
    'into the code that is specified for error handling
    Exit Sub
    'ErrorLabel gives the starting point. All error handling code follows.
    ErrorLabel:
```

```
        'Ask for the error we are expecting. The given value is less then zero
        If DoubleValue < 0 Then
            MsgBox("You can't use a divisor less then 0!",16,"An Error occurred" )
            'restart the action at label StartInput. Directly before the input box
            Resume StartInput
        'We have to handle all other errors too!
        'So we drop a generic error message and cancel the subprocedure
        Else
            MsgBox("The following error occurred" & chr(13) & Error() & chr(13) &_
                    "Error number: " & Err() & chr(13) &_
                    "In line: " & Erl() & " of the program",_
                    16,"Unknown Error")
        Endif
End Sub
```

As shown, this program is coded to handle an error you expect. You know of this error, and you also know that it is not critical. Therefore, you throw an error message and give the user another try. However, there could be other errors you are not expecting. To make your program robust, you need to handle every possibility of an error occurring. It's particularly important when you're testing new or altered procedures; you can get into serious trouble by not handling all possible errors.

PART

VIII

CH

38

It's helpful to the user if you generate a constructive error message giving a hint about the kind of error that occurred. In StarBasic, three functions offer information on errors; they're shown in Table 38.10.

TABLE 38.10   STARBASIC FUNCTIONS THAT RETURN ERROR INFORMATION

Function	Returns
Error()	A textual error message. sqr(-9) produces the error text Invalid procedure call.
Err()	The internal StarOffice error number. sqr(-9) produces the error number 5.
Erl()	The line in your StarBasic code that produced the error. This is the absolute line number in your module. If the example starts in the first line of the module, the line number is 14. The line is DoubleTheResult = sqr(DoubleValue).

You can use the error number Err() as a condition in a Select Case statement that handles different errors. Bear in mind that it is best to use the Case Else block.

→ You can find an overview of all the StarBasic error messages and numbers in Appendix E, "StarBasic Error Codes," **p. 1429**.

In the square root example, you used Resume <Label> to repeat the input of the value. Conveniently, you also can continue the code directly after the line that caused the error by using the Resume Next statement.

Just as you switch the error handling on with On Error Goto <Label>, you can switch it off by using On Error Goto 0. Having only one critical point in your program is very useful.

The `Error Goto <Label>` turns off the internal error handling of StarBasic. As a result, you get the control to handle errors directly before critical code in your program. After passing the critical point, you can give the control back to StarBasic.

> **Note**
>
> You may have programmed before but never heard about error handling statements. They are a modern concept with which you should become familiar because they are much more powerful than the classical error handling techniques. Using `On Error Goto` is recommended for every situation. For example, simply trying to open a file that doesn't exist causes an error. Trying to divide a number by zero causes an error. No big deal. You can handle these errors on your own. What makes this way of error handling so powerful is the fact that you can react to some errors in any way you like and pass the rest to the system. If you notice users falling into the same errors over and over again, you can simply add a new `Case` statement and direct them in the right direction.

With STATEMENTS

You can't create your own object hierarchy in StarBasic. Instead, you have to make heavy use of StarOffice objects. However don't panic, you'll learn more about them in the next chapter and begin using them in small tasks. If you want to perform a *search and replace* within a StarBasic program, you need to use the method `ReplaceAll()`—the method StarWriter itself uses in a document. Before you begin, though, you need to set the attributes of a search in StarWriter text.

The attributes are stored in the *properties* of the `SearchSettings` object. A subprocedure to exchange "Bug" with "Feature" could look something like this:

```
Sub ReplaceBugByFeature
   'Set search options first otherwise the default is the last search options used
   'Search backwards from cursor position
   ActiveWindow.SearchSettings.Backward = False
   'Search only in the current selection
   ActiveWindow.SearchSettings.InSelection = False
   'Search with respect to upper/lower case
   ActiveWindow.SearchSettings.CaseSensitive = True
   'Search with wildcards
   ActiveWindow.SearchSettings.RegExp = False
   'Search only entire words
   ActiveWindow.SearchSettings.WordOnly = True

   'Replace "Bug" by "Feature"
   ActiveWindow.ReplaceAll("Bug", "Feature") 'Search and Replace
End Sub
```

The use of the With statement in this program gives you a shortcut to refer to the properties of ActiveWindow.SearchSettings. The With statement sets a given object to the default object. In between the With...End With block, you can refer to the properties and methods of the object by beginning the expression with a period, as shown here:

```
Sub ReplaceBugByFeature
    'Set search options first.
    'Otherwise the default is the last search options used
    With ActiveWindow.SearchSettings
        .Backward = False       'Search backwards from cursor position
        .InSelection = False    'Search only in the current selection
        .CaseSensitive = True   'Search with respect to upper and lower case
        .RegExp = False         'Search with wildcards "regular expression"
        .WordOnly = True        'Finds the search string only as entire word
    End With

    'Replace "Bug" by "Feature"
    ActiveWindow.ReplaceAll("Bug", "Feature") 'Search and Replace
End Sub
```

PART

VIII

CH

38

You can use any object you like with the With statement. In the preceding example, you could have just written With ActiveWindow and then referred to each property by using .SearchSettings.Backward = False and so on. This isn't the correct use for the With statement; plus it doesn't really make any sense unless you have time to kill. You should use the With statement when you're operating with three or more properties or methods of an object; it shortens your code and increases the performance of your program. StarBasic needs to refer to the object only once.

CHAPTER 39

PROGRAMMING WITH STARBASIC

In this chapter

by Werner Roth

LEARNING DAY-TO-DAY SOLUTIONS WITH STARBASIC

As seen in the previous chapters, StarBasic macros can perform almost all operations in the methods and properties belonging to StarOffice.

The StarOffice object hierarchy is so expansive that it's outside the scope of this book to represent it all. In fact, unfolding the entire object hierarchy would take another book! Fortunately, you don't need to be acquainted with the entire hierarchy to use StarBasic successfully.

This chapter lets you in on some typical solutions for day-to-day work using StarBasic. You will learn about organizing the objects you need and about some of the many StarOffice objects not available for recording with the macro recorder. Finally, with your newly gained knowledge, you'll learn how to program an entire StarBasic dialog application.

INTRODUCING THE STAROFFICE APPLICATION OBJECT

As you will see, you can change the value of text or its color, enter formulas in StarCalc cells, add graphics, and carry out similar tasks with the help of StarOffice toolbars. However, sometimes you need to access the functionality or attributes of the entire StarOffice program. That's why an object representing StarOffice appears in the hierarchy of programming objects. This object is simply called `Application`.

You can use the `Application` object in a modest program, like the one shown here, to open your Address Book:

```
Sub OpenAddressBook
    Application.AddressBook()
end Sub
```

To refer to the properties and methods of each object, you need to place a period (.) between the object name and the name of the property or method. Now examine the following program. It displays address details you normally access by selecting Tools, Options and the category User Data in the General dialog. All the data at hand is stored in the properties of the object `Address`, which is owned by `Application`:

```
Sub ShowUserData
    MsgBox("The current user is:" & chr(13) &_
           "Name: " & Application.Address.FirstName & " " &_
                    Application.Address.LastName & chr(13) &_
            " ID: " & Application.Address.ID & chr(13) &_
           "Street: " & Application.Address.Street & chr(13) &_
           "City: " & Application.Address.City & chr(13) &_
           "ZIPCode: " & Application.Address.ZIPCode & chr(13) &_
           "E-mail: " & Application.Address.EMail & chr(13) &_
           "Phone (home): " & Application.Address.PhonePrivate, _
           48, "Informations")
End Sub
```

As demonstrated in the preceding code, the ownership of methods, properties, and objects is denoted by a period between the elements. The element to the left always represents the parent of the element to the right and so on, throughout the hierarchy, as you can see here:

```
Application.Address.FirstName
'  ^              ^     ^Property of the Address object
'  ¦              Address object
' Application object
```

If you need to refer repeatedly to a property belonging to an object, you can use the With statement, which is explained at the end of Chapter 38, "Understanding StarBasic Structures and Statements."

→ For details and examples of using the With statement, **see** "Jumps to Control Your Program," **p. 1302**.

The next program produces the same result as the previous version; instead, you use a shortcut to refer to the Application.Address object:

```
Sub ShowUserData
   With Application.Address
      MsgBox("The current user is:" & chr(13) &_
             "Name: " & .FirstName & " " & .LastName & chr(13) &_
             " ID: " & .ID & chr(13) &_
             "Street: " & .Street & chr(13) &_
             "City: " & .City & chr(13) &_
             "ZIPCode: " & .ZIPCode & chr(13) &_
             "E-mail: " & .EMail & chr(13) &_
             "Phone (home): " & .PhonePrivate, _
             48, "Informations")
   End With
End Sub
```

INTRODUCING COLLECTIONS

In the StarOffice object hierarchy, there are several Collection objects, such as Documents, Tables, and Windows. Any object in this category can have multiple instances open at a time. That is, several documents could can be opened at the same time in StarOffice—for example, say, a spreadsheet containing several tables or a Web site constructed with frames. A Collection object is a container for objects. Think of them as a way to access all objects of the same kind (like a display basket in a supermarket containing similar items).

To make this type of access possible, StarOffice provides several collection objects to access all the open objects of that type that can be found in the current session. For example, Windows(1) indicates the StarDesktop window, Documents("LetterToBoss") indicates a particular document, and Graphics(1) indicates the first graphic in a text document.

In the following examples, you'll work with collections. There, you'll learn what exactly a collection is and the tasks in which it is useful.

PART

VIII

CH

39

REFERRING TO ACTIVE OBJECTS

You access a new document window by using the phrase [Untitled1:1]. This phrase represents the first window of the document Untitled1 that appeared at the beginning of the session (not additional windows that you subsequently opened of the same document). This means you have access to an exclusive instance of a window object. To refer to the document object of the document Untitled1, you use the documents collection Documents("Untitled1"). Using Documents, you have access to all the items in the document.

If you want to write macros that can be used in different documents, it would be nice to be able to access the window or document actually opened. Therefore, StarBasic offers the objects ActiveWindow and ActiveDocument. They refer to the instance window of the document that the macro was executed in. You may have seen the macro recorder generate such objects.

It's always a good idea to retain access to objects by assigning them to object variables. Doing so provides faster access to their properties and methods. A bonus is that your macro still can access a particular object even if the user has positioned the focus on another window:

```
Sub WorkWithWindowsAndDocuments
    Dim oActiveWindow As Object
    Dim oActiveDocument As Object
    oActiveWindow = ActiveWindow
    oActiveDocument = ActiveDocument
    [...]
    'Do your actions here
End Sub
```

StarBasic has two other useful objects called Selection and ActiveCell. They refer to the selected object; typically, Selection is text in the actual StarWriter document, and ActiveCell is the currently selected cell in your StarCalc table. Be careful, however; the Selection object refers only to the "real" selected object. Selection.Insert("Hello") is valid only if the cursor is somewhere in a text document; it doesn't work if a picture is selected. To confirm the object Selection is referring to, ask for its class name like this:

```
Sub InsertHallo
    If Selection.ClassName <> "Text" Then
        MsgBox("Sorry, no Text selected.",16,"Error")
    Else
        Selection.Insert("Hello")
    Endif
End Sub
```

ASSIGNING MACROS TO EVENTS

StarOffice includes several *events* such as Start Program or Save Document that you can assign a macro to. The two main categories of events are StarOffice events and events belonging to particular documents or templates. For example, you can assign a macro to the event that is thrown by closing StarOffice. The macro can perform a backup of your work folder on closing. The templates generated by the Letter AutoPilot typically have a macro assigned to creating the letter document. The macro normally initializes the document, for example, by placing today's date at the top of the letter.

You can do a lot of handy things by assigning macros to StarOffice or Document events. You can automate your work by creating templates containing macros that run on creation of a new document. Think about filling out a standard form. Having to type all the information over and over again isn't anyone's idea of a good time. Instead, you can simply create a StarBasic dialog with an option button representing each standard case. Even after printing, your macro can save your form automatically in an archive. So, numerous opportunities await you when you're working with events.

AN EXAMPLE: RECORDING PRINTING HISTORY

Say you want detailed information every time a document is printed. To find it, you could select File, Properties and then open the Document tab, but this tab provides you only with the details of the last time the document was printed. To solve the problem, you can store the date of every print occurrence in the Comment field of the Description tab in the Properties dialog. You do so by assigning a macro to the `Print Document` event.

To get started, open a new text document, and save it under the name `DocumentWithEvent.sdw`. You now need to write a macro and store it in the standard StarBasic library of your text document. While you're still in the new document, select Tools, Macro and select the Standard library of `DocumentWithEvent.sdw`, as shown in Figure 39.1.

PART

VIII

CH

39

Figure 39.1
The first step in creating your macro is to open the Macro dialog and select its Standard library as the location for storing the macro. Make sure your text document is the active document when you choose your library.

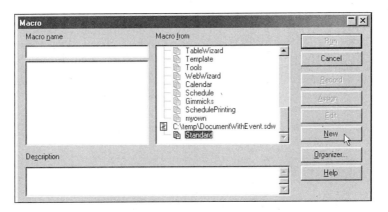

In the Macro dialog, first type the macro's name—`InsertPrintDate`—in the Macro Name box. (Otherwise, a non-descript name such as `Macro1` will be assigned.) Then click the New button to create a new module. The StarBasic IDE appears.

At this point, you can replace the empty subprocedure `Main` with the following macro:

```
Sub InsertPrintDate
    Dim StrStrComment As String
    'Save the contents of the StrComment field
```

```
   StrComment = ActiveDocument.DocumentInfo.Description
   'If it's empty the document was never printed before,
   'so generate a header to inform the reader
   If StrComment = "" Then
      StrComment = "Printing dates:" & chr(13)
   Endif
   'Pass today's date, time and the user's name to the StrComment
   StrComment = StrComment & Date() & " " & Time() & " " & _
            Application.Address.FirstName & " " &_
            Application.Address.LastName & chr(13)
   'Write new StrComment to description tab
   ActiveDocument.DocumentInfo.Description = StrComment
End Sub
```

When this macro is invoked, it will add today's date, time, and the username to the Comment field in the Description tab of the Properties dialog.

Next, you need to assign the Print function to this StarBasic macro you've just stored in your document. This means that you assign it to the Print Document event.

To assign this function, make sure DocumentWithEvent.sdw is still the active window, and then select Tools, Configure to open the Configuration dialog. Click the Events tab to bring it to the front (see Figure 39.2). (Alternatively, you can click the Assign button from within the Tools, Macro dialog, which also opens the Configuration dialog.)

Figure 39.2
In the Configuration dialog, you can assign the macros and programs you create to program events.

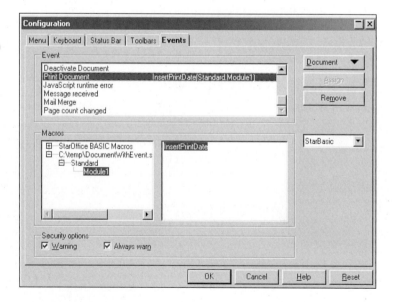

On the Events tab, follow these steps:

1. In the upper right of the dialog is a button labeled StarOffice. Click this button to open a drop-down list, and select Document. Otherwise, you'll assign your event globally to all StarOffice documents. (You can see the button after Document has been selected in Figure 39.2.)

2. Select the document `DocumentWithEvent.sdw` from the Macros list in the lower left.

3. Click the + (plus) sign to open the Standard library.

4. Select `Module1` from the Standard library.

5. Select the macro `InsertPrintDate`.

6. Select the event `Print Document` from the Events list.

7. Click the Assign button.

When `InsertPrintDate(Standard.Module1)` appears beside the event `Print Document`, click OK to close the Configuration dialog and save your document.

Now try the macro. Print the document. If you've selected the Security options (see the option boxes at the bottom of the dialog in Figure 39.2), a message box appears and gives a warning that a macro, configured to an event, will be run. Click the Execute button to print the document. See whether it worked by choosing File, Properties and then opening the Description tab. This tab should display details like the following in the Comment field:

```
Printing dates:
07/07/1999 21:02:19 Werner Roth
```

The next time the document is printed, a new line with the print details will be added to the Comment field:

```
Printing dates:
07/07/1999 21:02:19 Werner Roth
08/09/1999 08:53:33 Rachel van Maanen
11/11/1999 23:36:59 Michael Herger
```

EVENTS FOR STAROFFICE AND DOCUMENTS

As shown in Figure 39.2, the Events tab of the Configuration dialog enables you to switch between events for StarOffice as a whole and events for documents. Assigning a macro to an event of a document is document-specific. That means whenever a document or template is used and the specific event has occurred, the macro will start. Even if you pass this document on to a friend or colleague, that person's version of StarOffice will start the macro every time the event is started within the document. Storing the macros in the StarBasic libraries of this document is quite convenient.

StarOffice events are specific to your StarOffice installation. They are essentially global events. If you were to assign the `InsertPrintDate` macro to StarOffice, you would record the printing information of every StarOffice document printed from your system in each document's properties.

The list of events for documents and the list of events for StarOffice are identical; StarOffice doesn't adapt the list. Events that are never started appear in the Event list shown in Figure 39.2. Choosing the right event for your task is a judgment call. Assigning the `Start Application` event to a document makes no sense.

Surviving Everyday Tasks

The following sections focus on solving tasks that you'll find in everyday work. To achieve this goal, you examine general problem-solving strategies and learn how to solve them by using StarOffice objects. Of course, the best way to master the use of StarOffice objects is to experiment. You won't become a StarBasic expert by reading this book. You may, however, become a StarBasic expert by solving your everyday problems.

Unfortunately, not very many examples of everyday tasks require a macro in StarCalc. It's such a powerful spreadsheet program that you seldom need assistance from a StarBasic macro. Hence, these sections just show you how to fetch and place data in your spreadsheet. This knowledge can serve as the foundation for programming converters and routines that fill in cells.

General Routines for StarWriter and StarCalc

You can use the Documents collection to access all open documents by their index numbers. You'll use this principle in the next example. This example shows how to convert all open StarWriter and StarCalc documents to several document formats, closing them afterward. You can use the same techniques to manage your own work documents. For example, it's normal to edit documents on your local drive and, from time to time, transfer them concurrently to a Web server.

Say you want to convert all opened StarWriter and StarCalc documents into one common document type to archive them. To avoid overloading the folder the document is stored in, you can create a new subfolder (of the document folder) called Converted in which you store all the converted documents. You can cycle through each document with the collection `Application.Documents.Item(i)`. You start at the highest index because you close each document after converting it. If you were to start with the first document and then close it, the next document would take its place because no gaps are allowed with index numbers. The macro is as follows:

```
Sub ConvertOpenedDocuments
    Dim i As Integer
    Dim StrDocumentPath As String
    'Start with the highest index and go down to 2. No. 1 is the StarDesktop.
    For i = Application.Documents.Count to 2 step -1
        'Now we do everything with document No.i, we make a shortcut
        'to its Object using the with statement
        with Application.Documents.Item(i)
            'Check if we touched a StarWriter or StarCalc document. No other
            'documents or for example, StarBasic IDE are allowed.
            If (.classname = "TextDocument") or (.classname = "TableDocument") Then
                'create the new folder stemming from the old one. If the path
                'was "c:\temp" the path for the Converted documents is
                '"c:\temp\Converted"
                StrDocumentPath = .Path+"\Converted"
                'Check if the folder exists. The Dir run-time function will check
                'for its name. The argument 16 will only examine folders—
                'no ordinary files
                If Dir(StrDocumentPath,16)="" Then
```

```
            'Create a folder on your disk
            MkDir(StrDocumentPath)
        Endif
        'Now add the document name to the converted path. Name results
        'in the file name without an extention. The result is e.g.
        '"c:\temp\Converted\MyLetter"
        StrDocumentPath = StrDocumentPath + "\" + .Name
        'Now we can add different file extentions to the name in order
        'to save it in different formats.

        'Now convert the StarWriter document into HTML, RTF and plain text
        If .classname = "TextDocument" Then
            .SaveAs( StrDocumentPath+".html", _
                    "swriter: HTML (StarWriter)", "", "" )
            .SaveAs( StrDocumentPath+".rtf", _
                    "swriter: Rich Text Format", "", "" )
            .SaveAs( StrDocumentPath+".txt", _
                    "swriter: Text", "", "" )
        Else
            'Convert the StarCalc spreadsheet into SYLK and Excel format
            .SaveAs( StrDocumentPath+".slk", "scalc: SYLK", "", "" )
            .SaveAs( StrDocumentPath+".xls", "scalc: MS Excel 97", "", "" )
        Endif
        'Close the active document
        .Close( False, "" )
    Endif
    End With
    Next i
End Sub
```

Note

This program will not run on UNIX Systems because of the DOS-style Path-Separator "\".
Simply change it to "/" and enjoy.

PART

VIII

CH

39

MANIPULATING STARWRITER DOCUMENTS

StarWriter offers many more possibilities for handy everyday programs to automate and
speed your work than StarCalc, so in the following sections, you'll explore a number of
examples based on text documents.

KEYBOARD SHORTCUTS FOR STYLES

In StarWriter, you can't assign a keyboard shortcut to a paragraph or text style. You don't
have a great need for shortcuts here because you can use the Stylist in any document. It's
still handy, however, to have a shortcut for applying common styles such as Heading 1 to
Heading 10 or Text Body.

You can apply these styles by creating a macro and assigning it to a keyboard shortcut. In
this next example, you'll write a macro for the paragraph style Heading 1. To do so, open a
new text document, and create a macro by selecting Tools, Macro. Enter the macro name as
Heading_1, and start recording by clicking the Record button. Apply the paragraph style
Heading 1 by using the Stylist, and stop the recording of the macro.

If you open the StarBasic IDE, you see the following recorded macro:

```
Sub Heading_1
    Selection.StyleApply( "Heading 1", 2 ) '2 stands for the paragraph style
End Sub
```

Now assign the macro `Heading_1` to a keyboard shortcut of your choice—and that's it! It couldn't be simpler.

→ For information on assigning a macro to a keyboard shortcut, **see** "Assigning a Keyboard Shortcut," **p. 1245**.

KEYBOARD SHORTCUT FOR THE Format&Default FUNCTION

All major StarOffice programs have the powerful command Default (on the Format menu), which resets a selected object to the default value of its style. (Think of it as a giant eraser for direct formatting.) Say you want to reformat a Word document that has text with style formatting. You just need to choose a selection with paragraph styles and invoke the Default command. However, if you need to do so for a large number of text blocks, this process could quickly become annoying. But what if you could somehow create a macro with the Default command's underlying function, `Format&Default`?

If you look on the Tools, Configure, Keyboard tab, you won't find the function Format and Default because the contents of the Format menu are determined by the selected object. For example, if the cursor is in a text block, you see entries such as Character and Paragraph. If you select a picture or text box in a text document, you see entries such as Arrange and Alignment. You won't see an entry called Default.

The best thing to do in this case is to use the same trick as in the preceding section—record a macro and assign it to a keyboard shortcut:

1. Open a document, and choose the Tools, Macro command.
2. Type the macro name—`FormatDefault`—in the Macro Name text box.
3. Click Record to begin recording.
4. Select the Format menu and then the Default command.
5. Click the Stop button in the upper corner of the window.
6. Assign this macro to a keyboard shortcut of your choice.

Your recorded macro should look like this:

```
Sub FormatDefault
    Selection.ResetAttributes()
End Sub
```

This macro will continue to function perfectly until the day you select an object without the capability of `Format&Default`. StarBasic then throws the error message `Property or method not found`. You could analyze the `ClassName` of the selection object to find out whether the given object has a method called `ResetAttributes()`. Instead, you can use the effective error-handling capability of StarBasic.

What *should* happen when the user selects an object—say, a picture—and tries to run the macro? Ideally, nothing. This action is unavailable for the object; it's best to just give a warning message and leave it at that. So you can create a little program that asks whether the error is Property or method not found. If so, the program gives a friendly beep; otherwise, it throws a generic error message. This program looks like the following:

```
Sub FormatDefault
   'Error Handling is dealt with in this subprocedure
   On Local Error Goto ErrorLabel
   'Here is our function to set default style
   Selection.ResetAttributes()
   'Cancel the subprocedure here. Do not run into the error handling code
   Exit Sub
   'Error handling stuff follows
   ErrorLabel:
      'We are expecting the error "Property or method not found"
      'when a picture in a text document is selected.
      'This error has the number 423 (see Appendix F)
      If Err() = 423 Then
         'This error is not serious. Just give a warning tone to say
         'that the macro is functioning
         Beep
      Else
         'Throw a generic error message in case of other errors
         MsgBox("By deleting all hard formatting" & chr(13) &_
                "the following error occurred:" & chr(13) &_
                Error() & chr(13) &_
                "Error number: " & Err() ,_
                16,"Unknown Error")
      Endif
End Sub
```

REBUILDING SEARCH AND REPLACE FOR TEXT

In several situations, you might find you need to run through your document and visit all occurrences of a string. Let's see how you might solve such a problem. First, take a look at the simplest solution, which is rebuilding the search and replace function:

```
Sub SearchAndReplaceInGeneral
   'Declare two variables as arguments to make your subprocedure more flexible
   Dim StrSearchForWhat As String, StrReplaceItWith As String
   Dim oActiveWindow As Object
   'Saving the ActualWindow to an Object variable has some advantages,
   'you program will run faster and there are no problems in gaining
   'access to this document.
   oActiveWindow = ActiveWindow

   'First, set the settings of the search
   'otherwise the previous settings are taken.
   With oActiveWindow.SearchSettings
      .Backward = False        'Search backwards from cursor position
      .InSelection = False      'Search only in the current selection
      .CaseSensitive = False    'Search with respect to upper and lower case
      .RegExp = False           'Search with wildcards "regular expression"
      .WordOnly = True          'Finds the search String only as entire word
   End With
```

```
'Define attributes of the items to search and replace with the
'ReplaceAttributes and SearchAttributes class.
'Use the StarBasic Help system for further information

StrSearchForWhat = "NCC1701D"
StrReplaceItWith = "NCC1701"

'JumpToStartOfDoc brings us to the beginning of the document.
'Don't use GoToStartOfDoc. This moves the cursor to the beginning of
'the current Object e.g. the first cell of a table
oActiveWindow.JumpToStartOfDoc()

'The result of Search() will be true if the search was successful.
Do While oActiveWindow.Search(StrSearchForWhat)
   'We found the String. The text in the document is now selected.
   'By inserting new text, the old text will be deleted.
   oActiveWindow.Insert(StrReplaceItWith)
Loop
End Sub
```

SEARCHING FOR ITEMS TO APPLY PARAGRAPH STYLES The fundamental structure of this document scanning subprocedure can be applied to much more than just search and replace operations. Perhaps you've copied a plain text document from the Internet that has manual outline numbering, and you want to reformat it using the Heading 1 to 3 paragraph styles. Say the manual outline numbering was made in the following style:

```
1<tab>First chapter
1.1<tab>First section
1.1.1<tab>First sub section
```

As you can see, the format works in a pyramid fashion: The numbers are separated by points, followed by a tab and then some text. You have to locate such paragraphs and apply the corresponding paragraph style Heading 1 to 3. Your search structure would look something like this:

```
<begin of paragraph><number><point><number><tab>
```

StarOffice supports regular expressions; therefore, for the preceding structure, you can use the regular expression `^.\..\t`, where `^` stands for the beginning of a paragraph, `.` stands for any character, `\.` is the point character, and `\t` represents a tab. The regular expression for the chapter is `^.\t`, for a section it is `^.\..\t`, and for a subsection it is `^.\..\..\t`. You can begin your search for these structures and then apply the corresponding paragraph style.

To begin, create a user-defined function and call it `SearchAndReplaceStyles`. You do so because you need to perform the same search procedure with three different search expressions and insert three corresponding paragraph styles. To do so, you just call the `SearchAndReplaceStyles` function three times in your main program.

The argument list of SearchAndReplaceStyles is the search word, the name of one template, and its family, meaning you have adapted the arguments of the StyleApply() method to enhance the functionality of the function. The function can apply every style just like StyleApply() can. The basis of this search function is taken from the previous search and replace example. The difference is that you're no longer replacing the text but formatting it instead:

```
Sub CreateOutline
    'Declare variables for statistical information.
    Dim LongNumberOfHeading1 As Long
    Dim LongNumberOfHeading2 As Long
    Dim LongNumberOfHeading3 As Long

    'Search with regular expressions.
    With ActiveWindow.SearchSettings
        .Backward = False          'Search backwards from cursor position
        .RegExp = True             'Switch regular expressions on
    End With

    'The SearchAndReplaceStyles function will apply a given style and
    'record the number of items found
    LongNumberOfHeading1 = SearchAndReplaceStyles("^.\t",        "Heading 1", 2)
    LongNumberOfHeading2 = SearchAndReplaceStyles("^.\..\t",     "Heading 2", 2)
    LongNumberOfHeading3 = SearchAndReplaceStyles("^.\..\..\t", "Heading 3", 2)

    'Give information about what happened
    MsgBox( "Number of Chapters: "      & LongNumberOfHeading1 & chr(13) &_
            "Number of Sections: "      & LongNumberOfHeading2 & chr(13) &_
            "Number of Sub Sections: " & LongNumberOfHeading3 ,_
            64, "Information about Replacements")
End Sub

Function SearchAndReplaceStyles(StrSearchForWhat As String, _
              StrTemplate As String, LongFamily As Long) As Long
    Dim oActiveWindow As Object
    oActiveWindow = ActiveWindow
    oActiveWindow.JumpToStartOfDoc()

    'Count how often the items were found and formatted
    SearchAndReplaceStyles = 0
    Do While oActiveWindow.Search(StrSearchForWhat)
        'Apply the given style
        oActiveWindow.StyleApply( StrTemplate, LongFamily )
        'Increment the number of formatted items
        SearchAndReplaceStyles = SearchAndReplaceStyles + 1
    Loop
End Function
```

For further documentation of the search function, take a look at the code in the previous example, SearchAndReplaceInGeneral.

PART

VIII

CH

39

Note

In this particular example, you also could have used the method
`oActiveWindow.SearchAll(SearchForWhat)`. The `SearchAll` function finds all the expressions in text and highlights them, and then it automatically applies the paragraph style to every highlighted section.

USING SEARCH AND REPLACE TO REFORMAT TEXT The preceding examples of scanning text by searching bring us back to search and replace. The Search & Replace dialog in StarOffice is quite powerful. You can solve many complicated cases with it, especially when you're dealing with regular expressions and the Search All button. However, in some cases a more specific search and replace function is required.

If you want to search for α_+ and replace it with β_- you can't use the Search & Replace dialog. Naturally, you can search for an a+ using the Symbol font and replace it with a b- using the Symbol font, but the subscript format of the character - will be lost. It's useful to always keep a macro such as `SearchAndReplaceInGeneral` in your standard StarBasic library. This way, you just need to make small modifications to fit it to such a task.

You must search for the string a+ by using the Windows Symbol font. When you find it, you type in a b- from the same font and apply the correct subscript formatting to these characters. Then you need to set the search font attributes by entering the formatting instructions in the statement block of the Do...Loop statement as follows:

```
Sub SearchAndReplaceSpecial
    Dim oActiveWindow As Object
    oActiveWindow = ActiveWindow

    'We have to search for items in a specific font
    'Check the font by searching. Specify the attributes of the font
    oActiveWindow.SearchAttributes.IsFont = 2
    oActiveWindow.SearchAttributes.SetFont(,,,,"Symbol")

    '***Don't forget to specify the SearchSettings here

    'Make a shortcut to the Object oActiveWindow by using the With statement
    With oActiveWindow
        .JumpToStartOfDoc()

        'Search for "a+" i.e. "alpha subscript plus"
        'is an a+ out of the windows font "Symbol"
        Do While .Search("a+")
            'We found an "a+" and select it, overwrite it with a "b"
            'of the font "Symbol"
            .InsertSymbol( "b", "Symbol" )
            .GoLeft( 1, True )              'highlight the "b"
            .Font.SubScript = False        'turn subscript of the "b" off
            .GoRight( 1, False )           'go right beside the "b"
            .InsertSymbol( "-", "Symbol" ) 'type "-" beside the "b"
            .GoLeft( 1, True )             'highlight the "-"
            .Font.SubScript = True         'turn subscript on
        Loop
    End With
End Sub
```

Tip #603 from
Werner Roth

The best way to figure out which objects and methods are needed to replace the selected text with β is to select a piece of text, start recording a temporary macro, insert the beta symbol β and the hyphen, and then format them.

SEARCHING FOR TEXT AND REPLACING IT WITH GRAPHICS An acquaintance writing a children's book told me that he had no way in his word processor to search for the word *ball* in text and replace it with a picture of a ball. He pointed out that some word processors for kids have this feature. I told him that even grown-ups could replace text with graphics by using StarWriter—not by using the Search & Replace dialog, but with a macro. When you want to search and replace something and can't do it with the normal dialog, a macro is usually your answer.

In the following example, you'll search for the word *Australia* and replace it with a picture of the Australian flag. What you need is a small-scaled flag anchored *as character* to fit in the flow of the text. The method `InsertGraphic()` inserts every picture in full size and anchors it to a paragraph. You therefore have to play a little trick.

Before any other action occurs, you must jump to the start of the document, insert a linked picture, scale it down, anchor it as a character, and cut it to the Clipboard using the Cut command (Ctrl+X). Next, you use the search loop once again. At every occurrence of the word *Australia*, you paste the picture from the Clipboard. That's the little trick:

```
Sub SearchAndReplaceGraphic
    Dim oActiveWindow As Object
    Dim SingleSaveGraphicHeight As Single, SingleSaveGraphicWidth As Single

    oActiveWindow = ActiveWindow
    oActiveWindow.JumpToStartOfDoc()

    'Here we perform our little trick with the picture. Shhhh...
    'Insert a picture of the Australian flag as a link
    'Maybe you have to change the path of the graphic to your installation
    oActiveWindow.InsertGraphic( _
        "file:///C¦/Office51/gallery/flags/austral1.wmf",_
        "WMF - MS Windows Metafile", True )
    'Copy height and width to scale the picture
    SingleSaveGraphicHeight = Selection.GraphicHeight
    SingleSaveGraphicWidth = Selection.GraphicWidth
    'Scale it to 32% of the original
    Selection.Height = SingleSaveGraphicHeight * 0.32
    Selection.Width = SingleSaveGraphicWidth * 0.32
    'Change the anchoring to "as character"
    Selection.SetAnchorToChar()
    'Cut this picture (to the clipboard)
    oActiveWindow.Cut()

    'Don't forget to specify the SearchSettings here

    'Now search for "Australia"
```

```
      Do While oActiveWindow.Search("Australia")
         'When found paste the picture in place of the word "Australia".
         oActiveWindow.Paste()
      Loop
   End Sub
```

MOVING AHEAD BY STAYING IN PLACE

In the section on searching and replacing, you jumped to the beginning of a document, performed some actions, and finally left the cursor where it was. This situation isn't ideal if you're writing, want to execute a macro, and then continue with your work where you left off. If you want to perform a number of actions and then return the cursor position to your starting point, you can insert a bookmark as follows:

```
Sub StayWhereYouAre
   'Place the bookmark "MyBookmark" into the current cursor position
   Selection.InsertBookmark("MyBookmark")
   [...]
   'Do your actions here
   [...]
   'Return to the saved cursor position
   Selection.GotoBookmark("MyBookmark")
   'That's it. Delete the bookmark "MyBookmark"
   Selection.DeleteBookmark("MyBookmark")
End Sub
```

Essentially, this macro uses a bookmark named MyBookmark as a marker, performs the actions, jumps back to this bookmark, and then deletes it. Ensure that you delete the bookmark; otherwise, you only fool the user with a bookmark he or she never needed.

What happens if you already have a bookmark named MyBookmark? StarBasic tries to set this bookmark, fails without throwing an error message, performs the actions, jumps to the original bookmark MyBookmark, and deletes it. Not very funny. In any case, what can you do? Some people may not worry and just say, "Give the bookmark a seldom-used name." They're right. You'll rarely fall into this trap if you name your bookmark StarOfficeSpecialEditionBookmarkJustForMacros. If you consider this name just a tad long, you can make use of a more appropriate and even elegant solution for this problem.

The solution is to randomly generate a name for the bookmark and check whether this name is already in use. If so, you can generate another name and check it again. To create a solution that you can use in any like situation, I designed a user-defined function called EmptyBookMarkName(). This function requires you to keep the given bookmark name so that you can jump back and delete it afterward. The final solution for such a task is as follows:

```
Sub ImprovedStayWhereYouAre
   Dim StrGeneratedBookmark As String
   StrGeneratedBookmark = EmptyBookMarkName()
   Selection.InsertBookmark(StrGeneratedBookmark)
   [...]
   'Perform your actions here
   [...]
   Selection.GotoBookmark(StrGeneratedBookmark)
   Selection.DeleteBookmark(StrGeneratedBookmark)
End Sub
```

```
Function EmptyBookMarkName As String
    'i is a counter to cycle through all bookmark names
    Dim i As Long
    'BoolFoundAName is a help variable to control do...loop
    Dim BoolFoundAName As boolean
    Randomize 'initializes the random number generator Rnd().

    'Loop until a proper name is found
    Do
        'Calculate a bookmark name with the random number generator
        EmptyBookMarkName = "StrGeneratedBookmark" & _
                        Right("00000" & Fix(1000000 * Rnd()),6)
        'BoolFoundAName is true until we find out it is
        'an existing bookmark name
        BoolFoundAName = True
        'Cycle through all bookmark names and compare them
        'with our generated name
        For i = 0 To Selection.Bookmarkcount - 1
            'If an existing bookmark is equal to our new name
            'we have to loop again
            If EmptyBookMarkName = Selection.BookmarkName(i) Then
                BoolFoundAName = False
            Endif
        Next i
    Loop Until BoolFoundAName
End Function
```

Now take a closer look at the expression Right("00000" & Fix(1000000 * Rnd()),6). Rnd() generates a random floating-point number between 0 and 1. So 1000000 * Rnd() generates a random number between 0 and 1000000—for example, 1901.91351054415. The Fix() runtime function removes the fractional part of the number so that it results in 1901. The next move is to add leading zeros to ensure every generated string has the same length of six digits. You then place five zeros in front of the generated number 000001901. The Right function then returns the six rightmost characters, and the end result for the example is 001901.

Now that you've learned how to generate the bookmark name, you should be able to use the principle of the EmptyBookMarkName function in any case in which a temporary object is needed—for example, a temporary filename or different values for database fields.

PART

VIII

CH

39

Tip #604 from
Werner Roth

If you want to test such a function, it's a good idea to know what random numbers are created. You can pass a number as an argument to the Randomize function to create the same sequence of random numbers. This trick works because the StarBasic Rnd() function generates pseudo-random numbers. They are sequences of numbers that are, in essence, random yet at the same time determined depending on the start value. If no argument is given to the Randomize function, StarBasic uses the system timer of your computer for the start value.

MAKING FASTER MACROS

When StarWriter performs manipulations on your text document via a macro, it behaves exactly as it would in any normal editing situation. All actions are visible on the screen. There's no doubt that a macro's performance is very fast compared to classical formatting with the keyboard and mouse. Nevertheless, if your StarBasic program carries out a lot of formatting and insertions, you might want to turn off the visible formatting of a document. Turning it off improves the performance of your program and gets rid of the annoying flickering on the screen. The method you use to turn off visible formatting is called `ActionStart()`, and you need to turn it back on via `ActionEnd()`. You can nest `ActionStart()` and `ActionEnd()` blocks. Just make sure to have a corresponding `ActionEnd()` for each `ActionStart()` method:

```
Sub NoVisibleFormatting
    'ActionStart() and ActionEnd() are only available in text documents
    'check if text document is open
    If ActiveModule.Name <> "StarWriter" Then
        MsgBox("This program is only available in text documents.",16,"Error")
        Exit Sub
    Endif

    Application.EnterWait() 'switch to hourglass cursor

    ActiveWindow.ActionStart()
    [...]
    'Do your actions here
    [...]
    ActiveWindow.ActionEnd()

    Application.LeaveWait() 'display the regular cursor again
    'EnterWait() and LeaveWait() can also be nested.
End Sub
```

Adding the corresponding `ActionEnd()` to the `ActionStart()` is quite important. Otherwise, after you've finished testing and using your newly created macros, you'll end up scratching your head wondering why your screen won't refresh. You could also fool older versions of StarOffice; in earlier versions, the visible formatting was simply switched off. StarOffice 5.0 and 5.1 automatically turn the visible formatting back on after your StarBasic program ends. All the same, leaving out the last `ActionEnd()` is lazy programming practice. For your information, StarWriter doesn't mind executing an `ActionEnd()` method even if it doesn't have an `ActionStart()`.

Tip #605 from
Werner Roth

As you learned previously, StarBasic can improve the performance of your macro program by referring objects such as `ActiveWindow` to its own object variable. You can then use the `With` statement to access three or more properties or methods of an object.

Note

Being scant with help variables is not necessarily a good idea. You might not think such variables are needed from a logical point of view, but they make the code more readable and in turn maintainable. You win only milliseconds by omitting a few variables and lose nanoseconds by mucking around with buggy programs.

WAITING—FOR GOOD REASON

In StarBasic, you can use a runtime function called `Wait`. This function suspends the execution of your StarBasic program for a given number of milliseconds but does not block the execution of StarOffice. At first glance, waiting isn't necessary in a program, but in a lot of cases, you have to wait for an action performed by StarOffice to finish before you can go on with the next action.

In many cases, you can ask whether StarOffice has finished the invoked action. It makes no sense, however, to ask every millisecond if StarOffice is ready. Asking so frequently would only hog more time than the action itself. In the following example, you load a StarWriter document out of the work folder, "wait" until it's loaded, and make some changes to it when it arrives:

```
Sub OpenAFile
    Dim oDocument As Object
    Dim StrWorkFolder As String
    'Ask for the standard work folder
    StrWorkFolder = Application.DefaultFilePath
    'Open the document "temp.sdw" and pass a handle to it to
    'by way of an Object variable
    oDocument = Documents.Open( Application.DefaultFilePath & "\temp.sdw" )

    'Ask if the document is loaded.
    'Stop any further actions as long as StarWriter is still loading the text
    'or images
    Do While oDocument.IsLoading or oDocument.IsLoadingImages
        'Just ask every second
        Wait 1000
    Loop
    'Make another little pause here, to give StarWriter a chance
    'to initialize the document data
    Wait 100

    [...]
    'Do something with your document here
End Sub
```

PART

VIII

CH

39

Use `Wait` every time you deal with a StarOffice object using a method that takes a bit of time. Without it, your program causes errors that are difficult to recognize. In some instances, you can't ask whether the action has taken place. Waiting for an estimated amount of time is not an optimum solution; however, it's the only thing you're able to do.

Scanning Text Paragraph by Paragraph

On occasion, you might find that you need to make changes to a text document by cycling through all its paragraphs. This process is time consuming, so it's better to use another method, if possible—for example, altering the search macros described previously. Sometimes you don't have any option other than to cycle through every paragraph, row, or even every character. I'll at least show you a strategy that will work with paragraphs and can be easily adapted to scan rows or characters as well.

Often, plain text files are formatted with a paragraph sign at the end of each line and a blank paragraph sign to signify the actual paragraph end. Normally, you can use the AutoFormat function of StarWriter. However, if you have prior knowledge that a plain text file is formatted in this way, the following macro will give better results than AutoFormat because AutoFormat tries to recognize a paragraph using a more general strategy.

For this example, you can reformat the following piece of text:

```
Quaeramus aliquod non in speciem bonum, sed solidum et aequale
et a secretiore parte formosius; hoc eruamus.

Nec longe positum est: invenietur, scire tantum opus est, quo
manum porrigas; nunc velut in tenebris vicina transimus,
offensantes ea ipsa quae desideramus.

Sed ne te per circumitus traham, aliorum quidem opiniones
praeteribo (nam enumerare illas longum est coarguere): nostram
accipe.
```

You need to start in the first line of the text and then cycle through all the lines. At each line, you need to check whether it contains characters. If you find characters, you know you're in between a (real) paragraph and need to join it to the next line. If you find an empty line, the end of the (real) paragraph is reached. You use the following macro for this task:

```
Sub MakeCorrectParagraphs
    Dim oActiveWindow As Object
    oActiveWindow = ActiveWindow
    'We will only use methods of the ActiveWindow so we make good use
    'of the With statement
    With oActiveWindow
        .JumpToStartOfDoc() 'Start from the beginning
        'otherwise we have to go to the End of the actual paragraph
        'IsEndOfDoc() is false even if we are in the last paragraph
        'of a document
        .GoToEndOfPara()
        'Cycle through all paragraphs
        Do Until .IsEndOfDoc()
            'go right to check if the next paragraph is an empty one
            .GoRight()
            'If the beginning of this paragraph is also its End
            'we've found an empty one
            If (.IsStartOfPara() and .IsEndOfPara()) Then
                'Delete the paragraph End sign
                .Delete()
            Else
```

```
            'If the paragraph contains any characters join them together
            .Backspace() 'Delete the paragraph End sign of the former paragraph
            .Insert(" ") 'Insert a blank
         Endif
         'Now let's look for the next paragraph, but again we have to go
         'to the End of the actual paragraph to check if the End of the
         'document is reached
         .GoToEndOfPara()
      Loop
      'Perhaps our document produced some extra spaces; search for two spaces
      'and replace them with one
      .ReplaceAll("  ", " ")
   End With
End Sub
```

If you code such a scanning program for your own purposes, make sure it works in text documents that contain elements other than text, such as pictures, tables, and so on. After final testing, use `ActionStart()` and `ActionEnd()` to improve the performance of your program.

CYCLING THROUGH GRAPHICS AND TABLES

Now cast your thoughts to reformatting objects such as tables or graphics in your document. In such cases, you can work with StarOffice Collections such as Tables and Graphics, which give you access to individual objects by index or by name.

StarOffice numbers new pictures inserted in a document in their insertion order, with the names `Graphic1`, `Graphic2`, and so on. Because these names are so boring, you can rename them `Picasso No. 1`, `Picasso No. 2`, and so on, instead. You cycle through a text document with the collection object `Graphics`. It provides you with access to every picture object in the text document by using `Graphics(Index)`:

```
Sub RenameGraphics
   Dim IntNumberOfGraphics As Integer, i As Integer
   Dim oActiveWindow As Object
   'This macro is only designed for text documents
   If ActiveModule.Name <> "StarWriter" Then
      MsgBox("This program is only available in text documents.",16,"Error")
      Exit Sub
   Endif
   'Refer to the actual document by an object variable
   oActiveWindow = ActiveWindow
   'The property Count of Graphics collection contains the number of
   'pictures in the actual document.
   IntNumberOfGraphics = oActiveWindow.Graphics.Count
   If IntNumberOfGraphics = 0 Then
      MsgBox("There are no graphics in this document.",16,"Error")
      Exit Sub
   Endif
   'Cycle through all pictures
   For i = 1 To IntNumberOfGraphics
      'Change the Name of the i-th picture in the document
      oActiveWindow.Graphics(i).GraphicName = "Picasso No. " & i
   Next i
End Sub
```

Now cycle through all tables in your document. Such macros are often very handy. Think about editing the documentation for a project in which every item is explained in its own table. You could very well have over 100 tables that all need to look the same. They probably need to have identical column widths, borders, and so on. You would go mad trying to give the tables the same attributes manually. To solve this problem, the following macro sets the width of the first column in all tables to one inch:

```
Sub FormatAllTables
   Dim IntNumberOfTables As Integer, i As Integer
   Dim oActiveWindow As Object
   'Again check for the correct Staroffice program
   If ActiveModule.Name <> "StarWriter" Then
      MsgBox("This program is only available in text documents.",16,"Error")
      Exit Sub
   Endif
   oActiveWindow = ActiveWindow
   'The object collection for tables in documents is named Tables
   IntNumberOfTables = oActiveWindow.Tables.Count
   If IntNumberOfTables = 0 Then
      MsgBox("There are no tables in this document.",16,"Error")
      Exit Sub
   Endif
   'We know that there are tables in our document so let's reformat them
   For i = 1 To IntNumberOfTables
      'Set the width of the first column (left side) to one inch
      oActiveWindow.Tables(i).SetColumnWidth(0, "1in")
   Next i
End Sub
```

Naturally, you do not use these macros just to rename graphics and change column widths of tables in your document. You also can resize graphics, change the linked picture file, reformat columns and rows of tables, insert other values, and even delete them all.

Tip #606 from
Werner Roth

To find out more about changing graphics and tables in text documents, look at their base classes in the StarBasic Help system. The base class of a graphic in a text document is `BaseTextGraphic`, and the base class for a table is `BaseTextTable`. Choose Help, Contents; search the index for `StarBasic, contents`; and then double-click the `Class Structure` hyperlink to jump to the relevant pages.

WORKING WITH AND IN STARCALC SHEETS

As you learned earlier, StarCalc is full-featured and powerful enough not to require much programming. In fact, because of StarCalc's power, programming is somewhat complex. However, you can still do some useful things with macros in StarCalc. One of them is to automate data entry.

ADDRESSING ELEMENTS OF A SPREADSHEET

A macro for a StarCalc spreadsheet will work on entries in a spreadsheet table. In text documents, you worked with selected text. In order to find the right section of text we browsed through the text document using the Search and Replace function. StarCalc works with a grid. This makes life easier; you simply address a couple of cells in the grid.

→ For more information on searching documents **see** "Using Search and Replace," **p. 460**.

To address cells of a spreadsheet, you can use the Range object. It gives you the same access to cells that you're used to in a normal spreadsheet calculation:

```
ActiveDocument.Range("A1").Select()
ActiveDocument.Range("B1:B3").Select()
ActiveDocument.Range("Sheet1.C1").Select()
ActiveDocument.Range("Sheet1.D1:E3").Select()
```

You need to pass the address of the cells you intend as a string. You also can address the cells of a spreadsheet by number; to do so, you can use the Cells object:

```
ActiveDocument.Range("Sheet1.B3").Insert("I was here first")
ActiveDocument.Cells(2,3,1).Insert("No, I was here first")
```

Both of the preceding lines insert a value into the same cell. The arguments of the Cells object are <Column>, <Row>, and <Sheet>. You use the Cells object to cycle through a complete Sheet with two nested For loops, as shown in the example for nested loops in Chapter 38.

→ For more information on For loops, **see** the section "Loop Statements," **p. 1296**.

To insert a value, you use the Insert method. Its argument is a string that will be inserted as if it were passed to the cell by the keyboard. The following line inserts a formula:

```
ActiveDocument.Range("A4").Insert("=sum(A1:A3)")
```

So, there you have the basic functions to read and write data to a spreadsheet.

You can navigate on a sheet in several ways. Because there is no standard way to change a spreadsheet by navigating with a macro, you can use the macro recorder to record your own way of navigating through the sheet.

You already saw one example of manipulating data by transposing a sheet. The most common thing you'll do with a macro in a spreadsheet is change given values; the calculation is made by the spreadsheet program StarCalc.

PROGRAMMING STARCALC FUNCTIONS

StarCalc enables you to use user-defined functions for calculations in your spreadsheet. You would normally program a StarBasic function into one module of the library of your StarCalc document and use it like an ordinary StarCalc function.

If you have to fill in a time table with the IDs of employees, for example, you might be interested in their names. If only a few people are working in your company, you can easily realize this goal by using a macro.

To get started, open a new spreadsheet, save it under the name TimeTable.sdc, and add a new StarBasic module in its Standard library. Select Tools, Macro, and then select the Standard library of the TimeTable spreadsheet (at the bottom of the Macros From list). Click the New button to add a new module and open the StarBasic IDE.

The function itself simply tests the passed argument in a Select Case statement and returns the corresponding name, when it exists. If a name is not found, the StarBasic function gives a warning tone. The return in this case is ***not valid***.

Type this function in Module1 of the TimeTable spreadsheet, deleting the empty Main subprocedure:

```
Function LastName(ID as string) as string
    Select Case ID
        Case "445"
            LastName = "Kay"
        Case "446"
            LastName = "Harkey"
        Case "457"
            LastName = "Anderson"
        Case Else
            Beep

            LastName = "***not valid***"
    End Select
End Function
```

Now leave the StarBasic IDE, and return to the spreadsheet using the StarOffice taskbar. In cell A1, type the ID 445, and in cell B1, type =LASTNAME(A1). The function calculates the corresponding name Kay. Now if you change the value in cell A1 to 444, you receive the error message.

You can think of a StarBasic user-defined function in a spreadsheet as a way of opening up communication—for example, a macro you can connect to a database table produced by another application. Your macro could even ask the external application to produce new data.

Tip #607 from
Werner Roth

Using StarBasic functions instead of more complicated StarCalc functions results in a loss of performance in most cases. Use StarBasic functions only when you really need them.

Note

If you know how to program a dynamic link library (DLL), you can use the StarBasic Add-In interface to add new functions. Look in the Help system for further information.

BUILDING AN ENTIRE APPLICATION IN STARBASIC

If you want to add further functionality to StarOffice that requires its own window (for example, a complete calculator for calculating line spaces and margins in a text document), you first need to program a StarBasic dialog. No problem; in the following sections, you'll learn how.

EXAMPLE: DESIGNING A ManualComplete FUNCTION

StarWriter 5.1 comes with the AutoComplete function that suggests words you've typed previously in your text. By default, it recognizes words longer than 10 characters. This function is fine for people who are not very fast typists. However, sometimes the AutoComplete function disrupts more than it saves time. So how about a ManualComplete function? With it, you can add the word at the current cursor position to a list box and paste it into the text whenever you like.

To accomplish this task, you need a dialog with a list box containing all recently added words. Further, you need a feature to add words or complete phrases to enter new words in the list box. Finally, you need a button to insert selected words in the document. Your dialog might look something like the one shown in Figure 39.3.

PART

VIII

CH

39

Figure 39.3
This is the initial user interface design for the ManualComplete application you'll develop in this section.

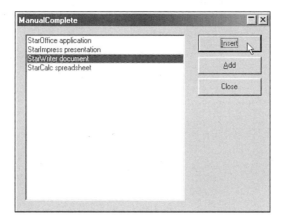

The following are the steps you take to create this StarBasic application:

1. Add a StarBasic module and a dialog module to the Standard library of a StarWriter document. This way, you create a place to put the dialog and its subprocedures.

2. Use the StarBasic IDE to paint the dialogs. This process barely differs from painting rectangles and circles in StarDraw.

3. Produce the subprocedures that give the program the required functions. This step demands careful design of the subprocedures' structure and necessary functionality.

4. Connect the StarBasic code produced to the dialog. A click on a button starts the function behind it.

GETTING STARTED

Get ready to build your application. First, you need a proper StarBasic library in which to store your project. To develop and test this new StarBasic application, you can use the standard StarBasic library of a StarWriter document. Using a standard library ensures you don't disturb the StarOffice libraries or hold up the building of StarBasic functions. The advantage of developing a StarBasic application in a StarOffice document is that you can easily control different versions of your application, make backups, and when you're finished, append them as a StarOffice library.

→ For more information on how to create, append, and work with StarBasic libraries and modules, **see** "Organizing Macros in Libraries and Modules," **p. 1252**.

Next, begin by opening a new text document. Save it under the name `InsertText.sdw`.

Tip #608 from *Werner Roth*	Naming your document after the application or macro is good practice if the primary purpose of the document is to store your program. This naming convention helps you and others to keep track.

Now you need a new module to store your source code. To create one, select Tools, Macro, and then select the library Standard on the document `InsertText.sdw` (see Figure 39.4). Next, click the New button.

Figure 39.4
Your first step in creating a dialog application is to create a new module in which to store it. Make sure you select your document, not the StarOffice Basic library.

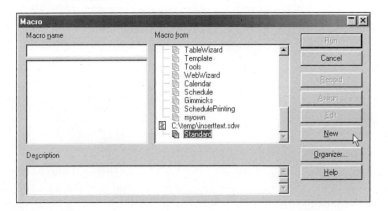

The StarBasic IDE appears with an almost empty module called `Module1`. Alt+click the tab Module1 at the bottom of the screen, and rename the module `ManualComplete`.

Next, you need a StarBasic dialog. Place the mouse cursor over the module tab now named ManualComplete, right-click to open its context menu, and choose Insert, BASIC Dialog (see Figure 39.5).

Tip #609 from
Werner Roth

You can also insert a new dialog by using the macro organizer. To do so, choose the Modules button in the macro bar.

Figure 39.5
You can "paint" your own dialog boxes by choosing the Insert, BASIC Dialog command in the StarBasic IDE.

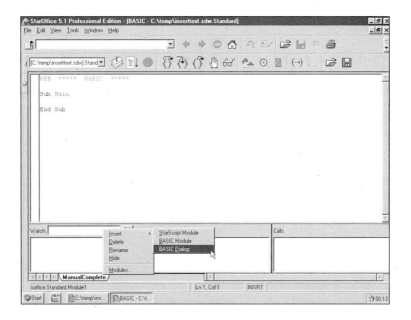

PART

VIII

CH

39

StarBasic adds a new dialog module to the library and displays an empty dialog form. Rename this dialog module MC_Dialog using the same Alt+click trick as with Module1. Names of StarBasic modules are not too important unless you call functions out of another module. It is important to remember that the name of a dialog module is the default name of the dialog object. If you want to follow this example, though, you need to rename it MC_Dialog.

PAINTING THE DIALOG

To create a dialog as shown in Figure 39.3, you need to place three buttons and a list box on your empty dialog. In other words, you need StarBasic controls. A click on the Controls button opens a floating toolbar that you can place anywhere you like on the screen (see Figure 39.6). This toolbar might look familiar if you've worked with forms before because many of the same tools are found on the Forms floating toolbar.

Figure 39.6

Your dialog box will initially look just like a big, blank window. You can draw your buttons and list box using tools from the Controls toolbar, open here on the right.

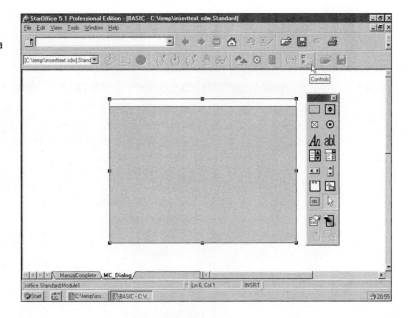

Drag the floating toolbar out of its starting position so that it's always available. Make sure Tips are turned on in the Help menu; you can then easily find out the type of control each button on the toolbar creates by moving your mouse pointer over the tool until the tip pops up.

In a nutshell, creating the dialog in Figure 39.3 can be broken down into four general steps, which are discussed in the following sections:

1. Give the dialog a title.
2. Draw and label the dialog buttons.
3. Paint and rename the list box.
4. Test the dialog.

STEP 1: GIVE THE DIALOG A TITLE

First, you need to give your dialog box a title as follows:

1. Click the Properties button at the bottom of the floating toolbar. An empty Properties window appears showing the properties of the selected control or dialog.

2. Select the dialog box (not the Properties window) by clicking its border. (If you are working with a high screen resolution, this step can be tricky.) After you select the dialog, you can view and edit its properties in the Properties window, as shown in Figure 39.7.

Figure 39.7
After you click the Properties button and select your blank dialog box, you can edit its properties, including its caption (title) and appearance. The Control toolbox, which you use to draw your buttons and list box, is open on the right.

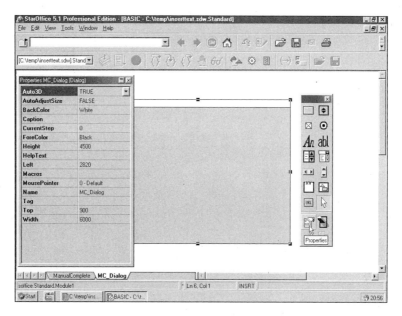

3. Click the cell directly beside Caption, and type ManualComplete. StarBasic assigns this name to the property Caption on leaving the edit box. Click another property, and you see the new title at the top of your dialog.

As you can see, several properties are shown in the Properties window. Most of them are self-explanatory, such as Height, Width, BackColor, and ForeColor. You can use the Help Agent and the Help contents to find the meaning of other properties.

One row in the Properties window isn't a property at all. Clicking the row Macros makes a button appear, and it, in turn, leads you to a dialog box in which you can assign subprocedures to events. You'll make use of this dialog box later in this example.

Note

If you're going to play around with the properties of the StarBasic dialog at this stage, you might fall into a little trap. If you want to change the backcolor or forecolor of the dialog, nothing happens until you switch off Auto3D.

Leave the Properties window open because you'll need it continually while developing this dialog.

STEP 2: DRAW AND LABEL THE DIALOG BUTTONS

If you refer to Figure 39.3, you'll see that the next thing you need to do is place your own buttons on the right side of the dialog. Just follow these steps:

1. Click the Command Button tool in the Control floating toolbar. The cursor changes into a little cross and lets you paint your own button.

2. Place the cursor somewhere on the right-hand side of the dialog, press the left mouse button, and draw a rectangle by dragging the mouse down and to the right. Then release the mouse button. StarBasic paints a button called CommandButton1.

Figure 39.8
After you draw and select your new command button, you can view its properties in the Properties window.

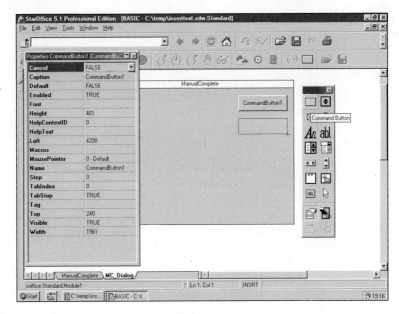

3. Click this new CommandButton1. Even though the mouse cursor is still in Drawing mode, the properties of this button are shown in the Properties window.

4. Click the cell to the left of Caption, and replace the default button caption with Insert (the name you want to appear on the button of your interface). After you rename the text value of this property from CommandButton1 to Insert and leave the edit box, the text on the Cursor changes to Insert.

5. Change the name of the button from CommandButton1 to InsertButton in the same way.

6. Following the same procedure, add two more buttons to the dialog, as shown in Figure 39.3. Give the middle button the caption Add and the name AddButton. Then give the third button the caption Close and the name CloseButton.

Tip #610 from
Werner Roth

You can place your buttons with great precision by changing the values of the Height, Left, Top, and Width properties.

If you want all your buttons to be the same exact size, just copy and paste them. You can use the regular Ctrl+C and Ctrl+V shortcuts.

STEP 3: PAINT AND RENAME THE LIST BOX

The last control field you need is a list box; you can create it as follows:

1. Click the List Box tool, and paint it on the left-hand side of the dialog box.
2. Click the cell next to the property Name, and replace the default name with WordsListBox.

The dialog itself is now finished.

If you want your list to be sorted alphabetically, don't forget to set the property Sorted to True. Setting this property allows for faster searching.

STEP 4: TEST THE DIALOG

You can test the dialog by clicking the Activate Test Mode button in the Control floating toolbar. The dialog appears in the form that is shown later in the StarBasic application. For now, none of the buttons you just drew are functioning. Close the dialog in test mode by clicking the Close button in the upper-right corner.

ASSIGNING INITIAL FUNCTIONALITY TO THE DIALOG

To assign functionality to your dialog, select the Close button you created on the dialog, and change the property Cancel to True. Changing the property assigns the same function to your Close button as you get when clicking the Close button in the box's corner or pressing the Esc key. Essentially, you've created a Cancel button. You can add a word to the list box or insert a selected word to the text, but nothing else. Thus, closing the dialog box is the same as canceling it.

Now click Activate Test Mode again. You'll find that you can click your own Close button to exit the dialog.

ASSIGNING SUBPROCEDURES TO THE ADD AND INSERT BUTTONS

The next step is to program the dialog so that it reacts accordingly when someone clicks the Add or Insert buttons. This reaction is performed by a StarBasic subprocedure assigned to an event of a control field. First, you must program a StarBasic subprocedure in the module ManualComplete that executes the desired task. Then you can assign this subprocedure to the OnClick event of the button. As a result, whenever the button is clicked, the corresponding subprocedure is called. At this point, now that the dialog box is ready, you need to step back and design your application.

PART
VIII
CH
39

DESIGNING THE APPLICATION BEHIND THE DIALOG

The initial purpose of this project was to add an often-used word to a list box and reinsert it in the text when needed. Why? To save keystrokes.

After you close a document and reload it again, certainly the collected list of frequently used words should still be available. However, using one list for all documents is bad planning. Your collection would continue growing until you needed more time to find the required word in the list box than simply to type it. Therefore, you need to save the list with each document.

PRINCIPAL APPLICATION DESIGN

The following are the major parts of the program:

- A subprocedure that adds a selected word or phrase to the list box (invoked by the Add button)
- A subprocedure that inserts a selected item of the list box in the current cursor position (invoked by the Insert button)
- A subprocedure that loads the words from the document into the list
- A subprocedure that saves all the words in the list to the document
- A main subprocedure that initializes and starts the dialog

Now think about how to save the list in a document. You could save it as a separate file in the same folder as your StarWriter document. StarBasic has low-level file capabilities, so this approach would pose no problem. However, extra files such as these are often forgotten when you're transporting your document to another computer. Adding the words to the regular text is also an undesirable solution because the user would always need to cut the list out of the document before printing. What about the description fields in the File, Properties dialog? You could use the user-defined fields Info 0 through Info 3 to store four words. But this solution is not really sufficient either.

Yet, what about storing more than one word to one description field? Not a bad idea! You can place a character between two words to separate them. The space character is not ideal because you might want to store little phrases. How about using the asterisk (*)?

Three words stored would look like this: Word1*Word2*Word3. The words are clearly separate from each other.

So you have all the parts of the main design of your application. Now you need to define names and the tasks for the subprocedures. Take a look at Table 39.1, which outlines the subprocedure names and tasks.

TABLE 39.1   OUTLINE OF SUBPROCEDURES AND TASKS USED BY *ManualComplete*

Subprocedure	Task	Called by
Sub ManualComplete	The Main procedure initializes the dialog, displays it to the screen, and removes it frommemory.	The user
Sub MC_LoadData	Loads the data out of the Comment field and passes it to the list box.	The initialization routine: ManualComplete
Sub MC_AddWord	Adds the selected text to the list box and saves the word list.	A click on the Add button
Sub MC_SaveData	Stores the words in the list box separated by * to the Comment field.	After each addition of a word: MC_AddWord
Sub MC_InsertWord	Inserts the highlighted item in the list box into the text.	A click on the Insert button

Note

StarOffice offers limited space for the description fields in the File, Properties dialog. For example the dialog will not accept more than 250 characters in the description field. If the description field is filled by a macro program, you can use as many characters as you like. However, if a document information field is written by a macro it can hold too much characters, which means you can no longer edit it manually.

REFERRING TO NEEDED OBJECTS

Throughout the program, you need to communicate with the StarWriter document. You need to load data into the Comment field and save it. You need to know the currently selected text and be able to insert text at the current cursor position. Therefore, you can use the following properties and method:

- `ActiveDocument.DocumentInfo.Description` gives you direct access to strings in the Comment field.

- `ActiveWindow.SelectionTextExt()` returns the currently highlighted text or, if no text is highlighted, the complete word at the cursor position.

- `ActiveWindow.Insert("Text")` inserts the given string argument at the current cursor position.

The next move is to work with the objects on the dialog. First, you need to add items to the list box. To refer to the properties or methods of your dialog, use the name of the dialog, `MC_Dialog`, followed by a period (.), and then the name of the property.

Remember how you changed the caption of the dialog using the Properties window? You can also change this property by using this command line in your program:

```
MC_Dialog.Caption = "My new Caption"
```

Note

Changing the properties using the Properties window means changing elements in the dialog module. They are saved with the dialog's StarBasic library. Changing properties with a command line changes them only for the lifetime of the program. Some properties, such as Cancel, are read-only at runtime.

You need three methods to control the dialog:

- `.Show()`—Brings the dialog to screen
- `.Hide()`—Closes the dialog after inserting a phrase into the text, or vice versa, placing a word from the text to the list box
- `.UnLoad()`—Removes the dialog from memory

If you're going to make heavy use of this application, you might want to leave the dialog in memory. In this case, place comments before the `MC_Dialog.UnLoad()` line in the module to explain your choice.

Because control fields are owned by their dialog, you refer to them with the dialog name. The address to a property or method of a control field is divided into three elements, each separated by a period (.):

```
<Dialogname>.<Control field name>.<Property name>
```

or

```
MC_Dialog.InsertButton.Caption = "Register"
```

In the application, you need to access only properties and methods of your list box. The list box's name is `WordsListBox`; hence, you refer to this control field as `MC_Dialog.WordsListBox`. Table 39.2 lists the properties and methods you need.

TABLE 39.2 PROPERTIES AND METHODS OF THE LIST BOX

Property or Method	Explanation
`.Clear`	Deletes all items from the list box.
`.ListCount`	Lists the number of items in the list box.
`.AddItem("Text")`	Adds the passed text to the list box.
`.ListIndex`	Lists the number of currently highlighted entries in the list box.
`.Text`	Returns the current highlighted item as a string.
`.List(IndexVariable)`	Returns the item at the given position. The first index is zero; the last is `MC_Dialog.WordsListBox.ListCount - 1`.

Property or Method	Explanation
`.Selected(IndexVariable) = true`	Highlights the item at a given position. This method appears to be a little bit complicated; you can also design list boxes with multiselection. There, you need to switch highlighting on or off for each item.

Tip #613 from
Werner Roth

You can drag and drop properties and methods of your control fields into your source code using the Object Catalog window. Open the Object Catalog window by clicking its button on the macro bar.

SAVING AND RESTORING PHRASES

To create the complete application, you need to store phrases and words given by a list to a single string and then restore them. For now, concentrate on storing them. This is the easy part. All phrases and words are items in a list box, which means you can cycle through all the items and concatenate them into a string separated by * symbols.

Dividing the given string into the original phrase or words later, however, is a bit more complex. You need to break apart the string at each occurrence of the asterisk separator, rescue the word, and add it to the list box. You do so by cycling through the complete string character by character. When you reach the asterisk character, the string before it should be added to the list box.

As you check each character to see whether it's the separator, you simply add to a string variable any character that is not an asterisk. When you reach the *, the string variable contains the complete word. You can then add it to the list box, clear the string variable, and continue. You keep collecting word for word until the end is reached.

ASSEMBLING THE BITS AND PIECES INTO AN ENTIRE PROGRAM

You've already designed the major structure of your program, found the methods and properties needed, and delved deeper into the save and load subprocedures. Now you can link all the parts together in a complete program by typing your code into the module `ManualComplete` of the StarBasic library in your document.

Don't get too excited, though; you still need to solve a lot of details in this program! One, for example, is how to refer to the StarWriter `ActiveWindow` and `ActiveDocument`. Take a careful look at the following source code; it's been documented in detail to give you the opportunity to explore it:

```
Option Explicit

'All of the stored words are separated by a Char. If you want to store
'words containing the asterisk char, choose a different char here
Const SeparatorChar = "*"

'We need references to two StarOffice objects declared as Module level
'variables, because we need them in three sub-procedures.
```

```
Dim oActiveWindow As Object
Dim oActiveDocument As Object

Sub ManualComplete
    'The macro only functions out of text documents, so check this
    If ActiveModule.Name <> "StarWriter" Then
        MsgBox("This program is only available in text documents.",16,"Error")
        Exit Sub
    Endif
    'Save a reference to the two StarOffice Objects as we need them later on
    oActiveWindow = ActiveWindow
    oActiveDocument = ActiveDocument
    'Call a subprocedure that puts the words in our list box.
    MC_LoadData()
    'Display our dialog to the screen
    MC_Dialog.Show()
    'All commands following will be executed after closing the dialog
    'Remove the dialog from memory
    MC_Dialog.UnLoad()
End Sub

Sub MC_LoadData
    'We stored the words for this document in the comment field
    'of the document properties (File, Properties).
    Dim IntCharNumber As Integer
    Dim StrData As String, StrWord As String, StrChar As String
    Dim BoolAddedWord as Boolean

    'Remove all entries in the list box that contain the words
    MC_Dialog.WordsListBox.Clear

    'We have to check that there is at least one word added to the list box,
    'as we want to highlight the first entry
    BoolAddedWord = False
    'Save the complete comment to a string
    StrData = oActiveDocument.DocumentInfo.Description
    'We need a variable to collect the actual word char by char
    StrWord = ""

    'The words or phrases for the list box are stored all in one string,
    'separated by an asterisk:
    'StrData = "Word1*Word2*Phrase No.1*Word3*"

    'We will cycle through this string char by char.
    'If the actual character is a * add the last word to the list,
    'otherwise add the character to the word we are collecting
    For IntCharNumber = 1 to Len(StrData)
        'We cycle through the String; StrData and StrChar store the actual character
        'Mid(<String>,<Starting point>,<Length>)
        StrChar = Mid(StrData,IntCharNumber,1)
        'If we reach a separator character, the collection of the actual word
        'is finished. Add this word to the list and continue on
        If StrChar = SeparatorChar Then
            'There is no need for empty words in our list.
            If StrWord <> "" Then
                'Add the actual word
                MC_Dialog.WordsListBox.AddItem(StrWord)
                'Keep in mind, that we added at least one word
```

```
              BoolAddedWord = True
              'Prepare for the next word. Therefore delete the old one.
              StrWord = ""
          Endif
      Else
          'We received a character so add it to the actual word
          StrWord = StrWord + StrChar
      Endif
  Next IntCharNumber

  'If there is at least one word added, we highlight the first item
  'in the list box
  If BoolAddedWord Then
      MC_Dialog.WordsListBox.ListIndex = 0
      MC_Dialog.WordsListBox.Selected(0) = true
  Endif
End Sub

Sub MC_AddWord
  'SelectionTextExt() returns the highlighted text or the whole word in
  'which the cursor stands. Add this to the list
  MC_Dialog.WordsListBox.AddItem(oActiveWindow.SelectionTextExt())
  'Call a sub-procedure to store the new word (and the others, too)
  MC_SaveData()
  'Close the dialog, there is nothing more to do
  MC_Dialog.Hide()
End Sub

Sub MC_SaveData
  'Let's store the words in the list box to the comment field of this document
  Dim i As Integer
  Dim StrData As String
  'StrData is a helper variable to store all words separated by "*".
  'Finally we will assign its value to the document comment field
  StrData = ""
  'Cycle through all Items in the list box and join all words to the string
  For i = 0 to MC_Dialog.WordsListBox.ListCount - 1
      'Concatenate the next word to the string followed by an "*"
      StrData = StrData + MC_Dialog.WordsListBox.List(i) &  SeparatorChar
  Next i
  'Save the Wordlist in the document.
  oActiveDocument.DocumentInfo.Description = StrData
End Sub

Sub MC_InsertWord
  'Insert the actual selected item in the list to the current cursor position.
  oActiveWindow.Insert(MC_Dialog.WordsListBox.Text)
  'Close the dialog, the users can continue to work with their text.
  MC_Dialog.Hide()
End Sub
```

PART

VIII

CH

39

Tip #614 from
Werner Roth

If you want to check whether methods that display no visible results are executed, such as `Unload()`, place the runtime function `Beep` directly before or behind them.

Note

You don't need to type the complete source code into your module. You can find the entire application on Werner's Web site at http://www.wernerroth.de/staroffice/.

GIVE ME CONTACT!

What you have now is a StarBasic module full of source code and a dialog module—separated from each other. If you were to activate the test mode for your dialog now, you still wouldn't get a reaction when clicking the Insert or Add button. As Table 39.1 shows (refer to the section "Principal Application Design"), you have to assign the subprocedures MC_AddWord and MC_InsertWord to the OnClick event of the buttons Add and Insert.

To begin, open the dialog module by clicking on the MC_Dialog tab at the bottom of the StarBasic IDE. Make sure the Properties window is still open, and then follow these steps:

1. Click the Insert button to select it.

2. Click in the cell beside Macro in the Properties window. A button with ellipses appears. Click this button to open the Assign Macro dialog, as shown in Figure 39.9.

Figure 39.9
In the Assign Macro dialog box, which you open from within the dialog box's Properties, you can connect your dialog buttons to the StarBasic code you've created.

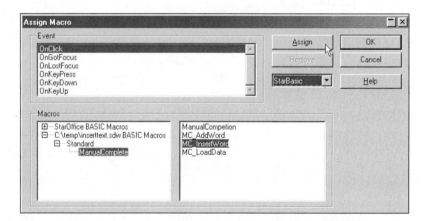

3. Select the event OnClick. By doing so, your code will be activated every time the button is clicked.

4. Open the module ManualComplete located in the Standard library of the document InsertText.sdw.

5. Select the subprocedure MC_InsertWord.

6. Click Assign to connect the clicking of the Insert button to the subprocedure MC_InsertWord. In the Event list box, the entry MC_InsertWord(Standard.ManualComplete) should appear beside the OnClick event to confirm this fact.

7. Click the OK button to close the Assign Macro dialog.

Repeat the same actions for the Add button, but associate the appropriate subprocedure: Select the Add button, and open the Assign Macro dialog by clicking the button beside `Macros` in the Properties window. Leave the event setting as `OnClick`, but open the `ManualComplete` method. Finally, assign the subprocedures `MC_AddWord` to the `OnClick` event.

RUNNING THE APPLICATION

Well, that's it! Your application is ready for its first run. Data is put into the list by the subprocedure `MC_LoadData`, and the buttons Add and Insert are connected to the appropriate subprocedures.

To give it a test drive, first select the module `ManualComplete` in the StarBasic IDE. (The program won't run if you're still in the dialog tab.) Make sure a text document is open, place the cursor into a word of your choice, and click the Run button in the macro bar.

Your dialog should open, containing an empty list box. Click the Add button to add a word as the first list box item. After adding the word, the dialog automatically closes. Place the cursor in another region of text, click the Run button again, and this time test the Insert button. If you want to add a complete phrase, highlight it in the text, run the application, and click the Add button.

After you play around with your StarBasic application, take a look at the properties of your text document. To do so, select File, Properties, and then open the Description tab. In the Comment field, you should it! Yoursee a string like `document*properties*StarBasic Application*`.

<table>
<tr><td>Tip #615 from
Werner Roth</td><td>To make your application easier to use, you can make it possible to insert a word in the list box simply by double-clicking it. To do so, select the list box, open the Assign Macro dialog, and assign the <code>OnDblClick</code> event it! Your to the subprocedure <code>MC_InsertWord</code>.</td></tr>
</table>

WHERE TO GO FROM HERE

StarBasic is a very powerful programming language, and it would take an entire book to cover it in detail. However, if you've worked through Chapters 37 through 39, you'll have a good foundation for your own journey of discovery into the power of StarBasic.

You have yet to discover many other StarBasic objects for spreadsheets. A comprehensive explanation is impossible because programming an entire spreadsheet with a StarBasic macro is so complex. I hope that you at least gained insight into its potential.

StarBasic dialogs also offer many more possibilities. Just take a look at the StarOffice AutoPilots; they are all StarBasic dialogs.

StarBasic can also be used quite successfully with databases. In fact, all the database wizards are programmed in StarBasic.

PART

VIII

CH

39

In general, StarBasic is yet rather scantily documented, so often the best source of information or troubleshooting advice is a more experienced StarOffice programmer or advanced user. If you're really interested in pursuing programming in StarBasic, you can explore newsgroups and Web resources. For example, if you're looking for a specific answer to a StarBasic question, consider posting a question to `stardivision.com.support.starbasic` or the German-based `stardivision.de.support.starbasic`. The following are a few points to remember when posting a message to this (or any other) newsgroup:

- Always send your messages in ASCII only (you might easily forget this advice when you're using StarMail because sending in other formats is so easy).
- Be as specific as possible about your problem or question, including code samples if relevant.
- Be polite.
- Be patient.

In addition, you might want to check out my StarOffice Web site at `http://www.wern-erroth.de/staroffice/`, which contains a lot of handy StarOffice information and macros, as well as complimentary downloads to accompany the StarBasic chapters in this book.

Note

If you find resources in German written by TEAM StarOffice members, you should first try asking a TEAM StarOffice member (newsgroup: `starnews.stardivision.com`) to translate for you before trying an automatic translator such as Babelfish, which often mangles the text.

You also can check out the English-language StarBasic newsgroup, which is part of the StarDivision StarOffice newsgroups, mentioned in the section "Internet Resources" in Chapter 2, "Stepping into StarOffice." That particular newsgroup doesn't have much traffic—yet. However, *you* can be part of the force that changes that situation.

Of course, now that you've made your way through this book, perhaps you're ready to join Team StarOffice, too!

TROUBLESHOOTING

Help! I assigned my macro to an event, but it doesn't run in the document to which I assigned it.

You probably made one of two common mistakes: You didn't have the correct document active at the moment you chose the Tools, Configure command; or you choose Tools, Configure from within the StarBasic IDE and thereby assigned the event to the StarBasic IDE, not your document.

I'm looking for some StarBasic information in the Help system and can't find it.

Although the StarBasic reference is fairly thorough, unfortunately not all the Help files on StarBasic have been translated into English yet. If you have a specific question, search the newsgroups using www.deja.com, or try posting it to a newsgroup. Currently, that's the best resource. If you know some German and have a fast Internet connection, you could also try to download the 1,800+ page StarBasic manual available for version 4.0. Some changes have been made, but it's still useful as a reference. Check the section "Finding Help in StarSpace" at the end of Chapter 2 for complete details.

I tried one of the programs in this book, and it's not running properly.

Now you're really becoming a programmer! All the code in this book was tested multiple times before inclusion and worked as described. However, many things may happen between the moment the fresh code was minted and the time you run a program on your computer. Some of the common, easy-to-overlook problems include making typos in the code, including extra spaces, and failing to include correct punctuation marks and other separators. Beyond that, the program may not have worked for a universe of possible reasons. If you've checked over your code and are sure it's correct, search for help on the Internet. Don't forget to include your source code.

I've created a macro that I've assigned to a keyboard command and also want to assign to an event, but when I look for the macro on the Events tab of the Configure dialog box, it's not there!

Your problem is likely a case of having saved the macro to the wrong library. By default, StarOffice selects the soffice library, Standard module, in which to store your recorded macros. If you don't actively select a different library, your macro is located there. If you then go to the Events tab planning to assign your macro to a specific document—as with some of the examples in this chapter—you won't find your macro there because it hasn't been saved to your document. You need to be sure to save the macro to the proper library.

When I'm using the Macro Editor while working on a dialog, I should be seeing a toolbar with all kinds of tools. However, even though this toolbar is activated (View, Toolbars, Main Toolbar), I can't see it.

The organization of toolbars in StarBasic differs somewhat from other modules. If you're looking at the dialog, you have to select the third button from the right to show the control fields.

How can I start a macro from inside a formula in StarClac?

Write a macro function, such as the following:

```
Function foo()
      ...
End Function
and call it up
if(a4="x";foo())
```

Do macro viruses affect StarOffice?

No. No such viruses have been discovered so far, nor have any known security leaks.

Can Microsoft macro viruses such as Melissa infect my StarOffice?

Because StarOffice does not import macros written with Visual Basic for Applications (VBA) from Microsoft documents, you do not face any danger of infecting your system using StarOffice. For further security, be sure to check your settings by selecting Tools, Options, Browser, Scripting.

I got an excellent macro from a friend who created it using StarOffice on his Linux box, but this macro doesn't work on my Windows computer.

If you have the time, take a deeper look at the code. Are the paths or even the path separator hard-coded? Linux, as other UNIX systems, does not use the backslash known from DOS-based systems. It uses the forward slash (/) instead. Also, no drive letters are available.

Whenever I'm working with a dialog I created in StarBasic, I can't access other StarOffice documents.

This limitation is particular to StarBasic dialogs; they are always so-called *modal dialogs*. The only way around this problem is to use forms based on a StarOffice document. Describing this solution, however, is far beyond the scope of this book.

Can I somehow access the serial port using StarBasic?

You should be able to do so on Windows-based systems. Just use the commands for file I/O. Instead of a filename, use com2:, for example, for the second serial port. Access restrictions on UNIX systems don't allow for direct hardware access.

APPENDIXES

INSTALLING STAROFFICE

In this appendix

Requirements and Recommendations

People commonly experience installation problems because they fail to read the documentation provided with the program they want to install. Although this appendix leads you through the StarOffice installation process, software products continually change, so it's inevitable that some of the information in this book will be out of date by the time you read it. You should therefore *always* view or print a copy of the installation documentation provided by the company *before* you begin the installation process.

Look for document files named

- `readme.txt`
- `setup.pdf`

(In earlier versions of StarOffice, `install.pdf` was used instead of `setup.pdf`.)

→ For more information on locating the installation documents, **see** "Finding the Included Installation Documents," **p. 1356**, in this appendix.

Although Star Division recommends that individual users install StarOffice using the standard setup procedure, we suggest that you install the program using the /net option even if you are not working on a network or using the program with multiple users. When the program is installed using a /net installation, the program files are stored separately from your user and data files. This makes backing up your work much easier.

→ For more information on installing StarOffice using the /net option, **see** "Installing StarOffice for Multiple Users or on a Network," **p. 1376**, in this appendix.

Hardware Requirements

The following are minimum hardware requirements for installation of StarOffice:

- Standard PC processor (Intel 'x86 type)
- 32MB of RAM
- CD-ROM drive (to run the installation CD)
- 120 to 140MB of hard drive space (depending on options you might choose during installation)
- 20MB (Windows users) during installation for temporary files (temporary files are automatically deleted after installation is complete)
- 35MB (Linux users) during installation for temporary files (temporary files are automatically deleted after installation is complete)
- 80MB of free disk space on the swap volume (Linux users)

> **Note**
>
> If you abort your installation, temporary files may remain in your /tmp directory. You should check your /tmp directory, and delete any files named sv###.tmp, where # stands for a number (for example, sv001.tmp). Otherwise, you might not have enough room in your /tmp directory to install the program.

> **Note**
>
>
>
> If you abort your installation, temporary files may remain in your windows/temp directory. You should check this directory and delete any files named sv###.tmp, where # stands for a number (for example, sv001.tmp).

If you're installing StarOffice on a network server, these hardware requirements apply only to the server. Each person who uses the program must also install the program individually. Each individual installation requires 2 to 4MB of hard drive space in the target directory.

HARDWARE RECOMMENDATIONS

Because StarOffice is an integrated desktop, by default it stores many files internally in the Office51 directory that you might expect to be stored elsewhere on your system. For example, the program saves deleted files in its own Recycle Bin. Mail, news, and FTP accounts are stored within the config/groups directory and can quickly grow very large. The cache files, kept in the Office51\store directory, also grow quickly.

We therefore recommend that you have a minimum of 20MB of additional storage space in the partition or drive on which you install StarOffice. You might also want to immediately check the path settings for storage when starting the program for the first time and make adjustments as appropriate for your system, redirecting some storage to other directories, partitions, or volumes.

→ For information on changing the path settings, see "Setting Your General Options," **p. 76** (Chapter 3, "Getting Ready for Work").

→ To understand the default path settings, look at the listing of program directories and their contents in Appendix C, "StarOffice Program Directories and Files," **p. 1405**.

APP

A

Although Star Division does not state any specific graphics card or display requirements, StarOffice makes intensive use of toolbars and floating tools windows and is a very graphics-oriented program (containing excellent drawing and image programs). You'll therefore find it most satisfying to run StarOffice with at least a 17-inch monitor set to display at a resolution of 1024×768 and a fast graphics card with at least 4MB of video memory.

SOFTWARE REQUIREMENTS: WINDOWS

To use StarOffice, you should be running Windows 95, Windows 98, or Windows NT.

While StarOffice runs on virtually every kind of operating system available today, it has been optimized for running on Windows-based systems. Certain features, like Font Work and the StarBase relational database format, are available only on the Windows platform.

Software Requirements: Linux

To use StarOffice, your Linux installation should have the following characteristics:

- Linux kernel 2.0.x or higher
- X Server with a minimum of 256 grayscales or colors
- X Window System installed with a window manager
- Libc version of Libc.so.6.x (glibc 2) or higher
- Java Runtime Environment (JRE) 1.17 or Java Development Kit (JDK) 1.1.7

Tip #616 from
Michael & Sarah

StarOffice offers menu integration with KDE and CDE window managers. KDE menu integration files are installed by default in the standard installation. If you're running KDE, they are also automatically integrated. CDE integration files can be selected with a custom installation.

A critical factor in successfully installing StarOffice on Linux is having the right glibc2 files installed. StarOffice 5.1 requires glibc 2.07; it also runs under the new glibc 2.1 libraries. The glibc 2.07 files are included on the program CD in the /linux/misc/glibc2 directory. If you are currently using libraries other than 2.07 or 2.1, , you first need to install the included files in a separate directory where only StarOffice can access them. Most Linux users encounter problems at this point on initial installation and setup, so be sure to read the section "Installing the Required libc Files" later in this appendix, which addresses installing these lib files in detail.

Caution

Don't load the included 2.07 libraries at all if you're running the 2.1 libraries. Even if you install them in a separate directory, your system will be unable to run with both 2.07 and 2.1 loaded.

Finding the Included Installation Documents

You should read the following three documents before you install StarOffice as a single user:

- The *readme file* (named readme), a text file created at the time the program was produced, contains last-minute updates on the product and important information on installation.

  You can find the readme file in the root directory of the product that you're installing on the StarOffice CD, or (if you're installing a copy you downloaded from the Internet) in the so51inst or so510 directory. Because it is a simple text file, you can open it in any word processor.

Note The readme file contains important information about the glibc2 files StarOffice requires to run. A separate readme file located in the `/linux/misc/glibc2` directory gives more details on installing the glibc2 files.

- The *installation manual* gives step-by-step instructions on installing the program. Some versions of the product include a printed copy of an installation guide. If not, you can find a complete installation guide for each operating system included on the StarOffice CD-ROM from Star Division. These guides are in `.pdf` format, which requires you to have the Adobe Acrobat Reader installed, or to use a viewing program like ghostview or xpdf (Linux).

  If you do not already have Adobe Acrobat or a suitable viewer on your computer, a copy of Adobe Acrobat has been included in the folder called `Reader`. You need to install this program before you can read the `.pdf` installation manual.

Note To install the Adobe Acrobat Reader for Windows, open the Acrobat folder in My Computer or in the Windows Explorer, and double-click the `.exe` file.

Note Acrobat is archived in a `.tar` file. Type `tar -xz` *filename* (where *filename* is the complete filename of the Acrobat tar file) and press Enter to decompress the program files. Then run the Acrobat setup program by typing `./setup` and pressing Enter.

After you have Adobe Acrobat installed, open the file `setup.pdf` (in the folder or directory named `Documentation`). Both manuals are fairly long and include pictures of the installation screens that you don't really need to print. However, you should at least read through the entire document online.

- The file `migration.pdf` explains how to migrate data from an existing StarOffice 5.0 installation to the new StarOffice 5.1 installation. It details each StarOffice directory that might contain files you want to copy into the new version and gives tips on migration. For a list of key points for a successful migration, see "Migrating from StarOffice 5.0," immediately following this section.

- If you're installing StarOffice on a network server, you should read a fourth document, `schedule.pdf`, which explains how to install the new StarSchedule Server application. This application is an optional component that enables you to run StarSchedule independently of the rest of StarOffice's modules.

APP

A

MIGRATING FROM STAROFFICE 5.0

Star Division has included a detailed and useful guide to migrating your StarOffice 5.0 data to StarOffice 5.1; it's called `migration.pdf`. A few key points on migrating are listed here; for more information, refer to the Star Division documentation.

Star Division Corporation's recommended method for migrating is to first install 5.1 in a new directory and then copy the data you want to continue to use from the 5.0 directory:

- You cannot reuse configuration files from 5.0. We don't recommend installing your new version into the same directory as an existing version; one of the authors of this book tested that scenario and experienced problems that required reinstalling the program.

- To transfer mail and news, first export your mail and news files from the Explorer by using the Export command; then import them by using the Import command into new accounts you have created in 5.1.

- If you are moving database files, be sure you copy the entire set of database files that comprise your database, as listed in Table A.1. Remember that the Address Book is a database file.

TABLE A.1   IDENTIFYING STARBASE DATABASE FILES

Database Files with This Extension	Contain This
.dbf and .dbt	Data files
.sdb	StarBase queries, forms, and reports
.rb1, .rb2, and so on	Database definition files

CHOOSING YOUR TYPE OF INSTALLATION

Although Star Division recommends the Standard installation, you should choose the Custom installation if you want to install some of the optional components, or languages other than U.S. English, British English (called UK English), and/or German.(Yes, of course, German is one of the default languages.) You should also choose the Custom installation if you want to deselect any of the default installation options.

Your other language choices are the following:

- French
- Spanish
- Italian
- Dutch
- Portuguese
- Swedish

You can install only three languages at a time.

You also must choose the Custom installation if you want to install any or all of the following options:

- StarCalc date function and other function add-ins
- Sample C++ program code for use with StarCalc
- Additional graphics import and export filters
- Palm synchronization
- PGP integration, if you don't already have PGP installed on your system and want to force the install (Windows only)
- WordPerfect, Interleaf, FrameMaker, Microsoft Works, Ami Pro, and Claris Works text import filters (plus a wide range of other text import filters) (Windows only)
- Phone dialer (Windows only)

If you don't want all the filters, fonts, sample documents, or help modules installed, or don't want StarOffice to integrate with Microsoft Internet Explorer 5, you must also choose the Custom installation and deselect these components.

Caution

Do not deselect any of the main program modules, even if you don't think you will use a particular application. StarOffice is an integrated program and does not run properly without all of them. If you want to save space, you can deselect the program module help, sample document, and/or template files.

The basic differences between the three installations are shown in Table A.2.

TABLE A.2 BASIC STAROFFICE INSTALLATION OPTIONS

Type of Installation	Approximate Storage Space Required	Description
Standard	Approximately 150MB installed, 170MB during installation	Installs all the StarOffice modules along with templates, samples, fonts, and a selection of filters
Custom	Between 80 and 185MB installed, and 83 to 200MB during installation, depending on your selections	Enables you to pick and choose what components to install and choose language dictionaries
Minimum	Approximately 93MB installed, 96MB during installation	Installs only the minimum files required to run StarOffice; does not include samples, templates, or fonts

APP

A

CONTENTS OF THE CD

Table A.3 lists the contents of the StarOffice 5.1 program CD, along with installation tips for the add-ons and miscellaneous components.

TABLE A.3 CONTENTS OF THE STAROFFICE 5.1 PROGRAM CD

This Directory...	Contains These Files	Description and Tips
\windows\office51 or /linux/office51	StarOffice 5.1 setup program installation files	Run the setup program in this directory to begin the installation process.
\windows\schedule or /linux/schedule	StarSchedule Server setup program and installation files	New to 5.1. Run the setup program to install the StarSchedule Server. For network installation only.
/linux/misc/glibc2	Documentation and installation files for installing the libraries needed to run StarOffice on Linux	Read the readme file *before* installing StarOffice. You must have the correct libraries installed to install StarOffice successfully. soprep is a script file that helps install the necessary libraries if you don't already have them installed.
\windows\misc\ dragon	Microsoft Speech API for Dragon NaturallySpeaking 3	This is an optional component that you install separately. It enables you to use StarOffice with NaturallySpeaking. You must already have the Dragon NaturallySpeaking program.
\windows\ documentation or /linux/ documentation	Installation reference materials in .pdf file format and a copy of the Acrobat Reader program	Contains essential setup information prepared by StarDivision. The Acrobat Reader program enables you to read .pdf files in the Acrobat subdirectory.

This Directory...	Contains These Files	Description and Tips
\addon\clipart	2000 clip art files	Install StarOffice first. Then click the Gallery icon in the Explorer, and choose the Import command. Next, navigate to this directory, and select the clip art you want to install. This directory is not available in the Internet download edition.
\addon\fonts_tt	200 TrueType fonts	TrueType is a Microsoft standard font type. If you're working on Linux, you can make these fonts work, but doing so requires extra configuration steps. See the readme file in this directory and tips in "Installing Fonts" in this appendix. This directory is not available in the Internet download edition.
\addon\fonts_ps	200 PostScript fonts	You can print with these fonts only if you have a PostScript printer. This directory is not available in the Internet download edition.

USING VOICE RECOGNITION WITH STAROFFICE

If you want to use voice recognition software, IBM's ViaVoice program has versions for both Linux and Windows and should run with StarOffice without significant problems. The Microsoft application programming interface (API) required to interface between ViaVoice and other programs is built into ViaVoice, so you don't need to install any additional components.

You also can use Dragon NaturallySpeaking with StarOffice on Windows if you install the API found in \windows\misc\dragon. To install it, just navigate to that directory, and double-click the setup program. An installation wizard guides you through the process.

Note

You might experience a time lag in the execution of some program commands when you use voice recognition software.

APP

A

FINDING ADDITIONAL INSTALLATION HELP

In this appendix, we have tried to cover the most common questions and problems about installing StarOffice, but you may well have questions or problems that are not answered here.

If you have downloaded StarOffice for free, you are not entitled to direct company support. Your only source of help is the Star Division online newsgroups and Web sites. You can, however, purchase a service contract from Star Division; see the company Web site (www.stardivision.com) for details.

If you have purchased the Personal Deluxe edition, the Professional edition, a site license, and/or have a service contract with Star Division, you can contact the company directly for support at the numbers listed in your readme file. You might still find it helpful to check out the newsgroups because many common questions are answered there.

KNOWLEDGE DATABASE ON THE WEB

Just recently, Star Division made a StarOffice knowledge database called the Support Information System available on the Web (www/stardivision.com/support). It provides answers to all known technical problems with StarOffice 5.1 and some for version 5.0 as well. It's not as useful as it could be, but it's a start.

STAR DIVISION NEWSGROUP SUPPORT

The Star Division installation newsgroups are two of many newsgroups run from the Star Division news server at starnews.stardivision.com.

The newsgroups that address installation issues are stardivision.com.support. installation and stardivision.international.support.installation. Most traffic takes place in the stardivison.com news group.

You might also check stardivision.com.support.announce; sometimes information about installation issues is posted there.

Old postings from all the newsgroups are archived on the DejaNews Web site (www.dejanews.com).

DOWNLOADING STAROFFICE FROM THE INTERNET

You can download a free copy of StarOffice for personal use from the company's Web site at www.stardivision.com. You first must register at the site. After completing the registration form, you jump to a page that lists links to HTTP and FTP download sites. Click the link to download from your site of choice. Note that FTP transfer is generally faster and more reliable.

The download copy is a full-featured version of the program, although it lacks a complete set of fonts, samples, templates, and filters for importing and exporting. (It contains the basic set of Microsoft Office filters; however, it does not contain WordPerfect text filters.)

Note

> If you want these additional add-ons, you can purchase the Personal Deluxe edition, available on CD-ROM from a variety of sites or direct from the company online store. If you purchase the CD, you also get a slim printed Installation Manual, a User's Guide, and 30 days of free installation support.

If you have a standard telephone modem and connection, the download takes several hours because the file is very large. You might want to download overnight. The Linux version, so51_lnx_01.tar, is 69MB; the Windows version, so51_win_49.exe, is 67MB.

Tip #617 from
Michael & Sarah

> You can reduce your download costs to a minimum if you use an FTP client that supports resuming. You can then fetch the zip file or tarball in a series of tiny slices when you are online browsing.

Because traffic on the Internet is just like traffic on a highway—a lot of different data going a lot of different places on the same roads, all at once—problems can occur. Your download could be interrupted. If you have an FTP program that enables you to restart an interrupted download from the place where it left off, you might still be able to download an uncorrupted copy. If you do not and your download is interrupted, sad to say, your best bet is to dump what you have and begin again. It's likely your file is corrupted and will not install and/or run properly.

The steps for downloading from the Web are simple:

1. Open your browser program.

2. Type http://www.stardivision.com into the URL field of your browser, and press Enter.

3. Follow the links for the free 5.1 download. Be sure to select the correct operating system.

4. You are asked to read a page with the License agreement and signify your acceptance of its terms by clicking the I Accept hyperlink. If you do not accept, click the other hyperlink, which exits you from the download sequence.

5. When you are presented with a registration page, choose the language version you want. You must also fill out the user data fields indicated in bold, which include your full name, street address, and email address, to download the program. If you have used previous versions of StarOffice and have a customer number, insert it into the Customer Number field. If you're a new user, don't worry about this field; just leave it blank.

   Be careful to enter this information accurately and without typos. You need to enter the same information again when you install the program. This information is used in configuring your StarOffice Internet accounts, in program templates, and in a number of other ways, so it's to your advantage to fill it out accurately.

6. After you have finished entering all the necessary data, click the hyperlink at the bottom of the page to continue the registration process.

APP

A

7. You then see a page like the one shown in Figure A.1. This page lists all the information you entered, along with your customer number and registration key. (The page shown is actually the page produced after online registration of a version installed from a CD.) You should print this page because you will need the customer number and registration key to install your program and complete your registration after you first launch it. (Star Division will also email you a copy of this information, but it's a good idea to print a copy now, just in case you don't receive the email.) After you print the page, click the button at the bottom of the page to proceed.

Figure A.1
When you register at the Star Division Web site, a Web page is produced with your customer number and registration key, numbers you'll need later to enable the installation program.

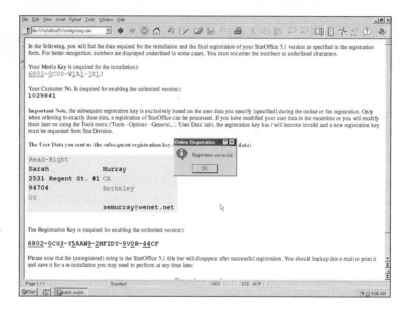

8. When you are presented with a list of FTP and HTTP download sites, click a hyperlink to go to your selected site, and follow the instructions for downloading.

Tip #618 from
Michael & Sarah

Downloading from an HTTP site is usually slower and more unreliable than downloading from an FTP site. If you're downloading over a regular telephone line, you're more likely to have a successful download from an FTP site.

Note

To install the download version, you must already have JRE or JDK installed on your system. The StarOffice setup program looks for a Java installation as given by your JAVA_HOME variable. You can download the appropriate Java installation from `http://www.blackdown.org/java_linux.html`.

For more information, see "Understanding StarOffice 5.1 and Java–Linux," later in this Appendix.

UNPACKING STAROFFICE AND RUNNING THE SETUP PROGRAM

Your downloaded file is a self-extracting zip file (Windows) or a tar archive file (Linux) that you must first unzip or expand (respectively) before you can run the setup program. If you've downloaded an English version, your filename should be so51_win_01.exe for the Windows version and so51_lnx_01.tar for the Linux version. (The 01 is country code for the American version.)

UNZIPPING YOUR FILE: WINDOWS

Your Windows download version of StarOffice is a self-extracting zip file. To unzip it, navigate to the directory where you downloaded it. Then double-click the icon next to the filename (so51_win_01.exe). You will be asked in which directory the unzipped files should be placed. Once you have selected the directory, click Unzip. The program then automatically unpacks itself and places the unzipped files in a folder called Office51.

EXPANDING THE ARCHIVE FILE: LINUX

To expand your file in Linux, navigate to the directory where you downloaded the StarOffice archive file. Then enter the following command:

```
tar xvf so51_lnx_01.tar
```

Your files are unpacked into a directory named so51inst. You should print and read the readme file you find here. This file contains essential information regarding the installation and configuration of glibc2 libraries. You need to have the correct libraries installed before you install StarOffice.

STARTING THE SETUP PROGRAM: WINDOWS

To start the setup program in Windows, navigate to the Office51 directory. Find the file called Setup, and double-click.

STARTING THE SETUP PROGRAM: LINUX

To start the setup program in Linux, you must first navigate to the so51inst directory. Then type ./setup and press Enter. The setup script will not work if you execute it from a different directory.

BEGINNING THE INSTALLATION PROCESS

At this point, you are greeted by the opening screen of the Setup Installation Wizard. The installation process is now essentially the same as installing StarOffice from a CD—with one exception. Users installing from a CD must enter a media key to install the program, whereas users installing a downloaded version are prompted to enter the customer number and registration key you were assigned after completing registration at the StarDivision Web site.

> **Note**
>
> A media key from an earlier version won't work.

If you are a single user, see the next section, "Installing StarOffice for a Single User," for steps to install the program. If you are installing StarOffice for multiple users or on a network, see the section "Installing StarOffice for Multiple Users or on a Network," later in this appendix. Note, however, that we highly recommend even single users install the program using the /net option for multiple and network users.

INSTALLING STAROFFICE FOR A SINGLE USER

You can choose from two ways to install StarOffice as a single user: You can download a zip file from one of the Star Division FTP or Web sites and unzip it, or you can install it from a CD.

You can purchase CD-ROM versions from the Star Division online Web store as well as a number of computer software resellers in the U.S. In addition, some commercial Linux packages bundle StarOffice on a CD.

> **Note**
>
> If you have version 5.0 on a CD that was bundled with another program, you need to upgrade to version 5.1 before you can install the program. Star Division is no longer issuing registration keys for this version, and you can't install the program without them.

A single user is considered someone running the program on a single machine. Multiple users can run the program on the same machine if they install with the network option.

If you are using StarOffice on more than one machine or for commercial purposes, you should be operating under a license from Star Division. If you pay the license fee, you'll receive the Professional version of the program on CD-ROM, which has additional filters and add-ons, a printed manual, and rights to additional phone and fax support.

> **Note**
>
> If you are installing StarOffice over an existing installation of the same version number, be sure to first delete the sversion (Linux) or `soffice.ini` (Windows) file. Otherwise, the installation will not work properly.

Tip #619 from
Michael & Sarah

StarOffice saves your user files over several directories. This is not only troublesome when you're upgrading, but also when you're backing up your data. To make your life easier, you can use the /net option for installing the program even on single user systems. Your files are then installed and maintained separately from the program's files.

INFORMATION REQUIRED TO INSTALL STAROFFICE FROM A CD

Although StarOffice is available for free download from the Internet, the surest and easiest way of installing is from a program CD because you know that all program components are present and the files have not been corrupted. You also get additional filters, clip art, templates, and sample files.

To install StarOffice from a CD-ROM, you must enter a media key, which is an alphanumeric number. This key should have been included on a sticker placed in your manual or CD-ROM jewel case; it may also be located on your invoice. Locate this number before you sit down to install the program. If you can't find your media key, you need to contact Star Division Customer Service to obtain one.

Note
You cannot obtain a media key through the www.stardivision.com Web site.

GENERAL INFORMATION REQUIRED TO INSTALL STAROFFICE

When you're installing StarOffice, you must enter certain personal data, including your phone number(s), address, and email address. Some portions of the Internet setup are now automated, so you are also prompted to enter information about your Internet accounts. Be prepared with the following information:

- Your current home address
- Your current home and work phone numbers
- Your fax number (if any)
- Your incoming mail server's name
- Your outgoing mail server's name
- Your news server's name
- Your logon name
- Your email address
- Your password (optional)

APP

A

Note
If you are installing an Internet download version, you should have your registration information handy. You need to enter the exact user data you used to register on the Star Division Web site.

Tip #620 from
Michael & Sarah
The simplest way to enter your registered user data is to save your email registration confirmation as a file, open the file when you need to enter your data, and cut and paste the data. You can then be sure you've entered it exactly as you did when registering online. Be

continues

continued

> sure to close your word processing application after entering your user data before proceeding to the next installation window, as you shouldn't have other programs running when StarOffice copies the program files to the hard drive.

INITIATING INSTALLATION: WINDOWS

Note

> If you have a previously installed version of StarOffice, and this version will replace it, first install the new version in a new directory. Then copy all the folders and files you want to reuse from your old version to your new version. Finally, run the setup.exe program of your old version, and uninstall it. For detailed information on migrating, see the program documentation MIGRATION.PDF.

To install StarOffice in Windows, follow these steps:

1. Place the CD in your CD-ROM drive.

2. Select Run from the Start menu.

3. Type X:\cdrom\windows\setup.exe, where X is the correct drive letter for your CD-ROM, and press Enter.

INITIATING INSTALLATION: LINUX

When you're ready to install StarOffice in Linux, begin by making sure the directory in which you want to install StarOffice has the required disk space and that you have write privileges (w) to that drive or partition. Also, make sure that your tmp directory has the required 35MB of space.

Note

> If you have previously installed another version of StarOffice as a single user and this version will replace it, first install the new version in a new directory. Then copy all the folders and files you want to reuse from your old version to your new version. Finally, run the setup.exe program of your old version, and uninstall it. (If you have previously installed StarOffice using the /net option—which is the recommended method of installation on Linux systems—you do not need to follow this procedure.)

CHECKING LIBRARIES

You can find information about the needed Linux libraries in the readme.txt files found in linux/office 51 and /linux/misc/glibc2.

StarOffice 5 uses the new glibc2 (= libc6), version 2.0.7, and Linux-Kernel-Threads. It also runs with the new 2.1 libraries; you should not install the 2.0.7 libraries if you are running the 2.1 libraries.

By entering the following commands, you can check to see whether your version of Linux makes the named lib files available:

```
ls -l /lib/ld-linux.so.2
ls -l /lib/libc-2.*.so
```

Your output should look something like this:

```
lrwxrwxrwx   1 root     root    11 Apr  9 17:01 /lib/ld-linux.so.2 -> ld-2.0.7.so
```

If your currently installed libraries are not versions 2.0.7 or 2.1, you need to install the required libc files. You can find them in the /misc/glibc2 directory on the StarOffice CD.

Caution

Replacing existing libraries on your system is not a good idea if the system is running stably. Instead, you can create a separate directory in which to install these libc files so that only StarOffice can access them. Do this only if you are running libraries previous to version 2.0.7. If you install the 2.0.7 libraries anywhere on a system running 2.1, your system will be unable to run.

INSTALLING THE REQUIRED libc FILES

To install the libc files, log in as root or superuser, and complete the following steps. (The /usr/home directory is a common choice for storing application programs, but you can substitute other directory locations.)

1. Create a directory for the StarOffice program files:
   ```
   mkdir /usr/home/Office51
   ```

2. Create a subdirectory to hold the libc files:
   ```
   cd /usr/home/Office51
   mkdir /lib
   ```

3. Copy the libc file on the CD to the directory you have just created:
   ```
   cp /libc.so.5.4.33 /usr/home/Office51/lib
   ```

4. If you have other versions of the version 5 library files installed on your system, you can create a symbolic link to version 5 in the directory:
   ```
   ln -s /usr/home/Office51/lib/libc.so.5.4.33 /usr/lib/libc.so.5
   ```

5. To run these libraries during setup and when running the program, you need to set the LD_LIBRARY_PATH variable to refer to the library subdirectory you've just created:
   ```
   export LD_LIBRARY_PATH=/usr/home/Office51/lib
   ```

You need to enter this command every time you launch StarOffice, whether you start it manually or via a startup script that simultaneously sets the library path and starts StarOffice. It's a good idea to add this line to the Office51/bin/soffice script that you use to start StarOffice.

APP

A

Tip #621 from
Michael & Sarah

Your startup script might look something like this:

```
!/bin/sh
export LD_LIBRARY_PATH=$export
LD_LIBRARY_PATH=":/usr/home/Office51/lib"
/usr/home/Office51/bin/soffice
```

Be sure to save this script in a file. You can enter the command

```
Chmod a+x nameofscriptfile
```

to make the script executable. Then you can always launch StarOffice with this script.

STARTING THE SETUP SCRIPT

Once you have the correct libraries installed, you can proceed with setup.

Note

To install the download version, you must already have JRE or JDK installed on your system. The StarOffice setup program looks for a Java installation as given by your JAVA_HOME variable. You can download the appropriate Java installation from http://www.blackdown.org/java_linux.html. For more information, see "Understanding StarOffice 5.1 and Java–Linux," later in this Appendix, and your StarOffice Setup guide.

To start your setup script, follow these steps:

1. Log on with your username.

2. Start the X Window system.

3. Open an xterm window from your window manager menu.

4. Mount your CD-ROM drive.

5. Nagivate to your CD-ROM mount directory and into the Linux directory. For example, type

   ```
   cd /mnt/cdrom/prod_linux
   ```

   Then press Enter.

7. Type `./setup` and press Enter to begin the installation script.

NAVIGATING THE INSTALLATION WIZARD

The Installation Wizard makes the StarOffice installation process easy. Using it is covered thoroughly in the installation documentation. The process is therefore reviewed only briefly in this section.

Throughout the setup, you can click the Back button to retrace your steps, one screen at a time, or you can click Cancel to cancel the setup process and return to your desktop or program prompt. If you cancel, installation is not completed, so you'll need to run Setup again to install the program.

The Installation Wizard steps are as follows:

1. You are greeted with a Welcome screen that recommends you close all other running programs before proceeding (see Figure A.2). When you have done so and are ready to proceed, click Next.

Figure A.2
If you have any other running programs, you should click Cancel on the Welcome screen, close out of those programs, and begin Setup again.

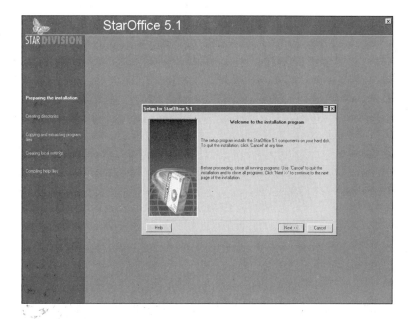

2. You are prompted to enter your program registration information (see Figure A.3). If you're installing from a CD, choose the Media Key option. The media key was included with your CD-ROM. Look for it on a sticker on your CD jewel case, inside the front cover of one of the manuals, or on your invoice. Be sure to place your cursor in the field before typing; StarOffice does not automatically move your cursor there. After you enter your key, click Next.

   If you are installing StarOffice from an Internet download, select the Registration Key option, and enter your customer and registration numbers in this screen. If you are installing a campus or business license version, select the Company/Campus Key option, and enter the key you received from your company or school representative.

3. The Enter User Data dialog box prompts you to enter personal data (see Figure A.4). You can use the Tab key to move between text entry fields. After you've entered all your data, click Next.

   Your user data is used in three ways:

   - Registering you as a StarOffice user
   - Automating your StarOffice setup (particularly with online settings)
   - Automating personal data entry into prebuilt program templates via the Sender database field

APP

A

Figure A.3
To initiate the installation program, you must first enter your media key or registration number.

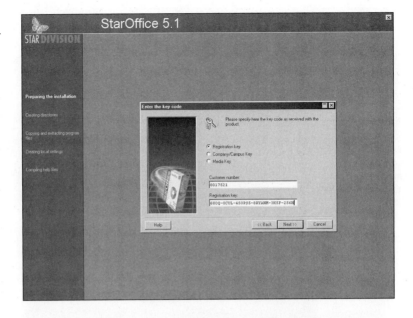

Figure A.4
Some of the information requested in the Enter User Data dialog box is required for program registration.

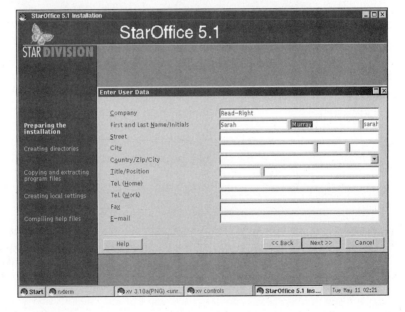

Note

You must enter at least your first and last name, street address, and email address to install the program successfully. If you are installing an Internet download version, be sure to enter the same data you entered when registering for the download. Otherwise, the setup program won't continue.

Tip #622 from
Michael & Sarah

If you don't have some of the information required or don't want to enter it, just enter **none** or some other word in the field's text box.

You can change this data from within the program later via the Tools, Options, General, User Data dialog box. If you change any portion of the critical data after registering the program, you need to re-register within 30 days. (If you are installing StarOffice from a CD, you can change it freely before registering without problem.)

4. When the readme file is displayed, use the scrollbars to read any hidden text. (If you've already printed and/or read the readme file, you can skip reading this file.) When you're done, click Next to proceed.

5. Read the License agreement carefully before clicking Next to proceed because it explains your terms of use for StarOffice. Note that StarOffice is neither freeware nor shareware. Registering the program as described later in this appendix is a condition of unrestricted use of the program.

6. Choose the type of installation you want. You have a choice of Standard, Custom, or Minimum installations. The Minimum installation is intended primarily for laptop computers, where space is at a premium. Note that you must run a custom installation to install certain add-ons (including CDE menu integration on Linux) or to select languages other than U.S. English, UK English, and German (which are the defaults). After you choose, click Next.

→ For a complete list of features that can be installed only with a custom installation, **see** "Choosing Your Type of Installation," **p. 1358**, in this appendix.

7. Select the directory into which you want to install StarOffice. The Windows default is /Office51; if you have logged on as root, the Linux default is /root/Office51. To change the installation directory, type in a new path; alternatively, you can click the Browse button, navigate to the directory, and select its name.

If you select a Standard or Minimum installation, click Next to begin copying program files to your hard drive. Then skip to the section "Installing the Java Runtime Environment (JRE)."

Note

If you are running a system with 2.1 libraries files, StarOffice setup generates an error message informing you that you don't have the libraries files needed to run StarOffice. Ignore this message and proceed with the installation. (The message is generated because Star Division has not yet updated the installation script to check for the 2.1 libraries; it checks only for the 2.0.7 libraries.)

If you choose a Custom installation, read on in the next section.

APP

A

SELECTING COMPONENTS IN A CUSTOM INSTALLATION

After you select Custom Installation and click Next, you see a window like the one shown in Figure A.5 that lists all available StarOffice components.

Figure A.5
If you select the Custom Installation option, you can select or deselect program components.

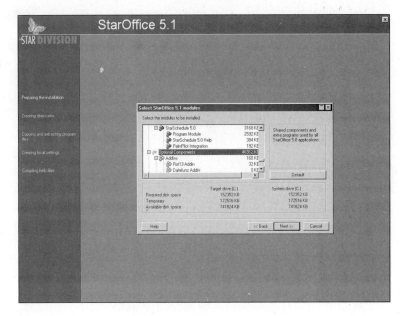

Components are listed in typical branching hierarchical view. Some contain subcomponents that you can reveal by clicking the plus sign (+) to the left of the component's name:

- A selected component is indicated by fully colored-in cubes to the left of its name. If it has subcomponents, these cubes indicate that all possible subcomponents are selected.
- A component in which only some of its subcomponents are selected is indicated by transparently colored cubes.
- A component that is not selected is indicated by white cubes with black outlines.

You can click a component's cube to select or deselect it. You can double-click a component name to simultaneously reveal any subcomponents and select or deselect the component and all its subcomponents.

Note

Some of the custom options are available only in Windows. They include extra text import and export filters, PGP integration, and a built-in phone dialer.

Caution

Do not deselect any of the main program modules, even if you don't think you will use a particular application. StarOffice is an integrated program and does not run properly without all of them. If you want to save space, you can deselect the program module help, sample document, and/or template files.

After you select all the components you want to install, click Complete. Program files are then copied to your hard drive; the dialog displays the progress of the installation.

INSTALLING THE JAVA RUNTIME ENVIRONMENT (JRE)

After the StarOffice program files have been copied to your hard drive, you see a dialog that lists any registered versions of the Java Runtime Environment (JRE) on your system.

Note

If you are installing a download version of StarOffice for Linux, you must already have JRE or JDK installed on your system to run the StarOffice setup program.

You can do the following:

- Choose an existing version.
- Choose to install the version provided with the StarOffice installation.
- Choose to work without Java or JavaScript support.

You need to use a JRE of version 1.1.6 or higher.

Note

The Java Runtime Environment (JRE) is a program that enables StarOffice to process JavaScript, a programming language, and Java applets. You cannot access certain Web pages (for example, some pages on Star Division's own www.stardivision.com) or certain features of some Web sites without the JRE. On Linux, where StarOffice makes use of Java native threads, StarOffice must have the JRE or JDK to run properly. On Windows, certain StarOffice features do not work without the JRE or JDK.

APP

A

Make your selection, and click OK. After StarOffice finishes this step, the installation is complete. Click Complete in the final dialog that appears to close the setup program.

Tip #623 from
Michael &
Sarah

You can add $HOME/Office51/bin/soffice to the program's path. If you do so, you can start StarOffice from any directory by using the soffice command.

Note

If you have installed KDE or CDE integration, log out and log in again to update the integration.

POST-INSTALLATION CONFIGURATION: LINUX

A number of post-installation configuration issues might arise for Linux users. Check out the following sections for more details.

ADDRESSING FONT ERROR MESSAGES

An error message like

```
SalFontStruct::Load !XLoadQueryFont()
```

means that a font that should exist on the X Server could not be loaded. Your system might have a memory problem, but it is more probable that the font has not been installed or has been uninstalled. You can verify this fact by using the commands xlsfonts, xfontsel, and xfd.

Any other error messages may be caused by a lack of X Server memory. If you experience such errors together with other errors in StarOffice, even after rebooting the system, you should contact Star Division Support.

INSTALLING STAROFFICE STARTUP ICONS

StarOffice for Linux comes with two XPM format icon files, L_soffice.xpm and S_soffice.xpm, which you can install on your user interface. You can then start StarOffice by activating the icon you install icon instead of typing a command at a shell prompt. Check your window manager documentation for instructions on installing icons.

INSTALLING STAROFFICE FOR MULTIPLE USERS OR ON A NETWORK

You should use the network option if you are installing StarOffice on a single Linux or Windows NT machine that will have multiple users or on a network server. We also highly recommend you use this option as a single user because you can then keep the StarOffice program files separate from your user files, making upgrading and creating backups much easier.

Installation for network users is a two-step process. First, you log on as the root or system administrator and install using the /net option. Then each individual user runs the setup program from the program directory to do an individual user installation of configuration files. The user installation requires 2 to 4MB of hard drive space.

The standard method of installation is to install the program files on the network, run StarOffice from the network server, and install the user files on the hard drives of the local machines.

If you are running an older network (10 MBit), this might not be your best option. The traffic generated by loading StarOffice from a server causes significant performance problems. Each time a user loads a document, several libraries have to be loaded from the server.

This not only slows you down working with StarOffice (since your hard disk is probably about 5 to 10 times faster than the slow network connection!), but hinders any other work on the network as well. You can reduce this problem by copying the server installation to the local hard disk (or just install StarOffice on the local machines in the first place). Of course, this results in additional installation and maintenance work. Your performance gains may well be worth it, however.

On the other hand, installing the user files on the client workstation creates inefficiencies in network administration and use. Backing up data is much more difficult when users save data on their local computers. Also, if a user gets a new machine, all the data must be copied from the old computer to the new one. You therefore might want to install the user files on the server, not on the user's local hard drive. If the user files are stored on the network, users can also easily access their personal StarOffice configurations and data files by just logging on to the network.

You can think of this variation on the standard method as the "upside down server/user installation."

Once you are logged on, you can run the setup script with the /net option as follows:

- If you're a Windows NT user, enter the following at a DOS prompt or Run command window, where d: is the CD-ROM's drive letter:

  `d:\windows\setup /net`

- If you're a Linux user, from an xterm window within the /mnt/cdrom/prod_lnx/: (or equivalent installation) directory, enter the following:

  `./setup /net`

The setup proceeds largely as described previously for the single user installation from a CD. You don't enter any user data, however; individual workstation users enter this information as they run the setup program for the individual user installation.

→ For details on steps in the installation process, **see** "Installing StarOffice for a Single User," **p. 1366**, in this appendix.

If you are installing the program files on a network drive, you should choose a Custom installation and install all available components so that individual users have access to all StarOffice components.

INDIVIDUAL INSTALLATION FROM A SERVER

Each network user is required to step through a brief installation process. This process creates personalized configuration files that can be accessed from any computer on the network with the user's logon name (if the files are stored on the network).

Note

If a new user tries to launch StarOffice , the setup program is automatically launched.

APP

A

During this process, each user is required to enter the following:

- User data
- A media key or other registration number, as provided by StarDivision

Each user must have a unique key, which means you must be sure you have as many licenses and keys as you will have users. When you are ready to start this process as a new user, follow these steps:

1. Log on to the system with your username.

Note

Switch to or initiate the X Window interface if you are not already in it.

2. Switch to the installation directory on the server.
3. Type ./setup and press Enter to start the setup process.

At this point, the installation process is similar to installing StarOffice for a single user, except that instead of a choice between Standard, Custom, and Minimum Installation, you choose between a Standard Workstation Installation or a Standard Installation (Local), as you can see in Figure A.6.

Figure A.6
When you're installing from a network, you can choose to run StarOffice off the network, which uses minimal space on your client machine, or to install a complete copy of StarOffice. On older, slower networks, you may be best off installing a complete copy on client machines and store only individual configuration and user files on the network.

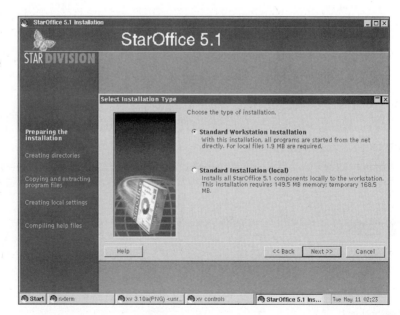

A Standard Workstation Installation creates only local configuration files, and you run StarOffice from the network. A Standard Installation (Local) installs the entire StarOffice program on your local drive.

→ For details on steps in the installation process, **see** "Installing StarOffice for a Single User," **p. 1366**, in this appendix.

UNDERSTANDING STAROFFICE 5.1 AND JAVA (LINUX)

A Java library that supports the required StarOffice native threads for the glib2 is now available. This library also supports the Java Native Interface (JNI).

You can download the Java installation you need from www.blackdown.org/java-linux.html. There, you can download one of three versions of the installation:

- Java Runtime Environment (JRE)
- The minimal Java Runtime Environment
- Java Development Kit (JDK)

Each contains two archived files.

To activate Java, you must first modify the initialization file, soffice, which is stored in the Office51/bin directory (single user installation) or in the corresponding server directory (network installation).

In this file, depending on the installation path of your Java components, you set the environment variable JAVA_HOME with a command like the following:

```
JAVA_HOME=/usr/jrel17_v1a; export JAVA_HOME
```

> **Note**
>
> In the string jrel17, the first character after the e is an l character, and the second is the number one (1).

You must then also change the LD_LIBRARY_PATH as follows:

```
sd_arch='uname -m'  # e.g. 'i5867
LD_LIBRARY_PATH=$JAVA_HOME/lib/$sd_arch/native_threads:$LD_LIBRARY_PATH
export LD_LIBRARY_PATH
```

> **Note**
>
> Use of Java can be turned off and on in the Other dialog box (which you open from the Tools menu's Options master dialog, Browser category). JavaScript can be turned off and on in the Scripting dialog in the same Browser category.

> **Note**
>
> For information on using the JDK with StarOffice, see the setup.pdf file or the Installation Guide (if one was included in your package).

INSTALLING THE STARSCHEDULE SERVER

In StarOffice version 5.1, you now can install an independent application, the StarSchedule Server, that enables you to run StarSchedule on a network even when StarOffice is not running, thus placing fewer demands on your system resources and enabling users to access common calendars at any time.

> **Note**
>
> Single users can run StarSchedule from within StarOffice. You should not install the StarSchedule Server, which is intended for use on a network only.

The StarSchedule Server has its own setup program in the `schedule` directory of the StarOffice 5.1 installation files.

INSTALLATION REQUIREMENTS

To install StarSchedule Server, you need the following:

- 18 to 40MB free hard drive space in the installation directory (depending on your operating system)
- 2MB free hard drive space on the drive of each user with access to the event calendar

STARTING SETUP

To install the Star Schedule, you must login to the system as administrator. Then, navigate to the `schedule` directory on the CD-ROM where the schedule server installation files are located. (The StarSchedule server is not included with the Internet download version of the program.)

Run the setup program in this directory.

You are greeted by a Welcome dialog. You can access installation help by clicking the Help button here; if you access Help, click the Back button when you are finished to return to the Welcome dialog. Don't click the Close button, as that cancels the installation.

Click Next to continue with installation.

A dialog appears that displays the readme file. (You can also choose to read this file later, after installation is complete.) After you are finished reading the file, click Next.

A window with the license agreement appears. Read the license carefully. If you accept the terms, click Next to continue with the installation.

SELECTING THE INSTALLATION DIRECTORY

> **Caution**
>
> Be sure to install the StarSchedule Server in a *different* directory than StarOffice. Otherwise, neither program will operate.

The installation program offers /windows/SdlSrvc51 (Windows) or /root/SdlSrvc51 (Linux) as the default directory. You can select another directory by typing the pathname in the text box or clicking the Browse button, navigating to the directory, and clicking to select it. Click Next to continue with the installation.

ENTERING STARSCHEDULE SETTINGS

At this point, a dialog appears to inform you that the files have been successfully copied. Click Complete, and a Schedule Server Setup dialog box appears. Default settings are already entered for the HTTP Port and Administration Port for the server. If you don't have any other StarSchedule Servers running, you can accept the default settings. If you have multiple servers, each server must receive its own port assignment. You can run up to 10 schedule servers on the same computer.

Make sure the start Administration Service box is checked, and click Complete to complete the installation.

RUNNING AND ADMINISTERING STARSCHEDULE

If you have set up a new StarSchedule Server or deleted an existing one, you have to restart the server through the Service Manager. After you do so, the StarSchedule Server runs automatically every time you start your computer.

In Windows, a new program group, StarSchedule Server 5.1, is placed in your Start menu with the entries Setup and Service Manager. The Service Manager enables you to supervise running services and to start, halt, and interrupt them.

In Linux, the subadmin program, located in your StarSchedule Server directory, gives you information on the currently running services. After the installation is finished, the server is started automatically. For administration, you should register the server by opening the pop-up menu of the Data Sources entry in your StarSchedule folder, which is located in the StarOffice Explorer. Now server administration can be performed directly through the server entry's pop-up menu.

The main server functions can be administered with Java- and JavaScript-enabled browsers using the TCP/IP protocol. In your browser, enter the name of the server in the URL Locator field. If you have chosen a port number other than the default of 80, enter the number after the server name and a colon (for example, http://localhost: portnumber).

Other functions can be administered from within the StarSchedule Server entries in the Explorer.

→ For information on administering and using StarSchedule, **see** "Getting Started with StarSchedule," **p. 1024**, and "Getting Organized with StarSchedule," **p. 1020**.

APP

A

INSTALLING YOUR PRINTER: LINUX

Installing a printer on Linux is more of a challenge than on the Windows platform, so we have included a special section on installing Linux printers. Even so, this book is not a Linux manual. The information provided here gives a general overview but does not go into the details of editing your printer files or getting GhostScript to work with StarOffice. If you need more information than is provided here, check the man pages for the lpd and lpq commands and any other Linux documentation on printing issues you might have, the Star Division newsgroups, and the sites listed in tips throughout the following sections.

➜ For information on installing and configuring a Windows computer, **see** "Setting Up Your Windows Printer," **p. 184**.

PRINTER SETUP BASICS

In Linux, you can print in two ways:

- You can send your file directly to the printer.
- You can spool your files in a print queue and print as a background process to other ongoing system tasks.

Spooling your print files takes advantage of Linux's multitasking capabilities to use system resources more efficiently during printing. It is the recommended method of printing. If you are printing to a non-PostScript printer from StarOffice, you have no choice; you must spool your data because your file must be translated from the PostScript language before it can be printed.

Spooled data is managed by a *print daemon* that normally is loaded at startup and runs constantly in the background, scanning for new files to print. This print daemon (in a file called lpd) is by default stored in the /usr/sbin directory. If, for some reason, your print daemon was not loaded at startup, you can load it now by entering the following command:

```
lpd [options]
```

Check the lpd man page for a list of available options.

The print daemon needs information about the printers attached to your computer and how to work with them. This information is stored in a file called /etc/printcap. If you are installing a PostScript printer and use the included printer setup utility, spadmin, StarOffice writes the necessary changes for you. If you are installing a non-PostScript printer, you need to either use your Linux distribution's print utility or edit the /etc/printcap file manually to define your printer(s).

SETTING UP A NON-POSTSCRIPT PRINTER

StarOffice directly supports only PostScript printers, the UNIX standard. If you want to print using a non-PostScript printer, you must *filter* your print file as generated by StarOffice into a language your printer can understand. GhostScript is the program most commonly used to do this. You may already have GhostScript installed because it is included in most distributions of Linux. You can also download it from http://www.cs.wisc.edu/~ghost/. This site also has documentation on using GhostScript.

To enable filtering, you must create a print *queue* so that your output is sent to a temporary file rather than sent directly to your printer. This process is called *spooling your data*. To create a queue, create a directory called spool (typically, you would create it in the /usr directory), and enter the path information in the /etc/printcap file so that the printer daemon knows where to store print data. You must also enter information about your printer in /etc/printcap so that the daemon knows where to send your data after it's filtered.

After you have edited your /etc/printcap file appropriately, you can run the StarOffice print manager (spadmin) from the Star Office desktop.

Finally, select the Generic PostScript driver as your printer.

SETTING UP A POSTSCRIPT PRINTER

StarOffice has built-in support to print output directly to PostScript printers. You can configure your printer using the StarOffice print manager, spadmin. To run spadmin, follow these steps:

1. Open an xterm window.
2. Navigate to the Office51/bin directory that contains the StarOffice program files.
3. Type ./spadmin and press Enter.

The Printer Installation dialog opens, from which you can do the following:

- Manage installed printers
- Install new print drivers
- Uninstall unneeded printer drivers
- Install and manage fonts
- Print test pages

App

A

> **Note**
> You can filter output to your PostScript device, but you cannot access additional paper trays or perform double-sided printing.

A PostScript printer uses a PostScript Printer Description (PPD) file (also referred to as a *print driver*) that describes the specific printer's features so that programs know how to communicate with it correctly. If you don't have the proper PPD for your printer, you may print garbage characters, have incorrect margins, be unable to print from alternate print trays or print double-sided documents, or encounter other printing problems.

The StarOffice print manager, spadmin, has PPD files for a large number of PostScript printers. Scroll through the list to see whether a PPD for your printer is listed. If you see your printer listed, select it and click Add New Printer (or double-click the printer name). The printer name appears in the Installed Printers list above. Then you can follow these steps:

1. Click Rename to open the Input dialog.

2. Enter a name for the printer, if you like. Choose a name that all users will easily recognize. Then click OK.

3. In the Printer Administration dialog that appears, select your printer in the Installed Printers list, and click the Connect button. The Connect dialog opens.

4. In the Existing Queues text box, enter the name of your printer (its default name or the name you have just assigned it) and an equals sign (=), followed by the command string needed to print to this queue and the name of your print queue. For example, if your printer is the HP 1200 and your queue is called HP1200PQ, you would enter the following:

   HP1200=lpr -P HP1200PQ

5. Click Add to confirm the new connection.

6. Click OK to return to the main spadmin dialog. (Alternatively, you can click Modify to edit an existing queue or Remove to delete one.)

7. In the spadmin dialog, select the printer in the Installed Printers list, and click Configure. The Configure dialog box opens.

8. Set your default page size, page orientation (portrait or landscape), and page margins in the Configure dialog. If you use an older PostScript printer, you might need to select PostScript level 1 to match your printer's older software. (Check the printer's documentation to determine whether it uses level 1 or level 2 PostScript.) Click OK when you're done.

9. In the spadmin dialog, click Test Page to see whether your printer settings result in satisfactory output. If not, refer to the StarDivision documentation, check your settings, and try again.

You can select more than one PPD, if you like. If you install multiple PPDs, select one to be the default, and click Default Printer.

Tip #624 from
Michael & Sarah

StarOffice stores printer information in the text file Xpedefaults (or ~/.Xpedefaults in a multi-user installation). If you are an experienced user, you may want to edit this file directly.

Tip #625 from
Michael & Sarah

If you want to use PostScript files to create PDF or EPS files, select the Generic PostScript driver.

If your printer is not listed, go to the Adobe site at www.adobe.com/prodindex/ printerdrivers/winpdd.html or www.adobe.com/prodindex/printerdrivers/linuxpdd.html or to your printer manufacturer's Web site, and download the correct PPD file. After you have expanded and/or decompressed the downloaded file (if necessary), click the Install New Driver button in the spadmin dialog. In the Driver Installation dialog that opens, click the Browse button, navigate to the directory with the PPD, and select the PPD in the Installable Drivers list. Then click OK.

INSTALLING FONTS

Font installation and management on Linux can be a complicated affair. The StarOffice setup.pdf guide includes detailed instructions on installing fonts, so you can refer to that guide for further information. The Star Division newsgroups also have many helpful postings on font installation issues.

If your printer has installed fonts other than the standard PostScript fonts, you need to load and install AFM files to be able to use these additional fonts. You may be able to download these AFM files from ftp://ftp.adobe.com/pub/adobe/type/win/all/afmfiles or ftp://ftp.adobe.com/pub/adobe/type/linux/all/afmfiles. If you are not using an Adobe font, you must request AFM files from the font provider or create them yourself. It is beyond the scope of this book to detail the process of creating AFMs; just be aware that it is not an easy process. If you do not have experience creating AFMs, you should search the StarOffice newsgroups and other Internet resources for assistance.

Tip #626 from
Michael &
Sarah

For a useful guide to installing TrueType fonts on Linux, go to http://www.mind-spring.net/~john_mcl/adding_fonts.html. Scroll down the page to find tips on installing fonts for version 5.1.

APP

A

CHECKING THE DIRECTORY STRUCTURE

Appendix C, "Program Directories and Files," lists the directory structure of StarOffice at installation, with brief descriptions of the contents of each directory. If you have problems running StarOffice after installation, you might want to check your installed directories against this list to see whether your installation was incomplete.

Take care in altering the default StarOffice directory structure because the program may depend on a folder or file having a particular name or location in order to function properly. If you change the name and/or location of folders or systems files, be sure to change the path to that location (if one exists), either by using the Tools, Options, General, Path tab, or by directly editing the appropriate systems files or environment variables.

REGISTERING THE PROGRAM

Star Division has changed and streamlined the registration procedures for version 5.1. If you have previously registered a different version, you will find that the process has changed. Note that your old customer number and registration key no longer work.

The registration process differs slightly depending on whether you have installed a free download edition, a Personal Deluxe or Professional edition, or a Business or Campus License edition.

If you have installed the free Internet version, registration of the program is now automatic upon installation and initial startup, based on the information you entered online when obtaining the program.

If you have installed a version from a CD, you are prompted to register by a dialog box at program startup. Registration requires you to submit certain personal data and transmit this data to the company. In response, you are given customer and registration numbers that enable you to fully register your copy of the program for unrestricted use.

Just as Star Division changed the registration process and key system for version 5.1, it's always possible that they might change the key system again in the future. If this happens, your registration may generate a key that doesn't actually work with your program, even though you enter it correctly. If you have problems with a key and do not know why, check the Star Division newsgroups at the `*.com.chat`, `*.com.announce`,or `*.com.misc` at `starnews.stardivision.de`.

REGISTERING IF YOU INSTALLED FROM A CD

If you installed StarOffice from a CD or network, you need to register the program to be able to use it for more than 30 days. (If you don't register within the 30 days, the program automatically disables critical files it needs to run and will no longer function. You will need to run the setup program—which still works—to uninstall the program files and then reinstall the program to use it again.)

To register, you need a customer number and a registration key. These numbers are generated only after you submit your personal data to the company. Because these numbers are generated based on your personal data (name, address, email address, and so on), if you change certain critical parts of your data, you might need to re-register the program. Also, if you reinstall the program, you need to enter your personal data just as you did on registering the program.

Note

Your customer number may change as you upgrade to new versions or change your user data, so don't assume an old customer number will work.

If you don't want to submit this data, you're out of luck because there's no way around it (unless you want to reinstall the program every 30 days). If you're concerned about Star

Division misusing this data, Star Division assures customers that it stores and uses your personal data for internal purposes only. Star Division has operated in Germany for almost 15 years without users complaining of misuse of this data, which is a good recommendation because both laws and customs concerning sharing of such personal information are much stricter in Europe.

To obtain your customer number and registration key, execute the Registration command. You can choose this command when prompted to register at program startup or by choosing Registration from the Help menu. A Registration Wizard takes over from there.

The easiest way to register is via email, in which case your numbers are automatically generated via the company's server and entered into your program. The numbers are also immediately sent back to you as a StarWriter document. You should save and print this message in case you ever need to install the program again.

Note

The registration document returned to you says at the bottom that Star Division will soon send you your customer number via email. In fact, your customer number is already listed on the same document, although a copy will also be sent by email.

Sometimes the online registration process is not successful, often for reasons that have nothing to do with you. For example, the Star Division server might be down, or your Internet connection may be faulty. Just try again.

If you're unable to register via email, you can register via fax or snail mail instead. If you choose to register by snail mail, you need to print the registration form generated by the Registration Wizard, so be sure that your printer is configured to work with StarOffice. Be forewarned that the registration process is considerably slower using these methods—sometimes not being completed within the 30-day period of initial use. If you don't have access to email yourself, you're better off trying to email from a friend's or colleague's machine—something you can do if you have the Personal Edition Deluxe or another higher level version.

Your numbers are then sent to you, and you must enter them manually. To do so, choose the Register command from the Help menu, enter your customer and registration numbers, and click OK.

Caution

Because the registration key combines numbers and letters, you can easily confuse the letter *O* with the number 0. Confusing the two is a common reason for registration to fail. Other common reasons are transposing characters, accidentally entering a blank space at the beginning or end of an entry, and making typing mistakes. To help you distinguish between the letter o and the number 0, all numbers on the registration form Star Division generates are underlined.

REGISTERING IF YOU DOWNLOADED FROM THE INTERNET

If you downloaded StarOffice via links you accessed through the Web site, you had to enter your personal data to be able to download the program. Your customer number and registration key were automatically generated as part of that process; a copy is also sent to your email address. When you install the program, you enter those two numbers as part of the process. In the new registration system, your version of StarOffice is automatically registered upon successful installation.

You should print and keep a copy of your customer number and registration key in a safe place; if you ever need to reinstall StarOffice, you'll need this information again, and obtaining a new key from Star Division is a slow and sometimes frustrating process.

> **Caution**
>
> If you have changed certain key parts of your user data since entering your personal data on the Web site, your numbers may not be valid. In this case, you need to return to the Web site and resubmit your new information.

MODIFYING, REPAIRING, OR REMOVING STAROFFICE

After you install StarOffice, a copy of the setup program remains in your Office51 directory. You can run this setup program if you want to modify, repair, or uninstall StarOffice. "Modify" means to install selected components, uninstall selected components, or both. The uninstallation process uninstalls the entire program at once.

To begin the setup program on Windows, navigate to the Office51 directory, and double-click the file named setup.

To begin the setup program on Linux, from within X, open an xterm window, navigate to the Office51 directory, type ./setup, and press Enter.

MODIFYING YOUR INSTALLATION

If you want to change your language dictionaries, add additional filters, or otherwise install or uninstall selected components of StarOffice, select Modify on the Setup's opening screen, and click Next. You are presented with a list of all the program components much like the one you encounter during a custom installation. Click the plus sign (+) to the left of the module names to reveal their contents just as you do with an Explorer folder:

- To select a new item to install, click the cube to its left so that it is filled in with color.
- To select a loaded item to uninstall, click in the cube to its left so that it is marked with a red X.
- For an item you want to leave as is, leave the cube to its left, blank.

You can select as many items as you want to install or uninstall.

After you've made your selections, click Complete, and StarOffice copies the selected program components to (or deletes them from) your hard drive.

> **Caution**
>
> Don't uninstall any core program modules—StarWriter, StarCalc, StarDraw, StarImpress, StarBase, StarMath, or the StarDesktop. If you do, your program will no longer function properly because the modules are interdependent.

REPAIRING STAROFFICE

If StarOffice starts acting strangely, such as crashing frequently, failing to start, or giving you repeated error messages, you should try running the Repair option of Setup. You can also run Repair to restore files that you accidentally deleted, such as samples, templates, or filters. Repair checks your currently installed files. If any are incomplete or damaged, the setup program reinstalls these files. This process doesn't endanger your saved data or change anything else about your StarOffice configuration.

To repair your installation, run Setup from the Office51 directory, choose the Repair option, and click Next. StarOffice checks your installed components and gives you a report. If it finds that any files are damaged, it does its repair work and returns you to your desktop when it's done.

If you have an Internet download version, and StarOffice tells you your files are damaged but running Repair doesn't solve your problems, you might need to download another copy of the program and install the new copy.

UNINSTALLING STAROFFICE FOR SINGLE USERS

If you want to remove StarOffice from your hard drive entirely, the safest and cleanest way to do that is to run Setup and choose the Deinstall option.

→ If you are uninstalling StarOffice on a network installation, **see** "Uninstalling StarOffice from a Network," **p. 1390**, in this appendix.

Running Deinstall removes all StarOffice components from your hard drive, most special StarOffice systems files, and most of the changes to non-StarOffice systems files that were made during the program's installation. It leaves intact any file or folder within the Office51 directory that you have created or to which you have made changes.

To use this feature, first make sure that you aren't running StarOffice. Then run Setup from the Office51 directory, choose the Deinstall option, and click Next. The uninstallation process begins immediately.

After you have completed the uninstallation, you should manually delete the sofficerc file (Linux) or the soffice.ini file in the Windows directory (Windows). If you do not delete this file, and you try to reinstall StarOffice again, you might experience problems.

APP

A

UNINSTALLING STAROFFICE FROM A NETWORK

The Deinstall option of the setup program does not work for network installations. To uninstall a network installation, you must log on as the administrator (Windows) or as superuser (Linux) and delete the entire server installation directory. Doing so deactivates all users' installations on individual workstations, which should then be deleted manually as well.

TROUBLESHOOTING

This troubleshooting section offers solutions to a number of commonly encountered problems. Although the installation wizard smoothes the installation process, users on all platforms commonly experience problems at a two key points in the process: Initiating the installation process, and registering the program.

TROUBLESHOOTING STAROFFICE 5.0 REGISTRATION

I have StarOffice 5.0, but I don't have a registration key. Can I get a registration key from the Web site that works with this version of the program?

No. StarDivision no longer supports versions 5.0 or 5.01 (the filter update), and because it has changed the registration process with 5.1, the registration keys generated by the Web site don't work with these versions. If you are using StarOffice via a campus or business license, contact your Star Division sales representative for assistance. Otherwise, you need to upgrade to version 5.1. In general, if you have an older version but lack the necessary personal, media, and/or registration keys, you're out of luck.

TROUBLESHOOTING INTERNET DOWNLOAD VERSIONS

When trying to download StarOffice, I can't get past the Registration Form. Every time I click Submit, the form reappears!

In your Web browser's configuration, you have to check the option that enables accepting cookies. If your browser doesn't accept cookies, it won't work.

I've read the StarDivision FAQ on registering 5.1, and I'm totally confused because it keeps talking about a personal key. I don't have a personal key. Is that why my registration isn't working?

No. This FAQ has not been properly updated. If you downloaded the program yourself from the Star Division Web site, you registered during that process. If you downloaded from elsewhere, you need to go to the Star Division site to register (www.stardivision.com). On completing the online registration process, you'll receive a customer number and a registration key. That's all you need to install and register the program. If you have these numbers and are still experiencing problems, refer to the other troubleshooting questions in this section.

I'm trying to install the StarOffice 5.1 I downloaded from the Internet, but I don't have a customer number and registration key.

Visit the Star Division home page (`www.stardivision.com`), and click the link for the StarOffice 5.1 Personal Edition download. From there, you can reach the registration page. Fill in the fields with the appropriate data. To submit and process the data, your browser must be set to accept cookies. Confirm the data you've entered. You then are given a customer number and registration key and should be able to install StarOffice without problems.

GENERAL TROUBLESHOOTING

I use the correct customer number and registration key or the correct media key, but I still can't install the program!

The following are three common reasons that installation fails:

- You have used special characters in your user data, such as # or accent marks on names. StarOffice can choke on them. Eliminate any such marks (except the @ symbol, which you should be able to use in your email address without problems).

- You have mistyped the registration or media key, mistaking the letter *O* for a zero (0) or vice versa. Note that all numbers on the registration form are underlined to help you distinguish between letters and numbers.

- (Internet download version) You have altered your user data in some way. Your user data must match *exactly* the data you entered in the online registration form. This includes things like an accidental space before or after a name, capitalization, and use of an initial in a name. One way to be sure you have entered the information correctly is to save the email with your registration information as a text file, open the file when you are at the Enter User Data dialog box, and the cut and paste your data from the file into the appropriate fields in the User Data form.

I installed the program without problem, but when I try to open a new document, I can't or the program crashes.

You might have this problem for many possible reasons. One is that you can experience conflicts if you have both Microsoft Internet Explorer (versions 4 or 5) and Netscape on your system. Installing MS Internet Explorer 5 after installing StarOffice can also cause conflicts.

This problem occurs because the File, New command does not open conventional templates but runs StarBasic scripts that generate new, blank documents. These scripts are called by a URL (path entry) that uses a special reference. For example, the StarWriter URL is `private:factory/swriter`. If StarOffice is not properly registered to execute this URL—if, for example, IE4, IE5, or Netscape are attempting to execute these URLs instead—none of the File, New commands will work.

If you have both IE and Netscape installed on your system, try uninstalling one of these programs.

If you have only IE on your system, try leaving IE on your hard drive, and then uninstalling and finally reinstalling StarOffice. This trick enables StarOffice to properly recognize and register the existence of IE to prevent conflicts.

I've been using StarOffice without problem for a while, but suddenly I'm getting messages that I need to re-register my program. What's going on?

You probably registered the program and then made changes to your user data in the User Data dialog box (opened from the Tools, Options, General master dialog box). StarOffice checks the user data in this dialog against an internal registration file every time the program starts. If the two sets of data don't match, it generates a registration request message. Star Division does this to enforce the terms of its license agreements, which require every user to submit certain data to the company.

To re-register with your new data, simply open the Help menu, and choose Registration.

TROUBLESHOOTING FOR LINUX USERS

Even though I installed the Java Runtime Environment as instructed, I can't get Java to work.

Try editing the sofficerc file in the StarOffice51 directory, and enter the following lines :

```
~~~~
[Java]
Java=1
UserClassPath=/usr/rt117_v1a/lib
[INet]
JavaScript=1
Applets=1
```

Also, be sure that your operating system can handle Java native threads because StarOffice 5.1 makes use of threads.

If you still experience problems, visit the Star Division installation newsgroups and/or browse back postings at the DejaNews Web site (www.dejanews.com).

The installation script complains that it can't find the 2.0.7 libraries, but I have 2.1 libraries, and I thought 5.1 worked with them.

StarOffice 5.1 is compatible with glibc 2.1 libraries. However, the installation startup script automatically checks your system for your default libraries files and generates a warning message if they are not version 2.0.7. It does not yet recognize the 2.1 libraries. Just select the option to continue anyway, and your installation should work without problem. Do not under any circumstances load the version 2.0.7 libraries; your system won't work properly if you do.

I have already installed the 2.0.7 library files in the StarOffice directory, but the installation program tells me it can't detect these files.

The installation startup script automatically checks your system for your default system libraries files and generates a warning message if they are not version 2.0.7. It does not check to see whether you have installed the necessary libraries in a separate directory where only StarOffice can access them. Just select the option to continue anyway, and your installation should work without problem.

Trying to install the program, I get a message that StarOffice can't create the needed temp file, or I get the message */tmp/sv001.tmp/shartup.sh: No such file or directory*.

You might not have enough room in your /tmp directory for StarOffice to do its business. Check your /tmp directory to see whether you have old temp files (left by StarOffice or other processes). Old StarOffice installation files have the name sv###.tmp, where ### stands for a number (for example, sv002.tmp). Delete any unneeded files, and try again. Alternatively, you can redirect the setup temp file to another directory. Using bash, enter these commands:

```
mkdir $HOME/tmp
export TEMP=$HOME/tmp
setup
```

Using csh, use the following

```
mkdir $HOME/tmp
setenv TEMP=$HOME/tmp
setup
```

Then run the setup script.

FILE FORMATS AND EXTENSIONS

Interested in finding out what file formats are supported by StarOffice for opening (importing) and saving (exporting) non-StarOffice documents? Look no further. The following tables list the most common file formats that you might encounter when working in StarOffice or exchanging files between StarOffice and other programs.

With the version 5.0 filter update, StarOffice added a huge number of new text import filters and can now import almost any flavor of text you might have hanging around, including many older formats such as Wang, WordStar, XyWrite, and MultiMate. It also imports some more specialized formats such as FrameMaker MIF and Interleaf. Most importantly, it includes a full set of WordPerfect import and export filters.

There are far too many of these new filters to list here. If you're looking for a specific filter that isn't listed, run Setup from the Office51 directory and choose the Modify option. When you click Next, a window appears listing the StarOffice 5.1 Program Modules and other program components. Click the plus sign next to the StarWriter 5.1 module and you'll see an item named Text Filter. Click its plus sign, and the entire list of text filters will cascade open. Click to the left of any text filters you want to add to select them, and follow the dialog box instructions to complete their installation.

Since StarOffice incorporates any plug-ins you may have installed in your Netscape or MS Internet Explorer browser, you might also be able to open file types other than those listed here.

Tip #627 from
Michael & Sarah

If you want to see what filters are installed on your system, locate the file `install.ini`, open it as a simple text file, print it, and close without saving.

IMPORTING AND EXPORTING NON-GRAPHIC FILES

Table B.1 lists the most common file formats for word processing and Web page (HTML) editing that StarOffice can handle. If you're importing text files to use in HTML pages, be sure to use the StarWriter Web text filters rather than the standard StarWriter text filters.

TABLE B.1 TEXT AND WEB PAGE IMPORT AND EXPORT FILTERS

File Type	Import	Export	Extension	Notes
HTML	X	X	.htm or .html	Hypertext Markup Language pages. Used to create Web pages and intranet documents as well as exchange documents across platforms. This filter is a general HTML filter, without special StarOffice coding.
HTML (StarWriter)	X	X	.htm or .html	The StarOffice native HTML format.
Text	X	X	.txt	Windows only—equivalent to Text ASNI on Linux.

File Type	Import	Export	Extension	Notes
Text ANSI	X	X	.txt	Linux only.
Text UNIX	X	X	.txt	Uses line feed only as line breaks.
Text Mac	X	X	.txt	Uses both carriage return and line feed as line breaks.
Text DOS	X	X	.txt	Text is ASCII-encoded. Uses both carriage return and line feed as line breaks.
Rich Text Format	X	X	.rtf	A Microsoft file format that saves all typographic formatting (but not all layout information) so you can exchange files among programs without losing all character and text formatting.
MS Word97	X	X	.doc	To be imported properly, files must be saved with Fast Save option turned off. Export filters seem to save in Word 95 format, not Word 97.
MS Word95	X	X	.doc	To be imported properly, files must be saved with Fast Save option turned off.
MS WinWord 6.0	X	X	.doc	To be imported properly, files must be saved with Fast Save option turned off.
MS Excel 4.0 (StarWriter)	X		.xls	Import as StarWriter tables.
MS Excel 5.0 (StarWriter)	X		.xls	Import as StarWriter tables.
MS Excel95 (StarWriter)	X		.xls	Import as StarWriter tables.
Lotus 1-2-3 1.0 (DOS)	X			Import as StarWriter tables. (StarWriter)
Lotus 1-2-3 1.0 (Windows)	X			Import as StarWriter tables. (StarWriter)
Text ANSI (StarWriter Web)			.ansi .txt	Linux only.
Text (StarWriter Web)	X	X	.txt	Windows only—equivalent to Text ASNI on Linux.
Text UNIX (StarWriter Web)	X	X	.txt	Uses line feed only as line breaks.
Text Mac (StarWriter Web)	X	X	.txt	Uses both carriage return and line feed as line breaks.

Cн

B

continues

TABLE B.1 CONTINUED

File Type	Import	Export	Extension	Notes
Text DOS (StarWriter Web)	X	X	.txt	Text is ASCII-encoded. Uses both carriage return and line feed as line breaks.
WordPerfect (Win) 6.1	X		.wpd	
WordPerfect (Win) 7.0	X		.wpd	
WordStar (Win) 1.x-2.0	X		.wsd	
WordStar 7.0	X		.wsd	
Ami Pro 1.1-1.2	X		.sam	
Ami Pro 2.0-3.1	X		.sam	
MS MacWord 5.x	X		.doc	

IMPORTING AND EXPORTING SPREADSHEETS AND DATABASE TABLES

Table B.2 lists common file formats that StarCalc and StarBase can handle. If a file format is not qualified with a module name afterward, it can be handled by both StarCalc and StarBase. StarBase can also import databases using OBDC and JDBC drivers. For more information on importing and exporting databases, see Chapter 30, "Working with Databases in StarBase."

TABLE B.2 SPREADSHEET AND DATABASE IMPORT AND EXPORT FILTERS

File Type	Import	Export	Extension	Notes
MS Excel 4.0 (StarCalc)	X		.xls	
MS Excel 5.0 (StarCalc)	X	X	.xls	
MS Excel95 (StarCalc)	X	X	.xls	For all Excel files, macros and VBA modules do not translate directly, although you can open them in StarBasic. With some tweaking, they can work. Formulas may also require manual editing. Before opening an Excel file, check to see what the base calculation data is for your version of Excel, versus that used by StarCalc. You can set the base date StarCalc uses in the General, Other dialog box

File Type	Import	Export	Extension	Notes
				that opens from within the Tools, Options master dialog box. If you don't set this base data to match that of Excel's, all your imported dates might be incorrect (depending on your version of Excel).
Lotus 1-2-3 1.0 (DOS) (StarCalc)	X			
Lotus 1-2-3 1.0 (Windows) (StarCalc)	X			
DBase	X	X	.dbf	dBase III format. Uses character set 435.
Text-txt-csv (StarCalc)	X	X	.csv	Delimited text file. Use to import databases in text formats. If you want to edit an imported text database, you must import it into StarCalc using this filter; text databases imported into StarBase are read-only.
Text-txt-csv (StarBase)	X		.csv, .txt	Delimited text file. Imports in read-only form.
Rich Text Format (StarCalc)	X		.rtf	A Microsoft file format that saves all typographic formatting (although not all layout information) so you can exchange files across platforms and still retain character and text formatting.
SYLK	X	X	.syk	Symbolic Link exchange database format.
DIF	X	X	.dif	Data Information Exchange database format.
HTML (StarCalc)	X	X	.htm .html	Hypertext Markup Language pages (Web).
MS Access97 (StarBase)	X	X	Windows only.	Cannot open directly through the Open dialog box, but can import into a StarBase database if you have the MS Jet Engine and DAO installed. You can then modify and save your database as well as enter and extract data. See Chapter 30 for more information.

IMPORTING AND EXPORTING GRAPHIC FILE FORMATS (STARDRAW/STARIMAGE AND STARIMPRESS)

File formats are often native to a specific application. For example, drawings created in StarDraw are stored as .sda files. StarOffice is capable of importing virtually every major graphic file format as well as some oddball ones. Table B.3 lists the most common file formats StarOffice can handle. Be aware when dealing with graphic file formats that some formats are better for certain uses (such as Web publishing, for example) than others.

TABLE B.3   GRAPHIC AND PRESENTATION FILE FORMATS SUPPORTED BY STAROFFICE

Extension	Name	Format	Import	Export	Comment
.bmp	Bitmap	Pixel	x	x	A computer graphics format created by Microsoft and supported by a variety of Windows, DOS, and OS/2 applications. StarOffice supports BMP images with up to 16 million colors. You also can use Run-Length Encoding (RLE), a lossless compression scheme specifically applicable to the BMP format. BMP images are often used to create images for help files and Windows wallpaper. Standard resolution is 96dpi. BMP files are typically very large.
.cgm	Computer Graphics Metafile	Vector	x		This format imports vector graphics.
.dxf	AutoCad	Vector	x		AutoCad Exchange. This opens files created with Autodesk's AutoCad program, the PC standard for 2D engineering and architectural drawings.
.gif	Graphics Interchange Format	Pixel	x	x	GIF is a standard developed by CompuServe for bitmap graphics of up to 256 colors per pixel. Originally developed as a means of compressing files so you could quickly transfer photographs via modem to and from the company's commercial bulletin boards, the GIF format has become a staple for WWW images and illustrations. Due to their low color depth, they are almost never used for professional printing.

Extension	Name	Format	Import	Export	Comment
.jpg	Joint Photographic Experts Group (JEPG)	Pixel	x	x	The most efficient compression format currently available. JPEG is a lossy compression scheme, which means it sacrifices quality to conserve disk space JPEG is best used when compressing continuous-tone images for the WWW.
.met	MET Metafile		x	x	This is IBM's presentation manager graphics format for OS/2.
.pbm	Portable	Raw/ binary	x	x	This format was originally developed for use with email.
.pcx	PC Paintbrush	Pixel	x		Very popular format for clip art that goes back to the old DOS days. StarOffice supports PCX images with up to 16 million colors. You can find an enormous amount of art, usually clip art, in this format.
.pgm	Portable Grayscale Map	Raw/	x	x	This format was originally developed for use with email.
.png	Portable Network Graphics	Pixel	x	x	Pronounced ping, the PNG format enables you to save 16 million color images without compression for the WWW However, there are only a few browsers that support PNG, including Netscape.
.pct	Mac	Vector/ PixelPict	x	x	Pict is one of the few file formats that handles both object-oriented and bitmapped images. It supports images in any bit depth, size, or resolution. StarOffice can open but not save in the PICT format.
.ppm	Portable Pixel Map	Raw/ binary	x	x	This format was developed for use with email.
.psd	Adobe Photoshop	Pixel	x		Adobe Photoshop native file format. PSD files can handle 1-bit, grayscale and color (up to 32-bit) images. Although StarOffice can open PSD files, it cannot export a file created or modified in StarDraw as a PSD file.
.PS or .EPS	Postscript; Encapsulated Postscript	Vector	x	x	StarOffice supports object-oriented files saved in EPS or PS format. EPS has been designed to save object-oriented graphics that you intend to print to a PostScript output device.

CH

B

continues

TABLE B.3 CONTINUED

Extension	Name	Format	Import	Export	Comment
.ras	Sun Raster-file	Pixel	x	x	RAS is the original bitmap format for the UNIX platform. The filter supports 1-, 2-, and 24-bit images with RLE.
.sda	StarDraw	Vector			StarDraw's native file format.
.svm	StarView Metafile	Vector	x	x	A StarDivision graphic format that can be used if you want to work across platforms or if you create graphics with StarImpress that you want to embed in StarWriter.
.tif	Tagged Image File Format (TIFF)	Pixel	x	x	TIFF is the most widely supported image printing format across both the Macintosh and the PC platforms.
.tga	Targa	Pixel	x		A file format developed by TrueVision to support images capable of displaying live video.
.wmf	Windows Metafile	Vector	x	x	A Windows GDI metafile extension.
.xpm		Pixel	x	x	The XPM filter supports up to 256 colors. XPM graphics have the advantage that they can be incorporated into the C source code.
.ppt	MS PowerPoint		x	x	MS PowerPoint 97 presentation files.

StarOffice Native Document Types and File Extensions

Table B.4 lists native StarOffice 5.0/5.1 formats and file extensions. Document file extensions are added by StarOffice when you save with the Automatic File Extensions option (on by default). We recommend you leave this option on. However, if you have turned it off, you can add the extensions manually.

TABLE B.4 NATIVE FILE FORMATS AND FILE EXTENSIONS

Extension	File Type/Module	Location/Comments
.$$$	Temporary StarBase files	If these files build up, you can delete them as long as you aren't currently using a StarBase database.

Extension	File Type/Module	Location/Comments
.bak	Backup files	\Office50\backup Saved if you have selected the save backup files option on the Save tab of the Tools, Options, General dialog box.
.bau	Autotext file (StarWriter)	\Office50\Autotext
.bmp	StarImage	MS bitmap format
.cal	StarSchedule	\Office50\store\schedule.cal \Office50\store\format.cal
.dat	Dictionary files	\Office50 \Office\autotext
.dbf	Database files in dBase III format	\Office50\database
.dic	Custom dictionary files	\Office\wordbook Can be manually edited.
.dnl	StarDownload	
.htm	StarWriter/Web	StarOffice HTML files do have some proprietary code and are not pure HTML, but fields are stored as plain HTML as well, so they are fully compatible with HTML standard.
.sbl	StarBasic program wizard	\Office50\basic StarOffice wizards are all in .sbl format.
.scc	StarOffice Explorer	\Office50\explorer Special Explorer objects including the Gallery, Workplace, and Recycle Bin.
.scs	StarOffice system files	Storage files used by StarOffice for many purposes, including mail, FTP, and scheduling. These files can therefore get very large. Be sure you leave enough room on your drive or partition for them.
.sda	StarDraw	
.sdb	StarOffice database	\Office50\explorer Should not be manually edited.
.sdc	StarCalc	Spreadsheet.
.sdd	StarImpress	Presentation.
.sdm	StarMail	Mail message.
.sds	StarChart	Chart.

continues

CH

B

TABLE B.4 CONTINUED

Extension	File Type/Module	Location/Comments
.sdw	StarWriter	Text documents. Some special features (for example, Master Pages, some aspects of table formatting) do not translate into Word or other WP programs.
.sfs	StarFrame	StarOffice native frame document.
.sgl	StarWriter	Master document; will not export into foreign formats.
.smd	StarMail	Mail document.
.smf	StarMath	Formula.
.sms	StarMath	Formula template
.sob-.soh		Office5.1\config. These files contain information about color palettes and various style elements within StarOffice.
.sob		Bitmap styles.
.soc		Color palettes.
.sod		Line styles.
.soe		Arrow styles.
.sog		Gradients.
.soh		Hatches.
.svh	StarOffice Help files;	\Office50\help\01 Should not be manually edited.
.vor	StarOffice templates	You can import them into Microsoft Word, but they share the normal limitations of importing across the programs.
*_hyph.dat, *_spell.dat, *_thes.dat	Dictionary Files (hyphenation and spelling dictionary and thesaurus).	\Office50 These files cannot be altered. To extend spelling options, create a custom dictionary.
sv.tmp	Temporary files	\usr\Office50\backup Backup file storage.

APPENDIX

C

StarOffice Program Directories and Files

If you want to know where to find a certain file, this appendix is for you. The following tables list the StarOffice directories and their contents and selected StarOffice program files. Although it's technically possible for you to move StarOffice directories or even delete them, unless you are an advanced user, we recommend that you don't. You can easily redirect StarOffice's attention through the Paths tab of the Tools, Options, General dialog box.

→ For more details, **see** "Setting Your General Options," **p. 76**.

> **Caution**
>
> When editing system or program files (including those noted here as "can be manually edited"), you should always backup the original file first or save it under a different name (such as *soffice.old*). In case you experience problems, you can then easily revert to the original file in order to get StarOffice running.

> **Note**
>
>
>
> A note on conventions: Windows and Linux use different slashes to mark directories—Windows uses the \ backslash while Linux uses the / forward slash. To be consistent (also with the StarOffice documentation), the \ backslash is used in the tables in this book. Linux users, don't let the different orientation of the slashes confuse you—the directory and filenames are the same for StarOffice on both operating systems unless otherwise indicated.

> **Note**
>
>
>
> Linux is case-sensitive (recognizes a difference between capital and lowercase letters), whereas Windows is not. We've rendered accurately the capitalization in all filenames so Linux users can find these files and directories without frustration; Windows users don't really need to worry about it.

STAROFFICE PROGRAM DIRECTORIES AND CONTENTS

Directory Name	Contents
\Office51	Root directory for all program files.
\Office51\addin	Some additional StarCalc functions that you can choose to add during a Custom installation; the Source subdirectory contains samples and other add-ons available during installation.
\Office51\autotext	Stores StarWriter AutoText (*.bau) files; each category has its own file.
\Office51\backup	The default directory for storing backup (*.bak) files. You must select the backup option on the Save tab of the Tools, Options, General dialog for backups to be saved. You can direct your backups to another directory through the Paths tab in the same dialog.
\Office51\basic	Contains wizards for StarOffice, created in StarBasic (*.sbl files); when updating SO, be sure to backup these libraries. This generally affects the \Office51\basic\soffice.sbl.

Directory Name	Contents
\Office51\bin (Linux only)	Contains binary program files.
\Office51\bookmark	Contains folders with bookmarks preset by StarDivision. Includes some handy links to Java Web sites and some StarOne programming documents. Depending on your system configuration at installation, this Bookmark folder might appear in the Explorer. (Alternatively, you may have a link to an existing Bookmarks folder that StarOffice encountered on your system during installation.)
\Office51\config	Contains basic configuration (*.cfg) files and many configuration subdirectories. You can customize a number of program menus by adding or deleting the appropriate shortcuts in the subdirectories here. It's a good idea to back up your *.SCS files (mail boxes and other Internet accounts) for emergencies (for example, reformatting your hard drive). If you remove *.cfg files, StarOffice will revert to its default settings. If you're experiencing problems running StarOffice, sometimes deleting your current .cfg file and restarting the program to allow a clean .cfg file to be created can solve your problems.
\Office51\groups	Contain links to those directories you define as groups in the Explorer.
\Office51\config\help	Contains program help configuration files. StarOffice distinguishes help files (as well as dictionary files) by country code. For example, the desktop help file is called desktop.01.
\Office51\config\ helpmenu	Contains hyperlinks to topics in the online help that appear on the StarOffice Start menu.
\Office51\config\more	Stores contents of the StarOffice Start menu More subfolder. Customize by adding and deleting links here.
\Office51\config\new	Stores contents of the File, New submenu. Customize by adding and deleting links here.
\Office51\config\ quickstart	Stores links to programs and documents that you have dragged and dropped into the Quickstart area of the taskbar. See Chapter 2, "Stepping into StarOffice," for more information.
\Office51\config\start	Contains elements that appear on the StarOffice Start menu. Customize by adding or deleting items.
\Office51\config\startup	Empty at installation. Place links or programs here that you want to start at the same time you start StarOffice. Beware, however: some programs don't work very well from startup, including some StarOffice programs.
\Office51\config\symbol	Contains bitmap images for all program tools buttons. If so inclined, you can add your own here.
\Office51\config\tasks	Contains links to StarOffice task shortcuts for the Explorer Tasks group. You can add your own links or template files here.
\Office51\config\wizard	Contains AutoPilot wizards for creating documents (Windows version only).

APP

C

continues

continued

Directory Name	Contents
\Office51\database	Contains links to all registered databases. If you have problems with the Address Book or Merge Mail functions, close StarOffice and look here if you see files similar to *@1 and if so, delete them and check on the contents of the Address Book with a text editor.
\Office51\Desktop	Stores the contents of the StarOffice desktop. Initial contents are all links only. Similar in concept to the Windows Desktop folder.
\Office51\download	The default directory for Internet downloads. Set any folder you like as target, through the Tools, Options, General, Path tab.
\Office51\explorer	Stores the contents of the Explorer—the control center of the StarOffice desktop.
\Office51\explorer\ Samples	Contains samples of every document type that can be created in StarOffice. The samples also show off StarOffice's wide range of uses and might give you some creative ideas. Use them as templates, if you like.
\Office51\explorer\ Workfolder	Depending on your system, this might be a link to a folder you have already designated as your default storage location (in which case you won't see a Workfolder directory here). Or it might be an empty directory provided for your convenience in the Explorer as your initial document storage folder. It's also the default location when you select File, Open, or File, Save As.
\Office51\filter	Contains import and export filters. Copy all filters from the SO Professional Edition into this folder; in addition, you also have to copy \Office51\Install.ini.
\Office51\fonts	Desktop installation: Linux only (Windows fonts are handled through the Windows OS); server installation: stores all StarOffice fonts for installation on client computers.
\Office51\gallery	Contains sound and graphics files that you can preview in the Beamer and insert into your StarOffice documents. Also contains SG*.SDG, SG*.SDV, and SG*.THM files, which contain thumbnail database and other information. You can import your own gallery files into the Gallery as well from inside the Explorer. Select Gallery and right-click to open its context menu and import.
\Office51\help	Contains program help files (*.svh) in the 01 subdirectory.
\Office51\kde (Linux only)	Contains icons for menu integration with the KDE window manager program.
\Office51\kino (Linux only)	Contains icons for menu integration with the kino window manager program.
\Office51\lib	Java Class Libraries. Extends the capabilities of StarWriter/Web and the desktop browser.
\Office51\palmpilot	Contains the starsync.prc file that is needed to synchronize a PalmPilot with StarSchedule. You'll see this only if you chose a Custom installation and selected the PalmPilot add-on as an option. If you want to add this after initial program installation, run Setup from the Office51 directory and choose Modify.

Directory Name	Contents
\Office51\service (Linux only)	Contains `sschdled.bin` file.
\Office51\store	Stores a number of important configuration files and your Recycle Bin folder, \trash. If you experience problems with the Recycle Bin, try deleting this directory and the file `\Office51\store\trashcan.scs`.
\Office51\template	Contains program templates. The structure of the category folders and files is stored in the `sfx.tlx` file. Information on the various templates is stored in the `sfx.tpl` files. If you copied template files (`.vor`) into this folder, you first have to update them using the Style Catalog, Document Templates Update command.
\Office51\wordbook	Stores all custom dictionaries you create as well as the program custom dictionary (`Standard.div`), and a StarDivision custom dictionary of computing terms (`stardiv`).
\Office51\xp3 (Linux only)	Contains font metrics and PostScript printer information.

SELECTED STAROFFICE PROGRAM FILES AND FILE EXTENSIONS

The file locations listed in this table assume that you have not altered the directory structure of StarOffice, except perhaps to select a different main directory name or location at installation. The default installation directories are `/usr/Office51` on Linux, and `\Office51` on Windows. Files that can be manually edited are so noted, along with tips about what aspects of the program can be controlled through such editing. Files that users are best off leaving alone are also noted. Most other files may be manually edited, but only advanced users should attempt this. Do so at your own risk, as editing these files might prevent StarOffice from running properly or even from running at all.

Note
Most filenames are the same on both Linux and Windows. However, a few filenames are system-specific and are so identified.

SELECTED STAROFFICE PROGRAM FILES

Filename	Location	File Type	Comments
install.ini	\Office51	Configuration	Configuration file for import and export filters.
soffice.cfg	\Office51\config	Configuration	Stores StarOffice configurations, such as keyboard shortcuts or toolbars. If you experience problems with SO, try deleting this file. SO will start a new file at restart. However, you will lose all your previous workspace settings (custom menus, keyboard assignments, and so on).

APP

C

continues

continued

Filename	Location	File Type	Comments
readme.txt	\Office51	Documentation	Information on installation and registration, including notes about installing speech recognition software and phone numbers for contacting StarDivision support.
sversion.ini	\Windows	Initialization	Contains information on the location of SO, as well as multiple user information (if applicable).
soffice.ini (Windows) s-office.xpm lsoffice.xpm sofficerc (Linux)	\Office51	Initialization	Basic desktop configuration information, including URL history list, user data, program paths, and browser security information. Can be manually edited. You can use this file to personalize SO for different users; just exchange the file before program start.
so.ini (Windows only)	\Office51	Initialization	Basic application configuration information. Should not be edited.
docmnu.ini	\Office51\ config	Initialization	Contains history list of recently opened documents that appears at the end of the File menu. Can be manually edited.
fntsubst.ini	\Office51\ config (Windows) \usr\51\config (Linux)	Initialization	Determines whether font substitution is turned on or off. Can be manually edited. This option can also be set through the Tools, Options, General, Substitute font tab.
gpm.ini	\Office51\ config	Initialization	In order to support the StarWriter PC 7.0 text import filter, contains a list of font settings for each printer driver. Can be manually edited.
hlpagent.ini	\Office51\ config	Initialization	Contains configuration information for Help Agent.
labels.ini	\Office51\ config	Initialization	Contains information for quick formatting and printing of printer labels. Can be manually edited in order to make StarWriter work with label formats of your own quickly and easily. Instructions are included at the beginning of the file.
defcal.ini	\Office51\ config	Initialization	Date and time settings for around the world.
defuser.ini	\Office51\ config	Initialization	Your personal date and time settings.
services.ini (Windows) servicesrc (Linux)	\Office51\ config	Initialization	Contains initial configuration information for the desktop and database elements.

Filename	Location	File Type	Comments
srcheng.ini	\Office51\ config	Initialization	Contains list of Web search engines that StarWeb searches by default. Can be manually edited. These settings can also be changed through the Tools, Options, Internet tab.
wizard.ini (Windows only)	\Office51\ config	Initialization	Contains template formatting information for templates made with AutoPilot.
sointgr.exe	\Office51	Program	A key program file that executes StarOffice's system integration. Due to technical problems with this file, some users might have problems with their system icon tray integration on the taskbar. If so, you can deactivate this integration by entering the following command in the StarOffice installation directory: sointgr.exe -u After restarting Windows, the service will not be reactivated. Enter the following command to make it available again: sointgr.exe -i
setup.exe	\Office51	Setup Program	An executable or binary file that runs StarOffice setup so you can uninstall or repair an installation, or install new components.
deinstall-kde file	\Office51 (Linux only)	Deinstallation	Uninstalls KDE icons and menu integration. The files for KDE icons and integration are copied to your drive by default, so if you didn't do a custom install, you'll find this file, along with an install-kde file, on your system. If you don't run KDE, you don't need any of them; if you do, you can run the install-kde program by itself. There is also a CDE menu integration option that you can install by running Setup, choosing Modify, and selecting CDE.

Caution

You should never terminate the running sointgr program!

APP

C

DEFAULT KEYBOARD SHORTCUTS

In this appendix

Although StarOffice provides virtually every command you could want on a context menu, it doesn't neglect users who prefer to use the keyboard.

This appendix lists the preset keyboard shortcuts by module because key assignments are module specific. If you don't like the default assignments, or find yourself missing shortcuts you use in other programs, you can reconfigure the shortcuts for all key combinations (except those using the Alt key) by using the Tools, Configure dialog box. The Alt key shortcuts are hard-coded through the program.

→ For more details on customizing keyboard shortcuts, **see** "Customizing Desktop Tools and Menus," **p. 115**.

However, before customizing the shortcut keys, you might want to wait until you've familiarized yourself with StarOffice's organization and context menus. You might find that, with a few exceptions, you already have everything you need at your fingertips.

COMMON STAROFFICE SHORTCUTS

TABLE D.1 GENERAL FILE COMMANDS AVAILABLE WITH MOST SO MODULES

Shortcut Combination	Action It Performs
Ctrl+N	Open new document from template
Ctrl+O	Open document
Ctrl+P settings	Print selected or current document, using current printer
Ctrl+S	Save document

TABLE D.2 GENERAL WINDOWS COMMANDS AVAILABLE WITH MOST SO MODULES

Shortcut Combination	Action It Performs
Alt+F4	Close application
Arrow keys	In dialog boxes: Move to other buttons
Ctrl+F4	Close current task
Ctrl+Q	Close application
Ctrl+Shift+B	Open Beamer; if Beamer is already open, jump between Beamer and active task
Ctrl+Shift+E	Open Explorer; if Explorer is already open, jump between Explorer and active task
Ctrl+Shift+I	Turn integrated desktop on/off (aka Desktop mode; available only with Windows)
Ctrl+Shift+J	Turn full screen mode on/off
Ctrl+Tab	Switch to next open document
Enter	In dialog boxes: Press default button

Shortcut Combination	Action It Performs
Esc	Cancel
F1	Turn on Help Agent
Shift+Ctrl+Tab	Switch to previous open document
Shift+F1	Show Extended Tips
Shift+F10	Open context menu
Shift+Tab	In dialog boxes: Move to previous field
Tab	In dialog boxes: Move to next field

TABLE D.3   COMMON EDITING AND FORMATTING SHORTCUTS AVAILABLE WITH MOST SO MODULES

Shortcut Combination	Action It Performs
Ctrl+A	Select all
Ctrl+C	Copy
Ctrl+V	Paste
Ctrl+X	Cut
Ctrl+Z	Undo
Ctrl+B	Apply bold
Ctrl+I	Apply italic
Ctrl+U	Apply underline
Ctrl+D	Apply double underline
Ctrl+E	Center-align
Ctrl+L	Left-align
Ctrl+R	Right-align
Ctrl+J	Justify
F5	Turn Navigator On/Off
F7	Check spelling
Ctrl+F7	Open Thesaurus
F11	Turn stylist On/Off
Ctrl+Y	Open Style Catalog
Ctrl+F	Open Search and Replace dialog
Ctrl+Shift+R	Redraw screen

COMMON STARWRITER SHORTCUTS

TABLE D.4   GENERAL STARWRITER SHORTCUTS

Shortcut Combination	Action It Performs
F2	Insert formula
Ctrl+F2	Open Fields dialog
F3	Insert AutoText entry
Ctrl+F3	Open AutoText dialog
F4	Open Beamer; display current database
Shift+F5	Jump to next frame
Ctrl+Shift+F5	Open Navigator, and place cursor in the To Page spinbox
F8	Turn on extended selection
Ctrl+F8	Turn field shadings on/off
Shift+F8	Turn on additive selection
F9	Update fields
Ctrl+F9	Turn field names on/off
Shift+F9	Calculate table
Ctrl+Shift+F9	Update input fields
Ctrl+F10	Turn nonprinting characters on/off
Shift+F11	Create style
Ctrl+Shift+F11	Update style
F12	Turn numbering on/off
Shift+F12	Turn bullets on/off
Ctrl+Shift+F12	Turn numbering/bullets off
Ctrl+F12	Insert table

D.5   FORMATTING SHORTCUTS FOR TEXT DOCUMENTS

Shortcut	Action it Performs
Ctrl+Shift+P	Make superscript
Ctrl+1	Apply single line spacing
Ctrl+2	Apply double line spacing
Ctrl+5	Apply 1.5 line spacing
Ctrl++	Calculate selection

Shortcut	Action it Performs
Ctrl+-	Insert soft hyphen
Ctrl+*	Execute macro field
Ctrl+Spacebar	Insert nonbreaking space
Shift+Enter	Insert manual line break
Ctrl+Enter	Insert manual page break
Ctrl+Shift+Enter	Insert column break
Shift+left arrow	Select character to the left
Ctrl+left arrow	Jump to beginning of word
Ctrl+Shift+left arrow	Select to left of word
Shift+right arrow	Select character to the right
Ctrl+right arrow	Jump to end of word
Ctrl+Shift+right arrow	Select to right of word
Shift+up arrow	Select up
Shift+down arrow	Select down
Home	Jump to beginning of line
Shift+Home	Select to beginning of line
End	Jump to end of line
Shift+End	Select to end of line
Ctrl+Home	Jump to document begin
Ctrl+Shift+Home	Select document beginning
Ctrl+End	Jump to document end
Ctrl+Shift+End	Select to document end
Ctrl+Page Up	Move to header and back
Ctrl+Page Down	Move to footer and back
Shift+Page Up	Select to previous page
Shift+Page Down	Select to next page
Ctrl+Delete	Delete to end of word
Ctrl+Backspace	Delete to beginning of word
Ctrl+Shift+Delete	Delete to end of sentence
Ctrl+Shift+Backspace	Delete to beginning of sentence

Table D.6 Moving Paragraphs and Changing Headings

Shortcut Combination	Action It Performs
Ctrl+up arrow	Move selected paragraph(s) up
Ctrl+down arrow	Move selected paragraph(s) down
Tab	Heading x; x = 1-4 demoted*
Shift+Tab	Heading x; x = 2-5 promoted*
Ctrl+Tab	Insert tab in front of heading text

Place cursor at beginning of heading

Table D.7 Shortcuts for Working in StarWriter Tables

Shortcut Combination	Action It Performs
Ctrl+A	If the current cell is blank: Marks the entire table
	If the current cell contains data: Marks the current cell; press Ctrl+A again to mark the entire table
Ctrl+Home	If the cursor is at the beginning of a cell: Jumps to the beginning of the table
	If the cursor is not at the beginning of a cell: Jumps to the beginning of the current cell; press Ctrl+Home again to jump to the beginning of the table; press Ctrl+Home a third time to jump to the beginning of the document
Ctrl+End	If the cursor is at the end of a cell: Jumps to the end of the table
	If the cursor is not at the end of a cell: Jumps to the end of the current cell; press Ctrl+End again to jump to the end of the table; press Ctrl+End a third time to jump to the end of the document
Ctrl+Tab	Enter a tab stop
Ctrl+Shift+up arrow	Move to the beginning of the table
Ctrl+Shift+down arrow	Move to the end of the table
Alt+left arrow+right arrow	Increase/decrease the column width from the right border
Alt+up arrow+down arrow	Increase/decrease the row height from the bottom of the cell
Alt+Shift+left arrow+right arrow	Increase/decrease the column width from the left border of the cell

Shortcut Combination	Action It Performs
Alt+Shift+up arrow+down arrow	Increase/decrease the row height from the upper border of the cell
Alt+Ctrl+left arrow	Increase/decrease the column width from the right column border in the current cell only
Alt+Ctrl+Shift+left arrow	Increase/decrease column width from left column border in current cell only
Alt+Insert; then up arrow or down arrow	Activate 3-second Insert mode; up arrow key or down arrow key inserts a new row
Alt+Insert; then left arrow or right arrow	Activate 3-second Insert mode; left arrow key or right arrow key inserts a new column; Ctrl+left arrow or right arrow inserts a new cell
Alt+Delete; then up arrow or down arrow	Activate 3-second Delete mode; up arrow key or down arrow key deletes row
Alt+Delete; then left arrow or right arrow	Activate 3-second Delete mode; left arrow key or right arrow key deletes column
	Ctrl+left arrow key or right arrow key merges current cell with adjacent one
Ctrl+Shift+T	Remove cell protection for the selected table; if no table is marked, protection for all tables is removed
Shift+Ctrl+Delete	If nothing is selected: Deletes the following cell content
	If cells are selected: Deletes all rows of the selected cells
	If all rows are partially or entirely selected: Deletes the entire table

GENERAL TEXT FRAME AND OBJECT SHORTCUTS

TABLE D.8   WORKING WITH TEXT FRAMES AND OLE OBJECTS

Shortcut Combination	Action It Performs
Alt+arrow keys	Move object in direction of arrow key
Alt+Ctrl+up arrow or down arrow	Change frame or object height from lower border
Alt+Ctrl+right arrow or left arrow	Change frame or object width from right border
Alt+Ctrl+Shift+ up arrow or down arrow	Change frame or object height from upper border
Alt+Ctrl+Shift+right arrow or left arrow	Change frame or object height from left border

COMMON STARCALC SHORTCUTS

Shortcut Combination	Action It Performs
Insert	Paste special
Backspace	Delete contents
Del	Open Delete Contents dialog
Ctrl+Home	Move to start of data
Ctrl+End	Move to end of data
Ctrl+Spacebar	Select column
Home	Move to beginning of row
End	Move to end of row
Enter	Move to next cell (direction set in Tools, Options dialog; default direction is down)
Ctrl+left arrow	Move to left margin block
Ctrl+right arrow	Move to right margin block
Ctrl+up arrow	Move to upper margin block
Ctrl+down arrow	Move to lower margin block
Ctrl+Page Up	Move to previous sheet
Ctrl+Page Down	Move to next sheet
Alt+Page Up	Scroll one screen to left
Alt+Page Down	Scroll one screen to right
F2	Set input mode
Ctrl+F2	Open AutoPilot
Ctrl+F3	Define area names
F4	Import data from table (open Beamer)
Ctrl+F4	Close window
Shift+F4	Toggle between relative and absolute reference
Shift+F5	Trace dependents
Shift+F6	Trace precedents
F8	Open Extended Selection mode

Shortcut Combination	Action It Performs
Shift+F8	Open Additive Selection mode
Ctrl+F8	Turn value highlighting on/off
F9	Recalculate
Ctrl+Shift+F9	Recalculate (hard)
Shift+F11	Save as template
F12	Create group
Ctrl+F12	Ungroup
Shift+Space	Select row
Shift+Backspace	Undo selection
Ctrl+D	Select list
Ctrl+Shift+T	Go to sheet area input field

TABLE D.10 STARCALC CELL FORMATTING SHORTCUTS

Shortcut Combination	Action It Performs
Ctrl+Shift+1	Use Decimal number format
Ctrl+Shift+2	Use Exponent number format
Ctrl+Shift+3	Use Date number format
Ctrl+Shift+4	Use Currency number format
Ctrl+Shift+5	Use Percent number format
Ctrl+Shift+6	Use Standard number format
Shift+Alt+Enter	If pressed after entering data in a selected block, switches to new number format if previous one is incompatible
Ctrl+*	Select data area
Alt+up arrow	Decrease row height in increments of default row height (.17 inch)
Alt+down arrow	Increase row height in increments of default row height (.17 inch)
Alt+right arrow	Increase current column width in increments of default column width (.17 inch)
Alt+left arrow	Decrease current column width in increments of default column width (.17 inch)
Alt+Shift+Arrow	Sets row height and column width to optimal size for current cell data

StarImpress/StarDraw Shortcuts

TABLE D.11   GENERAL StarImpress/StarDraw Shortcuts

Shortcut Combination	Action It Performs
F2	Select text tool
Ctrl+F2	Open presentation (StarImpress only)
F3	Enter group
Ctrl+F3	Exit group
Shift+F3	Duplicate
F4	Open Position and Size dialog of selected object
F8	Edit points
Ctrl+Shift+F8	Fit to size
F12	Enter Outline mode (StarImpress only)
Ctrl+F12	Enter Drawing mode (StarImpress only)

TABLE D.12   Keyboard Shortcuts for Running a Presentation

Shortcut Combination	Action It Performs
Esc	End presentation
Spacebar	Go to the next object (animation or slide)
Enter	Go to the next slide
nn Enter	Switch to the nth slide
Cursor left	Switch to the previous slide
Cursor right	Switch to the next Slide
Home	Jump to the first slide
End	Jump to the last slide
Page Up	Jump to the previous page
Page Down	Jump to the next page

TABLE D.13   StarImpress/StarDraw in Draw Mode/Drawing Keyboard Shortcuts

Shortcut Combination	Action It Performs
Page Up	Switch to previous page
Page Down	Switch to next page
+	Increase view

Shortcut Combination	Action It Performs
-	Decrease view
Ctrl+Shift+G	Group
Ctrl+Shift+Alt+G	Ungroup
Shift+left click	Group objects (press Shift until all objects have been selected)
Ctrl+left click	Edit group(ed) objects
Ctrl+Shift+K	Create combination
Ctrl+Shift+Alt+K	Remove combination
Ctrl+Shift++	Bring to front
Ctrl++	Bring forward
Ctrl+-	Send backward
Ctrl+Shift+-	Send back

TABLE D.14   SPECIAL KEY COMBINATIONS FOR PRESENTATIONS AND DRAWINGS

Shortcut Combination	Action It Performs
Cursor keys	Move selected objects in the direction of the cursor
Ctrl+cursor	Move the page view in the direction of the cursor
Shift+drag	Move the selected object horizontally or vertically in the desired direction
Ctrl+drag	If Snap to Grid is not selected: Temporarily activates the Snap to Grid option during dragging of object, and objects will snap to gridlines
	If Snap to Grid is selected: Object will not snap to gridlines during move
	If Copy When Moved option is on: Snap to Grid function is temporarily active during move, and a copy is made of the original
Alt	Cause changes to occur from the center of the object outward when building or changing the size of an object
Alt+click	Select overlapping objects; the object behind the selected object is also selected
Alt+Shift+click	Select overlapping objects; the object in front of the selected object is also selected
Shift while selecting	Add object to/removed object from the current selection, depending on whether it was previously part of the selection

continues

TABLE D.14 CONTINUED

Shortcut Combination	Action It Performs
Shift while increasing/building	Increase object proportionally; a straight line can only be enlarged linearly
Tab	Select individual objects in the order in which they were built, from first to last
Shift+Tab	Select individual objects in the order in which they were built, from last to first
Shift+drag (while in Edit Points mode)	Enable changing the length of a measured line
Esc	When a tool is active: Switch to Selection mode
	When object is selected: Cancel selection
	When object is in Text Entry mode: Cancel the Text Entry mode; the object remains selected

COMMON StarImage SHORTCUTS

TABLE D.15 STARIMAGE SHORTCUTS

Shortcut Combination	Action It Performs
F2	Flip horizontal
Shift+F2	Flip vertical
F3	Rotate 90 degrees to the left
Shift+F3	Rotate 90 degrees to the right
F4	RGB: Decrease red
Shift+F4	RGB: Increase red
F5	RGB: Decrease green
Shift+F5	RGB: Increase green
F6	RGB: Decrease blue
Shift+F6	RGB: Increase blue
F7	Decrease brightness
Shift +F7	Increase brightness
F8	Decrease contrast
Shift +F8	Increase contrast

Shortcut Combination	Action It Performs
F9	Apply charcoal sketch effect
Shift+F9	Apply poster effect
Ctrl+Shift+F9	Apply definition
F11	Apply mosaic effect
Shift+F11	Apply pop-art effect
Ctrl+F11	Apply solarization effect
Ctrl+Shift+F11	Apply smooth effect
F12	Apply relief effect
Ctrl+F12	Apply tile effect
Shift+F12	Apply aging effect
Ctrl+Shift+F12	Remove noise effect

COMMON StarMail/StarDiscussion Shortcuts

TABLE D.16   StarMail and StarDiscussion Shortcuts

Shortcut Combination	Action It Performs
Ctrl+left arrow	Move to next unread message, up
Ctrl+right arrow	Move to next unread message, down
Ctrl+M	Mark message as Marked
Ctrl+S	Mark message as Unread
Ctrl+H	Open Properties dialog of selected mail or news message
Ctrl+R	Reply to sender; open StarMail composition window with message quoted
Ctrl+F	Forward
Ctrl+T	Mark discussion thread as read
Ctrl++	Move to next unread message in thread (use + on numeric keypad, not on main keyboard)
Ctrl+-	Close posting and all subentries
Spacebar	Move to next unread message; when reading newsgroups, change to the next group with an unread message

COMMON STARSCHEDULE SHORTCUTS

TABLE D.17 GENERAL STARSCHEDULE KEYBOARD SHORTCUTS

Shortcut Combination	Action It Performs
Cursor right/left	Advance/go back by one day
Cursor up/down	When in day/week view: Browse up/down by time
	When in month view: Browse to the same day of the previous/next week
Ctrl+cursor right/left	When in day/week view: Browse to the next/previous week
	When in month view: Browse to the next/previous month
Ctrl+cursor up/down	When in day/week view: Toggle between day schedule and all hours
	When in month view: Browse to the previous/next month
Home or End	When in month view: Browse to the previous/next year (or the unit set in the context menu on the object bar)
Tab	Advance through all dates visible in the current filter, including the current selection
Shift+Tab	Go back through all dates visible in the current filter, including the current selection
Esc	Leave the text entry mode; the date remains selected
Delete	If date is selected in non-text-entry mode: Delete the appointment

TABLE D.18 KEYS IN STARSCHEDULE TASK WINDOW

Shortcut Combination	Action It Performs
Cursor right/left	Set entry focus one column forward/back
Cursor up/down	Browse up/down through the currently visible tasks (depends on filter used)
Ctrl+cursor up	Place insertion point in the blank entry line
Ctrl+cursor down	Move insertion point from the blank entry line to the previously selected entry

COMMON StarMath Shortcuts

TABLE D.19   GENERAL StarMath Shortcuts

Shortcut Combination	Action It Performs
F2	Go to next marker
Shift+F2	Go to previous marker
F3	Go to next error
Shift+F3	Go to previous error
F9	Refresh

STARBASIC ERROR CODES

If you're ever puzzled over an error code in StarBasic, this is the place to look. For your convenience, we've included the complete list of error codes in StarBasic. You won't find them documented elsewhere in StarOffice.

Error Number	Error Text
2	Syntax error
3	Return without Gosub
4	Incorrect entry; please retry
5	Invalid procedure call
6	Overflow
7	Not enough memory
8	Array already dimensioned
9	Index out of defined range
10	Duplicate definition
11	Division by zero
12	Variable not defined
13	Data type mismatch
14	Invalid parameter
18	Process interrupted by user
20	Resume without error
28	Not enough stack memory
35	Sub or function procedure not defined
48	Error loading DLL file
49	Wrong DLL call convention
51	Internal error
52	Invalid filename or file number
53	File not found
54	Incorrect file mode
55	File already open
57	Device I/O error
58	File already exists
59	Incorrect data record length
61	Disk or hard drive full

Error Number	Error Text
62	Reading exceeds EOF
63	Incorrect data record number
67	Too many files
68	Device not available
70	Access denied
71	Disk not ready
73	Not implemented
74	Renaming on some drives impossible
75	Path/file access error
76	Path not found
91	Object variable not set
93	Invalid string pattern
94	Use of zero not permitted
250	DDE error
280	Awaiting response to DDE connection
281	No DDE channels available
282	No application responded to DDE connect initiation
283	Multiple applications responded to DDE connect initiation
284	DDE channel locked
285	External application cannot execute DDE operation
286	Timeout while waiting for DDE response
287	Escape pressed during DDE operation
288	External application busy
289	Data not provided in DDE operation
290	Data in wrong format
291	External application has been terminated
292	DDE connection interrupted or modified
293	DDE method invoked with no channel open
294	Invalid DDE link format
295	Message queue filled; DDE message lost
296	Paste link already performed
297	Link mode cannot be set due to invalid link topic

continues

continued

Error Number	Error Text
298	DDE requires the DDEML.DLL file
323	Module cannot be loaded; invalid format
341	Invalid object index
366	Object is not available
380	Incorrect property value
382	This property is read-only
394	This property is write-only
420	Invalid object reference
423	Property or method not found
424	Object required
425	Invalid use of an object
430	OLE automation is not supported by this object
438	This property or method is not supported by the object
440	OLE automation error
445	This action is not supported by the given object
446	Named arguments are not supported by the given object
447	The current local setting is not supported by the given object
448	Named argument not found
449	Argument is not optional
450	Invalid number of arguments
451	Object is not a list
452	Invalid ordinal number
453	Specified DLL function not found
460	Invalid Clipboard format
951	Unexpected symbol
952	Expected
953	Symbol expected
954	Variable expected
955	Label expected
956	Value cannot be applied
957	Variable already defined

Error Number	Error Text
958	Sub or function procedure already defined
959	Label already defined
960	Variable not found
961	Array or function not found
962	Procedure not found
963	Label undefined
964	Unknown data type
965	Exit expected
966	Unterminated statement block missing
967	Parentheses do not match
968	Symbol already defined differently
969	Parameters do not correspond to procedure
970	Invalid character in number
971	Array must be dimensioned
972	Else/Endif without If
973	Not allowed within a procedure
974	Not allowed outside a procedure
975	Dimension specifications do not match
976	Unknown option
977	Constant redefined
978	Program too large
979	Strings or arrays not permitted
1000	Object does not have this property
1001	Object does not have this method
1002	Required argument lacking
1003	Invalid number of arguments
1004	Error executing method
1005	Unable to define property
1006	Unable to determine property

INDEX

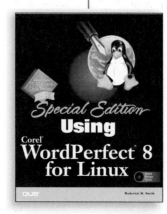

Other Related Titles

Caldera OpenLinux Installation and Configuration Handbook
Gary Wilson
ISBN:0789721058
$39.99 US/$56.95 CAN

The Complete Idiot's Guide to Linux
Manuel Ricart
ISBN:078971826x
$19.99 US/$28.95 CAN

Linux User Manual
Que
ISBN:0789718774
$19.99 US/$28.95 CAN

Platinum Edition Using HTML 4, XML, and Java 1.2
Eric Ladd
ISBN:078971759x
$59.99 US/$85.95 CAN

Using UNIX, 2nd Ed.
Steve Moritsugu
ISBN:0789716321
$29.99 US/$42.95 CAN

Using Networks
Frank Derfler
ISBN:0789715961
$29.99 US/$42.95 CAN

Windows NT Hints and Hacks
John Savill
ISBN:0789719185
$19.99 US/$28.95 CAN

Managing Multivendor Networks
John Enck
ISBN:0789711796
$29.99 US/$42.95 CAN

Upgrading and Repairing PCs, 11th Ed
Scott Mueller
ISBN:0789719037
$54.99 US/$78.95 CAN

Using Visual InterDev 6
Mike Amundsen
ISBN:0789716402
$29.99 US/$42.95 CAN

Working with Active Server Pages
David Merrick
ISBN:078971115x
$39.99 US/$56.95 CAN

Using Linux
Bill Ball
ISBN:0789716232
$29.99 US/$42.95 CAN

UNIX Hints and Hacks
Kirk Waingrow
ISBN:0789719274
$19.99 US/$28.95 CAN

www.quecorp.com

All prices are subject to change.